The Complete
WHO'S WHO OF TEST CRICKETERS

The Complete WHO'S WHO OF TEST CRICKETERS

Christopher Martin-Jenkins

Research by James Coldham

ORBIS PUBLISHING · LONDON

PICTURE CREDITS
Adrian Murrell/All-Sport 42, 47, 50, 60*r*, 61, 91, 145, 170, 209, 221, 337, 339, 347, 354, 364, 418, 420, 430, 432, 455, 461*b*, 463, 470, 471, 480*b*, 483, 484*t*, 484*b*, 485, 486, 487; Australian News and Information Bureau 235; BBC Hulton Picture Library 19, 45, 46, 49, 56*r*, 71, 72, 77, 101, 141, 151, 172, 200, 202*l*, 237, 241, 255, 260, 283, 360, 426; Central Press 8, 9, 10, 12, 18, 24, 51, 52, 60*l*, 68, 70*l*, 90*r*, 92*t*, 92*b*, 95, 97, 99, 103, 113*r*, 114, 122, 125, 128, 131, 139, 143, 144, 150, 152, 155, 156, 159, 168, 178, 180, 181, 183, 186, 189, 191, 196, 199, 202*r*, 204, 205*t*, 205*b*, 215, 216*l*, 220, 223, 226, 229*l*, 238, 243*l*, 243*r*, 246, 250, 268, 271, 272, 273, 275, 287, 290, 294, 296, 300, 302, 311, 316, 322, 329, 331, 342, 351, 397, 402, 405, 433, 434, 435, 437, 440, 445, 450, 461; J. Coldham Collection 63; Coloursport 123; Patrick Eagar 11, 13, 22, 25, 27, 38, 40, 44, 48, 53, 65, 75, 76, 83, 90*l*, 94, 105, 110, 116, 118, 120, 126, 129, 136, 137, 140, 146, 148, 163, 166, 184, 188, 193, 208, 222, 227*l*, 229*r*, 232, 233, 234, 247, 252, 253, 258, 263, 264, 267, 270, 306, 307, 336, 338, 341, 346, 350, 353, 362, 363, 368, 379, 381, 382, 391, 400, 406, 408, 417, 421, 423, 429, 442, 451, 452, 453, 458, 464, 466, 468, 472, 474, 475, 477, 480*t*, 482; Ken Kelly 64, 154, 256, 416; Kent County Cricket Club 33, 165; Lancashire County Cricket Club 119; Mansell Collection 62, 96, 98*l*, 124, 153, 190, 207, 261*l*; MCC 2, 28, 86, 98*r*, 115, 138, 158, 176, 216*r*, 225, 240; Popperfoto 35, 36, 70*r*, 82, 130, 132, 218; Press Association 14, 30, 56*l*, 78, 85, 109, 133, 175, 227*r*, 277, 345, 361; Sport and General 16, 41, 57, 59, 74, 108, 113*l*, 177, 201, 211, 332, 343, 357, 380, 386, 388, 390, 399, 460; Sussex County Cricket Club 17, 67, 121, 278, 303, 317; Roger Wood 374

First published in Great Britain by Orbis Publishing Ltd, London, 1980
Reprinted 1980
Revised 1983

Printed in Great Britain by Jarrold and Sons Ltd, Norwich
ISBN 0-85613-487-2

Title page: W.G. Grace (left) talking to F.S. Jackson

CONTENTS

PREFACE TO THE SECOND EDITION

Various changes have been made to the career statistics given in the first edition of this book due to the reclassification of certain matches after work by the Association of Cricket Statisticians. Some games played on 'private' tours are now deemed to be first-class, and the New Zealand Cricket Board has ruled as first-class the 1932/3 Wellington *v* MCC fixture, which was reduced by rain to one day and hitherto disregarded for the purpose of first-class records. In contrast, the Essex *v* Sir Julien Cahn's XI match of 1930 has been ruled not first-class by the MCC, although it was generally regarded as such at the time. My special thanks are due to Geoffrey Saulez for updating and adapting the career figures on the basis of recent research by himself and other members of the Association of Cricket Statisticians.

I am also grateful to the following for pointing out errors or omissions or making suggestions about entries in the first edition: R. L. Arrowsmith, K. T. Barrett, Anthony Bradbury, B. C. Dodd, L. R. Hill, John Hodkin, Douglas Miller, Colin Sansom, Peter Sellers (Dunedin) and George Thomas. The late Michael Fordham, that most modest and reliable of cricket statisticians, had already given willing help on updated career figures before his untimely death. Bill Frindall and Chris Rhys also helped me with checklists of recent Test career figures, and Brian Heald and Barry Macauley kindly answered some last-minute queries. S. S. Perera checked and updated the Sri Lankan figures to the end of September 1982, including the inaugural Test against India.

Career figures are given up to the end of the 1982 English season, except in the case of some Indians for whom it has not proved possible to check with absolute certainty beyond the end of 1980/81 season. Test figures for all countries are correct to the end of September 1982. For Pakistan and Australia the figures are further updated to include their series in Pakistan in 1982/3, which began in September 1982 and ended on only 19 October. The text updates all biographies to the end of September 1982. Where a cricketer has died during the process of publication (or, in a few cases, where a career has changed dramatically) reference has been made to this.

Since the publication of the first edition the increasing proliferation of Test matches has produced many new players and many new records. Most notable has been the welcoming into the international cricket community of Sri Lanka, with the country's first official Test being played against England (at Colombo) in February 1982. Some people may feel that the quantity of Tests played worldwide has produced a danger that the supreme form of cricket might be debased, but, apart from some deplorable shows of dissent towards umpires, the most recent series between England and Australia have been in the highest traditions of the game. Indeed the matches which took place at Headingley in 1981 and at Melbourne at the end of 1982 were so stirring, unpredictable and spectacular that they were enough in themselves to put a whole new generation under cricket's bewitching spell.

PREFACE TO THE FIRST EDITION

If it has in some respects been hard labour producing this volume, it has nevertheless been a genuine labour of love. I was privileged to be asked to write the book and, although I am aware of its shortcomings, I very much hope it will fill a gap as a work of cricket reference and at the same time give pleasure to the casual reader. Not only do the sheer facts of the performances of many Test cricketers amaze one but among those who have played this most complex and absorbing of all sports at the highest level there have been some rich characters, many of them distinguished in a wide variety of pursuits other than cricket.

I am both deeply indebted and immensely grateful to Jim Coldham for his assiduous, indeed fastidious research for this book. Literally nothing has been too much trouble for him, and his energy, enthusiasm and capacity for detail seemed to know no bounds. For well over a year the lines between his home and mine buzzed almost incessantly: What was Mordecai Sherwin's weight in his prime? When was Anwar Khan born? What is the second Christian name of Don Smith of Sussex? And so on. Jim has uncovered many hitherto unpublished first names and career figures, often after deep and painstaking digging.

Some career figures will, for simple lack of records, never be completed, particularly in India and Pakistan, but wherever possible the figures of any players who have reached a significant number of runs, wickets or catches have been given. For ease of reference players are shown in alphabetical order and in the case of those who played for two countries they are entered under the country for which they played first. This is of particular note with those Pakistan players who played for India before Partition. For those players who appeared in one Test only, the Test figures will be found in the body of the text and not at the end of the entry.

For reasons of space the pen portraits are largely factual and one has had to assume knowledge by the reader of certain aspects of cricket history. The uninitiated may not, for example, know that the Ashes had their origin in the defeat of England by Australia at The Oval in 1882, when the *Sporting Times* published an obituary of English Cricket, the body of which 'will be cremated and the Ashes taken to Australia'. When, the following Australian summer, England, under the captaincy of the Hon. Ivo Bligh (later Lord Darnley), won a three-match rubber against Murdoch's Australian team, a bail was burnt and the ashes were put into an urn and have been played for ever since. The term 'bodyline' also appears from time to time; this was the policy of systematic short-pitched bowling aimed by England's fast bowlers at the bodies of the Australian batsmen in 1932/3, when in a bitterly contested series many an Australian was caught in the leg-trap off the fast bowling of Larwood and Voce. Another incident, occasionally referred to in the text, is the row between players and the Australian Cricket Board in 1912. There were frequent arguments about the early tours the Board arranged, and on this occasion six leading players – Armstrong, Carter, Cotter, Hill, Ransford and Trumper – refused to tour England because they could not have the manager they wanted. Thus, discontent with the administration, which occurred again with the 'Packer Revolution' of 1977, has deep roots in Australian cricket.

The match that has become officially known as the first Test was played at Melbourne on 15, 16 and 17 March 1877 between Lillywhite's 'England' team and an 'Australian' team (made up of New South Wales and Victoria).

In South Africa the first Tests were played in 1888/9 against an England touring team, the first Tests in England against South Africa being played in 1907. Since 1970, however, South Africa have played no Test cricket for political reasons.

After South Africa it was some time before other countries started playing at Test level, beginning with the West Indies in 1928 (first match at Lord's), followed by New Zealand in 1929/30 (against an England touring team), then India in 1932 (also at Lord's) and finally Pakistan with a tour of India in 1952/3, after Partition in 1947.

ENGLAND

ABEL, Robert (1857-1936)

Surrey

With his faded, chocolate-coloured Surrey cap, waddling walk, upright stance, resourceful, patient and often punishing batting, Robert Abel, or 'The Guv'nor', was a great favourite, especially at The Oval. A diminutive opening batsman (5ft 4ins), he was reputedly afraid of fast bowling, yet he mastered all types of attack – and in 1901 scored 3,309 runs (55.15) after passing 2,000 for six consecutive seasons. Two years before he carried his bat for his highest score, 357 against Somerset at The Oval. In 1897, with William Brockwell, he put on 379 for the first wicket, for Surrey against Hampshire, also at The Oval, which was a record at that time. On his second visit to Australia, in 1891/2, he made 388 runs (38.80) in first-class matches, including 132 in the Test at Sydney, when he carried his bat. He toured South Africa with the first English team in 1888/9, and was, in figures if not in fact, head and shoulders above the other batsmen. He made 1,075 runs (48.19) in all matches, including 120 in the second Test at Cape Town, which was the first hundred in matches between the two countries. He was also a jack-in-the-box at slip and a useful slow bowler. Two sons played for Surrey, one going on to Glamorgan.

First-class career (1881-1904): 33,124 runs (35.46) including 74 centuries, 263 wickets (24.01) and 585 catches
Test matches (13): 744 runs (37.20) including 2 centuries, and 13 catches

ABSOLOM, Charles Alfred (1846-89)

Cambridge University, Kent and Essex

Known as 'the Cambridge navvy', Charlie Absolom was a large, bearded all-rounder who trained on haymaking and beer and could bowl a good medium pace, hit in lively fashion and field actively. He was a member of Lord Harris's team to Australia in 1878/9 and rescued England with 52 at Melbourne in his only Test. On forsaking first-class cricket soon afterwards, he travelled extensively and became a purser, dying in agony at Port of Spain, Trinidad, when a crane discharged a cargo of sugar on him. (Strangely, he was one of the few cricketers who had never worn a cap or hat.) In 57 matches for Kent he made 1,644 runs (16.60) and took 89 wickets (25.22).

ALLEN, David Arthur (b.1935)

Gloucestershire

With a comfortable amble to the crease of no more than four or five paces, David Allen could bowl accurately for long spells, turning his off-spinner substantially. His best batting came against the fastest

David Allen

bowling or when his side badly needed runs, and he was a very good outfield. He was Jim Laker's successor as the prime England off-spinner and proved his class on his first tour of the West Indies in 1959/60. He toured all the leading cricket countries within the next ten years, although several top-class off-spinners including Titmus, Illingworth and Mortimore challenged him for a place.

First-class career (1953-72): 9,291 runs (18.80) including 1 century, 1,209 wickets (23.64) and 252 catches
Test matches (39): 918 runs (25.50), 122 wickets (30.96) and 10 catches

'Gubby' Allen

ALLEN, George Oswald Browning (b.1902)

Cambridge University and Middlesex

A brave, forthright and determined character, 'Gubby' Allen has for many years been the *eminence grise* of English cricket. His actual home is within a six-hit of Lord's Cricket Ground and his spiritual home the Lord's Pavilion. A stubborn supporter of the traditional virtues of cricket, he has made enemies who have resented his 'backroom meddling' in England's cricket politics, but his undoubtedly strong influence has invariably been for the good of the game. 'Gubby' has had a wider experience than any predecessor in the practicalities of cricket in England, as player, captain, selector and administrator, although he was born in Australia and had an uncle, R.C. Allen, who played for Australia. Attacking like 'flaming fire', his right-arm fast bowling with a classical sideways-on action often touched greatness; in full measure he possessed rhythm and the ability to make the ball hurry from the pitch. His batting was strong, courageous and correct, and his outstanding close-in fielding completed his status as a genuine all-rounder. He was an amateur, with no time to play cricket full-time, whose career reached its zenith in his thirties when he toured Australia in 1932/3, taking 21 wickets in that series without resorting to bodyline, of which he disapproved. He led England to victory over India in 1936, taking 20 wickets (16.50) himself in the three Tests. Back in Australia in 1936/7, his exertions as captain were herculean, but after England had won the first two Tests, Australia recovered and retained the Ashes. First appointed a selector in 1955, he became a tough and inventive chairman of selectors, putting his faith in class rather than averages. He served as president of MCC in 1963/4 and as treasurer from 1964 until 1976, and was awarded the CBE in 1962.

First-class career (1921-54): 9,232 runs (28.67) including 11 centuries, 785 wickets (22.31) and 125 catches
Test matches (25): 750 runs (24.19) including 1 century, 81 wickets (29.37) and 20 catches

ALLOM, Maurice James Carrick (b.1906)

Cambridge University and Surrey

Maurice Allom was a huge but genial fast-medium right-arm bowler. He was a Cambridge blue and toured Australasia, 1929/30, securing 68 wickets (18.35) and, in the first ever Test between England and New Zealand at Christchurch, he took four wickets in five balls, including the hat-trick. In 1930/31 he toured South Africa. With Maurice Turnbull he wrote light-hearted accounts of these two tours in *The Book of the Two Maurices* and *The Two Maurices Again* respectively, but business curtailed his career. President of MCC in 1969/70, he is currently president of Surrey C.C.C. His son also (briefly) represented Surrey.

First-class career (1926-38): 1,953 runs (12.84) and 605 wickets (23.62)
Test matches (5): 14 runs (14.00) and 14 wickets (18.92)

ALLOTT, Paul John Walter (b.1956)

Cheshire and Lancashire

Six-foot-four, strongly built, fair-haired and bespectacled, Paul Allott showed promise at Altrincham

Grammar School, played for Cheshire in 1976 and for Lancashire from 1978 whilst studying at Durham University. A useful right-hand bat with a correct technique, he blossomed suddenly as a right-arm fast-medium bowler in 1981 when, with Michael Holding as an occasional new-ball partner, he bowled with stamina and determination to take 85 first-class wickets at 23.09. Not genuinely quick, his high action and strength enable him to move the ball, and he revealed a sound temperament too when playing a useful all-round part in his first Test at Old Trafford, when England retained the Ashes. He took four wickets for 88 and scored 52 not out – an inspired innings – and 14. He was left out of the next Test, but deservedly went to India in 1981/2. Injury restricted him to two Test appearances in 1982, and he was not picked to tour Australia in 1982/3.

First-class career (1978-): 577 runs (12.54) and 186 wickets (28.35)
Test matches (5): 119 runs (29.75), 6 wickets (69.00) and 2 catches

AMES, Leslie Ethelbert George (b.1905)

Kent

A cheerful, bubbling character, Les Ames has spent most of his life in professional cricket. He was a fine, strongly built, all-round wicket-keeper, equally at home taking Tich Freeman, Harold Larwood or Bill Voce, and responded admirably to the demands of the big occasion. He was first choice 'keeper for England from 1931 until 1938. The strength of the England sides in that period owes much to the fact that he was also an orthodox, free-scoring batsman who showed the full face of the bat and was good enough to play for England as a batsman alone. In 1934, particularly, his batting was invaluable against Australia, especially when he and Maurice Leyland were the sixth-wicket rescuers at Lord's adding 129, Ames scoring 120. He shared the record fifth- and eighth-wicket partnerships against New Zealand and the fourth against South Africa. His highest in Tests was 149 against the West Indies at Kingston, 1929/30, in which series he made 417 runs (59.57). Against the West Indies at The Oval in 1933, he had eight dismissals. In 1928 and 1929 he had 121 and 127 dismissals respectively in first-class games, besides making 1,919 and 1,795 runs. In 1932 his record was 2,482 runs and 100 dismissals. For many years he was hampered by fibrositis. He was an England selector from 1950 until 1956 and again in 1958, and latterly as the secretary/manager of Kent he has been a much-respected administrator.

First-class career (1926-51): 37,248 runs (43.56) including 102 centuries, and 1,113 dismissals (698 ct, 415 st.)
Test matches (47): 2,434 runs (40.56) including 8 centuries, and 97 dismissals (74 ct, 23 st.)

Les Ames

AMISS, Dennis Leslie (b.1943)

Warwickshire

Until his decision to secure his family's future by accepting 'an offer I could not refuse' from Kerry Packer's World Series Cricket (despite a record declared benefit of £34,947 from Warwickshire), the image of Dennis Amiss was one of a loyal and dedicated professional cricketer. But temporary bitterness resulting from this decision was quickly forgotten and he has continued to serve Warwickshire with honour. Such was his natural ability that, as a schoolboy, he became associated with Warwickshire at the age of only fifteen. At seventeen he played his first County Championship match and at twenty-three his first Test for England against the West Indies, who were to come to respect him as a formidable opponent. His batting reflected his character: calm, determined, disciplined, cautious. An affable, pipe-smoking family man with his heart very much set in his Birmingham home, his career has had more peaks and troughs than most, but only Boycott among English batsmen in the

1970s equalled his ability patiently to accumulate runs. It took Amiss a long time to establish a regular place in the England team, which he did towards the end of the 1972/3 tour of India and Pakistan, after reaching his first Test century in his thirteenth Test at Lahore. In his first twelve games for England he averaged only 18; in his next twenty he made over 2,000 runs with eight centuries at an average of 71.33. In 1974 alone he scored 1,379 runs, including his most famous innings, 262 not out at Sabina Park, a marathon of concentration and endurance which saved England from defeat in a truly heroic way. He followed this run of high scores with a series of depressing failures against Australia, frequently falling to Dennis Lillee. But after being hit on the head by a ball from Michael Holding in 1976, he returned to Test cricket with another double century at The Oval. Squarely built, his special hallmarks as a batsman have been a glorious cover-drive and the flick off the legs executed with wrists of steel. Before suffering a back injury he could bowl useful, medium-pace, left-arm seamers, and he is a reliable if not very athletic fielder. He started his career as a middle-order batsman but achieved a new consistency from the moment that he began regularly to open the Warwickshire innings. He scored two hundreds, 155 not out and 112, in the match against Worcestershire at Edgbaston in 1978 when he was the only batsman in the English season to pass 2,000 runs. His highest aggregate in an English season was his 2,110 runs at 65.93 in 1976. His highest score in England was his 232 not out against Gloucestershire at Bristol in 1979. Unlucky not to be restored to the England side in the post-Packer years, he burnt his last boats by joining the unofficial tour of South Africa in March 1982, but he has continued to play effectively for Warwickshire and he may well become the twenty-first batsman to score a hundred centuries.

Dennis Amiss watched by Majid Khan (left) and Wasim Bari

First-class career (1960-): 35,158 runs (43.24) including 82 centuries, 18 wickets (38.88) and 336 catches
Test matches (50): 3,612 runs (46.30) including 11 centuries, and 24 catches

ANDREW, Keith Vincent (b.1929)

Northamptonshire

Keith Andrew, in the face of much competition, played only twice for England, once on the tour to Australia, 1954/5. He was a neat, skilful, unobtrusive and very successful wicket-keeper in county cricket – once holding seven catches in an innings – and a stubborn, late-order batsman. He captained Northamptonshire with distinction for five years (1962-6), one of the most successful periods in the county's history. Successively a committee man with Northamptonshire and Lancashire, he is now the National Cricket Association's chief coach, a popular and respected figure.

First-class career (1952-66): 4,230 runs (13.38) and 903 dismissals (721 ct, 182 st.)
Test matches (2): 29 runs (9.66) and 1 dismissal (1 ct)

APPLEYARD, Robert (b.1924)

Yorkshire

Tall, with an ideal physique, smooth action and quiet, thoughtful manner, Bob Appleyard was a right-arm, medium-paced off-spin bowler, whose unusual pace combined with his high action enabled him to achieve extra bounce. Like a right-handed Derek Underwood, he was at his most devastating on a wet or damp wicket. His length was superb, and one of his greatest gifts was being able to make the ball dip. He was also an occasionally useful tail-end batsman and a safe catcher. He was dogged by ill-health for much of his career, but despite an attack of pleurisy took 200 wickets (14.14) and headed the averages in his first full season of first-class cricket in 1951, at the relatively advanced age of twenty-seven. In Australia and New Zealand, 1954/5, he was at his best, heading the averages in the Tests against Australia with 11 wickets (20.36) and in the two Tests against New Zealand with 9 wickets (8.88), including 4 for 7 in the second innings at Auckland; but his continual struggle against sickness caused his retirement in 1958.

First-class career (1950-58): 776 runs (8.52) and 708 wickets (15.48)
Test matches (9): 51 runs (17.00), 31 wickets (17.87) and 4 catches

Bob Appleyard

ARCHER, Alfred German (1871-1935)

Shropshire and Worcestershire

A wicket-keeper of occasional county experience, Alfred Archer toured South Africa with Lord Hawke's team, 1898/9, and in his sole Test at Cape Town batted at number ten scoring 7 and 24 not out, not keeping wicket and not bowling.

First-class career (1899-1903): 227 runs (11.35) and 12 dismissals (10 ct, 2 st.)

ARMITAGE, Thomas (1848-1922)

Yorkshire

Tom Armitage was a useful right-handed batsman and a round-arm, medium-pace or slow-lob bowler. He played in the first two Tests of all, both at Melbourne, 1877. Robust, tall and bulky, he prompted one of Tom Emmett's classic 'cracks': he likened the slender Louis Hall and Armitage to 'Law and Gospel', and when his fellow-cricketer, the Rev. E.S. Carter, asked him for an explanation, he replied, 'Shadow and Substance'. In 53 matches for Yorkshire between 1872 and 1878 he made 1,074 runs (13.59) and took 119 wickets (14.08). He died in Chicago.

Test matches (2): 33 runs (11.00) and 0-15

ARNOLD, Edward George (1876-1942)

Devon and Worcestershire

A long, loose-limbed all-rounder, Ted Arnold was a right-handed batsman, strong in defence and a powerful stroke-player all round the wicket; a right-arm bowler above medium pace, who would vary his speed intelligently; and a safe field. Starting with Devon at sixteen, he joined Worcestershire two years later and helped to raise his adopted county to first-class rank in 1899. In four consecutive seasons he achieved the 'double' of a thousand runs and a hundred wickets, and in 1903/4 was an integral part of P.F. Warner's team in Australia that regained the Ashes. Only Rhodes enjoyed greater success than Arnold, who secured 18 wickets (26.38) in the series.

First-class career (1899-1913): 15,853 runs (29.91) including 24 centuries, 1,069 wickets (23.14) and 187 catches

Test matches (10): 160 runs (13.33), 31 wickets (25.41) and 8 catches

ARNOLD, Geoffrey Graham (b.1944)

Surrey, Sussex and Orange Free State

Geoff Arnold – 'Orse' to his fellow players – was a master of the art of swing and cut, and for most of the period in which he played for England, 1967 to 1975, was as dangerous a new-ball bowler as any in the country. Strongly built, yet prone to injury, his effectiveness was reduced more drastically than most by clear blue skies and lifeless pitches. In these conditions, lacking extreme pace and despite exceptional accuracy, he could look ordinary and on three major overseas tours achieved little success apart from one outstanding return of 6 for 45 at Delhi, where the ball often swings a great deal. But in overcast conditions or on a green pitch his late out-swing and prodigious cut off the seam in either direction undermined the best batsmen: Boycott, for example, seldom survived long against him in these conditions. Against Australia at Old Trafford in 1972 he had three slip catches dropped off him in successive balls. His reaction was remarkably phlegmatic although on another occasion he was disciplined for abusing an umpire. A straightforward character and a friendly family man, he seldom gives the public the impression that cricket is anything other than a stern job of work. He was an outstanding all-round games player and had the batting ability to develop into a genuine all-rounder but seldom got enough opportunity at The Oval. Despite making 59 in only his second Test, against Pakistan in 1967, he became no more than an occasionally useful tail-ender. 'Orse made his debut for Surrey in 1963, was capped four years later and collected a £15,000 benefit in 1976. He played in the South African Currie Cup for the Orange Free State in 1976/7 and moved to Sussex in 1978. The pitches at

Geoff Arnold

Hove often proved more helpful to his skilful fast-medium bowling than the bland Oval pitches of the seventies and he enjoyed a successful extension to his career, helping considerably towards a sustained improvement in Sussex's fortunes and to victory in the 1978 Gillette Cup final. His best figures remain his 8 for 41 (13 for 128 in the match) for Surrey against Gloucestershire at The Oval in 1967 when he took 109 wickets (18.22). He did the hat-trick for Surrey against Leicestershire at Leicester in 1974.

First-class career (1963-82): 3,952 runs (13.67), 1,130 wickets (21.91) and 122 catches
Test matches (34): 421 runs (12.02), 115 wickets (28.29) and 9 catches

ARNOLD, John (b.1907)

Oxfordshire and Hampshire

John Arnold was Hampshire's outstanding opening batsman during the second decade of the inter-war period. He was a fine attacker, employing some brilliant strokes, and was undisturbed by fast bowling. He was also a quick mover in the field, especially at cover, as befitted an Association Footballer with Southampton and Fulham who was capped for England. A double international, he appeared once also for England at cricket, scoring 0 and 34 in the first Test against New Zealand in England, at Lord's in 1931. On retirement he became a first-class umpire.

First-class career (1929-50): 21,831 runs (32.82) including 37 centuries, and 17 wickets (69.52)

ASTILL, William Ewart (1888-1948)

Leicestershire

One of the best cricketers never to play a Test against Australia. Ewart Astill was a mainstay of the county side season after season and, indeed, with George Geary he virtually carried the side upon his shoulders between the two World Wars. He was an orthodox right-handed batsman without mannerism or oddity. As an off-spin bowler he had an enviable ease with a lolloping run and tireless wheel of the arm and could spin acutely even on true surfaces. He was also first-rate in the slips or gully. From 1921 until 1930 he achieved the double each season except 1927. In 1935 he was the first Leicestershire professional to be appointed county captain. He appeared in nine Tests, all abroad. An excellent pianist, vocalist, banjoist and billiard player, he was, especially on tour, an amusing singer of songs to his own ukulele accompaniment.

First-class career (1906-39): 22,731 runs (22.55) including 15 centuries, 2,432 wickets (23.76) and 464 catches
Test matches (9): 190 runs (12.66), 25 wickets (34.24) and 7 catches

ATHEY, Charles William Jeffrey (b.1957)

Yorkshire

A small, fair-haired right-handed batsman of wiry build, useful medium-paced bowler and brilliant outfielder, Bill Athey made an impressive start for Yorkshire in 1976, soon hitting form with 131 against Sussex. Four years later, he scored 1,000 runs for the first time during a consistent season for Yorkshire but made a disappointing start to his Test career, having been talked of as the next in line to Sutcliffe, Hutton and Boycott. After playing with great flair in a one-day international against Australia, he was selected for the 1980 Centenary Test but failed in trying circumstances. Not originally selected to tour the West Indies under Ian Botham early in 1981, he was called from a coaching job in Australia to join a team stricken by various tribulations. In four Test innings against ferocious fast bowling, he managed only seven runs but his speed in the field won frequent applause. Despite these initial failures, he remains respected in county cricket as a fine player of fast bowling, and he seems sure to come again.

First-class career (1976-): 6,045 runs (27.98) including 11 centuries, 18 wickets (52.77), 135 catches and 2 stumpings
Test matches (4): 17 runs (2.83) and 2 catches

ATTEWELL, William (1861-1927)

Nottinghamshire

William Attewell, a right-arm, medium-paced bowler of exceptional accuracy, could bowl for long spells without tiring. He was also a useful late-order batsman and a good field at cover-point. He played first for his county during the 'Nottingham Schism' of 1881 when many leading players went on strike; immediately he strengthened the attack and for sixteen years was an integral part of the side. He took a hundred wickets in a season ten times, and visited Australia three times, taking 53 wickets (11.05) in first-class matches on his second visit in 1887/8. He became an umpire on retirement.

First-class career (1881-1900): 8,086 runs (14.04) including 1 century, 1,949 wickets (15.34) and 349 catches
Test matches (10): 150 runs (16.66), 27 wickets (23.18) and 9 catches

BAILEY, Trevor Edward (b.1923)

Cambridge University and Essex

A cricketer and personality of immense character, Trevor Bailey, like his predecessor, J.H.W.T. Douglas, enjoyed a reputation as a tough competitor, but unlike Douglas never became England captain (except in a BBC computer Test!). Bailey played for Dulwich, Cambridge, Essex and England, and was an outstanding right-arm, fast-medium bowler. He was a brilliant fielder and a dour batsman (mainly by nature, partly through necessity) who earned the sobriquet 'Barnacle', though he could score quickly when the occasion demanded it. He positively relished crises and rearguard actions. At least twice during the 1953 series with Australia, England owed her survival to him – notably at Lord's where he and Watson batted for most of the last day, Bailey making 71 in four and a quarter hours. In the last Test at Sabina Park in the Caribbean, 1953/4, the West Indies were batting first on a fine wicket on a burning hot day, after Hutton had lost the toss, and this time Bailey was the destroyer, taking 7 for 34 in 16 overs. He achieved the double eight times and served his county as captain and secretary for many years. With his lovely high action and complete command of swing and cut he was better to watch as a bowler than as a batsman. He also got a Cambridge blue for soccer. Nowadays he is a popular, astringent authority on the game for the *Financial Times* and on the BBC's radio programme, 'Test Match Special'.

First-class career (1945-67): 28,642 runs (33.42) including 28 centuries, 2,082 wickets (23.13) and 425 catches
Test matches (61): 2,290 runs (29.74) including 1 century, 132 wickets (29.21) and 32 catches

Trevor Bailey

BAIRSTOW, David Leslie (b.1951)

Yorkshire and Griqualand West

Red-haired, a chunkily built but very acrobatic wicket-keeper in the Godfrey Evans mould, and a determined and hard-hitting right-handed batsman, David Bairstow is a wholehearted extrovert and enthusiast. After making his county debut in 1970 while still a Bradford schoolboy, he got his first chance at international level when he was called to Australia in 1978/9 to replace the injured Roger Tolchard. He won his first Test cap against India at The Oval in 1979, making 9 and 59 and taking 3 catches, doing quite enough to ensure a place as Bob Taylor's deputy wicket-keeper in Australia in 1979/80. Bairstow did not play in any of the three Tests on this tour but was a valuable member of the England side in the one-day internationals, making many useful contributions with his pugnacious batting. He again showed his value with the bat when making top score of 40 against the fierce West Indies attack in the fifth Test at Headingley in 1980 and played in the Centenary Test against Australia at Lord's, but after an untidy performance behind the stumps at Bridgetown on the tour of West Indies which followed, he was not considered again for England. In 1981 he became the first Yorkshire wicket-keeper since Arthur Wood to score 1,000 runs in a season. In the 1971 Roses match Bairstow caught six Lancashire batsmen in the first innings and three in the second. He played some professional soccer for Bradford City.

First-class career (1970–): 8,396 runs (23.25) including 3 centuries, and 785 dismissals (684 ct, 101 st.)
Test matches (4): 125 runs (20.83) and 13 dismissals (12 ct, 1 st.)

BAKEWELL, Alfred Harry (1908-83)

Northamptonshire

A great batsman and fielder was locked up inside 'Fred' Bakewell but, in some ways, he was his own worst enemy. His right-handed batsmanship had authority and, although his stance was ugly – wide, straggling, rather crouched and very open – he had no fear of bowlers. In a small innings of 30 he would reveal every stroke in the book. Essentially a stroke-maker, not a compiler of runs, his footwork was nimble and he was an especially strong and daring off-driver. A specialist short-leg, he was almost worth playing for his fielding alone. As a change-bowler he met with some success. On his county debut he held 5 catches against Essex at Kettering, 1928, and in the return at Leyton held 8 catches. In successive matches in 1933 he made the then record score by a Northamptonshire batsman – 246 against Nottinghamshire at Northampton and 257 against Glamorgan at Swansea. In that season he also hit the then highest aggregate, 1,952 runs, and over 2,000 in all matches including 107 in the Test against the West Indies at The Oval. Throughout his career he was consistently effective against touring sides and, although he never appeared in a Test against Australia, he represented England with success against other countries and toured India, 1933/4, in MCC's first Test-playing tour of the sub-continent. His last match of all was at Chesterfield against Derbyshire, the champions of 1936, when Northamptonshire were bottom of the Table. He hit a chanceless 241 not out, and the champion county very nearly lost. On the way home he was involved in a car accident, and was never able to play first-class cricket again.

First-class career (1928-36): 14,570 runs (33.98) including 31 centuries, 22 wickets (57.77) and 267 catches
Test matches (6): 409 runs (45.44) including 1 century, 0-8 and 3 catches

BALDERSTONE, John Christopher (b.1940)

Yorkshire and Leicestershire

Had the financial reward of cricket been greater, Chris Balderstone would probably have given less of the prime years of his athletic life to football, which he played professionally for Huddersfield, Carlisle and Doncaster, and as a result might have won more than his two Test caps. He was unlucky to be picked for England against one of the most fearsome fast bowling attacks in Test history – the 1976 West Indians. He is a brave, sound, dependable, right-hand bat with the ability to concentrate for long periods and has been a key member of the strong Leicestershire side of the 1970s in both three-day and one-day cricket. He is also an excellent fielder whose one catch in Test cricket was a brilliant diving effort following an unexpected lapse. A flighty, left-arm spinner who can be relied on to take wickets on a turning pitch, he was shrewdly used by Ray Illingworth, whom he followed to Leicester from his native Yorkshire in 1971. Chris Balderstone has always been a model professional, dedicated and untemperamental and he was therefore a sound choice to take on the duties of the chairman of the Cricketers' Association, the representative body of the professional players in Britain.

First-class career (1961–): 14,615 runs (33.98) including 23 centuries, 298 wickets (25.86) and 167 catches
Test matches (2): 39 runs (9.75), 1 wicket (80.00) and 1 catch

BARBER, Robert William (b.1935)

Cheshire, Cambridge University, Lancashire and Warwickshire

Bob Barber was one of the few England opening batsmen to spend a tour of Australia almost exclusively on the attack, but he retired early owing to the claims of business. He was a left-handed batsman with a superb array of strokes, a talented leg-break bowler and an excellent field in the leg-trap. At his school, Ruthin, he achieved the double and also played for Lancashire. He won blues at Cambridge for cricket and the javelin, endured a stormy passage as captain of Lancashire and reached his best form for Warwickshire. Utterly fearless against fast bowling, he changed quite suddenly from a cautious batsman into one who would attack from the start. He was an early hero of Gillette Cup cricket, winning four Man-of-the-Match awards and at one time making more runs in the competition than anyone else. For his new county, Warwickshire, he hit a brilliant hundred against the West Indies side who had humbled England in 1963, and the following year made a hundred before lunch on the first day against Australia. He had a Test average of 72.50 in South Africa in 1964/5, and in the Test at Sydney in 1965/6 hit a memorable 185, which remained his highest; on the latter tour he scored 1,001 runs (50.05). His best bowling was 7 for 35 for Lancashire against Derbyshire at Chesterfield in 1960. It was typical of his adventurous and independent

Bob Barber

spirit that he should have taken part, in 1980, in an arduous mountaineering expedition in the Himalayas.

First-class career (1954-69): 17,631 runs (29.43) including 17 centuries, 549 wickets (29.46) and 209 catches
Test matches (28): 1,495 runs (35.59) including one century, 42 wickets (43.00) and 21 catches

BARBER, Wilfred (1901-68)

Yorkshire

Wilf Barber, or 'Tiddley-push', was a text-book right-handed batsman. His speciality was to the off and, with his solid defence, he exercised a restraint typical of Yorkshire's opening batsmen. He was a first-rate outfield. During his years with the county Yorkshire were champions on eight occasions. His best year was 1935 when he exceeded 2,000 runs, hitting his highest score, 255 off Surrey at Bramall Lane, and playing for England twice against South Africa. That winter he was senior professional with MCC's 'goodwill' side to Australasia. On retirement he became a coach and groundsman to a school in Harrogate.

First-class career (1926-47): 16,402 runs (34.38) including 29 centuries, and 16 wickets (26.18)
Test matches (2): 83 runs (20.75), 1-0 and 1 catch

BARLOW, Graham Derek (b.1950)

Middlesex

Graham Barlow had an influence on England's Test cricket much stronger than his modest figures would suggest. The brilliance and aggressiveness of his fielding at cover and mid-wicket, in tandem with Derek Randall, saved countless runs and helped to usher in a period when much of England's success was due to the high standard of the fielding, giving extra confidence to the bowlers. An open, cheerful and amusing character, Barlow's cricket always has an engaging vitality, and at his best his rugged left-handed batting is punishing and authoritative. His rapid improvement in 1976 when he scored 1,478 runs at an average of just under fifty, and usually at a brisk pace, had much to do with Middlesex's first Championship win since 1947. On the tour to India, Sri Lanka and Australia the following winter he scored hundreds in his first two innings in India and finished top of the tour averages with 51, but unusual nervousness and a relatively loose defence have proved fatal in his three Test appearances to date. He gained further experience during coaching assignments in both Australia and South Africa, and in 1981 scored 1,233 runs in the Championship.

First-class career (1969-): 8,402 runs (34.15) including 15 centuries, 3 wickets (17.33) and 96 catches
Test matches (3): 17 runs (4.25)

BARLOW, Richard Gorton (1851-1919)

Lancashire

Cricket was the absorbing interest of Dick Barlow's life. He kept himself in first-rate condition and was always capable of doing his best; no day was too long for him. He was first among right-handed batsmen of the extremely steady or stonewalling school, using forward play excessively in defence. He was also a left-arm, medium-pace bowler, possessing implicit faith in accuracy of length, and he was a sure fieldsman. He and his captain, A.N. Hornby, were well-contrasted opening batsmen of some 'box-office' appeal, whose partnership was immortalized in verse. Barlow paid three visits to Australia and did not miss a single match. In Tests he was always doing something useful; his steadiness with the bat at Old Trafford in 1886 pulled England through on a crumbling wicket, and he took 7 for 44 in the second innings. At Trent Bridge in 1884, for North of England against the Australians, he had the game of his life, scoring 10 and 101 and taking 10 for 48 in the match. On retirement he became a much respected Test match umpire. A quiet, neighbourly man, his home was a complete cricket museum. His marriage, like that of many a wandering cricketer, was not a success.

First-class career (1871-91): 10,732 runs (20.11) including 4 centuries, and 805 wickets (14.67)
Test matches (17): 591 runs (22.73), 34 wickets (22.55) and 14 catches

BARNES, Sydney Francis (1873-1967)

Warwickshire, Staffordshire and Lancashire

A large proportion both of those who watched and of those who played against Sydney Barnes, especially on big occasions, have no hesitation in naming this dark, brooding, gaunt, almost cadaverous-faced man as the best bowler ever. In all Test match series in which he played and was free from illness or injury, his bowling was strong and subtle enough to settle matters in England's favour. Tall, with a back as straight as a shield, he was a right-arm, medium-fast bowler who made devastating use of the seam and shine of a new ball, and combined swing and cut so subtly with spin that few batsmen could distinguish one from the other. He made a name in the days when one new ball had to suffice for the whole innings. He had a splendid upright action after a shortish, springy approach, and his phenomenal successes stemmed from a powerful frame, immense stamina and large hands as strong as steel. An aloof man of independent outlook, he seemed more at home in League cricket. After several appearances for Warwickshire with moderate success, he served as a professional in the Lancashire League, and at the Old Trafford nets impressed A.C. Maclaren who invited him to tour Australia with his team, 1901/2. After a successful tour and despite some injury, he had two full seasons with Lancashire. Then, when relations fell short of cordiality, he returned to League cricket, devoting much time on home territory in Staffordshire Leagues, and returned at intervals to England's Test and touring teams straight from the League. In Australia, 1911/12, he took 34 wickets (22.88); in the 1912 Triangular Tournament against Australia and South Africa, he took 39 wickets (10.35); and in South Africa, 1913/14, in four of the five Tests, took 49 wickets (10.93) at the age of forty. Until his sixties he continued to achieve distinction in local League cricket and also appeared in the occasional first-class match for a variety of teams, including Wales. In 132 first-class matches he took five or more wickets in an innings on sixty-eight occasions.

Sydney Barnes

First-class career (1894-1930): 1,573 runs (12.78) and 719 wickets (17.09)
Test matches (27): 242 runs (8.06), 189 wickets (16.43) and 12 catches

BARNES, William (1851-99)

Nottinghamshire

A right-handed batsman, Billy Barnes was a strong off-side player who liked to keep things moving. He was also a medium-pace bowler, one of the best change-bowlers in England, besides being a fine close field. Over six feet tall, he had a long reach but an unbecoming style. He could be a brilliant batsman – in 1880 he became the first Nottinghamshire player to reach 1,000 runs in a season – but he was not as patient as Arthur Shrewsbury or William Gunn. He played in the first Test against Australia in England in 1880, and in the second in 1882, when England lost by 7 runs in the match that gave rise to the Ashes. Three times he visited Australia and until 1890 was nearly always a first choice for England. He found the discipline of county cricket irksome and was warned not to arrive at matches the worse for liquor. On one occasion he staggered out to the wicket and made a saving hundred for his county, and afterwards, on being reprimanded by the committee, said, 'How many of you gentlemen could make a hundred, drunk *or* sober?' On retiring from the game he became, perhaps appropriately, landlord of an inn.

First-class career (1875-94): 15,425 runs (23.20) including 21 centuries, 903 wickets (17.13), 334 catches and 3 stumpings
Test matches (21): 725 runs (23.38) including 1 century, 51 wickets (15.54) and 19 catches

BARNETT, Charles John (b.1910)

Gloucestershire

Charlie Barnett first appeared for his county at sixteen in 1927, coming to the fore in 1933 with 2,280 runs (40.71). An opening, right-handed batsman of vigour and imagination, he was specially adept at driving and square-cutting. Barnett shared in many brilliant and prolific partnerships with Walter Hammond. He was prepared to cut the ball in the first over of a Test; a little more caution, perhaps, would have stood him in better stead with the selectors. He hit eleven sixes in his 194 against Somerset at Bath, 1934. He visited Australia, 1936/7, and his century at Adelaide was a nobly aggressive innings. When he hit 126 against Australia at Trent Bridge, 1938, he reached his century off the first ball after lunch on the first day. He was a fast-medium change-bowler of no mean ability and a very reliable outfielder. His father, C.S., and uncle, E.P., both played for Gloucestershire.

First-class career (1927-53): 25,389 runs (32.71) including 48 centuries, 394 wickets (30.97) and 318 catches
Test matches (20): 1,098 runs (35.41) including 2 centuries, 0-93 and 14 catches

BARRATT, Frederick (1894-1947)

Nottinghamshire

Fred Barratt was a burly coal-miner turned right-arm fast bowler. After taking more than a hundred wickets in his initial season of first-class cricket, 1914, he was slow in finding his form again after the War, but he did so and, developing also as a powerful and effective hitter, achieved the double in 1928. Touring Australasia with MCC, 1929/30, he played in the first-ever Test matches against New Zealand; the previous season he appeared once against South Africa. Against Sussex at Trent Bridge in 1924, he sent a bail 38 yards in bowling a batsman out. At soccer he represented Aston Villa and Sheffield Wednesday as a full-back.

First-class career (1914-32): 6,445 runs (15.53) including 2 centuries, and 1,224 wickets (22.71)
Test matches (5): 28 runs (9.33), 5 wickets (47.00) and 2 catches

BARRINGTON, Kenneth Frank (1930-81)

Berkshire and Surrey

One of the true cricketing heroes of recent times, Ken Barrington devoted much of his life to the cause of English cricket. The son of a regular soldier, he batted for England as if the country's future depended on his success – and, in cricketing terms, it often did. A little under medium height, he was stockily built with features of considerable strength, notably a nose and a chin which might have been hewn from granite. He possessed a full array of powerful strokes, but used them only when he was sure it was safe to do so. He had to fight his way into both the Surrey and the England sides and seldom, if ever, returned to the pavilion as a result of an ill-judged shot, although he delighted often in reaching three figures with a six. Wally Grout said that he always seemed to walk to the wicket with a Union Jack trailing behind. He was a useful but under-used leg-break and googly bowler and on the 1964/5 tour took 7 for 40 for MCC against Griqualand West at Kimberley. He revelled in bowling as a coach when testing the England team in the nets. He was also a

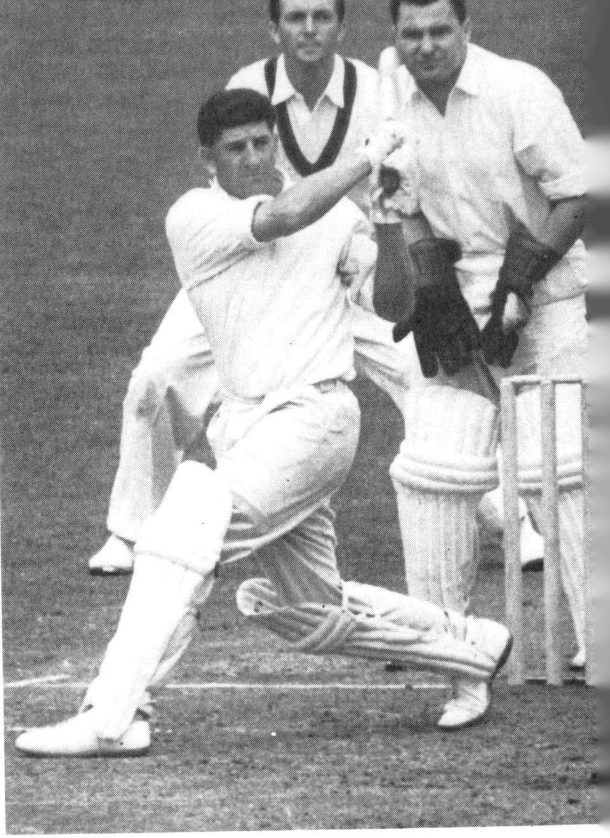

Ken Barrington – Australians Barry Jarman keeping wicket, and Richie Benaud at slip

thoroughly dependable fielder. He first played for England in 1955, the year he won his Surrey cap, making 0, 34 (top score) and 18 against South Africa. At this stage he was a flowing strokeplayer, but he disciplined himself and by the time that he returned to England colours (and no one ever wore them with greater pride) in 1959, he was one of the hardest men in the world to dig out. A regular tourist, he made 1,329 runs (69.94) in India and Pakistan, 1961/2, 1,763 runs (80.13) in Australia and New Zealand, 1962/3, and 1,128 runs (86.76) in South Africa, 1964/5. In England he exceeded 1,000 runs in a season twelve times. His highest score was 256 in eleven hours and twenty-five minutes against Australia at Old Trafford in 1964 – his first Test century in England after nine abroad and England's highest at Old Trafford – and in his next match, against Nottinghamshire at The Oval, he scored 207. A cheerful, witty man and skilful mimic, he was also thoughtful, sensitive and conscientious. He suffered a mild heart attack whilst competing in a double-wicket tournament in Australia in 1968, and retired from first-class cricket as a result. In later years he was an able Test selector and a popular manager of England touring teams. It was as assistant manager and coach of the England team in the West Indies in 1981 that he died suddenly in Barbados. It was a grievous blow to English cricket and he was mourned throughout the cricket world.

First-class career (1953-68): 31,714 runs (45.63) including 76 centuries, 273 wickets (32.61) and 511 catches
Test matches (82): 6,806 runs (58.67) including 20 centuries, 29 wickets (44.82) and 58 catches

BARTON, Victor Alexander (1867-1906)

Kent and Hampshire

Victor Barton was bought out of the army, where he was a bombadier in the Royal Artillery, to play county cricket. An attractive right-handed batsman, few men drove more powerfully to the on. He was also a useful change-bowler. He hit 205 for Hampshire against Sussex at Hove in 1900, but poor health made his retirement imperative two years later. In 1891/2 he toured South Africa with W.W. Read's side, scoring 23 in his sole Test at Cape Town.

First-class career (1889-1902): 6,387 runs (25.48) including 6 centuries, and 141 wickets (28.64)

BATES, William (1855-1900)

Yorkshire

Billy Bates's brilliant career was closed when he received a blow in the eye at net practice on the Melbourne ground in 1887; his sight was permanently injured. Then at the height of his powers, he was a brilliant, cavalier right-handed batsman and a first-rate slow, round-arm bowler, commanding both a high degree of spin and an immaculate length. It was only his uncertain catching that prevented him being chosen to play against Australia in his own country. He toured Australia five times and America once. He was the first Englishman to perform the hat-trick against Australia. This was in the second Test, at Melbourne, in 1882/3, for Hon. Ivo Bligh's side, when he took 14 for 102, England winning after two recent defeats. Sartorially elegant, he was a fine vocalist and his rendering of 'The Bonny Yorkshire Lass' fascinated the King of the Sandwich Islands so much that he asked him to sing it time and again on the voyage to Australia. His son was W.E. Bates (Yorkshire and Glamorgan) and his grandson was manager of Southampton F.C.

First-class career (1877-87): 10,214 runs (21.54) including 10 centuries, and 860 wickets (17.02)
Test matches (15): 656 runs (27.33), 50 wickets (16.42) and 9 catches

BEAN, George (1864-1923)

Nottinghamshire and Sussex

George Bean was a fast-scoring right-handed batsman, especially on dry wickets, and was well-suited to the Hove ground, where, due to short boundaries and a fast outfield, he obtained numberless fours. He was a useful medium-pace bowler and above average at cover-point. In 1891/2 he went to Australia with Lord Sheffield's side, playing in the three Tests. Except for one other season the remainder of his career was an anti-climax. At the time of his death, he was the senior member of MCC's ground staff.

First-class career (1885-98): 8,634 runs (20.71) including 9 centuries, 260 wickets (27.28) and 145 catches
Test matches (3): 92 runs (18.40) and 4 catches

BEDSER, Alexander Victor (b.1918)

Surrey

Alec Bedser was born within minutes of his identical twin brother, Eric, who was a talented county all-rounder. He began his illustrious Test career with 11 wickets from each of his first two Tests against India in 1946. Until 1954 he seemed to be carrying the burden of England's fortunes in the field on his broad shoulders, and willingly, too, for he loved bowling. He was a leading player in Surrey's run of Championship victories from 1952 to 1958. In a long career he left the field of play only once, during a Test match in a heat wave at Adelaide. He went to the edge of the boundary to vomit, then returned to carry on bowling. Bedser was a truly great medium-fast bowler, likened by many to Maurice Tate. He had a model action: a relatively short approach, late turn of a powerful body, high arm and full follow-through. His stock ball was

Alec Bedser

the in-swinger, often with his huge right hand cutting across the seam at the moment of release. The leg-cutter was his most feared delivery: on helpful pitches it became effectively a fast leg-break. Sir Donald Bradman considers him, in some conditions, the most difficult bowler he batted against. His batting was wooden but straight, and often useful, especially in the role of nightwatchman, as when he made 79 against Australia at Headingley in 1948. His catching was eminently safe. Intensely loyal, patriotic and committed, and with trenchant conservative views, he served England as a selector for a record period, starting as a member of the committee in 1962 and being chairman from 1969 until 1981, during which time England played seven Ashes series against Australia and lost only two of them. He was a popular assistant manager to the Duke of Norfolk during the MCC tour of Australia in 1962/3 and manager of the 1974/5 and 1979/80 teams in Australia. The ethics of hard work and clean living have never had a sterner champion, and they have served him well, both in his cricket career and as a successful businessman. He remains inseparable from his identical twin and only their friends can distinguish between them.

First-class career (1939-60): 5,735 runs (14.51) including 1 century, 1,924 wickets (20.41) and 289 catches
Test matches (51): 714 runs (12.75), 236 wickets (24.89) and 26 catches

BERRY, Robert (b.1926)

Lancashire, Worcestershire and Derbyshire

An orthodox, left-arm, spin bowler from the Lancashire and Cheshire League, Bob Berry harnessed length to flight and spin, and was a much better bowler than his figures suggested. Tired of fighting for a regular place alongside other spinners in the Lancashire team, he migrated to other counties. He was a deep field with a good arm. He toured Australia and New Zealand with Freddie Brown's side, 1950/51, but was not selected for any of the Tests.

First-class career (1948-62): 1,463 runs (7.58) and 703 wickets (24.73)
Test matches (2): 6 runs (3.00), 9 wickets (25.33) and 2 catches

BINKS, James Graham (b.1935)

Yorkshire and Lincolnshire

Jimmy Binks was a polished, unassuming professional playing in 412 consecutive Championship matches for Yorkshire. Possibly even better standing up to the wicket than he was standing back, he was a highly skilled but often underrated wicket-keeper, the Bob Taylor of his day. He dismissed 107 batsmen in 1960 (96 ct, 11 st.), his total of catches setting a new record for a season. Against India, 1963/4, in his only Tests, he opened the batting three times in four innings with J.B. Bolus. He was normally a useful lower-order batsman with his county, and his highest score was 95 against Middlesex, at Lord's. He flew out to India and Pakistan in 1961/2, as a replacement wicket-keeper for John Murray.

First-class career (1955-75): 6,910 runs (14.73) and 1,071 dismissals (895 ct, 176 st.)
Test matches (2): 91 runs (22.75) and 8 catches

BIRD, Morice Carlos (1888-1933)

Lancashire and Surrey

Scoring two separate centuries as Harrow's captain in the Eton and Harrow match, 1907, Morice Bird captained Surrey for two seasons and toured South Africa with MCC in 1909/10 and 1913/14. In his rather meteoric career he was a fine, forcing, right-handed batsman, strong on the off, both in driving and cutting, and a good medium-pace bowler. He later coached at Harrow and at The Oval.

First-class career (1907-21): 6,920 runs (23.94) and 149 wickets (25.69)
Test matches (10): 280 runs (18.66), 8 wickets (15.00) and 5 catches

BIRKENSHAW, Jack (b.1940)

Yorkshire, Leicestershire and Worcestershire

Jack Birkenshaw was a great team man and tourist. Fair-haired and small, he presented a neat appearance, whether as left-handed batsman with a fine cover-drive or when sidling up to the wicket to bowl his right-arm 'tweakers'. He was a safe slip field, but his main strength lay in bowling; an orthodox, right-arm, slow, off-break bowler, he had a light-footed, springy approach and a high action, combining accuracy with subtle variations of flight and spin. He played for Yorkshire between 1958 and 1960 without winning a cap but his move to Leicestershire in 1961 paid mutual dividends. His county captain, Ray Illingworth, unwittingly restricted his chances, first for Yorkshire and later for England. 'Birky's' handful of Tests have all been played abroad against the West Indies, India and Pakistan, and he never once let England down. He is a dry humorist off the field and a determined fighter on it. He was released by Leicestershire after the 1980 season and joined Worcestershire for one year before becoming a first-class umpire.

First-class career (1958-81): 12,780 runs (23.57) including 4 centuries, 1,073 wickets (27.28) and 318 catches
Test matches (5): 148 runs (21.14), 13 wickets (36.07) and 3 catches

BLIGH, Hon. Ivo Francis Walter (8th Lord Darnley) (1859-1927)

Cambridge University and Kent

A tall man, Bligh was a right-handed batsman with a fine drive and, until handicapped by illness, a first-rate outfield or point. He batted well at Eton and Cambridge, where he won his blue and was a member of the side that defeated the Australians in 1878. For Kent he hit a brilliant century against Surrey at The Oval in 1880 but his health allowed him to play for his county only from 1877 until 1883. He captained the team to Australia, 1882/3, which retrieved 'the ashes of English cricket' thus avenging the historic defeat at The Oval in 1882 when English Cricket 'died' and its body was cremated. The exact origins of the Ashes have been disputed by historians but Bligh met his future wife, Florence Morphy, during the tour and on his death she presented the famous urn to MCC. Bligh had succeeded to the title of Lord Darnley. A genial and kind-hearted man, he retained his intense interest in the game, serving as president of MCC (in 1900) and of Kent C.C.C.

First-class career (1877-83): 2,642 runs (20.64) including 2 centuries
Test matches (4): 62 runs (10.33) and 7 catches

BLYTHE, Colin (1879-1917)

Kent

'Charlie' Blythe was one of the greatest slow left-arm bowlers. In accuracy and flight he was masterly and in style he was rhythmic and graceful; there were a few dancing steps, a long last stride, left arm flung behind the back, right thrown high forward to balance it, long sensitive fingers wrapped round the ball and every inch of his height in use. He bowled to a full length, so could be driven on good wickets, but he made the fullest use of any turn in the pitch. In his second county season, 1900, he took over 100 wickets in county matches alone, and he hardly ever looked back, enjoying his best season in 1909 with 215 wickets (14.54). At Northampton in 1907 he obtained 17 wickets in a day (10 for 30 and 7 for 18) and he enjoyed many other extraordinary feats. Fourteen times he exceeded a hundred wickets in a season. Artistic, highly strung and subject to epileptic fits, he found Tests emotionally trying, but he toured Australia and South Africa twice each and, at home, had a big share in England's win over Australia at Edgbaston in 1909. Two years before he had captured 26 South African wickets in the three Tests. He was killed in action in France and is remembered by a monument on Kent's home ground at Canterbury.

First-class career (1899-1914): 4,455 runs (9.91), 2,506 wickets (16.81) and 189 catches
Test matches (19): 183 runs (9.63), 100 wickets (18.63) and 6 catches

BOARD, John Henry (1867-1924)

Gloucestershire and Hawkes Bay

A fearless and untiring wicket-keeper, Jack Board was a contemporary of Dick Lilley, Bill Storer and Joe Humphries and, therefore, his appearances in representative cricket were few. A long-term county 'keeper, he also developed his batting so well that, late in his career, he exceeded 1,000 runs in a season six times. He toured Australia, 1897/8, as understudy to Storer but did not reach the Test side. He had better fortune on two tours of South Africa.

First-class career (1891-1914): 15,674 runs (19.37) including 9 centuries, and 1,206 dismissals (852 ct, 354 st.)
Test matches (6): 108 runs (10.80) and 11 dismissals (8 ct, 3 st.)

BOLUS, John Brian (b.1934)

Yorkshire, Nottinghamshire and Derbyshire

A batsman of canny technique and great resource, Brian Bolus became the third player after Bob Berry and Roy Swetman to be capped by three different first-class counties. He was also the first to captain different counties (Nottinghamshire and Derbyshire in 1972 and 1973) in successive seasons. His distinguishing features were sleek, carefully combed dark hair which turned prematurely grey and a bulbous pair of pads which he sometimes seemed to use in defence as often as his bat. Indeed, before the law governing leg-byes acquired without playing a stroke was changed, he could sometimes be seen apparently kicking the ball to the boundary! But he was also a skilful and powerful stroke-player, good off his legs, and possessing a strong square-cut and a low-slung cover-drive. He showed great courage during his brief period as a Test player, notably in 1963 against the extreme speed of Griffith and Hall, whom he on-drove for four from the first ball he received in Test cricket. In the Oval Test he drove Hall back over his head to the pavilion, a stroke which revealed character as well as talent. He was an occasional left-arm, medium-pace bowler.

First-class career (1956-75): 25,598 runs (34.03) including 39 centuries, 24 wickets (36.91) and 201 catches
Test matches (7): 496 runs (41.33), 0-16 and 2 catches

BOOTH, Major William (1886-1916)

Yorkshire

Booth was tall, good-looking and popular, and a fine, punishing, right-handed batsman and fast-medium bowler. He possessed a free, natural action, making the ball come quickly off the pitch: occasionally, his off-break was formidable, but his main strength lay in his swerve and pace. Making 1,228 runs (27.28) and taking 181 wickets (18.46) in 1913, he toured South Africa with MCC that winter, making his Test debut. A native of Pudsey (hallowed in Yorkshire cricket annals), Second-Lieutenant Booth (West Yorkshire Regiment) was a player of the richest promise; but he fell on the Somme in July 1916.

First-class career (1908-14): 4,754 runs (23.30) including 1 century, and 603 wickets (19.82)
Test matches (2): 46 runs (23.00) and 7 wickets (18.57)

BOSANQUET, Bernard James Tindal (1877-1936)

Oxford University and Middlesex

Over six foot in height, Bosanquet was a fine, upstanding, right-handed batsman, who put power into his drives and other forcing strokes with apparently little effort. At first a fast-medium bowler, he was a capable all-rounder successively at Eton, Oxford – where he won a blue – and Middlesex. But his main fame is due to being remembered as the inventor of the 'googly'. Certainly he was the first cricketer to make the googly, or 'Bosie' as Australians refer to it, a practical proposition at the highest levels. The googly is an off-break, delivered with a leg-break action from the back, rather than the front, of the hand. Bringing the ball over from a great height, Bosanquet mystified the best batsman with its flight and uncertain break. He developed the ball playing billiard fives or 'twisty grab' and experimenting with bouncing a tennis ball on a table so that his opponent seated at the other end could not catch it. 'It was not unfair; only immoral,' he said of his 'Bosie'. Trying out his new style at Lord's for Middlesex against Leicestershire in 1900, he had Sammy Coe stumped at 98. In Australia, 1903/4 – his only Test-playing tour out of six tours he made – he won the deciding Test for the rubber at Sydney, taking 6 for 51; and at Trent Bridge against Australia in 1905, he captured 8 for 107: England won convincingly. Remaining a very talented all-rounder, he took 11 for 138 and scored 103 and 100 not out against Sussex at Lord's in the same year. His son is Reginald Bosanquet, the former ITV newsreader.

First-class career (1898-1919): 11,696 runs (33.42) including 21 centuries, 629 wickets (23.81) and 191 catches
Test matches (7): 147 runs (13.36), 25 wickets (24.16) and 9 catches

BOTHAM, Ian Terence (b.1955)

Somerset

The only man to have completed a Test double of over 3,000 runs and 250 wickets, Ian Botham gained too an undisputed place amongst the supreme all-round cricketers of the game's history when in 1981 England

Ian Botham

won three Tests against Australia largely by dint of this man's herculean performances with bat and ball. Not indeed since W.G. Grace has England produced such a colossus. He has a super-abundance of all the qualities needed for success in cricket: immense natural ability, physical strength, determination, confidence, courage, luck, and an instinctive common sense. Though he failed in an almost impossible task when asked to captain England against the West Indies before his carefree, sometimes wild spirit was ready for such heavy responsibility, he quickly bounced back and continued to live life his own way, making a small fortune from advertising endorsements, driving fast cars, learning to fly his own aeroplanes, going fishing or playing Fourth Division football for Scunthorpe United – in his youth he had been offered professional terms by Crystal Palace. Yet none of this interfered with a stream of matchwinning performances on the cricket field or with his determination to see as much as possible of his wife and two children. Six feet one inch, and powerfully built, he is a brilliant, natural, attacking batsman and a superb fielder, notably in the slips; he bowls with consistent hostility from fast to medium pace and can swing the ball exceptionally in helpful conditions as well as produce wickets by an extra turn of speed when things are not in his favour. He scored 3 centuries in his first seven Tests and reached the double of a 100 Test wickets and 1,000 runs in his twenty-first Test – the least number of Tests in which any bowler has reached this goal. Born in Cheshire of parents hailing from the East Yorkshire/North Lincolnshire area, Botham married a girl from the same area and now has a home near Doncaster as well as one in Somerset where his parents moved before he was three and where he was brought up. After proving an outstanding games player at school near Yeovil, he joined the MCC ground staff at Lord's and first played for Somerset in the John Player League in 1973 at the age of seventeen. The following year he played Somerset into the semi-finals of the Benson and Hedges Cup with an innings of brilliance and courage after being hit on the mouth by a ball from Andy Roberts. Three years later, at twenty-one, he was making his Test debut at Trent Bridge, taking five wickets against Australia on his first day at the top level. Those Australians who had seen Botham struggle to find any form in grade cricket while on a Whitbread scholarship in Melbourne the previous winter were surprised by his success and, by the time that England toured Australia, under Brearley in 1978/9, Botham was already the pivotal player in the successful England side. With 23 wickets, some superb slip catches and two outstanding attacking innings, which rescued a struggling team at Sydney and Adelaide in successive Tests, he fully justified his reputation. Known to his team mates as 'Guy the Gorilla', his toughness was already legendary. The following winter he scored a commanding 119 not out in a losing cause in the Melbourne Test and took 19 wickets in three Tests before moving to India to dominate the Jubilee Test in Bombay, scoring 114 when England were in trouble and taking 13 wickets for 106 in the match. In 1980 he was appointed England captain at the age of 24 in succession to Mike Brearley and during the season became the first England player to pass 1,500 runs and 150 wickets in Tests. But the burden of captaining England in successive series at home and away against the powerful West Indies proved too great. His phenomenal performances became ordinary, his whole demeanour lost its sparkle and aggression and off the field he was troubled by a charge of assault against a man who had provoked him in a night club: he was declared not guilty at a time when his year of misfortune had already been dramatically reversed. He continued to lead England for the first two Tests against Australia in 1981 but the first was lost and the second, in which he made a pair, was a dull draw. He resigned the captaincy which the selectors had already decided to take from him. At the same time he gave the opinion that Brearley should take over the reins again and under the latter's shrewd leadership he proceeded to transform the summer into one of the most memorable in the history of the game. The Ashes appeared to be on their way back to Australia in the third Test at Headingley when Botham, who had already taken six wickets for 95 in Australia's first innings and scored 50 of England's first innings 174, came in at 105 for five. England, who had followed on, were still 122 runs behind and soon they were 92 behind with only three wickets left. A furious assault by Botham on a difficult pitch against hitherto rampant fast bowlers now turned the match and the series upside down. A heroic, smiling figure, bare-headed and defiant on a grey Leeds afternoon, he took England to an eventual lead of 129 by driving of staggering power. His 149 not out included a six and 27 fours. England then bowled out Australia to win the game. The following Test at Edgbaston was finally decided by a spell of five wickets for one run in 28 balls by England's inspired all-rounder and in the fifth Test at Old Trafford he lifted the 'man of the match' award for the third successive Test by playing one of the great innings of history. This time on a very good wicket England's second innings lead of 205 was by no means certain to be enough when Botham came in to bat. He played himself in quietly for a time and then unleashed another volley of blistering strokes which owed nothing to luck and everything to rare strength and skill. Only Jessop could have equalled the power of his hitting as he moved from 28 to 100 in 37 minutes, reaching three figures off his 86th ball with his fifth six. Some huge hooks off Lillee and searing drives through the offside field, straight past or straight over the bowler, will live for ever in the memory of those who watched spellbound. His 118 included 13 fours and six sixes, the most in any Test innings. England won again and Botham, who also took many fine catches, was assured of immortality. Further successes against India away in 1981 (he hit 142 in the Kanpur Test) and at home the following summer maintained his reputation as the world's best all-rounder despite strong individual challenges by India's Kapil Dev and Pakistan's Imran Khan. He scored two more centuries against India, 128 at Old Trafford and 208 at The Oval. For Somerset against Warwickshire at Taunton in 1982 he hit a century in 52 minutes off 56 balls, the fastest in the county's history and a matchwinning performance. After playing himself in, he scored 114 off his last 44 balls, including 30 off one over. Gradually his batting was becoming even more impressive than his bowling, yet in his 54 matches for England before leaving for an unsuccessful tour of Australia in 1982 he had already taken five wickets in a Test innings on twenty occasions.

First-class career (1974-): 9,415 runs (32.80) including 20 centuries, 726 wickets (24.33) and 187 catches
Test matches (54): 2,996 runs (37.92) including 11 centuries, 249 wickets (23.32) and 60 catches

BOWDEN, Montague Parker (1865-92)

Surrey and Transvaal

An Old Alleynian, Monty Bowden's right-handed batting and wicket-keeping for Surrey raised hopes which were never quite realized, although in his last home season, 1888, he hit 797 runs (31.22), making 189 not out in only 3½ hours against Sussex at The Oval. He kept for Gentlemen v. Players at Lord's and at The Oval, and for Gentlemen v. Australians at Lord's. He toured South Africa with the first-ever team, led by Major Warton, 1888/9, and when he captained England in the second Test at Cape Town (in the absence of C. Aubrey Smith) he became, at twenty-three years and 144 days, England's youngest-ever Test captain. Remaining behind in South Africa, he formed a stock-broking firm with Aubrey Smith in Johannesburg, and they both played in the first Currie Cup Challenge match, for Transvaal v. Kimberley at Kimberley, when Monty scored 63 and 126 not out, his debut in South African first-class cricket. Bitten by the pioneering 'bug', he went to Rhodesia with the Pioneer Column of Cecil Rhodes. For three years he led a very adventurous life before falling heavily from his cart and dying at Umtali hospital, a primitive first-aid station little more than a mud hut. A man with a revolver had to stand guard over the body in case lions snatched it, and Monty Bowden was buried in a coffin knocked together out of whisky cases.

First-class career (1883-90): 2,316 runs (20.14) including 3 centuries, and 72 dismissals (66 ct, 6 st.)
Test matches (2): 25 runs (12.50) and 1 catch

BOWES, William Eric (b.1908)

Yorkshire

Bill Bowes, tall, raw-boned and bespectacled, was a bowler of great ability with the new ball, having control of swing either way, although not quite as fast as some of his contemporaries. He could make the ball kick and would bowl a few bumpers to test out a batsman's nerve and technique. Sometimes (in the early thirties) he bowled leg-theory to a packed leg-field and was involved in his share of controversy, but he spearheaded Yorkshire's attack during years of great Championship success. Touring Australia with MCC's 1932/3 side, he took only one wicket in the Tests, forcing Bradman to play on the first ball at Melbourne in the second Test. But in England, against Australia in 1934 and 1938, South Africa in 1935, and West Indies in 1939, he was an integral part of the attack. Bill had an air of remoteness on the field, but underneath lay an educated, intelligent and mathematical mind. His fielding was moderate and his batting such that he took more wickets than he scored runs. During the War, in which he reached commissioned rank, he was a POW and returned, not in full health, as a medium-paced bowler for two first-class seasons. He had a very good benefit and became a cricket journalist on Yorkshire newspapers. One of his books is his autobiography, *Express Deliveries*.

Bill Bowes

First-class career (1928-47): 1,529 runs (8.58) and 1,638 wickets (16.75)
Test matches (15): 28 runs (4.66), 68 wickets (22.33) and 2 catches

BOWLEY, Edward Henry (1890-1974)

Sussex and Auckland

One of the finest back-foot, right-handed batsmen of his time, Ted Bowley would raise his left elbow quite remarkably high, pushing the ball away with almost truculent force or leaning back to square-cut for four from right in front of his off-stump. Very quick on his feet, he could also drive powerfully off the front foot. He stiffened his county's batting and adapted himself as an opening batsman. A more than useful change-bowler, he was always liable to get wickets, tossing up deceptively flighted right-arm spinners; and as a slip field he was superb. He reached 1,000 runs in a season fifteen times and he shared in fifteen partnerships exceeding 200, most notably 490 with John Langridge, opening for Sussex against Middlesex at Hove in 1933. Several great opening batsmen – from Hobbs and Sutcliffe down – stood in his way for representative honours, and he never played against Australia. But, as a veteran, he appeared against South Africa in 1929, and that winter toured Australasia with MCC, appearing in three of the earliest Tests against New Zealand, and scoring 109 at Auckland. On retirement he became an outstanding coach at Winchester.

First-class career (1912-34): 28,378 runs (34.94) including 52 centuries, 741 wickets (25.99) and 373 catches
Test matches (5): 252 runs (36.00) including 1 century, 0-116 and 2 catches

BOYCOTT, Geoffrey (b.1940)

Yorkshire and North Transvaal

One of the greatest opening batsmen in cricket history, Geoffrey Boycott followed Herbert Sutcliffe and Len Hutton as the third Yorkshire opener to score 100 first-class centuries and, on an occasion which stirred deep emotions in every Yorkshire breast, he achieved this rare feat on his home ground at Headingley in a Test match against Australia. A model of the on-driven four which took him to his century has appropriately been cast into bronze in a limited edition of statuettes. A profoundly sensitive man for whom outstanding success and world-wide fame have created intense personal problems, Boycott has aroused extraordinary passions during a controversial career. His fan club has loyal members in many countries yet his single-minded and occasionally selfish approach to cricket has sometimes caused animosity among fellow players. He was dropped by England after scoring 246 not out against India at Leeds in 1967 because the selectors felt that the innings was compiled too slowly for the good of the side. Eleven years later, after a bitter civil war in which Boycott enjoyed considerable support among the Yorkshire C.C.C. members, the committee held firm in their decision to dismiss him as club captain after eight years under his leadership, during which Yorkshire were, for many reasons, unable to win any major competitions. At times Boycott has seen the middle of a cricket ground as the one place where he can escape from the intense publicity which has hounded him. One part of his nature enjoys the limelight; the other longs to run away and hide from it. Yet no one has set his mind towards success with equal dedication and his decision to replace spectacles with contact lenses symbolized the development of a carefully cultivated public personality. Every run he has scored in a long and prolific career has been the result of a conscious act of will. A deep study of the game, a frugal life-style and a fetish for daily practice in the nets have been the hallmarks of his approach to cricket. (For many years until his mother's death he lived with her in Fitzwilliam in a simple terraced house although he was long since a man of substantial wealth.) Faults, such as an early fallibility around the off-stump, a tendency to run partners out too often and moderate fielding performances, have all been ruthlessly eradicated. Bowling in a cap, he is a useful medium-pace, in-swing bowler, though restricted by a recurrent back injury, but his main business is batting. Right-handed, five feet ten inches and with a strong, spare frame, he is especially strong square on the off-side. His runs are churned out as from a highly reliable machine. All shots are at his command but only the safe ones are used often. His first Test innings was 48 against Australia in 1964 two years after his debut for Yorkshire. He became a more or less automatic selection as England's opening batsman until going into a self-imposed exile from Test cricket in 1974. He missed thirty Tests before returning against Australia in 1977, with scores of 107, 80, 191, 39 and 25. In the 1970/71 series against Australia he scored 657 runs and his total aggregate of Test runs for England has been exceeded only by Cowdrey, Hammond, Hutton and Barrington. He is one of a select group – Barrington, Cowdrey and Dexter are the other members – who have scored centuries against all the other six Test-playing countries. In 1971 he scored 2,503 runs at first-class level, becoming the only English batsman to average better than 100 (100.12) in a season. He repeated this feat (102.53) in 1979. His highest score is 261 not out for MCC against the West Indian Board President's XI at Bridgetown in 1974, a great though wicket-monopolizing performance early in the tour. Though his performances for Yorkshire became slightly less prolific, and he became involved in yet another controversy at the end of the 1981 season when Ray Illingworth suspended him for publicly complaining about being left out of Yorkshire's Sunday side, he continued to hold his own at Test level, scoring a particularly fine 137 against Australia in the sixth Test of 1981. This was his seventh Test hundred against Australia. He travelled to India despite some political objections because of his South African connections (he had often coached and holidayed there) but he publicly avowed his opposition to apartheid. In India in 1981/2 he scored 105 in the third Test at Delhi to pass the record of Gary Sobers and to become the highest scorer in Test history. Thereafter he seemed to lose interest in the tour and was sent home early, apparently ill. A few weeks later he appeared in shining health in South Africa as the early leader of a team of English 'mercenaries' who took on the South African team in a series disapproved of by the main governing bodies. The TCCB suspended Boycott, along with 14 other English players, for three years. Yet in 1982 this complex man

Geoff Boycott

and master batsman was once again the leading English batsman in the averages with 1,913 first-class runs (61.70).

First-class career (1962-): 42,269 runs (56.28) including 132 centuries, 44 wickets (30.90) and 220 catches
Test matches (108): 8,114 runs (47.72) including 22 centuries, 7 wickets (54.57) and 33 catches

BRADLEY, Walter Morris (1875-1944)

Kent

After doing remarkable things for Lloyd's Register – such as taking six wickets with consecutive balls against Mitcham – 'Bill' Bradley played for Kent as a protégé of Lord Harris. He had an aggressively long run with both arms flung above his thrown-back head prior to the right-arm delivery from the full reach of his six foot height. Pitching at the stumps and seldom short, he personified the attack in cricket. In a short career he played in two Tests against Australia, 1899; he was emphatically the best amateur bowler of the year with 156 wickets (19.10).

First-class career (1896-1903): 906 runs (6.09) and 624 wickets (22.64)
Test matches (2): 23 runs (23.00) and 6 wickets (38.83)

BRAUND, Leonard Charles (1875-1955)

Surrey and Somerset

Of Len Braund, C.B. Fry said, 'He was one of the greatest all-rounders – *and to think that Surrey let him go!*' Playing on and off for Surrey for three years, he joined Somerset and fought many a noble battle for them. At Taunton in 1901 Somerset were 239 in arrears when Braund and L.C.H. Palairet added 222 in two hours twenty minutes. An aggressive right-handed batsman with powerful strokes on the leg, a bowler who became much more effective on switching from fast-medium to slow-medium leg-spin, and the finest slip field in an era of remarkable slip fielders, he was a first choice for England from 1901 until 1908. There were many highlights; on his first tour of Australia, 1901/2, he averaged 36 with the bat and took 21 wickets in the Tests. In 1903/4 he hit a classic 102 at Sydney and took 8 for 81 at Melbourne. Against the South African googly attack, at Lord's in 1907, he scored 104. And in the field, darting across from slip to leg-side, he made an historic catch off George Hirst in the Edgbaston Test against Australia in 1902. Even in his last playing season he could pick slip catches off his toes, while discussing the Derby with the wicket-keeper. In retirement, a first-rate umpire for eighteen years, he was an arbiter of complete integrity, full of pleasant humour which turned away wrath. During the Second World War both his legs were amputated in turn, but such was his strength of body and spirit that he survived and attended play at Lord's in his bath chair. In 1949 he became one of the twenty-six retired professionals who were given honorary membership of MCC.

First-class career (1896-1920): 17,801 runs (25.61) including 25 centuries, 1,113 wickets (27.30) and 508 catches
Test matches (23): 987 runs (25.97) including 3 centuries, 47 wickets (38.51) and 39 catches

BREARLEY, John Michael (b.1942)

Cambridge University and Middlesex

A brain as sharp as barbed wire, allied to a sensitive and sympathetic nature and a passionate interest in the game, produced in Mike Brearley, OBE, almost the ideal captain. He was the first to acknowledge his good fortune in inheriting an improving England team at a time when some countries were weakened by the defection of leading players to Kerry Packer's World Series Cricket, and he led England to ten wins and five draws before first tasting defeat as captain against Australia at Melbourne in the New Year Test of 1979. He accepted defeat on that occasion with the same philosophical calm with which he had greeted the other of Kipling's 'two impostors' (triumph and disaster) and by the time that he had led England to an unprecedented 5-1 win in the series and come home with the Ashes, which had been regained under his leadership in England in 1977, he was being recognized as one of the greatest, if also one of the luckiest, of all captains. Clear thinking, calmness under pressure and decisiveness were his major qualities on the field, fair-mindedness and consideration for others the main ones off it. It was all the more remarkable that he retained the complete faith of his team mates despite failing to justify a place as a top England batsman. As a solid right-handed (usually opening) batsman he had the ability to stroke the ball effortlessly in his more felicitous moods as well as to work assiduously for long periods with rigid determination and concentration; he was good enough to be chosen for England in the first place as an opener capable of standing up squarely to one of the most fearsome fast bowling attacks in cricket history, the West Indies side of 1976, when Holding, Daniel, Roberts and Holder formed a truly formidable quartet. He was vice-captain to Tony Greig in the following winter and took over as captain when the latter defected to Packer. After he took on the extra responsibility, his batting became rather careworn, and, with his exaggerated early backlift and his belief in wearing copious protective 'armour', he sometimes seemed wooden. But his several useful innings at important times included a crucial 53 in a stand of 111 with Derek Randall in the fourth Test at Sydney, 1978/9, which led to England's unexpected victory and the retention of the Ashes. A wicket-keeper in his

Mike Brearley

younger days, Brearley developed into an outstanding catcher at first slip. In his four years as a Cambridge blue, 1961-4, he scored 4,348 runs, a record aggregate for a university career. He hit ten centuries and averaged 38.14. He captained Cambridge in 1963 and 1964. He won his Middlesex cap in 1964 and toured South Africa with scant success that winter. He captained MCC's Under 25 team in Pakistan in 1966/7 and averaged 132.16, scoring 312 not out against North Zone at Peshawar. But he played no cricket in England in 1966 and 1967 when he was pursuing an academic career at British and American universities. (At Cambridge he gained a first in Classics and an upper second in Moral Sciences.) From 1968 to 1970 he played only half a season's cricket but in 1971 he returned to captain Middlesex and their fortunes soon improved because Brearley was able to steer a talented, but hitherto rudderless, ship in the right direction. Middlesex won the Championship in 1976 and 1977 and the Gillette Cup in 1977. They were losing finalists in the Gillette and Benson and Hedges Cups in 1975. As a senior county captain he played a leading role in formulating policies in the administration of county cricket and, characteristically, he was fair but firm in his attitude to the formation of World Series Cricket. He opposed the victimization of those players who signed at the start for Packer but led moves to ensure that the Packer players did not have everything their own way. Brearley himself rejected a vague offer in 1977 to join Packer and recruit other members of the England team. He said of it, 'Kerry Packer is not my style. I prefer the chugging British coaster with a cargo of pig-iron to a monstrous supertanker, hurriedly constructed.' Anyone who doubted his capacity as a captain, or as a worthy Test cricketer, had to change his mind during the amazing 1981 season when Brearley was recalled to take over as captain from the beleagured Ian Botham. Largely by utilizing the latter's prodigious all-round powers, Brearley guided England from a one-nil deficit after two Tests to an eventual 3-1 win and thus again secured the Ashes. Twice, at Headingley and Edgbaston, in desperately tight, tense finishes, he pressurized the Australian batsmen by artful field-placing and by making the maximum use of his bowlers, notably of his main 'striker', Willis. The Australian barrackers who had ruthlessly harried and taunted him when England made an extra tour under his captaincy after the treaty with Kerry Packer in 1979/80 (England lost a series for which they were poorly prepared 0-3, although Brearley performed well personally as a batsman) must have squirmed as the scholar captain (and his brilliant protégé Botham) stole two matches which Australia had every right to win. Brearley's career came to an appropriate end in 1982 when he led Middlesex to another Championship, the fourth in his 11 years as captain. He left the game to develop a career as a psychotherapist, freelance writer and teacher. Having finished top in the 1964 Civil Service examination, he could have chosen almost any career but, as Rodney Hogg remarked, Brearley got a 'degree in People' and he wanted to make use of it.

First-class career (1961-82): 25,168 runs (37.84) including 45 centuries, 3 wickets (64.00), 418 catches and 12 stumpings
Test matches (39): 1,442 runs (22.88) and 52 catches

BREARLEY, Walter (1876-1937)

Lancashire

If ever a man bowled his heart, soul and fifteen stone weight, it was Walter Brearley, whose belligerency was his natural state. A right-arm fast bowler, he took a short run, with a rolling gait, and used his body to the full as he delivered. He believed that no batsman could bat – 'They are probably a lot of ruddy teetotallers, anyway!' – and he loved to see the middle stump fly. As a number eleven batsman himself, he was an inveterate jumper of pavilion gates on the way to and from his short lease of the crease. It was said that, when he hurried to the wicket at Old Trafford, the horse walked between the shafts ready to drag the heavy roller for use at the end of the innings. In the first of his handful of Tests against Australia and South Africa, spread between 1905 and 1912, he took 8 wickets at Old Trafford; Australia lost by an innings and England clinched the Ashes. He appeared for Gentlemen v. Players five times and became a notable coach.

First-class career (1902-21): 849 runs (5.97) and 844 wickets (19.31)
Test matches (4): 21 runs (7.00) and 17 wickets (21.11)

BRENNAN, Donald Vincent (b.1920)

Yorkshire

In a career sadly cut short by the claims of business, Don Brennan's brilliance in leg-side stumping rivalled that of Godfrey Evans and his talent behind the stumps was exceptional. He toured India with MCC, 1951/2, but his only Tests were in England against South Africa, 1951. One of the characters of the game, he has subsequently been a very active member on the committee of Yorkshire C.C.C.

First-class career (1947-64): 1,937 runs (10.52) and 434 dismissals (316 ct, 118 st.)
Test matches (2): 16 runs (8.00) and 1 stumping

BRIGGS, John (1862-1902)

Lancashire

Johnny Briggs was one of the best loved of Lancashire's characters, a little skip-jack of a man and a magnificent all-rounder. A cheerful, simple man, he thought life great fun and adored cricket. He was an aggressive right-handed batsman, with a penchant for a slashing drive into the vicinity of cover-point, a puzzling left-arm slow bowler with a beautifully easy action and much guile, and a swift-footed field at cover-point. He made his debut at sixteen, and hit his highest score, 186, against Surrey at Aigburth, three days after his marriage in 1885. A first choice for England, he toured Australia six times and South Africa once with the first team there, 1888/9; in the second Test at Cape Town he was unplayable with 15 for 28, England winning by an innings. He had a hat-trick and a century for England against Australia; when he took 11 for 74 in the Lord's Test of 1886, England triumphed by an innings. Also, he played a considerable part in England's story-book win at Sydney, 1894/5; Australia required only 64 to win with eight wickets standing, but England scraped home by 10 runs, thanks to the bowling of Johnny Briggs and Bobby Peel. His ending was sad. During the Test against Australia at Headingley, 1899, he suffered an epileptic seizure which is believed to have started with a blow over the heart from a drive of Tom Hayward's. He had to retire from the game and, though he

Johnny Briggs

returned to first-class cricket the following year, he had a further breakdown and died in an asylum. There, the story goes, he would imagine himself bowling up and down the ward and at the end of the day would proudly announce his bowling figures to the nurses.

First-class career (1879-1900): 14,092 runs (18.27) including 10 centuries, 2,221 wickets (15.93) and 223 catches
Test matches (33): 815 runs (18.11) including 1 century, 118 wickets (17.74) and 12 catches

BROCKWELL, William (1865-1935)

Surrey and Kimberley

An integral part of the Surrey Championship-winning side of the 1890s, Bill Brockwell was a stylish and often brilliant right-handed batsman, strong in back play and a free hitter in front of the wicket. He was also a useful medium-paced bowler, and very smart at second slip. Maturing slowly and first appearing for England against Australia in 1893, he headed the national batting averages in the wet summer of 1894 – 'Brockwell's year' – with 1,491 runs (38.23), and toured Australia that winter with A.E. Stoddart's team. He had one good Test, but generally disappointed. He continued as an excellent county player, in 1897 putting up 379 with Bobby Abel for the first wicket against Hampshire at The Oval, and in 1899 was again selected for England. An early coach overseas, he was employed both at Kimberley in South Africa and by the Maharajah of Patiala in India for some years. Though a man of parts – well-groomed, a theatregoer, photographer, writer and conversationalist – he fell on hard times after retirement and at the time of death was destitute.

First-class career (1886-1903): 13,285 runs (27.00) including 22 centuries, 553 wickets (24.74), 250 catches and 1 stumping
Test matches (7): 202 runs (16.83), 5 wickets (61.80) and 6 catches

BROMLEY-DAVENPORT, Hugh Richard (1870-1954)

Cambridge University, Cheshire and Middlesex

At Eton Bromley-Davenport was described by *Wisden* as 'the best Public School bowler of 1887'. Fast left-arm, he subsequently gained a blue at Cambridge, and played intermittently for Cheshire and Middlesex, as well as for Gentlemen v. Players. He toured the West Indies twice, Portugal once and South Africa with Lord Hawke's teams, 1895/6 and 1898/9, where he had his Test experience. He could be a useful batsman.

First-class career (1892-9): 1,540 runs (19.49) and 123 wickets (21.71)
Test matches (4): 128 runs (21.33), 4 wickets (24.50) and 1 catch

BROOKES, Dennis (b.1915)

Northamptonshire

A Yorkshireman, Dennis Brooke's beginnings with his lowly adopted county were unspectacular but, just after the Second World War, he developed into one of the finest batsmen ever to play for Northamptonshire. His stance was upright and his immaculate on-drive and elegant deflected strokes a joy to watch. He scored most of his runs in front of the wicket, largely with variations of the drive. He had 'the look of an England batsman' but he chipped a finger bone in the first Test of MCC's visit to the West Indies in 1947/8 at Barbados. This ended his participation in the tour, and he was never selected for England again. In the Test he had scored 10 and 7 and held 1 catch. He was the county's first official professional captain from 1954 until 1959, and, in his last season, captained Players against Gentlemen at Lord's. No one had made more runs for Northamptonshire alone – 28,980 (36.13), which includes at least one century off each of the first-class counties. In early days a superb outfield, latterly he fielded close in.

First-class career (1934-59): 30,874 runs (36.10) including 71 centuries, and 202 catches

BROWN, Alan (b.1935)

Kent

Alan Brown was a right-arm, fast-medium bowler with a pronounced 'drag' and an occasionally useful batsman. In his youth he was one of the fastest bowlers to have played for Kent for years, but did not fully live up to early promise. He toured India and Pakistan with MCC, 1961/2, and appeared in two of the Tests. He took four wickets in five balls against Nottinghamshire at Folkestone in 1959, and it was at Folkestone that he made his best score, 81 against Glamorgan in 1968.

First-class career (1957-70): 2,189 runs (9.72) and 743 wickets (24.64)
Test matches (2): 3 runs (—), 3 wickets (50.00) and 1 catch

BROWN, David John (b.1942)

Warwickshire

Six feet four inches tall, a great enthusiast with a never-say-die spirit, 'Big Dave' was a robust, hustling, right-arm, fast-medium bowler without a pretty action but with a suitably aggressive outlook and an ability to make the ball bounce. Red-faced and cheerful, he was popular with opponents as well as with his own team, and few bowlers tried harder. He was a safe fielder and played many stubborn tail-end innings. Many of his best performances were on five overseas tours, when hot weather and hard pitches brought out his best qualities of courage and determination. He was vice-captain of an MCC side in Pakistan in 1966/7 and captained Warwickshire from 1975 to 1977. In 1968 his 5 for 42 helped bowl out Australia for 78 at Lord's in the 200th Test between the two countries. In 1975 he took 8 for 60 for Warwickshire against Middlesex, also at Lord's, and he would have had more wickets had not most of his work been done on the benign pitch at Edgbaston. Off the field he became an enthusiastic horse-breeder and for some years acted as a wise and reasonable chairman of the Cricketers' Association. He became manager of Warwickshire in 1980 when the county won the John Player League, and briefly returned to first-class cricket in 1982 when Warwickshire were short of bowling.

First-class career (1961-82): 4,110 runs (12.26), 1,165 wickets (24.85) and 157 catches
Test matches (26): 342 runs (11.79), 79 wickets (28.31) and 7 catches

BROWN, Frederick Richard (b.1910)

Cambridge University, Surrey and Northamptonshire

Burly, red-faced, and jolly, Freddie Brown looks the archetypal country squire. A dynamic personality, he was once nicknamed 'Ginger' for pluck. He was a hard-hitting right-hand batsman, whose uninhibited straight-driving was worth a page from an Edwardian

Freddie Brown

text-book. He was also a bowler who proved effective on all sorts of wickets. Starting as a leg-spin and googly bowler, his medium-pace 'cutters' were a revelation later in his career. He was, too, an energetic and skilful fielder who as captain insisted on fielding of consistent excellence. Such was his zest for the game that, either in batting, bowling or fielding, he could transform a match. The revival of Northamptonshire cricket began after the Second World War under his captaincy. Previously, he had earned a high reputation as a Cambridge blue and Surrey amateur who had toured Australia with Douglas Jardine's side in 1932/3 and appeared in six pre-war Tests against New Zealand and India. He captained MCC to Australia in 1950/51 and, if luck had veered only once or twice in his direction, the margin in the rubber could have been 3-2 in England's favour rather than Australia's 4-1. There was a force and inspiration about his captaincy that was immortalized in the Sydney barrow-boy's cry: 'Fine lettuces, fine lettuces! Hearts like Freddie Brown's.' Since his retirement from cricket he has served as president of MCC, chairman of the Cricket Council and the National Cricket Association, and president of the English Schools Cricket Association. Father of four, he has done much good work for club and school cricketers and was awarded first an MBE then a CBE.

First-class career (1930-61): 13,325 runs (27.36) including 22 centuries, 1,221 wickets (26.21) and 212 catches
Test matches (22): 734 runs (25.31), 45 wickets (31.06) and 22 catches

BROWN, George (1887-1964)

Hampshire

Broad, tall and immensely strong, George Brown once deliberately 'chested' two successive balls from a fast bowler, while holding his bat aside and laughing. He was an all-rounder in the truest sense. Not only was he a top-class left-handed batsman with a long, free sweep of the bat, and a useful right-arm, medium-paced bowler, but he was a wicket-keeper good enough to be selected for England and a splendid, fearless fielder. He shared in a three-figure stand for every Hampshire wicket except the sixth and several of his partnerships still stand as county records, including his 344 with Phil Mead in 1927. In all his Tests he kept wicket, and was brought in to strengthen England's weak batting against Australia for the last three matches of 1921 hitting 250 runs in five innings. He toured South Africa in 1922/3, and the West Indies and India before those countries were given Test status. By his wish his ashes were scattered over the county ground at Southampton. For many years Brown, Mead, Alec Kennedy and Jack Newman had been the main substance of the Hampshire team.

First-class career (1908-33): 25,649 runs (26.71) including 37 centuries, 629 wickets (29.73), 528 catches and 68 stumpings
Test matches (7): 299 runs (29.90) and 12 dismissals (9 ct, 3 st.)

BROWN, John Thomas (1869-1904)

Yorkshire

Short but strongly built, Jack Brown could make runs under all conditions of weather and wicket. A neat, polished, right-hander specializing in the late cut, he was a pleasure to watch and, as an opening batsman, was a mainstay of the Yorkshire Championship-winning side at the turn of the century. With 'Long John' Tunnicliffe, he shared in nineteen opening partnerships exceeding a hundred, the highest being 554 against Derbyshire at Chesterfield, 1898, a record which stood for thirty-four years. Jack's score in this match was 300, but his highest was 311 against Sussex at Sheffield in 1897. His greatest day in Tests was in 1894/5 at Melbourne (on his only tour of Australia) when he and Albert Ward put on 210 together. England, after early disasters, won both this match and the rubber. A useful change-bowler, he cultivated the fashionable leg-break. A quiet, pleasant man, he was a heavy smoker and drinker but became a teetotaller. Nonetheless, he died tragically young of 'congestion of the brain'.

First-class career (1889-1904): 17,850 runs (30.46) including 29 centuries, 188 wickets (29.65) and 222 catches
Test matches (8): 470 runs (36.15) including 1 century, 0-22 and 7 catches

BUCKENHAM, Claude Percival
(1876-1937)

Essex

Tall and slim with a fine nose and a little dark toothbrush moustache, Claude Buckenham bowled very fast right-arm with a good high delivery and aimed straight for the stumps, but he suffered more than most from an Essex inability to hold catches. A hard-hitting batsman, he often played a useful innings when required. He went to South Africa in 1909/10, with H.D.G. Leveson Gower's MCC team, and enjoyed heartening success, but unfortunately he was considered a little too old for MCC's tour of Australia in 1911/12.

First-class career (1899-1914): 5,666 runs (14.98) including 2 centuries, and 1,152 wickets (25.31)
Test matches (4): 43 runs (6.14), 21 wickets (28.23) and 2 catches

BUTCHER, Alan Raymond (b.1954)

Surrey

A stocky fair-haired left-handed opening batsman, Alan Butcher has a full range of attractive strokes, and is especially strong off the back foot. He is also a fine fielder and occasional left-arm bowler at either medium or slow pace. He took time to establish himself in the Surrey side, having spent some of his youth in Australia where his keen cricketing parents had emigrated for a while with their three sons, all highly promising cricketers. He was selected for a Test trial in 1976 and in 1978 he attracted wide notice with an accomplished 188 against Sussex at Hove. After scoring consistently in 1979 he was awarded his sole Test cap to date in the final Test against India at The Oval. He scored 14 and 20 but did not look at ease and was left out of the Australia tour the following winter. In 1980 he was comfortably Surrey's top scorer with 1,713 runs in the season, hitting 216 not out against Cambridge. More consistent batting in 1981 and 1982 failed to win him another chance for England, but if such form continued it seemed certain that the opportunity to establish himself at Test level would come.

First-class career (1972-): 9,927 runs (33.09) including 19 centuries, and 94 wickets (39.46)

BUTCHER, Roland Orlando (b.1953)

Middlesex, Barbados and Tasmania

Born in Barbados, Roland Butcher, became, in 1981, the first black cricketer of West Indian extraction to play for England, thus giving hope to thousands more of Britain's post-war immigrants. He came to England at the age of 14 and was taken on from his school by Middlesex, who recognized a right-hand batsman of rare panache. He played with modest success for Barbados in the 1974/5 Shell Shield but was not capped for Middlesex until 1979. The following year he played two brilliant match-winning hundreds in the County Championship and also two spectacular innings in limited-overs games, for England in the Prudential Trophy and for Middlesex in the last Gillette Cup Final. The latter effort clinched a place on the England tour to the Caribbean early in 1981 and his first Test Cap was won in his native Barbados where he was warmly welcomed. But the fairy-tale ended there. In three Tests against fierce fast bowling he averaged only 14, with a top score of 32, and although not a complete failure (he also fielded brilliantly) it was clear that he needed to develop a sounder technique if he was to return to Test cricket. He played for Tasmania in 1982/3.

First-class career (1974-): 5,396 runs (29.01) including 8 centuries, and 140 catches
Test matches (3): 71 runs (14.20) and 3 catches

BUTLER, Harold James (b.1913)

Nottinghamshire

When Harold Larwood was partly disabled as a result of his exertions in Australia during the Bodyline Tour, Harold Butler was promoted to the county side, and on Larwood's retirement he shared the new ball with Bill Voce. Right-handed and genuinely pacey, Butler lost his best years to the War and tended to break down, but he played for England against South Africa in 1947, and toured the West Indies in 1947/8. Carrying considerable weight, his run-up was sag-kneed and uninspiring; but he was a highly respected opponent and his delivery was difficult to fault. His best performance for Nottinghamshire was 8 for 15 against Surrey at Trent Bridge, 1937 (six clean-bowled). In his first Test at Leeds in 1947 his analysis read: 52-24-66-7.

First-class career (1933-54): 2,962 runs (10.54) and 952 wickets (24.44)
Test matches (2): 15 runs (15.00), 12 wickets (17.91) and 1 catch

BUTT, Harry Rigden (1865-1928)

Sussex

An undervalued wicket-keeper, at a time of great 'keepers, Harry Butt let only six byes while 1,938 runs were being made at Hove in 1895. Year after year his hands were badly knocked about, but he quietly maintained his form, and possessed a great reputation for fairness. He toured South Africa with Lord Hawke's team, 1895/6. On retirement he became a highly valued umpire, standing in many Tests.

First-class career (1890-1912): 7,313 runs (12.94) and 1,262 dismissals (971 ct, 291 st.)
Test matches (3): 22 runs (7.33) and 2 dismissals (1 ct, 1 st.)

CALTHORPE, Hon. Frederick Somerset Gough (1892-1935)

Cambridge University, Sussex and Warwickshire

Described in 1911 at Repton as 'the backbone of a strong side's batting', the Hon. Freddie Calthorpe obtained his blue at Cambridge and, from 1920 until 1929, captained Warwickshire. Always enthusiastic, he was an attractive right-handed batsman, who went out to the half volley or cut the short ball with the panache of a true amateur. As a medium-paced bowler he had a peculiar corkscrew run, and his swerve with the new ball often worried batsmen. In 1920 he achieved the double, and in 1922 he took 4 for 4 when Hampshire were dismissed for 15 (and yet ultimately won an extraordinary match!). Captain of MCC teams to the West Indies in 1925/6 and 1929/30, he led England in the first-ever Tests played in the Caribbean. He founded the Cricketers' Golf Society.

First-class career (1911-35): 12,596 runs (24.04) including 13 centuries, 782 wickets (29.90) and 214 catches
Test matches (4): 129 runs (18.42), 1 wicket (91.00) and 2 catches

CARR, Arthur William (1893-1963)

Nottinghamshire

The prototype of Lovelace in Alec Waugh's *The Loom of Youth*, Arthur Carr was a fine right-handed attacking batsman, a splendid field and a strong and inspiring – if provocative – captain. There have been few fiercer straight-drivers, especially off the quicker bowlers; and in 1929 he led Nottinghamshire as Champion county (for the first time for twenty-two years). His team was devoted to him. He had a great year in 1925, when he made 2,338 runs (51.95), and two years before toured South Africa with MCC. Aggression was his essential characteristic and he was at the centre of several controversies. He lost the England captaincy to Percy Chapman against Australia in 1926, after four Tests, ostensibly because of tonsillitis; and, eight years later, his uncompromising and undiplomatic support of Harold Larwood and Bill Voce in the bodyline controversy brought his career as player and administrator to a premature close.

First-class career (1910-35): 21,051 runs (31.61) including 45 centuries, 31 wickets (37.10), 393 catches and 1 stumping
Test matches (11): 237 runs (19.75) and 3 catches

CARR, Donald Bryce (b.1926)

Oxford University and Derbyshire

After leaving Repton, Donald Carr played in one of the Victory 'Tests' of 1945, and, after National Service, successively captained Oxford, Derbyshire and an MCC 'A' team in Pakistan. He was a class right-handed batsman, particularly strong to the on and a very good hooker, often at his best against fast bowling. He was also a useful, if erratic, unorthodox, slow, left-arm bowler, and he was brilliant at either slip or short leg. He toured India and Pakistan in 1951/2, where he played his Test cricket. Since 1962 he has been successively assistant-secretary of MCC and secretary of the Cricket Council and Test and County Cricket Board. Thus, he is now immersed in the increasingly complex adminstration of the official game. He is a patient, fastidious and cautious administrator who cares deeply about the game and its players but is also blessed with a sense of humour. He managed three major MCC tours – to South Africa in 1964/5, to India and Pakistan in 1972/3 and to the West Indies in 1974.

First-class career (1945-68): 19,257 runs (28.61) including 24 centuries, 328 wickets (34.74) and 501 catches
Test matches (2): 135 runs (33.75) and 2 wickets (70.00)

CARR, Douglas Ward (1872-1950)

Kent

Douglas Carr was virtually unknown before he entered first-class cricket in 1909 at thirty-seven. Having developed and practised the googly, then not widely used in county cricket, he created consternation among batsmen. So successful was he for Kent that, in his first season, he was chosen for Gentlemen against Players at Lord's and played in the final Test at The Oval against Australia, where he took 7 for 282 in 414 balls (and failed to score – he was no batsman). This was his sole Test appearance, although he fully maintained his bowling form until 1914.

First-class career (1909-14): 425 runs (9.04) and 334 wickets (16.84)

CARTWRIGHT, Thomas William (b.1935)

Warwickshire, Somerset and Glamorgan

Tom Cartwright was a player's player. A slightly crude but effective batsman, he was good enough to make seven first-class hundreds including 210 for Warwickshire against Middlesex at Nuneaton in 1962. But he was respected by a whole generation of county cricketers as a medium-paced bowler who never made life easy for opponents and who, in the right conditions, could make it hellish. His action, with a high, rhythmic leap into the delivery stride, was smooth as velvet and his variety, like Cleopatra's, infinite. Generally speaking, medium-pace bowlers do not prosper in Test cricket where the broader canvas and better pitches tend to demand greater speed or subtle spin. Hence, in five Tests, against Australia in 1964, and against South Africa, home and away, in 1964/5, Cartwright could average only three wickets a match, six of these (for 94) in one innings against South Africa at Trent Bridge in 1965. But in county cricket he did a useful job day after day for three counties – primarily for Warwickshire where he first played in 1952, was capped in 1958 and remained until 1969. He did the double in 1962, when he took 8 for 39 in Somerset's first innings at Weston-super-Mare. He became coach at Millfield School, then played for Somerset before becoming coach at Glamorgan.

First-class career (1952-77): 13,710 runs (21.32) including 7 centuries, 1,536 wickets (19.11) and 332 catches
Test matches (5): 26 runs (5.20), 15 wickets (36.26) and 2 catches

CHAPMAN, Arthur Percy Frank
(1900-1961)

Cambridge University, Berkshire and Kent

Percy Chapman is remembered particularly as a person who brought *joie de vivre* and the dashing stroke-play associated with the Edwardian amateur to the first-class scene after the holocaust of 1914-18. Over six feet tall, with a mass of curly blond hair, his presence was towering, yet his features cherubic, and he radiated a debonair gaiety which captured the public's imagination. Dominating cricket at Uppingham and Cambridge before going to Kent, he was a polished left-handed batsman, excelling in exciting off-drives and leg-side strokes, almost invariably willing to attack the bowling, and often to loft the ball vast distances. He showed amazing speed and brilliance at silly point, cover, slip and, above all, gully, where his huge hands would swallow almost anything. In his first match as England captain, at The Oval in 1926, he led the team that won back the Ashes which had been lost in 1920/21, and in Australia in 1928/9 he retained the Ashes when England triumphed 4-1. He was dispossessed of the captaincy in the final match at The Oval against Australia in 1930, but took charge again in South Africa in 1930/31, after which his representative career ended, although he captained Kent from 1931 until 1936. He will remain the only player to have scored a century at Lord's in the University match, Gentlemen v. Players, and in a Test match against Australia. He married a sister of Tom Lowry, New Zealand's first Test captain. In later years he tended to drink more than was good for him and he became a sad shadow of the Adonis who had

Three Kent stalwarts of the twenties and thirties. From left to right: Les Ames, Percy Chapman and 'Tich' Freeman

once been a true national hero. People who had once flocked to be near, now avoided him.

First-class career (1920-39): 16,309 runs (31.97) including 27 centuries, 22 wickets (41.95) and 356 catches
Test matches (26): 925 runs (28.90) including 1 century, 0-20 and 32 catches

CHARLWOOD, Henry Rupert James
(1846-88)

Sussex

One of four Charlwoods who played for Sussex between 1860 and 1914, Henry was the most useful, and known as 'the hope of Sussex' and 'the most dashing batsman in the south'. For seven seasons he had the highest aggregate of runs for his weak county. He toured Australia with James Lillywhite's team in 1876/7, appearing in the first two Tests ever played.

First-class career (1865-81): 7,095 runs (28.81) including 4 centuries
Test matches (2): 63 runs (15.75)

CHATTERTON, William (1861-1913)

Derbyshire

It was largely due to William Chatterton's essentially watchful and steady right-handed batting that Derbyshire were reinstated among the first-class counties in 1894. For W.W. Read's team in South Africa in 1891/2 he was the most prolific run-getter with 955 runs in 31 innings (eight times not out), and in his sole Test, at Cape Town, he opened the batting and scored 48. Such was the strength of English cricket, he never toured again nor played in a Test in this country. A direct man, he called a spade a spade, whatever the company.

First-class career (1882-1902): 10,914 runs (23.17) including 8 centuries, 208 wickets (21.48), 239 catches and 4 stumpings

CHRISTOPHERSON, Stanley (1861-1949)

Kent

One of the ten brothers who, with their father, used to form a family eleven and play matches, mostly in the Blackheath district, Stanley Christopherson was one of the best fast bowlers in the 1880s. Right-handed he took a long run, made full use of his height and, with a natural swing, acquired much pace. In 1884, for the Gentlemen against the Australians, he took 8 wickets; for Kent, the only county to beat the tourists, he played a decisive part; and, for England in the Test at The Oval (his sole Test), he took 1 for 69 and scored 17. A man of great personal charm and an important figure in the City, he was president of MCC from 1939 until 1946, which, thanks to the War, was the longest period anyone has held the office.

First-class career (1883-90): 881 runs (9.57) and 240 wickets (22.25)

CLARK, Edward Winchester (1902-82)

Northamptonshire and Cambridgeshire

Tall and fair and a natural left-arm fast bowler, 'Nobby' Clark's action was literally a picture, for during the 1930s he was the anonymous subject of a Worthington beer advertisement, which showed him at the moment before delivery, right shoulder pointing at the batsman, left arm almost brushing the ear. His pace was tremendous, and he could produce the almost unplayable ball that came across the batsman like a fast leg-break. He was highly strung and temperamental, he would worry about his foothold, his feet blistered easily, and, when he was out of luck, the fire would leave his bowling. Should birds come flying overhead, chirping merrily, 'Nobby' would hurl oaths at them and ask what they had to sing about. He caused some controversy on tour in Ceylon in 1933/4 when, according to the opposition, he deliberately roughed up the pitch. He made his Test debut against South Africa at The Oval in 1929, and did well, but, as he tended to alternate between his county and the more lucrative Lancashire League, he could not always be considered for England. In the early thirties, however, he appeared against West Indies, India (while touring with MCC, 1933/4) and Australia. As late as 1946, he was considered for five overs as fast as any bowler in the country. Both as batsman and fielder he was moderate.

First-class career (1922-47): 1,971 runs (21.54) and 1,208 wickets (21.49)
Test matches (8): 36 runs (9.00) and 32 wickets (28.09)

CLAY, John Charles (1898-1973)

Glamorgan

John Clay was a right-arm, slow bowler of infinite cunning (after a spell as an enthusiastic fast-medium bowler) and a very useful late-order batsman. He acted towards his adopted county as a kind of Lord Palmerston; for many years he was either captain or captain-secretary, forming a most dedicated partnership with Maurice Turnbull in the 1930s, and playing a vital part in Glamorgan's first Championship title in 1948. In 1937 he captured 176 wickets (17.34) – including 17 for 212 against Worcestershire at Swansea. He had played in his sole Test against South Africa at The Oval two years previously, taking 0 for 75, holding one catch and not batting. After nearly thirty years as a player, he continued to give great service to the game both in Wales (especially as Glamorgan's president from 1961 until his death) and at Lord's (notably as an England selector). He was a shrewd, urbane and witty contributor to the *Glamorgan C.C.C. Year Book*.

First-class career (1921-49): 7,186 runs (15.45) including 2 centuries, and 1,337 wickets (19.46)

CLOSE, Dennis Brian (b.1931)

Yorkshire and Somerset

A tough, stubborn, likeable character, Brian Close will be remembered as a great captain and as an all-round cricketer who did not achieve what he might have done. He was a gifted, left-hand bat, versatile right-arm, medium-pace or off-spin bowler and a quite fearless close fielder. Born at Rawdon near Leeds, he achieved fame overnight at the age of eighteen when he did the double for Yorkshire in his first season and was picked for England against New Zealand. He has seldom been off the back pages of the newspapers for long thereafter and remains the youngest player to be capped by England. He toured Australia in 1950/51 while still on National Service, and made 108 not out in the opening first-class match but 0 and 1 in his only Test. Many disappointments followed and he seemed throughout his career to be plagued by ill-luck. He dabbled with professional football for a while and missed one cricket season due to a football injury. His appearances for England were sporadic, including one notorious innings in 1961 when England seemed to be sailing to victory against Australia at Old Trafford but

Brian Close in full cry

collapsed against Benaud. Close tried recklessly to hit England to success but perished to an ungainly leg-side heave which the selectors took a long time to forget. Yet against Hall, Griffith, Sobers, Gibbs and the other members of the strong West Indies side of 1963 he established himself at last, playing an heroic innings of 70 at Lord's, during which he drove Wes Hall to distraction by moving down the pitch towards him as he ran up to bowl. At times Close's courage was almost blind – the type which won V.C.'s in wartime. The unpredictable nature of his own play did not extend to his captaincy. He became Yorkshire captain in 1963 and at once proved strong, shrewd and able to lead by his own determined example. In 1966 he was asked to captain England in the last Test against the West Indies at The Oval. He did an outstanding job, England won, and he continued successfully as captain the following summer against India and Pakistan. But he lost the position as a disciplinary measure after using delaying tactics in a Championship match against Warwickshire. He was involved in controversy again when he lost the Yorkshire captaincy after 1970, but in 1971 he began a successful twilight career with Somerset, whom he captained with the old skill, audacity and occasional eccentricity from 1972 to 1977. In 1976 he played three more Tests for England, batting with his usual bravery against some ferocious fast bowling. He became a Test selector in 1979. Happily married, with two children, he was awarded the CBE for his services to cricket. He also became manager of Scotland's national team and in 1982 returned to captain his invitation eleven in a first-class game against the Pakistan touring team at the Scarborough Festival. His team won in two days. 'I wasn't showing 'em any mercy,' he remarked, with a characteristic chuckle.

First-class career (1949-82): 34,859 runs (33.26) including 52 centuries, 1,167 wickets (26.42), 811 catches and 1 stumping
Test matches (22): 887 runs (25.34), 18 wickets (29.55) and 24 catches

COLDWELL, Leonard John (b.1933)

Devon and Worcestershire

A medium-fast bowler in the Tate/Bedser mould, Len Coldwell was a strongly built, right-arm in-swing bowler with a whippy action, accurate length and considerable stamina. Nearly bowling his county to her first-ever Championship in 1962 – with 139 wickets from county matches alone – he was selected for MCC's tour of Australia in 1962/3. He achieved little on the tour, however, and, though he received further chances against Australia, it was only against Pakistan in 1962 that he had any real success at Test level. Later in the sixties he and Jack Flavell formed Worcestershire's attacking spearhead in Championship wins in two successive seasons.

First-class career (1955-69): 1,474 runs (5.96) and 1,076 wickets (21.18)
Test matches (7): 9 runs (4.50), 22 wickets (27.72) and 1 catch

COMPTON, Denis Charles Scott (b.1918)

Middlesex

One of the great artists and characters the game has known, Denis Compton is a warm-hearted, carefree, sometimes careless, genius. He was a dazzling right-handed batsman, a natural fielder with swift reactions, and occasionally a destructive bowler of left-arm unorthodox spin. He was a first choice for England, injuries permitting, from 1938 until 1956. His batting had a poetic quality mixed with the spirit of the eternal schoolboy. His most publicized stroke was the sweep, which he played perilously late, his most pleasing the cover-drive, placed exquisitely out of the reach of fielders; and, like all perfect timers of the ball, his leg-glance seemed not so much a stroke as a caress. He was a good hooker and cutter and was never tied to the crease; he loved to do battle, especially with the best wrist-spin bowlers. But for all his occasional unorthodoxy he had a sound basic technique. The only uncertainty about his batting lay in his running between wickets and, while he was in, the air tended to be filled with call and counter-call. As Trevor Bailey said: 'A call from Denis was merely the basis for negotiation!' Punctuality for the start of play was never his strong suit, and he was once surprised to hear from another motorist on Vauxhall Bridge that the last day's play in a Test match at The Oval, starting half an hour earlier than usual, was already in progress. But his skill, good looks, charm and natural generosity brought him a fan club of unrivalled proportions. He became the original 'Brylcream boy', feature of a thousand advertisements. The agent who organized him, Bagenal Harvey, founded a successful business around him, so much so that many subsequent sports 'stars' have called upon agents to look after their business affairs. Denis Compton first turned out for

Denis Compton

Middlesex against Sussex at Lord's in 1936, as a slow bowler batting at number eleven. Soon he was moving up the order and he made over 1,000 runs in his first season. He was to make at least 1,000 runs a season seventeen times (three times overseas). On his Test debut against New Zealand at The Oval in 1937 he hit 65 (run out); in his next Test, against Australia at Trent Bridge the following year, he hit his first century for England, 102. He could not tour South Africa in 1938/9 owing to his football contract with Arsenal. After the War and particularly in the halcyon summer of 1947 his cricket reached a breath-taking maturity. That year he scored 753 runs (94.12) against the South Africans in the five Tests; and in all first-class matches he made 3,816 runs (90.85), including 18 centuries, both of which constituted records for a first-class season. He also took 73 wickets (28.12)! Against Australia, the major power in those years, Compton was often England's mainstay, with 459 runs (51.00) in 1946/7 and 562 runs (62.44) in 1948. At Old Trafford he edged a ball from Ray Lindwall into his own face and had to retire before returning, still bleeding, to hit 145 not out (out of 363). About this time an old football injury to his knee flared up and the 'Compton knee' became a serious news topic. Some of his mobility was impaired, though not before he had slammed 300 in three hours for MCC against North-East Transvaal at Benoni in South Africa, 1948/9, the fastest triple-century known. But some of the old dash left his play, and he had a disastrous Test series in Australia in 1950/51, making 53 runs in 8 innings. He fought back and, with Bill Edrich at The Oval in 1953, made the winning hit which enabled England to win back the Ashes after twenty years. In his last Test against Australia, at The Oval in 1956, after an operation to remove his right knee-cap, Compton top-scored with 94 (and hit 35 not out in the second innings). His highest score in a Test was 278 against Pakistan at Trent Bridge in 1954 and his best bowling 5 for 70 against South Africa in 1948/9. He captained Middlesex jointly in 1951 and 1952 with Edrich. His benefit realized £12,200 in 1949. He was awarded the CBE and is now a P.R. consultant, occasional BBC commentator and cricket correspondent of the *Sunday Express*. He still plays charitable cricket for The Lord's Taverners. With Arsenal F.C. he won a League medal and Cup-winner's medal and earned fourteen wartime England soccer caps. His elder brother, Leslie, also played cricket for Middlesex and soccer for Arsenal and England.

First-class career (1936-64): 38,942 runs (51.85) including 123 centuries, 622 wickets (32.27) and 415 catches
Test matches (78): 5,807 runs (50.06) including 17 centuries, 25 wickets (56.40) and 49 catches

COOK, Cecil (b.1921)

Gloucestershire

'Sam' Cook was a left-arm slow bowler, whose accuracy and flat trajectory meant that he was very difficult to attack successfully but, except when the wicket was extremely helpful, he was a dependable rather than a deadly bowler. In nine seasons he took more than a hundred wickets. In his sole Test, against South Africa at Trent Bridge (of all places for his kind of bowling) in 1947, he scored 0 and 4 and took 0 for 127. He has been a highly esteemed umpire.

First-class career (1946-64); 1,964 runs (5.39) and 1,782 wickets (20.52) and 152 catches

COOK, Geoffrey (b.1951)

Northamptonshire and Eastern Province

Born in Middlesborough, Geoff Cook escaped the Yorkshire recruiting system and made his way instead to Northamptonshire for whom he had five times scored 1,000 runs in a season when he was made captain in 1981. It turned out to be a momentous season for this cheerful individual, a right-hand opening batsman with a very solid technique, an occasional slow left-arm bowler and brave short-leg fielder (twice in one season he was hit on the head and concussed when fielding short-leg). Cook first played for Northants in 1971 and was capped in 1975 when he established with Wayne Larkins one of the best and most attractive opening partnerships in county cricket. In 1978/9 he went to South Africa to captain Eastern Province in the Currie Cup and the following winter hit 172 against North Transvaal at Port Elizabeth. He was now showing confidence against all types of bowling and when the England selectors turned to him for the tour of India in 1981/2 – impressed by his century in the 1981 NatWest Trophy Final – they saw him as a potential replacement for Geoff Boycott.

Moreover, his captaincy of Northants had suggested that he had the qualities necessary for leading England and he reacted with good sense and maturity when for a time England's tour of India was threatened because of his connections with South Africa. Making his debut against Sri Lanka at Colombo in 1982 (Sri Lanka's first official Test) Cook scored 11 and 0, but against India in England in 1982 he scored 138 runs in five innings, making two fifties and sharing in two century opening stands. Though he was dropped for the second series of the summer he was selected to tour Australia in 1982/3 but failed in the Tests.

First-class career (1971–): 14,141 runs (29.89) including 23 centuries, 6 wickets (58.16) and 297 catches
Test matches (4): 149 runs (21.28), 0-4 and 8 catches

COPE, Geoffrey Alan (b.1947)

Yorkshire and Lincolnshire

An exceptionally accurate off-spin bowler, determined tail-end batsman and sound fielder, Geoff Cope has proved himself a cricketer of immense character. His career has twice been interrupted by official judgements declaring his action illegal. On the first occasion he remodelled his action successfully enough to earn a place on MCC tours to India and Australia in 1976/7 – he took 23 wickets (19.52) in India – and to Pakistan and New Zealand in 1977/8, when he played his three Tests. Prevented from bowling in county cricket again in 1978, he returned to the Yorkshire side at the end of 1979 and earned a benefit with the county in 1980. But further criticisms of his action forced his retirement from first-class cricket.

First-class career (1966–80): 2,383 runs (14.01) and 686 wickets (24.70)
Test matches (3): 40 runs (13.33), 8 wickets (34.62) and 1 catch

COPSON, William Henry (1908–71)

Derbyshire

Bill Copson was a link in his county's strong chain of fast or fast-medium bowlers; he bowled above medium-pace right-arm and, though his arm was not high, he could make the ball whip up or break back alarmingly. His fiery red hair matched his bowling, though he had a quiet and happy temperament. He left coal-mining during the General Strike of 1926, when he played cricket for the first time, and he worked up to the county eleven. He took a wicket with the first ball he bowled in first-class cricket, that of Andy Sandham at The Oval in 1932. From that point he improved steadily, developing his late swerve and pace off the pitch. His 160 wickets in 1936 contributed much towards Derbyshire's first Championship win, and in 1936/7 he toured Australia with MCC. Though he headed the averages for the tour, he did not make his Test debut until 1939, when he was selected against the West Indies. In his first match at Lord's he captured 5 for 85 and 4 for 67, and England won handsomely. In 1937 he had some startling performances: 8 for 11 against Warwickshire at Derby, including four wickets in four balls, and hat-tricks in two other matches. He appeared for England again after the War, against South Africa and, on retirement, became an umpire.

First-class career (1932–50): 1,711 runs (6.81) and 1,094 wickets (18.96)
Test matches (3): 6 runs (6.00), 15 wickets (19.80) and 1 catch

CORNFORD, Walter Latter (1900-1964)

Sussex

'Tich' Cornford was only just above five foot high. A wicket-keeper, he incredibly stood right up to all bowling, even that of Arthur Gilligan and Maurice Tate at their best, and one of his happiest memories was at Hastings, when he stumped Jack Hobbs twice on the leg-side and also took five catches. At Worcester in 1928 he had eight victims. He was 'keeper in the inaugural Tests against New Zealand in 1929/30, but had the doubtful distinction of being behind the stumps at Auckland (the fourth Test) when extras numbered 57, for many years the largest ever in a Test innings. A useful later-order right-handed batsman, he hit 82 at Eastbourne in 1928, against Yorkshire.

First-class career (1921-47): 6,554 runs (14.96) and 1,000 dismissals (656 ct, 344 st.)
Test matches (4): 36 runs (9.00) and 8 dismissals (5 ct, 3 st.)

COTTAM, Robert Michael Henry (b.1944)

Hampshire and Northamptonshire

A tall right-arm fast-medium bowler of fire, persistency and stamina, Bob Cottam took 9 for 25 for Hampshire against Lancashire at Old Trafford in 1965, the best bowling figures ever in an innings for Hampshire, and three times exceeded 100 wickets in a season, all for Hampshire. But he was not happy there and joined Northamptonshire in 1971. Reducing his pace and cutting the ball, he was part of a strong attack which made his new county Championship contenders for several years. He was also very effective in limited-over cricket. He toured India once and Pakistan twice, playing his only Test cricket on those tours. He is now the NCA's chief coach in the West Country.

First-class career (1963-76): 1,286 runs (7.02), 1,010 wickets (20.91) and 153 catches
Test matches (4): 27 runs (6.75), 14 wickets (23.35) and 2 catches

COVENTRY, Hon. Charles John (1867-1929)

Worcestershire

After assisting Worcestershire, then a minor county, and MCC, Charles Coventry toured South Africa with Major Warton's team in 1888/9, playing in the first two Tests against South Africa, batting at number ten and not bowling. In the first of these matches he made his debut in first-class cricket, and was described as a 'fair bat with a free style who can hit hard'. Returning to South Africa in 1896, he took part in the Jameson Raid. He was reported dead – having been seen under a blanket 'kicking like a shot hare' – and arrangements were made at his home in Worcestershire for a funeral service; but news came through shortly before the service began – with all the mourners in attendance – that he was alive. The funeral became a celebration, and dancing on the village green, top hats, frock coats and all, was hastily arranged.

Test matches (2): 13 runs (13.00)

Colin Cowdrey

COWDREY, Michael Colin (b.1932)

Oxford University and Kent

A great player, and a greatly loved one, Colin Cowdrey's life has centred around cricket. The youngest player ever to appear in a Public Schools match at Lord's at thirteen, he dominated Tonbridge cricket for five years, scoring 2,894 runs and, with leg-breaks and googlies, taking 216 wickets. The initials, M.C.C., given to him by a cricketing father after his birth in Ootacamund, continued to fit him well. He was a prolific run-getter at Oxford, making a century in the Varsity match and serving as captain in his last year, and he was the youngest player capped by Kent. His emergence at Oxford followed soon after Peter May's at Cambridge and led directly to many prosperous years for England's cricket. He was the most felicitous and effortless of stroke-players, yet few worked harder on their technique. Indeed there were times when he was too introspective, and, had he given fuller play to his natural genius, he could have been even greater. Plumply built, he was nonetheless a superlative first slip and in his early days a skilful, flighty leg-spinner. Perhaps only Jack Hobbs has been as popular in Australia, where he toured six times between 1954/5 and 1974/5 – the latter visit when he was called for as emergency replacement in the battered and shell-shocked England side. Though only moderately successful, his patience, technique and courage against Lillee and Thomson justified the choice. His first Test century was a saving 102 out of an innings of 191 at Melbourne, 1954/5, and he made three other centuries against Australia. For Kent at Canterbury against the Australians in 1961 he was at his best with a century in each innings, and his last century against the Australians in 1975, was also at Canterbury, a matchwinning innings. Among his twenty-two Test centuries one of the best remembered is his 154 at Edgbaston against the West Indies in 1957, when he and Peter May, by putting on 411 in eight hours twenty minutes, laid the Ramadhin bogey and deprived their opponents of victory. Another magnificent exhibition of stroke-play against South Africa at The Oval in 1960, when he hit 155, saved his side. Cowdrey captained England in the West Indies, 1967/8, a happy and successful tour, and on other occasions, but, to his chagrin, he was never appointed captain on any of his tours of Australia. He lost the job for the final time in 1969 because of an injury, and never regained it. He captained Kent from 1957 until 1971, leading the county to the Championship in 1970. He was and is revered by the legions of Kent cricket supporters. Gentle, friendly and polite, he has a way of charming young, old, rich and poor. Twenty-seven times he exceeded 1,000 runs in a season (six on tour). He has served on several Lord's committees, written a number of cricket books, been an active supporter of youth and charity cricket and has been awarded the CBE for his services to the game. He played in more Tests and Test innings and held more catches than any other player. His eldest son, Christopher, plays for Kent, much to Colin's delight, two other sons have been outstanding cricketers at Tonbridge, and the youngest, Graham, joined Kent in 1983 after scoring a century for the county second eleven at the age of 18 in 1982.

First-class career (1950-76): 42,719 runs (42.89) including 107 centuries, 65 wickets (51.21) and 638 catches
Test matches (114): 7,624 runs (44.06) including 22 centuries, 0-104 and 120 catches

COXON, Alec (b.1916)

Yorkshire and Durham

Alec Coxon was a hostile, whole-hearted, tireless, right-arm, fast-medium bowler and a well-equipped late-order batsman. In his sole Test against Australia at Lord's in 1948, he scored 19 and 0 and took 3 for 172.

First-class career (1945-50): 2,814 runs (18.15) and 473 wickets (20.91)

CRANSTON, James (1859-1904)

Gloucestershire and Warwickshire

Late in his career (in 1889 and 1890), despite greatly increasing weight, James Cranston was regarded as one of the best left-handed batsmen in county cricket, but he was seized with a fit on the field of play in 1891 and much of his old brilliance thereafter left him. In his sole Test, against Australia at The Oval, 1890, he scored 16 and 15 and held one catch.

First-class career (1876-99): 3,450 runs (19.71) including 5 centuries

CRANSTON, Kenneth (b.1917)

Lancashire

Ken Cranston had appeared for the Navy, Combined Services and Club Cricket Conference with distinction, but he was completely new to first-class county cricket when he accepted the captaincy of Lancashire in 1947. It was a great blow to the game when he had to resign at the end of the 1948 season owing to the claims of his dental practice, and subsequently his only appearances were in occasional Festival matches. He was a gifted all-rounder, a forcing right-handed batsman and a fast-medium opening bowler. In the two years he captained his county he played for England against South Africa in 1947 and against the West Indies in 1947/8, when he captained the side at Barbados in the first Test.

First-class career (1947-50): 3,099 runs (34.82) including 3 centuries, and 178 wickets (28.00)
Test matches (8): 209 runs (14.92), 18 wickets (25.61) and 3 catches

CRAPP, John Frederick (1912-81)

Gloucestershire

A Cornishman, Jack Crapp was a countryman of unruffled calm. He was an extremely sound left-handed batsman and a brilliant first slip. He provided the middle-order 'graft' for his county for twenty years. Altogether he reached 1,000 runs in a season fourteen times, and he captained the county in 1953 and 1954, the first professional to do so. He appeared in Test cricket between 1948 and 1949, against Australia at home and in South Africa on tour; he visited India with the Commonwealth side in 1953/4, but had to return home ill after two matches. On retirement he became a highly respected umpire. Once asked for his name at a hotel, he replied 'Crapp' and was directed to the second door on the left.

First-class career (1936-56): 23,615 runs (35.03) including 38 centuries
Test matches (7): 319 runs (29.00) and 7 catches

CRAWFORD, John Neville (1886-1963)

Surrey, South Australia, Otago and Wellington

A prodigy at Repton where, in four seasons, he scored 2,098 runs and took 224 wickets, Jack Crawford first appeared for his county at seventeen. He was, perhaps, the greatest school cricketer in the history of the game, and, at nineteen, was the youngest player until Brian Close to achieve the double in first-class cricket (in 1906). He was a fine, orthodox, firm-footed, right-handed batsman with an upright stance, who delighted in straight-driving. He was also a medium-pace bowler who possessed nearly every gift: an easy delivery, accuracy and ability to make the ball move considerably. He always played in spectacles. In his first season for his county in 1904 he bowled unchanged with H.C. McDonell in the match against Gloucestershire at Cheltenham, taking 10 for 78. Two years later he hit a ball on to the top balcony of the Pavilion at Lord's. He toured South Africa in 1905/6 – before he was twenty – and Australia in 1907/8, when he headed the bowling in the Tests with 30 wickets (24.79) and was considered by many to have been the finest orthodox medium-pace bowler ever on Australian shirt-front wickets. After a sharp dispute with Surrey over the composition of the county's eleven which he was captaining against the Australians in 1909, he settled in Australia, playing Sheffield Shield cricket with distinction and touring New Zealand with an Australian side in 1914, when, against Fifteen of Canterbury, he scored 354, 254 of which came from sixes and fours. Returning to England after the War, he had three more seasons with Surrey, and at The Oval in 1919 he hit impressively against the Australian Imperial Forces, driving Jack Gregory back over his head into the Pavilion and scoring 144. His father, an uncle and two brothers all played county cricket.

First-class career (1904-21): 9,488 runs (32.60) including 15 centuries, 815 wickets (20.66) and 162 catches
Test matches (12): 469 runs (22.33), 39 wickets (29.48) and 13 catches

CUTTELL, Willis Robert (1864-1929)

Yorkshire and Lancashire

Robert Cuttell was a first-rate all-rounder, a right-handed batsman who could defend strongly and hit hard, a slow bowler of good length who could turn the ball either way, and an excellent field. In 1898 he became the first Lancashire player ever to achieve the double. He toured South Africa in 1898/9 with Lord Hawke's team, where he had his Test match experience. His father also appeared for Yorkshire.

First-class career (1896-1906): 5,938 runs (21.83) including 5 centuries, and 791 wickets (19.47)
Test matches (2): 65 runs (16.25), 6 wickets (12.16) and 2 catches

DAWSON, Edward William (1904-79)

Cambridge University and Leicestershire

While still at Eton, where he made centuries against Harrow and Winchester in the same year, Eddie Dawson appeared for his county and, later, captained Cambridge. A very sound right-handed batsman – a visiting Australian said that he had never seen such a broad bat when he played forward – he was equally valuable in the field. County captain for four years, he was claimed by business after 1933. He toured South Africa in 1927/8, and Australasia in 1929/30, playing in the earliest Tests against New Zealand. His twin nephews, keen club cricketers, run a Prep school at Sunningdale.

First-class career (1922-34): 12,597 runs (27.09) including 14 centuries
Test matches (5): 175 runs (19.44)

DEAN, HARRY (1884-1957)

Cheshire and Lancashire

Suiting his methods to the conditions of pitch and play, Harry Dean would bowl either his left-arm, fast-medium with its deceptive swerve, or slow spinners. Eight times he took more than a hundred wickets in a season, and was generally at his best in the 'Roses' match. Against Yorkshire at Aigburth in 1913 – a special match arranged to coincide with the visit to Liverpool of King George V – he captured 17 for 91. His only Test appearances were in the Triangular Tournament of 1912 and at The Oval against Australia in the first 'timeless' Test in England, where he took 4 for 19 and the visitors were skittled out for 65. He was also a League cricketer of note.

First-class career (1906-21): 2,448 runs (10.28) and 1,301 wickets (18.14)
Test matches (3): 10 runs (5.00), 11 wickets (13.90) and 2 catches

DENNESS, Michael Henry (b.1940)

Scotland, Kent and Essex

Mike Denness was unfortunate to become England captain in an age when the conduct of the man in the hot seat is open to almost as much scrutiny from press and public as that of the prime minister. An outwardly tough but inwardly sensitive Scotsman with no flair for handling the demands of the press and not a natural 'man manager', he nevertheless captained Kent with outstanding success, notably in one-day cricket, and was a generally sound, orthodox and enthusiastic captain on the field who set a shining example with his athletic fielding in the covers. His batting limitations, like those of all his colleagues, were exposed by the exceptional pace and fury of Lillee and Thomson in Australia in 1974/5 but he was a player of high quality with a beautiful array of off-side strokes off front foot and back. A crowd pleaser, his batting exuded confidence, style and his own uninhibited delight in hitting a cricket ball hard to the boundary. He was an outstanding schoolboy player at Ayr Academy and made his debut for Scotland in 1959, playing his first game for Kent in 1962 and winning his cap in his third season. For much of his career at Kent he formed a successful opening partnership with Brian Luckhurst, although he batted most often at number four in his twenty-eight Tests for England, in nineteen of which he was captain. He often played skilfully against the Indian spinners when vice-captain on his first tour of India, Pakistan and Sri Lanka in 1972/3 but his form was mercurial in the two tours in which he captained England in the next two winters. He presided over some remarkable recoveries in the Caribbean which enabled England to draw a series against a much stronger West Indies side, but dropped himself at Sydney in the fourth Test in which Australia regained the Ashes in 1975. Yet in the last match of the rubber he made a brilliant 188 at Melbourne and on the tour

Mike Denness

overall averaged 54. He made 1,000 runs in a season 14 times in England and once abroad. Under his captaincy Kent won the John Player League three times, the Benson and Hedges Cup twice and the Gillette Cup once. He moved to Essex in 1977, and played a significant role in their winning of two competitions in 1979. A family man who still lives in Canterbury, he has worked in insurance, finance and as a manager for World Series Cricket teams and in 1981 took over responsibility for the coaching and management of the Essex 2nd XI, becoming an honorary cricketing Life Member of MCC.

First-class career (1959-80): 25,886 runs (33.48) including 33 centuries, and 411 catches
Test matches (28): 1,669 runs (39.69) including 4 centuries, and 28 catches

DENTON, David (1874-1950)

Yorkshire

'Lucky' Denton was so audacious in his right-handed batting that many people said that he was 'playing at Scarborough all the time' and taking too many risks, yet his aggregate of runs for Yorkshire alone (33,608) remained the highest until surpassed by Herbert Sutcliffe. Lightly built, of medium height, and possessing very flexible wrists, Denton was a stroke-maker of considerable power all round the wicket. On fast wickets he would cut brilliantly and, when the ground was slow, he employed the pull and the hook very effectively. In the field, especially in the deep and at third man, none of his contemporaries could chase the ball at greater speed, or return it more quickly and accurately. He played only once for England at home, against Australia at Headingley in 1905, J.T. Tyldesley generally being preferred to him. His other Test experience was with MCC in South Africa, 1905/6 and 1909/10, and on the latter occasion, at Johannesburg, he hit 104 in a hundred minutes, his sole Test century. He exceeded 1,000 runs in a season twenty-one times. On retirement he became a first-rate umpire.

First-class career (1894-1920): 36,440 runs (33.40) including 69 centuries, 34 wickets (27.58), 353 catches and 1 stumping
Test matches (11): 424 runs (20.19) including 1 century, and 8 catches

DEWES, John Gordon (b.1926)

Cambridge University and Middlesex

A sound left-handed batsman and fine outfield, John Dewes scored 1,000 runs in May 1945, for Cambridge University (all in minor matches) and played for England in the Lord's 'Victory' Test that year. One of the powerful Cambridge side after the War, he shared an unbeaten second-wicket partnership of 429 with Hubert Doggart against Essex at Fenner's in 1949, at that time an English record, and the following year made his highest score, 212 against Sussex at Hove, adding 349 for the first wicket with David Sheppard. In 1950 he scored 2,432 runs (59.31), including nine centuries. Though he also scored quite heavily for Middlesex, he proved a class below Test cricket. On his debut against Australia at The Oval in 1948, he opened with Len Hutton when England were routed for 52. He appeared against the West Indies in 1950 and toured Australia in 1950/51, but he was disappointing and his career faded. He was an assistant master at Tonbridge before becoming a headmaster in Australia.

First-class career (1945-57): 8,564 runs (41.78) including 18 centuries
Test matches (5): 121 runs (12.10)

DEXTER, Edward Ralph (b.1935)

Cambridge Univeristy and Sussex

A T.E. Lawrence of the cricket field, Ted Dexter is an adventurer who will try anything once. The sixth Cambridge blue to captain Sussex after the Second World War, he was known as Lord Edward, as befits

Ted Dexter

his naturally aristocratic air. A gifted all-round sportsman, born in Milan, he was one of the few 'box-office' draws in the 1960s, but retired while still in his prime to pursue an extraordinary variety of interests and careers, including flying private planes, riding motorbikes, playing brilliant amateur golf in high company, writing, broadcasting, modelling clothes, running a P.R. company, and owning first horses and then greyhounds. A handsome figure, he was a right-handed batsman who often demonstrated that the best answer to great bowling is attack, although he seldom did so recklessly and his defence was firm and clean. In the right mood he could destroy any attack by orthodox assault, driving with immense power off front and back foot. He was always at his best when challenged by outstanding bowling or a race against time. As a medium-pace bowler, though handicapped by injury, he was an effective partnership-breaker. In his last stride he was reminiscent of Keith Miller, the ball unleashed in a final orgy of muscular activity after a brief, languid approach. Although apt to practise golf shots in the outfield he was a fine cover-point and an athletic fielder anywhere. His air of apparent disdain and aloofness and a tendency to over-theorize limited his success as a captain, but his players and his opponents always respected him. In a few short years he captained England against Australia, India, New Zealand, Pakistan and the West Indies. In a Test career ranging from 1958 until 1968 it was sad that such a great attacking player should frequently have been forced to try to save matches rather than to win them. He came to the fore in the West Indies in 1959/60, heading the Test averages and making two centuries. His outstanding big innings were 180 at Edgbaston in 1961, and the even more remarkable 174 in eight hours at Old Trafford in 1964, both of which saved England against Australia. More characteristic were his brilliant, indeed breathtaking, innings of 76 against Australia at Old Trafford in 1961, and his daring 70 against the West Indies at Lord's in 1963. Against Pakistan he shared in the record partnerships for the second and fourth wickets, the former being 248 with Colin Cowdrey at The Oval, 1962, and the latter 188 with Peter Parfitt at Karachi in 1961/2, when Dexter scored 205 which was to remain his highest in first-class cricket. Curiously, he first made his mark as a bowler in a representative match, for Gentlemen v. Players at Lord's in 1957, when he took 5 for 8 and 3 for 47. At Headingley, 1962, he secured 4 for 10 against Pakistan. Captain of Sussex from 1960 until 1965, he made 1,000 runs or more in a season ten times (twice overseas). There were times when his heart was not in the game and he would give his wicket away. Although a brief sortie into politics turned out to be a failure – when he stood as a candidate in Cardiff against the future Prime Minister, James Callaghan – there are few things that he would not do better than the average mortal.

First-class career (1956-70): 21,150 runs (40.75) including 51 centuries, 419 wickets (29.92) and 230 catches
Test matches (62): 4,502 runs (47.89) including 9 centuries, 66 wickets (34.93) and 29 catches

DILLEY, Graham Roy (b.1959)

Kent

A six-foot-three-inch, blond-haired, right-arm fast bowler from Dartford, Graham Dilley emerged in the late 1970s as the first in a possible new crop of English fast bowlers after a lean period. A very determined competitor, sometimes given to overt aggression, he can be very fast despite a rather rough action with a very long final stride and an open chest. A good fielder anywhere and an effective hard-hitting left-hand batsman, many English hopes for the 1980s rest on him. Making his first appearance for Kent in 1977, he was still uncapped by his county when picked to tour Australia in 1979/80, when he became, at 20 years and 210 days, the youngest to play for England for 30 years. He excelled himself with the bat in his first Test in Perth (scoring 38 not out and 16) and generally bowled well on the tour but without stamina. The following winter he played in all four Tests on a tough tour of the West Indies, taking only 10 wickets at 45 each, yet impressing with his speed and aggression. In 1981 he took 7 for 62 in the two innings of the first Test

Graham Dilley

against Australia on a helpful pitch at Trent Bridge, and seven more wickets in the next two games. He also batted belligerently in all three games; indeed his 56 in the second innings at Headingley was the catalyst for Botham's match-winning performance. After this match, Dilley lost fitness and form, but Keith Fletcher insisted that he should go to India in 1981/2. Only a moderate performer on this tour, however, he returned to county cricket, some feeling that he did not have the fighting qualities to return, others that his talent was being wasted.

First-class career (1977-   ): 1,044 runs (15.58) and 228 wickets (29.60)
Test matches (16): 313 runs (17.38), 45 wickets (31.13) and 4 catches

DIPPER, Alfred Ernest (1886-1945)

Gloucestershire

Alfred Dipper came into his county's eleven by chance, as a last-minute substitute against Kent at Tonbridge in 1908. He was straight from village cricket but stemmed a disastrous collapse, and for twenty-four years remained a pillar, especially at number one, with his watchful right-handed batting. Having to bolster a weak batting side, he tended to become rigidly defensive, until the advent of Walter Hammond encouraged him to deploy more strokes. Five times he exceeded 2,000 runs in a season and ten other times exceeded 1,000 runs, but he was a poor fielder. 'There goes my whippet', would comment the laconic Charlie Parker as Alfred trotted after his ball at mid-on. He was a useful change-bowler. His sole Test was against Australia at Lord's in 1921, when he scored 11 and 40. On retirement he stood as an umpire for some years.

First-class career (1908-32): 28,075 runs (35.27) including 53 centuries, 161 wickets (30.32) and 197 catches

DOGGART, George Hubert Graham (b.1925)

Cambridge University and Sussex

A stylish and forcing right-handed batsman, useful right-arm off-break bowler and a fine slip fielder, Hubert Doggart made a sensational debut for Cambridge when he scored 215 not out against Lancashire in 1948. The following year his unbroken second-wicket stand of 429 with J.G. Dewes against Essex became an English record, and at the same time he made the highest score of his career, 219 not out. In all first-class matches that season he scored 2,063 runs at an average of 45.00, including a record 1,280 runs for Cambridge University. In 1950, while captain of Cambridge, he played in the first two Tests against the West Indies. He captained Sussex in 1954, but teaching at Winchester later curtailed his appearances. He became headmaster of King's School, Bruton, and in 1981/2 was President of MCC. Both his father, A.G., and his son, S.J.G., were Cambridge blues. Hubert himself also won a soccer blue.

First-class career (1948-61): 10,054 runs (31.51) including 20 centuries, 60 wickets (34.28) and 197 catches
Test matches (2): 76 runs (19.00) and 3 catches

D'OLIVEIRA, Basil Lewis (b.1931)

Worcestershire

An immensely talented and popular cricketer, Basil d'Oliveira moved from poverty in Cape Town to prosperity in Worcestershire with unwavering dignity. Few sportsmen in the public eye have given a better example of how to react to success, failure and the problem of being a controversial figure. Debarred, despite his ability, from playing cricket against the best in South Africa because of being a 'Cape Coloured', he nevertheless performed with such dazzling success in minor cricket on very poor grounds and matting wickets that word reached England via John Arlott and Peter Walker and he was offered £450 in 1960 to play for the Central Lancashire League Club, Middleton. Two hundred pounds were needed for the air-fare and the sum was partially raised by raffles, fêtes and matches held in the region of his tenement home, but for 'Dolly', as he affectionately became known, it was a wise investment. Already twenty-five years old, he had to leave his wife and first child behind in South Africa for his first season. It took him some time to adapt to English conditions but by the end of the season he was ahead of Garfield Sobers at the top of the league averages. He played with great success for Middleton for four years, made his first-class debut in Rhodesia on a Commonwealth XI tour in 1961/2 and on a later Commonwealth tour Tom Graveney persuaded him that he could make the grade in county cricket. He spent 1964 qualifying for Worcestershire, making a century against the Australians, and in 1965, at the age of thirty, was the only batsman in county cricket to score more than 1,500 Championship runs. He also took 35 wickets and some brilliant slip catches. In 1966 he played his first Test for England at Lord's, making an accomplished 27 before being unluckily run out. With a beautifully relaxed, sideways-on stance and a very short backlift, his powerful forearms nevertheless gave him command of all the strokes and after a steady, watchful start to an innings he would accelerate to score freely and attractively. His bowling, again with a classic sideways-on action, was steady, medium pace with swing either way and disconcerting wobble. He was more or less a regular England all-rounder until 1972, making three major overseas tours, playing many crucial innings and always taking useful wickets. But in 1968 he was the innocent cause of an international incident when, picked to replace Cartwright for the MCC tour of South Africa after he had been controversially omitted in the first place, he was refused entry and the tour was cancelled. Long after losing his place in the England team to Tony Greig he continued to display his class for Worcestershire, whose full-time coach he became when finally forced to stop regular county cricket because of age and injury at the end of 1979. Even in later years he was capable of anything when the mood was right, once almost winning a Benson and Hedges Cup Final at Lord's single-handed, despite a severe leg injury, and on another occasion keeping Yorkshire in the field for more than a day while compiling 227 (at Hull in 1974) purely because a Yorkshire bowler had annoyed him with a reference to his colour. He was awarded the OBE in 1969 for his services to cricket and his benefit in 1975 was worth £27,000. His son, Damian, who is also a right-handed batsman, has shown promise for Worcestershire.

First-class career (1961-80): 18,919 runs (39.57) including 43 centuries, 548 wickets (27.41) and 211 catches
Test matches (44): 2,484 runs (40.06) including 5 centuries, 47 wickets (39.55) and 29 catches

Basil d'Oliveira

DOLLERY, Horace Edgar (b.1914)

Berkshire and Warwickshire

Known as 'the schoolboy wonder' at Reading School, 'Tom' Dollery was playing for Berkshire at fifteen and Warwickshire at twenty. For many years the best and most consistent right-handed batsman in the county with a wide range of strokes, he was forceful in approach and eminently dependable; at number five he was prepared equally to push home the advantage already gained or to retrieve the disaster of a sudden collapse, and he was a fine slip field and useful deputy wicket-keeper. Fifteen times he exceeded 1,000 runs in a season. Always greatly respected, he extracted the best that each man had to give when he became the first-ever professional captain of Warwickshire (a post he held from 1949 to 1955) and was an outstanding success. In 1951 he led the county to her first Championship title for forty years. He was selected for England, however, in only a handful of Tests against South Africa, Australia and the West Indies between 1947 and 1950. On retirement he served as county coach.

First-class career (1933-55): 24,413 runs (37.50) including 50 centuries, 291 catches and 13 stumpings
Test matches (4): 72 runs (10.28) and 1 catch

DOLPHIN, Arthur (1885-1942)

Yorkshire

Contemporary with Herbert Strudwick, E.J. 'Tiger' Smith and George Brown, Arthur Dolphin played only once for England, against Australia at Melbourne, 1920/21, when he scored 1 and 0 and held 1 catch, but he was an outstanding wicket-keeper in a great tradition of Yorkshire 'keepers, and a member of eight Championship-winning sides. His playing days over, he became an efficient and popular umpire who never wore a hat, even on the hottest days.

First-class career (1905-27): 4,191 runs (10.76) and 719 dismissals (488 ct, 231 st.)

DOUGLAS, John William Henry Tyler (1882-1930)

Essex

Nearly six foot tall, strongly built, with dark hair parted down the middle, piercing blue eyes and a square jaw, Johnny Douglas was, mentally and physically, as tough as he looked. 'Johnny Won't Hit Today' – the initials were so converted in Australia – became an axiom. A born fighter, he became a dour right-handed batsman, blocking with obstinacy and only occasionally revealing his hitting powers; and the more he was barracked the more dour became his defence. With his rather cramped style and limited number of strokes, he was never an attractive player, though very effective. As a fastish bowler he worked untiringly, regularly rubbing the new ball vigorously against his left arm during the first overs with it. He could bowl for hours without losing either speed or length and, with a new ball, he imparted an awkward swerve both ways. 'J.W.H.T.' achieved the double five times. Always extremely fit, he was a rare fighter and had to be; England under his captaincy lost the first seven Tests off the reel against Australia after the First World War. Before 1914, however, he had led England in the regaining of the Ashes in Australia in 1911/12, standing in for P.F. Warner who was ill, and he was also the victorious captain against South Africa in 1913/14. He captained Essex from 1911 to 1928. A notable boxer, he won the Olympic Middleweight Championship in 1908, and also represented England in amateur Association Football. He was drowned at sea while trying to save his father, after their ship collided with another in fog.

First-class career (1901-30): 24,530 runs (27.90) including 26 centuries, 1,894 wickets (23.32) and 330 catches
Test matches (23): 962 runs (29.15) including 1 century, 45 wickets (33.02) and 9 catches

Johnny Douglas

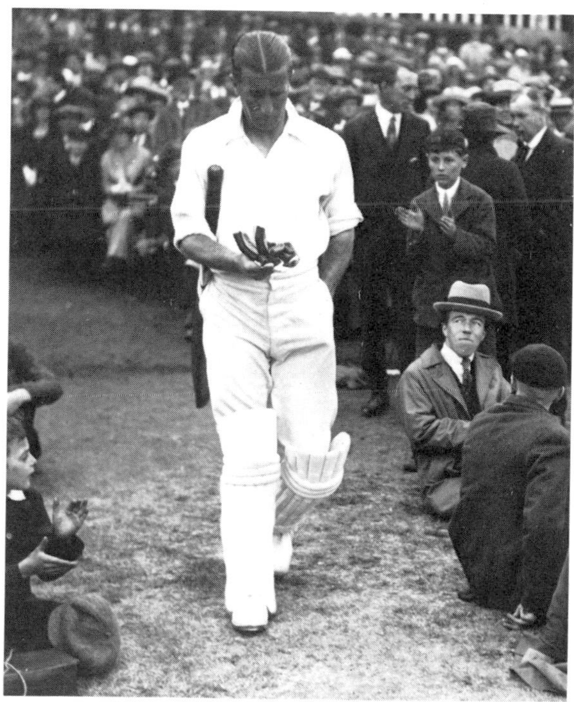

DOWNTON, Paul Rupert (b.1957)

Kent and Middlesex

The son of a noted club cricketer who played briefly for Kent, Paul Downton is an acrobatic wicket-keeper and a useful and determined right-hand batsman. Educated at Sevenoaks School and Exeter University, he may have suffered from being selected for England before he was ready for it. He toured the West Indies with the England Young Cricketers in 1976 and played for Kent the following year, winning a cap in 1979. The return of Alan Knott, however, persuaded him to move to Middlesex. Already he had so impressed J.T. Murray, then an England selector, that he was chosen to tour Pakistan and New Zealand as deputy to Bob Taylor in 1977/8, and after playing a major role in his first season with Middlesex in 1980, he toured the West Indies the following winter, winning his first Test Cap in Trinidad and playing two more games in the series. His 26 not out in the final Test in Jamaica helped England to save the game. In the first Test against Australia at Trent Bridge in 1981, however, he dropped a very easy catch which proved decisive in a low-scoring game. It cost him his place.

First-class career (1977-): 1,929 runs (17.69) and 288 dismissals (251 ct, 37 st.)
Test matches (4): 59 runs (9.83), and 8 catches

DRUCE, Norman Frank (1875-1954)

Cambridge University and Surrey

A right-handed batsman, Frank Druce captained Cambridge in 1897, averaging 66, an exceptional figure in those days. *Wisden* commented: 'He plays his own game without any rigid over-adherence to rule, scoring on the on-side from straight balls in a fashion only possible to a batsman with a genius for timing.' He toured Australia in 1897/8 with A.E. Stoddart's team and fared reasonably well in the Tests, but he retired from regular cricket after the tour, occasionally reappearing, with success, in such matches as the Free Foresters versus the Universities.

First-class career (1894-1913): 3,416 runs (35.21) including 9 centuries
Test matches (5): 252 runs (28.00) and 5 catches

DUCAT, Andrew (1886-1942)

Surrey

With his glistening, dark hair firmly parted and seemingly never out of place, Andy Ducat was a dapper and attractive right-handed, fast-scoring batsman, who used his height (five feet ten inches) well. An all-round stroke-maker, he was an occasional bowler and a fast-moving field. All his centuries were scored for Surrey, and when he received a telegram inviting him to play for England against Australia at

Headingley in 1921, he thought it was a leg-pull and asked his Surrey colleagues which of them had done it. The invitation was genuine, but in this, his sole Test, he scored 3 and 2 and held 1 catch. A double international, he appeared six times for England at Association Football as a half-back, and he led Aston Villa to victory in the 1920 Cup Final. Cricket coach at Eton for several years, he died at Lord's while batting in a match between Home Guard units.

First-class career (1906-31): 23,373 runs (38.31) including 52 centuries, 21 wickets (43.00) and 205 catches

DUCKWORTH, George (1901-66)

Lancashire

It was said that there was only one greater appealer than George Duckworth and that was Dr Barnardo. Built like a miniature and very mobile tank, he was indeed a very demonstrative and vocal 'keeper, his right hand going affirmatively on high, but he was likened to the quieter Herbert Strudwick for swiftness of execution. At his best for his county between 1926 and 1930, when Lancashire won the Championship four times, he took some remarkable leg-side catches standing back to Ted McDonald. He toured Australia with MCC in 1928/9, 1932/3 and 1936/7 – as second-string to Leslie Ames on the two latter tours – and South Africa in 1930/31. He was a very shrewd Lancastrian, always highly regarded for his cricket sense. He later became county scorer, a BBC commentator and a popular baggage-master for touring teams.

First-class career (1923-47): 4,945 runs (14.58) and 1,090 dismissals (751 ct, 339 st.)
Test matches (24): 234 runs (14.62) and 60 dismissals (45 ct, 15 st.)

DULEEPSINHJI, Kumar Shri (1905-59)

Cambridge University and Sussex

Born to the purple, Duleep was nephew of the great Ranji; cricket was in his blood, bones and sinewy wrists. An elegant and artistic right-handed batsman, lithe and quick on his feet, with the ability to sight the ball a fraction earlier than most other players, he combined a basically sound defence with a fascinating variety of stroke-play, rivalling his uncle in many ways. He was panther-like at slip. He owed much to the prince of coaches, G.A. Faulkner. Had his cricketing life not been harassed and cut short by ill-health, he might have risen to even greater heights. A Cambridge blue, he averaged some 2,000 runs a season for Sussex for several seasons, and was not afraid to go for the bowling. He hit 333 in a day at Hove, against Northamptonshire in 1930; but his greatest innings

K.S. Duleepsinhji

was at Lord's that year against Australia when he made 173 comfortably off the deadliest of Australia's bowlers. When caught off a big hit, Ranji, gnawing his umbrella handle in the Pavilion, muttered: 'The boy was always careless!' Duleep captained Sussex for two seasons before his health failed, and he toured Australasia with MCC's team in 1929/30, playing in the earliest Tests against New Zealand. He had appeared against South Africa in the first Test of 1929, but this was one of his few failures at representative level. In 1950 Duleep was appointed High Commissioner for India in Australia and, three years later, returned to India to take high office in the State of Saurashtra.

First-class career (1924-32): 15,485 runs (49.95) including 50 centuries, 28 wickets (48.03) and 243 catches
Test matches (12): 995 runs (58.52) including 3 centuries, 0-7 and 10 catches

DURSTON, Frederick John (1893-1965)

Middlesex

A ground-staff boy at Lord's in 1914, Jack Durston blossomed slowly as a right-arm fast bowler when peace returned. Six foot five inches tall and powerfully built, he commanded greater control of length as his career progressed and, with a speedy break-back, took many wickets on hard pitches at Lord's and elsewhere. He was a major influence in Middlesex's Championship victories of 1920 and 1921 and, in the latter year, having taken 11 wickets for the county against the Australians at Lord's, he played in the second Test there, scoring 6 not out and 2, and taking 5 for 136; this was his sole Test. Towards the end of his career, he put on a lot of weight, turning the scale at nearly 20 stone, and he changed from fast to off-break bowling.

First-class career (1919-33): 3,918 runs (11.91), 1,329 wickets (22.03) and 255 catches

EDMONDS, Phillippe Henri (b.1951)

Cambridge University, Middlesex and Eastern Province

A tall, strongly built, richly gifted cricketer, Edmonds is an orthodox slow, left-arm spinner, hard-hitting middle-order batsman and a brilliant all-round fielder. He was born of an English father and Belgian mother and brought up in Zambia (then Northern Rhodesia) before finishing his schooling at Cranbrook and proceeding to a Cambridge blue as a freshman. He captained Cambridge in 1973, and after success for Middlesex was picked for England against Australia at Headingley in 1975. In the match, which was ended when vandals poured oil on the pitch under cover of darkness on the fourth evening, Edmonds took 5 for 17 in his first 12 overs in Test cricket. He finished with 5 for 28 but took only one more Test wicket in three innings later in the series. It was not until Derek Underwood (who had bowled in harness with Edmonds in his first Test) decided to join World Series Cricket that Edmonds gained a regular place as England's left-arm spinner, but Underwood superseded him again for the tour of Australia in 1979/80. Against Pakistan and New Zealand, both away and at home in 1977/8, Edmonds developed into an exceptionally accurate bowler who would turn the ball given the slightest help from any pitch. He took 7 for 66 against Pakistan at Karachi in the third Test, 1977/8. His career was set back, however, in Australia, 1978/9, when he surprisingly lost his Test place and, getting too little match practice, played only a minor background role in the retention of the Ashes. He took disappointment philosophically – when asked once to explain why England had collapsed he remarked: 'I really don't know. Test cricket has changed so much since I used to play it.' It was felt that his independent spirit and somewhat argumentative manner at times (he and Mike Brearley had the occasional contretemps) had something to do with his being discarded by England's selectors again after winning back his place at home against India in 1982. In three Tests, played on good wickets, he bowled unadventurously but at Lord's made a valuable 64. Since, in the view of most county cricketers, he remained the best available English spinner, it was surprising when the selectors again overlooked him for the tour of Australia in 1982/3. With 80 wickets at 22 each he was the leading Middlesex bowler of 1982 when the county won the Championship. A man of wide interests, he is also a dedicated professional and it would be surprising if he did not re-establish himself as an effective cricketer in the highest company. He plays his cricket with a detached air that sometimes suggests aloofness or boredom, but the impression is false.

Phillippe Edmonds

First-class career (1971-): 5,758 runs (19.99) including 2 centuries, 852 wickets (24.85) and 251 catches

Test matches (21): 367 runs (19.31), 55 wickets (27.49) and 22 catches

EDRICH, John Hugh (b.1937)

Norfolk and Surrey

Small, chunky and strong, John Edrich was like a left-handed version of his first cousin, Bill, but he became a more prolific batsman and was only the third left-hander, after Phil Mead and Frank Woolley, to score a hundred first-class centuries. He achieved this feat in 1977, the same year as Geoff Boycott, batting against Derbyshire at The Oval in a County Championship match. Much less of a song and dance was therefore made about Edrich's milestone than about Boycott's and this was somehow typical, for Edrich was always a quiet, undemonstrative cricketer, his remarkably consistent success being based on a great natural ability, an iron self-discipline and unwavering concentration. Unlike most players he could shut everything from his mind except the advent of the next ball. Moving from his native Norfolk to London, John immediately made his mark for Surrey scoring a century in each innings of only his second Championship match, against Nottinghamshire at Trent Bridge in 1959. At the age of only twenty-one he averaged 52 that season and had already made twenty-four centuries by the time he played the first of his seventy-seven Tests, against the West Indies in 1963. The following summer, playing his first Test against Australia at Lord's, he demonstrated the ideal temperament which he possessed for cricket, scoring 120, the first of seven centuries against Australia, four of them on different grounds in Australia where he was a key member of three MCC touring teams in 1965/6, 1970/1 and 1974/5. On the last tour he captained England at Sydney after Mike Denness had dropped himself and, although England lost the match (the fourth Test of that rubber) and thereby relinquished the Ashes, he played an innings of immense courage on the final day of the match, making 33 not out in two and a half hours after suffering broken ribs from the first ball he had received from Lillee. Good looking, with dark eyebrows above piercing light-blue eyes and flashing white teeth, he was seldom satisfied or fully convinced that the odds were in his favour. The strong points of his technique were very powerful forearms, watchfulness, and a rigid adherence to the principle of getting in line with the ball. His most productive strokes were placements off his toes either side of square-leg (and, as the innings progressed, through mid-wicket), a controlled cut behind the wicket on the off-side and a decisively punched cover-drive. In difficult batting conditions he would never lose patience, but in top form he could also be a devastating attacking player, most notably in 1965 when in the course of nine innings he made 1,311 runs including 310 not out at Leeds against New Zealand when his 5 sixes and 52 fours amounted to more runs in boundaries than any other player has scored in a Test innings. His lofted straight driving at this time was a revelation. A few weeks later he was hit on the head by a ball from Peter Pollock of South Africa at Lord's, but was soon scoring freely again. He scored more than 1,000 runs in a season twenty-one times (once in Australia), and more than 2,000 six times. He scored centuries against all other countries and in all the overseas countries which he toured except New Zealand. He captained Surrey for five seasons between 1973 and 1977, a relatively lean period for the county although they won the Benson and Hedges Cup in 1974. Always safe and tidy in the field, he was an especially good gully. He retired after the 1978 season to concentrate on a number of business interests. He was awarded the MBE in 1977 and two separate testimonials by a grateful county club. He became an England selector in 1981 but resigned after one season to concentrate on his business activities.

John Edrich

First-class career (1959-78): 39,790 runs (45.47) including 103 centuries, and 311 catches
Test matches (77): 5,138 runs (43.54), 0–23 and 43 catches

EDRICH, William John (b.1916)

Norfolk and Middlesex

Still an active follower of first-class cricket, Bill Edrich, John's cousin, is remembered also for his great courage and determination, especially on the international scene. Short, chunky and alert, he was a right-handed batsman whose favourite shots were the pulled drive, the hook and the late cut. Watchfulness and grit were the keynotes, and his skill, especially on bad wickets in Australia, endeared him to the crowds. With his Middlesex 'twin', Denis Compton, he was a great box-office draw immediately after the Second World War. His fast bowling was explosive and tearaway. Operating from a short run, he was capable of great speed in short bursts, almost hurling himself at the batsman as he delivered the ball. Later in his career he bowled slow off-breaks. He was also a slip field and, therefore, always in the game. He scored 1,886 runs in five seasons for Norfolk, including 111 against the South Africans in 1935. In his first full season for Middlesex in 1937 he made 2,154 runs in all matches, and also exceeded 2,000 in the last two seasons before the War. He made over 1,000 runs for Lord Tennyson's side in India in 1937/8, but his early Test performances were disastrous. Before the end of May 1938 he hit 1,010 runs, all at Lord's, but in the Tests

Bill Edrich

that year he made only 67 in six innings, followed by consecutive scores of 4, 10, 0, 6 and 1, before he produced a magnificent 219 in the 'timeless' Test at Durban. In his earlier days he was frequently an opening batsman, but he settled down at first or second wicket down; and in Australia, 1946/7, he consolidated his place as a Test cricketer, especially at Sydney with 71 and 119, besides dismissing three of the first four batsmen. 1947 marked the zenith of his career as it did of his Middlesex 'twin', Denis Compton. The two of them seemed to be spending the whole summer at the crease, either for Middlesex, the county champions, or for England against South Africa. All bowling was put to the sword. Edrich scored 3,539 runs (80.43) with 12 centuries, took 67 wickets (22.58) and held 35 catches. In 1948 he battled against Australia, hitting 111 and 54 at Headingley (a match that England should have won). He did not tour Australia under Freddie Brown in 1950/51 – a glaring omission – but he was at the other end when Denis Compton hit the winning run at The Oval in 1953 by which England regained the Ashes. In the first Test of the 1954/5 tour he scored a fighting 88 at Brisbane. Generally, however, he never quite recaptured his 1947 form again, although he captained Middlesex from 1953 until 1957. He returned to his native Norfolk, and for more than a decade enjoyed minor county cricket again. During the War he served in the RAF and was awarded the DFC for daylight bombing over Germany as a Squadron Leader. Three of his brothers also played first-class county cricket.

First-class career (1934-58): 36,965 runs (42.39) including 86 centuries, 479 wickets (33.31), 526 catches and 1 stumping
Test matches (39): 2,440 runs (40.00) including 6 centuries, 41 wickets (41.29) and 39 catches

ELLIOTT, Harry (1891-1976)

Derbyshire

Harry Elliott made his county place secure as wicket-keeper, although his early promise as a batsman was not realized, despite the fact that he often played well in a crisis. He appeared in 194 consecutive matches for his county up to 1928, when his selection for the Test against West Indies at Old Trafford broke the sequence. Subsequently he made 232 consecutive appearances until he was injured in 1937. In an emergency he reappeared for Derbyshire aged fifty-six after the War, while he was senior coach. In 1936, when the county won the Championship for the first time, he conceded only one bye in twenty-five completed innings. He toured South Africa with MCC (when the skipper himself was a 'keeper) in 1927/8, and India, 1933/4, when he kept in the first Test on Indian soil. His nephew, Charlie Elliott, played for Derbyshire and became well known as an umpire.

First-class career (1920-47): 7,580 runs (13.93) and 1,206 dismissals (904 ct, 302 st.)
Test matches (4): 61 runs (15.25) and 11 dismissals (8 ct, 3 st.)

EMBUREY, John Ernest (b.1952)

Middlesex

Although he had been a capped Middlesex player for less than two years when he was picked for England in 1978, John Emburey was already generally recognized as potentially one of the best slow bowlers in the world. A tall off-spinner with a classical high action, he turns the ball sharply whenever conditions permit, can vary his speed and trajectory without losing control and curves the ball disconcertingly away from the right-hander. Forced to play much of his cricket in limited-over matches and thus to spend much of his time bowling to contain, he is a leading representative of the new school of tight, mean spinners that modern cricket demands. But that he can also be a destructive attacking bowler he amply proved in Australia in 1978/9 when he forced his way into England's Test team against all expectations and in four matches took 16 wickets at 19 each. Amazingly, he did not play any more Tests in 1979/80, despite joining the 1979/80 tour of Australia as a replacement. On England's next two tours, however, to the West Indies in 1980/81 and India and Sri Lanka in 1981/2, he was his country's first-choice spinner of any type. It was therefore ironic that, soon after taking 6 for 33 in the second innings of Sri Lanka's first Test in February 1982, a match-winning performance, he should have been banned from Test cricket for three years. The ban was imposed by the TCCB on 15 players who ignored a TCCB warning not to join a richly sponsored tour of the politically isolated Republic of South Africa. A modest character, he was used to disappointment –

John Emburey

his first four years at Middlesex were spent in the shadow of Fred Titmus – but he has the typically dry wit of a Londoner. He is also a determined late-order batsman and a brilliant catcher at gully.

First-class career (1973-): 3,113 runs (19.95) including 1 century, 606 wickets (23.69) and 167 catches
Test matches (22): 326 runs (12.07), 56 wickets (30.28) and 15 catches

EMMETT, George Malcolm (1912-76)

Devon and Gloucestershire

A short, slightly built man, George Emmett knew every shot in the book, and often, perhaps, tried to play too many of them. Extremely quick on his feet, he was never afraid to go down the wicket to slow bowlers. He was at a disadvantage against the really quick bowlers, but he was a fine hooker and cutter and he could hit the ball extremely hard. An occasional bowler, he was also a very safe field. After four seasons with Devon he joined Gloucestershire. He made his debut for his adopted county in 1936, and fourteen times exceeded 1,000 runs in a season, mainly as opening batsman. He toured India twice with Commonwealth teams, but his selection as opening batsman against Australia at Old Trafford in 1948 caused a sensation because he replaced Len Hutton. In this, his sole Test, George scored 10 and 0. Captain of Gloucestershire from 1955 until 1958, he became coach on retirement in 1959.

First-class career (1936-59): 25,602 runs (31.41) including 37 centuries, 60 wickets (44.01) and 299 catches

EMMETT, Thomas (1841-1904)

Yorkshire

Tom Emmett was a vigorous left-arm fast bowler with a round-arm action, who could pitch on the leg-stump and hit the off. In a long career he remained effective even after he had lost his pace, by imparting greater spin to the ball. A cheery and humorous professional, his verbal exchanges with W.G. and others were as belligerent as those of his contemporaries, Gladstone and Disraeli. Tom called his ball that pitched on the leg-stump his 'sostenuter' – 'What else would you call it?' he would ask. His motto was 'First a wide and then a wicket', and so it often proved. A useful, free-scoring batsman and good field, he captained Yorkshire from 1878 to 1882. Tom did not appear for England against Australia at home, but toured Australia with three teams, and appeared in the first Test at Melbourne in 1876. Later, he coached Leicestershire C.C.C. and at Rugby, where one of his pupils was P.F. Warner.

First-class career (1866-88): 8,734 runs (15.18) including 1 century, and 1,582 wickets (13.36)
Test matches (7): 160 runs (13.33), 9 wickets (31.55) and 9 catches

EVANS, Alfred John (1889-1960)

Oxford University, Hampshire and Kent

An Oxford blue who captained the University in 1911, John Evans was a tall, lissom, right-handed, hard-driving batsman and a lively medium-paced bowler. In 1921, on the strength of an innings of 69 not out for MCC against the overwhelming Australians at Lord's, he played for England in the Test at Lord's, but was not a success, scoring 4 and 14, and was not selected again. He escaped from POW camps in the First World War, about which he wrote *The Escaping Club*, a classic of its genre. His father played for Oxford University, Hampshire and Somerset.

First-class career (1908-28): 3,436 runs (24.36) including 6 centuries, and 110 wickets (27.73)

EVANS, Thomas Godfrey (b.1920)

Kent

An irrepressible extrovert and the outstanding wicket-keeper of his day, Godfrey Evans made nonsense of the convention that wicket-keepers should be sound rather than showy, for he was, on most big occasions, both sound as a bell *and* spectacular as a catherine wheel. Until Alan Knott surpassed him, he held the record for the most Test dismissals. Of stocky build and a quicksilver character, his darting movements flowed from his natural exuberance, and he made acrobatic catches which few others, and certainly no other contemporary, could have reached. He always kept a game alive, and he stood up to anything less than a genuinely fast bowler, most notably to Alec Bedser. It is doubtful if there has ever been a more brilliant wicket-keeper, though he had the occasional bad day. He was a talented batsman, being very quick on his feet and having a wonderful eye. Two of his seven centuries were made in Tests, 104 against West Indies at Old Trafford in 1950 and 104 against India at Lord's in 1952, when he failed by only two runs to complete the hundred before lunch. Yet in a crisis at Adelaide in 1946/7 he stayed in for ninety-five minutes without scoring. He scored more than 1,000 runs in a season four times and claimed his 1,000th victim in 1959. Having first played for Kent in 1939, he was England's automatic choice as wicket-keeper between 1946 and 1958/9, making four tours of Australasia and two each to South Africa and the West Indies. Whether keeping or batting, his name was synonymous with entertainment and he was awarded the CBE.

First-class career (1939-69): 14,882 runs (21.22) including 7 centuries, and 1,060 dismissals (811 ct, 249 st.)
Test matches (91): 2,439 runs (20.49) including 2 centuries, and 219 dismissals (173 ct, 46 st.)

FAGG, Arthur Edward (1915-77)

Kent

A very sound right-handed opening batsman, Arthur Fagg had strokes all round the wicket and, being a fine hooker, was particularly severe on fast bowlers. He was also a reliable slip field. After playing two Tests against India in 1936 he toured Australia with MCC in 1936/7, playing in two Tests, but had to be invalided home with rheumatic fever and missed the 1937 season. He recovered to perform the unique feat of scoring 244 and 202 not out for Kent against Essex at Colchester in 1938. He had to turn down the offer of a place in the side to South Africa that winter and played only one more Test, but he remained a first-rate county batsman, exceeding 1,000 runs thirteen times. For eighteen years he was one of the best umpires, standing in many Tests, although latterly he was troubled by the lack of good behaviour on the field; he temporarily walked out of a Test at Edgbaston in 1973 when the West Indian players complained at one of his decisions.

First-class career (1932-57): 27,291 (36.05) including 58 centuries, 421 catches and 5 stumpings
Test matches (5): 150 runs (18.75) and 5 catches

Godfrey Evans stumps Allan Rae (West Indies)

FANE, Frederick Luther (1875-1960)

Oxford University and Essex

For two decades Frederick Fane's attractive right-handed, front-foot style was a familiar feature on Essex grounds. As an opening batsman he enjoyed success against googly bowlers on matting in South Africa in 1905/6, when he more than held his own and headed the Test averages with 342 runs (38.00). He visited South Africa again in 1909/10, but without the same success. He led MCC in Australia in 1907/8, when A.O. Jones fell ill and, though he did not relish having the captaincy thrust upon him, made 774 runs on the tour. He captained Essex from 1904 to 1906 and went to New Zealand and the West Indies on minor tours. Curiously, both his father and he read their own obituaries, owing to confusion over family initials.

First-class career (1895-1924): 18,548 runs (27.39) including 25 centuries, and 179 catches
Test matches (14): 682 runs (26.23) including 1 century, and 6 catches

FARNES, Kenneth (1911-41)

Cambridge University and Essex

Ken Farnes was one of the most mourned of the international cricketers lost in the Second World War. Six feet five inches tall, but well proportioned, he took a run of eleven paces and, moving at a great pace at the moment of delivery, could bowl at a ferocious speed. His right-arm deliveries, with the ball coming down from a height of above eight feet, rose very sharply from a hard wicket and, to add extra nip, he flicked his wrist down at the last moment. On his day he bowled as fast as any man, but he had to cope with unresponsive pitches and powerful batting. He played in three series against Australia, one against the West Indies and one against South Africa, the last being the 'timeless' Test at Durban. After three years in the Cambridge side, he joined Essex and, by taking 11 for

131 at Southend against the all-powerful Yorkshire side, he enabled his county in 1934 to beat the Tykes for the first time for many years. Then chosen for England against Australia at Trent Bridge – his first Test – he captured five wickets in each innings. In the 1936 Gentlemen v. Players match at Lord's his bowling was reckoned the fastest seen at Lord's since the time of C.J. Kortright, and he took a sensational 8 for 43 in the first innings. His best bowling in Tests was 6 for 96 in a total of 604 in the fifth match against Australia at Melbourne in 1936/7, on a perfect wicket. He was a safe field near the wicket but rarely of much account as a batsman. Nevertheless he hit 97 not out for Essex against Somerset at Taunton in 1936, helping to add 149 for the last wicket, and laughed at just missing his century. Pilot Officer Farnes was killed on active service while flying during the Second World War.

First-class career (1930-39): 1,182 runs (8.32) and 690 wickets (21.45)
Test matches (15): 58 runs (4.83), 60 wickets (28.65) and 1 catch

Percy Fender

FARRIMOND, William (1903-79)

Lancashire

Second-string wicket-keeper at Lancashire to George Duckworth, Bill Farrimond was still good enough to represent England abroad against South Africa, 1930/31, against the West Indies, 1934/5 and, at home, against South Africa in 1935. On Duckworth's retirement he stepped into his shoes in 1938, but by the end of the War he was too old for county cricket. He was a very sound, quietly confident 'keeper, and a better batsman than Duckworth. In the present era, no doubt, he would simply have moved to another county to ensure a regular place in the first team.

First-class career (1924-45): 2,908 runs (23.64) and 333 dismissals (256 ct, 77 st.)
Test matches (4): 116 runs (16.57) and 7 dismissals (5 ct, 2 st.)

FENDER, Percy George Herbert (b.1892)

Sussex and Surrey

Percy Fender will be best remembered for his inspired captaincy. Tall, dark, with a long nose, moustache, glasses and a long sweater, he was a gift to cartoonists and a calculating showman. In private life his habit and speech were of a conventional, even serious turn, but on the field he was adventurous, loved a gamble, and possessed one of the most acute brains ever applied to cricket. Most of his career was with Surrey, whom he helped to the Championship in 1914 and captained from 1921 until 1931. His expert handling of a rather thin Surrey attack on the perfect wickets at The Oval was a source of mystery; and when he sighted victory on the horizon, he would ride straight for it. In eight seasons he achieved the double six times. A right-handed batsman, he lived on risk and his wrists, and could hit with tremendous power; as a bowler he sometimes lost himself in search of variety, but was at his best as a slow leg-breaker; and he was superb in the slips. His century in thirty-five minutes at Northampton in 1920 remains the world record – he and H.A. Peach added 171 in forty-two minutes – and at Lord's in 1927 he dismissed five Middlesex batsmen in seven balls. When he hit 185 against Hampshire at The Oval in 1922, the innings included three sixes, three fives and twenty-five fours. Surprisingly, he never captained England, although he appeared against Australia and South Africa. He bowled as successfully as any Englishman in Australia on the 1920/21 tour, taking 12 wickets in the Tests, and on matting in South Africa he took 4 for 29 at Cape Town, 1922/3. A writer with an analytical mind, he wrote several classic books about Test matches: *Defending the Ashes*, *The Turn of the Wheel*, *The Tests of 1930* and *Kissing the Rod*, besides a text-book, *The ABC of Cricket*. Still quick-witted in very old age, he lives in Horsham with his daughter, retaining an interest in his wine business and, although almost totally blind, he attended the 1977 Centenary Test in Melbourne as the oldest player able to travel.

First-class career (1910-36): 19,034 runs (26.65) including 21 centuries, 1,894 wickets (25.05) and 599 catches
Test matches (13): 380 runs (19.00), 29 wickets (40.86) and 14 catches

FERRIS, John James (1867-1900)

New South Wales, South Australia and Gloucestershire

See Australia section.

FIELDER, Arthur (1877-1949)

Kent

Arthur Fielder could bowl fast right-arm for hours without fatigue. He bowled off-cutters and out-swingers and he was fortunate in that Kent abounded with almost infallible slip fielders. He toured Australia twice and, in 1907/8, secured 25 wickets (25.08) in the Tests; all his Test cricket was confined to these tours. Taking 186 wickets (20.19) in 1906, he was prominent in Kent's winning of the Championship for the first time, and that year, uniquely for Players against Gentlemen at Lord's, he captured all 10 wickets (for 90) in the first innings. He rarely achieved much as a batsman, but still managed to set up an English record for the last wicket by assisting Frank Woolley to add 235 runs against Worcestershire at Stourbridge – his own share was his highest score, 112 not out.

First-class career (1900-1914): 2,290 runs (11.56) including 1 century, and 1,277 wickets (21.02)
Test matches (6): 78 runs (11.14), 26 wickets (27.34) and 4 catches

FISHLOCK, Laurence Barnard (b.1907)

Surrey

Laurie Fishlock was a left-handed stroke-maker with a style quite free from fuss. His emphasis was always on attack, whether batting or fielding – in his heyday he was a magnificent outfield – and he had a wonderfully consistent record for his county. Unfortunate with injuries in representative cricket, he perhaps did not quite have the patience for Test matches. As an opening batsman, he toured Australia with MCC in 1936/7, appearing in one Test, and again in 1946/7. His other Test cricket was at home against India. He toured India with the Commonwealth team in 1950/51, and made over 1,000 runs; in England he exceeded 1,000 runs in a season twelve times. He also gained an England Amateur Football Cap.

First-class career (1931-52): 25,376 runs (39.34), including 56 centuries, 11 wickets (45.81) and 216 catches
Test matches (4): 47 runs (11.75) and 1 catch

FLAVELL, John Alfred (b.1929)

Worcestershire

Jack Flavell, a strong, red-faced, red-headed man, was among the fastest right-arm bowlers in England in the fifties. Starting as something of a tearaway, whose control was rather suspect, he later slowed down a little and became a steadier and more consistently successful performer. His 101 wickets in eighteen matches in 1964 helped Worcestershire become County Champions for the first time. However, 1961 had been his best year – 171 wickets (17.79). In 1965, when the county won the Championship again, he took 132. Three times in his career he took nine wickets in an innings, all for his county. He appeared in Tests against Australia in 1961 and 1964, but seldom got helpful conditions and was a disappointment.

First-class career (1949-67): 2,032 runs (6.51) and 1,529 wickets (21.48)
Test matches (4): 31 runs (7.75) and 7 wickets (52.42)

FLETCHER, Keith William Robert (b.1944)

Essex

A likeable Londoner, Keith Fletcher (nicknamed 'the gnome') has a Test record of which any batsman could be proud, but the impression remains that he could have been even more successful given a greater determination to take the initiative from the bowlers. Test match atmosphere often sent his shy character into its shell, and he was usually at his best in the second innings rather than the first. Three of his finest innings were 178 against New Zealand at Lord's in 1973, 129 not out against the West Indies at Bridgetown in 1974, and 58 not out against India at Bombay in 1977 – defiant defensive innings which saved each match for his country. He also shone

Keith Fletcher

brightly in defeat at Lord's in 1973 against the West Indies, making 68 and 82 not out during the heaviest home defeat in England's history. From his youth this slightly built, fair-haired right-hander had a gift of perfect timing which aroused expectations of more matchwinning innings than he eventually achieved. But he became an accomplished craftsman and an especially fine player of spin. Born in Worcestershire of London parents whose home was bombed in the War, he was brought up in Cambridgeshire and played first for Royston, also Jack Hobbs' first club. He first played for Essex in 1962, was capped the following year and has been an astute and successful county captain since 1974 leading Essex to their first major triumphs in 1979. Always a valuable adviser to England captains, he has himself led skilfully on the field and kept his players happy off it with a philosophical approach to setbacks and a wry London humour. On seven overseas tours for MCC he was a key member of a frequently struggling batting side. In a stronger one he would have flourished more than he did. An occasional leg-spinner, he has taken many useful wickets. A fine all-round fielder for Essex, he caught some brilliant slip catches in Tests but also missed many important chances. He lost his appetite for Test cricket after the battering he received from Lillee and Thomson in 1974/5 but, though he was often a poking prodding shadow of the batsman he could be, one prefers to remember the days when, with a complete repertoire of glorious strokes, he would look too good for any attack, glancing the ball off his toes forward of square, driving through extra-cover or wide of mid-on, and, above all, square-cutting with punishing power and a brilliance which glittered. He was recalled to the England side as captain for the tour of 1981/2 and, although England lost a grim, dilatory series against India one-nil, he led England to success in the first-ever Test played against Sri Lanka, in February 1982. As a batsman he held his own with several timely innings.

First-class career (1962-): 32,880 runs (38.86) including 57 centuries, 50 wickets (43.34) and 549 catches
Test matches (59): 3,272 runs (39.90) including 7 centuries, 2 wickets (96.50) and 54 catches

FLOWERS, Wilfred (1856-1926)

Nottinghamshire

Wilfred Flowers was the last survivor of the Nottinghamshire eleven that in 1878 played the opening match with the first Australian touring team. He was a resolute right-handed batsman, a steady off-break bowler who was extremely difficult to play on a soft wicket, and a very safe field, either at third man or mid-wicket. In 1879 he demolished Middlesex at Lord's, taking 7 for 16 in 22 overs, 12 of which were maidens; and in 1883 he became the first professional ever to complete the double in a season (with 1,144 runs and 113 wickets). He played only once in a Test against Australia in England – in 1893 – but he toured Australia twice. On retirement he became a first-class umpire.

First-class career (1877-96): 12,891 runs (19.77) including 9 centuries, 1,187 wickets (15.92) and 216 catches
Test matches (8): 256 runs (18.14), 14 wickets (21.14) and 3 catches

FORD, Francis Gilbertstone Justice (1866-1940)

Cambridge University and Middlesex

Described as 'six feet two of don't care', Francis Ford, or 'Stork' as he was known, was the youngest of seven cricketing brothers (all Reptonians) and an elegant left-handed batsman, who used his height so effectively that, despite his very spare physique, he put exceptional force into his stroke-play. He turned many good-length balls into half-volleys. His most brilliant display was 191 for Cambridge against Sussex at Hove (out of 703 for 9) in 1890. A slow left-arm bowler, he caused trouble sometimes by dropping the ball on an accurate length from a great height, with plenty of spin and curl. He toured Australia with A.E. Stoddart's side in 1894/5, but did not enhance his reputation. He held strong views about 'leg before wicket', and his influence at Lord's was considerable in amending Law 39 (the Lbw Law) in 1937.

First-class career (1886-1908): 7,359 runs (27.06) including 14 centuries, and 200 wickets (23.78)
Test matches (5): 168 runs (18.66), 1 wicket (129.00) and 5 catches

FOSTER, Frank Rowbotham (1889-1958)

Warwickshire

In an age rich in genuine all-rounders, Frank Foster, no relation of the seven Foster brothers, was among the best. A natural hitter, he was a right-hand batsman who did not bother overmuch about technique yet was good enough to hit 305 not out against Worcestershire at Dudley in 1914. He bowled left-arm, medium-fast with a short run and beautifully easy action, his delivery seeming to hurry off the ground and rush batsmen into their strokes. He was also a fine slip. One of the pioneers of leg-theory bowling, he was consulted by Douglas Jardine before the Bodyline Tour of Australia in 1932/3. As captain of Warwickshire from 1911 until 1914 he was an inspiration and led his county to their first Championship triumph in 1911. He made 1,383 runs and took 116 wickets that season, topping both batting and bowling averages. In Australia in 1911/12 he and Sydney Barnes won the Ashes for England, Foster taking 32 wickets (21.62) in the series. Foster and Barnes formed one of the best bowling combinations England has ever had, and, incidentally, were a remarkable exception to the rule that all-out pace is the answer in Australian conditions. His career was finished by a crash on a motorcycle early in the First World War.

First-class career (1908-14): 6,540 runs (26.69) including 7 centuries, 721 wickets (20.66) and 118 catches
Test matches (11): 330 runs (23.57), 45 wickets (20.57) and 11 catches

FOSTER, Reginald Erskine (1878-1914)

Oxford University and Worcestershire

In the early years of the century Worcestershire were known as 'Fostershire' as the seven sons of a clergyman at Malvern all played for the county. It is said that when the family did the washing-up, the plates and cups were thrown from one to another to be dried and put away. R.E. Foster – 'Tip' – the third in age, was undeniably the greatest of the septet. His right-handed batting was of the cultured, polished kind associated with Malvern; he has been described by a contemporary as a more flexible and sounder version of Ted Dexter, hard on the latter perhaps but an indication of Foster's class and style. At Oxford he won his blue as a freshman, played four times against Cambridge at Lord's and hit 171 in 1900, the record score in the match up to that date. A few days later, for Gentlemen against Players at Lord's, he scored 102 not out and 136. On his Test debut, at Sydney in 1903/4, he held England's batting together in scoring 287, fours cascading from his bat. It was the highest score ever made by an Englishman in Australia. Although he captained England against South Africa in 1907, he had ceased to play regularly, business and illness successively curtailing his career. He died, sadly young, a victim of diabetes, three months before the First World War broke out. Also a brilliant footballer, he gained six full England soccer caps and is the only man to have captained England in both soccer and cricket.

First-class career (1897-1912): 9,076 runs (41.82) including 22 centuries, 25 wickets (46.16) and 175 catches
Test matches (8): 602 runs (46.30) including 1 century, and 13 catches

FOTHERGILL, Arnold James (1854-1932)

Northumberland and Somerset

A medium-paced left-arm bowler and hard-hitting batsman, Arnold Fothergill was employed by Somerset before they were elevated to first-class rank. He toured South Africa with Major Warton's team in 1888/9 and played in the first two Tests ever held against South Africa. He represented Players against Gentlemen at Lord's in 1882 and was on MCC's ground staff.

First-class career (1882-87): 430 runs (14.33) and 64 wickets (13.57)
Test matches (2): 33 runs (16.50) and 8 wickets (11.25)

FOWLER, Graeme (b.1957)

Lancashire

A neat, jaunty left-handed opening batsman and a fine athlete, as befits his other profession as a teacher of PE, Accrington-born Fowler took advantage of TCCB bans on Graham Gooch, Geoff Boycott, Wayne Larkins and others by scoring consistently for Lancashire throughout the 1982 season and earning a place in the England team for the last Test of the summer, the decisive third match at Headingley against Pakistan. He was bowled for nine in the first innings but, showing confidence and good technique against Imran Khan, he made 86 in the second innings to inspire an England win and make sure of his place on the plane to Australia. A useful reserve wicket-keeper but also a fine all-round fielder, he first played for Lancashire's second eleven in 1973 at the age of 16 and made his first appearance in a first-class match in 1979, but was not capped until 1981 when he hit 1,560 runs at an average of 40. Shrewdly advised by his friend David Lloyd, Fowler's three hundreds in his first full season were followed by five in 1982, including two in one match against Warwickshire at Southport when he batted with an injured leg and a runner in each innings. He hits the ball very hard, especially on the off-side.

First-class career (1979-): 3,233 runs (37.16) including 9 centuries
Test matches (1): 95 runs (47.50) and 1 catch

FREEMAN, Alfred Percy (1888-1965)

Kent

'Tich' Freeman must have bowled more balls that looked as if they could be hit for six than any bowler who ever lived, but his records in domestic cricket were simply fantastic. Regularly he took more than 200 wickets a season for Kent when the next most successful bowler managed about 60. In eight seasons between 1928 and 1935 he took more than 2,000 wickets. He bowled wonderfully well-controlled, right-arm leg-breaks, mixed with a skilfully disguised googly and top spinner. Against the best county batsmen he was a threat, against the worst a tyrant.

'Tich' Freeman

Only five feet two inches tall he had small hands but very strong fingers which enabled him to turn the ball sharply. Ian Peebles has described how after hitching up his trousers he would run up five paces and deliver the ball with a neat rotary action, 'like a spring snapping'. The quick feet beat him, however, and the Australians were not afraid of him. He took 304 wickets (18.05) in 1928, a record in first-class cricket, but that winter, in Australia, he did not appear in a single Test. In his first tour of Australia, 1924/5, he had taken eight wickets at 57.37 in two Tests. Such triumph set off by such failure is practically without parallel. He mesmerised the West Indies in their first Test series in 1928, heading the bowling with 22 wickets (13.72); and against South Africa, 1927/8 and 1929, he captured 14 and 22 wickets respectively. Only Wilfred Rhodes has taken more wickets in first-class cricket, and no one has taken more than his 3,151 in the County Championships.

First-class career (1914-36): 4,913 runs (9.40), 3,776 wickets (18.42), 249 catches and 1 stumping
Test matches (12): 154 runs (14.00), 66 wickets (25.86) and 4 catches

FRY, Charles Burgess (1872-1956)

Oxford University, Surrey, Sussex and Hampshire

One of the legendary figures of cricket, C.B. Fry was a man of such majesty that he was actually offered the Kingdom of Albania. Unfortunately for that country Fry declined and King Zog ruled in his stead. His talent as a batsman blossomed gloriously during the early years of this century. He studied with a scholar's application the technique of batting and had the concentration and determination, as well as the physical strength and fitness, to master most bowlers in most conditions; science applied to genius was formidable indeed. Pre-eminently a back-foot player, he had a powerful straight drive but scored mainly on the leg-side and he had a cast-iron defence. A critic once said he had only one stroke. 'True,' replied Charles Fry, 'but I can send it in twenty-two places.' Ranji and C.B. Fry were the twin champions of Sussex: on what one likes to think of as a typical day at Hove, Fry would win the toss, open with Joe Vine and, as a matter of course, have an exhilarating stand later with Ranji. At close of play Sussex would be 500 for 2, with Fry some 200 not out. Six times between 1899 and 1905 he scored more than 2,000 in a season, in 1901 reaching 3,147 runs (78.67) which included 13 centuries, six of them in succession. Although he could never spare the time for a tour of Australia, he played in Tests against 'the ancient enemy' in England in 1899, 1902, 1905, 1909 and 1912, in the latter year leading England to victory. He toured South Africa in 1895/6 and played against them at home in 1907 and 1912. He captained Sussex in 1904, 1905, 1907 and 1908. He made magnificent centuries against Australia and South Africa, 144 at The Oval in 1905, and 129 at The Oval in 1907, and as late as 1921, while playing for Hampshire, he was again invited to play against Australia, but declined on grounds of age. A fine field, he had a chequered career as a bowler, being labelled a 'thrower' and, for a time, had his bowling arm in splints. Fry himself insisted that all his deliveries were fair. Although it was his cricket that captured the public imagination, Charles Fry was the complete all-round man. He was a dazzling and, if Neville Cardus is to be believed, domineering conversationalist, and a brilliant scholar (placed above a future Lord Chancellor, F.E. Smith, on the scholarship roll to Wadham

C.B. Fry

College, Oxford). He held the world record for long jump for twenty-one years, played Association Football for England and also earned a Cup Final medal (with Southampton). He edited *Fry's Magazine*, wrote several books of permanent cricket interest, an autobiography and a novel (the latter with his wife), served on the League of Nations, stood as a Liberal candidate for Parliament and, the great purpose of his life, trained the young on T.S. *Mercury* on the Hamble. Only look at his photograph and you will see why H.S. Altham wrote of him, 'Fry could, alike in form and feature, have stepped out of the frieze of the Parthenon.'

First-class career (1892-1921): 30,886 runs (50.22) including 94 centuries, 165 wickets (28.68) and 218 catches
Test matches (26): 1,223 runs (32.18) including 2 centuries, 0-3 and 17 catches

GATTING, Michael William (b.1957)

Middlesex

Mike Gatting, a natural games player whose brother has played football for Arsenal, is one of a group of exceptionally talented batsmen who graduated from the England school sides of the early 1970s. A cheerful Londoner, short but very solidly built, he is a very straight, hard-hitting right-handed batsman, useful medium-pace bowler and good all-round field. Playing his first match for Middlesex in 1975, he won his cap in 1977 when he scored more than 1,000 runs despite not scoring a century and gained the last place in the England touring team to Pakistan and New Zealand, playing in a Test in each country without success. As soon as he had scored his initial championship hundred, 136 against Surrey in 1980, he added another immediately and developed into one of the few English batsmen who could be relied upon to trade blow for blow with the overseas stars in county cricket. In 1980, he made a determined 51 not out in the Centenary Test against Australia at Lord's and, although he failed against ferocious bowling in the West Indies in 1980/81, he played attractively and consistently for England throughout the 1981 Ashes series, scoring 370 runs in 12 innings at 30.83. He hit four fifties but his highest score was only 59. He held several crucial catches. In the season he scored 1,492 runs (55.23). In India the following winter he was given too little chance to bat high in the order and gained little from the tour. He was omitted from England's side at the start of 1982, but forced his way back with several commanding innings in county cricket. Alas, some careless shots against Pakistan prevented him from developing several promising starts and this gifted and enterprising all-rounder was unwisely omitted from England's team in Australia in 1982/3.

Mike Gatting

First-class career (1975-): 8,725 runs (38.95) including 16 centuries, 87 wickets (24.42) and 156 catches
Test matches (22): 797 runs (22.77), 0-1 and 17 catches

GAY, Leslie Hewitt (1871-1949)

Cambridge University, Hampshire and Somerset

In a rather short, irregular career, Leslie Gay won a blue at Cambridge and kept wicket in one Test, for England in Australia, 1894/5, scoring 33 and 4, catching 3 and stumping one. A Corinthian, he kept goal for England at Association Football in three matches in 1893/4, and is thus a double international.

First-class career (1891-1900): 1,004 runs (15.93) and 85 dismissals (66 ct, 19 st.)

GEARY, George (1893-1981)

Leicestershire

One of a family of sixteen, George Geary thought of emigrating. But fortunately he remained and, with Ewart Astill, carried Leicestershire on his shoulders for many seasons. Big, strong and cheerful, despite suffering some unpleasant injuries, he was a right-arm, fast-medium bowler with a high action and unwavering accuracy. He could also turn off-spinners if the conditions warranted. As a batsman he played many valiant innings with a good range of strokes; and he was a superb slip field, his long reach enabling him to hold some dazzling catches. Eleven times he took a hundred wickets in a season. In his first Test against Australia, at Headingley in 1926, he shared in an invaluable ninth-wicket partnership of 108 with George Macaulay; and the same year, at The Oval, his two excellent catches in the last innings helped England to win the rubber. In Australia in 1928/9 he broke his nose but played on and, in the first innings of the final Test at Melbourne, took 5 for 105 in 81 overs, 36 of which were maidens, a remarkable feat of endurance. At Sydney in the second match he captured 5 for 35 and scored 66, and he headed the bowling averages for the series, with 19 wickets (25.10). On matting in South Africa, 1927/8, he was quite deadly, taking 12 for 130 in the first Test at Johannesburg, when the South Africans considered him the best in the world under those conditions. Later, elbow trouble incapacitated him. For his county he took all 10 for 18 against Glamorgan at Pontypridd, 1929, which was a world record until eclipsed by Hedley Verity (10 for 10) three years later. In retirement he was coach at Charterhouse, where he put Peter May on the road to success.

First-class career (1912-38): 13,504 runs (19.80) including 8 centuries, 2,063 wickets (20.04) and 451 catches
Test matches (14): 249 runs (15.56), 46 wickets (29.41) and 13 catches

GIBB, Paul Anthony (1913-77)

Cambridge University, Yorkshire and Essex

Awarded his blue at Cambridge in 1935, Paul Gibb became, in the same year, the first Yorkshire amateur to make a century on his debut for the county, scoring 157 against Nottinghamshire at Bramall Lane. In 1938/9 he further proved his appetite for the big occasion when he scored 93 and 106 in his first Test against South Africa at Johannesburg. He was a right-handed batsman who defended stoutly and drove admirably, and also a very competent wicket-keeper. He toured Australia in 1946/7, but retired from the game on his return home. He reappeared in 1951 as a professional for Essex and played with success until becoming an umpire in 1956. He travelled the country in a caravan. At the time of his death he was a bus driver, and had been so reserved that none of his workmates knew of his origins.

First-class career (1934-56): 12,520 runs (28.07) including 19 centuries, and 544 dismissals (423 ct, 121 st.)
Test matches (8): 581 runs (44.69) including 2 centuries, and 4 dismissals (3 ct, 1 st.)

GIFFORD, Norman (b.1940)

Worcestershire and Warwickshire

With his relatively flat trajectory and low delivery, often from wide of the crease, Norman Gifford has never been a beautiful left-arm spinner to watch, but for twenty years he has earned the respect of county batsmen for his unerring accuracy and his ability to bowl sides out whenever the wicket helps him. He is also a determined and resourceful left-handed tail-ender. A Lancastrian from the Furness district, his career began when he answered an advertisement in *The Cricketer* placed by Worcestershire, who quickly saw his ability. Lancashire also offered him terms but he has not regretted his choice and in 1974 he captained Worcestershire to an exciting win in the County Championship. Ruddy-faced and curly-haired, he is a witty man with a cool temperament and astute cricket brain; his captaincy has been outstanding although marked at one point by a dispute between players and committee over pay. In his first full season he took 133 wickets. In 1964 he played in two Tests against Australia, doing creditably but, with Derek Underwood barring the way for other left-arm spinners after 1966, he did not play again until 1971. However, he bowled particularly well in India, Pakistan and Sri Lanka in 1972/3, and two England captains, Illingworth and Lewis, thought there was little to choose between Gifford and Underwood on good pitches. Worcestershire released him after the 1982 season when his appearances had been restricted because of his elevation to the England selection committee. Instead he was offered terms by Warwickshire for the 1983 season.

First-class career (1960-   ): 6,302 runs (13.70), 1,720 wickets (22.81) and 282 catches
Test matches (15): 179 runs (16.27) 33 wickets (31.09) and 8 catches

GILLIGAN, Arthur Edward Robert (1894-1976)

Cambridge University, Surrey and Sussex

The most famous of three brothers who gained distinction at the game, Arthur Gilligan was a happy ambassador for cricket in England, Australia, South Africa and India. A fighter but endlessly cheerful, he got the best out of Sussex, whom he captained from 1922 until 1929, by making the county one of the best fielding sides. He led England to success in the rubber against South Africa in 1924 and also to her first win over Australia after the First World War, at Melbourne in 1924/5. While his health lasted, he was a lively right-arm fast bowler, accurate and always bowling at the stumps or for catches in the slips. He was a courageous batsman anywhere in the order – his initial hundred in first-class cricket was made at number eleven – and believed that all bowlers were made to be hit. Fielding at mid-off he ranked among the best. In 1924 at Edgbaston he took 6 for 7, with Maurice Tate dismissing South Africa for 30 (and in the second innings he claimed 5 for 83), but some weeks later he was hit badly over the heart while batting and his doctor advised him to stop bowling fast. As a bowler he was never the same force again. He later became immersed in the administration of the game and was successively president and patron of Sussex C.C.C. and president of MCC (in 1967). He was popular as a radio commentator, especially in Australia, and, while teamed with Victor Richardson, 'What do you think, Arthur?' became a catch-phrase. He wrote a study of Sussex cricket and some well-received tour books, *Collins's Men, The Urn Returns* and *Australian Challenge*.

First-class career (1919-32): 9,140 runs (20.08) including 12 centuries, and 868 wickets (23.20)
Test matches (11): 209 runs (16.07), 36 wickets (29.05) and 3 catches

Arthur Gilligan leads out the England team to field at Melbourne in 1924/5. The players are, from left to right, Maurice Tate, Patsy Hendren, Arthur Gilligan, Herbert Sutcliffe and Harold Strudwick

GILLIGAN, Alfred Harold Herbert (1896-1978)

Cambridge University and Sussex

A determined right-handed batsman, often opening the batting, a useful change-bowler and a keen field, Harold Gilligan succeeded his brother Arthur as captain of Sussex in 1929 for two seasons. In 1929/30 he led England in the first-ever Tests against New Zealand, England winning the rubber. During the First World War, as a pilot in the Royal Navy Air Service, he piloted the first plane to fly over the German fleet at Kiel; engine trouble developed and he spent three days and nights in the North Sea before help came. One of his daughters, Virginia, married P.B.H. May.

First-class career (1919-31): 8,873 runs (17.96), 116 wickets (33.37) and 120 catches
Test matches (4): 71 runs (17.75)

GIMBLETT, Harold (1914-78)

Somerset

When only a young farmer, Harold Gimblett hit 123 against Essex at Frome in 1935, his first county match, treating the bowling with unbecoming levity for sixty-three minutes. A right-hander, he cut, drove, pulled and hooked in a manner which gave him fame overnight. He soon opened the batting and continued his swashbuckling way, once hitting three sixes in an over during which his partner appealed against the light. Also a versatile fielder, he blazed a trail in 1936 which many thought would lead to regular international honours, and, indeed, on his Test debut against India at Lord's he hit 67 not out on a frisky wicket. But he played in only two more Tests and never against Australia. His highest was 310 against Sussex at Eastbourne in 1948, and he exceeded 1,000 runs in twelve English seasons and once with a Commonwealth team in India. On retirement he held his county's record for runs and centuries in a career, and runs in a season. Latterly, he was dogged by ill-health.

First-class career (1935-54): 23,007 runs (36.17) including 50 centuries, and 41 wickets (51.80)
Test matches (3): 129 runs (32.25) and 1 catch

GLADWIN, Clifford (b.1916)

Derbyshire

Always remembered for his Derbyshire partnership with Les Jackson, Cliff Gladwin was a tall, rather gangling, lively right-arm in-dipping seam bowler, who achieved greater cunning and accuracy as the years went by, seriously begrudging the batsman every run. As a tail-end batsman, he was more light-hearted, his best efforts usually being saved for times of crisis. Generally a cheerful extrovert, he was given to impulsive gestures. He toured South Africa with MCC in 1948/9, and it was a leg-bye off his thigh that won the Durban Test off the last ball of the match. He took 100 wickets or more in a season twelve times.

First-class career (1939-58): 6,283 runs (17.36) including 1 century, and 1,653 wickets (18.30)
Test matches (8): 170 runs (28.33), 15 wickets (38.06) and 2 catches

GODDARD, Thomas William John (1900-1966)

Gloucestershire

Originally Tom Goddard was an undistinguished right-arm fast bowler for his county. But at twenty-nine he began bowling off-breaks and the effect was

Tom Goddard

dramatic. In his first season he took 184 wickets (16.38) and never looked back. Six foot three inches tall with enormous hands, he could turn the ball sharply, coming fast off the pitch, and was a master of flight. His appeal, a rolling, burring 'How wer're it?' was West Country incarnate. Tom played once for England against Australia in 1930 – his first Test – and occasionally against New Zealand, West Indies and South Africa; he toured South Africa in 1930/31 and 1938/9, when he achieved the hat-trick in the first Test at Johannesburg. His impressive statistics might have been better had he not already been thirty-five when the new Lbw Law from 1937 gave encouragement to off-spinners, and he was nearing fifty when off-spin began to replace leg-spin in Tests. Sixteen times he took over a hundred wickets in a season.

First-class career (1922-52): 5,224 runs (9.41) and 2,979 wickets (19.84)
Test matches (8): 13 runs (6.50), 22 wickets (26.72) and 3 catches

GOOCH, Graham Alan (b.1953)

Essex and Western Province

A big, dark, fresh-faced man whose trade-marks have become a droopy black moustache and a large, faded, cream-coloured sunhat, Graham Gooch needs only a bushy beard to give him, from a distance, the appearance of a youthful W.G. Grace. After an uncertain start in Test cricket he developed as a magnificent right-handed opening batsman who loves to attack and hits the ball immensely hard, especially excelling in the drive and hook. He is a useful medium-paced seam bowler and a fine fielder anywhere. After a distinguished schoolboy career in Essex and for the Young England side, with whom he toured the West Indies in 1972, he came to prominence with Essex. He played a commanding innings for MCC against the Australians in 1975, hitting both Jeff Thomson and Gary Gilmour for towering sixes into the grandstand, and was picked for England following his maiden Championship hundred against Kent. But he was out of his depth against Lillee and Thomson, scoring a pair on a spiteful rain-affected wicket in his first Test at Edgbaston. Dropped after one more match, he was retarded by this premature taste of life at the top but found form again as an opening batsman in 1978 and played consistently enough on his return to the England side to earn a place in Mike Brearley's successful touring team to Australia in 1978/9. There the extra bounce of Australian pitches, many of them unreliable, resulted in a succession of low scores but, dropping down the order to number four, he justified the selectors' faith with his fine 74 in the sixth Test which helped England to their historic 5-1 win in the series. By now he had established a fruitful partnership with Geoff Boycott, and it remained more or less undisturbed until March 1982 when both decided to join a commercially sponsored tour of South Africa against the wishes of the TCCB and the other ICC countries. Along with 14 others Gooch was suspended from Test cricket for three years. He was at the peak of his powers at the time and England could not afford to lose this talented and enterprising opener who had played such innings as 99 (not out) v. Australia at

Graham Gooch

David Gower

Melbourne in 1979/80, 123 v. West Indies at Lord's in 1980 (a magnificent exhibition of driving against fierce fast bowling), two more hundreds against West Indies in 1980/81, 116 at Bridgetown and 153 at Kingston (400 runs in 8 innings in this series at 57.50) and 127 against India at Madras in 1981/2 (487 runs in the series at 54.11). In South Africa he was elected captain of the 'rebel' side and played a number of brilliant innings. He played for Western Province in 1982/3, ironically as a replacement for the South African-born Allan Lamb, who had become an England player in Gooch's absence. Off the field the occasional dry comment delivered in a low London drawl reflects a keen sense of humour, and he delights in imitating other cricketers for the benefit of the crowd.

First-class career (1973-): 13,711 runs (39.39) including 31 centuries, 83 wickets (33.56) and 195 catches
Test matches (42): 2,540 runs (35.77) including 4 centuries, 8 wickets (43.50) and 36 catches

GOVER, Alfred Richard (b.1908)

Surrey

In retirement Alf Gover has been well known for his famous London cricket school near Clapham Junction, where many of the world's great players have practised in their time. A right-arm fast bowler, he spent half his career bowling on shirt-front wickets at The Oval. He had pace, length, direction and frequent 'devil'; what he lacked was co-operation in the Surrey slips. In his first Test, against India at Old Trafford in 1936, two catches were dropped off his bowling on the first morning. Running in like a man pursuing but not catching a bus, he would pound away with his arms working like pistons – his 'cocktail-mixing action' – culminating in some dangerous break-backs and late away-swingers. He took at least 100 wickets in eight seasons and in 1935 he took four wickets with successive deliveries at Worcester. The following year, by taking 200 wickets at 17.73, he was the first English fast bowler in thirty-nine years to take as many wickets in a season. His batting caused vast amusement; the crowd hoped for beefy, agricultural blows and often saw them, but he rarely stayed for long. He toured India with Lord Tennyson's team in 1937/8.

First-class career (1928-48): 2,312 runs (9.36), 1,555 wickets (23.63) and 171 catches
Test matches (4): 2 runs (—), 8 wickets (44.87) and 1 catch

GOWER, David Ivon (b.1957)

Leicestershire

A casual, friendly man, David Gower is a left-handed batsman of rare brilliance and a superb fieldsman. He has not achieved all that his ability suggested he would when first he arrived in Test cricket, partly through lack of concentration, partly through lazy footwork; but he is, like Frank Woolley, as much an entertainer as a breaker of records. Indeed he is one of the few players whom spectators, young and old, look forward to seeing every time he plays. There is a touch and elegance about his batting which is uniquely his. Tall, with fair curly hair and the body of a natural athlete who can play any game well, his timing has the exquisite touch of a Menuhin. He stands straight and still at the crease, moves easily into the line of the ball and plays it late with the relaxed air of a man always in control. His record in Test cricket has been reasonably consistent, since the day in 1978 when, still twenty-one, he calmly and instinctively hooked his first ball in Test cricket for four. Liaquat Ali was the bowler and Pakistan the first of many sides destined to suffer at the hands of perhaps the most gifted batsman to play for England since Denis Compton. His superlative cover fielding and occasional dazzling brilliance close to the wicket have been an added bonus. Born in Tunbridge Wells, he was educated at King's School, Canterbury, and with eight 'O' levels and three 'A' levels he began a Law course in London but abandoned it after a year to take up a professional career with Leicestershire who were quicker than Kent to offer him terms. Outstanding in the England Schools and young England teams, notably on tours to South Africa and the West Indies (1974/5), he first played for Leicestershire in 1975 and for some time scored more runs for them in limited-over cricket than he did in the Championship where he tended to get himself out to rash strokes outside the off-stump. He became England's outstanding player in his first home series against Pakistan and New Zealand in 1978 and also in Australia in 1978. His first Test century at The Oval against New Zealand was followed by another in Perth and by 200 not out against India at Edgbaston in 1979. A lean period followed, especially in home Tests, and he was dropped during the 1980 series against the West Indies. But on the tour of the Caribbean early in 1981 he played with a new maturity, hitting 187 against Young West Indies in the first match of the tour and 154 not out in the fourth and final Test, at Sabina Park. He did not add to his four Test hundreds in India and Sri Lanka in 1981/2, or at home against India and Pakistan in 1982 but, though he still succumbed to the occasional loose stroke, he was steadily becoming a more consistent batsman. He became vice-captain of England in 1982 and at the age of 25 led his country for the first time that season in the Lord's Test against Pakistan, when Willis, the officially appointed captain for the series, was injured. England were beaten but although Gower's batting in the match was unusually careworn, he still looked likely to become a successful captain in the future.

First-class career (1975-): 9,812 runs (38.17) including 17 centuries, 4 wickets (19.50) and 98 catches
Test matches (44): 2,897 runs (42.60) including 4 centuries, and 24 catches

GRACE, Dr Edward Mills (1841-1911)

Gloucestershire

Barring his younger brother, W.G., it would be hard to name anyone who was – in his time – a more remarkable matchwinner than Dr Edward Grace. 'The Coroner', as he was called, was primarily an attacking right-handed batsman, a lob-bowler who took thousands of wickets in club cricket, and an outstanding field at point (then a far more important position than it is today). Fame came early; in 1862 he was the most dangerous batsman in the country and a dominant all-rounder, and for MCC against Gentlemen of Kent he scored 192 not out and took all 10 wickets in an innings. In 1863 he made over 3,000 runs in all matches and, that winter, toured with George Parr's team to Australia, the second such side, but failed to enhance his reputation, a bad hand and reckless hitting being the main causes. Later he was put in the shade by W.G., but he played for Gloucestershire from 1871 until 1896, serving also as secretary from 1871 (when the club was founded) until 1909. He and his brothers G.F. and W.G. represented England in the first-ever Test in England, against Australia at The Oval in 1880, and he made 36 (putting on 96 with W.G. for the first wicket) and 0.

E.M. Grace

First-class career (1862-96): 10,025 runs (18.67) including 5 centuries, 305 wickets (20.37), 366 catches and 1 stumping

GRACE, George Frederick (1850-1880)

Gloucestershire

Frederick Grace was tall, handsome and muscular and the most charming of the Graces. His right-handed, free-hitting batting was more attractive to the eye than that of his elder brothers, though he did not have W.G.'s tremendous concentration and tempered-steel defence. The fifth and youngest of the brotherhood, he had a great career opening before him, but in 1880 a severe cold, caught while engaged in a club match, developed into congestion of the lungs, and he was dead within three days. A fortnight previously he had played with E.M. and W.G. in the first Test against Australia at The Oval and had failed to score in either innings, but his great catch off a soaring hit by George Bonnor is part of the legend of the game. The batsmen were on their third run when the steepler landed in Fred's hands, which his speed and judgement had brought precisely into the right position close on the boundary. He also held another catch in the match. He toured Australia with W.G.'s team in 1873. He was also successful for Gentlemen against Players, scoring 1,008 runs (31.50), including one century in twenty-four matches, and appeared for his county from 1870 to 1880, scoring 3,216 runs (30.6).

First-class career (1866-80): 6,910 runs (25.04) including 8 centuries, 328 wickets (19.98), 177 catches and 8 stumpings

GRACE, Dr William Gilbert (1848-1915)
Gloucestershire
'W.G.' is still, a century after his prime, the most famous cricketer of all. His tall, broad, bearded figure is still instantly recognized today wherever the game is played. No one else has ever dominated the field so long and indisputably by prowess and personality alike; he was for years, with W.E. Gladstone, the best-known of all Englishmen and, in a sense, he epitomized the British passion for sport, the seeds of which were sown in every part of the Empire. He possessed colossal physical energy and an unappeasable appetite for every department of the game; and he put cricket 'on the map' as a public spectacle. He played lustily and within the law, but at times, with a twinkle in his eye, he stretched the rules. In the 1870s and 1880s particularly, he was head and shoulders above his fellows. The fourth of five brothers, who were all devoted to the game and whose father and mother coached and encouraged them, he burst into first-class cricket early and retained his power for forty years. Tall and strong, he made his first century at fifteen – 170 for South Wales against Gentlemen of Sussex at Hove – and, at forty-six, bearded and burly, he made his hundredth in first-class cricket, 288 for Gloucestershire against Somerset at Bristol. In 1871 he became the first man ever to reach 2,000 runs in a season, 2,739 runs (78.25), which remained his own highest aggregate. In 1873 he was the first to achieve the double – 2,139 runs and 106 wickets – a feat he achieved each year until 1878, and twice in the 1880s. In 1876 he made 2,622 runs (62.42), including 344 for MCC against Kent at Canterbury. This innings was followed in the next week by scores of 177 against Nottinghamshire and 318 not out against Yorkshire. In 1895, his 'Indian Summer', he was the first to achieve 1,000 runs in May (the month in which he also hit his hundredth century), and so spontaneous was the public reaction that four testimonials were started. Many of these colossal performances were achieved on pitches which were dangerous and unpredictable. He captained Gloucestershire for twenty-five years and led them on the two occasions they have won the Championship. When he first played for Gentlemen in 1865, they had lost their last nineteen matches. When he last played in 1906 they had lost only four more. He took a side to Australia in 1872/3 and captained Lord Sheffield's Test-playing side in 1891. He hit the first century in Tests in England, 152 at The Oval in 1880, in the first match; and in 1886, in the Oval Test, his 170 was the highest of three centuries he made against the touring team that year. He led England most times between 1880 and 1899, with success. He retired from the Tests in the latter year because 'the ground was getting too far away'. A natural athlete in his younger days, he was a first-rate hurdler and runner. Grace's right-handed batting was based on a correct technique and an assertive attitude. At times he undoubtedly overawed his opponents as on the occasion when he was bowled early in a minor match but at once replaced the bails and batted on, pointing out that the crowd had come to watch him bat and not the unfortunate bowler! But his true genius is not in doubt; no one sighted the ball and assessed its length earlier, or timed it more truly than he did, and he was equally at home on the back or front foot – 'the faster they bowl, the better I like them'. As a bowler with a round-arm action, he varied his flight skilfully, his pace usually very slow, turning the ball in from leg. He was a magnificent catcher off his own bowling. In first-class cricket he exceeded 1,000 runs twenty-eight times and 100 wickets ten times. He kept up with club cricket to the last, played bowls for England, followed all sports and ran with the beagles. Stories of 'The Champion' abound, of course. Most are true. In his last great season, 1898, he suddenly 'declared', for no apparent reason, when 93 not out and on his way to his fourth century of the season. Asked why, he said that he had just remembered that 93 was the one score between nought and a hundred he had never got. On the day

W.G. Grace

that his wife produced their second child he was playing for the United South against twenty-two local players at Grimsby. He celebrated by making 400 out of his side's total of 681. Given out once at The Oval he remonstrated in his loud, squeaky voice: 'Shan't have it, can't have it, *won't* have it.' The riposte from Walter Read was: 'But you'll *have* to have it.' Once he had cooled down, W.G. would have seen the humour in this; he could always laugh at himself. He died of a heart attack after an air raid in 1915 and it was appropriate that this symbol of the British Empire should die during the war which marked the beginning of the end of Britain's dominant role in the world.

First-class career (1865-1908): 54,896 runs (39.55) including 126 centuries, 2,876 wickets (17.99) and 872 catches
Test matches (22): 1,098 runs (32.29) including 2 centuries, 9 wickets (26.22) and 39 catches

GRAVENEY, Thomas William (b.1927)

Gloucestershire, Worcestershire and Queensland

For many years the bearer of Gloucestershire's (and later Worcestershire's) post-War torch, Tom Graveney was a tall, stylish right-handed batsman with a complete array of elegant strokes played mainly off the front foot. He was also a good slip and occasionally useful leg-spin bowler. Whether making 0 or 90, he looked as if he enjoyed his cricket and such was his grace and touch that few batsmen have given more pleasure to spectators. Early in his Test career he would too often give his wicket away, and he did less well in Australia than elsewhere partly because the high bounce tended to undermine the effectiveness of his front-foot technique, yet he was the most prolific craftsman of his generation and the first of only six to have scored 100 centuries since the Second World War. Twenty-one times he exceeded 1,000 runs in a season (twice on tours), and four times scored two centuries in the same match. Two of these were overseas – 153 and 120 at Bombay in 1956/7 (for C.G. Howard's XI) and 164 and 107 not out at Lahore in 1963/4 (for a Commonwealth XI against Pakistan). Such performances in extreme heat proved his ability to concentrate. Against Australia he scored only one Test century – his superb 111 in about two hours in the fifth Test at Sydney, 1954, when the Ashes had already been decided. Against the West Indies, on the other hand, he was often outstanding when others struggled. His 258 against them at Trent Bridge in 1957 silenced those critics who had questioned his temperament. Three years earlier he had shared in a record partnership of 402 with Willie Watson against British Guiana and in 1966 he made a highly successful return to Tests with 459 runs in 7 innings at 76.50. He captained Gloucestershire in 1959 and 1960 and Worcestershire from 1968 to 1970; and he led England against Australia at Headingley in 1968 (in an emergency). He played for and coached Queensland where he lived for some time and, on returning to the U.K., became landlord of a pub near Cheltenham. He was awarded the OBE for his services to cricket, and he became an articulate and justly popular commentator on the game for the BBC.

Tom Graveney

First-class career (1948-72): 47,793 runs (44.91) including 122 centuries, 80 wickets (37.96), 547 catches and 1 stumping
Test matches (79): 4,882 runs (44.38) including 11 centuries, 1-167 and 80 catches

GREENHOUGH, Thomas (b.1931)

Lancashire

Tommy Greenhough (the second syllable pronounced 'hoff'), was one of the outstanding right-hand leg-break bowlers of the fifties and early sixties until he became handicapped by sundry injuries to fingers and feet. He was also unfortunate in that his was a dying art in England. He ran in a long way for a leg-spinner, with bouncing strides and the ball cradled in both hands until delivery, and spun the ball considerably. He played for England against India in 1959 and South Africa in 1960, taking 5 for 35 in the first innings against India at Lord's.

First-class career (1951-66): 1,913 runs (8.42) and 751 wickets (22.37)
Test matches (4): 4 runs (1.33), 16 wickets (22.31) and 1 catch

GREENWOOD, Andrew (1847–89)

Yorkshire

Andrew Greenwood had family associations with Lascelles Hall, a nursery of Yorkshire cricket. A small man, he was a plucky, sound batsman and a brilliant outfield. He toured Australia in 1873/4 and 1876/7, appearing in the first two Tests ever played. He was nephew of the more famous Luke Greenwood. For Yorkshire, from 1869 until 1880, he scored 2,780 runs (17.82).

Test matches (2): 77 runs (19.25) and 2 catches

GREIG, Anthony William (b.1946)

Border, Eastern Province and Sussex

Although an outsize man with an outsize influence on the game of cricket, Tony Greig may be judged less severely by posterity than by his contemporaries. He was born in South Africa, the son of a Scottish father and South African mother, and lived there until 1966 when he moved to Sussex. From the start of his always controversial career he has been a Jekyll-and-Hyde character, a dashing handsome man in a hurry to succeed, charming and multi-talented yet also ruthless and at times disingenuous. It is simply not in doubt that he was a brave, determined and skilful all-round cricketer who seldom failed in Tests and many times seemed to be holding England's fortunes on his shoulders. He was never happier, indeed, than when he was doing so, for few other cricketers have so relished a fight against odds. Coming in at number six in the order he would immediately impose his personality on any match; with his six foot seven inch figure, almost always topped with a cap, he marched out swinging his bat round his shoulders as he prepared for battle. After the 1972/3 tour of India he adopted a policy of lifting the bat beyond stump height as the bowler approached and from the first ball he would be looking to drive. His batting was based on the front foot and his particular glories were the off-drive and the lofted straight drive, which he could produce at a moment of tension in a Test match (like the monstrous hit off Ashley Mallett into the outer at Melbourne in 1974/5) or in up-country matches, when he would delight crowds of all nationalities with his ability to hit the ball immense distances with no concern for the risks he was taking with his own average. His Test average is much better, in fact, than his career average – a testimony to his flair for the biggest challenge and the biggest occasion. Many of his best innings were played on two tours of India and one each to the West Indies and Australia. In the five Tests in the West Indies in 1974 he made 430 runs, with two centuries, at an average of 47.77, took 24 wickets at 22.62 each – whereas England's next best bowler, Pocock, took 9 wickets at 61 – and held seven catches. Yet his copy-book was blotted by his notorious running out of Alvin Kallicharran after the final ball of the day had been bowled. Greig publicly apologised and Kallicharran was reinstated. He was normally a medium-fast bowler, unpredictable but able to swing the ball a great deal and to get steep bounce, but in the Caribbean tour he turned to quickish off-spinners, and with inspired bowling won the fifth Test at Port of Spain for England by taking thirteen wickets in the match. Later in 1974 he scored a buccaneering 110 at Brisbane against Lillee and Thomson in their primes. As a slip fielder he was superlative, the safest and also the most brilliant of his era. Unsuccessful as a captain of Sussex, he was an inspiring captain of England in fourteen Tests, although in the field he was inclined to make wildly inappropriate moves on a sudden impetuous whim and tended either to attack or to defend with no policy in between. Nevertheless he led England brilliantly on and off the field in India in 1976/7 and had the world of cricket at his feet when he accepted Kerry Packer's secret offer to become the catalyst for the cricket revolution of 1977. While already earning upwards of £50,000 a year from various cricket contracts and allied business activities, and while a hundred percent certain to be England's captain against Australia in 1977, he spent some of his time, between the Centenary Test in Melbourne, March 1977, and the new English season, in travelling the world on Mr Packer's behalf helping to sign up many of the world's best cricketers to play in a newly promoted cricket series known at first as Packer's Circus but later by its official name, World Series Cricket. Greig was well

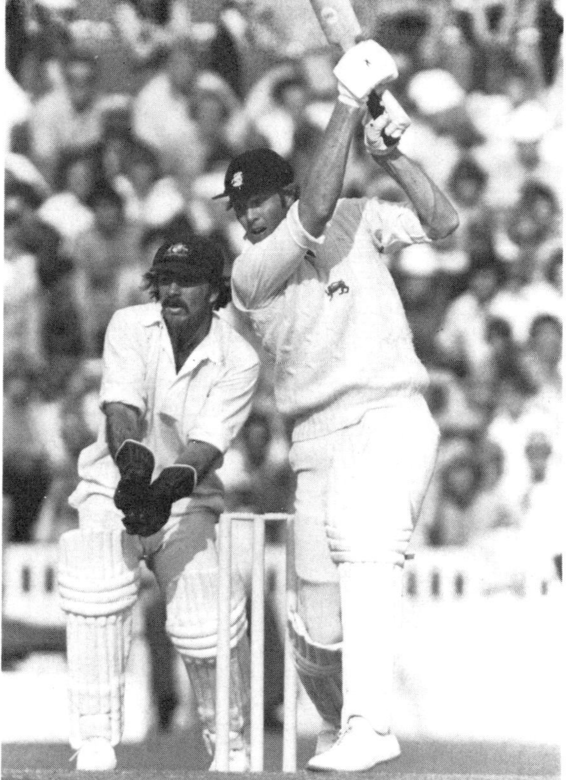

Tony Greig – Rodney Marsh (Australia) keeping wicket

aware that, by doing this in secret and by actually signing up members of his own England team for series which he knew would be bitterly opposed by the organizers of established cricket, he was burning the boats of his career in England. He was dismissed as captain of England for what was regarded as his betrayal of trust, but continued to play for England (successfully) under Mike Brearley in 1977. Banned for a time from playing for Sussex in 1978 because of his outspoken remarks in a newspaper article in breach of his county contract – he could never resist saying what he thought in public – he played only a few more matches for Sussex that year before emigrating to Australia and becoming a full-time executive with the Packer organization.

First-class career (1965-78): 16,660 runs (31.19) including 26 centuries, 856 wickets (28.85) and 345 catches
Test matches (58): 3,599 runs (40.43) including 8 centuries, 141 wickets (32.20) and 87 catches

GREIG, Ian Alexander (b.1955)

Cambridge University, Sussex, Border and Griqualand West

Destined in cricket always to live in the outsize shadow of his brother Tony, Ian Greig is a strong and capable right-handed all-round cricketer possibly a little below the high level of ability needed for sustained success at Test level. Personable, he was an outstanding captain at Cambridge in 1979 and led his team to an innings victory over Oxford at Lord's. He also won two blues at Rugby Union. He had to work hard for a regular place in the Sussex side. A medium-fast bowler with a good action, unexpected nip and a good command of swing and cut, he is also a determined middle-order batsman. An outstanding all-round season for Sussex in 1981 forced his name into the notebooks of England's selectors. In 1982 he won his first cap for England at Edgbaston against Pakistan, taking 4 for 59 in the first innings, identical figures to those returned by Tony Greig in *his* first official Test (4 for 59 in second innings v. Australia, 1972).

First-class career (1974-): 2,602 runs (24.09) including 2 centuries, 197 wickets (26.48) and 56 catches
Test matches (2): 26 runs (6.50) and 4 wickets (28.50)

GRIEVE, Basil Arthur Firebrace (1864-1917)

MCC

A member of the Harrow eleven of 1883 and of MCC for many years, and a wine merchant, Basil Grieve toured South Africa with Major Warton's team in 1888/9, and appeared in the two Tests, which were the first played on South African soil and also his earliest excursions in first-class cricket. He never represented a first-class county.

Test matches (2): 40 runs (40.00)

GRIFFITH, Stewart Cathie (b.1914)

Cambridge University, Surrey and Sussex

'Billy' Griffith was in the eleven at Dulwich for four years, keeping wicket in the last two, and making 1,300 runs. A Cambridge blue, he toured Australasia with MCC's 'goodwill' team in 1935/6 and, after a handful of county games, served as a glider pilot in the Airborne Division, being awarded the DFC for his services at Arnhem. He kept wicket in the five 'Victory' Tests against Australia in 1945. Appointed captain and secretary of Sussex, he toured the West Indies with MCC, 1947/8, as player and assistant-manager. Pressed into service as opening batsman in the second Test at Port of Spain, he hit his maiden century in first-class cricket, a resolute 140, which remained his career highest. In South Africa, 1948/9, he kept so well that he replaced Godfrey Evans in two Tests. Appointed assistant-secretary of MCC in 1952, he succeeded Ronald Aird as secretary in 1962, retiring in 1974. At a time of rapid change and many tensions (especially during the 'Stop the South African tour' campaign in 1970) it was fortunate that a man of his integrity, patience and expertise should have been the pilot of English cricket. His son Mike became a Cambridge blue and later Sussex captain. In 1979/80 Billy Griffith became president of MCC.

First-class career (1934-54): 4,846 runs (16.42) including 3 centuries, and 413 dismissals (329 ct, 84 st.)
Test matches (3): 157 runs (31.40) including 1 century, and 5 dismissals (5 ct)

GUNN, George (1879-1958)

Nottinghamshire

George Gunn was an original – a small, slim right-hander and for most of his long career an opening batsman. His style had sound classical foundations, but, as Sir Neville Cardus wrote, his mind and nature were whimsical, so that one day he would play an innings correct in every movement and principle, the next day produce something entirely unorthodox such as cutting a ball square from the leg-stump or walking out to the fastest bowling. Possessed of remarkable eyesight and judgment, he made his debut in Test cricket by chance. During the 1907/8 MCC tour he happened to be in Australia for health reasons; England's captain fell ill, and George was called in as reserve batsman. In the five Tests he included such scores as 119, 74, 65 and 122, heading the batting with

George Gunn

an average of 51.33 and making the 119 and 74 in his first Test match. An official member of MCC's team to Australia in 1911/12, he averaged 42.33 in the Tests, but he only appeared once against Australia in England. His only other tour was to the West Indies in 1929/30, and the season before he had celebrated his fiftieth birthday with a century off Worcestershire. Twenty times he exceeded 1,000 runs in a season. For several seasons with Nottinghamshire he appeared with his son, George Vernon Gunn, who predeceased him. His uncle William and elder brother John, were also Test cricketers.

First-class career (1902-32): 35,208 runs (35.96) including 62 centuries, 66 wickets (35.61) and 472 catches
Test matches (15): 1,120 runs (40.00) including 2 centuries, 0-8 and 15 catches

GUNN, John Richmond (1876-1963)

Nottinghamshire

A hard-working all-rounder, John Gunn was a stubborn left-handed batsman with a variety of strokes, a slow-medium bowler with skilful variation of flight and spin, and an excellent field at cover-point. He remains the only Nottinghamshire player to have scored 20,000 runs and taken 1,000 wickets for the county. In 1903 he shared with William Gunn in a record third-wicket stand of 369 against Leicestershire at Trent Bridge, his own share being his first county century and career highest, 294. Two years later he added 361 for the fourth wicket with A.O. Jones against Essex at Leyton, still also a record. In the same week in 1903 he took 14 for 142 against Surrey at The Oval and 14 for 174 against Essex at Leyton. He achieved the double four times but, in an age of great all-rounders, his sole tour was to Australia in 1901/2 with A.C. Maclaren's team. Like George Gunn he appeared only once in England, in 1905. Though he ceased playing for Nottinghamshire after 1925, he played further first-class cricket for Sir Julien Cahn's team.

First-class career (1896-1932): 24,557 runs (33.18) including 40 centuries, 1,243 wickets (24.56) and 239 catches
Test matches (6): 85 runs (10.62), 18 wickets (21.50) and 3 catches

GUNN, William (1858-1921)

Nottinghamshire

In organized county cricket Billy Gunn was perhaps the first of the great 'classic' batsmen, with a commanding height and reach, upright stance and whip-cord wrists. A right-handed batsman he set the pattern of beauty through technical perfection in English batting, and would exhibit a perfectly straight bat and finished style wherever he played. He was also a useful slow, round-arm bowler and a splendid, fast moving field in the deep. He had no sudden jump to fame, but he was at his best in the 1890s, when no England side was complete without him; and he enjoyed many great partnerships with Arthur Shrewsbury. He played a commanding innings of 228 for Players against Australians at Lord's in 1890 and his 102 not out for England against Australia in 1893 was the first Test century at Old Trafford. As a veteran, he shared with John Gunn in a record third-wicket stand of 369 against Leicestershire at Trent Bridge in 1903. Owing to the claims of his growing bat-making business, Gunn and Moore, he could afford to visit Australia only once. In earlier years a mainstay of Notts County, he represented England twice at soccer – one of the rare double internationals. He also became a director of Notts County. Starting his career with nothing, when he died he was worth £60,000.

First-class career (1880-1904): 25,840 runs (33.21) including 49 centuries, 76 wickets (23.68), 325 catches and 1 stumping
Test matches (11): 392 runs (21.77) including 1 century, and 5 catches

HAIG, Nigel Esmé (1887-1966)

Middlesex

Lean, wiry and enthusiastic, Nigel Haig would bowl tidy right-arm medium pace for long spells without showing any signs of fatigue. He was also a dangerous forcing batsman with strong wrists, whose upper-cut shocked the purists, and a fielder of feline prowess. He achieved the double three times, captained Middlesex with varying success from 1929 until 1934 – he was a member of the Championship-winning sides of 1920 and 1921 – toured the West Indies with MCC, 1929/30, appearing in the first Tests in the Caribbean, and represented England against Australia once in 1921. He was something of a sporting all-rounder and was also extremely well-read.

First-class career (1912-36): 15,224 runs (20.91) including 12 centuries, 1,117 wickets (27.48) and 221 catches
Test matches (5): 126 runs (14.00), 13 wickets (34.46) and 4 catches

HAIGH, Schofield (1871-1921)

Yorkshire

Dubbed 'the sunshine of the Yorkshire eleven', Schofield Haigh was a thorough sportsman, who loved the game. A member of the powerful side that won the Championship regularly at the turn of the century, he was a right-arm, medium-fast bowler whose off-cutters on sticky wickets would make him practically unplayable. He believed in bowling at the stumps and his observation after inspecting a sticky pitch remains embedded in the folklore of cricket, 'Methinks they'll deviate somewhat.' He developed as a good utilitarian batsman, able to defend stubbornly or attack briskly as the occasion demanded, and he was a keen field. In his four Tests against Australia he was not the force he was for Yorkshire, but on two tours of South Africa he had considerable success in all matches. In 1898/9 he captured 107 wickets (8.18), including 6 for 11 in the second innings of the Test at Cape Town when he and Albert Trott, unchanged, dismissed South Africa for 35. He took at least a hundred wickets in a season eleven times, and achieved the double once. After retiring from the county cricket he loved, he became a popular coach at Winchester.

First-class career (1895-1913): 11,715 runs (18.65) including 4 centuries, 2,012 wickets (15.94) and 274 catches
Test matches (11): 113 runs (7.53), 24 wickets (25.91) and 8 catches

HALLOWS, Charles (1895-1972)

Lancashire

'Good-looking in a sporting sort of way', as Sir Neville Cardus put it, Charlie Hallows was tall and slim, a stylish left-handed batsman and a fast fielder. He was opening batsman when Lancashire won the Championship three years in succession, 1926, 1927 and 1928. In 1928 he hit 1,000 runs in May – a feat which, up till then, had only been performed by W.G. and Walter Hammond – and, with effortless ease, he once hit a Nottinghamshire fast bowler over mid-on for six at Old Trafford, the ball dropping onto the platform at Warwick Road Station. Unlike many batsmen, he made it clear how much he was enjoying himself at the wicket. Although he scored heavily and passed 1,000 runs in a season six times, he was chosen only twice for England, both matches played at home, against Australia in 1921, and the West Indies in 1928. He earned the unique distinction of holding professional posts in Leagues in England, Scotland, Ireland and Wales.

First-class career (1914-32): 20,926 runs (40.24) including 55 centuries, and 19 wickets (41.26)
Test matches (2): 42 runs (42.00)

HAMMOND, Walter Reginald (1903-65)

Gloucestershire

Walter, or Wally, Hammond was simply one of the greatest cricketers ever. He was a product of Cirencester Grammar School and, although he had a chequered start to his career – appearing for Gloucestershire without birth or residential qualification and falling seriously ill in the Caribbean during his first tour with MCC – his immense natural talent was evident at once. Muscular and well-proportioned, he was from the beginning a daring and brilliant right-handed batsman: in 1927 at Old Trafford he put to the sword Champion county Lancashire's attack including McDonald, hitting 187 in three hours. His style ripened, as Sir Neville Cardus said, 'to an almost statuesque nobility, easy and powerful of stroke-play

Wally Hammond

but absolutely correct in its observance of first principles'. He reached 1,000 runs in the May of 1927 – only W.G. had previously achieved this in 1895 – and, on his first tour of Australia with MCC in 1928/9, he made 905 runs (113.12) in the series, which became a long-standing record. On his second tour in 1932/3 he hit 336 not out against New Zealand at Auckland, which remained for five years the highest in Tests. In addition, he hit six Test double centuries. He made three highly successful tours of South Africa, the last in 1938/39 as captain. Although often disappointing in Tests in England, no one who saw it will forget his classical and dignified batting against Australia at Lord's in 1938 when he scored 240, destroying the bowling with regal authority. Having turned amateur he captained England for the first time in this series. He also captained both Players and Gentlemen. During the Second World War he served in the RAF before playing with all his old freedom in the 'Victory' Tests against Australia in 1945. After a magnificent season in 1946, averaging 108 in the Championship, he led MCC in Australia that winter but, despite many successes outside the Tests, was very disappointing in the series itself and, on his return home, retired from regular first-class cricket. He had exceeded 1,000 runs in twenty-two seasons (five times overseas). Throughout, he was a nippy medium-fast bowler, especially effective with the new ball, and as a slip field he was swift and sure, one of the best ever. In 1929 he held 78 catches and, for more than a decade, 'c. Hammond b. Parker' was a regular feature of Gloucestershire's score-book. On retirement from English cricket he settled in South Africa, where he died, sadly rather a faded star and somewhat impoverished.

First-class career (1920-51): 50,551 runs (56.10) including 167 centuries, 732 wickets (30.58), 819 catches and 3 stumpings
Test matches (85): 7,249 runs (58.45) including 22 centuries, 83 wickets (37.80) and 110 catches

HAMPSHIRE, John Harry (b.1941)

Yorkshire, Derbyshire and Tasmania

John Hampshire (frequently called Jackie although he prefers his true name) is the only Englishman to have scored a century on his Test debut at Lord's, but most of his life has been devoted to Yorkshire cricket. He is a fine fielder and a powerfully built right-hander who always makes batting look relatively easy and hits the ball blisteringly hard, notably off the front foot. A failure to concentrate at times has kept down the number of really big scores, but by the time he was made Yorkshire captain in 1979 he had scored 1,000 runs or more in thirteen seasons, and all his runs had come at a healthy pace with the best interests of Yorkshire, rather than of himself, in mind. The one exception was his controversial 'go slow' at Northampton in 1978 when he blocked resolutely in order to draw public attention to what he considered to be selfish batting by his captain, Boycott. His debut Test innings was a courageous one of 107 against the West Indies in 1969 which helped to rescue his side after a poor start. But his appearances for England have been sporadic and, after his bright start, disappointing. He toured Australasia with Ray Illingworth's side of 1970/71, batting well without doing quite enough to win a regular Test place. He spent several winters in Tasmania, helping the island develop a team worthy of a place in the Sheffield Shield. Earlier in his career he was a useful leg-spin bowler. He was captain of Yorkshire for two seasons (1979-80), but could not hasten the county's longed-for new dawn and in 1982 he joined Derbyshire, making 1,264 runs (42.13) to underline his genuine quality.

First-class career (1961-): 26,666 runs (34.86) including 42 centuries, 30 wickets (54.43) and 420 catches
Test matches (8): 403 runs (26.86) including 1 century, and 9 catches

HARDINGE, Harold Thomas William (1886-1965)

Kent

Wally Hardinge was a sound and reliable right-handed opening batsman at a time of plenty. He made his debut at sixteen and was at his best in late Edwardian days when Kent were often Champion county. He reached 1,000 runs in a season eighteen times, but played only once for England, against Australia at Headingley in 1921, scoring 25 and 5. As a slow left-arm bowler he could break dangerous partnerships and he was a fleet-footed fieldsman, as befitted a soccer international, who played against Scotland as centre-forward in 1910. For many years he was on the staff of John Wisden & Co.

First-class career (1902-33): 33,519 runs (36.51) including 75 centuries, 371 wickets (26.37) and 293 catches

HARDSTAFF, Joseph, senior (1882-1947)

Nottinghamshire

Joseph Hardstaff earned the name 'Hotstuff' during MCC's Australian tour of 1907/8, when he was the most successful batsman, scoring 1,384 runs (51.25), including 311 in the Tests. A brilliant field in the deep, he was short but strongly built and a right-hander capable of scoring freely all round the wicket. Despite his successes in Australia and for his county, he never toured or played for England again, such was England's strength in the middle order. From 1927 until his death he stood as a first-class umpire, seventeen times in Tests until prevented by the selection of his son, 'Young Joe', for England.

First-class career (1902-26): 17,157 runs (31.36) including 26 centuries, 58 wickets (38.69), 183 catches and 2 stumpings
Test matches (5): 311 runs (31.10) and 1 catch

'Young Joe' Hardstaff

HARDSTAFF, Joseph, junior (b.1911)

Nottinghamshire and Auckland

'Young Joe' Hardstaff was a polished right-hander in the highest company and, although invaluable years were lost to the Second World War, he showed some magnificent form afterwards, notably in the first Test in peacetime, when he hit 205 not out against India at Lord's in 1946. His partnership of 215 with Len Hutton against Australia at The Oval in 1938 had revealed both the upstanding right-handed attacking style and the defensive qualities which augured so well. Joe toured Australia three times, 1935/6, 1936/7 and 1946/7, and the West Indies once, 1947/8. When he retired no one had made more runs for Nottinghamshire. He exceeded 1,000 runs fourteen times (once overseas) and his own son, another Joseph, has also appeared in first-class cricket.

First-class career (1930-55): 31,847 runs (44.35) including 83 centuries, and 35 wickets (60.00)
Test matches (23): 1,636 runs (46.74) including 4 centuries, and 9 catches

HARRIS, 4th Lord (1851-1932)

Oxford University and Kent

George Robert Canning, 4th Lord Harris, was perhaps the greatest administrator and 'missionary' in the history of cricket, remaining in the game all his life. After a thoroughly sound grounding at Eton and Oxford, he revived Kent C.C.C.; led a team to Canada and U.S.A. and the fifth team (1878/9) to Australia; collected and captained the team for the first Test in England; advanced the game in India while Governor of Bombay; befriended the professionals; opposed 'throwing' in bowling; upheld the Laws; contributed to the literature; served successively as president of Kent and of MCC and as a trustee and honorary treasurer of the Premier club; played from 1862 (his first net at Lord's) until 1930; appeared in four early Tests with success; and played for Gentlemen against Players for Kent from 1870 to 1889 when he was frequently captain. He appeared intermittently from 1895 to 1906 and once in 1911, against the first All Indian team. Of genuinely high rank as a player, he was a forcing right-handed batsman, especially severe on fast bowlers, a brilliant field and a useful change-bowler. Autocratic and unable to suffer fools gladly, he nonetheless promoted the honour and skill of the game at all levels. He served as Under-Secretary of State for India and Under-Secretary of State for War in the Administrations of the Marquess of Salisbury.

First-class career (1870-1911): 9,898 runs (26.75) including 11 centuries, and 75 wickets (23.72)
Test matches (4): 145 runs (29.00), 0-29 and 2 catches

Lord Harris

HARTLEY, Col. John Caborn (1874-1963)

Oxford University, Sussex and Devon

A right-arm slow-medium bowler, Col. John Hartley took a leading part in Oxford's win over Cambridge in

1896, with 11 wickets. During a career in which he could rarely play regularly, he toured America with Frank Mitchell's team in 1893, and South Africa with MCC in 1905/6, where he fared poorly in the Tests. He served during the Boer War and the First World War, being four times mentioned in despatches.

First-class career (1894-1926): 1,508 (13.58) and 69 wickets (22.81)
Test matches (2): 15 runs (3.75), 1-115 and 2 catches

HAWKE, 7th Lord (1860-1938)

Yorkshire

A great friend and colleague of Lord Harris, Martin Bladen, 7th Lord Hawke, played for Eton and Cambridge University (as captain in 1885) and was associated with Yorkshire from 1881 until his death. He served as captain from 1883 to 1910, leading eight Championship sides, and as president from 1898 to 1938. He was successively president, trustee and honorary treasurer of MCC, besides being an England selector and captaining teams to America, South Africa, India, the West Indies and Australia in 1887/8, when he had to return early owing to the death of his father. He was a very competent right-handed batsman, and represented England in some of the early Tests against South Africa. He was a far-sighted pioneer of winter payments and other benefits, helping to give cricketers the stability they would otherwise have lacked in their profession.

First-class career (1881-1911): 16,506 runs (20.25) including 13 centuries
Test matches (5): 55 runs (7.85) and 3 catches

HAYES, Ernest George (1876-1953)

Surrey and Leicestershire

One of the six aspirates that adorned the batting line-up at The Oval in Edwardian days – Hayward, Hobbs, Hayes, Holland, Harrison and Hitch – Ernie Hayes was an attractive right-handed batsman with a strong drive and fierce pull, a useful leg-break bowler and a brilliant slip. It was because he damaged his hands in the latter position – he had to field to such as Tom Richardson, Bill Lockwood and Bill Hitch – that he retired from Surrey in 1919. Sixteen times he exceeded 1,000 runs in a season, the best being 2,309 runs in 1906. His highest was 276 against Hampshire at The Oval in 1909, when he added 371 with Jack Hobbs for the second wicket, the year in which he made his only appearance in a Test against Australia. He toured South Africa 1905/6, and Australia in 1907/8. He captained Players against Gentlemen at The Oval in 1914. Serving with the Sportsman's Battalion in the First World War, he was commissioned, wounded and awarded the MBE. In 1924 he became coach to

Lord Hawke

Leicestershire after a period at Winchester and appeared as an amateur for his new county a few times in 1926, unfortunately being run out on 99 in his first innings. Later, he returned and coached at The Oval.

First-class career (1896-1926): 27,318 runs (32.21) including 48 centuries, 597 wickets (25.56) and 533 catches
Test matches (5): 86 runs (10.75), 1-52 and 2 catches

HAYES, Frank Charles (b.1946)

Lancashire

Frank Hayes, despite a very successful career by most standards, has been one of the major disappointments of modern English cricket. Fair-haired, of medium height, he is a right-handed batsman with a natural balance and flair, and an athletic cover fielder. He was for a while the 'great white hope' of English batting, following innings of 94 and 99 in his first two Championship matches for Lancashire in 1970. In 1973 he played a brilliant innings in a Test trial at Hove, hitting the ball impressively off the back foot. He was selected for England for the first time against the West Indies at The Oval that year and scored 106 not out in the second innings although England were soundly beaten. Hayes was destined to play all of his Test cricket against strong West Indian sides and for losing causes. The following winter in the Caribbean he had little luck, found no consistent form, was handicapped by nervousness to the point of physical sickness before going in to bat, and has never commanded a regular Test place again. Yet once or twice, as when he hit Malcolm Nash of Glamorgan for

34 runs in one over (the four came off the second ball), he has suggested a rare talent. An intelligent introvert with a science degree from Sheffield University, he became captain of Lancashire in 1978 when he was given sole power of first-team selection. But he was replaced after three relatively unsuccessful years as captain and the feeling that he is not a lucky cricketer was underlined when, in 1982, he suffered a complex fracture of an ankle when running between the wickets in a match at Lord's.

First-class career (1970-): 12,141 runs (36.24) including 20 centuries, and 163 catches
Test matches (9): 244 runs (15.25) including 1 century, and 7 catches

HAYWARD, Thomas Walter (1871-1939)

Cambridgeshire and Surrey

Tom Hayward, a powerful influence on the young John Hobbs, was himself one of the most prolific right-handed batsmen in the history of the game. He came from a famous Cambridgeshire cricketing family, son of Daniel and nephew of Thomas, regarded in the 1860s as the finest professional of the time. He was tallish and well built with a military moustache and bearing, and his off-drive and cut were handsome and correct. Patient and watchful, he reached his 1,000 runs for 20 successive seasons. Although he enjoyed several profitable years early in his career as a medium-pace off-break bowler, achieving the double in 1897 and the hat-trick twice in 1899, he felt he had to work too hard as both batsman and bowler and said so. In the field he was a reliable catcher. In 1906 he hit two separate centuries at Trent Bridge and Leicester in successive matches during Whitsun week, and altogether amassed 3,518 runs (66.37) in the season, which remained a record until Denis Compton and Bill Edrich beat it forty-one years later. In 1913 he became the first professional to reach his hundredth century in first-class matches. His opening partnerships with Hobbs were prolific; and he averaged 46 in thirty-three matches for Players against Gentlemen. A first choice for England from 1896 until 1909, he toured Australia three times and South Africa once, making 3 centuries in Tests. These included 122 against South Africa at Johannesburg in 1895/6 – his second match for England – and 137 at The Oval against Australia in 1899 when he put on 185 with F.S. Jackson for the first wicket. In retirement he returned to Cambridge but later became coach in the Parks at Oxford.

Tom Hayward

First-class career (1893-1914): 43,551 runs (41.79) including 104 centuries, 481 wickets (22.96) and 492 catches
Test matches (35): 1,999 runs (34.46) including 3 centuries, 14 wickets (36.71) and 19 catches

HEARNE, Alec (1863-1952)

Kent

A younger brother of George and Frank, both of whom, like himself, appeared in early Tests between England and South Africa, Alec Hearne was a right-arm, medium-paced, leg-break bowler with an excellent command of length, flight and spin. A neat batsman, he was strong in back play, a precise cutter and, particularly on slow pitches, a quick and accurate hooker. Most of his best work was done for his county and he was prominent in Kent's victories over the Australians in 1884, 1886, 1890 and 1893. Yet he was never selected for a Test against Australia, despite the fact that his highest-ever score was 168 for W.G. Grace's side against the Australians at Crystal Palace in 1893. He toured South Africa with W.W. Read's team in 1891/2, and appeared in his sole Test at Cape Town in company with brother, George, and cousin, John Thomas, although his other brother Frank was representing South Africa; he scored 9, held one catch and did not bowl. In retirement Alec Hearne was coach at Kent's Nursery and later scorer to the club for many years.

First-class career (1884-1910): 16,346 runs (21.65) including 15 centuries, 1,144 wickets (20.03) and 372 catches

HEARNE, Frank (1858-1949)

Kent and Western Province

Brother of George and Alec Hearne, Frank had the rare experience of representing both England and South Africa in Tests. Only five foot five inches he was a sound, defensive right-handed batsman, with many fine off-side strokes, and a useful, fast round-arm bowler who enjoyed ten good years (1879-89) with Kent before ill-health forced him to retire. He toured South Africa with Major Warton's team in 1888/9 and appeared in the first Tests between the two countries. Subsequently he settled in South Africa and represented his adopted country against England in 1891/2 and 1895/6. In 1894 he was a member of the first South African team to visit England, scoring 508 runs in 33 completed innings. His son, George Alfred Lawrence Hearne, was a member of the 1924 team to England.

First-class career (1879-1904): 4,553 runs (18.06) including 4 centuries, and 59 wickets (21.96)
Test matches (England - 2): 47 runs (23.50) and 1 catch. (South Africa - 4): 121 runs (15.12), 2 wickets (20.00) and 2 catches

HEARNE, George Gibbons (1856-1932)

Kent

The eldest of three brothers – Frank and Alec being the others – George Hearne was primarily a left-arm medium-pace bowler with a round-arm action, who could bat correctly and whose batting improved as he got older. Throughout his career he was a very good field at point or mid-wicket. He was a participant in the Lord's match in May 1878 which established the reputation of Australian cricket, when a strong MCC eleven was defeated in a day. With W.W. Read's team in South Africa, 1891/2, he failed to score and did not bowl in his sole Test at Cape Town.

First-class career (1876-1903): 8,772 runs (17.96) including 6 centuries, and 658 wickets (17.01)

HEARNE, John Thomas (1867-1944)

Middlesex

Brother of Herbert and Walter who played for Kent, J.T., Jack, or 'Old Jack' Hearne had twenty years as a loyal and successful servant of Middlesex. He bowled right-arm medium pace with considerable nip, and his action was perfect with left arm thrust out and left shoulder pointing towards the batsman. At times a useful batsman, he was also a reliable fielder. He captured 257 wickets (14.72) in 1896, including 56 wickets in all games against the Australians (15 in the three Tests): and on fourteen other occasions he took a hundred wickets in a season. In Australia, 1897/8, he headed the Test averages with 20 wickets (26.90). In 1899 he made history in the Test at Headingley with a hat-trick, accounting for Clem Hill, Syd Gregory and Monty Noble. His life-aggregate of wickets is the fourth highest in the history of the game. Quiet, dignified and controlled, he was considered by his old Middlesex captain, A.J. Webbe, to have 'a wonderfully kind nature'. On retirement 'Old Jack' was elected to the county committee, in those days an almost unprecedented honour for a professional. He was a cousin of George, Frank and Alec Hearne of Kent.

First-class career (1888-1923): 7,205 runs (11.99), 3,061 wickets (17.76) and 421 catches
Test matches (12): 126 runs (9.00), 49 wickets (22.08) and 4 catches

HEARNE, John William (1891-1965)

Middlesex

A distant cousin (it is said) of J.T. Hearne, 'Young Jack' was slightly built, a serious and prolific all-rounder. As a right-hand batsman he was patient, business-like and undemonstrative. As a leg-break and googly bowler he was at his very best from 1911 to 1914 and, after the War, was both one of the most erratic but also most potent leg-break bowlers around. 'Joe' Murrell who kept to him for many years said, 'You can have 'em all, here and overseas. When he was pitching the leg-break "Nutty" Hearne was away on his own.' Before his twenty-third birthday Hearne had already played for England against either Australia or South Africa thirteen times. He toured Australia three times, and South Africa once, opening his Test career with 76 and 43 at Sydney and 114 at Melbourne in 1911/12 when he was twenty. Largely self-taught, he started his career as a ground-boy at Lord's and would have gone further had he not suffered from indifferent health. As it was, he reached 1,000 runs in a season nineteen times, a hundred wickets five times and achieved the double on five occasions. After the war he relied increasingly on the off-spinner.

First-class career (1909-36): 37,252 runs (40.98) including 96 centuries, 1,839 wickets (24.44) and 349 catches
Test matches (24): 806 runs (26.00) including 1 century, 30 wickets (48.73) and 13 catches

HEMMINGS, Edward Ernest (b.1949)

Warwickshire and Nottinghamshire

Eddie Hemmings was 33 when he won his first Test cap after a career with many vicissitudes. A smallish, slightly plump man with a lively sense of humour and liable to clown during the most serious match, he is the son of a good club cricketer from Leamington Spa. A useful right-hand batsman, he began as a medium-paced bowler but developed his main skill as an off-spinner and he had learnt all the tricks of his trade by the time that he began bowling for England in 1982. Running in mechanically, he bowls at subtly varied paces from close to the stumps with a good action and curves the ball away from the right-hander in the air as well as turning the off-spinner sharply enough when conditions allow. Yet when he left Warwickshire, for whom he had first appeared against Scotland at the age of 16 in 1966, he did so in some disillusionment after becoming the butt of the Edgbaston crowd on more than one occasion. He moved to Nottinghamshire in 1979 and there began to make the most of a tough apprenticeship on the bland Edgbaston pitches. In Nottinghamshire's Championship winning year of 1981 he took 90 wickets at 20 each and he was by now an effective bowler in limited-overs matches too. The first chances for England came in two one-day internationals against Pakistan in 1982. He did well and confirmed his growing confidence with a maiden hundred for Notts against Yorkshire. Ironically, his first Test was at Edgbaston where he took three wickets against a strong Pakistan batting side. He had less success in the following Test, at Lord's, and was omitted from the final game of the rubber but still went to Australia in 1982/3 as England's first-choice off-spinner. Playing for an international eleven against a West Indies XI in September 1982 in Kingston, Jamaica, he took all ten wickets for 175.

First-class career (1966-): 5,995 runs (20.81) including 1 century, 746 wickets (28.75) and 129 catches
Test matches (2): 41 runs (10.25), 3 wickets (49.66) and 2 catches

HENDREN, Elias Henry (1889-1962)

Middlesex

A Cockney with Irish blood, 'Patsy' Hendren was a true immortal with 170 centuries, though a largely self-taught cricketer. His outstanding early talent was his speed and skill in the field. Only when cricket was resumed in 1919 did he really establish himself as a county batsman. He was a stocky scrum-half of a figure and Ian Peebles has recalled how he 'stood at the wicket with a slight crouch, a sharply protruding rump proclaiming his resolution'. He was a nervous starter but, as his innings lengthened, so his stance grew more upright and he seemed to achieve in his determined right-handed forward strokes a height and reach not in fact possessed. Very quick-footed, he was a skilled player of slow bowling and weaker against speed. With his short, strong fore-arms he made the hook his finest shot but all strokes were at his command, reinforced by a strong and orthodox defence. The crowd loved his short, square build, busy movements and low-slung run, and he enjoyed the occasional piece of slapstick for their amusement. He toured Australia in 1920/21, 1924/5 and 1928/29, South Africa once and the West Indies twice. For Middlesex he reached 1,000 runs in a season twenty-one times, fifteen times exceeding 2,000, and three times exceeding 3,000. His highest score was 301 not out for Middlesex against Worcestershire at Dudley in 1933. He was inconsistent

Patsy Hendren hitting out

for England until 1924 when he hit 132 and 142 at Headingley and The Oval respectively against South Africa, then a succession of fifties in Australia that winter and 127 not out against Australia at Lord's in 1926. From that point, he was considered genuine England material and hit his highest score, 205 not out, against the West Indies at Port of Spain in 1929/30. In 1934 against Australia he made 132 at Old Trafford, stabilizing the middle batting with a stand of 191 for the fifth wicket with Maurice Leyland, and, earlier at Trent Bridge, enabled England to save the follow-on by adding 101 for the seventh wicket with George Geary. In retirement he coached at Harrow and, later, at Lord's and at Hove (for Sussex). As a footballer, he was a wing-forward who played for Brentford, Manchester City and other clubs and was capped for England in a 'Victory' international in 1919. His brother Denis played cricket for Middlesex and Durham and became a first-class umpire.

First-class career (1907-38): 57,611 runs (50.80) including 170 centuries, 47 wickets (54.77) and 755 catches
Test matches (51): 3,525 runs (47.63) including 7 centuries, 1-31 and 33 catches

HENDRICK, Michael (b.1948)

Derbyshire and Nottinghamshire

With a truly model action, high and sideways-on, Mike Hendrick is one of the finest fast-medium bowlers of his generation yet in an era of very strong competition in his department he only made certain of his England place at the age of thirty during his fourth major overseas tour. Although six feet three inches tall and strongly built, in his youth he was not physically fit enough to bowl at his best throughout the demanding county season. He first came to prominence with Derbyshire (that great breeding-ground of fast bowlers) in 1969 when Alan Ward looked more likely to become a regular England fast bowler. Hendrick, under the guidance of the England physiotherapist Bernard Thomas, had already decided that he must drive himself to go through a daily running and exercise routine when he experienced a humiliating moment in Australia in 1974/5. He had enjoyed a successful start to the tour and was running in to bowl his first over in the third Test at Melbourne when a hamstring snapped. The rest of the tour was a miserable anti-climax for him, but when, after some fine performances in England against Australia in 1977, his chance came again overseas, he took it with the eagerness of a man presented with a feast after a long and weary journey without food. Playing in five successive Tests against Australia in 1978/9 he was a key figure in England's success, driving the young Australian batsmen almost to despair with his remorseless accuracy. He took 19 wickets at 15 each in the series, but actually took credit for several more at the other end because the batsmen were forced to play rash shots against other bowlers in order to break the stranglehold imposed by 'Hendo'. Not only is he accurate, but he also gets bounce and movement off the pitch. Thus, five years after his Test debut against India in 1974 (when he took a wicket with his third ball at Old Trafford, and followed with figures of 4 for 28 at Edgbaston), he could mentally relax and consider himself established. Although a genuine tail-end batsman who thoroughly enjoys a hearty long-handled swing, his value to any side as a bowler is enhanced by his exceptional brilliance in any close-fielding position, and also by his quick-witted repartee in the dressing-room. He left Derbyshire after his benefit season of 1981, having helped his native county to a thrilling victory in the first final of the NatWest Trophy. Injury, his constant bugbear, restricted his appearances for his new county in 1982. By now, however, he was out of the reckoning for the England side, having been banned for three years for joining the 'rebel' tour of South Africa in March 1982.

Mike Hendrick

First-class career (1969-): 1,474 runs (10.16), 696 wickets (20.94) and 156 catches
Test matches (30): 128 runs (6.40), 87 wickets (25.83) and 25 catches

HESELTINE, Lt-Col. Christopher (1869-1944)

Cambridge University and Hampshire

Neither in the eleven at Eton nor winning a blue at Cambridge, Christopher Heseltine was twenty-seven before making a name as a right-handed fast bowler. Fully utilizing his height, he brought the ball over at the extreme extent of his arm, sometimes with deadly effect, but he required careful nursing, being apt to tire. Three times he dismissed Bobby Abel (Surrey and England) for a duck. Touring India, South Africa and the West Indies with teams captained by Lord Hawke, he appeared in two Tests against South Africa, 1895/6. 'The Colonel' was president of Hampshire from 1936 until his death. He was in the Boer War and the First World War, when he was mentioned in despatches.

First-class career (1890-1914): 1,372 runs (15.24) and 165 wickets (24.54)
Test matches (2): 18 runs (9.00), 5 wickets (16.80) and 3 catches

HIGGS, Kenneth (b.1937)

Lancashire, Leicestershire and Staffordshire

A quiet, undemonstrative cricketer, Ken Higgs has had two separate careers, each in its own way equally successful. He is a very sturdily built right-arm, medium-fast bowler, and his short, well-grooved approach is the economical launching pad for a strong, thrusting body-action. The result is a jarring pace off the pitch. This, allied to formidable accuracy, made

Ken Higgs

him one of the most respected and successful bowlers in county cricket for Lancashire between 1958 and 1969 and he won fifteen England caps between 1965 and 1968, touring Australia and the West Indies. After two seasons of league cricket in his native Staffordshire Higgs was persuaded back into county cricket with Leicestershire where he became captain after Ray Illingworth in 1979. A fine slip fielder and stubborn tail-end left-hander, he showed what can be done with a straight bat and a front foot technique by making 63 and sharing a last wicket stand of 128 with John Snow for England against the West Indies in 1966 (two short of England's record for the tenth-wicket partnership) and again by putting on a record 228 with Illingworth for Leicestershire's last wicket against Northants at Leicester in 1977 when he made 98. Remarkably he also has three first-class hat-tricks to his credit – two for Lancashire and one for Leicestershire – plus one in the 1974 Benson and Hedges Cup final.

First-class career (1958-): 3,637 runs (11.29), 1,531 wickets (23.64) and 311 catches
Test matches (15): 185 runs (11.56), 71 wickets (20.74) and 4 catches

HILL, Allen (1845-1910)

Yorkshire

The man who took the first ever Test wicket, Allen Hill was one of the best right-arm 'seamers' of his day and, with a far shorter run-up than most bowlers of his type, he could deliver a sharp break-back from the off. For Yorkshire against Surrey at The Oval in 1871 he took 12 wickets, all bowled. For Players against Gentlemen at Lord's in 1874 he performed a memorable hat-trick, dismissing three of the best amateurs of the day with successive balls. He was a good slip but an erratic batsman, who captained his county occasionally. He toured Australia with James Lillywhite's side in 1876/7, and appeared in the two Tests, hitting 49 and taking 4 for 27 in the first innings of the second. For Yorkshire (1871–83) he took 563 wickets (12.70).

Test matches (2): 101 runs (50.50), 7 wickets (18.57) and 1 catch

HILL, Arthur James Ledger (1871-1950)

Cambridge University, Wiltshire and Hampshire

A Cambridge cricket blue, Arthur Hill was a true sporting all-rounder, being also a fine player at rugby, hockey, boxing, rackets and tennis, a good man to hounds and an expert fisherman. Tall and stylish, he was a splendid right-handed batsman with a free, natural approach to the game, a useful fast bowler before taking up lobs, and a reliable slip. He toured India, America and South Africa with teams captained by Lord Hawke, and went with MCC to Argentina. He appeared in the Tests against South Africa in 1895/6, and in the last at Cape Town he hit 124 and took 4 for 8 in forty balls in the second innings; remarkably the only occasion he ever bowled in a Test! In 1920 he and his son, A.E.L. Hill, turned out to play for Hampshire together and in 1929 he became president of Hampshire.

First-class career (1890-1921): 10,141 runs (27.93) including 18 centuries, and 278 wickets (29.60)
Test matches (3): 251 runs (62.75) including 1 century, 4 wickets (2.00) and 1 catch

HILTON, Malcolm Jameson (b.1928)

Lancashire

A devastating slow left-arm spinner on a turning wicket, Malcolm Hilton hit the headlines when he dismissed Don Bradman twice for Lancashire at Old Trafford in 1948. The great man was among the ten Test batsmen who constituted Hilton's first ten wickets in first-class cricket and he could never live this down, although he formed with Roy Tattersall one of the most effective spin-bowling partnerships in county cricket. He was disappointing on the tour of India under Nigel Howard in 1951/2, except at Kanpur where he and Tattersall bowled England to victory. At home he played against both the West Indies and South Africa. His best year was 1956, when he secured 158 wickets (13.96). For Lancashire Second Eleven in

1949 he took more than a hundred wickets, a very unusual feat in minor county cricket. One of the best close-in fields, and a fast runner and accurate thrower from the deep field, he was selected several times as twelfth man for England because of these skills. He was also an aggressive right-handed, tail-end batsman with a slashing off-drive (he hit 100 not out against Northamptonshire at Northampton in 1955). His best bowling was 8 for 19 for his county against the New Zealanders at Old Trafford in 1958.

First-class career (1946-61): 3,416 runs (12.11) including 1 century, 1,006 wickets (19.41) and 204 catches
Test matches (4): 37 runs (7.40), 14 wickets (33.64) and 1 catch

HIRST, George Herbert (1871-1954)

Yorkshire

George Hirst was one of the legends of Yorkshire cricket, a fighter on the field and a friendly soul both on and off it. 'The happy warrior, this is he', read a caption on a contemporary photograph. The exploits of Hirst and Wilfred Rhodes, both from Kirkheaton, have a story-book quality about them. George combined toughness and loyalty with a sense of humour, kindness and integrity and was a great influence for good over young people. He was a fastish, left-arm bowler with nip off the pitch and devastating late in-swing. As a right-handed batsman his remarkable quickness of eye and feet enabled him to hook and pull magnificently. He frequently gave of his best when the pitch helped bowlers. He was a dauntless field, notably at mid-off. In nineteen seasons he made over 1,000 runs and in fifteen took over a hundred wickets; he achieved the double fourteen times, a feat surpassed only by Rhodes. In the years of Yorkshire's Championship 'hat-trick', 1900-1902, he made 5,323 runs and took 328 wickets. No one has exceeded or will exceed his record of 2,385 runs (45.86) and 208 wickets (16.50) in 1906. His highest score, 341 against Leicestershire at Leicester including 54 boundaries, in 1905, remains unbeaten by any other Yorkshire batsman. In his first match after the First World War he made 180 not out against MCC at Lord's, aged 48. He toured Australia twice, 1897/8 and 1903/4, and, although his overall Test record was comparatively modest, two of his performances were outstanding. At Edgbaston in 1902 Rhodes and he bowled out Australia for 36 and, in the next match for Yorkshire against the tourists, he and F.S. Jackson dismissed them for 23, Hirst capturing 5 for 9. At The Oval in the same year his unbeaten 58 rescued England from a desperate position and with Rhodes he made the famous 15 runs for the last wicket to win the match; he always disclaimed the famous remark, 'We'll get 'em in singles', attributed to him on this occasion. On retirement he coached at Eton for eighteen years. His benefit from Yorkshire in 1904 amounted to £3,703 and was the highest for twenty-one years.

George Hirst

First-class career (1891-1929): 36,323 runs (34.13) including 60 centuries, 2,739 wickets (18.72) and 550 catches
Test matches (24): 790 runs (22.57), 59 wickets (30.00) and 18 catches

HITCH, John William (1886-1965)

Surrey

John Hitch, called 'Bill' or 'Billitch', was a firm favourite at The Oval. Despite a hesitant run-up punctuated by two or three hops, he became one of the fastest right-arm bowlers in England. Always a spectacular hitter in the lower order, he more than once hit a ball out of The Oval. He was quite outstanding at short-leg, where he stood perilously close to the bat. He toured Australia twice, in 1911/12 and 1920/21, and also appeared in Tests against Australia and South Africa in England before and after the First World War. On leaving Surrey, he became a professional in the Lancashire League and later coach to Glamorgan.

First-class career (1907-25): 7,698 runs (17.92) including 3 centuries, 1,398 wickets (21.48) and 212 catches
Test matches (7): 103 runs (14.71), 7 wickets (46.42) and 4 catches

HOBBS, Sir John Berry (1882-1963)

Cambridgeshire and Surrey

A model cricketer in the widest sense, Jack Hobbs is remembered with affection not just as a master batsman but also as a man of natural dignity and charm, who through years of success remained unspoilt and unselfish. His father was a groundsman at Fenner's and his boyhood idol was a fellow Cambridge man, Tom Hayward, who led the youthful Hobbs to Surrey. Hayward was the first of his opening partners in first-class cricket and together they shared in four three-figure opening stands in one week in 1907. In his first two matches for Surrey in 1905, Hobbs hit 88 against Gentlemen of England (captained by W.G.) and 155 against Essex, both at The Oval, and was awarded his county cap. He never looked back. Hobbs saw the ball early and moved into each stroke calmly and comfortably. Before the First World War he was quick to attack, on springing feet, playing strokes all over the field. After the War, his batting lost any rough edges and he scored his centuries with serene poise. Ninety-eight of his 197 centuries were made after the age of forty. Though appearing to be a frail man, his strength, fitness and powers of concentration were considerable. A magnificent field in the covers and a master of the art of luring batsmen into a run by his apparent lethargy, he ran out fifteen batsmen on MCC's tour of Australia, 1911/12. He was only an occasional bowler, but with an easy and rhythmic action he could nevertheless make the ball swing away late and, in 1909/10 in South Africa, he opened both batting and bowling in three of the Tests. In 1920 he headed the national first-class bowling averages – with 17 wickets (11.82)! But it is his batting records which still make statistical minds boggle. No one has scored more runs in first-class cricket; his 316 not out for Surrey against Middlesex in 1926 remains the highest-ever at Lord's; his 266 not out at Scarborough in 1925 was the highest in the Gentlemen and Players match, and his aggregate of 4,052 runs is unbeaten in that fixture; no one has exceeded 12 centuries in Tests against Australia; and, until Denis Compton exceeded it, his 16 centuries in 1925 were a record for a season. He was the first man to score more centuries than W.G. – in a season when, aged forty-two, he made 3,024 runs. In fourteen Test series between 1907 and 1930 he made 2,493 runs in Australia alone, including 9 centuries. Andy Sandham succeeded Tom Hayward as his opening partner for Surrey, and they shared sixty-three opening three-figure stands, the highest being 428 against Oxford University at The Oval in 1926. In Tests Hobbs shared in twenty-three opening partnerships of over 100, eight with Wilfred Rhodes and fifteen with Herbert Sutcliffe, the most memorable being his 323 with Rhodes at Melbourne in 1911/12, which remained the record for thirty-seven years. His batting mastery was revealed in the challenge of a really difficult wicket, formidable bowling or a crisis, as at The Oval in 1926 or at Melbourne in 1929, when he and Sutcliffe led England from the prospect of inevitable defeat to victory on a treacherous pitch. With Sutcliffe he shared twenty-six opening stands of more than 100, including three in succession against Australia in 1924/5. Twenty-six times in a season (twice overseas) Hobbs himself exceeded 1,000 runs. Jack Mercer recalls how Glamorgan decided one day to try to run him out rather than bowl him out. A trap was laid on the off-side, with cover-point lurking closer than usual to cut off the off-side push with which Hobbs was wont to start an innings. Mercer bowled the first ball just outside the off-stump, but Hobbs moved across, pushed to mid-wicket and took an easy single! He received three benefits from Surrey which he used to finance a sports outfitters business which still flourishes. Honorary life member of Surrey and honorary member of MCC, he was knighted for his services to cricket in 1953.

Jack Hobbs

First-class career (1905-34): 61,237 runs (50.65) including 197 centuries, 113 wickets (23.97) and 317 catches

Test matches (61): 5,410 runs (56.94) including 15 centuries, 1-165 and 17 catches

HOBBS, Robin Nicholas Stuart (b.1942)

Essex, Glamorgan and Suffolk

Robin Hobbs would have been a typical county spinner if he had been born sixty years earlier. As it happened he was for much of his career unique: the only English leg-spinner good enough to command a regular place in a county side. Red-faced and jovial with large ears, sharp blue eyes and a fondness for a drink, he has been a popular character wherever he has travelled. Not only was he a convivial companion on four overseas tours, but also a skilful and flighty leg-spinner with a useful, if not baffling, googly, as well as a superb, irrepressibly enthusiastic cover-fielder and a spirited hitter. He scored a century in forty-four minutes' against the Australians in 1975 at Chelmsford, then the fourth fastest ever. He left Essex at the end of 1975 but returned to first-class cricket in 1979 as Glamorgan's captain.

First-class career (1961-81): 4,940 runs (12.10) including 2 centuries, 1,099 wickets (27.09) and 294 catches

Test matches (7): 34 runs (6.80), 12 wickets (40.08) and 8 catches

HOLLIES, William Eric (1912-81)

Warwickshire and Staffordshire

A sturdy and exceptionally accurate right-arm, leg-break bowler, Eric Hollies was for many years the pivot of the Warwickshire attack. Although his googly was unexceptional, his top-spinner was devastating. He exceeded 100 wickets in a season fourteen times. In his first county match he took 1 for 150, delivering a plethora of no-balls, and in his fourth match was often hit out of the Gloucester ground by Walter Hammond. Thereupon Hollies decided to accelerate his pace a little and so counteract the movements of quick-footed batsmen. This method made him one of the brisker slow bowlers of his time and he would no doubt have prospered equally well in one-day cricket. He toured the West Indies in 1934/5 and next played for England against South Africa in 1947, when he was preferred to Doug Wright. Hollies was the bowler when Don Bradman came out at The Oval to play his last Test innings against England. The first ball was a leg-break, which the Don played with a dead bat. The second, a googly of perfect length, bowled the great man and so deprived him of a glorious exit and reduced his Test career average to a mere 99! Though this was Eric Hollies' most famous moment, he preferred to talk about the rare occasions when he made runs. His best bowling was 10 for 49 in an innings against Nottinghamshire at Edgbaston in 1946, all without assistance from the field.

First-class career (1932-57): 1,673 runs (5.01), and 2,323 wickets (20.94)

Test matches (13): 37 runs (5.28), 44 wickets (30.27) and 2 catches

HOLMES, Errol Reginald Thorold (1905-60)

Oxford University and Surrey

A tall right-hander, Errol Holmes batted as one would have expected an Oxford Malvernian to bat: with style and panache – and in a Harlequin cap. His hallmark was the drive through the covers with the left leg well out and the bat following right through, but he could hit all round the wicket delightfully. Especially while at Oxford he had some triumphs with his medium-fast bowling; his was a tearaway action with a long run which did not produce quite as speedy a ball as promised. Succeeding Douglas Jardine as Surrey captain in 1934, he was a revitalizing influence. He believed that everyone should *enjoy* the game. He toured the West Indies as vice-captain, 1934/5, and led MCC's 'goodwill' tour of Australia, 1935/6. Retiring in 1938, he returned as Surrey captain for two seasons after the War. Some idea of his approach may be gained from his conversation with some Oxford cricketers long after he had retired. He was recalling the virtues of Harold Larwood: his searing pace, ferocious bounce, formidable accuracy etc. 'How on earth did you play him, then?', asked a timid undergraduate. 'Drove him through the covers, me boy,' replied Holmes 'drove him through the covers.'

First-class career (1924-55): 13,598 runs (32.84) including 24 centuries, and 283 wickets (33.67)

Test matches (5): 114 runs (16.28), 2 wickets (38.00) and 4 catches

HOLMES, Percy (1886-1971)

Yorkshire

Chiefly remembered as Herbert Sutcliffe's opening partner, Percy Holmes seldom got the credit due to him. Technically, he was possibly Sutcliffe's equal, but he was an attacking right-hander without the monumental calm and concentration which made Sutcliffe so exceptional. Good footwork made Holmes a particularly successful hooker and cutter and he was a good fielder. A jaunty character, he was always on the look out for runs. With Sutcliffe he set up the record first-wicket partnership of 555 against Essex at Leyton in 1932. In all they shared eighteen partnerships exceeding 250, and sixty-nine exceeding 100. His highest score was 315 not out for Yorkshire against Middlesex at Lord's in 1925, and he exceeded 1,000 runs in a season fifteen times – once overseas when he made 1,200 runs (51.14) for MCC in South Africa, 1927/8, his sole Test-playing tour for MCC. In England he appeared once against Australia in 1921, and against India in 1932, but was not selected again.

First-class career (1913-35): 30,574 runs (42.11) including 67 centuries, and 221 catches

Test matches (7): 357 runs (27.46) and 3 catches

HONE, Leland (1853-96)

Ireland

An old Rugbeian and member of a famous Irish cricketing family, Leland Hone was the first player to represent England in Tests who never played for a first-class county. He was a wicket-keeper/batsman and, when Lord Harris found himself short of a 'keeper at the last moment to tour Australia in 1878/9, he invited Hone. He acquitted himself well as a 'keeper, but failed with the bat, in the sole Test at Melbourne scoring 7 and 6 and holding 2 catches. He played with success for Phoenix, Dublin and All Ireland.

HOPWOOD, John Leonard (b.1903)

Lancashire

Len Hopwood was a very competent right-handed batsman and a left-arm medium-pace bowler. Patient and determined, he took several years to establish himself in the strong Lancashire Championship-winning side, but in 1933 he made 1,972 runs (46.95), and in 1934 and 1935, his peak years, he achieved the double. Chosen for England against Australia in 1934, he played at Old Trafford and Leeds but was disappointing. Ill-health prevented his return to first-class cricket in 1946.

First-class career (1923-39): 15,548 runs (29.90) including 27 centuries, and 671 wickets (22.47)
Test matches (2): 12 runs (6.00) and 0-155

HORNBY, Albert Neilson (1847-1925)

Lancashire

Small, truculent, bellicose, adventurous, rash, and a poor runner between wickets, 'Monkey' Hornby was a right-handed batsman with an attractive front-foot style and splendid punishing powers which he used freely. He was a magnificent field, but when he played for Harrow against Eton in 1864 he was of such slight physique that he weighed – 'bat and all' – less than six stone. Captain of Lancashire from 1880 until 1891 and again in 1897 and 1898, he was firm, keen and genial, generally getting the best out of his men. He led the county to the Championship in 1881 and 1897, and to tied first place in 1882 and 1889. He opened the batting for many years with Dick Barlow – a partnership that has been immortalized in verse by Francis Thompson. Barlow said of him, 'First he runs you out of breath; then he runs you out; then he gives you a sovereign; then he runs out of sovereigns.' A double international, he appeared nine times for England at Rugby football and three times at cricket against Australia. He was involved in a serious incident during a match between Lord Harris's team and New South Wales at Sydney, 1878/9, when Lord Harris was struck on the field of play by a 'larrikin' because of an umpire's decision on a run out; 'Monkey' was something of a pugilist, seized the offender and, despite being hit in the face and having his shirt nearly torn off his back, conveyed his prisoner to the pavilion. He captained England in the legendary 1882 Oval Test and in the Test at Old Trafford in 1884, and also captained England against Scotland in his last Rugby international.

First-class career (1867-99): 15,763 runs (23.91) including 15 centuries
Test matches (3): 21 runs (3.50) and 1-0

HORTON, Martin John (b.1934)

Worcestershire and Northern Districts

Martin Horton was a strongly built and effective all-rounder. As a right-handed opening batsman he could hit powerfully on both sides of the wicket and his cutting was devastating despite a somewhat ungainly stance and short backlift. He was also a valuable off-break bowler and versatile field. He achieved the double twice, and, when making his highest score, 233 against Somerset at Worcester in 1962, he added 314 for the third wicket with Tom Graveney. His best bowling performance was 9 for 56 in an innings against the South Africans at Worcester in 1955. He appeared in two Tests against India in 1959 and, on leaving his county in 1966, became National Coach in New Zealand.

First-class career (1952-71): 19,944 runs (29.55) including 23 centuries, and 825 wickets (26.94)
Test matches (2): 60 runs (30.00), 2 wickets (29.50) and 2 catches

HOWARD, Nigel David (1925-79)

Lancashire

One of the two sons of Major Rupert Howard (sometime secretary of Lancashire and manager of MCC touring teams) who appeared for the county, Nigel Howard was a stylish and forcing right-handed batsman and a fine, zealous field. Soon after his debut he was opening the batting with Cyril Washbrook and captained Lancashire unselfishly from 1949 until 1953. He captained MCC to India, Pakistan and Ceylon in 1951/2 when, although he struggled to justify his place in the side as a batsman, he did a good job on and off the field, relieving his players of most of the diplomatic chores which, so soon after partition, were considerable.

First-class career (1946-54): 6,152 runs (24.70) including 3 centuries
Test matches (4): 86 runs (17.20) and 4 catches

HOWELL, Henry (1890-1932)

Warwickshire

Taking a fairly long run, 'Harry' Howell bowled distinctly fast right-arm with a nice easy action. At his best in the early twenties, he enjoyed such hauls as 161 and 152 wickets in a season. In 1923 he took all 10 for 51 in Yorkshire's first innings at Edgbaston and, in 1922 on the same ground, captured 6 for 7, when Hampshire fell for 15, but eventually won the match. He visited Australia with MCC in 1920/21, when the slip fieldsmen often failed him lamentably, and in 1924/5.

First-class career (1913-28): 1,679 runs (7.81) and 975 wickets (21.23)
Test matches (5): 15 runs (7.50) and 7 wickets (79.85)

HOWORTH, Richard (1909-80)

Worcestershire

A versatile and canny all-rounder, Dick Howorth was a left-handed batsman of uncompromising style based on the straight bat in defence and solid front-foot strokes in attack. He drove powerfully and batted anywhere either as an opener or as low as number nine; he usually bowled slow left-arm, turning the ball from a steady length but could also bowl seamers if required; and he could field near the wicket or in the deep. There was an air of competence about everything he did. Off the field he was a notable raconteur. In 1947 he scored 1,510 runs, took 164 wickets, made his Test debut against South Africa – securing a wicket with his first ball at The Oval – and toured the West Indies with MCC. He achieved the double three times and nine times took more than 100 wickets in a season.

First-class career (1933-51): 11,479 runs (20.68) including 4 centuries, and 1,345 wickets (21.87)
Test matches (5): 145 runs (18.12), 19 wickets (33.42) and 2 catches

HUMPHRIES, Joseph (1876-1946)

Derbyshire

A feature of Joe Humphries's wicket-keeping was the way he stood up to fast bowlers like Arnold Warren and Bill Bestwick. At one time he seemed destined for the highest honours but, though he kept in three Tests in Australia, 1907/8, and at Melbourne added 34 for the ninth wicket with Sydney Barnes to enable England to win, ultimately, by one wicket, he was not selected again. But at home he performed admirably for his county until 1914. He returned for a benefit match in 1920, but rain prevented a single ball from being bowled.

First-class career (1899-1914): 5,464 runs (14.19) and 674 dismissals (564 ct, 110 st.)
Test matches (3): 44 runs (8.80) and 7 dismissals (7 ct)

HUNTER, Joseph (1855-91)

Yorkshire

Though never taking the same rank as such contemporaries as Richard Pilling and Mordecai Sherwin, Joe Hunter was a good enough wicket-keeper for any county team. He toured Australia with Shaw and Shrewsbury's side, 1884/5, when he played for England. Ill-health caused his retirement and he was succeeded by his brother, David.

First-class career (1878-88): 1,336 runs (7.95) and 309 dismissals (200 ct, 109 st.)
Test matches (5): 93 runs (18.60) and 11 dismissals (8 ct, 3 st.)

HUTCHINGS, Kenneth Lotherington (1882-1916)

Kent

Although Kenneth Hutchings did not fulfil all the expectations for him after his brilliant years at Tonbridge, he was an outstanding right-handed batsman amid a galaxy of amateur talent the like of which has never been seen since. His driving was outstanding, and his fielding in the slips or the deep equally so. He was a regular choice for England for several years, touring Australia with MCC in 1907/8 and playing against Australia again in 1909. He hit 126 at Melbourne, when England eventually won by one wicket. He was killed in action in France at the height of the First World War.

First-class career (1902-12): 10,054 runs (33.62) including 21 centuries, 22 wickets (39.50) and 166 catches
Test matches (7): 341 runs (28.41) including 1 century, 1 wicket (81.00) and 9 catches

HUTTON, Sir Leonard (b.1916)

Yorkshire

A dour and painstaking character with a whimsical sense of humour, Len Hutton will perhaps be best remembered for two among many great achievements: as the maker of the record score in England and Australia Tests – 364 at The Oval in 1938 – and, as the first professional to be regularly appointed captain of England, the man who won back the Ashes in the Coronation year of 1953. He was also the first professional to be elected to membership of MCC before his career had finished and the second (after Jack Hobbs) to be knighted for his services to cricket. A product of Pudsey St Lawrence and a protégé of Herbert Sutcliffe, Len Hutton (together with Denis Compton) towered above contemporary England batsmen. Tenacity, concentration and perfect balance marked his play. The stylist always, with a wide repertoire of strokes, he did not venture anything unreasonably risky, but he could, according to the conditions, be either austerely defensive or a versatile handsome stroke-player. In the latter vein he played one of the most regal innings ever seen at Lord's, when he made 145 against Australia in 1953. Controversially, however, he was almost the first great player who habitually, after 1945, played slow bowling from the crease. He was a good close fielder and a useful leg-break bowler who often obtained valuable wickets. In his first Test, against New Zealand at Lord's in 1937, he made 0 and 1, but in the next match at Old Trafford he hit 100 and did not look back. In 1938 against Australia he averaged 118.25, and, in 1939, 96.00 against the West Indies. After the war an operation left his left arm permanently shorter and weaker than his right but, except for one occasion when he was controversially dropped from the England side against Australia in 1948, he was at the forefront of England's gradual revival after 1946. Head and shoulders above anyone else in Australia, 1950/51, he averaged 88.83 (the next best being 38.77); and he was captain in the 1953 and 1954/5 series, when the Ashes were won back and retained. In 1953 he averaged 55.37 (the next best being 39.00). Against Australia alone he made 2,428 runs (54.46). Altogether he captained England twenty-three times – more than any other player previously – and did not lose a rubber. He twice shared in three-figure stands with Cyril Washbrook in each innings of Tests against Australia, at Adelaide in 1946/7 and at Headingley in 1948. They made the then highest opening stand in Tests, when they scored 359 together at Johannesburg in 1948/9, Len's contribution being 158. Despite three successive ducks, he hit 1,294 runs in June 1949, the highest aggregate for a batsman in any one month. In retirement he became a successful businessman and was for a time an England selector.

First-class career (1934-60): 40,140 runs (55.51) including 129 centuries, 173 wickets (29.42) and 387 catches
Test matches (79): 6,971 runs (56.67) including 19 centuries, 3 wickets (77.33) and 57 catches

HUTTON, Richard Anthony (b.1942)

Cambridge University, Yorkshire and Transvaal

Born, like his father, at Pudsey, Richard Hutton inevitably lived in his father's illustrious shadow. Yet he had the independence of character to forge his own career inside and outside cricket and is now a chartered accountant and banker. An outstanding schoolboy all-rounder at Repton, he was a Cambridge blue from 1962 to 1964 and was for ten years a respected and aggressive Yorkshire all-rounder. Although a powerful driver, his batting had little of his father's exceptional balance, but he played an outstanding innings of 81 against India at The Oval in 1971 when he appeared in five of the six Tests of the summer.

Len Hutton – Ron Archer (Australia) fielding

Tall, strong and belligerent (not incapable of some earthy language on the field) he was a steady fast-medium bowler in all conditions and a dangerous swinger and cutter of the ball in helpful ones. His opposition to the Yorkshire captain Geoff Boycott hastened his retirement.

First-class career (1962-76): 7,561 runs (21.48) including 5 centuries, 625 wickets (24.01) and 216 catches
Test matches (5): 219 runs (36.50), 9 wickets (28.55) and 9 catches

IDDON, John (1902-46)

Lancashire

Jack Iddon was a right-handed hard-driving batsman, a natural who reached 1,000 runs in twelve successive seasons up to 1939 (thirteen in all). Also a slow left-arm bowler, he was particularly effective on a wearing pitch at Bramall Lane in 1937, when he took 9 for 47 in Yorkshire's second innings. He toured the West Indies with MCC in 1934/5 and represented England against South Africa in 1935. He was killed in a car accident.

First-class career (1924-45): 22,681 runs (36.76) including 46 centuries, and 551 wickets (25.08)
Test matches (5): 170 runs (28.33) and 0-27

IKIN, John Thomas (b.1918)

Staffordshire and Lancashire

A lantern-jawed left-hander, Jack Ikin was a player of lion-hearted courage, whose career was cut short by ill-health. He fought to uphold England's middle batting in the crucial years immediately after the Second World War, and was also a useful right-arm leg-break and googly bowler, and a brilliant and daring field in the short-leg area. He played for England against India in 1946, before receiving his county cap, and toured Australia with MCC in 1946/7.

He also toured the West Indies, 1947/8, and India with the Commonwealth side, 1950/51. He exceeded 1,000 runs in a season eleven times – 1952 was his best year with 1,912 runs (45.52) – and in 1946 he held 55 catches. He last appeared for England in 1955 against South Africa and later became a notable coach.

First-class career (1938-64): 17,968 runs (36.81) including 27 centuries, 339 wickets (30.27) and 419 catches
Test matches (18): 606 runs (20.89), 3 wickets (118.00) and 31 catches

ILLINGWORTH, Raymond (b.1932)

Yorkshire and Leicestershire

Never has an Indian summer burned so brightly or so long as in the case of Ray Illingworth. A shrewd and polished craftsman, he was a flawlessly accurate off-spinner, sound batsman and safe field, especially good in the gully. He might easily have ended his career merely as an oustanding county all-rounder with a moderate record as an England player. Yet he became captain of England and was one of the few players whose personal form has been enhanced by the responsibility of captaining a Test side. The opportunity came when he left Yorkshire (like Len Hutton he was Pudsey born) after eighteen years to become captain of Leicestershire in 1969. For ten years under his leadership Leicestershire were always among the top counties, winning the Championship in 1975 and four other major trophies. In his momentous year of 1969 he took over the England captaincy from the injured Colin Cowdrey and, although he was envisaged originally as merely a caretaker, 'Illy' proved himself so tough a leader and so skilful a tactician that he was to lead England in thirty-one Tests, plus five games against the Rest of the World when the South African tour of 1970 was cancelled through political pressure. The pinnacle of his career was reached the following winter when England beat Australia by two Tests to nil to regain the Ashes which had been lost twelve years before. Popular alike with players and with press, Illingworth was every inch a professional both in his fastidious attention to his own and his players' legitimate interests and in his approach to the game itself. A formidable opponent, stubborn and fearless, he was also a loyal and considerate friend. His batting was solid, rugged, utilitarian and determined, especially in a crisis. His bowling action started with a chassé, followed by a poised, relatively lengthy run and a classic delivery reminiscent of Laker. He varied his pace and mixed his stock off-break with the ball which floated away to slip. He took 100 wickets or more in a season ten times and scored more than 1,000 runs eight times. His highest Test score was 113 against the West Indies at Lord's in 1969 and his best bowling 6 for 29 against India in 1967, but it was for

Ray Illingworth

the useful, business-like performance rather than the spectacular one that he was treasured – this and for his skill as a captain. He practically never lost his grip on any match and his competence improved the record of a moderate England side under his command. Awarded the CBE in 1973, he became Yorkshire manager in 1979. This was not the panacea all Yorkshiremen had sought, however, and in 1982, at the age of 50, he took over the Yorkshire captaincy, the oldest man to be officially appointed a county captain for any substantial period. A steady improvement followed and Illingworth was reappointed as both captain and manager in 1983.

First-class career (1951-): 24,063 runs (28.37) including 22 centuries, 2,040 wickets (20.13) and 435 catches
Test matches (61): 1,836 runs (23.24) including 2 centuries, 122 wickets (31.20) and 45 catches

INSOLE, Douglas John (b.1926)

Cambridge University and Essex

Douglas Insole was a powerfully built, right-handed batsman with no frills but plenty of courage and resolution. He was one of the most prolific run-getters in the first two decades after the Second World War, a useful medium-pace change-bowler and a fine all-round field, especially at slip. He captained Cambridge University in 1949 and Essex from 1950 until 1960. A resourceful captain with up-to-date ideas, he had a first-class cricketing brain and his sense of humour and lack of pomposity kept the game in proper perspective. As Essex captain he pulled the county up from the bottom of the Championship to a regular position in the top half. His best season was 1955 with 2,427 runs (42.57), and he exceeded 1,000 runs in a season thirteen times. At Clacton against Surrey in 1956 he scored 8 runs off one ball from Tony Lock. He appeared in occasional Tests in the fifties against Australia, South Africa and the West Indies in England, and in South Africa, 1956/7, when he was MCC's vice-captain, scoring 110 not out at Durban. He was a Test selector for many years from 1959, chairman of the TCCB when the controversy over Kerry Packer's World Series Cricket arose, and manager of the 1978/9 and 1982/3 teams to Australia, where he did an ideal job in awkward circumstances. Also a football blue, he played in the 1955/6 F.A. Amateur Cup Final.

First-class career (1947-63): 25,237 runs (37.61) including 54 centuries, 138 wickets (33.95), 363 catches and 6 stumpings
Test matches (9): 408 runs (27.20) including 1 century, and 8 catches

JACKMAN, Robin David (b.1945)

Surrey, Western Province and Rhodesia

Robin Jackman was born in Simla, the son of a British colonel in the Indian army. Never was there a more determined cricketer than this short, stocky, red-faced, fast-medium bowler with the strident appeal who loves the game with a rare devotion and achieved his great ambition when asked to play for England at last after 17 seasons in the game. Educated at St Edmunds, Canterbury, Jackman deliberately became 'just one of the lads' in the Oval dressing room. His apprenticeship was long and hard as he worked to make the most of modest abilities. Accuracy, the ability to swing the ball away from the bat and delivery from close to the stumps helped him to pick up a healthy harvest of wickets every year after winning his cap in 1970, six seasons after his debut. Also a capable fielder and useful tail-end batsman, he played for Western Province in 1971/2 and for Rhodesia between 1972/3 and 1979/80, taking 8-40 against Natal in 1972/3. These connections, and his marriage to a South African girl, created political problems in Guyana when Jackman was flown out to join England's team in the West Indies in 1980/81. But he achieved his ambition when chosen for the Third Test in Barbados, getting a wicket with the fifth ball of his first over. He has taken three first-class hat-tricks, against Kent, Yorkshire and Natal, and in 1980 took 121 wickets at 15.40. He made sure of achieving another ambition, a tour to Australia, by taking three wickets for 74 in Pakistan's first innings in the Headingley Test of 1982. With characteristic doggedness Jackman bowled unchanged for 35 overs. However, he retired at the end of the 1982/3 tour of Australasia and emigrated to South Africa.

First-class career (1964-83): 5,593 runs (17.58), 1,399 wickets (22.66) and 175 catches
Test matches (4): 42 runs (7.00) and 14 wickets (31.78)

JACKSON, Sir Francis Stanley (1870-1947)

Cambridge University and Yorkshire

Tall and well-built, Sir Stanley Jackson was a graceful right-handed batsman with superb timing, a medium-paced bowler with a model run-up and action who varied his pace subtly, and a keen field especially at cover. In many ways he personified the late Victorian and Edwardian approach to the game. From the time that 'Jacker' (fagmaster of Winston Churchill) enabled Harrow to overwhelm Eton at Lord's in 1888, he went from strength to strength. Son of Lord Allerton, a member of the Cabinet in Lord Salisbury's second Government, he led Cambridge to decisive victory in the 1893 University match. He also played for Yorkshire and England against Australia that year, making 91 and 103 in his first two Tests, at Lord's and The Oval respectively. He hit 118 at The Oval in the 1899 Test. After war service in South Africa he returned to cricket and in 1902 he was the best batsman in the series against Australia, redeeming the dreadful England start in the famous 'three run match' at Old Trafford. His career was crowned in 1905 – 'Jackson's Year' – when he led England to victory in the rubber, winning the toss in all five matches against Australia, and heading the batting averages with 70.28 and the bowling with 15.46. He appeared regularly for the Gentlemen, and for Yorkshire he was prolific. Subsequently, 'Jacker' was M.P. for a Yorkshire constituency, Lieutenant-Colonel of a West Yorkshire Regiment, Governor of Bengal (where he narrowly escaped an assassin's bullet), chairman of the Conservative Party, president of MCC and Yorkshire, and chairman of the England selectors (1934 and 1946).

First-class career (1890-1907): 15,824 runs (34.03) including 31 centuries, and 770 wickets (20.26)
Test matches (20): 1,415 runs (48.79) including 5 centuries, 24 wickets (33.29) and 10 catches

JACKSON, Herbert Leslie (b.1921)

Derbyshire

After Cliff Gladwin's retirement in 1958 Les Jackson took over the extra responsibility and labour of 'stock' as well as 'shock' bowler, even though he was at an advanced age for a right-arm, fast-medium bowler. But his skill seemed to increase and, when he retired five years later, he held all the main records for a Derbyshire bowler. Strong, with a slingy action, he was accurate, hostile and moved the ball wickedly off the seam; the game was never dull or negative when he was bowling on a 'green 'un' and he had a few in Derbyshire. For many years he was among the meanest and best seam bowlers in England. A miner who started in first-class cricket at the late age of twenty-seven, he exceeded 100 wickets in a season ten times, twenty times took 10 or more wickets in a match, and nineteen times 7 or more wickets in an innings. He was not chosen for an overseas tour with MCC and appeared only twice for England at home – against New Zealand in 1949 and Australia in 1961. This was scant honour for so good a bowler.

First-class career (1947-63): 2,083 runs (6.19) and 1,733 wickets (17.36)
Test matches (2): 15 runs (15.00), 7 wickets (22.14) and 1 catch

JAMESON, John Alexander (b.1941)

Warwickshire

John Jameson was a modest man off the field but assertive and dominating on it. Barrel-chested and strong, he was a right-handed opening batsman with a brutal approach to the new ball. He got many a Warwickshire innings off to an exceptionally fast start, notably in 1974 when he dominated a world-record stand of 465 for the second wicket with Rohan Kanhai against Gloucestershire at Edgbaston, hitting 240 not out. His opening partnerships with Dennis Amiss were often prolific. On ten occasions he exceeded 1,000 runs in a season, but his tendency to inconsistency deterred the England selectors. He toured the West Indies in 1973/4, and his first ball in the Test at Kingston, a Boyce bouncer, he mis-hooked for six over fine third man. His best Test innings was 82 against India at The Oval in 1971, a characteristic effort including two straight-driven sixes off Bedi into the pavilion.

First-class career (1960-76): 18,941 runs (33.34) including 33 centuries, 89 wickets (42.49), 255 catches and 1 stumping
Test matches (4): 214 runs (26.75) and 1-17

JARDINE, Douglas Robert (1900-58)

Oxford University and Surrey

Douglas Jardine was an austere character of iron will with an inflexible self-discipline which extended to his captaincy. His name will forever be linked with bodyline. 'The Iron Duke' was a remarkably mature batsman and captain at Winchester before becoming – like his father – an Oxford blue. For Surrey he finished at the head of the national averages in 1927 and 1928 with 91 and 87 respectively; and he captained Surrey in 1932 and 1933. As England's captain he was a cold authoritarian figure, who yet inspired the loyalty of his team and the grudging admiration of most opponents – the 1932/3 Australians *not* included! As a right-handed batsman he was upright and correct, especially strong on the leg side, a solid defender and a particularly fine player of fast bowling – invariably wearing his Oxford Harlequin cap. He was a heavy scorer in Australia in 1928/9 and in 1932/3 (as captain), on the former tour hitting centuries in his first three innings. After talking with bowlers like Harold Larwood, he devised the bodyline method of attack – short fast bowling aimed at the body with a ring of short-leg fielders – both to counteract the menace of Don Bradman in Test cricket and as a concerted plan to bring back the Ashes in 1932/3. The campaign was successful but the tactics widely condemned. Despite much hostility, Jardine stuck to his convictions that such bowling was not unlawful, and in 1933 he scored 127 for England against the West Indies at Old Trafford facing and overcoming the fast leg-theory (or bodyline) of Learie Constantine and Manny Martindale. He captained MCC in the first Test-playing tour of India, 1933/4, but thereafter he

Douglas Jardine

appeared in very little first-class cricket.

First-class career (1920-48): 14,848 runs (46.83) including 35 centuries, 48 wickets (31.10) and 188 catches
Test matches (22): 1,296 runs (48.00) including 1 century, 0-10 and 26 catches

JENKINS, Roland Oliver (b.1918)

Worcestershire

A sound right-handed batsman but better known as one of the last outstanding English leg-spinners, 'Roley' Jenkins was the local boy made good *par excellence.* He had immense energy, every ounce of which went into every ball he bowled, and when he batted he did it with the same cheerful determination. He approached the stumps with a nautical roll, taking a childlike pleasure in capturing a wicket. He achieved the double twice in 1949 and 1952, and performed the hat-trick three times, two of them in the same match, and all against Surrey. He played at home for England against the West Indies and India, and toured South Africa with MCC, 1948/9, when he took 15 wickets in the Tests with his leg-breaks.

First-class career (1938-58): 10,073 runs (22.23) including 1 century, 1,309 wickets (23.62) and 210 catches
Test matches (9): 198 runs (18.00), 32 wickets (34.31) and 4 catches

JESSOP, Gilbert Laird (1874-1955)

Cambridge University and Gloucestershire

The most famous hitter in cricket history, Gilbert Jessop, 'The Croucher', unfortunately seems to prove the case for a sterner approach to the business of batting in Test cricket. Although he won one Test with his century at The Oval in 1902 his overall average was only 21. Yet for twenty years before the First World War he was the most exciting figure in the game. A right-handed batsman, he was short and compact with great strength about the shoulders, large, strong hands and exceptionally long arms. He would sight the ball very early from his crouched stance, and by daring and speedy footwork completely invalidate the bowler's length and field-placings. Most of his shots were unorthodox, played with a straight bat, and he was consistent as well as pulverizing. Away from Tests he topped 1,000 runs in a season fourteen times. In five innings of over 200 – the highest being 286 against Sussex at Hove in 1903 – he maintained a scoring-rate of only just under 100 runs an hour. Each of his 53 centuries averaged an almost unbelievable 82.7 runs an hour. A fast but unremarkable bowler, he opened the bowling in his first Test against Australia at Lord's in 1899, when he was captain of Cambridge University. In 1897 and 1900 he achieved the double. His most famous performance came in the Oval Test of 1902. Seeking 273 to win, England were 48 for 5 when he went in on a none-too-easy pitch. In seventy-five minutes against bowling of the highest class he hit 104, making it possible for England to win amid almost unbearable tension with the last pair together. The previous winter in Australia he had met with only moderate success. He was one of the greatest fielders and throwers there has ever been, and few dared to take risks with 'Jessopus' at cover. He captained Gloucestershire from 1900 until 1912. His son, Rev. G.L.O. Jessop, played for Hampshire and Dorset.

Gilbert Jessop

First-class career (1894-1914): 26,698 runs (32.63) including 53 centuries, 873 wickets (22.79) and 453 catches
Test matches (18): 569 runs (21.88) including 1 century, 10 wickets (35.40) and 11 catches

JONES, Arthur Owen (1872-1914)

Cambridge University and Nottinghamshire

Despite a rather cramped stance, Arthur Jones was a brilliant but sometimes impetuous opening batsman, especially strong on the off-side. He was also a very useful leg-break bowler and one of the finest all-round fieldsmen ever seen – said to be unequalled in the slips and to have invented the position of gully. A Cambridge blue, he led Nottinghamshire to the Championship in 1907, and that winter led MCC to Australia, where he had a serious illness. He had also toured Australia in 1901/2 with Archie Maclaren's team but his real *métier* was county cricket and, with James Iremonger, shared in twenty-four opening stands of 100 or more for Nottinghamshire. He captained his county from 1900 until within a few months of his death from tuberculosis in 1914.

First-class career (1892-1914): 22,955 runs (31.57) including 34 centuries, 333 wickets (32.62), 574 catches and 2 stumpings
Test matches (12): 291 runs (13.85), 3 wickets (44.33) and 15 catches

JONES, Ivor Jeffrey (b.1941)

Glamorgan

A well-built, strapping Welshman, Jeff Jones was a fast and graceful left-arm bowler, who had immense fire, speed and sustained hostility. He matured into a first choice England bowler between 1963 and 1967 and toured Australia and New Zealand in 1965/6, taking 15 wickets in four Tests against Australia, and also the West Indies, India and Pakistan. His best bowling was 8 for 11 at Leicester in 1965, and in his last full season, 1967, he took 100 wickets (19.49). But in May 1968, he tore the ligaments in his elbow, and he never bowled effectively again.

First-class career (1960-68): 513 runs (3.97) and 511 wickets (25.98)
Test matches (15): 38 runs (4.75), 44 wickets (40.20) and 4 catches

JUPP, Henry (1841-89)

Surrey

Henry Jupp or 'Young Stonewall' of Dorking was once clean-bowled first ball in a local match. Instead of going out, he coolly turned, replaced the bails and prepared to receive the next ball. 'Ain't you going, Juppy?' asked the umpire. 'No,' replied Juppy, 'not at Dorking I ain't' – and he did not! Short, broad-shouldered, powerful and a rough diamond, Harry Jupp was at his best defending, but he was a stylish and sound right-handed batsman, who could drive powerfully. He opened for Surrey for about twenty years. He was very good at cover-point or in the outfield. Touring Australia with James Lillywhite's team in 1876/7, he appeared in two Tests, top-scoring in the first at Melbourne with 63.

First-class career (1862-81): 15,319 runs (23.78) including 12 centuries, 229 catches and 19 stumpings
Test matches (2): 68 runs (17.00) and 2 catches

JUPP, Vallance William Crisp (1891-1960)

Sussex and Northamptonshire

A short, prematurely bald man, Vallance Jupp or 'Juppy' had broad shoulders, long arms, great strength, and a rough humour. He was an enterprising right-handed batsman of blazing energy, a penetrating slow-medium off-break bowler with a rolling gait, and a very agile field at cover. Starting as a professional with Sussex – his first century was against Northamptonshire – he turned amateur after the First World War and went to live in Northampton, where he had a business. He became secretary/captain of his new county and, during years of cricket depression at Northampton, was always ready to carry on the fight. He achieved the double ten times, more than any other amateur, and eight of them while with his new county, and, although he was unable to tour Australia with MCC in 1920/21 or 1924/5, he went to South Africa in 1922/3, taking 14 wickets in the four Tests. He appeared twice against Australia in 1921 and against the West Indies in 1928.

First-class career (1909-38): 23,278 runs (29.39) including 30 centuries, and 1,658 wickets (23.01)
Test matches (8): 208 runs (17.33), 28 wickets (22.00) and 5 catches

KEETON, William Walter (1905-80)

Nottinghamshire

Walter Keeton was a quick-footed right-handed opening batsman, stylish, wristy and consistent, who shared 45 century opening stands with Charlie Harris. His highest score was 312 not out at The Oval against Middlesex in 1939, the only triple hundred ever scored for Notts. He scored at least one century against each of the other first-class counties. With Reg Simpson he added 318 for the first wicket against Lancashire at Old Trafford in 1949 and besides his 312 he hit six other double centuries. He played twice for England, against Australia in 1934 and against the West Indies five years later. He also played soccer for Sunderland and Nottingham Forest.

First-class career (1926-52): 24,276 runs (39.53) including 54 centuries
Test matches (2): 57 runs (14.25)

KENNEDY, Alexander Stuart (1891-1959)

Hampshire

One of the most durable and consistent of all county all-rounders, Alex Kennedy was a dapper little man with sleek, dark hair and an india-rubber physique, which nothing seemed to tire. He was a right-handed batsman, who could be either studious or violent and who appeared in every position from one to eleven. As a dedicated right-arm medium-fast bowler he varied his pace subtly and could swing the new ball very late either way. His accuracy, freshness and intelligence were remarkable. He took a relatively long run-up, which included a sort of chassé in the middle. For years Newman and Kennedy *were* Hampshire's bowling and often, with Phil Mead, the batting too! Kennedy took 100 wickets in fifteen seasons and did the double five times, in 1922 taking 205 wickets and scoring 1,129 runs. He took all 10 for 37 for Players against Gentlemen at The Oval in 1927; but represented England only in South Africa, 1922/3, when his bowling was very effective on the matting. (For Lord Tennyson's team in South Africa, 1924/5, he took 21 wickets in the unofficial Tests.)

First-class career (1907-36): 16,586 runs (18.53) including 10 centuries, 2,874 wickets (21.24) and 523 catches
Test matches (5): 93 runs (15.50), 31 wickets (19.32) and 5 catches

KENYON, Donald (b.1924)

Worcestershire

A right-handed, opening batsman, Don Kenyon was a craftsman with a shrewd cricket brain. He scored more runs and centuries than any other Worcestershire player, nineteen times exceeding 1,000 runs in a season. His highest score was 259 against Yorkshire at Kidderminster in 1956; and three years previously, in the opening match of the tour, he hit 122 off the Australians. He toured India in 1951/2 and represented England against Australia and South Africa occasionally at home. He led Worcestershire for nine years, and was at the helm when the county won the Championship in 1964 and again in 1965. He served for several years as a Test selector.

First-class career (1946-67): 37,002 runs (33.63) including 74 centuries, and 327 catches
Test matches (8): 192 runs (12.80) and 5 catches

KILLICK, Rev. Edgar Thomas (1907-53)

Cambridge University and Middlesex

A graceful right-handed stroke-player, Tom Killick's first-class career was all too short. Few contemporaries executed the off-drive and square-cut with such ease and he was a swift mover in the outfield. A Cambridge blue, he enjoyed a short but distinguished career as opening batsman for Middlesex. In 1931, in his only game for the county that season, he shared in an opening stand of 277 with G.T.S. Stevens against Warwickshire at Lord's, his own score being 206. In 1929 he went in first with Herbert Sutcliffe in two Tests against South Africa, as successor to Jack Hobbs. He died while batting in a match between the diocesan clergy of St Albans and Coventry at Northampton.

First-class career (1926-46): 5,730 runs (40.35) including 15 centuries
Test matches (2): 81 runs (20.25) and 2 catches

KILNER, Roy (1890-1928)

Yorkshire

With his long chin, merry eyes and cap askew, Roy Kilner said of a typical Roses match – which he relished – 'What we want is no umpires and fair cheating all round!' He was a man of rare charm, humour and generosity. A left-hander, he could not only drive powerfully on the off-side and pull very hard, but he could also play a dogged game and, as a slow bowler, his spin and accuracy made him at times unplayable. On true pitches he would plug away on a length for long spells with slight variations of flight and pace. A member of Yorkshire's Championship winning sides of the early twenties, he achieved the double three times, and his benefit in 1925 realized £4,014, a record for many years. He played for England against Australia and South Africa at home, and against Australia in Australia in 1924/5, when he was prominent in England's win at Melbourne in the fourth match, scoring 74 and taking 5 for 70. He died of enteric fever, contracted on his way home from India after a coaching engagement.

First-class career (1911-27): 14,422 runs (29.73) including 17 centuries, 991 wickets (18.48) and 225 catches
Test matches (9): 233 runs (33.28), 24 wickets (30.58) and 6 catches

KING, John Herbert (1871-1946)

Leicestershire

John King had a long and honourable career as player and umpire. A grand left-handed batsman, strong on the leg side and gifted with a powerful square-cut, a left-arm slow bowler and reliable in the field, he was the pivot of his county's cricket for thirty years, scoring 205 against Hampshire at the age of fifty-two. He exceeded 1,000 runs in a season fourteen times and twice he took 100 wickets. For Gentlemen v. Players at Lord's in 1904, he hit 104 and 109 not out against some terrific fast bowling. In his sole Test, against Australia at Lord's in 1909, he scored 60 and 4. In the absence of a fast bowler, he also opened the bowling and took 1 for 99 (but Ransford and Trumper were both dropped off him in the same over).

First-class career (1895-1925): 25,122 runs (27.34) including 34 centuries, 1,204 wickets (25.16) and 340 catches

KINNEIR, Septimus (1871-1928)

Wiltshire and Warwickshire

Coming into first-class cricket at twenty-seven, 'Paul' Kinneir was an orthodox left-handed batsman who rivalled Willie Quaife at the head of Warwickshire's batting averages for more than a decade. Touring Australia with MCC in 1911/12, he appeared in one Test at Sydney, scoring 22 and 30, but did not represent England again, partly because his fielding was considered poor.

First-class career (1898-1914): 15,641 runs (32.72) including 26 centuries, and 48 wickets (31.08)

KNIGHT, Albert Ernest (1872-1946)

Leicestershire

An outstanding character among the professionals of his day, Albert Knight was a very good hard-wicket player. A right-handed batsman, strong on the off-side with a favourite square-drive, he was also a good cover who threw in belligerently. He scored 1,000 runs in ten seasons, making his highest score, 229 not out, against Worcestershire at Worcester in 1903. He toured Australia in 1903/4, and played a heroic part in the fourth and critical match of the rubber at Sydney, making 70 not out after an early collapse. A Methodist lay preacher, he would pray before going in to bat and, sometimes, at the wicket – Walter Brearley threatened to report him to MCC for taking unfair advantage! He tended to forget the name of his batting partner to everyone's confusion. Once, a puzzled George Hirst, ball in hand, said to Knight's partner 'Won't you tell him your name, sir? Then we'll all be happy!' A widely read man, Knight became coach successively at Highgate School and Belvedere College, Dublin.

First-class career (1895-1912): 19,357 runs (29.24) including 34 centuries
Test matches (3): 81 runs (16.20) and 1 catch

KNIGHT, Barry Rolfe (b.1938)

Essex and Leicestershire

A vigorous all-rounder who enjoyed life off the field as well as on it, Barry Knight was an attractive forcing right-handed batsman, dangerous right-arm fast-medium bowler and an excellent field. Capable of hard work despite his slim, trim build, he achieved the double four times between 1962 and 1965. Leaving Essex after a dispute in 1966, he had three years with Leicestershire and then went to live in Sydney, where he established an indoor cricket school. He had toured Australia twice, India once and Pakistan once. By scoring 125 against New Zealand at Auckland in 1962/3 he shared in the record sixth-wicket stand of 240 with Peter Parfitt, and he hit 127 against India at Kanpur in 1963/4.

First-class career (1955-69): 13,336 runs (25.70) including 12 centuries, 1,089 wickets (24.06) and 260 catches
Test matches (29): 812 runs (26.19) including 2 centuries, 70 wickets (31.75) and 14 catches

KNIGHT, Donald John (1894-1960)

Oxford University and Surrey

Donald Knight was an amateur opening batsman of high distinction and his classic right-handed method, learned at Malvern, made him one of the outstanding players in immediate post-1918 cricket. After a bad blow to his head in 1920 when fielding at short-leg he was never quite the same although he played in the first two Tests of 1921 against Australia with some success before dropping out of the regular first-class game and becoming a highly respected cricket master at Westminster.

First-class career (1911-37): 6,231 runs (30.84) including 13 centuries
Test matches (2): 54 runs (13.50) and 1 catch

KNOTT, Alan Philip Eric (b.1946)

Kent

Alan Knott surpassed all previous records for an England wicket-keeper during the eleven hectic years between 1967 and 1977, when he played in eighty-nine Tests. Soon after the Centenary Test at Melbourne he became one of the first recruits to Kerry Packer's World Series Cricket. Small, nimble and dark-eyed, he is a serious family man off the field and an impish genius on it. He was preferred to all his wicket-keeping rivals, notably his immediate succcessor Bob Taylor, because of his exceptional batting ability. At his best in a crisis (and England faced many a crisis in his era) 'Knottie' applied hawk-eyed defence, an instinct for survival and formidable powers of concentration, and with brilliant attacking flair was often able to turn the course of a game. His right-handed batting was shrewd, increasingly unorthodox (his top hand holding the bat with the palm facing the bowler) and often outrageous, as when he repulsed the dangerous swing bowling of Bob Massie by carting him to all parts of the leg-side field in 1972, or on two tours of India when he broke the stranglehold imposed by the Indian spinners by moving his feet to the pitch of the ball and hitting it over the top. He was an even better player of fast bowlers. Against Lillee and Thomson in 1974/5 he was England's second highest scorer. His wicket-keeping was as quick and dazzling as the flight of a hornet. He ignored the advice of wicket-keepers of other eras to stand up to the wicket to medium-paced bowlers, believing he got far more catching chances standing back. He frequently dived to pick up the half-chance,

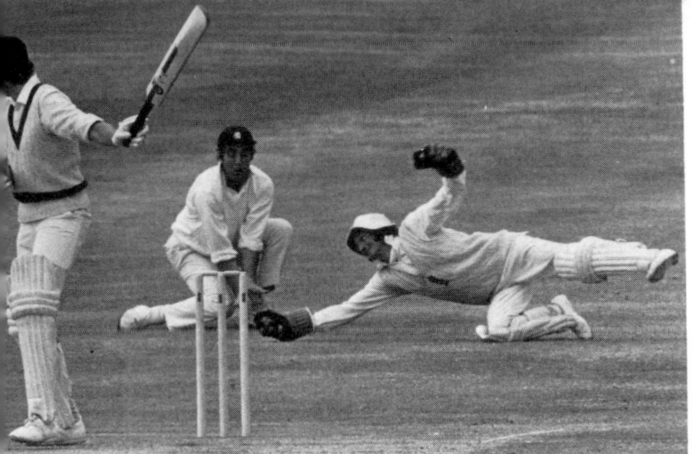

Alan Knott catches Rick McCosker (Australia) – Mike Brearley covering

sometimes with positively demonic dexterity; up to the stumps he could be equally brilliant although he was undoubtedly more fallible. Much of his keeping for Kent and England was to the awkward bowling of Derek Underwood – the two were an almost inseparable partnership. Knott's fetish for fitness included sticking to a careful diet. He was prone to stiff muscles and therefore exercised constantly to keep his limbs supple. Off the field he was almost paranoiacally suspicious of breezes and draughts. He went on six major overseas tours, and scored more than a 1,000 runs twice, hitting 127 not out and 118 not out in one Championship match against Surrey at Maidstone in 1972. Only Rodney Marsh has bettered his total of 269 Test victims which began with seven catches in his first Test against Pakistan at Trent Bridge in 1967. Yet he only began to dedicate himself to his keeping when he joined the Kent staff, having been a successful schoolboy off-spinner.

First-class career (1964-): 16,583 runs (30.09) including 17 centuries, 2 wickets (43.50) and 1,213 dismissals (1,090 ct, 123 st.)
Test matches (95): 4,389 runs (32.75) including 5 centuries, and 269 dismissals (250 ct, 19 st.)

KNOX, Neville Alexander (1884-1935)

Surrey

From Dulwich College Neville Knox burst into Surrey cricket and had a big share in bringing the county out of a deep depression. Over six foot tall and loose-limbed, he was probably the fastest bowler in England for several years. With a long and peculiar run, which started from near deep mid-off, he bowled at a great pace with a sharp break-back, and his good length deliveries often reared up straight *à la* Jeff Thomson. He took twelve Players wickets for Gentlemen at Lord's in 1906 – seven clean-bowled – and appeared the following year in two Tests against South Africa. His career ended rather abruptly: he had developed an acute form of shin soreness and was struggling against chronic lameness. Only sheer pluck enabled him latterly to keep going.

First-class career (1904-19): 831 runs (9.89) and 411 wickets (21.55)
Test matches (2): 24 runs (8.00) and 3 wickets (35.00)

LAKER, James Charles (b.1922)

Surrey and Essex

Jim Laker will forever be remembered for his amazing analysis of 19 for 90 against Australia in 1956. In his prime he was perhaps the best of all off-spinners, with a model high action, sharp spin, great accuracy, flight and the intelligence to think batsmen out. A Yorkshireman of few words, his approach to cricket and to life is independent, detached, cool. His figures do his talking for him. Eleven times he exceeded 100 wickets in a season. His best season was 1950, when he took 166 wickets (15.32), including 8 for 2 in the Test Trial at Bradford; and, from 1952 until 1958 when Surrey reigned as Champions, he shared the main attack with Alec Bedser, Peter Loader and Tony Lock, personally taking 327 wickets (15.62). Partly because he had been punished heavily by the 1948 Australians, he could not find a regular place for England until 1956, but in this *annus mirabilis* his revenge was fearsome. In seven games against the Australians, many on rain-affected pitches, he took 63 wickets, including 46 at 9.60 in the Tests, the record against Australia. His performance at Old Trafford (9 for 37 and 10 for 53) is unique.

Jim Laker

Leaving Surrey in 1959, he reappeared after three years for Essex, finally retiring in 1964. He is now a popular cricket commentator for BBC Television and has written several books, one of which got him into trouble with Surrey and MCC, but his sins have long since been forgiven and he is now an active member of Surrey's Cricket Committee. Throughout his playing career, he was a useful, sturdy tail-end batsman and a reliable catcher.

First-class career (1946-65): 7,304 runs (16.60) including 2 centuries, 1,944 wickets (18.40) and 270 catches
Test matches (46): 676 runs (14.08), 193 wickets (21.24) and 12 catches

LAMB, Allan Joseph (b.1954)

Western Province and Northamptonshire

Born of English parents in the Cape Province in South Africa, Allan Lamb had already attracted several plaudits for his batting for Western Province when he came to England in 1977 and qualified to play for Northamptonshire by special registration in 1978. Despite breaking an arm in his first season he immediately impressed as a compact, naturally gifted right-hand batsman with a simple method and a desire to take the initiative from bowlers whenever possible. Debarred from playing Test cricket by the boycott of South Africa, he set his heart on playing for the land of his parents instead. He acquired a British passport, bought a cottage in Northamptonshire and in 1982 won a place in the England side immediately he became available. Having averaged 66.55 in 1980 and 60.26 in 1981 in English first-class cricket, he had already proved himself a class above the run-of-the-mill county player. Dark, stocky and assertive, he confirmed his ability with an innings of 99 on his second representative appearance in a one-day international against India and in his Third Test, at The Oval, scored 107 against India before being run out. He failed in the second 1982 series, against Pakistan, but toured Australia with England in 1982/3.

First-class career (1972-   ): 11,458 runs (50.92) including 27 centuries, 4 wickets (22.75) and 113 catches
Test matches (6): 255 runs (25.50) and 1 catch

LANGRIDGE, James (1906-66)

Sussex and Auckland

A genuine all-rounder, Jim Langridge was a fine fielder, a very sound, fighting, but rather slow batsman, and a formidable left-arm bowler with flight, accuracy and spin, despite an odd action which had the suggestion of a curtsy about it. The first of the modern professional Sussex captains, he led the county from

Allan Lamb

1950 until 1952, but Hedley Verity barred his way to regular Test cricket. Langridge played against the West Indies, South Africa and India in England, and toured India in 1933/4, the first Test-playing tour to the Sub-Continent, appearing in the three Tests. He also toured Australia, 1946/7, without playing a Test. He was called 'a fine, sturdy character, a real part of Sussex'. Twenty times he exceeded 1,000 runs in a season, and he did the double six times. He became county coach, his son Richard also played for Sussex and his brother John was another Sussex stalwart who was certainly amongst the best batsmen never to play for England.

First-class career (1924-53): 31,716 runs (35.20) including 42 centuries, and 1,530 wickets (22.56)
Test matches (8): 242 runs (26.88), 19 wickets (21.73) and 6 catches

LARKINS, Wayne (b.1953)

Northamptonshire

A cheerful character from Bedfordshire, Wayne Larkins is a right-handed opening batsman of medium height and wiry build who possesses a rare gift of timing. Also a fine fielder and occasional medium-pace swing bowler, he undoubtedly had the ability to establish himself at Test level but a batting average of 16 after six Tests did not do him justice. He took a long time even to cement a regular place in the Northants side, making his first appearance in 1972 but not being capped until 1976. Once established, he became a consistently high scorer, forming an attractive opening partnership with Geoff Cook and putting on a county record of 322 for the second wicket with Richard Williams against Leicestershire in 1980. He toured Australia in 1979/80, played his first Test at Melbourne and his second against India in Bombay on the way home. He had three further opportunities against the West Indies in England in 1980, achieving a top score of only 33 but occasionally driving or playing the ball off his legs with crisp strokes which bore the hallmark of true class. He was recalled for the last Test of 1981 against Australia, scoring 34 and 24 at The Oval, and he was distinctly unlucky to be left out of the team for the subsequent tour of India. His disappointment no doubt persuaded him to take a hefty financial inducement to play on the officially disapproved-of South African tour of March 1982. This earned him a three-year ban from Test cricket, but he underlined what might have been by scoring 5 hundreds and 1,863 runs in first-class cricket in 1982.

First-class career (1972-): 10,558 runs (33.30) including 24 centuries, 27 wickets (39.66) and 93 catches
Test matches (6): 176 runs (16.00) and 3 catches

David Larter

LARTER, John David Frederick (b.1940)

Northamptonshire

An extremely tall man (6ft $7\frac{1}{2}$ins), David Larter approached the crease with ten easy strides in a run of twenty yards, generally maintaining control over his length and mixing his pace. But his build was not ideal and he did not possess either the dynamism or speed of his predecessor, Frank Tyson. He took 121 wickets (16.76) in 1963 and in his first Test, against Pakistan at The Oval in 1962, he captured 9 wickets. He toured Australia and New Zealand in 1962/3 and 1965/6 and India in 1963/4, but he broke down frequently through injuries, the last time during a Gillette Cup match in May 1967, and he retired from the game that year, briefly returning in 1969. His best bowling was 8 for 28 against Somerset at Northampton in 1965.

First-class career (1960-69): 639 runs (6.08) and 666 wickets (19.53)
Test matches (10): 16 runs (3.20), 37 wickets (25.43) and 5 catches

LARWOOD, Harold (b.1904)

Nottinghamshire

A gentle, modest character, Harold Larwood is linked forever with one of the most violent episodes in cricket history. Of a little below medium height and wiry rather than powerful, he remains, perhaps, the most heroic England right-arm fast bowler. With a run-in of about eighteen yards and with accelerating yet controlled rhythmical strides, his action built up like a long-jumper's to the explosive moment of delivery. He appeared to have abnormally long arms and in his prime his right hand would swing through from low on his right leg to a point so low after delivery that, according to D.R. Jardine and other contemporaries, his knuckles would actually touch the pitch on his follow-through. He was exceptionally fast – his

Harold Larwood

contemporaries believe the fastest of all. Representing England against Australia in his first full season in 1926, he toured with Percy Chapman's team, 1928/9, and appeared again on the next Australian visit in 1930, but it was not until his second tour of Australia with Douglas Jardine, 1932/3, that he reached his best. He was at the centre of the bodyline controversy, the man who made the ruthless policy work. Bowling his short-pitched balls to a packed leg-side field with great pace and accuracy, he reduced Bradman to a mere mortal and in the five Tests he took 33 wickets at 19.51. He did not play for England again after this tour; as a result of the constant pounding on the hard pitches, he received an injury to his left foot from which he never fully recovered. In 1936, however, he headed the national first-class averages with 119 wickets at 12.97 runs each. A useful but underrated hard-hitting batsman, he hit 98 at Sydney in his last Test. In eight full domestic seasons he exceeded 100 wickets each time. After the Second World War he took his wife and five daughters to Australia, and settled in Sydney.

First-class career (1924-38): 7,290 runs (19.91) including 3 centuries, 1,427 wickets (17.51) and 204 catches
Test matches (21): 485 runs (19.40), 78 wickets (28.35) and 15 catches

LEADBEATER, Edward (b.1927)

Yorkshire and Warwickshire

Eddie Leadbeater was that Yorkshire rarity, a right-arm leg-break bowler. Accurate, his 'wrong 'un' was usually a top-spinner instead of a googly. He was also a very useful batsman and a zealous field anywhere. He joined the MCC team in India in 1951/2 as replacement for the injured 'Dusty' Rhodes, playing in two Tests. He did not maintain his early success in county cricket, however, and had a short career for Warwickshire, without enhancing his figures.

First-class career (1949-58): 1,548 runs (15.18) including 1 century, and 289 wickets (27.50)
Test matches (2): 40 runs (20.00), 2 wickets (109.00) and 3 catches

LEE, Harry William (1890-1981)

Middlesex

During the First World War, Harry Lee, who had been an ordinary right-handed batsman and off-spinner, was seriously wounded, reported killed, and taken prisoner by the Germans. On returning to England with a permanent limp, he became Middlesex's opening batsman and a member of two Championship-winning sides, hit two centuries against Surrey at The Oval in 1919, and for fifteen years played third string to Patsy Hendren and 'Young Jack' Hearne. A very sound opener, he exceeded 1,000 runs in a season thirteen times. His highest score was 243 not out against Nottinghamshire at Lord's in 1921. While coaching in South Africa, he was co-opted by MCC in 1930/31, after Andy Sandham had been injured in a car accident; and, playing in the fourth Test at Johannesburg, he scored 18 and 1. Often a useful change bowler, he took 6 for 53 against the 1921 Australians. He was the elder brother of Frank and Jack (killed in action, 1944), both of whom played for Middlesex and Somerset. Frank became an umpire.

First-class career (1911-34): 20,069 runs (30.17) including 37 centuries, 376 wickets (31.12) and 178 catches

LEES, Walter Scott (1875-1924)

Surrey

On the quick side of right-arm medium pace, Walter Lees had an easy, untiring action and plenty of 'devil' under all conditions, and he was also a dashing and fearless batsman, who won nearly all his fame playing for Surrey. He toured South Africa with MCC in 1905/6, when the whole team was baffled by googly bowlers on matting, but he added to his laurels in the Tests, the only ones he played.

First-class career (1896-1911): 7,642 runs (17.23) including 2 centuries, and 1,402 wickets (21.39)
Test matches (5): 66 runs (11.00), 26 wickets (17.96) and 2 catches

LEGGE, Geoffrey Bevington (1903-40)

Oxford University and Kent

A former Oxford captain, Geoffrey Legge led Kent ably for three seasons from 1928 and, in a short career, off-drove and cut effectively as a right-handed batsman as well as catching almost anything within reach in the slips. He toured South Africa in 1927/8, and Australasia in 1929/30. He played in the earliest Tests against New Zealand, hitting 196 in the fourth match at Auckland. Unable to play much cricket after 1930, he was killed in action in 1940.

First-class career (1924-31): 4,955 runs (24.89) including 7 centuries, 8 wickets (22.52) and 118 catches
Test matches (5): 299 runs (49.83) including 1 century, 0-34 and 1 catch

LESLIE, Charles Frederick Henry (1861-1921)

Oxford University, Middlesex and Shropshire

A capable all-rounder, Charles Leslie's career was all

too short. He toured Australia in 1882/3 with Hon. Ivo Bligh's team, making 54 (run out) in the second Test at Melbourne and 144 against New South Wales.

First-class career (1881-88): 1,860 runs (22.96) including 4 centuries, and 8 wickets (20.62)
Test matches (4): 106 runs (15.14), 4 wickets (11.00) and 1 catch

LEVER, John Kenneth (b.1949)

Essex

After being for many years a respected county opening bowler, John Lever, known as 'J.K.', seized with both hands his chance to break through at the highest level. Steady bowling and stamina earned him selection in the first Test against India at Delhi in 1976/7 but no-one was prepared for his matchwinning performance. On his first active day in Test cricket he made 53 and took 4 for 16 in his opening spell, undermining India with late in-swing. He finished the match with 10 for 70, and the series with 26 wickets at 14.61. Tallish, fair-haired and lithe, a fast left-arm bowler, brilliant outfielder and staunch right-hand tail-ender, he has not been able to live up to that remarkable start but has been unfortunate in having to fight for an England place against some outstanding rivals, notably Willis, Old, Botham and Hendrick. But on five major England tours between 1976 and 1982 Lever never let anyone down. He never seems to be worried by minor injuries, can bowl long spells despite an excessively long run-up, is always accurate and can swing the ball both ways in helpful conditions. In both 1978 and 1979 he took 106 wickets and was the chief inspiration in Essex's first County Championship title in 1979.

First-class career (1967-): 2,607 runs (10.72), 1,213 wickets (24.05) and 151 catches
Test matches (20): 306 runs (12.24), 67 wickets (26.64) and 11 catches

LEVER, Peter (b.1940)

Lancashire and Tasmania

A wholehearted and aggressive right-arm fast bowler, 'Plank' Lever was an important member of the 1970/71 side in Australia which brought back the Ashes, and four years later his bowling in the sixth Test at Melbourne (6 for 38 in the first innings) restored some lost prestige for a battered team. Back trouble restricted him in his last few seasons and hastened his retirement, but he possessed a dangerous late out-swing and fierce pace. He was at his best when he pitched the ball up and used the seam, rather than trying to dig the ball in, and he restricted his use of the bouncer after very nearly killing the New Zealand tail-ender, Ewan Chatfield, with a short ball in 1975. After years as a respected county opener, notably in partnership with Ken Shuttleworth, he was picked for England against the Rest of the World in 1970 and took 7 for 83 in the World XI's first innings. He was thirty by the time he reached Australia for the first time but he proved the ideal support for John Snow. His batting successes in Tests included a merry innings of 88 not out against India at Old Trafford in 1971. He could be a determined and useful right-hand batsman.

First-class career (1960-76): 3,534 runs (14.25), 796 wickets (25.59) and 106 catches
Test matches (17): 350 runs (21.87), 41 wickets (36.80) and 11 catches

LEVESON GOWER, Sir Henry Dudley Gresham (1873-1954)

Oxford University and Surrey

Known as 'Shrimp', Leveson Gower was for about sixty years a considerable personality in English cricket. Short and slight but effervescent, he was a right-handed batsman with a good eye and supple wrists, who revelled in the cut and, as a slow-medium bowler, he could make the ball drift. As both player and administrator, he was a naturally friendly and cheerful character. Successively captain of Winchester, Oxford, Surrey and England in South Africa in 1909/10, he had a long playing career and afterwards served as president of Surrey for ten years

John Lever

and chairman of the England Selection Committee. He frequently toured with private teams, and for nearly fifty years ran the popular Scarborough Cricket Festival. In 1953 he was knighted for his services to the game.

First-class career (1893-1931): 7,638 runs (23.72) including 4 centuries, and 46 wickets (29.96)
Test matches (3): 95 runs (23.75) and 1 catch

LEVETT, William Howard Vincent (b.1909)

Kent

One of the characters of the game, a tireless conversationalist behind the stumps or in the pavilion, 'Hopper' Levett brought a store of nervous energy to everything he undertook, and had days of brilliance when he was the best wicket-keeper in the land. He appeared four times for Gentlemen against Players, but the presence of Les Ames limited his opportunities for Kent. He toured India with MCC in 1933/4, and appeared in a sole Test at Calcutta, scoring 5 and 2 not out and holding 3 catches. After a 'heavy' night he is once said to have remained totally motionless whilst the first ball of the match whistled by him for four byes. The batsman tickled the next delivery down the leg-side, Hopper dived, caught it and came up triumphantly with the ball in his hand saying, 'Not bad for the first ball of the morning, eh?'

First-class career (1930-47): 2,524 runs (12.25) and 467 dismissals (272 ct, 195 st.)

LEWIS, Anthony Robert (b.1938)

Cambridge University and Glamorgan

Darkly good-looking, with a smile which would charm a statue, Tony Lewis is a man of many talents. An attacking right-hand batsman he drove impeccably, cut well, and could work the ball anywhere on the leg-side with easy timing. An occasional leg-break bowler, he once had 3 for 18 against Somerset. Captain of Cambridge in 1962, he scored 2,198 runs (41.47) in 1966 and led Glamorgan to her second Championship title in 1969. He was captain from 1967 to 1972. His belated chance to play for England came when he replaced Ray Illingworth, who was not available on the tough tour of India and Pakistan in 1972/3. He made 0 and 70 not out in his maiden Test at Delhi and 125 at Kanpur – and he included two half-centuries during the three drawn Tests with Pakistan. He failed in the first home Test against New Zealand in 1973 but it was because of injury that he did not represent England again. A gifted cricket writer and broadcaster, he also won a Rugby blue and was a violinist with the Welsh National Youth Orchestra.

First-class career (1955-74): 20,495 runs (32.42) including 30 centuries, and 6 wickets (72.00)
Test matches (9): 457 runs (32.64) including 1 century

LEYLAND, Morris or Maurice (1900-1967)

Yorkshire

Few men have relished a fight more than Leyland, whose Christian name was registered as Morris but usually published as Maurice. A tough and cheerful Yorkshireman with one of the best records against Australia of any English batsman (1,705 runs at 56.83 in 20 matches), he was a left-hander with a wide stance and great strength, his strokes being weighty and decisive. He particularly liked hitting powerful skimming drives and, before the ball had thumped into the boundary fence, he would be standing still as a statue, his right arm at his side and his bat close to his body. He also bowled left-handed chinamen, which were a little less friendly than they looked – he once performed a hat-trick at Headingley. Apart from holding England together in many Tests – usually at number four – he was part of twelve Yorkshire Championship-winning sides. He exceeded 1,000 runs in 17 seasons with a highest score of 263 against Essex at Hull in 1936. After making 0 in his first Test innings against West Indies in 1928, he scored 137 and 53 not out in his second Test at Melbourne in 1928/9. He made two further tours of Australia, averaging 55.12 in the Tests of 1936/7. In his prime against Australia in 1934 he made 109 at Lord's and 110 at The Oval. He also toured South Africa and the West Indies. In his

Maurice Leyland

last Test – against Australia at The Oval in 1938 – he contributed 187, his highest score for England, to England's record 903 for 7.

First-class career (1920-48): 33,660 runs (40.50) including 80 centuries, and 466 wickets (29.28)
Test matches (41): 2,764 runs (46.06) including 9 centuries, 6 wickets (97.50) and 13 catches

LILLEY, Arthur Frederick Augustus (1866-1929)

Warwickshire

From 1896 until 1909 'Dick' Lilley monopolized the position as England's wicket-keeper; and he toured Australia twice. He took the infinitely varied bowling of his period calmly, soundly and without fuss. For his county against MCC at Lord's in 1896, he took eight catches and, though he kept continuously for 23 years, he was such an artist that at the end of his career his hands and fingers showed scarcely a trace of the heavy strain to which they had been subjected. As a right-handed batsman, he was often invaluable and he continued to play for Warwickshire as a batsman when 'Tiger' Smith replaced him as 'keeper.

First-class career (1891-1911): 15,597 runs (26.30) including 16 centuries, 41 wickets (36.22) and 899 dismissals (709 ct, 190 st.)
Test matches (35): 903 runs (20.52), 1-23 and 92 dismissals (70 ct, 22 st.)

LILLYWHITE, James, junior (1842-1929)

Sussex

The last survivor of the team which he captained in the first two Tests ever against Australia, 1876/7, Jim Lillywhite came from a notable cricketing family. His uncle was William, the 'Nonpareil'. Five of the family played for Sussex and in one match three generations – father, son and grandson – took part. From 1862 until 1881 Jim appeared in every match played by the county. A left-arm slowish bowler with a high and exceptionally accurate delivery, he was also a vigorous left-handed batsman and a good field, either at slip or mid-on. Altogether, he visited Australia six times, the first being as a member of W.G. Grace's 1873/4 side, and four being in business partnership with Alfred Shaw and Arthur Shrewsbury, when he tended to have his fingers burned financially. He also toured America in 1868 and for some years was secretary of the United South of England Eleven. He became an efficient umpire.

First-class career (1862-81): 1,140 wickets (15.38)
Test matches (2): 16 runs (8.00), 8 wickets (15.75) and 1 catch

Dick Lilley

LLOYD, David (b.1947)

Lancashire

A chirpy, intelligent Accrington lad, affectionately known as 'Bumble' (he talks a lot and with an engaging Lancashire burr), David Lloyd had a high promise but this was blighted in mid-career by being a front-line batsman against Thomson and Lillee on the daunting 1974/5 tour of Australia, and by the responsibility of being county captain between 1973 and 1977, a job which on the whole he relished little. A neat, strong left-hander with all the shots and sometimes exceptional flair in attack, he is also an under-used, slow, left-arm orthodox spinner and a brilliant close fielder. For several seasons he was a specialist in the dangerous short-leg position. He made an immediate impact on Test cricket in 1974, scoring 214 not out in only his second Test against India at Edgbaston, an innings full of handsome driving, pulling and cutting, all based on quick, incisive footwork. But like all the England batsmen who had to face the ferocious pace of Thomson and Lillee the following winter, sometimes on difficult pitches, he seemed to be shell-shocked by the experience. Not that it affected his humour. Seeing Keith Fletcher signing an autograph the day after he had painfully 'headed' a bouncer far into the covers, Lloyd asked: 'What are you signing, Keith, Nat Lofthouse?' Under Lloyd's cheerful captaincy Lancashire reached three successive Gillette Cup Finals, winning in 1975. In 1982 he hit 5 hundreds and scored 1,371 runs. He also had much to do with the development of the career of Graeme Fowler.

First-class career (1965-): 18,762 runs (33.14) including 37 centuries, 220 wickets (30.78) and 326 catches
Test matches (9): 552 runs (42.46) including 1 century, 0-17 and 11 catches

LOADER, Peter James (b.1929)

Surrey and Western Australia

A hostile, wiry, right-arm fast bowler with a long, high-stepping run, Peter Loader spearheaded Surrey's attack with Alec Bedser during the triumphant Championship years of 1952-8. When the swing went from the new ball he varied his pace cleverly. Against West Indies at Headingley, 1957, he achieved the first hat-trick in post-War Test cricket. He took 9 for 17 against Warwickshire at The Oval in 1958, and 9 for 28 against Kent at Blackheath, 1953 – each in an innings – and seven times exceeded 100 wickets in a season. He toured Australia in 1954/5, 1958/9, South Africa 1956/7, and it was only because England had a cache of fast bowlers that he received so few chances in Test cricket. On leaving Surrey in 1963, he emigrated to Western Australia, where he is now a family man, businessman and cricket broadcaster.

First-class career (1951-63): 2,314 runs (8.51) and 1,326 wickets (19.04)
Test matches (13): 76 runs (5.84), 39 wickets (22.51) and 2 catches

LOCK, Graham Anthony Richard (b.1929)

Surrey, Leicestershire and Western Australia

Tony Lock's remarkable career had as many dramatic turning points as an epic family saga. Sturdily built, with reddish sandy hair which thinned early, he was an orthodox slow left-arm spinner possessed of an aggression seldom found in the fastest of bowlers. Fiery, rash and quick-witted, he was quite phenomenal fielding at short-leg. At The Oval in 1957 he caught eight Warwickshire batsmen. Starting as a sixteen-year-old slow, left-arm bowler with a good flight, Tony Lock, or 'Beau', first altered his technique to suit the slow turning wickets at The Oval, fizzing the ball at the batsman with sharp spin accompanied by shouts and gestures. He played a prominent part when England recovered the Ashes against Australia at The Oval in 1953, taking 5 for 45 in the second innings, and the partnership of Lock and Laker kept the Ashes in England in 1956. His quicker ball, however, was suspected as a 'chuck' and – after seeing a film of his action during MCC's tour of Australia in 1958/9 – he decided to end any controversy by returning to his slower style. He became notably more successful on hard overseas pitches by giving the ball more air. He had seven overseas tours, only one to Australia. Fourteen times he took more than 100 wickets in a season. He took four hat-tricks and reached his thousandth wicket at the age of only twenty-six – the fourth youngest ever. He was also the most prolific catcher among his contemporaries and always a useful, hard-hitting batsman. The final phase of his career began when he emigrated to Western Australia in 1963, although he returned to join Leicestershire in 1965, becoming captain the following year. His exuberant personality brought out the best in every member of the side both at Leicester and at Perth, where he captained Western Australia to success in the Sheffield Shield and broke their wicket-taking record.

Tony Lock

First-class career (1946-71): 10,342 runs (15.88), 2,844 wickets (19.24) and 830 catches
Test matches (49): 742 runs (13.74), 174 wickets (25.58) and 59 catches

LOCKWOOD, William Henry (1868-1932)

Nottinghamshire and Surrey

A 'rough diamond' with an impressive high action, Bill Lockwood was noted for a tremendous body-swing in delivery, followed by a sharp off-cutter or break-back, so that the ball often pitched outside the off-stump and caused the wicket-keeper to jump to take it on the leg-side. He had a chequered career. He was a great bowler for Surrey and England for three seasons, but on tour in Australia with A.E. Stoddart's team in 1894/5 he failed badly and the slide continued until 1897, when he lost his place in the county side. A narrow escape from being maimed by a shark and the tragic death of his wife and one of his children had led him to try to find too great a solace in alcohol. He made a courageous comeback, however, in 1898 when he took 134 wickets, scored nearly 1,000 runs and regained his place for England against Australia, not retiring until 1904. Against Australia at Old Trafford in 1902 he captured 11 for 76, one of the greatest feats in Anglo-Australian matches. Had he not done so much bowling, he would have been an impressive run-getter; he seven times took more than 100 wickets in a season, and twice achieved the double.

Bill Lockwood

First-class career (1886-1904): 10,673 runs (21.96) including 15 centuries, and 1,376 wickets (18.34)
Test matches (12): 231 runs (17.76), 43 wickets (20.55) and 4 catches

LOHMANN, George Alfred (1865-1901)

Surrey and Western Province

Before he died of tuberculosis in South Africa, where he had gone in search of health six years before, George Lohmann had built a magnificent reputation as a cricketer's cricketer who always threw himself into a game. A fair, blue-eyed, square-shouldered and altogether handsome man, he had jumped to the top early and remained there. He was a right-handed, quick-footed, matchwinning batsman, a fielder who held slip catches no one else would have thought possible and, above all, a graceful medium-pace bowler with an occasional fast ball, who used every variety of deception. He was an integral part of Surrey's Championship-winning side of the late 1880s and early 1890s. He toured Australia three times between 1886 and 1892 and South Africa in 1895/6 when in the three Tests he was complete master on the matting with 35 wickets (5.80), taking 15 for 45 (7 for 38 and 8 for 7) at Port Elizabeth. Against Australia at The Oval in 1886 he took 7 for 36 in the second innings, bowling unchanged with Johnny Briggs to help England win by an innings. At Sydney he took 8 for 25 in 1886/7 and 8 for 58 in 1891/2. Altogether he took 8 or more wickets in an innings twenty times (four times in Tests) and fourteen times thirteen or more wickets in a match. He managed the South African team to England in 1901.

First-class career (1884-97): 7,247 runs (18.68) including 3 centuries, 1,841 wickets (13.74) and 336 catches
Test matches (18): 213 runs (8.87), 112 wickets (10.75) and 28 catches

LOWSON, Frank Anderson (b.1925)

Yorkshire

Frank Lowson was a quiet, compact and stylish right-handed opening batsman who produced some superb innings for his county, notably his highest score – 259 against Worcestershire at Worcester in 1953. At its best his batting was marked by firm driving and attractive cutting, but somehow lacked the spark which would have turned him from an extremely competent performer into an outstanding one. He received several chances for England and toured India with MCC in 1951/2, reaching 1,000 runs on the tour. In England he exceeded 1,000 in a season eight times.

First-class career (1949-58): 15,321 runs (37.18) including 31 centuries, and 191 catches
Test matches (7): 245 runs (18.84) and 5 catches

LUCAS, Alfred Perry (1857-1923)

Cambridge University, Surrey, Middlesex and Essex

A classic, though defensive, batsman who had a long career, 'Bunny' Lucas captained MCC against Australia at Lord's in 1902 having toured Australia with Lord Harris's team in 1878/9, and played in the first

George Lohmann

two Tests in England at The Oval in 1880 and 1882. Normally a change-bowler, he performed wonders for Lord Harris's team, having to do practically all the bowling with the two professionals, Tom Emmett and George Ulyett.

First-class career (1874-1907): 10,263 runs (26.38) including 8 centuries, and 155 wickets (18.38)
Test matches (5): 157 runs (19.62), 0-54 and 1 catch

LUCKHURST, Brian William (b.1939)

Kent

Brian Luckhurst was a staunch, loyal, honest cricketer and a determined right-handed opening batsman with a particularly fierce square-cut. He had been a solid performer for Kent for many years when he was selected for England against the Rest of the World in 1970 at the age of thirty-one. In the second match of the series, at Trent Bridge, he made his reputation, his 113 not out steering England to victory against formidable opposition. Luckhurst's official Test career began in Australia the following winter when he was a stalwart of Illingworth's Ashes-winning side, making 455 runs at 56.87 in five Tests and hitting determined centuries at Perth and Melbourne. Four years later against much fiercer fast bowling he was a sad failure but the story of his career is one of consistent run-getting with an occasional purple patch. He scored 1,000 or more runs in a season fourteen times and was a key member of the successful Kent side in limited-over cricket, not least because of his excellent athletic fielding in any position. On his day he could also be a useful, slow, left-arm bowler; at Gravesend in 1962 he took 4 for 32 against Somerset. His highest score was 215 against Derbyshire at Derby in 1973. He is now manager of Kent.

First-class career (1958-76): 22,293 runs (38.17) including 48 centuries, 64 wickets (42.87) and 392 catches
Test matches (21): 1,298 runs (36.05) including 4 centuries, 1-32 and 14 catches

Brian Luckhurst watched by Surrey's Arnold Long (wicket-keeper) and Stewart Storey

LYTTELTON, Rt Hon. Alfred (1857-1913)

Cambridge University and Middlesex

A member of a strong cricketing family – his seven brothers also played either first-class or good class cricket – Alfred Lyttelton was in the Cambridge side that defeated the 1878 Australians, and was a right-handed, front-foot batsman in the classical mould. Moreover, he was the foremost amateur wicket-keeper of his day, standing up without a long stop, and he appeared in four of the first five Tests played against Australia in England. At The Oval in 1884, after the regular bowlers had been mastered by the Australian batsmen, he bowled in his pads and, with lobs, finished off the innings, taking 4 for 19 in twelve overs. Alfred Lyttelton was the best contemporary tennis player, excelled also at racquets and played for England at Association Football. A lawyer, politician and philanthropist, he held office as Colonial Secretary in A.J. Balfour's Conservative administration, 1903-5.

First-class career (1876-87): 4,429 runs (27.85) including 7 centuries, and 206 dismissals (135 ct, 71 st.)
Test matches (4): 94 runs (15.66), 4 wickets (4.75) and 2 dismissals (2 ct)

MACAULAY, George Gibson (1897-1940)

Yorkshire

Relentless and self-confident, George Macaulay was a versatile right-arm bowler. After a short, breezy run to the wicket, he could open the attack with lethal swing and then turn to off-spin, bowling round the wicket to utilize his vast break from the off. A tenacious batsman, he showed his fighting spirit in his only Test against Australia, at Leeds in 1926 when the two Georges, Macaulay and Geary, came together for the ninth wicket, added 108 and saved the game. Macaulay was also a daring close field. He was an integral part of Yorkshire for fifteen years, eight years of which the county was Champion. In 1925 he took 211 wickets (15.48). His sole MCC tour was to South Africa in 1922/3 – he took 16 wickets in four Tests – and he took a wicket with his first ball in Tests at Cape

Town as well as making the stroke which brought victory by one wicket. He appeared in two Tests against the West Indies.

First-class career (1920-35): 6,212 runs (18.00) including 3 centuries, 1,837 wickets (17.65) and 348 catches
Test matches (8): 112 runs (18.66), 24 wickets (27.58) and 5 catches

MacBRYAN, John Crawford William (b.1892)

Cambridge University and Somerset

Taken prisoner in August 1914, Jack MacBryan played much cricket in Holland when interned there as a POW. A Cambridge blue, he became a mainstay of Somerset as a neat and polished right-handed batsman. His sole Test appearance at Old Trafford against South Africa in 1924 was ruined by rain, and he did not bat. He deserved many more opportunities.

First-class career (1911-36): 9,379 runs (26.41) including 17 centuries

McCONNON, James Edward (b.1922)

Glamorgan

A tall right-arm off-spinner with an ideal action, Jim McConnon, or 'Mac', had long, strong fingers and impressive flight. Rather highly strung, he needed encouragement to produce his best. He was an excellent gully and a late-order batsman who once scored 95 against Middlesex at Cardiff in 1951. In the same season he took 136 wickets (16.07) and performed the hat-trick against the South Africans at Swansea. He toured Australia with MCC, 1954/5, and India with a Commonwealth team, but had to return home early with injury each time. His only Tests were against Pakistan in 1954.

First-class career (1950-61): 4,661 runs (14.38) and 819 wickets (19.88)
Test matches (2): 18 runs (9.00), 4 wickets (18.50) and 4 catches

McGAHEY, Charles Percy (1871-1935)

Essex

A cheerful, careless extrovert, Charlie McGahey was a tall, right-handed, hard-hitting, front-foot batsman, a useful, slow, leg-break bowler and a good field. The crowd loved him. His highest score was 277 against Derbyshire at Leyton in 1905, and he six times shared stands of over 200 for his county. He made more than 1,000 runs in a season ten times. Early in his career he suffered a threat of tuberculosis, and partly for medical reasons toured Australia with Archie McLaren's team in 1901/2. There he appeared in his only Tests and came home cured. Over 6 foot and weighing 14 stone, he played full-back for Arsenal and Millwall.

First-class career (1894-1921): 20,723 runs (30.20) including 31 centuries, and 328 wickets (31.00)
Test matches (2): 38 runs (9.50) and 1 catch

MacGREGOR, Gregor (1869-1919)

Cambridge University and Middlesex

Edinburgh-born, Gregor MacGregor or 'Mac' was famous before the age of twenty. A wicket-keeper of extraordinary ability, he played for Cambridge for four years, becoming captain in the fourth when Oxford were defeated. He first played for England against Australia in 1890, while still an undergraduate. He would stand up close to the fastest deliveries of such as Sammy Woods and Charles Kortright, gathering the ball with an air of ease on either side of the wicket. He led Middlesex from 1899 until 1907. Sometimes a very useful batsman, he toured Australia with Lord Sheffield's team in 1891/2. He was also a Scottish Rugby international.

First-class career (1888-1907): 6,381 runs (18.03) including 3 centuries, and 560 dismissals (410 ct, 150 st.)
Test matches (8): 96 runs (12.00) and 17 dismissals (14 ct, 3 st.)

McINTYRE, Arthur John William (b.1918)

Surrey

Originally a leg-spinner, Arthur McIntyre first kept wicket in an emergency. In 1947 he became Surrey's regular 'keeper and played a principal part in Surrey's unrelenting triumphs of the 1950s. He is specially remembered for some brilliant stumpings off Alec Bedser's cutters, though he was also a sound right-handed batsman. Only Godfrey Evans stood in the way of a regular England place. He appeared in only three Tests, once each against the West Indies, South Africa, and Australia in 1950/51, when he was played as a batsman. In 1947 he claimed 95 victims; and three times he exceeded 1,000 runs in a season.

First-class career (1938-63): 11,145 runs (22.83) including 7 centuries, and 797 dismissals (639 ct, 158 st.)
Test matches (3): 19 runs (3.16) and 8 dismissals (8 ct.)

MacKINNON, Francis Alexander (The 35th MacKinnon of MacKinnon) (1848-1947)

Cambridge University and Kent

Francis MacKinnon played for Cambridge in the

historic 'Cobden's Match' of 1870 and was a good, steady batsman who, from 1875 until 1885, appeared for Kent in 78 matches, scoring 2,184 runs (16.42), including 2 centuries. He toured Australia with Lord Harris's team in 1878/9 and, in his sole Test at Melbourne, made 0 and 5. He was president of Kent in 1889 and always kept in close touch with the game.

MacLAREN, Archibald Campbell
(1871-1944)

Lancashire

Archie MacLaren was the true model of the classic batsman. A right-hander with a handsome face and figure, a high backlift, and an array of strokes all round the wicket (his particular glory being the off-drive and straight drive), he was in charge from the moment he got to the crease. He led Lancashire from 1894 until 1896, and again from 1899 until 1907. He succeeded W.G. Grace as England captain against Australia in 1899, took his own team to Australia in 1901/2 – he had been there with A.E. Stoddart's teams, 1894/5 and 1897/8 – and was captain in England in 1902 and 1909. He led Lancashire to Championship victory, but failed to win a rubber for England. He was a calculating attacker and sound tactician but his leadership was authoritarian. He reached 1,000 runs eight times in a season in England, and once in Australia. Throughout, he was an opening batsman. He made 108 on his debut in first-class cricket, for Lancashire against Sussex at Hove in 1890; 228 on his debut in Australia, for A.E. Stoddart's team against Victoria at Melbourne in 1894/5; 149 on his debut in a first-class match in America; and 200 not out for MCC against A New Zealand Eleven at Wellington in 1922/3, his last first-class match. His 424 against Somerset at Taunton in 1895 remains the highest score in a first-class match in England. He hit five Test hundreds, four in Australia and one, his highest – 140 – at Trent Bridge in 1905. In 1921, at the age of forty-nine, he raised and captained the famous amateur side which at Eastbourne defeated Warwick Armstrong's hitherto undefeated Australians. But away from cricket he found little pleasure or success in business.

Archie MacLaren

First-class career (1890-1922): 22,022 runs (34.03) including 47 centuries, and 411 catches
Test matches (35): 1,931 runs (33.87) including 5 centuries, and 29 catches

McMASTER, Joseph Emile Patrick
(1861-1929)

An Irishman, McMaster toured South Africa with Major Warton's team of 1888/9 and appeared in the second Test at Cape Town. Going in at number nine he failed to score and did not bowl. This Test is believed to have been his only experience of first-class cricket!

MAKEPEACE, Joseph William Henry
(1882-1952)

Lancashire

A thoughtful, right-handed opening batsman, 'Harry' Makepeace relied chiefly upon placing the ball and seldom put much power into his strokes. He was masterly against the turning ball on a difficult pitch. To him defence was the best method of attack. He was also an excellent cover-point. In 1926, when Lancashire won the Championship for the first time in twenty-two years, he made 2,340 runs (48.75) and in all he made more than 1,000 runs in thirteen seasons. He toured Australia with MCC in 1920/21, hitting 117 in the fourth Test at Melbourne, but never appeared for England at home. In retirement he served as county coach. A double international, he played soccer for England four times, against Scotland and Wales, and with Everton won an F.A. Cup Winner's medal.

First-class career (1906-30): 25,799 runs (36.23) including 43 centuries, 41 wickets (46.87) and 183 catches
Test matches (4): 279 runs (34.87) including 1 century

MANN, Francis George (b.1917)

Cambridge University and Middlesex

The elder son of F.T. Mann, George was a superb fielder and a very competent right-handed batsman who had established himself as one of the most popular and successful England captains when the demands of the family brewery forced him to leave the first-class game. More slightly built than his father, he was a balanced, attacking batsman, particularly strong on the leg. He captained Middlesex in 1948 and 1949 but his greatest triumph came in the fifth Test in South Africa at Port Elizabeth in 1948/9 when, as skipper, he saved England with 136 not out and turned a possible defeat into victory. This team remained unbeaten and was one of the finest fielding sides of modern times. His integrity and experience have made him an invaluable chairman of the TCCB.

First-class career (1937-58): 6,350 runs (25.92) including 7 centuries
Test matches (7): 376 runs (37.60) including 1 century, and 3 catches

MANN, Francis Thomas (1888-1964)

Cambridge University and Middlesex

Remembered as a popular captain and massive hitter, Frank Mann, in fact, did not always score fast – his highest score, 194 against Warwickshire at Edgbaston in 1926, took five hours – but, when he did open out, the results were startling. A powerful right-hander, his most notable display of 'fireworks' was against Nottinghamshire at Lord's in 1921 when he hit 53 in nineteen minutes. Burly and a delightful personality, he captained Middlesex from 1921 until 1928 – leading them to the Championship title in 1921 – and also MCC in South Africa, 1922/3, when the rubber was won. He was a Test selector and Middlesex president.

First-class career (1908-33): 13,237 runs (23.43) including 9 centuries, and 176 catches
Test matches (5): 281 runs (35.12) and 4 catches

MARKS, Victor James (b.1955)

Oxford University and Somerset

Vic Marks has made increasingly good use of relatively modest abilities. At Blundells, and at Oxford, where he was a popular and determined captain in 1976 and 1977, he was mainly a middle-order batsman, effective in a rugged and rough sort of way. But for Somerset he has become steadily more useful as an off-break bowler, giving the ball an almost old-fashioned amount of air and, despite this, proving highly effective in limited-overs cricket. He first represented England in a one-day international against the West Indies in 1980 and, after considerable practice at carrying out drinks, won his first Test cap against Pakistan in the decisive third Test at Headingley in August 1982. He was bowled for 7, padding up to Abdul Qadir's googly in the first innings, an embarrassing start, but made an important 12 not out in the second and also took a vital wicket with a disputed 'bat and pad' catch. He was subsequently picked to tour Australia in 1982/3.

First-class career (1975-): 5,663 runs (27.35) including 1 century, 339 wickets (33.42) and 69 catches
Test matches (1): 19 runs (19.00)

MARRIOTT, Charles Stowell (1895-1966)

Cambridge University, Lancashire and Kent

Charles Marriott (known as 'Father') learned his cricket in Ireland and was a skilful right-arm, leg-break bowler with a rare googly. A schoolmaster, he played most of his cricket for Kent in the month of August. His style was odd: starting in the region of mid-off, he would prance up to the wicket with high, finnicky steps, but his length was immaculate, and his leg-break deadly on any responsive wicket. He played for England once, against the West Indies at The Oval in 1933, when he made a duck, held 1 catch but took 11 for 96, England winning by an innings. He toured India with MCC, 1933/4, performing the hat-trick against Madras.

First-class career (1919-38): 574 runs (4.41) and 711 wickets (20.11)

MARTIN, Frederick (1861-1921)

Kent

Frederick Martin (known as 'Nutty') had a long career as a left-arm, medium-pace bowler with a high, easy action that seemed part of himself. Most of his best work was done for Kent and MCC, on whose groundstaff he served for many years. He captured 436 wickets in three seasons from 1889 until 1891. In 1890 his haul was 190 wickets (13.11) and against Australia at The Oval he took 12 for 102, yet never represented England against Australia again. He toured South Africa with W.W. Read's team in 1891/2, bowling unchanged with J.J. Ferris in the second innings of the only Test at Cape Town.

First-class career (1885-1900): 4,456 runs (13.54) and 1,317 wickets (17.38)
Test matches (2): 14 runs (7.00), 14 wickets (10.07) and 2 catches

MARTIN, John William (b.1917)

Kent

A right-arm, fast-medium, in-swing bowler and a

hard-hitting, tail-end batsman, Jack Martin was regarded as an England 'hope' at a time of dearth of fast bowlers. He appeared in the first Test at Trent Bridge against South Africa in 1947, taking 1 for 129 and scoring 0 and 26, but he was not selected again.

First-class career (1939-53): 623 runs (11.53) and 162 wickets (24.00)

MASON, John Richard (1874-1958)

Kent

One of the best amateur all-rounders who never played in a Test in England, Jack Mason stood over six foot and was essentially a right-handed, front-foot player, possessing a drive rarely surpassed for cleanness and power, and a most effective cut. A fast-medium bowler with a model action and high arm, he moved the ball away from the batsman; he was also a high-ranking slip fielder. He was a popular Kent captain from 1898 until 1902, and toured Australia with A.E. Stoddart's 1897/8 team.

First-class career (1893-1919): 17,337 runs (33.27) including 34 centuries, 845 wickets (21.85) and 340 catches
Test matches (5): 129 runs (12.90), 2 wickets (74.50) and 3 catches

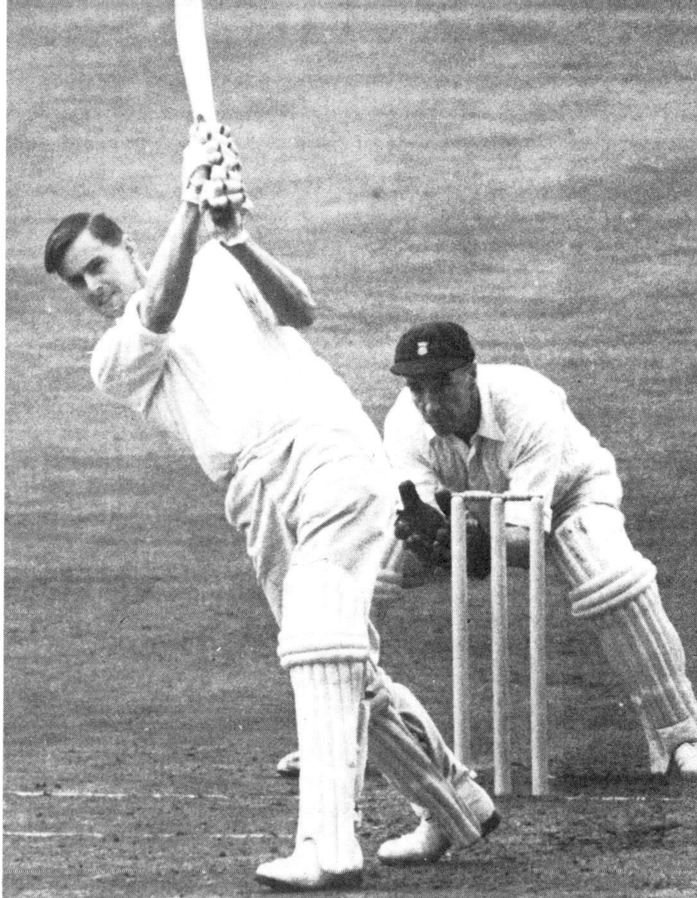

Peter May driving – John Murray is the wicket-keeper

MATTHEWS, Austin David George (1905-77)

Northamptonshire and Glamorgan

Tall and with powerful shoulders, Austin Matthews was a right-arm bowler who could make the ball do a little both ways, a hard-hitter and a fine slip. After taking 14 for 132 on a batsman's wicket at Hastings for Glamorgan against Sussex, he played for England against New Zealand at The Oval in 1937 scoring 2 not out, taking 2 for 65 and holding 1 catch. This was his sole Test appearance.

First-class career (1927-47): 5,919 runs (16.48) including 2 centuries, and 816 wickets (23.40)

MAY, Peter Barker Howard (b.1929)

Cambridge University, Berkshire and Surrey

Perhaps the finest English batsman since the Second World War, Peter May was a prodigy at Charterhouse, where he was coached by George Geary, and was a prolific run-getter at Cambridge for three years amid a galaxy of talent never since equalled. During his National Service he played for the Royal Navy and Combined Services. He made his debut for Surrey in 1950. Six foot tall, with broad and strong shoulders, he was exceptionally straight in defence, and a quite superb driver anywhere between cover and mid-wicket, but especially wide of mid-on and straight back past, or over, the bowler. He was an effortless timer of the ball and his approach to batting, as indeed to all his affairs, was disciplined and fastidious. Gentle, good-mannered and self-effacing in character, he always had a hard, almost ruthless streak as a cricketer – very much an amateur with a professional approach. He captained Surrey from 1957 until 1962, and England against Australia and New Zealand, 1958/9, against the West Indies, 1959/60, and against South Africa, 1956/7. Altogether he led England forty-one times in only six years. A regular England player during the fifties, he toured Australasia and the West Indies twice each and South Africa once with MCC. On his Test debut he made an impressive 138 against South Africa at Headingley in 1951, when England were chasing a large total. He overcame Ray Lindwall eventually in 1953, and was a key figure in England's victory at The Oval which regained the Ashes. Thereafter, he was the chief thorn in Australia's flesh, in twenty-one Tests against them making 1,566 runs (46.05) including 3 centuries, each scored when runs were badly needed. At Edgbaston against the West Indies in 1957, England were 288 behind on the first innings, when May and Cowdrey added 411 superbly for the fourth wicket, May's share being 285 not out, his highest score. In that series he averaged 97.80. Such was the responsibility that always seemed to rest on his shoulders that he seldom allowed himself to 'let loose', although for MCC against An Australian Eleven at Sydney in 1958/9 he made his second hundred of the match between lunch and tea on the third day, with batting which only a few players in history could have equalled. He exceeded 1,000 runs in a season fourteen times (three times overseas), five times exceeding 2,000. Illness forced him to withdraw from the tour of the West Indies in 1959/60 and this, together with the need to give more attention to his insurance business in the City, caused his premature retirement from the first-class game. He married Virginia, daughter of Harold Gilligan, and has four daughters one of whom was European Three-Day-Event Junior Champion in 1979. He has been chairman of the TCCB's Cricket Committee, was President of MCC in 1980/1 and became chairman of England's selectors in 1982.

First-class career (1948-63): 27,592 runs (51.00) including 85 centuries, and 282 catches
Test matches (66): 4,537 runs (46.77) including 13 centuries, and 42 catches

MEAD, Charles Philip (1887-1958)

Hampshire and Suffolk

Phil Mead was the imperturbable and unbowlable backbone of Hampshire's batting for some thirty years. His 48,892 runs for Hampshire is a record number for any county. Left-handed, his defence was strong and his strokes firm and clean. A tall, heavily-built man, he would, wrote Ian Peebles, 'move deliberately into a wide range of strokes, sound, safe and unspectacular . . . Between each ball he would glance round the field, pluck his cap as if in salutation and shuffle his feet into a somewhat crouching stance.' Twenty-seven times he exceeded 1,000 runs in a season, eleven times 2,000 and twice 3,000. His best year was 1921 when he made 3,179 runs (69.10), including his highest score, 280 not out against Nottinghamshire at Southampton. In 1921, when English batsmen were generally failing against Australia, he scored 182 not out at The Oval in the fifth Test. He toured Australia in 1911/12 and again in 1928/9. He visited South Africa twice also, averaging 54 in the Tests of 1913/14 and hitting 181 at Durban in 1922/3. He was hardly a sprightly wit, but one little quip gave him constant pleasure. The county offered £1 in talent money to every scorer of 50 runs and, as Phil reached his inevitable half-century, he would murmur: 'Well, that's another ton of coal for the winter!' Latterly, he became totally blind.

First-class career (1905-36): 55,061 runs (47.67) including 153 centuries, 277 wickets (34.46) and 668 catches
Test matches (17): 1,185 runs (49.37) including 4 centuries, and 4 catches

MEAD, Walter (1869-1954)

Essex

'The Essex Treasure', Walter Mead was a short man with a drooping moustache who bowled right-arm, slow-medium with a deceptively easy action and a remarkable command of length; he could make the ball turn on the best of pitches, generally off-breaking but sometimes sending down a leg-break or a googly to good effect. He was excellent at cover and occasionally a useful tail-end batsman, who made 119 against Leicestershire at Leyton in 1902. Twice he took 17 wickets in a match, against the Australians at Leyton in 1893 for 205 runs, and against Hampshire at Southampton in 1895 for 119 runs. His sole Test was against Australia at Lord's in 1899, when he took 1 for 91 in fifty-three overs (twenty-four of them maidens), scored 7 and 0 and held one catch. His son, Harold, who died of war wounds, played with him for Essex in 1913.

First-class career (1892-1913): 4,948 runs (10.41) including 1 century, and 1,916 wickets (18.99)

MIDWINTER, William Evans (1851-90)

Victoria and Gloucestershire

See Australia section.

MILBURN, Colin (b.1941)

Durham, Northamptonshire and Western Australia

A massively built Geordie, as jolly as he is large, Colin or 'Ollie' Milburn was both a right-handed, scientific hitter, and a character who, in his short career, became a 'box office' draw. Rotund as Billy Bunter he first attracted attention by making a century for Durham against the Indians in 1959, while still in his teens, and, on joining Northamptonshire, became a refreshing attacking opening batsman. Technically sound and straight, he was a fearless hooker, savage square-cutter and drove as immaculately as anyone through the cover region. He was also a useful medium-pace bowler and a reliable, forward short-leg, although his relative lack of mobility in the field certainly restricted his appearances for England. His best year was 1966: he scored 1,861 runs (48.97), including 203 against Essex at Clacton, hit a century before lunch on three occasions, and made his Test debut, against the West Indies at Old Trafford, scoring 0 and 94. In the next Test, at Lord's, he scored 6 and 126 not out. He showed his mettle against India, Pakistan and Australia – in his first Test against the latter, at Lord's in 1968, he hit a ferocious 83 – but he was disappointing in the West Indies in 1967/8. The following winter he played with success for Western Australia, scoring 243 against Queensland at Brisbane, an innings of rare brilliance, and joined MCC in Pakistan, hitting 139 at

Karachi. He opened 1969 with 158 (including five sixes) for his county against Leicestershire at Northampton but, a few days later, he was involved in a car accident and lost his left eye. Reacting with incredible good humour to this shattering misfortune, he fought back and reappeared for Northamptonshire in 1973, but his batting was severely handicapped and his bowling not quite good enough to justify a regular place. He retired after the 1974 season and his benefit realised £20,000. He was greatly missed. In 1979 he became coach to Oxford University.

First-class career (1960-74): 13,262 runs (33.07) including 23 centuries, 99 wickets (32.03) and 226 catches
Test matches (9): 654 runs (46.71) including 2 centuries, and 7 catches

MILLER, Audley Montague (1869-1959)

Wiltshire and MCC

An all-rounder, Audley Miller captained Wiltshire for twenty-five years and served also as honorary secretary. He played many times for MCC (mainly in minor matches) and toured South Africa in 1895/6 with Lord Hawke's team, in his sole Test at Port Elizabeth scoring 4 not out and 20 not out at number ten, and not bowling.

First-class career (1896-1903): 104 runs (13.00) and 1-18

MILLER, Geoffrey (b.1952)

Derbyshire

Geoff Miller, known as Dusty, had a long apprenticeship at Test level which he thoroughly justified by emerging as a key all-rounder during England's five to one win in Australia in 1978/9. Tallish, slim and dark with a droopy moustache, he toured both India and the West Indies with the England Young Cricketers, first playing for Derbyshire in 1973. A tidy off-spinner, reliable fielder and a right-hand batsman with a natural gift of timing and a greater willingness than most English contemporaries to play strokes off the back foot, he made only a modest start in county cricket. But the arrival of the ebullient and dynamic Eddie Barlow as Derbyshire captain proved the catalyst he needed. He played promisingly in his first Test for England in 1976, but on two official tours in the next two winters he was often starved of opportunity as a bowler, though he seldom let anyone down with bat or ball. Against Australia in 1977 he was still not an established member of a strong team, but from the start of the 1978/9 series he bowled with greater confidence and even tighter control than before. He used the Australian breezes skilfully to flight the ball and took more wickets than any bowler on the tour, including 23 in the Test series. A frugal eater and assiduous trainer, he is also a thoughtful and witty character. He took over the captaincy of Derbyshire in 1979. His form suffered and he was relatively unsuccessful on tours of Australia in 1979/80 (he returned early with an injury) and the West Indies in 1980/81. He relinquished the Derbyshire captaincy during the 1981 season, but in 1982 a return to form earned him a place in the England side at Old Trafford against India. He scored 98, the second time he had missed a Test hundred by two runs. The first occasion had been at Lahore in the first Test of 1977/8 when he was left 98 not out as the last wicket fell, having batted for six hours with a heavy cold. In 1982 it was chickenpox which kept him out of the team for one Test and he was twelfth man in two others, suffering from not being quite good enough as either batsman or bowler to earn a place on merit, yet always liable to be useful at both. He was chosen for his third tour of Australia in 1982/3.

Geoff Miller

First-class career (1973-): 7,332 runs (26.85), 542 wickets (24.90) and 154 catches
Test matches (27): 978 runs (28.76), 46 wickets (28.69) and 12 catches

MILLIGAN, Frank William (1870-1900)

Yorkshire

Frank Milligan was very much the ideal of the nineteenth-century amateur cricketer. He bowled fast, batted aggressively, if somewhat impatiently, and fielded superbly. But he was also a national symbol, for he was killed in action whilst serving as a lieutenant under Colonel Plumer in a bid to relieve Mafeking in the Boer War. He toured South Africa with Lord Hawke's team in 1898/9, playing in two Tests.

First-class career (1895-9): 2,151 runs (19.03) and 136 wickets (23.12)
Test matches (2): 58 runs (14.50), 0-29 and 1 catch

MILLMAN, Geoffrey (b.1934)

Bedfordshire and Nottinghamshire

Joining Nottinghamshire after playing for Bedfordshire and Combined Services, Geoff Millman was a most accomplished wicket-keeper and a useful, stubborn batsman, who often opened. He captained Notts from 1963 until 1965, when he left cricket to concentrate on his business career. He toured India and Pakistan in 1961/2 and also appeared in Tests, against Pakistan in England in 1962. However, John Murray and Jim Parks both had the edge on him.

First-class career (1956-65): 7,770 runs (18.85) including 3 centuries, and 652 dismissals (556 ct, 96 st.)
Test matches (6): 60 runs (12.00) and 15 dismissals (13 ct, 2 st.)

MILTON, Clement Arthur (b.1928)

Gloucestershire

Small and fair-haired, Arthur Milton was a neat and accomplished right-hand opening batsman, a steady and skilful accumulator of runs. Watching each ball with the greatest care, he always appeared to have plenty of time to play his strokes, preferring the back foot. An occasional medium-pace bowler, he was also a brilliant short-leg, extremely agile, with a very safe pair of hands. He exceeded 1,000 runs in a season sixteen times, and twice made 2 centuries in a match. In his first Test, against New Zealand at Headingley in 1958, he made 104 not out, a real scrambler's innings, full of luck but also of character. He toured Australia with MCC in 1958/9 but suffered a finger injury after playing in two Tests, although he reappeared against India the following year. Also a soccer international, he played with success for Arsenal. He captained Gloucestershire in 1968, but the extra responsibility did not suit him.

First-class career (1948-74): 32,150 runs (33.73) including 56 centuries, 79 wickets (45.94) and 759 catches
Test matches (6): 204 runs (25.50) including 1 century, 0-12 and 5 catches

MITCHELL, Arthur (1902-76)

Yorkshire

Arthur or 'Ticker' Mitchell – so named because of his habit of 'ticking-on' (nattering) while play was in progress – often carried 'caution to excess' (as *Wisden* put it), although he could drive as well and as hard as anyone. His right-handed batting was generally grave and determined. In the slips he became a legend. On ten occasions he exceeded 1,000 runs in a season, including 1933, when he made 2,300 runs (58.97), 508 of them coming in a purple patch between 30 August and 7 September. He toured India with MCC in 1933/4 and appeared in the first Test series in that country without distinction, but as a late replacement in the Test against South Africa at Headingley in 1935 – he was literally called from his garden to take part – he made 58 and 72. On retirement he became county coach, guarding the traditional values with an endearing severity.

First-class career (1922-47): 19,523 runs (37.47) including 44 centuries, and 462 catches
Test matches (6): 298 runs (29.80), 0-4 and 9 catches

MITCHELL, Frank (1872-1935)

Cambridge University, Yorkshire and Transvaal

A triple blue at Cambridge, Frank Mitchell played cricket for both England and South Africa and Rugby football for England. While captain of Cambridge in 1896 he helped to make history by instructing E.B. Shine to give away extras so that Oxford should not follow on. Despite the uproar it caused, his action helped the law to be changed so that the enforcement of the follow-on became voluntary. A heavy scorer in a strong Yorkshire side, Mitchell toured South Africa with Lord Hawke's team in 1898/9, served there in the army during the Boer War, returned to Yorkshire, then went back to South Africa, captaining the teams to England in 1904 and 1912. He also played for MCC, earned distinction in the First World War and was a prolific journalist on war, cricket and rugby.

First-class career (1894-1914): 8,668 runs (31.31) including 16 centuries, and 35 wickets (23.17)
Test matches (England – 2): 88 runs (22.00) and 2 catches. (South Africa – 3): 28 runs (4.66)

MITCHELL, Thomas Bignell (b.1902)

Derbyshire

A bespectacled former coal-miner, Tommy Mitchell was a resourceful right-arm leg-break and googly bowler who spun the ball as much as any bowler and could make it turn on any wicket. He flighted the ball well and could bowl the off-spinner for variety. His quirks and quips could make a batsman lose his balance with laughter. He took more than 100 wickets in ten of his twelve seasons of first-class cricket, including 116 in Derbyshire's first Championship year, 1936. He toured Australia and New Zealand in 1932/3, playing against Australia and New Zealand once each; he also appeared against Australia and South Africa in England.

First-class career (1928-39): 2,431 runs (7.97), 1,483 wickets (20.59) and 132 catches
Test matches (5): 20 runs (5.00), 8 wickets (62.25) and 1 catch

MITCHELL-INNES, Norman Stewart (b.1914)

Oxford University, Somerset and Scotland

Norman Mitchell-Innes was a stylish and confident, right-handed batsman and a medium-pace change-bowler. His first-class cricket was limited by severe hay-fever and by his career in the Sudan Civil Service. He captained Oxford and Somerset occasionally. In his sole Test innings against South Africa at Trent Bridge in 1935 he scored 5, and he toured Australasia with the MCC 'goodwill' side of 1935/6.

First-class career (1931-49): 6,944 runs (31.42) including 13 centuries, and 82 wickets (34.70)

MOLD, Arthur Webb (1863-1921)

Northamptonshire and Lancashire

A great humorist and betting man, Arthur Mold was one of the deadliest right-arm fast bowlers of his day, but, even while he was with his native Northamptonshire, his action was suspect. Qualifying for Lancashire, he spearheaded the attack so well that he took 13 or more wickets in a match fourteen times, taking 4 wickets in four balls at Trent Bridge in 1895. He was selected for the three Tests against Australia in 1893. In 1900, however, when the county were playing Nottinghamshire at Trent Bridge, umpire Jim Phillips no-balled him for throwing, and he sent down only one over in the match. Later, the county captains condemned his delivery by eleven votes to one, and his first-class career was over.

First-class career (1889-1901): 1,814 runs (6.81) and 1,673 wickets (15.54)
Test matches (3): 0 runs (—), 7 wickets (33.42) and 1 catch

MOON, Leonard James (1878-1916)

Cambridge University and Middlesex

One of the many amateurs of quality who flourished in Edwardian days, Leonard Moon was a vigorous right-handed batsman, whose speciality was the cut, and a useful wicket-keeper. A prolific run-getter at Westminster and Cambridge – where he hit 138 against the 1899 Australians – he was equally at home with Middlesex, sharing in two opening stands in excess of 200 with Sir Pelham Warner. He toured America in 1905 and South Africa in 1905/6; on the latter tour he made 826 runs and had his Test experience. He died of wounds in France in 1916.

First-class career (1897-1913): 4,223 runs (26.72) and 88 dismissals (70 ct, 18 st.)
Test matches (4): 182 runs (22.75) and 4 catches

MORLEY, Frederick (1850-84)

Nottinghamshire

A left-arm fastish bowler, Fred Morley was the first Nottinghamshire player to take 100 wickets in a season, when in 1878 he captured 126 at 9.92. In America in 1879 he took 100 wickets for 354 runs! His success lay in his length and direction. 'If Morley bowled like a machine,' said his captain, Richard Daft, 'he certainly resembled a machine that was well oiled and in perfect working order.' He played in the first Test in England at The Oval in 1880, opening the attack and taking 8 for 146, the best analysis of the match. In 1882/3 he was a member of Hon. Ivo Bligh's team to Australia but he was knocked out and badly hurt in a collision at sea on the way out. A simple soul, he struggled on throughout the tour but it turned out that he had fractured a rib. On his return home his health deteriorated and he died of 'congestion and dropsy'.

First-class career (1872-83): 1,396 runs (5.76) and 1,270 wickets (13.45)
Test matches (4): 6 runs (1.50), 16 wickets (18.50) and 4 catches

MORTIMORE, John Brian (b.1933)

Gloucestershire

A tall, slim all-rounder, John Mortimore was a right-arm off-break bowler, who spun the ball enough to be dangerous on helpful pitches and kept batsmen quiet at other times by dint of considerable accuracy and a good away-drifter. He was a contemporary of another Gloucestershire and England off-spinner, David Allen, with whom he made a formidable partnership. Mortimore was also a solid middle-order batsman, who loved to drive, and a very reliable field. His usefulness on hard wickets was proved in Australia in 1958/9, when he went as a reinforcement for a side hard pressed by injuries. Mortimore took four wickets in five balls against Lancashire at Cheltenham in 1962 and was always coming up with useful performances, achieving the double three times between 1959 and 1964. He led his county from 1965 to 1967, doing the job well in his studious, undemonstrative way.

First-class career (1950-75): 15,891 runs (18.32) including 4 centuries, 1,807 wickets (23.18) and 346 catches
Test matches (9): 243 runs (24.30), 13 wickets (56.38) and 3 catches

MOSS, Alan Edward (b.1930)

Middlesex

Alan Moss, or 'Amos', was the spearhead of the Middlesex attack in the fifties and early sixties. Tall and strong, he was a very competent right-arm, fast bowler, who could always be relied on to do a steady job and was very quick indeed for a few overs, once hitting the sight screen first bounce with a bumper at Sabina Park. He was a great trier, working hard and learning how to move the ball about and increase his accuracy. He toured the West Indies twice and Pakistan once with MCC and, at home, played against Australia, South Africa and India.

Alan Moss

First-class career (1950-68): 1,671 runs (6.99) and 1,301 wickets (20.78)
Test matches (9): 61 runs (10.16), 21 wickets (29.80) and 1 catch

MURDOCH, William Lloyd (1855-1911)

New South Wales and Sussex

See Australia Section.

MURRAY, John Thomas (b.1935)

Middlesex

John Murray, or 'J.T.', was a stylist – indeed a perfectionist – both as a right-handed batsman and wicket-keeper. Immaculately turned-out always, he went through a careful ritual of touching his gloves together and describing a graceful curve with his hands before settling onto his haunches. His very passing of the ball to the slips when he had taken it was a graceful and studied performance and he was a 'keeper of exceptional agility, bringing off some spectacular diving catches. He scored 1,025 runs and took 104 dismissals in 1957, only one other (Leslie Ames) having ever achieved this double in a season. Unfortunate injuries, both in India in 1961/2 and Australia in 1962/3, deprived him of a regular England place after he had done well against Australia in 1961, as virtual heir-apparent to Godfrey Evans. At his best he was a batsman of very high class, a lovely driver both to off and on, and a brave hooker. He made a timely and memorable hundred for England against the West Indies at The Oval in 1966. In 1975, his final season, he established the world record for the most dismissals in a career, broken by R.W. Taylor in 1982/3.

First-class career (1952-75): 18,872 runs (23.50) including 16 centuries, and 1,527 dismissals (1,270 ct, 257 st.)
Test matches (21): 506 runs (22.00) including 1 century, and 55 dismissals (52 ct, 3 st.)

NEWHAM, William (1860-1944)

Sussex

Of medium height and well built, Billy Newham drove hard on either side of the wicket, cut brilliantly, and was specially adept, when playing back, at forcing strokes past mid-on or turning the ball to leg. At Leyton in 1902 he and Ranji added 344 against Essex, which remains the record seventh-wicket stand in England. As amateur player, captain, secretary or assistant-secretary, his connection with his county lasted sixty-three years. Touring Australia with

John Murray

Shaw's and Shrewsbury's team in 1887/8, he appeared in his sole Test, at Sydney, scoring 9 and 17.

First-class career (1881-1905): 14,657 runs (24.42) including 19 centuries, and 10 wickets (57.70)

NICHOLS, Morris Stanley (1900-1961)

Essex

Morris Nichols was a fast right-arm bowler who never knew when he was beaten. He kept the ball up, either moving it away or bringing it back, and sometimes pitched in a yorker. He was a left-handed batsman, not elegant but businesslike and a shrewd hitter. His walk back for his run-up had something of the rollicking gait of a sailor. He always looked relaxed and proved it was no illusion by prospering in many a crisis. Eight times, between 1929 and 1939, he achieved the double. In 1935 at Huddersfield he took 11 for 54 and scored 146, the county champions, Yorkshire, losing by a large innings margin. He toured New Zealand, 1929/30, and India, 1933/4, playing in the first Test series in those countries. He appeared only once against Australia in 1930, and twice against the West Indies. But he played four times against South Africa in 1935 and at Trent Bridge in the first Test, took 6 wickets for only 35 runs.

First-class career (1924-39): 17,827 runs (26.56) including 20 centuries, 1,833 wickets (21.63) and 332 catches
Test matches (14): 355 runs (29.58), 41 wickets (28.09) and 11 catches

OAKMAN, Alan Stanley Myles (b.1930)

Sussex

Exceptionally tall and gangling, Alan Oakman was a right-handed batsman, at his best on hard wickets against medium and fast-medium bowling when, using his immense reach, he would unleash a stream of drives. His coolness in a crisis often served Sussex well. A useful off-break bowler, he took 99 wickets in 1954 (his best season) and, superb as a close field, held 57 catches in 1958. He appeared in two Tests against Australia in 1956, when his catching in Laker's leg-trap was outstanding, and he toured South Africa in 1956/7, where he was hampered by back trouble. He became a respected coach at Warwickshire.

First-class career (1947-68): 21,800 runs (26.17) including 22 centuries, 736 wickets (27.63) and 594 catches
Test matches (2): 14 runs (7.00), 0-21 and 7 catches

O'BRIEN, Sir Timothy Carew, Bart. (1861-1948)

Oxford University, Middlesex and Ireland

A fiery Irishman, Tim O'Brien went up to Oxford only to obtain a blue for cricket but he was dismissed for a pair in his first University match. He was a dashing right-handed batsman, who loved the pull, at his best on 'sticky' wickets. His great resource and splendid physique made him at times a terror to the best of bowlers. Hitting 92 in Oxford's win against the Australians in 1884, he played in two Tests that year. Amid a galaxy of Middlesex amateur talent, his most notable performance was against Yorkshire at Lord's in 1889, when he hit 92 and 100 not out, his last 83 runs coming in thirty-five minutes, allowing Middlesex to win very unexpectedly. He toured Australia with G.F. Vernon's team in 1887/8 and South Africa with Lord Hawke's in 1895/6.

First-class career (1881-1914): 11,397 runs (27.01) including 15 centuries, 172 catches and 2 stumpings
Test matches (5): 59 runs (7.37) and 4 catches

O'CONNOR, Jack (1897-1977)

Essex and Buckinghamshire

A small man from a notable cricketing family, Jack O'Connor was a right-handed batsman, quick on his feet, a good driver on both sides of the wicket and a fine hooker. He exceeded 1,000 runs in sixteen seasons, reaching 2,000 runs four times between 1928 and 1934. He bowled a mixture of off- and leg-breaks which looked simpler than they were. A mainstay of Essex during the inter-War years, he toured the West Indies in 1929/30 and, in England, appeared once against South Africa in 1929.

First-class career (1921-39): 28,778 runs (34.92) including 72 centuries and 557 wickets (32.91), 210 catches and 1 stumping
Test matches (4): 153 runs (21.85), 1-72 and 2 catches

OLD, Christopher Middleton (b.1948)

Yorkshire and Northern Transvaal

Tall, strongly built and the brother of an international Rugby Union player, Chris Old is immensely gifted in all three departments of cricket. But although in, or on the fringe of, the England side between 1972 and 1981, he achieved less than he might have done because of persistent injuries. He had operations on both knees in 1970 and 1971 and frequently suffers from strains in the shoulders or side. Often injuries have come just before a Test match, suggesting that they might be psychosomatic, yet once involved in an important match he has often shown exceptional determination and has seldom failed to justify his selection. A modest, charming, friendly and amusing companion and prolific imbiber of ale, he talks eloquently about his own ills but never has a bad word to say about anyone else. A left-handed batsman, he is effective against all but top-class fast bowling and he drives gloriously: in 1977 he made the second fastest first-class century ever, in 37 minutes against an indifferent Warwickshire attack (his second 50 came in nine minutes). He is also a brilliant fielder, athletic in the deep and superb in the slips, but his main value to Yorkshire and England has been as a right-arm, fast-medium bowler. Approaching the wicket with heavy tread but lissom rhythm, he delivers with a classical sideways-on action, moving the out-swinger late and often bringing the ball back in wickedly off the pitch. Genuinely fast in his early years, he has recently slowed his pace to fast-medium and can now bowl long and accurate spells, as in 1978 against Pakistan at Edgbaston when his 7 for 50 included four wickets in five balls. If he lacks anything (apart from that elusive fitness) it is the mean or malicious streak which turns some fast bowlers into devils. In 1981 he became captain of Yorkshire in difficult circumstances and played a valuable all-round role in two exciting Test victories over Australia at Headingley and Edgbaston. But a year later his career went into a sudden decline. Having spent the 1981/2 winter playing for Northern Transvaal, he joined the so-called 'rebel' tour of South Africa and, along with the other English players concerned, was banned from Test cricket for three years. He did little for Yorkshire the following season, was deposed from the captaincy and replaced by Ray Illingworth and then harshly discarded by his county at the end of the season. He moved to Warwickshire. He visited all the main cricket countries, making seven major MCC or England tours.

Chris Old

First-class career (1966-): 6,828 runs (21.00) including 6 centuries, 941 wickets (22.57) and 196 catches
Test matches (46): 845 runs (14.82) 143 wickets (28.11) and 22 catches

OLDFIELD, Norman (b.1911)

Lancashire and Northamptonshire

Had he not lost his best years to the Second World War, 'Buddy' Oldfield would no doubt have appeared in more Test cricket. In his sole Test, against the West Indies at The Oval in 1939, he scored 80 and 19, rippling the ground with lovely strokes. Short but stylish, a right-handed batsman rich in natural gifts, he was a versatile stroke-maker all round the wicket. Specially registered for Northamptonshire in 1948, he toured India with the Commonwealth team of 1949/50, making a century in three successive matches against India.

First-class career (1935-54): 17,811 runs (37.89) including 38 centuries

PADGETT, Douglas Ernest Vernon (b.1934)

Yorkshire

A Yorkshire stalwart, Doug Padgett played for England twice against South Africa in 1960. At sixteen the youngest man ever to play for Yorkshire, he became a very successful county batsman at a time of transition. He was a dapper, neat right-hander with an exemplary technique which he passes on to the present generation as the Yorkshire coach. He exceeded 1,000 runs in a season twelve times and toured New Zealand in 1960/61.

First-class career (1951-71): 21,124 runs (28.58) including 32 centuries, and 261 catches
Test matches (2): 51 runs (12.75) and 0-8

PAINE, George Alfred Edward (1908-78)

Middlesex and Warwickshire

A slow left-arm bowler, George Paine thought much about his craft and, when he was practising, he would place white tape round the ball so that he could see how much he was spinning it. His Test match experience was for England in the West Indies in 1934/5 but, despite his success he never represented his country at home.

First-class career (1926-47): 3,430 runs (11.95), 1,021 wickets (22.85) and 155 catches
Test matches (4): 97 runs (16.16), 17 wickets (27.47) and 5 catches

PALAIRET, Lionel Charles Hamilton (1870-1933)

Oxford University and Somerset

A tall and graceful right-handed opening batsman, Lionel Palairet combined strong defence with elegant cutting and driving. After four years in the Oxford eleven, two as captain, he joined Somerset as an undergraduate, and his drives into the river and churchyard at Taunton are still remembered. In 1892 he shared a then record opening partnership of 346 with H.T. Hewett against Yorkshire at Taunton. His highest score was 292 against Hampshire at Southampton in 1896 and seven times he exceeded 1,000 runs in a season, but his sole Test appearances were against Australia at Old Trafford and The Oval in 1902, when England lost by 3 runs and won by one wicket respectively. A useful change-bowler and deputy wicket-keeper, 'Stork' captained Somerset in 1907.

First-class career (1890-1909): 15,777 runs (33.63) including 27 centuries, 136 wickets (33.91) and 260 dismissals (236 ct, 24 st.)
Test matches (2): 49 runs (12.25) and 2 catches

PALMER, Charles Henry (b.1919)

Worcestershire and Leicestershire

Diminutive and bespectacled but a cricketer of character, Charles Palmer was an attractive right-handed batsman, his cutting and driving on the off-side being particularly effective. His size was deceptive, for he had very strong wrists and could hit very hard. As captain of Leicestershire from 1950 until 1957, he underrated himself as a bowler, delivering useful medium-pacers of immaculate length and – occasionally – 'donkey drops'. Against Surrey, the Champion county, at the Oval in 1955 he wreaked havoc, taking 8 for 7. In making two centuries for Gentlemen against Players he joined a select band. He toured South Africa in 1948/9 and the West Indies in 1953/4 as player/manager. In his sole Test, against the West Indies at Barbados, he scored 22 and 0, and took 0 for 15. He has served both as secretary and chairman of Leicestershire and was president of MCC in 1978/9.

First-class career (1939-59): 17,458 runs (31.74) including 33 centuries, 365 wickets (25.15) and 146 catches

PALMER, Kenneth Ernest (b.1937)

Somerset

Ruddy faced and very much a 'Zomerset' man with a rich West Country burr, Ken Palmer was a hard-working, right-arm, fast-medium bowler and a useful batsman. He was coaching at Johannesburg when he was brought to Port Elizabeth and used as the new ball spearhead in the fifth Test against South Africa in 1964/5 after England's team had been weakened by injuries. He scored 10 and took 1 for 189. The previous winter he had toured Pakistan with a Commonwealth side. He achieved the double in 1961 with 1,036 runs and 114 wickets. Against Notts at Trent Bridge in 1963 he took 9 for 57 in an innings. He has become a first-class and Test umpire of high repute. His brother, Roy, and son, Gary, both played for Somerset.

First-class career (1955-69): 7,771 runs (20.66) including 2 centuries, 866 wickets (21.34) and 157 catches

PARFITT, Peter Howard (b.1936)

Norfolk and Middlesex

Following the Edrich path from Norfolk to Middlesex, Peter Parfitt was a left-handed batsman of high class, a useful off-spinner and a superb close fielder. A chirpy character, he broke through with 2,007 runs in 1961, including 8 centuries. In form like this he was a handsome and complete player with a very straight bat which seemed unusually broad. He represented England periodically between 1962 and 1972, visited Australia, New Zealand and India twice and South

Africa and Pakistan once. He scored 3 centuries in successive innings against Pakistan in 1962, as part of a sequence of 7 consecutive fifties. He scored two centuries in a match twice, including 122 and 144 against Pakistan at Lord's in 1962, and fifteen times exceeded 1,000 runs in a season, including the tour of India and Pakistan in 1961/2. From 1968 until 1970 he captained Middlesex. He now runs a pub on the Yorkshire moors and is an eager and amusing raconteur.

First-class career (1956-74): 26,924 runs (36.33) including 58 centuries, 277 wickets (30.32) and 565 catches
Test matches (37): 1,882 runs (40.91) including 7 centuries, 12 wickets (47.83) and 42 catches

PARKER, Charles Warrington Leonard (1882-1959)

Gloucestershire

Charlie Parker, or 'Parlie Charker', became with A.E. Dipper one of the 'grand old men' of his county's cricket. He was a left-arm slow bowler with an immaculate length and enough spin to catch the edge of the bat, so that 'c. Hammond b. Parker' became a frequent entry in the score-book. He performed some extraordinary feats: 10 for 79 in an innings against Somerset at Bristol in 1921; 17 for 56 against Essex at Gloucester in 1925; 9 wickets in an innings on eight occasions; 5 wickets in successive balls (one a no-ball) against Yorkshire at Bristol during his benefit match in 1922, and many more. There was always guile and accuracy in his bowling, and no-one loved a sticky wicket more. He was underrated by England selectors, playing only one Test, against Australia at Old Trafford in 1921, when he made 3 not out and took 2 for 32 in twenty-eight accurate overs. Having taken over 100 wickets for the sixteenth year in succession he became coach at Cranleigh School. Only two bowlers in history have taken more first-class wickets.

First-class career (1903-35): 7,951 runs (10.48), 3,278 wickets (19.47) and 248 catches

PARKER, Paul William Giles (b.1956)

Cambridge, Sussex and Natal

An outstandingly brilliant fieldsman and attractive right-handed middle-order batsman, Paul Parker comes from a large and talented family based near Horsham. His father was a journalist in Rhodesia when Paul was born in Bulawayo. His career had a spectacular start with two big innings as a freshman at Cambridge against Yorkshire, and Essex, whom he hit for 215 at Fenner's. He made his debut for Sussex the same year and has been a regular member of the side since coming down from Cambridge for whom he also played Rugby, missing a blue only because of injury. Inconsistency and an apparent frailty against fast bowling early in an innings held him back, but overseas experience first in South Australia then in South Africa matured him enough to make him a candidate for England throughout 1981, when he scored 1,416 runs (45.67) and hit four championship hundreds. Eventually picked for the final Test of the summer against Australia, his only Test to date, he was out for 0 and 13 and was not selected for the subsequent tour of India. He bowls only rarely, right-arm, medium-pace. His form declined seriously in 1982, although as vice-captain, he had much to do with Sussex's success in the John Player League.

First-class career (1976-): 8,047 runs (34.38) including 18 centuries, 8 wickets (58.87) and 104 catches

PARKHOUSE, William Gilbert Anthony (b.1925)

Glamorgan

Gilbert Parkhouse was a sound right-handed opening batsman. He was also a brilliant slip field. For England he hit 69 against the West Indies at Trent Bridge in 1950 and – recalled to the Test arena after nine years – a memorable 78 against India at Headingley in 1959, putting on 146 with Geoff Pullar for the first wicket. But his failure in Australia in 1950/51 hung like a cloud over his career. For Glamorgan he shared many a long opening stand with Bernard Hedges. He exceeded 1,000 runs in a season fifteen times.

First-class career (1948-64): 23,508 runs (31.68) including 32 centuries, and 323 catches
Test matches (7): 373 runs (28.69) and 3 catches

PARKIN, Cecil Harry (1886-1943)

Durham, Yorkshire and Lancashire

Although born in County Durham, 'Ciss' Parkin played once for Yorkshire before joining Lancashire, and also devoted much time to Staffordshire and other league cricket. Of medium height and rather slim, he was a splendid natural bowler. A clown and an eccentric, he relied mainly on the off-break, cleverly varying pace and spin. He toured Australia in 1920/21 with MCC and, although England were outplayed, Parkin took most wickets – 16 (41.87) – in the series. He headed the bowling against the almost equally devastating Australians in 1921, with 16 wickets (26.25) from four Tests. But, after criticizing his captain, Arthur Gilligan, in the Test against South Africa at Edgbaston in 1924 (in a national newspaper), he was dropped from the England side and, two years later, returned full-time to league cricket. Cricket's chief comedian at that time, he could talk almost as well as he bowled, and was forever playing to the gallery, conjuring the ball out of his pocket or flicking it from his toe to his head.

First-class career (1906-26): 2,456 runs (11.47) and 1,048 wickets (17.58)
Test matches (10): 160 runs (12.30), 32 wickets (35.25) and 3 catches

PARKS, James Horace (1903-80)

Sussex and Auckland

Short and stocky, James Parks was a solid and fearless right-handed opening batsman, a medium-pace in-swing bowler and a brilliant fielder. Although generally a workaday all-rounder, he made 3,003 runs (50.89) in 1937, including 11 centuries, and took 101 wickets (25.83), besides holding 21 catches – a performance which will never be repeated. His sole Test was against New Zealand at Lord's in 1937, when he scored 22 and 7 and took 3 for 36 (all lbw). He toured Australasia in 1935/6. In 1937 he added 297 for the fifth wicket with his brother, Harry, against Hampshire at Portsmouth, a long-standing Sussex record. His son, Jim, played for Sussex and England and his grandson, Bobby, for Hampshire.

First-class career (1924-52): 21,369 runs (30.74) including 41 centuries, 852 wickets (26.74) and 291 catches

PARKS, James Michael (b.1931)

Sussex and Somerset

A sunny character, Jim Parks was a brilliant right-handed stroke-maker, especially quick on his feet to slow bowlers, who scored more than 2,300 runs in 1955 and 1959. He put the wicket-keeper's gloves on for the first time to help out when the regular Sussex 'keeper was injured and proved so safe and efficient standing back that he took over the post the following year, 1959. He played for England as batsman against Pakistan in 1954, and ten years later was picked as first choice wicket-keeper. He dismissed 93 batsmen in both 1959 and 1961. A replacement for MCC in the West Indies, 1959/60, he came into the Test side at the eleventh hour and hit a match-saving 101 not out. When John Murray was injured in 1963, he established himself as England's 'keeper, taking some brilliant catches standing back, doing an adequate job to the spinners and making many useful runs. Between 1963 and 1967 he toured Australia, New Zealand, India, South Africa and the West Indies. On twenty occasions he exceeded 1,000 runs in a season and he was a prolific scorer in limited-over matches. In 1967 and 1968 he captained Sussex and later he played a few games for Somerset.

First-class career (1949-76): 36,673 runs (34.76) including 51 centuries, 51 wickets (43.82) and 1,182 dismissals (1,089 ct, 93 st.)
Test matches (46): 1,962 runs (32.16) including 2 centuries, and 114 dismissals (103 ct, 11 st.)

PATAUDI, NAWAB OF (Iftiqar Ali Khan) (1910-52)

Oxford University, Worcestershire and Southern Punjab

Coached by Frank Woolley when he came to England

Peter Parfitt and Jim Parks (behind the stumps)

The Nawab of Pataudi (senior)

at the age of sixteen, Pataudi's fluent right-handed stroke-play was based on a patient and correct technique. Naturally gifted, he loved a challenge. He scored 238 not out for Oxford against Cambridge at Lord's in 1931, the record innings in the contests, a typical response to Alan Ratcliffe's double hundred for Cambridge in the same game. In his first Test, against Australia at Sydney in 1932/3, he made 102. In a short career for Worcestershire he scored heavily, making 224 not out, 231 not out and 222 against Kent, Essex and Somerset respectively in 1933, and having an average of 91 in 1934. He represented England against Australia at Trent Bridge in 1934. Thereafter, he was handicapped by ill-health. Returning to India, he appeared in only one Ranji Trophy match, but captained the Indian team to England in 1946, when he reached 981 runs (46.71), including 4 centuries, on the tour, but achieved little in the Tests. He died of a heart attack while playing polo. His son also captained India.

First-class career (1928-46): 8,750 runs (48.61) including 29 centuries, and 15 wickets (35.26)
Test matches (England – 3): 144 runs (28.80) including 1 century. (India – 3): 55 runs (11.00)

PAYNTER, Edward (1901-79)

Lancashire

A perky left-handed batsman with an unquenchable Lancastrian spirit, Eddie Paynter had a perfect temperament. Amazingly enough, for a batsman with a Test average of 59, he only played his first game for his county at twenty-five and did not gain a regular place until he was thirty. Small and wiry, he invested his strokes with remarkable power and drove, cut and pulled with delightful facility. Against Australia in seven Tests he averaged 84.42, his highest score being 216 not out at Trent Bridge in 1938, when he was a natural counter to the prevailing Australian leg-spin. In that series he averaged 101.75. In South Africa in 1938/9, he made 243 at Durban and 653 runs (81.62) in the series. Paynter's most legendary performance, however, was during his only tour of Australia in 1932/3, when he rose from a sick-bed at Brisbane, played a heroic first innings of 83, and in the second hit the winning six just before rain began falling heavily. Between 1932 and 1938 he exceeded 2,000 runs in a season four times; his career highest was 322 (in five hours) against Sussex at Hove in 1937. Although he had lost the tops of the first and second fingers of his right hand in an accident, he was a good cover-point and deep field.

Eddie Paynter – Ben Barnett (Australia) keeping wicket

First-class career (1926-50): 20,075 runs (42.35) including 45 centuries, and 30 wickets (45.70)
Test matches (20): 1,540 runs (59.23) including 4 centuries, and 7 catches

PEATE, Edmund (1856-1900)

Yorkshire

Although Ted Peate began with a troupe of Treloar's 'Clown Cricketers', he graduated in Yorkshire circles as the first of that county's line of famous left-arm slow bowlers. His bowling was extremely accurate and marked by just enough break to beat the bat. He toured Australia in 1881/2; and in the classic Oval Test of 1882 he opened the bowling and had a match record of 8 for 71. Until 1886 he was a first choice for Tests in England. Six times he took more than 100 wickets in a season. His career was brilliant but short. According to *Wisden*, 'he would have lasted longer if he had ordered his life more carefully.'

First-class career (1879-90): 2,327 runs (10.92) and 1,076 wickets (13.48)
Test matches (9): 70 runs (11.66), 31 wickets (22.00) and 2 catches

PEEBLES, Ian Alexander Ross (1908-80)

Oxford University, Middlesex and Scotland

Ian Peebles was a tall and talented leg-spinner from Scotland, and became one of the most brilliant and humorous of all cricket writers. He toured South Africa in 1927/8 – and played in Tests – before appearing for Middlesex and Oxford. He learned his trade as secretary of the Aubrey Faulkner School of

Cricket. There he developed a bowling action which was a model of its kind, flowing and easy. He was educated at Glasgow Academy and joined Middlesex in 1928, taking his first 100 wickets the following year. In the University match at Lord's in 1930 he captured 13 Cambridge wickets. Always a severe test for batsmen with his deceptive googly and looping flight, he dismissed Don Bradman for 14 at Old Trafford in 1930, after the great man had been floundering against him, and at The Oval took 6 for 204 in seventy-one overs. He revisited South Africa with MCC in 1930/31 and emerged with honour. Subsequently, he toured India, America, Ceylon, Malaya, and Egypt (usually with Sir Julien Cahn's team), enjoying a vast amount of cricket. He captained Middlesex successfully in 1939, but played less regularly after the war. Cricket correspondent of *The Sunday Times* for many years, his writing was always witty, shrewd and polished whether it appeared in newspapers or in the many books he wrote.

First-class career (1927-48): 2,213 runs (9.66) and 923 wickets (21.38)
Test matches (13): 98 runs (10.88), 45 wickets (30.91) and 5 catches

PEEL, Robert (1857-1941)

Yorkshire

Small and sturdy, Bobby Peel (no relation of the Prime Minister) was second in line to the great Yorkshire left-arm spin bowlers. To him length was the key; and he kept it no matter how severely he was attacked. Moreover, he was a punishing left-handed batsman, and an excellent cover-point. He visited Australia four times between 1884 and 1895 and never had a poor tour. In 1894/5 he took 27 wickets (26.70) in the five matches. In England he was equally successful. At Old Trafford in 1888 his 11 for 68 won the match, and at The Oval in 1896 Australia collapsed for 44 in the second innings, Peel taking 6 for 23. He achieved the double once, in 1896, when he hit his career highest, 210 not out against Warwickshire at Edgbaston, adding 292 for the eighth wicket with Lord Hawke. But one day in 1897 he came on the field under the influence of alcohol, and misbehaved himself on the pitch in front of his lordship, who thereupon banished him from the Yorkshire eleven. Years later, Lord Hawke said: 'He never bore me any malice.'

Bobby Peel

First-class career (1882-99): 12,191 runs (19.44) including 7 centuries, 1,754 wickets (16.21) and 203 catches
Test matches (20): 427 runs (14.72), 102 wickets (16.81) and 17 catches

PENN, Frank (1851-1916)

Kent

Although his career in first-class cricket was cut short by a heart disorder, Frank Penn achieved some very good performances for his county and the Gentlemen as a free, commanding batsman who hit to all parts of the field, a good cover-point or long-leg and a useful slow, round-arm bowler. He toured Australia with Lord Harris's team in 1878/9, but his only Test was the first Test in England at The Oval, 1880, when he bowled three overs for 2 runs and hit 23 and 27 not out, cutting for four the ball which gave England victory. The following year he retired from first-class cricket. In 1905 he was president of Kent; and his two brothers and son, Frank, also played for the county. In sixty-one matches for Kent between 1875 and 1881, he scored 2,906 runs (29.35), including 6 centuries, and took 8 wickets (38.87).

PERKS, Reginald Thomas David (1911-77)

Worcestershire

Tall and broad-shouldered, Reg Perks bowled right-arm fast-medium with very good control. Attacking the stumps, he had a long smooth run, a perfect high action with a sweeping follow-through and a sharp late in-swing. He took at least 100 wickets in a season sixteen times, taking more wickets for his county than anyone else. As a left-handed batsman, he was a bold and sometimes effective hitter. He toured South Africa with MCC in 1938/9 and played in the last Test against the West Indies in 1939 which was his best year with 159 wickets (19.22). Still a force after the war, he captured 14 for 96 (including 9 for 42) against Gloucestershire at Cheltenham in 1946.

First-class career (1930-55): 8,956 runs (12.20), 2,233 wickets (24.08) and 244 catches
Test matches (2): 3 runs (—), 11 wickets (32.27) and 1 catch

PHILIPSON, Hylton (1866-1935)

Oxford University, Middlesex and Northumberland

An Old Etonian, 'Punch' Philipson was a competent and versatile batsman and an excellent wicket-keeper who, standing up to most bowlers, took the ball with easy grace. Though only an irregular with Middlesex, he toured Australia with Lord Sheffield's and A.E. Stoddart's teams of 1891/2 and 1894/5. He also got blues for racquets, tennis and soccer.

First-class career (1887-98): 1,951 runs (17.26) including 2 centuries, and 149 dismissals (102 ct, 47 st.)
Test matches (5): 63 runs (9.00) and 11 dismissals (8 ct, 3 st.)

PILLING, Richard (1855-91)

Lancashire

Dick Pilling was, perhaps, the outstanding professional wicket-keeper of his day. He was known as 'The Prince of Wicket-Keepers' and his style was described as 'the perfection of neatness and rapidity'. He visited Australia with Shaw's and Shrewsbury's teams of 1881/2 and 1887/8 (besides appearing in three Tests in England) and, when his never robust health was seen to be failing, he went there on medical advice in 1890. His case, however, was hopeless and he returned home to die.

First-class career (1877-89): 2,696 runs (9.91) and 597 dismissals (417 ct, 180 st.)
Test matches (8): 91 runs (7.58) and 14 dismissals (10 ct, 4 st.)

PLACE, Winston (b.1914)

Lancashire

Winston Place was a discovery of 1946. Before the Second World War he was just an ordinary right-handed batsman, but when the game was resumed he became the perfect foil to Cyril Washbrook as Lancashire's opener. Dependable, self-effacing, conscientious, he could drive high over the bowler's head, indulge in a hefty pull and produce a classic cover-drive. Sure defence against the turning ball was another characteristic of his batting. In 1947/8 he toured the West Indies with MCC, scoring 107 in the fourth Test at Kingston (when the West Indies won the rubber) and in 1949/50 he visited India with the Commonwealth team. Place passed 1,000 runs in a season eight times, his best year being 1947 when he made 2,501 runs (62.52).

First-class career (1937-55): 15,609 runs (35.63) including 36 centuries
Test matches (3): 144 runs (28.80) including 1 century

POCOCK, Patrick Ian (b.1946)

Surrey and Northern Transvaal

Both as a gauche teenager on the Surrey staff and as a mature Test player, Pat, or 'Percy', Pocock has remained the same cheerful, open, friendly, talkative character. It was obvious from an early age that he had outstanding ability as an off-spinner. Tall and strong, he is a sharp spinner of the ball despite persistent bother from blisters on his spinning finger, and possesses a perfect, high, sideways-on action, but he has disappointingly failed to develop his full potential at the highest level. He bowled impressively on the demanding pitches of the Caribbean on his first tour of 1967/8, taking over from F.J. Titmus when the latter was injured, but was dropped despite taking 6 for 79 in the second innings of the first Test against Australia in

Pat Pocock, and umpire John Langridge, who was most unlucky never to play Test cricket

1968. (Lawry had punished him in the first innings.) In helpful conditions Pocock will bowl a side out quicker than most off-spinners in the world, but overseas he has tended to experiment too much rather than just wheel away and let his action take wickets for him. Equally effective for Surrey in both three-day and one-day cricket, he has taken two hat-tricks, one during an amazing spell against Sussex in 1972 when he took four wickets in four balls, five in six, six in nine and seven in 11 – the last two are records. Significantly this was at Eastbourne, not The Oval where wickets have given him little assistance. He is a capable fielder and a stylish, sometimes useful right-hand batsman. He went on five MCC tours, though never to Australia, a disappointment to him and a mistake by the selectors.

First-class career (1964-): 4,321 runs (11.58), 1,375 wickets (25.88) and 159 catches
Test matches (17): 165 runs (6.60), 47 wickets (43.04) and 13 catches

POLLARD, Richard (b.1912)

Lancashire

Dick Pollard was a right-arm, fast-medium bowler with a long, padding, flat-foot run, who could move the ball either way and seemed to bowl faster as he warmed to his task; and his stamina was immense. But he lost his best years to the War. In his first Test, against India at Old Trafford in 1946, he took 5 for 24 (in twenty-seven overs) in the first innings. He toured Australasia in 1946/7, appearing in one Test in New Zealand, and played twice against Australia in 1948. He dismissed Don Bradman twice for low scores.

First-class career (1935-50): 3,505 runs (13.27) and 1,119 wickets (22.52)
Test matches (4): 13 runs (13.00), 15 wickets (25.20) and 3 catches

POOLE, Cyril John (b.1921)

Nottinghamshire

At his peak in the fifties, Cyril Poole was one of the best left-handed attacking stroke-makers in county cricket and, as befitted a professional footballer, he was brilliant in the deep. He toured India with MCC in 1951/2, making two fifties in three Tests, and made his highest score, 222 not out, for his county against the Indians at Trent Bridge in 1952, an uncharacteristically grim effort. In contrast he reached a century in sixty minutes (154 not out in ninety-seven minutes) against Leicestershire at Trent Bridge in 1949.

First-class career (1948-62): 19,364 runs (32.54) including 24 centuries, 220 catches and 5 stumpings
Test matches (3): 161 runs (40.25), 0-9 and 1 catch

POPE, George Henry (b.1911)

Derbyshire

Tall and spare, George Pope was one of three brothers who played for Derbyshire, Alfred and Harold being the others. He was a lively, right-arm, medium-pace bowler and, as a batsman, seemed a natural hitter who had schooled himself into a necessary restraint, without overdoing it. He possessed considerable speed in the field and when he 'bent' to pick up a ball from the ground, his back was completely straight. He achieved the double twice and in 1937 he hit 3 centuries in a month. In his sole Test, against South Africa at Lord's in 1947, he scored 8 not out and, as opening bowler, took 1 for 85. He also played in the three 'Victory' Tests against the Australian Services in 1945, and toured India with the Commonwealth team in 1949/50.

First-class career (1933-50): 7,518 runs (28.05) including 8 centuries, and 677 wickets (19.92)

POUGHER, Arthur Dick (1865-1926)

Leicestershire

An all-rounder, Dick Pougher achieved much of his best work before his county became first-class in 1894. Bowling right-arm medium-pace with a high action, his stock ball was the off-break which came sharply off the pitch; he could also turn enough from leg to beat the bat. As a batsman, he used his height, reach and straightness of bat to play many useful innings. For MCC at Lord's in 1896 Pougher and Jack Hearne dismissed the Australians for 18; Pougher took 5 for 0 in fifteen balls, coming on to bowl with the score at 18 for 3 ! Yet he never represented England against Australia. He toured Australia with Shrewsbury's team in 1887/8 and South Africa with W.W. Read's in 1891/2. At Cape Town in his sole Test he scored 17, took 3 for 26 and held 2 catches. He became owner of the pub which adjoined the county cricket ground at Leicester.

First-class career (1886-1902): 4,553 runs (18.58) including 5 centuries, and 535 wickets (19.02)

PRICE, John Sidney Ernest (b.1937)

Middlesex

Strongly built, John Price was a determined, right-arm fast bowler with a long, crescent-shaped run-up who, unhappily was never free from injury for long. He was a willing work-horse, however, distinctly sharp when firing on all cylinders and lacking only an especially steep bounce. He toured India and South Africa, but his appearances for England were spread over nine years and he never made his place secure. His best performance was at Calcutta in 1963/4 when he took 5 for 73 in India's first innings in his second Test.

John Price

In the previous match he had taken 3 for 66 and 2 for 47 and, normally a left-hand batsman of no account, scored 32 going in at number eight for a team stricken by illness and injuries.

First-class career (1961-75): 1,108 runs (8.39) and 817 wickets (23.55)
Test matches (15): 66 runs (7.33), 40 wickets (35.02) and 7 catches

PRICE, Wilfred Frederick Frank (1902-69)

Middlesex

A very safe wicket-keeper, Fred Price became a distinctly useful batsman – known as the 'Rock of Gibraltar' because of his defensive methods – and he often opened his county's batting. In 1937 he created a then world record by taking 7 catches in Yorkshire's first innings at Lord's. Afterwards a lady congratulated him. 'I was so thrilled with your performance, Mr Price, that I nearly fell over the balcony.' 'If you had, Madam,' replied Fred, 'I would have caught you as well!' He joined MCC as a replacement in the West Indies in 1929/30 and India in 1937/8, but his sole Test was against Australia at Headingley in 1938, when he scored 0 and 6 and held 2 catches.

First-class career (1926-47): 9,035 runs (18.33) including 3 centuries, and 977 dismissals (665 ct, 312 st.)

PRIDEAUX, Roger Malcolm (b.1939)

Cambridge University, Kent, Northamptonshire, Sussex and Orange Free State

A gifted, natural, right-handed opening batsman, Roger Prideaux was outstanding both at Tonbridge and at Cambridge. He had an attractive upright style, was particularly strong off the front foot and played with an air of calm authority. Indeed it is surprising that he played in only three Tests. He scored two centuries in the match between Cambridge and Somerset at Taunton in 1960 and again for Northamptonshire against Nottinghamshire at Trent Bridge in 1966. His century in fifty-two minutes (118 in sixty minutes), for South against North at Blackpool in 1961, was the fastest in first-class cricket since 1937. His highest score was 202 not out for Northamptonshire against Oxford in the Parks in 1963. He played for Northamptonshire from 1961 until 1970, and as captain from 1967. In his first Test, against Australia at Headingley in 1968, he hit an outstanding 64, adding 123 for the first wicket with John Edrich. But he was unfit for the next match at The Oval, being replaced by Basil d'Oliveira and, because of the events which followed, Prideaux missed the chance to tour South Africa the following winter, when the tour was cancelled for political reasons. He did, however, tour Pakistan in 1968/9, and Canada and New Zealand with non-Test playing MCC sides. Thirteen times he exceeded 1,000 runs in a season.

First-class career (1958-75): 25,136 runs (34.29) including 41 centuries, and 301 catches
Test matches (3): 102 runs (20.40) and 0-0

PRINGLE, Derek Raymond (b.1958)

Cambridge University and Essex

An all-round cricketer of great strength and ability, Derek Pringle is a broadly built man of a fraction under six foot five who has used his physical advantages to good effect. He was given sudden promotion to the England side in 1982 after captaining Cambridge with flair early in that season. He played for Cambridge for four years (1979-82) as a hard-striking right-hand batsman and a right-arm fast-medium bowler with an excellent action. When he went on his first tour for England in 1982/3 he was already experienced overseas, having been to Australia with Oxford and Cambridge in 1979/80 and to India with the English Schools team the previous year. He also toured South Africa with an Oxbridge side in 1981/2. Troubled by the spinners, he was disappointing with the bat in his first Test appearances in England against India and Pakistan in 1982 when he missed two matches because of a back injury, the second sustained when stretching after writing a letter! But his bowling was impressive and the figures he produced on slow pitches did not tell how tidily he bowled. If luck goes his way, he has much to offer to English cricket in the 1980s. He is the son of Donald Pringle, who played for East Africa, where Derek was born, in the 1975 Prudential World Cup.

First-class career (1978-): 2,514 runs (32.64) including 5 centuries, 133 wickets (29.03) and 26 catches
Test matches (4): 58 runs (11.60), 7 wickets (40.14)

PULLAR, Geoffrey (b.1935)

Lancashire and Gloucestershire

A tall, strong left-handed batsman, Geoff Pullar was known as 'Noddy' because of his ability to fall asleep in almost any situation. But he was awake enough at the crease, playing mainly off the front foot and accumulating runs assiduously on the leg-side. He started as a middle-order batsman but his solid technique and phlegmatic temperament persuaded the England selectors to choose him as an opening batsman in 1959. He responded with 75 against India at Headingley, followed by 131 at Old Trafford, the latter being the first Test century scored by a Lancastrian batsman at Old Trafford. After withstanding the West Indian fast bowlers calmly and successfully in 1959/60, he made 175 against South Africa at The Oval in 1960 (his career-highest), sharing in an opening stand of 290 with Colin Cowdrey. He toured India and Pakistan in 1961/2 – reaching 1,000 runs – and Australia in 1962/3. But both in the latter series and in the 1961 series in England he failed against Australia, his highest score being 63 from nine matches. His twenty-eight Tests were concentrated between 1959 and 1963. Giving up opening, he found form again. He played for Gloucestershire in 1969 and 1970. Ten times he exceeded 1,000 runs in a season.

Geoff Pullar

First-class career (1954-70): 21,528 runs (35.34) including 41 centuries, 10 wickets (38.70) and 126 catches
Test matches (28): 1,974 runs (43.86) including 4 centuries, 1-37 and 2 catches

QUAIFE, William (1872-1951)

Sussex, Warwickshire and Griqualand West

Adding the initial 'G' to differentiate between his elder brother, Walter, and himself when they were both with Sussex, Willie Quaife joined Warwickshire after one season and played for them for thirty-five years. In his first match for the Midland county he made 115 not out against Durham in 1893, and in his last, 115 against Derbyshire in 1928. A model right-handed batsman, a slow leg-break bowler and a fine cover-point, he was, perhaps, the smallest man to play for England against Australia. Very sound in defence, he played with a very straight bat, demonstrating perfect balance, footwork and control. On twenty-five occasions he exceeded 1,000 runs in a season, his best year being 1905 with 2,060 runs (54.21) including his career-highest, 255 not out against Surrey at The Oval. However he was rarely successful in Tests, his best performance being 68 and 44 at Adelaide in 1901/2, as a member of Archie MacLaren's team.

First-class career (1894-1928): 36,016 runs (35.38) including 72 centuries, 931 wickets (27.38), 346 catches and 1 stumping
Test matches (7): 228 runs (19.00), 0-6 and 4 catches

RADLEY, Clive Thornton (b.1944)

Middlesex

A small, chunkily built right-handed batsman from Norfolk, Clive Radley has always been a consistent accumulator of runs. Effective rather than attractive, he watches the ball intently, cuts well, and plays skilfully within his limitations, often inventing his own strokes and running brilliantly between the wickets. Although a natural fighter, he proved suspect against the fast lifting ball in Australia. He is a fine close field. He has reached 1,000 runs in a season fourteen times and he shares the sixth-wicket partnership record for the county, 227 with Fred Titmus, against the South Africans at Lord's in 1965. He toured Pakistan and New Zealand 1977/8 and Australia 1978/9 and in his second Test, against New Zealand at Auckland in 1977, he made a marathon score of 158. His second century was 106 against Pakistan at Edgbaston in 1978.

First-class career (1964-): 21,886 runs (35.30) including 38 centuries, 6 wickets (18.50) and 442 catches
Test matches (8): 481 runs (48.10) including 2 centuries, and 4 catches

RANDALL, Derek William (b.1951)

Nottinghamshire

Of few cricketers can it be said with more truth that figures do not tell the full story. Derek Randall, first called 'Arkle' (after the great steeplechaser) when he lapped some of his Nottinghamshire colleagues on a training run, averaged only 26 after sixteen Tests for England before the tour of Australia in 1978/9, yet had already had an extraordinary effect on English cricket. In Australia, often faced with poor wickets, he made more runs (763 at 47.68) than anyone in the touring party and scored 385 Test runs at 38.50, returning home an established member of the side for the first time. Although he is a dedicated right-hand batsman with immense natural flair and a gift of timing, captains have always been tempted to pick him for his fielding alone and he has achieved many phenomenal run-outs. There has never been a keener cover-point and it is difficult to think of any faster ones. Moreover his throwing has become increasingly accurate. Covering some fifteen yards towards the stumps as the bowler delivers Randall is actually running as the batsman plays his stroke and his acrobatics in the field inspired his colleagues in the MCC side on his first tour, to India and Australia in 1976/7. Thanks to Randall other fielders also began to perform superhuman feats, the bowlers were themselves lifted and, although his own form was mercurial, England's success in the next four years owed much to his influence. Although normally a somewhat diffident and self-conscious character, he becomes a natural clown with an audience to play to, and, despite being a very nervous starter of an innings, thrives on the big occasion. In March 1977 he played one of the great Test innings, cutting, driving and hooking his way to a brilliant and audacious 174 in the second innings of the Centenary Test in Melbourne. Almost single-handed Randall took the fight to Dennis Lillee and turned potential anti-climax into a classic finish. A modest series against Australia at home in 1977, interrupted by an injury, was followed by failure on the winter tour of Pakistan and New Zealand but his second Test hundred, a staunch and patient innings of 150 in the second innings of the fourth Test at Sydney in 1978/9, turned a series which was delicately balanced decisively England's way. Though he still gets himself out sometimes with rash strokes, and fidgets about at the crease as the bowler delivers the ball, he remains a character, an entertainer and a batsman sometimes touched by genius, perhaps the spiritual son of another great but eccentric Nottinghamshire cricketer, George Gunn. He had a disastrous tour of Australia in 1979/80 and lost his place, but his Test career took on a new lease in 1982 when he hit entertaining and valuable hundreds for England against India at Lord's, going in at number six, and against Pakistan at Edgbaston when, against his will, he was tried as an opener. Subsequent efforts were less successful and he batted lower in the order in Australia in 1982/3, when he played consistently and well.

Derek Randall – Rodney Marsh (Australia) keeping wicket

First-class career (1972-): 14,787 runs (35.97) including 25 centuries, 3 wickets (47.33) and 169 catches
Test matches (33): 1,514 runs (30.28) including 4 centuries, 0-3 and 22 catches

RANJITSINHJI, Kumar Shri (H.H. Jam Sahib of Nawanagar) (1872-1933)

Cambridge University, Cambridgeshire and Sussex

The legendary Ranji came from ancient Rajput stock, and brought Eastern magic to the cricket fields of England, America and Australia. Individual and distinctive in style, he possessed exceptionally keen eyesight besides flexibility and power of wrist, and he could glance the good length ball off the middle stump to leg in a way that no one else has equalled. His cutting and driving, too, were superb, models of feline grace. He was a useful change-bowler and a safe catcher in the slips. Throughout, he suffered from hay-fever. Awarded his blue at Cambridge by F.S. Jackson (and known in his university days as 'Smith') he soon announced his genius to the world. He made 77 and 150 on his debut for Sussex against MCC at Lord's; and in his first Test against Australia at Old Trafford, 1896, he made 62 and 154 not out, rescuing England from two shaky starts. He was first in the national averages in 1896 with 2,780 runs (57.91), including 10 centuries; in 1900 with 3,065 runs (87.57), including 11 centuries; and again in 1904 with 2,077 runs (74.17), including 8 centuries. In 1899 he made 3,159 runs

(63.18), including 8 centuries. He passed 1,000 runs in all twelve seasons he was able to appear regularly, including his tour of Australia in 1897/8 with A.E. Stoddart's team, when he averaged 50.77 in the Tests. His highest score in Tests was 175 in the first match at Sydney in 1897, and his career-highest, 285 not out for Sussex against Somerset at Taunton in 1901. He captained Sussex for five seasons and somehow always seemed to be engaged in a stand at Hove with C.B. Fry, with whom he later served on the League of Nations. Ranji played his last match for Sussex in 1920 but by then he had lost an eye in a shooting accident, was overweight and no longer a force. K.S. Duleepsinhji was his nephew.

First-class career (1893-1920): 24,692 runs (56.37) including 72 centuries, 130 wickets (34.06) and 232 catches
Test matches (15): 989 runs (44.95) including 2 centuries, 1-39 and 13 catches

READ, Holcombe Douglas (b.1910)

Essex and Surrey

'Hopper' Read took a long run with a somewhat tearaway right-arm action and his length was often erratic, but there was no doubt about his speed. A surprise choice for England against South Africa at The Oval in 1935 – though earlier in the season he had been prominent in the debacle of the champions, Yorkshire, at Huddersfield – he took 6 for 200 on a batsman's paradise and did not bat. He toured Australasia with MCC's 'goodwill' team of 1935/6, but he was unable to spare much time afterwards for first-class cricket.

First-class career (1933-48): 158 runs (3.67) and 219 wickets (22.93)

K.S. Ranjitsinhji

READ, John Maurice (1859-1929)

Surrey

Nephew of a prominent early player H.H. Stephenson, Maurice Read represented a new 'school' of professionals: well-groomed, well-mannered, articulate, sober and thrifty. He was a free, hard-hitting, right-handed batsman with a sound defence, a useful fast-medium change-bowler and a reliable outfield. For fifteen years he was an integral part of the successful Surrey side and for more than a decade a regular choice for England against Australia and for Players against Gentlemen. He had a large part in England's two-wicket victory at The Oval in 1890, on a sticky wicket making 35 of a total 95 for eight. He toured Australia four times between 1884 and 1892, and in all hit three centuries against the Australians, notably 186 for Surrey at The Oval in 1886, his career-highest, adding 241 with Bobby Abel for the fourth wicket. He toured South Africa with Major Warton's pioneer team of 1888/9, playing in the first Tests against that country.

First-class career (1880-95): 14,010 runs (24.66) including 11 centuries, and 73 wickets (24.71)
Test matches (17): 463 runs (17.14) and 8 catches

READ, Walter William (1855-1907)

Surrey

A former school-teacher, Walter Read or 'W.W.' was a bold and dashing character, no respecter of very important persons, and often in a high fury about something or other. He was a prime mover in the revival of Surrey cricket in the early 1880s, and for more than a decade one of the two best batsmen in the eleven. He was a punishing front-foot player, with tremendous power in his right-handed off-drive. He was a safe field at point and purveyed lobs occasionally even in Tests. His career-highest score was 338 for Surrey against Oxford University at The Oval in 1888. In the previous season he had exceeded 200 in an innings twice. He toured Australia twice – captaining England in the sole Test of 1887/8 at Sydney, as the compromise leader agreed to by two rival touring teams. He also led his own team to South Africa in 1891/2. (Both Tests in which he was captain were won.) He represented England at home in each series from 1884 until 1893. In The Oval Test of 1884 he was furious at Lord Harris sending him in at number ten instead of three or four and 'took it out of' the Australian bowlers, slamming 117 in just over two hours.

First-class career (1873-97): 22,349 runs (32.06) including 38 centuries, 108 wickets (32.25), 318 catches and 20 stumpings
Test matches (18): 720 runs (27.69) including 1 century, 0-63 and 16 catches

RELF, Albert Edward (1874-1937)

Norfolk, Sussex and Auckland

Coming to Sussex from Norfolk at the age of twenty-five, A.E. Relf was an immediate success and remained a mainstay of the team for twenty-one years, achieving the double eight times in ten seasons. Taking a short run with an easy, natural right-arm action, he bowled medium pace with perfect command of length and could keep an end going all day without becoming tired. He was also a prolific run-getter and brilliant in the slips. He toured Australia with the first MCC team of 1903/4, and his diary revealed his sore disappointment at receiving so few chances in the series. He appeared in two Tests, adding 115 for the ninth wicket with R.E. Foster in the first at Sydney. In his only Test against Australia in England, at The Oval in 1909, he took 5 for 85 in a total of 350. He toured South Africa in 1905/6 and 1913/14 with more satisfaction. For most of his life he was a happy, popular man but, while coach at Wellington College, he shot himself through the head in a mood of depression caused by the serious illness of his wife. He died a wealthy man and his wife recovered.

First-class career (1900-1921): 22,176 runs (26.68) including 26 centuries, 1,897 wickets (20.94) and 493 catches
Test matches (13): 416 runs (23.11), 25 wickets (24.96) and 14 catches

RHODES, Harold James (b.1936)

Derbyshire and Nottinghamshire

Harold or 'Dusty' Rhodes first appeared for Derbyshire at sixteen as a right-arm spin bowler, but subsequently altered his style, becoming a fast seam bowler in the rich Derbyshire tradition. He represented England against India in two Tests in 1959, but his career was blighted. Doubts were expressed about his action, especially when he delivered his faster ball, and at Derby in 1960, while bowling against the South Africans, he was no-balled six times by umpire Paul Gibb. Both Gibb and Sid Buller called him in later matches; MCC investigated the matter and eventually decided that Rhodes had a 'hyper-extended arm'. He was officially cleared in 1968 but he did not play for England again. Three times he captured 100 wickets in a season, with 119 wickets (11.04) in 1965. After 1969 he went into League cricket and appeared for Nottinghamshire in several Gillette Cup and John Player League matches. He is the son of another Derbyshire cricketer, A.E.G. Rhodes, who is now a Test umpire.

First-class career (1953-75): 2,427 runs (9.48) and 1,073 wickets (19.70)
Test matches (2): 0 runs (—) and 9 wickets (27.11)

RHODES, Wilfred (1877-1973)

Yorkshire

The exploits of Wilfred Rhodes and George Hirst are legendary in Yorkshire. As with Hirst, Rhode's integrity was a prime quality but his character was even tougher and more complex. The third in his county's great tradition of slow left-arm bowlers, he was a natural psychologist. In his career of thirty-two years he learned and explored the weaknesses, rashnesses and timidities of virtually every batsman in the Commonwealth. His action was balanced and economical with a natural flow. Formidably accurate, he would turn the ball on most surfaces but it was in the air that, by subtle variations of flight, he beat most of the 4,187 batsmen he dismissed. No man has equalled that gargantuan haul. Beginning with his county as a number eleven batsman, he rose to open for England against Australia and South Africa with Jack Hobbs. A tenacious, right-hander, he was thorough in defence

Wilfred Rhodes

and calculated and certain in attack, notably so with a leaning off-drive which placed the ball accurately into the cover gaps. Apart from his bowling record only thirteen batsmen have exceeded his total of runs; only six fieldsmen (excluding wicket-keepers) have held more catches. He passed 1,000 runs twenty-one times and took 100 wickets twenty-three times. His success was immediate, with 154 wickets in his first season, 1898, and 1,251 wickets in his first five seasons. He played in his first Test against Australia at Trent Bridge in 1899 (taking 7 wickets) and his last at The Oval in 1926, when his 4 for 44 on the final day enabled England to regain the Ashes after fourteen years. He toured Australia four times between 1903 and 1921; he visited South Africa twice; and his last tour was to the West Indies in 1929/30, when he appeared in the first Test series in the Caribbean. He captured 31 wickets (15.74) against Australia in 1903/4, when England won back the Ashes. Opening the batting for England for only the second time, in the first Test against South Africa at Johannesburg in 1909/10, he put on 159 with Jack Hobbs. In the fifth match at Capetown these two added 221 and, in the fourth Test against Australia at Melbourne two years later, they created England's (then) first-wicket record of 323, Rhodes making 179. His most successful bowling returns were 8 for 68 at Melbourne in 1903/4 (15 for 124 in the match) and 7 for 17 at Edgbaston in 1902 when Australia were all out for 36. In later years he coached at Harrow before turning gradually blind. But he never repined and would attend matches regularly, 'reading' the game with remarkable accuracy by the familiar sounds around him. Of the many stories told about Rhodes one by Sir Neville Cardus stays in the mind. Rhodes and Emmott Robinson went out one day to inspect a rain-affected wicket. 'That'll be turning by four o'clock,' said Robinson sagely. 'Nay Emmott,' was the reply, '*half-past* four.'

First-class career (1898-1930): 39,802 runs (30.83) including 58 centuries, 4,187 wickets (16.71) and 708 catches
Test matches (58): 2,325 runs (30.19) including 2 centuries, 127 wickets (26.96) and 60 catches

RICHARDSON, Derek Walter (b.1934)

Worcestershire

Fair-haired and with a countryman's complexion, 'Dick' Richardson was an attractive left-hand, middle-order batsman, who had a high backlift and a style quite unlike his brother Peter, his strokes tending to be more fluent. Possibly through rather careless stroke-play, he failed to fulfil his early great promise. He was a fine close fielder. He passed 1,000 runs in a season nine times and, in his sole Test against the West Indies at Trent Bridge in 1957, he scored 33 and held 1 catch.

First-class career (1952-67): 16,303 runs (27.40) including 16 centuries, 8 wickets (44.25) and 419 catches

RICHARDSON, Peter Edward (b.1931)

Worcestershire and Kent

A patient and canny left-handed opening batsman, Peter Richardson was the eldest of three brothers to play county cricket. He established himself with 2,294 runs (39.55) in 1953, his second full season for Worcestershire. Three further times he exceeded 2,000 runs in a season, and twelve times altogether passed the 1,000 mark. Fair-haired and stocky with strong forearms, he pushed and deflected the ball with the minimum of backlift and loved to steal a quick single. Captain of Worcestershire from 1956 until 1958, he also achieved much success in Tests. In his first match at Trent Bridge in 1956 he hit the Australian bowling for 81 and 73, putting on 151 for the first wicket with Colin Cowdrey in the second innings. At Old Trafford he made 104, again opening with Cowdrey, and adding 174 on the first day. England won by an innings. Richardson, however, was one of the disappointments of the 1958/9 tour of Australia. Moving afterwards from Worcestershire to Kent, he hit 111 and 115 for Kent against the Australians at Canterbury in 1964. He appeared in eight Tests during the 1961/2 tour to India and Pakistan and one more at home against the West Indies in 1963. A humorist, Peter had a penchant for sending deliberately faked cricket records to E.W. Swanton, for publication in the *Daily Telegraph*. On

Peter Richardson

one occasion he also complained about excessive noise from Mr Swanton in the commentary box!

First-class career (1949-65): 26,055 runs (34.60) including 44 centuries, 11 wickets (45.36) and 220 catches
Test matches (34): 2,061 runs (37.47) including 5 centuries, 3 wickets (16.00) and 6 catches

RICHARDSON, Thomas (1870-1912)

Surrey and Somerset

One of the immortal fast bowlers, Tom Richardson was a black-haired, black-moustached gypsy of a fellow; lithe and supple, he pounded away with heart, hand and magnificent muscle, not for a few overs with the new ball, but over after over all day. During his career Surrey were champions in four seasons. When asked if he approved of increasing the number of balls in an over from five to six, Tom said, 'Give me *ten*!' A glutton for work, he took 809 wickets in only three seasons from 1895 to 1897, in the former year taking 290 wickets (14.37), which is the largest number ever taken by a fast bowler and remained the highest by any bowler for thirty-three years. Seven times he passed 150 wickets in a season, ten times altogether 100 wickets. In his first Test against Australia, at Old Trafford in 1893, he took 5 wickets in each innings. On the first of his two tours in 1894/5 he headed the bowling with 32 wickets (26.53); in the second, also with A.E. Stoddart's team, he again took most wickets, capturing 22 (35.27). In the 1896 series he was again the most effective bowler, securing 24 wickets (18.29), and his great-hearted bowling at Old Trafford, when he took 13 for 244, one of the greatest sustained spells in the history of Test cricket, very nearly brought victory to England. At his peak, for some four or five years, he was certainly one of the greatest of fast bowlers. After a long run-up and high right-arm delivery, the combination of sheer pace with a pronounced off-break made him irresistible. Neville Cardus described his action memorably as being 'like a great wave of the sea about to break'. He died of a heart-attack while on holiday walking in France; there was no question of the suicide that has sometimes been alleged.

First-class career (1892-1905): 3,424 runs (9.65) and 2,105 wickets (18.42)
Test matches (14): 177 runs (11.06), 88 wickets (25.22) and 5 catches

Tom Richardson

RICHMOND, Thomas Leonard (1890-1957)

Nottinghamshire

A right-arm, leg-break and googly bowler, who spun the ball considerably, Tom Richmond was under medium height and began to lose his skill when his increasing weight, combined with his lack of inches, made him very rotund indeed. Both as batsman and fielder he was a passenger. From 1920 until 1926, however, he never took fewer than 113 wickets in a season. Eight times he had more than 12 wickets in a match. His sole Test was against Australia at Trent Bridge in 1921, when he scored 4 and 2 and took 2 for 86.

First-class career (1912-32): 1,644 runs (9.96) and 1,176 wickets (21.22)

RIDGWAY, Frederick (b.1923)

Kent

A hard-working, right-handed, fast-medium bowler, Fred Ridgway was in his prime when many other fastish bowlers were available for England, and consequently his only tour for MCC was India in 1951/2 where his Test cricket was played. His short stature meant that some of his deliveries kept rather lower than the batsman expected. His best season was 1949 with 105 wickets (23.32) and he once took 4 wickets in

4 balls for Kent against Derbyshire at Folkestone in 1951. He was an excellent close field and could be a useful lower-order batsman.

First-class career (1946-61): 4,081 runs (11.00). 1,069 wickets (23.74) and 233 catches
Test matches (5): 49 runs (8.16), 7 wickets (54.14) and 3 catches

ROBERTSON, John David Benbow (b.1917)

Middlesex

A man of modesty and natural dignity, Jack Robertson was a right-handed opening batsman of high class who would have played many more Tests had it not been his misfortune to be a contemporary of Len Hutton and Cyril Washbrook. He never failed England. He was a correct, consistent and handsome batsman, and one of the best players of the new ball anywhere. Opening with Sid Brown for Middlesex during the 'Golden Summer' of 1947, he helped to wear down the bowling for Denis Compton and Bill Edrich to follow. When Brown and Robertson put on 310 against Nottinghamshire at Lord's that summer, it was a new record for the county and, although one thinks of 1947 as the year of the Middlesex twins, Robertson himself made 2,760 runs (52.47), including 12 centuries. His best season was 1951 when he scored 2,917 runs (56.09), including 7 centuries. His highest score, 331 not out at Worcester in 1949, was made in the course of a day. Fifteen times (once overseas with MCC in India) he exceeded 1,000 runs in a season and nine times between 1947 and 1957 he passed 2,000 runs. Robertson's first Test was against South Africa in 1947. He headed the averages in the West Indies in 1947/8 with 390 runs (55.71), including 133 at Port of Spain. Against New Zealand at Lord's in 1949, when he replaced the injured Washbrook, he hit 121, putting on 143 for the first wicket with Hutton but was omitted for the rest of the series! His last Test series was against India in 1951/2, when he made over 300 runs. He was never selected against Australia. Also a useful off-break change-bowler and a fine field, he slid almost unnoticed from a game which his cultured and consistent play had graced for such a long time and became joint county coach with Jim Sims.

First-class career (1937-59): 31,914 runs (37.50) including 67 centuries, 73 wickets (34.74) and 351 catches
Test matches (11): 881 runs (46.36) including 2 centuries, 2 wickets (29.00) and 6 catches

ROBINS, Robert Walter Vivian (1906-68)

Cambridge University and Middlesex

A forceful, dynamic and influential cricketer, Walter

Walter Robins

Robins was an outstanding player at Highgate school, then a successful Cambridge blue, later a captain of both Middlesex and England, and finally an administrator as lively and enterprising as he had been player. Quick, short, with the walk and build of a cavalryman and a cheeky manner of batting, he used his feet freely and would go down the pitch to both fast and slow bowling. When he struck a length with his leg-breaks and googlies, he could go through any side. He was irrepressible, a believer in attack, whether batting, bowling or fielding with energetic hostility in the cover. He led Middlesex from 1935 until 1938, in 1946 and 1947 and again in 1950, the county gaining the Championship in 1947. An old Middlesex player was once asked: 'What difference did Walter Robins make to a match?' He replied: 'The difference between the quick and the dead.' His first Test was against South Africa at Lord's in 1929. The following year he played against Australia twice, taking 7 wickets in the match at Trent Bridge. Against the West Indies at Lord's in 1933, he took 6 for 32 in the first innings (West Indies falling for 97). He rescued England with 108 in just over two hours against South Africa at Old Trafford in 1935. He toured Australia in 1936/7, but was handicapped by injury. He led England victoriously against New Zealand in 1937. He achieved the double once, had a highest score of 140 against Cambridge at Fenners in 1930 and best bowling figures of 8 for 34 (13 for 115 in the match) against Lancashire at Lord's in 1929. He produced two hat-tricks at Lord's. He became honorary treasurer to Middlesex, a Test selector, manager of MCC in the West Indies, 1959/60 – a rather too dogmatic one for the liking of some of his players – and served on the Cricket Inquiry Committee set up in 1960. A soccer blue at Cambridge, he played for Corinthians and Nottingham Forest.

First-class career (1925-58): 13,884 runs (26.40) including 11 centuries, 969 wickets (23.30) and 220 catches
Test matches (19): 612 runs (26.60) including 1 century, 64 wickets (27.46) and 12 catches

ROOPE, Graham Richard James (b.1946)

Berkshire, Surrey and Griqualand West

Tall, raw-boned and curly haired, Graham Roope is a gifted, all-round games player, probably just below the highest class as a right-hand, middle-order batsman, but he nevertheless did a useful job in twenty-one Tests for England between 1973 and 1978. He was also a noted goalkeeper in amateur football and it was his brilliant close fielding, especially at second slip, which often gave him the edge over others, when England teams were being picked. A genial character off the field, he is a determined and tough competitor in any match and, although he did not make a century for England, 7 fifties and 35 catches bear testimony to his usefulness. A right-hander, he is capable on his day of dominating an attack with glorious driving, but his batting for England was more often a question of a dogged struggle, as in 1975 when his solid 77 at The Oval helped to save England from defeat against Lillee, Thomson and the other Australians. A consistent county cricketer, Roope gave Surrey long and loyal service until 1982, often taking useful wickets with his medium-fast bowling.

First-class career (1964-): 19,037 runs (36.96) including 26 centuries, 225 wickets (37.31), 599 catches and 2 stumpings
Test matches (21): 860 runs (30.71), 0-76 and 35 catches

Graham Roope

ROOT, Charles Frederick (1890-1954)

Derbyshire and Worcestershire

Fred Root was shot in the chest while serving as a dispatch-rider in the First World War, but he lived to become a leading exponent of right-arm, leg-theory bowling and a master of spin. Powerful and enduring in physique, he was contemptuous of adversity and pettiness, being himself a cheerful toiler. He delivered his in-swinger at a brisk medium pace, the ball dipping in at the toes unpleasantly late, and he had a complement of close leg-fielders. As a batsman, he loved to drive high and hard, and his defence was solid enough in a rough sort of way. He started first-class cricket with Derbyshire, where a familiar scoreboard line would be the suitably agricultural 'c Beet b Root', but he earned most of his fame with Worcestershire after the War. From 1923 until 1931 he took more than 100 wickets in every season, and in 1925 his haul was 219 wickets (17.21), a county record. Three times he took 9 wickets in an innings, including 9 for 23 against Lancashire at Worcester in 1931. In 1928 he achieved the double. He toured the West Indies in 1925/6 and coached in South Africa, but his only Tests were against Australia in 1926. In retirement he played Lancashire League cricket for Todmorden. He became a journalist and his book, *A Cricket Pro's Lot*, expresses admirably the view of the professional then.

First-class career (1910-33): 7,911 runs (14.73) including 1 century, 1,512 wickets (21.11) and 243 catches
Test matches (3): Did not bat, 8 wickets (24.25) and 1 catch

ROSE, Brian Charles (b.1950)

Somerset

A tall, fair-haired, left-handed batsman and product of Millfield school, Brian Rose is likely to be remembered as the man who captained Somerset to their first wins in any major competitions: the Gillette Cup and John Player League in 1979. He first led the county in 1978 after playing his first Test cricket the previous winter on the England tour of Pakistan and New Zealand. Although he scored a century in both countries, he scored few runs in the five Tests in which he played. Lacking in neither courage nor application, he is at his best an attractive batsman with a pleasant, leaning, straight drive and a savage square-cut. A charming, rather dozy character, he is a captain who is popular both with opponents and with his own team, although he created a furore in 1979 by declaring the Somerset innings after one over to take advantage of a technicality in the rules of the Benson and Hedges Cup. Somerset were expelled from the competition but Rose was soon forgiven. His finest hour as a Test player came against the powerful West Indies attack of 1980 when, returning to England's team at Old

Trafford, he hit a dashing 70 out of England's first-innings total of 150. He finished this series with 243 runs from six innings at an average of 48.60, but in the West Indies the following winter he could find no form, returning early with an eye defect. He later batted in glasses.

First-class career (1969-): 11,156 runs (33.80) including 22 centuries, 6 wickets (36.33) and 111 catches
Test matches (9): 358 runs (25.57) and 4 catches

ROYLE, Rev. Vernon Peter Fanshawe Archer (1854-1929)

Oxford University and Lancashire

Brilliant fielding at cover-point brought Vernon Royle his fame; he was ambidextrous, very quick on his feet and in return. 'Woa, mate, there's a policeman,' called out Tom Emmett to his batting partner in a 'Roses' match as Royle pounced on a shot in the cover. Just above average height, he was a right-handed batsman who got well over the ball, often hit powerfully and scored quickly. As a slow change-bowler, he helped Oxford to win the University match of 1875. He toured Australia with Lord Harris's team in 1878/9, and in his sole Test at Melbourne he scored 3 and 18, took 0 for 6 and held 2 catches.

First-class career (1873-91): 2,298 runs (15.64)

RUMSEY, Frederick Edward (b.1935)

Worcestershire, Somerset and Derbyshire

Fred Rumsey was a large and enthusiastic left-arm fast bowler with a long run and a comfortable figure. He had two seasons with Worcestershire and, in his first full season for Somerset in 1963, took over 100 wickets and was prominent in what was then the county's most successful season. Against Nottinghamshire at Taunton he took 13 for 104. His best year, 1965, saw him take 119 wickets (16.18), but he left the county after 1968 to become Derbyshire's Public Relations Officer and for five years he appeared mainly in limited-over matches. He played for England against Australia at Old Trafford in 1964 and in four more Tests against South Africa and New Zealand in 1965.

First-class career (1960-70): 1,015 runs (8.45) and 580 wickets (20.29)
Test matches (5): 30 runs (15.00) and 17 wickets (27.11)

RUSSELL, Charles Albert George (1887-1961)

Essex

Born within a stone's throw of the Leyton ground, Charles Russell or 'Jack' was a master of on-side strokes. Although not specially attractive to watch, he became, soon after the First World War, one of the most dependable batsmen in the country. From 1919 until his retirement he never failed to reach 1,000 runs in a season, five times exceeding 2,000. His best year was 1922 when he was the most prolific batsman in England, scoring 2,575 runs (54.78), with 9 centuries, including 273 against Northamptonshire at Leyton. On tour with MCC in Australia, 1920/21, he made 135 not out and 59 in the third Test at Adelaide (on the same ground he also made 156 and 201 against South Australia). In his first Tests in England, at Old Trafford and The Oval in 1921, he made 101 in the first and 13 and 102 not out in the second. On tour with MCC in South Africa, 1922/3, he made 9 and 96 in the fourth Test at Johannesburg and 140 and 111 in the fifth at Durban, the first time an English batsman had made two centuries in the same Test. A tree was planted to commemorate this feat. Remarkably, he was battling illness at the time and he played no further Test cricket. He was also one of the best slips of his time and a useful change-bowler.

First-class career (1908-30): 27,546 runs (41.73) including 71 centuries, 285 wickets (27.17) and 292 catches
Test matches (10): 910 runs (56.87) including 5 centuries, and 8 catches

RUSSELL, William Eric (b.1936)

Middlesex and Berkshire

Eric Russell was the natural successor to Jack Robertson as Middlesex opener: a similarly modest man and often an equally handsome player. His right-handed, off-side hitting off either foot and his leg-glancing were, for a decade, among the delights of the game. In thirteen seasons he exceeded 1,000 runs, with 2,342 runs (45.92) in 1964. With 'Pasty' Harris he put on 312 for the first wicket against the Pakistanis at Lord's in 1967, which was a county record. His major tours were to India and Pakistan in 1961/2, and Australia and New Zealand in 1965/6, when he played many fine innings, and in the mid-sixties he represented England against South Africa, West Indies and Pakistan at home.

First-class career (1956-72): 25,525 runs (34.87) including 41 centuries, 22 wickets (45.14) and 304 catches
Test matches (10): 362 runs (21.29), 0-44 and 4 catches

SANDHAM, Andrew (1890-1982)

Surrey

Andy Sandham was the first batsman ever to make a triple century in a Test, 325 for England against the

Andy Sandham – George Duckworth keeping wicket

West Indies at Kingston, 1929/30. He was a skilful opening batsman, small, neat, assured, a strong cutter and hooker, and deft deflector. Overshadowed by his county partner, Jack Hobbs, he was unlucky that Herbert Sutcliffe was also available to open for England. A self-effacing character who, paradoxically, drew attention to himself when batting, he shared in an opening stand of 428 with Jack Hobbs against Oxford University at The Oval in 1926, the highest ever for Surrey's first wicket, and one of sixty-six century stands he shared with Hobbs. Twenty times (twice overseas) he exceeded 1,000 runs in a season, eight times exceeding 2,000 between 1921 and 1931. Besides his visit to the West Indies, he toured South Africa, 1922/3 and 1930/31, and Australia, 1924/5, and represented England at home against Australia once in 1921, and South Africa twice in 1924. He was also a fine outfield.

First-class career (1911-37): 41,284 runs (44.82) including 107 centuries, and 18 wickets (26.44)
Test matches (14): 879 runs (38.21) including 2 centuries, and 4 catches

SCHULTZ (later STOREY), Sandford Spence (1857-1937)

Cambridge University and Lancashire

A Cambridge blue who played occasionally for Lancashire, Schultz was more prominent in club cricket as a fast, round-arm bowler, good batsman and smart slip. A member of Lord Harris's team to Australia in 1878/9, he batted last, scoring 0 not out and 20, and taking 1 for 26 in his sole Test at Melbourne – but he helped to avert an innings defeat. As his German name 'Schultz' offended, he changed it to 'Storey'.

First-class career (1876-84): 1,012 runs (16.59) and 15 wickets (51.13)

SCOTTON, William Henry (1856-93)

Nottinghamshire

From 1884 until 1886 he was the best – or certainly the most successful – professional left-handed batsman in England, and he was an accomplished outfield. Few have ever played with so straight a bat or possessed such a strong defence but, as *Wisden* said, 'he carried caution to such extremes that it was often impossible to take any pleasure in seeing him play'. His finest hour – or rather five and three quarter hours – was in the Oval Test in 1884. England's batsmen had faltered, confronted by a large Australian total, but Scotton, going in first, was ninth out for 90, a great chanceless defensive innings, adding 151 with the more dashing Walter Read for the ninth wicket, which made a respectable England total possible. Again, in the Oval Test of 1886, Scotton with W.G. put on 170 for the first wicket, taking about four hours over 34. The stand was immortalized in verse in *Punch*. Scotton visited Australia three times in the 1880s. He killed himself in a fit of depression due to domestic troubles and to losing his place in the Nottinghamshire eleven.

First-class career (1875-91): 6,527 runs (18.97) including 4 centuries, and 120 catches
Test matches (15): 510 runs (22.17), 0-20 and 4 catches

SELBY, John (1849-94)

Nottinghamshire

A first-rate right-handed batsman, especially on difficult wickets, Selby was at his best just before the Test era, although he appeared in the first two matches at Melbourne in 1876/7 with James Lillywhite's England eleven, and top-scored with 38 in the second innings of the first Test. He revisited Australia in 1881/2, with Shaw's and Shrewsbury's side, but came home under a cloud, and never represented England again. There is some evidence that he misbehaved with his colleague's, W.H. Scotton's, wife. 'It is probable', said *Wisden*, 'that the stroke of paralysis which ended his life was partially due to a criminal charge . . . of which he was acquitted.'

First-class career (1870-87): 6,215 runs (18.83) including 4 centuries, 12 catches and 4 stumpings
Test matches (6): 256 runs (23.27) and 1 catch

SELVEY, Michael Walter William (b.1948)

Cambridge University, Surrey, Middlesex, Glamorgan and Orange Free State

A dark, hirsute, hostile and immensely strong, fast-medium bowler, Mike Selvey has developed from modest beginnings with Cambridge and Surrey into one of the most consistent opening bowlers in England. Able to swing the ball both ways in the air, he often gets a waspish pace and bounce off the pitch: a horrible man to face on a moist and cloudy morning at Lord's. He had a sensational start to his Test career: because of injuries to numerous other fast bowlers he was called up at the eleventh hour to play at Old Trafford against the immensely gifted West Indian team of 1976, and proceeded to dismiss Fredericks, Richards and Kallicharran with his first twenty balls, finishing with 4 for 41. He toured India the following winter and bowled well without doing enough to earn more than one further Test cap. A safe, but by modern standards, ponderous fielder, he plays with a straight bat and has made some useful scores. He became captain of Glamorgan in 1983. He is an intense and intelligent man who cares deeply about social problems.

First-class career (1968-): 2,044 runs (12.85) and 685 wickets (25.66)
Test matches (3): 15 runs (7.50), 6 wickets (57.16) and 1 catch

SHACKLETON, Derek (b.1924)

Hampshire and Dorset

A model professional, Derek Shackleton or 'Shack' was an apparently tireless right-arm stock bowler of uncanny accuracy who could both swing the ball in at medium pace and get it to leave the bat late. As a young player he was a batsman who could bowl erratic leg-spinners. But Hampshire were short of seam bowlers and Shackleton became, for two decades, an awesome phenomenon of modern cricket, bowling 1,500 overs or so annually as though he were playing them on the pianola. Slim, trim and immaculate, his action was light and easy. In his fortieth year (according to his captain, Desmond Eagar) he actually bowled a long-hop. In 1955, against Somerset at Weston-super-Mare, he took 14 for 29, including figures of 8 for 4 in the first innings. Twenty times consecutively he took more than 100 wickets in a season, a record, and no one has captured more wickets for Hampshire – 2,669. Only Wilfred Rhodes has taken 100 wickets in more seasons. He took 9 wickets in an innings on four occasions and 10 or more in a match thirty-eight times. 'Shack' never represented England against Australia. However, he toured India in 1951/2, and appeared occasionally against South Africa and the West Indies at home. As a right-handed batsman, he added many runs when some of the acknowledged batsmen failed. His son, Julian, has played for Gloucestershire. A modest, friendly man, he became coach at Canford School and from 1979 to 1981 a first-class umpire.

First-class career (1948-69): 9,561 runs (14.69), 2,857 wickets (18.65) and 223 catches
Test matches (7): 113 runs (18.83), 18 wickets (42.66) and 1 catch

Derek Shackleton

SHARP, John (1878-1938)

Lancashire

Short and thickset, Jack Sharp was a right-handed batsman who scored freely with hard, punching off-drives and powerful cuts and pulls. A good fast-medium bowler, he was also a brilliant field at cover-point. Ten times he exceeded 1,000 runs in a season and once – in 1901, a batsman's year – took more than 100 wickets. But against Australia at The Oval in 1909 he was chosen primarily as a fast bowler on a wicket hard and true. He took 3 good wickets and scored 105. He appeared in two other Tests that year. He also played soccer for Everton and England. Becoming an amateur cricketer, he captained Lancashire from 1923 until 1925, and was an England selector.

First-class career (1899-1925): 22,715 runs (31.11) including 38 centuries, 440 wickets (27.46) and 223 catches
Test matches (3): 188 runs (47.00) including 1 century, 3 wickets (37.00) and 1 catch

SHARPE, John William (1866-1936)

Nottinghamshire and Surrey

'One-eyed' Sharpe – he had lost an eye while a youth – came to Surrey as there was no room for him in his native Nottinghamshire eleven. His right-arm, fast-medium bowling, with its remarkable break from the off and extra fast yorker, earned him two great seasons – 1890 (139 wickets) and 1891 (108 wickets) – with the Champion county. After his tour of Australia, however, with Lord Sheffield's team, 1891/2, his talent evaporated as suddenly as it had developed. He returned to Nottinghamshire but, after a handful of matches, he was dropped. Of slight build, he had tried to bowl too fast, and had consequently worn himself out very quickly. He was an excellent field, with a good throw.

First-class career (1889-94): 657 runs (8.53) and 338 wickets (16.06)
Test matches (3): 44 runs (22.00), 11 wickets (27.72) and 2 catches

SHARPE, Philip John (b.1936)

Yorkshire, Derbyshire and Norfolk

A cheerful, stocky, right-hand batsman renowned for his skill at hockey, cards, Gilbert and Sullivan performances and witty repartee, Philip Sharpe was one of those players who was more impressive as a Test batsman than he was at county level. His outstanding claim to fame is as one of the greatest of all slip fielders, one amazing catch very close to the stumps off a full blooded slash by Joey Carew of the West Indies at Old Trafford in 1969 living ineradicably in the memory. Sharpe's reactions were as his name and he so often got two sure hands to chances which others might have dived for in vain. His batting was full of enterprise: a good cover-driver, he was a particularly good hooker and cutter and many of his best innings for England were against the fast bowlers of the West Indies sides of 1963 and 1969. His defence was less impressive, hence perhaps his somewhat unpredictable form for Yorkshire. A brilliant boy cricketer at Worksop, he was capped by Yorkshire in 1960 and toured India with MCC in 1963/4. He passed 1,000 runs in a season twelve times. He moved to Derbyshire for two seasons in 1975, hitting his highest score, 228, against Oxford University in his final season and also pleasing himself with a fine 126 against his old county colleagues. He then played minor county cricket for Norfolk for two more seasons.

First-class career (1956-76): 22,530 runs (30.73) including 29 centuries, and 616 catches
Test matches (12): 786 runs (46.23) including 1 century, and 17 catches

SHAW, Alfred (1842-1907)

Nottinghamshire and Sussex

In old portraits Alfred Shaw looked the epitome of Victorian uncles: grave, portly, benign, a small cap perched on the top of rather a large head and a short avuncular beard round his chin. He was *the* master of right-arm, slow-medium, good length bowling. He never delivered a wide in his life and in a long career bowled more overs than he had runs hit off them (25,699 overs and 5 balls, 24,873 runs). Nine times between 1870 and 1880 he took 100 wickets or more in a season; 1878 brought him 202 wickets (10.88) and his 186 wickets in 1880 cost only 8.54 runs each. He and Arthur Shrewsbury were the prime movers of a strike by the Nottinghamshire professionals against the county's committee; but in 1882 he was appointed county captain and, in the five years of his leadership, the county finished top of the Championship each time. He was shrewd, honest, obliging and acquisitive. He toured Australia with James Lillywhite's team, 1876/7, captured 198 wickets (3.95) in all matches and appeared in the first Tests at Melbourne, taking 3 for 51 and 5 for 38 in 89.3 overs in the inaugural match. Later, he took three teams out to Australia as business ventures with either Lillywhite or Shrewsbury, though overall the ventures were financial failures. He appeared in the first Test in England at The Oval,

Alfred Shaw

1880. He visited America with Edgar Willsher's side of 1868, and Richard Daft's of 1879. On the latter tour he was phenomenal, taking 178 wickets at the absurd average of 2.70. With his patron, Lord Sheffield, Shaw continued to tour the world, even playing cricket by the light of the midnight sun on the Ice Fiord at Spitzbergen. His professional connection with the game lasted more than forty years, latterly as Sussex coach and a first-class umpire; at fifty-three he appeared for the weak Sussex side with some success.

First-class career (1864-97): 6,585 runs (12.83), 2,021 wickets (12.11) and 364 catches
Test matches (7): 111 runs (10.09), 12 wickets (23.75) and 4 catches

SHEPPARD, Rt Rev. David Stuart (b.1929)

Cambridge University and Sussex

As a schoolboy at Sherborne, David Sheppard was a relatively modest batsman but mental tenacity drove him to the top. A tall, right-hand batsman he possessed many graceful off-side shots and limitless power of concentration, and became a leading figure in what one might term the 'Cambridge Movement' of the early 1950s. He shared opening partnerships with John Dewes of 343 against the West Indies at Fenner's and 349 against Sussex at Hove in 1950, both records. From 1951 to 1953 he scored 24 centuries, each season exceeding 2,000 runs. In 1952, as Cambridge captain, he hit 127 in the University match and topped the national first-class averages with 2,262 runs (64.62), including his career-highest, 239 not out for Cambridge at Worcester. Captain of Sussex in 1953, he was firm but kind and steered his team to second place in the Championship. He was selected for England in the final Test against the West Indies at The Oval in 1950, and toured Australia with MCC in 1950/51, but was disappointing. Against India at The Oval in 1952, he scored 119; and he led England in two Tests against Pakistan in 1954. In 1956, now ordained to the ministry of the Church of England, he was recalled for the fourth Test against Australia at Old Trafford and hit a memorable 113. He was the first ordained minister to play in Test cricket. Inevitably, his appearances in first-class cricket became fewer, but in 1962 he made a 100 at Lord's in the last Gentlemen versus Players match, and that winter toured Australasia again, his 113 at Melbourne in the third Test contributing to England's only victory in the series. He made 1,074 runs (38.35) on the tour. One or two unfortunate dropped catches, however, led to Fred Trueman's affectionate jibe: 'It's a pity Reverend don't put his hands together more often in t'field.' Now Bishop of Liverpool, David Sheppard was an inspiring organizer of the Mayflower Centre in London and it would surprise few if he were one day to become Archbishop of Canterbury.

First-class career (1947-63): 15,838 runs (43.51) including 45 centuries
Test matches (22): 1,172 runs (37.80) including 3 centuries, and 12 catches

SHERWIN, Mordecai (1851-1910)

Nottinghamshire

Less than 5ft 10ins tall but weighing around 17st., Mordecai Sherwin was jocular, physically powerful and very hard-working. A surprisingly agile wicket-keeper, whose fleshy hands did not often suffer damage behind the stumps, he was quoted as saying: 'O'm not much with my pen myself, but Oi'd loike to bung my fist into the face of anyone wot says aught be wrong with my stumping.' He was the last of the old-time professionals of the county (1887 and 1888), and an ardent but unsuccessful Conservative candidate in Nottingham Municipal elections. For Players against Gentlemen at Lord's in 1888 he dismissed 5 batsmen in an innings; and represented England for the only time against Australia at home that year. In 1886/7 he toured 'down under' with Shaw and Shrewsbury's team. He also kept goal for Notts County for many years.

First-class career (1876-96): 2,339 runs (7.61) and 834 dismissals (607 ct, 227 st.)
Test matches (3): 30 runs (15.00) and 7 dismissals (5 ct, 2 st.)

SHREWSBURY, Arthur (1856-1903)

Nottinghamshire

In the 1880s and 1890s Arthur Shrewsbury held a position of honour in the cricket world similar to that held by Jack Hobbs thirty to forty years later. He stood head and shoulders above his fellow-professionals in

David Sheppard – Arthur McIntyre keeping wicket

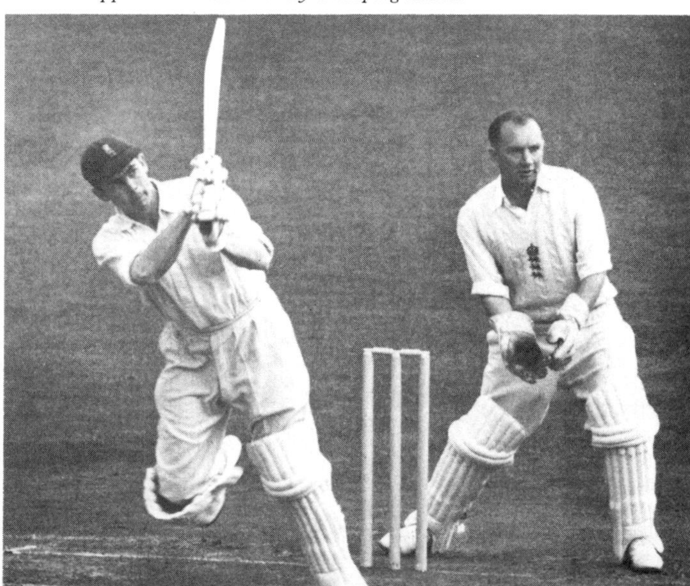

Arthur Shrewsbury

artistry and attainments on the field and second to none in the respect which his personal character had gained. He was one of the first right-handed batsmen to develop an impregnable quality in defence and combine it with powers of steady scoring. 'Bring me out a cup of tea at four o'clock,' he would say to the Trent Bridge pavilion attendant, in days before the interval was introduced, and he was generally still in when the time for his favourite beverage came round. When W.G. picked a Test team, Arthur was always his first choice – 'Give me Arthur' has gone down in cricket lore. Sound rather than spectacular, he was a perfectionist, wanting every stroke to be played precisely right. Many of his finest innings were played on treacherous wickets, when he would go right forward, or right back to play the ball as late as possible. He was an excellent field either in the deep or, latterly, at point. A precise man, neat as a new pin, he was completely bald, but it was a joke among his colleagues that nobody had ever seen the top of his head. On the field he wore his cap, off it a neat bowler hat, and in bed a nightcap! Thirteen times he exceeded 1,000 runs in a season, his best year being 1887, when he made 1,653 runs (78.71), including 8 centuries and headed the national averages. He hit no fewer than 10 double centuries, his highest being 267 for Nottinghamshire against Middlesex in 1887, and the same score against Sussex in 1890, both at Trent Bridge. He carried his bat through an innings nine times. Shrewsbury visited Australia with four teams in the 1880s, three times in partnership with Alfred Shaw, and also took a football team there. He played many fine Test innings. At Sydney in 1881/2 he top-scored each time with 82 and 47 in a losing contest. He made 164, a dominant innings, at Lord's in 1886 and in his last series in 1893 he made 106 and 81 at Lord's and 66 at The Oval. He shot himself through the mouth because he believed he was suffering from an incurable disease.

First-class career (1875-1902): 26,439 runs (36.66) including 59 centuries, and 317 catches
Test matches (23): 1,277 runs (35.47) including 3 centuries, 0-2 and 29 catches

SHUTER, John (1855-1920)

Kent and Surrey

A short man – 5ft 6ins – who did not care for averages or personal glory, John Shuter led Surrey from 1880 until 1893 and during the last seven seasons the county won the Championship five times and tied once. He was a popular leader and a singularly graceful right-handed batsman, with remarkable power on the off-side. He represented England once against Australia, at The Oval in 1888, scoring 28. On retiring from the Surrey captaincy he received, as a testimonial, a grand piano and a brace of pistols. Shortly before his death he had been appointed secretary to Surrey.

First-class career (1874-1909): 10,206 runs (21.26) including 8 centuries

SHUTTLEWORTH, Kenneth (b.1944)

Lancashire and Leicestershire

A dark and well-built fast bowler with an action surely modelled on Fred Trueman's, Ken Shuttleworth has been restricted by injuries throughout a career which has never quite taken off as it might have done. At the brief peak of his powers he was distinctly quick with a dangerous out-swing, flowing from a fine action with long, final stride and sideways-on delivery. Also a capable batsman, he first played for Lancashire, a county with considerable fast bowling talent, in 1964, but did not establish himself until 1968. In 1970 he played an unofficial Test for England against the Rest of the World and was an important member of Illingworth's successful MCC side in Australia the following winter, taking 5 for 47 in the first Test at the Gabba ground in Brisbane. His best Championship performance is 7 for 41 for Lancashire against Essex in 1968. Lancashire grew tired of his persistent misfortune with injuries but he had his successes for Leicestershire after 1977.

First-class career (1964-80): 2,589 runs (16.80), 623 wickets (24.32) and 128 catches
Test matches (5): 46 runs (7.66), 12 wickets (35.58) and 1 catch

Reg Simpson

SIMPSON, Reginald Thomas (b.1920)

Sind and Nottinghamshire

Making his debut in first-class cricket in India, 1944/5, while serving with the RAF, Reg Simpson was already a well-equipped, right-handed batsman when he first played for Nottinghamshire in 1946. An opener, he was tall and slim with short, curly dark hair. Possessing a neat, upright stance, he was a beautiful striker of the ball and a good player off the back foot, who had less trouble than most with the bouncer. He fielded superbly, usually at cover or in the deep. On fourteen occasions he exceeded 1,000 runs in a season (once overseas), and scored over 2,500 runs in both 1949 and 1950. At one period in 1949 Reg Simpson and Walter Keeton shared four successive century opening partnerships for Notts. From 1951 until 1960 he captained the county. He shared the record first-wicket partnerships for England against New Zealand with Len Hutton – 147 at The Oval in 1949 – and against the West Indies with Cyril Washbrook – 212 at Trent Bridge in 1950. His most memorable innings, however, was 156 not out in the fifth Test at Melbourne in 1950/51, which was a major factor in England's first win over Australia for thirteen years. He toured Australia twice, New Zealand and South Africa, and represented England against all the Test-playing countries at home but never fully established himself at the highest level. He is now a director of Gunn and Moore Ltd and a shrewd observer of modern batting techniques.

First-class career (1944-63): 30,546 runs (38.32) including 64 centuries, 59 wickets (37.74) and 189 catches
Test matches (27): 1,401 runs (33.35) including 4 centuries, 2 wickets (11.00) and 5 catches

SIMPSON-HAYWARD, George Hayward Thomas (1875-1936)

Cambridge University and Worcestershire

George Simpson-Hayward was the last and one of the most successful lob-bowlers to represent England. He was very effective on the matting with H.D.G. Leveson-Gower's team in South Africa, 1909/10, which was his third, and only major, MCC tour. In 1909 he had taken 6 for 132 (in a total of 289) and top-scored when Worcestershire played the Australians; but he did not play for England at home.

First-class career (1899-1914): 5,582 runs (18.55) including 3 centuries, and 510 wickets (21.46)
Test matches (5): 105 runs (15.00), 23 wickets (18.26) and 1 catch

SIMS, James Morton (1903-73)

Middlesex

Jim Sims was lank, solemn and lugubrious in the style of Alfred Lester, a master of understatement and a lively humorist, centre of many stories and a lovable character who spoke out of the side of his mouth. Starting in first-class cricket as a right-handed batsman, he developed more as an unusually consistent leg-break bowler with a tricky googly. He took all 10 for 90 in an innings for East against West at Kingston in 1948, and on eight occasions took more than 100 wickets in a season. As a lower-order batsman, he was sometimes invaluable. He toured Australia with MCC's 'goodwill' side of 1935/6 and the full side in 1936/7, and represented England at home against South Africa and India, his best performance being 7 wickets in the match against India at The Oval in 1936. In retirement he became county scorer and died during a match at Canterbury.

First-class career (1929-53): 8,984 runs (17.31) including 4 centuries, 1,581 wickets (24.92) and 253 catches
Test matches (4): 16 runs (4.00), 11 wickets (43.63) and 6 catches

SINFIELD, Reginald Albert (b.1900)

Hertfordshire and Gloucestershire

Year after year, Reg Sinfield served Gloucestershire with his mild-looking but persistent slow-medium, right-arm bowling and his obstinate and defensive batting, generally as an opener. Sometimes, however, he would attack to great effect. Ten times he exceeded 1,000 runs in a season and four times 100 wickets; twice he achieved the double. In 1938 in his sole Test, against Australia at Trent Bridge, he scored 6 and took 2 for 123. On retirement he became coach at Clifton.

First-class career (1921-39): 15,674 runs (25.69) including 16 centuries, 1,173 wickets (24.49) and 178 catches

SMAILES, Thomas Francis (1910-70)

Yorkshire

Frank Smailes was a right-arm, fast-medium bowler who could make the ball move either way. He was also capable of bowling useful off-breaks at slower speed and he was a hard-hitting, late-order, left-handed batsman. In the powerful Yorkshire side of the thirties – seven times Champions – he took more than 100 wickets in a season four times and once reached 1,000 runs. In 1939 he captured all 10 for 47 in an innings against Derbyshire at Bramall Lane and he took 6 for 29 and 4 for 45 at Bramall Lane when his county nearly defeated the 1938 Australians; but his sole Test was against India at Lord's in 1946, when he scored 25 and took 3 for 62. He was picked in England's squad of 13 for the 1938 Manchester Test, which never started because of rain.

First-class career (1932-48): 5,892 runs (19.25) including 3 centuries, 823 wickets (20.77) and 154 catches

SMITH, Alan Christopher (b.1936)

Oxford University and Warwickshire

Three years in the Oxford University side and captain for two, Alan Smith or 'A.C.' was a 'complete cricketer'. He was a sound right-handed batsman always on the lookout for runs, a medium-pace bowler with an extraordinary knock-kneed run and a windmill action, and a top-class wicket-keeper. In 1962 he scored 1,201 runs (31.60) and had 82 dismissals (79 ct, 3 st.) and in the following winter was first-choice 'keeper for England in Australia and New Zealand, as well as sharing in the second partnership of 163 unbroken for the ninth wicket with Colin Cowdrey against New Zealand at Wellington. He hit two centuries for Oxford against Hampshire at Bournemouth in 1959, held 6 catches in one innings against Derbyshire at Derby in 1970 and, on taking off his pads and going on to bowl against Essex at Clacton in 1965, he took a hat-trick. He was a keen, indeed hostile, captain who believed completely in himself and he led his county from 1968 until 1974, winning the Championship in 1972. He also had a flair for one-day cricket, and led Warwickshire to victory in the Gillette Cup in his first year as captain. Now secretary of Warwickshire, he has been a director of Aston Villa F.C., a Test selector, assistant manager of the MCC touring team to Australia in 1974/5, and manager of England in the West Indies in 1980/81. This was a tour fraught with problems, but so well did he overcome them that he was publicly praised by the TCCB.

First-class career (1958-75): 11,027 runs (20.92) including 3 centuries, 131 wickets (23.46) and 776 dismissals (715 ct, 61 st.)

Test matches (6): 118 runs (29.50) and 20 dismissals (20 ct)

SMITH, Sir Charles Aubrey (1863-1948)

Cambridge University, Sussex and Transvaal

As well known in Hollywood as he was at Lord's, Aubrey Smith was an old Carthusian and a Cambridge blue who appeared four times in the University match. Over six feet tall, he was primarily a right-arm, fast-medium bowler whose sobriquet was 'Round the Corner', because he approached the wicket on a parabolic curve. He had a high action and persistent accuracy, cutting the ball in from the off. He was also a long-reaching batsman of both vigilance and power and excellent at slip. He played for Sussex for thirteen years, as captain in 1887, 1888 and 1890. Against Cambridge at Fenner's in 1885 he took 5 for 8 and, five years later, 7 for 16 against MCC at Lord's. He toured Australia in 1887/8 and in 1888/9 he captained the first team (Major Warton's) to visit South Africa. In the first Test (his sole Test appearance) he scored 3 and took 5 for 19 and 2 for 42, thus playing a considerable part in England's victory. He remained in South Africa, stockbroking in Johannesburg for some years and played in the first Currie Cup tournament. Returning to London, he made his debut on the London stage in 1896, and in the 1920s went to Hollywood, where in many films he typified the English gentleman – as he did in life. He became a one-man MCC in Hollywood, cricket in California revolving around him; he revitalized the game in the USA. His house at Beverly Hills was called 'The Round Corner'. He was knighted for his services to Anglo-American friendship and came to Lord's as often as he could to watch Test cricket.

First-class career (1882-96): 2,715 runs (13.37) including 1 century, and 312 wickets (23.56)

SMITH, Cedric Ivan James (1906-79)

Wiltshire and Middlesex

At 6ft 4ins 'Big Jim' Smith was a burly man, who bowled fast and hit faster. A right-arm bowler he had stamina and a good action made his deliveries lift, swing and cut. In his first season for Middlesex in 1934 he took 172 wickets (18.88), and in six brief seasons for the county alone secured 676 wickets (17.75). His reputation as a smiter was richly deserved, and he was a great favourite at Lord's and elsewhere. He was as if 'hewn out of English oak', the personification of the village blacksmith. The violence of his favourite stroke between square-leg and mid-on was terrifying; at Lord's his hits would take the ball into the 'Q' stand, or over the Tavern into St John's Wood. Against Gloucestershire at Bristol in 1938 he hit 50 not out in eleven minutes (66 in eighteen minutes), against Kent at Maidstone in 1935, 50 not out in fourteen minutes; and his sole century, also against Kent at Canterbury, took eighty-one minutes. He appeared in one home Test against New Zealand in 1937, and toured the

West Indies with MCC in 1934/5. At Bridgetown he took 5 for 15, enabling England to win her only match of the series.

First-class career (1930-9): 4,007 runs (14.68) including 1 century, and 845 wickets (19.25)
Test matches (5): 102 runs (10.20), 15 wickets (26.20) and 1 catch

SMITH, David Robert (b.1934)

Gloucestershire

David Smith was a right-arm, medium-fast bowler with a very short run-up, whose pace was often considerably quicker than the batsman expected. Able to move the ball both ways, he was also able to maintain accuracy for long periods. He tended to be over-worked; in 1960, a rather wet season, he bowled not only 500 overs more than any of his colleagues, but more overs than any Gloucestershire seam bowler since 1945. Moreover, he captured more wickets in a season, 143, than any other seam bowler since that time. He was a useful tail-end batsman and, as befitted a professional footballer with Bristol City and Millwall, a reliable field. He toured India with MCC in 1961/2 and did a useful job in the Tests on wickets totally unsuited to his style.

First-class career (1956-70): 4,970 runs (12.30), 1,250 wickets (23.72) and 290 catches
Test matches (5): 38 runs (9.50), 6 wickets (59.83) and 2 catches

SMITH, Denis (1907-79)

Derbyshire

A left-hander, Denis Smith became one of the most aggressive, stylish and successful batsmen in Derbyshire's history. At his best around the mid-thirties, he headed the batting averages with 42.42 when the county finished second in the Championship Table in 1935, and he was very prominent when they won the Championship for the first time in modern history the following year. His catching close to the wicket was invaluable throughout and he was a good deputy 'keeper. In 1935 he played two Tests against South Africa, in his first, at Headingley, putting on 128 for the first wicket with Arthur Mitchell. That winter he averaged 47.40 for MCC in the 'goodwill' tour of Australasia. He remained a county bulwark for many years, although no further Test honours came his way and on retirement he became county coach. He scored more than 1,000 runs in a season twelve times.

First-class career (1927-52): 21,843 runs (31.65) including 32 centuries, 20 wickets (36.70), 378 catches and 5 stumpings
Test matches (2): 128 runs (32.00) and 1 catch

SMITH, Donald Victor (b.1923)

Sussex

Donald Smith spent several seasons when he was unable to consolidate himself in the Sussex side, but he suddenly found his form and runs flowed thereafter with great regularity. A left-handed opener, he struck 166 in less than three hours at Hove in 1957, an innings of electrifying brilliance, in which he hit 9 sixes and 11 fours, winning the match unexpectedly against Gloucestershire. That season he scored 2,088 runs (42.61), playing in three Tests against the West Indies, although with scant success. He passed 1,000 runs in a season eight times with a highest score of 206 not out against Nottinghamshire at Trent Bridge in 1950. A useful left-arm medium-pace bowler, he took 7 for 40 for MCC against Oxford University at Lord's in 1956, including a hat-trick.

First-class career (1946-62): 16,960 runs (30.34) including 19 centuries, 340 wickets (28.44) and 232 catches
Test matches (3): 25 runs (8.33) and 1-97

SMITH, Ernest James (1886-1979)

Warwickshire

For many years the oldest-living Test cricketer, 'Tiger' Smith was the doyen of Edgbaston. He was wicket-keeper/batsman in 1911, when the county won the Championship for the first time, and he soon became England's 'keeper, standing up to the waspish bowling of Sydney Barnes and Frank Foster. In 1926 he dismissed 7 batsmen in an innings (4 caught and 3 stumped) against Derbyshire at Edgbaston and, overall, his record is similar to that of his predecessor and mentor, Dick Lilley. A fine, confident, right-handed batsman, he opened the county's batting for many years, six times exceeding 1,000 runs in a season. He toured Australia in 1911/12 and South Africa in 1913/14, and represented England at home in 1912. He became a Test umpire and a much respected Warwickshire coach. For many years after retirement he would sit in the Edgbaston pavilion, telling cricket stories or demonstrating batting techniques.

First-class career (1904-30): 16,997 runs (22.39) including 20 centuries, and 878 dismissals (722 ct, 156 st.)
Test matches (11): 113 runs (8.69) and 20 dismissals (17 ct, 3 st.)

SMITH, Harry (1890-1937)

Gloucestershire

As a Bristol colt before the First World War, Harry Smith was asked to go behind the stumps in an emergency – and he blossomed as a consistently reliable 'keeper, besides being a sound batsman. His best work was in 1927 when in four consecutive innings he allowed only one bye while 1,374 runs were scored; and the following year he kept for England in the first match – his sole Test – against the West Indies at Lord's, scoring 7 and holding 1 catch.

First-class career (1912-35): 13,413 runs (22.35) including 10 centuries, and 722 dismissals (457 ct, 265 st.)

SMITH, Michael John Knight (b.1933)

Oxford University, Leicestershire and Warwickshire

Mike Smith was a modest but prolific and universally popular cricketer better known perhaps by his initials 'M.J.K.' He always played in spectacles. He had three memorable years at Oxford – captain in his last year in 1956 – hitting 201 not out, 104 and 117 against Cambridge in successive seasons at Lord's. His number of centuries and aggregate for these matches, 477, are records. A tall right-hander with great powers of improvisation and concentration he was always a prolific run-scorer, difficult to bowl to and especially punishing to the on-side where he unerringly found gaps. Once, batting for Warwickshire and going well, he expressed his concern to his partner, Ray Hitchcock, that the latter was getting bogged down. 'I don't seem to be able to find any gaps for the singles,' Ray complained. 'Well, chip them for threes instead,' Smith replied. To him this was no problem. He captained Warwickshire from 1957 until 1967, and in six consecutive seasons (1957-62) exceeded 2,000 runs each time, with 3,245 runs (57.94) in 1959. Twenty times he exceeded 1,000 runs in a season (once overseas). A brilliant short-leg field, he held 52 catches in 1961. He retired after 1967, but returned in 1970 to play regularly for another six seasons and was recalled for England against Australia in 1972. Taking longer to play himself in than most top-class players, he was particularly susceptible to the yorker early on in an innings. He toured Australia, South Africa, the West Indies, New Zealand, India and Pakistan, captaining England in 25 Tests. Three times he was dismissed in the nineties but perhaps the best of his three Test centuries was 108 in the second Test against the West Indies at Port of Spain in 1959/60. A double blue and double international, he played Rugby once for England at fly-half against Wales.

First-class career (1951-75): 39,832 runs (41.84) including 69 centuries, and 593 catches
Test matches (50): 2,278 runs (31.63) including 3 centuries, 1-128 and 53 catches

SMITH, Thomas Peter Bromley (1908-67)

Essex

Peter Smith was a right-arm, leg-break and googly bowler, who captured many wickets and seldom lost his length even when receiving heavy punishment. As a batsman, usually at number eight, he was a hitter who kept to rational laws. Four times he captured 9 wickets in an innings, once against New South Wales for MCC in 1946/7. For Essex against Middlesex at Colchester in 1947 – the season in which he achieved the double for the only time – he took 16 for 215, and against Derbyshire at Chesterfield, batting at number eleven, he hit 163, his own top score and the highest-ever in that position, adding 218 with Frank Vigar for the last wicket, a record for Essex. In 1933 he arrived at The Oval prepared to play for England against the West Indies, only to learn that the invitation telegram was a hoax. He did not represent his country until thirteen years later.

M.J.K. Smith

First-class career (1929-52): 10,161 runs (17.98) including 8 centuries, 1,697 wickets (26.55) and 359 catches
Test matches (4): 33 runs (6.60), 3 wickets (106.33) and 1 catch

SMITHSON, Gerald Arthur (1926-70)

Yorkshire, Leicestershire and Hertfordshire

While doing his National Service as a 'Bevin Boy', Gerald Smithson was selected for the MCC team to the West Indies in 1947/8, playing in two Tests. An attractive left-handed batsman, he had hit 169 for

Yorkshire at Leicester. He injured his arm badly on the tour, however, missed the 1948 season, and could not consolidate his place with Yorkshire.

First-class career (1946-56): 6,940 runs (22.68) including 8 centuries
Test matches (2): 70 runs (23.33)

SNOW, John Augustine (b.1941)

Sussex

Moody and intense, John Snow was the despair at times of even the most sympathetic captain, and quite unpredictable even to those who thought they knew him well. Yet he was unquestionably among the greatest of post-war English fast bowlers, on his day an irresistibly hostile matchwinner. He is the son of a Sussex vicar and was educated at Christ's Hospital, joining Sussex first as a right-hand batsman. He continued even as a lower-order batsman to play many a useful innings both for his county and his country, and would sometimes open the batting for Sussex in limited-over matches. He is of wiry build and his action, though far from classical, had a lovely rhythm. He approached the wicket with a relatively short run but with long, loping, relaxed strides and delivered the ball with a slightly open chest and a faint sway away from the stumps, all the force of a strong body going into the moment of propulsion. He varied his pace cleverly, bowling only a few really quick deliveries an over, but these few were genuinely fast. He could bowl the bouncer at will, but seldom overdid its use, even though he fell foul of umpires from time to time on the 1970/71 tour of Australia. He also moved the ball away from the bat and brought it back meanly from the off to right-handers or across the body and past the groping bat of left-handers. He seldom saw eye to eye with captains and had a habit of switching himself off and looking bored, though even in this mood he would swoop on the ball in deep field and throw it flat and hard to the top of the stumps or come on to bowl grudgingly and still produce a spell of devastating hostility. He played his first two Tests in England in 1965, but the first of many matchwinning performances in Tests came at Sabina Park in 1967/8 when he took 7 for 49 in the second Test. He finished the series with 27 wickets in four Tests, quite outdoing his rival fast bowlers in the West Indies side. He was now England's first-choice fast bowler, reaching his peak under Illingworth in Australia in 1970/71 when his 31 wickets in six Tests did more than anything to regain the Ashes. The following summer he was dropped from the England side after knocking India's Gavaskar off his feet as the latter went for a quick run and he did not go on any more MCC tours, although he had made a successful home return against Australia in 1975. He called the book he wrote at the end of his career *Cricket Rebel*, a role he rather relished. He was one of the first to join the Kerry Packer organization and he strongly criticized the status quo in the High Court case. Two volumes of his poetry have been published.

John Snow

First-class career (1961-77): 4,832 runs (14.17), 1,174 wickets (22.72) and 125 catches
Test matches (49): 772 runs (13.54), 202 wickets (26.66) and 16 catches

SOUTHERTON, James (1827-80)

Surrey, Sussex and Hampshire

Short and sturdy, James Southerton was a student of cricket and a slow round-arm bowler, who spun his off-breaks considerably. He had an easy action and with the years, contrary to normal practice, his arm got higher and higher so that he developed from round-arm to over-arm. He was also a good middle-order batsman and a safe slip. He used to play for all his three counties in the same season before birth and residential qualifications became law. On ten occasions he took more than 100 wickets in a season. He toured Australia in 1876/7 with James Lillywhite's team and appeared in the first two Tests ever played, at 49 years 119 days the oldest ever to make a Test debut.

First-class career (1854-79): 3,159 runs (9.03), 1,681 wickets (14.45), 215 catches and 3 stumpings
Test matches (2): 7 runs (3.50), 7 wickets (15.28) and 2 catches

SPOONER, Reginald Herbert (1880-1961)

Lancashire

An outstanding schoolboy player at Marlborough, Reggie Spooner was one of the most handsome-looking right-handed batsmen of the Edwardian amateur heyday. Although he handled his bat as a lady would have handled her fan, there was a steely strength beneath his ease and rhythmic style. His superb off-drive had many a spectator purring with pleasure, many a fielder rubbing his hands. When he hit 224 against Surrey at The Oval in 1911, he drove Bill Hitch so straight and powerfully that Neville Cardus recalled Hitch having to 'leap into the air to save his shins time and again'. Rarely able to play a full season, Spooner exceeded 1,000 runs in a season six times, his highest score being 247 against Nottinghamshire at Trent Bridge in 1903. Unable because of injury or business to visit Australia, he appeared in seven Tests against them in England in 1905, 1909 and 1912. As one of the first batsmen to find the answer to the googly as perfected by the South Africans, he made 119 for England against South Africa at Lord's in 1912. A double international, he played Rugby for England against Wales in 1902/3.

First-class career (1899-1923): 13,681 runs (36.28) including 31 centuries
Test matches (10): 481 runs (32.06) including 1 century, and 4 catches

SPOONER, Richard Thomas (b.1919)

Durham and Warwickshire

As wicket-keeper and left-handed opening batsman, Dick Spooner was among the best since the Second World War, but being of the same generation as Godfrey Evans he was at a disadvantage. First playing for Warwickshire at twenty-nine, he exceeded 1,000 runs in a season six times, 1,767 runs (43.09) in 1951 being the best. He toured India in 1951/2, and the West Indies in 1953/4, with MCC, and India with the Commonwealth side in 1950/51. He made 319 runs in the series against India in 1951/2, but represented England only once at home against South Africa in 1955, failing to score in both innings.

First-class career (1948-59): 13,851 runs (27.27) including 12 centuries, and 765 dismissals (585 ct, 180 st.)
Test matches (7): 354 runs (27.23) and 12 dismissals (10 ct, 2 st.)

Reggie Spooner

STANYFORTH, Lt-Col. Ronald Thomas (1892-1964)

Yorkshire

An amateur wicket-keeper, Captain Stanyforth (as he was then) played much Army cricket and, although born in London, played for Yorkshire in three matches in 1928. He toured South America with 'Plum' Warner's MCC team in 1926 and captained MCC in South Africa in 1927/8, when illness compelled the original selection, Captain G.R. Jackson, to withdraw. He also visited the West Indies with MCC in 1929/30 until injury forced him to return home early. His sole Tests were played in South Africa. A man of engaging enthusiasm, he wrote a text-book on the subject of wicket-keeping, and was a trustee of MCC.

First-class career (1914-32): 1,092 runs (17.33) and 93 dismissals (72 ct, 21 st.)
Test matches (4): 13 runs (2.60) and 9 dismissals (7 ct, 2 st.)

STAPLES, Samuel James (1892-1950)

Nottinghamshire

A right-arm, medium-pace bowler with a rather jumpy, shuffling run, Sam Staples bowled cutters on an excellent length for long spells, and was able to break the ball either way. A useful lower-order batsman, he was also a splendid field. At Canterbury in 1927 he took 9 for 141 in an innings against Kent. He toured South Africa with MCC in 1927/8, playing his only three Tests, and visited Australia with MCC in 1928/9, only to return home before playing a single game, because of severe rheumatism. On retirement he was successively coach to Hampshire and a first-class umpire. His younger brother, Arthur, was also a Nottinghamshire stalwart.

First-class career (1920-34): 6,470 runs (17.03) including 1 century, 1,331 wickets (22.85) and 345 catches
Test matches (3): 65 runs (13.00) and 15 wickets (29.00)

STATHAM, John Brian (b.1930)

Lancashire

Honest, loyal, reliable and the most undemonstrative of the great fast bowlers, Brian or 'George' Statham was a part of two outstanding partnerships within a decade. Both of them allowed England to recover constantly from the problems provided by a promising batting line-up which often disappointed in actual performance. First, with Frank Tyson, Statham tore through the Australians in the last four Tests of 1954/5, and he was later equally effective with Fred Trueman. Because of his remorseless accuracy, Statham was at least as much feared as his more ferocious partners. Known also as 'The Whippet', he was loose-limbed, indeed double-jointed and his action was beautifully fluid and smooth. He was content to bowl fast and straight, moving the ball both ways off the seam but working on the theory that if the batsman missed, *he* generally hit. He first burst into first-class cricket in 1950, and that winter flew to Australia as reinforcement for the MCC team, making his Test debut against New Zealand. This was the first of four visits to Australia; and he also toured India,

Brian Statham

South Africa and the West Indies. Only two England bowlers have taken more wickets than he in Tests. Thirteen times he took more than 100 wickets in a season. He had 15 for 89 against Warwickshire at Coventry in 1957 and 15 for 108 against Leicestershire at Leicester in 1964; and he performed the hat-trick three times. Very occasionally a useful tail-end, left-handed batsman, he was an outstanding fielder in the deep. He captained Lancashire from 1965 until 1967 and was awarded the CBE for his services to cricket.

First-class career (1950-68): 5,424 runs (10.80), 2,260 wickets (16.36) and 230 catches
Test matches (70): 675 runs (11.44), 252 wickets (24.82) and 28 catches

STEEL, Allan Gibson (1858-1914)

Cambridge University and Lancashire

A member of the 'golden' Cambridge University eleven that defeated the 1878 Australians, Allan Steel was reckoned in his day the greatest amateur all-rounder after W.G. Outstanding at Marlborough and a member of four good Cambridge sides, he was a first choice for Gentlemen against Players, and for England in the early home Tests from 1880 until 1888. Though never regularly captaining his county, he had a remarkable sequence as a winning skipper: Marlborough over Rugby, Cambridge over Oxford, Gentlemen over Players, Lancashire over Yorkshire and England over Australia. In fact, he led England to victory in all three Tests of 1886. A remarkably accurate, right-arm, slow bowler, he spun the ball either way and kept a full length. He was also a quick-footed batsman and a superb driver on both sides of the wicket. He made 135 not out for England against Australia at Sydney in 1882/3, and 148 at Lord's in 1884 – the former innings saved England and the latter helped to win the match.

First-class career (1877-95): 6,759 runs (29.25) including 7 centuries, and 781 wickets (13.50)
Test matches (13): 600 runs (35.29) including 2 centuries, 29 wickets (20.86) and 5 catches

STEELE, David Stanley (b.1941)

Staffordshire, Northamptonshire and Derbyshire

Grey-haired and bespectacled, David Steele is a right-hand batsman, fine close fielder and slow left-arm bowler. Even if it had occurred in the pre-television age, his Test debut in 1975 at Lord's at the age of thirty-three would have captured the national imagination. Only the regular followers of county cricket knew what a staunch and dependable player he was, until, coming in to bat against Australia in an all-too-familiar atmosphere of crisis (and after losing his way in the Pavilion as he left the dressing room to bat), he

David Steele – Rodney Marsh (Australia) keeping wicket

made a heroic 50, putting on 96 with Tony Greig. That summer he topped England's averages with 365 runs from six innings at 60.83, playing Lillee and Thomson as if they were just another pair of county professionals. With a solid technique based on a firm forward defensive, plenty of shots once his eye is in, and limitless concentration and determination, he continues to be one of the hardest of batsmen to dig out. Coming with further credit through a tough home series against the West Indies in 1976, making 106 at Nottingham, he was unlucky to be omitted thereafter as England rebuilt for the future; this was harsh but realistic and it meant that the unknown who became a household name overnight never played for England abroad. He moved to Derbyshire in 1979, starting as captain, soon resigning the post but doing well with bat and ball. After four seasons with Staffordshire from 1958 to 1962, he had played for Northants for fifteen years, in nine of which he scored more than 1,000 runs, with 1,756 (48.7) in 1975 his highest aggregate. A cautious, moderate man, with printing as a secondary trade, Steele kept his feet firmly on the ground during his brief spell in the limelight. His 1975 benefit at Northants brought him £25,000 and a meat chop for every run he scored from a grateful local butcher. His brother, John Steele, and cousin, Brian Crump, have both played regular county cricket. He rejoined Northants in 1982, taking 70 wickets at 26.37, six times taking 5 or more wickets in an innings, and suggesting that England ought to have made much more of his bowling.

First-class career (1963-): 21,138 runs (33.18) including 30 centuries, 494 wickets (24.19) and 488 catches
Test matches (8): 673 runs (42.06) including 1 century, 2 wickets (19.50) and 7 catches

STEVENS, Greville Thomas Scott (1901-70)

Oxford University and Middlesex

One of the greatest of all schoolboy prodigies, Greville Stevens was a right-handed batsman who, despite his short backlift, hit with surprising power. A leg-break and googly bowler, he foxed even the best batsmen when they failed to differentiate between his top-spinner and googly (let alone his well disguised, fast, straight delivery) and he was also a safe field near the wicket. A member of the Middlesex Championship winning sides of 1920 and 1921, he was the only schoolboy of modern times to play for Gentlemen against Players. His highlight as a batsman was 149 at number one for Middlesex against the Australians at Lord's in 1926 and, as a bowler, when he snatched victory by four runs over Yorkshire at Bradford in 1920. He was a member of the England team that regained the Ashes at The Oval in 1926, and he toured South Africa twice and the West Indies once.

First-class career (1919-33): 10,376 runs (29.56) including 12 centuries, 684 wickets (26.85) and 216 catches
Test matches (10): 263 runs (15.47), 20 wickets (32.40) and 9 catches

STEVENSON, Graham Barry (b.1955)

Yorkshire

A right-handed all-rounder who bowls fast-medium, hits hard in an uncomplicated fashion and fields athletically with a powerful throw, 'Stevo' is a down-to-earth character who had not made the most of his considerable ability by 1982, when he ought to have been at his peak. Strongly built with a good, busy, orthodox action, he can be a matchwinner on a helpful pitch and is a consistently useful performer in limited-overs cricket. First playing for Yorkshire in 1973, he was capped in 1978 and joined the England touring team to Australia as a replacement in 1979/80, playing his first Test against India in Bombay on the way home. The following winter he toured the West Indies but was selected for only one of the four Tests. In 1980 he took 8-57 in an innings against Northamptonshire and hit a rapid 111 against Derbyshire at Chesterfield. In 1982, going in at number eleven, he hit 115 not out against Warwickshire and put on 149 with Geoff Boycott, a county record.

First-class career (1973-): 3,230 runs (21.53) including 2 centuries and 403 wickets (28.26)
Test matches (2): 28 runs (28.00) and 5 wickets (36.60)

STEWART, Michael James (b.1932)

Surrey

'Micky' Stewart became a regular member of the Championship-winning Surrey side in the late fifties, as opening batsman and specialist short-leg fieldsman. A cheerful, steady character, he was a neat and well-organized right-hander. His enthusiasm and agility in the field helped him to create a world record (since equalled) when he took 7 catches in an innings at Northampton in 1957; that season he held 77 catches (one less than Walter Hammond's all-time record). His highest score was 227 not out against Middlesex at The Oval in 1964, and he passed 1,000 runs in a season fifteen times. He captained Surrey from 1963 until 1972 and visited India in 1963/4 as vice-captain of MCC but had to return early owing to illness. Between 1962 and 1964 he represented England against the West Indies, India and Pakistan. As a footballer, he played for Charlton Athletic, Wimbledon, Hendon and Corinthian Casuals, usually at inside-right. He returned to The Oval in 1979, as manager of Surrey, the county's fortunes instantly improving.

First-class career (1954-72): 26,492 runs (32.90) including 49 centuries, and 634 catches
Test matches (8): 385 runs (35.00) and 6 catches

STODDART, Andrew Ernest (1863-1915)

Middlesex

England's captain at both cricket and Rugby football, Andrew Stoddart, or 'My dear victorious Stod' of the ballad, was a sporting Titan who led England to victory over Australia in 1894/5. He also scored 352 runs in the Tests, including 173 in the second Test at Melbourne, when he led a fight back that resulted in a win, but was not so successful the next time in 1897/8. 'Stod' or 'Stoddie' was a dominating right-handed batsman with all the strokes, especially strong in driving and hitting to leg. He came into cricket seriously for the first time in 1885, when he made his debut for Middlesex, and he hit 485 for Hampstead against Stoics the year after, then the highest score on record anywhere. He hardly knew a poor season and his last innings for Middlesex was a mammoth score of 221 against Somerset at Lord's in 1900; it was also his highest first-class score. He was a useful change-bowler and very reliable field. He toured Australia

Andrew Stoddart

four times and the West Indies and America once each. His later years saw his hopes and health in decline, and he shot himself through the head in 1915.

First-class career (1885-1900): 16,738 runs (32.13) including 26 centuries, 278 wickets (23.63) and 260 catches
Test matches (16): 996 runs (35.57) including 2 centuries, 2 wickets (47.00) and 6 catches

STORER, William (1867-1912)

Derbyshire

One of the most polished wicket-keepers, Bill Storer was one of the first to stand up coolly to the fastest bowling, including that of Charles Kortright. Though he bent – without squatting – he appeared to be upright at the moment of receiving the ball. He would collect the ball off the edge of the bat as delicately as though picking a moth off a mink coat; and he had much experience facing fastish bowlers in Derbyshire's matches. He maintained a high reputation as a sound right-handed batsman always looking for runs. Twice he averaged over 50 in a season, scored 100 and 100 not out against Yorkshire at Derby in 1896, made his highest score, 216 not out against Leicestershire at Chesterfield in 1899, and seven times exceeded 1,000 runs in a season. He could take off his pads and become a useful change-bowler. Bill played in one Test against Australia in 1899 and toured there in 1897/8, but his career coincided with that of Dick Lilley, who was almost invariably given the preference as England's 'keeper. He spoke his mind and enjoyed his cricket, but his later years were dogged by ill-health.

First-class career (1887-1905): 12,966 runs (28.87) including 17 centuries, 232 wickets (33.89) and 431 dismissals (376 ct, 55 st.)
Test matches (6): 215 runs (19.54), 2 wickets (54.00) and 11 dismissals (11 ct)

STREET, George Benjamin (1889-1924)

Sussex

George Street joined MCC's team in South Africa in 1922/3 as a late replacement and played in his one and only Test at Durban, scoring 4 and 7 not out and making one stumping. He was then in his prime as a very competent county 'keeper – in 1923 having eight victims against Worcestershire at Hastings – and a useful tail-end batsman, but he was killed in a motor-cycle accident just before the 1924 season started.

First-class career (1909-23): 4,031 runs (17.22) including 1 century, and 419 dismissals (304 ct, 115 st.)

STRUDWICK, Herbert (1880-1970)

Surrey

Bert Strudwick, or 'Struddie', held the world record, until beaten by John Murray in 1975, for the most dismissals in a career by a wicket-keeper. Neat, agile, dependable and accomplished, he had 91 'scalps' in his first full season in 1903. Throughout his career Surrey had few spinners and he had to keep mainly to fastish bowlers, as most of his successors do today. As a right-handed batsman, he played some determined innings. He toured Australia with MCC four times between 1903 and 1924 and South Africa twice before the First World War. At Johannesburg in 1913/14 he dismissed seven in the match. His last Test was against Australia at The Oval in 1926, when England regained the Ashes after a long wait. He held a partnership in Alf Gover's Cricket School, and served Surrey for sixty years, latterly as scorer. During one of his Australian tours, a letter was addressed: 'Struddy, 'Stralia' – and it reached him safely without delay! There have been few more popular or respected cricketers.

First-class career (1902-27): 6,445 runs (10.89) and 1,495 dismissals (1,241 ct, 254 st.)
Test matches (28): 230 runs (7.93) and 72 dismissals (60 ct, 12 st.)

STUDD, Charles Thomas (1860-1931)

Cambridge University and Middlesex

Charles Studd was the youngest and most famous of three brothers – the others were George and Kynaston – all of whom played for Eton, Cambridge (successively as captain) and Middlesex. Possessing a fine upright style, C.T. was a right-handed batsman, particularly strong on the off-side, and a medium-fast bowler who brought the ball over from a good height. While still at Cambridge, he played for England in the historic Oval Test of 1882 – the year in which he became the second man ever (after W.G.) to achieve the double, with 1,249 runs and 128 wickets – and that winter he was a member of the Hon. Ivo Bligh's party to Australia which came home with the original Ashes. Studd achieved the double again in 1883, but a year later, greatly influenced by the evangelists, Moody and Sankey, he retired from regular first-class cricket to devote himself to overseas missionary work: he endured great hardship in China, Africa and India.

First-class career (1879-1903): 4,391 runs (30.49) including 8 centuries, and 455 wickets (17.30)
Test matches (5): 160 runs (20.00), 3 wickets (32.66) and 5 catches

STUDD, George Brown (1859-1945)

Cambridge University and Middlesex

The eldest of the three brothers – George, Kynaston and Charles – George Studd hit 120 against Oxford at Lord's, when he was captain in 1882. Essentially a front-foot player, he was a skilful and powerful driver, but in the field he was an uncertain catcher, though his picking-up was clean and quick. He toured Australia in 1882/3 with Hon. Ivo Bligh's team in search of the Ashes, but was very disappointing in the Tests. Called to the Bar, he did not practise but like his brother Charlie became a missionary; and from 1891 until his death he lived and worked in a notorious and squalid area of South Los Angeles in California.

First-class career (1879-86): 2,892 runs (21.91) including 3 centuries
Test matches (4): 31 runs (4.42) and 8 catches

SUBBA ROW, Raman (b.1932)

Cambridge University, Surrey and Northamptonshire

Raman Subba Row was a key member of one of the last powerful Cambridge elevens. A tallish left-handed batsman, he was at first predominantly an on-side player but developed his off-side strokes and was particularly adept at placing the ball for singles. His high-flighted leg-breaks and googlies could break a stubborn stand – he took 5 for 21 against Oxford at Lord's in 1951 – and, in the field, he alternated successfully between slips, gully and the deep. On joining Northamptonshire – whom he captained from 1958 until 1961 – he became a consistently heavy run-getter, with a strong defence. He made the highest-ever score for the county, 260 not out against Lancashire at Northampton in 1955, and in 1958 he broke his own record with 300 against Surrey at The Oval – adding 376 for the sixth wicket with Albert Lightfoot, the best for any wicket for the county. Six times he exceeded 1,000 runs in a season. After a rather disappointing start in Test cricket, he was pressed into service as an opening batsman against India at The Oval in 1959, scoring 94, and was an England regular until 1961, when he headed the batting against Australia with 468 runs (46.80), including his Test highest, 137 (in seven hours forty minutes) at The Oval. He resigned suddenly for business reasons after the 1961 season, and has subsequently been a strong voice for reform within the establishment. A public relations executive, he has been closely involved on various Lord's committees, is chairman of Surrey and managed England's tour of India in 1981/2.

First-class career (1951-68): 14,182 runs (41.46) including 30 centuries, 87 wickets (38.65) and 176 catches
Test matches (13): 984 runs (46.85) including 3 centuries, 0-2 and 5 catches

Herbert Sutcliffe with Jack Hobbs (left)

SUGG, Frank Howe (1862-1933)

Yorkshire, Derbyshire and Lancashire

A fine all-round games player, Frank Sugg stood six feet tall and was an enterprising right-handed batsman, hitting astoundingly hard off the back foot and never troubling himself about what the wicket was like, belonging to the hit-or-miss brigade. He was also a magnificent outfield. Five times he exceeded 1,000 runs in a season. His best work was for Lancashire, and he hit his highest score, 220, for Lancashire against Gloucestershire at Bristol. He appeared in only two Tests against Australia, both in 1888, making 31 at The Oval and 24 at Old Trafford, England winning by an innings each time.

First-class career (1883-99): 11,859 runs (24.45) including 16 centuries, 10 wickets (27.30), 167 catches and 1 stumping
Test matches (2): 55 runs (27.50)

SUTCLIFFE, Herbert (1894-1978)

Yorkshire

One of the game's immortals, Herbert Sutcliffe did not play for Yorkshire's first team until he was twenty-four, due to the First World War. In his first season, 1919, he made 1,839 runs (44.85) and by 1924 he had eclipsed all rivals as opening partner for Jack Hobbs in Tests. Debonaire, well-groomed and unruffled, he was essentially a practical batsman, with a superb judgment of length, pace and direction. He lacked the polished elegance of Hobbs but certainly not his appetite for runs. He stood with the face of the bat very open, presenting its full width always, making few classical strokes, but hitting the ball firmly off the front foot especially to the off-side and cutting and hooking efficiently. A clever runner between wickets, he stole many a cheeky single with Jack Hobbs or Percy Holmes. Never flustered or intimidated, he had great courage, determination and concentration, and was at his best on the big occasion. He shared in 145 first-wicket partnerships of 100 runs or more, 74 of them with Holmes and twenty-six with Hobbs. He first opened with Hobbs against South Africa in 1924, and they put on 136 together at Edgbaston and 268 at Lord's in his first two Tests. In the first Test in Australia, 1924/5, they put up 157 and 110 together at Sydney in the first match, followed by 283 in the second at Melbourne, when they batted all day facing a total of 600; at Melbourne Herbert made 176 and 127; and again at Melbourne, in the fourth Test, he scored 143 in another century opening partnership. He headed the Test averages with 734 runs (81.55). At The Oval in 1926, when England went in again, behind on the first innings, Hobbs and Sutcliffe put up 172, Sutcliffe going on to 161, thus laying the foundation for the victory that brought back the Ashes to England. In 1928/9 they remained reliable, Sutcliffe averaging 50.57 in the series. In 1930 he headed the England batting against Australia (who recovered the Ashes) with 436 runs (87.20); and against Australia, 1932/3 and 1934 (with a variety of opening partners), he still averaged over 50 per series, at Sydney, 1932/3, making his Test highest, 194. He hit centuries against New Zealand and South Africa, two in the match at The Oval in 1929; and his last Test of all was against

South Africa in 1935. His stand of 555 with Holmes against Essex at Leyton in 1932 stood as the world record for forty-five years, his score of 313 on this occasion remaining his highest, although it was only one of seventeen scores above 200. He reached 1,000 runs in a season twenty-four times (including three times abroad). From 1922 until 1935 he scored over 2,000 runs each season, including 3,336 runs (74.13) and 14 centuries in the wet season of 1932. His average in Tests exceeds his overall average by nearly nine runs! Later a very successful businessman, he was also a Test selector and his son, christened William Herbert Hobbs, played for, and captained, Yorkshire. Herbert himself had been offered the Yorkshire captaincy; as a professional, he declined it. However, he became a major in the Second World War and later he deliberately took on the accents and manners of a 'gentleman'.

First-class career (1919-45): 50,138 runs (51.95) including 149 centuries, and 469 catches
Test matches (54): 4,555 runs (60.73) including 16 centuries, and 23 catches

SWETMAN, Roy (b.1933)

Surrey, Nottinghamshire and Gloucestershire

Slightly built, neat and compact. Roy Swetman kept wicket confidently and creditably for three counties, and was also a useful batsman. He toured Australia and New Zealand with MCC in 1958/9, and the West Indies in 1959/60, but could not quite clinch the regular place as England's 'keeper.

First-class career (1953-74): 6,495 runs (19.21) including 2 centuries, and 597 dismissals (531 ct, 66 st.)
Test matches (11): 254 runs (16.93) and 26 dismissals (24 ct, 2 st.)

TATE, Frederick William (1867–1943)

Sussex

The tragedy of Fred Tate's or 'Chub's' missed catch and mishandled innings in his sole Test, against Australia at Old Trafford in 1902, is well known to cricket students. He scored 5 not out and 4, took 2 for 51 and held one other catch in England's narrow defeat. 'I've a little lad at home who'll make up for that,' said the tearful Fred after the match – and so it proved twenty-two years later! Fred, however, was outstanding for Sussex. A slow to medium, right-arm, off-break bowler, with an easy action and good command of length, Chub remained the stock bowler for seventeen years and, in the short programmes, exceeded 100 wickets in a season five times. His best (and most fateful year) was 1902, when he secured 180 wickets (15.71), his feats including 15 for 68 in a day against Middlesex at Lord's. On retirement he became coach to Derbyshire. Besides Maurice, one other son, C.F., played county cricket.

First-class career (1887-1905): 2,891 runs (10.17), 1,331 wickets (21.55) and 216 catches

TATE, Maurice William (1895-1956)

Sussex

Maurice Tate – who like his father was nicknamed 'Chub' – began as a right-handed batsman, but developed as one of England's greatest bowlers. At the outset he bowled right-arm, slow-medium, off-breaks like his father, interspersed by the occasional fast ball. But on being asked to concentrate on bowling fast-medium, he advanced overnight and in 1923 took 219 wickets (13.97). He was a big man with heavy shoulders and powerful thighs, whose feet delighted Tom Webster and other cartoonists but, when he turned to bowl, all was grace and co-ordination. His brisk run-up was a mere eight yards, leading up to a high action as he leant back on his right leg with a fully extended left arm; his right arm catapulting over with a smooth elasticity, which gave an impression of immense momentum. He would swerve late from leg or bring the ball back from outside the off-stump; and it appeared that the ball gained pace off the pitch. From 1922 until 1925 inclusive he captured 848 wickets; and he exceeded 100 wickets in a season fourteen times. As a good, workmanlike, free-hitting batsman, who often opened for the county (besides being opening bowler) he exceeded 1,000 runs in a season twelve times; and he achieved the double eight times, seven seasons in succession in the twenties. He toured Australia (three times), New Zealand and

Maurice Tate

South Africa. On his first tour in 1924/5 he took 38 wickets (23.18) in the five Tests, a record against Australia not broken until 1956. He took 13 wickets (18.92) in the first three Tests against the West Indies, and headed the bowling against South Africa in 1930/31 with 14 wickets (24.35). His best series at home was against South Africa in 1924, when he headed the bowling with 27 wickets (15.70) and in the first Test at Edgbaston he bowled unchanged with his England and county captain, Arthur Gilligan, to dismiss the visitors for 30 in seventy-five minutes. At The Oval in 1926 he was prominent in England's defeat of Australia when the Ashes were regained.

First-class career (1912-37): 21,717 runs (25.04) including 23 centuries, 2,784 wickets (18.16) and 242 catches
Test matches (39): 1,198 runs (25.48) including 1 century, 155 wickets (26.13) and 11 catches

TATTERSALL, Roy (b.1922)

Lancashire

Although he was never a vicious finger-spinner, Roy Tattersall's height combined with subtle variations of pace and great accuracy made him a first-rate, right-arm, off-break bowler. Emphatically the bowler of 1950 – taking 193 wickets (13.59), which remained his career-best – he also headed the national averages. He was flown out as a replacement to Australia that winter. In the fifth Test at Melbourne his last-wicket stand of 74 with Reg Simpson, the left-handed Tattersall contributing 10, assured an English victory; and his 1 for 16 and 6 for 44 in the second Test against New Zealand at Wellington enabled England to win comfortably. Subsequently he toured India in 1951/2 and appeared in occasional Tests against South Africa, Australia and Pakistan but Jim Laker was usually preferred. Against South Africa, on a rain-affected wicket at Lord's in 1951, he took 7 for 52 and 5 for 49, the outstanding performance of an underrated bowler. He exceeded 100 wickets in a season eight times and he performed the hat-trick while taking 9 for 40 in an innings against Nottinghamshire in 1953.

First-class career (1948-64): 2,040 runs (9.35), 1,369 wickets (18.04) and 143 catches
Test matches (16): 50 runs (5.00), 58 wickets (26.08) and 8 catches

TAVARÉ, Christopher James (b.1954)

Oxford University and Kent

A correct and determined right-handed batsman of phlegmatic temperament and a brilliant slip-fielder, Chris Tavaré has a chance to prove himself in the 1980s to be the solid and reliable batsman England were seeking throughout the 1970s. Educated at Sevenoaks School and Oxford, he was obviously

Chris Tavaré

destined for a cricket career and at Oxford quickly earned the respect of the professionals with his studious and disciplined approach to batting. An ability to get his head down and graft for runs, however, sometimes conceals the fact that he has a full array of attacking shots which are more often displayed in the one-day game. In the Lambert and Butler Floodlit Cup at the Crystal Palace Football Club in 1981, he hit a hundred off 27 balls. Tavaré scored a century for England Schools against All-India Schools at Birmingham in 1973 and won blues from 1975 to 1977, having made his first appearance for Kent in 1974. His first full season for Kent brought him 1,534 runs (45.11), and an innings of 150 not out in the Tunbridge Wells week against Essex, the 1979 county champions, underlined his ability to concentrate for long periods. His first chance at higher level came in a one-day international against the West Indies in 1980 when he played a fine innings of 82 not out at Headingley and won selection for the first two Test matches. A staunch innings of 42 in his second match at Lord's was considered too slow and strokeless, but England were thankful when he batted in much the same way against Australia in 1981, playing two dull but valuable innings of 69 and 78 on his recall at Old Trafford. He batted for nearly twelve hours in the match and his second 50 was the slowest in a Test in England, a 'record' he broke against Pakistan at Lord's in 1982 when, in a brave rearguard action, he took 350 minutes to reach 50. His 82 in 404 minutes very nearly saved England and underlined Tavaré's skill, courage and concentration. He toured India in 1981/2 and scored his first Test hundred, a patient and valuable 149, at Delhi, finishing the series with 349 runs (38.77) before scoring a vital 85 in the second innings to steer England to success in the inaugural Test with Sri Lanka in Colombo. In England in 1982 the selectors asked him to open the innings and he did so with success, despite continuing at number three for Kent whose captain he became in 1983, on his return from an unsuccessful 1982/3 tour of Australia.

First-class career (1974-): 10,539 runs (40.84) including 21 centuries, 2 wickets (136.00) and 183 catches
Test matches (17): 1,072 runs (36.96) including 1 century, 0-11 and 13 catches

TAYLOR, Kenneth (b.1935)

Yorkshire, Auckland and Norfolk

Ken Taylor served Yorkshire effectively either as an opening right-handed batsman or the middle-order and, in his best innings, played with such fluency and authority that he looked to be of the highest quality. A bowler of 'little seamers' as he called his medium-pace swing bowling, he was also a cover fielder of uncommon mobility, as befitted a professional footballer. His highest score was 203 not out against Warwickshire at Edgbaston in 1961. He represented England against India in 1959 and against Australia in 1964. He now teaches art at Gresham's School.

First-class career (1953-68): 13,053 runs (26.74) including 16 centuries, 131 wickets (28.72) and 148 catches
Test matches (3): 57 runs (11.40), 0-6 and 1 catch

TAYLOR, Robert William (b.1941)

Derbyshire and Staffordshire

Of all the good and bad repercussions of the 'Packer Revolution', the happiest was that this perfect craftsman and ideal sportsman suddenly acquired a status which his exceptional ability warranted. Such a perfectionist as a wicket-keeper that he gave up the captaincy of his county the moment that he felt he was not keeping wicket as well as he could (though no one else had noticed any decline), Bob Taylor manages to be at once as keen as mustard and totally undemonstrative. A capable, orthodox batsman, lacking any great power of stroke, he was second choice to Alan Knott for almost a decade. He has toured Australia with four England sides and once with a Rest of the World side, the West Indies, Pakistan, India and New Zealand. He has three times dismissed 80 or more batsmen in a season (1962, 1963 and 1965). At Chesterfield in 1963 he dismissed 10 Hampshire batsmen in the match and in 1966 at Derby caught 7 Glamorgan batsmen in one innings. He had played just one Test in New Zealand in 1971 before his chance came to become England's regular 'keeper in Pakistan in 1977/78. He seized that opportunity unerringly and was a valuable member of the England team which defeated Australia 5–1 in 1978/9. At Adelaide England were in severe danger of losing the fifth Test when Taylor and his Derbyshire colleague, Geoff Miller, rescued England with a stand of 135, Taylor going on to make 97, equalling his highest score. In 1981, to his great delight, he scored a maiden first-class hundred in his 21st season, against Yorkshire at Abbeydale Park. He was twice discarded by England after a relatively disappointing tour of Australia in 1979/80, amazingly enough after taking 10 catches, 7 in one innings, and scoring a priceless 43, in the Jubilee Test in Bombay. He re-established himself and in Australia in 1982/3 he broke J.T. Murray's all-time record of 1,527 first-class victims. At the age of 41 he looked as fit and agile as ever. He was awarded the MBE in 1981.

Bob Taylor

First-class career (1960-): 10,967 runs (16.82) including 1 century, and 1,526 dismissals (1,359 ct, 167 st.)
Test matches (42): 875 runs (17.85) and 138 dismissals (131 ct, 7 st.)

TENNYSON, Hon. Lionel Hallam (3rd Baron Tennyson) (1889-1951)

Hampshire

Originally a fast right-arm bowler and heavy hitter in

the lower rungs of the Eton batting order, Lionel Tennyson eventually made 19 centuries. He was a Regency figure and refused consistently to be trammelled by many of the considerations that bind most of humanity to a more prosaic existence. Captain of a depressed England for three Tests of 1921 and of Hampshire from 1919 until 1933 (the county's wicket-keeper, Walter Livsey, was his butler), he split a hand trying to stop an unstoppable shot from Charles Macartney in the Test at Leeds and batted one-handed against the thunderbolts of Gregory and MacDonald. He did not flinch in scoring 63 in just over an hour, while the other batsmen were hard pressed. He toured South Africa with MCC in 1913/14 and took his own team to the West Indies, India and elsewhere. Seven times he reached 1,000 runs in a season. His two uninhibited and amusing volumes of autobiography are entitled *From Verse to Worse* and *Sticky Wickets.*

First-class career (1913-37): 16,828 runs (23.33) including 19 centuries, 55 wickets (54.18) and 172 catches
Test matches (9): 345 runs (31.36), 0-1 and 6 catches

THOMPSON, George Joseph (1877-1943)

Northamptonshire

A big, burly all-rounder with a drooping moustache, George Thompson or 'The Northampton Nugget', bowled and batted Northamptonshire into first-class cricket. At Wellingborough School he bowled himself into the first eleven at thirteen and became one of the first public schoolboys to turn professional cricketer; he first played for the county at seventeen as an amateur. Bowling right-arm medium to fast, rather at the pace of Tate or Bedser, his run was short but his delivery was high and whirling, like a windmill. His batting was solid and he was a great fighter in a tight corner. The first minor county cricketer to take 100 wickets in a season, he performed this feat eight times in first-class cricket between 1905 and 1913. He achieved the double twice, in 1906 and 1910, and was prominent in the county's rise to second place in the Championship in 1912. He hit 125 for Players against Gentlemen at Scarborough in 1900; and, for an England eleven against the Australians at Eastbourne in 1902, took 8 for 88 in one innings. But, such was the talent available, he represented England once only at home, against Australia at Edgbaston in 1909. His sole major tour was to South Africa in 1909/10 when, for a losing team, he came second to Jack Hobbs in the Test batting, averaging 33.37, and took 23 wickets (26.91). He toured Australasia with Lord Hawke's team in 1902/3 and the West Indies with Lord Brackley's in 1904/5, on the former tour routing the opposition with 177 wickets (6.50). He captained Northants occasionally in 1913 – the first professional to do so.

First-class career (1897-1922): 12,018 runs (21.97) including 9 centuries, 1,591 wickets (18.89) and 226 catches
Test matches (6): 273 runs (30.33), 23 wickets (27.73) and 5 catches

THOMSON, Norman Ian (b.1929)

Sussex

Ian Thomson was the best right-arm, medium-fast seam bowler produced by Sussex since Maurice Tate, though not in Tate's exalted class. He took more than 100 wickets in a season twelve times. After a shuffling, unimpressive approach, his right arm came over high; his natural delivery was the in-dipper and, on a green top, he was able to make the ball dance off the seam bewilderingly, often bowling a good leg-cutter. He took all 10 for 49 in an innings (15 for 75 in the match) against Warwickshire at Worthing in 1964. A useful tail-end batsman, he hit 77 at Leicester in 1959. He was flown out to Pakistan, 1954/5, as a replacement, and in 1964/5 toured South Africa, where his only Tests were played. He won the 1964 Gillette Cup Final almost single-handed, taking 4 for 23.

First-class career (1952-72): 7,120 runs (14.74), 1,597 wickets (20.57) and 137 catches
Test matches (5): 69 runs (23.00), 9 wickets (63.11) and 3 catches

TITMUS, Frederick John (b.1932)

Middlesex, Surrey and Orange Free State

Fred Titmus's long and distinguished career began with a first match for Middlesex at the age of sixteen in 1949 and effectively ended with Middlesex winning the county championship for the first time since 1947 in his final full season, 1976. Small, dark, with twinkling brown eyes underneath prominent eye-brows, Fred was loved as a cheerful character with a quick if sometimes caustic wit, and revered as a master off-spinner and courageous batsman, with an effective method based upon a sound technique. He was good enough to open the batting for England in an emergency and, late in his career, his technique stood the searching test of the speed of Thomson and Lillee better than that of some more vaunted batsmen. Titmus first took 100 wickets in 1953, when he established himself in the Middlesex side on his return from National Service. He did the double of 100 wickets and 1,000 runs eight times, the last in 1967. He took 100 or more wickets in a season a further fifteen times, twenty-six times taking more than 10 wickets in a match and 168 times 5 or more wickets in an innings. Keeping a perfect length, his special skill lay in his use of the air, making the ball float, drift and dip like a bird on the wing. But when a pitch was allowing the ball to turn he would bowl sides out as quickly as most –

against New Zealand in 1965 at Headingley he took 4 wickets in 6 balls. First playing for England in 1955, he was on his sixth major MCC tour, as vice-captain, in 1967/8 when he lost four toes as his foot was caught in the propeller of a motor boat in the West Indies. If this accentuated his rather rolling gait, it hardly seemed to impair his skill and he was justifiably selected for a seventh tour (his third tour of Australia) in 1974/5, when he was more than forty. However he had less success with the ball than in 1962/3, when with 21 wickets he was England's leading wicket-taker in the Tests, and less success with the bat than in 1965/6, when he made 258 Test runs at an average of 64. That tour saw his highest score – 137 not out against South Australia at Adelaide. In first-class cricket his best bowling returns were 9 for 52 against Cambridge in 1962, and 9 for 57 against Lancashire at Lord's in 1967. In Tests his best efforts were 7 for 79 at Sydney in 1962/3, and 84 not out against India at Bombay in 1963/4. He became Surrey's coach in 1977 but stayed in the job for only two seasons, feeling that he was not given enough independence. He retired to run a post office in Hertfordshire with his wife. All the time Fred was itching to play again and he did indeed play one game for Surrey in 1978, his thirtieth season in first-class cricket, and two for Middlesex in 1979. Still this was not the end, for he made further appearances in 1980 and 1982, in both of which years Middlesex won the Championship. He thus joined a small and select band of those who have played first-class cricket in five decades.

First-class career (1949-): 21,588 runs (23.11), including 6 centuries, 2,830 wickets (22.37) and 474 catches
Test matches (53): 1,449 runs (22.29), 153 wickets (32.22) and 35 catches

Fred Titmus

TOLCHARD, Roger William (b.1946)

Devon and Leicestershire

Roger Tolchard is a natural games player, although his wicket-keeping, judged by the highest standards, was good but not great. His batting form during MCC's tour of India and Pakistan in 1972/3 entitled him to a chance for England, but it did not come until four years later when he played a major role in England's first ever Test win in Calcutta. Normally a brilliant and often unorthodox strokemaker with nimble footwork as his main asset, he was forced on this occasion to defend grittily, and did so for five and a half hours to make 67 on a pitch which was rapidly deteriorating. He retained his place for the remainder of the series and shone, even in a brilliant fielding side, with his speedy work at short-leg or in the covers. In 1978/9 he toured Australia and again batted well in very different conditions. He was unlucky not to be chosen for more Tests before his tour was abruptly ended by a bouncer which caused a severely fractured cheek-bone. Coming from a Devonian family (his elder brother Jeff played for Leicestershire and younger brother Ray for Devon) he was an outstanding schoolboy player at Malvern and was capped by Leicestershire in his second season, 1966. He became captain of his county in 1981 and the following year led them to second place in the Championship. He has been outstanding in limited-over cricket.

First-class career (1965-): 14,513 runs (31.34) including 12 centuries, and 985 dismissals (869 ct, 116 st.)
Test matches (4): 129 runs (25.80) and 5 catches

TOWNSEND, Charles Lucas (1876-1958)

Gloucestershire

A lean and lanky schoolboy at Clifton, Charlie Townsend first played for his county at sixteen. A right-arm slow bowler and left-handed batsman, he was an immediate success in 1895. Such was his tidy length and exceptional degree of spin even the best batsmen were in serious trouble with his leg-breaks. He once did the hat-trick, all three victims being stumped. He frequently opened the bowling, and in the two matches against Nottinghamshire in 1895, he took 16 for 122 and 13 for 110. He achieved the double in 1898 when he took 101 wickets (29.06) and made 2,440 runs (51.91), including 9 centuries, among which was his highest score of 224 not out against Essex at Clifton. He again did the double in 1899, when he made his only appearances in Tests against Australia. Although he was never able to appear regularly after 1900, as late as 1909 he hit 129 out of 169 in two hours for his county against the Australians at Cheltenham. His father was Frank Townsend, who played in the early years of the county club. His son, D.C.H., also represented England (see below) and his grandson, J.R.A., played for Oxford and Durham.

First-class career (1893-1922): 9,512 runs (30.29) including 21 centuries, 725 wickets (23.12) and 193 catches
Test matches (2): 51 runs (17.00) and 3 wickets (25.00)

TOWNSEND, David Charles Humphrey (b.1912)

Oxford University and Durham

David Townsend is the last man to have represented England without ever having played for a first-class county. From Winchester he went to Oxford, and played against Cambridge in 1933 and 1934. Of fine physique, he was strong in defence and a powerful stroke-player. He hit 193 against Cambridge at Lord's in 1934, and toured the West Indies in 1934/5, opening the batting in three Tests.

First-class career (1933-48): 1,801 runs (29.04) including 4 centuries, and 6 wickets (83.50)
Test matches (3): 77 runs (12.83), 0-9 and 1 catch

TOWNSEND, Leslie Fletcher (b.1903)

Derbyshire, Northumberland and Auckland

One of a posse of all-rounders who were prominent in Derbyshire's first Championship win of 1936, Leslie Townsend was an attractive right-handed batsman, especially strong in front of the wicket and on the off-side. He was also a medium-pace, off-spin bowler and a very good field. Nine times he exceeded 1,000 runs in a season, four times took 100 wickets, and three times achieved the double, notably in 1933 when he made 2,268 runs (44.47) and took 100 wickets (18.71). He toured the West Indies with MCC in 1929/30 when he first represented England. He went to India with MCC in 1933/4, appearing in all three Tests on another inaugural tour, and altogether made 829 runs and took 65 wickets. He was never selected for a Test in England, however, and after the Second World War emigrated to New Zealand where he played for Auckland and later coached in Nelson (South Island).

First-class career (1922-39): 19,555 runs (27.50) including 22 centuries, 1,088 wickets (21.12) and 234 catches
Test matches (4): 97 runs (16.16), 6 wickets (34.16) and 2 catches

TREMLETT, Maurice Fletcher (b.1923)

Somerset and Central Districts

On his debut for Somerset against Middlesex at Lord's in 1947, Maurice Tremlett impressed as a right-arm fast-medium bowler, taking 8 for 86 in the match. Well built and looking every inch a cricketer, he toured the West Indies that winter with MCC because of the great promise he had shown. Relatively inexperienced, however, he was always liable to be erratic and his bowling was severely mauled in the Caribbean. He again toured with MCC the following winter in 1948/9, and in South Africa, although he achieved little with the ball, his batting improved. Subsequently, while he lost his control as a bowler, he was worth playing for his batting alone. He passed 1,000 runs in a season ten times and his hard, straight driving, either lofted or along the ground, was most exhilarating. From 1956 until 1959 he served as the county's first professional captain. His son Tim has played for Hampshire.

First-class career (1947-60): 16,038 runs (25.37) including 16 centuries, 351 wickets (30.63) and 257 catches
Test matches (3): 20 runs (6.66) and 4 wickets (56.50)

TROTT, Albert Edwin (1873-1914)

Victoria and Middlesex

See Australia section.

TRUEMAN, Frederick Sewards (b.1931)

Yorkshire and Derbyshire

'I 'ear things about myself I'd never 'ave dreamt of in a million years, Sunshine, and I don't reckon to be short on imagination.' Thus did Fred Trueman, sitting back in a BBC commentary box, in affluent middle age, for once disclaim one of the numerous outrageous stories which have attached themselves to the game's greatest modern character. If ever a man deserved his affluence it is F.S.T. He has achieved international fame, first as one of the greatest fast bowlers of all time (only Lance Gibbs has taken more than Trueman's 307 Test wickets), secondly as a character who gave life and humour to every game he played, and thirdly as a naturally gifted radio commentator and raconteur. As his bowling developed from that of the wild young tearaway into the mature artist, so has his character developed from the raw, reckless, boastful but fearless youth to a canny, positively diplomatic maturity in his present position as international celebrity. For 'Fiery Fred', born at Stainton, cricket was the probable alternative to life down a coal mine. His early days in the Yorkshire side – he was picked for nine matches in 1949 when just eighteen – showed him to be a hungry fighter. He always believed himself to be the best man for any job

Fred Trueman

he wanted to do and after being left out of the Yorkshire side for the more experienced Bill Foord he was determined, as his colleague Bill Bowes has recorded, to 'bloody well show 'em'. Much of the blustering talk, which accompanied his bowling and the overuse of bouncers in his early days, stemmed, Bowes believes, from a certain inferiority complex. At times this proved expensive, but hardly so during his dramatic entry onto the Test arena against India in 1952 when in three Tests he took 24 wickets, plainly terrifying some of his opponents. At Leeds four Indian wickets fell before a run was scored: they were bowled out in an hour and twenty minutes for 58, Trueman taking eight for 31. National Service interrupted his career; he fell foul of authority on Len Hutton's tour of the West Indies in 1953/4 and he was left out of the MCC sides which toured Australia in 1954/5 and South Africa in 1956/7. However, for ten consecutive seasons between 1957 and 1966 he took 100 wickets or more, including 175 in 1960 at 13.98, and became a more or less automatic selection for England. Neil Hawke, in 1964, was his 300th Test victim, pouched by Cowdrey at slip, the victim like countless others of a deadly, late out-swing. Trueman is 5ft 10ins tall and he had the ideal physique for fast bowling with immensely strong arms, legs, back and shoulders. Added to this, he had mental aggression, sheer courage, and a beautiful, rhythmic action which built up from a rolling approach into an unforgettable long final stride with the body sideways-on. His fastest speed was genuinely quick, his length and line were good and his swing formidable. In addition he was an effective right-hand batsman who hit the ball tremendously hard on the leg-side and scored 3 centuries. A brilliant natural fielder, he specialized at short-leg but also threw in hard and flat from the boundary with either hand. But it is as a bowler that he is immortal. He took four hat-tricks, 10 or more wickets in a match twenty-five times and 5 wickets or more in an innings 126 times. After retiring from Yorkshire in 1968, he played successfully in a few limited-over matches for Derbyshire.

First-class career (1949-69): 9,231 runs (15.56) including 3 centuries, 2,304 wickets (18.29) and 438 catches
Test matches (67): 981 runs (13.81), 307 wickets (21.57) and 64 catches

TUFNELL, Col. Neville Charsley
(1887-1951)

Cambridge University, Surrey and Norfolk

An Old Etonian and a talented wicket-keeper, Col. Neville Tufnell was a Cambridge blue who turned out occasionally for Surrey (when Bert Strudwick was not playing). While still at Eton, he toured New Zealand with Major E.G. Wynyard's team in 1906/7. He visited South Africa with MCC in 1909/10 and, deputizing for the injured Strudwick in the fifth Test at Cape Town – his sole Test – he made a stumping and scored 14.

First-class career (1906-24): 1,514 runs (14.28) including 1 century, and 99 dismissals (59 ct, 40 st.)

TURNBULL, Maurice Joseph Lawson
(1906-44)

Cambridge University and Glamorgan

To Maurice Turnbull batting was a gay adventure. He was a gifted right-hander who made runs when they were wanted and whose value could not always be assessed on figures. Initially an on-side player, he developed all the recognized strokes and added some of his own, and he was also a fine short-leg fielder. Always associated in the public mind with Glamorgan, he first appeared for them as a schoolboy in 1924. He captained Cambridge in 1929 and Glamorgan from 1930 until 1939. He passed 1,000 runs in a season ten times and three times hit double centuries, the highest being 233 against Worcestershire at Swansea in 1937, a season in which Glamorgan finished higher than ever before thanks to his bold leadership and devoted example. For ten years he was an outstanding secretary to the Club. He toured Australia in 1929/30 and South Africa in 1930/31, and with Maurice Allom, wrote a lighthearted account of each tour. At home he represented England against the West Indies and India; and he was an England selector in 1938 and

1939. A Major in the Welsh Guards, he was killed in action in Normandy. A brilliant all-round sportsman, he also played for Wales at Rugby Union and hockey.

First-class career (1924-39): 17,543 runs (29.78) including 29 centuries, and 277 catches
Test matches (9): 224 runs (20.36) and 1 catch

TYLDESLEY, George Ernest (1889-1962)

Lancashire

The first Lancastrian to score 100 centuries, Ernest Tyldesley was the younger brother of J.T. He was an elegant right-handed stroke-player, fine hooker and engaging cutter whose chivalrous manner concealed a ruthless and belligerent approach. He reached 1,000 runs in a season nineteen times (once overseas), six times exceeding 2,000. His best years were 1928 with 3,024 runs (79.57), including 10 centuries, and 1926 with 2,826 runs (64.22), again including 10 centuries, 4 coming in successive innings. In July 1926 alone he scored 1,024 runs (128.00). His highest was 256 not out against Warwickshire at Old Trafford in 1930 (the season when Lancashire won the Championship for the fourth time in five years). In and out of the England team, he appeared in five Tests against Australia between 1921 and 1928/9, making 257 runs (42.83); and against South Africa in 1927/8, against vicious spin on matting, he achieved great things, making 520 runs (65.00) including 122 at Johannesburg, when he added 230 with Herbert Sutcliffe for the second wicket. He appeared against the West Indies in the first three Tests in England in 1928, scoring 122 in the first at Lord's.

First-class career (1909-36): 38,874 runs (45.46) including 102 centuries, and 287 catches
Test matches (14): 990 runs (55.00) including 3 centuries, 0-2 and 2 catches

TYLDESLEY, John Thomas (1873-1930)

Lancashire

J.T., or Johnny, Tyldesley brought to the battle the trained skill and aggressive spirit of a good professional soldier. Only 5ft 6ins tall, not only was he a fine, attacking right-handed batsman on all wickets, particularly on the off-side, but he could also defend strongly. Moreover, he was a fine outfielder. He hit 152 in his second match for the county against Warwickshire at Edgbaston in 1895, and never looked back. Nineteen times he exceeded 1,000 runs in a season, five times the 2,000, 1901 bringing 3,041 runs (55.29), including 9 centuries. He scored thirteen double centuries, all for Lancashire, the highest being 295 not out against Kent at Old Trafford in 1906. Three times he hit two centuries in a match. For several years, amid a rich profusion of amateur talent, he held the coveted post of number three in England's team. He toured Australia with A.C. MacLaren's team in 1901/2 and with the first MCC team in 1903/4 and South Africa with Lord Hawke's side of 1898/9. He was a regular against Australia in England between 1899 and 1909, and appeared in the first home series against South Africa in 1907.

Johnny Tyldesley

First-class career (1895-1923): 37,897 runs (40.66) including 86 centuries, and 355 catches
Test matches (31): 1,661 runs (30.75) including 4 centuries, and 16 catches

TYLDESLEY, Richard Knowles (1897-1943)

Lancashire

Dick Tyldesley's skill as a right-arm slow bowler increased like his bulk; he was a Falstaff from Westhaughton. Carrying his weight with remarkable ease, he toiled for long spells without tiring. Above medium height, he flighted the ball naturally and often got lbws with his top-spinner. His leg-break turned little under normal conditions but, on a responsive pitch, could be devastating. From 1922 until 1931 he took at least 100 wickets a season, his best being 1924, with 184 (13.98). At Derby in 1929 he dismissed two men with the last two balls of the first innings and two more with the first two balls he sent down in the second. He toured Australia in 1924/5, but played against Australia and South Africa at home with more success. He was one of four brothers – not related to G.E. or J.T. – who all played for Lancashire, the others being William, James and Harry; all died young.

First-class career (1919-35): 6,424 runs (15.04) including 1 century, 1,509 wickets (17.21) and 328 catches
Test matches (7): 47 runs (7.83), 19 wickets (32.57) and 1 catch

TYLECOTE, Edmund Ferdinando Sutton (1849-1938)

Oxford University, Kent and Bedfordshire

While at Clifton, where he was in the eleven for five years, finishing as captain, Edmund Tylecote made 404 not out in a house match. He led Oxford to victory in the University match. Besides his remarkably steady and free-hitting batting, he was a quiet and unobtrusive wicket-keeper who stood close-up unless the bowling was exceptionally fast, and he was one of the first to dispense with a long-stop. For Kent he hit a splendid 100 not out against the Australians at Canterbury in 1882; and that winter he toured Australia with Hon. Ivo Bligh's side in search of the Ashes, hitting 66 at Sydney in the match that decided the rubber. He hit a century at Lord's for Gentlemen against Players, and in the same fixture in 1876 he stumped two batsmen and caught five. He appeared twice for England against Australia in 1886, at Lord's and The Oval. In 22 matches for Kent from 1875 until 1883 he made 927 runs (24.39), including 2 centuries.

Test matches (6): 152 runs (19.00) and 10 dismissals (5 ct, 5 st.)

TYLER, Edwin James (1864-1917)

Worcestershire and Somerset

Playing a prominent part i Somerset's promotion to first-class rank in 1891, Edwin Tyler was a left-arm bowler of such slow pace that, had he not possessed a good head and great command of length, first-rate batsmen would have hit him all over the field. As it was, even the best batsmen respected him, and he achieved some outstanding performances. He captured all 10 for 49 in an innings against Surrey at Taunton in 1895, 9 for 33 against Nottinghamshire at Taunton in 1892 and 9 for 83 against Sussex at Hastings in 1907. Match figures included 15 for 95 against Sussex at Taunton in 1895 and 15 for 96 against Nottinghamshire at Taunton in 1892. There was some doubt about the legality of his action, but, as he was too slow to hurt anybody, his action passed muster. For Lord Hawke's team in South Africa in 1895/6, he appeared in his sole Test at Cape Town, failing to score and taking 4 for 65.

First-class career (1891-1907): 2,952 runs (11.35) and 895 wickets (21.88)

TYSON, Frank Holmes (b.1930)

Northamptonshire

Frank Tyson was perhaps the only great fast bowler capable of quoting from Shakespeare or Wordsworth in between knocking stumps out of the ground. On his debut for Northamptonshire at the county ground against the 1952 Indians, he swung his first ball so far that it went to first slip – and the slips moved back five yards! He was in the public eye thereafter as the fastest bowler in England. After trials for his native Lancashire, he had qualified for Northamptonshire and was soon to earn the designation 'Typhoon Tyson': his pace, originally after a run-up of more than seventy yards from the 'keeper, made spectators gasp and chatter, and batsmen turn to the wicket-keeper with a resigned smile after the first ball had whistled through. Although quite tall and immensely strong, Tyson tended to put excessive strain on his frame with his long final stride and a not quite fluent action and this, plus the need to bowl on too many featherbeds at Northampton, caused frequent injuries and a short career. But his partnership with Brian Statham, especially in Australia in 1954/5, has passed into the legend of the game. In the first Test at Brisbane he took 1 for 160 in twenty-nine overs; the rest was a tale of unending success. There can have been few faster spells in cricket history than Tyson's in the second innings of the third Test at Melbourne. He skittled the opposition, taking 7 for 27 and, bowling downwind off a shorter run, was literally as fast as a typhoon. He took most wickets in the series on either side: 28 (20.82). Against South Africa at Trent Bridge, in the first Test of 1955, he was almost equally devastating, taking 6 for 28 (off 21.3 overs) in the second innings. He toured Australia and New Zealand again, in 1958/9, with less

Frank Tyson

success, and South Africa in 1956/7. Plagued by injuries, he played no more than a sprinkling of Tests in England between 1954 and 1956. A graduate of Durham University, he emigrated to Australia and has been assistant master and headmaster, as well as making an erudite author, journalist and commentator. He gave up teaching to become the chief cricket coach in Victoria.

First-class career (1952-60): 4,103 runs (17.09) and 766 wickets (20.92)
Test matches (17): 230 runs (10.95), 76 wickets (18.56) and 4 catches

George Ulyett

ULYETT, George (1851-98)

Yorkshire

George Ulyett, or 'Happy Jack', said of himself that Yorkshire played him for his whistling and good behaviour and that England played him to go in first with W.G. Grace, to give the doctor confidence. A tall, well-built man, he had the fun and zest of his generation of carefree professionals; and he was one of the foremost all-rounders of his day. His batting motto was high, wide and handsome: at Edgbaston he off-drove a ball 130 yards and at Lord's straight-drove a ball over the old Pavilion. His bowling was fast, the ball breaking sharply from the off and often rising uncomfortably, and he was a very reliable fielder, especially to his own bowling. Nine times he exceeded 1,000 runs in a season. His highest score was 199 not out against Derbyshire at Sheffield in 1887, when he carried his bat through the innings. A regular England player for a decade, he appeared in the first two Tests against Australia at Melbourne in 1876/7, taking 3 for 39 in the first Test and top-scoring with 52 and 63 in the second. Uniquely, he also played in the first Test against South Africa in 1888/9. At Lord's in 1884 he took 7 for 36 (in 39.1 overs) in the second innings, Australia being beaten by an innings. Altogether, he toured Australia five times, heading the batting averages as well as doing most of the bowling with 'Bunny' Lucas and Tom Emmett for Lord Harris's team in 1878/9, and hitting 149 and 64 at Melbourne in 1881/2. He also toured America with Richard Daft's team of 1879, when he frustrated a well-known baseball-pitcher by scoring 160 not out against him.

First-class career (1873-93): 20,484 runs (23.46) including 18 centuries, and 619 wickets (20.17)
Test matches (25): 949 runs (24.33) including 1 century, 50 wickets (20.40) and 18 catches

UNDERWOOD, Derek Leslie (b.1945)

Kent

When Derek Underwood decided in 1977 to join World Series Cricket, he voluntarily interrupted one of the most remarkable of all Test careers. He left the Test arena after helping England to win the Jubilee series of 1977 against Australia and having taken 265 wickets in 74 Tests, but returned to play in 12 more Tests and to make two further tours – to Australia in 1979/80 and India in 1981/2 – before joining an officially disapproved-of tour of South Africa in March 1982 which ended his Test career 3 wickets short of 300. A left-arm spin bowler, his pace is normally slow-medium but varies from brisk medium to slow according to conditions. His walk is rather flat-footed, the feet pointing towards mid-off and mid-on as he goes back to bowl, and there is no beauty about the plodding approach to the stumps – seven or eight paces – but the delivery is at once mechanical and fluid. What is exceptional is the totally unfailing length and carefully calculated direction, which has driven thousands of batsmen to strokeless distraction and an often self-inflicted doom. Intensely dedicated, 'Deadly' first played for Kent in 1963 when not yet eighteen and became the youngest player to take 100 wickets in his maiden season. By the age of twenty-five he had taken his 1,000th first-class wicket; only Wilfred Rhodes and George Lohmann had achieved this landmark at a younger age. He first played for England against the West Indies in 1966 and, as well as impressing as a bowler, he played the first of many determined and useful tail-end innings. He is a right-handed batsman with a strictly limited range of strokes, though cannily used. By sheer will-power, he has also made himself into a reliable outfielder with safe hands and an accurate throw. Although it took him a long time to become as effective a bowler overseas as he is in England (he was for many years reluctant to give the ball the necessary extra air on good pitches) he has travelled on eight overseas tours with official MCC teams. Among his many match-winning performances for Kent and England are his 7 for 50 against Australia in 1968 at The Oval (when he proved totally unplayable after a thunderstorm appeared to have deprived England of victory), 8 for 51 against Pakistan at Lord's in 1974 (again on a wet wicket), 9 for 28 against Sussex at Hastings in 1964 and 9 for 32 against Surrey at The Oval in 1978. Though his attack is based upon his miserly hatred of any batsman scoring any runs off him at any time, his bowling has endless subtle variations of pace, often of trajectory too, and his 'arm ball', which swings in to the right-hander, has claimed many a victim. A dogged, steady character and an avid reader, he is a highly disciplined professional who still has many bowling records within his compass.

First-class career (1963-): 3,990 runs (9.41), 2,118 wickets (19.81) and 233 catches
Test matches (86): 937 runs (11.56), 297 wickets (25.83) and 44 catches

Derek Underwood

VALENTINE, Bryan Herbert (1908-83)

Cambridge University and Kent

Like his contemporary Percy Chapman, Bryan Valentine was a cheerful and sometimes great batsman. He often started hitting as soon as he went in, and averaged some fifty runs in an hour. Right-handed, he was essentially an in-front-of-the-wicket player with a penchant for the leg-side, and he could be a matchwinner; he was also a brilliant fielder. He captained Kent from 1932 until 1934, jointly in 1937, and from 1946 until 1948. In 1946 he led a cavalry charge at Gillingham against Nottinghamshire, hitting 95 and 114, including nine sixes (seven in the century), allowing Kent to earn their first post-War points. He toured India and South Africa with MCC teams in 1933/4 and 1938/9 respectively, and made 136 on his Test debut against India at Bombay, the first Test in that country. In his first two Tests against South Africa, he made 97 and 112. He did not represent England at home. He made 1,000 runs in a season nine times with a highest score of 242 against Leicestershire at Oakham in 1938. Also a brilliant lawn-tennis player, he won the Public Schools doubles with H.W. (Bunny) Austin. During the Second World War he was awarded the MC in North Africa.

First-class career (1927-50): 18,306 (30.15) including 35 centuries, 27 wickets (41.29) and 309 catches
Test matches (7): 454 runs (64.85) including 2 centuries, and 2 catches

VERITY, Hedley (1905-43)

Yorkshire

Following in the great Yorkshire tradition of Peate, Peel and Rhodes, Hedley Verity was one of the most skilful left-arm spin bowlers in history. His easy, springing run-up to the wicket suggested a cat preparing for the kill and his sheer accuracy of length and viciousness of spin reduced the best of batsmen to uncertainty and impotence. His average pace was slow-medium, on fast wickets about medium, and he could send down a virulent in-swinging yorker; on wet, crumbled or sticky wickets he reduced his pace and tossed the orthodox spinner higher. He was a great student of the game and, with Bill Bowes, the pivot of Yorkshire's attack in the great Championship-winning years of the thirties. From 1935 to 1937 he exceeded 200 wickets each season. Twice he took all 10 wickets in an innings, against Warwickshire at Headingley for 36 runs in 1931 and against Nottinghamshire on the same ground for 10 runs in 1932 – a world record. Against Essex at Leyton in 1933 his match haul was 17 for 91. In his last match of all he took 7 for 9 against Sussex at Hove on 1 September 1939. A regular for England for seven years, he toured Australia twice and South Africa, India and New

Hedley Verity

Zealand once each; and at home played in two series against Australia, the West Indies and New Zealand, and once each against South Africa and India. He was irresistible after rain at Lord's in 1934, when in one day he took 14 for 80 (15 for 104 in the match). Yet more than one witness has observed that he was almost happier bowling on a batsman's pitch than a bowler's: he loved a challenge. As a batsman, he was usually in the lower order. He had grit and technique and a casual observer could have mistaken him for Herbert Sutcliffe out of form. He was a sound all-round fielder, who could be brilliant to his own bowling or at backward point. During the 1936/7 Test series in Australia few regular opening batsmen could remain together for long. In the fourth match, at Adelaide, he was promoted to open with Charles Barnett, and they put up 53 and 45 together, the best first-wicket stands for England in the five Tests! A kindly, thoughtful, clean-living man, Captain Verity of the Green Howards died as a POW in Italy, having been wounded in an 8th Army attack in Sicily. There was no 'breaking-point' for him and his last reported words to his Company, 'Keep going', were characteristic.

First-class career (1930-39): 5,603 runs (18.13) including 1 century, 1,956 wickets (14.87) and 244 catches
Test matches (40): 669 runs (20.90), 144 wickets (24.37) and 30 catches

VERNON, George Frederick (1856-1902)

Middlesex

George Vernon was a splendid, natural hitter, whose quickness of eye to some extent made up for his playing with a bat that was never quite straight. Clean, powerful driving was his forte. He toured Australia with the Hon. Ivo Bligh's team in 1882/3, and in his sole Test, the first at Melbourne, he batted number eleven, scoring 11 not out and 3 and not bowling. He took his own side to Australia five years later, in conjunction with the Melbourne club, but Shaw and Shrewsbury took out another team at the same time, and the financial results were disastrous. He also took a team to India in 1889/90. He died young in West Africa. He also played rugby for England.

First-class career (1876-98): 7,070 runs (19.11) including 4 centuries

VINE, Joseph (1875-1946)

Sussex

Originally a forcing right-handed batsman, the sturdy Joseph Vine curbed his natural instincts while partnering Charles Fry or Ranji and, in the early years of this century, was quite a stonewaller. Fry, his captain, told him that his job was to keep up one end and break the bowler's heart. Six times between 1901 and 1904, these two shaped double century stands for the first Sussex wicket, each time the captain dominating the scoring. In a cartoon Joe was once likened to a snail. Late in his career, however, he emerged from his shell: in 1920 at Hastings against Northamptonshire he hit his highest score, 202, in five hours. Fourteen times he exceeded 1,000 runs in a season. He was also a useful slow leg-break bowler (he achieved the double in 1901) and an outfield of rare speed and certainty. He toured Australia in 1911/12 with MCC and appeared in two Tests. After retiring, he coached at Brighton College.

First-class career (1896-1922): 25,171 runs (29.94) including 34 centuries, 683 wickets (29.99) and 228 catches
Test matches (2): 46 runs (46.00)

VOCE, William (b.1909)

Nottinghamshire

In a long career Bill Voce was three separate bowlers – slow left-arm, fast left-arm bowling over the wicket, and even faster bowling leg-theory round the wicket. At his peak he was the best fast left-arm bowler of his time: the famous foil to Harold Larwood, both for Nottinghamshire and, immortally, for England in Australia in 1932/3, the highly controversial Bodyline Tour. Tall and strong, Voce had a beautiful action and his loose left arm made him also a glorious thrower from the deep. A more than useful batsman, he made several centuries for his county, and scored 1,020 runs in 1933. He took more than 100 wickets in a season six

Bill Voce

times, the first being 1929 when his county won the Championship. He toured the West Indies in 1929/30 and took most Test wickets – 17. In South Africa, 1930/31, he was again chief bowler with 23 Test wickets. In the Bodyline Series he took 15 wickets in four Tests; and four years later the first two Tests, at Brisbane and Sydney, both of which England won, brought him analyses of 6 for 41, 4 for 16, 4 for 10 and 3 for 66. In the five Tests he took more wickets than anyone on either side, 26 (21.53). In the second match he began by taking O'Brien, Bradman and McCabe in four balls! After the Second World War England were short of bowlers and Bill Voce, hard-working as ever, but overweight, played against India and toured Australia in 1946/7. He finished his county career as he began it – as a slow bowler.

First-class career (1927-52): 7,583 runs (19.19) including 4 centuries, 1,558 wickets (23.08) and 280 catches
Test matches (27): 308 runs (13.39), 98 wickets (27.88) and 15 catches

WADDINGTON, Abraham (1893-1959)

Yorkshire

Abe Waddington was a lively left-arm, fast-medium bowler, who gave no quarter and asked for none. His length was good, his action flowed, he made the ball swerve and rear awkwardly from the pitch, and he exceeded 100 wickets in six of his nine seasons with Yorkshire (the county winning the Championship four years in succession). A tail-end batsman, he hit his only century, 114 against Worcestershire at Headingley, in his last season. He was a very reliable close field. He toured Australia with MCC in 1920/21 where he played his only Test cricket.

First-class career (1919-27): 2,529 runs (12.90) including 1 century, 857 wickets (19.75) and 217 catches
Test matches (2): 16 runs (4.00), 1-119 and 1 catch

WAINWRIGHT, Edward (1865-1919)

Yorkshire

Ted Wainwright belonged to Lord Hawke's great Yorkshire eleven. Tall, craggy, and blunt of tongue – but, to C.B. Fry, 'a charming character' – he was a fine right-handed batsman, a deadly off-break bowler on any wicket giving him assistance (although sometimes erratic) and an excellent field. In his first season, 1888, he took 105 off the Australians for his county at Bradford; and for more than a decade he was always scoring runs or taking wickets. He achieved the double in 1897. When he made his highest score, 228 against Surrey at The Oval in 1899, he added 340 for the fifth wicket with George Hirst in three and a half hours. He played once for England against Australia in 1893, and in the following season he took 166 wickets (12.73). He toured Australia with A.E. Stoddart's unsuccessful side in 1897/8.

First-class career (1888-1902): 12,485 runs (21.82) including 19 centuries, 1,062 wickets (18.20) and 339 catches
Test matches (5): 132 runs (14.66), 0-73 and 2 catches

WALKER, Peter Michael (b.1936)

Glamorgan, Transvaal and Western Province

Peter Walker is an all-rounder on and off the cricket field. He was a very tall (6ft 4ins) left-arm, orthodox, slow bowler, a hard-driving right-hand batsman and brilliant specialist short-leg fieldsman with octopus-like arms. Capped by Glamorgan in 1957, he won three caps for England against South Africa in 1960. In all he scored more than 1,000 runs in eleven seasons, doing the double in 1961 with 101 wickets, 1,347 runs and 73 catches. His total in 1959 was 1,564 runs, 80 wickets and 65 catches. He continued to be a key all-rounder in the Glamorgan side for a decade or more, taking more catches for the county than any other player, including eight in the match against Derbyshire at Swansea in 1970. A modest, personable man of wide interests, he lives in Cardiff and is now a cricket author and a broadcaster on cricket and current affairs.

First-class career (1954-72): 17,650 runs (26.03) including 13 centuries, 834 wickets (28.63) and 697 catches
Test matches (3): 128 runs (32.00), 0-34 and 5 catches

WALTERS, Cyril Frederick (b.1905)

Glamorgan and Worcestershire

Joining Worcestershire as secretary after five seasons with Glamorgan, in which his overall batting average was 17, Cyril Walters blossomed as a flowing right-handed stroke-player. Slightly built, he played with wristy elegance and was admirably consistent, although he too often got out when he was well set. First playing for Worcestershire in 1928, he captained his new county from 1931 until 1935, scoring more than 2,000 runs in 1933 and 1934. His highest score was 226 against Kent at Gravesend in 1933. He made 51 in his first Test against the West Indies at Lord's in 1933. In India in 1933/4 he partnered Fred Bakewell and made 59 and 102 in the third Test at Madras. Against Australia in 1934 he captained England in the first Test at Trent Bridge because Bob Wyatt was injured and, partnering either Sutcliffe or Walter Keeton, was very successful throughout the series (401 runs at 50.12). Part way through the 1935 season, however, owing to ill-health and domestic commitments, he suddenly retired from first-class cricket.

First-class career (1923-35): 12,145 runs (30.74) including 21 centuries
Test matches (11): 784 runs (52.26) including 1 century, and 6 catches

WARD, Alan (b.1947)

Derbyshire, Border and Leicestershire

Not many very tall fast bowlers have survived for long in top class cricket, and Alan Ward is a case in point. On his day he could be very fast indeed, and one often felt that his spirit was willing but his flesh weak. His height, relatively slim build, and a right-arm action which somehow never looked natural – he almost seemed to over-balance as he delivered the ball – conspired to cause numerous injuries, especially in the legs. Derbyshire nursed him gently after a promising debut in 1966. He was capped in 1969 and played for Derbyshire until 1976, when he moved to Leicestershire for two seasons without being able to command a regular place. His five Tests were spaced between 1969 and 1976, but injury plagued him when he had his big chance in Australia in 1970/71, and he had to return home early without sharing in the success of John Snow and England's other fast bowlers. His best bowling return in a Test was 4 for 61 against New Zealand at Trent Bridge in his second Test match. He took 10 wickets in that short series at 21 each but the auspicious start was deceptive. For Derbyshire he took 7 for 42 against Glamorgan in 1974 and he also once took 4 wickets in four balls in a John Player league match. He was often useful as a tail-ender.

First-class career (1966-78): 928 runs (8.43) and 460 wickets (22.81)
Test matches (5): 40 runs (8.00), 14 wickets (32.35) and 3 catches

WARD, Albert (1865-1939)

Yorkshire and Lancashire

While an assistant schoolmaster, Albert Ward had some outings for Yorkshire, but was soon snatched for Lancashire by John Stanning, who was 'a naughty old boy', according to Lord Hawke, 'being an inveterate cricket poacher'. Thus Ward, a right-handed opening batsman, began a long, splendid and honourable career for Lancashire. Six feet tall and of an ideal temperament – cool, patient and persevering – he had a very sound defence and could drive powerfully and cut well. He seldom dropped a catch in the deep, and was a useful slow bowler. He carried his bat through an innings on five occasions (the best being 140 out of 281 against Gloucestershire at Bristol in 1893). His highest score was 219 for A.E. Stoddart's team against South Australia at Adelaide in 1894/5. He was prominent in England's success in Australia in 1894/5. In the first Test at Sydney he top-scored in both innings with 75 and 117 – England winning by a mere 10 runs. In the fifth match at Melbourne which decided the rubber, England, seeking 297 to win, lost two early wickets, but Ward, defending stoutly, scored 93, added 210 with J.T. Brown and victory was secured. He scored more runs than anyone else in the series, 419 (41.90) but never played for England again.

First-class career (1886-1904): 17,783 runs (30.08) including 29 centuries, 71 wickets (25.59) and 159 catches
Test matches (7): 487 runs (37.46) including 1 century, and 1 catch

WARDLE, John Henry (b.1923)

Yorkshire and Cambridgeshire

Johnny Wardle could bowl slow, left-arm orthodox *and* the chinaman and googly with equal facility. He was probably the best wrist spinner of his generation, and, excepting perhaps Tony Lock and Alf Valentine, the best orthodox left-arm spinner too. He was a hard-hitting batsman and zealous close field, whose clowning would delight the crowd. He took his bowling seriously, however, and in 1954 he was very successful, taking 9 for 25 against Lancashire at Old Trafford, 9 for 48 against Sussex at Hove, and 16 for 112 against Sussex at Hull; and in ten seasons of his rather short career he captured at least 100 wickets, six times exceeding 150 wickets, 1955 bringing him 195 wickets (16.14). He had an outstanding tour for MCC in South Africa in 1956/7, taking 90 wickets (12.25), including 12 for 89 in the second Test at Cape Town. He toured Australia and New Zealand once and the West Indies twice; and occasionally represented England at home from 1950 until 1957. His career ended under a cloud: ill-advised articles in a national newspaper criticizing the Yorkshire captain and the other members of his team led to his being dropped by Yorkshire and the withdrawal by MCC of the invitation to tour Australia in 1958/9. Wardle retired to the Lancashire league, and later played for Cambridgeshire.

First-class career (1946-68): 7,333 runs (16.08), 1,846 wickets (18.97) and 257 catches
Test matches (28): 653 runs (19.78), 102 wickets (20.39) and 12 catches

'Plum' Warner

WARNER, Sir Pelham Francis (1873-1963)

Oxford University and Middlesex

'Plum' in his gracious old age was the very reverend dean of Cricket's Cathedral, but at the turn of the century he was young 'Plum' Warner, a polished batsman and the keenest of captains. 'Cricket's gentil knight', he became Sir Pelham for his services to the game world-wide in 1937. He was born in Trinidad where his father had been attorney-general, became captain of cricket at Rugby, earned a blue at Oxford, and played for Middlesex from 1894 until 1920, captaining the county between 1908 and 1920. He captained the first official MCC team to Australia in 1903/4, recovering the Ashes, and the first MCC team to South Africa in 1905/6. He was elected to the committee of MCC in 1904 and remained on it for most of the rest of his life. He founded and for many years edited *The Cricketer*, served as deputy-secretary of MCC from 1939 to 1945, and became president in 1950. In between, he travelled to many countries as an ambassador of the game. A neat, brave, balanced and determined right-hand batsman of frail physique, 'Plum' first toured with Lord Hawke's team in the West Indies in 1896/7, and made his debut in Tests for his Lordship's England side in South Africa in 1898/9. He was bitten by the travel bug and claimed to have made a duck in every British Dominion except India, as well as in Portugal. In successive Tests on the triumphant 1903/4 tour he made 68, 48 and 79. On his second tour of Australia in 1911/12, as captain, he was taken ill after scoring 151 against South Australia in the opening game and could play no more on the tour. He represented England against Australia at home in 1909 and 1912, and against South Africa in 1912; and was joint manager of MCC's team to Australia in 1932/3, the Bodyline Tour, when he did not emerge from the controversy as a decisive figure. Well read and scholarly, he wrote or edited some twenty books on tours, history and autobiography and was cricket correspondent of *The Morning Post* for nearly twenty years. His success as a batsman was as much due to concentration and will-power as to innate ability. He made 1,000 runs in a season fourteen times, his best season being 1911 with 2,123 runs (46.15), including his highest score of 244 for the Rest of England against Warwickshire at The Oval. On his Test debut he carried his bat through the innings, making 132 (out of 237). He made three successive centuries at Lord's in 1910. In his last season as Middlesex captain, he led his county after a late burst to a sensational Championship win over Surrey at Lord's in his last match. It was said of Warner that he knew every blade of grass at Lord's: he certainly loved the game, and when he died his ashes were scattered at Lord's.

First-class career (1894-1929): 29,028 runs (36.28) including 60 centuries, 15 wickets (42.40) and 187 catches
Test matches (15): 622 runs (23.92) including 1 century, and 3 catches

WARR, John James (b.1927)

Cambridge University and Middlesex

John Warr was discovered bowling in a humble match

on Parker's Piece by a Cambridge captain desperate to find a fast bowler. He was something of a tearaway at University, captaining Cambridge in 1951, but developed into a much more controlled opening bowler, who could move the ball away from the bat from the extreme edge of the crease. As an undergraduate he was an unexpected choice for MCC's team to Australia, 1950/51, and failed in the Tests. Subsequently, he was a shrewd captain of Middlesex from 1958 until 1960; he took 116 wickets (18.17) in 1956, in which year he took 9 for 65 (14 for 92 in the match) against Kent at Lord's. A raconteur and wit, he has written entertainingly on the game in *The Sunday Telegraph* and other publications; he is also a very successful City businessman, a steward of the Jockey Club, and has acted as Australia's representative on the ICC.

First-class career (1949-60): 3,838 runs (11.46) and 956 wickets (22.80)
Test matches (2): 4 runs (1.00) and 1-281

WARREN, Arnold (1875-1951)

Derbyshire

Over six feet and taking a long, bounding run, Arnold Warren was a fast right-arm bowler in the Derbyshire tradition. He was the first player ever to take 100 wickets in a season for the county – 124 wickets (20.94) in 1904, including 15 for 112 against Nottinghamshire at Welbeck. In 1905 he represented England against Australia in the third Test at Headingley, scoring 7, taking 5 for 57 and 1 for 56 – numbering Trumper (twice), Noble, Armstrong and Darling among his victims – and holding one catch, but this was his sole appearance for England.

First-class career (1897-1920): 5,441 runs (14.02) including 1 century, and 939 wickets (24.55)

WASHBROOK, Cyril (b.1914)

Lancashire

Shortish and strong around the chest and shoulders, Cyril Washbrook invariably wore his cap at a jaunty angle, and always put character as well as sound technique into his batting. He was neat and quick on his feet and a ruthless attacker of anything short, either with perfectly timed square-cuts or daring hooks. In the field he was a swift and accurate cover-point. In his second match for his county, against Surrey at Old Trafford in 1933, he hit 152. He made his Test debut for England against New Zealand at The Oval in 1937. Despite losing invaluable years to the War, he enjoyed his best seasons straight after it, in 1946 and 1947 making 2,400 runs (68.57) including 9 centuries, and 2,662 runs (68.25) including 11 centuries, one of which, 251 not out against Surrey at Old Trafford, remained his career-highest. He became Len Hutton's regular partner in Tests. They put on three successive century opening partnerships against Australia in 1946/7. Washbrook saved England in the third match at Melbourne with 62 and 112. Against Australia in England in 1948 he made 356 runs (50.85), including 143 and 65 in the fourth Test at Headingley, when he put on 168 and 129 with Hutton for the first wicket. In the second Test against South Africa, at Johannesburg in 1948/9, he made his highest Test score, 195, and with Hutton hit 359 for the first wicket, which became the new England record for the first wicket. In the five Tests he made 542 runs (60.22). He toured Australia in 1950/51 and, at home, appeared with success against India, New Zealand and the West Indies. Recalled to the England side in 1956 against Australia at Headingley, he came in when the score was 17 for 3, and shared in a stand of 187 with Peter May. When Washbrook was lbw to Benaud for 98 there were tears in many eyes. In all he made 996 runs in 17 Tests against Australia. He was the first professional Lancastrian captain, from 1954 to 1959. He had made 1,000 runs in a season twenty times (three times overseas) when he retired. He has since served as a Test selector.

Cyril Washbrook

First-class career (1933-64): 34,101 runs (42.67) including 76 centuries, and 206 catches
Test matches (37): 2,569 runs (42.81) including 6 centuries, 1-33 and 12 catches

WATKINS, Allan John (b.1922)

Glamorgan

A balding and genial 'Friar Tuck' of cricket, Allan Watkins was the first Glamorgan player to represent England against Australia (at The Oval in 1948, when England were dismissed on the first morning for 52, and eventually lost heavily by an innings). A genuine all-rounder, he was a sound and enterprising left-handed batsman, who often rallied his county, a penetrating, left-arm, medium-pace bowler and a dynamic field. He was an invaluable member of Glamorgan's first Championship-winning side in 1948. He achieved the double in both 1954 and 1955, and thirteen times exceeded 1,000 runs in a season. His highest score was 170 not out against Leicestershire at Swansea in 1954; and his best bowling feats were 7 for 28 against Derbyshire at Chesterfield and 7 for 29 against Gloucestershire at Gloucester, both in 1954. He toured South Africa, India and Pakistan. In South Africa, 1948/9, he made 111 in the fourth Test at Johannesburg; and he played especially well against India, 1951/2, when he was the foremost run-getter on either side, hitting 451 runs (64.42). Because of asthma, his doctor advised him to give up the game at first-class level, but he still plays cricket for charity from time to time.

First-class career (1939-63): 20,362 runs (30.57) including 32 centuries, 833 wickets (24.48) and 461 catches
Test matches (15): 810 runs (40.50) including 2 centuries, 11 wickets (50.36) and 17 catches

WATSON, William (b.1920)

Yorkshire and Leicestershire

A natural left-handed batsman, Willie Watson was both graceful and patient. Making batting look supremely easy, he was also a speedy runner between wickets. His bat met the ball with the measured straightness and certainty of a pendulum. He played for Yorkshire until 1956 and spent the rest of his career at Leicester as assistant-secretary and captain from 1958 until 1961. He represented England regularly from 1951 until 1958 against Australia, South Africa, the West Indies, New Zealand and India. He toured Australasia in 1958/9 and the West Indies in 1953/4. In his first two Tests against South Africa in 1951, he hit 57 and 79, immediately strengthening the previously suspect English middle-batting. On his debut against Australia, at Lord's in 1953, he made 109 and, with England facing defeat, he batted five and three quarter hours, adding 163 with Trevor Bailey for the fifth wicket, one of the epic Test match stands. On his debut against the West Indies, at Kingston in 1953/4, he made 116. He was vice-captain of the MCC non-Test playing tour of New Zealand in 1960/61. When Yorkshire allowed him to join Leicestershire, he was an immediate success. He headed the averages of his new county each year, his best being 1959 with 2,212 runs (55.30). Altogether, he made 1,000 runs in a season fourteen times with a highest score of 257 for MCC against British Guiana at Georgetown in 1953/4. Throughout, he was brilliant in the outfield, as befitted an international footballer. He played for Huddersfield Town and Sunderland, winning four caps for England, and he was a member of the World Cup side in 1950. He emigrated to South Africa in 1968, becoming coach at the Wanderers club in Johannesburg.

First-class career (1939-64): 25,670 runs (39.86) including 55 centuries, and 293 catches
Test matches (23): 879 runs (25.85) including 2 centuries, and 8 catches

WEBBE, Alexander Josiah (1855-1941)

Oxford University and Middlesex

Perhaps the best batsman produced by Harrow, and captain of Oxford, Alexander Webbe or 'Webbie' crouched in ungainly fashion with legs wide apart at the wicket, but his defence was masterly and his cutting and driving outstanding. An opening right-handed batsman and useful change-bowler, he captained Middlesex from 1885 until 1898 and remained until his death the county's guide, philosopher and friend. His highest score was 243 not out against Yorkshire at Huddersfield in 1887 when he carried his bat through the innings. Altogether he carried his bat eight times, seven for his county. For Gentlemen against Players, at Lord's in 1875, he shared in an opening partnership of 203 with W.G. To W.G. on that occasion Webbe's defence and patience seemed perfect. He toured Australia with Lord Harris's team in 1878/9, and in his sole Test at Melbourne scored 4 and 0 and held 2 catches.

First-class career (1875-1900): 14,466 runs (24.81) including 14 centuries, 109 wickets (25.20), 227 catches and 10 stumpings

WELLARD, Arthur William (1902-80)

Somerset

Arthur Wellard was a valuable all-rounder, but is remembered largely as a hitter of 500 sixes. The record season was 1935 with 72 sixes and in both 1936 and 1938 he slammed 57; in 1933 he numbered 51; in 1935 he hit 5 off consecutive balls from T.R. Armstrong of Derbyshire and two years later he did the same to Frank Woolley. However, he was no rustic slogger, but a serious batsman with a respectable defence. Three times in 1933, 1935 and 1937, he achieved the double. A right-arm fast bowler with a fierce break-back, he varied his deliveries with medium-pace off-spinner. He was also a fine close field. Eight times he exceeded 100 wickets in a season, his best years being 1938 with 172 wickets (20.29) and 1937 with 156 wickets (23.55), and those years he represented England against Australia and New Zealand. He toured India in 1937/8 with Lord Tennyson's team. A native of Kent, Arthur as a young man asked the county club whether he could join the staff: he was told he would do better to go and be a policeman! He was still playing effective club cricket well into his sixties.

First-class career (1927-50): 12,515 runs (19.73) including 2 centuries, 1,614 wickets (24.35) and 375 catches
Test matches (2): 47 runs (11.75), 7 wickets (33.85) and 2 catches

WHARTON, Alan (b.1923)

Lancashire and Leicestershire

A left-handed batsman who liked to attack, Alan Wharton had a full range of strokes and was also a more than useful, right-arm, medium-pace bowler. He made his reputation with Lancashire (1946-60) and then had a short – but prolific – stay with Leicestershire. Eleven times he exceeded 1,000 runs in a season, his best year being 1959 with 2,157 runs (40.69), including his highest score of 199 against Sussex at Hove. He made a century in each innings against Middlesex at Leicester in 1961. His best bowling was 7 for 33 in an innings against Sussex at Old Trafford in 1951. In his sole Test, against New Zealand at Headingley in 1949, he scored 7 and 13. He had to drop out of the Lord's Test through injury. A schoolteacher and J.P., he was also a Rugby League footballer.

First-class career (1946-63): 21,796 runs (32.24) including 31 centuries, 237 wickets (31.59) and 289 catches

WHITE, David William (b.1935)

Hampshire and Glamorgan

Unlucky to be a contemporary of Trueman, Statham and Tyson, 'Butch' White was powerfully built, and a genuinely fast right-arm bowler whose action was basically sound, although he was once no-balled for throwing, in 1960. A variable, inspirational performer, his career was sprinkled with fine achievements, including more than 100 wickets in a season four times, 9 for 44 in an innings against Leicestershire at Portsmouth in 1966, and 4 for 8 in a Gillette Cup contest. Although he toured India and Pakistan in 1961/2, playing in two Tests, he never represented his country at home. He joined Glamorgan in 1972, to play mainly in one-day matches. He was a cheerful and popular cricketer.

First-class career (1957-72): 3,080 runs (10.58) and 1,143 wickets (23.54)
Test matches (2): 0 runs (0.0) and 4 wickets (29.75)

WHITE, John Cornish (1891-1961)

Somerset

A serene and cheerful character, looking, with his rosy cheeks and blue eyes, exactly like the yeoman farmer he was, Jack or 'Farmer' White was England's slow left-arm bowler between the reigns of Wilfred Rhodes and Hedley Verity. Remarkably, he spun the ball very little and succeeded instead by means of subtle variations of pace and trajectory. Nevertheless, he could make the ball 'do a little' each way on the truest pitch, and he often opened the attack for his county with the new ball. He developed into a competent batsman. He took 100 wickets in a season fourteen times, his best year being 1929 with 168 wickets (15.76). He captured all 10 for 76 against Worcestershire at Worcester in 1921, took 9 wickets in an innings on four occasions and three times had 15 or more wickets in a match. He twice did the double. He captained Somerset from 1927 until 1931, often coming from a morning's haymaking to play at Taunton. Playing fourteen of his fifteen Tests after the age of thirty-seven, he played for England against Australia in 1921 and 1930. He played against South Africa – as captain in 1929 – and against the West Indies in 1928. He toured Australia in 1928/9 and exploded the theory that slow left-arm bowlers are of little use on Australian wickets; he was England's most successful bowler with 25 wickets (30.40) on the generally prevailing batsmen's pitches. In the blazing hot sun at Adelaide in the fourth Test his record was 124.5 overs, 37 maidens, 256 runs and 13 wickets, England winning by 12 runs. 'Farmer' White was an England selector in 1929/30, and became president of Somerset in 1960.

First-class career (1909-37): 12,202 runs (18.40) including 6 centuries, 2,356 wickets (18.57) and 423 catches
Test matches (15): 239 runs (18.38), 49 wickets (32.26) and 6 catches

WHYSALL, William Wilfrid (1887-1930)

Nottinghamshire

After slow development as a right-handed batsman, 'Dodger' Whysall forged ahead after 1919 and he was at his peak by the time of his early death – he had fallen on a dance floor, injured his elbow, and died of septicaemia. Not a graceful batsman, he possessed unlimited patience, a strong defence and all the strokes. For nine years he opened with George Gunn, and they shared in forty three-figure stands together. He made 1,000 runs or more in ten seasons, reaching 2,000 between 1926 and 1930 inclusive. His best year, 1929, brought him 2,716 runs (51.24) – 2,620 for Nottinghamshire alone, which remains a county record. His highest score was 248 against Northamptonshire at Trent Bridge in 1930, his last season. He played in one Test against Australia in 1930 having toured Australia with MCC in 1924/5 as batsman and emergency wicket-keeper. On his Test debut, the third Test at Adelaide, he made 75 in the second innings, which nearly brought victory. In the next Test he made 76 at Melbourne.

First-class career (1910-30): 21,592 runs (38.74) including 51 centuries, 325 catches and 16 stumpings
Test matches (4): 209 runs (29.85), 0-9 and 7 catches

WILKINSON, Leonard Litton (b.1916)

Lancashire

A fair-haired, right-arm, leg-break bowler with a lively action, Len Wilkinson lost little time in making his presence felt in first-class cricket, taking 151 wickets (23.38) in 1938. He headed the bowling averages in all matches for MCC in South Africa, 1938/9, but he was very disappointing thereafter.

First-class career (1934-47): 321 runs (7.64) and 282 wickets (25.25)
Test matches (3): 3 runs (3.00) and 7 wickets (38.71)

WILLEY, Peter (b.1949)

Northamptonshire

A cool, self-possessed and philosophical north-easterner, Peter Willey is an exceptionally talented, right-hand, middle-order batsman. After beginning as a useful medium-pace bowler, severe knee injuries caused him to take up off-spin, which he has developed with considerable success. Born in Durham, he first played for Northamptonshire in 1966 at the age of sixteen years and five months, making 78 against Cambridge in the second innings. A brilliant natural timer of the ball, his batting has been inconsistent despite some electrifying innings in one-day cricket and several memorable first-class centuries, including his highest score of 227 against Somerset at Northampton in 1976, when he shared a record sixth-wicket stand for Northants of 370 with Roy Virgin. Making 1,115 runs (41.29) in this season, and playing a prominent part in Northamptonshire's victory in the Gillette Cup, Willey was selected for England against the immensely powerful West Indies side. He acquitted himself well in the circumstances, falling to a brilliant catch when well set on 45 in the second innings of his first Test at Headingley. After scoring 36, 45, 33 and 1 in matches which England lost, he was harshly treated when omitted from the MCC tour of India and Australia the following winter. But he earned a second chance against India at The Oval in 1979, played well and toured Australia in 1978/9. On a difficult tour he was a great success in the one-day internationals, hitting hard and handsomely and bowling usefully, but he failed in the Test matches. His wristy strength, determination and glorious offside strokes were seen to better advantage against the West Indies fast bowlers, however. He scored 100 not out, his maiden Test century against them at The Oval in 1980 and saved England from possible defeat by adding 117 for the last wicket with Bob Willis. Eight months later he hit the same fierce West Indian attack for 102 not out, including a slashed square-cut six over third man. It was the first Test hundred ever scored in Antigua. He finished the four-Test series with an average of 48. However, he had lost his place in the England team when in March 1982 he joined a group of English cricketers for a lucrative unofficial tour of South Africa, a decision which earned him a three-year ban from Test cricket. His response was to hit 1,783 runs for Northants in 1982 at an average of 50 with five hundreds. Every run seemed to say, 'I'll show 'em.'

First-class career (1966-): 13,274 runs (28.54) including 20 centuries, 491 wickets (28.97) and 131 catches
Test matches (20): 923 runs (27.96) including 2 centuries, 6 wickets (73.50) and 4 catches

WILLIS, Robert George Dylan (b.1949)

Surrey and Warwickshire

It is not easy to define what has made Bob Willis, at his best, a great fast bowler. Will-power, intelligence, in recent years exceptional fitness, and a belief in bowling as fast and as straight as possible have all played a part in his success. Unusually tall at 6ft 5ins, with his mop of brown, curly hair, he presents a hostile image to timid batsmen. He can bounce the ball awkwardly and at will on most pitches and the unorthodox nature of his open-chested action has made him that much more awkward and unpleasant for batsmen to face. He runs in a long way off a straight approach, moves the ball only a little but unpredictably – bowls a good yorker and an especially mean bouncer. On the field he locks himself into a cocoon of concentration, showing scant facial reaction in either triumph or dismay. He had proved himself a sensible, even astute captain when leading England as Brearley's deputy on two tours.

Bob Willis

Then, in 1982, he became England captain in his own right. Willis bowled effectively against India and Pakistan despite the cares of leadership, and by winning both series earned himself the crown of his career, the chance to captain England in Australia. The Ashes were lost but Willis lost none of his reputation as a staunch cricketer and an honourable sportsman. He had made his first visit to Australia as a slim youth of twenty-one in 1970/71 when he flew out late to replace Alan Ward and established himself as an important member of the Test side, bowling accurately and fielding brilliantly close to the wicket. Returning home he was dissatisfied with Surrey's unwillingness to give him his county cap and moved to Warwickshire in 1972. For several seasons he was handicapped by various injuries, notably to both knees, but he bowled with great consistency and courage on his second tour of Australia in 1974/5, taking 17 wickets (30.70). His recent spell of success began with his recall to the England side in 1976, when he took 5 for 42 in the second innings, and 8 wickets in the match, on a perfect Headingley pitch against the immensely powerful West Indies side. By now he was engaging in a daily routine of running and exercises and, during the Centenary Test in Australia in 1977, his rehabilitation was completed when a hypnotherapist taught him how to condition his mind for a major sporting occasion. In India, earlier in this tour, Willis had taken 20 Test wickets (16.75). At home against Australia in 1977 he took 27 wickets at 19.77 and in Australia in 1978/9 20 wickets (23.05), despite pain from blistered feet and a viral infection. His loyal support for Brearley and his own intelligent approach to the problems of touring had much to do with the team's well-being. Things did not go nearly so well in the hastily arranged tour of Australia the following winter when Willis could take only three Test wickets at 74 each when plagued by various ailments. But after returning home early for another knee operation, having taken little part in the 1980/81 tour of the West Indies, he bounced back into the limelight in 1981 to capitalize on Botham's famous innings at Headingley and, by taking 8 for 43 in Australia's second innings, he bowled England to a win which had seemed impossible. It was one of the great fast bowling spells of Test history. He ran down the slope from the Kirkstall End like a man possessed, achieving great pace and wicked lift. Australia, needing only 130 to win on a worn pitch, were 56 for one when Willis began bowling with the wind. They were bowled out for 111. Willis finished the series with 29 wickets to confirm the impression that his best efforts have always tended to come against Australia. In 1977 he took 8 for 32 against Gloucestershire at Bristol, but his performances for Warwickshire have seldom been half as inspirational as some of those for England. He took hat-tricks for his county, however, against Derbyshire in 1972 and the West Indies in 1976, both at Edgbaston where pitches are seldom helpful to the fast bowler. Off the field Willis's interests include music and such was his admiration for the American folk singer Bob Dylan that he took Dylan as a third name. He is not a quick man in the field, but has an unfailing pair of hands and has taken many superb catches. An eccentric but determined tail-end batsman, he can be difficult to dig out and occasionally hits effectively with a great whirl of the bat. No batsman has ever been not out in so many Test innings as Willis. Even as a number eleven he has made use of every ounce of ability, though as captain against Pakistan at Edgbaston in 1982, he got so carried away by a team talk he was giving that he walked out to bat after tea – *without* his bat!

First-class career (1969-): 2,358 runs (14.64), 796 wickets (24.51) and 113 catches
Test matches (74): 645 runs (11.72), 267 wickets (25.13) and 29 catches

WILSON, Rev. Clement Eustace Macroe (1875-1944)

Cambridge University and Yorkshire

Outstanding at Uppingham, Clem Wilson soon gained his blue at Cambridge, and in his fourth University match in 1898 made 118. His brother Rockley also scored a century three years later, the only instance of brothers achieving this feat for Cambridge. Clem could bowl with either arm and, at The Oval against Surrey in 1895, ended a stand of 306 by holding a return catch when bowling left-arm. He played a little for Yorkshire, but the calls of the Ministry curtailed his appearances. He toured South Africa with Lord Hawke's team in 1898/9 when he played his Tests.

First-class career (1895-1900): 1,454 runs (23.93) including 1 century, and 121 wickets (20.23)
Test matches (2): 42 runs (14.00)

WILSON, Donald (b.1937)

Yorkshire

A tall, slow, left-arm bowler, Don Wilson was in the Yorkshire tradition that stretches back to Edmund Peate, although he was not quite as dominant as his great predecessors. He took 100 wickets in a season five times. For Yorkshire against MCC at Scarborough in 1969, he took 7 for 19, and in the John Player League took 6 for 18 against Kent at Canterbury in 1969. He toured India 1963/4 and Australia and New Zealand in 1970/71, where he had his Test match experience. On a lesser tour, MCC to Sri Lanka in 1969/70, he took 8 for 36 (14 for 71 in the match) against the national side at Colombo. A left-handed, hard-hitting batsman, he hit his sole first-class century of 112 for MCC against South Zone at Hyderabad in 1963/4. For Yorkshire against MCC at Scarborough in 1966 he hit Robin Hobbs for 30 in one over. A highly regarded coach, who did notable work for non-white players in South Africa, he became chief coach at Lord's.

First-class career (1957-74): 6,230 runs (14.09) including 1 century, 1,189 wickets (21.00) and 250 catches
Test matches (6): 75 runs (12.50), 11 wickets (42.36) and 1 catch

WILSON, Evelyn Rockley (1879-1957)

Cambridge University and Yorkshire

Rockley Wilson was a fine all-round cricketer and a unique character, whose conversation was full of anecdotes and wit. A remarkably accurate, slow-medium, right-arm bowler who could spin the ball a little either way, he was also a sound, determined batsman. At Cambridge he made 117 not out and 70 on his debut in first-class cricket against A.J. Webbe's eleven at Fenner's in 1899, and two years later scored 118 against Oxford at Lord's thus equalling the feat of his brother, Clem, in the University match three years before. For many years he ran the cricket at Winchester where he was a teacher, and played no first-class cricket from 1902 until 1913. He toured the Argentine with MCC and from 1913 until 1923 assisted Yorkshire regularly during August, when his bowling was very effective. He toured Australia in 1920/21 with MCC and in his sole Test, the fifth at Sydney, he scored 5 and 5 and took 3 for 36.

First-class career (1899-1923): 3,121 runs (22.13) including 4 centuries, and 397 wickets (18.32)

WOOD, Arthur (1898-1973)

Yorkshire

As a wicket-keeper, Arthur Wood was a master of the unexpected, full of uproarious humour, which, however, never interfered with his skill as a first-rate stumper or as a competent, right-handed batsman. His best season as a batsman was 1935, when he made 1,087 runs (36.23) for the Champion county; and his best-known story concerns Yorkshire's game with the South Africans that year at Sheffield. Horace Cameron punished Hedley Verity for 30 runs in one over, at the end of which Arthur turned to Hedley and said: 'You've got him in two minds. He doesn't know whether to hit you for six or four!' As Leslie Ames was incapacitated, Arthur made his Test debut against Australia at The Oval in 1938. Going in at 770 for 6 he hit 53 and stated afterwards: 'I'm always at my best in a crisis!' He kept in the three Tests against the West Indies in 1939, and at The Oval in the last match he took a most astounding catch; the ball soared up from the bat of Learie Constantine very high and Arthur sprinted, taking the catch at long-leg. 'By gow,' he panted, 'it's a good job I were standing back!'

First-class career (1928-48): 8,842 runs (21.20) including 1 century, and 878 dismissals (621 ct, 257 st.)
Test matches (4): 80 runs (20.00) and 11 dismissals (10 ct, 1 st.)

WOOD, Barry (b.1942)

Yorkshire, Lancashire, Derbyshire and Eastern Province

Very short, fair-haired, sturdy and gutsy, Barry Wood is a correct and patient opening batsman, fine gully field, and useful slow-medium bowler who will swing the ball exceptionally in cloudy conditions. In all three roles he has been outstanding for Lancashire in limited-over cricket, winning no fewer than six Gillette Cup Man-of-the-Match awards and eight Benson and Hedges Gold awards for the outstanding individual performance in a match. Moreover he shared in all of Lancashire's Gillette Cup triumphs in the early 1970s after winning his cap in 1968, two years after crossing the border from Yorkshire, for whom he played in 1964. Wood's Test career began promisingly against Australia in 1972 when he made a good looking 90, his highest Test score, against Dennis Lillee at his best at The Oval, driving immaculately through the covers. But a weakness against spin was cruelly exposed by the Indian spinners when he toured the

East with MCC the following winter and his Test appearances since have been sporadic, although he was flown out very late in the winter of 1977/8 to reinforce the England team in New Zealand. After a successful benefit for Lancashire in 1979, he moved to Derbyshire and soon became an effective captain.

First-class career (1964-): 17,431 runs (33.91) including 30 centuries, 298 wickets (30.48) and 283 catches
Test matches (12): 454 runs (21.61), 0-50 and 6 catches

WOOD, George Edward Charles (1893-1971)

Cambridge University and Kent

Standing right up to the stumps for even the fastest bowlers, George Wood was a wicket-keeper who played for Cambridge both before and after the First World War, and a member of Archie MacLaren's amateur team which defeated the mighty Australians at Eastbourne in 1921. He had to decline a place in the MCC side to Australia in 1920/21 but was able to represent England in Tests against South Africa in 1924, and also played for Gentlemen against Players.

First-class career (1913-36): 2,773 runs (19.66) and 170 dismissals (118 ct, 52 st.)
Test matches (3): 7 runs (3.50) and 6 dismissals (5 ct, 1 st.)

WOOD, Henry (1854-1919)

Kent and Surrey

Harry Wood was the third of four long-serving wicket-keepers who sustained Surrey for seventy years. He played during years when Surrey were either Champion county or close to the leaders. He was painstaking to a degree and his hands often suffered horribly, but he never complained. He made the initial tour of South Africa in 1888/9, with Major Warton's team, appearing in the first Tests against that country and returned there in 1891/2. He was a useful batsman whose sole century in first-class cricket was 134 not out for England against South Africa at Cape Town on the second tour. His only appearance against Australia was at The Oval in 1888.

First-class career (1876-1900): 5,523 runs (16.94) including 1 century, and 673 dismissals (555 ct, 118 st.)
Test matches (4): 204 runs (68.00) including 1 century, and 3 dismissals (2 ct, 1 st.)

WOOD, Reginald (1860-1915)

Lancashire and Victoria

When William Barnes was injured – he had aimed a blow at the Australian captain, Percy McDonnell, but connected with a wall instead – Reginald Wood, a native of Cheshire resident in Australia, was asked to play in the second Test at Sydney in 1886/7. Batting at number ten, he scored 6 and 0 and was not required again. Between 1880 and 1884 he had appeared with some success for Lancashire, scoring 166 runs (23.71) and taking 4 wickets (18.00) in six matches. Educated at Charterhouse, he played for Lancashire as an amateur but for Victoria as a professional. As a bowler he was left-handed, medium-paced.

WOODS, Samuel Moses James (1867-1931)

Cambridge University and Somerset

See Australia section.

WOOLLEY, Frank Edward (1887-1978)

Kent

Without question Frank Woolley rests among the half dozen or so great all-rounders of cricket history, although he did not dominate in Tests against Australia quite as much as he might have done. H.S. Altham has described how with his 'tall and graceful figure, his quiet air and unhurried movements, he brought to his left-handed batting an unmistakable air of majestic, almost casual, command. With his long reach and great gift for timing, he would with fascinating ease drive or force off the back foot what to other men was good-length bowling.' Neville Cardus managed at once to be romantic and succinct in his description: 'There was all summer in a stroke by

Frank Woolley

Woolley.' His left-arm slow bowling was equally natural and elegant. His height enabled him to get bounce, his large hands considerable spin and he was accurate too. In the field he became outstanding at slip – 'c Woolley b Freeman' was a regular entry in the score-books, and no fielder has taken more catches. Only Sir Jack Hobbs has scored more runs. In four of the thirteen seasons in which he made 2,000 runs, Woolley also took 100 wickets, a feat no one else has achieved more than twice. In all he scored 1,000 runs in 28 seasons and took 100 wickets in eight of them. His highest aggregate was 3,352 runs (60.94), including 12 centuries. His highest score, 305 not out for MCC against Tasmania at Hobart in 1911/12, remained for more than fifty years the highest by an Englishman in Australia. His last wicket stand of 235 with Arthur Fielder, against Worcestershire at Stourbridge in 1909, remains the record for county cricket. Woolley toured Australia and South Africa three times each, and New Zealand once. He represented England from 1909 until 1934. His debut was against Australia at The Oval in 1909, and his first Test century was 133 in the fifth Test at Sydney in 1911/12. In the first 'timeless' Test, against Australia at The Oval in 1912, he won the game with 62 and 10 for 49 in the match; and again in 1912, at The Oval against South Africa, he took 5 for 41 in the first innings. After the War he disappointed in Australia in 1920/21, but at Lord's the following season he held England together against Gregory and MacDonald with the historic 95 (out of 187) and 93 (out of 283), two amazing performances against the irresistible Australian tide. One of only two English players to appear in all five Tests of 1921, he scored 343 runs (42.87). He hit hundreds against South Africa in 1924 and against Australia in 1924/5, his 123 at Sydney in the first Test coming in two and a half hours. In the 1924/5 series he made 325 runs (36.11). He was, deservedly, a member of the England team at The Oval in 1926, which won back the Ashes after a long wait. His highest score in Tests was 154 against South Africa at Old Trafford in 1929, a series when he made 378 runs (128.00). Woolley was a sober, cautious, introverted character. On retirement he coached at King's School, Canterbury.

First-class career (1906-38): 58,969 runs (40.75) including 145 centuries, 2,068 wickets (19.85) and 1,018 catches
Test matches (64): 3,283 runs (36.07) including 5 centuries, 83 wickets (33.91) and 64 catches

WOOLMER, Robert Andrew (b.1948)

Kent and Natal

Bob Woolmer's Test career was blossoming handsomely when he took the decision to join Kerry Packer's World Series Cricket. A rosy-cheeked and genial man with great confidence in himself, Woolmer

Bob Woolmer

is a graceful right-handed batsman with a casual air and a delightful 'touch' – the comparison with Colin Cowdrey has often been made – who drives fluently on the off-side and deflects with a delicate sense of timing. He is also a useful medium-fast bowler who swings the ball considerably in cloudy conditions, and a safe close fielder. His apprenticeship in the strong Kent side was a relatively long one and his break-through came when he began opening their batting after a long spell late in the order. Son of a British business executive who had captained Uttar Pradesh at cricket, Woolmer lived in India until he was seven, but was educated at Tunbridge Wells and first played for Kent in 1968. Capped in 1970, he began opening in 1976 when he made 1,749 runs (47.27). The previous year he had taken a hat-trick for MCC against the Australians at Lord's and also played his first Test as an all-rounder on the same ground. He was left out until the final match of the series when, going in at number five, he scored 149, reaching the slowest century for England against Australia in six hours thirty-six minutes. Two modest series followed, against the West Indies in 1976 and in India, 1976/7, but in 1977 he scored hundreds in successive Tests against Australia at Lord's and Old Trafford. Thus in only seven Tests against Australia (including the Centenary Test) he had already scored three centuries – as many as May, more than Washbrook, Woolley, Grace, Graveney. What he gained financially by joining World Series Cricket he lost in the momentum of his Test career. He played four more Tests for England at home, in 1980 and 1981, but could not establish himself again.

First-class career (1968-): 14,350 runs (32.76) including 29 centuries, 405 wickets (26.28), 228 catches and 1 stumping
Test matches (19): 1,059 runs (33.09) including 3 centuries, 4 wickets (74.75) and 10 catches

WORTHINGTON, Thomas Stanley (1905-73)

Derbyshire and Northumberland

Stan Worthington began as a right-arm, medium-fast bowler of accurate length and a late-order batsman, who indulged in the fast bowler's traditional 'dip'. He gradually learned to hit with more discrimination. When he made his first century, against Essex in 1928, he included four towering sixes. *Wisden* called him 'a serious-minded fellow'. Between 1928 and 1939 he reached 1,000 runs ten times, and in 1936 hit his highest score, 238 not out, against Sussex at Derby. Stan Worthington toured New Zealand in 1929/30 with MCC, playing in the earliest Tests against that country. In his next series, against India in 1936, he made 87 at Old Trafford, quickly adding 127 with Walter Hammond for the third wicket, and 128 at The Oval, this time adding a record 266 for the fourth wicket with Hammond in just over three hours. He toured Australia with MCC in 1936/7, playing and opening in three Tests, but was disappointing.

First-class career (1924-47): 19,221 runs (29.07) including 31 centuries, 682 wickets (29.22) and 340 catches
Test matches (9): 321 runs (29.18) including 1 century, 8 wickets (39.50) and 8 catches

WRIGHT, Charles William (1863-1936)

Cambridge University and Nottinghamshire

'Chawles' Wright played four times for Cambridge against Oxford at Lord's, winning a medal for his faultless 102 in the 1883 match. After playing intermittently for Nottinghamshire for some eighteen years, he lost the sight of an eye in an accident while shooting partridges. He was a very steady batsman who usually went in first, and his strong back-foot play on treacherous wickets often averted a collapse; he was also a good reserve wicket-keeper. He was one of the few county players given out 'handled ball', against Gloucestershire at Bristol in 1893, when the ball lodged in his pads and he picked it out, and, as captain of Notts (though never officially appointed) against Kent at Gravesend in 1890, he was the first ever to declare an innings closed. He toured with four teams led by Lord Hawke, two to America, and one each to India and South Africa in 1895/6 (his Tests).

First-class career (1882-1901): 6,976 runs (15.86) including 2 centuries, 183 catches and 41 stumpings
Test matches (3): 125 runs (31.25)

WRIGHT, Douglas Vivian Parson (b.1914)

Kent

Doug Wright was one of the enigmas of post-1945 cricket. At his destructive best, his impact on batsmen was devastating, as his record number of seven hat-tricks showed. His action was unusual, with skips and jumps in a long springy run, and he bowled much faster than the average leg-spinner, often turning and lifting the ball so sharply that it missed the stumps and even the wicket-keepers. It was this ability to beat even great batsmen when well set which kept him in Test cricket; his relatively modest figures do not reveal his ability to bowl the unplayable ball. Ten times he took more than 100 wickets in a season, the best being 177 wickets (21.12) in 1947, and twice he took 9 wickets in an innings, his best match record being 16 for 80 against Somerset at Bath in 1939. He toured Australia and New Zealand twice and South Africa twice; from 1938 until 1951 he was an integral part of the England eleven. In Australia, 1946/7, he took more wickets than anyone on either side, but at heavy cost – 23 wickets at 43.04. Though he took his fair toll himself, Don Bradman had a tremendous regard for him. Again the most successful on both sides in 1947, he secured 19 wickets (25.47) from four Tests against South Africa, at Lord's taking 10 for 175 in the match. Time after time he bowled with skill and stubbornness, magnificent but – generally – ill-rewarded. Also a useful tail-end batsman and a good field, he became a much respected coach at Charterhouse, where Richard Gilliat and many other good players flourished in his care.

First-class career (1932-57): 5,903 runs (12.34), 2,056 wickets (23.93) and 165 catches
Test matches (34): 289 runs (11.11), 108 wickets (39.11) and 10 catches

WYATT, Robert Elliott Storey (b.1901)

Warwickshire and Worcestershire

Cousin of the noted MP, Woodrow Wyatt, Bob Wyatt made runs, took wickets and held catches in every quarter of the globe. He still holds strong, independent and shrewd views on the game. Though he often opened the batting, he is best remembered as a solid and dependable middle-order right-hander, who also bowled useful medium-pace swing. For sheer determination and concentration on all aspects of the game, he has had few equals; his study was scientific and intense. He captained Warwickshire, Worcestershire and England. Instead of tossing the ball to a bowler and saying, 'All right, have a go,' he would at great length and with some eloquence outline the strategic masterplan. He toured India with MCC in 1926/7 and South Africa in 1927/8, making his first Test appearances. He hit 113 against South Africa at Old Trafford in 1929, toured the West Indies in 1929/30 with some success, and displaced Percy Chapman (against frantic newspaper disapproval) as England captain in the fifth Test against Australia at The Oval

Bob Wyatt leading out the England team in 1934

in 1930. He made 64, but England lost. He toured South Africa in 1930/31, as vice-captain to Chapman, and Australia the following year, as vice-captain to Douglas Jardine, making 51 and 61 not out in the fifth Test at Sydney. Captain against Australia in 1934, he was the less successful captain of two strong sides, and he lost series to the West Indies in 1934/5, and to South Africa in 1935. He hit 149, however, in the first Test at Trent Bridge. No longer captain, he appeared against India in 1936, and toured Australia with MCC in 1936/7. Bob Wyatt exceeded 1,000 runs in a season eighteen times (once overseas), five times reaching 2,000, his best being 2,630 runs (53.67) in 1929, including 10 centuries. His highest score was 232 for Warwickshire against Derbyshire at Edgbaston in 1937. Among his writings is the widely acclaimed *The Ins and Outs of Cricket*. He served as a Test selector from 1949 to 1953 (chairman in 1950).

First-class career (1923-57): 39,404 runs (40.04) including 85 centuries, 901 wickets (32.88) and 417 catches
Test matches (40): 1,839 runs (31.70) including 2 centuries, 18 wickets (35.66) and 16 catches

WYNYARD, Major Edward George (1861-1936)

Army and Hampshire

Over six foot and finely built, Teddy Wynyard was a brilliant player of most games, excellent at cricket. A splendid right-handed forcing batsman using a wide variety of strokes, and an occasional lob-bowler, he stated that he had made 150 centuries in all kinds of cricket. For Hampshire against Somerset at Taunton in 1899, he made 225. He was a member of the winning England team, against Australia at The Oval in 1896, and he toured South Africa with MCC sides in 1905/6 and 1909/10, but his Test record was poor. A rather irascible man, he was not always popular and fell out with Ranji when the young Indian prince inadvertently ate some of his grapes!

First-class career (1878-1912): 8,407 runs (34.73) including 14 centuries, and 66 wickets (28.03)
Test matches (3): 72 runs (12.00) and 0-17

YARDLEY, Norman Walter Dransfield (b. 1915)

Cambridge University and Yorkshire

A kindly, genial, unflappable character, Norman Yardley was a reliable cricketer who did valuable service during lean years for English cricket. A right-handed batsman, he was primarily an on-side player but had strokes all round the wicket. As a right-arm medium-pace bowler, he bowled at the wicket to a full length, and came through quicker than expected. After captaining Cambridge in his fourth year he toured South Africa with MCC in 1938/9 and, although he was wounded in the Western Desert in the Second World War, he returned to be vice-captain of MCC in Australia in 1946/7, and to captain England at home against South Africa in 1947, against Australia in 1948 and against the West Indies in 1950. He was Yorkshire skipper from 1948 until 1955, considered to be too nice a person at times and not severe enough on some of his senior professionals. In Australia against a very powerful side, he averaged 31.50 with the bat in the Tests and headed the bowling with 10 wickets (37.20), dismissing Bradman three times running, twice before the great man had made a large score. He also came top of the bowling averages in 1948 with 9 wickets (22.66), all accredited Australian batsmen. His highest Test score was 99 at Trent Bridge in 1947 against South Africa, after England had followed on and, with Denis Compton, he helped to save the day. For Yorkshire his highest was 183 not out against Hampshire at Headingley in 1951, and his best bowling was 6 for 29 for MCC against Cambridge at Lord's in 1946. Eight times he exceeded 1,000 runs in a season. He was a good, versatile fielder. Chairman of the England Test selectors from 1951 to 1952 and again a selector from 1953 to 1954, he became a popular broadcaster on BBC radio. An all-round athlete, he was also North of England squash champion six times.

First-class career (1935-55): 18,173 runs (31.17) including 27 centuries, 279 wickets (30.48) and 320 catches
Test matches (20): 812 runs (25.37), 21 wickets (33.66) and 14 catches

YOUNG, Harding Isaac (1876-1964)

Essex

While serving in the Royal Navy, 'Sailor' Young bowled so well in minor matches and in the nets at Leyton that the Essex president, C.E. Green, bought him out of the Service to play for the county. A well-built man, he was a left-arm medium-pace bowler with 'a deceptive curl'. His best season was 1899, taking 139 wickets (21.79) and making 607 runs; against Warwickshire at Edgbaston he secured 15 for 154; and in his only two appearances in Tests, against Australia, he headed the England bowling averages, taking 4 for 30 in the first innings at Headingley. He also helped Essex beat the Australians at Leyton, taking 11 for 74. He toured the West Indies with MCC, 1910/11, and was on the ground staff at Lord's for many years, before becoming a first-class umpire from 1921 until 1931 and, latterly, a school coach.

First-class career (1898-1912): 2,328 runs (11.69) and 477 wickets (23.00)
Test matches (2): 43 runs (21.50), 14 wickets (21.83) and 1 catch

YOUNG, John Albert (b. 1912)

Middlesex

Small, dapper and smiling in the style of a polished light comedian, Jack Young was a lively humorist and an orthodox, left-arm, spin bowler with a perky run-up and an excellent action. Like other slow spinners of his generation, his command of length and direction was complete. He could spin the ball considerably and if there was not quite enough guile in his flight to make him outstanding in Tests – although he bowled eleven consecutive maidens against Australia at Trent Bridge in 1948 – he took many wickets for his county. Eight times he took more than 100 wickets in a season, four times between 1947 and 1952 exceeding 150 wickets, the best haul being 163 (19.88) in 1952. He toured South Africa in 1948/9, and played for England against Australia, South Africa and New Zealand at home. His best bowling in an innings was 9 for 55 for England against Commonwealth at Hastings in 1951.

First-class career (1933-56): 2,485 runs (8.93), 1,361 wickets (19.68) and 147 catches
Test matches (8): 28 runs (5.60), 17 wickets (44.52) and 5 catches

YOUNG, Richard Alfred (1885-1968)

Cambridge University and Sussex

One of the few players to wear spectacles – the thickest conceivable – while representing England at both cricket and Association Football, 'Dick' Young established a high reputation as a batsman/wicket-keeper at Repton and won his blue at Cambridge, playing four times against Oxford, and in his last year, 1908, as captain. First in and last out in 1906, he had hit 150. From 1905 until 1925 he assisted Sussex in the holidays. For 30 years he taught mathematics at Eton, where he was also cricket master. Though inclined to take risks, he got most of his runs in front of the wicket and in 1921 obtained one of the few centuries off the triumphant Australians, for Sussex at Eastbourne. He toured Australia with MCC in 1907/8, when he made his sole, disappointing, appearances in Tests. A fanatical theorist about cricket, he wrote a pamphlet, *Time for Experiment*, in which he suggested that captains should have the right to pour a hundred gallons of water on any part of the pitch.

First-class career (1905-25): 6,502 runs (28.76) including 6 centuries, and 105 dismissals (82 ct, 23 st.)
Test matches (2): 27 runs (6.75) and 6 dismissals (6 ct)

AUSTRALIA

A'BECKETT, Edward Lambert (b.1907)

Victoria

A right-handed batsman, Edward A'Beckett could attack or defend quite resolutely, but as a fast-medium bowler he lacked fire and that little extra which makes the true Test player. On his Test debut, against England at Melbourne, 1928/9, he opened the bowling and his first wicket was that of Jack Hobbs. He toured England with Woodfull's team in 1930, and appeared against South Africa in 1931/2. Work as a barrister caused his early retirement.

First-class career (1927-31): 1,636 runs (29.21) including 2 centuries, and 105 wickets (29.16)
Test matches (4): 143 runs (20.42), 3 wickets (105.66) and 4 catches

ALDERMAN, Terence Michael (b.1956)

Western Australia

A tall and good-looking right-arm fast-medium bowler with fine control of swing and cut, the only surprise about Terry Alderman, who was selected for Australia in England in 1981, was that recognition had not come earlier. As long before as 1974/5 he had taken 5-65 in the first innings of his first Sheffield Shield match and he had given another impressive performance against the MCC touring team in the same season, but such was the competition from bowlers of similar type it was not until 1977/8 that he established himself in the West Australian side in the Sheffield Shield. In that season he took 28 wickets, in the following one 26, and in 1979/80 42, the third biggest haul in first-class cricket that season. In England in 1981 he was an immediate success, moving the ball both ways through the air and off the pitch and doing so at a pace liable to make batting a nightmare on pitches such as that at Trent Bridge, where Alderman's figures of 9-130 in his first Test were instrumental in a narrow Australian victory. Later he met his match – as did his partner Lillee – in Ian Botham and Australia lost a close series despite his 42 wickets (21.26) in the six Tests. No Australian has taken more wickets in a Test series in England. At home the following season he continued to bowl with stamina and skill, taking 37 first-class wickets (16.94) including 7 for 28 against Queensland at Brisbane. A modest fellow with a good sense of humour, he is no batsman but a very accomplished slip fieldsman. His career was badly set back in the first Test of the 1982/3 series against England when he damaged his right shoulder as he tried to apprehend a spectator invading the ground. He missed the rest of the season.

Terry Alderman

First-class career (1974-): 236 runs (6.37) and 271 wickets (23.08)
Test matches (15): 51 runs (5.10), 65 wickets (27.78) and 16 catches

ALEXANDER, George (1851-1930)

Victoria

A hard-hitting right-handed batsman, a useful fast-medium change-bowler and a smart field, George

Alexander was player/manager of the Australian teams in 1880 and 1884 and manager of Hon. Ivo Bligh's team in Australia in 1882/3. He played in the first-ever Test in England, at The Oval in 1880, when his steadfast innings of 33 in a last wicket stand of 88 with W.H. Moule enabled Australia to avoid an innings' defeat. For Victoria against New South Wales in 1879/80 he made 75, the highest score on either side and took 5 for 64.

First-class career (1875-84): 466 runs (15.53) and 33 wickets (18.39)
Test matches (2): 52 runs (13.00), 2 wickets (46.50) and 2 catches

ALEXANDER, Harry Houston (b.1905)

Victoria

A right-arm fast bowler, Harry Alexander toured India in 1935/6 with Jack Ryder's Australians. His sole Test was against England in the fifth match at Sydney in 1932/3, as something of a reply to Harold Larwood. He scored 17 not out, and took 1 for 154.

First-class career (1928-35): 228 runs (6.16) and 95 wickets (33.91)

ALLAN, Francis Erskine (1849-1917)

Victoria

Known as 'The Bowler of the Century', he was the first of the great Australian bowlers. Left-arm medium-pace with abundant spin and a remarkable 'curl' (or swerve), he was immediately famous in inter colonial matches. Not fully fit when coming to England with the first Australian team in 1878 – though in the whole length of the tour he took no fewer than 217 wickets for 1,832 runs – his sole Test was at Melbourne in 1878/9, when he scored 5 and took 4 for 80.

First-class career (1867-82): 371 runs (10.91) and 123 wickets (13.31)

ALLAN, Peter John (b.1935)

Queensland

A tall, strongly built, right-arm fast bowler, Peter Allan took 10 for 61 in an innings for Queensland against Victoria at Melbourne in 1965/6 – the only occasion this feat has been accomplished on the Melbourne ground. By the time of his retirement he was Queensland's highest wicket-taker. He toured the West Indies in 1964/5 and played his sole Test against England at Brisbane in 1965/6, not batting and taking 2 for 83.

First-class career (1959-69): 689 runs (10.59) and 206 wickets (26.10)

ALLEN, Reginald Charles (1858-1952)

New South Wales

An uncle of 'Gubby' Allen, himself an Australian by birth, Reginald Allen was a competent batsman whose sole Test was against Shaw and Shrewsbury's team in 1886/7, the second match at Sydney; he scored 14 and 30 and held 2 catches.

First-class career (1878-87): 382 runs (12.32)

ANDREWS, Thomas James Edwin (1890-1970)

New South Wales

Rather thickset and a right-handed stylist with powerful wrists and a straight bat, Tommy Andrews was not a good starter, but once settled in could play attractively and entertainingly with a wide range of strokes. He was also a high-ranking close-to-the-wicket field. He toured England in 1921 and 1926 and South Africa in 1921/2, in the former year hitting 92 and 94 in the Tests at Headingley and The Oval respectively. He made 1,358 runs (33.95) on the 1921 tour and, though he achieved little in the 1926 Tests, he hit a magnificent 164 against Middlesex at Lord's in about three hours, and reached an aggregate of 1,234 runs (38.56). He scored 224 for his State against Arthur Gilligan's MCC team in 1924/5 at Sydney, adding 270 for the second wicket with Herbie Collins. In the Sheffield Shield he scored 3,072 runs (42.08).

First-class career (1912-30): 8,095 runs (39.49) including 14 centuries, and 95 wickets (32.10)
Test matches (16): 592 runs (26.90), 1-116 and 12 catches

ARCHER, Kenneth Allan (b.1928)

Queensland

The elder brother of Ron Archer, Ken had grace of style and some good strokes including a liking for the deflection. He opened the batting for his State from 1946 to 1957 and was also an excellent field. He toured South Africa in 1949/50 and, although he did not make the Test side, scored 826 runs in twenty-four innings. In a short Test career he played against England in 1950/51 and West Indies in 1951/2.

First-class career (1946-57): 3,774 runs (29.95) including 3 centuries, and 13 wickets (53.69)
Test matches (5): 234 runs (26.00)

ARCHER, Ronald Graham (b.1933)

Queensland

A vigorous all-rounder, Ron Archer relied on a strong right arm and a keen eye to attack. Of fine physique, he used his height and reach to punch the ball hard in front of the wicket. As a fast-medium stock bowler he bowled at the stumps and was often successful with the new ball. He toured England twice, in 1953 and 1956, also the West Indies and Pakistan, and represented his country at home against England and South Africa. In the 1956 series, he captured 18 wickets (25.05), including a remarkable spell in the third Test at Headingley when, on the first morning, he dismissed Colin Cowdrey, Alan Oakman and Peter Richardson in nine overs for 3 runs; he took no more wickets in the innings but his fifty overs yielded only 68 runs. At The Oval in 1953 he struck hard, top-scoring with 49. In the West Indies he made 364 runs (60.66) in the Tests, including 128 in the fifth Test in Kingston, when his was one of five centuries in the innings! In the Sheffield Shield he made 1,766 runs (29.43) and took 115 wickets (24.08). He is now a high-ranking commercial television executive.

First-class career (1951-58): 3,768 runs (31.93) including 4 centuries, and 255 wickets (23.36)
Test matches (19): 713 runs (24.58) including 1 century, 48 wickets (27.45) and 20 catches

Warwick Armstrong

ARMSTRONG, Warwick Windridge (1879-1947)

Victoria

Tall and slim when he first appeared for his country against England during the 1901/2 tour, Warwick Armstrong weighed twenty-two stone at the end of his playing days twenty years later. 'The Big Ship' was a highly successful captain, leading Australia to eight successive wins against England in 1920/21 and 1921. His manner was haughty, even bossy, but a kind heart lay beneath. Not a graceful or cultured right-handed batsman, he was nonetheless completely assured, certain in defence, confident in attack, and terribly difficult to shift even when he seemed to be floundering against spin. As a bowler he took an exceptionally long run for one of his slow pace, but he had uncanny gifts of length and control. On helpful pitches he would turn his leg-break quickly and he could keep going for hours. Touring England in 1902, 1905, 1909 and 1921, he was outstanding all round, altogether making 5,974 runs (40.36), taking 443 wickets (16.45) and holding 150 catches. He put up 428 with Monty Noble against Sussex at Hove in 1902 for the sixth wicket, an Australian record; and his 'double' record in 1905 was 2,002 runs (48.82), including his highest score, 303 not out against Somerset at Bath, and 130 wickets (17.60). He headed Australia's batting averages in 1907/8 with 410 runs (45.55) and 1911/12 with 324 runs (32.40); and he hit three of his four Test centuries against England in 1920/21 when he made 464 runs (77.33). His highest in Tests was 159 not out against South Africa at Johannesburg in 1902/3, and he reached 410 runs (51.25) against South Africa in 1910/11. His best series as a bowler was 1909, when he took 16 wickets, including 5 for 27 in the first innings of the first Test at Edgbaston, which Australia lost, and 6 for 35 in the second innings of the second Test at Lord's, which Australia won. He was independently minded, strong-willed and caustic; when a draw was certain in the last Test at The Oval in 1921, 'The Big Ship' rested his regular bowlers and retired to the deep field, where he started reading a newspaper. Asked what he was reading, he replied that he was trying to find out who his opponents were. A whisky merchant and journalist, he died a wealthy man. In the Sheffield Shield he made 4,993 runs (49.93) and took 117 wickets (24.16).

First-class career (1898-1921): 16,158 runs (46.83) including 45 centuries, 832 wickets (19.71) and 274 catches
Test matches (50): 2,863 runs (38.68) including 6 centuries, 87 wickets (33.59) and 44 catches

BADCOCK, Clayvel Lindsay (1914-82)

Tasmania and South Australia

'Jack' Badcock played for Tasmania at 15, the second youngest Australian to play first-class cricket, but his career was linked mostly with his adopted State, South Australia. He once hit a century in each innings against Victoria, scored 325 in another game against Victoria, 271 not out against New South Wales and 236 against Queensland. He could drive magnificently on either side of the wicket, and his square-cut was so hard and clean that cover-point had little chance of getting a hand to it. In the Sheffield Shield he hit 2,473 runs (58.88) from thirty matches. Against England in 1936/7 he opened without success in the first Test at Brisbane, and in the fifth at Melbourne made 118 at number five, adding 161 with Ross Gregory. In England in 1938 he was often devastating against the counties, overall making 1,859 runs (45.35), but he failed completely in the Tests, with scores of 9, 5, 0 and 0 (at Lord's), 4, 5 not out, 0 and 9. Recurring lumbago brought his career to a close.

First-class career (1929-41): 7,371 runs (51.54) including 26 centuries
Test matches (7): 160 runs (14.54) including 1 century, and 3 catches

BANNERMAN, Alexander Chalmers (*c.* 1854-1924)

New South Wales

Alec Bannerman, younger brother of Charles, was a member of the Australian eleven which defeated MCC at Lord's in 1878. He played in the first Test in England in 1880 and in the classic match at The Oval in 1882 which gave birth to the Ashes. The catch by which he disposed of W.G. in the second innings was the turning-point of the latter epic struggle. He paid three other visits to England, 1884, 1888 and 1893, and, short and dour, became the most famous (or infamous) of Australian stonewallers: his patience was inexhaustible. He took seven and a half hours to make 91 in the Test at Sydney in 1892, when his side won the rubber, scoring from only 5 of 204 balls bowled to him by William Attewell. Though such a slow run-getter, he made many large scores and was invaluable as a partner for bigger hitters. In the field, he was superb at mid-off – fast, safe and untiring. In England he scored 4,881 runs (19.44), including two centuries, and for New South Wales against Victoria 1,209 runs (29.29). In five Sheffield Shield matches he made 197 runs.

First-class career (1876-93): 7,816 runs (22.14) including 5 centuries, 22 wickets (29.81) and 154 catches
Test matches (28): 1,108 runs (23.08), 4 wickets (40.75) and 21 catches

BANNERMAN, Charles (1851-1930)

New South Wales

Immortal as the man who made the first century in Test cricket, Charles Bannerman was a fine, upstanding and polished batsman. A native of Kent, he was master of most strokes and, unlike his brother, delighted in playing them. He was also a first-rate, versatile field. In the first-ever Test at Melbourne in 1877 his chanceless 165 (before retiring hurt) in four and three quarter hours, came off a reputable professional attack and none of his colleagues reached 20 in the innings. Never before had an Australian made a century off an English team. In the bowlers' summer of 1878 he scored 770 runs (34.06), including 133 at Leicester. In the whole tour, including New Zealand and Canada, he reached 2,630 runs (23.90). Ill-health prevented him visiting England again, but at various times he coached in Australia and New Zealand and served as an umpire in Tests.

First-class career (1870-87): 1,687 runs (21.62) including 1 century
Test matches (3): 239 runs (59.75) including 1 century

BARDSLEY, Warren (1882-1954)

New South Wales

A stylish left-handed opening batsman, accomplished on all wickets, Warren Bardsley played with an exemplary straight bat, had an upright stance, quick and shrewd footwork and employed a wide variety of strokes. He drove easily off the front foot, was ready to go back on his stumps to force the ball from his pads by means of powerful wrists and forearms, and was a fine outfield. At a bumper he would toss his head backwards with a contemptuous sniff of the nose. He toured England in 1909, 1912, 1921 and 1926, on his first tour heading the batting with 2,180 runs (46.39), including 136 and 130 in the fifth Test at The Oval, putting up a record 180 for the first wicket of the second innings with Sid Gregory, and becoming the first player to hit two centuries in a Test. In two other tours he exceeded 2,000 runs – reaching 2,441 runs (51.98), including eight centuries in 1912 – and in the Test at Lord's in 1926 he carried his bat through the first innings for 193 not out in six and a half hours on a turning wicket against a superb attack. He headed the batting averages against England in 1921 (46.83), and against South Africa and England in the Triangular Tournament he was the most prolific batsman on the three sides, with 392 runs (65.33), including 164 against South Africa at Lord's, adding 242 with Charles Kelleway for the third wicket after an early collapse. In 1910/11 he made 573 runs (63.66) against the visiting South Africans. Although considered to be better in England than at home – he made 7,974 runs (49.83) in England – he still represented his country at home in each series from 1910 until 1925.

First-class career (1903-26): 17,025 runs (49.92) including 53 centuries
Test matches (41): 2,469 runs (40.47) including 6 centuries, and 12 catches

BARNES, Sidney George (1916-73)

New South Wales

A colourful, bizarre personality, from the outset Sid

Barnes was renowned for his glorious right-handed off-side strokes. On board ship coming to England with the 1938 team, he fractured a wrist – an accident which developed his one-side play amazingly. After the Second World War he became sounder and tougher and, getting on to his back foot more and more, was dogged and defiant, a particularly hard man to dislodge. He set himself to accumulate runs in large quantities. Generally an opening batsman, he shared a world record partnership for the fifth wicket of 405 with Don Bradman in the second Test at Sydney against England in 1946/7, each man making 234. He averaged 73.83 for the series. In England in 1948 he finished second in the averages with 82.25, hitting 141 at Lord's. It was at Lord's too that he was criticized for fielding so close in at point or short-leg five yards from the bat and, at Old Trafford, the beefy Dick Pollard hit him in the ribs from a full-blooded stroke. Barnes had to spend the next ten days in hospital. Following that tour, he dropped out of cricket for two years and began writing controversial pieces for the newspapers. His great days were behind him. His eccentricities increased, and he eventually took his own life. He could, however, be a man of real wit. In a match during the 1948 tour, after a strong appeal had been turned down by Alec Skelding, the umpire, a dog ran on to the field. Sid captured it and carried it to the umpire with the caustic comment: 'Now all you want is a white stick!' In the Sheffield Shield he scored 2,655 runs (47.41) and took 29 wickets (28.65).

First-class career (1936-52): 8,333 runs (54.11) including 26 centuries, and 57 wickets (32.21)
Test matches (13): 1,072 runs (63.05) including 3 centuries, 4 wickets (54.50) and 14 catches

BARNETT, Benjamin Arthur (1908-79)

Victoria and Buckinghamshire

Ben Barnett was a cricketer of great charm. Although a model wicket-keeper and steady left-handed batsman, he was overshadowed by Bert Oldfield for several years. He toured England in 1934 and South Africa in 1935/6, without playing in any of the Tests, but his chance came on his second visit to England in 1938, when he played in all four Tests, hitting 57 at Headingley – a low-scoring match – and effecting five dismissals; and he came fourth in the Test batting averages with 27.85. Subsequently, he settled in England, playing for and captaining Buckinghamshire. He acted as Australia's ICC representative in London before returning to Australia where he died in 1979.

First-class career (1929-61): 5,531 runs (27.51) including 4 centuries, 358 dismissals (216 ct, 142 st.)
Test matches (4): 195 runs (27.85) and 5 dismissals (3 ct, 2 st).

BARRETT, Dr John Edward (1866-1916)

Victoria

A patient left-handed batsman and useful medium-paced change-bowler with a high action, Jack Barrett was eighteen when, on his debut for his State against South Australia at Melbourne, he took 5 for 31 and 6 for 49 in the two innings. He came to England with the 1890 side and in the Test at Lord's carried his bat through the innings of 176 against Lohmann, Peel, Attewell, Barnes, Ulyett and W.G. Grace. A busy medical practitioner, he had a relatively short first-class career.

First-class career (1884-92): 2,039 runs (25.81) and 21 wickets (16.00)
Test matches (2): 80 runs (26.66) and 1 catch

BEARD, Graeme Robert (b.1950)

New South Wales

A versatile all-round cricketer who could bowl either medium pace or slow off-spin and batted usefully in the middle-order, Graeme Beard made only slow progress after his first appearance for New South Wales in 1975/6, starting with a pair against the West Indies. But in 1979/80 he scored 230 runs (38.33) and took 23 wickets (22.17) in the Sheffield Shield, and was chosen to tour Pakistan at the end of the season, playing in all three Tests on the short tour. He gained only one expensive wicket, but at Lahore in the third Test scored 39 and 49. He was a surprising choice for Australia's 1981 tour of England but was given little chance to shine and he announced his retirement in 1982 to concentrate on his job as an Industrial Officer in the Australian Workers' Union.

First-class career (1975-82): 1,441 runs (23.62), and 125 wickets (28.19)
Test matches (3): 114 runs (22.80) and 1-109

BENAUD, John (b.1944)

New South Wales

A punishing right-handed batsman, John Benaud's aggressive leadership of his State during 1969/70 won him considerable respect until a two-match suspension marred his season following his insistence on wearing ripple-heeled boots against the directions of the State Association. Like his elder brother, Richie, he revealed a flair for captaincy, and again led his State with success in 1972/3, when he made his Test debut. In his second Test, against Pakistan at Melbourne, he hit 142 after learning that the selectors had left him out of the third Test. He toured the West Indies in 1973 with less success. He made a powerful 134 for his State against Victoria in 1969/70 which all but won the match when the cause looked hopeless for New South Wales. For Australia against Rest of the World at

Adelaide, 1971/2, he hit 99. Like his brother he is a prominent journalist.

First-class career (1966-73): 2,888 runs (36.56) including 4 centuries
Test matches (3): 223 runs (44.60) including 1 century, and 2-12

BENAUD, Richard (b.1930)

New South Wales

One of the great Test captains, Richie Benaud has remained a household name through his work as a cricket journalist and broadcaster. His father was an Australian first-grade player, who once took twenty wickets in a match, and Richie himself first played for his State at eighteen and for Australia in Tests against the West Indies in 1951/2, aged twenty-one. He became a notable all-rounder, a tough competitor and an enterprising, adroit leader who captained his country in four successive and triumphant series – against England twice, and West Indies and Pakistan once each. His efforts lifted the game in Australia out of the doldrums. As a lithe and forcing right-handed batsman he was always worth watching. His drives, powerfully hit with a full follow-through, were often lofted. At Scarborough in 1953, against T.N. Pearce's eleven, he hit eleven sixes and nine fours while making 135. As a leg-spinner he touched the heights. An advocate of regular practice, he drove himself to the top. From a rhythmical, high action, he was more accurate and had greater variety than most of his kind. He bowled the leg-break, the googly, the top-spinner and his speciality, the 'flipper': in effect an off-spinning top-spinner. With clever changes of pace and a teasing flight, he was a more fearsome prospect on the hard wickets in Australia and overseas than he was in England. A magnificent close fielder, able to leap with cat-like agility, he brought off some spectacular catches, notably one left-handed in the gully in 1956, to dismiss Cowdrey off a full-blooded drive at Lord's. He came to England in 1953 and 1956, and appeared in the home series against England in 1954/5 and in the West Indies in 1955, but it was not until the tour of South Africa in 1957/8 that he established himself as an all-rounder of the highest class, with 817 runs, including four centuries, and 106 wickets, a record number in that country. Against India and Pakistan in 1959/60 he took 47 wickets (20.19) in the eight Tests. With 31 wickets (18.83) against England in 1958/9 – his first series as captain – he was largely instrumental in Australia's winning back the Ashes. His co-operation with Frank Worrell in the exciting series against the West Indies in 1960/61 captured the imagination of the whole cricket world. On his last tour England looked set to win the Test at Old Trafford in 1961, when they needed little more than a hundred runs to win with nine wickets in hand. Benaud took the

Richie Benaud

ball and (despite pain in his shoulder) bowled round the wicket into the rough, first dismissing the rampant Ted Dexter, and then Brian Close, Peter May and Raman Subba Row in the space of five overs. From 150 for 1, England were all out for 201, Benaud taking 6 for 70, saving the Ashes for Australia. When his shoulder trouble hastened his retirement, he had taken a record number of wickets for Australia, and also for his State (266 from 73 matches). He was awarded the OBE for his services to Australian cricket. A journalist, he has written several cricket books, mainly about tours. As a public relations officer he was the key adviser to those who set up Kerry Packer's World Series Cricket.

First-class career (1948-68): 11,719 runs (36.50) including 23 centuries, 945 wickets (24.73) and 255 catches
Test matches (63): 2,201 runs (24.45) including 3 centuries, 248 wickets (27.03) and 65 catches

BLACKHAM, John McCarthy (1854-1932)

Victoria

Jack Blackham was an outstanding wicket-keeper who generally stood up to fast bowling without a long-stop – although he invariably went back when 'The Demon' Spofforth was bowling his fastest. He was neat, quick and accurate, a stumper who would gather the ball and whip off the bails in a flash. He was a very useful right-handed batsman, but (like most of the early Australians) had no pretentions to style. Coming to England with each of the first eight teams, he captained that of 1893. He kept in the first Test at Melbourne in 1876/7 when Spofforth refused to take part 'because his own wicket-keeper, W.L. Murdoch, did not play'. By 1878, however, Jack Blackham was established and his most notable achievement on this historic tour was to stump six and catch four of an Eighteen of Stockport on a rough, bumpy pitch. A bank clerk, Jack grew a beard (suitably black) as a young man of twenty-three and kept it all through his life.

First-class career (1874-94): 6,395 runs (16.78) including 1 century, and 451 dismissals (272 ct, 179 st.)
Test matches (35): 800 runs (15.68) and 60 dismissals (36 ct, 24 st.)

BLACKIE, Donald Dearness (1882-1955)

Victoria

At forty-six the oldest player to represent Australia for the first time, against England in 1928/9, Don Blackie headed the bowling averages in this, his only series. Tall and spare and somewhat bow-legged, he was a vintage right-arm off-spin bowler, starting his run near mid-off (where he could joke with the fieldsman), curving his way to the stumps, and often making the ball curl in the breeze. For his State he took 157 wickets (23.59).

First-class career (1924-33): 548 runs (12.17) and 211 wickets (24.10)
Test matches (3): 24 runs (8.00), 14 wickets (31.71) and 2 catches

BONNOR, George John (1855-1912)

Victoria and New South Wales

Six feet six inches tall, around sixteen stone in weight and known as either 'The Australian Giant' or 'The Australian Hercules', George Bonnor was a hitter of extraordinary power. Finely proportioned, he was no mere slogger, indeed was able to play quite an orthodox game at times, much to the disgust of some colleagues who argued that his business was to hit hard and often. He toured England in 1880, 1882, 1884, 1886 and 1888. During the first Test in England at The Oval in 1880 he hit a ball to such a tremendous height that the batsman had turned for the third run when Fred Grace caught it. Bonnor, like all hitters, was as inconsistent as he could be explosive, but at Sydney in 1884/5 he slammed 128 after Australia had lost 7 wickets for 134.

First-class career (1880-90): 4,820 runs (21.23) including 5 centuries, 12 wickets (39.16), 127 catches and 1 stumping
Test matches (17): 512 runs (17.06) including 1 century, 2 wickets (42.00) and 16 catches

BOOTH, Brian Charles (b.1933)

New South Wales

A very slim right-handed batsman with a great gift of timing, Brian Booth was an elegant stroke-player who looked taller than his 5 feet 11½ inches. His unruffled effortless style owed much to unhesitating footwork right to the pitch of spin-bowling. Besides a full range of graceful on-side shots, his cover-drives and square-drives were placed to advantage and he cut well. He was a useful change-bowler and versatile field. After playing hockey for Australia in the 1956 Olympic Games in Melbourne, he visited New Zealand with the Australian 'A' side in 1959/60, opening the tour with 105 against Auckland. A permanent member of Australia's middle-order between 1961 and 1965, he toured England twice (in 1964 as vice-captain), India, Pakistan and the West Indies and played in series at home against England, South Africa and Pakistan. He was in this period probably Australia's most consistent scorer, reaching 1,000 runs after eleven Tests. He made 112 at Brisbane and 103 at Melbourne in 1962/3 against England; and 169 at Brisbane and 102 not out at Sydney in 1963/4 against South Africa, the former on his debut against that country. Moreover, he frequently made his runs when they were most needed.

George Bonnor with Jack Blackham (keeping wicket)

He substituted as Bob Simpson's captain in two Tests against England in 1965/6 but, displaced by changes in a beaten side, was never chosen for Australia again, although he continued for several years successfully for his State and was vice-captain of the Australian 'A' tour to New Zealand in 1967. A cricketer respected and liked by opponents and team-mates, he is now a teacher, Anglican lay-reader and a member of the New South Wales Parliament.

First-class career (1954-68): 11,265 runs (45.42) including 26 centuries, 16 wickets (59.75) and 119 catches
Test matches (29): 1,773 runs (42.21) including 5 centuries, 3 wickets (48.66) and 17 catches

Allan Border hits out

BORDER, Allan Robert (b.1955)

New South Wales, Queensland and Gloucestershire

A stocky left-hand batsman, specialist slip fielder and steady, slow left-arm orthodox spin bowler, Allan Border looks likely to be a force in Test cricket for many years. He advanced quickly after a season in the Lancashire League in 1978 and, showing himself in the Sheffield Shield to be a cool, decisive and impressive stroke-player with a good technique, quick to pull or cut the short ball but also a confident driver, he soon made his way into a struggling Australian team in 1978/9, his first Test and also England's first and only defeat in the series. In his second Test at Sydney, Border scored 45 not out and 60 not out, batting with remarkable authority against the England spinners on a turning pitch on the last day. Against Pakistan later in the season he scored 20, 105, 85 and 66 not out to establish himself as Australia's number three, and he again batted well at times in India in 1979. He scored 521 runs in six Tests in India, starting the series with scores of 162 and 50 in the first match at Madras. Back at home during the hectic season of 1979/80 he was a regular member of the reconstituted Australian team which now included those players who had been out of Test cricket during the two seasons of World Series Cricket. He was punished for a weakness outside the off-stump by the accurate and remorseless West Indies fast bowlers, but in the three Tests against England he averaged 49, scoring 115 in the Perth Test, probably the decisive innings of the game. Though the West Indies had caused his first real setback at the highest level he worked with rare determination to overcome the flaw in his technique and, during the short tour of Pakistan which completed a season in which he had played in 15 Tests, he enjoyed a great triumph in the final Test at Lahore, scoring 150 not out in the first innings and 153 in the second. In the previous match he had hit 178 against the Punjab Eleven at Multan. When he came to England in 1980 for the Centenary Test he hit with impressive power to score 77 undefeated runs in a match ruined by rain. Soon after he played for Queensland, where he had moved on attractive terms from New South Wales. His form at home against India and New Zealand in 1980/81 was modest until in the last Test of another busy season he made 124, his sixth Test century, against India at Melbourne. He was an automatic choice for the 1981 tour of England, when he was easily the leading batsman in either side with 533 runs (59.22) in the six Tests including a remarkable 123 not out at Old Trafford when he batted throughout with a broken finger, a rare example of courage, concentration and resolution. In the next Test, at The Oval, he hit 106 not out and 84.

First-class career (1976-): 6,680 runs (46.71) including 17 centuries and 42 wickets (35.28)
Test matches (45): 3,175 runs (46.69) including 9 centuries, 14 wickets (30.79) and 51 catches

BOYLE, Henry Frederick (1847-1907)

Victoria

More than anyone else, the full-bearded 'Harry' Boyle made the fame of the first Australian touring team of 1878. As a right-handed overarm bowler, he relied much on intelligence and accuracy; he could peg away at medium pace for an hour without bowling a bad ball, and was satisfied if he could make the ball do just enough to beat the bat. A tall man, his very high delivery made the ball rise quickly off the pitch. Spofforth, Allan and he dismissed MCC at Lord's in 1878 twice in one day, Boyle's record being 3 for 14 and 5 for 3 (when MCC made 19). He toured England again in 1880, 1882, 1884, 1888 and 1890 (in the last tour he was player/manager). He appeared at home against England in 1878/9, and through the early 1880s. In England he appeared in the first two Tests, when he was at his peak. At The Oval in 1882 it was

Don Bradman in action, cutting. Godfrey Evans (England) is the wicket-keeper

Harry Boyle who took the last wicket to give Australia her victory by 7 runs. In first-class matches in England he secured 311 wickets (13.48), 144 coming in 1882. He was one of the most daring of fieldsmen at short mid-on.

First-class career (1871-90): 1,711 runs (10.24) including 1 century, 370 wickets (15.38) and 125 catches
Test matches (12): 153 runs (12.75), 32 wickets (20.03) and 10 catches

BRADMAN, Sir Donald George (b.1908)

New South Wales and South Australia

The son of a farmer and carpenter, the young Don Bradman revealed precocious skill in games and athletics in the country town of Bowral and through the logical organization of Australian sport eventually made his way to the Sydney Cricket Ground for trials, to grade cricket in Sydney, into the New South Wales eleven, and into the Australian side he was to dominate for some twenty years. The mental approach of the man – the resolve, the patience, the concentration, the discipline, the shrewd assessment of any cricketing situation, and the terrier-like desire to worry the bowlers to death – was as remarkable as his natural genius. Although quite small (5ft 7ins), he is physically unexceptional, and scientific tests on his eyesight suggested nothing abnormal. Yet the impression he gave was that he saw the ball earlier in flight than most mortals, and with a clear, unerring judgment, always had the right stroke at his immediate command. He became the greatest run-getter the game has ever known: in twenty-one years of first-class cricket he was to average a century once in every three innings played. If his actual run-scoring was mechanical, the method employed to get the runs had as much variety as any great player and the pace of his innings was almost always appropriate to the position of the match. His declared aim, indeed, was to dictate the terms of any cricketing situation in which he found himself. The little man was invariably the master and how the bowlers must have loathed him, despaired against him, but grudgingly admired him! His footwork was swift and sure, the timing of his driving, hooking and cutting perfect. Though he six times scored more than 300, only on twelve occasions did he bat for six hours or more. His fielding in the deep or the covers was brilliant. He scored 118 on his debut for New South Wales against South Australia at Adelaide, in 1927/8; the following season he appeared for Australia for the first time, at Brisbane in the first Test, but was relegated to twelfth man for the second match. He returned for the third at Melbourne, when he made 79 and 112, invaluably for a side in transition, and was never again left out. He toured England in 1930, 1934, 1938 and 1948; the first year he made 2,960 runs (98.66), including 10 centuries; the second, 2,020 runs (84.16), including 7 centuries; the third, 2,429 runs (115.66), including 13 centuries; and the final tour, as captain, 2,428 runs (89.92), including 11 centuries. In the 1930 series he set a record of 974 runs (139.14), including 334 at Headingley, 254 at Lord's and 232 at The Oval. Against the West Indies and South Africa at home he was also virtually unbowlable. Against the latter, in 1931/2, he made 806 runs (201.50), including 4 centuries. When MCC were in Australia in 1932/3, bodyline bowling was devised to halt 'the Don's' progress; it was half successful as he averaged a mere 56.57 in four Tests! In 1934, with Bill Ponsford, he amassed 451 for the second wicket against England at The Oval and 388 for the fourth wicket at Headingley. In the series he scored 758 runs (94.75). Away from Tests he struck the then highest score ever in first-class cricket, 452 not out for New South Wales against Queensland at Sydney in 1929/30, and the previous season compiled the record aggregate in Australia of 1,690 runs (93.88), including seven centuries in thirteen matches, the highest being 340 not out against Victoria at Sydney. Becoming Australia's captain against England in 1936/7, he was as astute, as tough and as mercilessly efficient as he was as a batsman, and his own batting performances lost nothing to the extra responsibility. Leading his country in five series between 1936 and 1948 he did not lose one, and, indeed, won four decisively. In 1936/7, after a quiet start, he finished with 810 runs (90.00), including 270 at Melbourne, when he added 346 for the sixth wicket with Jack Fingleton, another record, and 212 at Adelaide. He was injured while bowling his leg-breaks during England's marathon innings of 903 runs for 7 at The Oval in 1938, but he averaged 108.50 in the series. He became unfit through fibrositis and there was some doubt about his return to post-War cricket, but he continued to lead Australia. In the first Test against England at Brisbane in 1946/7 he made 187, adding 276 with Lindsay Hassett for the third wicket, and 234 in the second at Sydney, adding 405 for the fifth wicket with Sid Barnes, a record-breaking stand. He made 680 runs (97.14) in the five Tests. In 1947/8 he totalled 715 runs (178.75) against the first Indian side in Australia, including 132 and 127 not out in one match at Melbourne. On his final visit to England he led an unbeaten Australian side. He made 138 in the first Test at Trent Bridge and 173 not out at Headingley in the fourth match. But in his last Test of all at The Oval, cricket proved its power to humble even the immortal: 'the Don' was bowled by Eric Hollies for 0, second ball. He had scored over 200 in an innings on thirty-seven occasions. In sixty-two Sheffield Shield matches for New South Wales from 1927 to 1934 and for South Australia after 1935 (he captained his second State until 1948) he made 8,896 runs (109.82). On retirement in Adelaide he became the first Australian cricketer to be knighted and at different times chairman of the Board of Control and chairman of the selectors. A public figure of immense significance – he is a businessman and writer of considerable expertise – he remains a devoted family man, though his son, a barrister, protested at the burden of being the son of the most famous of all Australians by changing his surname to 'Bradson'.

First-class career (1927-49): 28,067 runs (95.14) including 117 centuries, 36 wickets (37.97), 131 catches and 1 stumping
Test matches (52): 6,996 runs (99.94) including 29 centuries, 2 wickets (36.00) and 32 catches

BRIGHT, Raymond James (b.1954)

Victoria

Ray Bright is one of the best orthodox left-arm spinners to have been produced by Australia since the Second World War, but by international standards is no more than a moderate performer. Forced largely by the modern Australian emphasis on fast bowlers to become economical first and a wicket-taker second, Bright has developed into a very steady, tight bowler, his orthodox spinner away from the right-hander being cleverly mixed with a dangerous in-swinging 'arm ball'. However, the surfeit of one-day cricket which he played during the two seasons of World Series Cricket caused his trajectory to get flatter and he lacks the curve and dip of the great slow left-handers. He is a determined and capable right-handed batsman, and an excellent gully fielder. Some useful performances for Victoria in Sheffield Shield cricket led to his selection for two tours of New Zealand, where he performed well, especially in 1976/7 when he took 25 wickets at 14.64 on the short tour to finish top of the bowling averages. With 39 wickets at 20.35 he was again top of the averages in England in 1977 when he played in three Tests. He was only on the fringes of the Australian team after the treaty between World Series Cricket and the Australian Cricket Board, playing in one match against the West Indies and one against England in 1979/80, taking only one wicket in each game. Against Pakistan on the short tour at the end of that season, however, he put in an outstanding Test performance at Karachi where Australia were defeated on a turning pitch. He took 7 for 87 in the first innings and the 3 Pakistan wickets to fall in the second for 24, finishing the series with 15 wickets (23.60). He was chosen for the Centenary Test at Lord's where he bowled tidily without taking a wicket and, having been ignored for the home Tests in 1980/81, he was selected as the main spinner in England in the 1981 Ashes series. Playing in all but one of the six Tests, he took 12 wickets (32.50) and in all first-class matches on the tour took 40 wickets (26.40).

First-class career (1972-): 2,445 runs (20.37) including 1 century, 289 wickets (28.82) and 74 catches
Test matches (16): 303 runs (13.77), 37 wickets (36.30) and 8 catches

BROMLEY, Ernest Harvey (1912-67)

Western Australia and Victoria

An attractive left-handed batsman whose game was built on attack, Ernest Bromley could hit with terrific power, but his defence was suspect; he was also a superb field, fleet of foot and a sure catch. He toured England in 1934, but made only 416 runs in twenty-two innings. It was his fielding that won him a place in the Test at Lord's after representing Australia once previously in the 1932/3 series. In six years with Victoria he averaged 35.71 for the State, hitting three centuries. He appeared in the Bombay Quadrangular Tournament in December 1936.

First-class career (1929-38): 2,055 runs (28.54) including 3 centuries, and 39 wickets (42.33)
Test matches (2): 38 runs (9.50), 0-19 and 2 catches

BROWN, William Alfred (b.1912)

New South Wales and Queensland

A right-handed opening batsman of undoubted charm but rather slow in unfolding his array of strokes, Bill

Brown was unruffled and assured at the wicket and a prolific scorer in Tests. An excellent field, he trained regularly with professional sprinters. Although he made a duck on his debut for his adopted State, New South Wales, he made 154 in his seventh match and 205 in his thirteenth against Queensland and Victoria respectively; against Queensland he shared in a stand of 294 with Don Bradman. He was chosen in preference to Jack Fingleton for the 1934 tour of England, and among his 5 centuries was 105 in the Test at Lord's, when he opened for his country for the first time. In South Africa, 1935/6, he averaged 59.57 in the Tests, and, returning to England in 1938, enjoyed his best season. Coming second to Bradman in the overall tour averages with 1,854 runs (57.93), including his career-highest, 265 not out against Derbyshire at Chesterfield, he was second also in the Tests, making 512 runs (73.14). At Trent Bridge he made a stolid 133, and at Lord's carried his bat through the first innings of 422, amassing 206 in six and a quarter hours. Returning to his native Queensland in 1936/7 as player-coach, he scored 1,057 runs in eleven innings in 1938/9; and he captained Australia successfully in the first post-War Test, against New Zealand at Wellington. For Australia against India in 1947/8, he was run out controversially by Mankad, when backing up too far; and in the fifth Test at Melbourne he was run out again – for 99. He later served as a Test selector.

First-class career (1932-49): 13,838 runs (51.44) including 39 centuries, and 110 catches
Test matches (22): 1,592 runs (46.82) including 4 centuries, and 14 catches

BRUCE, William (1864-1925)

Victoria

The first left-handed batsman sent to England with an Australian team – in 1886 and again in 1893 – William Bruce was free and attractive in style, a brilliant hitter either as an opener or in the middle-order, but he lacked a sound defence. More successful on his second trip, he made 60 and 37 against Surrey at The Oval, when Tom Richardson was at his best; and he headed the averages in the Tests with 39.75. To a huge record total of 843 against Oxford and Cambridge Past and Present at Portsmouth, he contributed his career-highest, 191, adding 232 in two hours twenty minutes with Hugh Trumble. In very good form against Lord Sheffield's side, 1891/2, he averaged 37.66 in the Tests; and in the third Test at Adelaide in 1894/5 he made his highest against England, a charming 80. His left-arm, medium-paced bowling brought him 69 wickets for his State, but it was infrequently used in Tests. Falling on hard times, he was found drowned near Melbourne in 1925. He was sixty-one years old at time of death.

First-class career (1882-1903): 5,732 runs (23.98) including 4 centuries, 143 wickets (29.68) and 101 catches
Test matches (14): 702 runs (29.25), 12 wickets (36.66) and 12 catches

BURGE, Peter John Parnell (b.1932)

Queensland

A tall, rugged, strong right-handed batsman who loved a fight. Peter Burge was one of the most dangerous batsmen of the sixties. A powerful driver and natural attacker, he was an exceptionally good hooker for a tall man, and many fast bowlers had cause to regret bowling short at him. On his debut for his State, against South Australia in 1952/3, he hit 54 and 46, when runs were badly needed each time. The next year he made 103 off a powerful New South Wales attack. He represented Australia for the first time at Sydney in the fifth Test against England in 1954/5 when, at his first touch of the ball, he caught Len Hutton at leg-slip off Ray Lindwall. He toured the West Indies in 1955, with his father managing the side, but did little other than make 177 against British Guiana, and then fared moderately in England in 1956. Dropped first ball, he went on to score 210

Peter Burge – Murray keeping wicket and Barrington behind

against Victoria in 1956/7, but continued to be erratic for Australia, despite touring New Zealand, South Africa, India and Pakistan. It was after 1960/61 that he emerged as a dominant figure. From two Tests he headed the averages against the West Indies with 53.75. On the England tour of 1961 he appeared in all five Tests for the first time. At The Oval, in the last Test, he struck hard for 181. Against England in 1962/3 he came back superbly with 103 and 52 not out in the fifth match at Sydney and headed the averages with 61.25. He made his career-highest score of 283 against New South Wales at Brisbane in 1963/4 and, after a foot operation, came to England again in 1964 when he finished second to Bobby Simpson in the Test averages. He hit a magnificent 160 at Headingley, turning the match with a daring assault on the second new ball. Burge always considered he batted better against England than anyone else. His last Test century was in the second Test at Melbourne in 1965/6 when he hit 120, another decisive knock, after Australia had followed-on. He made 8,443 runs (50.86) in Sheffield Shield matches alone. He is still a prominent and popular figure in Queensland cricket. He has lost weight after becoming, the locals said, the 'fastest growing sport in Queensland'.

First-class career (1952-67): 14,640 runs (47.53) including 38 centuries, 166 catches and 4 stumpings
Test matches (42): 2,290 runs (38.16) including 4 centuries, and 23 catches

BURKE, James Wallace (1930-79)

New South Wales

Dark-haired, lantern-jawed and with his baggy cap tugged down over one eye, Jim Burke was an obdurate opening batsman who exuded a healthy dislike of English cricketers on the field. Enthusiastic but ultra-cautious and stodgy at times, he toured New Zealand with the Australian 'A' team in 1949/50 and, as runs continued to come, made his debut against England at Adelaide in 1950/51, scoring 101 not out in the second innings. He toured England (in 1956), South Africa, India and Pakistan – scoring 161 at Bombay in 1956/7 and 189 at Cape Town in 1958/9. On his sole tour of England he topped the Test averages with 30.11, in 'Laker's year'. In the Test at Brisbane in 1958/9 Burke followed an incredibly slow innings by Trevor Bailey with an even slower one – 28 not out in 250 minutes. As an occasional off-break bowler, his action was described by Ian Peebles as looking like a policeman applying his truncheon 'to a particularly short offender's head'. At the height of the 'throwing' controversy in 1958/9, when Peter May was scoring a brilliant century at Sydney, a voice bellowed from the Hill: 'Put Burke on – he can throw straight!' In fifty-eight Sheffield Shield matches he made 3,399 runs

Jim Burke

(44.14), including his highest, 220 against South Australia at Adelaide in 1956/7. Although he had domestic and financial worries, and was facing a major hip operation which threatened to prevent him from playing golf, a sport he loved, it was a great shock to his friends when he bought a gun one morning in Sydney early in 1979 and shot himself with it that afternoon.

First-class career (1948-58): 7,563 runs (45.01) including 21 centuries, and 101 wickets (29.11)
Test matches (24): 1,280 runs (34.59) including 3 centuries, 8 wickets (28.75) and 18 catches

BURN, Edwin James Kenneth (1862-1956)

Tasmania and Wellington

Ken Burn, 'The Scotsman', was a sound, painstaking batsman who made many runs for Richmond, East Hobart, Wellington and Tasmania: he hit forty-one centuries, two above 350, reached three figures in six successive innings in 1895/6 and three years later scored 1,200 runs at an average of 133 in club cricket. He was chosen as second-string wicket-keeper for the 1890 Australian tour of England, and it was only when they were in the Red Sea that his colleagues learnt that he had never put on the gloves in his life. During the tour he made only 355 runs (10.14), but appeared in two Tests. At time of death he was the oldest surviving Test cricketer.

First-class career (1883-1909): 1,750 runs (21.34) including 2 centuries, and 14 wickets (22.85)
Test matches (2): 41 runs (10.25)

BURTON, Frederick John (c.1866-1929)

New South Wales and Victoria

A wicket-keeper, Frederick Burton played in two Tests against England, both at Sydney, in 1886/7 and 1887/8, though Jack Blackham kept during the second match. He toured New Zealand with a New South Wales team in 1895 and settled there.

First-class career (1885-95): 376 runs (13.42) and 32 dismissals (25 ct, 7 st.)
Test matches (2): 4 runs (2.00) and 2 dismissals (1 ct, 1 st.)

CALLAWAY, Sydney Thomas (1868-1923)

New South Wales, Queensland and Canterbury

A splendid batsman when in form and a medium-fast bowler with a good length, Sydney Thomas represented Australia against Lord Sheffield's 1891/2 team and A.E. Stoddart's of 1894/5. In the third Test at Adelaide in 1894/5, he took 5 for 37 (England being dismissed for 124) and added 81 with Albert Trott for the last wicket. He visited New Zealand twice with teams from New South Wales, each time heading the bowling averages. Later he settled there, playing for Canterbury as well as for New Zealand against English and Australian teams. He took 167 wickets in New Zealand from 1896 to 1907. He died in New Zealand after two years of ill health.

First-class career (1888-1906): 1,747 runs (16.79) and 321 wickets (17.00)
Test matches (3): 87 runs (17.40) and 6 wickets (23.66)

CALLEN, Ian Wayne (b.1955)

Victoria

Ian Callen made an impressive start in the Sheffield Shield in 1976/7, taking 25 wickets in three matches. His Test career was soon blighted after a promising start against India in 1977/8. He took 6 wickets (31.83), scored 22 and 4, both times not out, and held one catch in his first Test at Adelaide, when Australia's inexperienced side won a high-scoring game, but on the arduous tour of the Caribbean which followed, he could take only 11 wickets at 50 each and did not get another Test cap. Tall and wiry, with a fine action and an ability to swing the ball away from the bat, he was hardly able to give a fair reflection of his potential. A back injury reduced his chances of playing further Tests but he came back into the reckoning by doing well for Victoria in 1981/2 when he took 31 wickets at 25.45 runs each in six matches (besides averaging more than 20 with the bat). He toured Pakistan in 1982/3, but did not get a chance in the Tests.

First-class career (1977-): 464 runs (12.88), 155 wickets (27.41) and 17 catches

CARKEEK, William (1878-1937)

Victoria

William Carkeek toured England in 1909 as second-string wicket-keeper, but was first choice in 1912, the year of the Triangular Tournament. Short and sturdily built, he was sound rather than brilliant and not in the tradition of the great Australian 'keepers. Nicknamed 'Barlow' because of his stonewalling propensities, his left-handed batting remained moderate and he averaged only 13.28 for his State.

First-class career (1903-14): 1,388 runs (12.17) and 159 dismissals (114 ct, 45 st.)
Test matches (6): 16 runs (5.33) and 6 dismissals (6 ct)

CARLSON, Philip Henry (b.1951)

Queensland

Phil Carlson made an outstanding start to his Sheffield Shield career, scoring a century for Queensland at the age of eighteen, but he was unfortunate in starting his Test career against such a strong England bowling attack as that of the 1978/9 team. Tall, strong and Scandinavian in appearance, with a military bearing, he was a gifted batsman who loved to drive straight and hard, a good fielder (who held a superb slip catch in his first Test) and a useful, medium-pace, swing bowler. His selection against England followed a succession of high scores in Sheffield Shield cricket – in 1977/8 he scored 591 runs at 45.46 and in 1978/9 he made 448 runs (40.33) as well as taking 28 wickets at 11.00 each – but he proved vulnerable against fast bowling in Test cricket.

First-class career (1969-81): 4,167 runs (28.34) including 5 centuries, and 124 wickets (24.06)
Test matches (2): 23 runs (5.75), 2 wickets (49.50) and 2 catches

CARTER, Hanson (1878-1948)

New South Wales

Born in Halifax, 'Sammy' or 'Sep' Carter was rather short and slightly built and he did not stand as close to the stumps as some other noted wicket-keepers have done, but he took the ball comfortably, even when Albert Cotter, Jack Gregory and Ted McDonald bowled their fastest and very few byes swelled England's totals. He toured England in 1902, 1909 and 1921, and in the Test at Headingley in 1921 found himself the only Yorkshire-born player in the match! Generally of small account as a batsman, he could be dangerous and prolific in his own way. His chief delight was a stroke by which he lifted the ball over his left shoulder just as a labourer shovels the dirt out of a drain he is digging. An authority on the Laws of Cricket it was Sep Carter who pointed out at Old Trafford in 1921 that England's captain had erred in closing his innings, a revelation which sent the Australians back on the field, where the Australian captain Warwick Armstrong unwittingly committed a breach of the Laws by bowling two successive overs. An undertaker by profession, Sammy sometimes came to matches in a hearse. At the age of 54, in 1932, he went on Arthur Mailey's lengthy private tour of Canada, the USA and New Zealand.

First-class career (1897-1924): 2,897 runs (20.11) including 2 centuries, and 271 dismissals (182 ct, 89 st.)
Test matches (28): 873 runs (22.97) and 65 dismissals (44 ct, 21 st.)

CHAPPELL, Gregory Stephen (b.1948)

South Australia, Queensland and Somerset

The Chappell family has provided something of an Australian answer to the Grace family. The three grandsons of Victor Richardson, Ian, Greg and Trevor Chappell, have all played Test cricket, and the elder two have been amongst their country's finest batsmen as well as providing the only instance of brothers captaining Australia. Greg, who took over from Ian in 1976/7 as captain of Australia (his brother, elder by five years, had carefully groomed him for the job), is the more brilliant. A tall, naturally graceful right-hander, his batting is cool and composed, without being casual: he has mastered even the best bowlers in the worst batting conditions. At the crease he appears instantly and permanently at ease, rarely betraying excitement or emotion. He is quick to judge whether he should defend with a bat perfectly straight, or attack with an array of strokes which range from a crisp and fearless hook, through majestic drives on either side of the wicket, to delicate cuts and deflections. Starting in the Sheffield Shield with his native South Australia, he later toughened his attitude and broadened his experience by playing for Somerset. In the Championship of 1968 he made 1,108 runs and took 26 wickets, in addition to making one spectacular century in a televised John Player Sunday League game – typical of his flair for the big occasion. He had already shown such flair when only eighteen in a Sheffield Shield match against his later adopted State, Queensland, scoring a century when still in his first season, and at twenty-two he revealed it again in his first Test at Perth in 1970 when, coming in at 107 for 5 in a reply to an England total of 397, he made 108. The high Test average which he later built up would have been even higher had Australia's unofficial series against the Rest of the World in 1971/2 been taken into account: Chappell made 115 not out at Sydney, 197 not out at Melbourne, and 85 at Adelaide. In England in the closely fought Ashes series of 1972 he made two beautiful centuries at Lord's and The Oval. Against New Zealand at Wellington in 1973/4 he scored 247

Greg Chappell

not out and 133 in a match at which another fraternal record was established when Ian too scored two centuries. Brilliant performances rolled off his bat in the ensuing years. Against England, 1974/5, he scored 608 runs (55.27) and caught brilliantly at second slip. Tired and unwell, he was much less successful in England the following summer, but in his first match as captain of Australia in 1975/6 he scored 123 and 109 against the powerful West Indies at Brisbane. He went on to lead Australia to a 5-1 victory in the series, scoring 702 runs at an average of 117. Chappell's experience as a captain had begun with his move to Queensland in 1973/4. He was a less successful motivator of men than his brother Ian, but it is perhaps unfair to lay much of the blame for Australia's failures in England in 1977 at the door of their captain, who scored most runs for his team (371 at 41.22), including a memorable century against the tide of English success at Old Trafford, and who by then had decided to join most of his fellows in Kerry Packer's World Series Cricket. In addition to his genius as a batsman, Greg Chappell is a more than useful, medium-pace, swing bowler, always capable of turning in an inspirational spell, and one of the most brilliant slip fielders of modern times. He held 7 catches at second slip in the Perth Test against England in 1974/5, setting a world record (subsequently equalled by

India's Yajurvindersinh). Chappell's 14 catches in that series is the second highest in a Test series by a non wicket-keeper. After the disbandment of World Series Cricket, Greg Chappell, who had hitherto announced his retirement from Test cricket, returned to the fray as captain of Australia in sixteen more Tests from 1979 to 1981 before deciding against touring England in 1981. There were times when his health was in doubt during this intense period but his cricket throughout was superb. Against the West Indies he made 124 at Perth and against England 98 not out at Sydney and 114 at Melbourne. In the many one-day internationals he was still Australia's key batsman although in the field his captaincy sometimes lacked resource. He took the Australian team to Pakistan where the short series was lost despite the captain's 235 in the second Test at Faisalabad. Chappell's third Test double century came less than a year later against India at Sydney where his 204 out of 406 was decisive. For the 1980/81 season he led Australia, at last, to success in a one-day tournament, the triangular series with India and Pakistan, but in the third match of the best of five finals he created an international furore by ordering his brother Trevor to bowl an underarm grubber with New Zealand requiring six runs off the last ball of the match to tie the game. It was an uncharitable piece of captaincy, described by the New Zealand Prime Minister as cowardly, and it was certainly unworthy of a cricketer normally exemplary and gracious in triumph or failure. In 1981/2 he had a run of unaccustomed failures, but kept his place as captain on the short tour of New Zealand at the end of the season, scoring 176 at Christchurch, his 20th Test century. In 1982/3 he at last achieved his ambition to captain Australia to victory in an Ashes series, hitting centuries at Brisbane and Adelaide, significantly the two games which Australia won.

First-class career (1966-): 22,786 runs (52.74) including 68 centuries, 282 wickets (28.59) and 336 catches
Test matches (76): 6,291 runs (53.31) including 20 centuries, 46 wickets (37.21) and 106 catches

CHAPPELL, Ian Michael (b.1943)

South Australia

Ian Chappell will be remembered for many reasons: as one of Australia's best post-War batsmen, as one of her greatest captains of any era, and as a fiercely determined man who led a players' revolt against the cricket administrators of Australia. Educated like his brothers at Prince Alfred College in Adelaide, Ian was playing for South Australia at the age of eighteen and for his country at twenty-one. He became quickly established as a tough competitor, a right-handed batsman both gritty and attractive, a brilliant slip fielder and useful leg-spin bowler. Unlike that of his younger brother Greg, Ian Chappell's apprenticeship in Test cricket was tough. After making 348 runs against England in 1968, when he established himself in the Australian team, he scored 138 and 99 in successive Tests in India in 1969/70, but was then brought to earth as Australia were humiliated under Bill Lawry's captaincy in South Africa, losing 4-0. Chappell (whom Lawry had called at the start of the tour 'the best batsman in the world') had a top score of only 34. But from the moment that he replaced Lawry as captain, for the final Test of the 1970/71 series against England, Ian Chappell made a lasting reputation. He lost that match to the wily Illingworth, but a new spirit and new players – notably Dennis Lillee – were to transform Australian fortunes in the next few years. Although Australia failed to regain the Ashes in 1972, the match in which they squared the series at The Oval, with the Chappell brothers both making centuries and sharing a stand of 201, marked the turning point. It was Chappell's good fortune to have at his command one of Australia's greatest-ever fast bowlers, Dennis Lillee, and when he was joined by Jeff Thomson in 1974/5, there was never any doubt that he would restore the Ashes to Australian hands. He used his major assets shrewdly, never relaxing the relentless pressure on the unfortunate English batsmen and setting a fine example in the other departments of the game – batting with his characteristic concentration and dedication to the cause of victory, as well as fielding brilliantly at first slip where

Ian Chappell – Alan Knott (England) keeping wicket

he has always been outstanding. The following season in England he retained the Ashes, making 192 at The Oval in his final Test as captain. Under his brother's subsequent captaincy he continued to score freely. With Greg he shares a record unlikely to be equalled – both scored centuries in each innings of the first Test against New Zealand at Wellington in 1973/4, Ian making 145 and 121 (yet the match was drawn). Much of Ian Chappell's temperament and character was infused into the men under him, and his players were sometimes accused of excess arrogance and bluntness. It was this very matter-of-fact approach of his, refusing to pay lip service to the niceties of the establishment, which not only resulted in his various brushes with the authorities of cricket, but also contributed to the formation of World Series Cricket. Having played a leading role, both as player and adviser, in World Series Cricket, he returned to Test cricket when WSC was disbanded, but the controversies continued to follow him. He was suspended for abusing an umpire in a Sheffield Shield match and also carried out two petulant public protests when playing for South Australia against England. He nevertheless played three more Tests in 1979/80, failing in both innings against the West Indies at Adelaide but making 152 (50.66) in four innings against England when his experience, application and determination proved invaluable. It appeared, however, that his enthusiasm for the game had turned sour and his retirement at the end of the season came as no surprise despite the fact that his final year had brought him 890 runs (40.25) and that he had led South Australia into second place in the Sheffield Shield. Thus this stormy character departed the playing scene, knowing that he was loved by few but that he had achieved much and feeling, rightly or wrongly, that he had sinned less than he had been sinned against.

First-class career (1961-79): 19,680 runs (48.35) including 59 centuries, 176 wickets (37.13), 312 catches and 1 stumping
Test matches (75): 5,345 runs (42.42) including 14 centuries, 20 wickets (65.80) and 105 catches

CHAPPELL, Trevor Martin (b.1952)

South Australia, Western Australia and New South Wales

The youngest of the Chappell brothers, Trevor, like Ian and Greg, set his heart on playing for Australia and eventually achieved his ambition in England in 1981, after a long struggle to establish himself in Sheffield Shield cricket. Small, tough, curly-haired and determined, a nuggety right-handed batsman, useful medium-paced bowler and fine cover fielder, he eventually proved himself a valuable member of the New South Wales side, scoring 550 runs with two centuries in 1980/81 and thus earning a place on the tour of England. He played in the first three Tests, sharing the pleasure of victory at Trent Bridge, where his staunch 20 not out in the second innings helped to stop a sudden slide of Australian wickets, and the humiliation of unexpected defeat at Headingley. After this match, however, he was dropped and took a back seat on the tour. Not called on at home the following season, he maintained steady form with 533 Sheffield Shield runs. Though he shared with his brothers the distinction of the only instance of three (or more) brothers playing for their country, he was never quite the batsman Greg or Ian was.

First-class career (1972-): 3,201 runs (31.38) including 4 centuries, 25 wickets (24.00) and 34 catches
Test matches (3): 79 runs (15.80) and 2 catches

CHARLTON, Dr Percie Chator (1867-1954)

New South Wales

Showing promise as batsman and fast-medium bowler – for Eighteen of Sydney Juniors he took 7 wickets against Shaw and Shrewbury's team in 1887/8 – Percie Charlton toured England with the 1890 team when he took 42 wickets (19.04) but averaged only 14.30 with the bat. But due to ill-health he soon retired from first-class cricket and became a medical practitioner.

First-class career (1888-97): 648 runs (13.69) and 97 wickets (19.96)
Test matches (2): 29 runs (7.25) and 3 wickets (8.00)

CHIPPERFIELD, Arthur Gordon (b.1905)

New South Wales

Of average height, thickset and rather slow in his movements, 'Chipper' was a solid batsman, busy and competent, essentially a front-foot player. He was also a slow spin bowler who collected useful wickets (although he often toiled more than he spun) and a good slip field. A surprise choice for the 1934 tour – he had played only three times for his State, though he had hit a century for Northern Districts of N.S.W. against the 1932/3 MCC team – he soon justified his selection by making 99 on his Test debut at Trent Bridge. He played in all five Tests. He averaged 37.58 on this tour, and 38.56 in the 1936/7 series against England. When Gubby Allen and Bill Voce bundled Australia out for 58 at Brisbane in the first Test, he alone stood his ground with 26 not out. On the 1938 tour his activities were greatly curtailed by appendicitis. His one Test century was 109 in the first Test at Durban in 1935/6.

First-class career (1933-9): 4,295 runs (38.34) including 9 centuries, and 65 wickets (39.72)
Test matches (14): 552 runs (32.47) including 1 century, 5 wickets (87.40) and 15 catches

CLARK, Wayne Maxwell (b.1953)

Western Australia

A strongly built, fast-medium right-arm swing bowler with an action very reminiscent of Graham McKenzie's Wayne Clark was a pivotal member of the young Australian side formed under Bobby Simpson's captaincy in the wake of the defections to Kerry Packer. But after taking 43 wickets in nine successive Tests, suspicions about the legality of his action when he delivered his bouncer (certainly a mean and dangerous one) and a general loss of form at the start of the 1978/9 season led to his replacement by Rodney Hogg as Australia's opening bowler. A back injury had caused his omission from the final Test of the 1978 tour of the West Indies, but with 15 wickets in four Tests and 34 on an arduous tour at an average of 23 each, Clark performed manfully.

First-class career (1974-): 530 runs (12.32) and 158 wickets (29.06)
Test matches (9): 89 runs (5.93), 43 wickets (27.02) and 5 catches

COLLEY, David John (b.1947)

New South Wales

A right-arm fast-medium bowler with a long run-up and a more than useful late-order batsman, David Colley was a surprise choice for the 1972 tour of England. He appeared in three Tests without distinguishing himself as a bowler, but he hit a daring 54 at Trent Bridge. He played another remarkable hitter's innings in 1974/5 when, in a losing cause, he hit MCC for 90 off 67 balls while only 19 runs came at the other end.

First-class career (1969-77): 2,374 runs (23.74) including 1 century, and 236 wickets (31.60)
Test matches (3): 84 runs (21.00), 6 wickets (52.00) and 1 catch

COLLINS, Herbert Leslie (1889-1959)

New South Wales

Herbie or 'Horseshoe' Collins – a bookmaker by profession – was a right-handed batsman with unlimited patience and concentration, of practically impregnable defence, almost strokeless, seemingly without power, and yet highly effective and a regular choice in Tests from 1920 until 1926. As a slow left-arm bowler, he often broke irritating partnerships. Opening with Warren Bardsley, he made 70 and 104 in his first Test at Sydney in 1920/21, and 162 in his third at Adelaide; in that series he totalled 557 runs in nine completed innings. In South Africa, 1921/2, he hit 203 in the Test at Johannesburg. His last major successes against England were in the first Test at Sydney in 1924/5 when he scored 114 and 60. A shrewd captain who understood his men, Herbie Collins led Australia to a 4-1 victory in the 1924/5 series, but when he led the team that lost the Ashes in 1926 he was handicapped by neuritis. In Sheffield Shield matches he scored 2,040 runs (41.63).

Herbie Collins (left) and Warren Bardsley

First-class career (1909-26): 9,924 runs (40.01) including 32 centuries, and 181 wickets (21.38)
Test matches (19): 1,352 runs (45.06) including 4 centuries, 4 wickets (63.00) and 13 catches

CONINGHAM, Arthur (1866-1939)

Queensland and New South Wales

A left-handed batsman and fast bowler, Arthur Coningham ranked high in Australia as an all-rounder and came to England with the 1893 team but was surprisingly given little to do. His career-highest score was 151 for Queensland against New South Wales at Sydney in 1895/6; and his sole Test was the second at Melbourne in 1894/5, when he scored 10 and 3 and took 2 for 76. Volatile and over-confident, he was no-balled when bowling to England's captain, A.E. Stoddart, and, in annoyance, deliberately threw the next ball at the batsman. Adept at billiards, rowing, shooting and Rugby football, he earned a medal saving a boy's life in the Thames in 1893. But this was dull fare compared with the conspiracy sensation of 1900: 'Conny', revolver at his hip, conducted his own scandalous and unsuccessful divorce case with an eminent priest as the alleged 'other man'. In eleven Sheffield Shield matches he made 203 runs and took 41 wickets.

First-class career (1892-8): 896 runs (15.71) including 1 century, and 112 wickets (23.24)

CONNOLLY, Alan Norman (b.1939)

Victoria and Middlesex

A tall and powerfully built, right-arm, fast-medium bowler, Alan Connolly's swerve, cut and clever changes of pace set the batsmen of several nations some insoluble problems. He toured England twice in 1964 and 1968, suffering a back injury on the former tour, but in the latter headed the Test averages with 23 wickets (25.69). He toured India twice and South Africa once. During his last tour, one of several as partner for 'Garth' Mackenzie, he took 20 wickets (26.10) in the four Tests against the victorious South Africans in 1969/70, heading the averages. Seven Tests against England brought him 25 wickets, but his finest feat was 6 for 47 in the first innings of the fourth Test at Port Elizabeth – in the last Test to be played by South Africa – before Australia were overwhelmed by 323 runs. Connolly signed for Middlesex for three years, but after two not entirely successful seasons, partly because of back trouble, he returned home. No one has taken more wickets for Victoria than his 330 at 27.04 in 83 matches.

First-class career (1959-70): 1,073 runs (8.79) and 676 wickets (26.58)
Test matches (29): 260 runs (10.40), 102 wickets (29.22) and 17 catches

COOPER, Bransby Beauchamp (1844-1914)

Middlesex, Kent and Victoria

Bransby Cooper was an outstanding right-handed batsman at Rugby school – attractive hard-hitting, patient and defensive when necessary. In 1869 he opened with W.G. at The Oval for Gentlemen against Players, putting on 105, and three weeks later – going in against a total of 475 – they put on 283 in three hours and forty minutes for Gentlemen of the South against Players of the South. Soon afterwards he left England for the USA and then spent the rest of his life in Australia. He hit 83 for Eighteen of Victoria against W.G.'s England team in 1873/4, and he represented Australia in the first-ever Test at Melbourne in 1876/7, scoring 15 and 3 and holding two catches. He was also a useful wicket-keeper.

First-class career (1863-77): 1,610 runs (20.64) including 1 century, 41 catches and 20 stumpings

COOPER, William Henry (1849-1939)

Victoria

Born at Maidstone in Kent, William Cooper was, at the time of death, the oldest Australian Test player. Starting serious cricket late, at twenty-seven, he became an effective right-arm, slow, leg-break bowler, and in his initial Test at Melbourne, in the 1882 New Year's match, took 9 for 200 (in 98.2 overs). He toured England with the 1884 team but could not grip the ball properly because of a finger injured on the voyage over. He was successively captain of his State, a State selector and vice-president of Victoria Cricket Association. Paul Sheahan, who also played for Victoria and Australia, is his great-grandson.

First-class career (1878-86): 247 runs (10.29) and 71 wickets (24.49)
Test matches (2): 13 runs (6.50), 9 wickets (25.11) and 1 catch

CORLING, Grahame Edward (b.1941)

New South Wales

On the small side for an opening right-arm fast-medium bowler, Grahame Corling had admirable stamina and, after one season of first-class cricket, toured England in 1964 as the youngest member of the team, appearing in all the Tests. Thereafter, his first-class career fell away though he remained a keen and cheerful grade cricketer. In forty Sheffield Shield matches he took 111 wickets (33.45).

First-class career (1963-8): 484 runs (10.52), 173 wickets (32.05) and 11 catches
Test matches (5): 5 runs (1.66) and 12 wickets (37.25)

COSIER, Gary John (b.1953)

Victoria, South Australia and Queensland

Red-haired, burly and merry, like a reincarnation of the youthful Henry VIII, Gary Cosier was a cricketer of character who never quite established himself in the Australian side, either before or after the Packer Revolution. An outstanding teenage cricketer in Victoria, he moved to South Australia for whom he scored two hundreds against the 1975/6 West Indians. Rewarded with a place in the third Test at Melbourne, he scored 109, but though he played some fine innings afterwards, including 168 against Pakistan in 1976/7, technical deficiencies, and a desire to play his shots even when it was indiscreet to do so, led to a disappointing inconsistency. He batted with virtually no backlift, but very powerful arms made him a good hooker and square-cutter and in limited-over cricket he could be a dynamic exponent of the lofted drive: a whirlwind knock helped Australia defeat England in a one-day international at his favourite Melbourne in 1978/9. A cheerful, happy-go-lucky character, he was also a good close fielder and a very useful slow-medium bowler who could swing the ball alarmingly in humid conditions. A property company in Queensland insured his future with the 'Sunshine State' by offering him a long-term contract said to be worth some £30,000 a year, but his career faded.

Gary Cosier

First-class career (1971-80): 5,005 runs (32.92) including 7 centuries, and 75 wickets (30.68)
Test matches (18): 897 runs (28.93) including 2 centuries, 5 wickets (68.20) and 14 catches

COTTAM, John Thomas (1867-*c.* 1897)

New South Wales

A right-handed batsman, John Cottam represented Australia once against England at Sydney, 1886/7, scoring 1 and 3 and holding one catch. He did not appear in any Sheffield Shield matches.

First-class career (1886-90): 273 runs (22.75)

COTTER, Albert (1883-1917)

New South Wales

Once he gained command over his length and shortened his run, 'Tibby' Cotter, whose style was similar to that, later, of Jeff Thomson, could be a fearsome fast bowler. From 1904 until 1912 he was the spearhead of his country's attack. In the fifth Test at Melbourne in 1903/4, after England had regained the Ashes, he took 8 for 65, earning Australia a convincing win. He toured England in 1905 and 1909; in 1905 he took 124 wickets (including 12 for 34 at Worcester) when his pace was terrific, and in 1909 he had a large hand in the winning of the Headingley Test, taking 5 for 38 in the second innings. Two years later he took 4 wickets in 4 balls for Glebe versus Sydney. Tibby was killed in action by a sniper at Beersheba while serving in the Australian Light Horse.

First-class career (1901-13): 2,484 runs (16.89) and 442 wickets (24.27)
Test matches (21): 457 runs (13.05), 89 wickets (28.64) and 8 catches

COULTHARD, George (1856-83)

Victoria

On the staff of the Melbourne club, George Coulthard accompanied Lord Harris's 1878/9 team in Australia as umpire, and adjudicated in the sole Test at Melbourne to general satisfaction. Then, during the match between the tourists and New South Wales at Sydney, all hell broke loose. Rivalry between Victoria and New South Wales was bitter and when George gave W.L. Murdoch out on an appeal for run out, the crowd grew angry and invaded the playing area. George appearing to be in danger, Lord Harris moved to help him but was struck by a 'larrikin' wielding a stick. The trouble subsided, and the match continued. George became the first umpire who *later* played in a Test, for Australia at Sydney in 1881/2, when he made 6 not out at number eleven and did not bowl. He died of consumption a year later.

First-class career (1880-81): 92 runs (11.50) and 5 wickets (25.00)

COWPER, Robert Maskew (b.1940)

Victoria and Western Australia

Known as 'Wallaby' because, like his father, he played Rugby Union in an Australian Rules stronghold, Bob Cowper was a well-built left-handed batsman who scored readily with skilful leg-side deflections, square-cuts, hooks and drives. Though not spectacular, he was remarkably consistent either as an opener or in the middle-order. A useful off-spin bowler, he was a little quicker than most bowlers of this type and was rarely collared; and he was also a first-rate slip field. He toured England in 1964 and 1968, and South Africa, the West Indies, India and Pakistan once each. On his first tour in 1964 he scored 1,287 runs (51.48) but did not establish himself as a Test player until his visit to the West Indies in 1965 when he headed the Test aggregates with 417, including two centuries, creating a fine impression against the fast bowlers. He was recalled for the fifth Test against England at Melbourne in 1965/6 and scored 307, the highest innings in a Test in Australia and the fourth longest in history, lasting in all twelve hours and seven minutes. Less successful against South Africa in 1966/7, he was back to his best when India toured Australia in 1967/8, scoring most runs in the four Tests, 485 (69.28), including two centuries, and taking 13 wickets (18.38).

Bob Cowper

He also played as a professional in the Lancashire League. In Sheffield Shield matches, he scored 4,067 runs (53.51) and took 59 wickets (40.83). He was a very keen and studious cricketer, with an extensive knowledge of the game. He acted as adviser to Kerry Packer during his first negotiations with the Australian Cricket Board and is now a respected figure in Melbourne business circles and a fine player of real tennis.

First-class career (1959-69): 10,595 runs (53.78) including 26 centuries, 183 wickets (31.19) and 151 catches
Test matches (27): 2,061 runs (46.84) including 5 centuries, 36 wickets (31.63) and 21 catches

CRAIG, Ian David (b.1935)

New South Wales

At sixteen years five months, Ian Craig became the youngest player to appear in inter-State cricket, against South Australia at Sydney, when he made a sedate 91. The following season, 1952/3, an innings of 213 not out for his State against the South Africans gained him a place in the fifth Test at Melbourne, when he scored 53 and 47, as Australia's youngest player in Test cricket. Touring England in 1953, however, he averaged only 16.50, and on returning home he resumed his studies as a chemist, not coming back to first-class cricket for three years. But his skill was never in doubt: his cover-driving could be a model of perfection and his on-side play crisp and certain, with feet in the right place all the time. Though small and apparently quite slight, he had deceptive strength and timing and once hit Ian Johnson for four sixes in five balls in Lindsay Hassett's benefit match. But he had weaknesses, especially against the good-length ball just outside the off-stump, and he lacked the ruthlessness of Don Bradman, with whom in his youth he was compared. On his second visit to England in 1956 he made only 55 runs (being dismissed by Jim Laker three times out of four); he was still the youngest member of the Australian party. On the way home he did well against India and Pakistan and he captained the Australians in South Africa in 1957/8 with much success: the newly confident team won three Tests out of five and lost none. Beyond a 52 in the third Test at Durban, which saved his side in the first innings, he did little in the Tests, but averaged 36.93 for the whole tour. A serious and pleasant man by nature, Ian was being groomed for leadership against England on his return to Australia, but he contracted hepatitis the following season and was rarely in the running for a Test place subsequently. He continued to captain his State, however, and against Queensland at Sydney in 1960/61 Neil Harvey and he added 323 for the second wicket.

First-class career (1951-61): 7,328 runs (37.96) including 15 centuries
Test matches (11): 358 runs (19.88) and 2 catches

CRAWFORD, William Patrick Anthony (b.1933)

New South Wales

A tall, gangling right-arm fast bowler, Pat Crawford burst on the scene in 1954/5, heading the Sheffield Shield averages with 25 wickets (12.96). He was regarded as the logical successor to Ray Lindwall in Australia's ranks and was an improving batsman. He toured England, India and Pakistan in 1956 and captured some inexpensive wickets against India, but throughout was subject to muscular injuries, and soon dropped out of first-class cricket. He had some experience of the Lancashire League.

First-class career (1954-7): 424 runs (19.27) and 110 wickets (21.27)
Test matches (4): 53 runs (17.66), 7 wickets (15.28) and 1 catch

DARLING, Hon. Joseph (1870-1946)

South Australia

Of medium height, thickset, powerful of frame and personality, his brown moustache and tanned face making him look older than he was, Joe Darling was a batsman who never seemed out of form. Frequently opening the innings, he was one of the great left-handers, who could either defend with stubborn steadiness or pull a game round by determined forcing tactics; and he was a fine mid-off. His greatest impact, however, was as a leader. He toured England in 1896, 1899, 1902 and 1905, as the inspiring captain of the last three teams. On these tours he led two Ashes-winning

Joe Darling

sides – 1899 and 1902 – and made, altogether, 6,377 runs (33.56) and held 109 catches. At home he led the winning side of 1901/2. In 1905, however, England were triumphant, the captain F.S. Jackson winning all five tosses in the Tests. When the two skippers met again at the Scarborough Festival at the end of the tour, Joe, with a towel round his waist, waited in the dressing-room and received 'Jacker' with the remark: 'I'm not going to risk the toss this time except by wrestling' – but the spin of the coin again favoured 'Jacker'. In the 1897/8 series Joe made 101 in the first Test at Sydney, 178 in the second at Adelaide and 160 in the fifth at Sydney, heading the batting with 537 runs (67.12). His highest in first-class cricket was 210 for his State against Queensland at Brisbane in 1898/9. Farming and politics occupied his time outside cricket. Settling in Tasmania, he became a member of the Legislative Assembly, being awarded the CBE for public services in 1938. His father had been a member of the Legislative Assembly of South Australia and had inaugurated the Adelaide Oval, one of the most beautiful Test grounds.

First-class career (1893-1907): 10,637 runs (34.42) including 21 centuries
Test matches (34): 1,657 runs (28.56) including 3 centuries, and 27 catches

DARLING, Leonard Stuart (b.1909)

Victoria

A left-handed batsman born to attack but lacking solidity, Len Darling had no outstanding successes for Australia; he is best remembered for his superb catches on the leg-side which disposed of Walter Hammond and Maurice Leyland on the 'sticky' wicket at Melbourne in 1936/7. He appeared occasionally for his country against England in 1932/3 and 1934 – when he made over 1,000 runs on the tour – and again in 1936/7. He also played in all five Tests against South Africa in 1935/6. His highest Test score was 85 at Sydney in the last match of 1932/3. For his State he made 3,451 runs (47.93).

First-class career (1926-36): 5,780 runs (42.50) including 16 centuries, and 32 wickets (47.00)
Test matches (12): 474 runs (27.88), 0-65 and 8 catches

DARLING, Warrick Maxwell (b.1957)

South Australia

Given his chance in Test cricket earlier than might have been the case if so many senior players had not played World Series Cricket for two years, 'Rick' Darling had a stern baptism against the varied skills of India (1977/8 and 1979), West Indies (1978) and England (1978/9), but his ability to shine in the highest company was clear, for all his inconsistency. Bursting with youthful keenness, this fair-haired, right-handed opening bat and brilliant cover fielder from the Murray River country, a great-nephew of Joe Darling, scored 65 and 56 in his first Test against India, and made two hundreds on his first tour, to the West Indies – although he failed in the Tests. He often threatened to disrupt the supremacy of England's bowlers in 1978/9 with his brilliant and audacious hooking and cutting. His 221 runs in the series (27.62) included a highest score of 91 at Sydney. But his flair has so far not been exploited to the full because of accompanying rashness. Time is on his side, and the potential is clearly immense. He nearly died after being hit on the heart by a ball from Bob Willis in the fifth Test at his home ground, Adelaide. The gum he was chewing lodged in the back of his throat but he was revived by England's John Emburey who administered the 'pre-cordial thump' to get him breathing again. Modest performances in five more Tests in India unfortunately seemed to suggest that his early promise would never be entirely fulfilled; he batted sometimes as an opener and sometimes in the middle order and although he made 59 in the third Test at Kanpur, an innings of great resolution, he made only one other fifty on the tour, illness and injury more than once obstructing this unlucky cricketer. He had to retire hurt in the last innings of the tour, having been hit on the head again, this time by a ball from Kapil Dev. He came back to form with a vengeance in 1981/2, hitting

1,011 runs (72.21) with 3 centuries, but he was overlooked for Test matches.

First-class career (1975-): 4,730 runs (37.53) including 8 centuries
Test matches (14): 697 runs (26.80) and 5 catches

DAVIDSON, Alan Keith (b.1929)

New South Wales

Now president of the New South Wales Cricket Association, Alan Davidson was a left-handed all-rounder of the highest class. Turning from left-arm 'chinamen' to fast bowling to make full use of his height and barrel-chested power, he ran a lively fifteen yards, culminating in a strong wheeling action. He moved the new ball very late in the air, and off the pitch in either direction. As a left-handed batsman, he had tremendous power in his attacking strokes; and in the field he moved sharply, equally brilliant in the deep or close to the wicket. He toured England in 1953, 1956 and 1961, India and Pakistan twice, and South Africa once; and at home he had three series against England and one against the West Indies. He never knew a poor series. In 1958/9 against England he scored 180 runs and took 24 wickets (20.00). In 1960/61, far and away the best bowler on either side, he took 33 wickets (18.54), besides scoring 212 runs against the West Indies. In the unique Test tie at Brisbane, he became the first player to score 100 runs and take 10 wickets in a Test (44 and 80 – his own Test highest – and 5 for 135 and 6 for 87). His most productive bowling in a Test innings was 7 for 93 against India at Kanpur in 1959/60. In twenty-five Tests against England alone he made 750 runs, took 84 wickets and held 23 catches. A modest family man, but an amusing raconteur, he has been successively bank clerk, manager and director. His autobiography, *Fifteen Faces*, which was published in 1963, was well received.

Alan Davidson

First-class career (1949-63): 6,804 runs (32.86) including 9 centuries, and 672 wickets (20.91)
Test matches (44): 1,328 runs (24.59), 186 wickets (20.53) and 42 catches

DAVIS, Ian Charles (b.1953)

New South Wales and Queensland

Something of an enigma, Ian Davis is a slightly built, fair-haired, neat, right-handed opening (or middle-order) batsman, who first played Test cricket for Australia at the age of twenty. He faded for a time, spending one season with Queensland before returning to his native Sydney, but seemed to be re-establishing himself in the Australian team before joining the Kerry Packer troupe. He was given an extended trial in the Australian side first, performing only modestly in six Test matches at home and abroad against New Zealand in 1973/4. A good innings of 91 against the 1974/5 MCC team did not regain him his Test place but after a maiden Test century against Pakistan at Adelaide (105) he was back in favour by the time of the Centenary Test, scoring a solid 68 in the second innings at Melbourne. In three Tests in England in 1977, he could make only 107 runs (17.83) and in thirteen matches on the tour averaged a modest 30. He held his own, however, in the highly competitive World Series Cricket events. An outstanding fielder, his batting has a pleasant touch at its best, with neat cutting and glancing and some sweet driving as its chief attractions.

First-class career (1973-): 4,508 runs (33.89) including 7 centuries
Test matches (15): 692 runs (26.61) including 1 century, and 9 catches

De COURCY, James Harry (b.1927)

New South Wales

Although possessing the ability to charm and play all the strokes, Jim de Courcy never took the high place his ability indicated. An attacking right-handed batsman, he frequently obtained a good start without reaching big figures. He toured England in 1953, scoring 1,214 runs (41.86), including 204 against Combined Services at Kingston, but disappointed in the Tests, the only series in which he represented his country. Fifty matches for his State realized 2,362 runs.

First-class career (1947-57): 3,778 runs (37.04) including 6 centuries
Test matches (3): 81 runs (16.20) and 3 catches

DELL, Anthony Ross (b.1947)

Queensland

A heavily built left-arm fast-medium bowler, born in Hampshire of English parents, Tony Dell joined Dennis Lillee in the attack for the final Test of 1970/71 against England, and made another Test appearance against New Zealand in 1973/4. But he was unable to secure a Test match place in the face of such competition as Jeff Thomson, Max Walker, Gary Gilmour, Lillee himself and his own Queensland opening partner Geoff Dymock.

First-class career (1970-74): 169 runs (5.63) and 137 wickets (26.70)
Test matches (2): 6 runs (—) and 6 wickets (26.66)

DONNAN, Henry (1864-1956)

New South Wales

Harry Donnan's patience as a right-handed batsman was monumental. He was extremely difficult to dislodge and his style was not unattractive: watching the ball right on to his bat, he could cut and drive admirably. He hit centuries against all the other States, in thirty-two Sheffield Matches alone making 1,784 runs. His fielding, however, was against him. Touring England in 1896, he made 1,000 runs but was disappointing in the Tests. He first represented Australia against Lord Sheffield's team in 1891/2. He was brother-in-law of Syd Gregory.

First-class career (1887-1900): 4,262 runs (29.19) including 6 centuries
Test matches (5): 75 runs (8.33), 0-22 and 1 catch

DOOLAND, Bruce (1923-80)

South Australia and Nottinghamshire

A tall, right-arm, leg-break and googly bowler, Bruce Dooland performed the first post-War hat-trick, for his State against Victoria at Melbourne in 1945/6, and was tried in Tests against England in 1946/7 and India in 1947/8. At this stage of his career, however, he lacked the subtleties of flight and the ability to beat the best batsmen off the pitch. He later became a great, rather than just good, leg-spinner but it was as a batsman that his most effective Test performances occurred: in 1946/7 at Adelaide he batted doggedly, helping to restore his country's morale in the first innings. Not selected for the team to England in 1948, he came to England on his own account and played in league cricket until Nottinghamshire specially registered him in 1953 – and he was such a success that he just failed to achieve the double in his first season. Five times he captured 100 wickets in a season, twice achieving the double, the second time in his last county season, 1957, when he made 1,604 runs (28.64) and captured 141 wickets (23.21). Throughout he was a great success for his adopted county – he had 16 for 83 against Essex at Trent Bridge in 1954 and took 8 for 20 in an innings against Worcestershire on the same ground in 1956. It was a heavy blow when he decided to return to his native South Australia. He represented Australia also at baseball.

First-class career (1945-57): 7,141 runs (24.37) including 4 centuries, 1,016 wickets (21.98) and 180 catches
Test matches (3): 76 runs (19.00), 9 wickets (46.55) and 3 catches

DUFF, Reginald Alexander (1878-1911)

New South Wales

Of sturdy medium height and cheerful disposition, Reggie Duff was a very punishing right-handed batsman who watched the ball closely and drove powerfully. On his Test debut, against England in the second Test at Melbourne in 1901/2, he hit 104, sharing in a last-wicket partnership of 120 with Warwick Armstrong – a strange last-wicket pair! – and averaged 44.42 for the series. Coming to England as opening partner for Victor Trumper in both 1902 and 1905, he was very successful, exceeding 1,400 runs each time. In his last Test innings, at The Oval in 1905, he made 146 – the highest of the series on both sides – and headed the averages with 41. 'He was never the same man after his second visit', said *Wisden*, 'quickly losing his form' – in fact he fell on hard times. At the turn of the century he was one of the half-dozen best batsmen in Australia – twenty-six Sheffield Sheild matches brought him 2,149 runs (49.97), including his highest, 271, against South Australia at Sydney in 1903/4. At Sydney for his State against South Australia in 1902/3 he and Trumper put up 298 together for the first wicket; and against Victoria their stand was worth 367. Back in 1900/1901 he contributed a modest 119 to his State's record 918 against South Australia at Sydney.

First-class career (1898-1907): 6,589 runs (35.04) including 10 centuries
Test matches (22): 1,317 runs (35.59) including 2 centuries, 4 wickets (21.25) and 14 catches

DUNCAN, John Ross Frederick (b.1944)

Queensland and Victoria

An accurate fast-medium right-arm bowler with considerable powers of swing, Ross Duncan played in the fifth Test against England at Melbourne in 1970/71, scoring 3 and taking no wickets for 30. That season he took 34 wickets for Queensland, including 13 in the match against Victoria at Melbourne. He moved to Victoria in 1971/2, but played for only one more season.

First-class career (1964-72): 649 runs (8.42) and 218 wickets (31.19)

DYMOCK, Geoffrey (b.1945)

Queensland

A thoroughly genuine medium-fast left-arm opening bowler, strongly built and with an economical action of some twelve paces, Geoff Dymock was the pivot of Queensland's attack for many years, but his role in Test cricket was that of a stock bowler. His first Test cricket was against New Zealand, at home and away in 1973/4. He took 7 wickets in his first Test match at Adelaide and appeared in two Tests in New Zealand before losing his place to Gary Gilmour, whose bowling was of similar style but whose batting was superior. However, after taking 35 wickets at 24.66 in nine Shield matches in 1976/7, Dymock was rather surprisingly preferred to Gilmour for the 1977 tour of England on which he took only 15 wickets in ten matches at an average of 31.20. Restored to a side weakened by World Series Cricket defections in 1978/9, he did a much more effective and useful job for Australia than his 7 wickets in three Tests at 38.42 suggest. A cheerful, sunny-tempered character, he bowled without histrionics and enjoyed cricket whatever the results. By far the most memorable year in a worthy career came in 1979/80 when he followed a successful tour of India with some fine performances on home soil. In India 24 of his 32 wickets came in the five Tests in which he played. At Kanpur, in great heat, he took 12 wickets in the match for 166 from 63 overs. His success against England in Australia was less expected and consistent performances earned him a place ahead of some of the former World Series Cricket stars and he produced a decisive spell with the new ball in the second innings of the Perth Test to finish with 6 for 34. Helped by Lillee's fire at the other end, he took 17 wickets (15.29) against England and 11 (26.27) in the two Tests in which he played against the West Indies, having been omitted in his native Brisbane. At the end of this busy season he toured Pakistan, taking only one wicket for 128 on the unresponsive pitches on which the three Tests were played. His service was rewarded with another visit to England for the Centenary Test but he was unsuccessful and his Test days were over. Nevertheless, he had much to tell his own children and those he teaches in Queensland as his profession.

Geoff Dymock

First-class career (1971-82): 1,518 runs (14.45) including 1 century, and 425 wickets (26.91)
Test matches (21): 236 runs (9.44), 78 wickets (27.13) and 1 catch

DYSON, John (b.1954)

New South Wales

John Dyson made a modest start to his Sheffield Shield career in 1976/7, but two centuries by this patient and resolute right-hand opening batsman the following season earned him a place in the Australian team against India and he began well with 53 in his first Test innings at Perth. He failed later against the Indian spinners and although he batted well for New South Wales against the England touring team of 1978/9 making a solid 67 out of a total of 165, he was struggling to hold his place in the State side by the end of the season. The selectors, however, had not forgotten him and he toured England in 1980, although making only 66 in six innings and missing selection for the Centenary Test. It was an injury to Bruce Laird which enabled him to earn the place as opening partner to Graeme Wood in all six home Tests of 1980/81. The big score eluded him, against both New Zealand and India, but his 'stickability' persuaded the selectors to give him another tour of England in 1981. He made his mark with an excellent hundred in the Leeds Test and also by some spectacular fielding.

First-class career (1975-): 4,976 runs (38.27) including 11 centuries and 1 wicket (20.00)
Test matches (22): 999 runs (27.00) including 2 centuries, and 6 catches

EADY, Charles John (1870-1945)

Tasmania

Over six feet tall and weighing fifteen stone, Charles

Eady was best known for scoring 566 out of 911, made in less than eight hours for Break O'Day against Wellington at Hobart in 1902. For Tasmania against Victoria at Hobart, 1894/5, he hit 116 and 112 not out and against the same State at Melbourne in the same year he took 8 for 35. During his sole visit to England in 1896 – a rare experience for a Tasmanian – he was handicapped by ill-health, his powerful batting and pacey bowling bringing only 290 runs and 16 wickets from sixteen matches (including one Test). He represented his country once at home in 1901/2. Sometime president of the Australian Board of Control, he was also a member of the Tasmanian Legislative Council.

First-class career (1889-1907): 1,490 runs (22.92) including 3 centuries, and 135 wickets (23.13)
Test matches (2): 20 runs (6.66), 7 wickets (16.00) and 2 catches

EASTWOOD, Kenneth Humphrey (b.1935)

Victoria

A solid left-handed opening batsman, strong on the leg-side, Ken Eastwood was a shock choice for the seventh Test against England at Sydney in 1970/71, in place of his own State captain, Bill Lawry who had the experience of 67 Tests but was two years younger; in an intermittent first-class career this was the first and only time he appeared for a team other than Victoria. He scored 5 and 0 and took 1 for 21.

First-class career (1959-71): 2,722 runs (41.87) including 9 centuries

EBELING, Hans Irvine (1905-80)

Victoria

A right-arm fast-medium bowler, turning the ball usually from the off but sometimes from the leg, an occasionally useful batsman but an ordinary field, Hans Ebeling had an irregular career with his State for fourteen years. He made two tours, with his State side to New Zealand in 1924/5 and with Australia to England in 1934. In England he took 62 wickets (20.80) and appeared in his sole Test, the fifth at the Oval, scoring 2 and 41 and taking 3 for 89. Associated with Melbourne C.C. since his youth, he was the originator of the Melbourne Centenary Test Match celebrations in March 1977.

First-class career (1923-37): 1,005 runs (14.15) and 217 wickets (26.58)

EDWARDS, John Dunlop (1862-1911)

Victoria

Not an elegant right-handed batsman, Jack Edwards was a good middle-order man, able to play steadily, hitting and defending wisely. Shortly before leaving Australia with the 1888 team to England he hit 254 and 104, both undefeated, for Sandhurst in club cricket, but did not enjoy the wet English summer and the slow pitches, averaging 12 for the whole tour and achieving very little in the three Tests.

First-class career (1880-89): 961 runs (13.72)
Test matches (3): 48 runs (9.60) and 1 catch

EDWARDS, Ross (b.1942)

Western Australia and New South Wales

Fair-haired, strongly built and a genial pipe-smoker, Ross Edwards was a sound and steady middle-order right-handed batsman and a superb cover fielder, swift as a hawk to swoop on the ball; at the outset of his career he was also a very competent wicket-keeper. His batting improved with age and, after scoring 4 centuries for his State in 1971/2, he toured England with the 1972 side as a batsman. Opening the innings in an emergency, he hit a chanceless 170 not out at Trent Bridge in the third Test, displaying a fine array of off-side strokes mainly off the back foot. He toured the West Indies in 1972/3, acting as reserve wicket-keeper, and was recalled to the Test side against England for 1974/5, hitting 115 in the second Test. Back in England he made 80 not out against Pakistan and 58 against the West Indies in the 1975 Prudential World Cup – the latter score being Australia's highest, but insufficient to ward off defeat – and averaged 50.60 in the Tests which followed. At Lord's he stemmed a first innings collapse with a bold 99 (out lbw). He became a Packer-contracted player in 1977, although his main employment is as an accountant. In 1979 he moved to New South Wales.

First-class career (1964-79): 7,345 runs (39.27) including 14 centuries, 107 catches and 11 stumpings
Test matches (20): 1,171 runs (40.37) including 2 centuries, 0-20 and 7 catches

EDWARDS, Walter John (b.1950)

Western Australia

Playing for the same State as Ross Edwards, but not related to him, Wally Edwards was an attractive left-hand opening batsman, who proved disappointing in Test company. In his three Tests against England in 1974/5 he twice helped Ian Redpath to put on more than 60 at the start of an innings, but his own top score was only 30. That season, however, in all first-class matches he made 731 runs (30.46).

First-class career (1973-8): 1,381 runs (30.68) including 2 centuries
Test matches (3): 68 runs (11.33)

EMERY, Sidney Hand (1886-1967)

New South Wales

A right-arm googly bowler of lively medium-pace, Sid Emery could make the ball fizz from the pitch, but his length was uncertain. If he could have gained consistent control, he would have been a real matchwinner. He toured England in 1912, taking 67 wickets, including 12 for 110 against Northamptonshire at the county ground, but enjoyed little success against either England or South Africa in the Triangular Tournament. In fifteen Sheffield Shield matches he scored 371 runs (16.13) and took 60 wickets (24.65).

First-class career (1908-13): 1,192 runs (18.33) and 183 wickets (23.79)
Test matches (4): 6 runs (3.00), 5 wickets (49.80) and 2 catches

EVANS, Edwin (1849-1921)

New South Wales

In his prime, a very accurate right-arm spin bowler with a high action, who could pitch on a sixpence, Edwin Evans was in his thirty-eighth year when he toured England for the first and only time in 1886, and, past his best, he held no terrors for English batsmen during a summer of hard wickets. He also appeared for Australia in 1881/2, 1882/3 and 1884/5. At home his career for his State was brilliant, and with 'The Demon' Spofforth he often did great things in the 1870s. He was also a useful tail-end batsman.

First-class career (1874-87): 1,016 runs (12.26) and 201 wickets (16.69)
Test matches (6): 82 runs (10.25), 7 wickets (47.42) and 5 catches

FAIRFAX, Alan George (1906-55)

New South Wales

Tall and dark-haired, Alan Fairfax was a sound right-handed stroke-player who used his long reach extremely well. He was also a lively fast-medium bowler. Coming into Australia's rebuilt Test side for the fifth match of 1928/9 at Melbourne, he scored 65, sharing in a fifth-wicket record stand of 183 with young Don Bradman. On his tour of England in 1930, when he generally shared the new ball with Tim Wall, he averaged 50 with the bat in four Tests, besides taking 12 wickets; and in Australia's first-ever series against the West Indies in 1930/31, he averaged 48.75 with the bat in the five Tests and took seven wickets. Lost to Australian cricket thereafter, he returned to England in 1932 as a professional in the Lancashire League. He later organized an indoor cricket school in London and after the War became a newspaper columnist. A serious injury during the War led to his early death. In seventeen Sheffield Shield matches he scored 804 runs (29.77) and took 60 wickets (24.73).

First-class career (1928-34): 1,910 runs (28.93) including 1 century, and 134 wickets (27.87)
Test matches (10): 410 runs (51.25), 21 wickets (30.71) and 15 catches

FAVELL, Leslie Ernest (b.1929)

South Australia

A stocky, hard-hitting right-handed opening batsman, Les Favell tended to attack merrily from the start, believing that the new ball could be hit just as hard and as often as the old one. In particular he was a daring hooker. He made 80 and 40 for his State against MCC in 1954/5 but he never did himself full justice against England, often getting himself out by chasing the ball wide of the off stump. He appeared occasionally against England and the West Indies at home, and toured the West Indies, India and Pakistan, and New Zealand in 1957 and 1967 (as captain). His sole century in Tests was 101 in the fourth Test at Madras when Australia beat India by an innings. Latterly, he captained his State, for whom he made 8,983 runs (38.38) in 130 Sheffield Shield matches. Now closely involved in the administration of South Australian cricket, he is also a shrewd and interesting commentator on cricket for ABC Radio in Adelaide. His career aggregate is the highest by an Australian who never toured England.

First-class career (1951-70): 12,379 runs (36.63) including 27 centuries, and 110 catches
Test matches (19): 757 runs (27.03) including 1 century, and 9 catches

FERRIS, John James (1867-1900)

New South Wales, South Australia and Gloucestershire

A left-arm medium-fast bowler of immaculate length who could vary his pace admirably, 'J.J.' Ferris was a member of the Australian teams to England in 1888 and 1890 when he formed a phenomenally successful partnership with C.T.B. Turner, 'The Terror'. On the two tours he captured 435 wickets (13.19) in all matches. In 1888 they bowled unchanged against Middlesex at Lord's and an England eleven at Stoke. On his Test debut at Sydney in 1886/7 he and Turner were unchanged in the first innings, bundling out England for 45, J.J. having a match record of 9 for 103, and in the second match, also at Sydney, he took 9 for 140. In his last Test for Australia, at The Oval in 1890, he took 9 for 74 in all. He then settled in England and had three disappointing seasons for Gloucestershire. He toured South Africa with W.W. Read's side in 1891/2, representing England for the only time and taking 13 for 91 in the sole Test at Cape Town.

Altogether, he took 235 wickets on this tour. He died while serving with the British Forces during the Boer War.

First-class career (1886-97): 4,264 runs (15.67) including 1 century, and 813 wickets (17.52)
Test matches (Australia – 8): 98 runs (8.16), 48 wickets (14.25) and 4 catches. (England – 1): 16 runs (16.00) and 13 wickets (7.00)

FINGLETON, John Henry Webb (1908-81)

New South Wales

A right-hand opening batsman, often associated with Bill Brown at either Sheffield Shield or international level, Jack Fingleton had a strong defence and great courage. Solid rather than fluent, he hit hard and could score quickly. Like many of his colleagues his effectiveness was reduced by Harold Larwood and Bill Voce in the 1932/3 Bodyline series and, although he hit 83 in the second Test at Melbourne, he made 'a pair' in the third, was dropped and later omitted from the 1934 tour of England. In South Africa, however, in 1935/6 he was highly successful, making 478 runs (79.66)in the Tests. This included three successive centuries in the third, fourth and fifth matches – 118 at Cape Town (putting on 233 with Bill Brown), 108 at Johannesburg and 118 at Durban. The runs continued, with 100 in the first Test against England at Brisbane in 1936/7. Then, in the third Test at Melbourne, he made 136, adding a record 346 for the sixth wicket with Don Bradman. Visiting England at last in 1938, his defence was often invaluable although he did not score highly in the Tests; on the tour he made 1,374 runs (38.16). A wise and kindly man with a mischievous sense of humour, he was a professional journalist of the highest calibre, also employed by the Government in Canberra. He wrote ten cricket books in an informed, literary and scholarly way, including *Cricket Crisis*, *Brightly Fades the Don*, *The Ashes Crown the Year* and *The Immortal Victor Trumper*. In thirty-seven Sheffield Shield matches Fingleton scored 2,263 runs (39.70).

Jack Fingleton (left) and Bill Brown

First-class career (1928-39): 6,816 runs (44.54) including 22 centuries
Test matches (18): 1,189 runs (42.46) including 5 centuries, and 13 catches

FLEETWOOD-SMITH, Leslie O'Brien (1910-71)

Victoria

'Chuck' Fleetwood-Smith was a left-arm back-of-the-hand spin bowler who changed his style after breaking his arm as a schoolboy; he had exceptional powers of spin and made the ball twist and turn on the hardest pitches at near medium pace. After a few short steps he would deliver his natural off-break to a right-hander; the leg-break was his 'wrong 'un' and he was not easy to bat against, though Walter Hammond disagreed, thrashing his bowling in Australia in 1932/3 and at Lord's in 1938. In the late thirties the Australian strategy revolved round 'Chuck' and Bill O'Reilly. He toured England in 1934, taking 119 wickets (18.06), yet not gaining a Test place. In 1938, however, he was an integral part of Australia's attack, taking 14 wickets (though at high cost) in the four Tests. He also toured South Africa in 1935/6. At home in 1936/7 he took 19 wickets in Tests against England. Lacking the killer instinct, much of his talent was wasted in Tests, but he had some amazing performances for his State, twice dismissing nine batsmen in an innings, and taking 295 wickets (24.38).

First-class career (1931-9): 617 runs (7.34) and 597 wickets (22.64)
Test matches (10): 54 runs (9.00) and 42 wickets (37.38)

FRANCIS, Bruce Collin (b.1948)

New South Wales and Essex

A genial and intelligent man, a graduate of Sydney University and a strapping right-handed opening batsman who loved to attack, Bruce Francis was a popular cricketer with both players and spectators. If he got going at the start of an innings, there was no likelihood of dull cricket, for he was a handsome striker of the ball, especially to the on-side, and with his burly strength the lofted straight drive was often brought into use against even the fastest bowlers. Coming to England in 1970 to play in the Lancashire League for

Accrington, he later had three successful seasons for Essex between 1971 and 1973, scoring 1,578 runs (38.48) with four centuries, plus another in the Sunday League, in his first year, and 1,384 (38.44) in his last. In between he toured England with the Australian side, but at Test level one or two inadequacies in his defensive technique were uncovered, notably by John Snow. He had first represented Australia (unofficially) in two matches against the Rest of the World in 1971/2 scoring 34 runs in three innings before breaking a thumb. His highest score was 210 not out against the Combined Oxford and Cambridge side in 1972. Seldom suffering physical injury, he sometimes had to leave the field because of bad migraines.

First-class career (1968-74): 6,183 runs (33.97) including 13 centuries
Test matches (3): 52 runs (10.40) and 1 catch

FREEMAN, Eric Walter (b.1944)

South Australia

A husky and combative cricketer, Eric Freeman had a meteoric rise in first-class cricket, even though he was originally more involved in Australian Football. A right-arm fast-medium bowler, hard-hitting batsman and excellent field, he took 7 for 52 for his State against Queensland in 1966/7; he toured New Zealand with an 'A' team; and when a visiting New Zealand side played South Australia in 1967/8 at Adelaide, he hit 50 and 39 (at number 10) and took 3 for 50 and 8 for 47, his State winning by 24 runs. Between 1967 and 1970 he toured England, South Africa and India and represented his country at home against India and the West Indies. He took some useful wickets, but was not the penetrative opening bowler Australia was looking for and he was dropped after his drubbing at the hands of the South Africans in the 1969/70 series. His hitting brought two fifties in Tests; but he soon dropped out of Sheffield Shield cricket.

First-class career (1964-74): 2,244 runs (19.17) including 1 century, and 241 wickets (27.76)
Test matches (11): 345 runs (19.16), 34 wickets (33.17) and 5 catches

FREER, Frederick William (b.1915)

Victoria

A hardworking right-arm fast-medium bowler and very useful lower-order batsman, Fred Freer replaced Ray Lindwall, who was unfit for the second Test at Sydney against England in 1946/7, scoring 28 not out and taking 3 for 74. He was not selected again when Lindwall recovered but toured India with the Commonwealth team of 1949/50. His three first-class centuries were hit on this tour, the highest being 132 against India at Bombay.

First-class career (1945-9): 1,284 runs (32.10) including 3 centuries, and 104 wickets (27.75)

GANNON, John Brian (b.1947)

Western Australia

A fast-medium left-arm bowler and athletic fielder 'Sam' Gannon effectively had two first-class careers, the second bringing him Test honours in the wake of the defections to Kerry Packer. First playing for Western Australia against Victoria in 1966/7, he took 6 for 107 in that season against South Australia at Adelaide, but although a useful member of the Western Australia side for several more seasons with his often hostile new-ball bowling, he was overshadowed in a strong team by Lillee, Massie and Brayshaw (one of the best Australian bowlers never to be capped). Gannon did not play for Western Australia between 1973/4 and 1976/7 but the following year he bowled himself into the Australian side for the second Test against India, after taking four second innings wickets against them for Western Australia. In his first Test on his home ground at Perth he took 3 for 84 and 4 for 77, but he was dropped after failing to take a wicket in the fourth Test, which India won easily.

First-class career (1966-79): 141 runs (6.40) and 117 wickets (30.79)
Test matches (3): 3 runs (3.00), 11 wickets (32.82) and 3 catches

GARRETT, Thomas William (1858-1943)

New South Wales

At the time of his death the oldest living Australian Test cricketer, Tom Garrett played in the first two matches against England in 1876/7. He toured England with the first team in 1878, again in 1882 (playing in the historic Ashes match) and 1886. A good right-arm medium-fast bowler, a fine fielder (he was an expert sprinter) and a hard-hitting, but undependable, batsman, he improved as he got older. Having an easy action, he used his height (about six feet) well, came fast off the pitch, could move the ball either way and send down a telling yorker. On hard grounds many considered he was more effective than Spofforth or Boyle. On the 1882 and 1886 tours he took more than a hundred wickets each time – in the former year, *four* matches against Yorkshire bringing him 27 wickets at 9 runs each. He represented Australia in seven series at home, having his best return in 1881/2, when he headed the bowling with 18 wickets (20.38), including 9 for 163 in the third match at Sydney.

First-class career (1876-97): 3,673 runs (16.18) including 2 centuries, and 445 wickets (18.77)
Test matches (19): 339 runs (12.55), 36 wickets (26.94) and 7 catches

GAUNT, Ronald Arthur (b.1934)

Western Australia and Victoria

A right-arm fast-medium bowler, Ron Gaunt was a determined cricketer but he bowled countless no-balls during his short career and came under the eye of the umpires for dragging. He toured New Zealand twice on 'A' tours, South Africa in 1957/8 and England in 1961. He played at home against South Africa in 1963/4. He was a moderate left-handed batsman.

First-class career (1955-63): 616 runs (10.44) and 266 wickets (26.85)
Test matches (3): 6 runs (3.00), 7 wickets (44.28) and 1 catch

GEHRS, Donald Raeburn Algernon (1880-1953)

South Australia

Tallish, thickset and athletic, Algy Gehrs was an attractive right-handed batsman who could hook superbly against any type of bowler; he had many strokes and much audacity, although he was rather disappointing at representative level. He appeared once against England at home in 1903/4, and once on tour in 1905, when he averaged 21.77. Against South Africa in 1910/11 he had some glory, hitting 67 and 58 in Tests at Sydney and Melbourne respectively. In thirty-four Sheffield Shield matches he made 2,168 runs (35.54) and in all matches for his State he hit 3,387 runs, including thirteen centuries.

First-class career (1902-21): 4,377 runs (33.67) including 13 centuries
Test matches (6): 221 runs (20.09), 0-4 and 6 catches

GIFFEN, George (1859-1927)

South Australia

Known as 'the W.G. Grace of Australia', George Giffen was a highly gifted all-rounder. A determined, attacking right-handed batsman, he stooped a little but possessed a variety of strokes, including some exceptionally powerful drives; he was also a slow-medium bowler of great accuracy who delivered very effectively a high-tossed slow ball, which resulted in many caught and bowled victims. Overshadowed on his first tour in 1882, when he played in the Ashes match at The Oval, he came to England again in 1884, 1886, 1893 and 1896 when he was usually the dominant figure, though he did not always reproduce his Australian form. Minor tours included visits to the United States, Canada and New Zealand. He headed both batting and bowling in 1886, with 1,454 runs and 162 wickets. He hit four double centuries for South Australia, the highest being 271 against Victoria at Adelaide in 1891/2. His highest score in England was 180 against Gloucestershire at Bristol, where he also captured 7 for 11. Although England won, his best series was 1894/5, when he scored most runs and took most wickets – 475 runs (52.77) and 34 wickets (24.11). He led Australia in four Tests in all. His finest feat was in the first Test at Sydney, when he scored 161 and 41 and took 8 wickets (in 118 overs) – yet was on the losing side! Like W.G., he retained his fitness for many years: in his forty-fourth year, he made 81 and 97 not out and took 15 for 185 against Victoria at Adelaide. In thirty-eight Sheffield Shield matches he scored 2,318 runs (36.21) and took 192 wickets (29.55). No other Australian has made over 10,000 runs and taken over 1,000 wickets in first-class cricket. On retirement from the Civil Service (Post Office branch) he delighted in coaching schoolboys. One of the main stands at the Adelaide Oval bears his name.

First-class career (1877-1903): 11,757 runs (29.61) including 18 centuries, and 1,022 wickets (21.31)
Test matches (31): 1,238 runs (23.35) including 1 century, 103 wickets (27.09) and 24 catches

GIFFEN, Walter Frank (1863-1949)

South Australia

Walter Giffen was a sound defensive batsman and a good outfield. He was perhaps fortunate in being chosen to tour England in 1893, although he had been a prolific scorer in Adelaide club cricket. At home he appeared for Australia three times against England in 1886/7 and 1891/2 (with little success). He averaged 13.77 in England but did not play in a Test; it was said that his famous elder brother, George, had insisted on his coming. In 1886 Walter lost the top of two of his fingers at the Brompton Gasworks, Adelaide, in an accident involving a pair of cog-wheels. In thirteen Sheffield Shield matches his batting average came to 11.77.

First-class career (1882-1902): 1,178 runs (15.92)
Test matches (3): 11 runs (1.83) and 1 catch

GILMOUR, Gary John (b.1951)

New South Wales

A highly talented and natural cricketer, Gary Gilmour is a left-handed all-rounder – fast-medium over-the-wicket bowler, hard-hitting batsman and athletic fielder. Fair haired, burly and a genial character, he was bred in the wine-growing area of the Hunter Valley of New South Wales and came to Sydney to develop his cricket skills, soon making his mark in the New South Wales side. His Test career started against New Zealand at Melbourne in 1973/4 when he made 52 and took 4 for 75 in each first innings. An injury led to him temporarily losing his place to Geoff Dymock, a similar bowler, but, after New Zealand had beaten

Australia for the first time at Christchurch in March 1974, Gilmour returned for the third Test at Auckland and with sharp late-swing undermined New Zealand's batting with a twelve-over spell in the first innings which brought him 5 wickets and led to swift Australian revenge. The emergence of Jeff Thomson in 1974/5 and further rivalry from Dennis Lillee and Max Walker meant that, of ten Tests against England in 1974/5, Gilmour played only one, although he bowled Australia into the final of the 1975 Prudential World Cup with a devastating spell of swing bowling on a humid, cloudy day at Headingley. He lacks only the pace of several contemporary Australian fast bowlers. He was a surprise omission from Australia's 1977 side to England, after which he played two seasons of World Series Cricket with success but again was not selected for the Australian team in 1979/80.

First-class career (1971-9): 3,126 runs (30.64) including 5 centuries, and 233 wickets (31.52)
Test matches (15): 483 runs (23.00) including 1 century, 54 wickets (26.03) and 8 catches

John Gleeson

GLEESON, John William (b.1938)

New South Wales and Eastern Province

Short and sinewy, with the weather-beaten face of a jockey, John Gleeson was a right-arm spin bowler who propelled the ball off a bent middle finger in the manner of Jack Iverson. He produced a greater spin variety than Iverson, making more use of the leg-break, though perhaps his staple ball was the off-break. Although he was tidy, there were enough loose balls for experienced players, even those who could not 'read' him, to feed on. Making his first-class debut at the age of twenty-eight and taking 23 wickets (18.22) in his first season, he played first for Australia against India in 1967/8. He toured England in 1968 and 1972, as well as India and South Africa. He did well generally in England in 1968 and was one of the few successes in South Africa in 1969/70, taking 59 wickets (19.49), including 19 wickets in four Tests. However, against England in 1970/71 he took 14 very expensive wickets; and in England again in 1972 he was disappointing, claiming only 3 wickets from three Tests. He did not represent his country again. In 1974/5 he played with success for Eastern Province in the South African Currie Cup.

First-class career (1966-74): 1,095 runs (11.06) and 430 wickets (24.95)
Test matches (29): 395 runs (10.39), 93 wickets (36.20) and 17 catches

GRAHAM, Henry (1870-1911)

Victoria, South Island and Otago

Although 'Harry' Graham did not play with a perfectly straight bat, he was a splendid right-handed hitter with plenty of dash and vigour. In England in 1893 he hit 219 at Derby and 107 in his first Test, at Lord's: in this Test he came in with the score faltering at 75 for 5 and immediately flayed the bowling. He headed the batting for the tour with 1,435 runs (28.7), and at Sydney in 1894/5 his 105 was equally valuable against England; but on his second tour three years later he showed a marked decline and, though he recovered some of his lost skill on his return home, his career was left half-fulfilled. He went to live in New Zealand, where he died young. *Wisden* commented: 'Had he ordered his life more carefully, he might have had a much longer and more successful career.'

First-class career (1892-1906): 5,054 runs (26.32) including 7 centuries
Test matches (6): 301 runs (30.10) including 2 centuries, and 3 catches

GREGORY, David William (1845-1919)

New South Wales

With a full, flowing beard and Ned Kelly looks, Dave Gregory appeared much older than his years. He captained Australia in the first three Tests (two in 1876/7 and one in 1878/9) – winning the first and third comprehensively – and was in charge again on the first tour of England in 1878, when MCC were overwhelmed at Lord's in a day. Except as a tactful leader among rugged types, he did not earn much distinction on English cricket grounds – it was a wet summer, the slow, treacherous wickets were too much for him and his batting average was only 11. As a batsman, he had no grace or style to commend him – a common failing amongst his contemporaries – but he could defend stubbornly and did not lack grit. In inter-colonial matches against Victoria he scored 445 runs (17.80) on wickets which did not approach their later perfection. For some years he was honorary secretary of the N.S.W. Cricket Association. His brothers, Ned, Walter, Charles and Arthur also played for New South Wales, as did his nephews, Sydney, Charles and Jack. Several nieces were keen lady cricketers.

First-class career (1866-82): 889 runs (14.59) and 29 wickets (19.06)
Test matches (3): 60 runs (20.00) and 0-9

GREGORY, Edward James (1839-99)

New South Wales

A useful right-handed forcing batsman and latterly custodian of the Association ground at Sydney, Ned Gregory played for Australia in the first-ever Test at Melbourne in 1877, under the captaincy of brother Dave, scoring 0 and 11 and holding one catch. He was the first man to make a duck in Test cricket. He was father of the future captain, Syd, and the eldest of five brothers to play for N.S.W.

First-class career (1862-77): 470 runs (17.40)

GREGORY, John Morrison (1895-1973)

New South Wales

Jack Gregory was, in the words of Ian Peebles, 'towering, tanned and powerfully lithe', and, according to R.C. Robertson-Glasgow, 'tall, strong and raw-boned, like one of his native kangaroos'. As the descriptions suggest, Jack Gregory was a spectacular as well as great all-rounder. He was a left-handed batsman, who, with great confidence and without a pair of batting gloves, could hit with tremendous power, using his long reach to attack, often with low, skimming drives. He could cover the length of the pitch with a few long strides. Primarily, however, a right-arm fast bowler, he took a long run, starting with a shuffle, then moved his fourteen-stone weight forward like an avalanche to finish with a huge bound as he let go of the ball. His speed came from sheer strength, and, although he bowled a good out-swinger with the new ball, it was speed itself rather than any subtle movement or variety which got him wickets. He simply frightened many a batsman into submission. He was also a quite superb slip fielder with marvellous anticipation and long reach. He first came to public notice with the Australian Imperial Forces Team in 1919, scoring 942 runs and taking 131 wickets. In partnership with Ted McDonald in Australia 1920/21, England 1921, and South Africa 1921/2, he was magnificent; in the first Test series he took 23 wickets (24.17) and scored 442 runs (73.66), including 100 (at number nine) and 7 for 69 in the first innings of the second Test at Melbourne; in the second 'Gregory and McDonald' were the scourge of England, Jack securing 19 wickets in the Tests; and in the third series, on matting, he took 15 wickets (18.93) in the three matches and hit 119 in 70 minutes at Johannesburg, which still remains the fastest Test century. In England in 1921 he achieved the double with 1,135 runs (36.61) and 116 wickets (16.58). Subsequently, he was not quite the same power. It is true he took 22 wickets in 1924/5 but they were gained expensively. On the 1926 England tour he broke down physically; and he had to leave the field during the first Test at Brisbane in 1928/9 after sending down 41 overs. Now plagued by muscle injuries, he never represented his country again. But for a time Jack Gregory had been the personification of young dynamic physical power and gusto for life. In eleven Sheffield Shield matches he made 476 runs (31.73) and took 38 wickets (28.97). He was the son of Charles Gregory and cousin of Syd Gregory.

Jack Gregory

First-class career (1918-28): 5,661 runs (36.52) including 13 centuries, and 504 wickets (20.99)
Test matches (24): 1,146 runs (36.96) including 2 centuries, 85 wickets (31.15) and 37 catches

GREGORY, Ross Gerald (1916-42)

Victoria

One of the youngest ever to play in Test cricket, Ross

Gregory was chosen for his State while still a schoolboy. He made 128 for Victoria against MCC in 1936/7 and in the last two Tests of the series made 23, 50 and 80. He was passed over, however, for the 1938 England tour. In his last season he averaged 44.72 for his State yet had a top score of only 77. A very quick-footed right-hander, he could produce brilliant front-of-the-wicket forcing strokes, pull confidently, send down a useful slow leg-break and field cleanly. As Sgt Observer Gregory (R.A.A.F.) he died while on active service in Assam. He was not related to the N.S.W. Gregory family.

First-class career (1933-8): 1,874 runs (38.24) including 1 century, and 50 wickets (35.34)
Test matches (2): 153 runs (51.00), 0-14 and 1 catch

GREGORY, Sydney Edward (1870-1929)

New South Wales

Born on the site of the present Sydney Cricket ground and son of Ned Gregory, Syd Gregory, of the curling moustache and text-book style, visited England with the teams of 1890, 1893, 1896, 1899, 1902, 1905, 1909 and 1912. What the Graces and the Walkers were to English cricket, the Gregories were to Australian, and Syd was the second most distinguished. For many years his fifty-eight Tests constituted an Australian record. Little more than five feet tall, his quick footwork compensated for lack of inches. Right-handed, possessing a keen eye and strong wrists, and particularly strong on the off-side, he was also brilliant at cover-point, quick and deadly accurate with his returns. He helped maintain the supremacy of New South Wales in the Sheffield Shield – hitting eight centuries – and his earliest great achievement in Tests was 201 in the first Test played at Sydney in 1894/5, when he added 154 with Jack Blackham for the ninth wicket – yet the match was lost! In the first Test at Lord's in 1896, after Australia had been routed for 53 in the first innings and were 62 for 3 in the second, Syd made 103, putting on 221 for the fourth wicket with Harry Trott in just over two and a half hours – again in a losing cause. At The Oval in 1899 he scored a brave 117. He also toured South Africa in 1902/3 but did not prosper on matting. He returned to Test cricket in 1912, captaining a weakened side in the Triangular Tournament in England. In 53 Sheffield Shield matches he scored 3,626 runs (43.68).

Syd Gregory

First-class career (1889-1912): 15,192 runs (28.55) including 25 centuries, and 174 catches
Test matches (58): 2,282 runs (24.53) including 4 centuries, 0-33 and 25 catches

GRIMMETT, Clarence Victor (1891-1980)

Victoria, South Australia and Wellington

Small, stringy, prematurely bald and wizened in the face, Clarrie Grimmett was a New Zealander by birth. With his short, jerky approach and almost round-arm action, 'the Gnome' or 'Scarlet' (after the Pimpernel whose enemies sought him here and there without much result) was a slow leg-break bowler, exceptionally accurate, with an obvious googly but a wicked dipping top-spinner. Prolific in Australia, he was nevertheless more consistent in England where the softer pitches were more responsive to his 'infinite variations'. On his belated Test debut at the age of thirty-four in the final Test at Sydney in 1924/5, he took 5 for 45 and 6 for 37, routing England, and after this sensational start he toured England in 1926 in harness with his flightier leg-spin partner, Arthur Mailey. They took 27 of the 39 wickets that fell to bowlers in the Tests and they both took over a hundred wickets on the tour. Clarrie was the pivot of Australia's attack against England in 1928/9, capturing 23 wickets in 398.2 overs from the five Tests; 29 wickets from 349.4 overs in 1930; and 28 wickets in 1934, bowling in tandem with Bill O'Reilly. Against other countries he was often even more deadly. He took 33 wickets against the West Indies in 1930/31, the first series in Australia; 33 against South Africa in 1931/2; and in South Africa, 1935/6, 44 wickets – at 14.59 each! This tour of South Africa witnessed his swan-song, as he was not selected for Australia against England in either 1936/7 or 1938. Sometimes a useful tail-end batsman, his all-round record in seventy-nine Sheffield Shield matches was 1,989 runs (19.50) and 513 wickets (25.29).

Clarrie Grimmett

First-class career (1911-40): 4,720 runs (17.67), 1,424 wickets (22.28) and 139 catches
Test matches (37): 557 runs (13.92), 216 wickets (24.21) and 17 catches

GROUBE, Thomas Underwood (1857-1927)

Victoria

Tom Groube was a steady right-handed batsman and good field at cover-point or long-on. He toured England in 1880, playing in the first-ever Test in England at The Oval, scoring 11 and 0. His highest score in first-class cricket was a mere 61 against Yorkshire at Huddersfield. He did not represent Australia again but ran up some fantastic averages for East Melbourne, for example 155.33 in 1879/80.

First-class career (1878-81): 179 runs (8.52)

GROUT, Arthur Theodore Wallace (1927-68)

Queensland

A universally popular cricketer, Wally Grout was a very agile wicket-keeper who missed very few chances and his diving catches down the leg-side will be long remembered. He was also a good enough right-hand batsman to open for his State. He represented Australia in four home series between 1958 and 1964; in England in 1961 and 1964, and in South Africa, the West Indies and India and Pakistan. On two occasions he claimed eight victims in a Test and his six (all caught) in an innings against South Africa at Johannesburg in 1957/8 was then a Test record; also in this match his stand of 89 for the eighth wicket with Richie Benaud remains an Australian record against South Africa. On five other occasions he disposed of five men in an innings. Against the West Indies in 1960/61 he had 23 dismissals and the world record of eight catches in an innings, for Queensland against Western Australia at Brisbane, 1959/60, stands to his name. He showed true sportsmanship when refusing to take off the bails during a Test against England when Fred Titmus became stranded after colliding with Neil Hawke during a run. He died after a heart attack.

First-class career (1946-65): 5,168 runs (22.56) including 4 centuries, and 587 dismissals (473 ct, 114 st.)
Test matches (51): 890 runs (15.08) and 187 dismissals (163 ct, 24 st.)

GUEST, Colin Ernest James (b.1937)

Victoria and Western Australia

Colin Guest was one of the army of right-arm fast bowlers competing for a place in Australia's team in succession to Lindwall and Miller. In his sole Test against England in the third Test at Sydney in 1962/3, he scored 11 and took 0 for 59 (eighteen overs, no maidens). Most of his Sheffield Shield cricket was

Wally Grout leaps to stop a high return. Bill Lawry fielding

played for Victoria; once he took 10 wickets in a match and five times 5 or more wickets in an innings.

First-class career (1958-66): 922 runs (19.20) and 115 wickets (27.13)

HAMENCE, Ronald Arthur (b.1915)

South Australia

A shortish, compact figure, Ron Hamence possessed strong back-foot strokes and liked to attack. Although he had the big match temperament, he was rarely impressive against genuine pace. He was a good outfield. A long-serving, dependable State player, often as opening batsman, he made 30 not out on his debut in the fifth Test at Sydney in 1946/7 when Doug Wright was making short work of his partners, and the following season he made two 25s against India. On coming to England in 1948 he became a familiar figure with the drinks tray and was unable to force his way into the strong Test side. For his State he hit centuries against MCC touring sides in 1946/7 and 1950/51. He also hit 130 and 103 not out against Victoria at Melbourne and 132 and 101 against New South Wales at Adelaide in 1940/41 and 1946/7 respectively, the only South Australian player to have achieved this.

First-class career (1935-50): 5,285 runs (37.75) including 11 centuries
Test matches (3): 81 runs (27.00) and 1 catch

HAMMOND, Jeffrey Roy (b.1950)

South Australia

An enthusiastic right-arm, fast-medium bowler with a good action, Jeff Hammond took 34 wickets (20.26) in his second season for his State in 1970/71, and looked a fine prospect for Australia in the search for fast bowlers. He was unlucky not to play in the series against the Rest of the World in 1971/2 but toured England in 1972, the youngest member of the side. He took 6 for 15 by sheer speed in the first innings of the match against the Minor Counties at Stoke, but did not appear in the Tests. He was handicapped by an earlier back strain. In the West Indies in 1972/3 he was selected for all five Tests, and showed much promise. On his return home, however, he broke a foot and then a further back injury forced him to retire temporarily.

First-class career (1969-80): 922 runs (16.46) and 184 wickets (28.88)
Test matches (5): 28 runs (9.33), 15 wickets (32.53) and 2 catches

HARRY, John (1857-1919)

Victoria

John Harry was an above-average all-rounder – very good right-handed batsman, useful off-break change-bowler, good wicket-keeper and brilliant mid-off. Several times he was nearly chosen as reserve wicket-keeper to tour England, and in 1896 was actually selected, only to be discarded at the last moment ostensibly owing to a knee injury. Thereupon he came to England on his own account and joined the ground staff at Lord's but was only moderately successful. For Victoria he made many good scores and at Adelaide against South Australia in 1891/2 he bowled both left- and right-handed. In his sole Test at Adelaide in the third match of 1894/5, he scored 2 and 6 and held a catch. In club cricket, for either East Melbourne or Bendigo, he made over 11,000 runs and took 250 wickets. He was also a skittles player and an inter-State baseballer.

First-class career (1883-97): 1,466 runs (25.71) including 2 centuries, 26 wickets (23.76) and 21 dismissals (18 ct, 3 st.)

HARTIGAN, Roger Joseph (1879-1958)

New South Wales and Queensland

A bright and attractive right-handed batsman and a brilliant slip, Roger Hartigan, in a short career, was Queensland's star batsman long before Sheffield Shield status was attained. He played in two Tests against England in 1907/8 and scored 116 in the second innings of his first at Adelaide when runs were badly needed. He toured England in 1909 but rarely found his form and did not play in a Test. An able administrator, he served on the Australian Board of Control for thirty-five years as a Queensland representative. He represented New South Wales at baseball and Queensland at lacrosse.

First-class career (1903-20): 1,901 runs (25.01) including 2 centuries
Test matches (2): 170 runs (42,50) including 1 century, 0-7 and 1 catch

HARTKOPF, Albert Ernst Victor (1889-1968)

Victoria

One of the most powerful of right-handed hitters and a talented slow leg-break bowler, Albert Hartkopf was a superb athlete and was selected for the second Test at Melbourne in 1924/5 to strengthen the bowling. He took 1 for 134 (Bert Strudwick's wicket) and hit 80 out of a total of 600. Australia won by 81 runs but he did not appear in another Test. He toured New Zealand with his State in 1924/5. He was a good player, but not sufficiently outstanding for the period in which he lived.

First-class career (1911-28): 1,758 runs (34.47) including 2 centuries, and 121 wickets (30.79)

HARVEY, Mervyn Roye (b.1918)

Victoria

Usually an opening batsman, Mervyn Harvey was a delightfully free right-handed stroke-maker, at his happiest when the ball was coming through to him from the faster bowlers. His career was seriously interrupted by the Second World War, and in his sole Test, the fourth at Adelaide against England in 1946/7, he scored 12 and 31, putting on 116 for the first wicket with Arthur Morris. He was the eldest of four cricketing brothers who all played for Victoria, the others being Mick (now a first-class umpire), Ray and Neil.

First-class career (1940-48): 1,147 runs (38.23) including 3 centuries

HARVEY, Robert Neil (b.1928)

Victoria and New South Wales

Between 1948 and 1963 Neil Harvey played in more Tests than any other Australian, scored more runs in Tests than all but Don Bradman, and was preceded only by Bradman in Australian Test centuries and averages. The sight of his trim figure coming through the gate – short, stocky and with his neat, dark hair always capless – invariably spelt danger to opponents. One of the greatest of all left-handers, he was continually looking for runs, a clinical destroyer of the bad ball. A strong driver and cutter, it was said that when he hooked, the sound of the ball hitting the fence was like an explosion from Bikini. His footwork was brilliant, but if he was vulnerable anywhere it was outside the off-stump. Against spin he often danced down the pitch to balls an ordinary batsman would have played defensively. In the field, swooping on the ball and flicking it back to the 'keeper accurately with a minimum of effort, he was superb, usually in the covers, but sometimes on the boundary or in the slips.

Neil Harvey

He burst into cricket brilliantly with a century in his first club match, another in his first game for Victoria, one in his second Test, against India in 1947, and 112 on his first appearance against England, at Headingley, in 1948, when he was the youngest member of the touring side. He made four tours of England, scoring 1,129 runs (53.76) and 2,040 runs (65.80) in 1948 and 1953 respectively. In South Africa in 1949/50 he hit eight centuries, four in the Tests and averaged 76.30 on the tour. When the South Africans visited Australia in 1952/3 he made 834 runs in the Tests, again hitting four centuries, including his Test highest, 205 at Melbourne, and beating Bradman's record of 1931/2. To crown all this, he married a South African girl. In thirty-seven Tests against England between 1948 and 1961, he made 2,416 runs (38.34), including six centuries, the highest being 167 at Melbourne in 1958/9. A specially memorable innings was 92 not out (out of 184) at Sydney in 1954/5 when Tyson and Statham were carrying all before them. On the uncertain pitches against the dominant Jim Laker in 1956 he hit 69 (out of 140) at Headingley, resisting with superb footwork and concentration for four and a half hours. He toured the West Indies, India and Pakistan – making 204 at Kingston and several other centuries. His highest score in first-class cricket was 231 not out for New South Wales against South Australia at Sydney in 1962/3; in all he made seven scores in excess of 200. In seventy-five Sheffield Shield matches he made 5,853 runs (50.46). In one such match he made 52 in forty-eight minutes before being caught. 'Why did you get out?' asked a selector, 'You could have made 300 today.' Neil's reported reply was, 'Who on earth ever wants to make 300?' Latterly he has been a Test selector.

First-class career (1946-62): 21,699 runs (50.93) including 67 centuries, 30 wickets (36.86) and 228 catches

Test matches (79): 6,149 runs (48.42) including 21 centuries, 3 wickets (40.00) and 64 catches

HASSETT, Arthur Lindsay (b.1913)

Victoria

One of the smallest men ever to represent Australia, Lindsay Hassett was a glorious right-handed attacking batsman by nature who often became dour and watchful at the wicket in his country's service. Not only could he hook and cut the short ball and drive the half-volleys but he would also force the good-length ball 'on the up'. His footwork was superbly quick. Poker-faced, he is both a wit and a practical joker, at home as much with 'larrikins' as with princes and prime ministers, possessing a charm and personality all his own. The game has never been for him a matter of life and death and, until recently from the ABC commentary box, he watched it with dispassionate

Lindsay Hassett – Godfrey Evans keeping wicket

fairness. He toured England in 1938, 1948 and 1953, when he succeeded Bradman as captain. He found English pitches much to his liking, on his initial tour making 1,589 runs (54,79), on his second 1,563 runs (74.42), when vice-captain, and 1,236 runs (44.14) on his final tour. Like all his contemporaries, he was overshadowed by Bradman, but when he retired only Bradman among Australians had made more runs. In his first post-War Test, at Brisbane, he hit 128 in six and a half hours, adding 276 for the third wicket with Bradman. Against India in 1947/8 he came second to Bradman with an average of 110.66, which included his Test highest score of 198 not out at Adelaide. At Trent Bridge in 1948 he made 138 and, when he took over the captaincy in South Africa in 1949/50, he scored two centuries and averaged 67.00. He never had a poor series. When he scored 163 at Adelaide against South Africa in 1952/3 he put on 275 for the second wicket with Colin McDonald, and in his last series in 1953, against England, he headed the batting with 365 runs (36.50), becoming an opening batsman to help steady the side. He made eight scores above 200, the highest being 232 for Victoria against MCC at Melbourne in 1950/51. In fifty-eight Sheffield Shield matches he made 5,535 runs (63.62). Happily married, he retired to the New South Wales coast where fishing is his great hobby.

First-class career (1932-53): 16,890 runs (58.24) including 59 centuries, 18 wickets (39.05) and 170 catches
Test matches (43): 3,073 runs (46.56) including 10 centuries, 0-78 and 30 catches

HAWKE, Neil James Napier (b.1939)

Western Australia, South Australia and Tasmania

A renowned Australian Rules footballer, Neil Hawke was a dark, powerfully built right-arm fast-medium bowler who cut the ball off the pitch and bowled a good late in-swinger from an economical, open-chested action. He was also a useful late-order batsman. His debut was against England, 1962/3, in the final match of the series; and he replaced Ian Meckiff against South Africa in 1963/4, after the latter was no-balled for 'throwing' in the first Test. He took 14 wickets (33.78) in the series. In 1967/8 he took 48 wickets in Australia, including 7 for 46 for his State against the Indians and 8 for 62 against New South Wales. He toured England in 1964 and 1968, and 12 Tests against England brought him 37 wickets, his best piece of bowling being 7 for 105 when England reached 488 in the third Test at Sydney in 1965/6. His finest hour was, however, in the West Indies in 1965, when, for a losing side, he was the best bowler with 24 wickets (21.83) in the Tests – besides earning a batting average of 28.60. Although Australia lost heavily at Georgetown, he took 10 for 115 in the match. He had success with Nelson in the Lancashire League and settled in Lancashire for some years. He made a courageous recovery from a very severe illness.

First-class career (1959-71): 3,383 runs (23.99), and 458 wickets (26.39)
Test matches (27): 365 runs (16.59), 91 wickets (29.41) and 9 catches

HAZLITT, Gervys Rignold (1888-1915)

Victoria and New South Wales

Although Gerry Hazlitt was a very useful batsman, it

Neil Hawke

was his bowling which gained him his reputation. He bowled right-arm off-breaks at swerving medium-pace, though there were some doubts at times about his action. He first appeared for Victoria at 17. He played in Tests against England in 1907/8 and 1911/12, and came to England for the Triangular Tournament in 1912, taking 19 wickets (20.94) in the Tests, including 7 for 25 in the second innings against England at The Oval, at one time ensnaring 5 for 1 in seventeen balls. Despite having to have an eye operation, he took 101 wickets (18.96) on the tour. In Sheffield Shield matches he made 390 runs (16.25) and took 60 wickets (31.98). He was a master at the King's School, Parramatta, where he died.

First-class career (1905-13): 876 runs (12.69) and 188 wickets (26.09)
Test matches (9): 89 runs (11.12), 23 wickets (27.08) and 4 catches

HENDRY, Hunter Scott Thomas Laurie (b.1895)

New South Wales and Victoria

Tall and slim, 'Stork' Hendry was a right-handed batsman who cut and drove effortlessly, a fast-medium change-bowler and a fine slip field. He toured England in 1921 and 1926, disappointing in the Tests on the former tour and being kept out of them by illness on the latter. He hit 112 in the second Test at Sydney in 1928/9 and opened the bowling in two of the matches, but he had lost his place by the end of the series. Although he rarely revealed his true ability for his country, he made 325 not out for Victoria against the New Zealanders at Melbourne in 1925; and in fifty-two Sheffield Shield matches (mostly for Victoria) he made 3,305 runs (42.37) and took 101 wickets (29.53). He toured South Africa in 1921/2 and India in 1935/6.

First-class career (1918-35): 6,799 runs (37.56) including 14 centuries, 229 wickets (29.02) and 152 catches
Test matches (11): 335 runs (20.93) including 1 century, 16 wickets (40.00) and 10 catches

HIBBERT, Paul Anthony (b.1952)

Victoria

A dark, quite tall left-handed opening batsman, Paul Hibbert played for Victorian Colts for four years and much was expected of him, but he has not developed as hoped and was perhaps fortunate to be selected for Australia against India for the first Test of 1977/8 after making 100 not out (his only first-class century) against the touring team for Victoria. Curiously, this was an innings without any boundaries. On the other hand, he was somewhat harshly dropped after only one Test, in which he scored 13 and 2, and held one catch. A useful change-bowler, he took 4 for 28 against South Australia at Melbourne in 1977/8 with his left-arm medium pace.

First-class career (1974-): 2,214 runs (32.55) including 3 centuries, 15 wickets (15.06) and 14 catches

HIGGS, James Donald (b.1950)

Victoria

Probably the best Australian leg-spinner since Richie Benaud, and a cheery, straightforward character, Jim Higgs has long since lived down his first main claim to fame, that of being bowled by the only ball he faced on the fifteen-match tour of England in 1975. Red-faced on the coolest days, he is a dedicated cricketer who has worked hard to turn himself into a respectable batsman (in 1978/9 he was promoted to number ten) and into a serviceable fielder. But if these two departments of the game have not come easily to him, leg-spinning seems to do so. With a good, high, comfortable action, he gives the ball a strong flip and has a useful googly. These qualities allied to exceptionally good control have made him an economical as well as an effective Test bowler, anything but a luxury in an attack, although Australia's selectors have sometimes been unwise enough to leave him out of their team. His selection for the 1975 tour owed much to a return of 8 for 66 against the powerful West Australian side the previous season (11 for 118 in the match), but not until the cream of Australian cricketers had left to join World Series Cricket did Jim Higgs make his belated Test debut. In four Tests in the West Indies in 1978 he took 15 wickets (25.60) and on the tour 42 wickets at 22.21, including 12 for 163 in the match against the Leeward islands. Against England in 1978/9 he demanded respect in all the five games he played, finishing the series with 19 wickets (24.63) though the pitches were seldom quick enough to suit his spin, which can be extremely sharp. Touring India in 1979, Higgs took 29 wickets on the tour (32.86) but his 14 wickets in the six Tests cost 50 runs apiece. He played one Test each against the West Indies and England in 1979/80, taking 3 for 122 against the former at Melbourne but suffering the misery against England at Sydney of bowling only one over in the entire game. The feeling was growing that he might be one of the last of a dying breed but he bowled Victoria to success in the Sheffield Shield in 1979/80 and played in the first four Tests of 1980/81 (three against New Zealand and one against India) taking 4 wickets in an innings on three occasions. Then he was dropped and left out of the tour to England in 1981.

First-class career (1970-): 383 runs (5.71) and 397 wickets (29.12)
Test matches (22): 111 runs (5.55), 66 wickets (31.16) and 3 catches

HILDITCH, Andrew Mark Jefferson (b.1956)

New South Wales and South Australia

A confident and determined young solicitor and graduate of Sydney University, Andrew Hilditch is an unflappable, right-handed, opening batsman with a thoroughly sound, front-foot technique and limitless concentration. He was made captain of New South Wales at the age of twenty-one. Lean, sallow-complexioned and combative in the true Australian tradition, he was appointed State captain after he had played only two first-class matches; only Ian Craig was younger when first leading N.S.W. After several failures at the start of 1978/9 season N.S.W. were said to be captained by Andrew 'Who?' But after scoring a determined 93 against the England touring team he batted consistently enough to earn a place as opening batsman for the sixth Test against England and for two games against Pakistan (1978/9), in the second of which he was appointed deputy to Australia's new captain, Kim Hughes. He remained vice-captain during the Prudential World Cup in 1979 when he was a conspicuous success. He is also a good slip fielder. In the second Test against Pakistan at Perth in 1979 he was the victim of an appalling mockery of the spirit of cricket. Picking up the ball after it had been fielded, he handed it to the bowler Safraz Nawaz, who appealed successfully for 'handling the ball'. Australia went on to win the match. He fell swiftly from grace, despite a not unsuccessful tour of India later in 1979. He opened the batting in all six Tests, passing fifty three times and making 313 runs (26.08). But the return of the World Series Cricket players, and of Rick McCosker in particular, caused him to lose the captaincy of New South Wales and his place as well for a time. He was married during the 1979/80 season to the daughter of R.B. (Bobby) Simpson. Making no progress in Sydney, however, he moved to South Australia and scored 79 against the 1982/3 England touring team.

First-class career (1976-): 1,998 runs (32.75) including 1 century
Test matches (9): 452 runs (25.11) and 9 catches

HILL, Clement (1877-1945)

South Australia

Shortish, square and sturdy, Clem Hill was one of the greatest of left-handed batsmen. He had an ugly wide stance, with the hands held low on the bat handle, but saw the ball early and positioned himself easily for a wide variety of strokes. Strong on the leg side, and quick into position to hook or pull, he could also drive anywhere and was an explosive cutter. With his bottom-handed grip he was merciless on anything short. Although normally an attacking player, he was also a natural fighter, who saved many a lost cause. The son of H.J. Hill, who scored the first century at Adelaide Oval, Clem at sixteen hit 360 in an inter-College match – the highest innings hit in Australia at that time – and visited England with the 1896, 1899, 1902 and 1905 sides. He headed the Test averages with 60.20 in 1899, his 135 at Lord's being important in helping to win the only match decided that year. A fine fielder, especially in the deep, he made a legendary catch at Old Trafford in 1902: running from long-on to square-leg, he held a skier hit by Dick Lilley, and soon afterwards Australia won by 3 runs. Hill's highest score in Tests was 191 against South Africa at Sydney in 1910/11, but perhaps the best innings was his 188 against England at Melbourne in 1897/8, when he was twenty-one. Coming together at 58 for 6, he and Hugh Trumble added 165, a stand which won the match. At Adelaide in 1907/8 he and Roger Hartigan put on 243 for the eighth wicket. When Australia retained the Ashes in 1901/2, Hill was the heaviest run-getter with 521 runs (52.10), which included 99, 98 and 97 in successive innings! He captained Australia in 1910/11 and 1911/12. During the latter series, he was involved in a 'punch-up' with another Test selector, Percy McAlister, which was a prelude to the great 'Board of Control versus Players' row. He did not tour England

Clem Hill

therefore in 1912. In sixty-eight Sheffield Shield matches he made 6,274 runs (52.28), a record until beaten by Don Bradman. His career-highest score was 365 not out for South Australia against New South Wales at Adelaide in 1900/1901.

First class career (1892-1923): 17,216 runs (43.47) including 45 centuries
Test matches (49): 3,412 runs (39.21) including 7 centuries, and 33 catches

HILL, John Charles (1923-74)

Victoria

Jack Hill was an inelegant right-arm leg-break bowler who turned the ball little but made the top-spinner especially bounce awkwardly at a brisk pace. He toured England in 1953 and the West Indies in 1955, but did not represent his country at home. In the West Indies he headed the bowling in all matches with 18 wickets (21.11), and was also successful in England with 63 wickets (20.98). Seven of his eight Test wickets were recognized batsmen. He was a great Rules footballer until he twice fractured his skull.

First-class career (1945-55): 867 runs (16.05) and 218 wickets (23.11)
Test matches (3): 21 runs (7.00), 8 wickets (34.12) and 2 catches

HOARE, Desmond Edward (b.1934)

Western Australia

Des Hoare was a tall, strong right-arm fast bowler who represented Australia in one Test, at Adelaide against the West Indies in 1960/61. In a particularly exciting game his match analysis was 29–0–156–2. He scored 35 and 0 and held two catches.

First-class career (1955-66): 1,276 runs (18.49) including 1 century, and 225 wickets (26.91)

HODGES, John Henry (1856-1933)

Victoria

John Hodges was a left-arm fast-medium bowler renowned for his straightness and pronounced break, but was too inclined to bowl short. An erratic batsman, he was not remarkable in the field. Much of his best cricket was played for Richmond (Victoria) and he appeared for Australia in the first two Tests of 1876/7.

First-class career (1876-7): 75 runs (12.50) and 12 wickets (16.50)
Test matches (2): 10 runs (3.33) and 6 wickets (14.00)

HOGG, Rodney Malcolm (b.1951)

Victoria and South Australia

Rodney Hogg

After a long struggle to establish himself in first-class cricket, Rodney Hogg burst into Test matches like one of his own express deliveries. Blue-eyed, with fair curly hair, six foot but strongly built around the shoulders and rump, he aims to bowl fast and straight in short, electric spells, putting all his energy into most deliveries, except when bowling off a shorter run. Even then he is decidedly sharp. The approach from little more than twenty yards is a fine example of smoothly gathered momentum, the body leaning forward and gathering speed into the final leap and long stretch of the delivery stride. Only a certain stiffness of movement and a lack of stamina, sometimes due to a mild asthmatic condition, prevented him taking even more than his 41 wickets at a remarkable average of 12.85 against England in 1978/9. Only three bowlers (Barnes, Laker and Grimmett) have taken more in the history of Tests in one series, and none more in his first series. Yet before this dramatic performance Hogg had played first-class cricket in only two seasons. Time and time again, with hostile three- or four-over bursts, he undermined the confidence of the England batting, reducing the menace of the hitherto consistently successful Geoff Boycott (whom he often defeated by sheer speed) and generally saving Australia from a much heavier defeat. A serious, determined character, sometimes petulant, he had a number of jobs while struggling, first in his native Victoria and then in South Australia, to make his mark in the game. He toured England for the Prudential World Cup in 1979, and India later that year. Hogg was a grave disappointment on the Indian tour, bowling an excessive number of no-balls and taking only 11 wickets in the Tests at 53.72. He played in only one home Test in 1979/80 but won his place back the following Australian season, bowling effectively as the back-up fast bowler to Lillee and Pascoe and winning selection for a tour of England in 1981. Sadly, however, a serious back injury restricted him to two Test appearances.

First-class career (1975-): 736 runs (9.31) and 219 wickets (22.88)
Test matches (22): 246 runs (7.68), 82 wickets (23.62) and 5 catches

HOLE, Graeme Blake (b.1931)

New South Wales and South Australia

A tall right-handed middle-order batsman, Graeme Hole had an awkward knock-kneed stance and was too fond of the sweep for his own good, but he could be a powerful right-handed driver, attractive and punishing. A brilliant slip field, he twice caught four men in Tests against South Africa, at Adelaide and Sydney in 1952/3. His other series were against the West Indies and England. His sole overseas tour to England was in 1953, when, despite many opportunities, he never really established himself. He top-scored with 63 in the second innings of his first Test, against the West Indies at Melbourne in 1951/2, but, although he opened his England tour with 112 at Worcester, his ten Test innings brought only 273 runs, with 66 at Old Trafford as his best effort. He made his career-highest score of 226 against Queensland at Adelaide in 1953/4, and the following season made his last Test appearances, scoring 85 runs in three matches. A prolific run-getter for his States, in 44 Sheffield Shield matches he made 3,060 runs (42.50), besides taking 34 wickets (50.35).

First-class career (1949-57): 5,647 runs (36.66) including 11 centuries, and 61 wickets (44.04)
Test matches (18): 789 runs (25.45), 3 wickets (42.00) and 21 catches

HOOKES, David William (b.1955)

South Australia

David Hookes has made an indelible impression by hitting five centuries in six innings during three successive Sheffield Shield matches for South Australia at the age of twenty-one in 1976/7, and then hitting five successive fours off Tony Greig during an innings of 56 in the Centenary Test in Melbourne (Hookes's first). A fair-haired left-hander, he has a wonderful gift of timing, plus self-confidence and courage; Sir Donald Bradman said of his Test debut, 'I thought Frank Woolley had been born again.' Hookes owed his selection to his inspired run of scores against Victoria, Queensland and New South Wales. The innings, all played at Adelaide Oval, were 163, 9, 185, 101, 135 and 156. He had already made a mark in minor cricket in England, hitting six sixes in one six-ball over when playing club cricket for Dulwich, but his phenomenal start was followed by anti-climax in England in 1977 when, sometimes let down by impetuosity and a rather fiery temperament, he scored only 283 runs in nine innings, hitting only one hundred on the tour. However, despite breaking his jaw when trying to hook a bumper from Andy Roberts, he played some outstanding innings during two seasons of World Series Cricket, having unsuccessfully tried to obtain a release from his contract. The seasons which followed the disbandment of World Series Cricket suggested that it would have been better for him in the long run had he stayed with the 'Establishment'. Turned into a star, even an idol, by the marketing men now so powerful in Australian cricket, he lost the ability to apply himself for long periods at the crease and was ditched after only one Test in 1979/80, despite scoring 43 and 37 against the West Indies at Brisbane. Poor form in the many limited-over internationals seemed to hasten his downfall and although he toured Pakistan at the end of the 1979/80 season he made a pair in the only Test in which he played. 'Hooksey' remained in the cold in 1980/81 but in 1981/2 he returned to the international arena and proved a very successful captain of South Australia, who won the Sheffield Shield. Hookes himself scored 703 runs (43.93).

David Hookes

First-class career (1975-): 3,503 runs (38.07) including 7 centuries and 7 wickets (64.57)
Test matches (8): 436 runs (29.07), 0-15 and 2 catches

HOPKINS, Albert John Young (1876-1931)

New South Wales

A right-arm slow-medium bowler with a pronounced swerve and break from the off, a forceful batsman and a brilliant field, Bert Hopkins toured England with the 1902, 1905 and 1909 teams – passing 1,000 runs on each of the first two tours and taking 38 wickets (17.60) in 1902. He also went to South Africa in 1902/3, and at home played in two series against England, without really establishing himself. In the second Test at Lord's in 1902 he opened the bowling (to everyone's surprise bar his captain's) and immediately disposed of C.B. Fry and K.S. Ranjitsinhji. He did not get another wicket in the series. His highest score in England was 154 against Northamptonshire at Northampton in 1905. Usually opening the batting for his State, he made his career-highest score of 218 against South Australia at Adelaide in 1908/9, adding 283 for the second wicket with M.A. Noble in two hours and fifty minutes. In thirty-five Sheffield Shield matches he made 1,594 runs (30.65) and took 96 wickets (22.57).

First-class career (1896-1914): 5,563 runs (25.40) including 8 centuries, and 271 wickets (24.40)
Test matches (20): 509 runs (16.42), 26 wickets (26.76) and 11 catches

HORAN, Thomas Patrick (1854-1916)

Victoria

A native of Ireland, Tom Horan was for more than a decade the 'crack' batsman for his State. He was not a stylist, but his defence was strong and he excelled against fast bowling. He was also a round-arm, medium-pace change-bowler. He played in the first-ever Test at Melbourne in 1876/7 and was a member of the 1878 and 1882 teams to England, playing in the historic Ashes match at The Oval. He was second to the captain, W.L. Murdoch, in 1882 with 1,197 runs (25.00) on the tour, including his career-highest score of 141 not out against Gloucestershire at Clifton and 112 against the United Eleven at Chichester. In the first Test at Melbourne in 1881/2 he made 124, adding 124 for the fifth wicket with George Giffen – the first century stand in Australia. A good judge of the game and a first-rate journalist, he wrote on cricket for many years under the pseudonym 'Felix' in the *Australasian*. For his State alone, in forty-two matches, he made 2,101 runs (30.01).

First-class career (1874-91): 4,027 runs (23.27) including 8 centuries, and 35 wickets (23.68)
Test matches (15): 471 runs (18.84) including 1 century, 11 wickets (13.00) and 6 catches

HORDERN, Dr Herbert Vivian (1884-1938)

New South Wales and Philadelphia

A googly bowler of exceptional merit and a useful batsman, 'Ranji' Hordern (so-called because of his dark complexion) was prevented by the claims of his medical career from visiting England with an Australian side, but in the Tests of 1911/12 he was sensational, taking 32 wickets (24.37), besides making 173 runs (21.62), for a losing team. The previous season he had captured 14 wickets in two Tests against South Africa. In the first Test against England at Sydney in 1911/12, opening the bowling in both innings, he took 12 for 135, Australia winning her only match of the series. In the last match, also at Sydney, he had 10 for 161. In England, on tour with Pennsylvania University in 1907, he was extraordinarily successful, capturing 110 wickets (9.68) and making 391 runs (21.72).

First-class career (1905-13): 721 runs (16.38) and 217 wickets (16.79)
Test matches (7): 254 runs (23.09), 46 wickets (23.36) and 6 catches

HORNIBROOK, Percival Mitchell (1899-1976)

Queensland

A tall, left-arm slow-medium bowler, loose-armed and with an easy action, Percy Hornibrook often opened the attack with swingers and then, after a few overs, reduced his pace, to spin and flight the ball. He suffered more than most through the inability of slip fielders to hold catches off his bowling; moreover, he was selected for Australia in Tests far too late in his career. He took 81 wickets at less than ten runs apiece on an Australian tour of New Zealand in 1921, but was not selected for visits to England in 1921 and 1926, and did not make his Test debut until the fifth Test of 1928/9. Touring England in 1930 he took 96 wickets (18.77) but accomplished nothing in the Tests until the last at The Oval, when he took 7 for 92 in the second innings on a turning wicket, England losing the match and Ashes after making 405 in the first innings. After 1931 he played only once more for Queensland, taking 4 for 43 in 1934 against South Australia. In twelve Sheffield Shield matches he took 36 wickets (31.97).

First-class career (1919-33): 754 runs (10.77) and 279 wickets (23.32)
Test matches (6): 60 runs (10.00), 17 wickets (39.05) and 7 catches

HOWELL, William Peter (1869-1940)

New South Wales

Heavily built and genial, Bill Howell spun the ball at medium pace from a strong right hand. His command of length was excellent and his off-break could be deadly. A left-handed batsman who hit hard, high and often, he was a great entertainer. On his Test debut at Adelaide in 1897/8 he bowled Archie MacLaren, who had been in great form, very cheaply (taking 4 for 70 in

54 overs). On his first match in England in 1899 he created a sensation by dismissing Surrey in the first innings – capturing all 10 for 28 in 23.2 overs – and taking 5 for 29 in the second. He toured England, again successfully, in 1902 and 1905. In the 1903/4 series he took 14 wickets (21.14), including 4 for 43 in 34.5 overs when England made 315 in the second Test at Melbourne. On matting he took 14 wickets (12.42) from two matches against South Africa, 1902/3, opening the bowling at Cape Town and taking 4 for 18 and 5 for 81. In thirty-six Sheffield Shield matches he scored 1,029 runs (22.86) and took 159 wickets (23.55).

First-class career (1894-1905): 2,228 runs (14.85) including 1 century, 520 wickets (21.45) and 124 catches
Test matches (18): 158 runs (7.52), 49 wickets (28.71) and 12 catches

HUGHES, Kimberley John (b.1954)

Western Australia

Considerable natural ability took a long time to mature in Kim Hughes, a modest and charming man who became captain of his country at the age of twenty-five in his eleventh Test. A fine all-round fielder and gifted right-hand batsman with a complete array of attractive strokes, he made 119 and 60 in his first first-class match for Western Australia in 1975/6 against New South Wales, but was a long time on the fringe of the Australian Test side (several times being twelfth man) before finally establishing himself against England in 1978/9. Until the moment of his breakthrough he had travelled with official Australian teams to New Zealand and England (both in 1977) and the West Indies in 1978, yet for various reasons, including an appendix operation, had played in only three Tests, which had brought him a mere 65 runs in five innings. Then, in an hour of great Australian need, he scored 129 in the second innings of the first Test at Brisbane, his stand of 170 with Graham Yallop saving Australia from a much heavier defeat after a humiliating first innings failure. By batting for only four minutes less than eight hours he showed that he had concentration as well as natural and technical ability. A full blooded stroke-maker when he commits himself to attack, his defence is solid. Taking over the captaincy from Yallop when the latter was injured at the end of the 1978/9 season, Hughes led Australia to a convincing seven-wicket victory over Pakistan and captained the Prudential World Cup side in 1979 and the touring team to India later that year. He returned from India with his reputation enhanced. His inexperienced team lost the Test series 2-0 but the captain made 858 runs (53.62) on the tour and led by example in the Tests, hitting 594 runs (59.40) including 100 at Madras and 92 not out and 64 at Calcutta. At home in 1979/80 he played some sparkling innings against England and

Kim Hughes

the West Indies in both Test and limited-over cricket, scoring 130 not out in a bold innings against the West Indies fast-bowling battery in the Brisbane Test and a beautiful 99 against England at Perth in conditions favouring swing bowling. He was even more impressive during the Centenary Test at Lord's in 1980 when his brilliant footwork and flamboyant, inventive stroke-play in innings of 117 and 84 proved the most memorable features of the match. At home in 1980/81 his form was relatively modest until, on a perfect wicket at Adelaide, he became the third Australian after Bradman and Greg Chappell to score a double century against India, making 213 out of 528. When Chappell decided not to tour England for the 1981 Ashes series, Hughes was appointed captain in his place. The tour began well for him, with a thrilling victory in a low-scoring Test at Trent Bridge, but turned sour with Australia's defeat at Headingley after England had followed on. Hughes had little luck personally in a series eventually won 3-1 by England, scoring 300 runs at an average of 25. His 89 in the first innings of the Leeds Test was his top score of the whole tour. He was displaced as captain by Greg Chappell for the home series against West Indies and Pakistan, in which he scored further Test hundreds against each country; but then, in Chappell's absence, he captained Australia again on a disastrous short tour of Pakistan in the early part of the 1982/3 season. All three Tests were lost and not a fixture won. Yet none of these misfortunes could fairly be laid at his door.

First-class career (1975-): 7,244 runs (35.33) including 14 centuries, 2 wickets (24.50) and 96 catches
Test matches (51): 3,275 runs (37.64) including 7 centuries, 0-28 and 38 catches

HUNT, William Alfred (b.1908)

New South Wales

A left-arm medium-pace bowler, Bill Hunt spent several years with Rishton in the Lancashire League. Before leaving Australia, he represented his country in the fourth Test against South Africa at Adelaide in 1931/2, scoring 0, taking 0 for 39 and holding one catch. A genial raconteur, he has furnished incidental material for several cricketing biographies. In eleven Sheffield Shield matches he scored 192 runs (14.76) and took 48 wickets (20.70).

First-class career (1929-31): 301 runs (14.33) and 62 wickets (23.00)

HURST, Alan George (b.1950)

Victoria

A tall, dark and strapping right-arm fast bowler, Alan Hurst was considered to be almost as fast as Dennis Lillee when he made his first tour to England in 1975, taking 21 wickets at 31 each as reserve for Lillee, Thomson and Walker. A series of injuries delayed his arrival as a regular Test cricketer but in 1978/9 he finally established himself with a vengeance, taking 40 wickets in eight Tests, 25 in six matches against England, including 5 for 28 in England's first innings in the fourth Test at Sydney, and 15 in two games against Pakistan, including 9 for 155 at Perth. A modest man, he had hitherto seemed to have everything needed to make himself a success at the top level except luck, sustained fitness and the killer instinct. But with his strength and a model action – cheeks puffing during a short, rhythmical approach and then a rapid but fluent sideways-on delivery – it was no surprise that he should have proved his true worth after modest success in two isolated Test appearances, against New Zealand in 1973/4 and India in 1977/8. Against England and Pakistan, however, he bowled genuinely fast, swung the ball both ways, and only occasionally lost control. Merely an adequate fielder by modern high standards, he is a genuine number eleven batsman: he suffered no fewer than three Test pairs in the one 1978/9 season! His best performance for Victoria was 8 for 84 in Queensland in 1977/8. He toured India in 1979/80 but a serious back injury forced him to return home after playing in only the first two Tests.

First-class career (1972-81): 504 runs (8.68) and 280 wickets (26.28)
Test matches (12): 102 runs (6.00), 43 wickets (27.91) and 3 catches

HURWOOD, Alexander (b.1902)

Queensland

A tall, right-arm medium-pace bowler, Alec Hurwood toured England with the 1930 team, but was not called upon in the Tests. He represented his country only in the first and second Tests, at Adelaide and Sydney, against West Indies, 1930/31, when he met with encouraging success against the leading batsman. He took 4 for 22 when West Indies fell for 90 in the second innings at Sydney, but was then dropped.

First-class career (1925-31): 575 runs (11.27) and 113 wickets (27.62)
Test matches (2): 5 runs (2.50), 11 wickets (15.45) and 2 catches

INVERARITY, Robert John (b.1944)

Western Australia and South Australia

A born leader, John Inverarity achieved greater fame for Western Australia than he did for his country, leading his State to the Sheffield Shield title in four of his five seasons as captain. He would undoubtedly have been an effective captain of Australia, and deserved to be so in 1978/9 when he alone, perhaps, could have matched Brearley's leadership of England. A calm, thoughtful and astute captain, Inverarity knew how to react under pressure and how best to put pressure on opposing sides. He was himself a talented all-rounder, a neat and patient right-hand batsman, good fielder and useful slow left-arm spin bowler. He is the son of a former West Australian stalwart, Mervyn Inverarity. John first attracted national attention with an innings of 177 against South Australia in 1965/6. He toured England in 1968 and 1972 and New Zealand in 1969/70. He scored a determined 56 against England at The Oval in 1968, being last out, lbw to Underwood, who had routed Australia on a wet wicket. When Underwood again destroyed Australia at Leeds in 1972, 'Invers' took 3 for 26 with his own left-arm spin. He became deputy headmaster of a school in Adelaide, marking his final season with Western Australia in 1978/9 with 187 against New South Wales at Sydney and 124 not out against Tasmania at Devonport. However, he continued to be an exceptionally valuable cricketer for South Australia and it was his slow left-arm spin which had much to do with the Shield victory of his adopted State in 1981/2, taking 30 wickets (21.30) in nine games.

First-class career (1962-): 10,297 runs (35.75) including 24 centuries, 141 wickets (29.36) and 228 catches
Test matches (6): 174 runs (17.40), 4 wickets (23.25) and 4 catches

IREDALE, Francis Adams (1867-1926)

New South Wales

Tall, lean, cool, collected and a resourceful right-handed batsman, Frank Iredale combined sound defence with good hitting power: he was a particularly graceful off-side player. In the outfield he was a quick mover and a sure catch. On his Test debut, at Sydney in 1894/5, he scored 81 and he finished the series with 337 runs (37.44). Touring England in 1896 and 1899, he passed 1,000 runs on both visits and had a blaze of success during the first tour, in quick succession scoring 94 not out, 114, 106, 171, 108 (in the Test at Old Trafford), 73 and 62. He headed the Test batting averages in 1896 with 38.00 and in the 1897/8 series averaged 43.20. In thirty-eight Sheffield Shield matches he made 2,466 runs (38.53).

First-class career (1888-1901): 6,794 runs (33.63) including 12 centuries, and 111 catches
Test matches (14): 807 runs (36.68) including 2 centuries, 0-3 and 16 catches

IRONMONGER, Herbert (1881-1971)

Victoria

Heavily-built, slow-moving and awkward, 'Dainty' Ironmonger was a left-arm medium-pace bowler relying on spin which broke sharply from the leg on all pitches, most of which had surfaces like glass. He had lost the top joint of his middle finger and the stump enabled him to twist the ball; his leg-break looked sometimes as if it were an off-spinner. He never went to England – there was some doubt about the legality of his action – and he was, at 45 years 237 days, the second (and still the fourth) oldest cricketer to make his Test debut, at Brisbane in the first Test against England in 1928/9, when he delivered 94.3 overs (4 for 164). At Melbourne in the fifth Test against South Africa in 1931/2 he was unplayable on a soft pitch, taking 5 for 6 and 6 for 18, the visitors collapsing for 36 and 45. In that series he was supreme with 31 wickets (9.67); and the previous season against the West Indies he took 22 wickets (14.68) in four Tests, including 7 for 23 in 20 overs (11 for 79 in the match), the West Indies falling for 99 on the first day. Although he often wreaked havoc with the ball, he was no asset in the field, and as a batsman, as A.G. Moyes wrote, 'He went to the wickets mostly as a gesture to convention.' It was said of Bert Ironmonger that his wife once rang him at the Melbourne ground and, on being told that he had just gone in to bat, replied, 'Oh, that's alright. I'll hold on!' In forty-two Sheffield Shield matches 'Dainty' took 215 wickets (24.74). He toured New Zealand in 1920/21 with an Australian side and India with Frank Tarrant's in 1935/6. In 1932/3 he became the only Australian to play Test cricket when past the age of fifty.

First-class career (1909-35): 476 runs (5.95) and 464 wickets (21.50)
Test matches (14): 42 runs (2.62), 74 wickets (17.97) and 3 catches

IVERSON, John Brian (1915-73)

Victoria

Six feet two inches tall and weighing fifteen stone, 'Big Jack' Iverson was Australia's Bosanquet, creating something of a sensation during his brief first-class career. At first he bowled fastish, but while on Army Service in New Guinea during the Second World War he developed a peculiar method of spinning the ball, which he gripped in his right hand between his thumb and bent middle finger, using the bent finger as a spring to discharge 'the missile'. Batsmen with experience of Iverson came to know that if the thumb pointed straight, it was a top-spinner and if the thumb pointed to the leg-side the ball would turn from the off, a peculiar 'wrong 'un' bowled with the wrist over the ball instead of underneath it. He could bowl his wide variety of deliveries – off-breaks, leg-breaks and googlies – without any change of action. He attracted great attention when he took 46 wickets (16.12) for Victoria in 1949/50, and 75 wickets (7.00) for Bill Brown's Australian side in New Zealand later that season. Inevitably dubbed the 'mystery bowler' when he was selected against England in 1950/51, he took 6 for 27 in England's second innings (a mere 123) at Sydney in the third match, but in the fourth match at Adelaide he suffered an ankle injury when treading on a ball and played in only one game in each of the next two years. Thereupon he gave up the game altogether in Australia. He toured India, however, with the Commonwealth team of 1953/4.

First-class career (1949-53): 277 runs (14.57) and 157 wickets (19.22)
Test matches (5): 3 runs (0.75), 21 wickets (15.23) and 2 catches

JACKSON, Archibald (1909-33)

New South Wales

Had Archie Jackson lived longer, some authorities believe he would have gone further than Don Bradman. With his bat held high on the handle and his cap brim drooping like a guardsman's, his leg glances were casually elegant, subtle wrists steering the ball square and late. His footwork was light and as he cover-drove his body would incline like a ballet dancer's. In short he was an artist with a genius for timing and placing. As an outfield he was superb. At seventeen he made his debut for his State, and his first season, 1926/7, brought him 464 runs (58.00). The following year, promoted to opening batsman, he made 131 and 122 – the latter century coming in two hours – against South Australia at Sydney. He toured New Zealand with an Australian side in 1927/8, averaging 49.50. Australian cricket was in a transitional state and young class batsmen were being eagerly accepted. Only nineteen on his Test debut in the fourth match against England at Adelaide in

1928/9, he opened with Bill Woodfull and hit a brilliant 164. His career-highest score of 182 in the Test Trial for Ryder's XI against Woodfull's XI ensured his selection for the 1930 England tour. Possibly the sickness which carried him off less than three years later was already affecting him, but he was rarely at his best in England, though he reached his 1,000 at The Oval in the final Test, when he made 73, helping Bradman to add 243 for the fourth wicket, then a record. He appeared against the West Indies on the first Australian tour of 1930/31, but he was by now regularly fighting poor health. While in hospital on his death-bed, he became engaged. In twenty-three Sheffield Shield matches he made 1,858 runs (54.64).

First-class career (1926-30): 4,383 runs (45.65) including 11 centuries
Test matches (8): 474 runs (47.40) including 1 century, and 7 catches

JARMAN, Barrington Noel (b.1936)

South Australia

For years in the shadow of Wally Grout, Barry Jarman emerged as his country's number one wicket-keeper, a very good right-handed batsman and vice-captain on the England tour of 1968. A cheerful character, he toured England three times, India and Pakistan and New Zealand twice each and the West Indies and South Africa once each. Except for his first Test against India at Kanpur in 1959/60 he was understudy for twenty-seven Tests in six series. Bulkily built – 5 feet $7\frac{1}{2}$ inches and $13\frac{1}{2}$ stone – he was, nevertheless, agile. In his first match against England (Grout being out because of a broken jaw) at Melbourne in 1962/3, he made a fantastic one-handed, diving, leg-side catch from Geoff Pullar off 'Garth' McKenzie. During the Test at Lord's in 1968 a ball from McKenzie broke his right forefinger in three places, but he came in to bat most gamely – only for a fast ball from David Brown to strike the damaged finger. The following month he led Australia for the first time in the absence of Bill Lawry (injured) at Headingley. He had ten New South Wales victims at Adelaide in 1962/3; and 1963/4 saw him dismiss 45 batsmen in eleven first-class matches. Only two Australian 'keepers have taken more wickets – Bert Oldfield and Grout himself. A hard-hitting batsman who could have held his place in some sides as such, he struck 26 off one over from David Allen against T.N. Pearce's side at Scarborough in 1961. His best score in Tests was 78 against India at Calcutta in 1964/5. His career-highest score was 196 against New South Wales at Adelaide in 1965/6.

First-class career (1955-69): 5,615 runs (22.00) including 5 centuries, and 560 dismissals (431 ct, 129 st.)
Test matches (19): 400 runs (14.81) and 54 dismissals (50 ct, 4 st.)

JARVIS, Arthur Harwood (1860-1933)

South Australia

The exceptional ability of Jack Blackham as wicket-keeper limited 'Affie' Jarvis's opportunities in representative cricket, but he toured England as second-string in 1880, 1886, 1888 and 1893, and had a long career for his State from 1877 until 1901. In the third Test at Sydney in 1884/5 he caught five and stumped one, helping Australia to win by six runs. A dogged batsman not often among the runs, he hit 98 not out for his State against New South Wales in 1894/5, and 82 – top-score for a losing side – for Australia against England in the second Test at Melbourne in 1884/5.

First-class career (1877-1901): 3,161 runs (15.57) and 198 dismissals (115 ct, 83 st.)
Test matches (11): 303 runs (16.83) and 18 dismissals (9 ct, 9 st.)

JENNER, Terence James (b.1944)

South Australia, Western Australia and Cambridgeshire

Ashley Mallett's 'spin-twin', Terry Jenner was a right-arm leg-break bowler with a good googly who toured New Zealand in 1969/70 and the West Indies in 1972/3. He played in Tests against England in 1970/71 and 1974/5, and when he was not selected for any tours of England came over and joined a minor county. Sometimes he bowled impressively in Tests: in the fifth match against West Indies at Port of Spain in 1972/3 he took 5 for 90 in conditions favouring the bat. A useful late-order batsman, his aggressive 74 in the fifth Test at Adelaide in 1974/5 enabled Australia to recover (after losing five wickets for 84) and win.

First-class career (1963-77): 3,580 runs (22.23) and 389 wickets (32.18)
Test matches (9): 208 runs (23.11), 24 wickets (31.20) and 5 catches

JENNINGS, Claude Barrows (1884-1950)

South Australia and Queensland

A neat right-handed opening batsman, sound and able to adapt his game to the circumstances but lacking real power in his strokes, Claude Jennings visited England in 1912 for the Triangular Tournament, opening the batting in all six Tests. He was fortunate to make the team as a substitute, six famous players, in dispute with the Board of Control, refusing to make the trip. In a wet summer he reached his 1,000 runs. In sixteen Sheffield Shield matches for South Australia he made only 617 runs (20.56). Sometime South Australian correspondent of the British Department of Overseas Trade and secretary of the Adelaide Chamber of Commerce, he was appointed a delegate to the Australian Cricket Board of Control in 1938.

First-class career (1902-12): 2,452 runs (25.54) including 1 century
Test matches (6): 107 runs (17.83) and 5 catches

JOHNSON, Ian William (b.1918)

Victoria

A very slow off-spinner with a teasing flight, Ian Johnson is one of the few high-class, right-arm, off-spin bowlers to emerge from Australia. He would use a wind skilfully, making the ball float away as a change from the off-break. His action was unusual with a rather staccato swing of the bowling arm, but he was not quick enough to use wet wickets effectively and was no answer to Laker in 1956. As a right-handed batsman, he had a sound defence and, able to hit very hard when necessary, was very useful in the middle order. He was a brilliant slip field. Making his first-class debut at seventeen and succeeding Lindsay Hassett as Australian captain in 1954/5, he did not always enjoy his team's confidence – there were those who believed that Keith Miller, not Johnson, should have got the job. But he was a cheerful captain, generous in defeat in 1956. He also toured England in 1948 and, over eight years, South Africa, the West Indies, New Zealand and India and Pakistan. The first time he bowled against England, in the second Test at Sydney in 1946/7, he was virtually unplayable, taking 6 for 42 in 30.1 overs. In the third Test at Georgetown in 1955 he took 7 for 44 in the second innings. In South Africa in 1949/50 he was the leading bowler with 79 wickets (16.82), including 18 in the Tests. In the third Test at Durban, when Australia were 236 behind on the first innings, Johnson took 5 for 34, and South Africa were bundled out for 99. Amazingly, Australia won handsomely by five wickets. His highest score in Tests was 77 against England in the third Test at Sydney in 1950/51, and his career-highest, 132 not out against Queensland at Melbourne in 1948/9. His best bowling was 7 for 42 at Leicester in 1948. He has for many years been secretary of Melbourne Cricket Club and was awarded the MBE for his services to the game. His father-in-law was Dr. R.L. Park, who played once for Australia.

First-class career (1935-56): 4,905 runs (22.92) including 2 centuries, 619 wickets (23.30) and 138 catches
Test matches (45): 1,000 runs (18.51), 109 wickets (29.19) and 30 catches

JOHNSON, Leonard Joseph (1919-77)

Queensland

One of the many right-arm fast bowlers who came and went while Ray Lindwall and Keith Miller remained in harness, Len Johnson was also a useful hitter in the lower order. He played in the fifth Test against India at Melbourne in 1947/8, scoring 23 not out, taking 3 for 66 and 3 for 8 and catching Lala Amarnath; this was his sole Test. His tally of 171 wickets (24.59) from forty-two Sheffield Shield matches was a record for his State.

Ian Johnson

First-class career (1946-52): 1,139 runs (16.75) and 218 wickets (23.17)

JOHNSTON, William Arras (b.1922)

Victoria

A sporting and good-humoured cricketer but a tough competitor, Bill Johnston was a tall, strongly built, left-arm fast-medium bowler. With a bucking and plunging run-up of ten paces, he bowled a good length, would cut and swing the ball late either way and make the ball lift disconcertingly. His batting afforded rich entertainment. He played with limbs seemingly independent of each other, aiming his bat at the ball with arms and legs flying and, on contact, prancing down the pitch in bounding good spirits. Occasionally he would connect with a really bit hit. He was an extremely good catcher and had a strong throw which reflected earlier baseball training. He toured England in 1948 – taking 102 wickets (16.42) – and in 1953. He also toured South Africa and the West Indies. At home he was a regular (when free of injury) in five series from 1947 until 1955. On his first tour of England he was the invaluable link between Ray Lindwall and Keith Miller in the Tests, taking 27 wickets (23.33), including 9 for 183 in 84 overs in the first Test at Trent Bridge. In South Africa in 1949/50, despite an early injury in a car accident, he topped the bowling in all first-class matches with 56 wickets (13.75) and took 23 Test wickets (17.04), his best haul being 6 for 44 at Johannesburg in the first Test. In two successive seasons in Australia from 1950 to 1953 he took 22 wickets (19.18) and 23 wickets (22.08). At that time he had taken 100 Test wickets faster than any other bowler in history – four years and a few days. In thirty-eight Sheffield Shield matches he took 147 wickets (28.78), with a best innings analysis of 8 for 52 against Queensland at Melbourne in 1952/3.

First-class career (1945-54): 1,129 runs (12.68) and 554 wickets (23.35)
Test matches (40): 273 runs (11.37), 160 wickets (23.91) and 16 catches

Bill Johnston

JONES, Ernest (1869-1943)

South Australia

Barrel-chested Ernie Jones or 'Jonah' was the best Australian right-arm fast bowler of his day. Originally a miner, he was below medium height but very powerfully built and, after a fairly short run, would put all his bodily strength behind the delivery, the intense force of which often made the ball rise very unpleasantly, especially if pitched short. No-balled twice in Australia for throwing, once in the opening match of the 1897/8 tour between South Australia and A.E. Stoddart's team at Adelaide and later in a Test, he subsequently concentrated more on length and control, to very good effect. From 1894 until 1902 he represented his country regularly. In his tours of England, 1896, 1899 and 1902, he took 121, 135 and 71 wickets respectively at an average of 19 runs a wicket. In the first match of the first tour, against Lord Sheffield's Eleven at Sheffield Park, he allegedly bowled a ball through Dr W.G. Grace's beard, and to W.G.'s querulous, 'What do you think you're at, Jonah?' made the classic reply, 'Sorry, Doctor, she slipped.' He was especially effective against Yorkshire, taking 6 for 74 at Sheffield and 7 for 36 at Headingley, and An England Eleven at Crystal Palace lost the last four wickets to him for no runs, Jonah finishing with 8 for 39. Not until the 1897/8 and 1899 series did he fulfil his promise in Tests, taking 22 wickets (25.13) and 26 wickets (25.26) respectively, the chief wicket-taker each time. For South Australia at Adelaide against A.E. Stoddart's 1897/8 side he captured 14 for 237, a record for the ground. In 38 Sheffield Shield matches he took 209 wickets (26.35). Of little account as a batsman, he was a fine mid-off. Stories abound about Jonah, who called a spade a spade in a genial way. He was introduced to the Prince of Wales, later Edward VII, who asked him whether he had attended St Peter's College, Adelaide, to which he replied, 'Yes, I take the dust-cart there regularly!'

Ernie Jones

First-class career (1892-1907): 2,405 runs (13.07) and 645 wickets (22.75)
Test matches (19): 126 runs (5.04), 64 wickets (29.01) and 21 catches

JONES, Samuel Percy (1861-1951)

New South Wales, Queensland and Auckland

The last survivor of both sides in the Ashes match at The Oval in 1882, Sammy Jones was a determined and watchful right-handed batsman, a fast scorer when in the mood, a pleasing stroke-maker confident on difficult pitches, a versatile field and useful change-bowler. Before he was twenty he had hit a century; and he toured England in 1882, 1886, 1888 (when he became dangerously ill with smallpox) and 1890. At his very best in 1886, he finished second in the averages, making 1,530 runs (23.90), including 151 against the Gentlemen at The Oval and, in the first Test at Old Trafford, 87, which remained his Test highest. Settling in Queensland, he toured New Zealand with the State's team in 1896/7, and lived in New Zealand for his last forty-seven years, playing for Auckland from 1904 until 1908. During the 1882 Oval Test he was batting with W.L. Murdoch who played a ball to leg and ran. Sammy Jones completed the first run and, thinking the ball was dead, went out of his ground to pat the wicket. W.G. whipped the bail off and the umpire, Robert Thoms, gave him out. Sammy was furious, but did not retain ill-will for the Doctor, whose ethics on this occasion hardly bear scrutiny.

First-class career (1880-1908): 5,189 runs (21.03) including 5 centuries, and 55 wickets (33.52)
Test matches (12): 432 runs (21.60), 6 wickets (18.66) and 12 catches

JOSLIN, Leslie Ronald (b.1947)

Victoria

Bursting into first-class cricket, Les Joslin was an aggressive left-handed batsman of brilliant potential, not alas fulfilled. Scoring 565 runs (51.36) in Australia in 1967/8, he made a Test appearance against India in the fourth match, scoring 7 and 2. He toured England in 1968, but was disappointing, averaging only 21.60 with the bat and not being selected for the Tests. He dropped out of first-class cricket after the 1969/70 season.

First-class career (1966-9): 1,816 runs (29.77) including 2 centuries

KELLEWAY, Charles (1889-1944)

New South Wales

A very sound right-handed batsman, Charles Kelleway possessed unlimited patience – he was named 'Rock of Gibraltar' – and was invaluable opening the innings or facing a crisis. He also bowled fast-medium with a swerve that troubled the best batsmen. Coming to England in 1912 with an Australian team weakened by internal politics, he scored 360 runs in the six Tests, including 114 against South Africa at Old Trafford and 102 at Lord's; his only superior was Warren Bardsley. He captained the Australian Imperial Forces in 1919, but at the outset of the tour – and after scoring 505 runs in nine innings – he left the side and, indeed, never came to England again as a player. In the 1920/21 series he made 330 runs (47.14) and took 15 wickets (21.00), heading the bowling averages in a powerful side. At Adelaide, after England had gained a lead of 93, he was missed before scoring but stayed nearly seven hours for 147, showing solid defence in an uphill struggle. He finished his Test career in 1928/9, falling ill during the first match at Brisbane which England were to win by 675 runs. For his State against South Australia at Sydney in 1920/21, he made his career-highest score of 168, and added 397 for the fifth wicket with Bardsley – a world-record for nearly thirty years. Awkward but indomitable, and deaf to the opinion of others, Charles Kelleway was one of the toughest cricketers produced by Australia. He sometimes brought his defensive tactics to the verge of inhumanity. Bardsley said of him that he 'only got out so that he could go away, have a good long bite on it, and tell you a month later, "Thought that one the other day would break from the off."' In thirty-nine Sheffield Shield matches he made 2,304 runs (40.42) and took 126 wickets (27.73).

First-class career (1907-28): 6,389 runs (35.10) including 15 centuries, 339 wickets (26.32) and 103 catches
Test matches (26): 1,422 runs (37.42) including 3 centuries, 52 wickets (32.36) and 24 catches

KELLY, James Joseph (1867-1938)

New South Wales

An outstanding wicket-keeper, James Kelly left Victoria – where Jack Blackham held sway – and joined New South Wales two years before touring England for the first time in 1896. He made other tours in 1899, 1902 and 1905. He was particularly adept at taking very fast bowlers like Ernest Jones and Albert Cotter. A useful batsman, he was able to defend or attack as the game demanded. In the Old Trafford Test of 1896, he and Hugh Trumble batted an hour for the last 25 runs, bringing victory by 3 wickets after a terrific struggle against the fast bowling of Tom Richardson. He hit 105 against Warwickshire at Edgbaston in 1899, and 74 out of 112 in an hour against Gloucestershire at Bristol in 1905. He gave up first-class cricket after his last tour largely because of a damaged finger and a blow over the heart by a ball from Walter Brearley at Old Trafford.

First-class career (1894-1906): 4,108 runs (19.94) including 3 centuries, and 355 dismissals (243 ct, 112 st.)
Test matches (36): 664 runs (17.02) and 63 dismissals (43 ct, 20 st.)

KELLY, Thomas Joseph Dart (1844-93)

Victoria

Playing in the second and third Tests at Melbourne in 1876/7 and 1878/9, Thomas Kelly was a good right-handed batsman and outstanding at point.

First-class career (1863-82): 543 runs (20.11)
Test matches (2): 64 runs (21.33) and 1 catch

KENDALL, Thomas (1851-1924)

Victoria and Tasmania

Tom Kendall played purely as a left-arm slow bowler in the first Test at Melbourne in 1876/7 and, next to Charles Bannerman, had the biggest share in beating England, capturing 8 for 109. Taking two walking strides to the wicket, he bowled orthodox left-arm spin with considerable flight and command of length and, for variety, a ball which went with his arm. He was a surprising omission from the 1878 side. Although a poor batsman and slow in the field, he was a safe catcher. Living latterly at Hobart, he toured New Zealand with a Tasmanian side in 1883/4.

First-class career (1876-88): 141 runs (12.81) and 40 wickets (16.65)
Test matches (2): 39 runs (13.00), 14 wickets (15.35) and 2 catches

KENT, Martin Francis (b.1953)

Queensland

Cricket fate was never very kind to Martin Kent, a tall man, who batted right-handed with aggressive intent and a handsome, upright style. He scored freely for Queensland after his debut for them in 1974/5 and was one of the few men signed up to play World Series Cricket for Kerry Packer without having established himself in Test cricket. In his first Shield match, against New South Wales, he hit 140. He added to his experience by touring West Indies on an unofficial World Series tour, and made his first Test appearance in England in 1981, making 171 runs in three Tests and hitting fifties at Old Trafford, batting number five, and as a makeshift opener in the final Test at The Oval. A very good slip fielder, he lost his place the following Australian season only because of a serious back injury caused by a disc protruding into the spinal cord. He was obliged to retire prematurely from the game.

First-class career (1974-82): 3,567 runs (36.03) including 7 centuries
Test matches (3): 171 runs (28.50) and 6 catches

KIPPAX, Alan Falconer (1897-1972)

New South Wales

Tallish, rather slim, with his shirt-sleeves rolled just like Victor Trumper's, Alan Kippax was a charming, cultured, right-handed batsman, orthodox in his stroke-play but never dull or boring. He was very quick-footed and could get to the pitch of the ball when facing the spinner or walk inside the line of flight when the short one came along. Not always well treated by Test Selection Committees, he remained a brilliant and prolific batsman, and captained his State for several years. He made his Test debut against England in 1924/5 but was a surprise omission from the 1926 team to England, although he toured in 1930 and 1934, making 329 runs (54.83) in the Tests of the former year, and averaging more than 50 in all first-class matches on each tour. He scored 100 in the third Test against England at Melbourne in 1928/9, adding 161 with Jack Ryder after three wickets had fallen cheaply. Against the first West Indian tourists of 1930/31 he made 146 at Adelaide, top-scoring in the first Test between the two countries; and the following season he was quite effective against South Africa. In sixty-one Sheffield Shield matches he made 6,096 runs (70.88), his career-highest being 315 not out against Queensland in 1927/8. He made 260 not out against Victoria at Melbourne the following year, adding 307 for the last wicket with J.E.H. Hooker, which remains a world record. Altogether, he passed two hundred four times and twice scored a century in each innings.

First-class career (1918-35): 12,762 runs (57.22) including 43 centuries, and 21 wickets (52.53)
Test matches (22): 1,192 runs (36.12) including 2 centuries, 0-19 and 13 catches

Alan Kippax

KLINE, Lindsay Francis (b.1934)

Victoria

A left-arm off-break and googly bowler and dogged tail-end batsman, Lindsay Kline took 37 wickets (24.89) for his State in his second season in 1956/7, which led to tours to New Zealand (with an 'A' team) and South Africa in 1957/8. In his second Test, at Cape Town, he performed one of the rare hat-tricks. He headed the Test bowling averages in that series with 15 wickets (16.33). Again heading the averages against India and Pakistan in 1959/60, he collected 16 wickets (14.45) from four Tests, including 7 for 75 in the Pakistan second innings at Lahore on an easy turf pitch, clinching victory for Australia. He appeared twice against England, in 1958/9 without success, and went on the 1961 tour of England but was not selected for the Tests. In the fourth Test at Adelaide against the West Indies in the unforgettable series of 1960/61, Kline batted a hundred minutes for 15 not out in a last wicket stand of 66 with Ken Mackay which denied victory to the visitors. The whole nation listened to the commentary of the final stages.

First-class career (1955-61): 559 runs (8.60) and 276 wickets (27.39)
Test matches (13): 58 runs (8.28), 34 wickets (22.82) and 9 catches

LAIRD, Bruce Malcolm (b.1950)

Western Australia

A gritty, fair-haired, right-hand opening batsman, Bruce Laird was unlucky to make his Test debut as late as he did and to make it, moreover, against one of the fiercest fast-bowling attacks in history – the West Indians Holding, Roberts, Croft and Garner. He had played his first match for Western Australia in 1972/3 and toured England in 1975, batting consistently without earning a cap. He scored four first-class hundreds, the highest, 171 against Queensland in 1976/7, before signing for World Series Cricket, where he gained valuable experience against high-class fast bowling which stood him in good stead when WSC was disbanded in 1979/80. In that season Laird assured himself of Test selection with a fighting 117 in his State's first Sheffield Shield game against New South Wales, and his first innings for Australia was outstanding: 92 at Brisbane, scored during five hours of determined batting which deserved at least eight more runs. His 75 in the second innings helped Australia to draw the game and throughout the season he continued to display pluck and concentration which, allied to a compact and correct technique, made him Australia's most successful batsman with 340 runs (56.66) against the West Indies. Against England he was less successful until he made 74 and 25 in the Melbourne Test, and on the short tour of Pakistan in 1979/80 he disappointed on the slow pitches apart from scoring 63 in the third Test in Lahore. He did not get going, either, in the Centenary Test at Lord's and further appearances at Test level were prevented by a serious rupture to an Achilles' tendon which kept him out of the 1980/81 season and the 1981 England tour. He reclaimed a regular place against Pakistan and West Indies at home in 1981/82 and toured Pakistan in 1982/3. He was consistent, but a major innings eluded him.

First-class career (1972-): 4,499 runs (34.87) including 8 centuries
Test matches (21): 1,341 runs (35.29), 25 wickets (28.60) and 16 catches

LANGLEY, Gilbert Roche Andrews (b.1919)

South Australia

At one time Speaker of the South Australian parliament, Gil Langley was for several years Australia's number one wicket-keeper. Genial and burly, he was also a stolid right-handed batsman, extremely sound though hardly a stylist, his most useful scoring strokes being past square-leg and point. His first tour was to South Africa in 1949/50, followed by trips to England in 1953 and 1956, and to the West Indies, India and Pakistan. His Test experience was packed into the years between 1951 and 1956, and, in achieving twenty-one dismissals in the series at home against the West Indies in 1951/2, he equalled the then world-record in a rubber. Nine Tests against England brought him 37 victims (35 caught). At Lord's in 1956 he had nine in the match, a record, and nineteen in the three matches in which he kept that year. His career-highest score was 150 not out for his State against New Zealand at Adelaide in 1953/4.

First-class career (1945-57): 3,236 runs (25.68) including 4 centuries, and 369 dismissals (293 ct, 76 st.)
Test matches (26): 374 runs (14.96) and 98 dismissals (83 ct, 15 st.)

LAUGHLIN, Trevor John (b.1951)

Victoria

An aggressive all-rounder, hard-hitting left-hand batsman, steady medium-pace right-arm bowler and fine close fielder, Trevor Laughlin had a good tour of the West Indies for Bobby Simpson's reconstituted Australian team early in 1978. But his subsequent form was disappointing. He was dropped from the team after Australia had lost the first Test to England in 1978/9 (when Laughlin brought off one brilliant catch in the gully) and thereafter only shone for his country in limited-over cricket. He was a useful member of Australia's Prudential World Cup side in

England in 1979. In two tests against the West Indies he made 24 priceless runs in a crisis to help his side win the third Test narrowly, and then took 5 for 101 in the first innings of the fifth Test, sharing the new ball with Jeff Thomson. Laughlin played cricket in the Scottish and Lancashire Leagues in 1976 and 1977 to broaden his experience. In seven matches for Victoria, 1977/8, he scored 497 runs (49.70) and took 20 wickets (29.10)

First-class career (1974-81): 2,770 runs (32.58) including 1 century, and 99 wickets (31.92)
Test matches (3): 87 runs (17.40), 6 wickets (43.66) and 3 catches

LAVER, Frank (1869-1919)

Victoria

A tall, powerful man, Frank Laver's right-handed batting was so ungainly that, even when he did well, little was thought of him. As a medium-pace bowler, however, he had an excellent command of length and a deceptive flight. On his first England tour in 1899 he made 859 runs and, having ten not outs, averaged 30, but, except in the Test at Lord's when he quickly disposed of Tom Hayward, Johnny Tyldesley and Gilbert Jessop (Australia ultimately winning), he had little chance to shine as a bowler. Coming to England in 1905 and, as player/manager, in 1909, he enjoyed greater success in the former year, virtually winning the first Test at Trent Bridge by taking 7 for 64 in the first innings. In all first-class matches on the tour he captured 115 wickets (18.19). In 1909 he headed the averages for both Tests with 17 wickets (13.50), and for all matches with 70 wickets (14.97) from eighteen games. In the first innings of the Old Trafford Test, flattered by some inept batting, he took 8 for 31. Although he hit 143 against Somerset at Taunton in 1899, he was generally a more effective batsman at home, hitting five centuries there. In fifty-nine Sheffield Shield matches he made 2,760 runs (28.75) and took 108 wickets (36.58). He was also player/manager on two tours of New Zealand. It was partly because the Board of Control refused to appoint him as manager in 1912 that six important players declined to make the trip to England. A photographer and writer, he wrote a well-illustrated book of his first two tours of England, *An Australian Cricketer on Tour*.

First-class career (1891-1913): 5,431 runs (25.02) including 6 centuries, 404 wickets (24.72) and 148 catches
Test matches (15): 196 runs (11.52), 37 wickets (26.05) and 8 catches

LAWRY, William Morris (b.1937)

Victoria

Six feet two inches tall, lean, with a sharp jaw, prominent nose and ready smile, Bill Lawry bore the nickname 'The Phantom' because of his youthful addiction to a comic strip character of that name. A left-handed opening batsman with a short back-lift which did not prevent him from driving well and scoring greedily on the on-side, his major quality was his quite exceptional concentration. A very fine player of fast bowling, he hooked with authority. He was also a fast outfielder with a good arm, but opposing bowlers will recall only his broad, straight bat and his endless patience. Bill Lawry came to England comparatively unknown in 1961 and had a triumphant summer: all first-class matches brought him 2,019 runs (61.18), including nine centuries, and in the Tests he made 420 runs (52.50). This was his first Test series. In his first match at Edgbaston he made 57 and in his second, at Lord's, a memorable 130 out of 238 in six hours ten minutes against the hostile fast bowling of Brian Statham and Fred Trueman on a fiery wicket. Largely due to him Australia won. At Old Trafford his 74 and 102 were also fighting matchwinning innings. On return home he became captain of his State and led Australia from 1968 to 1971 against England (twice), West Indies, India and South Africa. He was in charge of a relatively weak side who were heavily mauled by South Africa in 1970 and lost the Ashes in 1970/71 when Lawry lost the captaincy to Ian Chappell for the final Test. He toured England three times and, in twenty-nine Tests against England alone, made 2,233 runs (48.54). At home in 1965/6 he three times stood between England and the decisive advantage that presages victory, scoring more runs than anyone else in the series: 592 (84.57). In the first Test at Brisbane he made 166, adding 187 with Doug Walters after four

Bill Lawry

wickets had fallen very cheaply; and in the fourth, at Adelaide, he put on 244 for the first wicket with his captain Bobby Simpson (by themselves they passed England's 241). In his day the hardest Australian batsman to dismiss, Lawry averaged 55.11 in the series against South Africa in 1963/4, his 157 in the second Test at Melbourne being an especially good innings. His highest Test score was 210 against West Indies in the fourth Test at Bridgetown in 1964/5 when he put on 382 with Bobby Simpson for the first wicket; they were the first opening pair in Test history to score double centuries in the same innings. He averaged 52.57 for the Tests and 65.92 for the tour. His career-highest score was 266 for Victoria against New South Wales at Sydney in 1960/61. Highly effective he was, as all these figures prove, but he was often a rather colourless cricketer to watch. Originally a plumber, he has devoted more time to his hobby of racing pigeons, since retiring from cricket.

First-class career (1955-71): 18,734 (50.90) including 50 centuries, and 121 catches
Test matches (67): 5,234 runs (47.15) including 13 centuries, 0-6 and 30 catches

LAWSON, Geoffrey Francis (b.1957)

New South Wales and Lancashire

A tall, slim, raw-boned fast bowler and hard-hitting batsman, Geoff Lawson interrupted his degree course in optometry at the University of New South Wales to tour India (as a replacement) and Pakistan at each end of the 1979/80 season. He had come to prominence with some lively performances in the previous season. He dismissed Geoff Boycott in the match between New South Wales and England at Sydney in 1979/80 and also unleashed a series of bouncers at him in the second innings, earning a reprimand from the umpire. In that season he took 34 wickets (20.97) and five times took 4 or more wickets in an innings. He had little opportunity in Pakistan but won his first cap against New Zealand at Brisbane in 1980/81. Despite taking 1 for 39 and 2 for 26 in a comfortable Australian win he was considered to have sacrificed accuracy for hostility and lost his place immediately, but he was picked to tour England in 1981 as a replacement for the injured Len Pascoe. He had already had experience in England, having taken 94 wickets for Heywood in the Central Lancashire League in 1979, and he played in one first-class match for Lancashire against Cambridge University. This experience stood him in good stead on the 1981 tour until a back injury ruled him out of the remainder of the tour after three Tests. Perhaps he overstrained himself at Lord's where, in the first England innings, he took 7 for 81, figures only surpassed in a Lord's Test for Australia by Bob Massie. He was fast, persistent and hostile. He played only one Test at home in 1981/2 when his back had mended, but on a disastrous Australian tour of Pakistan in 1982/3 he was the outstanding bowler, taking 9 wickets in the three Tests at 33 each.

First-class career (1977-): 568 runs (12.08), 176 wickets (24.21)
Test matches (8): 146 runs (13.27), 25 wickets (28.60) and 1 catch

Geoff Lawson

LEE, Philip Keith (1904-80)

South Australia

A batsman who liked to attack and an off-spin bowler with good control and shrewd knowledge of flight, Phil Lee was particularly successful for his State against the first West Indian tourists in 1930/31. His Tests, however, were limited to one each against South Africa in 1931/2 and England in 1932/3. In forty Sheffield Shield matches he scored 1,053 runs (15.48) and took 115 wickets (30.41). He was also a gifted football and baseball player.

First-class career (1925-35): 1,669 runs (18.54) including 2 centuries, and 152 wickets (30.16)
Test matches (2): 57 runs (19.00), 5 wickets (42.40) and 1 catch

LILLEE, Dennis Keith (b.1949)

Western Australia

Indisputably Dennis Lillee is one of the greatest fast bowlers in history and no one has taken so many Test wickets. A glorious action has been at the heart of his

Dennis Lillee

success. In addition, Lillee has a fine physique, courage and burning determination, exceptional stamina and a belligerence which sometimes amounts almost to hatred. Some fast bowlers go about their business with a silent menace – Andy Roberts, Brian Statham, Jeff Thomson, Lindwall himself – some with histrionics and occasional invective, although with the likes of a Fred Trueman the ostentatious fire and brimstone is part bluff, part acting for the gallery. Lillee too is a great showman, but all too often has appeared to show a really vicious streak. Starting with Western Australia in 1969/70, he took 32 Shield wickets in eight matches, then 18 wickets at 16 each on the tour of New Zealand which followed. As Australia rebuilt with the loss of the Ashes imminent in 1970/71 he bowled with hostility, but without his later control, in his first two Test matches, the last two of that series, starting with 5 for 84 on his debut at Adelaide. In 1971 he broadened his experience playing for Haslingden in the Lancashire League, and in 1971/2 showed his growing maturity by taking 23 wickets in four matches against the Rest of the World in Australia, including a devastating 8 for 29 in 7.1 overs downwind on the fast Perth pitch. He was now approaching the first of his peaks, a controlled fast bowler with a long run leading to a magnificent final leap and a full-blooded, no-holds-barred delivery. Dark, moustached, with an eagle's eyes and an eagle's beak for a nose, he provided a splendid spectacle for watchers, a fearsome one for batsmen. Moreover he varied the direction of his swing and his speed intelligently. He took 31 wickets in the five Tests in 1972, a record for an Australian bowler in England. At The Oval he took 10 for 81 in an Australian victory which ushered in a new era of success. However, he broke down in the West Indies with stress fractures in the back and, after spending six weeks in plaster, had a long fight back to fitness before joining forces with Jeff Thomson in 1974/5 to demoralize England with one of the most destructive fast-bowling partnerships in history. Making ferocious use of the bouncer, he took 25 wickets (23.84) and 21 wickets (21.90) in the Tests in England in 1975. He also won the Centenary Test for Australia at Melbourne in 1977, with 6 for 26 and 5 for 139. A useful tail-end batsman who plays very straight, he scored a fine 73 not out to rescue Australia at Lord's in 1975. After the disbandment of World Series Cricket, in which he played such a prominent part, Lillee returned to the Test arena and to new triumphs. Superbly fit, he seemed to have lost very little pace, and his control of swing and cut, allied to his bristling aggression at all times, discomforted batsmen of all nationalities (but especially English ones), as he passed Richie Benaud in 1980/81 to become the highest wicket-taker in Australian Test history. His chief successes in 1979/80 were against England. He took 23 wickets (16.86) in the three Tests but spoilt this fine bowling with a public display of arrogant ill-humour at Perth when the umpires ordered him to change the aluminium bat he was using for a wooden one. The match was held up for ten minutes, and the episode ended with Lillee throwing the bat twenty yards. He was widely believed to be deliberately seeking publicity for the new bat, which he was involved in promoting. He escaped with an official reprimand. Against the West Indies he was less successful (12 wickets at 30.41) and on the short tour of Pakistan his 3 Test wickets cost 101 runs apiece. But in England for the Centenary Test his 4 for 43 helped to bowl England out cheaply in the first innings and in the 1980/81 season he was consistently successful with 16 wickets in three Tests against New Zealand and 21 wickets in three more against India. He passed Benaud's 248 wickets in the third Test against India at Melbourne in his forty-eighth match for Australia. The next landmark, Lance Gibbs's all-time Test record of 309 wickets, was reached with remarkable rapidity. Despite suffering a bout of viral pneumonia at the start of the 1981 tour of England, he took 39 wickets (22.30) in the six Tests and in the first Test against West Indies in Melbourne in 1981/2 – his 58th Test for Australia – he dismissed his 310th victim, Larry Gomes. A tour to New Zealand at the end of another crowded season enabled him to take his haul to 328. Sadly he marred these admirable performances by again losing his temper in the middle of a Perth Test, aiming a public kick at the Pakistan captain Javed Miandad. Further controversy surrounded his admission that he and Rodney Marsh had placed a bet on Australia to lose the 1981 Headingley Test. The odds against an England win at the time were 500 to one. Lillee won £5,000 having, as usual, played his heart out for his beloved country. His earnings from the game, considerable since the intervention of Kerry Packer, were further boosted by a national testimonial in 1981/2.

First-class career (1969-): 2,038 runs (14.25) and 747 wickets (22.38)
Test matches (63): 872 runs (13.62), 328 wickets (23.07) and 19 catches

LINDWALL, Raymond Russell (b.1921)

New South Wales and Queensland

In his youth Ray Lindwall and his friends bowled vigorously at paraffin-tins in the street down which Bill O'Reilly made his way home, hoping to catch the great man's eye; and he also watched Harold Larwood bowling in the 1932/3 series. Five feet ten inches, with broad chest and shoulders, he rose to rank with the great fast bowlers and, for a decade after the Second World War, his partnership with Keith Miller became legendary. His low-slung run to the wicket had a slow start, then an arm-pumping acceleration which brought him smoothly to his delivery and follow-through. He had genuine pace, a great variety of swing and speed, good control and the 'killer' spirit, though he bowled the bouncer relatively rarely – a surprise weapon, which was often lethal. His 'stock' delivery was the late out-swinger. He was also a distinctly useful batsman, who could hit the ball effectively through the covers and who played some invaluable innings. In Tests his return of wickets was the best by any Australian fast bowler this century. He toured England in 1948, 1953 and 1956, also South Africa, the West Indies and New Zealand; and from 1946 until 1958 he was a first choice at home. In twenty-nine Tests against England alone he took 114 wickets (22.44), besides scoring 795 runs (22.08). On the 1948 England tour crowds who had been starved of a really great fast bowler gave him a tumultuous reception and in the Tests he captured 27 wickets (19.62), including one of the most remarkable spells of bowling in the whole series between the two countries, 6 for 20 at The Oval in the fifth match, England falling for 52. When England were fighting back in the third Test at Melbourne in 1946/7, Lindwall hit 100, adding 154 with Don Tallon for the eighth wicket in eighty-eight minutes. Against India in 1947/8 he took more wickets than anyone on either side, 18 (16.88) including 7 for 38 in the second innings of the fourth match at Adelaide. His 7 for 43 in the second innings at Madras won Australia's first Test in India, 1956/7. Against West Indies in Australia in 1951/2 he took 21 wickets (23.04) and made 211 runs in the five matches. In the West Indies his twenty Test wickets were expensive, but in the fourth match at Bridgetown he slammed the wilting bowlers for 118. Most of his cricket was played at the highest level, on the best wickets and against strong opposition. His skill, unaccompanied by histrionics, was something for the connoisseur to savour. He reached his first hundred Test wickets after twenty-six matches and his second hundred after fifty-two matches. He led Australia once against India in 1956/7 and Queensland from 1955 until 1960. He was awarded the MBE for his services to Australian cricket, and now partners his wife in a flourishing florist business in Brisbane.

Ray Lindwall

First-class career (1941-61): 5,042 runs (21.82) including 5 centuries, 794 wickets (21.35) and 123 catches
Test matches (61): 1,502 runs (21.15) including 2 centuries, 228 wickets (23.03) and 26 catches

LOVE, Hampden Stanley Bray (1895-1969)

Victoria and New South Wales

'Hammy' Love was a very sound wicket-keeper and safe right-handed batsman who dealt largely in deflections. Replacing Bert Oldfield, who had been disabled in the previous Test, he played once for Australia, against England in the fourth match at Brisbane in 1932/3, scoring 5 and 3 and holding 3 catches.

First-class career (1919-35): 2,906 runs (35.01) including 7 centuries, and 102 dismissals (73 ct, 29 st.)

LOXTON, Samuel John Everett (b.1921)

Victoria

Looking like a boxer, with a chin jutting out belligerently not unlike Humphrey Bogart's, Sam Loxton played some glorious swashbuckling innings. His reply when told the fast bowlers would bounce the ball at his head was characteristic: 'If they do I'll hit them over the fence.' A right-hander, he also bowled as fast as he could – fast-medium – for long periods; he could move the ball in the air and was a useful accessory to a powerful Australian attack. In the field he was a fast mover and an accurate thrower. He toured England in 1948 and South Africa in 1949/50, and managed the team to India and Pakistan in 1959/60 (playing one match). At home he played against India and England. In England in 1948 he made 973 runs (57.23), including three forceful centuries; and he appeared in three Tests primarily as a batsman. In the fourth at Leeds he struck five sixes in his first innings score of 93 which occupied only two and a quarter hours, when runs were badly needed. In his first Test against South Africa, at Johannesburg in 1949/50, he hit 101 in two and a half hours, again when runs were needed. He toured India with the Commonwealth team in 1953/4. Sam Loxton entered national politics, becoming a member of the Australian Parliament as a Liberal-Country member. He has served as a member of the Test Selection Committee since 1972. In sixty-six Sheffield Shield matches he made 3,157 runs (36.28) and took 133 wickets (23.57).

First-class career (1946-59): 6,249 runs (36.97) including 13 centuries, and 232 wickets (25.73)
Test matches (12): 554 runs (36.93) including 1 century, 8 wickets (43.62) and 7 catches

LYONS, John James (1863-1927)

South Australia

'J.J.' Lyons was a very hard-hitting right-handed opener, a quick-footed driver, especially on a hard, true wicket. But when the ball was turning, he was generally an easy victim for a spin bowler. He toured England in 1888, 1890 and 1893, and was at his best during his last tour. He made 1,605 runs (28.37) and at Lord's in May he played the most brilliant innings of his career. The touring team needed 181 against a powerful MCC eleven, and got them without losing a wicket, J.J. scoring 149 in ninety minutes, his century coming in an hour. He had a penchant for Lord's: during the Test of 1890 he hit 55 out of 66 in forty-five minutes on the first morning and, later, took 5 for 30 with his change-bowling; against MCC he struck 99 out of 117 in seventy-five minutes; and in 1893, in two games against MCC, he scored 149 out of 181 in ninety minutes and 83 out of 117 in a hundred minutes respectively. At home he appeared in Tests between 1886 and 1898, heading the averages in 1891/2 with 287 runs (47.83) in the three matches, including a quick 134 in the second innings at Sydney. Australia, 162 behind and batting again, were indebted to J.J. and A.C. Bannerman for putting on 174 for the second wicket – and the match was ultimately won; J.J. reached his hundred out of 129 and batted for about three hours altogether. In twenty-nine Sheffield Shield matches he made 1,826 runs (33.20).

First-class career (1884-1900): 6,792 runs (25.53) including 11 centuries, and 107 wickets (21.14)
Test matches (14): 731 runs (27.07) including 1 century, 6 wickets (24.83) and 3 catches

McALISTER, Percy Alexander (1869-1938)

Victoria

A Test selector, Percy McAlister toured England in 1909 as vice-captain and opening batsman. A veteran, he had appeared six times against England in 1903/4 and 1907/8, and on tour scored 816 runs though he achieved little in the Tests. A tall, spare, right-handed batsman, he played in forty Sheffield Shield matches and made 2,398 runs (32.40). Active for many years in cricket administration, he sided with the Board of Control in the 1911/12 controversy and was involved in a fist-fight in the Selection Committee room, the provoked Australian captain, Clem Hill, punching him on the nose. His career-highest was 224 for Victoria against New Zealand at Melbourne in 1898/9.

First-class career (1898-1910): 4,552 runs (32.74) including 9 centuries
Test matches (8): 252 runs (16.80) and 10 catches

MACARTNEY, Charles George (1886-1958)

New South Wales and Otago

A little man but a great batsman, Charles Macartney, known as the 'Governor General', developed an artistry which charmed spectators and drove bowlers to distraction. A right-handed batsman, he was a brilliant improviser, though his risks were calculated and even Bradman did not dominate bowlers more ruthlessly than Macartney in his prime. He was short, square-shouldered, with forearms formidably strong, chin aggressive and eyes perpetually alive. He would dart down the pitch to drive, or go right back to hook or cut. By nature confident and a little cocky, he was always looking for runs and never resisted a challenge. 'I can't bear watching luscious half-volleys being nudged gently back to bowlers!' he would exclaim when he became a spectator. At the outset he was played more for his bowling than his batting. On his first tour of England in 1909, he took 71 wickets (17.46) and scored only 638 runs in forty innings. Taking a long run for one of his slow left-arm pace, he had excellent control and could produce an unexpected faster one. He was an excellent fielder, with few equals at mid-off. Besides 1909, he toured England in 1912, 1921 and 1926 and South Africa in 1921/2; and between 1907 and 1921 played in four series at home, three times against England and once against South Africa. He won the third Test at Headingley in 1909 by taking 11 for 85; but against the 1910/11 South Africans he first blazed as a batsman. He hit a century in each innings for New South Wales against the tourists, and in the fifth Test at Sydney, opening the batting for the first time, scored 137 and 56. At Lord's in the first Test of 1912 he struck hard for 99. A year later he hit 2,390 runs and captured 180 wickets in an unofficial Australian visit to America; and after the First World War, usually at first wicket down, he rarely failed at the highest level. Against England in 1920/21 he headed the averages with 86.66 from two Tests, including 170 in the fifth match at Sydney. In England in 1921 he averaged 42.85 in the five Tests and in all first-class matches made 2,335 runs (58.37), including eight centuries, the highest being a punishing 345 in one day (less than four hours) against Nottinghamshire at Trent Bridge, the third of four centuries in successive innings. In reaching 115 in the third Test at Headingley, he hit a century before lunch on the first day. That winter in South Africa he averaged 73 in the Tests. Back in England for the last time in 1926 he headed the batting with 473 runs (94.60) in the Tests, including 133 not out, 151 and 109 in successive innings. Missed by the England captain before he had scored in the third match at Headingley, he added 235 with Bill Woodfull for the second wicket – again scoring his century before lunch on the first day (going on to 151).

Charles Macartney

First-class career (1905-35): 15,019 runs (45.78) including 49 centuries, 419 wickets (20.96) and 102 catches

Test matches (35): 2,131 runs (41.78) including 7 centuries, 45 wickets (27.55) and 17 catches

McCABE, Stanley Joseph (1910-68)

New South Wales

A right-hander of the highest class, Stan McCabe's batting had a daring and cavalier gaiety about it; his great innings lived on in the imagination. He was short, stockily built, strong and extremely agile. His stance and strokes were perfectly balanced and he specialized in the drive, late-cut and hook. An all-rounder, he was an accurate fastish-medium bowler, who occasionally produced a googly, and he opened the bowling in a Test on several occasions. He fielded magnificently anywhere until suffering, late in his career, from sore feet. By then, he had been the cause of many sore feet amongst his opponents! First representing his State at the age of eighteen, he toured England in 1930 (as the 'baby' of the side), 1934 and 1938, and South Africa in 1935/6; and he appeared at home in four series between 1930 and 1937. On the first tour he averaged 35 in the Tests and took eight inexpensive wickets. His first-class matches in 1934 brought him 2,094 runs (67.54), including eight centuries, only twelve runs less than Bradman, the headline-stealer. In his short Test career he continued to shine. In the Bodyline Series he was second to Bradman, averaging 42.77, in the 1934 series third to Bill Ponsford and Bradman when he made 483 runs (60.37). In 1936/7 he was second to Bradman with 491 runs (54.55) and in the 1938 series, his last, he averaged 45.25. Usually batting at number four, Stan McCabe played three innings which will never be forgotten, such was their heroic stature. In the first Test at Sydney, 1932/3, he defied the fearsome Larwood with 187 not out. In South Africa, 1935/6, in the second Test at Johannesburg he scored 189 not out. And in the first Test at Trent Bridge in 1938 he scored 232 (out of 300) in less than four hours in the face of a huge England total. This was the famous occasion when Bradman begged his team not to miss a ball for, he said, they would never again see batting to equal it. On Stan's return to the pavilion Bradman said to him, 'If I could play an innings like that, I'd be a proud man, Stan!' He had the phenomenal average of 438 in the Sheffield Shield matches of 1931/2. He hit 229 not out against Queensland at Brisbane. In thirty-seven Sheffield Shield matches he made 3,031 runs (55.10) and took 49 wickets (24.08). He did not return to first-class cricket after the Second World War, becoming a successful seller of sporting equipment until dying tragically in a fall from a cliff near his home in Sydney.

Stan McCabe

First-class career (1928-41): 11,951 runs (49.39) including 29 centuries, and 159 wickets (33.72)
Test matches (39): 2,748 runs (48.21) including 6 centuries, 36 wickets (42.86) and 41 catches

McCOOL, Colin Leslie (b.1915)

New South Wales, Queensland and Somerset

Short but powerful, Colin McCool was a right-handed stroke-playing batsman, at his best when playing his natural attacking game, a leg-break bowler with something of a round-arm delivery but a shrewd control, and a safe catcher at slip. He was handicapped by the tendency of the skin to rub off his spinning finger. He took the last New Zealand wicket at Wellington with his second ball in Tests to give Australia the victory in the first post-War Test of 1946; and against England in 1946/7 he scored 272 runs (54.40) and took 18 wickets (27.27) in the five matches, his 104 not out in the third match at Melbourne saving Australia from collapse, and his 5 for 44 in England's second innings of 186 in the fifth match at Sydney bringing the victory. He appeared against India in the first series between the two countries; toured England in 1948, doing well all round but not appearing in a Test; and toured South Africa in 1949/50. He came to England as a professional in the East Lancashire League and qualified for Somerset in 1956, when a new, highly successful, career began. In five seasons he exceeded 1,000 runs four times, his 1,966 runs (37.80) in 1956 being the best, and his best bowling feat was 8 for 74 against Nottinghamshire at Trent Bridge in 1958. His career-highest score was 172 for Queensland against South Australia at Adelaide in 1945/6.

First-class career (1939-60): 12,420 runs (32.85) including 18 centuries, 602 wickets (27.48), 262 catches and 2 stumpings
Test matches (14): 459 runs (35.30) including 1 century, 36 wickets (26.61) and 14 catches

McCORMICK, Ernest Leslie (b.1906)

Victoria

Tall and slim, Ernie McCormick measured out a run of thirty-one paces. He had real, venomous pace when creaking joints or lumbago left him free to bowl at his top speed, and he brought the ball very awkwardly into the batsman but never mastered away-swing. His approach was unusual in that he carried the ball as he ran without swinging his arms. He toured South Africa in 1935/6, taking 15 wickets (27.86) in the Tests; and in his first Test against England, at Brisbane in 1936/7, he was menacing and hostile in the opening overs – sending back Stan Worthington with the first ball of the match and soon afterwards Walter Hammond for a duck. Then lumbago took charge and never again, except briefly at Lord's in 1938, was he able to bowl with such fire. He was no-balled (for overstepping) thirty-five times during his first match in England, at Worcester in 1938. An inveterate joker, he told a sympathizer at lunch that day at Worcester, 'It's all right. The umpire is hoarse; he can't call any more!' The English turf did not suit him and it was said in 1938 that he was faster through the air than off the pitch. He batted left-handed and moderately.

First-class career (1929-38): 582 runs (8.68) and 241 wickets (27.74)
Test matches (12): 54 runs (6.00), 36 wickets (29.97) and 8 catches

McCOSKER, Richard Bede (b.1946)

New South Wales

A tall, dark, broad-shouldered opening batsman from the diamond-mining area of Inverell in northern New South Wales, Rick McCosker came to Sydney to take a job in a bank and advance his cricket career. He is a player with a solid defence, considerable powers of concentration and unerring ability to hit away any ball straying towards the leg-side. After a long struggle to get into the State side, he made four centuries in four successive Shield matches and two fifties against MCC, to earn a Test cap at the age of twenty-eight in the fourth game at Sydney in 1974/5 when Australia regained the Ashes. Opening the batting (having gone in first wicket down for New South Wales) he made a solid 80 in his first Test innings and 202 runs (40.40) in five innings overall. Thereafter he was a regular member of the Australian side until he left to join World Series Cricket. Perhaps troubled by the unsettling nature of the controversy, and by memories of breaking his jaw when missing a hook at Bob Willis during the Centenary Test (coming back with his jaw wired up he made some courageous runs late in Australia's second innings which helped to decide the game), he was disappointing in England in 1977, apart from a fine innings of 107 at Trent Bridge. But in 1975 he topped the Test averages with 414 runs in four matches (82.80) and he hit four centuries on the tour, scoring 1,078 runs at 59.88. A quiet and modest character, clean-shaven and short-haired, he stood out in an Australian side which tended to be hirsute and extrovert. After two years with World Series Cricket Rick McCosker returned to captain New South Wales and play in three more Tests in 1979/80, two against England and one against the West Indies. In these matches he did not seem quite the player he had been but for New South Wales he hit two Shield hundreds and looked, as ever, a difficult man to dislodge, seldom pretty but highly effective.

First-class career (1973-): 7,107 runs (43.33) including 23 centuries, and 109 catches
Test matches (25): 1,622 runs (39.56) including 4 centuries, and 21 catches

Rick McCosker

Colin McDonald – David Sheppard (England) fielding

McDONALD, Colin Campbell (b.1928)

Victoria

A fighter, but a true 'sport', Colin McDonald was a most able right-handed opening batsman. Despite a short backlift he was strong off the back foot, and a shrewd judge of when to play a shot to the swinging ball. He was a regular choice for his country from 1951 until 1961. He toured England in 1953, 1956 and 1961, South Africa, the West Indies, India and Pakistan; and he appeared in five series at home, two against England. He had a first poor tour of England, but averaged 34.34 and 48.05 respectively in all first-class matches on his second and third tours. Indeed he developed into a scourge of England. His opening stand of 137 with Jim Burke in the 1956 Lord's Test set Australia on the way to victory and he alone threatened to prevent Jim Laker from performing his miracle at Old Trafford, when he scored 32 out of 84 and 89 out of 205. He was ahead of everyone else with 519 runs (64.87) in 1958/9, including 170 in the fourth Test at Adelaide, his Test-highest. He had another highly successful series against South Africa in 1952/3, when he made 437 runs (48.55), including 154, again in the fourth Test at Adelaide. His final home series, against West Indies in 1960/61, saw him bearing the brunt of Wesley Hall's speed with great courage. His 91 in the fifth match was valuable in deciding the rubber for Australia. He captained his State from 1958 until 1963 and in forty-nine Sheffield Shield matches made 3,237 runs (43.16), including his career-highest of 229 against South Australia at Adelaide in 1953/4. In fifteen Tests against England alone he made 1,043 runs (38.62). After retiring he worked for some time in north Queensland, before taking a senior job with the Australian Lawn Tennis Association.

First-class career (1947-62): 11,375 runs (40.48) including 24 centuries
Test matches (47): 3,107 runs (39.32) including 5 centuries, 0-3 and 14 catches

McDONALD, Edgar Arthur (1892-1937)

Tasmania, Victoria and Lancashire

A natural athlete, tall, strongly but not heavily built, 'Ted' McDonald ran some sixteen yards easily to the crease, and with his rhythmical action, accurate length, exceptional pace and ability to move the ball either way was one of a dominating pair of fast bowlers, the other being Jack Gregory, who proved altogether too good for England in 1921. After taking 8 for 42 for Victoria against New South Wales at Sydney in 1918/19, in conditions favourable to the bat, McDonald took only six very expensive wickets in the 1920/21 series; but, in the following summer, 'Gregory and McDonald' were the bane of practically all England's batsmen. In the first Test at Trent Bridge he had a match record of 8 for 74, and at Lord's and Headingley his early break-throughs led to decisive victories. He took 27 wickets (24.74) in the series, and in South Africa in 1921/2 collected 10 wickets from three Tests. But, in accepting a professional post with Nelson in Lancashire, he deserted Australian cricket, and qualified for Lancashire, spearheading the attack with great aplomb when the county was Champion in 1926, 1927, 1928 and 1930. In eight seasons (1924-31) he collected 1,040 wickets for Lancashire, also representing Players against Gentlemen. He took 205 wickets (18.67) in 1925, and 190 wickets (19.75) in 1928. Usually of small account as a batsman, he made a century in a hundred minutes against Middlesex at Old Trafford in 1926. A calm, detached cricketer of few words, he would often merely go through the motions of bowling fast against modest opposition but when a class player such as Hobbs or Bradman was at the other end he would suddenly produce a spell of bowling as fast as anything seen before or since. He was killed in the aftermath of a car accident: having accidentally crashed his car, he staggered into the road waving for traffic to stop and was run down by another car.

First-class career (1909-35): 2,663 runs (10.44) including 1 century, and 1,395 wickets (20.76)
Test matches (11): 116 runs (16.57), 43 wickets (33.27) and 3 catches

McDONNELL, Percy Stanislaus (1860-96)

Victoria, New South Wales and Queensland

The only captain of Australia who was also a Greek scholar, 'Percy Greatheart' McDonnell was an attacking right-handed batsman with a strong defence. With a keen eye and remarkable footwork he was regarded as an even better batsman on bad wickets than on good. Contemporary critics considered that his sterling performances on wickets ruined by rain had never been equalled. He toured England in 1880, 1882, 1884 and finally as captain in 1888. Between 1881 and 1887 he represented his country fairly regularly at home when his medical studies allowed. When he was captain – 1886/7, 1887/8 and 1888 – England's cricket was in the ascendent, but McDonnell's fearless hitting frequently turned the tide; his greatest achievement being an innings of 82 with which he won the game against North of England at Old Trafford in 1888. His 147 in a low-scoring game against England in the third Test at Sydney in 1881/2 earned a six-wicket victory. In successive Tests in 1884 he hit 103 at The Oval and 124 and 83 at Adelaide in the first Test of the next series. His Test averages were quite prodigious for those years. He made 302 runs (50.33) in 1881/2, 230 runs (57.50) in 1884/5 and in England in 1884 he averaged 39.75. His career-highest score was 239 for New South Wales against Victoria at Melbourne in 1886/7.

First-class career (1877-95): 6,470 runs (23.52) including 7 centuries, and 99 catches
Test matches (19): 950 runs (28.78) including 3 centuries, 0-53 and 6 catches

McILWRAITH, John (1857-1938)

Victoria

A hard-hitting right-handed batsman, John McIlwraith toured England in 1886 when he averaged only 15 and in his sole Test, the third at The Oval, scored 2 and 7 and held one catch. He had made 133 on his debut in first-class cricket, for Victoria against New South Wales at Melbourne in 1885/6.

First-class career (1884-9): 1,468 runs (24.06) including 2 centuries

MACKAY, Kenneth Donald (1925-82)

Queensland

A left-hander of infinite patience and solid skill despite an ungainly style, 'Slasher' Mackay was for a decade the most difficult batsman in Australia to dismiss. He was at his best and most frustrating when Australia were in trouble. He was also a useful right-arm medium-pace bowler with a strange, almost furtive approach to the wicket. He was one of the earliest and most vigorous of gum-chewers. While at school, he had shown outstanding promise, in one match scoring 364 not out and taking 10 wickets. His career-highest score, 223 for his State against Victoria at Brisbane in 1953/4, took him nine hours and forty-five minutes; and his next innings was an almost equally patient 198

'Slasher' Mackay during his match-saving innings at Adelaide in 1961 – West Indians Gerry Alexander keeping wicket and Gary Sobers at leg-slip

against Western Australia on the same ground. He toured England in 1956 and 1961 and South Africa, India and Pakistan; and at home played in the series against England in 1958/9 and 1962/3, and against the West Indies in 1960/61. He took 6 for 42 against Pakistan at Dacca in 1959/60 and, although he never scored a Test century, made thirteen Test fifties. He was very good at the 'bits and pieces'. On the first visit in 1956 he could make little of Jim Laker – but fought well and headed the averages for the whole tour, 52.52 for 1,103 runs. Resisting valiantly in the Test at Lord's which Australia won, he took 264 minutes over his 35, and he saved Australia with another long innings against the West Indies at Adelaide in 1961. In a hundred Sheffield Shield matches he made 6,341 runs (44.97) and took 122 wickets (37.54).

First-class career (1946-63): 10,823 runs (43.64) including 23 centuries, and 252 wickets (33.18)
Test matches (37): 1,507 runs (33.48), 50 wickets (34.42) and 17 catches

McKENZIE, Graham Douglas (b.1941)

Western Australia and Leicestershire

Truly a 'gentle giant', Graham or 'Garth' McKenzie was a Rolls-Royce amongst modern fast bowlers – smooth and classy. He was a modest but often useful right-hand batsman and a safe and athletic fielder in the deep. About six feet and of superb physique – he was nicknamed after the sizeable comic strip character – he had an economical run-up that seemed all muscular ease and a classic final stretch in his sideways-on delivery. He swung the ball late, away from the right-hander and he was often at his best on good wickets where he was able to combine genuine fast bowling with a deceptive change of pace. He 'hit the deck' hard and the lift off the pitch was often too much for the best batsmen. Geoff Boycott had his forearm broken by his bowling, and the West Indian Jackie Hendriks had to be taken to hospital for brain surgery after being struck by one of his deliveries. But they were accidents; he was a gentleman on and off the field who never abused his strength and speed. He toured England in 1961, 1964 and 1968, South Africa twice, India twice, and the West Indies and Pakistan once each. Between 1962 and 1971 he appeared in seven series at home, including three against England. He also toured India, South Africa and Rhodesia with the International Cavaliers. At twenty-three he became the youngest Australian bowler ever to take 100 wickets in Tests and in the shortest time – three years 165 days. He was also the youngest to reach 150 wickets (against South Africa in 1966/7) and, at twenty-seven, the youngest to take 200 wickets (against the West Indies in 1968/9). His number of wickets in Tests was only two short of the record held by Richie Benaud and these he would surely have obtained if he had not been dropped for the last two Tests against India in 1967/8. He had taken 10 for 151 in the third Test at Melbourne and was then rested because Australia's selectors wanted to give others a chance. McKenzie had many memorable performances. He took 7 for 153 out of an England total of 611 at Old Trafford in 1964. In Australia's victory at Lord's in 1961 he took five wickets in each innings and

Graham McKenzie

was at the crease when the last two wickets put on 149, himself making 34 vital runs. It was not his only important innings: in the same series at Old Trafford he put on 98 for the last wicket with Alan Davidson to turn the match; and in the third Test at Sydney against South Africa in 1963/4 he made 76. From 1969 until 1975 he was registered for Leicestershire and in his last season his adopted county won the Championship for the first time. Altogether, he took 465 wickets and scored 1,830 runs for Leicestershire in first-class cricket.

First-class career (1959-75): 5,662 runs (15.39), 1,218 wickets (26.98) and 200 catches
Test matches (60): 945 runs (12.27), 246 wickets (29.78) and 34 catches

McKIBBIN, Thomas Robert (1870-1939)

New South Wales

A man of frank, happy character and the possessor of a flowing moustache, Tom McKibbin toured England in 1896, and his delivery raised such criticism that it was written 'there can be little doubt that he continually threw when putting on his off-break'; but he played for Australia from 1894 until 1898 and does not appear to have been actually called by the umpire for 'throwing'. Of medium height but powerfully built, he could be legitimately deadly with his right-handed slow to medium bowling when he kept a length. In England he took 101 wickets (14.27), including 11 wickets in the two Tests he played. Against Lancashire at Aigburth, bowling unchanged with Hugh Trumble, he took 13 for 38, Lancashire falling for 28 in the second innings, when his analysis was 7 for 11, including a hat-trick. (Frank Sugg did not attempt to play one that came back a prodigious amount on to the stumps, which he thought was a palpable throw.) In eighteen Sheffield Shield matches his tally was 136 wickets (20.50).

First-class career (1894-98): 686 runs (10.04) and 319 wickets (19.73)
Test matches (5): 88 runs (14.66), 17 wickets (29.17) and 4 catches

McLAREN, John William (1887-1921)

Queensland

A fast bowler, John McLaren toured England with the weakened Australian team of 1912, as replacement for Albert Cotter, but took only 27 wickets and did not appear in any of the Tests. His sole Test appearance was in the fifth match at Sydney against England in 1911/12: he was 0 not out in both innings and took 1 for 70. He died young of diabetes.

First-class career (1906-14): 564 runs (12.53) and 107 wickets (26.74)

MACLEAN, John Alexander (b.1946)

Queensland

A product of the University of Queensland and a civil engineer, John Maclean was unfortunate to be selected for Australia when he was past his best, and as a wicket-keeper/batsman it was touch-and-go whether he or Rodney Marsh would be chosen in 1970/71. Throughout the seventies Maclean gave Queensland staunch service, captaining them with enterprise and by fine example in 1972/3 and between 1977 and 1979. Solidly built, he is a limited but determined right-hand batsman, a particularly good cutter, and a surprisingly agile wicket-keeper. First playing for Queensland in 1968/9 he toured New Zealand with the Australians in 1969/70, playing in three representative games not recognized as Tests. But his Tests were played against a confident and all-conquering England side in 1978/9 and, though he brought off some very good catches, his batting proved vulnerable against the off-spinners.

First-class career (1968-79): 3,888 runs (24.45) including 2 centuries, and 385 dismissals (354 ct, 31 st.)
Test matches (4): 79 runs (11.28) and 18 dismissals (18 ct)

McLEOD, Charles Edward (1869-1918)

Victoria

A right-handed batsman of the ultra-careful school, strong in defence but undistinguished in style, Charlie McLeod was also a steady, persistent medium-paced bowler. He played for his country with fair regularity from 1894 until 1905. He toured England with the 1899 and 1905 teams, making 545 runs and taking 81 wickets in the former year and 722 runs and 91 wickets in the latter. In the fifth Test at The Oval in 1899 his 31 not out and 77 did much to save the match. Promoted to opening batsman, he put on 116 with Jack Worrell for the first wicket, when Australia had to follow on 224 behind. In the 1897/8 series, when he opened several times, he came second in the batting with 352 runs (58.66), making 112 in 245 minutes in the second Test at Melbourne, very slow by contemporary but not modern standards. In thirty-three Sheffield Shield matches he made 1,281 runs (23.29) and took 108 wickets (24.63). He was the younger brother of R.W. McLeod.

First-class career (1893-1905): 3,321 runs (21.15) including 2 centuries, and 334 wickets (24.32)
Test matches (17): 573 runs (23.87) including 1 century, 33 wickets (40.15) and 9 catches

McLEOD, Robert William (1868-1907)

Victoria

A steady left-handed batsman and right-arm medium-paced bowler who hurried the ball from the pitch, Bob McLeod toured England with the 1893 side but generally did not enhance his reputation, although at Lord's against MCC he took 5 for 29 in the second innings, the premier club saving the game narrowly. On the tour he averaged 17 with the bat and took 47 wickets. One of his experiences is said to be unique: batting for Melbourne against North Melbourne in the competition final, he was run out in each innings without having a ball bowled to him. His Test cricket was confined to the 1891/2 and 1893 series. In his first Test at Melbourne he took 5 for 55 in the first innings, but achieved little subsequently. He had real ability but, according to some contemporary writers, lacked enthusiasm.

First-class career (1889-99): 1,701 runs (22.38) including 1 century, and 141 wickets (22.73)
Test matches (6): 146 runs (13.27), 12 wickets (32.00) and 3 catches

McSHANE, Patrick George (1857-1903)

Victoria

A contemporary described McShane as 'a very fine left-hand bowler, with great command over the ball, a splendid batsman who had made some fine scores; and a good field'. He achieved some good performances in inter-State matches but never came to England; his short Test career was spread over the 1884/5, 1886/7 and 1887/8 series. Indeed, he umpired the fourth Test in 1884/5 and played in the fifth. While curator (groundsman) to St Kilda C.C. in Melbourne, he became mentally afflicted and had to receive treatment at an asylum.

First-class career (1880-92): 1,117 runs (18.31) and 72 wickets (25.37)
Test matches (3): 26 runs (5.20), 1-48 and 2 catches

MADDOCKS, Leonard Victor (b.1926)

Victoria and Tasmania

Now one of the most influential men on the Australian Cricket Board, Len Maddocks was a very competent wicket-keeper, the best second-string for Australia of his time, and a very useful right-handed batsman. Always a cheerful cricketer, he had the size and appearance of a racehorse jockey. In his first Test innings against England, in the third Test at Melbourne in 1954/5, he top-scored with 47 against Brian Statham and Frank Tyson, enabling his country to take an unexpected first innings lead, and in the next Test at Adelaide he again top-scored with 69, by robust methods and good running adding 92 in ninety-five minutes with his captain Ian Johnson for the ninth wicket. He toured England (in 1956), the West Indies and India without gaining a regular Test place. He toured South Africa with the International Cavaliers. He had the thankless task of managing the team to England in 1977, when he discovered early in the tour that most of his team had secretly signed contracts with Kerry Packer. It was thereafter an unhappy and unsuccessful tour but Maddocks kept smiling and did his best to maintain a united front.

First-class career (1946-67): 4,106 runs (32.84) including 6 centuries, and 277 dismissals (209 ct, 68 st.)
Test matches (7): 177 runs (17.70) and 19 dismissals (18 ct, 1 st.)

MAILEY, Arthur Alfred (1886-1967)

New South Wales

Although of slight physique, Arthur Mailey was a man of many talents and one of the great right-arm leg-break and googly bowlers. He sometimes paid the penalty for poor length, but he had abnormally strong fingers which enabled him to impart tremendous spin. He gave the ball a generous amount of air, cheerfully prepared to 'buy' his wickets. He toured England in 1921 and 1926, and South Africa in 1921/2. At home he played against England in the 1920/21 and 1924/5 series. In his first series of 1920/21 he took 36 wickets (26.27) which remained the largest-ever for an Australian until exceeded by Rodney Hogg in 1978/9. In the fourth match at Melbourne he captured 9 for 121 in the second innings (13 for 236 in the match). In 1924/5 he again had a large, though expensive, haul of 24 wickets (41.62). In England he took 146 wickets (19.61) and 141 wickets (18.70) respectively on his two tours. Outside the Tests his most noteworthy achievement was 10 for 66 in the Gloucestershire second innings at Cheltenham in 1921 which inspired the title of his autobiography *Ten for 66 and All That*, written thirty-seven years later. He also took 9 for 86 in an innings against Lancashire at Aigburth in 1926. Starting his working life as a labourer, Arthur was a wit, philosopher, a very clever cartoonist, painter (in oils) and journalist. He frequently revisited England and South Africa and was one of the best-loved of cricketers. In thirty-seven Sheffield Shield matches he took 180 wickets (24.10).

First-class career (1912-30): 1,529 runs (12.33), 779 wickets (24.10) and 157 catches
Test matches (21): 222 runs (11.10), 99 wickets (33.91) and 14 catches

MALLETT, Ashley Alexander (b.1945)

South Australia

Known as 'Rowdy' because he usually kept his thoughts to himself – although he is now a successful journalist – Ashley Mallett is the best Australian off-

Ashley Mallett

spinner since the War, judged by his success on different types of pitches in different countries – although on three tours of England his tallies were modest. Tall and sinewy, with thin rather strained-looking features, he was a limited right-hand batsman, often difficult to remove, and a fine close fielder, who held 95 catches in first-class cricket including some unbelievable ones in the gully against England in 1974/5. He toured England in 1968, 1972 and 1975 and India and South Africa in 1969/70, taking 28 wickets in five Tests in India. He bowled with a rather flat trajectory but with excellent control of line and length; he deployed a sharp off-break whenever conditions permitted, often with an awkward bounce, and he had a useful away-drifter. It took him a surprisingly long time to establish himself in the Australian Test side, partly because, when he did play, Bill Lawry was reluctant to use him in long spells. After a season in the Scottish Western Union in 1967, during which he took 111 wickets for Ayr, he took 32 wickets in eight games in his first season for South Australia in 1967/8. He played only one Test in 1968, the last at The Oval. But, after an analysis of 13 for 122 against Western Australia in a Shield game at Adelaide in 1971/2, as well as a score of 92 against Western Australia in the season before, he was recalled to the Test side and became virtually a fixture in the successful Ian Chappell side, taking 10 wickets against England in 1972, 17 (19.94) in 1974/5 and 9 (42.88) in 1975. At Adelaide in 1972/3 he took 8 for 59 against Pakistan. His best Test match analysis came during his highly successful tour of India when he took 10 for 144 at Madras. Although not one of those who joined World Series Cricket, Mallett left the first-class game after the 1976/7 season to work as a journalist in South Australia. But he returned in 1979/80 and took 48 wickets (23.75) for his State, winning back the spinning place in the national team for the last two Tests against the West Indies and England. Against the former he bowled with his old control, taking 4 significant wickets on a delightful batting pitch at Adelaide, and although he opted out of the subsequent tour of Pakistan he earned a farewell tour of England in 1980 for the Centenary Test in which he played and took a wicket in each innings. It seemed out of character for him, but in 1981 he was banned for life by the Queensland Cricketers Club for telling blue jokes within the hearing of ladies.

First-class career (1967-81): 2,326 runs (13.60), 693 wickets (26.27) and 105 catches
Test matches (38): 430 runs (11.62), 132 wickets (29.85) and 30 catches

MALONE, Michael Francis (b.1950)

Western Australia and Lancashire

Though he made a very good living from joining World Series Cricket from 1977 to 1979, 'Mick' Malone did himself a grave disservice by missing two years of Test cricket just as he was breaking through. A dark and strapping, right-arm, medium-fast swing bowler with the strength and will to bowl all day, he emerged in 1975/6 when he took 31 Sheffield Shield wickets at 20.58. Next season he took 40 Sheffield Shield wickets (16.13) for Western Australia and 49 wickets in the season, and he was unlucky not to gain selection for more than one Test in England in 1977, for he often bowled better than Max Walker. In this, his sole Test, he took 5 for 63 in England's first innings at The Oval in a fine demonstration of his stamina, strength and ability to swing the ball late away from the bat. In the match he took 6 wickets (12.83) and scored 46 runs (46.00). His action is high and classical, and he can hit the ball effectively. After two years of relative obscurity with WSC, he joined Lancashire at the end of 1979, but his success was limited.

First-class career (1974-): 914 runs (16.03) and 260 wickets (24.77)

MANN, Anthony Longford (b.1945)

Western Australia

A fair-haired all-rounder, slow right-arm leg-break bowler, vigorous left-hand bat and fine fielder, Tony Mann hit an electrifying hundred in his second Test match at Perth against India in 1977/8. Coming in as night-watchman at number 3, he hit 105 and helped win a thrilling game by 2 wickets. But his leg-breaks were ineffective against Indian batsmen used to slow bowling of greater subtlety and he had lost his place by the end of the series. He was a key man in several Western Australian triumphs in the Sheffield Shield.

First-class career (1963-): 2,397 runs (24.21) including 2 centuries, and 188 wickets (23.85)
Test matches (4): 189 runs (23.62) including 1 century, 4 wickets (79.00) and 2 catches

MARR, Alfred Percy (1862-1940)

New South Wales

A useful batsman and bowler, Alfred Marr was one of the 'might have beens': chosen three times to come to England, he was never able to do so. When New South Wales were defeated unexpectedly by Queensland in 1884, he took 8 for 28 unavailingly in the second innings. In his sole Test, the second at Melbourne in 1884/5, he scored 0 and 5 and took 0 for 14. He remained so fit that at 67 he hit 101 in a Sydney grade competition match.

First-class career (1882-90): 304 runs (11.26) and 14 wickets (32.42)

MARSH, Rodney William (b.1947)

Western Australia

Rodney Marsh revealed his quality in his very first match for Western Australia, scoring 106 against the West Indies. Burly and tending in his youth to be distinctly podgy, he survived a baptism of fire in his first Test series of 1970/71 to become one of Australia's finest wicket-keeper/batsmen. In that first series the Australian public dubbed him 'Irongloves' because of the amount of times he dropped the ball, but the germs of a great cricketer were evident even then in his agility, aggressive attitude and rugged strength as a left-hand batsman. He became a regular and vital member of Ian Chappell's successful Australian side, throwing his formidable weight in all directions to take the thunderbolts of Lillee and Thomson, and then coming in at number seven, chewing gum as if he meant to grind it into oblivion, shirt half-open to reveal a hairy chest, to bludgeon often weary bowlers with calculated hitting. An immensely forceful driver, often hitting straight back over the bowler's head, and a ruthless square-cutter of anything short, he can also defend if necessary. Of his three Test hundreds perhaps his best was 110 not out in the Centenary Test in Melbourne. He toured England in 1972, dismissing 45 batsmen and scoring 664 runs (242 in the Tests), also in 1975 (28 dismissals, 464 runs), 1977 (30 dismissals, 477 runs) and 1981 (28 dismissals, 368 runs). It was partly the huge discrepancy between Marsh's earnings as a Test cricketer and those of his brother Graham, a wealthy and successful professional golfer, which persuaded Mr Packer and his associates that cricketers would willingly respond to generous financial offers. Marsh duly joined World Series Cricket then returned to Test cricket, where this indestructible bear of a man continued to be an integral part of the national team. Certainly he remained the outstanding wicket-keeper in Australia although his batting seemed to have lost its assurance and it was not until the eighth match after his return that he scored a fifty. This was in the high scoring second Test against Pakistan at Faisalabad, when Marsh also bowled 10 overs in a match in which only 10 wickets fell to the bowlers. Against India at Sydney in 1980/81 he took 5 catches in the first innings, a record for an Australian wicket-keeper against India. Earlier in the season on his home pitch at Perth he helped to rescue Australia against New Zealand with a fighting 91. Having captained Western Australia for a season, he was replaced by Kim Hughes and became vice-captain to Hughes for the 1981 tour of England. During the momentous Headingley Test of that summer he overtook Alan Knott as the most successful wicket-keeper in Test history. Appropriately enough his 264th victim, Ian Botham, was caught behind off Dennis Lillee, who had accounted for 74 of Marsh's catches. This was the Test in which Marsh and Lillee took bets on an England victory at 500 to one. Australia lost the Test but their two senior players, hard though they tried for their side, won the money. Marsh continued indestructibly through more Test series against Pakistan, West Indies and New Zealand in 1981/2 and against Pakistan and England in 1982/3. Unlike others such as Lillee and Chappell, Marsh

Rodney Marsh

never made himself unavailable for unattractive tours, continuing to fight through thick and thin.

First-class career (1968-): 9,986 runs (31.70) including 10 centuries, and 742 dismissals (684 ct, 58 st.)
Test matches (86): 3,434 runs (27.25) including 3 centuries, and 306 dismissals (294 ct, 12 st.)

MARTIN, John Wesley (b.1931)

South Australia and New South Wales

Short, enthusiastic and jaunty, Johnny Martin was an unorthodox left-arm off-break and googly bowler inclined to be somewhat erratic, an aggressive right-handed batsman and good fielder. A prolific wicket-taker in Australia, he took 45 wickets (23.64) for his State in Sheffield Shield matches in 1959/60, which was the largest number taken in the competition for ten years. Making his Test debut against the West Indies in 1960/61, he scored 55, helping 'Slasher' Mackay add 97 for the ninth wicket in seventy-two minutes; and he also took 3 wickets in 4 balls – those of Rohan Kanhai, Gary Sobers and Frank Worrell – these being his first three wickets in Test cricket. Not selected to tour England in 1961, he instead came over as professional for Colne in the Lancashire League, taking 70 wickets (12.04) and scoring 706 runs (35.30). When he toured England in 1964 he did not make the Test side and, although he represented his country against South Africa and India and Pakistan in the early sixties, he never repeated his initial Test successes. He joined only three other bowlers who had taken 200 wickets for New South Wales; and he travelled 470 miles each week-end from his home to play in Sydney district cricket. In seventy-seven Sheffield Shield matches he made 2,701 runs (27.84) and took 273 wickets (31.92).

First-class career (1956-67): 3,970 runs (23.77) including 1 century, 445 wickets (31.17) and 114 catches
Test matches (8): 214 runs (17.83), 17 wickets (48.94) and 5 catches

MASSIE, Hugh Hamon (1855-1938)

New South Wales

Nearly six feet tall, Hugh Massie was a magnificent right-handed forcing batsman, moving forward to the pitch of the ball whenever possible. Making his Test debut modestly in 1881/2, he was the last man chosen for the 1882 England tour. In the first match, however, at Oxford he opened the batting and thrashed the University's bowling for 206 in three hours – his only century in first-class cricket – scoring his second hundred while his partners were scratching only 12 runs. Later he won undying fame in the Ashes match at The Oval when he flayed the bowling in the second innings on a slowish pitch. Australia had made but 63 and England 101, when Massie struck 55 out of 66 for the first wicket in about forty-five minutes. This fine piece of attacking cricket won the match for Australia by seven runs. He scored 1,403 runs (24.64) on the tour. At home he appeared in the 1882/3 and 1884/5 series, but his duties as a banker prevented him touring again. He was selected to captain Australia in the third Test at Sydney in 1884/5, after two leaders had failed, but he did no better. In 1895 he played some more first-class cricket in England.

First-class career (1877-95): 2,485 runs (23.00) including 1 century
Test matches (9): 249 runs (15.56) and 5 catches

MASSIE, Robert Arnold Lockyer (b.1947)

Western Australia

A right-arm medium-fast bowler, who could swing and cut the ball either way, Bob Massie came like a comet into Test cricket as opening partner for Dennis Lillee. For a while it was believed that Ray Lindwall and Keith Miller would be replaced at last by an established matchwinning pair but Massie faded almost as quickly as he had shone. Coming to England in 1972 after taking 6 for 27 in eleven overs for Australia against the Rest of the World at Sydney, he made an astounding Test debut at Lord's, taking 8 for 84 and 8 for 53, swinging the ball about in humid conditions as if he had string attached to it. Bowling round the wicket, he mesmerized the English batsmen with the late swerve of the ball, and only Jim Laker and

Bob Massie

Sydney Barnes have taken more wickets in a Test. It was the performance of his life. He took only seven wickets in the remaining three Tests and eight wickets in two Tests at home the following season against Pakistan. Although he toured the West Indies in 1973 he could not swing the ball in the thin atmosphere, took only 18 wickets in six games, and his Test career was over. He lost his place in his State side in 1973/4. For some reason he could never recapture the magical power of swing. He unwisely tried to compensate by pushing the ball through faster and this made him easier to play. It was rumoured that he used lip-salve to keep the shine on the ball and that Sir Donald Bradman ordered the practice to stop, but Sir Donald has publicly denied the truth of the story. Two years before Massie achieved fame, he had been rejected by Northamptonshire after being offered a trial when playing in the Scottish League.

First-class career (1965-75): 385 runs (9.62) and 179 wickets (24.83)
Test matches (6): 78 runs (11.14), 31 wickets (20.87) and 1 catch

MATTHEWS, Thomas James (1884-1943)

Victoria

Pint-sized, his skin tanned by continual exposure to the sun, 'as tough as a piece of jarrah', Jimmy Matthews was an honest-to-goodness, right-arm, leg-break bowler, who was accurate, persistent and kept the ball well up to the bat, and a right-handed batsman difficult to shift, tough and without frills. He made his Test debut in 1911/12, making 53 in the third match at Adelaide, and toured England in 1912, the year of the Triangular Tournament, earning his place in history by achieving a hat-trick in each South African innings at Old Trafford: a unique feat in Test cricket. He took 85 wickets (19.37) on the tour. In a short career he played in nineteen Sheffield Shield matches, making 915 runs (29.51) and taking 39 wickets (38.71). After the First World War he became curator of the Williamstown ground, the home of Victoria cricket.

First-class career (1906-14): 2,149 runs (24.98) and 177 wickets (25.46)
Test matches (8): 153 runs (17.00), 16 wickets (26.18) and 7 catches

MAYNE, Edgar Richard (1884-1961)

South Australia and Victoria

A tall and fluent right-handed stroke-maker excelling with the cut and drive, Edgar Mayne needed a fast wicket to display his powers to the full. An opening batsman, he lived for cricket, never shirking his responsibility. He toured England in 1912 and 1921 and South Africa in 1921/2, but only played in four Tests altogether with moderate success. Such was Australia's batting strength in 1921 that, although he averaged 36.33 for the tour, he could not make the Test eleven. He captained both South Australia and Victoria, exceeding 2,300 runs for each State. Making 209, his career-highest, he put on 456 for the first wicket with Bill Ponsford for Victoria against Queensland at Melbourne in 1923/4, which remains the record stand for any Australian wicket in Australia.

First-class career (1906-25): 7,620 runs (32.70) including 14 centuries
Test matches (4): 64 runs (21.33), 0-1 and 2 catches

MAYNE, Laurence Charles (b.1942)

Western Australia

All through the 1960s the Australian opening attack remained unsettled, and briefly Laurie Mayne was tried as opening partner with Graham McKenzie. A right-arm fast-medium bowler, he toured the West Indies in 1965, and South Africa and India in 1969/70, but he was then eclipsed by Dennis Lillee.

First-class career (1961-70): 667 runs (12.83) and 203 wickets (30.35)
Test matches (6): 76 runs (9.50), 19 wickets (33.05) and 3 catches

MECKIFF, Ian (b.1935)

Victoria

A controversial left-arm fast bowler with a strong

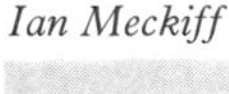

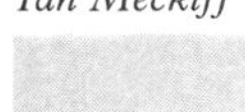

Ian Meckiff

physique, whose casual approach to the crease belied the speed of his delivery, Ian Meckiff toured South Africa in 1957/8, and India and Pakistan in 1959/60 and at home played against England in 1958/9, West Indies in 1960/61, and South Africa in 1963/4. He never toured England – torn tendons in an ankle followed by loss of form caused him to be left out of the 1961 side. It was also believed that his action might not have been passed by English umpires. Certainly there was something unusual about his action and some players and journalists were convinced that he sometimes threw rather than bowled the ball. He took 17 wickets (17.17) in four Tests against England in 1958/9, taking 9 for 107 in the second Test at Melbourne when the suspicions were aired very loudly. This was a disastrous tour for MCC, and Meckiff was not the only bowler accused of an unfair action. Eventually, against South Africa at Brisbane in 1963/4, he was called by umpire Colin Egar for throwing his second, third, fifth and ninth balls, and he was taken off at the end of this his first over, never to play first-class cricket again.

First-class career (1956-63): 778 runs (11.27) and 269 wickets (23.35)
Test matches (18): 154 runs (11.84), 45 wickets (31.62) and 9 catches

MEULEMAN, Kenneth Douglas (b.1923)

Victoria and Western Australia

A sound right-handed opening batsman, very unlucky to miss regular international honours, Meuleman toured New Zealand – the first post-Second World War tour – where he played his sole Test, at Wellington in 1946, being bowled for 0 and holding one catch. He visited New Zealand again in 1949/50, and India with the Commonwealth team in 1953/4. For Western Australia against the South Africans at Perth in 1952/3 he scored 103, assisting in adding 170 for the third wicket, a record for the State. Later he captained Western Australia. His highest score was 234 not out against South Australia at Perth in 1956/7 and he made 206 for Victoria against Tasmania at Melbourne in 1947/8. He was a prolific scorer in Sheffield Shield games, seventy matches bringing him 4,916 runs (48.19).

First-class career (1945-60): 7,855 runs (47.60) including 22 centuries, and 19 wickets (50.31)

MIDWINTER, William Evans (1851-90)

Gloucestershire and Victoria

Born in Gloucestershire, Billy Midwinter is the only cricketer to have played both for and against Australia. He emigrated and became professional at Melbourne. Also an extremely good billiards player, he was known as 'the Bendigo Infant'. A steady right-handed batsman who could hit hard, he was a medium-paced bowler who spun the ball quite considerably and a first-rate outfielder. He appeared in the first-ever Test for Australia at Melbourne, taking 5 for 78 in England's first innings. He commuted between Victoria and Gloucestershire for some years, playing for the county from 1877 until 1882 and for Players against Gentlemen. A member of the first Australian side of 1878, he was virtually kidnapped by W.G. Grace after arriving at Lord's to represent the tourists against Middlesex; the great cricketer took him by cab to The Oval to play for his native county against Surrey, and Billy did not play for the Australians again on the tour! He toured Australia with Alfred Shaw's team in 1881/2, opening the bowling for England with Edmund Peate in two Tests; but he represented Australia again in 1882/3 and 1886/7 and toured England again (without being kidnapped) in 1884. For several years he was a professional on the Lord's ground staff. His ending was tragic: his wife and two children died, he became insane and was confined to an asylum where he died.

First-class career (1874-86): 4,493 runs (19.11) including 3 centuries, 418 wickets (17.38) and 122 catches
Test matches (Australia – 8): 174 runs (13.38), 14 wickets (23.78) and 5 catches. (England – 4): 95 runs (13.57), 10 wickets (27.20) and 5 catches

MILLER, Keith Ross (b.1919)

Victoria, New South Wales and Nottinghamshire

One of the greatest natural all-round cricketers in history, and certainly one of the most popular, Keith Miller was a wartime pilot in Britain, capable of crash-landing at 11 a.m. and joining in a game of cricket at noon. Red-faced and generous, he loves life and still lives it to the full. Matured by playing for the Australian Services side in 1945, he was brilliant in the Victory Tests and scored an unforgettable 185 in 165 minutes at Lord's for a Dominions eleven. He was a right-handed batsman in the grand manner, an especially powerful driver, who could also be a delicate late-cutter, but his success often depended on his mood: he was a somewhat wayward genius. As a natural bowler, his action was a model of co-ordination, classically high. With his height – above six feet – and athlete's physique, he bowled an occasional ball faster than Ray Lindwall, his regular destructive opening partner in international matches. His speed (and the length of his run-up) depended on his state of health, which often had something to do with how he had spent the previous evening. He was at once an aggressive but also a magnificently casual cricketer, a crowd-pleaser whose long black hair would

Keith Miller

drop over his eyes as he bowled and be sent back into place with a flick of the head. He played in the first Test after the Second World War, against New Zealand at Wellington in 1945/6, and from then until 1956 was an integral part of Australia's side. He toured England in 1948, 1953 and 1956; and South Africa, the West Indies and Pakistan; and at home appeared in six series, including three against England. In twenty-nine Tests alone against England, he made 1,511 runs (33.57) and took 87 wickets (22.40). In his first Test against the 'ancient enemy' at Brisbane in 1946/7 he scored 79 and took 7 for 60 in the first innings, which remained his best piece of bowling for his country. His first Test hundred was 141 not out in the fourth match at Adelaide, adding a bright 150 for the fifth wicket with Ian Johnson. He finished second in the batting averages to Don Bradman with 384 runs (76.80) and second to Ray Lindwall in the bowling with 16 wickets (20.87). Often unfit to bowl in England in 1948, he had a decisive hand in the victory in the first Test at Trent Bridge, taking 7 wickets. In the third match at Sydney in 1950/51 he captured 4 for 37, breaking the back of the early batting, and then slammed 145 not out. He headed the batting in the series with 350 runs (43.75), besides taking 17 wickets (17.70). In the second Test at Lord's in 1953 his 109 was invaluable. In the West Indies in 1955 he came second in the averages with 439 runs (73.16), which included three hundreds, his 147 in the first Test at Kingston, when he added 224 for the third wicket with Neil Harvey, remaining his highest for Australia. He never made runs for the sake of it (when the Australians scored more than 700 in a day against Essex in 1948, Keith was bored and allowed himself to be dismissed for a duck) but he was always in the game at some point or another as a potential matchwinner. Seven times he exceeded 200 in an innings, the highest being 281 not out against Leicestershire at Leicester in 1956. In fifty-two Sheffield Shield matches he made 3,803 runs (57.62) and took 109 wickets (26.13). He appeared for MCC and Nottinghamshire in 1959, in his sole match for the county making 62 and 102 not out against Cambridge University at Trent Bridge. In collaboration with R.S. Whitington, he wrote several books and is now a journalist and commentator. He was awarded the MBE for his services to the game.

First-class career (1937-59): 14,183 runs (48.90) including 41 centuries, 497 wickets (22.30) and 136 catches
Test matches (55): 2,958 runs (36.97) including 7 centuries, 170 wickets (22.97) and 38 catches

MINNETT, Dr Roy Baldwin (1888-1955)

New South Wales

One of three brothers who played for the State, Minnett was essentially a right-handed forward player with a fine, free swing of the bat, and a fast-medium bowler with a longish run, his arms revolving like a windmill as he ran in to deliver the ball. He toured England in 1912 but without much success, scoring 734 runs in forty-two innings and taking 41 expensive wickets. He was unfortunate not to have made a hundred in his first Test, against England at Sydney in 1911/12. He often told the story of how Sidney Barnes – 'that wily old fox' – enticed him into flashing at one outside the off-stump with his score at 90. In ten Sheffield Shield matches he made 621 runs (44.35), including his career-highest, 216 not out against Victoria at Sydney in 1911/12, and took 26 wickets (20.03).

First-class career (1906-14): 2,203 runs (28.98) including 2 centuries, and 86 wickets (25.02)
Test matches (9): 391 runs (26.06) and 11 wickets (26.36)

MISSON, Francis Michael (b.1938)

New South Wales

A blond, very determined right-arm fast-medium bowler, useful batsman and good field, Frank Misson was one of the many fastish bowlers tried fleetingly for Australia in the 1960s. He toured New Zealand in 1959/60 and, on his Test debut in the second match against West Indies at Melbourne in 1960/61, dismissed C.C. Hunte with his second ball. In England in 1961 his chief virtues were stamina and accuracy, but at Lord's he scored 25 not out in a vital last wicket stand of 49.

First-class career (1958-63): 1,052 runs (17.53) and 177 wickets (31.13)
Test matches (5): 38 runs (19.00), 16 wickets (38.50) and 6 catches

MORONEY, John (b.1917)

New South Wales

Powerfully built and a fine right-handed opening batsman who tended to carry caution to extremes, Jack Moroney had a curious career in Test cricket. He toured South Africa in 1949/50, scoring 1,487 runs in thirty-one innings, including six centuries, and scoring 352 runs in the Tests. In the fourth Test at Johannesburg he made 118 and 101 not out, the first time an Australian had achieved the feat against South Africa. However, in the first Test against England at Brisbane in 1950/51, he failed to score in either innings (dismissed by Trevor Bailey each time) and was promptly dropped from the side. Although he continued to be a prolific if laborious run-getter for his State, he appeared in only one further Test, against West Indies in 1951/2, and was again dropped, this time for good. His career-highest score was 217 for A.R. Morris's XI against A.L. Hassett's XI (Test Trial) at Sydney in 1948/9.

First-class career (1945-51): 4,023 runs (52.25) including 12 centuries
Test matches (7): 383 runs (34.81) including 2 centuries

MORRIS, Arthur Robert (b.1922)

New South Wales

A charming and relaxed person, for whom cricket was never a matter of life and death, Arthur Morris scored 148 and 111 on his first-class debut for his State against Queensland at Sydney in 1940/41, the first player in any country to score two centuries on his debut. He was only eighteen. After war service he became Australia's regular opening batsman for a decade. Of medium height and compact build he was an elegant left-hander, at his most brilliant when facing spin, when he would sometimes move yards down the pitch to break up a length. A certain fallibility against the swinging ball around the leg-stump caused some loss of confidence and Alec Bedser exploited the weakness, dismissing him eighteen times in Tests. Nonetheless, he scored six hundreds in his first ten Tests against England; and in 24 Tests against England between 1946 and 1955 he made 2,080 runs (50.73), including 7 centuries. He toured England in 1948 and 1953, South Africa and the West Indies; and at home had three series against England and one each against India, West Indies and South Africa. Only Don Bradman scored more runs in the 1946/7 series; Morris made 503 runs (71.85). He scored 155 in the third Test at Melbourne, and 122 and 124 not out in the fourth at Adelaide. He made another century off the 1947/8 Indians and in England in 1948 he had a sequence of 105 and 62 in the second Test at Lord's; 51 and 54 not out in the third at Old Trafford; 6 and a matchwinning 182 at Headingley, where Australia scored 404 to win in the fourth innings, and 196 in the fifth at The Oval. In this series he made 696 runs (87.00), far more than anyone else. In South Africa at Port Elizabeth and Johannesburg in 1949/50 he scored further Test centuries. In 1950/51 Alec Bedser dismissed him four times for scores of 25 or less. The fourth dismissal occurred on Morris's twenty-ninth birthday and that evening Bedser presented him with a book entitled *Better Cricket* by Lindsay Hassett and Ian Johnson, saying, 'I hope this will help you.' Morris promptly made his highest Test score – 206 – in the fourth Test at Adelaide! He held his place until his retirement in 1955, and his last major Test innings was 153 in the first Test against England at Brisbane in 1954/5 when he added 202 for the third wicket with Neil Harvey, before Frank Tyson and Brian Statham

Arthur Morris

began to dominate the series. Captain of New South Wales at twenty-five, he led Australia when the regular captain was unable to play through injury, once against West Indies in 1951/2 and once against England in 1954/5. In thirty-seven Sheffield Shield matches he made 3,517 runs (65.12). In all, he made four double-centuries, his career-highest being 290 against Gloucestershire at Bristol in 1948. Now a successful businessman, he has been a member and vice-chairman of the Sydney Cricket Ground Trust.

First-class career (1940-63): 12,614 runs (53.67) including 46 centuries, and 12 wickets (49.33)
Test matches (46): 3,533 runs (46.48) including 12 centuries, 2 wickets (25.00) and 15 catches

MORRIS, Samuel (1856-1931)

Victoria

Born at Hobart of West Indian parents attracted by the gold rush, the lissom and good humoured Sam Morris remains the only black man to have represented Australia in Tests. In the 1880s the country's cricket was rent by disputes and at times well-known players refused to play for their country, but when Sam Morris appeared in his sole Test, the second at Melbourne in 1884/5, opening the batting and scoring 4 and 10 not out and taking 2 for 73, he was genuinely considered to be 'among the best twenty-two in Australia'. His right-handed batting was 'first-class, of a taking, wristy kind, scientific, strong on the off'; his medium-paced bowling was generally very accurate; and he fielded with characteristic West Indian zest; at a pinch, too, he could also keep wicket. He played for Victoria for eleven years irregularly and became curator of the St Kilda ground until afflicted by blindness. He learned the game at Daylesford, and the Cricket Association there play annually for 'The Sam Morris Cup'.

First-class career (1881-92): 623 runs (18.32) and 31 wickets (26.09)

MOSES, Henry (1858-1938)

New South Wales

The first of a long line of famous left-handed batsmen produced by Australia, 'Harry' Moses had great defensive powers, monumental patience and exquisite skill in on-side play, notably the leg-glance, but business prevented him from visiting England with an Australian side. He appeared occasionally in Tests during the 1886/7, 1887/8, 1891/2 and 1894/5 series, but he was disappointing. For his State against Victoria at Sydney he hit 297 not out in 1887/8, one of the highest scores ever registered in the country. In the same season he made 58 and 109 against Arthur Shrewsbury's England team. A batsman of special gifts, he was placed next to W.L. Murdoch in ability among the batsmen of his day. He was chairman of the Sydney Cricket Ground Trust for many years.

First-class career (1881-94): 2,898 runs (35.77) including 4 centuries
Test matches (6): 198 runs (19.80) and 1 catch

MOSS, Jeffrey Kenneth (b.1947)

Victoria

A hard-hitting and uncomplicated left-handed batsman, who stands up straight and keeps the blade straight too, Jeff Moss scored 748 runs at 68 in 1978/9 when his consistency had much to do with Victoria's winning of the Sheffield Shield. Although overlooked by the selectors while the England bowlers were causing havoc, he was called in for the final Test of the season in March 1979, making 22 and 38 not out against Pakistan in his sole Test to date, when Australia won by seven wickets at Perth. A fine fielder, Moss toured England for the 1979 Prudential World Cup but was not picked to tour India later that year. In 1981/2 he scored 200 against Western Australia, sharing a record third-wicket stand of 390 with Julien Wiener.

First-class career (1976-): 3,416 runs (43.79) including 9 centuries

MOULE, William Henry (1858-1939)

Victoria

A member of the 1880 team, Moule was a good right-handed batsman and medium-pace change-bowler. In his sole Test – the first in England, at The Oval – he scored 6 and 34, took 3 for 23 (in a total of 420) and held one catch. As the number eleven batsman, he assisted his captain W.L. Murdoch in a last wicket stand of 88 after Australia had followed-on, which saved an innings defeat and made England bat again.

First-class career (1878-85): 137 runs (11.41) and 5 wickets (21.20)

MURDOCH, William Lloyd (1855-1911)

New South Wales and Sussex

Of fine physique, Billy Murdoch, a great friend of W.G. Grace, was the first Australian to rank with England's best batsmen. Although a wicket-keeper – he came as deputy-keeper with the first 1878 side – he was usually played for his batting. Right-handed, he had a good style, plenty of strokes, good eyes and superb footwork, especially on difficult wickets. He made his Test debut in the second match at Melbourne in 1876/7, and captained the 1880 Australians in the first Test in England, at The Oval, going in first wicket down in the second innings and carrying his bat for 153

Billy Murdoch

(exceeding W.G.'s century by one run). Altogether, he led his country in five further campaigns: 1881/2, 1882, 1882/3, 1884 and 1890. In the low-scoring classic Ashes match at The Oval in 1882, his 13 and 29 were invaluable; and in 1884 he became the first batsman to register a double century in Tests – 211 in the third match at The Oval, when he batted eight hours. Old photographs show his contented round face and Charlie Chan moustache. Genial and full of bonhomie, he was genuinely and unaffectedly amusing: the dressing-room was always relaxed while he was there. His 321 for New South Wales against Victoria at Sydney in 1881/2 remained the highest in first-class cricket in Australia for twenty years. Settling in Sussex, he captained the county from 1893 until 1899, hitting 226 against Cambridge University at Hove in 1895. He toured South Africa with W.W. Read's team in 1891/2, keeping wicket for England against South Africa at Cape Town in the sole Test match; thus, he represented both Australia and England. Finally, he appeared for W.G.'s London County Eleven for six seasons until 1904. He died, however, in Australia, suffering an apoplectic fit during a Test between Australia and South Africa.

First-class career (1875-1904): 16,953 runs (26.86) including 19 centuries, 10 wickets (43.00), 218 catches and 25 stumpings
Test matches (Australia – 18): 896 runs (32.00) including 2 centuries, and 14 dismissals (13 ct, 1 st.). (England – 1): 12 runs (12.00) and 1 dismissal (1 st.)

MUSGROVE, Henry (*c.*1860-1931)

Victoria

Born at Surbiton (Surrey), Harry Musgrove was the tactful, courteous and popular manager of the 1896 Australian team. Though never a distinguished player, he played for Australia as a late replacement in the second Test at Melbourne in 1884/5, when many prominent players refused to take part because they disagreed with the financial terms offered. He scored 4 and 9.

First-class career (1881-96): 99 runs (8.35)

NAGEL, Lisle Ernest (1905-71)

Victoria

Very tall (6 feet 6 inches) Lisle Nagel was a right-arm fast-medium swing bowler, who took 8 for 32 – with an elastic bandage around his elbow after a mishap with a crank handle – for an Australian Eleven against MCC (all out 60) at Melbourne in 1932/3. He appeared in the first Test at Sydney, scoring 0 and 21 not out and taking 2 for 110. That was his sole Test. He toured India with Frank Tarrant's side in 1935/6, and established a Melbourne Pennant record in 1939/40 by taking 86 wickets (13.45). His twin brother, Vernon, also played for Victoria.

First-class career (1927-38): 407 runs (12.33) and 67 wickets (28.35)

NASH, Laurence John (b.1910)

Tasmania and Victoria

A right-arm fast bowler and hard-hitting batsman, Laurie Nash took 7 for 50 for Tasmania against the South Africans at Hobart in 1931/2 and was selected for the fifth Test at Melbourne, taking 4 for 18 in South Africa's first innings debacle of 36. He had appeared only once for Victoria – taking 4 for 37 against the visiting MCC – before being chosen for his second (and last) Test, the fifth against England at Melbourne in 1936/7, and he took 4 for 70 in the first innings. He never appeared in a Sheffield Shield match. A magnificent athlete, he was one of the most accomplished footballers under the Australian Rules.

First-class career (1929-36): 953 runs (28.02) including 1 century, and 69 wickets (28.33)
Test matches (2): 30 runs (15.00), 10 wickets (12.60) and 6 catches

NITSCHKE, Holmesdale Charles (1906-82)

South Australia

Never happier than when driving a fast bowler back over his head into the pavilion, 'Jack' or 'Slinger' Nitschke, as the opening batsman of his State, went to the wickets breathing fire and slaughter. He was known as the 'Don Quixote' of the bat. For his State he averaged 39.85 in Sheffield Shield matches, though he was often on the beaten side; but he appeared only in two Tests, both against South Africa in 1931/2. He became a noted race-horse breeder. A left-hander, he hit five of his nine hundreds against New South Wales, including 130 not out, out of a South Australian total of 246 at Sydney in 1933/4.

First-class career (1929-35): 3,320 runs (42.03) including 9 centuries
Test matches (2): 53 runs (26.50) and 3 catches

NOBLE, Montague Alfred (1873-1940)

New South Wales

Regarded by many as the greatest all-rounder produced by Australia, Monty Noble, also known as 'Alf' or 'Mary Ann' was over six feet, powerfully built and with sharp, clean-shaven features; he was a right-handed batsman of rare style and execution. Beautifully positioned and relaxed, he was able to hit very hard or play with heart-breaking patience, using his height and reach fully in driving, forcing the ball off his legs, pulling and cutting, either square or late. As a bowler, he was an off-spinner with a fairly long run-up, good control, and the ability to swerve the ball: he varied his pace considerably from slow to medium-fast. He was also a good fielder, usually at point, and an astute captain who drilled his side like a Cromwell – though off the field he was quite a genial companion. Noble toured England in 1899, 1902, 1905 and, as captain, in 1909. At home he appeared in 1897/8, 1901/2 and, as captain, in 1903/4 and 1907/8. He toured South Africa in 1902/3. He was very successful all round on each England tour: 1,608 runs and 82 wickets (1899); 1,416 runs and 98 wickets (1902); 2,084 runs and 59 wickets (1905); and 1,109 runs and 25 wickets (1909). In his whole career he made seven double centuries. His highest score was 284 against Sussex at Hove in 1902, when he added 428 for the sixth wicket with Warwick Armstrong, which remains Australia's record for this wicket; and he hit 267 against Sussex again in 1905. He headed the Test bowling averages in 1897/8, with 19 wickets (20.26). On his debut in the second Test at Melbourne he took 6 for 49 on a difficult wicket in the second innings, winning the match for his country. Perhaps his greatest achievement was in taking 7 for 17 and 6 for 60 in the second Test at Melbourne against a strong England batting side in 1901/2. In the third Test at Sheffield in 1902 he took 11 for 103. He made his sole Test century, 133 (out of a total of 285) in the first Test at Sydney in 1903/4, and on several occasions held the batting together in that series. Five of his double centuries came in Sheffield Shield matches, in fifty-one of which he made 4,996 runs (69.38) and took 158 wickets (22.70). He was in turn banker, dentist, manufacturer's agent, writer and broadcaster, and his books *Gilligan's Men, The Game's the Thing, Those Ashes* and *The Fight for the Ashes 1928-29* are classics on the game.

Monty Noble

First-class career (1893-1919): 13,975 runs (40.74) including 37 centuries, and 625 wickets (23.11) and 191 catches
Test matches (42): 1,997 runs (30.25) including 1 century, 121 wickets (25.00) and 26 catches

NOBLET, Geoffrey (b.1916)

South Australia

Six feet three inches and very thin, Geoff Noblet's endurance was remarkable. Bowling a lively right-arm medium pace, he started his long run with a peculiar hop, as in a barn-dance, and finished with a seven-foot stride, delivering the ball with a flick which some purists thought was a throw; he could move the ball either way and his control was excellent. He toured

South Africa in 1949/50 and also represented his country at home against the West Indies in 1951/2 and South Africa in 1952/3. Thirty-five Sheffield Shield matches brought him 190 wickets (17.90), but Ray Lindwall, Keith Miller and Bill Johnston kept him out of the Australian side against England. He is president of the Cricket Union of South Australia.

First-class career (1946-54): 975 runs (13.92) and 282 wickets (19.26)
Test matches (3): 22 runs (7.33), 7 wickets (26.14) and 1 catch

NOTHLING, Dr Otto Ernest (1900-65)

Queensland and New South Wales

Otto Nothling could bowl right-arm medium pace and swing a heavy bat effectively; he appeared in one Test, the second at Sydney against England in 1928/9, scoring 8 and 44 and taking 0 for 72. A notable Rugby full-back, he represented Australia against New Zealand; and for many years he was president of the Queensland Cricket Association.

First-class career (1922-9): 882 runs (24.50) including 1 century, and 36 wickets (41.06)

O'BRIEN, Leo Patrick Joseph (b.1907)

Victoria

A small, neat, left-handed opening batsman, Leo O'Brien had a good defence and tons of courage, but a disappointing Test record. He appeared against England in 1932/3 and 1936/7, and South Africa in 1935/6, his only overseas tour. In the final match of the Bodyline Series at Sydney, after Vic Richardson, Bill Woodfull and Don Bradman had gone rather cheaply on the opening morning, he hit 61, adding 99 with Stan McCabe for the fourth wicket off Larwood, Voce and company, but he was unable to consolidate his place.

First-class career (1929-37): 3,303 runs (36.70) including 7 centuries
Test matches (5): 211 runs (26.37) and 3 catches

O'CONNOR, John Denis Alphonsus (1875-1941)

New South Wales and South Australia

Right-arm fastish medium in pace, with immaculate length, good control, able to make the ball lift and swing towards leg, Jack O'Connor played against England in 1907/8 – having a match record of 8 for 150 on his debut in the third Test at Adelaide. He toured England in 1909, taking 85 wickets (19.04) in all first-class matches. His best performance was 7 for 36 for South Australia against Victoria at Melbourne in 1908/9, enabling his State to snatch an unexpected victory. In seventeen Sheffield Shield matches his left-handed batting was of little account, but he took 80 wickets (29.13).

First-class career (1904-9): 695 runs (11.78) and 224 wickets (23.45)
Test matches (4): 86 runs (12.28), 13 wickets (26.15) and 3 catches

OGILVIE, Alan David (b.1951)

Queensland

A tall, bearded schoolmaster, red-haired and a right-hand batsman, David Ogilvie earned a place in Australia's fledgling side against India (at home) and the West Indies (away) in 1977/8, but was disappointing despite a pleasing upright technique. He simply could not go wrong in the Sheffield Shield, however. In the 1977/8 season he scored 1,060 runs (66.25) with six centuries which only Bradman and Ponsford have exceeded in the Shield. He played straight and hit hard but a blow on the head from a ball by Bob Willis at Brisbane in 1978/9 did nothing to help his confidence. A late replacement on the tour of the Caribbean, he scored 296 runs (26.91).

First-class career (1974-9): 3,006 runs (34.15) including 8 centuries
Test matches (5): 178 runs (17.80) and 5 catches

O'KEEFFE, Kevin James (b.1949)

New South Wales and Somerset

A tall fair-haired all-rounder, right-arm leg-break bowler and right-hand batsman, Kerry O'Keeffe has never quite fulfilled his early potential, and in an era dominated by fast bowlers he has often been the man left out of an Australian twelve. He is a brisk leg-spinner, with a good high action who bowls as many top-spinners and off-breaks as he does leg-spinners. As a batsman he possesses exceptional determination and a sound technique and he can field well anywhere, especially in the slip or gully. He has had wide English experience, although he has made only one official tour of England, in 1977, when he averaged 50 with the bat in all matches and took 36 tour wickets (28.75) but his Test bowling, three wickets at 101.66, was very disappointing. In 1971 he took 77 wickets for Somerset (but only 19 in 1972) and in 1975 scored over 1,000 runs and took 68 wickets for the League Club, East Lancashire. In Tests generally he was often chipping in with good all-round efforts at important times, but he only once took five wickets in an innings.

First-class career (1968-79): 4,169 runs (26.05), 476 wickets (28.11) and 112 catches
Test matches (24): 644 (25.76), 53 wickets (38.07) and 15 catches

Bert Oldfield

OLDFIELD, William Albert Stanley (1894-1976)

New South Wales

Very small, but wiry as a weasel, Bert Oldfield was an artistic wicket-keeper who did his job with quiet efficiency, stumping batsmen with the speed and stealth of a cat and then appealing with a polite conviction. His right-handed batting was also neat and business-like. He had a good defence and could force the pace when necessary. After front-line service near Ypres, he came to notice as a member of the Australian Imperial Forces team in 1919. He toured England in 1921, 1926, 1930 and 1934 and South Africa in 1921/2 and 1935/6. Establishing himself in Tests in 1924/5 against England, he showed amazing skill in the fourth Test at Melbourne, stumping Hobbs, Woolley, Chapman and Whysall and catching Gilligan, all in the same innings. In the fifth Test at Sydney he caught Hobbs for 0 in the first innings and stumped him for 13 in the second. He played in seven home series between 1920 and 1937, five against England. On his five tours of England he caught 155 batsmen and stumped 111. He was the unwitting cause of much Australian fury when, batting at Adelaide in the third Test of the Bodyline Series, he was hit on the head as he ducked into a ball from Larwood and had to be carried off the field. On recovering consciousness he said, 'It was my own fault,' and he and Larwood became great friends. He was awarded the MBE.

First-class career (1919-37): 6,135 runs (23.77), including 6 centuries, and 661 dismissals (400 ct, 261 st.)
Test matches (54): 1,427 runs (22.65) and 130 dismissals (78 ct, 52 st.)

O'NEILL, Norman Clifford (b.1937)

New South Wales

Heralded as 'the new Don Bradman', Norman O'Neill had a brilliant but also rather mercurial career. Without doubt he was a superb right-handed stroke-maker. Strongly built, and much taller than the Don, he was a back-foot player of the highest class, a powerful driver, very quick on his feet to the spinners, and was practically never tied down. But he was a nervous starter who had none of Bradman's air of invincibility. A useful leg-spin bowler, he was also a brilliant cover field with a superb throw. He averaged 43.61 at the age of eighteen in his first season of first-class cricket. He toured New Zealand with the 'A' team in his second season, averaging 72.66, and in his next season, 1957/8, made 1,005 runs (83.75) – only the third player to have totalled 1,000 runs in the Sheffield Shield in a season. He played his first Test against England in 1958/9 when he batted with admirable consistency to average 56.40. He toured England in 1961 and 1964, India twice, the West Indies and Pakistan. On his first England tour he was highly successful with 1,981 runs (60.03), including seven centuries, but on his second less so, although he averaged 45.63. His first Test century was 181 in the tied Test against the West Indies at Brisbane in 1960/61. His first century against England was in his tenth Test against them, 117 in the final match at The Oval in 1961. His superb footwork and powerful driving provided the best batting of that series. Soon after he lost form and confidence, but he redeemed himself with a memorable 143 against MCC at Sydney and

Norman O'Neill pulls a four watched by Roy Booth

100 in the fourth Test at Adelaide in 1962/3, adding 194 for the fourth wicket with Neil Harvey after a poor Australian start. He was even more successful against other countries, scoring 163 at Bombay and 113 at Calcutta against India in 1959/60 and 134 against Pakistan at Lahore on the same tour. The tour also saw his career-highest score of 284 against the Indian President's Eleven at Ahmedabad. By the mid-sixties, however, the glory had departed from his batting; and at the close of his last series against the West Indies in the Caribbean controversial articles appeared under his name bitterly condemning the bowling action of Charlie Griffith. His handsome stroke-play was still in evidence in Sheffield Shield matches, however, and he was the chief run-getter in 1966/7, heading the table with 741 runs (74.10). But late in the season after a poor tour with an Australian 'A' team of New Zealand, he announced his retirement from big cricket because of recurring knee trouble. In sixty-one Sheffield Shield matches he made 4,749 runs (50.52).

First-class career (1955-68): 13,859 runs (50.95) including 45 centuries, 99 wickets (30.31) and 104 catches
Test matches (42): 2,779 runs (45.55) including 6 centuries, 17 wickets (39.23) and 21 catches

O'REILLY, William Joseph (b.1905)

New South Wales

In Sir Donald Bradman's view the greatest bowler of his time, Bill O'Reilly played his cricket with the fierce zeal of a fire-and-brimstone missionary. Known as 'Tiger', he had a meteoric rise to fame. He played for his State in two matches in 1927/8, without any pronounced success, and nothing more was heard of him in first-class cricket until 1931/2, when the South Africans were touring Australia. In five Sheffield Shield matches he took 25 wickets and he was selected for the fourth and fifth tests – in the fifth at Melbourne helping to demolish South Africa's second innings for 45 (taking 3 for 19). From then until the outbreak of the Second World War he was an integral part of his country's fearsome spin attack, especially in company with Clarrie Grimmett. Over six feet tall, he bowled right-arm. His run-up and action formed an ungraceful whirl of arms and legs but the result was deadly. His stock delivery was a leg-break rolled out of the hand with no great turn, but he spun his googly sharply and almost every ball he bowled had abnormal bounce. His pace was such that few batsman could move out to the pitch of the ball, and both his accuracy and his hostility were unremitting; he had more the temperament of a fiery fast bowler than of a patient spinner. As a left-handed batsman he had no style but he could hit tremendously hard. In the Bodyline Tour of 1932/3 he consolidated his place as the outstanding Australian bowler, with 27 wickets (26.81) taking 10 for 129 in his country's sole victory, in the second Test at Melbourne. Against England in 1934 and South Africa in 1935/6, Grimmett and O'Reilly were a host in themselves – in the former series they collected 53 wickets (O'Reilly 28) and in the latter 71 wickets (O'Reilly 27). At Trent Bridge in 1934 O'Reilly took 11 for 129 and at Old Trafford took three wickets in four balls (Walters, Wyatt and Hammond). Although England reached 627 for 9, 'Tiger's' analysis was 7 for 189 in 59 overs. Against South Africa in 1935/6 he was consistently successful with 95 wickets (13.56). Both England tours brought him 100 wickets and first place in the averages. At Leeds in 1938, in a low-scoring match, his 10 for 122 was decisive. He appeared in the first post-War Test, against New Zealand at Wellington in 1945/6, taking 5 for 14 and 3 for 19, then retired. Originally a schoolmaster he turned to journalism and produced two tour books, besides much characteristically well-informed, honest, and forthright newspaper comment. A kind heart lies beneath his fiery exterior.

First-class career (1927-45): 1,655 runs (13.13) and 774 wickets (16.60)
Test matches (27): 410 runs (12.81), 144 wickets (22.59) and 7 catches

OXENHAM, Ronald Keven (1891-1939)

Queensland

Perhaps the best all-rounder produced by his State, Ron Oxenham made his name comparatively late. Not a stylist, he was a much better right-handed batsman than he looked and was a right-arm medium-paced bowler who flighted the ball well and had a jerky action, 'like a toy which functions when the strings are pulled.' His best delivery was a slower ball which floated from off to leg. He was a smart slip. In his late thirties and early forties he appeared in Tests against England in 1928/9, West Indies in 1930/31 and South Africa in 1931/2. His best feat in Tests was to take 4 for 39 in 30 overs as one of the opening bowlers in the third Test against West Indies at Brisbane in 1930/31. He toured India with the Maharajah of Patiala's Australian team in 1935/6, managed by Frank Tarrant, taking 101 wickets at 8 runs each. In forty-six Sheffield Shield matches he made 2,314 runs (30.72) and took 167 wickets (22.14). Suffering serious injury in a car accident in 1937, he never fully recovered.

First-class career (1911-36): 3,693 runs (25.64) including 4 centuries, and 369 wickets (18.67)
Test matches (7): 151 runs (15.10), 14 wickets (37.28) and 4 catches

PALMER, George Eugene (1860-1910)

Victoria and Tasmania

At nineteen, playing for Victoria against Lord Harris's

team at Melbourne in 1878/9, George or 'Joey' Palmer took 9 for 94 in the match, greatly impressing his opponents. A right-arm medium-paced spin bowler, with the necessary command of length and direction, he was considered Australia's best bowler in the early 1880s on batsmen's wickets – 'and when the wicket was sticky, he was a nasty one to face'. He toured England in 1880 – playing in the first Test in England at The Oval, taking 3 of the 5 wickets to fall in England's second innings – and again in 1882, 1884 and 1886. At home he played in the 1881/2, 1882/3 and 1884/5 series. On his last England tour he achieved the double with 1,028 runs and 106 wickets, his batting having developed greatly; this was the first Australian double in England. In the second Test at Sydney in 1881/2 his match analysis, 11 for 165 in 124 overs, enabled his country to win convincingly, and in the next match at Sydney he took 9 for 90 in 85.2 overs. The four Tests brought him 24 wickets (21.75). Again the chief bowler in 1882/3, he took 21 wickets (18.90). His highest score against England, 48, was made defiantly at Lord's in 1886. On his four trips to England he captured 449 wickets (15.80).

First-class career (1878-96): 2,728 runs (16.14) including 1 century, 594 wickets (17.71) and 108 catches
Test matches (17): 296 runs (14.09), 78 wickets (21.51) and 13 catches

PARK, Dr Roy Lindsay (1892-1947)

Victoria

Small in stature, Roy Park was generally a right-hand batsman of sound defence, who went on his way relentlessly. He made 586 runs (83.71) for his State in 1919/20 and the following season made his sole Test appearance, against England at Melbourne in the second match, when in Australia's only innings he was bowled first ball, and never received another chance. His career-highest score was 228 against South Australia at Melbourne in 1919/20.

First-class career (1912-24): 2,514 runs (39.28) including 9 centuries

PASCOE, Leonard Stephen (formerly Durtanovich, Len) (b.1950)

New South Wales

The son of Yugoslavian immigrants to Australia, Len Pascoe is a very determined right-arm fast bowler with little subtlety but plenty of strength and hostility. He was just challenging for a regular Test place at the outbreak of the Packer Revolution which he joined. After a successful season for New South Wales in 1976/7 he toured England, taking 41 wickets on the tour at 21.78. England's players were surprised and relieved when he was left out of the Australian team at Old Trafford after a promising Test debut at Lord's, where he took five wickets in the match. Later in the series he took 4 for 80 on a good pitch at Trent Bridge. He is an enthusiastic fielder, but a genuine tail-end batsman. Hostile fast bowlers thrived during the two years of World Series Cricket and Len Pascoe emerged from his time in the 'circus' a more confident and determined competitor. Looking an even more dangerous bowler than Lillee in the many one-day internationals of 1979/80 and the following season, he was not an automatic selection for the Test team but took 10 wickets (24.10) in two home Tests against England and then bowled outstandingly well in England's first innings in the Centenary Test, taking 5 for 59, 4 of his wickets being lbws. By now he had learned the virtues of bowling straight, fast and to a good length. He took 12 wickets in three Tests against New Zealand in 1980/81 and 16 in three Tests against India. But a knee injury was increasingly troubling him and he decided to miss the tour to England in 1981 in order to have an operation.

First-class career (1974-): 430 runs (9.34) and 262 wickets (24.56)
Test matches (14): 106 runs (10.60), 64 wickets (26.06) and 2 catches

PELLEW, Clarence Everard (1893-1981)

South Australia

Of average height, with strong shoulders and broad chest, 'Nip' Pellew could drive hard and straight, had a fine stroke past point – a mixture of cover-drive and cut – and was always looking for runs. He was nephew of the Shield player J.H. Pellew, also known as 'Nip'. He was a most accomplished field, sprinting round the boundary at even-time rate. 'Nip' toured England with the Australian Imperial Forces team in 1919, making 1,260 runs and returned home to hit 271 for his State against Victoria at Adelaide. In the 1920/21 series against England he made 319 runs (53.16) from four Tests, including 116 in the second at Melbourne and 104 in the third at Adelaide. He disappointed in the 1921 England tour, not even reaching 1,000 runs and appeared in only one more Test, against South Africa the following winter. In eighteen Sheffield Shield matches he made 1,343 runs (39.50).

First-class career (1913-29): 4,531 runs (33.56) including 9 centuries, and 12 wickets (72.33)
Test matches (10): 484 runs (37.23) including 2 centuries, 0-34 and 4 catches

PHILPOTT, Peter Ian (b.1934)

New South Wales

A right-arm leg-break bowler and very useful

batsman, Peter Philpott toured the West Indies in 1965 and, in his first Test series, took 18 wickets (34.94). In his first Test against England in 1962/3, at Brisbane, he took 5 for 90 in the first innings. He was a member of Denis Compton's side to the Transvaal in 1959 and played in the Lancashire League, but he never toured England and retired in his prime. He became captain of New South Wales for the 1964/5 season. He is now a noted coach.

First-class career (1954-66): 2,886 runs (31.36) including 4 centuries, and 245 wickets (30.31)
Test matches (8): 93 runs (10.33), 26 wickets (38.46) and 5 catches

PONSFORD, William Harold (b.1900)

Victoria

Though he was humbled by Larwood in 1928/9 and again in 1932/3, there were times during his career when Bill Ponsford scored runs with the relentless efficiency of a machine. He was an opening right-handed batsman regularly associated first with Bill Woodfull, then with the even more remorseless Don Bradman. Sturdy of frame, Ponsford's movements looked heavy, but in fact his footwork was quick. Bat and pad were always close together and even in defence he was perfectly positioned to push the ball for ones and twos. He was master particularly of spin bowling, sidling down the pitch and playing strokes into gaps all round the wicket, though he was especially good around the leg-stump. He toured England in 1926, 1930 and 1934, and appeared in five series at home between 1924 and 1933, three against England. On his three England tours he made 4,110 runs (54.80). On his Test debut, the first match at Sydney in 1924/5, he made 110 and 128 in the second match at Melbourne. He failed, relatively, in the 1926, 1928/9 and 1932/3 series, Harold Larwood being the main bogey-man; but he was a tower of strength against England in 1930 with 330 runs (55.00); against the West Indies in 1930/31 with 467 runs (77.83), including 183 in the second Test at Sydney; and in his final series in England in 1934 when, with Bradman, he dwarfed everyone else. Ponsford headed the averages with 569 runs (94.83), although the Don made more runs. At Headingley he scored 181, adding 388 in five and a half hours with Bradman for the fourth wicket after a batting collapse. Then, in what was to be his final Test, at The Oval, he scored 266, adding 451 with Bradman for the second wicket in only five and a quarter hours, which remains an Australian record. Against MCC at Lord's in 1934 Ponsford added 389 for the third wicket with Stan McCabe, another record stand, his own share being 281 not out, the record for an Australian at Lord's. He retired from first-class cricket at the end of the 1934 tour. He made thirteen scores exceeding 200, nine for his State. He scored 429 against Tasmania at Melbourne in 1922/3, then the world's highest score in a first-class match; and exceeded it with 437 against Queensland on the same ground in 1927/8. Also against Queensland at Melbourne, 1923/4, he put on 456 for the first wicket with Edgar Mayne, which remains the Australian record for the first wicket. In forty-three Sheffield Shield matches his remarkable record was 5,413 runs (84.57).

Bill Ponsford (left) with Bill Woodfull. They were associated together in many huge stands

First-class career (1920-34): 13,819 runs (65.18) including 47 centuries
Test matches (29): 2,122 runs (48.22) including 7 centuries, and 21 catches

POPE, Roland James (1864-1952)

New South Wales and Scotland

Roland Pope, or 'The Doc', travelled to England with touring teams from Australia with an array of luggage and medicines and was an honoured and welcome visitor though only as a player at the last resort! After hitting 170 for Melbourne I Zingari against Richmond in 1884/5, he represented New South Wales in two matches and Australia, depleted by disagreements over pay, called on him to play in the second Test at Melbourne in the same season, when he scored 0 and 3. He played some first-class cricket for Scotland.

First-class career (1884-1902): 318 runs (12.23)

RANSFORD, Vernon Seymour (1885-1958)

Victoria

A very attractive left-handed batsman, strong on the

leg-side and with a brilliant cover-drive, Vernon Ransford had a rather crouching stance, but moved rapidly into position, and was never afraid of lifting the ball into the open spaces. He was one of the best outfielders of his day. Unlucky, he once had an arm broken during a game and on another occasion deflected a full-toss on to his nose, with unpleasant results. After the First World War he was handicapped by ill-health and could not recapture his form of earlier days. He did not play in Test cricket again, although he toured New Zealand in 1921, 1925 and 1927. He appeared against England at home in 1907/8 and 1911/12, and South Africa in 1910/11. He toured England in 1909 but missed the 1912 tour owing to the dispute with the Australian Board. He paid five visits to New Zealand. In England he made 1,783 runs (43.48), including six centuries, one of 190 against MCC at Lord's being his highest-ever score. He led the Test averages with 353 runs (58.83). On a difficult wicket in the Lord's Test he hit 143 not out. In forty-nine Sheffield Shield matches, spread over twenty-two years, he made 3,061 runs (39.24). Against New South Wales at Sydney in 1908/9 he hit 182 and 110, the first Victorian to make a century in each innings of a first-class match. His career-highest, however, was the 190 against MCC at Lord's in 1909. From 1938 to 1957 he was Melbourne C.C. secretary.

First-class career (1903-27): 8,268 runs (42.40) including 25 centuries, and 29 wickets (30.62)
Test matches (20): 1,211 runs (37.84) including 1 century, 1-28 and 10 catches

REDPATH, Ian Ritchie (b.1941)

Victoria

For more than a decade Ian Redpath was one of the hardest Test batsmen in the world to dig out and an outstanding ambassador for his country, a charming, modest and amusing man, though his batting was often pedestrian. Very lean, sallow skinned, with a prominent Adam's apple and bandy-legged walk, 'Redders' was a right-hander with immense powers of concentration who accumulated his runs doggedly, mainly off the back foot, though he could also drive vigorously. He played straight and got behind the ball, often looking discomforted by bouncers, but usually managing to duck back out of reach and never flinching when the next ball came down. He was also a brilliant fielder close to the wicket, especially at short-leg. He succeeded Colin Macdonald as Victoria's opening batsman in 1962 and with Bill Lawry provided a highly productive opening partnership for many years, although until the initial retirement of Bobby Simpson he had to struggle to establish himself lower down the order for Australia. He toured England in 1964 and 1968, scoring 1,075 runs (32.57) in 1964 and 1,474 runs (43.35) in 1968, by which time

Ian Redpath

he was a much more positive player. He was still a thorn in English flesh in 1974/5 when he played with all his old solidity to score 472 runs (42.90). In the fourth Test of this series, at Sydney, he shared a record second-wicket partnership of 220 for Australia against England and, during the course of this innings of 105, his fifth century in Test cricket, he reached 4,000 runs in his fifty-eighth match for Australia. Against the West Indies fast bowlers the following season he was again consistency itself, scoring 575 runs (52.27) and hitting Test centuries at Melbourne (twice) and Adelaide as well as a fourth century against the touring side for Victoria. His highest Test innings was 171 against England at Perth in 1970/71, when he added 219 with Greg Chappell for Australia's sixth wicket. In this series he scored 497 runs (49.70) against John Snow at his peak. Despite these efforts at home he was left out of the Australian team touring England in 1972. Instead 'Redders' spent the summer teaching cricket at Charterhouse School in Surrey and, in his spare time, engaging in his hobby of fishing. Redpath played in some of the early World Series Cricket matches before injuring himself severely as he leapt in the air to celebrate taking a rare wicket! He is now back at his business as a Melbourne antique dealer, and has been active in politics.

First-class career (1961-75): 14,993 (41.99) including 32 centuries, 13 wickets (35.84) and 211 catches
Test matches (66): 4,737 runs (43.45) including 8 centuries, 0-41 and 83 catches

REEDMAN, John Cole (1865-1924)

South Australia

A postman, John Reedman's batting lacked polish, but never faith or courage. Known as 'Dinny' he was difficult to shift because he was prepared to take all the knocks rather than lose his wicket. His medium-pace change-bowling broke partnerships. He was held in high regard in his State during a very long career. His sole Test was the first at Sydney in 1894/5, when he scored 17 and 4, took 1 for 24 and held one catch.

First-class career (1887-1909): 3,337 runs (23.34) including 1 century, and 118 wickets (32.10)

RENNEBERG, David Alexander (b.1942)

New South Wales

A tall, dark and enthusiastic right-arm fast bowler, David Renneberg improved steadily during the early to mid-sixties. At first erratic, especially while using the new ball, he developed excellent control. In the second innings of his first Test, against India at Adelaide in 1967/8, he took 5 for 39. As Graham McKenzie's opening partner in the Tests in South Africa in 1966/7, he took only 11 expensive wickets, but in Australia, the following season, he had 47 wickets (19.20). He took 41 wickets in England in 1968 and had several spectacular bursts of success in Sheffield Shield cricket afterwards, but was not selected for his country again.

First-class career (1964-70): 466 runs (7.06) and 291 wickets (29.30)
Test matches (8): 22 runs (3.66), 23 wickets (36.08) and 2 catches

RICHARDSON, Arthur John (1888-1973)

South Australia and Western Australia

A tall, dark, rather lean, bespectacled figure, slow in his movements like a man accustomed to following the plough, Arthur Richardson was a right-handed opening batsman who played mainly in front of the wicket, being a powerful driver, and a medium-pace off-break bowler. He used a heavy bat with a piece of cow-hide fastened around it. He appeared against England at home in 1924/5, and on tour in 1926. In the second innings of his Test debut, at Sydney in 1924/5, he went in first and made 98 before giving a return catch to Tich Freeman. In the Test at Headingley in 1926 he made 100; and throughout the series bowled economically if not very penetratively, generally pitching on middle or middle-and-leg to four short-legs. He made 111 for his State against MCC at Adelaide in 1920/21. In 1922/3, in two matches for his State against Archie MacLaren's MCC side, he scored 150 in the first and 280 in the second, reaching his first hundred before lunch on the first day. This remains the highest for a State side against MCC. In thirty-two Sheffield Shield matches he made 2,355 runs (39.25) and took 74 wickets (39.04). He became a professional in the Lancashire League, coached in Australia, New Zealand and the West Indies, and even umpired Tests in the Caribbean.

First-class career (1919-33): 5,233 runs (41.57) including 13 centuries, and 209 wickets (31.41)
Test matches (9): 403 runs (31.00) including 1 century, 12 wickets (43.41) and 1 catch

RICHARDSON, Victor York (1894-1969)

South Australia

Full of life and vigour, Vic Richardson – grandfather of the Chappell brothers – was a courageous and forcing right-handed batsman, being despite his awkward stance an excellent driver on both sides of the wicket and a fine hooker. His speed, agility and safe hands made him a remarkable fielder in any position. A cheerful, enterprising and unorthodox leader, he captained his State for many years, was vice-captain of the 1930 Australians to England and captain of Australia in South Africa in 1935/6. At home he represented his country in the 1924/5, 1928/9 and 1932/3 series, just failing to win a permanent place at Test level. He toured America in 1932. He hit 138 in his second Test, at Melbourne in 1924/5, and 83 in the fourth Test at Brisbane, putting on 138 for the first wicket with Bill Woodfull. In seventeen years for his State he usually opened the batting, making 7,698 attractive runs (42.53), including 21 centuries. In making his career-highest score of 231 against MCC at Adelaide in 1928/9, he caused tremendous excitement by hooking Larwood into the Pavilion. He was also an outstanding athlete, representing Australia at baseball and his State at baseball, golf and tennis. He was also good at lacrosse, basketball and swimming. He became a journalist and highly regarded radio commentator with the ABC, especially in partnership with Arthur Gilligan, whence the catchphrase, 'What do you think, Arthur?'

First-class career (1918-37): 10,714 runs (37.59) including 27 centuries
Test matches (19): 706 runs (23.53) including 1 century and 24 catches

RIGG, Keith Edward (b.1906)

Victoria

A tall-right-hander with a fluent style, Keith Rigg had both strokes and courage but lacked opportunities at the highest level. He hit 126 for his State against the West Indians at Melbourne in 1930/31 and appeared in the fifth Test at Sydney but achieved little. The following season against South Africa, in the second Test at Sydney, he added 111 quickly for the third wicket with Don Bradman. In that series he made 253 runs (50.60). Subsequently, he appeared against England in three matches during 1936/7, but did not tour. He hit a century against MCC's 'goodwill' side in 1935/6.

First-class career (1926-38): 5,544 runs (42.00) including 14 centuries
Test matches (8): 401 runs (33.41) including 1 century, and 5 catches

RING, Douglas Thomas (b.1918)

Victoria

A happy philosopher, a tall right-arm leg-break bowler who did not mind being hit, and a fearless and unorthodox hitter, Doug Ring toured England in 1948 and 1953, appearing in one Test on each visit – although he took altogether 60 and 68 wickets, respectively. He played at home against India in 1947/8, West Indies in 1951/2 and South Africa in 1952/3. In Tests his main successes were at Brisbane in 1951/2 when he broke through to take 6 for 80, and again in the first Test at Brisbane in 1952/3 when he took 6 for 72. Against West Indies, with scores of 65, 67 and 32 not out, his swashbuckling batting was invaluable.

First-class career (1938-53): 3,418 runs (22.25) including 1 century, and 451 wickets (28.48)
Test matches (13): 426 runs (22.42), 35 wickets (37.28) and 5 catches

RITCHIE, Gregory Michael (b.1960)

Queensland and Buckinghamshire

Greg Ritchie toured Pakistan in 1982/3 as a replacement for Australia's senior batsman, Greg Chappell, and filled his shoes admirably on what was otherwise a disastrous tour for Australia. At Faisalabad, where Pakistan won by an innings, he scored 106 not out in only his third Test innings, hitting three sixes and nine fours. A tall, confident and aggressive right-handed batsman with fair, curly hair, Ritchie made his first appearance for Queensland in 1980/81 and that season scored 140 not out against Victoria. In 1981 he gained further experience with Buckinghamshire, scoring 433 runs from eight innings (54.12), and in 1982 he played for the Middlesex second eleven. His trip to Pakistan was thoroughly earned by a series of commanding innings in the 1981/2 Sheffield Shield. In all first-class cricket that season he hit 833 runs (59.50) with three centuries.

First-class career (1980-): 1,265 runs (48.65) including 4 centuries
Test matches (3): 206 runs (41.20) including 1 century, and 1 catch

RIXON, Stephen John (b.1954)

New South Wales

A neat and lively wicket-keeper and useful right-hand batsman, Steve Rixon played ten Tests in succession under the captaincy of Bobby Simpson in the reconstituted Australian side which played series against India at home and West Indies away in 1977/8. He was dropped, however, for the series against England in 1978/9 and a broken arm, suffered while batting at Perth, made this an unhappy season for a keen and personable cricketer. Rixon made the position of New South Wales wicket-keeper his own in 1974/5 when, after making a mere fifty runs in his first eleven innings in first-class cricket, he scored 115 against Queensland at Sydney, starting his innings as a night-watchman. Against the West Indies he made his major batting contribution in the fourth Test, scoring 54 and 39 not out, and although his keeping was inconsistent his subsequent rejection was harsh.

First-class career (1974-): 2,502 runs (21.56) including 4 centuries, and 287 dismissals (251 ct, 36 st.)
Test matches (10): 341 runs (21.31) and 35 dismissals (31 ct, 4 st.)

ROBERTSON, William Roderick (1861-1938)

Victoria

In a rather fleeting career 'Digger' Robertson, a useful right-handed batsman and leg-break bowler, took 8 wickets in the tied match between his State and Alfred Shaw's team in 1884/5. He filled a place in the second Test at Melbourne, after several outstanding players had defected owing to disagreements over pay and conditions. He scored 0 and 2 and took 0 for 24.

First-class career (1884-7): 109 runs (13.62) and 15 wickets (31.06)

ROBINSON, Rayford Harold (1914-65)

New South Wales, South Australia and Otago

Slim and slightly built, Ray Robinson was a right-handed batsman of tremendous natural ability and charm. He had made handsome centuries against South Australia and Queensland when he represented his country against England at Brisbane in the first Test of 1936/7, scoring 2 and 3 (being 'c. Hammond b. Voce' each time) and catching Hammond in the first innings before the great man had scored. This was his sole Test, however, though in twenty-three Sheffield Shield matches he made 1,539 runs (38.47). He played for South Australia in 1940 and after the Second World War he played in New Zealand.

First-class career (1934-48): 2,441 runs (31.70) including 4 centuries, and 44 wickets (37.59)

ROBINSON, Richard Daryl (b.1948)

Victoria

Tall for a wicket-keeper but also very capable and an attacking right-handed batsman, 'Richie' Robinson earned three Test caps in England in 1977 as a batsman. (Rodney Marsh kept wicket.) A popular and enterprising captain of Victoria, he had finished top of the Sheffield Shield batting averages in the previous Australian season and he was also successful against the English counties, scoring 715 runs (37.63). He also claimed more victims (34) on the tour than Marsh achieved from three more matches. But in the Tests the England fast bowlers exposed some technical frailties and, apart from a buccaneering 70 in a one-day international at The Oval, he was disappointing. He also toured England as Marsh's deputy in 1975, scoring 223 runs at 37.16 in seven matches.

First-class career (1971-): 4,776 runs (39.80) including 7 centuries, and 329 dismissals (289 ct, 40 st.)
Test matches (3): 100 runs (16.66) and 4 catches

RORKE, Gordon Frederick (b.1938)

New South Wales

A giant right-arm fast bowler, handsome, blond-haired and nicknamed 'Lothair', Gordon Rorke played with some success against England in 1958/9 and toured India and Pakistan in 1959/60. He was one of several controversial bowlers in international cricket at that time. Dragging his rear foot several feet over the bowling crease, he bowled the ball from such a height and at such a pace that even the tallest batsmen had difficulty in doing more than prodding off the chest. His accentuated drag precipitated moves in official quarters for the front foot Lbw Law. Unhappily, he fell victim to hepatitis, which curtailed his career. In twenty-five Sheffield Shield matches he took 58 wickets (31.01).

First-class career (1957-63): 248 runs (10.77) and 88 wickets (24.60)
Test matches (4): 9 runs (4.50), 10 wickets (20.30) and 1 catch

RUTHERFORD, John W. (b.1929)

Western Australia

A careful, defensive right-handed opening batsman, Jack Rutherford toured England, Pakistan and India in 1956, but appeared in only one Test, the second against India at Bombay, in which he made 30 and took 1 for 15. He was the first Western Australian to be selected for an important overseas tour and the first to be capped for Australia. In thirty-three Sheffield Shield matches he made 2,200 runs (37.92), including a career-highest 167.

First-class career (1952-61): 3,367 runs (31.79) including 6 centuries, and 29 wickets (45.27)

RYDER, John (1889-1977)

Victoria

A tall, slim, attacking right-handed batsman, Jack Ryder was largely a front-of-the-wicket player with a powerful drive. As a fast-medium change-bowler, he would get lift and movement away from the bat. He was also a good fielder. He toured England in 1921 and 1926 and South Africa in 1921/2. At home he appeared in the 1920/21, 1924/5 and 1928/9 series against England, the last as captain. He visited India as skipper of Frank Tarrant's side in 1935/6; and led his State for many years. Before the First World War he was outstanding as a bowler: in his first season for his State in 1912/13, he captured 30 wickets (15.40), including 13 for 155 against South Australia, but after the War his main forte was batting. His career-highest score of 295 against New South Wales at Melbourne in 1926/7 included six sixes, his second hundred coming in seventy-four minutes – the total innings of the team was the record 1,107 runs! He did not represent Australia in any of the 1921 Tests, although he made 1,032 runs (38.22) and took 24 wickets on the tour. Against South Africa he hit 334 runs (111.33) in the three Tests of 1921/2, including 142 in the third at Cape Town. In the third Test at Adelaide in 1924/5, coming in at 119 for six, he made 201 not out in six and a half hours – slow for him, but very responsible in the circumstances – and 88 in the second innings, Australia just managing to defeat England by 11 runs.

Jack Ryder

As captain for 1928/9, he made more runs than anyone else, 492 runs (54.66), which included 112 in the third Test at Melbourne, when he added 161 with Alan Kippax after three wickets had gone for 57. By now one of the Test selectors, there was much surprise and resentment that he was not selected for the team to England in 1930. The first of three teetotallers to captain Australia in the eleven years before the Second World War, he was well-liked as a straightforward, unpretentious, slow-spoken man. A great helper of young players, he was a selector again from 1946 until 1970, working closely with Sir Donald Bradman. Known as 'the King' in his native Collingwood, he proudly led the parade of old Australian Test players at the Centenary Test Match celebrations in March 1977, dying only a few days later.

First-class career (1912-35): 10,499 runs (44.29) including 24 centuries, 238 wickets (29.68) and 132 catches
Test matches (20): 1,394 runs (51.62) including 3 centuries, 17 wickets (43.70) and 17 catches

SAGGERS, Ronald Arthur (b.1917)

New South Wales

An accomplished second-string wicket-keeper to Don Tallon in England in 1948, Ron Saggers became the regular 'keeper during the tour of South Africa in 1949/50. His style was quiet and neat and reminiscent of Bert Oldfield. He was an attractive batsman, good enough early in his career for a place in his State eleven on his batting alone. He captained his State for some years. He dismissed seven (all caught) in an innings for New South Wales against a Combined Eleven at Brisbane in 1940/41 and six (4 ct, 2 st.) in an innings against Queensland at Sydney in 1946/7.

First-class career (1939-50): 1,888 runs (23.89) including 1 century, and 221 dismissals (147 ct, 74 st.)
Test matches (6): 30 runs (10.00), and 24 dismissals (16 ct, 8 st.)

SAUNDERS, John Victor (1876-1927)

Victoria and Wellington

Tall and spare, like the pen-pictures of Daniel Boone, Jack Saunders had a large moustache and a corkscrew run to the wicket. Starting from around mid-on, he came round the wicket, brought his left arm over close to his ear and spun the ball viciously at near medium pace. He was a holy terror on sticky wickets. A mainstay of the 1902 side to England, taking 127 wickets (17.07) in the wet summer, he was the man who bowled out Fred Tate at Old Trafford, thus ensuring the famous three-run victory. On his Test debut against England in the fourth match at Sydney in 1901/2, he took 9 for 162 in the match, bowling unchanged with Noble in the second innings. He took seven wickets at Old Trafford and six at The Oval in 1902 – having 18 wickets (26.27) in the series – and in South Africa in 1902/3 he took 15 wickets at 11.73 in two Tests, including 7 for 34 in the second innings at Johannesburg. Against the losing England 1907/8 side he took 9 for 104 in the fourth Test at Melbourne and 8 for 196 in the fifth at Sydney, which was his farewell appearance. In this last series he took more wickets than anyone else on either side and at lower cost, 31 wickets (23.09). In thirty-seven Sheffield Shield matches he took 196 wickets (26.16) four times taking ten or more wickets in a match. Jack Saunders settled in New Zealand, playing in representative matches for Wellington and New Zealand from 1910 to 1914, and helped Clarrie Grimmett enter Australian cricket.

First-class career (1899-1914): 586 runs (4.76) and 553 wickets (21.81)
Test matches (14): 39 runs (2.29), 79 wickets (22.74) and 5 catches

SCOTT, Dr Henry James Herbert (1858-1910)

Victoria

'Tup' Scott was a right-handed batsman and – like many of his colleagues – never a stylist, but his defence was assured, and he could hit when he liked. In a career that lasted less than ten years he represented Australia in the 1884/5 series, and toured England in 1884 and as captain in 1886. He gained golden opinions from those who played with him but there is little doubt that the cares of captaincy weighed heavily on him. His more prolific tour was 1886, when he made 1,289 runs in 59 completed innings; but his peak as a Test batsman was 1884 when he averaged 73.33 in the three matches. At Lord's, when England won by an innings, he top-scored each time with 75 and 31 not out; and at The Oval he made 102, adding 207 in a run-feast for the third wicket with Billy Murdoch. During the 1886 tour the players argued among themselves and sometimes blood-stained carriages bore witness to blows having been struck. 'Tup' remained in England to pursue his medical studies, played no more big cricket and became a pioneer country doctor.

First-class career (1877-86): 2,863 runs (22.72) including 4 centuries, and 18 wickets (27.44)
Test matches (8): 359 runs (27.61) including 1 century, 0-26 and 8 catches

SELLERS, Reginald Hugh Durning (b.1940)

South Australia

A tall, leg-spin bowler, Rex Sellers took 48 wickets for

his State in 1963/4, which earned him a place in the team to England in 1964, but he damaged his bowling hand in one of the preliminary games on the tour and did not appear in the Tests. He toured India in 1964/5 and made his sole Test appearance in the third match, at Calcutta, scoring 0, taking 0 for 17 and holding one catch.

First-class career (1959-67): 1,089 runs (18.15) and 121 wickets (38.45)

SERJEANT, Craig Stanton (b.1951)

Western Australia

A tall and strongly built right-hand batsman, Craig Serjeant is a powerful hitter of the ball, especially to the on-side, and such was his consistency after breaking into the strong Western Australian side in 1977/8 that he was making his first Test appearance at Lord's after only eighteen first-class innings. He had scored 730 runs at an average of 66 in his first ten innings for Western Australia, including an impressive century against MCC on their way via Perth to play in the Centenary Test at Melbourne. At Lord's in his first Test innings he played a determined innings of 81 marked by powerful leg-side hitting, but England's bowlers got the measure of him thereafter and it was only in his tenth Test, when he hit 124 against West Indies at Georgetown in 1978, that he appeared to have established himself in the Australian team. However his form was topsy-turvy the following season and he was not picked to play against England. A quiet, modest friendly man, he is a pharmacist by trade.

First-class career (1976-): 3,994 runs (35.66) including 9 centuries
Test matches (12): 522 runs (23.72) including 1 century, and 13 catches

SHEAHAN, Andrew Paul (b.1946)

Victoria

Although in the early part of his career Paul Sheahan was regarded as the most exciting batsman to emerge in Australian cricket since Norman O'Neill, he did not quite live up to that early reputation. Tall, good-looking, charming and erudite, he was, nevertheless, a classy and stylish right-handed batsman and brilliant cover-point. In his second season with Victoria, 1966/7, he came second in the overall Sheffield Shield averages with 66, making his career-highest score of 202 against South Australia at Melbourne. He was sparkling, and, making his Test debut against India in 1967/8 at Adelaide, he hit 81 and 35. Between 1967 and 1971 he appeared in twenty-five consecutive Tests: in England, South Africa and India, and at home against India, West Indies and England. He was then

Paul Sheahan

dropped, until making his second tour to England in 1972 and appearing against Pakistan and New Zealand in 1972/3 and 1973/4. With a highest score of 51 he averaged 36.71 against the West Indies in 1968/9, not able to build a long innings. In India in 1969 he made his first Test century, 114 in the second match at Kanpur. The previous year he had disappointed on his first tour of England, failing to reach 1,000 runs, and in the Tests excelling only with 88 in the first Test at Old Trafford when his fourth-wicket stand with Bill Lawry took Australia from danger at 174 for 4 to the safety of 326 for 5. On his second England visit in 1972 he performed quite well, making 788 runs (41.47) and in one of the two Tests he played, the last at The Oval, his 44 not out saw Australia safely home. His 127 in the second Test against Pakistan in 1972/3 helped to lay foundations for victory. His Test career ended quietly against New Zealand in 1973/4. For his State alone he made 3,988 runs (59.52) in forty-seven matches. A schoolmaster at Geelong College, specializing in mathematics, he spent two years teaching at Winchester.

First-class career (1965-73): 7,987 runs (46.16) including 19 centuries
Test matches (31): 1,594 runs (33.91) including 2 centuries, and 17 catches

SHEPHERD, Barrie Kenneth (b.1938)

Western Australia

A burly and very consistent left-handed batsman, who

scored 5,340 runs in eleven seasons, Barrie Shepherd narrowly missed the 1964 tour of England. He toured the West Indies in 1964/5 and at home, between 1962 and 1965, played a sprinkling of Tests, against England, South Africa and Pakistan. On his debut against England, in the third Test at Sydney in 1962/3, he made 71 not out, holding the middle-order batting together. In his first Test against South Africa, the second at Melbourne in 1963/4, he struck hard for 96, but in the fourth Test at Adelaide his 70 and 78 could not prevent South Africa winning handsomely. In four Tests of that series he averaged 38.28. Against Pakistan at Melbourne in 1964/5 he made 55 and 43 not out. Such was Australia's batting power that he had fewer chances than he deserved. He captained Western Australia for several seasons.

First-class career (1955-66): 6,838 runs (41.19) including 13 centuries
Test matches (9): 502 runs (41.83), 0-9 and 2 catches

SIEVERS, Morris William (1912-68)

Victoria

Six feet four inches, Morris Sievers was a right-arm fast-medium bowler with the invaluable lift which great height gives to a bowler, and a useful batsman. He appeared in three Tests as an opening bowler against England in 1936/7, in the third of which (his last) he was virtually unplayable on a Melbourne 'glue-pot' pitch, when the ball rose from a good length almost vertically. He took 5 for 21 in the first innings and headed the Test bowling averages. He toured South Africa in 1935/6 without, however, appearing in the Tests.

First-class career (1933-45): 2,075 runs (29.64) and 116 wickets (33.36)
Test matches (3): 67 runs (13.40), 9 wickets (17.88) and 4 catches

SIMPSON, Robert Baddeley (b.1936)

New South Wales and Western Australia

One of Australia's finest all-round cricketers, Bobby Simpson owes his success to a rigorous dedication to cricket allied to great natural ability. A sturdily built right-hand batsman at home against all bowlers except at times the very fastest, he was also a good leg-spin and googly bowler and one of the finest slip fielders of all time. His ability was evident very early. He made his initial first-class appearance for New South Wales in 1952/3 against Victoria when still a month short of his seventeenth birthday. To further his career, he played Lancashire League cricket in England in 1959 and moved to Western Australia between 1956/7 and 1960/61. Brilliant footwork and lightning reflexes took him into the right position to play any stroke but, like

Bobby Simpson

all prolific batsmen, he had the self-discipline not to play shots involving too great a risk until he was thoroughly established at the crease. New South Wales were reminded of what they had (temporarily) lost in 1959/60 when, playing for Western Australia against them, he scored 236 not out and then took three wickets in five balls while taking 5 for 45. His highest score, 359 for New South Wales against Queensland in 1963/4, is the highest score in Australia since the Second World War. Simpson has toured all the other Test playing countries: England (twice), New Zealand (twice), South Africa (twice), the West Indies (twice) and India and Pakistan. He captained Australia in twenty-nine Tests between 1963/4 and 1967/8, and again in a further ten in 1977/8 after accepting the invitation of the Australian Board to come back to lead the young side which had to be rebuilt after the defections to World Series Cricket. At Old Trafford in 1964 he hit 311 against England, the third highest by an Australian in Test cricket – a typically painstaking effort designed to make sure of the Ashes. He hit twenty-three fours and a six in this innings which stretched into the third morning of the match and which was, strangely enough, his first hundred in thirty Tests, although as opening partner to Bill Lawry he had already been a consistent run-scorer. With Lawry in 1965 he scored 382 for the first wicket against the West Indies at Bridgetown, the highest opening partnership in Australia's history, Simpson making 201. Like all their partnerships together this one was notable for a perfect understanding in their running between the wickets. Simpson always believed in taking as many short singles as possible. As a captain he was firm, decisive, always in control, but sometimes lacking imagination. His 110 catches in Test cricket is a record for Australia; practically nothing escaped him at first slip. His leg-spinners were good enough to bring him 5 for 57 against India at Sydney in 1967/8, his last season in his 'first' career. Always superbly fit, Simpson conducted the game sportingly but toughly, and he was always quite immaculately turned out, with his dark hair swept back neatly above square, tough and determined features. He now has a highly successful public relations business.

First-class career (1952-77): 21,029 runs (56.22) including 60 centuries, 349 wickets (38.07) and 383 catches

Test matches (62): 4,869 runs (46.81) including 10 centuries, 71 wickets (42.26) and 110 catches

SINCOCK, David John (b.1942)

South Australia

A red-haired left-arm googly bowler, David Sincock was able to spin the ball on any wicket but, like many of his type, tended to lack control and direction. He toured the West Indies in 1965 and played at home against Pakistan in 1964/5, and England in 1965/6 with expensive results. His debut in first-class cricket, however, had been notable: he took 6 for 52 in the first innings of the strong New South Wales side at Adelaide in 1960/61.

First-class career (1960-66): 838 runs (17.45) and 159 wickets (36.87)

Test matches (3): 80 runs (26.66), 8 wickets (51.25) and 2 catches

SLATER, Keith Nichol (b.1935)

Western Australia

An all-rounder, usually a slow off-spinner, sometimes a medium-pacer with the new ball, Keith Slater's action did not meet with general satisfaction, but later his sound batting enabled him to open the innings for his State. In taking 4 for 8 in one spell for Western Australia against MCC at Perth in 1958/9, he became the first of Australia's alleged 'chuckers' of the period. In his last season, 1964/5, he was called for throwing at Sydney, while playing against New South Wales, but this was only the second time he had been called. In his sole Test, the third at Sydney against England that season, he made 1 not out and took 2 for 101. He toured New Zealand in 1959/60 and was also a noted Australian Rules footballer.

First-class career (1955-65): 2,198 runs (21.13) including 1 century and 140 wickets (42.30)

SLEEP, Peter Raymond (b.1957)

South Australia

A highly promising right-arm leg spinner with a good high action and an attacking middle-order batsman, Peter Sleep, known as 'Sounda', belies his name because he is a thoroughly lively cricketer. Establishing himself in the South Australia side in 1977/8, he scored 105 not out against Queensland and took 4 for 41 against New South Wales. Performances like these the following season took him into the national side for the first Test against Pakistan at Melbourne in March 1979. He scored 10 and 0, took 1 for 16 in the first innings and 1 for 62 in only eight overs in the second, and was promptly dropped, but he gained further Test experience in India in 1979. His tour to India was disappointing, although in the fourth Test his determined 64 in the second innings helped to save the game for Australia. He was less successful in the other Test in which he played, the sixth, and he did not take a wicket in either game. Selection for the Test team eluded him in the following two seasons but he continued to be a considerable force for South Australia with batting becoming increasingly the strongest of his all-round qualities. Unfortunately for him the leg-spinner was becoming unfashionable, even in the country which has produced more outstanding exponents of the art than any other. However, he got another chance when playing a Test in Pakistan in 1982/3. He took only one wicket and was dropped again.

First-class career (1976-): 2,899 runs (32.21) including 4 centuries, and 149 wickets (32.06)

Test matches (4): 124 runs (15.50) and 3 wickets (127.33)

SLIGHT, James (1855-1930)

Victoria

Jim Slight was a right-handed batsman with a sound defence and a free style, and a good field at point or long-on. Impaired health, which necessitated an operation, handicapped him while in England with the 1880 team. In the first-ever Test in England at The Oval he scored 11 but did not represent Australia again.

First-class career (1874-87): 415 runs (12.57)

SMITH, David Bertram Miller (1884-1963)

Victoria

A fast-scoring right-handed batsman, being a splendid cutter and driver, Dave Smith toured New Zealand in 1909/10 and England in 1912 as a replacement for one of the six major players who had refused to tour. He was a big disappointment, 'living it up' and making only 316 runs (17.73), although he did hit a century off Surrey at The Oval, adding 176 for the sixth wicket in less than two hours with Claude Jennings. Even then an error of judgment on his part threw away his partner's wicket – and Surrey won. He played in two Tests on this tour and also toured America in 1912.

First-class career (1908-12): 1,764 runs (23.83) including 3 centuries
Test matches (2): 30 runs (15.00)

SPOFFORTH, Frederick Robert (1853-1926)

New South Wales, Victoria and Derbyshire

'The Demon' Spofforth was the greatest figure in early Australian Test cricket, the man who finally humbled W.G. Grace. In May 1878 at Lord's he captured 6 for 4 and 5 for 16, MCC being routed in one day. He studied the methods of all the famous bowlers he had seen and put to useful effect all their lessons, but he was still an original, mixing speed, cut and swerve with devilish accuracy. His basic pace was fast-medium. He was tall – over six feet – and lean, could run a hundred yards in less than eleven seconds and, unlike most of his contemporaries, studied the strengths and weaknesses of his opposing batsmen. He refused to play in the first-ever Test at Melbourne in 1876/7 as W.L. Murdoch had not been selected to keep wicket but he appeared in the second. At Melbourne in 1878/9 he was the main instrument of victory in taking 13 for 110. After his dramatic start in 1878 he toured England again in 1880 (injury prevented him appearing in the first Test at The Oval), 1882, 1884 and 1886. At The Oval in 1882 – the first Ashes match – he bowled Australia to victory with his 14 for 90. In the 1886 series he was still the most effective bowler with 14 wickets (18.57). In Australia he took 18 wickets (22.66) in the 1882/3 series, including 7 for 44 in the second innings of the third match at Sydney (11 for 117 in the match), which still could not bring victory; and he was still the best bowler in the 1884/5 series with 19 wickets (16.10). In all eleven-a-side matches in England he took 123 wickets (11.37) in 1878, 188 wickets (12.12) in 1882 and 216 wickets (12.23) in 1884. Only injuries prevented similar records in 1880 and 1886. Settling in England, 'The Demon' became a director of the Star Tea Company and played for Derbyshire with success from 1889 until 1891, taking 15 for 81 against Yorkshire at Derby in the former year. It is said that in 1881 he rode 400 miles to play in a minor match in Australia and then took all 20 wickets – clean-bowled!

'The Demon' Spofforth

First-class career (1874-97): 1,928 runs (9.88) and 853 wickets (14.95)
Test matches (18): 217 runs (9.43), 94 wickets (18.41) and 11 catches

STACKPOLE, Keith Raymond (b.1940)

Victoria

Squarely built and red-faced, Keith Stackpole was a lusty right-handed opening batsman who almost always attacked, and often hooked and cut so hard at the new ball that his occasional edges were just too hot for fielders to hold. He was an entertainer who, in full flow, would bat with tremendous confidence, often leaving the crease to drive straight or over mid-on. As he matured, he extended his range with many more front-foot strokes. He was a useful leg-break bowler in his early days and a fine close fieldsman. His sole tour of England in 1972 was as vice-captain. From 1966 until 1973 other tours were to South Africa (twice), India, the West Indies and New Zealand. At home he appeared in two series against England, 1965/6 and 1970/71, and against West Indies, Pakistan and New Zealand. He had a long haul to the top after making his first-class debut for his State against Tasmania in 1959/60. On his Test debut against England in 1965/6 he batted down the order. His first Test century was 134 against South Africa in the Cape Town match in 1966/7. He lost his place against the Indian tourists and was not selected for England in 1968, but he regained his place against the West Indies in 1968/9 and became established as an opening batsman. From then until the end of the 1970/71 England series, in which he headed the Australian averages with 627 runs (52.25) including his career-highest score of 207 in the first match at Brisbane, he played in twenty consecutive Tests. In England in 1972 he made more runs than anyone on either side and headed the averages again with 485 runs (55.88), including a fine 114 at Trent

Keith Stackpole

Bridge, when runs were badly needed against John Snow at his best. In all first-class matches on the tour he scored 1,309 runs (43.63). His last Test century was 122 in the first match against New Zealand at Melbourne in 1973/4, and in his final Test, against New Zealand at Auckland the same season, he was dismissed without scoring in either innings.

First-class career (1959-73): 10,100 runs (39.29) including 22 centuries, 148 wickets (39.28) and 166 catches
Test matches (43): 2,807 runs (37.42) including 7 centuries, 15 wickets (66.73) and 47 catches

STEVENS, Gavin Byron (b.1932)

South Australia

Gavin Stevens was a very competent opening batsman for his State, scoring 666 runs and 951 runs in 1957/8 and 1958/9 respectively, including his top-score, 259 not out against New South Wales at Sydney in 1958/9. He toured India and Pakistan in 1959/60 but had moderate success in the Tests.

First-class career (1954-60); 3,061 runs (38.26) including 7 centuries
Test matches (4): 112 runs (16.00) and 2 catches

TABER, Hedley Brian (b.1940)

New South Wales

A small, dark, neat, unobtrusive 'keeper, Brian Taber held some fine catches standing back and supported the slow bowlers very well. In his first season for his State in 1964/5 he made thirty-one dismissals, including eight victims against South Australia at Sydney, and thirty-five the following season. He toured England in 1968 as second-string to Barry Jarman, but visited South Africa (twice) and India as the first-string. His sole home Test was against the West Indies in 1968/9. His entry into Test cricket was most striking. At Johannesburg in 1966/7 he held seven catches and made one stumping, the most victims by an Australian 'keeper against South Africa. He became a senior coach.

First-class career (1964-74): 2,648 runs (18.01) including 1 century, and 395 dismissals (345 ct, 50 st.)
Test matches (16): 353 runs (16.04) and 60 dismissals (56 ct, 4 st.)

TALLON, Donald (b.1916)

Queensland

A strident appealer, Don Tallon was also a quick and brilliant wicket-keeper. He equalled a long standing world record by capturing twelve wickets in a match (9 caught, 3 stumped) for his State against New South Wales at Sydney in 1938/9. He was a stylish middle-order batsman with a pleasing array of strokes, making his name as a powerful driver; he hit centuries against all the other Sheffied Shield States. Against England at Melbourne in 1946/7 he hit 92 and added 154 with Ray Lindwall for the eighth wicket in eighty-seven minutes. He had twenty victims in this series. He toured New Zealand in 1946, and England in 1948 and 1953 and, at home, played against India in 1947/8 and England in 1950/51.

First-class career (1933-53): 6,034 runs (29.14) including 9 centuries, and 432 dismissals (303 ct, 129 st.)
Test matches (21): 394 runs (17.13) and 58 dismissals (50 ct, 8 st.)

TAYLOR, John Morris (1895-1971)

New South Wales

A schoolboy phenomenon, Johnny Taylor was a smallish man and a polished right-handed batsman, happiest when chasing runs and giving full rein to his varied array of strokes. His on-side play was excellent and he would stand back and, with certainty and power, force away anything short of a length. A brilliant fielder at cover, he was a spectacular runner and thrower. He was a member of the Australian Imperial Forces side in 1919, scoring 1,187 runs (32.23), and toured England again with the 1921 and 1926 teams, besides South Africa in 1921/2. It was in the 1924/5 home series against England that he rose to stardom, scoring 541 runs (54.10) and, in the second innings of the first Test at Sydney, saving his side with 108, when he added 127 for the last wicket with Arthur Mailey, a record for these contests. Taylor batted with the handicap of a boil on the back of the knee, just where the strap of the pad was rubbing. In the fourth Test at Melbourne, when England won handsomely, he top-scored each time with 86 and 68. On his last tour of England he was in poor health and achieved little. In twenty-one Sheffield Shield matches he made 1,299 runs (39.36).

First-class career (1913-26): 6,274 runs (33.37) including 11 centuries
Test matches (20): 997 runs (35.60) including 1 century, 1-45 and 11 catches

THOMAS, Graeme (b.1938)

New South Wales

Dark, thickset and a beautiful stroke-player, Graeme Thomas toured New Zealand in 1959/60, West Indies in 1965, and South Africa in 1966/7. Such was his country's batting strength, however, that he could never establish himself as a Test player. He represented Australia at home against England and on a tour of the West Indies, when his overall average was 40.91 in first-class matches. His highest Test score was 61 at Port of Spain in the second Test. In fifty-nine Sheffield Shield matches he made 3,992 runs (46.41), including his career-highest, 229 against Victoria at Melbourne. With Neil Marks he added 332 for the sixth wicket against South Australia at Sydney in 1958/9, a Shield record. He is of part-Aborigine extraction.

First-class career (1957-66): 5,726 runs (40.32) including 17 centuries
Test matches (8): 325 runs (29.54) and 3 catches

THOMPSON, Nathaniel (1838-96)

New South Wales

Nat Thompson was a considerable figure in early Australian cricket, playing twenty-one times for his State against Victoria between 1858 and 1879, achieving a batting average of 13.41 and 20 wickets. He was also a good reserve wicket-keeper. Against Twenty-Two of Queensland in 1864 he returned analyses of 7 for 9 and 7 for 25. He played against all the England sides which visited Australia up to and including Lord Harris's in 1878/9 – five in all – and, in eleven-a-side matches against them, averaged 18.8 with the bat. He appeared in the first two Tests of 1876/7 as an opening batsman, but was unable to make the first tour of England in 1878. He was the first player to be dismissed in Tests – 'b. A. Hill 1'.

First-class career (1857-79): 705 runs (14.10), 23 wickets (22.22) and 28 dismissals (21 ct, 7 st.)
Test matches (2): 67 runs (16.75), 1-31 and 3 catches

THOMS, George Ronald (b.1927)

Victoria

A right-handed opening batsman, George Thoms' sole Test was the fifth against West Indies at Sydney in 1951/2, when he scored 16 and 28.

First-class career (1946-53): 1,137 runs (35.53) including 3 centuries

THOMSON, Alan Lloyd (b.1945)

Victoria

Alan or 'Froggy' Thomson bowled with enthusiasm and a curious wrong-foot action which gave him some extra bounce. He was heralded as the new fast-bowling terror when MCC toured Australia in 1970/71 – especially when he took 9 for 181 for Victoria against the touring team at Melbourne in an early match – but he was not genuinely fast and his performances in the Tests were very disappointing.

First-class career (1968-74): 260 runs (8.12) and 184 wickets (26.72)
Test matches (4): 22 runs (22.00) and 12 wickets (54.50)

THOMSON, Jeffrey Robert (b.1950)

New South Wales, Queensland and Middlesex

A happy-go-lucky character, Jeff Thomson made one unsuccessful Test appearance against Pakistan in 1972/3 when it was subsequently discovered he played with a broken bone in his foot. Then, after showing his ability in his first season for Queensland in 1974/5, the selectors gambled with him for the first Test of that season and the result was one of the most awesome performances of fast bowling in cricket history. On a Gabba pitch unprepared because of tropical thunderstorms, Thomson got the ball to lift off the length after delivering it at a speed somewhere between 90 and 100 mph. Immensely strong and a former surf rider from the Sydney suburb of Bankstown, he bowls with a slinging action involving a powerful twist of the body in delivery. With the ball brought from behind his back at the last moment, he has the approach of a javelin thrower once his target is sighted. The action, however, demands much of his body, and he has never consistently achieved the ferocious pace which brought him 33 wickets (17.93) in his first five Tests against England. The bane of Thomson's life since this magnificent display of bowling, in which he earned success by sheer speed and exceptional bounce, has

Jeff Thomson

been a suspect right shoulder, which first caused him trouble while playing tennis at Adelaide during the fifth Test in 1974/5. When Thomson missed the last Test and his partner Lillee was injured at the start of the sixth Test in Melbourne, England who had been demoralized by the fire of these two won the final game by an innings! Of all the great fast bowling partnerships, perhaps none has been as crucial to their team's success as this one. The slow wickets in England in 1975 reduced Thomson's effectiveness: he took 16 Test wickets (28.56) in the four Tests. But the following winter he and Lillee outbowled an almost equally fearsome West Indian fast bowling combination, Thomson taking 29 wickets (28.65). However, on the first day of the first Test against Pakistan at Adelaide (his unlucky ground) in 1976/7, Thomson crashed into his team-mate Alan Turner as they went for a high catch and tore his right shoulder muscle so severely that he missed the remainder of the series, and the Centenary Test. During this match Thomson signed for World Series Cricket, only to withdraw from his contract when he realized that it contravened another. He played against England in 1977, taking 23 wickets in the series (25.34) (easily the leading Australian bowler), against India in 1977/8 (22 wickets at 23.45), and West Indies in 1978 (20 wickets at 28.85). However, getting into financial trouble, he accepted a second offer to join World Series Cricket, missed the 1978/9 series with England, and played for WSC in the West Indies when the Australian Board released him early from his contract. A capable fielder, he is a right-handed batsman who occasionally hits effectively. The prospect of Jeff Thomson resuming his partnership with Dennis Lillee was eagerly awaited after the disbandment of World Series Cricket in 1979/80. Thomson began that season well, with 10 wickets in the opening Shield encounter with Victoria, but at international level he was unhappy bowling in limited-over games in which containing the batsman is as important as getting him out and his 2 wickets in the Benson and Hedges World Series Cup cost him 95 runs each. He played in the first two Tests of the season, against the West Indies in Brisbane and England in Perth, but although he took 7 wickets the extraordinary pace and lift of five seasons before had gone, never, it seemed, to return. He toured England in 1980, playing in several of the warm-up games but not the Centenary Test itself, and despite some good performances at home in 1980/81 he was overlooked for the national team and omitted from the 1981 touring team to England when two younger fast bowlers were preferred. Instead Thomson signed a contract for Middlesex. He went home early, however, after an appendix operation, and in 1981/2 got back into the national side, bowling heroically against the West Indies at Adelaide after Lillee had been injured. He toured New Zealand at the end of the season, taking 4-51 in New Zealand's first innings at Christchurch, and bowled admirably in 1982/3. Thomson's decline was steady and only slight, but he was not quite the bowler who for two seasons at least had been amongst the fastest and best of all time.

First-class career (1972-): 1,600 runs (13.79) and 481 wickets (24.69)
Test matches (45): 599 runs (12.48), 175 wickets (26.94) and 18 catches

THURLOW, Hugh Motley (1903-75)

Queensland

A fast bowler, 'Pud' Thurlow attracted notice by taking 6 for 60 for his State against Victoria at Melbourne in 1929/30, in the course of which he broke the finger of Australia's future captain, Bill Woodfull, putting him out of action for the rest of the season. Then in 1931/2 Alan Kippax of New South Wales attempted to hook him too early and had to have his eyebrow treated in hospital. That season 'Pud' played in his sole Test, the fourth against South Africa at Adelaide, failing to score and conceding 86 runs without taking a wicket.

First-class career (1928-34): 202 runs (5.31) and 80 wickets (42.88)

TOOHEY, Peter Michael (b.1954)

New South Wales

A small, right-handed middle-order batsman, Peter Toohey had an impressive start in Test cricket in 1977/8 but failed most disappointingly against the strong England bowling attack the following season. At his best he is a fine stroke-player who drives extremely hard, and bears a strong resemblance in style to Doug Walters, whose role he took on in the New South Wales side. He is also a quick runner with a fine throw from the deep field. After scoring 1,149 runs at an average of 54 in Grade cricket in Sydney in 1973/4, the sixth highest seasonal aggregate ever recorded in that competition, Toohey soon showed his ability in first-class cricket the following season and played in all the Tests against India (home) and West Indies (away) in 1977/8, scoring 705 runs at 47.00 in his first eight Tests with a highest score of 122 against the West Indies at Sabina Park where he also made 97 in the second innings. He scored 954 first-class runs in the Australian season of 1977/8 and a further 566 at 51.46 in the West Indies, but the English fast bowlers uncovered, and mercilessly exploited, a weakness outside his off-stump and in five Tests he totalled only 149 runs (16.55), including a fine innings of 81 not out in the first innings of the second Test at Perth. In 1979/80 he hit three hundreds in the Sheffield Shield and finished the season in eighth place in the national averages with 697 runs from 19 innings. The four knocks which he had in Test cricket, however, brought down the average considerably, for he was out of luck in his one game each against the West Indies and England. Despite his eclipse at international level he continued to be a valuable batsman for New South Wales.

First-class career (1974-): 4,909 runs (39.27) including 11 centuries
Test matches (15): 896 runs (32.00) including 1 century, 0-4 and 9 catches

TOSHACK, Ernest Raymond Herbert (b.1917)

New South Wales

Tall, dark-haired and with a look of world-weariness, Ernie Toshack bowled a lively left-arm medium pace and, when he concentrated on the leg-stump, his main value lay in nagging accuracy of a kind which would have made him highly suitable for limited-over cricket. In a high scoring era he conceded approximately two and a half runs an over. He toured New Zealand in 1945/6 and England in 1948. At home he appeared against England in 1946/7 and India in 1947/8. With Lindwall, Miller, Johnston and Toshack to contend with, England's batsmen had little respite in 1948. Toshack himself took 50 wickets (21.12) on his England tour, including 11 in Tests (in which, incidentally, he made 51 of the 78 runs he hit on the tour and had some inspired and comical last-wicket stands with Bill Johnston). In his first Test, against New Zealand at Wellington in 1945/6, Toshack delivered 29 overs and took 6 for 18. On his debut against England, at Brisbane in 1946/7, his match record was 9 for 99; in the series he had 17 wickets (25.70). The following season, against India, he had his last major triumph: 5 for 2 (in two overs and three balls) and 6 for 29 (11 for 31 in the match) at Brisbane. A troublesome knee curtailed his career.

First-class career (1945-9): 185 runs (5.78) and 195 wickets (20.37)
Test matches (12): 73 runs (14.60), 47 wickets (21.04) and 4 catches

TRAVERS, Joseph Patrick Francis (1871-1942)

South Australia

A shrewd, slow left-arm bowler of the Wilfred Rhodes school, Joe Travers took 9 for 30 in the first innings of Victoria at Melbourne in 1900/1 and captured 28 wickets in Sheffield Shield matches that season. He appeared in the fifth Test at Melbourne against England in 1901/2, scoring 9 and 1, taking 1 for 14 and holding one catch; this was his sole Test. In 28 Sheffield Shield matches he took 90 wickets (33.06).

First-class career (1895-1906): 760 runs (16.52) and 116 wickets (31.66)

TRIBE, George Edward (b.1920)

Victoria and Northamptonshire

A genuine all-rounder, but best remembered as a back-of-the-hand left-arm spinner, George Tribe achieved great feats for Northamptonshire from 1951 until 1959, achieving the double seven times for his adopted county. He could bowl either slow left-arm orthodox or chinamen, spinning the ball quickly and often, and not giving the ball as much air as most bowlers. He was also a sound left-handed defender and front-of-the-wicket hitter liable to change the course of a game, and a brilliant fielder, especially at short-leg. He played in three Tests against England in 1946/7 after a season in which his 33 wickets had been largely instrumental in his State winning the Sheffield Shield, but there was a plethora of talent in Australia and he did not receive adequate recognition. Thus, he became a professional in the Central Lancashire League in 1947, capturing 426 wickets in three seasons. The rest is mainly the story of great, all-round work for Northamptonshire. Three times in his career he took 9 wickets in an innings (twice for Northamptonshire). He toured India with Commonwealth teams in 1949/50 and 1950/51.

First-class career (1945-59): 10,177 runs (27.35) including 7 centuries, 1,378 wickets (20.55) and 239 catches
Test matches (3): 35 runs (17.50) and 2 wickets (165.00)

Albert Trott

TROTT, Albert Edwin (1873-1914)

Victoria and Middlesex

Tall, strong, moustached and confident, 'Alberto' Trott burst into Test cricket in 1894/5 against A.E. Stoddart's England side. On his debut in the third match at Adelaide he scored 38 not out and 72 not out and took 8 for 43 in the second innings, and in the next match at Sydney his contribution was 85 not out. Both times Australia won handsomely (yet lost the Ashes) – and in all matches against the English teams on the tour he made 331 runs in nine innings and took 19 wickets. 'Alberto' was omitted, however, from the 1896 team to England captained by his elder brother, Harry. Thereupon, the most promising young Australian of his generation came to England on his own account, joined Lord's ground staff and qualified for Middlesex and from 1899 until 1904 enjoyed great all-round success. He scored 1,175 runs and took 239 wickets in 1899, and scored 1,337 runs and took 211 wickets in 1900. Though his arm was low, he could bowl just about anything from fast to slow and spun the ball vigorously. Six of his eight centuries were scored at Lord's and some tremendous hits were recorded there. For MCC against Sussex in May 1899 he drove Fred Tate so hard that the ball hit the left-hand emblem of the MCC Coat-of-Arms crowning the highest pinnacle on the top of the towers of the Pavilion and, two months later, for MCC against the Australians, came his unique hit: he struck a ball from Monty Noble over the top of the Pavilion. The wine went to his head: he was always trying to repeat these performances, and he eventually became a mere slogger. He took all ten wickets in an innings for Middlesex against Somerset at Taunton in 1900 and on ten occasions took thirteen or more wickets in a match. After 1904 he fell away, becoming heavy and muscle-bound, but in 1907, in his benefit match for Middlesex against Somerset at Lord's, he took four wickets in five balls, then finished the game early by doing the hat-trick a second time in the same innings. Thus he deprived himself of more gate money! His wry comment was that he was bowling himself 'into the workhouse'. From 1911 to 1913 he was a first-class umpire, but his health steadily worsened and he finally shot himself through the head at his lodgings at Willesden Green. Touring South Africa with Lord Hawke's team in 1898/9, he appeared in two Tests for England, very successfully.

First-class career (1893-1911): 10,696 runs (19.48) including 8 centuries, 1,674 wickets (21.09) and 449 catches
Test matches (Australia – 3): 205 runs (102.50), 9 wickets (21.33) and 4 catches. (England – 2): 23 runs (5.75) and 17 wickets (11.64)

TROTT, George Henry Stephens (1866-1917)

Victoria

'Harry' Trott, a genial fellow, was an elegant and forcing right-handed batsman who could also play the barn-door game if necessary, indeed was at his best in a difficult situation. An effective leg-spin change bowler, he was also a fine fielder at point. He toured England in 1888, 1890, 1893 and 1896; and at home played against England in 1891/2, 1894/5 and 1897/8. He captained Australia in 1896 and 1897/8, winning the rubber in the latter series by four games to one. Despite little early education he was a born leader. In the Test at Lord's in 1896 he was at his best. Australia were dismissed for 53 in the first innings and, 239 runs behind, lost three quick wickets in the second, but then Trott scored 143 and, with Syd Gregory, added 221 in just over two and a half hours. He averaged 34.33 in this series. Away from cricket he was a postman, but his later life was marred by mental breakdowns.

First-class career (1885-1907): 8,804 runs (23.54) including 9 centuries, 386 wickets (25.12) and 183 catches
Test matches (24): 921 runs (21.92) including 1 century, 29 wickets (35.13) and 21 catches

TRUMBLE, Hugh (1867-1938)

Victoria

Tall and slim with long bones, prominent nose and ears, Hugh Trumble made the most of his height by bringing the ball over at the full extent of his right arm. A medium-paced off-spin bowler of the highest class, he kept an impeccable length, flighted the ball skilfully, turned it a little on the hard pitches and a great deal on the poor ones. Highly intelligent, he would buy the wicket of the best players if necessary.

Hugh Trumble

He was a more than useful right-handed batsman at times, with abundant concentration, and also a fine slip fielder. He toured England in 1890, 1893, 1896, 1899 and 1902. After a quiet first tour he took 123 wickets (16.39), 148 (15.81), 142 (18.43) and 140 (14.27) respectively, and scored 1,183 runs (27.51) in 1899, thus achieving the double that year. At home he represented his country in 1894/5, 1897/8, 1901/2 and 1903/4. He took 12 for 89 in The Oval Test in 1896; 10 for 128 at Old Trafford in 1902, when Australia won by three runs; and 12 for 173 at The Oval the same year, when England triumphed by one wicket. In the 1901/2 series he took 28 wickets (20.03), in 1902 26 wickets (14.26), and in 1903/4 24 wickets (16.58). Twice he performed the hat-trick, each time at Melbourne, and in his final match in first-class cricket he captured 7 for 28 at Melbourne in 1903/4, Australia beating England by 218 runs. He also toured South Africa in 1902/3 and North America twice. From 1911 until 1938 he was secretary of Melbourne C.C. and, with his tall figure, broad-brimmed hat and kindly nature, he was a popular and respected official. He was younger brother of J.W. Trumble.

First-class career (1887-1903): 5,395 runs (19.47) including 3 centuries, 929 wickets (18.44) and 329 catches
Test matches (32): 851 runs (19.78), 141 wickets (21.78) and 45 catches

TRUMBLE, John William (1863-1944)

Victoria

John Trumble was a useful all-rounder. Tall, and bowling with a high delivery, he was noted for his accurate length. He toured England in 1886, but showed only moderate form, and at home represented his country in 1884/5. On his Test debut, in the second match at Melbourne in 1884/5, he made 59.

First-class career (1883-93): 1,761 runs (18.93) and 109 wickets (24.10)
Test matches (7): 243 runs (20.25), 10 wickets (22.20) and 3 catches

TRUMPER, Victor Thomas (1877-1915)

New South Wales

A genius, and the greatest Australian batsman before Bradman, Victor Trumper had the ability to make big scores in 'impossible' conditions. 'He moved into his strokes', wrote H.S. Altham, 'with effortless and perfectly balanced ease. There was no limit to their range, or flaw in their fluency or timing.' Those who saw him bat have never forgotten the extreme suppleness which gave peculiar grace to everything he did and the marvellous union of his hand and eye. Unlike Bradman, it was the style and grace of Trumper, rather than the figures he produced, which marked the man's greatness as a cricketer. Yet the figures themselves were impressive enough. His first three-figure score was 292 not out for his State against Tasmania at Sydney in 1898/9. The following English season he hit 135 not out at Lord's in his second Test and, against Sussex at Hove, contributed a chanceless

Victor Trumper

300 not out in six hours and twenty minutes. On this tour Trumper made 1,556 runs (34.57) and he remained an integral part of the Australian team until 1912. He came to England again in 1902, 1905 and 1909; and, at home, he appeared in the 1901/2, 1903/4, 1907/8 and 1911/12 series against England and the 1910/11 against South Africa. He established himself as the finest Australian batsman in the wet summer of 1902, making 2,570 runs (48.49) – 956 runs more than his nearest rival in the team – including eleven centuries, the greatest of which was 104 on a sticky wicket at Old Trafford, when England were beaten by a mere 3 runs. At Sydney, in the first Test of the 1903/4 series, Trumper scored 185 not out, and in the second, on a pig of a pitch at Melbourne, he hit a superlative 74 out of a total of 122. In this series he headed the averages of both sides with 574 runs (63.77). He dominated the 1910/11 series against South Africa with 661 runs (94.42), including 214 not out in the third match at Adelaide, his Test highest. By 1914 he had scored 3,627 runs (47.72) in forty-six Sheffield Shield matches, but he had never been robust and he was struck down by Bright's disease at the age of thirty-seven. When this modest, unspoilt, kindly and popular cricketer died, it was announced on newspaper placards even though it was during the First World War.

First-class career (1894-1913): 16,939 runs (44.57) including 42 centuries, 64 wickets (31.29) and 171 catches
Test matches (48): 3,163 runs (39.04) including 8 centuries, 8 wickets (37.62) and 31 catches

TURNER, Alan (b.1950)

New South Wales

A sturdy, pigeon-chested, dark-haired left-hand opening batsman, Alan Turner was a determined player with a good temperament who did not quite have the sound technique needed for consistent success at the highest level. A steady player for several seasons in the Sheffield Shield he was picked to tour England in 1975 and hit 158 against Kent at Canterbury, earning himself a Test place. He had toured New Zealand in 1969/70 and he did so again during 1976/7 by which time he was a regular contender for a Test place. His sole Test hundred was 136 against the West Indies at Adelaide in 1975/6. He was an especially rugged square-cutter and on his day he could be a highly effective attacker of anything but the most accurate bowling, as he showed in making a century before lunch against Sri Lanka during the 1975 Prudential World Cup.

First-class career (1968-77): 5,744 runs (30.88) including 7 centuries
Test matches (14): 768 runs (29.54) including 1 century, and 15 catches

TURNER, Charles Thomas Biass (1862-1944)

New South Wales

Shortish and thickset, Charlie Turner bowled fast-medium with a chest-on action. At nineteen he took 17 for 69, including all ten in the first innings, for Twenty-Two of Bathurst against Alfred Shaw's England team in 1881/2. Against Arthur Shrewsbury's team in 1886/7, playing for Eleven of New South Wales, he took 13 for 54. Then, on his Test debut at Sydney in the same season, he dismissed 6 for 15, England falling for 45, which remains their lowest against Australia. Thus was born the legend of 'Turner the Terror'. Touring England in 1888, 1890 and 1893, he found the wickets, especially after rain, just to his liking. He was coupled with J.J. Ferris on the first two tours as one of the great bowling partnerships in history. In 1888 they took 534 wickets between them (Turner 314), and in 1890 430 (Turner 215) in all matches. Yet they were invariably on the losing side. Two of the three Tests in 1888 England won by an innings margin – yet Turner took 21 wickets (12.42) in the series, including 10 for 63 at Lord's in the only game won (and against An England Eleven at Hastings he captured 17 for 50). At Sydney in 1887/8 he had 12 for 87. In the second and fourth Tests of 1894/5 he took 8 wickets each time and was then dropped from the side! He pleaded pressure of business when receiving his delayed invitation to tour in 1896, and thus passed out of Test cricket. He was the first man to take a hundred wickets in an Australian first-class season – 106 wickets (13.59) in 1887/8 – and his 283 wickets (11.68) in first-class matches in 1888 remains the record for a touring bowler.

First-class career (1882-1909): 3,856 runs (15.49) including 2 centuries, and 992 wickets (14.26)
Test matches (17): 323 runs (11.53), 101 wickets (16.53) and 8 catches

VEIVERS, Thomas Robert (b.1937)

Queensland

A cheerful Queenslander, Tom Veivers came to England in 1964 as the first genuine right-arm off-break bowler selected by Australia for some years. He also visited South Africa, India and Pakistan; and at home played against South Africa, Pakistan and England between 1963 and 1966. His vigorous but also responsible left-handed batting helped his country considerably on several occasions. In his third Test against South Africa in 1963/4 his defiant batting at Sydney on the last day of the series in a smallish innings prevented Australia coming to England a beaten side. At Lord's in 1964 he top-scored with 54 out of 176; and at The Oval he struck 67 not out. In his next two Tests, against India, he hit further half-centuries; and in the first Test against South Africa at the New Wanderers ground in Johannesburg in 1966/7 he held the middle-order together with 55. His top score in Tests was 88 against Pakistan at Melbourne in 1964/5. He proved his stamina at Old Trafford in 1964 when he bowled 95.1 overs to take 3 for 155. He was generally a tidy and economical off-spinner but one who lacked penetration at the highest level. In forty-nine Sheffield Shield matches he made 2,726 runs (37.86) and took 86 wickets (37.97). Dark and thickset, Tom Veivers emerged originally from Queensland country cricket.

First-class career (1958-68): 5,100 runs (36.96) including 4 centuries, and 191 wickets (38.71)
Test matches (21): 813 runs (31.26), 33 wickets (41.66) and 7 catches

WAITE, Mervyn George (b.1911)

South Australia

An honest type of batsman and medium-paced bowler without any special trimmings – 'good at the bits 'n pieces' – Mervyn Waite toured England in 1938, scoring 684 runs and taking 56 wickets. He opened the bowling with Stan McCabe in the fifth Test at The Oval, when England made 903 for 7 declared. In forty-eight Sheffield Shield matches he made 2,167 runs (31.86) and took 76 wickets (36.93).

First-class career (1930-46): 3,888 runs (27.77) including 1 century, and 192 wickets (31.62)
Test matches (2): 11 runs (3.66), 1-190 and 1 catch

Max Walker

WALKER, Maxwell Henry Norman (b.1948)

Victoria

A cheerful Tasmanian, Max Walker moved to the mainland to further his cricket and Rules Football careers and broke through as Victoria's main strike bowler in 1972/3, the year which also saw his emergence as a Test-class bowler. Six foot four, pigeon-chested and thoroughly revelling in the hard work of bowling, he bowled right arm 'off the wrong foot' at fast-medium pace, usually swinging the ball into the bat with an open-chested delivery but also getting the ball to cut sharply away from the batsman in the manner of Alec Bedser. He was also a willing and determined batsman who played some highly effective and important innings against England in 1974/5. As a fielder he was relatively ponderous by modern Test standards but his hands were safe, as befitted a noted jumper and catcher on the football field. After two home Tests against Pakistan, in the second of which he took 6 for 15 in the second innings to bowl Australia to victory at Sydney, 'Tanglefoot', as he was nicknamed as a result of his criss-crossing feet in the pre-delivery stride, went on to surpass Lillee and Massie in the Caribbean, taking 26 wickets (20.73) in the series and 41 (20.48) on the tour – outstanding figures on pitches which gave him little help. He was tirelessly hostile and enthusiastic. At home against England in 1974/5 he played third fiddle to Lillee and Thomson, but was nonetheless vital to the success of Australia, for he ensured that the England batsmen should be allowed no respite. In the six Tests he took 23 wickets (29.73) including 8 for 143 in England's first innings of 529 when, minus Lillee and Thomson, Walker had the stage to himself. In England he was less successful, taking 14 wickets (34.71) in 1975 and again 14 wickets (39.35) in 1977.

First-class career (1968-81): 2,014 runs (15.49) and 499 wickets (26.47)
Test matches (34): 586 runs (19.53), 138 wickets (27.47) and 12 catches

WALL, Thomas Welbourne (1904-81)

South Australia

One of the two outstanding Australian fast bowlers of

the 1930s, 'Tim' Wall had a long, flowing approach and a vigorous kicking action like a frisky colt as he reached the crease, but his length and direction tended to be faulty. His right arm was high and he often had nasty lift and movement. He toured England in 1930 and 1934, and played at home against England in 1928/9 and 1932/3, West Indies in 1930/31 and South Africa in 1931/2. In his first Test against England, the fifth at Melbourne in 1928/9, his stamina was magnificent; he bowled 75 overs in the match, taking 8 for 189, Australia winning after five successive Test defeats. He took 13 wickets (20.23) in three Tests against South Africa in 1931/2, and in the Bodyline Series of 1932/3 he headed Australia's averages with 16 wickets (25.56) from four Tests. On his two English tours his overall figures were unimpressive; spin bowlers tended to dictate policy. He took 56 wickets (29.25) and 42 wickets (30.71) respectively. For his State in 1932/3 he devastated New South Wales at Sydney, capturing all 10 for 36 in an innings where Bradman made the top score of 56.

First-class career (1924-36): 1,063 runs (10.52) and 328 wickets (29.83)
Test matches (18): 121 runs (6.36), 56 wickets (35.89) and 11 catches

WALTERS, Francis Henry (1860-1922)

Victoria and New South Wales

Although Frank Walters had height and reach and always seemed to be on the verge of something exceptional, over-caution prevented him from achieving anything of note on the slow wickets during the 1890 England tour, other than a valuable 53 not out against Surrey at The Oval. In his sole Test at Melbourne against Arthur Shrewbury's 1885/6 England side he scored 7 and 5 and held two catches. In inter-State games, however, he could cut loose and reveal a superb array of strokes.

First-class career (1880-95): 1,755 runs (20.17) including 4 centuries

WALTERS, Kevin Douglas (b.1945)

New South Wales

Only on English and South African pitches was Doug Walters anything less than a superb batsman and an inspiring all-round cricketer. On hard pitches his incisive footwork, crisp cutting, bold hooking and devastating driving made him a scourge of bowlers, a matchwinner who scored runs so quickly that many a game was transformed by his brilliance. He was also a useful medium-pace swing bowler with a knack of coming on to take important wickets, and a dazzling fielder in the covers who could catch with the best close to the wicket. For once, a 'new Bradman' did not

Doug Walters

disappoint when he reached Australian first-class cricket. In his first two Test matches, played against England in 1965/6, he scored 155, 22 and 115. A star was born and he finished the series with 410 runs at 68.33. However, National Service prevented him from going to South Africa the following season, and, although he was released to play on the England tour of 1968, there are many who claim that his technique was looser on his return. In a miserably wet summer he scored 933 runs (31.10), 343 in the five Tests at 38.11. He fared little better on his subsequent visits to England, scoring only 54 in seven Test innings in 1972, 125 in five innings in 1975, although in 1977 on his fourth visit he improved to make 223 runs in five Tests at 24.77, including a dashing 88 at Old Trafford, though these were nothing like the scores that a batsman of his talents should have been capable of producing. Like the South Africans a year earlier, England's bowlers, led by John Snow, had worked out his weaknesses in 1970/71, when it was realized that he would soon perish in the gully area if a fast attack was directed exclusively at his off-stump, and Walters did not have the discipline to reform his technique. Yet, even against the confident English bowlers, he made 373 runs (37.30) in 1970/71, including 112 at Brisbane, and 383 (42.53) in 1974/5, including a superb 103 in a fraction over two hours at Perth. If Walters blew hot and cold against England, he has been more consistently brilliant against other countries. In 1968/9 against the West Indies at home he made 699 runs in four Tests including 242 and 103 at Sydney. In West Indies in 1973 he hit 497 runs in five Tests at 71.00, including a century between lunch and tea at Port of

Spain. In 1976/7 he hit his second Test double century, 250 against New Zealand at Christchurch. He joined Kerry Packer's World Series Cricket, but did not meet with much success in cricket dominated by fast bowlers. When Doug Walters reappeared for Australia in one or two limited-over internationals in 1979/80 after a relatively unsuccessful sojourn with World Series Cricket, it looked rather like a case of a job for one of the boys for old time's sake. But the following season he returned to Test cricket and thoroughly justified his selection, hitting a fluent 107 in the third Test against New Zealand at Melbourne and batting steadily at number six in the order against India. The selectors must have thought long and hard before deciding against offering him a fifth major tour of England in 1981. On hearing the news, he decided to retire.

First-class career (1962-80): 16,180 runs (43.84) including 45 centuries, 190 wickets (35.69) and 149 catches
Test matches (74): 5,357 runs (48.26) including 15 centuries, 49 wickets (29.08) and 43 catches

WARD, Francis Anthony (1909-74)

South Australia

An honest toiler, full of courage but lacking inspiration, Frank Ward was a right-arm leg-break bowler contemporary with such masters as Clarrie Grimmett and Bill O'Reilly, and a dogged tailender. On his Test debut, against England in the first match at Brisbane in 1936/7, he captured 6 for 102 in the second innings (bowling 82 overs in the match). He toured England in 1938 as a controversial replacement for Grimmett and, although he took 92 wickets (19.27) in first-class matches, he appeared in only one Test.

First-class career (1935-40): 871 runs (13.83) and 320 wickets (24.68)
Test matches (4): 36 runs (6.00), 11 wickets (52.18) and 1 catch

WATKINS, John Russell (b.1943)

New South Wales

A right-arm leg-break bowler, he played against Pakistan in the third Test at Sydney in 1972/3 after only five first-class games in which he had taken a mere 11 wickets (37.18); his fame had been achieved for Newcastle. In this, his sole Test, he scored 3 not out and 36, sharing in a record ninth-wicket stand of 83 with Bob Massie, held one catch and took 0 for 21. He toured the West Indies in 1973, taking 10 wickets in four matches.

First-class career (1971-2): 70 runs (10.00) and 20 wickets (36.30)

WATSON, Graeme Donald (b.1945)

Victoria, Western Australia and New South Wales

An attractive right-handed batsman who sometimes opened and a vigorous medium-fast bowler, Graeme Watson was the keenest of cricketers. Hit on the bridge of the nose by a full-toss from Tony Greig while batting for Australia against the Rest of the World at Melbourne in 1971/2, he was in an intensive-care ward for days and received fourteen blood transfusions (forty pints of blood). He ignored the advice of surgeons never to play again and toured England in 1972, scoring 915 runs (36.60) and taking 25 wickets. Against Hampshire at Southampton he hit 176 (including five sixes), putting on 301 for the first wicket with Keith Stackpole in less than four hours. He did little in the Tests, but on his first tour, to South Africa in 1966/7, he had hit 50 on his debut at Cape Town.

First-class career (1964-76): 4,674 runs (32.68) including 7 centuries, and 186 wickets (25.31)
Test matches (5): 97 runs (10.77), 6 wickets (42.33) and 1 catch

WATSON, William James (b.1931)

New South Wales

A sound right-handed opening batsman, Bill Watson hit his maiden century in only his second first-class match – 155 in six and a quarter hours against MCC at Sydney in 1954/5. He played in the fifth Test at Sydney that season but achieved little, and a few months later toured the West Indies. He had a string of good scores against the Islands but disappointed in the Tests and was not tried again. In twenty-seven Sheffield Shield matches he made 1,233 runs (30.82).

First-class career (1953-61): 1,958 runs (32.09) including 6 centuries
Test matches (4): 106 runs (17.66), 0-5 and 2 catches

WELLHAM, Dirk Macdonald (b.1959)

New South Wales

A small, bespectacled, fair-haired man of neat movement and quiet, studious mien, Dirk Wellham was the surprise choice on the 1981 Australian tour of England. He justified his selection by scoring a hundred in his first Test, the sixth at The Oval, when his scores were 24 and 103. A qualified schoolmaster, and graduate of Sydney University, he impressed when scoring 95 against the 1979/80 England touring team for Combined Universities, though the first-class status of the game was later denied. The following season he forced his way into the New South Wales side and scored 408 runs in 8 innings, including 100 on his debut against Victoria and 128 not out against Tasmania. A compact, orthodox right-hander with the ability to concentrate and build an innings, and a complete variety of shots, he did consistently well during the 1981 tour of England, despite limited opportunities. Playing his first Test at The Oval, he seized his chance with both hands, although after his captain had delayed the declaration in order to give him his chance of glory a sudden attack of nerves made him play like a novice as his hundred came close. Dropped off a 'sitter', he recovered his poise and reached his goal. At home against the West Indies the following season, however, he was out of his depth against the non-stop attack of high-class fast bowling, in five innings scoring only 94.

First-class career (1980-): 1,058 runs (42.32) including 4 centuries
Test matches (4): 221 runs (31.57) including 1 century, and 1 catch

WHATMORE, Davenell Frederick (b.1954)

Victoria

A compact and strong right-handed batsman, born in Ceylon, 'Dav' Whatmore was a cricketer of wide experience when he appeared in both Tests against Pakistan, at Melbourne and Perth, in March 1979. As a club cricketer in England in 1975 and 1977, he represented Middlesex Second Eleven and toured South Africa with D.H. Robins' XI in 1975/6. The same year he appeared for Victoria for the first time and by 1977/8 was captaining the side with imagination in the absence of Graham Yallop on Test duty. He again led the side in several matches in 1978/9, when Victoria won the Shield. He can bowl medium pace, and was briefly used in this role during the 1979 Prudential Cup in England. Later that year he toured India. For much of the Indian tour his form was modest – 411 runs at 24.17 from 17 innings – but he played in all but one of the Test matches and was at his best in the fourth game at Delhi when his 77 and 54 helped save the match after a huge Indian first innings total. After this tour he faded from Test cricket.

First-class career (1975-80): 2,773 runs (31.35) including 4 centuries
Test matches (7): 293 runs (22.54), 0-11 and 13 catches

WHITNEY, Michael Roy (b.1959)

New South Wales and Gloucestershire

A very solidly built fast left-arm bowler and right-handed tail-ender, Mike Whitney had the sort of call-up for Test cricket that all young cricketers dream about. After just six first-class matches, four for New South Wales and two for Gloucestershire he was playing as a professional for Fleetwood (Lancashire) in the Northern League when a series of injuries to fast bowlers picked for the official Australian touring team caused him to be selected as an almost complete unknown for the vital Ashes Test at Old Trafford. In a dramatic match his was no fairy-tale success story, but he took four worthily earned wickets for 124 in the match, bowling with some speed and hostility for one of such scant experience. This sudden opportunity at the highest level had clearly come too early, but although Whitney was brought back to earth with a bump on his return to Australia (9 wickets in 6 matches at 51 apiece in the 1981/2 Sheffield Shield season) there is no reason why he should not bounce back into Test cricket.

First-class career (1980-): 13 runs (1.08) and 44 wickets (34.95)
Test matches (2): 4 runs (1.00) and 5 wickets (49.20)

WHITTY, William James (1886-1974)

New South Wales and South Australia

Six feet and with good shoulders, Bill Whitty was a left-arm fast-medium bowler with a high and graceful action, who swung the new ball prodigiously (like George Hirst). With the ball no longer new, he would bowl slow left-arm orthodox. He toured England in 1909 and 1912 and, at home, played against South Africa in 1910/11 and England in 1911/12. On his first tour he took 77 wickets, but was chosen for only one Test. Against South Africa he was almost unplayable, taking 37 wickets (17.08): 8 wickets in the first Test, 6 for 17 off 16 overs in the second innings of the second at Melbourne (routing the tourists for 80 when they needed only 161 to win) and 8 wickets in the third. In all five matches he opened the bowling with 'Tibby' Cotter. In the Triangular Tournament of 1912 he was again dominant, with 25 wickets (19.80), including 5 for 55 in the first innings against South Africa at Old Trafford. In all first-class matches in 1912 he took 109 wickets (18.08). He had a ready tongue. Once, refused an appeal for caught behind, he bowled a rather wide ball well clear of the batsman and appealed again. The umpire rebuked him, but Bill came back with an acid, 'Just thought you might make two mistakes in one day.' In thirty-seven Sheffield Shield matches he took 154 wickets (32.64).

First-class career (1907-25): 1,464 runs (11.52) and 491 wickets (23.39)
Test matches (14): 161 runs (13.41), 65 wickets (21.12) and 4 catches

WIENER, Julien Mark (b.1955)

Victoria

The fair-haired, well-built son of Austrian immigrants to Melbourne, Julien Wiener dedicated himself to the idea of opening the batting for Australia at an early age. A season of cricket for Kent second eleven had an ironic twist when Graham Dilley, the young Kent player with whom he had stayed, ran him out in his first Test innings. A solid right-handed opener with a good range of strokes and no fear of playing them, Wiener made a century in his first Shield game for Australia in 1977/8, scoring 31 and 106 against Queensland. In his first two seasons he hit four centuries. In addition, his occasional slow off-spin brought him 2 wickets for 31 for Victoria against England in 1978/9. It was no great surprise therefore when he overcame strong opposition from bigger names to win his first Test cap against England the following season. After his first innings run-out at Perth he made an impressive 58 in the second but this was his highest score in four Tests against the West Indies and England that season, although he top-scored with 40 against the fierce West Indies fast bowling in the first innings of the Melbourne Test. In Pakistan at the end of that season he played in two more Tests (March 1980) scoring 93 at Lahore. An outstanding 1981/2 season (847 runs at 52.93) included an innings of 221 not out against Western Australia at Melbourne: with Jeff Moss he added 390, an Australian third-wicket record.

First-class career (1977-): 2,920 runs (33.18) including 7 centuries, and 10 wickets (76.50)
Test matches (6): 281 runs (25.54), 0-41 and 4 catches

WILSON, John William (b.1922)

South Australia and Victoria

A left-arm orthodox spinner of relatively brisk pace, Jack Wilson took 40 wickets (24.32) for South Australia in 1953/4 and toured England and India in 1956. His sole Test came towards the end of that long tour when he took 1 for 64 and did not bat in the second Test against India at Bombay. In first-class matches in England his figures were respectable: he took 43 wickets (23.06) but his performance was never quite sufficient to demand a Test place.

First-class career (1949-58): 287 runs (5.74) and 230 wickets (30.51)

WOOD, Graeme Malcolm (b.1956)

Western Australia

A neat left-handed opening batsman with a cool temperament and determined approach, Graeme Wood made his first-class debut against MCC in 1976/7, scoring 37 and 1, and, a year later, as a result of the defections to World Series Cricket, was being tried as a Test cricketer. His start was auspicious: in his first six Tests, one at Adelaide against India followed by all five against the West Indies in the Caribbean, he scored 521 runs at 43.42, hitting 126 in the Georgetown Test and sharing a stand of 251 for the fourth wicket with Craig Serjeant. However, though

Graeme Wood hooks Andy Roberts – Deryck Murray keeping and Clive Lloyd at slip (all West Indies)

Wood's sound technique, wide variety of strokes and rather taciturn determination were clearly in evidence against England in 1978/9, he spoilt a respectable record of 344 runs (28.66) by dreadful misjudgments when running between the wickets. Constantly taking risks with the speed of the England fielders, he was involved in all but one of the run-outs which accounted for the dismissal of at least one of the opening batsmen in every Test of the series. They nicknamed Wood the 'Kamikaze Kid', and he lost his Test place for the series against Pakistan and for the Prudential World Cup. But he returned against India later in 1979. In India he was a grave disappointment, not getting to fifty in four Test innings and scoring only 138 runs (13.80) on the whole tour and for a time he lost his place in the Western Australia side. A promising career was in danger of being blighted but Wood showed the character to fight back and make the most of his ability. His chance came again when he was picked to tour England for the Centenary Test of 1980. He was a marginal selection and success was crucial. Shortly before the end of the first day he completed a determined and painstaking hundred. Significantly it was a spinner who eventually dismissed him for 112, for he is more at ease against fast bowling. He followed this effort with another century – 111 in Australia's next Test, against New Zealand at Brisbane but the balance was restored with a pair in his next Test! Indeed in three of the four innings he played in the last two Tests against New Zealand he was caught behind the wicket cheaply off Hadlee. He came back with his fifth Test hundred – 125 against India in the second Test at Adelaide, thus booking his passage to England in 1981. He had a relatively disappointing tour, scoring 310 Test runs (28.18) but had a good home series against Pakistan in 1981/2, scoring 100 at Melbourne. He made his seventh Test hundred against New Zealand in Auckland in March 1982. A somewhat taciturn character, Wood is a smart fielder and occasional slow left-arm bowler.

First-class career (1976-): 5,502 runs (35.72) including 13 centuries, and 5 wickets (25.40)
Test matches (40): 2,521 runs (34.53) including 7 centuries, and 31 catches

WOODCOCK, Ashley John (b.1948)

South Australia

A sound and stylish right-handed batsman for his State for a decade, Ashley Woodcock represented his country against Rest of the World in 1971/2 and toured New Zealand in 1973/4. Earlier in 1973 he appeared in his sole Test, against New Zealand, in the third match at Adelaide, scoring 27 and holding 1 catch.

First-class career (1967-79): 4,550 (30.95) including 5 centuries

WOODFULL, William Maldon (1897-1965)

Victoria

Bill Woodfull would hardly have appreciated the modern emphasis on limited-overs cricket. Variously known as 'The Rock', 'The Unbowlable' and 'The Worm-Killer', his backswing was a staccato bending of the wrists. But he had an imperturbable temperament, very strong defence and great patience; he built on firm foundations, learning to swing the bat harder and to place the ball firmly to one side or the other of the field with a variety of pushes and deflections. As right-handed opening partner of 'the other Bill', the heavy scoring W.H. Ponsford, for both state and country, he was never far behind as he gathered runs patiently and consistently. He toured England in 1926, 1930 and 1934, the last two occasions as captain, and played at home against England in 1928/9 and, as captain, in 1932/3. He also toured South Africa in 1931/2 (captain). He led Australia in twenty-five of his thirty-five Tests, winning back the Ashes in 1930 and 1934, and winning the series against West Indies and South Africa. A man of great moral and physical courage, he was a firm and understanding captain. He was at the heart of the bodyline controversy, both as captain and, in the more physical sense, being hit about the chest several times. He strongly denounced this form of attack as being contrary to the true spirit of cricket. At Adelaide, when Plum Warner, the MCC manager, went to the Australian dressing-room to enquire how he was, the solid Woodfull replied: 'There's two teams out there, and only one of them's playing cricket.' In England in 1926 he headed the batting overall with 1,672 runs (57.65), including eight centuries, scoring 201 against Essex at Leyton in his initial first-class match on English soil. At Headingley in the third Test he made 141, adding 235 for the second wicket with Charlie Macartney; in the series his record was 306 runs (51.00). Thereafter he never had a poor series with the bat: 1928/9, 491 runs (54.55); 1930, 345 runs (57.50); 1930/31, 195 runs (32.50); 1931/2, 421 runs (70.16) (including his Test highest, 161, in the third match at Melbourne); 1932/3, 305 runs (33.88); and 1934, 228 runs (28.50). Woodfull shared in nine three-figure stands in Tests, three with Ponsford in the 1930 series. His most prolific opening partnership was 375 with Ponsford for Victoria against New South Wales at Melbourne in 1926/7. Of seven double centuries his highest was 284 for An Australian Eleven against A New Zealand Eleven at Auckland in 1927/8. He received the OBE for services to education.

First-class career (1921-34): 13,392 (65.00) including 49 centuries

Test matches (35): 2,300 runs (46.00) including 7 centuries and 7 catches

Bill Woodfull

WOODS, Samuel Moses James (1867-1931)

Cambridge University and Somerset

A native of Glenfield, New South Wales, Sammy Woods was a player of grand physique, cheery disposition and unflinching courage: in both senses he was 'a sport'. Academic requirements were more charitable at Cambridge University in his day and he was able to appear four times against Oxford, being three times on the winning side. He captured 36 wickets in these games. He was an accurate and genuinely fast right-arm bowler with subtlety as well as speed, also bowling a skilful slower ball. He was a fighting and vigorous batsman and fine fielder. While an undergraduate, he was selected to play for the 1888 Australian team in the Tests but was disappointing. He settled in Taunton – in time developing the 'Zummerzet' brogue – playing for the county for twenty-one years, from 1894 until 1906 as a popular, determined captain, and serving as secretary for some thirty years. Four times he exceeded 1,000 runs in a season and twice a hundred wickets in the relatively short programmes of those years. For Somerset against Sussex at Hove in 1895 he hammered 215 – his career-highest – out of 282 in two hours and a half! A regular for Gentlemen against Players, he bowled unchanged in both innings with F.S. Jackson at Lord's in 1894. He toured South Africa in 1895/6 with Lord Hawke's team and represented England in the three Tests there, thus appearing for both Australia and England at cricket. He also played thirteen times for England at Rugby football!

First-class career (1886-1910): 15,352 runs (23.43) including 19 centuries, 1,040 wickets (20.82) and 282 catches
Test matches (Australia – 3): 32 runs (5.33), 5 wickets (24.20), and 1 catch. (England – 3): 122 runs (30.50), 5 wickets (25.80) and 4 catches

WORRALL, John (1863-1937)

Victoria

Short and thickset, Jack Worrall was a right-handed hitter, full of courage and ready to fight his way out of any trouble. Touring England twice in 1888 and 1899, he did not strike form on the earlier visit but, in 1899, he generally opened the batting with his captain, Joe Darling, scoring 1,202 runs (35.35) in all matches. In the Tests, with a highest score of 76 (out of 172) on a wet pitch at Headingley, he averaged 45.42. At home he played in the series of 1884/5, 1887/8, 1894/5 and 1897/8. In the fifth Test at Sydney in 1897/8, although Australia were 96 behind on the first innings, Jack Worrall hit 62 not out in the second, adding 193 with Darling for the third wicket in a homeric struggle which Australia managed to win. His 417 not out for Carlton against Melbourne University in 1896 was the then highest in Australian club cricket.

First-class career (1883-1901): 4,660 runs (20.99) including 7 centuries, 105 wickets (23.10) and 101 catches
Test matches (11): 478 runs (25.15), 1-127 and 13 catches

WRIGHT, Kevin John (b.1956)

Western Australia and South Australia

A red-headed wicket-keeper and left-handed catcher, although he bats capably right-handed, Kevin Wright comes from the same Western Australian club as Rodney Marsh. Trim, fit, neat, agile and with great determination, he received his first Test opportunities sooner than he would have done but for Marsh's involvement with World Series Cricket. Wright took over from John Maclean as Australia's wicket-keeper for the last two Tests against England in 1979 and for two games against Pakistan, taking seven catches in both these last two games. He toured England for the Prudential World Cup in 1979 and India later that year. In India he batted usefully, scoring a fighting and attractive 55 not out in the fourth Test at Delhi, and he claimed 3 stumpings as well as 10 catches in the six Tests. But when he got home the broad figure of Rodney Marsh barred his way, for Western Australia as well as for the national team. The consolation was that the international games were so many, Wright was able to play in the majority of Shield matches, and an innings of 88 not out against Queensland in the last match of 1979/80 took him to 322 runs for the season at an average of 35.77. Time was on his side but it must have been a big disappointment to this personable young man, who helps run a sports outfitting business off the field, when Steve Rixon was preferred to him as Marsh's deputy in England in 1981. In 1981/2 he moved to South Australia.

First-class career (1974-): 1,932 runs (27.60) including 2 centuries, and 231 dismissals (210 ct, 21 st.)
Test matches (10): 219 runs (16.84) and 35 dismissals (31 ct, 4 st.)

YALLOP, Graham Neil (b.1952)

Victoria

Not unlike Mike Denness in 1974/5, Graham Yallop had the misfortune to be a losing Test captain four years later in an era of intense and at times cruel publicity. Like Denness a fine batsman, and like him a sensitive man who hides his feelings and found it difficult to inspire his team, Yallop does, however, have time to re-establish his reputation in modern cricket. A determined, vigorous and orthodox left-hander, who hits the ball very hard, he toured Ceylon with the Australian schoolboys in 1971/2 and a year later was proving his ability by scoring 55 in his first Shield innings for Victoria. To widen his experience, he played for Walsall in the Birmingham League in 1973 and 1975 and also represented Glamorgan 2nd XI in 1977, having married a Welsh girl. The following Australian season he became only the tenth Victorian batsman to score two centuries in a match, hitting 105 and 114 not out against New South Wales at Sydney. His Test career began promisingly in 1975/6 against the West Indies. Dropped the following season, he returned for the final Test against India at Adelaide and scored 121. He followed by batting consistently in the West Indies, with 317 runs in the Tests at 45.29 and 660 runs (55.00) on the tour, including a brilliant 118 against Guyana before having his jaw broken by a ball from Colin Croft. When Bobby Simpson announced his second retirement after the tour, Yallop succeeded him for the 1978/9 Ashes series. His leadership was unimaginative, but he was captaining an inferior side. His own batting stood the stern test of the England bowlers well and he made a defiant century in the first Test at Brisbane and a brilliant 121 in the last. He scored more runs in the series (391) than any other batsman on either side. In India, under the captaincy of Kim Hughes, Yallop scored consistently throughout, scoring 729 runs at an average of 48.60 and reserving his highest score of 167 for the fifth Test. Yet when he returned home he found himself out of favour and out of form and he played in only one of the limited-over internationals in 1979/80 and in none of the Tests. His consolation was to lead Victoria to the Sheffield Shield for the second year running. When others were not available he answered the call to go to Pakistan – a lesser man might not have done so – and at Faisalabad scored 172, his fifth century in 23 Tests. He played in the Centenary Test at Lord's but never hit form on the short tour and played in none of the 1980/81 Tests. However, he was selected for the 1981 Ashes series, when, in a mixed tour, his personal highlight was a brilliant 114 at Old Trafford.

First-class career (1972-): 7,598 runs (40.41) including 18 centuries, 7 wickets (81.00), 91 catches and 1 stumping
Test matches (32): 2,101 runs (36.22) including 6 centuries, 1-116 and 16 catches

Graham Yallop

YARDLEY, Bruce (b.1947)

Western Australia

A lively, amusing, enthusiastic and highly strung character, Bruce Yardley is a slim and swarthy, right-handed all-rounder who hits very hard in an unorthodox way and bowls off-spinners at a brisk pace with considerable bounce and spin. Given greater control he could have been a world-beater. His apprenticeship was a long one, before the advent of World Series Cricket gave him the chance to break into Test cricket. He played one game for Western Australia in 1966/7 while still a teenager but did not establish a place in his strong State side until 1974/5. After a promising start to his Test career against India at Adelaide (22, 26 and 4 for 134 in the second innings) Yardley was a central figure in the Australian team in the West Indies, taking 15 Test wickets and making an aggressive 74 against the West Indies fast bowlers at Bridgetown. A senior West Indian umpire was unhappy about the legality of his bowling action. Against England in 1978/9 he was mercurial, never sure of a place and never quite sustaining his efforts with bat or ball, although in defeat in the final Test at Sydney he hit the spinners effectively in a defiant innings of 61 not out. Touring India in 1979/80, Yardley was disappointing, although 8 of his 17 wickets came in the two Tests in which he played – at Bangalore and Calcutta. In the latter Test, the fifth, he hit a spirited 61 not out in the first innings, all the more meritorious for the fact that he had missed the fourth Test because of a broken toe suffered when being lbw to Kapil Dev in the third. Having played in only three Shield matches for Western Australia after the return of the Packer cricketers in 1979/80, he burst back the following season and earned two more Test caps, both against India, at Adelaide and Melbourne. He bowled a great deal in both matches, taking 2 for 90 from 44.4 overs in India's first innings at Adelaide, but though the two games brought him 7 more Test wickets in all, he did not quite do enough to persuade the selectors to send him to England, a pity because he has always seemed likely to be a match-winner on damp wickets. (But the decision to cover pitches in all first-class matches in England in 1981 made the latter unlikely.) His career took on a new lease of life, however, at home in 1981/2 when he was voted cricketer of the year. In three Tests against Pakistan he took 18 wickets at 22 each and against the powerful West Indies a further 20 wickets in three more Tests, also at 22 each. He continued to play with customary zest in New Zealand towards the end of a tiring season, bowling 56 overs in the first innings of the Auckland Test (4 for 142) and taking 13 wickets in the three Tests. He was less successful in Pakistan early in the 1982/3 season but retained his place for the Ashes series.

First-class career (1966-): 2,154 runs (20.71) and 258 wickets (26.49)
Test matches (27): 837 runs (19.46), 97 wickets (31.20) and 24 catches

SOUTH AFRICA

ADCOCK, Neil Amwin Treharne (b.1931)

Transvaal and Natal

Tall, wiry and fit, Neil Adcock is one of only two South African fast bowlers to have exceeded a hundred wickets in Test cricket. He had a smooth, rhythmic run, and a right-arm, upright delivery which involved little strain on the body. Fiery and hostile, he frequently bowled short and even off a length could make the ball lift to an awkward height. By comparison, his batting was boyishly lighthearted. He was an immediate success in Tests. In his first series against New Zealand in 1953/4 he took 24 wickets (20.21), being at his best in the second match at Ellis Park, Johannesburg, when he took 8 for 87 in the match, South Africa winning comfortably. Although he bowled fast but fairly, he hit Bert Sutcliffe and Laurie Miller before either had scored and they had to retire to hospital. He went on to tour England in 1955 and 1960, and to play at home against England in 1956/7, Australia in 1957/8 and New Zealand again in 1961/2. Handicapped by various injuries, he took special exercises to improve his performance, and on his second England tour in 1960 captured 26 wickets (22.57) in the Tests, equalling Hugh Tayfield's record, and 108 wickets (14.02) overall. He was a tower of strength when his colleague, Geoff Griffin, was no-balled out of the game for throwing. Four times during this season Adcock took two wickets with successive balls, yet he never performed the hat-trick. Earlier in his career, he and Peter Heine were a formidable opening pair. Against England in 1956/7, they took 39 wickets between them; in the final Test at Port Elizabeth they routed England's strong batting side in the first innings for 110, Adcock taking 4 for 20. He had mixed fortune against Australia in 1957/8 but in the third Test at Durban he broke the batting in the first innings with 6 for 43, his best single innings performance. In Currie Cup matches, his best feat was 13 for 65 for Transvaal against Orange Free State at Johannesburg in 1953/4. He is now an incisive radio commentator on the game.

Neil Adcock

First-class career (1952-63): 451 runs (5.50) and 405 wickets (17.25)
Test matches (26): 146 runs (5.40) 104 wickets (21.10) and 4 catches

ANDERSON, John Henry (1874-1926)

Western Province

A fast-scoring batsman, in his sole Test against Australia at Johannesburg in 1902/3, 'Biddy' Anderson scored 32 and 11 and held 1 catch.

First-class career (1894-1908): 511 runs (23.22) including 1 century

ASHLEY, William Hare (1862-1930)

Western Province

A left-arm slow-medium bowler, in his sole Test, the second-ever against England at Cape Town in 1888/9, 'Gobo' Ashley scored 1 and 0 and took 7 for 95, but South Africa lost by an innings and 202, runs.

First-class career (1888-91): 17 runs (4.25), and 20 wickets (14.10)

BACHER, Dr Aron (Ali) (b.1942)

Transvaal

Ali Bacher made his first-class debut at the age of eighteen and, in the following season, 1960/61, hit impressive centuries off Rhodesia and Natal. A small, stocky and swarthy right-hander, he was mainly a back-foot player, very strong on the leg-side, partly as a result of his closed grip. He was a brilliant field and a competent second-string 'keeper. (Against a side of International Cavaliers, he held five catches and made one stumping in a single innings.) He toured England in 1965 and played in two series against Australia at home, captaining South Africa in the second of these in 1969/70, when Australia were routed. It was to be South Africa's final Test series, for political reasons. Bacher was selected to lead the attractive South African side to England in 1970, a tour that was cancelled at the eleventh hour after government intervention. In his second Test against England at Trent Bridge in 1965 his 67 helped materially in the victory; and in the third match against Australia at Durban in 1966/7, he was in at 'the kill' with 60 not out, having added 127 unbroken with Graeme Pollock for the third wicket. In South Africa's last Test innings of all, at Port Elizabeth in 1969/70, he hit 73 before giving 'Garth' McKenzie his sole wicket of the series. His highest score was 235 for Transvaal against the Australians at Johannesburg in 1966/7. Ali Bacher is now a senior house-doctor in a Johannesburg multi-racial hospital.

Ali Bacher

First-class career (1959-73): 7,894 runs (39.07) including 18 centuries, 110 catches and 1 stumping
Test matches (12): 679 runs (32.33) and 10 catches

BALASKAS, Xenophon Constantine (b.1910)

Griqualand West, Western Province, Border, Transvaal, and North-Eastern Transvaal

A thickset Greek, 'Bally' took a short run-up and, for a right-arm slow leg-spin bowler, brought the ball off the ground unusually fast: he used a well disguised googly sparingly. He was also a very useful lower-order batsman. His career was full of ups and downs. He first played for Griqualand West at fifteen, and in the 1929/30 Currie Cup matches took most wickets, 39, and scored most runs, 664. The following year he played in two Tests against England without success, and then toured Australia and New Zealand in 1931/2 without appearing in any Tests against Australia, but he hit 122 not out against New Zealand at Wellington. When he toured England in 1935, he could appear in only one Test because of injury, but his performance was memorable. He had exploited a worn spot at Bramall Lane to take 12 for 154 against Yorkshire and, just prior to coming to Lord's for the second Test, had collected 5 for 23 against Staffordshire. At Lord's in conditions favourable to bowlers, he took 5 for 49 and 4 for 54, and South Africa won her first-ever Test against England in England. It was his finest hour because he achieved little against Australia in 1935/6 or England in 1938/9. At home he made two double-centuries, 206 for Griqualand West against Rhodesia at Kimberley in 1929/30, and 200 not out for Rest of South Africa against Western Province at Cape Town in 1932/3. He took 9 wickets against Australia in 1935/6 but at high cost and played in only one Test against England in 1938/9.

First-class career (1926-47): 2,696 runs (29.68) including 6 centuries, and 276 wickets (24.11)
Test matches (9): 174 runs (14.50) including 1 century, 22 wickets (36.63) and 5 catches

Eddie Barlow

BARLOW, Edgar John (b.1940)

Transvaal, Eastern Province, Western Province and Derbyshire

Known in his youth as 'Bunter' because of his spectacles and stout build, Eddie Barlow was supposed to be so short-sighted that he never saw further than the front wheel of his bicycle when he rode to school. But he developed into a magnificent all-round cricketer who positively revels in every challenge the game sets him. Burly and strong, he became a determined right-handed opening batsman with a solid defence, who was especially strong off the back foot, a right-hand medium-pace bowler who could make the ball swing prodigiously, and a brilliant slip fielder. Born in Pretoria, Barlow first played for the Transvaal in 1959/60. He later represented Eastern Province in the Currie Cup from 1964/5, before moving back to Transvaal from 1966 to 1968, then on to Western Province, where he now runs a pig farm when he is not playing cricket. In 1976 Derbyshire invited him to join them, paying what was then an unusually high salary of five figures, and he repaid them handsomely with inspiring all-round cricket during his three years at the county. Taking over the captaincy midway through his first year, during which he hit 216 against Surrey at Ilkeston, he drove the team to new standards of fitness. When he left he had taken them to a final at Lord's, three of their players were in the England side, and the club was imbued with the spirit of success. Barlow was a vital member of the strong South African side during the 1960s, scoring 1,900 runs at an average of 63.33 on the tour of New Zealand and Australia in 1963/4. He scored 201 against Australia at Adelaide. In England in 1965, on a short tour, he made 971 runs (38.84) in sixteen matches, but had a rather modest Test series. Back in England, however, playing for the Rest of the World in 1970 when the scheduled South African tour was cancelled, he was his usual dynamic self, doing the hat-trick and taking four wickets in five balls against England at Headingley. (His final figures were 7 for 64.) At Cape Town in 1966/7 he took 5 for 85 against Australia. On the field Barlow bubbles with self-belief and bristles with belligerence. Off it he is a modest and charming character who has been a great ambassador for the game and for his country.

First-class career (1959-82): 17,740 runs (39.07) including 42 centuries, 562 wickets (24.22) and 331 catches
Test matches (30): 2,516 runs (45.74) including 6 centuries, 40 wickets (34.05) and 35 catches

BAUMGARTNER, Harold Vane (1883-1938)

Bedfordshire, Orange Free State and Transvaal

A tiny but tenacious left-arm slow bowler, Harold Baumgartner scored 16 and 3, took 2 for 99 (clean-bowling Jack Hobbs and J.W.H.T. Douglas) and caught one in his sole Test, the first against England at Durban in 1913/14.

First-class career (1903-14): 173 runs (7.86) and 70 wickets (18.51)

BEAUMONT, Rolland (1884-1958)

Transvaal

When he played his natural game Rolland Beaumont would hit with positive brilliance but he tended to be over-cautious, especially in Tests, and failed to do himself justice. He came to England in 1912, playing against both England and Australia, and in the wet summer scored 510 runs (18.21) in all first-class matches. He also played against England in 1913/14.

First-class career (1908-14): 1,086 runs (25.25) including 1 century
Test matches (5): 70 runs (7.77), 0-0 and 2 catches

BEGBIE, Denis Warburton (b.1914)

Transvaal

A quick-scoring but rather inconsistent batsman and change-bowler, Denis Begbie toured England in 1947, without reaching the Test side. On the tour he made 612 runs (30.60), including 132 against Essex at Southend. He played in Tests at home against England in 1948/9 and Australia in 1949/50, without quite fulfilling expectations.

First-class career (1933-50): 2,727 runs (35.88) including 6 centuries, and 88 wickets (23.69)
Test matches (5): 138 runs (19.71), 1-130 and 2 catches

BELL, Alexander John (b.1906)

Western Province and Rhodesia

A right-arm fast bowler of considerable grit – he once bowled on a hard wicket in a Test at Adelaide with a badly sprained foot – 'Sandy' Bell toured England in 1929 and 1935 and Australasia in 1931/2. At home he played against England in 1930/31. Although not outstanding generally on his England tours his Test debut was impressive. In his first innings at Lord's, maintaining an excellent length and making the ball swerve appreciably, he took 6 for 99. His best series, however, was against Australia in 1931/2 when he headed the bowling with 23 wickets (27.13). Four times he took four or more wickets in an innings but Australia won all five Tests, and 'Sandy' never dismissed Don Bradman! At Sydney, when he was hot and dripping with perspiration, and the scoreboard showed his figures to be no wickets for 96 runs, he said in trepidation to Herbie Taylor: 'What shall I do now, Herb?' The tongue-in-cheek reply was: 'Give him a fast one', and such was Bell's response that he finished his 46.5 eight-ball overs with 5 for 140. In Currie Cup cricket his best analysis was 8 for 34 in an innings for Western Province against Eastern Province at Cape Town in 1929/30.

First-class career (1925-39): 311 runs (9.14) and 228 wickets (23.29)
Test matches (16): 69 runs (6.27), 48 wickets (32.64) and 6 catches

BISSET, Sir Murray (1876-1931)

Western Province

Sir Murray Bisset, who captained Western Province with verve for several seasons, appeared in Tests against Lord Hawke's England side in 1898/9 and MCC in 1909/10. While the Boer War was still raging in 1901, he led a South African team to England. Controlling the side with skill and tact, he remained popular, despite some public criticism of the tour taking place at such a time, and reached 1,000 runs as a fine, forcing batsman. His highest score was 184 against Derbyshire at Derby. Also reserve wicket-keeper, he would stand right up to the fiery pace of the Boer fast bowler, J.J. Kotze, and execute stumpings at lightning speed. His final Test appearance was eleven years after his previous one. Sometime Chief Justice of Rhodesia, at the time of death he was Acting-Governor of that country.

First-class career (1894-1910): 1,436 runs (23.54) including 2 centuries, and 64 dismissals (51 ct, 13 st.)
Test matches (3): 103 runs (25.75) and 3 dismissals (2 ct, 1 st.)

BISSETT, George Finlay (1905-65)

Griqualand West, Western Province and Transvaal

Of wiry build and a right-arm fast bowler who could be devastating, George Bissett had a short career, but in his only Test series, against England in 1927/8, he did much to enable South Africa to draw the rubber after being two matches down. In the final match at Durban, he took a matchwinning 7 for 29 in the second innings. He toured England in 1924 but a foot injury prevented him appearing in any of the Tests.

First-class career (1922-29): 294 runs (15.47) and 67 wickets (27.10)
Test matches (4): 38 runs (19.00) and 25 wickets (18.76)

BLANCKENBERG, James Manuel (1893-presumed dead)

Natal and Western Province

Jimmy Blanckenberg was a right-arm medium-paced bowler who could bowl for hours on end to a perfect length. A formidable proposition on matting, he was considered the best bowler in South Africa for several years. Against England in 1913/14 he was the most successful bowler with 19 wickets (22.52), as he was also in the three Tests against Australia in 1921/2 with 12 wickets, and again against England in 1922/3 with 25 wickets (24.52). At Johannesburg in 1922/3 his first innings analysis of 6 for 76 was his best in Tests and largely instrumental in South Africa's victory. Failure in the Tests on the 1924 England tour, although he was dominant generally, taking 119 wickets (22.40), was followed by a felicitous spell playing in the Lancashire League.

First-class career (1912-24): 2,232 runs (22.32) including 1 century, and 293 wickets (21.26)
Test matches (18): 455 runs (19.78), 60 wickets (30.28) and 9 catches

BLAND, Kenneth Colin (b.1938)

Rhodesia, Eastern Province and Orange Free State

Colin Bland's fielding will never be forgotten by those who watched him. His speed at cover, perfect balance and phenomenally accurate throwing caught the

Colin Bland

breath of spectators and often created panic amongst opposing batsmen. Six foot one and strong without being heavy, he was a crowd-puller, too, as a right-handed forcing batsman, though his penchant for lifting the ball, particularly in the arc between long-off and long-on, was often his downfall. Whatever he scored with the bat, his fielding was worth 50 runs to his side in any match. First playing in Tests against New Zealand at home in 1961/2, he toured Australasia in1963/4 and England in 1965, besides appearing at home against England in 1964/5, and Australia in 1966/7. In his fourth Test against New Zealand at Johannesburg, the catch he held to dismiss John Reid, hurrying towards a century, was considered the finest seen in a representative match for many years. In Australia in 1963/4 he hit 126 in the final match at Sydney and made 367 runs (61.16) in the series. Against New Zealand he headed the batting with 207 runs (69.00) from the three matches. Against England in 1964/5 he was the dominant batsman, scoring 572 runs (71.50), including 144 not out in the second match at Johannesburg after South Africa had followed on 214 runs behind, which saved the match. In the short England tour of 1965, he made 906 runs (37.75) overall, hitting 286 runs (47.66) in the Tests, including 127 in the final Test at The Oval, which was to prove the last Test played to date between the two countries. It was his fielding, however, that captivated the public in England. At Lord's, England were 240 for 4 and heading for a matchwinning lead, when Barrington, at 91, played perhaps the most fateful stroke in the series. He pushed the ball to leg and scampered down the pitch. Bland ran from mid-wicket towards mid-on and in one thrilling movement scooped up the ball, twisted and threw down the stumps at the bowler's end. He followed by running out Jim Parks, after which the match and the series changed course. England never again won a commanding position. Only Derek Randall, and for a time Clive Lloyd, have in recent times equalled the exploits of this lean, rangy, powerful Rhodesian who practised regularly by throwing at a single stump. In domestic cricket he excelled in 1964/5, when he created a new record of 1,048 runs from ten first-class matches. His highest score was 197 for Rhodesia against Border in 1967/8. Born at Bloemfontein, though his grandparents were Scots, the man who had been a national hero in England in 1965 was a few years later refused entry to the United Kingdom.

First-class career (1956-74): 7,208 runs (37.73) including 13 centuries, and 43 wickets (35.16)
Test matches (21): 1,669 runs (49.08) including 3 centuries, 2 wickets (62.50) and 10 catches

BOCK, Ernest George (1908-61)

Griqualand West

A slow bowler, in his sole Test against Australia in the second match at Johannesburg in 1935/6, Ernest Bock scored 9 and 2, both times not out, and took 0 for 91.

First-class career (1928-39): 281 runs (14.05) and 32 wickets (27.78)

BOND, Gerald Edward (1909-65)

Western Province, Transvaal and North-Eastern Transvaal

A fighting batsman, Gerald Bond scored 170 when Western Province faced Natal's record 664 for 6 wickets declared at Durban in 1936/7, 424 runs behind, but in his sole Test, against England in the first match at Johannesburg in 1938/9, he failed to score in his only innings and took 0 for 16.

First-class career (1929-39): 1,604 runs (41.12) including 1 century, and 20 wickets (35.35)

BOTTEN, James Thomas (b.1938)

North-Eastern Transvaal

'Jackie' Botten was a right-arm medium-pace bowler, with subtle change of pace and the ability to make the ball run away to the slips. Also a useful batsman, he burst into Currie Cup cricket with 55 wickets in his first full season, 1958/9, a Cup record. He was also a star professional with Arcadia in the National Football League. He toured England in 1965, meeting with reasonable success, taking 33 wickets and scoring 227 runs in twelve matches.

First-class career (1957-72): 1,775 runs (15.84) and 399 wickets (20.36)
Test matches (3): 65 runs (10.83), 8 wickets (42.12) and 1 catch

BRANN, William Henry (1899-1953)

Eastern Province

A right-handed batsman, William Brann's sole Test experiences were against England in 1922. In his first match at Johannesburg, he scored 50 in the second innings, putting on 98 with Herbie Taylor in a fifth-wicket partnership, which did much towards winning the match. He represented his Province from 1920 until 1934 in the Currie Cup, doing nothing as memorable as hitting 97 and 83 not out against Western Province at Port Elizabeth in 1921/2.

First-class career (1920-34): 1,045 runs (22.23)
Test matches (3): 71 runs (14.20) and 2 catches

BRISCOE, Arthur Wellesley (1911-41)

Transvaal

A prolific scorer in Currie Cup matches, 'Dooley' Briscoe made such scores as 191 and 140 but could not reproduce such form in Tests, although for Transvaal he did hit 60 against the Australians in 1935/6 and 80 (for once out) against MCC in 1938/9. He was killed in action during the Abyssinian campaign.

First-class career (1931-40): 2,189 runs (45.60) including 6 centuries
Test matches (2): 33 runs (11.00) and 1 catch

BROMFIELD, Henry Dudley (b.1932)

Western Province

A competent right-arm off-spin bowler with a military appearance, and a fine close in field, 'Brom' received many chances in Tests, appearing at home against New Zealand in 1961/2, and England in 1964/5. He also toured England in 1965. In the third Test at Cape Town in 1964/5, when England amassed 442, he took 5 for 88 in 57.2 overs, 26 of which were maidens. In England he enjoyed days of success outside the Tests, especially against Lancashire at Old Trafford, taking 8 for 69 in the match.

First-class career (1956-69): 374 runs (6.33) and 205 wickets (25.63)
Test matches (9): 59 runs (11.80), 17 wickets (35.23) and 13 catches

BROWN, Lennox Sidney (b.1910)

North-Eastern Transvaal, Transvaal and Rhodesia

A right-arm leg-spin bowler, Lennox Brown toured Australia and New Zealand in 1931/2, playing one Test in each country.

First-class career (1930-48): 778 runs (16.91) and 147 wickets (24.77)
Test matches (2): 17 runs (5.66) and 3 wickets (63.00)

BURGER, Christopher George de Villiers (b.1935)

Natal

Chris Burger was a gifted stroke player who was unlucky not to be selected for an overseas tour. His sole Tests were against the visiting 1957/8 Australians.

First-class career (1955-66): 2,073 runs (30.04) including 2 centuries
Test matches (2): 62 runs (20.66) and 1 catch

BURKE, Sydney Frank (b.1934)

North-Eastern Transvaal and Orange Free State

A sporting, philosophical cricketer, Sydney Burke made his Test debut in the third match against New Zealand at Cape Town in 1961/2, and, spearheading the bowling with his right-arm fast-medium deliveries, bowled 81 overs in taking 11 for 196. Despite this he was relegated to the position of purveyor of drinks and towels for the next Test and he had to wait until 1964/5 for his second and final Test appearance, against England. He managed the South African Universities team in England in 1967.

First-class career (1954-68): 2,334 runs (26.52) including 1 century, and 241 wickets (21.38)
Test matches (2): 42 runs (14.00) and 11 wickets (23.36)

BUYS, Izak D. (1895-presumed dead)

Western Province

A slow to medium-paced bowler, Izak Buys' sole Test was the first against England at Johannesburg in 1922/3 when he scored 0 and 4 not out and took 0 for 52.

First-class career (1921-25): 37 runs (3.70) and 48 wickets (22.97)

CAMERON, Horace Brakenridge (1905-35)

Transvaal and Western Province

A high-ranking wicket-keeper/batsman, who learned his art on matting wickets, 'Jock' Cameron's stumping of a batsman was likened to the 'nonchalant gesture of a smoker flicking the ash from a cigarette'. Some of his

Jock Cameron

stumping efforts dazzled the eye: he was neither flamboyant nor noisy and he took the ball cleanly. His style was described as 'the perfection of ease and rapidity without unnecessary show'. He was essentially a fast-scoring right-handed batsman, who could adapt his game and discipline his methods if necessary. Soon coming to the front in Currie Cup matches, he first represented South Africa against England in 1927/8: he toured England in 1929 and 1935; Australia and New Zealand in 1931/2; and played against England again at home in 1930/31. He began the 1929 tour with 102 at Worcester and, later, secured seven victims behind the stumps against Somerset at Taunton. In the second Test at Lord's, however, he was felled by a terrible blow on the head from a ball bowled by Harold Larwood. Although he missed the next Test, he appeared to make a full recovery, and in all matches reached 1,000 runs. Captaining his country once against England in 1930/31, he led the team to Australia in 1931/2 but found captaincy very burdensome. His wicket-keeping remained splendid and, on his second England tour, 1935, under Herbert Wade, he was at his peak. His powerful driving and pulling in the Test at Lord's, hitting 90 out of 126 in 105 minutes after four wickets had fallen cheaply, caught the public imagination: South Africa went on to win her first Test in England. He made headlines again when he hit Hedley Verity for 30 in an over at Sheffield in the game with Yorkshire. It was said that Verity had him in two minds – whether to hit him for four or six! A charming and strong personality, Jock Cameron died of enteric fever shortly after his return home from the tour in which he had scored 1,458 runs (41.65), including three centuries, and made 48 dismissals.

First-class career (1924-35): 5,396 runs (37.47) including 11 centuries, and 224 dismissals (155 ct, 69 st.)
Test matches (26): 1,239 runs (30.21) and 51 dismissals (39 ct, 12 st.)

CAMPBELL, Thomas (1882-1924)

Transvaal

A competent wicket-keeper though of small account as a batsman, Tom Campbell first appeared for his province at twenty-four. He played against England in 1909/10 as the front-line 'keeper and also in 1912. While in England that year, however, rheumatism in the hands prevented him from showing his best form. He had toured Australia in 1910/11 without appearing in the Tests. He was killed in a Natal railway accident involving a mail train. This was uncanny for some years previously he had fallen out of a mail train.

First-class career (1906-12): 365 runs (12.16) and 51 dismissals (40 ct, 11 st.)
Test matches (5): 90 runs (15.00) and 8 dismissals (7 ct, 1 st.)

CARLSTEIN, Peter Rudolph (b.1938)

Orange Free State, Natal, Transvaal and Rhodesia

Making his first-class debut at sixteen years two months and scoring 56 for Orange Free State against Natal at Bloemfontein in 1954/5, Peter Carlstein is now the senior player in South African first-class cricket. A fine fielder and a slim, right-handed batsman, he could play some sparkling innings and seemed to have both the ability and the right temperament to succeed but consistency has eluded him. He toured England in 1960, and Australia in 1963/4, and played once in a Test at home against Australia in 1957/8. He had a torrid time against the fast bowlers in Australia and in England, although he made nearly 1,000 runs overall, including a magnificent 151 against Hampshire at Southampton. His best score in the Tests was 42. It cannot be said that he really 'came off' in Test cricket but he proved what he could do in the domestic first-class season of 1962/3 when he made 852 runs (71.00), including two double centuries in three matches, the highest being 229 for Transvaal against the International Cavaliers at Johannesburg.

First-class career (1954-80): 7,554 runs (31.60) including 9 centuries
Test matches (8): 190 runs (14.61) and 3 catches

CARTER, Claude Paget (1881-1952)

Natal, Transvaal and Cornwall

One of the most effective left-arm slow bowlers on matting, Claude Carter took 5 for 17 in nineteen overs on making his debut in first-class cricket at the age of sixteen against Transvaal. Twenty-three years later he routed Border for 23, the lowest total recorded in Currie Cup matches: his analysis was 6 for 11. He toured England in 1912 and 1924 – heading the bowling on his second visit with 65 wickets – and at home played against England in 1913/14 and Australia in 1921/2. When Australia amassed 450 at Johannesburg in 1921/2, he was at his best, taking 6 for 91. Also a hard-hitting batsman, he was professional to Cornwall for some years. For Natal he took 155 wickets.

First-class career (1897-1924): 1,333 runs (11.69) and 366 wickets (18.56)
Test matches (10): 181 runs (18.10), 28 wickets (24.78) and 2 catches

CATTERALL, Robert Hector (1900-61)

Natal, Orange Free State, Transvaal and Rhodesia

Though he was rarely a good starter, Bob Catterall's right-handed batting was delightfully free, marked by beautiful driving and strong hitting to leg, and he was also a fleet-footed and efficient deep field. Forthright and crinkly-haired, he was originally an opening batsman but later batted in the middle order though he opened again throughout the 1929 series in England. All his Test cricket was against England between 1922 and 1931. He toured England in 1924 and 1929, and at home was an integral part of the 1922/3, 1927/8 and 1930/31 series. On his first tour, he was the only consistent batsman in the Tests, scoring 471 runs (67.28). In the first Test at Edgbaston, after South Africa had been routed for 30 and were following on 408 runs behind, he hit a handsome 120. At Lord's his second successive innings of 120 could not prevent another innings defeat. At The Oval he was again top scorer with 95: no other South African hit a century in this series. On his second tour, he again did well at Edgbaston, scoring 67 and 98 and sharing in first-wicket partnerships of 119 and 171 with Bruce Mitchell. His best Test innings in South Africa was a matchwinning 119 in the fifth match at Durban in 1927/8. Not always in harmony with officialdom, he not only captained Natal at cricket, but excelled also at soccer, hockey, tennis, golf, billiards and baseball.

Bob Catterall

First-class career (1920-34): 5,849 runs (29.99) including 9 centuries, and 53 wickets (30.73)
Test matches (24): 1,555 runs (37.92) including 3 centuries, 7 wickets (23.14) and 12 catches

CHAPMAN, Horace William (1890-1941)

Natal

A useful right-handed batsman and googly bowler for Natal from 1911 until 1922, Horace Chapman played in two Tests, against England in 1913/14, and Australia in 1921/2, both at Durban.

First-class career (1910-22): 587 runs (20.96) and 30 wickets (25.23)
Test matches (2): 39 runs (13.00), 1-104 and 1 catch

CHEETHAM, John Erskine (1920-80)

Western Province

A cheerful sportsman, respected captain and very capable batsman whose straight drive was dominant, Jack Cheetham was also a superb versatile field. But it is as a captain who never allowed his men to lose faith in themselves that he is specially remembered. He toured England in 1951 and 1955, and Australasia in 1952/3; and at home played against England, Australia and New Zealand between 1948 and 1953. He captained South Africa in England in 1955, when the touring team levelled the rubber after being two matches down. Never before had a South African team been so successful in England though, strangely, Cheetham was unfit to play in either victory. He led his country to a 4-0 victory over New Zealand in 1953/4. Against Australia in 1952/3, his team left home virtually written off as 'no hopers' but his firm, confident leadership, with its special emphasis on the value of first-rate fielding at all times, produced a side that very unexpectedly drew the series 2-2; and, as a bonus, New Zealand were defeated later in the tour. Although he hit 271 not out against Orange Free State at Bloemfontein in 1950/51, which remained a short-lived highest-ever in the Currie Cup competition – and averaged 83.14 that season – he was not prolific in Tests. He made five fifties, with a highest of 89 in the third Test against New Zealand at Cape Town in 1953/4. On his first tour of England, 1951, he finished second in aggregate and average, 1,448 runs (38.10); and on his tour of Australasia he was second in the averages with 601 runs (40.06). President of the South African Cricket Association, 1969–72, he fought hard for the cause of South Africa in international cricket.

First-class career (1939-55): 5,697 runs (42.20) including 8 centuries
Test matches (24): 883 runs (23.86), 0-2 and 13 catches

CHEVALIER, Grahame Anton (b.1937)

Western Province

A left-arm slow bowler, Grahame Chevalier took the wicket of Paul Sheahan with the fifth ball he bowled in Test cricket, the first match at Cape Town against Australia in 1969/70. In this, his sole Test – the first that South Africa won at Newlands against Australia, the previous six having been lost – he scored 0 and 0 not out, took 5 for 100 and held 1 catch.

First-class career (1966-74): 84 runs (4.94) and 154 wickets (23.72)

CHRISTY, James Alexander Joseph (1904-71)

Transvaal and Queensland

A tall, powerful right-handed batsman and accomplished player of fast bowling, Jim Christy hit 68 and 107 not out in his first two matches for Transvaal in 1925/6. He toured England in 1929 and Australasia in 1931/2; and at home played against England in 1930/31. In the Lord's Test he impressed with 70 and 41 against Harold Larwood and Maurice Tate. After hitting 148 and 50 against Nottinghamshire at Trent Bridge, he suffered a finger injury which curtailed his appearances. His form was moderate in Australia, but he made 103 against New Zealand at Christchurch and 62 and 53 at Wellington, opening the batting each time, and in all first-class matches on the tour scored 1,178 runs (41.78).

First-class career (1925-36): 3,670 runs (37.07) including 11 centuries, and 32 wickets (27.93)
Test matches (10): 618 runs (34.33) including 1 century, 2 wickets (46.00) and 3 catches

CHUBB, Geoffrey Walter Ashton (1911-82)

Border and Transvaal

A bespectacled right-arm medium-pace bowler who moved the ball either way very late in flight or off the wicket, Geoff Chubb could bowl for long spells without losing accuracy. Originally an opening batsman, he turned to bowling after a rugby injury, and generally batted with the 'tail'. He toured England in 1951, taking 76 wickets (26.38), and, on making his Test appearance at Trent Bridge at the age of forty years fifty-six days became the oldest South African on debut. He had a very good series, taking 5 for 77 in the first innings at Lord's and 6 for 51 in the first innings at Old Trafford. After retirement at the end of the tour, he became involved in the management of the game. He has served two terms as president of the South African Cricket Association.

First-class career (1931-51): 835 runs (18.15) and 160 wickets (23.91)
Test matches (5): 63 runs (10.50) and 21 wickets (27.47)

COCHRAN, John Alexander Kennedy (b.1909)

Griqualand West and Transvaal

A fast bowler, in his sole Test, the fifth against England at Durban in 1930/31, John Cochran scored 4 and took 0 for 47.

First-class career (1929-32): 25 runs (4.16) and 15 wickets (24.06)

COEN, Stanley Keppel (1902-67)

Western Province, Orange Free State, Transvaal and Border

For several years, 'Shunter' Coen was at the fringe of the Test eleven. When Currie Cup matches were played on turf for the first time in 1926/7, he made 737 runs (73.70) for Orange Free State – a record for twenty years in the Cup – sharing in a stand of 305 for the second wicket with J.M.M. Commaille against Natal at Bloemfontein, a record for forty years in South Africa. His sole Test appearances were against England in 1927/8. With a highest score of only 41 not out he averaged over 50!

First-class career (1921-39): 2,808 runs (32.65) including 6 centuries, and 22 wickets (49.40)
Test matches (2): 101 runs (50.50), 0-7 and 1 catch

COMMAILLE, John McIllwain Moore (1883-1956)

Western Province, Orange Free State and Griqualand West

'Mick' Commaille represented South Africa at both cricket and Association Football. Very popular throughout a long career, he was a consistently effective batsman, generally opening the innings, in Currie Cup cricket. After some twenty years with Western Province, he joined Orange Free State and shared in a stand of 305 for the second wicket with S.K. Coen against Natal at Bloemfontein in 1926/7, a record for forty years. Though never very prominent in Tests, he played against England at home in 1909/10 and 1927/8, and in England in 1924 was vice-captain to Herbie Taylor. He toured Australia in 1910/11. On his England tour he made 1,202 runs (25.04).

First-class career (1905-30): 5,026 runs (32.21) including 9 centuries
Test matches (12): 355 runs (16.90) and 1 catch

CONYNGHAM, Dalton Parry (b.1897)

Natal, Transvaal and Western Province

Though handicapped by ill-health, 'Conky' Conyngham was one of Natal's best bowlers in the early 1920s. In his sole Test, the fifth against England at Durban in 1922/3, he scored 3 and 3 (both times undefeated), took 2 for 103 (in 61 overs) with his right-arm medium pace bowling and held 1 catch.

First-class career (1921-31): 348 runs (15.13) and 86 wickets (20.67)

COOK, Frederick J. (1870- presumed dead)

Eastern Province

A useful batsman, in his sole Test, the first against England at Port Elizabeth in 1895/6, Frederick Cook scored 7 and 0.

First-class career (1893-1905): 172 runs (17.20)

COOPER, Alfred Henry Cecil (1893-1963)

Transvaal

A heavy scorer for Transvaal, hitting 171 not out against Western Province at Johannesburg in 1923/4, Alfred Cooper's sole Test appearance was against England at Durban in 1913/14, when he scored 6 and 0 and held 1 catch.

First-class career (1912-29): 1,788 runs (31.92) including 4 centuries, and 15 wickets (39.73)

COX, Joseph Lovell (1886-1971)

Natal

Bowling a sharp right-arm fast-medium pace with a high action, Joe Cox achieved fame in the Currie Cup competition in 1910/11. Taking 8 for 20 (7 clean-bowled) against Transvaal in the second innings at Durban, he finished with 36 wickets from six matches, his province winning the trophy for the first time. He toured England in 1912 but was disappointing and his only Tests were played against England at home in 1913/14. He was an indifferent batsman and fielder.

First-class career (1910-22): 357 runs (8.30) and 120 wickets (22.53)
Test matches (3): 17 runs (3.40), 4 wickets (61.25) and 1 catch

CRIPPS, Godfrey (1865-1943)

Western Province

An old Cheltenham boy and a dashing right-handed batsman, Godfrey Cripps hit 102 against Griqualand West at Kimberley in 1892/3 when his province carried off the Currie Cup at their first attempt. In a handful of Cup games he held the then high average of 39.20. His sole Test was against W.W. Read's England side at Cape Town in 1891/2 when he scored 18 and 3 and took 0 for 23. He was vice-captain of the first South African team to England in 1894, making 394 runs (14.59).

First-class career (1891-94): 217 runs (31.00) including 1 century

CRISP, Robert James (b.1911)

Rhodesia, Western Province and Worcestershire

Debonair and good-looking, twice *Victor Ludorum* at school in Salisbury, Bob Crisp could swing the new ball either way and, bringing it down from a good height, make it lift awkwardly. In England in 1935 he took 107 wickets (19.58), including 13 in the five Tests. In the Currie Cup he twice took 4 wickets in 4 balls, respectively for Western Province against Griqualand West at Johannesburg in 1931/2, and against Natal at Durban in 1933/4, but after a season with Worcestershire in 1938, when he captured 42 wickets from eight matches, and a tour with Sir Julien Cahn, his activities were increasingly outside cricket. He climbed Kilimanjaro twice; became a reporter with the London *Daily Express*; ran a duck farm; as a tank commander in the Western Desert was wounded and awarded the D.S.O. and M.C.; published a book about his wartime experiences; and then, while living in England, 'opted out' and went to live a rather hermit-like life on a Greek island, suffering from an incurable disease. He never lacked guts, however; in the 1935 Test at Trent Bridge, when Maurice Leyland and Bob Wyatt were in command at the crease in a record stand, Crisp limped off the field with a foot inflamed from a blood blister. The doctor warned him not to bowl again that day but he returned to take the wickets of both batsmen.

First-class career (1929-38): 888 runs (13.06) and 276 wickets (19.88)
Test matches (9): 123 runs (10.25), 20 wickets (37.35) and 3 catches

CURNOW, Sydney Harry (b.1907)

Transvaal

Syd Curnow was an impressive batsman for several seasons in a strong Transvaal line-up. His career-highest score was 224 for North against South at Cape Town in 1932/3. He never toured England, but visited Australia in 1931/2, achieving little in the Tests. In three Tests at home against England in 1930/31, he had a highest score of 13. His cousin was a well-known statistician and record-keeper of South African cricket.

First-class career (1928-46): 3,409 runs (42.09) including 9 centuries
Test matches (7): 168 runs (12.00) and 5 catches

DALTON, Eric Londesbrough (1906-81)

Natal

More often than not a bad starter, at his best Eric Dalton was a determined and hard-hitting right-handed batsman and useful change bowler. He toured England in 1929 and 1935, and Australasia in 1931/2. At home he played against England in 1930/31 and Australia in 1935/6. On his second England tour he made 1,446 runs (37.07) and in the final Test at The Oval played a magnificent innings of 117, adding a record 137 for the ninth wicket with 'Chud' Langton. Again against England, in the first Test at Johannesburg in 1938/9, he came to the rescue with 102 and in the tremendously high scoring 'timeless Test' at Durban he took 4 for 59 in the first innings. On the Australian tour of 1931/2, playing against Tasmania at Hobart, he was hit first ball by a delivery from Laurie Nash which broke his jaw in two places and for more than a month his teeth were bound together with wire while he took liquid meals through a tube. A brilliant all-round sportsman, Dalton was South African amateur golf champion in 1950, and good at tennis and table tennis. He was also a musician with a fine baritone voice, and an accomplished pianist.

First-class career (1924-47): 5,333 runs (33.12) including 13 centuries, and 139 wickets (25.81)
Test matches (15): 698 runs (31.72) including 2 centuries, 12 wickets (40.83) and 5 catches

DAVIES, Eric Quail (1909-76)

Eastern Province, Transvaal and North-Eastern Transvaal

A tall, athletic man – he was a hurdles champion – Eric Davies bowled right-arm fastish out-swingers and, but for several dropped catches, might have achieved a sensational bowling analysis against Australia in his first Test at Johannesburg in 1935/6 when he spear-headed the attack and finished with 4 for 75 in a total of 439. For Transvaal against MCC in 1938/9, he took 6 for 82, but in the Tests that season achieved little.

First-class career (1929-46): 64 runs (3.55) and 47 wickets (27.70)
Test matches (5): 9 runs (1.80) and 7 wickets (68.71)

DAWSON, Oscar Charles (b.1919)

Natal and Border

Tall, broad-shouldered, fleet and easy of movement, Ossie Dawson was a right-handed batsman of the classic upstanding school, a medium-pace bowler who could deliver the outswinger from a smooth, long-striding run up and a high delivery, and a fielder who would sprawl after catches and chase the ball to the last gasp. He toured England in 1947, opening the bowling in four of the Tests and hitting 55 in the final Test at The Oval, and at home played against England in 1948/9. His overall record on his England tour was 1,002 runs (32.32) including his career-highest score of 166 not out against South of England at Hastings, and 54 wickets (26.07), but ultimately, although a power in Currie Cup matches, he disappointed in Tests.

First-class career (1938-62): 3,804 runs (34.58) including 6 centuries, and 123 wickets (27.87)
Test matches (9): 293 runs (20.92), 10 wickets (57.80) and 10 catches

DEANE, Hubert Gouvaine (1895-1939)

Natal and Transvaal

A fine leader of South Africa against England in 1927/8, 1929 and 1930/31, 'Nummy' Deane – so called because of the loss of a finger-joint in boyhood, causing his hand to be numbed for some time – was an attractive, fast-scoring right-handed batsman and a brilliant field at cover. An experienced leader of Currie Cup-winning Transvaal sides, he won two Tests against England in 1927/8 largely through shrewd tactics and under his guidance the young 1929 side to England did much better than expected. In the fifth Test at The Oval he added 214 for the fourth wicket with Herbie Taylor, his share being 93. His first England tour, 1924, had been a moderate one for him. Prominent in the administration of the game, he was a member of the Selection board from 1929 until 1932.

First-class career (1919-31): 3,795 runs (30.11) including 6 centuries
Test matches (17): 628 runs (25.12) and 8 catches

DIXON, Cecil Donovan (1891-1969)

Transvaal

A very good right-arm medium-paced off-spin bowler but a moderate batsman, in his sole Test, the third at

Johannesburg against England in 1913/14, Cec Dixon failed to score in either innings, took 3 for 118 (including Jack Hobbs twice) and held one catch. Touring England in 1924, he took 37 wickets (25.97) but was disappointing. For the victorious Transvaal side, in 1923/4, however, he had 33 wickets (10.00).

First-class career (1912-25): 184 runs (5.93) and 106 wickets (24.11)

DOWER, Robert Reid (1876-1964)

Eastern Province

A fine batsman on matting and, at the time of death the oldest surviving South African Test cricketer, Robert Dower's sole Test was the first against England at Johannesburg in 1898/9, when he scored 0 and 9 and held 2 catches.

First-class career (1896-1907): 82 runs (6.83)

DRAPER, Ronald George (b.1926)

Eastern Province and Griqualand West

A wicket-keeper but primarily a fast-scoring right-handed opening batsman, Ronald Draper scored a century before lunch on four occasions: one for Eastern Province and three for Griqualand West in successive matches in 1951/2 and 1952/3. He had made 114 for Eastern Province against Orange Free State at Port Elizabeth in 1945/6 on his debut in first-class cricket, and he became the first batsman to make two centuries in one Currie Cup match when he scored 129 and 177 for Griqualand West against Border at Kimberley in 1952/3. Despite this, his Tests were confined to two against Australia in 1949/50.

First-class career (1945-60): 3,290 runs (41.64) including 11 centuries and 42 dismissals (32 ct, 10 st.)
Test matches (2): 25 runs (8.33)

DUCKWORTH, Christopher Anthony Russell (b.1933)

Natal and Rhodesia

For much of his career, Chris Duckworth was second-string wicket-keeper to John Waite, but he was also, like Waite, a capable batsman, having a sound defence and being a strong driver and puller. He toured England in 1955 and 1960 and, although not chosen for any of the Tests, played a magnificent 158 against Northamptonshire. His sole Tests were against England in 1956/7 when he was played for his batting.

First-class career (1952-62): 2,572 runs (21.98) including 3 centuries, and 104 dismissals (91 ct, 13 st.)
Test matches (2): 28 runs (7.00) and 3 catches

DUMBRILL, Richard (b.1938)

Natal and Transvaal

A genuine all-rounder, Richard Dumbrill was born in London and was taken to South Africa at a very early age. His right-handed batting was naturally free, his medium-pace bowling steady and quicker than it appeared and his fielding good. He toured England with success in 1965, on his Test debut at Lord's – the hundredth match between the two countries – taking 3 for 31 and 4 for 30. He played two more Tests against England and, at home, two against Australia in 1966/7, without repeating such a good performance.

First-class career (1960-68): 1,761 runs (23.48) and 132 wickets (22.03)
Test matches (5): 153 runs (15.30), 9 wickets (37.33) and 3 catches

DUMINY, Jacobus Petrus (1897-1980)

Transvaal, Western Province and Oxford University

A good right-hand opening batsman, Duminy played in two Tests against England in 1927/8 without distinguishing himself and, while on a business trip to Europe in 1929, was called on to play in the third Test at Headingley because the touring team was stricken with injury and illness: again he achieved little.

First-class career (1919-29): 557 runs (29.42) including 1 century, and 12 wickets (30.66)
Test matches (3): 30 runs (5.00), 1-39 and 2 catches

DUNELL, Owen Robert (1856-1929)

Eastern Province

Not in the eleven at Eton or a cricket blue at Oxford, Owen Dunell became a useful batsman and good field. He appeared for South Africa in the first Tests against Major Warton's side in 1888/9, and was the country's first captain at Port Elizabeth. South African born, he died in France.

First-class career (1888-90): 79 runs (15.80)
Test matches (2): 42 runs (14.00) and 1 catch

Du PREEZ, John Harcourt (b.1942)

Rhodesia

A fine all-rounder, being a very capable right-handed batsman and leg-break bowler, 'Jackie' Du Preez completed the Currie Cup 'double' of 2,000 runs and 100 wickets in 1973/4 (having made his debut in 1961/2). Only eleven other players achieved this distinction. He made more than a hundred appearances for Rhodesia, scoring over 3,000 runs and taking over 200 wickets, which were all records for Rhodesia. His sole Test appearances were made against Australia in 1966/7.

First-class career (1961-80): 4,063 runs (23.76) including 1 century, and 296 wickets (31.07)
Test matches (2): 0 runs (0.00), 3 wickets (17.00) and 2 catches

Du TOIT, Jacobus Francois (1868-1909)

Orange Free State

A natural leg-break bowler with a curly flight, 'Flooi' Du Toit appeared in a sole Test against England – and his only first-class match – at Cape Town in 1891/2, scoring 0 not out and 2 not out, taking 1 for 47 and holding 1 catch.

DYER, Dennis Victor (b.1914)

Natal

Powerfully built with a good eye, Dennis Dyer, an opening batsman, had immense patience and could hit quite majestically through the covers. He was a very serious and conscientious cricketer who suffered badly from the seven year gap in high class cricket caused by the Second World War. He hit 185 against Western Province at Durban in 1939/40 on his first-class debut. He toured England in 1947 and in his first Test, the third at Old Trafford, defended doggedly for three hours for 62. Otherwise, his tour was disappointing; and at the end of the season, he underwent an operation for appendicitis.

First-class career (1939-49): 1,725 runs (37.50) including 3 centuries
Test matches (3): 96 runs (16.00)

ELGIE, Michael Kelsey (b.1933)

Natal

A very good right-handed batsman and useful change slow left-arm bowler, 'Kim' Elgie played three Tests against New Zealand in 1961/2, hitting 56 in his second at Johannesburg. A prolific scorer in Currie Cup cricket, he was better known as a Rugby footballer. He studied at the Universities of St Andrews and London and was capped for Scotland eight times.

First-class career (1957-62): 1,834 runs (36.68) including 3 centuries, and 10 wickets (40.50)
Test matches (3): 75 runs (12.50), 0-46 and 4 catches

ENDEAN, William Russell (b.1924)

Transvaal

A fine batsman and all-round fielder with very quick reflexes, Russell Endean toured England in 1951 and 1955 and Australasia in 1952/3. At home he played against New Zealand in 1953/4, England in 1956/7 and

Russell Endean (left) with Headley Keith

Australia in 1957/8. His 'keeping, although always very sound, never approached the brilliance shown by John Waite, but his batting developed so well that he became the sheet anchor of many a Springbok innings. Showing very good judgment against the new ball, his defence was sound and, although seldom a fluent stroke-maker, he dealt capably with the bad ball. During the 1952/3 Australian tour, he was the mainstay of South Africa's Test batting with 438 runs (48.66) including 162 not out in the second Test at Melbourne, and in all first-class matches he headed the batting with 1,496 runs (55.40) in Australia and New Zealand. He was also the best of an outstanding fielding side, holding 29 catches on the tour, some of them miraculous, in many different positions. He was known as 'Endless Endean'. Rather moderate in England in 1951, he was in excellent form in 1955, scoring 1,242 runs (34.50); at Headingley, his 41 at number eight and 116 not out at number six were important factors in South Africa's victory by 224 runs. His other Test century, 116, was off New Zealand at Auckland in 1952/3. He averaged 50.50 for Transvaal, his career-highest being 247 for his province against Eastern Province at Johannesburg in 1955/6. He was also a hockey international. Resident in England for some twenty years, he has captained Malden Wanderers C.C. and this quietly-spoken man has been very popular in a wide range of cricket. He is remembered also for two of Test Cricket's oddities. In the second Test at Newlands in 1956/7 he was given out for 'handling the ball'. Having padded away a ball from Laker, the ball spun up towards the stumps and Endean used his hands to deflect it. He was also involved in the unique dismissal of Len Hutton in 1951 when Hutton was out 'obstructing the field' by deflecting a 'ballooned up' catch to the wicket-keeper.

First-class career (1945-64): 7,757 runs (37.83) including 15 centuries, and 171 dismissals (158 ct, 13 st.)

Test matches (28): 1,630 runs (33.95) including 3 centuries, and 41 catches

FARRER, William Stephen (b.1936)

Border

A hard-hitting right-handed batsman, 'Buster' Farrer made 77 on his debut for Border against North-Eastern Transvaal in 1954/5, but was torn between cricket and tennis. Indeed, he dropped completely out of cricket between 1956 and 1960 during which time he reached number seven in South African tennis ranking and played at Wimbledon. But he returned to cricket, playing at home in three Tests against New Zealand in 1961/2, and touring Australasia in 1963/4. He captained his province on his return from tennis; made 888 runs (63.42) in nine matches in 1962/3; and hit his career-highest, 211, against Eastern Province at East London in his last first-class season, 1968/9.

First-class career (1954-69): 4,815 runs (43.37) including 12 centuries

Test matches (6): 221 runs (27.62) and 2 catches

FAULKNER, Major George Aubrey (1881-1930)

Transvaal

During the South African War, Aubrey Faulkner received professional coaching in Cape Town. During his career he was to become himself one of the great coaches and, as both player and coach, one of the dominating figures in South African cricket. One of the earliest exponents of the googly at slow-medium pace, he also used a well-concealed, and swift, yorker. At his best, with perfect length, spin in both directions and a puzzling variation of flight, he was master of some of the greatest batsmen. He bowled with a lively wheeling action. As a right-handed batsman he was solidity itself, and as a fielder versatile and reliable. He toured England in 1907 and 1912 and was called upon to strengthen the 1924 side in one Test. He toured Australia in 1910/11, and at home played against England in 1905/6 and 1909/10. On his Test debut in the first match at Johannesburg in 1905/6, his 4 for 26 led to a victory by one wicket, South Africa's first Test win. With his googly-bowler companions, Vogler and Schwarz, he created something of a sensation in 1907. In the three Tests he took 12 wickets (18.16), besides averaging 23.40 with the bat in the low-scoring series. On the tour he took 64 wickets (15.82) and headed the batting with 1,163 runs (29.82). In the Headingley Test, he took 6 for 17 (England falling for 76) and 3 for 58. He was complete master against England in 1909/10, heading the batting with 545 runs (60.55) and sharing most of the bowling with Vogler, taking 29 wickets (21.89). In the first Test at Johannesburg – narrowly won by South Africa by 19 runs – he scored 78 and 123 and took 8 for 160 in the match. Now in his prime, he was an astounding success in Australia in 1910/11, taking 49 wickets (27.06) and amassing 1,651 runs (61.14), including four centuries. Head and shoulders above anyone else in the Tests, he made 732 runs (73.20), the record aggregate in a series at that time, which included 204 in the second Test at Melbourne and 115 in the third match at Adelaide, the first won by South Africa against Australia. He was not so successful against Sidney Barnes in the Triangular Tournament, though he made 122 not out against Australia at Old Trafford, and secured 17 wickets (26.70) in the six matches; in all first-class matches he achieved the double with 1,075 runs (23.88) and 163 wickets (15.42). Virtually his last bowl in Tests was at The Oval when he took 7 for 84 in England's first innings of 176. He did little when briefly recalled to the Test side in 1924. He had a distinguished record in the First World War, being awarded the D.S.O., and, after settling in England, opened his famous School of Cricket, later employing and bringing to the fore the young Ian Peebles. For Archie MacLaren's side at Eastbourne in 1921, he scored 153 and in the two innings took 6 for 63, helping to defeat the hitherto invincible Australians. He was subject to melancholia and died tragically by his own hand.

First-class career (1902-24): 6,392 runs (36.31) including 13 centuries, and 449 wickets (17.42)

Test matches (25): 1,754 runs (40.79) including 4 centuries, 82 wickets (26.58) and 20 catches

FELLOWS-SMITH, Jonathan Payn (b.1932)

Oxford University, Northamptonshire, Transvaal and Hertfordshire

Very strong and very competitive, 'Pom-Pom' Fellows-Smith toured England in 1960, playing in four Tests. One of the great modern hitters, he batted with immense gusto and freedom, specializing in stinging off-drives and rustic leg-swings. As a stock bowler, he could be waspish and he also bowled leg-spin. From Natal University he passed to Oxford, where he became a cricket and rugger blue. Making his championship debut for Northants against Sussex at Hove in 1957, he rescued his adopted county by slamming 109 and 65 not out, innings which included six sixes and two sixes respectively. This century remained his career-highest. He disappointed in the Tests of 1960, but, on the tour, made 863 runs (31.96) besides taking 32 wickets.

First-class career (1953-64): 3,999 runs (29.40) including 5 centuries, and 149 wickets (29.62)
Test matches (4): 166 runs (27.66), 0-61 and 2 catches

FICHARDT, Charles Gustav (1870-1923)

Orange Free State

One of three cricketing brothers and educated at Bloemfontein, in Scotland and at Hamburg, Charles Fichardt was a vigorous batsman and useful lob-bowler. Once in a minor match at Bloemfontein he shared in a stand of 401 for the second wicket. He appeared in the third and fourth Tests played by his country, against England in 1891/2 and 1895/6.

First-class career (1891-1907): 87 runs (7.25)
Test matches (2): 15 runs (3.75) and 2 catches

FINLASON, Charles Edward (1860-1917)

Griqualand West and Transvaal

Author, journalist, tennis champion and a 'father' of Kimberley cricket, Charlie Finlason was a quick-scoring right-handed batsman and originally a fast bowler who later developed 'scientific break bowling'. He played in the first-ever Test at Port Elizabeth in 1888/9, scoring 0 and 6 at number ten and taking 0 for 7. As a journalist when not on the field, he incurred the wrath of England's players with his acid comments. Undaunted, he became editor of the Johannesburg *Star*. He hit 154 not out for Kimberley against Transvaal in the second Currie Cup Tournament in 1890/91, his last innings in first-class cricket.

First-class career (1888-91): 213 runs (26.62) including 1 century, and 14 wickets (20.50)

FLOQUET, Claude Eugene (1884-1963)

Transvaal

An opening right-handed batsman for his province, Floquet in his sole Test, the third match against England at Johannesburg in 1909/10, batted at number eight, scoring 1 and 11 not out and taking 0 for 24.

First-class career (1904-11): 104 runs (26.00)

FRANCIS, Howard Henry (1868-1936)

Gloucestershire and Western Province

As a right-handed batsman, Howard Francis appeared generally with rather moderate success for Gloucestershire from 1890 until 1894, although he added 137 with Jack Board for the ninth wicket against Middlesex at Clifton in 1894, when he made 55. He emigrated to South Africa and from 1895 until 1902 often appeared in Currie Cup matches. He appeared in both Tests against England in 1898/9.

First-class career (1890-1902): 529 runs (12.90) and 14 dismissals (13 ct, 1 st.)
Test matches (2): 39 runs (9.75) and 1 catch

FRANCOIS, Cyril Matthew (1897-1944)

Griqualand West

A hard-hitting right-handed batsman and fast-medium bowler, 'Froggy' Francois represented his Province from 1920 until 1928. He gained prominence in 1922/3 when he took 7 for 114 for Griqualand West against MCC and he was selected for all five Tests that season. He had little return generally as a bowler, although he dismissed Frank Woolley, Arthur Carr and Greville Stevens in the first innings of the first match at Johannesburg at a cost of 23 runs, but he enjoyed successive scores of 72, 41, 3 not out and 43. In his last two appearances in first-class cricket in 1927/8, he hit 54 against MCC and 97 and 54 against Orange Free State. He was killed in a motor accident.

First-class career (1920-28): 1,232 runs (22.81) and 101 wickets (28.44)
Test matches (5): 252 runs (31.50), 6 wickets (37.50) and 5 catches

FRANK, Charles Newton (1891-1961)

Transvaal

The diminutive Charlie Frank had been badly gassed during the First World War but fought his way back to fitness and, for several seasons, opened the batting for his province. He made 108 on his debut in first-class cricket for Transvaal against Australia Imperial Forces at Johannesburg in 1919/20. He appeared in the three Tests against Australia in 1921/2 – the tourists had been 'sweeping through South Africa like a raging veldt fire' – and in the second at Johannesburg he played an epic innings against Jack Gregory, Ted McDonald and Arthur Mailey. His country had followed on 207 behind whereupon he batted for 8 hours 38 minutes to score 152, one of the slowest Test innings ever recorded, but Australia were thwarted.

Test matches (3): 236 runs (39.33) including 1 century

FRANK, William Hughes Bowker (1872-1945)

Transvaal

An all-rounder, Billy Frank took part in only one first-class match: the second Test against England at Johannesburg in 1895/6 when he scored 5 and 2 and took 1 for 52.

FULLER, Edward Russell Henry (b.1931)

Western Province

Fair-haired, well-built and determined, Eddie Fuller bowled an energetic right-arm fast-medium. He toured Australia in 1952/3 and England in 1955 and at home played against Australia in 1957/8. In the days before three seamers were automatically required in a Test team, he had to compete for a place with Neil Adcock and Peter Heine. Supported by superlative fielding in Australia, however, he headed the bowling averages both for the tour with 32 wickets (26.62) and for the Tests: appearing in two, he took 10 wickets (27.10). In the fifth Test at Melbourne, which South Africa won handsomely, he had a haul of 8 for 140. In England he had 49 wickets (19.51), including 6 in two Tests. He clinched a narrow victory over Transvaal at Johannesburg in 1955/6 by taking 11 for 70, Western Province winning the Currie Cup.

First-class career (1950-58): 1,062 runs (15.17), and 190 wickets (26.45)
Test matches (7): 64 runs (8.00), 22 wickets (30.36) and 3 catches

FULLERTON, George Murray (b.1922)

Transvaal

Short and almost delicate in build, George Fullerton was one of three wicket-keepers in the South African team to England in 1947, and the second in ranking. Neither spectacular nor stylish he, nonetheless, discharged this onerous task with credit. A right-handed batsman, his bat meticulously straight in defence, he was a handsome player on the off-side. He toured England again in 1951 and appeared at home against Australia in 1949/50. On his first England tour he made 698 runs (31.72) and had 24 dismissals; on his second tour he played as a batsman only, scoring 1,129 runs (31.36), including 167 against Essex at Ilford, his career-highest. He kept wicket during the last two Tests against Australia in 1949/50, hitting his highest Test score, 88, in the fourth match at Johannesburg. He hit two fifties against England in 1951.

First-class career (1942-51): 2,768 runs (31.10) including 3 centuries, and 82 dismissals (64 ct, 18 st.)
Test matches (7): 325 runs (25.00) and 12 dismissals (10 ct, 2 st.)

FUNSTON, Kenneth James (b.1925)

North-Eastern Transvaal, Transvaal and Orange Free State

A right-hander, Ken Funston always had the urge to hit but was not always at home against the rising ball and never quite realized his potential as a batsman. He was a magnificent outfield. He toured Australasia in 1952/3 and at home played against New Zealand in 1953/4, England in 1956/7 and Australia in 1957/8. In Australia he came third in the Test averages with 365 runs (36.50) and on the whole tour scored 673 runs (32.04), with a highest score of 92 in the fourth Test at Adelaide which remained his best in all Tests. On his debut at Brisbane he hit 33 and 65 during a heatwave. He was a consistent scorer in Currie Cup matches.

First-class career (1946-61): 4,164 runs (30.39) including 5 centuries
Test matches (18): 824 runs (25.75) and 7 catches

GAMSY, Dennis (b.1940)

Natal

At an early age Dennis Gamsy showed himself to be an outstanding natural wicket-keeper. Bespectacled, he made his first-class debut at nineteen. In his first Currie Cup match for Natal, against Transvaal at Johannesburg in 1959/60, he had nine victims – eight caught and one stumped. On two further occasions he collected nine 'scalps', and twice eight, in Currie Cup matches. Stockily built, he was always efficient. He toured England in 1965, having 25 victims in eleven matches but Denis Lindsay, a better batsman, kept him out of the Tests. His only Tests were two against Australia in 1969/70, the last series ever played by South Africa.

First-class career (1958-73): 3,106 runs (23.70) including 2 centuries, and 310 dismissals (277 ct, 33 st.)
Test matches (2): 39 runs (19.50) and 5 catches

GLEESON, Robert Anthony (1873-1919)

Eastern Province

A useful batsman, Robert Gleeson played against England in the first Test at Port Elizabeth in 1895/6, scoring 3 and 1 not out and holding 2 catches.

First-class career (1893-1905): 312 runs (18.35)

GLOVER, George Keyworth (1870-1938)

Griqualand West

Yorkshire-born, a slow right-arm bowler and steady batsman, George Glover was a member of the first South African team to tour England in 1894, scoring 337 runs (13.26) and taking 56 wickets (17.40). He played in the third Test at Cape Town in 1895/6, scoring 18 not out and 3 and taking 1 for 28. In a Currie Cup match against Eastern Province at Cape Town in 1893/4, he took 15 for 68: he also made several fifties in the competition.

First-class career (1889-98): 621 runs (23.88) and 71 wickets (18.18)

Trevor Goddard

GODDARD, Trevor Leslie (b.1931)

Natal and North-Eastern Transvaal

A left-handed opener whether batting or bowling, and an excellent close-to-the-wicket fielder, Trevor Goddard was the outstanding South African all-rounder of his period. Tall, with short hair, his batting was firmly based on the back foot and his medium-paced new ball or stock bowling was naggingly accurate. He toured England in 1955 and 1960, and Australasia in 1963/4; and at home between 1956 and 1969 played against England in two series and Australia in three. He captained South Africa in thirteen Tests, winning one and losing two. On his England tours, he made 1,163 runs (30.60) and took 60 wickets (21.85) in 1955 and 1,377 runs (37.21) and 73 wickets (19.71) in 1960. He also held 21 and 26 catches respectively. In each series Goddard scored more than 200 runs, often giving his country a sound start, and making 99 at The Oval in 1960. But his bowling was even more effective. He took 25 wickets (21.12) in 1955, taking 5 for 69 in 62 overs, 37 of which were maidens, in the second innings at Headingley, and 5 for 31 in the first innings at The Oval. His haul in 1960 was 17 wickets at 24.35. As captain in Australia in 1963/4, he scored 454 runs (64.86), with a top score of 93, and took 11 wickets (38.18) in the five Tests, South Africa drawing the series. In New Zealand he made 233 runs (46.60) and took 7 wickets (20.28). Well over half the overs he bowled in this series were maidens. His best bowling in Tests was 6 for 53 (in 32.5 overs) in the second innings of the first Test against Australia in 1966/7 at Johannesburg, winning the match for South Africa handsomely after they had been 126 behind on the first innings. In this series he collected 26 wickets (16.23) topping the averages, besides making 294 runs. In his last series as captain, against England in 1964/5, South Africa lost the first Test but, though they were at least as strong a side thereafter, at no time did he show himself prepared to take the slightest risk. For once his bowling failed, but he made 405 runs (40.50), including his sole Test century, 112, in his sixty-second Test innings, in the fourth match at Johannesburg. In the same match he asked for an appeal against Mike Smith to be revoked after the England captain had been 'run out' when down the wicket 'gardening'. A heavy scorer and wicket-taker in the Currie Cup competition, Goddard's best season at home was 1966/7 with 830 runs and 45 wickets from ten matches. He was the first South African to have reached 10,000 runs and 500 wickets in first-class cricket and the only one to have reached 2,000 runs and 100 wickets in Tests.

First-class career (1952-70): 11,279 runs (40.57) including 26 centuries, 534 wickets (21.65) and 174 catches
Test matches (41): 2,516 runs (34.46) including 1 century, 123 wickets (26.22) and 48 catches

GORDON, Norman (b.1911)

Transvaal

Towards the end of the 1930s, Norman Gordon made enough impression in the Currie Cup competition with his right-arm bowling to suggest that he would have done well in England had not the 1940 tour been aborted. His Test experience was limited to the five heavy-scoring matches against England in 1938/9 when he bowled tirelessly. In four innings he conceded at least a hundred runs but he took more wickets – 20 – than anyone else on either side.

First-class career (1933-49): 109 runs (5.19) and 126 wickets (22.24)
Test matches (5): 8 runs (2.00), 20 wickets (40.35) and 1 catch

GRAHAM, Robert (1877-1946)

Western Province

An all-rounder, Robert Graham played in two Tests against England, at Johannesburg and Cape Town in 1898/9.

First-class career (1897-1901): 260 runs (10.83) and 61 wickets (23.04)
Test matches (2): 6 runs (1.50), 3 wickets (42.33) and 2 catches

GRIEVESON, Ronald Eustace (b.1909)

Transvaal

Ronnie Grieveson showed splendid form as wicket-keeper/batsman against England in the fourth and fifth Tests at Johannesburg and Durban respectively in 1938/9 but the Second World War robbed him of his best years. He scored 75 in the 'Timeless Test' at Durban.

First-class career (1929-40): 1,130 runs (33.23) including 1 century, and 36 dismissals (25 ct, 11 st.)
Test matches (2): 114 runs (57.00) and 10 dismissals (7 ct, 3 st.)

GRIFFIN, Geoffrey Merton (b.1939)

Natal and Rhodesia

An all-round athlete, the blond Geoff Griffin had an accident at school which left him with a distinct crook of the right elbow and he was totally unable to straighten the arm naturally. He persevered, however, as a fast bowler and in his second full season in the Currie Cup competition, 1959/60, headed the national averages with 35 wickets (12.23), despite some rumblings about his action. In England in 1960 he became the first touring player to be no-balled for throwing. This was at Lord's against MCC when he was called by Frank Lee and John Langridge. He was called again at Trent Bridge against Nottinghamshire, at Southampton against Hampshire and in the second Test at Lord's. At first, in this Test, he had done very well, achieving the first-ever hat-trick by a South African in a Test and, moreover, the first by anyone in a Test at Cricket's headquarters. He was no-balled eleven times, by Frank Lee again, for throwing, and in an exhibition match played after the match, which finished early, he was persistently no-balled by Sid Buller and had to finish his last over underhand. This was the end of his career as a bowler in Test cricket: he completed the tour as batsman, making 353 runs in 22 innings, and as fielder.

First-class career (1957-63): 892 runs (18.20) and 108 wickets (21.51)
Test matches (2): 25 runs (6.25) and 8 wickets (24.00)

HALL, Alfred Ewart (1896-1964)

Transvaal and Lancashire

A Lancastrian, Alf Hall was a left-arm fast-medium bowler who represented South Africa against England in the home series of 1922/3, 1927/8 and 1930/31. He also played for Lancashire in nine matches as a professional in 1923 and 1924 and for Transvaal for several seasons in the Currie Cup, capturing 52 wickets from six games in 1926/7 and 128 wickets (14.18) altogether in this competition. He loved matting, and on his Test debut in the second match at Cape Town in 1922/3, was almost unplayable. When England were seeking 173 to win, he took 7 for 63 in the innings (11 for 112 in the match) and South Africa won by one wicket. Again, when South Africa won narrowly by four wickets in the fourth Test at Johannesburg in 1927/8, he took 9 for 167.

First-class career (1920-31): 134 runs (3.72) and 234 wickets (19.23)
Test matches (7): 11 runs (1.83), 40 wickets (22.15) and 4 catches

HALL, Glen Gordon (b.1938)

North-Eastern Transvaal and Eastern Province

A capable right-arm leg-break bowler and occasionally useful batsman, Glen Hall made a memorable first-class debut in 1960/61, taking 9 for 122 in the first innings (13 for 146 in the match) for South African Universities against Western Province. His sole Test was in the third match at Cape Town against England in 1964/5 when he scored 0 and took 1 for 94.

First-class career (1960-68): 306 runs (7.84) and 110 wickets (29.66)

HALLIWELL, Ernest Austin (1864-1919)

Transvaal and Middlesex

Ealing-born, 'Barberton' Halliwell returned to England with the first South African team in 1894, the second in 1901 and the third in 1904, in the days before Tests were played in England between the two countries. At home he played for South Africa against England in 1891/2, 1895/6 and 1898/9, and against Australia in 1902/3. Captaining his adopted country in the first two Tests of 1895/6, he lost both. He ranked as one of the best wicket-keepers of the day, however, often standing up skilfully at the stumps to take the very fast bowler, J.J. Kotze. He considered that on South African matting it was better policy to stand up, whereas on English turf one could take more catches standing back. It was 'Barberton' who introduced the practice of having a piece of raw steak in the palm of the hand while keeping. A more than useful batsman, his highest score in Tests was 41 in the second match at Johannesburg in 1895/6. Having a birth qualification for Middlesex, for whom his father, R. Bissett Halliwell, had kept wicket in the early years, he appeared once for the county and also for Gentlemen against Players at Hastings in 1901.

First-class career (1891-1909): 1,702 runs (19.34) and 112 dismissals (75 ct, 37 st.)
Test matches (8): 188 runs (12.53) and 11 dismissals (9 ct, 2 st.)

HALSE, Clive Gray (b.1935)

Natal

Born in Zululand and making his first-class debut as a

schoolboy, Clive Halse was a right-arm fast bowler who toured Australasia in 1963/4 in a team packed with fastish bowlers. He was expensive on the tour, but played in the last three Tests against Australia: at Adelaide when South Africa won by 10 wickets, he took 3 for 50, including Bob Simpson and Norman O'Neill. His other sports were baseball and golf.

First-class career (1952-65): 321 runs (12.84) and 83 wickets (31.30)
Test matches (3): 30 runs (—), 6 wickets (43.33) and 1 catch

HANDS, Philip Albert Myburgh (1890-1951)

Western Province

As a right-handed batsman noted for his fearless hitting, Philip Hands toured England in 1924 but was disappointing, scoring only 436 runs in 26 innings. His best performance in a Test was a chanceless 83 against England in the fifth match at Port Elizabeth in 1913/14, made out of 98 in 105 minutes (but Sid Barnes was not playing!). In that series, he scored more runs, 281, than anyone other than Herbie Taylor. He represented his province in the Currie Cup competition from 1912 until 1927, hitting three centuries. Like his brothers, R.H.M. – with whom he appeared in the same Test – and K.C.M., he won a Rugby blue at Oxford. He was awarded the D.S.O. and M.C. in the First World War.

First-class career (1906-27): 2,034 runs (25.11) including 3 centuries
Test matches (7): 300 runs (25.00), 0-18 and 3 catches

HANDS, Reginald Harry Myburgh (1888-1918)

Western Province

A Rugby blue at Oxford and a good right-handed batsman, Reginald Hands made a sole Test appearance, against England in the fifth match at Port Elizabeth in 1913/14, scoring 0 and 7. His brother Philip also appeared in this match. He died of war wounds in France.

First-class career (1912-14): 289 runs (28.90)

HANLEY, Martin Andrew (b.1918)

Western Province and Border

A right-arm off-break bowler who turned the ball at Newlands even more than Athol Rowan, Martin Hanley took 128 wickets (18.86) in the Currie Cup competition alone. He wore the skin off his fingers in imparting his exceptional spin and, as he flighted the ball into a north-easter at Newlands, even the best batsman would grope like novices to cope with his 'bite' and flight. In his sole Test, against England in the third match at Cape Town (Newlands) in 1948/9, he achieved little, however, taking 1 for 88 and failing to score.

First-class career (1939-54): 308 runs (9.62) and 182 wickets (21.69)

HARRIS, Terence Anthony (b.1916)

Griqualand West and Transvaal

A boy wonder without parallel in South Africa, Tony Harris rode a horse at three, shot wonderfully well at five, drove a lorry at seven, played tennis at nine, started Rugby at twelve, won his province's junior tennis championship at the same age (for the first time out of five), represented his province at cricket at sixteen (three times as a schoolboy) and went on to play soccer, squash and golf, and to become one of four men only to have represented South Africa at both cricket and rugby. Aged seventeen years four months, he hit 114 not out in his first match in the Currie Cup for Griqualand West against Orange Free State at Kimberley in 1933/4. Only five feet six inches, he was an aggressive, right-handed fast-scoring batsman. On the tour of England in 1947, though he lacked consistency, he made 701 runs (36.89). His sole century, against Glamorgan at Swansea, was masterly, with conditions favouring the bowlers. On his Test debut, at Trent Bridge, he hit 60 in a general run-feast. Very light on his feet, he was a splendid outfield and turned many a certain four into a quick single. During the Second World War he became a Spitfire pilot; his engine failed after action in the air and he bailed out to be taken POW.

First-class career (1933-49): 3,028 runs (41.49) including 6 centuries
Test matches (3): 100 runs (25.00) and 1 catch

HARTIGAN, Gerald Patrick Desmond (1884-1955)

Border

A very competent right-handed batsman and fast-medium bowler, Gerald Hartigan shone like a beacon for the generally weak Border province side from 1903 until 1927, his highest score being 176 not out against Eastern Province in 1910/11. He toured England in 1912, playing in two of the Tests, but, in returning the ball from the deep, he fractured his arm and was out for the rest of the tour. He appeared in the first three Tests against England in 1913/14, top-scoring with 51 out of 160 in the second at Johannesburg (the match in which Sid Barnes took 17 wickets).

First-class career (1903-26): 1,544 runs (29.13) including 3 centuries, and 92 wickets (21.08)
Test matches (5): 114 runs (11.40) and 1-141

HARVEY, Robert Lyon (b.1911)

Natal

Sometime captain of his province, Robert Harvey was a very consistent right-handed batsman who, in a rather short career, made 740 runs (43.52) in the Currie Cup competition. He appeared in two Tests against Australia in 1935/6 without distinguishing himself, but for his province at Durban scored 104 in the first match and 138 in the second against the touring team.

First-class career (1933-40): 1,298 runs (38.17) including 2 centuries, and 37 wickets (26.10)
Test matches (2): 51 runs (12.75)

HATHORN, Christopher Maitland Howard (1878-1920)

Transvaal

A very sound right-handed batsman, usually at first or second wicket down, Maitland Hathorn toured England in 1901, 1904 and 1907 and Australia in 1910/11. At home he played against Australia in 1902/3 and England in 1905/6. He was very successful on his first two England tours (on neither of which Tests were played). He made 1,261 runs (35.02) in 1901 and 1,339 runs (37.19) in 1904. His sole Test century was 102 in the third match against England at Johannesburg in 1905/6. His health was never robust.

First-class career (1897-1911): 3,541 runs (26.62) including 9 centuries
Test matches (12): 325 runs (17.10) including 1 century, and 5 catches

HEARNE, Frank (1858-1949)

See England section.

HEARNE, George Alfred Lawrence (1888-1978)

Western Province

A fast-scoring right-handed opening batsman, George Hearne made a promising start to his Test career against England at Johannesburg in 1922/3, making 28 and 27, but in the next Test he made 'a pair' and he was dropped for the rest of the series. He toured England in 1924 but his success was moderate and he appeared in only one Test. He was the son of Frank Hearne.

First-class career (1910-27): 1,981 runs (28.30) including 2 centuries, and 14 wickets (28.64)
Test matches (3): 59 runs (11.80) and 3 catches

HEINE, Peter Samuel (b.1928)

Orange Free State and Transvaal

Always associated with his new-ball partner Neil Adcock, Peter Heine was a well-built, six feet five inches tall, right-arm, genuinely fast bowler with a 'killer' streak. He first made news when he devastated the 1953/4 New Zealanders, taking 7 for 29 for Orange Free State. He toured England in 1955, securing 74 wickets (19.86), including 21 wickets (23.52) in four Tests. On his debut, at Lord's, he took 5 for 60 on the first day, England collapsing for 133. In the next Test, at Old Trafford, Heine and Adcock collected 14 wickets between them, South Africa winning by 3 wickets. At home he played against England in 1956/7, Australia in 1957/8 and New Zealand in 1961/2. In the drawn rubber with England in 1956/7, the two fast bowlers took 39 wickets between them, Heine finishing with 18 (28.72). In the fifth match, at Port Elizabeth, they bowled out England for 110, Heine taking 4 for 22. Against Australia in 1957/8, he was more dominant than his partner, taking 17 wickets (18.88) and twice taking 6 wickets in an innings, certainly among his finest performances.

First-class career (1951-65): 1,255 runs (15.12) and 277 wickets (21.38)
Test matches (14): 209 runs (9.95), 58 wickets (25.08) and 8 catches

Peter Heine

HIME, Charles Frederick William (1869-1940)

Natal

Charles Hime was a reliable right-handed batsman and effective medium-paced bowler who, aged only nineteen, took 6 for 40 for Twenty-Two of Pietermaritzburg against the first England touring team in 1888/9. Amongst other good performances he also took 5 for 18 when captaining Natal against MCC in 1905/6 and added a very brisk 184 for the second wicket with Major R.M. Poore for Natal against Lord Hawke's England eleven in 1895/6. His sole Test, however, was the first at Port Elizabeth in 1895/6 when he scored 0 and 8 and took 1 for 31.

First-class career (1889-1906): 358 runs (12.34) and 24 wickets (22.41)

HUTCHINSON, Philip (1861-1925)

Natal

One of the best right-handed batsmen in Natal and a useful bowler, Philip Hutchinson performed very well as an all-rounder in preliminary matches against the first England team and was one of the first two Natal men to receive international honours when he represented South Africa in the first two Tests at Port Elizabeth and Cape Town in 1888/9. These were his only first-class matches.

Test matches (2): 14 runs (3.50) and 3 catches

INNES, Albert Rose (1868-1946)

Transvaal

A polished and reliable batsman and a slow left-arm bowler who 'terrorized most batsmen' (as a contemporary report put it), Bertie Innes made 55 and took 5 for 98 for Kimberley against Transvaal at Kimberley in the first Currie Cup Tournament of 1889/90. A year before he had appeared in the two Tests against England at Port Elizabeth and Cape Town and took 5 for 43 in the first innings of the first match.

First-class career (1888-94): 70 runs (7.77) and 18 wickets (17.27)
Test matches (2): 14 runs (3.50), 5 wickets (17.80) and 2 catches

IRONSIDE, David Ernest James (b.1925)

Transvaal

David Ironside swung the ball at medium-pace and was able to bowl for long spells without losing accuracy. An effective seam bowler for his province in a short career, he made an impressive Test debut in the second match at Johannesburg against New Zealand in 1953, proving irresistible in partnership with Neil Adcock, taking 5 for 51 and 3 for 37 in a winning cause. But after playing in two more matches in the series, he did not represent his country again.

First-class career (1947-56): 135 runs (6.42) and 130 wickets (21.13)
Test matches (3): 37 runs (18.50), 15 wickets (18.33) and 1 catch

IRVINE, Brian Lee (b.1944)

Natal, Transvaal and Essex

Son of a Natal baseballer, Lee Irvine was a marvellously free left-handed batsman with all the strokes and a versatile fielder who could keep wicket admirably. Trim and short-haired, he always cut a neat, dashing figure on the field. He burst suddenly into full flower in 1967/8 with 504 runs (56.00). He signed a three-year contract with Essex (although, in the event, he served only two years) and was a great success. He became known as a hitter of sixes, winning a competition in his first English season, 1968, with 26. A twenty-seven minute fifty brought him another prize. He made 1,439 runs (32.70) and 1,235 runs (37.42) in his two seasons with Essex and would assuredly have toured with South Africa had the 1970 visit gone ahead. Returning to his homeland, he continued to tear into bowling: he made 872 runs (54.50) in 1969/70, 882 runs (51.88) in 1972/3, and 890 runs (46.84) in 1974/5. He is one of the players who lost very severely when South Africa was banned from Test cricket. In his only series – the last played by his country – against Australia in 1969/70, he showed splendid form, hitting 79 and 73 in the third Test at Johannesburg and 102 in the fourth at Port Elizabeth. His career-highest was 193 for Transvaal against Eastern Province at Johannesburg in 1972/3.

First-class career (1962-76): 9,919 runs (40.48) including 21 centuries, 240 catches and 7 stumpings
Test matches (4): 353 runs (50.42) including 1 century, and 2 catches

JOHNSON, Clement Lecky (1871-1908)

Transvaal

A well-known Irish cricketer – a good right-handed batsman and fast bowler – 'Boy' Johnson was five years in the Dublin University eleven and toured America with Gentlemen of Ireland. He settled in South Africa for health reasons but, within a year, was touring England with the first South African side of 1894 when he scored 508 runs and took 50 wickets: among his scores was 79 at the expense of Gentlemen of Ireland! His sole Test was the second at Johannesburg against England in 1895/6 when he made 3 and 7, took 0 for 57 and caught 1.

First-class career (1893-99): 117 runs (16.71)

JONES, Percy Sydney Twentyman (1876-1954)

Western Province

A sound right-handed batsman, Percy Jones top-scored with 33 and 50 (in a total of 80!) for his province against the Australians in 1902/3 on a treacherous pitch, and he was selected for the third Test at Cape Town (his sole Test), when he was dismissed without scoring in either innings. It was enough, however, for he had joined the select band of Springboks who had represented their country at both cricket and Rugby football.

First-class career (1897-1906): 306 runs (18.00)

KEITH, Headley James (b.1927)

Natal

A forceful left-handed batsman, strong in square-cutting and driving, and part of the powerful line-up of his province in the early fifties, Headley Keith never quite made the grade in Tests. He toured Australasia in 1952/3 and England in 1955, and at home played against England in 1956/7. In the former tour he made 608 runs (33.77), including 111 and 113 not out against Victoria at Melbourne – the first South African to have achieved the feat in Australia – and in the latter tour he made 682 runs (24.35). On his Test debut against England, at Lord's in 1955, he scored 57, and at Headingley 73, playing his part in a South African victory, but otherwise he was disappointing. His career-highest was 193 for Natal against Transvaal at Johannesburg in 1951/2. His left-arm bowling was rarely used in Tests but he was often a partnership breaker in Currie Cup matches. Before he made his first-class debut he took 5 for 14 and 5 for 91 for Natal Country Districts against the visiting Australian team in 1949/50.

First-class career (1950-58): 3,203 runs (30.50) including 8 centuries, and 79 wickets (27.51)
Test matches (8): 318 runs (21.20), 0-63 and 9 catches

KEMPIS, Gustav Adolph (1865-90)

Natal

Many judges have affirmed that Gus Kempis was one of the best bowlers South Africa has ever possessed: a left-arm medium-pacer who possessed great control over his length and turn, he could break either way with equal facility. His sole Test was the first between South Africa and England at Port Elizabeth in 1888/9 when he scored 0 and 0 not out and took 4 for 76. On tour with Natal through Cape Colony in 1889/90, he took 49 wickets (12.10), but he died some months later of fever at Chiloane on the East Coast. His brother, G.S., visited England with the first South African team in 1894.

First-class career (1888-90): 60 runs (6.00) and 46 wickets (12.71)

KOTZE, Johannes Jacobus (1879-1931)

Western Province and Transvaal

A Boer farmer who preferred cricket to war, 'Kodgee' toured England with three South African teams in 1901 (while the Boer War was still raging), 1904 and 1907. Right-arm, and one of the fastest bowlers produced by South Africa, he could make the ball move even on the hardest pitches. Despite a vigorous body action and a very long run, he was able to keep going for long periods; he hated being punished by the batsman. 'Kodgee's' best year was 1904 when he took 104 wickets (20.50) – he had taken 79 wickets in 1901 – but it was not until 1907 that Tests were played in England and, as the googly bowlers were dominant that year, he appeared in only one Test. He had played twice against Australia, in 1902/3. A poor batsman, he was also a clumsy field. Remaining close to the game thoughout his life, he was, perhaps, more responsible than anyone else for the introduction of turf wickets in South Africa, at Newlands in 1927/8. His most impressive bowling in an innings was for his province against Griqualand West at Port Elizabeth when he took 8 for 18 in 1902/3. His best home season was 1906/7 – 54 wickets (10.83) from six matches. He twice performed the hat-trick.

First-class career (1901-11): 688 runs (8.60) and 348 wickets (17.86)
Test matches (3): 2 runs (0.40), 6 wickets (40.50) and 3 catches

KUYS, Frederick (1870-1953)

Western Province

An all-rounder, Frederick Kuys played in one Test, the second against England at Cape Town in 1898/9, when he scored 26 and 0 and took 2 for 31.

First-class career (1896-99): 229 runs (16.35) and 11 wickets (18.72)

LANCE, Herbert Roy (b.1940)

North-Eastern Transvaal and Transvaal

Tall, strongly built, determined and with the look of a G.I. with his crew-cut hairstyle, 'Tiger' Lance was a fine, upstanding right-handed stroke-player and a useful change medium-fast bowler. He toured England in 1965 and at home played against New Zealand in 1961/2 and Australia in 1966/7 and 1969/70. In England he made 475 runs (26.38), running into form in the third Test at The Oval with 69 and 53, adding 96 with Colin Bland in the second innings for the fifth wicket in a very closely-fought contest. His best series, however, was his first against Australia when he made 261 runs (37.28) including 44 and 70 in the first match at Johannesburg, which South Africa won handsomely after being 126 behind on the first innings. A heavy scorer in domestic cricket – he made 729 runs (66.27) in seven matches in 1965/6 – he scored 101 and 112 for Transvaal against Eastern Province at Johannesburg in 1966/7, becoming the third player to register two centuries in a Currie Cup match. His second knock included 10 sixes and 7 fours. He shared in the record tenth-wicket partnership in South Africa of 174 with D. Mackay-Coghill for Transvaal against Natal at Johannesburg in 1965/6.

First-class career (1958-71): 5,336 runs (34.87) including 11 centuries, 167 wickets (25.65) and 101 catches
Test matches (13): 591 runs (28.14), 12 wickets (39.91) and 7 catches

LANGTON, Arthur Beaumont Chudleigh (1912-42)

Transvaal

The tallest – six feet three inches – and the youngest of the 1935 South African team to England, 'Chud' Langton took more wickets – 115 (21.16) – than any of his colleagues and scored 537 runs. He bowled accurate right-arm medium-pace and always needed careful watching for lift, break or change of speed. As a batsman, he could defend when necessary, but was at his best forcing the pace – pulling, driving and cutting. He was a fine field in any company. He played an important part in South Africa's first victory over England in England, at Lord's, when he took 6 for 89 and added 101 in two hours with Bruce Mitchell for the seventh wicket; and in the final Test at The Oval, he added 137 in seventy minutes with Eric Dalton, then a record, for the ninth wicket. In the 1935 series he took 15 wickets (41.53) and made 121 runs (30.25). He continued to put in useful all-round efforts against Australia in 1935/6 and England in 1938/9.

First-class career (1931-42): 1,218 runs (19.96) and 193 wickets (25.74)
Test matches (15): 298 runs (15.68), 40 wickets (45.67) and 8 catches

LAWRENCE, Godfrey Bernard (b.1932)

Natal and Rhodesia

A six feet five inch giant, the tallest player in South African cricket, 'Goofy' Lawrence was a right-arm opening fast bowler who, by dint of sheer hard graft, impressed successively the Mashonaland, Rhodesian and Test match selectors. Also a useful batsman, it was unfortunate for him that his career should commence when Neil Adcock and Peter Heine were at peak form. He was sensational, however, in his sole Test series against New Zealand in 1961/2. He took 8 for 53 in the first innings of the second match at Johannesburg, and in the fourth Test, again at Johannesburg, his match analysis was 9 for 109. He only opened the bowling in one Test but in the fifth at Port Elizabeth he opened the batting in the first innings with Eddie Barlow, scoring 43. In ten first-class matches in 1961/2, he took 51 wickets (17.49). For more than a decade, he was Rhodesia's spearhead.

First-class career (1952-67): 1,079 runs (12.69) and 342 wickets (17.97)
Test matches (5): 141 runs (17.62), 28 wickets (18.28) and 2 catches

Le ROUX, Frederick Louis (1882-1963)

Transvaal and Eastern Province

An all-rounder and captain of Transvaal for several seasons, Fred Le Roux's sole Test was the fourth against England at Durban in 1913/14 when he scored 1 and 0 and (opening the attack) took 0 for 24. Before retiring officially, he captained a First League team in Durban at the age of fifty; and in 1950, acted as convener of the National Selection Committee.

First-class career (1908-29): 1,258 runs (28.59) including 2 centuries, and 93 wickets (19.75)

LEWIS, Percy Tyson (1884-1976)

Transvaal and Western Province

At the time of death the oldest surviving Springbok Test cricketer, 'Plum' Lewis was a right-handed batsman who could be brilliant at his best. He hit 151 for Western Province against MCC in the opening match of the 1913/14 tour, and was selected for the first Test at Durban, but was 'c. Woolley b. Barnes' in each innings without scoring. This was his sole Test. He won the M.C. and bar as a Lieutenant-Colonel in France during the First World War and, being severely wounded in the leg, could play only club cricket on his return, using a runner.

First-class career (1907-14): 507 runs (26.68) including 1 century

LINDSAY, Denis Thomson (b.1939)

North-Eastern Transvaal and Transvaal

As wicket-keeper/batsman for the Fezelas in England in 1961, Denis Lindsay played the first ball from Bill Greensmith circumspectly back to the bowler in the opening match against Essex at Chelmsford. Then, opening his shoulders, he sent the last five deliveries soaring over the fence for six and, scoring 83 not out, won the match for his side. A year later he hit 48 and 84 for a Rhodesian Invitation eleven against the Commonwealth tourists at Salisbury, the attack being of international calibre, and before long he was playing Test cricket. An upstanding right-handed attacking stroke-player, he was also a class wicket-keeper who had to wait for a Test place until John Waite retired, so for a time specialized as a batsman. He toured Australasia in 1963/4 and England in 1965, and at home played against England in 1964/5 and Australia in 1966/7 and 1969/70. In his first match on Australian soil, he hit a sparkling 104 (at number nine) against South Australia at Adelaide, but his sole notable Test innings was 65 in the fifth match at Sydney in a run-feast. On his England tour, when he was the first-string wicket-keeper, he made 779 runs (27.82) and had 24 dismissals, but he could not make runs in the Tests. He averaged only 22.80 against England in 1964/5, but in the home series against Australia in 1966/7 he blossomed as a well-organized as well as aggressive attacking force at the highest level. He hit 606 runs (86.57) in the series, more than anyone else on either side, the highest individual contribution by any wicket-keeper in a Test rubber. He also held 24 catches as South Africa beat Australia for the first time at home. Usually batting at number six, he hit 69 and 182 (including five sixes after the Springboks had been 126 behind) in the first match at Johannesburg; 81 in the second at Cape Town; 137 in the third at Durban; and 131 in the fourth at Johannesburg. His career-highest was 216 against Transvaal B at Johannesburg in 1966/7, his most prolific season, when he made 1,014 runs (72.42) in ten matches, including four centuries. The same season he had 46 dismissals (45 ct, 1 st.), a South African record. He is son of J.D. Lindsay.

First-class career (1958-74): 7,074 runs (35.54) including 12 centuries, and 333 dismissals (292 ct, 41 st.)
Test matches (19): 1,130 runs (37.66) including 3 centuries, and 59 dismissals (57 ct, 2 st.)

LINDSAY, John Dixon (b.1909)

North-Eastern Transvaal and Transvaal

A neat, business-like wicket-keeper, Johnny Lindsay toured England in 1947 and although he began shakily on the early wet wickets he always gave the impression of much natural skill. On the tour he earned 27 dismissals and played in three of the Tests.

First-class career (1933-49): 346 runs (11.16) and 55 dismissals (39 ct, 16 st.)
Test matches (3): 21 runs (7.00) and 5 dismissals (4 ct, 1 st.)

LINDSAY, Neville Vernon (1886-1976)

Orange Free State and Transvaal

An all-round sportsman, outstanding at rugby, hockey, golf and bowls, Neville Lindsay was a sound right-handed batsman and brilliant cover field who

Wicket-keeper Denis Lindsay catches Brian Booth (Australia). Graeme Pollock also dives for the ball

represented either of his two provinces from 1906 until 1927, scoring 2,030 runs (33.00). He shared the South African ninth-wicket record partnership of 221 for Transvaal against Rhodesia at Bulawayo in 1922/3 with G.R. McCubbin. His sole Test was the second against Australia at Johannesburg in 1921/2 when he scored 6 and 29 and caught 'Horseshoe' Collins after he had made 203.

First-class career (1906-27): 2,030 runs (33.27) including 5 centuries, and 24 wickets (27.83)

LING, William Victor Stone (1891-1960)

Griqualand West

Beginning as a promising right-arm googly bowler, William Ling developed into a very useful batsman in the Currie Cup competition, becoming the most effective batsman of his province for a decade. He appeared in the three Tests against Australia in 1921/2 and the first three against England in 1922/3, being marked 'absent' in the sole South African innings in the third match. He had been summoned home to Kimberley when his mother became seriously ill, and it proved to be his last Test.

First-class career (1910-30): 2,618 runs (31.76) including 3 centuries, and 72 wickets (31.52)
Test matches (6): 168 runs (16.80), 0-20 and 1 catch

LLEWELLYN, Charles Bennett (1876-1964)

Natal and Hampshire

A notable all-rounder, being a left-handed forcing batsman, a left-arm slow to medium-paced bowler and a fine fielder, especially at mid-off, Charlie or 'Buck' Llewellyn first played for Natal at eighteen and represented South Africa in five Tests against England and ten against Australia. His Test debut was against

England in the second match at Johannesburg in 1895/6; then from 1899 until 1910 he was a highly valued professional with Hampshire – ironically his career-highest was 216 for the county against the 1901 South Africans at Southampton. For Hampshire he achieved the double in a season three times and twice registered two centuries in a match: he was among the fourteen players chosen for the first Test for England against Australia in 1902 but was omitted in the final selection. Before qualifying for championship matches, he had created a sensation by taking 8 for 132 and then hitting 72 and 21 for Hampshire against the Australians at Southampton in 1899. He played for South Africa in the three Tests against Australia in 1902/3, taking 25 wickets (17.92), including 9 for 216 and scoring 90 in the first at Johannesburg, and 10 for 116 in the second, also at Johannesburg. After he had left Hampshire he toured Australia in 1910/11 and England in 1912. When South Africa defeated Australia for the first time, in the third match at Adelaide, he made 43 and 80 and clean-bowled Macartney, Ransford and Trumper. In the Triangular Tournament, he hit fifties off England and Australia, but in his final Test, against England at The Oval, he was dismissed for 'a pair'. Subsequently, he played League cricket in England and died in Surrey where he had lived for many years. A story that 'Buck' was a coloured man ostracized by Jimmy Sinclair and other members of the South African team to Australia in 1910/11 was scotched by his daughter in *The Cricketer* a few years ago. She confirmed that her father, though born at Pietermaritzburg, was of Welsh and English extraction and had no coloured blood. Moreover, he had been on good terms with all his cricket colleagues.

First-class career (1894-1912): 11,425 runs (26.75) including 18 centuries, 1,013 wickets (23.41) and about 200 catches
Test matches (15): 544 runs (20.14), 48 wickets (29.60) and 7 catches

LUNDIE, Eric Balfour (1888-1917)

Western Province, Eastern Province and Transvaal

A right-arm fast bowler, whose sole Test was against England in the fifth Test at Port Elizabeth in 1913/14, when he bowled 46 overs into the wind without being collared, 'Bill' Lundie took 4 for 107 and scored 0 not out and 1. He was killed in the First World War.

First-class career (1908-14): 126 runs (8.40) and 26 wickets (25.34)

MACAULAY, Michael John (b.1939)

Transvaal, Western Province, Orange Free State, North-Eastern Transvaal and Eastern Province

A left-arm medium-paced seam bowler, Mike Macaulay appeared in one Test, the fifth against England at Port Elizabeth in 1964/5, scoring 21 and 12 and taking 2 for 73. He toured England in 1965, but took 25 wickets rather expensively and did not appear in any Tests, although he performed the hat-trick against Kent at Canterbury. He retired from first-class cricket with knee trouble after the 1968/9 season, but made a remarkable comeback in 1977/8, taking 42 wickets (23.14) for Eastern Province. He is the only player to have represented five provinces.

First-class career (1957-79): 888 runs (13.05) and 234 wickets (22.89)

McCARTHY, Cuan Neil (b.1929)

Natal, Cambridge University and Dorset

At six feet two inches, the tallest cricketer and fastest bowler of his time produced by South Africa, Cuan McCarthy tended to be very erratic in length, although he always maintained a good pace, and in his first Test series, against England, he took 21 wickets (26.71). In his first Test, at Durban, when England won by 2 wickets off the last ball, he had torn through most of the second innings batting, taking 6 for 43 out of 128 for 8. When Australia toured in 1949/50, however, this answer to Ray Lindwall had eleven catches dropped off his bowling in the Tests, and his figures failed to do him justice. In England in 1951 he was too erratic, and his persistence in bowling the bumper on a lively pitch probably cost his country the Test at Old Trafford. He collected only 10 wickets (41.30) in the Tests and 59 wickets (23.96) in all first-class matches. Unfortunately, his fastest ball had in it some semblance of a throw and when he went up to Cambridge and played for the University as the attacking spearhead, rumblings grew about the legality of his action. Against Sussex his fiery bowling brought 8 for 36 including a hat-trick. He was no-balled only once, by Paddy Corrall, while bowling against Worcestershire at Worcester for Cambridge in 1952. He was also a boxing blue.

First-class career (1947-52): 141 runs (4.27) and 176 wickets (25.85)
Test matches (15): 28 runs (3.11), 36 wickets (41.94) and 6 catches

McGLEW, Derrick John (b.1929)

Natal

A dour and determined little opening batsman, 'Jackie' McGlew was appropriately named because there have been few tougher 'stickers' than he. He was also a brilliant fielder in the covers and an astute leader who captained his country in fourteen Tests, winning six of them and losing four. A right-hander, he had a good range of scoring strokes, but became noted instead for his concentration and powers of endurance. He toured England in 1951, 1955 and, as captain, in

1960; and Australasia in 1952/3. At home he played against New Zealand in 1953/4 and, as captain, in 1961/2; England in 1956/7; and Australia in 1957/8 (he captained South Africa against England and Australia in some earlier years when the regular leader was unable to play). He exceeded a thousand runs in each of his England tours – 1,002 runs (38.53) in 1951, 1,871 runs (58.46) including 5 centuries in 1955 and 1,327 runs (42.80) in 1960, heading the averages again. 1955 was by far his best Test series in England: he finished with 476 runs (52.88), including hundreds at Old Trafford and Headingley. In the third Test at Durban against Australia in 1957/8, two wickets had fallen very cheaply when McGlew 'stuck' there for 105 in 575 minutes: it was one of the slowest hundreds ever made, the first fifty taking 313 minutes, but his third-wicket partnership of 231 with John Waite was the highest to date for any South African wicket against Australia. He had made 108 in rather quicker time in the first match of the series at Johannesburg when he set up his country's first-wicket record stand of 176 against Australia with Trevor Goddard. His career-highest was 255 not out in the first Test against New Zealand at Wellington in 1952/3 when he carried his bat through an innings of 524 for 8 wickets declared, shared in the record seventh wicket stand of 246 with A.R.A. Murray and was on the field throughout the match. Moreover, until it was exceeded by Graeme Pollock, this was the highest score for South Africa. On the 1952/3 tour, he made 1,138 runs (47.41). His best season at home was 1957/8 when he made 953 runs (50.15) including eight scores above fifty in twelve matches. He captained Natal for many years.

Jackie McGlew

First-class career (1947-67): 12,170 runs (45.92) including 27 centuries, 35 wickets (26.62) and 103 catches
Test matches (34): 2,440 runs (42.06) including 7 centuries, 0-23 and 18 catches

McKINNON, Atholl Henry (b.1932)

Eastern Province and Transvaal

A wily left-arm spin bowler and off-the-field humorist, Atholl McKinnon took 278 wickets in Currie Cup matches alone. He toured England in 1960 and 1965; and at home played against New Zealand in 1961/2, England in 1964/5 and Australia in 1966/7. As successor to the late 'Tufty' Mann, he took 53 wickets (20.88) and 37 wickets (20.51) respectively on his England tours, while achieving very little in the Tests. In the high-scoring fourth Test against England at Johannesburg in 1964/5, he stuck manfully to his task, returning the following analysis: 86 overs – 30 maidens – 172 runs – 7 wickets. In his early days, batting left-handed at net practice, he almost decapitated that famous old Springbok, Dave Nourse, at the next net. 'Son', growled the old man, 'turn round and bat the other way'. Atholl followed this instruction and, thus converted into a right-handed batsman of aggressive intent, he became a useful lower-order player!

First-class career (1952-68): 1,687 runs (15.06) and 470 wickets (21.14)
Test matches (8): 107 runs (17.83), 26 wickets (35.57) and 1 catch

McLEAN, Roy Alastair (b.1930)

Natal

Ebullient and a superb right-handed stroke-maker, Roy McLean was a beautifully balanced player and a cutter and hooker of immense power. A striking exception to the run of defensive-minded batsmen produced by South Africa from 1947 until 1960, he was, naturally, a great favourite with the crowds. Either on the boundary or close to the wicket, he was an outstanding fielder. He toured England in 1951, 1955 and 1960, and Australasia in 1952/3; and at home played against New Zealand in 1953/4 and 1961/2, England in 1956/7 and in two matches in 1964/5 and Australia in 1957/8. He was a potential matchwinner whenever he played but he was also unreliable at times because of over impetuosity and in two series in South Africa was actually omitted from the side. He learned much of value from some ten century partnerships he enjoyed for Natal with Dudley Nourse, under whose captaincy he first toured England in 1951, when in the fourth Test at Headingley, he repeatedly pierced the deep-set fields, hitting 67, 50 coming from sixes and fours. He finished second in the averages each time to Jackie McGlew in 1955 and 1960, finishing with 1,448 runs (38.10) and 1,516 runs (37.90) respectively, including eight centuries. Not prolific in the Tests, he managed to score 142 in the second Test at Lord's in 1955 when he took charge on a lively wicket in a dashing display, though he was missed several times; and in the third at Old Trafford, when South Africa sought 145 to win in two and a quarter hours, he hit 50 out of 72 with McGlew in fifty minutes, helping to ensure a narrow victory. In the 1960 Tests, he made 269 runs (33.62), more than anyone else. In a rain-restricted match at Old Trafford he hit 109 in a total of 229 in two hours forty minutes. He hit the fastest century of that season, in seventy-five minutes against A.E.R. Gilligan's eleven at Hastings after making only 6 in the first half-hour of his remarkable innings. He made his career-highest, 207, at fifty an hour, in the opening match at Worcester. On his tour of Australia in 1952/3, he had scored steadily before playing a decisive role in the six wicket win in the fifth Test at Melbourne, where he made 81 and 76 not out. His first Test century was against New Zealand at Durban in 1953/4 – 101 in two hours twenty-five minutes – South Africa going on to win by an innings. He also made 100 against England in the third match at Durban in 1956/7, and 113 in the third match at Cape Town against New Zealand in 1961/2. This was a superb almost solo fight against speed and spin, his century coming in less than three hours, but it could not prevent New Zealand winning her first-ever Test abroad. He scored 356 runs (39.55) in the series. In contrast to these occasional outstanding innings, McLean failed to score in eleven of his Test innings. Throughout his career, however, his fielding was superb. He represented Natal at Rugby football until 1953.

First-class career (1949-66): 10,969 runs (36.68) including 22 centuries, and 132 catches
Test matches (40): 2,120 runs (30.28) including 5 centuries, 0-1 and 23 catches

McMILLAN, Quintin (1904-48)

Transvaal

A right-arm slow leg-spin and googly bowler and free-scoring batsman, Quintin McMillan packed a tremendous amount into his four years of first-class cricket. In his first two matches for his province, he scored 61 and took 9 wickets against Eastern Province and scored 185 against Orange Free State, both at Cape Town in 1928/9. He toured England in 1929, making 749 runs (26.75) and taking most wickets, 91 (25.45), including Hobbs, Carr and Ames at low cost in the Oval Test. He played in all five Tests against England in 1930/31, top-scoring on the first day of the first match at Johannesburg with 45 not out in a total of 126: and he toured Australasia in 1931/2 taking 71 wickets in first-class matches, including 16 (20.18) in the two Tests against New Zealand. In the first Test played between the two countries, at Christchurch, he took 9 for 127 in the match, South Africa winning by an innings. Against South Australia at Adelaide, he took 9 for 53 in an innings. He retired for business reasons.

First-class career (1928-32): 1,607 runs (26.78) including 1 century, and 189 wickets (26.63)
Test matches (13): 306 runs (18.00), 36 wickets (34.52) and 8 catches

MANN, Norman Bertram Fleetwood (1920-52)

Natal and Eastern Province

The bespectacled 'Tufty' Mann was a left-arm slow bowler who had no difficulty in pinning down English batsmen – his first spell of bowling in Tests, at Trent Bridge in 1947, consisted of eight successive maiden overs to Denis Compton and Bill Edrich in their peak year – but, as he admitted, he did not quite know where to bowl to Australians, although in the Tests against Australia in 1949/50, he headed the bowling averages with 17 wickets (25.29). He tended to seal up one end when conditions favoured batsmen and to extract full advantage when they offered him the slightest assistance. On the seven occasions when he bowled fifty or more overs in a Test, he only once gave away more than a hundred runs. On both England tours, 1947 and 1951, well over a third of his overs were maidens: he took 74 wickets (25.25) on the former tour and, when his health was indifferent, 44 wickets (26.38) on the second. He headed the averages in both series of Tests – with 15 wickets (40.20) and 10 wickets (26.40) respectively from four matches. Against England at home in 1948/9 he again finished at the top with 17 wickets (25.29). His 4 for 24 in the second innings of the first Test at Trent Bridge in 1951 helped South Africa to her first victory for sixteen years; and he also captured 6 for 59 in the first innings of the first match against England in 1948/9 at Durban – one of the most exciting of all Tests when England won by 2 wickets off the last ball. Despite indifferent eyesight, Mann could swing the bat to good purpose, hitting 97 in fifty-five minutes against Glamorgan at Cardiff in 1947. He made over 500 runs on the tour. In a short Currie Cup career, he took 75 wickets from twelve matches. During the Second World War, he was taken prisoner in Italy and escaped, being hidden by peasants. During the 1951 tour, he was taken ill and he died the following year after two operations.

First-class career (1939-51): 1,446 runs (17.42) and 251 wickets (23.71)
Test matches (19): 400 runs (13.33), 58 wickets (33.10) and 3 catches

MANSELL, Percy Neville Frank (b.1920)

Rhodesia

Percy Mansell wore spectacles, looked vague and distracted and reminded people of a country vicar. An all-rounder of potentially high quality, he was a consistent right-handed batsman, being a fine driver, an inexpensive leg-break bowler and a most reliable slip field. He never represented his country at home, but toured England in 1951 and 1955 and Australasia in 1952/3. On his first England tour he held 21 catches and on his Test debut, at Headingley, he hit 90 in seventy minutes. On his second tour, he was again the most reliable slip with twenty-seven catches, but as a batsman did not approach his form in the Currie Cup: over twenty-five years in this competition, from his debut at sixteen, he made 2,245 runs (41.57) and took 160 wickets (19.83). He made 571 runs (43.92) and took 52 wickets (17.63) in 1951/2. With Hugh Tayfield in such prime form his opportunities in Tests were blocked. For many years, he was prominent in the administration of the game in Rhodesia.

First-class career (1936-61): 4,598 runs (29.66) including 5 centuries, 299 wickets (26.08) and 156 catches
Test matches (13): 355 runs (17.75), 11 wickets (66.90) and 15 catches

MARKHAM, Lawrence Anderson (b.1924)

Natal

'Fish' Markham was an all-rounder who could bowl a prodigious leg-break and whose sole Test was against England in the fourth match at Johannesburg in 1948/9 when he scored 20 and took 1 for 72.

First-class career (1946-51): 268 runs (15.76) including 1 century, and 53 wickets (16.84)

MARX, Waldemar Frederick Eric (1895-1974)

Transvaal

An old Malvernian, Eric Marx scored a brilliant 240 on his debut for his province against Griqualand West at Johannesburg in 1920/21, including one six and thirty fours: it remains the highest first innings in first-class cricket anywhere. Although he made 119 against Orange Free State in the same season, his initial innings produced nearly half his total runs in an all too short first-class career. He was a useful right-arm medium-pace change bowler. This meteor appeared in all the Tests against Australia in 1921/2.

First-class career (1920-22): 656 runs (41.00) including 2 centuries, and 13 wickets (30.84)
Test matches (3): 125 runs (20.83) and 4 wickets (36.00)

MEINTJES, Douglas James (1890-1979)

Transvaal

A very good all-rounder from a powerful province, Doug Meintjes played against England in two Tests in 1922/3. He was primarily a right-arm fast-medium bowler and in the second innings of his first Test at Johannesburg, he disposed of Arthur Carr, Philip Mead and Percy Fender in quick succession and caught the next man, the captain, Frank Mann.

First-class career (1910-26): 1,146 runs (16.14) and 91 wickets (29.64)
Test matches (2): 43 runs (14.33), 6 wickets (19.16) and 3 catches

MELLE, Michael George (b.1930)

Transvaal and Western Province

Son of a former Western Province, Oxford University, Hampshire and Transvaal cricketer who was one of the first exponents of leg-theory bowling, Michael Melle was a genuinely fast right-arm bowler in days when South Africa's attack could be as fast as any. He toured England in 1951 and Australasia in 1952/3 and at home played against Australia in 1949/50. On his Test debut against Australia in the fourth match at Johannesburg in 1949/50, he captured 5 for 113 in the first innings of 465 for 8; but in England, where he was hampered by an operation, he was rather disappointing, although he headed the bowling averages with 50 wickets (20.28). In his only Test at The Oval he took 4 for 9 (three tail-enders). In Australasia he tended to lack the extra life and fire required there but took 14 Test wickets (37.92). Against Tasmania at Launceston, he shone with 9 for 22 (12 for 56 in the match). His best effort was at Johannesburg in 1950/51: he took 8 for 8 for Transvaal against Griqualand West, who fell for 29.

First-class career (1948-54): 544 runs (11.33) and 160 wickets (24.93)
Test matches (7): 68 runs (8.50), 26 wickets (32.73) and 4 catches

MELVILLE, Alan (1910–83)

Oxford University, Sussex, Natal and Transvaal

A graceful right-handed batsman with a classical upright method, Alan Melville was a commanding player against fast bowling, his driving and hooking possessing a special grandeur. A cool and astute captain, he led South Africa in ten of his eleven Tests. After playing as a schoolboy for Natal, he went up to Oxford for whom he played in four University matches, captaining the 1931 and 1932 sides. He captained Sussex in 1934 and 1935. Immediately on his return home, he was appointed captain of South Africa for the series against England in 1938/9; and he was the very popular leader of the 1947 side to England. Brought up with cricket on the mat, and never having played on a turf wicket before, he nevertheless made an immediate impact in England with 132 not out in the Freshmen's match, 78 against Kent and 118 against Yorkshire in his first three innings in the Oxford Parks. He scored a memorable 114 for Sussex at Hove against the West Indian fast bowlers in two and a half hours in 1933. The highlights of his first Test series were innings of 78 and 103, in the 'Timeless Test' at Durban. In his next two Tests, in 1947, he made 189 (his career-highest) and 104 not out at Trent Bridge, and 117 at Lord's. Thus he achieved four centuries in successive Test innings. In the first innings at Trent Bridge he shared in the then-record partnership of 319 for the third wicket with Dudley Nourse. In this series he made 569 runs (63.22) and in all first-class matches on the tour 1,547 runs, (40.71) including six centuries. His final Test appearance was against England in 1948/9. For many years he served as a Test selector.

First-class career (1928-49): 10,598 runs (37.85) including 25 centuries, 132 wickets (29.99) and 156 catches
Test matches (11): 894 runs (52.58) including 4 centuries, and 8 catches

MIDDLETON, James (1865-1913)

Western Province

'Bonnor' Middleton was the most prominent left-arm bowler in South Africa from 1894 until 1906, although he had a birth qualification for County Durham, and he revelled in his nickname as his batting efforts resembled those of the famous Australian hitter, at least in style if not in effect and quantity. Bought out of the Army by Cape Town C.C., his best feat was 12 for 100 for Western Province against Transvaal at Cape Town in 1897/8. He toured England with the 1894 and 1904 teams. In the former year, he took 83 wickets (15.79), including 12 for 83 against MCC and Ground at Lord's and 8 for 48 at Leicester. He played at home against England in 1895/6 and 1898/9, and Australia in 1902/3. On his Test debut, the first match at Port Elizabeth in 1895/6, he took 5 for 64 and 4 for 66, England nevertheless winning handsomely. In the first Test at Johannesburg in 1898/9, he took 5 for 51 in the second innings and, in the next match at Cape Town, had 4 for 18, England falling for 92 but again winning comfortably as South Africa's batting was even more ineffective. Eight years later he was completely overshadowed by the gaggle of googly bowlers and did not go on the first England Test tour.

First-class career (1890-1906): 176 runs (6.06) and 140 wickets (18.02)
Test matches (6): 52 runs (7.42), 24 wickets (18.41) and 1 catch

MILLS, Charles (1866-1950)

Surrey and Western Province

An all-rounder who appeared occasionally for Surrey in 1887 and 1888, Charles Mills emigrated to South Africa as professional to Kimberley C.C. His sole Test was against England at Cape Town in 1891/2 when he scored 0 and 21, took 2 for 83 and held two catches. He toured England with the first-ever South African team in 1894, scoring 452 runs (14.18) and taking 28 wickets (23.20)

First-class career (1888-94): 160 runs (12.30) and 29 wickets (15.55)

MILTON, Sir William Henry (1854-1930)

Western Province

An Old Marlburian, William Milton was a hard-hitting right-handed batsman with a good defence – especially intolerant of loose bowling – and a fine fielder. He became a very prominent figure in the administration of the game in South Africa. He captained his province from 1885 until 1896 and was largely responsible for the first England team visiting the country in 1888/9. He appeared in the first three Tests – as captain in the second and third, both played at Cape Town in 1888/9 and 1891/2 respectively. He also represented England at rugby against Scotland and Ireland. Sometime parliamentary secretary to Cecil Rhodes, he served as administrator of Southern Rhodesia for many years.

First-class career (1888-92): 152 runs (13.81)
Test matches (3): 68 runs (11.33), 2 wickets (24.00) and 1 catch

MITCHELL, Bruce (b.1909)

Transvaal

A neat, perfectly balanced right-handed opening batsman, Bruce Mitchell was a complete player who relished the Test match atmosphere. On his first tour of England in 1929, at the age of twenty, he scored more runs in first-class matches – 1,615 (32.95) – than any other member of the side. He toured England again in 1935 and 1947, and Australasia in 1931/2. At home he played against England in 1930/31, 1938/9 and 1948/9, and Australia in 1935/6. He played with a

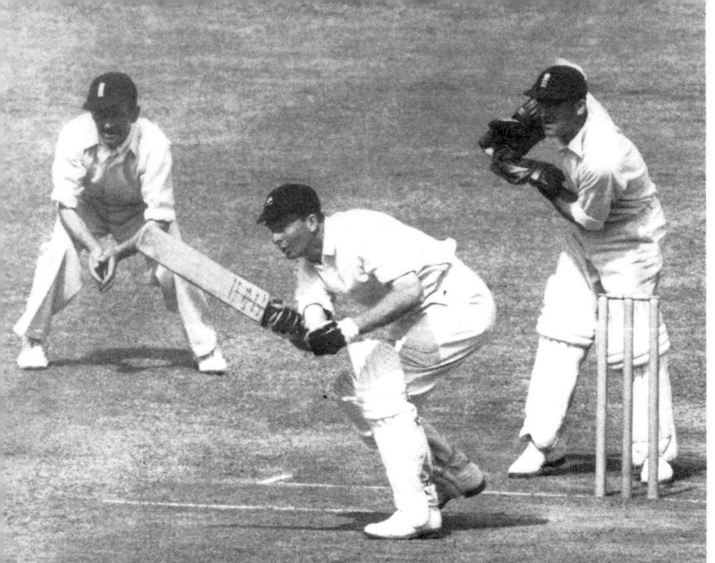

Bruce Mitchell – Godfrey Evans keeping wicket and Dick Howorth fielding (England)

quiet, calm deliberation, making the most of his five feet ten inches to get well over the ball, and his footwork was superb. A useful experimental slow bowler, he was also a reliable close field. Originally he gained his place for his province for his bowling, taking 11 for 95 against Border at East London in 1925/6 at the age of seventeen, but he scarcely maintained this form in first-class matches. On his Test debut at Edgbaston in 1929 he scored 88 and 61 not out, adding 119 and 171 respectively for the first wicket with Bob Catterall: he batted very slowly, however, and in later Tests went in first wicket down. He was reinstated as an opener against England in 1930/31, however, and he headed the batting averages with 455 runs (50.55) which included 123 in the second match at Cape Town when he put on 260 with I.J. Siedle for the first wicket. Although his overall record in Australia in 1931/2 was not outstanding, he headed the averages in the Tests, all five of which South Africa lost, with 322 runs (32.20). In the first Test played by South Africa against New Zealand, at Christchurch, he made 113, putting on 196 for the first wicket in two hours with J.A.J. Christy, his country winning by an innings. Mitchell's best match against Australia was the fourth at Adelaide, in which he made 75 and 95 in a losing cause. On his second England tour, in 1935, he scored 1,451 runs (45.34), including 195 (his career-highest) against Surrey at The Oval, when he put on 330 with Eric Rowan for the first wicket, a long-standing record, in three hours forty minutes, and 488 runs (69.71) in the Tests, when he was far ahead of anyone else. He hit 128 in the final match at The Oval and at Lord's he had a major hand in South Africa's first victory in England, scoring a masterly 164 not out in the second innings out of a total of 278 for 7 declared. He could rarely get going against Australia in 1935/6 but headed the bowling averages with 10 wickets (33.00). In 1938/9 he again scored most runs in the series against England, 466 (58.25), including 109 in the third match at Durban and three other scores in excess of fifty. Back in England in 1947, he was supreme, heading the tour averages with 2,014 runs (61.03), including 8 centuries, the only time a South African has topped two thousand runs in England. In the Tests, opening the batting, he made 597 runs (66.33), including 120 and 189 not out in the final Test at The Oval, when he was on the field for practically the entire match. In his final series against England in 1948/9 he opened in only two matches, scoring 120 at Cape Town and 99 (caught behind) and 56 in his last Test at Port Elizabeth. In this series he made 475 runs (52.77). Bruce Mitchell was South Africa's most accomplished batsman of his time. Quiet and retiring though he was, neither the fiercest fast bowler nor the worst wet wicket ever dampened his determination.

First-class career (1925-49): 11,395 runs (45.39) including 30 centuries, 249 wickets (25.63) and 229 catches
Test matches (42): 3,471 runs (48.88) including 8 centuries, 27 wickets (51.11) and 56 catches

MITCHELL, Frank (1872-1935)

Cambridge University, Yorkshire and Transvaal

See England section.

MORKEL, Denys Paul Beck (1906-80)

Western Province

Over six feet tall, good-looking with broad shoulders and sleek black hair, Denys Morkel made excellent use of his reach and strength and, as a right-handed batsman, could defend soundly or hit very hard as the occasion demanded. Bowling fast-medium with a high delivery, he would make the ball nip off the pitch and always seemed likely to get two or three wickets cheaply at the start of an innings. He was also a very good versatile field. He toured England in 1929 and Australasia in 1931/2, and at home played against England in 1927/8. The best all-rounder on the England tour, he made 1,443 runs (34.35) and took 69 wickets (26.01), including 321 runs (45.85) and 14 wickets (32.71) in the Tests, more Test runs and wickets than anyone else. In the second Test at Lord's, he top-scored with 88 and took 7 for 156 in the match (all accredited batsmen) and in the final match at The Oval he hit 81. Soon after hitting 208 not out – not his career-highest, which was 251 for Cahn's XI – for his province against Natal at Cape Town in 1929/30, he settled in England – although he toured Australasia rather disappointingly a year later. Joining Sir Julien Cahn's team and doing extremely well in business under the aegis of Sir Julien, he was a considerable loss to South African cricket. He played for Gentlemen versus Players in 1931, 1932 and 1934. With S.S.L. Steyn he put on a record 222 for Western Province's eighth wicket against Border in 1929/30.

First-class career (1924-38): 4,494 runs (34.30) including 6 centuries, and 174 wickets (28.58)
Test matches (16): 663 runs (24.55), 18 wickets (45.61) and 13 catches

MURRAY, Anton Ronald Andrew (b.1922)

Eastern Province

Although he was a nervous starter, Anton Murray used his six feet three inches to good effect as a right-handed batsman and was also an impressive right-arm slow-medium bowler with shrewd variations. In the field he was astonishingly agile for such a big man, chasing the ball with knees high in the air like a wing three-quarter making for the line. He toured Australasia in 1952/3 and England in 1955, and at home played against New Zealand in 1953/4. He did not make the Test side in England but in Australasia made 592 runs (31.15) and took 39 wickets (30.97) in fourteen matches. In the second Test at Melbourne, when South Africa defeated Australia for the first time for forty-two years, he top-scored in the first innings with 51, a solid rescue knock. Moreover, in the first Test against New Zealand at Wellington, when South Africa won even more comfortably, he hit 190, adding a record 246 for the seventh wicket with Jackie McGlew, and taking 5 for 49 in 51 overs in the match.

First-class career (1947-56): 2,685 runs (29.83) including 4 centuries, and 188 wickets (24.90)
Test matches (10): 289 runs (22.23) including 1 century, 18 wickets (39.44) and 3 catches

NEL, John Desmond (b.1928)

Western Province

A right-handed opening batsman, a fine player of fast bowling and a very reliable outfield, Jack Nel was chosen for all five Tests against Australia in 1949/50 to face Ray Lindwall and Keith Miller, but they were too good and his highest score was only 38. He made one further Test appearance, against Australia in 1957/8, and was then discarded, but he remained a true stalwart of Western Province whom he captained with much success for several years. He scored 217 not out against Eastern Province at Port Elizabeth in 1952/3.

First-class career (1947-61): 1,839 runs (31.70) including 4 centuries
Test matches (6): 150 runs (13.63) and 1 catch

NEWBERRY, Claude (1890-1916)

Transvaal

Always a trier, with plenty of dash in the field, Claude Newberry erred in trying to bowl too fast and tended to throw his wicket away when batting in his short Test career against England in 1913/14. He was killed in the First World War.

First-class career (1910-14): 251 runs (11.95) and 49 wickets (24.75)
Test matches (4): 62 runs (7.75), 11 wickets (24.36) and 3 catches

NEWSON, Edward Serrurier (b.1910)

Transvaal

A hard-working right-arm fast-bowler, 'Bob' Newson appeared in Tests against England in 1930/31 and 1938/9 without taking many wickets, but in his first Test at Johannesburg, the first of the rubber, he added 45 invaluable runs for the last wicket with Quintin McMillan in the second innings, and South Africa won narrowly by 28 runs.

First-class career (1929-50): 553 runs (17.83) including 1 century, and 60 wickets (26.03)
Test matches (3): 30 runs (7.50), 4 wickets (66.25) and 3 catches

NICHOLSON, Frank (1909-82)

Griqualand West

A competent opening batsman and wicket-keeper, 'Nipper' Nicholson played his sole Tests against Australia in 1935/6, when South Africa were looking for a successor to the recently deceased H.B. Cameron. He totalled 54 Currie Cup victims and hit four first-class hundreds including 185 against Orange Free State. He played for Griqualand West from 1927/8 to 1946/7, for several seasons as captain.

First-class career (1927-47): 2,353 runs (24.76) including 3 centuries, and 69 dismissals (32 ct, 37 st.)
Test matches (4): 76 runs (10.85) and 3 dismissals (3 ct.)

NICOLSON, John Fairless William (1899-1935)

Natal and Oxford University

At Oxford, John Nicolson failed to win his blue, despite undoubted talent. A very competent left-handed batsman, strong on the leg-side and possessing an excellent defence, he became famous by putting up 424 for Natal's first wicket with I.J. Siedle against Orange Free State at Bloemfontein in 1926/7, which remains a South African record for any wicket: his share was 252 not out. His Test experience was limited to three matches against England in 1927/8. On his debut, the third match at Durban, he made 39 and (top-scoring) 78, sharing in several sizeable partnerships. A schoolmaster, he died young in Ireland.

First-class career (1923-30): 1,543 runs (37.63) including 3 centuries
Test matches (3): 179 runs (35.80) and 0-17

NORTON, Norman Ogilvie (1881-1968)

Border and Western Province

A capable all-rounder and captain of a weak province, Border, 'Pompey' Norton played in a sole Test, the fifth match against England at Durban in 1909/10, scoring 2 and 7 and taking 4 for 47. He got Jack Hobbs out when the batsman hit his wicket after making 187!

First-class career (1902-14): 347 runs (15.08) and 49 wickets (15.75)

NOURSE, Arthur Dudley (1910-81)

Natal

Dudley Nourse received no more coaching from his illustrious father, 'Old Dave', than a few words: 'I learned to play cricket with a paling off a fence. Now you go and do the same.' Dudley Nourse achieved even more than the old man. He was a talented right-handed batsman with all the strokes, built four-square with broad shoulders and blacksmith forearms. He seldom went right forward except when moving out to drive the slow bowlers, but off his back foot he hit exceedingly hard, whether hooking, forcing to the off or square-cutting. He was naturally bold and aggressive. He toured England in 1935, 1947 and 1951; and at home played against England in 1938/9 and 1948/9, and Australia in 1935/6 and 1949/50. Although he made 1,681 runs (41.00) including four centuries, on his first England tour, it was not until the powerful Australian side visited South Africa the following winter that he established himself in Tests. Australia won the series overwhelmingly but Dudley Nourse was the backbone of his country's batting, easily heading the averages with 518 runs (57.55) including 231 in the second Test in only four hours. He again headed the averages against England in 1938/9, scoring 422 runs (60.28) which included 120 in four and a half hours in the second match at Cape Town, after England had topped 550. He hit an even more solid 103 in over six hours in the fifth, the 'Timeless Test' at Durban. A bout of pneumonia while serving in the Western Desert nearly cost him his life in the Second World War but he toured England as vice-captain in 1947 and made 1,453 runs (42.73), including four centuries, the highest being 205 not out against Warwickshire at Edgbaston. In the Tests he was supreme, with 621 runs (69.00), only Denis Compton scoring more runs in 'Compton's Year'. In the first Test at Trent Bridge, when he made 149, he added 319 for the third wicket with Alan Melville in just over four hours, a record that stood for sixteen years. Succeeding Melville as captain, he led his country against England in 1948/9, scoring 536 runs (76.57), making 112 and 129 not out (in a total of 257 for 9 wickets declared) in successive matches at Cape Town and Johannesburg. For the fifth successive time in a series he headed the averages against Australia in 1949/50

Dudley Nourse

with 405 runs (45.00), in the second match at Cape Town making 65 and 114 for a beaten side. On his final England tour of 1951, again as captain, he had the misfortune to break a thumb early in the tour and was no longer the master. Yet in the first Test at Trent Bridge, the only one South Africa won and their first victory in sixteen years, he made 208 in the first innings of 483 for 9 wickets declared, batting with a 'pinned' thumb. When the following year he retired, only his father and Herbie Taylor, both in longer careers, had scored more runs than Dudley Nourse. Altogether, he scored six double-centuries, the highest being 260 not out for Natal against Transvaal at Johannesburg in 1936/7. A born ball player, there were few better fieldsmen and safer catchers anywhere in the world.

First-class career (1931-52): 12,472 runs (51.53) including 41 centuries, and 134 catches
Test matches (34): 2,960 runs (53.81) including 9 centuries, 0-9 and 12 catches

NOURSE, Arthur William (1878-1948)

Natal, Transvaal and Western Province

The 'Grand Old Man' of South African cricket, 'Dave' Nourse was born at Croydon in Surrey and went to Africa as a seventeen-year-old trumpeter with the West Riding Regiment. From 1902 until 1924 he made forty-five consecutive Test appearances. A left-handed batsman of rocklike stability and nerve, he could score all round the wicket. His swinging left-arm cutters were often useful – frequently he opened the bowling in Tests – and his enormous hands helped him to be a brilliant slip fielder. He toured England in 1907,

'Dave' Nourse

1912 and 1924, and Australia in 1910/11; and he appeared at home against England in 1905/6, 1909/10, 1913/14 and 1922/3 and Australia in 1902/3 and 1921/2. He scored 72 against Australia at Johannesburg in 1903/4 in his first Test and 18 not out and 93 not out in his first against England at Johannesburg in 1905/6, being in at the death when South Africa recorded their first Test victory by 1 wicket. A host in himself, Nourse contributed 62 out of a total of 140 in the first Test at Lord's in 1907; 92 out of 205 against Australia in the fourth match at Melbourne in 1910/11; 42 out of 93 in the third match at The Oval in 1912; and 64 and 111 (his only Test century) in the third match against Australia at Johannesburg in 1921/2, in the second innings adding 206 for the fourth wicket with C.N. Frank. In the 1905/6, 1907, 1910/11, 1921/2 and 1922/3 series he averaged 48.16, 31.75 (top), 38.00, 56.00 (top) and 33.77 respectively. Equally successful overseas, he made 1,762 runs (35.24) in England in 1912; and 1,928 runs (39.34) in England in 1924, one of the few successes. In Australia in 1910/11 he made 1,454 runs (60.58). On these three tours alone, he hit thirteen centuries and twenty half-centuries. In the Currie Cup competition, he made 3,482 runs (51.57), including twelve centuries, the highest being his career-best, 304 not out for Natal against Transvaal at Johannesburg in 1919/20. He scored more runs than anyone else in South African domestic cricket or for South African teams overseas.

First-class career (1896-1936): 14,216 runs (42.81) including 38 centuries, 305 wickets (23.36) and 172 catches
Test matches (45): 2,234 runs (29.78) including 1 century, 41 wickets (37.87) and 43 catches

NUPEN, Eiulf Peter (1902-77)

Transvaal

Of Norwegian parentage and despite the loss of an eye – as a youngster, he was knocking two hammers together and a splinter flew off – 'Buster' Nupen was regarded as one of the greatest bowlers on matting there has ever been. Tall and strongly built, he bowled right-arm fast medium round the wicket and, on the mat, his off-cutter would nip off quickly and lift sharply. His leg-cutter was more obvious, but also obtained many wickets. He toured England in 1924, proving to be very disappointing on turf and he played at home against England in 1922/3, 1927/8 and 1930/31 (as captain in the first Test) and against Australia in 1921/2 and 1935/6. In the three Tests on matting in 1930/31 he captured 21 wickets (19.66) but was omitted from the other two on turf. In four 'unofficial Tests' against Hon. Lionel Tennyson's team in 1924/5 he took 37 wickets (11.45). In twenty-seven Currie Cup matches, he took 184 wickets (12.75) – not all on matting – taking 10 or more wickets in a match nine times: he is one of only two South Africans to have taken 16 wickets in a match (for 136 against Griqualand West at Johannesburg in 1931/2). Rarely of much account as a batsman, he managed to hit 51 and 69 in the third Test at Durban in 1927/8, sharing in a new record stand with 'Nummy' Deane – 95 for the eighth wicket and 123 for the seventh.

First-class career (1920-37): 1,635 runs (17.96) and 334 wickets (18.19)
Test matches (17): 348 runs (14.50), 50 wickets (35.76) and 9 catches

OCHSE, Arthur Edward (1870-1918)

Transvaal

At nineteen years and one day, the youngest-ever to represent South Africa, Arthur Ochse played in the first two Tests against Major Warton's England team in 1888/9. He was not closely related to A.L. Ochse.

First-class career (1888-95): 231 runs (23.10)
Test matches (2): 16 runs (4.00)

OCHSE, Arthur Lennox (1899-1949)

Eastern Province

Muscle-bound and thickset, 'Oosh' Ochse was a hostile right-arm fast bowler who headed the Test averages in England in 1929 with 10 wickets (31.70) from two matches: he took 52 wickets (35.36) on the tour. He made his Test debut in 1927/8, the same season taking 5 for 31 for his province against MCC when they collapsed for 49, only to win eventually by 10 wickets! Coming from deep country, he was shocked by his first sight of England, exclaiming outside Waterloo Station: 'There are more people in this street than in the whole of Graaff-Reinet!'

First-class career (1921-37): 564 runs (10.44) and 140 wickets (28.33)
Test matches (3): 11 runs (3.66), 10 wickets (36.20) and 1 catch

O'LINN, Sydney (b.1927)

Western Province, Transvaal and Kent

A left-handed batsman of strong defensive outlook and endless concentration, Sid O'Linn was also a capable deputy wicket-keeper and fleet-footed fielder in any position. After a season in which he made 619 runs (68.78) for Transvaal, he toured England in 1960, making 261 runs (32.62) in the five Tests. He made 98 in just under six hours in the third Test at Trent Bridge, when nearly everyone else was failing. He also played at home against New Zealand in 1961/2. From 1951 to 1954, he was deputy to Godfrey Evans for Kent, scoring 1,275 runs (31.09), catching twenty-two and stumping three. A good footballer, he played for Charlton Athletic with distinction and represented the Springboks at soccer against Australia in 1947.

First-class career (1945-66): 4,525 runs (35.62) including 4 centuries, and 103 dismissals (97 ct, 6 st.)
Test matches (7): 297 runs (27.00) and 4 catches

OWEN-SMITH, Dr Harold Geoffrey (b.1909)

Western Province, Oxford University and Middlesex

Full of fun and adventure, 'Tuppy' Owen-Smith who was later to qualify at St Mary's Hospital in London as a doctor of medicine, did not remain long in the Currie Cup competition. At twenty, after only five first-class matches, he became the most exhilarating member of the South African team to England in 1929 and, though on his return he took 11 for 185 against a strong Natal side at Newlands, he was soon back in England as a Rhodes Scholar, going on to win three blues at Oxford for cricket, rugby and boxing, captaining England at rugby and playing cricket for Middlesex. A dynamic personality, a daring and plucky right-handed batsman who drove, cut and hit to leg brilliantly, he bowled slow leg-breaks successfully and fielded with speed and accuracy either at cover-point or in the deep. On the 1929 tour he made 1,168 runs (35.39) and took 30 wickets (25.80), in the third Test at Headingley scoring a heroic 129 in the second innings in a hopeless situation and putting on 103 in sixty-three minutes with the last man, 'Sandy' Bell, which remains the country's record for the last wicket. England nevertheless won by 5 wickets.

First-class career (1927-50): 4,059 runs (26.88) including 3 centuries, and 319 wickets (23.23)
Test matches (5): 252 runs (42.00), 0-113 and 4 catches

PALM, Archibald William (1901-66)

Western Province

A consistent batsman, who shared the unbroken sixth wicket Currie Cup record stand of 244 with J.M.M. Commaille (after 5 wickets had fallen for 27) against Griqualand West at Johannesburg in 1923/4, Palm appeared in one Test, the second against England at Cape Town in 1927/8, when he scored 2 and 13 and held 1 catch.

First-class career (1921-34): 1,958 runs (32.09) including 3 centuries

PARKER, George Macdonald (1899-1969)

The bowling was not making much impact for the South Africans in England in 1924, so George Parker, who was born at Capetown but a professional in the Bradford League, was asked to represent his country in the first Test at Edgbaston and the second at Lord's. He had played only one match previously in first-class cricket. In the first match he worked like a Trojan, taking 6 for 152 in England's only innings, becoming so exhausted that he had to leave the field before close of play on the first day. In the second match he took 2 for 121 (in 24 overs), being hit unmercifully by Jack Hobbs and Herbert Sutcliffe, though he obtained both their wickets in due course.

First-class career (1924): 3 runs (1.50) and 12 wickets (28.58)
Test matches (2): 3 runs (1.50) and 8 wickets (34.12)

PARKIN, Durant Clifford (1870-1936)

Eastern Province, Transvaal and Griqualand West

A medium-paced bowler, 'Dante' Parkin played in a sole Test against England at Cape Town in 1891/2, scoring 6 and 0, taking 3 for 83 (in a total of 369) and holding 1 catch. He toured England with the first South African team in 1894 but failed on the turf wickets, taking only 5 wickets (50.00).

First-class career (1889-1903): 334 runs (15.18) and 48 wickets (20.29)

PARTRIDGE, Joseph Titus (b.1932)

Rhodesia

Sturdy, but bespectacled and looking like the bank official he was, Joe Partridge was a right-arm seam bowler of much honest endeavour who for more than a decade was a mainstay of Rhodesia's attack. After twelve years in first-class cricket, he made his belated Test debut against Australia in 1963/4, on his only overseas tour, and he played at home against England in 1964/5. In 1962/3 he had set up a new record for the number of wickets taken in a South African season – 64 wickets (16.68) from eleven matches. 1961/2 had brought him 53 wickets (13.98) from seven matches, including 14 for 101 against Natal at Salisbury. Against Border at Bulawayo in 1959/60 he had taken 7 for 9 in an innings. His was a long struggle for recognition at the highest level. In Australasia in 1963/4, however, he took more wickets than anyone else, 62 (25.91), relying on accuracy, stamina and swing. In the five Tests against Australia he took 25 wickets (33.32), the same number as his opening partner, Peter Pollock, and against New Zealand he had 13 wickets (19.00) from three matches. In the third Test at Sydney, his match record was 9 for 211, and in the fifth at Sydney, swinging the ball in the heavy atmosphere, he took 7 for 91 in the first innings, his best Test performance. In the first innings of the third Test against New Zealand, he captured 6 for 86. His performances against England, however, were an anti-climax. He was unfortunate in that, while in his prime, he was overshadowed by such fast bowlers as Neil Adcock and Peter Heine.

First-class career (1951-67): 523 runs (9.17) and 376 wickets (20.77)
Test matches (11): 73 runs (10.42), 44 wickets (31.20) and 6 catches

PEARSE, Charles Ormerod Cato (1884-1953)

Natal

A stylish batsman and useful change bowler, 'Ormy' Pearse toured Australia in 1910/11 but was not very successful, making 407 runs (20.35) and taking 10 wickets (26.80). He played in three of the Tests; and represented his province at intervals from 1905 until 1924.

First-class career (1905-24): 973 runs (23.73) and 11 wickets (31.18)
Test matches (3): 55 runs (9.16), 3 wickets (35.33) and 1 catch

PEGLER, Sidney James (1888-1972)

Transvaal

A right-arm medium-pace leg-break bowler with a high delivery, well-varied pace, and quick break from leg, Sid Pegler was the last choice for the team to tour England in 1912 and was not an original selection to tour in 1924, but South Africa would have been in dire straits without him each time. On the former tour he sprang to the front rank taking 189 wickets (15.26) – the record for a South African on tour – and making 643 useful runs with his careful batting. In the latter tour he took 111 wickets (23.18). He headed the bowling in the 1912 Triangular Tournament Tests with 29 wickets (20.48), frequently opening the attack with his leg-breaks, and he took nine wickets in the 1924 series, more than anyone else in another unduly rain-affected summer. Against England in the first Test at Lord's in 1912 he took 7 for 65 in the total of 337, only for South Africa to lose by an innings, and also at Lord's against MCC he captured 4 wickets in five balls, including the hat-trick, and finished with 11 for 119 in another losing cause. He appeared against England at home in 1909/10 and toured Australia in 1910/11, but did not meet with the same degree of success. He was manager of South Africa's team to England in 1951.

First-class career (1908-30): 1,677 runs (12.70) and 425 wickets (19.58)
Test matches (16): 356 runs (15.47), 47 wickets (33.44) and 5 catches

PITHEY, Anthony John (b.1933)

Western Province and Rhodesia

A Rhodesian whose cricket was developed at Cape Town University, Tony Pithey was a tall right-handed batsman, either as an opener or later in the order. He had correct technique but scored slowly in Tests. On the other hand, he could withstand the most ferocious onslaught from fast bowlers. He toured England in 1965, and Australasia in 1963/4; and at home played against England in 1956/7 and 1964/5. Disappointing as an opener in England he batted lower in Australia, scoring 736 runs (33.45), including 170 (his career-highest) against Tasmania at Launceston. In the Tests, he made 208 runs (41.60), including a much needed 76 in the second Test at Melbourne. His final Test series was his best, against England in 1964/5, when he made 462 runs (51.33). He tended to dawdle however, and took over six hours to score 154 in the third Test at Cape Town. In the next Test at Johannesburg, again in favourable conditions, he scored a sedate 95. In the Currie Cup competition he scored 2,786 runs (32.77), including five centuries, and captained Rhodesia for seven years.

First-class career (1950-68): 7,073 runs (35.90) including 13 centuries
Test matches (17): 819 runs (31.50) including 1 century, 0-5 and 3 catches

PITHEY, David Bartlett (b.1936)

Natal, Transvaal, Rhodesia, Oxford University and Northamptonshire

Tony Pithey's younger brother David was a good all-rounder, a right-handed forceful batsman and off-break bowler who won a Rhodes Scholarship to Oxford University in 1959 and was a cricket blue in 1961 and 1962, hitting 67 against Cambridge at Lord's in the latter year. After making fleeting appearances for Northamptonshire in 1962, he returned to Rhodesia, toured Australasia with the South African side in 1963/4 and at home played against Australia in 1966/7. He made his first-class debut in 1956/7 against Transvaal and in a career of some ten years was spasmodically brilliant. His career-highest score was 166 in four hours against North-Eastern Transvaal at Pretoria in 1962/3; and for Oxford he hit 133 against Glamorgan in The Parks in 1961, the same year taking 7 for 47 against the Australians. In three Tests against New Zealand in 1963/4, he took 12 wickets (18.66) including 6 for 38 in the second innings of the second match at Dunedin which was a major factor in South Africa's win. In the second Test against Australia at Cape Town in 1966/7 he made an invaluable 55 against periodic onslaughts from 'Garth' McKenzie.

First-class career (1956-68): 3,420 runs (23.26) including 3 centuries, and 240 wickets (30.78)
Test matches (8): 138 runs (12.54), 12 wickets (48.08) and 6 catches

PLIMSOLL, John Bruce (b.1917)

Western Province

Often looking like a Douglas Fairbanks pirate, lean, sun-tanned, with a thin moustache and a flicker of a grin, Jack Plimsoll was a left-arm fast-medium bowler who toured England in 1947, taking 68 wickets (23.32) and meeting with considerable success when the wicket gave him any help. His sole Test appearance was at Old Trafford, the third match, when he scored 8 and 8 not out and took 3 for 143. A successful manager of the 1965 team to England, he would also have managed the 1970 side if the tour had taken place.

First-class career (1939-50): 386 runs (11.35) and 155 wickets (23.10)

POLLOCK, Peter Maclean (b.1941)

Eastern Province

A strapping six-foot two-inch, fair-haired fast bowler, good fielder and more than useful right-handed tail-ender, Peter Pollock, elder brother of the even more talented Graeme, played his initial first-class match at the age of seventeen and at the age of twenty took 3 for 61 and 6 for 38 in his first Test at Durban against New Zealand. Genuinely fast with a good high action after a long, straight approach, he had mean bounce and a good away swinger. He continued to be successful throughout his Test career, taking 40 wickets in eight Tests on one tour of Australia and New Zealand in 1963/4. He reached 100 wickets in only his twenty-sixth first-class match, and in 1965 in England took 20 wickets in three Tests and 50 in only twelve games on the tour. He was relatively unsuccessful in two series at home, taking 12 wickets in each, against England in 1964 and Australia in 1966/7, but after taking 44 wickets in ten domestic matches in 1968/9 (when the

Peter Pollock

England tour was cancelled, see Basil d'Oliveira), he and Mike Procter formed a fearsome new-ball attack against Bill Lawry's Australians in 1969/70. Pollock took 4 for 20 in the first Test, 5 for 39 in the third and 15 in four Tests as he and Procter took 41 of the 80 Australian wickets to fall in a four-nil whitewash. By the time that South Africa had been 'blackballed' out of Test cricket, Peter Pollock had taken 116 wickets in twenty-eight Tests, his country's third largest haul. He showed his character when, in a losing cause against Australia at Cape Town in 1966/7, he scored 41 and 75 not out, going in at his customary position of number ten. In the first innings he shared a ninth-wicket stand against Australia, putting on 85 with his brother, and his second innings effort only just failed to save the game.

First-class career (1958-72): 3,028 runs (22.76) and 485 wickets (21.89)
Test matches (28): 607 runs (21.67), 116 wickets (24.18) and 9 catches

POLLOCK, Robert Graeme (b.1944)

Eastern Province and Transvaal

Although he is tall, tough and muscular, Graeme Pollock hits a cricket ball with the delicate touch and finesse of a surgeon. The sight of this fair-haired left-hander leaning effortlessly towards the path of the ball and sending it skimming through the covers or wide of mid-on with a relaxed swing through of a heavy bat has been one of the most glorious sights of modern cricket and, since 1970, one sadly reserved for South African crowds only. Undoubtedly a genius, Pollock has been an exceptionally heavy scorer throughout his carer. In a mere twenty-three Tests he scored seven centuries, two of which were double hundreds and two more innings of more than 150. Like Gary Sobers, the only comparable post-war left-hander, Pollock does not need a half-volley or a long-hop to score fours: he will drive on the up, or cut, force or pull anything even fractionally short of a good length. Said by his father, who kept wicket for Orange Free State, to have walked when he was eight months, Graeme Pollock was in his school side at the age of thirteen and at the age of sixteen became the youngest player to score a hundred in the Currie Cup. By the time that he had arrived in Australia in 1963/4 he was broad shouldered and over six feet tall and his inexperience meant little as he hit more than 1,000 runs on the tour at 53.27 and scored centuries in the Sydney and Adelaide Tests. He was not yet twenty and during his magnificent 175 at Adelaide he and Eddie Barlow added 341 for the third wicket in four hours and forty-three minutes, a record South African stand. His performances the following season in South Africa were relatively modest yet, although he often faced two top-class English off-spinners in Titmus and Allen on turning wickets, he made 137 and 77 not out in the final Test at his home ground in Port Elizabeth and reached 459 runs in the series. In England a few months later he scored 1,147 runs in fourteen matches, including a breathtaking 125 in the Trent Bridge Test, scored in two hours twenty minutes out of 160 in cloudy, humid conditions when an acknowledged master of seam and swing, Tom Cartwright, had reduced the rest of South Africa's top batsmen to 43 for 4. Against Australia in 1966/7 he made 90 at exactly a run a minute in the first Test at Johannesburg, helping South Africa's talented side to gain the first home victory against Australia. A mere week later he was forced to bat with a runner because of a pulled thigh muscle and also to limit himself for much of his innings to strokes off the back foot. Coming in at his usual number four when South Africa, confronted by Graham McKenzie in top form, were 12 for 2, and soon after 85 for 5 in reply to Australia's 542, Pollock scored 100 off 139 balls and went on to score 209 out of 353 in 350 minutes, adding 85 with his brother for the ninth wicket. He later helped South Africa to win the rubber with 105 in the fifth Test at Port Elizabeth and when the countries next met in 1969/70 he savaged Lawry's bowlers to the tune of 517 runs in four Tests at 73.85. Since the isolation of his country from international sport, he has continued to bat prolifically in South Africa, being some 2,000 runs ahead of the next highest scorer in Currie Cup cricket, and once hitting a record 222 not out at Port Elizabeth in a 60-over Gillette match. In 1974/5 he hit 1,097 runs (78.35) and he holds the record for a season's aggregate for both Eastern Province (984 runs in 1974/5) and Transvaal (961 runs at an average of 96.10 in 1978/9). A naturally gifted fielder, he has also bowled effective leg-spinners from time to time.

Graeme Pollock

First-class career (1960-): 17,534 runs (56.01) including 54 centuries, 43 wickets (47.95) and 204 catches
Test matches (23): 2,256 runs (60.97) including 7 centuries, 4 wickets (51.00) and 17 catches

POORE, Brigadier-General Robert Montagu (1866-1938)

Hampshire and Natal

Before going to India as a young Lieutenant, Robert Poore had not taken seriously to cricket. Thereupon, he studied textbooks avidly, practised strokes in front of his mirror and played in Army matches. Six feet four inches tall and with a large frame, his drive was one of the most powerful ever known. From 1892 until 1895, while A.D.C. to Lord Harris, then Governor of Bombay, he averaged 80 for Government House. On going to South Africa, he hit centuries for Natal against Lord Hawke's eleven in 1895/6 and appeared for South Africa in the three Tests that season, but with little success. On returning to England in 1898, after scoring nine centuries for Natal, Major Poore, as he was always known, became the most successful batsman in the country in 1899. He hit 1,399 runs (116.58) for Hampshire, including seven centuries, and in all first-class matches averaged 91.23 – an average not exceeded in English cricket until thirty-two years later. With Captain Wynyard, he set up the English record for the sixth wicket – 411 against Somerset at Taunton, the Major reaching 301, his career-highest. Military duties called him back to

South Africa before the end of the season and, after occasional appearances, his career for Hampshire ceased in 1906. He had a distinguished record in the First World War, kept fit and continued to play and coach cricket into old age. When told about the iniquities of body-line bowling in 1933, he exclaimed, 'By gad, if they did that to me I'd fix bayonets and charge the blighters!'

First-class career (1892-1913): 3,441 runs (38.66) including 11 centuries
Test matches (3): 76 runs (12.66), 1-4 and 3 catches

POTHECARY, James Edward (b.1933)

Western Province

A powerfully built right-arm fast-medium bowler, Jim Pothecary, who could swing a ball either way almost at will, shared the new ball with Neil Adcock for much of the England tour of 1960 but did not quite fulfil expectations, securing only 53 wickets (29.52). He played in three Tests on this tour, taking 4 for 58 in the first innings of the final Test at The Oval.

First-class career (1954-65): 1,039 runs (15.74) and 143 wickets (28.34)
Test matches (3): 26 runs (6.50), 9 wickets (39.33) and 2 catches

POWELL, Albert William (1873-1948)

Griqualand West

A good all-rounder, in his sole Test, the second at Cape Town against England in 1898/9, Albert Powell scored 5 and 11, took 1 for 10 and held 2 catches.

First-class career (1892-1905): 297 runs (9.90) and 12 wickets (34.33)

PRINCE, Charles Frederick Henry (1874-1948)

Western Province, Border and Eastern Province

A useful batsman, Charles Prince in his sole Test, the second at Cape Town against England in 1898/9, scored 5 and 1. He also appeared for London County.

First-class career (1894-1905): 730 runs (17.80), 14 catches and 14 stumpings

PROCTER, Michael John (b.1946)

Natal, Western Province, Rhodesia and Gloucestershire

One of the great all-rounders, an outstanding captain and a brave and admirable character, Mike Procter would have achieved colossal feats in Test cricket but the politics of his country and rest of the cricket world's reaction to them deprived him of the opportunity to add to the 226 runs and 41 wickets he had gained in seven Tests against Australia in 1966/7 and 1969/70. In the latter four-match series he took 26 wickets at 13.57 and devastated the opposition with his furious pace. Nearly six foot tall, but built like the trunk of an oak tree, Procter bowls straight and very fast, generally swinging the ball in to the right-hander after running in like a charging bull and delivering the ball before his front foot lands with a windmill twirl of his right arm, the chest facing the batsman but the arm coming past his right ear absolutely straight. On the quietest pitch he can suddenly produce an inspired spell of irresistible fast bowling which will tear apart the opposing batting as a sudden hurricane sweeps through a tropical village. When the wicket is taking spin he can also be a matchwinner, bowling orthodox off-spinners which turn sharply. As a batsman he is a glorious orthodox right-hander of the highest class, a commanding driver and a superb striker off the back foot. Again, with rare dynamism, he can transform a match with a flurry of majestic strokes. As a twelve year old at his prep. school in Natal, Procter scored five centuries, including 210 not out against a Transvaal under-thirteen side. Vice-captain of the South African Schools team to England in 1963, he returned in 1965 to qualify for Gloucestershire, top-scoring in his initial match for the first eleven against the touring South Africans and from 1968 to 1981 was the pivot of the Gloucestershire side, their captain from 1977 to 1981. In the various county limited-over competitions, he has frequently been an irresistible matchwinner and in the Championship, which Gloucestershire only narrowly missed winning under Procter's inspired leadership in both 1976 and 1977, he nine times passed 1,000 runs and twice took more than 100 wickets, despite recurring injuries to his knees. In South Africa, he scored six centuries in consecutive innings in 1970/71 to equal a world record, and, two seasons later, again playing for Rhodesia, scored two centuries in the match against the International Cavaliers. In 1972, 1977 and 1979 (twice in successive matches) he performed the hat-trick in Championship matches and in 1977 against Hampshire in the Benson and Hedges Cup, a competition which Gloucestershire went on to win. Against Worcestershire in 1977 he scored 108 and took 13 wickets in the match for 73. His highest score has been an innings of 254 for Rhodesia against Western Province in 1970/71 and his best bowling figures, 9 for 71 also for Rhodesia, against Transvaal in 1972/3. But he has time and again taken more than five wickets in an innings for many different teams in different countries and different competitions. Amongst all these performances with bat and ball may also be numbered many brilliant catches.

First-class career (1965-): 21,622 runs (36.33) including 47 centuries, 1,383 wickets (19.18) and 319 catches
Test matches (7): 226 runs (25.11), 41 wickets (15.02) and 4 catches

PROMNITZ, Henry Louis Ernest (b.1904)

Border, Griqualand West and Orange Free State

A right-arm spin bowler, Henry Promnitz appeared twice for South Africa against England in 1927/8 and in the first innings of his first Test at Johannesburg, he took 5 for 58 in 37 overs. In his career, for a weak side, Border, in the Currie Cup competition, he took 125 wickets (22.80).

First-class career (1924-37): 592 runs (11.84) and 150 wickets (23.80)
Test matches (2): 14 runs (3.50), 8 wickets (20.12) and 2 catches

QUINN, Neville Anthony (1908-34)

Griqualand West and Transvaal

A left-arm medium-pace bowler who could make the ball swerve and spin but was happier on matting than on turf, Neville Quinn toured England in 1929, coming top of the bowling averages, though not taking most wickets, with 65 (23.89). In the first innings of the third Test at Headingley he took 6 for 19, including the first three batsmen. He played against England once at home in 1930/31, and in Australasia in 1931/2 he again headed the bowling averages with 42 wickets (23.90), including 13 in the Tests. Don Bradman held a high opinion of his capabilities, especially during the third Test at Melbourne when he took 4 for 42 in 31 overs in the first innings, including 'the Don' for 2. He died suddenly two years later.

First-class career (1927-34): 438 runs (9.12) and 186 wickets (20.78)
Test matches (12): 90 runs (6.00), 35 wickets (32.71) and 1 catch

REID, Norman (1890-1947)

Western Province

A zestful all-rounder in a first-class career lasting four years, Norman Reid played in a sole Test against Australia, the third match at Cape Town in 1921/2, mainly because of his brilliant fielding, usually at cover-point. He scored 11 and 6 and took 2 for 63. An Oxford rugby blue in 1912 and 1913, he was awarded the D.S.O. and M.C. during the First World War, but died in tragic circumstances.

First-class career (1920-24): 395 runs (21.94) and 20 wickets (23.15)

RICHARDS, Alfred Renfrew (1868-1904)

Western Province

A useful batsman, Alfred Richards appeared in a sole Test, the third at Cape Town against England in 1895/6, when he scored 6 and 0.

First-class career (1889-96): 346 runs (23.06) including 1 century, 13 catches and 2 stumpings

RICHARDS, Barry Anderson (b.1945)

Natal, South Australia, Gloucestershire and Hampshire

One of the most gifted batsmen in the history of cricket, Barry Richards finds the difficult business of batting quite absurdly easy and all that has prevented him from piling up records like a Bradman has been his tendency to be bored if his supreme talent is not being fully tested by the mere mortals bowling at him. Forced by politics to play his cricket away from the Test arena during his prime, Richards became a wandering mercenary, playing only a little cricket in his native South Africa and instead revealing his magic in England and Australia. Born at Durban the year before Mike Procter, Richards came to England as captain of the 1963 South African schools side and five years later, in his first season for Hampshire, scored 2,395 runs (47.90). The following winter, in his only Test series, he dominated Bill Lawry's Australians, scoring his first Test hundred in his native Durban and reaching three figures in the first over after lunch. A tall fair-haired right-handed opening batsman with a casual and distracted air, Richards is separated from other batsmen by the almost unique amount of time he seems to have to pick up the line and length of the ball. With a high backlift, full flow through of the blade and quick movement of the feet either forward or back to get himself into the perfect position to play the ball, he has been a technical paragon. He has scored more than 1,000 runs in nine seasons in England and six in South Africa, twice scoring two hundred in a match (against Northants in 1968 and Kent in 1976). Playing for South Australia in 1970/71 he was at his brilliant best, scoring 1,538 runs (109.86) and making 356 against Western Australia at Perth, including 325 in a single day. In 1977/8 and 1978/9 he returned to Australia to play with success in World Series Cricket and in 1978 abruptly left county cricket because he was bored with the workaday grind. From time to time, as at Bournemouth against the Rest of the World team in 1968, when he took 7 for 63, he has proved devastating as an off-spin bowler, and he has consistently picked up brilliant catches in the slips with minimum effort or fuss. Ironically, since the politics of their two countries have prevented any form of dialogue, the West Indies cricket team of recent years owe a great debt to South Africa, for Richards had an immense influence on the batting of his Hampshire opening partner Gordon Greenidge, who developed into a magnificent batsman of world stature partly thanks to the example set by the graceful and regal presence at the other end. Hampshire crowds in the 1970s were privileged to see one of the most brilliant opening partnerships in cricket history. Generally smiling and charming, sometimes moody, even petulant, Barry Richards has been an individual, determined to earn the money his talents merited. The genius is seldom a straightforward or an equable character, and never a dull one.

First-class career (1964-): 27,768 runs (55.31) including 79 centuries, 77 wickets (37.38) and 361 catches
Test matches (4): 508 runs (72.57) including 2 centuries, 1-26 and 3 catches

RICHARDS, William Henry Matthews (1862-1903)

Western Province

A useful batsman, 'Dicky' Richards played in the second Test against Major Warton's England side at Cape Town in 1888/9, scoring 0 and 4. It was his only first-class match.

ROBERTSON, John Benjamin (b.1906)

Western Province

With his accurate and sustained spin bowling, Jack Robertson took 8 for 96 in the Australian innings of 318 for his province at Cape Town in 1935/6, thus earning Test selection for the first three matches.

First-class career (1931-37): 450 runs (18.00) and 65 wickets (24.20)
Test matches (3): 51 runs (10.20), 6 wickets (53.50) and 2 catches

ROUTLEDGE, Thomas William (1867-1927)

Transvaal

A fine right-handed batsman with a very forceful approach and a useful change-bowler, Tommy Routledge played in Tests against England in 1891/2 and 1895/6 without living up to his reputation. On the day the meeting was held to select the first-ever South African side to visit England in 1894, he made a century and clinched his place.

First-class career (1889-97): 492 runs (21.39)
Test matches (4): 72 runs (9.00) and 2 catches

ROWAN, Athol Matthew Burchell (b.1921)

Transvaal

With his shambling run – because of war wounds in the Western Desert he sometimes bowled with his leg in irons – Athol Rowan delivered right-arm slow-medium off-breaks from a good height. His grip was unusual in that he laid his index finger on, rather than across, the seam of the ball, which he delivered with a sharp and complete turn of the wrist; he imparted genuine spin and 'bite', varying these with a deceptive leg-cutter. He was also a very useful late-order batsman. For five post-War years he was a major factor in South Africa's attacking strategy. He toured England in 1947 and 1951 and played at home against England in 1948/9, not missing a Test. On his first tour he was the bowling mainstay, taking 102 wickets (24.97) in 1,075.4 overs. Although his 12 Test wickets were very expensive, most of his victims were the best batsmen. On the second tour his results were better in the Tests – 18 wickets (34.44) – although he had a poor tour as a whole with 53 wickets (26.58). He made 432 runs (24.00) as some compensation. Often he was in pain with his leg and retired from first-class cricket at the end of the tour. In the in-between series at home he was the pivot of the attack with 24 wickets (33.08).His best performance was 9 for 19 (15 for 68) for Transvaal against the Australians at Johannesburg in 1949/50. The pitch took sharp spin and he baffled everyone in a match in which he also made 31 out of 125 and top-scored with 15 not out when Transvaal, seeking a mere 69 to win, lost by 15 runs. Through his exertions in this match he injured himself and could not play in any of the Tests in that series. He is Eric's younger brother.

First-class career (1939-51): 1,492 runs (24.06) including 1 century, and 273 wickets (23.47)
Test matches (15): 290 runs (17.05), 54 wickets (38.59) and 7 catches

ROWAN, Eric Alfred Burchell (b.1909)

Transvaal

Superbly confident, a colourful, forthright character and a teetotaller and non-smoker, Eric Rowan had an insatiable appetite for runs, which he collected with patience and an often dogged defence. His right-handed batting, however, could be entertaining. He loved to carry on a running commentary as he was batting. His stance was easy and, very quick-footed, he could drive fearlessly and fluently against the fastest bowlers, chop or cut through the slips and spoon strokes impudently from off-spinners safely over the heads of the leg-trap. Despite having broken his right arm when young, he was a first-rate field in any position. He toured England in 1935 and 1951, and in South Africa played against England in 1938/9 and 1948/9, and Australia in 1935/6 and 1949/50. On his first England tour he amassed 1,948 runs (44.27) which included 6 centuries, more runs than anyone else, but he averaged only 27.33 in the Tests. Although he made 66 and 49 in the first Test against Australia at Durban in 1935/6, he was dropped after the third match and did not have an impressive series until 1938/9 when in four Tests he made 284 runs (47.33). In trouble with the authorities, he did not play another series against England till 1948/9. He opened the batting in the first

Eric Rowan

two Tests but during the course of the second at Johannesburg the selectors announced that he had been dropped for the third match – only for Rowan to make an invaluable 156 not out on the last day in six hours, adding 162 unbroken with Dudley Nourse for the third wicket and saving South Africa after they had been 293 behind on the first innings. He was back for the fourth match at Johannesburg, scoring 86 not out, when things again were looking difficult for his country. Against Australia in 1949/50 he came second to Dudley Nourse with 404 runs (44.88), facing Ray Lindwall, Keith Miller and Bill Johnston as the opening batsmen in all five Tests. Mainly on the losing side, he made 60 in a total of 137 in the first match at Johannesburg, and, in the third, 143 in a total of 311 at Durban. On his final England tour in 1951, he headed the batting with 1,852 runs (50.05) which included 5 centuries. In the Tests he scored 515 runs (57.22), including 236 and 60 not out at Headingley. In his first-class career he exceeded the double hundred five times, his highest being 306 not out for Transvaal against Natal at Johannesburg in 1939/40 which remains the highest score by anyone in South Africa. Prolific in the Currie Cup competition, his best season was 1952/3 with 899 runs (74.91) from eight matches shortly before he retired. In hitting 176 against Rhodesia at Salisbury in 1950/51, he reached a century before lunch on the first day. He is the elder brother of Athol.

First-class career (1929-54): 11,710 runs (48.58) including 30 centuries
Test matches (26): 1,965 runs (43.66) including 3 centuries, 0-7 and 14 catches

ROWE, George Alexander (1874-1959)

Western Province

A left-arm slow bowler in early Currie Cup days, George Rowe was one of the first consistently successful bowlers in representative cricket. He played against England in 1895/6 and Australia in 1902/3. On his debut in the second Test at Johannesburg he opened the bowling and took 5 for 115 in an innings of 482. Touring England in 1894 with the first South African side, he was the outstanding bowler in a wet summer, securing 136 wickets (12.87) in all matches and he was again the most successful on his second tour in 1901 in a warm, dry summer taking 136 wickets again (18.54). Bowling unchanged with George Lohmann for Western Province against Griqualand West at Johannesburg in 1896/7, he took 10 for 48 – and in the next match, against Natal, 10 for 103, but perhaps his best feat was 13 for 155 against Cambridge University at Fenner's in 1901.

First-class career (1893-1907): 303 runs (7.04) and 170 wickets (21.12)
Test matches (5): 26 runs (4.33), 15 wickets (30.40) and 4 catches

SAMUELSON, Sivert Vause (1883-1958)

Natal

A slow bowler, Sivert Samuelson played in only one Test against England, the fifth at Cape Town in 1909/10, scoring 15 and 7, taking 0 for 64 and holding a catch. The following season he was devastating in the Currie Cup competition, taking 13 for 111 and 13 for 147 for Natal against Griqualand West and Orange Free State respectively at Durban, and finishing with 41 wickets (13.87).

First-class career (1908-23): 193 runs (12.06) and 57 wickets (21.05)

SCHWARZ, Reginald Oscar (1875-1918)

Oxfordshire, Middlesex and Transvaal

Few men did so much to establish the reputation of South African cricket as Reggie Schwarz. A quiet, retiring character, he learned the game in England at St Paul's School and played for Middlesex occasionally – averaging a mere 17.80 with the bat and taking 7 wickets in fourteen matches for the county – before going to South Africa. He returned to England with the 1904 team and from that tour dates his fame. Studying the methods of B.J.T. Bosanquet, he learned most successfully the art of bowling off-breaks out of the back of the hand and then taught his fellow South Africans. He himself was unusual in that he bowled the googly only, without mixing in any leg-breaks. The ball moved slowly through the air, fast off the pitch, and often lifted awkwardly. Schwarz headed the averages in 1904 and in 1907, taking 65 wickets (18.26) and 137 wickets (11.79) respectively, and with six men on the leg-side he was very difficult to play, although he was not so successful in 1912. At home he appeared against England in 1905/6 and 1909/10; and he toured Australia in 1910/11. In Australia he took 59 wickets (25.00), heading the bowling in the Tests with 25 wickets (26.04). In the first Test at Sydney, when South Africa were completely outplayed, he took 5 for 102 in a total of 528 and scored 61, coming in at 49 for 7 and adding 100 with Aubrey Faulkner. In the fifth match at Sydney, again in a losing situation, he secured 6 for 47 in a total of 364. Often opening the bowling, he took 18 wickets (17.22) in the 1905/6 series. He was often a useful batsman. He was also an England Rugby football international.

First-class career (1901-14): 3,798 runs (22.60) including 1 century, 398 wickets (17.58) and 111 catches
Test matches (20): 374 runs (13.85), 55 wickets (25.76) and 18 catches

SECCULL, Arthur William (1868-1945)

Transvaal and Western Province

A competent right-handed batsman and useful change-bowler, Arthur Seccull visited England with the first South African side in 1894, making 355 runs (15.10). His sole Test was the third against England in 1895/6 when he scored 6 and 17 not out, took 2 for 37 and held 1 catch.

First-class career (1889-97): 229 runs (22.90) and 15 wickets (16.86)

SEYMOUR, Dr Michael Arthur (b.1936)

Western Province

A right-arm off-break bowler who made his first-class debut in 1960/61, 'Kelly' Seymour toured Australasia in 1963/4 and at home played against England in 1964/5 and Australia in 1969/70. On the tour he was expensive, taking 32 wickets (34.90), and none of his Test performances equalled the feat for South African Universities against New Zealand at Pretoria in 1961/2, when his accuracy helped him to figures of 7 for 80 in the first innings and 12 for 152 in the match.

First-class career (1960-70): 569 runs (14.22) and 111 wickets (29.52)
Test matches (7): 84 runs (12.00), 9 wickets (65.33) and 2 catches

SHALDERS, William Alfred (1880-1917)

Griqualand West and Transvaal

A very impetuous right-handed opening batsman possessing strokes all round the wicket, William Shalders toured England with the 1901, 1904 and 1907 teams, often helping to give the side a good start before getting himself out in the twenties and thirties. On each tour he made over 700 runs in the first-class matches but he was disappointing in the first Test series in England in 1907. At home he played against England in 1898/9 and 1905/6, and against Australia in 1902/3. His highest score in Tests was 42 in the second match against Australia at Johannesburg in 1902/3, but his most invaluable knock was 38 in the first Test at Johannesburg in 1905/6 when South Africa beat England by one wicket. He was a useful change-bowler and very good fielder.

First-class career (1897-1909): 3,351 runs (23.27) including 2 centuries
Test matches (12): 355 runs (16.13), 1-6 and 3 catches

SHEPSTONE, George Harold (1876-1940)

Transvaal

In the eleven at Repton as a free hitter and fast bowler, George Shepstone returned to South Africa to play later in Tests against England in 1895/6 and 1898/9. He came back to England with the South African side in 1904 but illness curtailed his appearances. He represented his province with some distinction from 1898 until 1905, hitting 104 against Griqualand West at Cape Town in 1897/8 and taking 10 for 39 in the match against Border at Port Elizabeth in 1902/3.

First-class career (1895-1905): 693 runs (21.00) including 1 century, and 42 wickets (16.23)
Test matches (2): 38 runs (9.50), 0-47 and 2 catches

SHERWELL, Percy William (1880-1948)

Cornwall and Transvaal

Although born in Natal, Percy Sherwell came to England in childhood for his education and he played cricket for Cornwall before going to the Transvaal as a mining engineer. Slight, but well-built, with a clear-eyed face, Kitchener moustache and kindly expression, he was a wicket-keeper specially adept at taking googly bowling and a good batsman in a crisis. As South Africa's captain he managed his battery of googly bowlers admirably and batted heroically, leading South Africa to her first Test victory over England in 1905/6. In fact, he led South Africa in all the Tests he played – against England in 1905/6 and 1907, and in Australia in 1910/11. His first Test, at Johannesburg in 1905/6, was one of the legendary contests: South Africa, 95 behind on the first innings, needed 48 for victory when Sherwell came in as last man to join Dave Nourse. Amid great excitement the match was won by one wicket. Promoting himself to opening batsman at Lord's in 1907, the first Test in England, he made a sparkling 115 after South Africa had followed on 288 runs behind and saved the game. In Australia, while 1,479 runs were being made in two of the Tests, he allowed only 4 byes (all off one ball). In the 1907 Tests he made more runs than any of his colleagues – 154 runs (30.80). He served on the Test Selection Committee from 1907 until 1924, was South Africa's Lawn Tennis singles champion in 1904, and represented his country against England at tennis in 1908/9. He was one of several brothers who made their mark at cricket, the best known being Noel, of Tonbridge, Cambridge University and Middlesex, also a wicket-keeper.

First-class career (1902-13): 1,808 runs (29.10) including 3 centuries, and 119 dismissals (67 ct, 52 st.)
Test matches (13): 427 runs (23.72) including 1 century, and 36 dismissals (20 ct, 16 st.)

SIEDLE, Ivan Julian (1903-82)

Natal

A solid right-handed opening batsman, 'Jack' Siedle never looked an easy man to get out. He watched the ball intently and had a good variety of strokes. He toured England in 1929 and 1935, each time being beset by illness and injuries to a knee, and at home played against England in 1927/8 and 1930/31, and Australia in 1935/6. On both England tours he was an admirable partner for Bruce Mitchell, scoring 1,579 runs (35.88) and 1,346 runs (39.58) respectively – including 5 centuries – though achieving little in the Tests. In South Africa, however, it was a different story: he made 384 runs (42.66) in the 1930/31 series, in the second Test at Cape Town putting on 260 with Mitchell for the first wicket, which remains the first-wicket record. Against Australia in 1935/6 he was the only batsman besides Dudley Nourse to show any degree of consistency, making 332 runs (33.20) in the series, with a highest score of 59. A heavy scorer in domestic cricket, he hit 3 double centuries and shared in the record South African partnership of 424 with J.F.W. Nicolson for Natal against Orange Free State at Bloemfontein in 1926/7. His career-highest was 265 not out against Orange Free State at Durban in 1929/30. He made centuries in his last three innings in first-class cricket in 1936/7, including 207 against Western Province at Durban. His son, John, made a century for Western Province against Eastern Province at Newlands on his first-class debut in 1955/6.

First-class career (1922-37): 7,730 runs (40.05) including 17 centuries
Test matches (18): 977 runs (28.73) including 1 century, 1-7 and 7 catches

SINCLAIR, James Hugh (1876-1913)

Transvaal

Big and strapping, one of the first men to make South African cricket famous, Jimmy Sinclair was a prodigious right-handed hitter and an excellent fast bowler, combining a nice variety of pace with a high delivery. He first attracted attention against Lord Hawke's team in 1898/9 with scores of 86 (as an opening batsman) and 106 in a total of 177 – the first Test century by a South African – in the Tests at Johannesburg and Cape Town respectively, together with 9 for 89 at Cape Town. Touring England in 1901, 1904 and 1907, he rather disappointed overall with the bat, though his great hitting remained a special feature – once he smote Wilfred Rhodes so hard out of the Harrogate ground that a cabby was knocked off his cab. But his bowling was very successful on the first two tours. He took 107 wickets (16.69) and 100 wickets (22.85) respectively in all matches. Twice in 1901, he took 13 wickets in a match and four times 7 or more wickets in an innings. Taken prisoner by the Boers in the war, he escaped from the PoW camp and reached the British lines thoroughly dishevelled but in time for the 1901 tour! Against the 1902/3 Australians he hit 101 in the second Test at Johannesburg and 104 (which included 10 sixes and 8 fours) in an innings of 225 in the third at Cape Town, heading the batting with an average of 47.66. In 1905/6 he took 21 wickets (19.90) against England. In England in 1907 his bowling was completely overshadowed by the quartet of googly bowlers but at times his hitting was as brilliant as ever. His Australian tour showed moderate results, but two years later he was dead. He also represented both South Africa and England at Rugby football and he was highly skilled at hockey and soccer.

First-class career (1892-1911): 4,483 runs (21.55) including 6 centuries, and 491 wickets (21.43)
Test matches (25): 1,069 runs (23.23) including 3 centuries, 63 wickets (31.68) and 9 catches

SMITH, Charles James Edward (1872-1947)

Transvaal

A useful middle-order right-handed batsman, Charlie Smith represented his province for twelve years. Against the Australians in 1902/3 he made 58 and 71 not out for a Transvaal Fifteen and was selected for the three Tests against the touring team.

First-class career (1893-1905): 409 runs (24.05)
Test matches (3): 106 runs (21.20) and 2 catches

SMITH, Frederick W. (No details available)

Kimberley and Transvaal

Successively captain of Kimberley and Transvaal, Fred Smith collided with another player on the field in

1894 and broke his collar bone. A competent middle-order batsman, his first Test was also the first-ever played by South Africa, against Major Warton's England side in 1888/9. He appeared in the second Test and also in the second match at Johannesburg in 1895/6, by which time he was fully recovered.

First-class career (1888-96): 140 runs (15.55)
Test matches (3): 45 runs (9.00) and 2 catches

SMITH, Vivian Ian (b.1925)

Natal

A very steady right-arm leg-break bowler but without the googly, Ian Smith could be deadly on a helpful wicket. He toured England in 1947 and 1955 and at home played against Australia in 1949/50 and 1957/8. At Derby on his first England tour, he took 13 for 66, including a second innings analysis of 4.5-1-1-6 (including a hat-trick). He took 7 for 189 in 78.1 overs on his Test debut at Trent Bridge (when England had to fight her way out of trouble) and on the tour headed the bowling averages with 58 wickets (23.17). When he visited England again he had fewer opportunities with Hugh Tayfield available. In the Currie Cup competition he took 190 wickets (19.53).

First-class career (1945-58): 547 runs (10.32) and 365 wickets (22.58)
Test matches (9): 39 runs (3.90), 12 wickets (64.08) and 3 catches

SNOOKE, Sibley John (1881-1966)

Border, Western Province and Transvaal

A stylish right-handed stroke-playing batsman, a useful fast-medium bowler and a reliable fielder, 'Tip' Snooke was a bulwark of his country for nearly twenty years. He made his first-class debut in the Currie Cup competition at sixteen, toured England in 1904, 1907 and 1912, and Australia in 1910/11. At home he played against England in 1905/6, 1909/10 and 1922/3. His first Test triumph was in the third match at Johannesburg in 1905/6 when he took 8 for 70 in the first innings (12 for 127 in the match), South Africa winning handsomely, and in the series he took most wickets, 24 (15.37). He helped his side avert defeat at The Oval in 1907 (when he appeared with his brother, Stanley) scoring 63 and 36. In the third Test at Adelaide in 1910/11, when South Africa beat Australia for the first time, he hit 103. In his last series, 1922/3, he opened South Africa's batting and bowling in three Tests, securing 3 for 17 and 2 for 41 in the fifth match at Durban, his final Test, and he headed the bowling averages.

First-class career (1897-1923): 4,821 runs (25.91) including 7 centuries, and 120 wickets (25.14)
Test matches (26): 1,008 runs (22.40) including 1 century, 35 wickets (20.05) and 24 catches

SNOOKE, Stanley Delacourte (1878-1959)

Western Province and Transvaal

A competent batsman, and captain of Western Province for some years, Stanley Snooke toured England in 1907, and in his sole Test at The Oval, batting at number eleven, failed to score in his single innings but held 2 catches. In the wet summer and on turf wickets, he was a great disappointment, averaging only 11.30 for the tour. He was elder brother of 'Tip' – S.J. – with whom he was often confused.

First-class career (1904-21): 798 runs (16.62) and 19 wickets (11.78)

SOLOMON, William Rodger Thomson (1872-1964)

Transvaal and Eastern Province

Largely because of two courageous innings, 64 for a Johannesburg Fifteen and 52 for Transvaal against Lord Hawke's team in 1898/9, William Solomon played in the first Test at Johannesburg about a fortnight later, his sole Test appearance. He scored 2 and 2 and held 1 catch.

First-class career (1892-1906): 73 runs (9.12)

STEWART, Major Robert Bernard (1856-1913)

Eastern Province

Captain of cricket at Wellington, the Major was stationed in South Africa for many years and was a stylish batsman and brilliant cover-point. His only first-class match was a Test, the first-ever for South Africa against Major Warton's England team at Port Elizabeth in 1888/9, in which he scored 4 and 9 and held 2 catches.

STRICKER, Louis Anthony (1884-1960)

Transvaal

A forcing right-handed opening bat, Louis Stricker toured Australia in 1910/11 and England in 1912. At home he played against England in 1909/10. Despite his opportunities, he failed to reach a fifty in Tests, his highest score being 48 in the third match against Australia at Adelaide in 1910/11. However, he hit a fine 101 for Transvaal against MCC at Johannesburg in 1909/10, putting on 215 in two hours and twenty minutes with J.W. Zulch for the first wicket, which constituted a record at that time against a touring team.

First-class career (1906-12): 2,105 runs (22.88) including 2 centuries, and 8 wickets (37.87)
Test matches (13): 342 runs (14.25), 1-105 and 3 catches

SUSSKIND, Manfred Julius (1891-1957)

Middlesex, Cambridge University and Transvaal

A tall right-handed batsman, often cramped in style, whose proneness to pad-playing caused much criticism, 'Fred' Susskind went to Cambridge, where he failed to win his blue, although, in his teens, he played in six matches for Middlesex (averaging 9.90). On returning home, he had a long and prolific career with Transvaal, making 2,595 runs (49.90) in the Currie Cup alone. He toured England in 1924 and although his method of batting did not arouse enthusiasm, he made 1,469 runs (32.64) in the wet summer, being one of the few successes. In this, his only Test series, he hit four scores between 51 and 65. He was a useful deputy wicket-keeper. As late as 1931/2 he made 769 runs (64.08) including 4 centuries for Transvaal.

First-class career (1909-37): 4,775 runs (34.60) including 11 centuries
Test matches (5): 268 runs (33.50) and 1 catch

TABERER, Henry Melville (1870-1932)

Oxford University, Essex, Natal, Rhodesia and Transvaal

Although he represented Oxford against Cambridge at athletics and Rugby football, 'Tabs' Taberer did not win his cricket blue and, after playing for Essex very usefully all-round, being a good batsman and fast bowler, he returned to South Africa. In his sole Test, the first against Australia at Johannesburg in 1902/3, he was appointed captain, scored 2 and took 1 for 48 (clean-bowling Victor Trumper). An exceedingly powerful man, he once, for a wager, threw a cricket ball 100 yards while standing in a tub.

First-class career (1891-1902): 222 runs (13.05) and 22 wickets (20.37)

TANCRED, Augustus Bernard (1865-1911)

Griqualand West and Transvaal

The eldest of the well-known brotherhood of five in the earlier annals of South African cricket, Bernard Tancred was regarded by some contemporaries as the first of the 'great' batsmen produced by his country. At least, in the first two Currie Cup Tournaments, 1889/90 and 1890/91, he averaged 74.75 with the bat in the generally rather low-scoring matches. An opening batsman, he had a sure defence and a splendid range of strokes. He was also an outstanding fielder at point. He played in the first-ever Tests against Major Warton's England side. He was unable to visit England in 1894 with the first touring team, owing to the claims of business.

First-class career (1888-98): 708 runs (35.40) including 1 century
Test matches (2): 87 runs (29.00) and 2 catches

TANCRED, Louis Joseph (1876-1934)

Transvaal

The best-known of the brotherhood of five, Louis Tancred possessed abundant patience as an opening batsman and could wear down the bowling for others to punish. Although a pronounced crouch spoilt his style, he could hit powerfully, being especially good against fast bowling. He toured England in 1901, 1904, 1907 and 1912, the year of the Triangular Tournament, taking over the captaincy from Frank Mitchell in three of the six Tests on the last visit. At home he played against England in 1905/6 and 1913/14, and Australia in 1902/3. On his four tours he made 3,526 runs (25.18) in first-class matches, his best being in 1904 when he reached 1,217 runs (41.96). Not consistently successful in Tests – he was dismissed for a 'pair' in his first Test in England at Headingley in 1907 – he did make 97 in the first innings of his first Test against Australia at Johannesburg in 1902/3, adding 173 for the second wicket with 'Buck' Llewellyn. In the third match against England at Johannesburg in 1905/6 he hit 73. In the Currie Cup he scored 1,231 runs (38.46), including four centuries, being the first man to reach a thousand runs in the competition.

First-class career (1896-1920): 5,695 runs (27.51) including 11 centuries
Test matches (14): 530 runs (21.20) and 3 catches

TANCRED, Vincent M. (1875-1904)

Transvaal

A member of the well-known brotherhood, Vincent Tancred was a useful batsman, bowler and wicket-keeper whose sole Test appearance – as an opening batsman like his other two brothers who represented their country – was in the first match against England at Johannesburg in 1898/9 when he scored 18 and 7. He took his own life in June 1904, while the South African team was in England.

First-class career (1897-99): 292 runs (24.33)

TAPSCOTT, George Lancelot (1889-1940)

Griqualand West

A hard-hitting right-handed batsman who enjoyed his cricket, 'Dusty' Tapscott scored 106 quickly against Natal and 111 (in sixty-five minutes) and 60 for Rest of South Africa against Transvaal in 1911/12. But he was not selected for the 1912 England tour and his sole Test appearance was at Durban in the first match against England in 1913/14 when he made 4 and 1 and held one catch. He was the elder brother of 'Doodles'.

First-class career (1910-23): 934 runs (26.68) including 2 centuries, and 47 wickets (21.40)

TAPSCOTT, Lionel Eric (1894-1934)

Griqualand West

A sparkling right-handed batsman and a fleet-footed fielder without a superior in South Africa, 'Doodles' Tapscott first played for his province in 1911/12 and was almost selected for the 1924 England tour. He played twice against England in 1922/23, hitting 50 not out on his debut in the fourth match at Johannesburg. He represented South Africa also at lawn tennis.

First-class career (1910-29): 1,759 runs (26.25) including 2 centuries, and 34 wickets (23.91)
Test matches (2): 58 runs (29.00) and 0-2

TAYFIELD, Hugh Joseph (b.1928)

Natal, Rhodesia and Transvaal

In the 1950s, Hugh or 'Toey' Tayfield – so-called because of his habit of stubbing his toe into the ground before bowling or receiving a ball – was in the top flight of right-arm off-spin bowlers and a major figure in the renaissance of South African cricket. Tall, trim and with immaculate black hair, he would kiss his cap for luck before each over. His greatest assets were meticulous accuracy, mastery of subtle flight and pace variations and the ability to bowl to his field. He hated being hit. He was a very useful lower-order batsman, especially in a crisis, and a brilliant field. A nephew of S.H. Martin (Natal, Rhodesia and Worcestershire), he made his debut at seventeen in first-class cricket and was soon among the wickets. He toured England in 1951, 1955 and 1960, and Australasia in 1952/3; and at home played against Australia in 1949/50 and 1957/8, and New Zealand in 1953/4. Four times in the series against Australia in 1949/50 he conceded at least a hundred runs in an innings – in the five matches his 17 wickets were very expensive – but in the first innings of the third match at Durban, he routed the tourists for 75 on a 'sticky dog', capturing 7 for 23 in 8.4 overs. Australia won, however, Tayfield being 'pasted' in the second innings. He established himself in Australasia in 1952/3. Despite breaking a thumb (and falling in love) he took 30 wickets (28.10) in the Tests against Australia as the pivot of the attack, and 84 wickets (26.14) in all first-class matches: two Tests against New Zealand yielded 10 wickets. He was the matchwinner when South Africa won the second Test at Melbourne by 82 runs, taking 13 for 165. He took 26 wickets (21.84) in the Tests and 143 wickets (15.75) in all first-class matches in England in 1955. During this tour he collected his hundredth wicket in only his twenty-second Test. In the fourth Test at Headingley he bowled remarkably well on a batsman's wicket taking 9 for 164 in 78.1 overs in the match, South Africa earning an unexpected victory. He took 14 for 126 against Hampshire at Southampton and 13 for 98

Hugh Tayfield

against Surrey at The Oval. Against England in 1956/7 he was even more dominant, taking 37 wickets (17.18) in the series – the most ever taken by a South African. His returns included 8 for 69 in the second innings at Durban and match figures of 13 for 192 at Johannesburg. When England wanted only 189 to win in the final match at Port Elizabeth, he took 6 for 78 and England lost decisively. On his last tour of England in 1960, however, he was almost innocuous in the Tests, although in all first-class matches he was as dangerous as ever with 123 wickets (21.65). More batsmen were using their feet to him but South African fielding around this period was brilliant. Three times he took 50 or more wickets in a home season, and he twice did the hat-trick. He has taken more wickets for South African teams, including Test teams, than anyone else.

First-class career (1945-62): 3,668 runs (17.30), 864 wickets (21.86) and 149 catches
Test matches (37): 862 runs (16.90), 170 wickets (25.91) and 26 catches

TAYLOR, Alistair Innes (b.1925)

Transvaal

Sometime captain of his province and a sound opening

batsman, 'Scotch' Taylor played in one Test against England, the first on the new Wanderers' ground at Johannesburg in 1956/7, scoring 12 and 6.

First-class career (1949-61): 2,717 runs (31.59) including 6 centuries, and 32 wickets (30.81)

TAYLOR, Daniel (1887-1957)

Natal

A sound batsman, Dan Taylor played in the fourth and fifth Tests at Durban and Port Elizabeth respectively against England in 1913/14. In the first, he batted effectively for two scores of 36, when Sydney Barnes with 14 wickets was the menace. He also batted courageously for his province when MCC were beaten by 4 wickets. His father, Daniel, was a South African cricketing pioneer and his younger brother was the gifted Herbie.

First-class career (1907-20): 394 runs (21.88)
Test matches (2): 85 runs (21.25)

Herbie Taylor

TAYLOR, Herbert Wilfred (1889-1973)

Natal, Transvaal and Western Province

Herbie Taylor was the undisputed master on matting wickets. Of average height, strong in defence and off the back foot, he blossomed as a free-scoring right-handed opening batsman with a perpendicular swing of the bat and all the orthodox scoring strokes: imperturbable, he was one of the most cultured batsmen of his time, his footwork so quick and sure that he was seldom forced into a hurried stroke. He displayed remarkable powers of concentration as a twenty-one-year-old in making 173 for Natal against Griqualand West at Durban in 1910/11 and he hit 250 not out, his career-highest in 1912/13 against Transvaal at Johannesburg in three hours forty-five minutes. He toured England in 1912, 1924 (captain) and 1929, and Australasia in 1931/2. At home he played against England in 1913/14 (captain), 1922/3 (captain), 1927/8 and 1930/31, and Australia 1921/2 (captain). In his three tours of England, he amassed 5,249 runs (34.30) including seven centuries: his aggregate in 1924 was 1,898 runs (42.17) and in 1929, 1,575 runs (38.41). From the day he hit a fighting 93 against Australia at Lord's in 1912 in nearly three hours, he never knew a poor series. Against England in 1922/3 and 1927/8 he made 582 runs (64.66) and 412 runs (41.20) respectively, by far the best batsman each time, in the former series scoring 176 in the first match at Johannesburg (helping in South Africa's then-highest against England), and 101 in the fourth and 102 in the fifth matches respectively: in the latter innings he batted solidly for 270 minutes but he received little support and his country lost the rubber. His 101 in the fourth match at Johannesburg in 1927/8, however, was a major factor in his country's victory. As late as 1929 he averaged 55.25 for the three Tests he played, making 121 at The Oval in the final Tests, and adding 214 for the fourth wicket with 'Nummy' Deane after the scoreboard read 20 for 3 in face of a good total by England. In his last full series in Australia in 1931/2, he finished second to Bruce Mitchell in the Tests with 314 runs (31.40), in the fourth match at Adelaide making 78 and 84, only for South Africa to lose convincingly. His final Test was the first-ever by South Africa against New Zealand in 1931/2 at Christchurch. It was the 1913/14 series against England that established his fame. Captain for the first time at twenty-four, he was the only batsman Sydney Barnes (49 wickets from four Tests) could not subdue, making 508 runs (50.80), including a chanceless 109 in the first Test at Durban. When Natal at Durban inflicted the only defeat on MCC (including Barnes), he was dominant with 91 out of 153 (the next highest score being 11), and 100 out of 216 for 6. In one match the mercurial Barnes dashed the ball to the ground: 'It's Taylor, Taylor, Taylor, all the time!' he exclaimed. The ideal model for all aspiring batsmen, in retirement he coached several generations of schoolboys. During the First World War he served in the Royal Field Artillery and the Royal Flying Corps, was commissioned and awarded the M.C. His aggregate of runs in Test cricket has only been exceeded in South Africa by Bruce Mitchell and Dudley Nourse junior.

First-class career (1909-36): 13,105 runs (41.86) including 30 centuries, and 22 wickets (25.45)
Test matches (42): 2,936 runs (40.77) including 7 centuries, 5 wickets (31.20) and 19 catches

THEUNISSEN, Nicolaas Hendrik (1867-1929)

Western Province

A right-arm fastish bowler with a good length and disconcerting off-break and a hitter who often succeeded when others failed, Nicolaas Theunissen played in a sole Test, the second against Major Warton's England side at Cape Town in 1888/9, scoring 0 and 2 not out and taking 0 for 51. In all matches against the touring team that season, he took 36 wickets (11.20).

First-class career (1888-90): 66 runs (22.00) and 20 wickets (12.35)

THORNTON, Dr Patrick George (1867-1939)

Yorkshire, Middlesex, Scotland, Transvaal and Ceylon

A much-travelled general medical practitioner, George Thornton was a left-handed batsman and slow left-arm bowler of considerable skill. He played occasionally for Yorkshire and Middlesex, being at his best for the latter county in 1895 when he took 9 for 72 in the match against Gloucestershire (including W.G.). One of the first doctors to volunteer for service when the South African War broke out, he was made head of the Government Hospital at Pretoria and spent nine years in South Africa, representing Transvaal at cricket. His sole Test appearance was in the first match against Australia at Johannesburg in 1902/3 when he scored 1 not out, took 1 for 20 and held one catch.

First-class career (1891-1903): 1,263 runs (22.55) including 1 century, and 32 wickets (31.47)

TOMLINSON, Denis Stanley (b.1910)

Rhodesia and Border

A right-arm slow leg-break bowler and useful batsman, Denis Tomlinson toured England in 1935 but did not receive many opportunities to shine, though he took 52 wickets (28.53). In his sole Test, the first at Trent Bridge, he scored 9 and took 0 for 38. In a long career, he was a very effective bowler for Rhodesia.

First-class career (1927-48): 912 runs (16.88) including 1 century, and 156 wickets (28.32)

TRAICOS, Athanasios John (b.1947)

Rhodesia and Zimbabwe

Born in Egypt and a right-arm off-break bowler, John Traicos was selected for his first Test against Australia in 1969/70 while he was a student at Natal University. On touring England in 1967 with South African Universities, he made his first-class debut against Cambridge University at Fenner's, taking 5 for 54 in 30.4 overs in the first innings. He twice took 8 wickets in a match for Rhodesia in 1968/9.

First-class career (1967-): 722 runs (12.89) and 176 wickets (31.54)

Test matches (3): 8 runs (4.00), 4 wickets (51.75) and 4 catches

TRIMBORN, Patrick Henry Joseph (b.1940)

Natal

A lively right-arm fast-medium bowler and fine close catcher, Pat Trimborn was twenty-six years old when he made his Test debut against Australia in the third match at Durban in 1966/7 to be one of his country's *six* seam bowlers. In the fifth Test at Port Elizabeth, he removed the 'bogeyman' Bob Cowper in the first innings and captured 3 for 12 in 10.1 overs of sustained effort in the second, South Africa winning the match and their first rubber against Australia. His last Test appearance was against Australia in 1969/70. His best season was 1966/7 when he took 36 wickets (18.94) in nine matches. Professional for East Lancashire in 1969, he took 91 wickets (7.89) and scored over 500 runs; and he also played for the International Cavaliers.

First-class career (1961-76): 880 runs (11.89) and 314 wickets (22.61)

Test matches (4): 13 runs (6.50), 11 wickets (23.36) and 7 catches

TUCKETT, Lindsay (b.1919)

Orange Free State

A right-arm fast-medium bowler with a run of twelve yards, covered with a loping, almost lolling, lazy stride and his eyes half-closed, Lindsay Tuckett had a high, smooth and easy action, and his main danger to the batsmen lay not in his swing but in his pace off the wicket and his tirelessness. He toured England in 1947, and at home played against England in 1948/9. The Second World War robbed him of precious years. In England, his lift, sustained hostility and in-swingers troubled many batsmen on the prevailing good batting wickets, but a groin injury minimized his effectiveness later in the tour: he captured 69 wickets (25.78) including 15 at high cost in the Tests. He was ineffective in the series in South Africa; but in domestic cricket he took 13 wickets in a match twice – for 66 runs against Griqualand West at Kimberley in 1951/2 and for 105 runs against North-Eastern Transvaal at Bloemfontein in 1946/7. His father 'Len' also played for South Africa.

First-class career (1934-55): 1,496 runs (17.60) including 1 century, and 225 wickets (23.07)
Test matches (9): 131 runs (11.90), 19 wickets (51.57) and 9 catches

TUCKETT, Lindsay Richard (1885-1963)

Orange Free State and Natal

A persevering right-arm stock bowler who from 1910/11 bowled tirelessly for his state, 'Len' Tuckett did not make his name until 1925/6, and then as a more than useful tail-end batsman: he shared in a century stand for the last wicket in each innings of a match, a unique performance. Playing for Orange Free State against Western Province at Bloemfontein, he added 115 with L. Fuller in the first and 129 with F. Caulfield in the second innings. In the same season he returned his best bowling feat, 13 for 136 against Griqualand West, also at Bloemfontein. In his sole Test, the third match against England at Johannesburg in 1913/14, he made 0 and 0 not out, took 0 for 69 and held one catch. In Currie Cup matches, he took 111 wickets (20.06).

First-class career (1909-30): 1,219 runs (18.19) and 167 wickets (30.07)

VAN DER BIJL, Pieter Gerhart Vintcent (1907-73)

Oxford University and Western Province

A lanky six feet four inches, Pieter van der Bijl won a Rhodes Scholarship to Oxford and was awarded his cricket blue in 1932, making 540 runs (45.00) for the University. A very patient opening batsman, he returned home in time for the 1933/4 season. He scored 603 runs in the 1937/8 Currie Cup matches and the following season was opening batsman for the Test series against England. In the fifth 'Timeless Test' at Durban and despite bodily punishment from Ken Farnes, he made 125 – at 17 runs an hour – and 97, sharing in opening stands of 131 with his captain, Alan Melville, and 191 with Bruce Mitchell who opened the second innings. During the Second World War he was badly wounded in Italy and was awarded the M.C. His six-foot seven-inch son, Vintcent, captains Natal and represented Middlesex with outstanding success in 1980.

First-class career (1925-43): 2,692 runs (40.17) including 5 centuries
Test matches (5): 460 runs (51.11) including 1 century, and 1 catch

VAN DER MERWE, Edward Alexander (1904-71)

Transvaal

A versatile sportsman who represented Witwatersrand University at rugby, soccer, cricket and athletics and, later, Transvaal at rugby, Edward van der Merwe was a very good wicket-keeper who toured England in 1929 and Australasia in 1931/2 as second-string to H.B. Cameron. He played in one Test in England and, on Cameron's death, one against Australia in 1935/6.

First-class career (1927-38): 287 runs (10.62) and 59 dismissals (33 ct, 26 st.)
Test matches (2): 27 runs (9.00) and 3 catches

VAN DER MERWE, Peter Lawrence (b.1937)

Western Province and Eastern Province

Well-built and bespectacled, Peter van der Merwe made his mark originally as a left-arm slow bowler and his solid, reliable right-handed batsmanship developed rather later: going in late in the middle order, he could defend or attack as the occasion demanded. His fielding was versatile and brilliant. He captained the University of Cape Town and Western Province and – quietly and without fireworks – led his country against England in 1965 and Australia in 1966/7, winning both rubbers, the second being the first-ever victory over Australia. A chartered accountant, he was a thoughtful and shrewd captain who inspired a zealous team-spirit. He also toured Australasia in 1963/4 and at home played against England in 1964/5, learning much about leadership from Trevor Goddard. He first toured England in 1961 with the Fezelas when he earned the nickname 'Murphy' after the team's sponsor. On his Australian tour he made 506 runs (29.76), but accomplished little in the Tests. His best series as a batsman, by which time he had practically given up bowling, was in 1966/7 when he scored 225 runs (32.14) against Australia, including his Test highest, 76, which he made in the first match at Johannesburg.

First-class career (1956-68): 4,086 runs (29.18) including 4 centuries, and 82 wickets (25.82)
Test matches (15): 533 runs (25.38), 1-22 and 11 catches

VAN RYNEVELD, Clive Berrange (b.1928)

Oxford University and Western Province

An outstandingly versatile sportsman, Clive van Ryneveld was generally regarded as the greatest natural athlete produced by South Africa since 'Tuppy' Owen-Smith. By the time he was twenty-three he had won nine international caps – four as a Rugby footballer for England (as a brilliant three-quarter) and five as a cricketer for South Africa. Modelling his batting style on that of Herbie Taylor, he was an enterprising batsman with a long reach, and a particularly good player of slow bowling. His leg-breaks were sometimes erratic but often unplayable. He was an outstanding field anywhere because of his quick reflexes. He toured England in 1951 and at home played against New Zealand in 1953/4, England in 1956/7 (captain) and Australia in 1957/8 (captain for four Tests). Before touring England he had earned a double blue. For South Africa on his England tour, he made 983 runs (29.78), including a faultless 150 against Yorkshire at Bramall Lane, his career-highest. His best innings in the Tests was at Headingley when he hit 83, adding 198 for the second wicket with Eric Rowan. Against New Zealand in 1953/4 he was consistency personified, with a highest score of 68 not out, averaging 46.80 for 234 runs, besides taking 10 wickets (30.50). By this time, he was hard at work on his profession, in due course gaining admission as an advocate at the Cape Bar. He was able to lead his country, however, in four Tests of a shared series with England in 1956/7, his boyish enthusiasm permeating to his players; but in his final series, against Australia the following season, South Africa lost 3-0. He retired from first-class cricket and entered politics, being elected to the House of Assembly.

First-class career (1946-63): 4,803 runs (30.20) including 4 centuries, and 206 wickets (30.24)
Test matches (19): 724 runs (26.81), 17 wickets (39.47) and 14 catches

VARNALS, George Derek (b.1935)

Natal, Eastern Province and Transvaal

A mature right-handed batsman and fine close-in field, Derek Varnals scored 111 in four and a quarter hours when several of his colleagues were in trouble for Natal against MCC at Durban in 1964/5, and subsequently appeared in the Test series without enhancing his career. His best seasons were 1957/8 when he made 519 runs (51.90) and 1964/5, 447 runs (40.63).

First-class career (1955-65): 2,628 runs (30.20) including 4 centuries
Test matches (3): 97 runs (16.16) and 0-2

VILJOEN, Kenneth George (1910-74)

Griqualand West, Orange Free State and Transvaal

A youthful prodigy who played his first game for Griqualand West at sixteen, Ken Viljoen became a confident and stylish right-handed batsman, possessing a remarkably sound defence, and very strong on his legs. He was also a brilliant outfield. He toured Australasia in 1931/2, England in 1935 and 1947, and at home played against England in 1930/31, 1938/9 and 1948/9, and Australasia in 1935/6. His first Test success was 111 in the third Test at Melbourne in 1931/2 when all his colleagues made double-figures but only he exceeded 47 – in the next two Tests he made 0, 1, 1 and 0! On his first England tour in 1935 he ended the wettish season in a blaze of run-getting, heading the averages with 1,454 runs (46.90) which included five centuries; 280 runs came in four Tests, including 124 at Old Trafford when runs were badly needed. Twelve years later in England, he had a rather similar record – 1,441 runs (49.68), including six centuries and 270 in five Tests, his best effort again being at Old Trafford when he made 93, with runs still badly needed. He was rather disappointing against the varied attacks of Australia in 1935/6 and England in 1938/9. He was consistently successful in the Currie Cup competition, making 2,658 runs (59.07), his best domestic season being 1936/7 with 743 runs (92.87). The highest of his three double-centuries was 215 for Griqualand West against Western Province at Kimberley in 1929/30. Ken Viljoen was a very significant figure in the administration of the game.

First-class career (1926-49): 7,964 runs (43.28) including 23 centuries, and 29 wickets (24.89)
Test matches (27): 1,365 runs (28.43) including 2 centuries, 0-23 and 5 catches

VINCENT, Cyril Leverton (1902-68)

Transvaal

In the tradition of top-class left-arm spin bowlers, and a competent batsman, Cyril Vincent flourished in provincial competitions and in Tests both at home and abroad, but for twelve years he never appeared in a Currie Cup match because his employer refused to allow him the time to play. After two feats for Transvaal against MCC in 1927/8 – 18 wickets from two games and, subsequently, 23 wickets (22.47) and 134 runs (33.50) in the Tests – he took leave again to play in two trial games at Durban and was selected for the 1929 England tour, when he took 13 wickets from four Tests and made a belligerent 60 in the third Test at Headingley. He toured Australasia in 1931/2 and England again in 1935, and at home played against England in 1930/31. In the latter series, he took 18 wickets (20.77), which included 6 for 51 in the first innings of the fifth match at Durban. On his second visit to England, at thirty-three the veteran of the side he took 111 wickets (20.19) in all matches, including 18 (33.38) from four Tests. On this his last tour, he continued to be a model of accuracy, highly skilful in flighting and spinning the ball. In the third Test at Headingley, he took 8 for 149 in the match, all recognized batsmen. He was sometime chairman of the South African and Transvaal selection committees. He also once represented South Africa at baseball against Australia.

First-class career (1920-43): 1,582 runs (17.97) and 293 wickets (23.91)
Test matches (25): 526 runs (20.23), 84 wickets (31.32) and 27 catches

VINTCENT, Charles Henry (1866-1943)

Griqualand West and Transvaal

An Old Carthusian and left-handed both as batsman and bowler, Charles Vintcent played in the first three Tests for South Africa, against England in 1888/9 and 1891/2, without distinguishing himself.

First-class career (1888-1905): 119 runs (11.90) and 11 wickets (33.09)
Test matches (3): 27 runs (4.50), 4 wickets (48.25) and 1 catch

VOGLER, Albert Edward Ernest (1876-1946)

Natal, Eastern Province, Middlesex and Aberdeenshire

Bert Vogler was a high-class right-arm leg-break and googly bowler. After a jerky approach his delivery was very difficult to read and he could vary his stock-in-trade with a top-spinner and a deceptive slow yorker. A useful hard-hitting batsman, he was also a good fielder. On his first-class debut at twenty-seven for Natal against Transvaal at Johannesburg in 1903/4 in the Currie Cup competition, he took 5 for 86 (four of them top-class batsmen). He turned professional, came to England and joined the MCC ground staff, bowling several times in MCC matches with brilliant success. He intended qualifying for Middlesex but appeared only once for the county in 1906, scoring 87 and taking 5 for 91, as the county already had two colonial players. There was some friction and Sir Abe Bailey found a position for him in South Africa. He met with startling success in domestic cricket. He took all 10 for 26 in twelve overs (16 for 38 in the match) all in one day for Eastern Province against Griqualand West at Johannesburg in 1906/7. A regular member of South Africa's winning team against England in 1905/6, though he only took 9 wickets in the five Tests (but scored 137 runs at 34.25), he toured England in 1907 as one of the 'googly quartet' and was called by England's captain, R.E. Foster, 'the best bowler in the world'. Second to Reggie Schwarz in the averages, he took 119 wickets (15.62) and scored 723 runs (21.26): in the three Tests he was supreme with 15 wickets (19.66). In the first Test at Lord's, he captured 7 for 128 in the total of 428. Against England in 1909/10 he was at his peak with 36 wickets (21.75) in the five Tests, a record that stood until Hugh Tayfield broke it forty-seven years later. He took 12 for 181 in the first and 8 for 207 in the third matches, both at Johannesburg. But in Australia in 1910/11 he fell away considerably. Later he was associated with various Scottish, Irish and English clubs and in 1912 even appeared against the South African tourists for an Irish club.

First-class career (1903-12): 2,375 runs (20.13) including 1 century, and 401 wickets (18.14)
Test matches (15): 340 runs (17.00), 64 wickets (22.73) and 20 catches

WADE, Herbert Frederick (1905-80)

Natal

Herby Wade was a tower of strength to Natal as a dashing right-handed batsman and captain. In representative cricket it was his great gift of leadership that was his greatest asset. Moreover, he was a fearless close-in field. He played in ten Tests, against England in 1935 and Australia in 1935/6, in each as captain. At Lord's in 1935 he led the eleven that registered the first-ever victory in a Test in England. On this tour, he made 1,042 runs (28.94) and showed an understanding knack of being able to 'read' the character of turf pitches. He inspired loyalty amongst all his team. His experience against Australia, however, was not quite so happy. For some years he played cricket and Rugby football in Yorkshire. He was elder brother of W.W. His highest score was 190 for Natal against Eastern Province in 1936/7. In all he scored 1,912 Currie Cup runs (44.46).

First-class career (1924-37): 3,858 runs (35.39) including 9 centuries
Test matches (10): 327 runs (20.43) and 4 catches

WADE, Walter Wareham (b.1914)

Natal

A very competent wicket-keeper/batsman, 'Billy' Wade was unable to tour, but kept wicket at home against England in 1938/9, and Australia in 1949/50. When England amassed 559 for 9 wickets declared in the second Test at Cape Town in 1938/9, he did not allow a single bye, an outstanding performance. In the 1948/9 series, he made 407 runs (50.87), including 125 in the fifth Test at Port Elizabeth. He had eight victims (1 ct, 7 st.) for Natal against Griqualand West at Durban in 1947/8. His highest score was 208 against Eastern Province at Pietermaritzburg in 1939/40.

First-class career (1935-50): 2,859 runs (48.45) including 8 centuries
Test matches (11): 511 runs (28.38) including 1 century, and 17 dismissals (15 ct, 2 st.)

WAITE, John Henry Bickford (b.1930)

Eastern Province and Transvaal

Perhaps the best wicket-keeper/batsman to have represented South Africa, John Waite was a quiet, self-effacing perfectionist, neat though relatively tall for his trade, taking the slow bowlers unobtrusively and efficiently and capable of the spectacular diving catch standing back. As a right-handed batsman he was very sound defensively, had a complete range of strokes despite a limited backlift, and was particularly strong off his legs. His powers of concentration were intense. He is the only player to have appeared in fifty Tests for South Africa and his representative career

John Waite, with Jim Parks and Colin Cowdrey (slip)

was spread between 1951 and 1965. He toured England in 1951, 1955 and 1960, Australasia in 1952/3 and 1963/4, and at home played against New Zealand in 1953/4 and 1961/2, England in 1956/7 and 1964/5, and Australia in 1957/8. On his first England tour he came as reserve 'keeper, but was selected for the first Test at Trent Bridge and never looked back, opening the batting on his debut (later he strengthened the middle order) and hitting 76. He scored 1,011 runs (33.70) on this tour and had 148 victims (124 caught and 24 stumped). He had the record 26 dismissals against New Zealand in 1961/2; 23 against New Zealand in 1953/4; and 16, 15 and 15 against England in 1956/7 and 1955 and against Australia in 1957/8 respectively. No other South African 'keeper has had as many, either in Tests or first-class cricket generally. In the fifth Test at Melbourne in 1952/3 he did not concede a bye in a total of 520. In two Tests against New Zealand, the fifth at Port Elizabeth in 1953/4 and the third Test at Cape Town in 1961/2, he had seven dismissals. His first Test century was 113 in the third Test at Old Trafford in 1955, a very patient effort, after a middle-order collapse. He headed the averages and scored most runs against Australia in 1957/8 with 362 runs (40.22), including 115 in the first match at Johannesburg and 134 in the third match at Durban when he added 231 for the third wicket with Jackie McGlew. In England in 1960 he headed the Test averages with 38.14, though his highest score was only 77. His fourth and last Test century was 101 in the second match against New Zealand at Johannesburg in 1961/2. Prolific in Australasia in 1963/4, he scored 552 runs (42.46) in all first-class matches; and his last dominant role as a batsman in Tests was in the fourth match against England at Johannesburg in 1964/5 when, in making 64, he added 157 for the fifth wicket with Tony Pithey in three hours forty minutes, a South African record.

First-class career (1948-65): 9,812 runs (35.04) including 23 centuries, and 510 dismissals (427 ct, 83 st.)
Test matches (50): 2,405 runs (30.44) including 4 centuries, and 141 dismissals (124 ct, 17 st.)

WALTER, Kenneth Alexander (b.1939)

Transvaal

A right-arm fast-medium bowler who took 165 wickets (19.55) in the Currie Cup competition in nine years, Ken Walter played in two Tests at home against New Zealand in 1961/2.

First-class career (1957-66): 594 runs (13.50) and 217 wickets (21.22)
Test matches (2): 11 runs (3.66), 6 wickets (32.83) and 3 catches

WARD, Thomas Alfred (1887-1936)

Transvaal

A wicket-keeper who was at times badly knocked about, and a dogged batsman with a strong defence, Tommy Ward toured England in 1912 and 1924, and at home played against England in 1913/14 and 1922/3, and Australia in 1921/2. While opening the batting he made a rugged 64 in the fourth Test against England at Johannesburg in 1922/3 and 50 in the fourth Test at Old Trafford. He was electrocuted while working in a gold-mine.

First-class career (1909-27): 1,651 runs (15.43) and 175 dismissals (107 ct, 68 st.)
Test matches (23): 459 runs (13.90) and 32 dismissals (19 ct, 13 st.)

WATKINS, John Cecil (b.1923)

Natal

Of lean and hungry appearance, John Watkins was a right-handed batsman with a fine range of scoring strokes – his batting, like the man himself, was cavalier and joyous. He was a medium-paced swing bowler who could keep all but the most gifted batsmen quiet, and a fine slip fielder. He toured Australasia in 1952/3, and played at home against Australia in 1949/50, New Zealand in 1953/4 and England in 1956/7. The pinnacle of his career was the tour of Australasia with the team of 'no hopers' who performed so valiantly. He made 679 runs (28.29) and took 31 wickets (27.74) on the tour. Supported by tigerish fielding, he secured 4 for 41 in the first Test at Brisbane; hit 76 in the fourth at Adelaide; and in the fifth at Melbourne, despite the large Australian total of 520, he struck hard for 92 and

50, and was prominent in the victory by 6 wickets. In this series, he scored 408 runs (31.38) and took 16 wickets (29.06); and in the first Test against New Zealand at Wellington, which South Africa won by an innings, he captured 4 for 22 in 23.5 overs in the second innings. With Neil Adcock, he broke the back of New Zealand's first innings of the fifth Test in 1953/4 at Port Elizabeth, taking 4 for 34, and ensured victory by adding 107 in seventy-five minutes with Ken Funston.

First-class career (1946-58): 2,158 runs (24.80) including 2 centuries, and 96 wickets (28.52)
Test matches (15): 612 runs (23.53), 29 wickets (28.13) and 12 catches

WESLEY, Colin (b.1937)

Natal

A squat left-handed opening batsman and a brilliant field 'Tich' Wesley was chosen for the 1960 England tour for his aggression, but he proved uncertain against the best bowlers. Brian Statham dismissed him first ball in each innings of the third Test at Trent Bridge. His career-highest was 131 for Natal against New Zealand at Pietermaritzburg in 1961/2.

First-class career (1956-66): 1,892 runs (27.02) including 3 centuries, and 15 wickets (23.60)
Test matches (3): 49 runs (9.80) and 1 catch

WESTCOTT, Richard John (b.1927)

Western Province

Dick Westcott was a stylish and fluent right-handed opening batsman who played his best cricket at Newlands: he was also a useful medium-paced change-bowler. Early in his career he was seriously injured in a car accident, but despite considerable damage to his left arm, he fought his way back to health and international honours. He played in Tests at home against New Zealand in 1953/4 and Australia in 1957/8. In his initial Test, the third at Cape Town in 1953/4, he scored 62 after New Zealand had forced South Africa to follow on.

First-class career (1949-62): 3,225 runs (36.23) including 4 centuries, and 10 wickets (31.40)
Test matches (5): 166 runs (18.44) and 0-22

WHITE, Gordon Charles (1882-1918)

Transvaal

Around 1910 Gordon White was considered to be South Africa's leading right-handed batsman. He had a sound defence and perfect timing, besides possessing a great variety of strokes, notably clean drives to both sides and crisp late cuts. He was also one of his country's battery of leg-break and googly bowlers. He never quite lived up to his reputation as a batsman on tour in England in 1904, 1907 and 1912. On his first visit to England, he scored 773 runs (29.73) in first-class matches and did the hat-trick against Kent at Canterbury, but three years later he found the prevailing soft wickets not to his liking. His experience was similar in 1912. He took 56 wickets (14.73) in 1907, as one of the googly quartet who carried most before them (except in the Tests). At home in 1905/6, however, when South Africa first won a Test rubber, he headed the batting with 437 runs (54.62), hitting 147 in four hours at Johannesburg in the third match when the rubber was decided; and he averaged 35.50 in the 1909/10 Tests, making 118 in the second match at Durban. In Currie Cup matches he averaged 38.10 with the bat and took 27 wickets. Gordon White died of war wounds a month before the Armistice.

First-class career (1902-12): 3,773 runs (27.74) including 4 centuries, and 158 wickets (20.29)
Test matches (17): 872 runs (30.06) including 2 centuries, 9 wickets (33.44) and 10 catches

WILLOUGHBY, Joseph Thomas (1874-presumed dead)

Western Province

A useful bowler, Joseph Willoughby played for South Africa in two Tests against England in 1895/6, which were his only first-class matches. In his first match at Port Elizabeth he dismissed George Lohmann for 'a pair', and when he batted George did the same to him.

Test matches (2): 8 runs (2.00) and 6 wickets (26.50)

WIMBLE, Clarence Skelton (1864-1930)

Transvaal

Generally regarded as a consistent run-getter and superior field, Clarence Wimble's sole Test was against England at Cape Town in 1891/2 when he did not score in either innings or hold a catch.

First-class career (1890-92): 108 runs (27.00)

WINSLOW, Paul Lyndhurst (b.1929)

Sussex, Transvaal and Rhodesia

One of the most effective right-handed hitters seen in South African cricket, Paul Winslow once hit 'Toey' Tayfield for two consecutive sixes in a Currie Cup match and was caught by the same spectator each time. Six feet three inches and lean, this aggressive batsman played a few games for Sussex in 1949, having been coached by 'Patsy' Hendren, but was unable to qualify and, on returning to South Africa, was selected for two Tests against the 1949/50 Australians because of his bold methods and also his exceptionally versatile fielding. He was not a success, however. Touring

England in 1955, though his overall figures were rather moderate – 758 runs (23.68) – he hit magnificently in two matches at Old Trafford. Against Lancashire, he struck 40 off eight balls, including 30 off an over of Jack Ikin's, and in the third Test, coming in after a severe middle-order collapse, he scored 108 in 3 hours 10 minutes, reaching his century with a hit over the sightscreen, one of the biggest ever seen on the ground – before waving joyfully to his fellows in the pavilion. He added 171 with John Waite for the sixth wicket. During this tour, he hit no fewer than twenty-seven sixes. In his first match for Rhodesia, he hit 81 and 139 against Australia at Salisbury in 1957/8 showing greater discernment in his selection of balls to punish; but he did not represent his country again. He also excelled in golf, tennis, rugby and hockey.

First-class career (1949-62): 2,755 runs (23.34) including 2 centuries
Test matches (5): 186 runs (20.66) including 1 century, and 1 catch

WYNNE, Owen Edgar (1919-75)

Transvaal and Western Province

A solid right-handed opening batsman, Owen Wynne was primarily an on-side player. He scored his career-highest of 200 not out for Transvaal against Border at Johannesburg in 1946/7. In the first match of MCC's tour in 1948/9, he made 108 for Western Province at Cape Town and, a few days later on the same ground, 105 for Cape Province against the tourists. Selected for the first three Tests, he accomplished nothing until the third at Cape Town when he scored 50 and 44 – and was then dropped from the side! The following season he was the only man to face Ray Lindwall with confidence, while batting for a South African Eleven at Salisbury, and played in three Tests against Australia, but failed to distinguish himself. He was tragically lost at sea when yachting.

First-class career (1937-59): 2,268 runs (37.18) including 7 centuries
Test matches (6): 219 runs (18.25) and 3 catches

ZULCH, John William (1886-1924)

Transvaal

An excellent right-handed opening batsman, with a wide range of strokes and sound defence, a very good field and useful change-bowler, 'Billy' Zulch, surprisingly, never came to England, his sole overseas tour being to Australia in 1910/11. At home he played against England in 1909/10 and 1913/14 and Australia in 1921/2. In Australia he scored 354 Test runs (39.33), including 105 in the third Test at Adelaide. In the fifth match at Sydney he made 150, which prevented a runaway Australian victory. Against England in 1913/14 he made 239 runs (39.83) in four Tests, sharing two century opening stands with Herbie Taylor. He scored an invaluable 80 in the first Test against Australia at Durban in 1921/2. In the next match, at Johannesburg, he was dismissed 'hit wicket' in an unusual manner – a splinter from his bat was sliced off by a ball from Ted McDonald and dislodged a bail. Consistently successful with Transvaal, in Currie Cup matches alone he averaged 59.33. He died young after a severe nervous breakdown.

First-class career (1908-24): 3,558 runs (41.85) including 9 centuries
Test matches (16): 985 runs (32.83) including 2 centuries, 0-28 and 4 catches

WEST INDIES

ACHONG, Ellis Edgar (b.1904)

Trinidad

Of Chinese extraction, 'Puss' Achong was a slow left-arm bowler of immaculate length. He toured England in 1933 and played at home against England in 1929/30 and 1934/5. Although working hard on the tour, he accomplished little in the Tests and was generally expensive, taking 71 wickets (36.14) in nearly 1,000 overs. He had a long experience of Lancashire League cricket in which he secured over 1,000 wickets. Possibly the expression 'Chinaman' for the left-arm bowler's 'wrong 'un' originated with 'Puss' in mind.

First-class career (1929-35): 503 runs (14.37) and 110 wickets (30.23)
Test matches (6): 81 runs (8.10), 8 wickets (47.25) and 6 catches

ALEXANDER, Franz Copeland Murray (b.1928)

Cambridge University and Jamaica

An aggressive right-handed batsman and sound, sometimes brilliant, wicket-keeper, 'Gerry' Alexander was a Cambridge blue in 1952 and 1953. His initial first-class match in the West Indies was for Jamaica versus the Duke of Norfolk's XI in March 1957. He toured England in 1957, India and Pakistan in 1958/9 (captain) and Australia in 1960/61, and at home played against Pakistan in 1957/8 (captain) and England in 1959/60 (captain). The first-choice wicket-keeper for several years, he was a popular and astute leader, especially against England in 1959/60 when he secured 23 victims, thus equalling the world record, though he lost the rubber. In Australia in 1960/61 he did not once fail to register at least one 50 in the Tests, his best score being 108 in the third match at Sydney, and he headed the batting with 484 runs (60.50), besides dismissing 16 (including 6 in the fourth match at Adelaide). In all first-class matches on this tour he made 734 runs (52.42). He was also a blue at Association Football and he won an England cap and an F.A. Amateur Cup Winner's medal.

First-class career (1952-61): 3,238 runs (29.17) including 1 century, and 256 dismissals (217 ct, 39 st.)
Test matches (25): 961 runs (30.03) including 1 century, and 90 dismissals (85 ct, 5 st.)

ALI, Imtiaz (b.1954)

Trinidad

A slim right-arm leg-spin and googly bowler with a fine action and a distinct loop in his flight, Imtiaz Ali looked an outstanding prospect in the Trinidad spin attack in the early 1970s but was tried in only one Test, the third against India at Port of Spain in 1975/6, when he scored 1 not out and took 2 for 89.

First-class career (1971-80): 558 runs (11.16) and 157 wickets (26.24)

ALI, Inshan (b.1949)

Trinidad

A small, left-hand back-of-the-hand spinner, Inshan Ali never quite turned out to be the matchwinner the West Indies selectors hoped he would be. He was a most unusual bowler, difficult to read, with a deceptive flight, but he lacked the control to trouble Test batsmen consistently. Cricket was never dull with Inshan for he seemed either to beat the bat or to be punished with a boundary for a full toss or long hop. Like all unorthodox spinners he seldom seemed to have much luck. He did, however, have one real Test triumph, figures of 5 for 59, against New Zealand in the first innings of the fifth Test at Port of Spain in 1971/2. He was certainly no failure on his two major tours, to England in 1973, when he took 38 wickets in eleven matches, and Australia in 1975/6, where he finished second in the tour averages with 22 wickets at 25.54. But on both tours he played only one Test.

First-class career (1965-80): 1,308 runs (13.62) and 324 wickets (29.06)
Test matches (12): 172 runs (10.75), 34 wickets (47.67) and 7 catches

ALLAN, David Walter (b.1937)

Barbados

Fair-haired and strong, David Allan came to England as a first-string wicket-keeper in 1963, but lost his place to Deryck Murray for all the Tests, despite a successful haul of 45 catches and 8 stumpings. On his second visit in 1966 he shared duties with Jackie Hendriks, playing in two Tests. He played once against Australia in 1964/5 when Hendriks was out through injury. In his first two Tests, against India at Bridgetown and Kingston in 1961/2, he had 10 victims and hit 40 not out in the first match. He could be a very useful batsman.

First-class career (1955-66): 764 runs (14.69) and 141 dismissals (117 ct, 24 st.)
Test matches (5): 75 runs (12.50) and 18 dismissals (15 ct, 3 st.)

ASGARALI, Nyron (b.1922)

Trinidad

A sound right-hand opening batsman though a late developer, Nyron Asgarali established himself by scoring 103, 128 and 83 in successive matches for Trinidad against British Guiana in 1951/2. Touring England in 1957, he disappointed in the Tests, but in all first-class matchcs madc 1,011 runs (29.73). Hc became a professional in the Lancashire League.

First-class career (1940-63): 2,761 runs (32.86) including 7 centuries, and 23 wickets (42.00)
Test matches (2): 62 runs (15.50)

ATKINSON, Denis St Eval (b.1926)

Barbados and Trinidad

A very sound right-handed batsman and medium-pace bowler of off-cutters and off-breaks, Denis Atkinson toured India in 1948/9, Australasia in 1951/2 and 1955/6 and England in 1957, and at home played against England in 1953, Australia in 1954/5 and Pakistan in 1957/8. He captained the West Indies in three Tests against Australia in 1954/5 in the absence of Jeff Stollmeyer through injury, losing two of them; and he led in the series against New Zealand in 1955/6, winning the rubber by three to one. His finest hour came in the fourth Test against Australia at Bridgetown in 1954/5. Facing a total of 668, West Indies collapsed and were 146 for 6 when Atkinson and C. Depeiaza came together and, in more than a day, added 348 for the seventh wicket, which remains a world record: Denis Atkinson contributed 219, his career-highest. He also took 7 for 164 in this match, which was drawn. In the series he headed the bowling with 13 wickets (35.30) and made 311 runs (44.42). In the fourth Test against New Zealand at Auckland in 1953/4 he took 7 for 53 (in 40 overs) in the second innings. On his sole tour of England in 1957 he began memorably taking 10 for 62 in the first match at Worcester with his off-cutters, but later he was overworked and a strained shoulder affected his performance. He achieved little in the Tests, but took 55 wickets (22.45) in all first-class matches and averaged 17.05 with the bat. Against England in the West Indies three years before, he had made 259 runs (43.16) in the Tests. He is the younger brother of Eric Atkinson.

First-class career (1946-60): 2,812 runs (28.40) including 5 centuries, and 200 wickets (26.73)
Test matches (22): 922 runs (31.79) including 1 century, 47 wickets (35.04) and 11 catches

ATKINSON, Eric St Eval (b.1925)

Barbados

A right-handed batsman and fast-medium bowler, Eric Atkinson toured India and Pakistan in 1958/9, and at home played against Pakistan in 1957/8. In the third Test against Pakistan at Kingston (dominated by batsmen, including the innings of 365 not out by Gary Sobers) he took 8 for 78 in the match. In the two Tests in Pakistan he took 9 wickets (13.22).

First-class career (1949-59): 696 runs (21.75) and 61 wickets (26.72)
Test matches (8): 126 runs (15.75), 25 wickets (23.56) and 2 catches

AUSTIN, Richard Arkwright (b.1954)

Jamaica

A sound and stylish right-handed batsman and adaptable bowler who can turn from medium pace to off-spin, Richard Austin had just found a place in the West Indies side when he signed for Kerry Packer in controversial circumstances. He was then omitted from the West Indies Test side for the third Test against Australia at Georgetown in 1977/8, causing other Packer players to withdraw from the side on the eve of the match. He was the outstanding batsman in the Shell Shield that season, starting the season as Jamaica's opening batsman with scores of 74, 127, 88 and 56, and finishing with an average of 61.50. He also took 18 Shield wickets, including 4 for 45 and 8 for 71 against Trinidad.

First-class career (1974-): 1,963 runs (33.84) including 4 centuries, and 73 wickets (30.72)
Test matches (2): 22 runs (11.00), 0-5 and 2 catches

BACCHUS, Sheik Faoud Ahumul (b.1954)

Guyana

After showing exceptional promise from an early age in cricket in Guyana, Faoud Bacchus was capped against Australia in 1977/8 after the World Series

Cricketers had withdrawn. In the last two Tests of this series his achievements were modest but as a right-handed opening or middle-order batsman and superb cover fielder he was outstanding on the tour of India in 1978/9, finishing second in the Test averages with 472 runs (47.20). On a batsman's paradise at Kanpur he hit 250 in 512 minutes, the highest score ever made in a Test on this ground. Even then he contributed to his own downfall, slipping and hitting his stumps as he attempted a sweep. He toured England in 1979 with the victorious West Indies Prudential World Cup squad, and during 1981/2 toured England, Pakistan and Australia without establishing a regular place in a powerful team. He captained the West Indies Under 26 team to Zimbabwe in 1981.

First-class career (1971-): 4,345 runs (36.20) including 6 centuries
Test matches (19): 782 runs (26.06) including 1 century, 0-3 and 17 catches

BAICHAN, Leonard (b.1946)

Guyana

A cautious left-handed opening batsman possessing unwavering concentration, Len Baichan toured India and Pakistan in 1974/5 and Australia in 1975/6. On his first tour he made 711 runs (50.78), scoring two centuries in his first two innings in India, but, unfortunately, he was injured in a car accident and missed several matches, including the Tests. Back in time for the first Test against Pakistan at Lahore – his debut in Test cricket – he made a very confident 105 not out. His tour of Australia was an anti-climax.

First-class career (1968-): 4,216 runs (49.60) including 11 centuries
Test matches (3): 184 runs (46.00) including 1 century, and 2 catches

BARRETT, Arthur George (b.1944)

Jamaica

A good and accurate if relatively straightforward right-arm leg-break bowler, Arthur Barrett toured India and Pakistan in 1974/5 and at home played against India in 1970/71 and England in 1973/4, but, in an age of fast bowling dominance, his leg-spinning talents were rarely reflected in his figures.

First-class career (1966-81): 1,086 runs (17.51) including 1 century, and 169 wickets (31.21)
Test matches (6): 40 runs (6.66) and 13 wickets (46.38)

BARROW, Ivan (1911-79)

Jamaica

A neat, sound and unobtrusive wicket-keeper and steady right-handed opening batsman, Ivan Barrow did not have a wealth of strokes but watched the ball closely and could drive powerfully when necessary. He toured Australia in 1930/31 and England in 1933 and 1939 and played at home against England in 1929/30 and 1934/5. He made 54 dismissals and scored 1,046 runs (23.77) on his first visit to England but on his second, after he had lived for several years in the United States, he averaged only 13.21. His third wicket partnership of 248 for Jamaica with George Headley against Lord Tennyson's side in 1932 at Kingston remains a Jamaican first-class record. Barrow scored 169 – his highest innings. In the second Test at Old Trafford in 1933 he scored 105, showing a greater range of stroke-play than usual, and putting on 200 for the second wicket with George Headley.

First-class career (1928-46): 2,551 runs (23.84) including 3 centuries, and 100 dismissals (73 ct, 27 st.)
Test matches (11): 276 runs (16.23) including 1 century, and 22 dismissals (17 ct, 5 st.)

BARTLETT, Edward Lawson (1906-76)

Barbados

A slightly built right-handed batsman, quick-footed, a hard-hitter in front of the wicket and a neat cutter, 'Barto' Bartlett toured England in 1928 and Australia in 1930/31. His best effort in Tests was 84 against Australia in the first match at Adelaide. He added 216 for the eighth wicket with C.R. Browne when Barbados registered 715 for 9 against British Guiana at Bridgetown in 1926/7.

First-class career (1923-39): 1,581 runs (23.25) including 1 century
Test matches (5): 131 runs (18.71) and 2 catches

BETANCOURT, Nelson (1887-1947)

Trinidad

A wicket-keeper and useful right-handed batsman, Nelson Betancourt did not keep wicket in his sole Test, against England at Port of Spain in 1929/30. But he batted soundly in a losing cause, scoring 39 and 13. He captained West Indies for this match because of a policy of there being a different captain for each match in the series.

First-class career (1905-30): 444 runs (17.07)

BINNS, Alfred Phillip (b.1929)

Jamaica

A competent right-handed batsman and wicket-keeper, Alfred Binns toured New Zealand in 1955/6, and played at home against India in 1952/3 and Australia in 1954/5, but rarely produced his best form in Tests.

First-class career (1949-57): 1,446 runs (37.07) including 4 centuries and 65 dismissals (47 ct, 18 st.)
Test matches (5): 64 runs (9.14) and 17 dismissals (14 ct, 3 st.)

BIRKETT, Lionel Sydney (b.1905)

Barbados, British Guiana and Trinidad

An attractive right-handed batsman and a useful medium-pace change-bowler, Lionel Birkett first attracted wide attention by his splendid 253 for Trinidad against British Guiana at Georgetown in 1929/30. He was vice-captain of the first team to Australia in 1930/31 and on his debut in the first Test at Adelaide scored 64, but did little in the others.

First-class career (1924-45): 1,295 runs (33.20) including 3 centuries
Test matches (4): 136 runs (17.00), 1-71 and 4 catches

BOYCE, Keith David (b.1943)

Barbados and Essex

Truly a dynamic cricketer, right-handed as a batsman and bowler, Keith Boyce was an exciting all-rounder who played much of his best cricket for Essex but who also proved himself at Test level as a hostile fast bowler, volatile hitter of the ball and a superb all-purpose field. Strongly built, with a lithe athletic approach, he put everything into his fast bowling, and his muscular hitting from a high backlift was truly spectacular. He adored hitting sixes and was a master in limited-over cricket, the first man in England to reach 1,000 runs and 100 wickets in this class of game. After playing with Trevor Bailey for the International Cavaliers, he joined Essex and from 1966 until 1977 was always a potential matchwinner for them. His highest score was 147 not out against Hampshire at Ilford in 1969. He reached a century in fifty-eight minutes and had a match double of 113 and 12 for 73 against Leicestershire at Chelmsford in 1975. His 8 for 26 against Lancashire at Old Trafford in 1971 is the record for the John Player League. He toured England with West Indian teams in 1973 and 1975, India and Pakistan in 1974/5, Australia in 1975/6, and at home played against India in 1970/71, Australia in 1972/3 and England in 1973/4. In the Prudential World Cup Final in 1975 he was a major factor in the West Indies defeat of Australia at Lord's. He had shattered England in 1973, taking 19 wickets (15.47) in the three Tests. His highest Test score was 95 not out in the fifth match at Adelaide in 1975/6, a brilliant innings.

First-class career (1964-77): 8,800 runs (22.39) including 4 centuries, 852 wickets (25.02) and 215 catches
Test matches (21): 657 runs (24.33), 60 wickets (30.01) and 5 catches

BROWNE, Cyril Rutherford (1890-1964)

Barbados and British Guiana

'Snuffy' Browne was a right-handed hard-hitting batsman and medium-pace leg-break bowler of quality. He toured England in 1923 and 1928 and played at home in the 1929/30 series, playing in the earliest West Indies Tests in both England and the Caribbean. he took 75 wickets (22.29) in 1923, and five years later, though past his best, took 8 for 81 at Derby, and against Kent at Canterbury had – literally – an hour of glory in which he hit a matchwinning 103. Despite a severe blow on the head from a rising ball, he hit 102 not out for the West Indies against MCC at Georgetown in 1925/6, in pre-Test days. In 1937/8 he took 7 for 13, Barbados collapsing for 99. A magistrate, 'Snuffy' Browne was the first black West Indian to be elected to honorary life membership of MCC.

First-class career (1908-39): 2,077 runs (19.97) including 3 centuries and 278 wickets (22.40)
Test matches (4): 176 runs (25.14), 6 wickets (48.00) and 1 catch

BUTCHER, Basil Fitzherbert (b.1933)

Guyana

A supple, wristy and resolute right-handed batsman and an occasional leg-break bowler, Basil Butcher became a consistently reliable performer at four or five in the West Indies order. In his first Test against India at Bombay in 1958/9, he made 28 and 64 not out and in the whole series he made 486 runs (69.42), including 103 in the third match at Calcutta and 142 in the fourth at Madras. Thereupon, he had a chequered career in representative cricket until the 1963 England tour when his 1,294 runs (44.62), including 383 in eight completed Test innings, one of which was 133 in a total of 229 in the memorable draw at Lord's, established him in the side. During an interval in the Lord's match he opened a letter which advised him that (against a background threat of civil war) his wife back home had had a miscarriage. Very upset, Butcher continued to play a solid and masterly innings which saved his side. Against Australia in 1964/5 he made 405 runs (40.50), including 117 at Port of Spain in the second Test; Richie Benaud considered he was the most difficult of all the West Indians to get out. This was confirmed in Australia in 1968/9 with an identical Test record, 405 runs (40.50), including 2 centuries, and in all first-class matches he made 1,505 runs (51.89). He remained at his best on two further tours of England in 1966 and 1969. In the former year he scored 1,105 runs (48.04), including 420 (60.00) in the Tests; his 209 not out at Trent Bridge in the third match was an heroic innings in seven and three-quarter hours, which won the match after West Indies had been 90 behind on the first innings. In the short tour in 1969 he headed the batting with 984 runs (61.50), including 3 centuries.

Basil Butcher

The only Test wickets he took were 5 for 34 (4 coming in 3 overs), when he finished off England's total for 414 at Port of Spain in 1967/8. He was a reliable outfielder with a remarkably powerful and accurate underarm throw. For many years he was a professional in the Lancashire League.

First-class career (1954-72): 11,628 runs (49.90) including 31 centuries, and 40 wickets (30.42)
Test matches (44): 3,104 runs (43.11) including 7 centuries, 5 wickets (18.00) and 15 catches

BUTLER, Lennox Stephen (b.1929)

Trinidad

A right-arm fast-medium bowler, 'Bunny' Butler took 5 for 93 for his island against Australia at Port of Spain in 1954/5, and his bowling was compared so favourably with that of Ray Lindwall that he played in the second Test on the same ground, when he took 2 for 151 in a run-feast, scored 16 and was not selected again.

First-class career (1948-56): 161 runs (14.63) and 29 wickets (33.34)

BYNOE, Michael Robin (b.1941)

Barbados

A stylish right-handed opening batsman and left-arm medium-pace change bowler, Robin Bynoe toured India and Pakistan in 1958/9, scoring 515 runs (34.33) and made his Test debut as an eighteen-year-old schoolboy against Pakistan. After being left in the background, he toured India again in 1966/7, but achieved little in the Tests and, because of a marked vulnerability against spin bowling, was not selected again.

First-class career (1957-72): 1,572 runs (41.05) including 6 centuries
Test matches (4): 111 runs (18.50), 1-5 and 4 catches

CAMACHO, George Stephen (b.1945)

Guyana

A very sound, bespectacled right-handed opening batsman, normally rather sober, steady and slow in uncharacteristic West Indian vein, Steve Camacho's first innings in the Shell Shield Tournament in 1965/6 was 106 against Trinidad at Port of Spain. Two years later he made 328 runs (32.80) against England in his first Test series, including 87 in the fourth match at Port of Spain. He toured England in 1969 as the opening partner to Roy Fredericks, heading the batting in the Tests with 187 runs (46.75). But in Australia in 1968/9 he did not quite come up to expectations. His last Tests were at home against India in 1970/71 when he made 68 runs in four innings.

First-class career (1964-79): 4,019 runs (34.86) including 7 centuries
Test matches (11): 640 runs (29.09), 0-12 and 4 catches

CAMERON, Francis James (b.1923)

Jamaica

A right-handed batsman and off-break bowler, who played much club cricket in England, Jimmy Cameron toured India and Pakistan in 1948/9, scoring 330 runs (25.38) and taking 18 very expensive wickets. His best performance was a punishing 75 not out in the second Test against India at Bombay.

First-class career (1946-60): 551 runs (25.04) and 29 wickets (48.65)
Test matches (5): 151 runs (25.16) and 3 wickets (92.66)

CAMERON, John Hensley (b.1914)

Cambridge University, Jamaica and Somerset

Something of a cricketing prodigy at Taunton School, John Cameron went on to be a Cambridge blue, playing in the University matches in 1935, 1936 and 1937 and putting Cambridge on the road to victory in his first year with 7 for 73 in the first innings. He also appeared with success for Somerset. A punishing right-handed batsman and reliable field, he bowled off-breaks and, in his earlier years, back of the hand spin as well. He was selected as vice-captain of the 1939 side to tour England but he had lost his googly by this time and he achieved little. He is F.J. Cameron's brother.

First-class career (1932-48): 2,772 runs (18.11) including 4 centuries, and 184 wickets (30.77)
Test matches (2): 6 runs (2.00) and 3 wickets (29.33)

CAREW, George McDonald (1910-74)

Barbados

A sound right-handed batsman, George Carew came to the fore in 1934/5 with impressively consistent scores of 46, 43 and 68 against MCC. His Test appearances were scattered: against England in 1934/5 and 1947/8 at home, and against India on tour in 1948/9. In the second Test at Port of Spain in 1947/8 he played the innings of his life. Wearing his chocolate-coloured felt hat and chewing gum rhythmically, he smashed into England's attack with some high-class batsmanship and hit 107, sharing in an opening stand of 173 with Andy Ganteaume.

First-class career (1934-49): 2,131 runs (34.37) including 3 centuries, and 13 wickets (46.15)
Test matches (4): 170 runs (28.33) including 1 century, 0-2 and 1 catch

CAREW, Michael Conrad (b.1937)

Trinidad

An attractive left-handed opening batsman, who struck the ball cleanly, notably through the covers off the back foot, 'Joey' Carew first impressed with 114 against Jamaica at Georgetown in 1958/9 and the following season hit 102 not out and 70 in two matches against MCC. He toured England in 1963, 1966 and 1969 and Australasia in 1968/9. At home he played against England in 1967/8 and India in 1970/71. He was not an overall success in English conditions, though in 1969 he made 677 runs in twelve matches, including 3 centuries, despite a damaged finger. By far his best season in representative cricket was 1968/9. In the fourth Test against Australia at Adelaide, he demonstrated to his colleagues the answer to John Gleeson's mysterious spin: hitting him straight, he made 90. In the fifth Test at Sydney he and Roy Fredericks put on 100 for the first wicket and at Auckland in the first Test against New Zealand he made a studious 109, adding 172 for the second wicket with Seymour Nurse. In the six Tests on the tour he made 643 runs (49.94) and in all first-class matches 1,222 runs (45.25). He was a useful right-arm leg-break bowler and later became a Test selector.

First-class career (1956-74): 7,810 runs (38.47) including 13 centuries, and 108 wickets (29.76)
Test matches (19): 1,127 runs (34.15) including 1 century, 8 wickets (54.62) and 13 catches

CHALLENOR, George (1888-1947)

Barbados

George Challenor was the originator of the great tradition of West Indian batsmanship. An opening batsman of medium height and powerful build, he was essentially an off-side player of perfect timing and a punisher of any loose balls with pulls or on-drives; he had everything – style, hitting power and strength of defence, all based on superb footwork. He toured England in 1906 (at eighteen), 1923 and 1928, the year Tests were first played between the two countries. On his second tour he made 1,556 runs (51.86), his 6 centuries including a matchwinning 155 against Surrey at The Oval. He was specially elected to membership of MCC in 1923. Past his best in 1928, he made 1,074 runs (27.53). In his early days Barbados was already a home of brilliant batting. Against the strong 1912/13 MCC team he scored 118 and 109. Seven years later in two successive club finals he made 261, 204 and 133; and as late as 1926/7, after C.A. Wiles (a Barbadian batting for Trinidad) had hit the highest-ever in Inter-Colonial cricket, Challenor responded with 220. A schoolteacher, he influenced the play of young Frank Worrell.

First-class career (1905-30): 5,822 runs (38.55) including 15 centuries, and 54 wickets (23.87)
Test matches (3): 101 runs (16.83)

CHANG, Herbert Samuel (b.1952)

Jamaica

A diminutive left-hander with considerable powers of concentration and plenty of strokes, Herbert Chang was rewarded for several years of consistent batting in the Shell Shield with a tour to India in 1978/9 but was disappointing in his sole Test, the fourth at Madras, scoring 6 and 2. Despite his size, he is a brave player of fast bowling, and after nine years in first-class cricket he was still looking one of Jamaica's best batsmen, in the 1981/2 Shell Shield scoring 426 runs in 10 innings (47.33).

First-class career (1972-): 3,187 runs (35.02) including 5 centuries, and 31 catches

CHRISTIANI, Cyril Marcel (1913-38)

British Guiana

Cyril Christiani toured England in 1933 as a very promising wicket-keeper/batsman. When MCC visited West Indies in 1934/5, he kept in all four Tests to a hostile and penetrating attack, and his 7 dismissals helped to win the series. He and one of his brothers, E.S. Christiani, put on 196 for the first wicket for British Guiana against East India C.C. in 1936/7, a British Guiana record. Little more than a year later, he died of malaria. He was the elder brother of R.J. Christiani.

First-class career (1931-8): 658 runs (16.45) and 63 dismissals (43 ct, 20 st.)
Test matches (4): 98 runs (19.60) and 7 dismissals (6 ct, 1 st.)

CHRISTIANI, Robert Julian (b.1920)

British Guiana

A bespectacled and attractive stroke-playing right-handed batsman, quick-footed and specially strong in front of the wicket, an occasional off-break bowler, a brilliant close field and a reserve wicket-keeper, Robert Christiani narrowly missed the 1939 England tour. On his Test debut, the first match against England at Bridgetown in 1947/8, he made 1 and 99 and the following season, in India, scored 107 in the first Test at Delhi. On this tour he made 785 runs (41.31). On his sole visit to England in 1950 he batted usually at number seven and made 1,094 runs (45.58), with 30 catches, mostly as 'keeper, and 3 stumpings. He toured Australasia in 1951/2, making 261 runs in the five Tests against Australia and at home played against India in 1952/3 and England in 1953/4.

First-class career (1938-54): 5,103 runs (40.50) including 12 centuries, 18 wickets (60.44), 97 catches and 12 stumpings
Test matches (22): 896 runs (26.35) including 1 century, 3 wickets (36.00), 19 catches and 2 stumpings

CLARKE, Dr Carlos Bertram (b.1918)

Barbados, Northamptonshire and Essex

Tall and lanky, 'Bertie' Clarke was a right-arm slow leg-break bowler with a high delivery and a pronounced 'loop' and a googly that nipped quickly off the pitch, a batsman who could hit very hard and a brilliant and versatile field. He was a surprise selection for the 1939 England tour but he proved to be one of the few successes with 87 wickets (21.81). After the War he appeared from 1946 until 1949 for Northamptonshire – taking 156 wickets – and for Essex in 1959 and 1960.

First-class career (1937-61): 1,292 runs (12.30) and 333 wickets (26.37)
Test matches (3): 3 runs (1.00) and 6 wickets (43.50)

CLARKE, Sylvester Theophilus (b.1954)

Barbados and Surrey

Tall and strapping, Sylvester Clarke is a right-arm fast bowler with a strange, inswinger's action in which the arm comes over rapidly and very high, despite the fact that the batsman sees the chest instead of the left shoulder in the delivery stride. Very fast and hostile when fit and firing, he played a prominent part in Surrey's first success in a county competition for several years, in the Benson and Hedges Cup, 1982. He first played for Barbados in 1978 and against Trinidad that season his six for 39 in an innings included a hat-trick. In his first Test, against Australia in 1977/8, he took 3 for 58 and 3 for 83, and only injury (to which he is prone) prevented him from playing further games in the series. In India in 1978/9 he headed the Test bowling averages with 21 wickets (33.85) and he made further tours of Pakistan (1980/81) and Australia (1981/2). He did well in Pakistan, taking 14 wickets (17.28) in four Tests and hitting an important 35 not out in 30 balls with three consecutive sixes at Faisalabad. But he seriously blotted his copybook when, furious at being pelted by oranges and other missiles when fielding on the boundary during the last Test in Multan, he picked up a brick being used as a boundary marker and hurled it at a spectator, who happened to be a student leader, and who was taken to hospital, seriously injured. Fortunately for Clarke he recovered and the bowler, normally a genial man, escaped with a short suspension by the West Indies Cricket Board. An unashamed hitter as a batsman, he made a rapid 100 not out for Surrey against Glamorgan in 1981. In the 1982 season he took 85 wickets (19.95).

First-class career (1977-) 1,537 runs (15.52) including 1 century, and 409 wickets (21.13)
Test matches (11): 172 runs (15.63), 42 wickets (27.88) and 2 catches

CONSTANTINE, Sir Learie Nicholas (Lord, Baron of Maraval and Nelson) (1902-71)

Trinidad and Barbados

A compelling, magnetic and inspiring cricketer of extraordinary zest and dynamism, Learie or 'Connie' Constantine was the son of Lebrun Constantine, a plantation foreman and son of a slave, who had toured England with the first two West Indian teams of 1900 (when he scored the first century by a West Indian in England) and 1906. Learie himself played with his father for Trinidad in 1922 and some months later toured England with the third West Indian team,

Learie Constantine sweeping to leg

where he impressed with some amazingly good fielding at cover-point. Coming here again in 1928, he established himself as a great and volatile all-rounder; he always became the centre of attraction and could change the course of a match by startling brilliance but in Test cricket he was inconsistent. Muscular, lithe, stocky but long-armed, and with distinctly beady eyes, he was a brilliant, if unpredictable and unorthodox, right-handed hitter with powerful drives, pulls and hits to leg. As a bowler he had a bounding run, a high smooth action and, in his prime, considerable pace, sometimes bowling bodyline. Later he used every variation of medium pace, with an occasional fast ball. As a fielder, his contemporaries believe that he was the best of all time; by anticipation, feline reflex and elastic movement, he brought off close catches no other fielders could have reached, and in the deep he picked up while going like a sprinter and threw with uncanny accuracy. He made 1,381 runs (34.52), took 107 wickets (22.95) and held 33 catches on the 1928 England tour. Only in the three Tests – 89 runs in six innings and 5 expensive wickets – did he fail. His essential quality was seen at Lord's against Middlesex. The West Indians were 122 behind on the first innings, although Learie had slammed 86 in half an hour, going in at 79 for 5. In the Middlesex second innings he took 7 for 57, thirty-nine balls bringing him 6 for 11. Set 259 to win, the touring team were 121 for 5 wickets when he hit 103 out of 133 in a hour, including 2 sixes and 12 fours and the West Indians won by 3 wickets. In the first series in the West Indies in 1929/30 he took 18 wickets (27.61) including 9 for 122 at Georgetown when West Indies beat England for the first time. In the first tour of Australia in 1930/31 he made 708 runs (30.78), took 47 wickets (20.23) and fielded brilliantly, but he again failed in the Tests. By now a professional with Nelson in the Lancashire League, Learie was permitted to appear in a handful of matches on the 1933 tour; in his only Test, at Old Trafford, he hit a confident 64 in the second innings and prevented an England victory. His highest score in Tests was 90 in the second match against England at Port of Spain in 1934/5, and his 3 for 11 (in 14.50 overs) in the second innings put the West Indies on the road to handsome victory. In the fourth match at Kingston he captured 6 for 68 and in the series took 15 wickets (13.13). Appearing regularly on the 1939 tour, making 614 runs (21.17) and heading the bowling with 103 wickets (17.77), he was scintillating in his last Test of all at The Oval, hitting 79 – the last 78 coming in fifty-seven minutes – and taking 5 for 75 in England's first innings. Prominent in welfare work among coloured people in England during the Second World War, he captained the Dominions team that defeated England at Lord's in 1945; he wrote books and broadcast; he studied doggedly and was called to the Bar by the Middle Temple; he returned to Trinidad and became an MP and the Minister of Works in the Trinidadian Government. Later he came back to England as High Commissioner for Trinidad and Tobago; he was awarded the MBE, knighted and created a Life Peer. Posthumously, Trinidad awarded him the Trinity Cross, the country's highest honour.

First-class career (1922-45): 4,451 runs (24.32) including 5 centuries, 424 wickets (20.61) and 133 catches
Test matches (18): 635 runs (19.24), 58 wickets (30.10) and 28 catches

CROFT, Colin Everton Hunte (b.1953)

Guyana and Lancashire

A tall, strong, hostile right-arm fast bowler with a chest-on, in-swing action, Colin Croft had a sensational start to his Test career, forming a devastating fast-bowling partnership with Joel Garner and Andy Roberts. Starting with 3 for 85 and 4 for 47 in his first Test against Pakistan at Bridgetown in 1976/7, he followed up with 8 for 29 in 18.5 overs in the first innings of the next Test at Port of Spain, the best analysis by a West Indian fast bowler in Test cricket. He took 33 wickets at 20.48 in the series, and began his second series the following season against Australia equally well until withdrawing with other players who had signed for Kerry Packer. In the first Test at Port of Spain he dismissed three Australians in his first eight overs for 9 runs on the first morning of the match, and finished with 4 for 15, Australia collapsing for 90.

Colin Croft

Later on the same tour he drew a strong protest from the Australian manager after bowling an excess of bouncers when playing for Guyana against the touring team, hitting one batsman on the head and fracturing the jaw of another. In England in 1978 and 1979 he played for Lancashire, with a total of 56 wickets in first-class games in 1978 at 22.60. He returned to the county in 1982. He was steadily successful in two years of World Series Cricket. He toured Australia and New Zealand in 1979/80, England in 1980, Pakistan in 1980/81 and Australia again in 1981/2. In all these tours he was one of the most feared members of a powerful four-man West Indies fast attack, his three main partners being Roberts, Holding and Garner. Against England at home in 1980/81 he was easily the most successful of the four, taking 24 wickets in four Tests (18.45). He disgraced himself, under provocation, in New Zealand in 1979/80, deliberately barging into an umpire as he ran in to bowl after a controversial decision had gone against him. A qualified airline pilot, he may settle in the United States. He left Lancashire after 1982 with a back injury which threatened his career, a fact that may have made him accept a big pay-off for touring South Africa in 1982/3.

First-class career (1971-): 853 runs (10.53) and 419 wickets (24.52)
Test matches (27): 158 runs (10.53), 125 wickets (23.30) and 8 catches

DA COSTA, Oscar C. (1907-36)

Jamaica

A very talented all-rounder, being a reliable right-handed batsman, useful medium-pace bowler and versatile field, Oscar da Costa appeared in the fourth Test against England in 1929/30 with some success. On the 1933 England tour he made 1,046 runs (26.82), including his maiden century, 105 against Essex at Leyton, and took 31 wickets (34.03), but did little in the Tests. He was, however, the comedian of the party: he had a rubber stamp made so that no autograph-hunter should be disappointed. He appeared in one Test against England in 1934/5.

First-class career (1928-35): 1,563 runs (29.49) including 1 century, and 44 wickets (40.13)
Test matches (5): 153 runs (19.12), 3 wickets (58.33) and 5 catches

DANIEL, Wayne Wendell (b.1956)

Barbados and Middlesex

The 'Black Diamond', as Wayne Daniel is known, came to England in 1976 as a raw young fast bowler and took 13 wickets in four Tests as part of a formidable quartet of fast bowlers who gave their opponents no respite. On this tour Wayne Daniel took 52 wickets (21.26) and Middlesex eagerly signed him on to their staff. A massively built, good looking man, friendly off the field but hostile (though fair and sensible) on it, Daniel has a fine, muscular action after a long and heavy-footed approach. Relatively predictable, he is very fast indeed, generally bowling straight and keeping the ball well up to the bat but testing the courage and technique of the finest players. In 1977 he was a key figure in Middlesex's retaining a share of the County Championship title, taking 75 wickets at 16.44. A year later his figures were still better, 76 at 14.65 and he twice took 7 cheap wickets in the Benson and Hedges Cup. In World Series Cricket in Australia, however, he was not consistently successful and, after a poor season in the Shell Shield in 1979, he was surprisingly omitted from the West Indies squad which won the Prudential World Cup in England in 1979 and, against formidable competition, could not regain his Test place.

First-class career (1975-): 945 runs (12.60) and 522 wickets (20.25)
Test matches (5): 29 runs (9.66), 15 wickets (25.40) and 2 catches

DAVIS, Bryan Alan (b.1940)

Trinidad and Glamorgan

A sound right-handed batsman, who often opened the batting, an occasional leg-break bowler and excellent close-in field, Bryan Davis carried his bat through the innings when he scored 188 for North against South of Trinidad at Port of Spain in 1966/7. In this same season he toured India without playing in any of the Tests. When Australia toured in 1964/5, however, he appeared in four Tests, hitting 54 and 58 in the second Test at Port of Spain and on his debut putting on 116 and 91 for the first wicket with Conrad Hunte. In two full seasons for Glamorgan in 1969 and 1970 he made well over 1,000 runs each time. He is the elder brother of Charlie Davis.

First-class career (1959-71): 6,231 runs (34.81) including 5 centuries
Test matches (4): 245 runs (30.62) and 1 catch

DAVIS, Charles Alan (b.1944)

Trinidad

A sound but slow right-handed batsman and useful medium-pace bowler, Charlie Davis was a schoolboy when he scored 115 in the Beaumont Cup match for North Trinidad in 1960/61. After prolific scoring for Trinidad against Guyana and the 1964/5 Australians, followed by a half-century for Trinidad and 158 not out for The President's XI against MCC in 1967/8, he was selected for the Test team at last to tour Australasia in 1968/9, only to fail with the bat. Although a change-bowler at home, he did nevertheless head the overall bowling averages with 24 wickets

(32.58), including 7 for 106 against South Australia at Adelaide, his career-best. In England in 1969 he proved himself with the bat, making 103 in the second Test at Lord's in a stay of six and a quarter hours, the only West Indian century of the series. Altogether, he made 848 runs (42.40). Although India won the rubber in the West Indies in 1970/71, Davis headed the batting with 529 runs (132.25) in four Tests, being almost unbowlable. He reached at least 50 in five innings out of seven, including 125 not out in the third match at Georgetown and 105 in the fifth at Port of Spain. When the New Zealanders toured in 1971/2, he made 466 runs (58.25) in the series, including 183 in the third match at Bridgetown, his career-highest, when he added 254 with Gary Sobers for the sixth wicket. He played his last Test in 1972/3.

First-class career (1960-76): 5,538 runs (41.32) including 14 centuries, and 63 wickets (39.36)
Test matches (15): 1,301 runs (54.20) including 4 centuries, 2 wickets (165.00) and 4 catches

DE CAIRES, Francis Ignatius (b.1909)

British Guiana

A sound right-handed batsman, Frank de Caires was masterly with 80 and 70 in the first-ever Test in the West Indies, against England at Georgetown in 1929/30. He toured Australia in 1930/31, but was not selected for the Tests.

First-class career (1928-39): 945 runs (28.63) including 1 century
Test matches (3): 232 runs (38.66), 0-9 and 1 catch

DEPEIAZA, Cyril Clairmonte (b.1927)

Barbados

Played mainly as a wicket-keeper in the West Indies, Clairmonte Depeiaza is remembered primarily for his historic seventh-wicket stand of 348 with his captain, Denis Atkinson, in the fourth Test against Australia at Bridgetown in 1954/5; it remains the world record and was made when West Indies, in facing a total of 668, were 146 for 6 wickets. The two batsmen were defiant for more than a day, and Depeiaza's contribution was 122. He appeared in a handful of Tests against Australia and New Zealand in the mid-fifties.

First-class career (1951-7): 623 runs (32.78) including 1 century, and 40 dismissals (31 ct, 9 st.)
Test matches (5): 187 runs (31.16) including 1 century, 0-15 and 11 dismissals (7 ct, 4 st.)

DEWDNEY, David Thomas (b.1933)

Jamaica

A tall, well-developed right-arm fast bowler, Tom Dewdney maintained a good control of length and possessed great stamina. His Test debut against Australia in 1954/5 was only his third first-class match, and in a total of 668 he returned impressive figures of 33-7-125-4. He toured New Zealand in 1955/6 and, generally used sparingly, took 5 for 21 in the fourth Test at Auckland in 19.5 overs. He was disappointing on the 1957 England tour and when Pakistan visited the West Indies in 1958/9 he met with little success. He was injured in a car accident (also involving Gary Sobers) in England in September 1959, in which 'Collie' Smith was killed.

First-class career (1954-61): 171 runs (5.70) and 92 wickets (30.73)
Test matches (9): 17 runs (2.42) and 21 wickets (38.42)

DOWE, Uton George (b.1949)

Jamaica

A solidly built right-arm fast-medium bowler, with a fierce appearance and long run, Uton Dowe played at home against India in 1970/71, New Zealand in 1971/2, and Australia in 1972/3, without establishing himself in the Test team. So wild was he when bowling against Australia that the Jamaican crowd was driven to inventing an eleventh commandment: 'Dowe shalt not bowl'.

First-class career (1969-77): 128 runs (7.11) and 97 wickets (27.86)
Test matches (4): 8 runs (8.00), 12 wickets (44.50) and 3 catches

DUJON, Peter Jeffrey (b.1956)

Jamaica

A natural cricketer, a right-handed batsman and wicket-keeper, Jeffrey Dujon is a product of Collyer's School in Kingston. He made an impressive start to his international career on tours to Zimbabwe and Australia in 1981/2. In Australia he scored 227 runs in three Tests (45.40), though his highest score was only 51. He scored 104 not out against New South Wales at Sydney and in the one-day internationals kept wicket competently as well as playing some spectacular innings. An aggressive player who times the ball well, he likes to drive and hook. Having done well since his debut for Jamaica in 1975, his recognition by the national selectors was surprisingly delayed. His temperament for the big occasions was emphasized in 1980/81 when he hit 105 not out for the President's XI at Pointe-à-Pierre in the opening game of the England tour.

First-class career (1975-): 2,225 runs (38.36) including 5 centuries, and 61 dismissals (55 ct, 6 st.)
Test matches (3): 227 runs (45.40) and 9 catches

EDWARDS, Richard Martin (b.1940)

Barbados

A lively right-arm fast-medium bowler, 'Prof' Edwards toured Australasia in 1968/9 but lacked penetration on the Australian leg of the tour, taking only 14 wickets (57.71). In New Zealand, however, he captured 6 for 129 in the first Test at Auckland and 7 for 126 in the second at Wellington, taking most wickets, 15 (23.48).

First-class career (1961-70): 389 runs (11.78) and 78 wickets (36.29)
Test matches (5): 65 runs (9.28) and 18 wickets (34.77)

FERGUSON, Wilfred (1917-61)

Trinidad

A short, burly man who caused much merriment among spectators when, occasionally, he removed his cap and revealed a bald head, Wilf Ferguson was a purveyor of slow, right-arm well-pitched leg-breaks and a hard-hitting late-order batsman. The pivot of the attack against England in 1947/8, he took 23 wickets (24.65), in the second Test at Port of Spain securing 11 for 229 in 73.2 overs, when, on an easy-paced matting wicket, he tossed his deliveries skilfully into the wind. In the fourth match at Kingston he hit a spectacular 75 in one and three-quarter hours. He toured India in 1948/9 and played once against England at home in 1953/4 without distinction.

First-class career (1942-56): 1,225 runs (23.55) and 165 wickets (31.55)
Test matches (8): 200 runs (28.58), 34 wickets (34.26) and 11 catches

FERNANDES, Marius Pachaco (1898-1981)

British Guiana

A right-handed batsman of class, with a strong defence and strokes all round the wicket, and a safe catcher, 'Maurice' Fernandes was a lynchpin of the 1923 side to England, despite an attack of malaria contracted in Ireland, scoring 523 runs (34.86). Back again in 1928, in a longer tour he made only 581 runs (18.15), but played in the first Test between the two countries, at Lord's. He led West Indies in the third Test against England at Georgetown in 1929/30, the first West Indian Test victory. For British Guiana he scored centuries against Barbados and Trinidad.

First-class career (1922-32): 2,087 runs (28.20) including 4 centuries
Test matches (2): 49 runs (12.25)

FINDLAY, Thaddeus Michael (b.1943)

Windward Islands

A genial and intelligent man from St Vincent, competent both as a wicket-keeper and right-handed batsman, Mike Findlay made his debut in first-class cricket against Australia in 1964/5, and toured Australasia in 1968/9 as reserve wicket-keeper. He toured England in 1969, superseding Jackie Hendriks as first-string wicket-keeper during the series, but when India toured in 1970/71 he was replaced by Deryck Murray after the first Test against Australia in 1972/3 and did not represent his country again.

First-class career (1964-78): 2,927 runs (20.18) and 252 dismissals (209 ct, 43 st.)
Test matches (10): 212 runs (16.30) and 21 dismissals (19 ct, 2 st.)

FOSTER, Maurice Linton Churchill (b.1943)

Jamaica

A cheerful character, Maurice Foster is a determined right-handed batsman, who often opens, and a flat but accurate off-break bowler. He has been captain of Jamaica for several years. He made his debut in three matches against International Cavaliers in 1963/4, scoring 136 not out in the second game. He toured England in 1969 and 1973 and at home played against India in 1970/71, New Zealand in 1971/2, Australia in 1972/3 and 1977/8, England in 1973/4 and Pakistan in 1976/7. Not so brilliant or flamboyant a player as many of his contemporary batsmen, Foster in Tests often provided the solid ballast in the middle order. Against Australia he scored 125 in the first Test at Kingston in 1972/3 when he made 210 for the fifth wicket in even time with Rohan Kanhai, and scored 262 runs (43.66) in the series.

First-class career (1963-78): 6,731 runs (45.17) including 17 centuries, and 132 wickets (30.72)
Test matches (14): 580 runs (30.52) including 1 century, 9 wickets (66.66) and 3 catches

FRANCIS, George Nathaniel (1897-1942)

Barbados

On the 1923 England tour George Francis established himself with George John as a first in the long line of outstanding fast-bowling partnerships from the West Indies. A professional cricketer, he was a right-hander who, avoiding any theory, unemotionally and undemonstratively bowled fast at the stumps. He fielded with characteristic West Indian zest. He was far and away the best bowler on the 1923 tour, collecting 96 wickets (15.32) and he put the touring team on the road to a brilliant victory against Surrey at The Oval, taking 10 for 76 in the match. When Test status was attained in 1928, he was a little past his best, taking 60 wickets (31.33), including only 6 in the Tests. Able to play only once in the first Caribbean Test series in 1929/30, he took 4 for 40 in 21 overs in England's first innings of 145 in the third match at Georgetown, which witnessed West Indies' first-ever victory. Touring Australia in 1930/31, he captured 11 wickets (31.81) in the first series there and, while engaged as a professional by Radcliffe in the Bolton League, he appeared in the first Test at Lord's in 1933 but was not a success. A truer reflection of his ability was his performance for Barbados against MCC in 1925/6 when he took 9 for 56 in an innings victory.

First-class career (1922-33): 874 runs (12.85) and 223 wickets (23.11)
Test matches (10): 81 runs (5.78), 23 wickets (33.17) and 7 catches

FREDERICK, Michael Campbell (b.1927)

Barbados, Jamaica and Derbyshire

A sound opening batsman, Michael Frederick made a sole Test appearance in the first Test against England at Kingston in 1953/4, scoring 0 and 30. He made two appearances as an amateur for Derbyshire in 1949.

First-class career (1944-54): 294 runs (29.40)

FREDERICKS, Roy Clinton (b.1942)

Guyana and Glamorgan

Roy Fredericks was a small but very tough left-handed opening batsman of high class who hit the ball exceptionally hard, an occasional slow left-arm bowler and a brilliant close fielder, especially on the leg-side. Both dashing and dependable he hit 26 fifties and 8 centuries in his fifty-nine Tests between 1968 and 1977. He played for Glamorgan between 1971 and 1973, scoring 1,377 runs (45.90) in his first season of county cricket and in his second sharing in a record opening stand of 330 with Alan Jones against Northants at Swansea when Fredericks scored 228 not out. He tended, indeed, to run into inspired bursts of form as when he hit two hundreds in a match against MCC for Guyana in 1973/4, a feat he had already achieved against Barbados in 1966/7. He toured Australasia in 1968/9 and 1975/6, England in 1969, 1973, 1975 (for the Prudential Cup) and 1976, and India, Pakistan and Sri Lanka in 1974/5. From his first tour of Australia and New Zealand in 1968/9 when he made 1,131 runs, he never had a bad tour or an unsuccessful series, although he had to wait until February 1972 and the first Test at Kingston to record his maiden Test century, 163 against New Zealand. A score of 150 against England at Edgbaston in 1973 was followed by two hundreds against India, at Calcutta and Bombay, and then in 1975/6 came one of the great innings of Test history. On the fast pitch at Perth the West Indies, already a Test down in the series, batted

Roy Fredericks; Gordon Greenidge is the non-striker

second against the all-conquering combination of Lillee and Thomson supplemented by Walker, Gilmour, Mallett and Ian Chappell. Fredericks reached his hundred in four minutes under two hours, off only 71 balls, with a six and 18 fours, and when he was out he had scored 169 out of 258. In such moods there was no stopping this pocket Hercules, who played every shot from the late cut to the leg-glance with immense gusto. He became Minister for Sport.

First-class career (1963-80): 16,064 runs (45.25) including 38 centuries, 75 wickets (37.94) and 176 catches
Test matches (59): 4,334 runs (42.49) including 8 centuries, 7 wickets (78.28) and 62 catches

FULLER, Richard L. (b.1913)

Jamaica

A useful right-handed batsman and fast-medium bowler, Dickie Fuller's sole Test was the fourth match against England at Kingston in 1934/5 when he scored 1 and took 0 for 12. For Jamaica against MCC, also at Kingston, he had struck hard for 113 not out, hitting Jim Smith for 4 fours in succession.

First-class career (1934-47): 280 runs (28.00) including 1 century, and 12 wickets (43.66)

FURLONGE, Hammond Alan (b.1934)

Trinidad

A right-handed opening batsman, given the forename

'Hammond' by keen cricket parents, Furlonge staved off defeat for Trinidad at the hands of Australia at Port of Spain in 1954/5 by scoring 57 and 150 not out, his maiden first-class century. He played Test cricket against Australia that season and the following, when he toured New Zealand with West Indies. He made a painstaking 64 (in a total of 145) in the fourth Test at Auckland, but won no more Test caps.

First-class career (1954-62): 808 runs (32.32) including 2 centuries
Test matches (3): 99 runs (19.80)

GANTEAUME, Andrew George (b.1921)

Trinidad

A diminutive, consistent right-handed opening batsman and deputy wicket-keeper, Andy Ganteaume marked his Test debut against England at Port of Spain in the second match in 1947/8 with a dogged 112. Not only was he discarded for the rest of the series, but he was never selected for another Test, such was the power of West Indian batting at the time. However, he toured England in 1957 without playing in a Test.

First-class career (1940-63): 2,785 runs (34.81) including 5 centuries

GARNER, Joel (b.1952)

Barbados, Somerset and South Australia

At 6ft 8ins one of the tallest Test cricketers of all time, Joel 'Big Bird' Garner is not just a *fast* bowler but a very accomplished one with a good action off a relatively short run and remarkable control for one whose stature might easily make him ungainly. Strongly built as well as very tall, high bounce comes naturally and he also swings and cuts the ball to present batsmen with very exceptional problems. He first appeared for the West Indies at home against Pakistan in 1976/7, taking 25 wickets at 27.52, including 8 for 148 in the match in the third Test at Georgetown. In the first two Tests against Australia in 1977/8 he took 13 wickets, including 8 for 103 at Bridgetown, but missed the remainder of the series following the split which resulted from Packer players' being unavailable for the official West Indies tour the following winter. In Australia Garner was consistently successful in World Series Cricket and in England in 1979 he ensured that West Indies retained the Prudential World Cup by taking 5 for 38 in the final at Lord's against England, 4 of them bowled. In England, after representing Somerset part-time in 1977 and 1978, he joined the county full-time in 1979. His devastating yorker ('the only consolation,' wrote Scyld Berry, 'of being bowled by Garner is that you haven't been hit on the boot') was frequently a

Joel Garner

matchwinner for his county on the big occasion. Between 1979 and 1982 he was always one of the first men chosen in the West Indies team, bowling with success in Australia (twice), New Zealand, England and Pakistan. A sunny character, popular wherever he plays, he is also a big-hitting late-order batsman who scored 104 against Gloucestershire for the 1980 West Indies touring team and made an impressive 60 against Australia in the Brisbane Test of 1979/80.

First-class career (1975-): 1,605 runs (17.44) and 490 wickets (17.32)
Test matches (28): 400 runs (11.76), 124 wickets (20.64) and 22 catches

GASKIN, Berkeley Bertram McGarrell (1908-79)

British Guiana

A steady right-arm medium-pace bowler, Berkeley Gaskin – in his fortieth year – played in two Tests against England in 1947/8, opening the attack.

First-class career (1928-54): 782 runs (14.21) and 138 wickets (31.89)
Test matches (2): 17 runs (5.66), 2 wickets (79.00) and 1 catch

GIBBS, Glendon Lionel (1925-79)

British Guiana

A consistent left-handed opening batsman and occasional slow left-arm bowler, Glendon Gibbs made 216 for British Guiana against Barbados at Georgetown in 1951/2, putting on 390 with Leslie Wright for the first wicket, still an overall West Indian first-class record. He appeared in his sole Test, the first match at Kingston against Australia, in 1954/5, scoring 12 and 0, taking 0 for 7 and holding 1 catch.

First-class career (1949-63): 1,730 runs (38.91) including 5 centuries, and 23 wickets (53.47)

GIBBS, Lancelot Richard (b.1934)

Guyana, South Australia and Warwickshire

For some years the highest wicket-taker in Test history, Lance Gibbs was a lithe, lean right-arm off-spinner with long fingers which gave him exceptional spin and bounce. With an unorthodox chest-on action and with the left arm down by his side as the right arm came over good and high, he exploited every conceivable change of pace, flight and length and eventually developed the essentially English off-spinner's art of being able to bowl the ball which drifts away from the right-handed batsman. His stamina and courage were virtually unlimited, despite such handicaps as a painfully sore spinning finger and a nagging groin injury, and he was a very loyal team-man. He was a negligible batsman but a fine fielder in the gully. Only Gary Sobers has appeared in more Tests for the West Indies. Lance Gibbs toured India in 1958/9, 1966/7 and 1974/5, Australia in 1960/61, 1968/9 and 1975/6, Pakistan in 1958/9 and 1974/5, England in 1963, 1966, 1969 and 1973, and New Zealand in 1968/9; and at home he played against Pakistan in 1958/9, India in 1962/3 and 1970/71, Australia in 1965/6 and 1972/3, New Zealand in 1971/2, and England in 1967/8 and 1973/4. He played his cricket with a quiet, dignified air, only rarely showing much emotion. In his first Test series, against Pakistan in 1957/8, he headed the bowling averages with 17 wickets (23.05) from four Tests. He was top again in Australia in 1960/61 with 19 wickets (20.78) from three Tests, including 3 wickets in four balls in the second innings at Sydney. In the next Test at Adelaide he performed the hat-trick. In 1961/2 he captured 24 wickets against the visiting Indians, in the third Test at Barbados assuring his country of the rubber by taking 8 for 38 in the second inings; he took these 8 wickets for 6 runs in a spell of only 15.3 overs, 14 of these being maidens. This was to remain his best Test performance. In England in 1963 he secured 26 wickets (21.30) in the Tests – 78 wickets (20.05) in all first-class matches – and in 1966, 21 Test wickets (24.76). Despite the plethora of fast bowling, he more than held his own in later years, always liable to bowl a side out in the later stages of the match. In Tests he took 5 or more wickets in an innings on eighteen occasions and twice 10 or more wickets in a match. Though generally of little account as a batsman, he and Gerry Alexander added 74 for the eighth wicket against Australia at Sydney in 1960/61, a West Indian record against Australia. In England, after experience in the Lancashire and Durham Leagues, he qualified for Warwickshire in 1968, remaining with the county until 1973, enjoying his best season in 1971, with 131 wickets (18.89). He was a popular club-man, his expertise at forecasting horse-racing results being almost on a par with his knowledge of cricket strategy. He is a cousin of Clive Lloyd.

Lance Gibbs

First-class career (1953-76): 1,729 runs (8.55), 1,024 wickets (27.22) and 203 catches

Test matches (79): 488 runs (6.97), 309 wickets (29.09) and 52 catches

GILCHRIST, Roy (b.1934)

Jamaica and Hyderabad

Stockily built, 'Gilly' Gilchrist was a mean and hostile fast right-arm bowler with a smooth effortless action, considered to be the most able fast bowler since 'Manny' Martindale. He briefly formed a formidable partnership with Wes Hall. Gilchrist toured England in 1957 and India in 1958/9, and at home played against Pakistan in 1957/8. In England, despite his venomous bouncer, he was not particularly successful, but he unsettled Pakistan, taking 21 wickets (30.28) in the five Tests. In India he collected 71 wickets (13.57) from all first-class matches. In four Tests he took 26 wickets (16.11), including 9 for 73 in the third match at Calcutta. He was sent home in disgrace from this tour for bowling fast 'beamers' (full tosses around the batsman's head) and other misdemeanours. He seemed to attract conflict and abuse, even in the Lancashire League, where he took hundreds of wickets and numerous hat-tricks. He played no more Test cricket after 1959.

First-class career (1956-63): 255 runs (7.72) and 167 wickets (26.00)
Test matches (13): 60 runs (5.45), 57 wickets (26.68) and 4 catches

GLADSTONE, George (1901-78)

Jamaica

A useful left-arm slow bowler and moderate batsman, Gladstone's 'bag' for Jamaica Colts Fifteen against MCC at Kingston in 1929/30 was 4 good wickets. A few days later, for Jamaica, he took 9 for 252 in 75.3 overs, also against MCC. Thereupon, he made his sole Test appearance at Kingston (a nine-day affair), scoring 12 not out and taking 1 for 189. His birth certificate states his name as George Gladstone Morais.

First-class career (1929-30): 26 runs (—) and 10 wickets (44.10)

GODDARD, John Douglas Claude (b.1919)

Barbados

A considerable figure for many years in Barbados and West Indies cricket, John Goddard was a vigilant and determined left-handed batsman, usually batting at number eight in strong Test sides and a useful right-arm medium-pace in-swinging or off-break bowler. Also an excellent fielder notably at silly mid-off, he was captain in twenty-two of his twenty-seven Tests. A formidable but popular leader, he was capable of pressing home every advantage his men had gained, and he will be remembered particularly for his captaincy of the 1950 side to England when West Indian cricket 'came of age' and won a rubber in England for the first time. In India in 1948/9 he won all five tosses and the rubber. He also toured England in 1957, besides Australasia in 1951/2 and New Zealand alone as player-manager in 1955/6; and at home he played against England in 1947/8. He not only let his batsmen and bowlers have their head, but also repeatedly brought off the boldest and most difficult catches, made runs and took wickets when needed. Making his debut in first-class cricket at sixteen in 1936/7, he shared in a large unbroken stand of 502 for the fourth wicket with Frank Worrell for Barbados against Trinidad at Bridgetown in 1943/4, his own score of 218 not out remaining his career-highest. In the third Test against England at Georgetown in 1947/8 he took 5 for 31 in the first innings, taking 11 wickets (26.09) in the series. Against India in 1948/9 with a highest score of only 44 he averaged 47.50 for the series; and against New Zealand in 1955/6 he headed the batting in the three Tests with 147.00, thanks to three not outs. He hit his highest Test score of 83 not out in the second match at Christchurch.

First-class career (1936-57): 3,769 runs (33.35) including 5 centuries, and 146 wickets (26.33)
Test matches (27): 859 runs (30.67), 33 wickets (31.81) and 22 catches

GOMES, Hilary Angelo (b.1953)

Trinidad and Middlesex

A slim, shy, artistic cricketer, 'Larry' Gomes is a left-handed batsman who times the ball with natural ease, a good fielder and useful, bustling medium-paced bowler. The brother of Sheldon Gomes, who has also played for Trinidad, Larry made his first appearance for the island in 1971/2. He was a member of one of the strongest touring teams, the formidable West Indies side to England in 1976. Although making 1,393 runs on the tour, including 5 centuries, of which the highest was 190 against Derbyshire, he was unable to gain a

Larry Gomes

regular Test place, indeed failed in two Tests when the England bowlers (who had little success generally) exposed some technical frailties around Gomes's off-stump. Moreover, in three years on the Middlesex staff between 1973 and 1976 he did not score more than 93 not out and never entirely established himself in another very strong team. Yet in 1977/8 he showed what he might have done in an era when West Indies cricket was less powerful, becoming a regular member of the Test team in the brief Packer interregnum, scoring 265 runs (44.16) against Australia in 1977/8 and 405 runs (40.50) in five Tests in India in 1978/9. Proper recognition came when he established a regular place in the full West Indies team at home against England in 1980/81, scoring 199 runs in four Test innings (49.75). Thus encouraged, he convinced everyone of his quality by scoring two Test hundreds in Australia in 1981/2, at Sydney and Adelaide. He finished top of both the tour and Test averages, scoring 200 not out against Queensland at Brisbane and in the Test scoring 393 runs (78.60) in six innings.

First-class career (1971-): 9,509 runs (42.45) including 23 centuries and 77 wickets (37.98)
Test matches (22): 1,418 runs (42.96) including 4 centuries, 5 wickets (53.20) and 4 catches

GOMEZ, Gerald Ethridge (b.1919)

Trinidad

A dependable middle-order right-handed batsman, an energetic fast-medium swing bowler who cantered in to bowl with his head nodding, and a superb close catcher, Gerry Gomez toured England in 1939 and 1950, India in 1948/9 and Australasia in 1951/2, and at home played against England in 1947/8 and 1953/4, and India in 1952/3. In his 1939 tour he did not bowl a ball but scored 719 runs (25.67) and, during and immediately after the Second World War, scored heavily at home. He shared in a partnership of 434 for the third wicket with Jeffrey Stollmeyer for Trinidad against British Guiana at Port of Spain in 1946/7, which remains the highest for that wicket in the Caribbean. Against England in 1947/8 he made 232 runs (46.40) and served as captain in the second match at Trinidad. In India in 1947/8 he began to come into his own as an all-rounder, scoring 256 runs (36.57), including 101 in the first Test at New Delhi – the first-ever Test between the two countries – and he sometimes shared the new ball, taking 16 wickets (28.58) in all first-class matches. In England in 1950 he made 1,116 runs (42.92) and took 55 wickets (25.58) in all first-class matches, including 207 runs in four Tests, and held 32 catches. At his best for a losing side in Australia in 1951/2, he headed the batting in the Tests with 324 runs (36.00), besides taking 18 wickets (14.22), which included 7 for 55 and 3 for 58 in the fifth match at Sydney, a magnificent performance in sweltering heat, when he bowled faster than usual and made the ball swing appreciably either way in the humid atmosphere. Gerry Gomez has been a sage and active administrator on the West Indies Cricket Board of Control for many years, and also an able radio commentator. He also stood as a Test umpire.

First-class career (1937-57): 6,764 runs (43.63) including 14 centuries, and 200 wickets (25.26)
Test matches (29): 1,243 runs (30.31) including 1 century, 58 wickets (27.41) and 18 catches

GRANT, George Copeland (1907-78)

Cambridge University, Trinidad and Rhodesia

A Cambridge cricket and Association football blue, 'Jackie' Grant played against Oxford at Lord's in 1929 and 1930. He later captained the team in Australia in 1930/31 (the first visit to Australia), in England in 1933, and at home against England in 1934/5. A good and plucky right-handed batsman, whose spirits were never depressed, and a brilliant field in the gully where he brought off some amazing catches, he was an enthusiastic and astute captain. He played the game in the most sporting spirit and also insisted on those under him doing the same. In his first Test, against Australia at Adelaide, he made 53 not out and 71 not out, and headed the averages in the series with 255 runs (42.50). In all first-class matches he made 738 runs (36.90) and was a sound leader. On his England tour he achieved little as a player in the Tests, but altogether scored 1,195 runs (30.64), including 115 against An England Eleven at Folkestone, when he added 226 with George Headley for the third wicket. He had the great pleasure of leading an underrated West Indian team to victory in the rubber against England in 1934/5. For many years he was engaged in missionary work in Africa.

First-class career (1928-35): 3,831 runs (32.19) including 4 centuries, and 19 wickets (51.00)
Test matches (12): 413 runs (25.81), 0-18 and 10 catches

GRANT, Rolph Stewart (1909-77)

Cambridge University and Trinidad

Tall and handsome, Rolph Grant was an all-round sportsman who won blues at Cambridge for cricket and Association football and a half-blue for boxing, later becoming goal-keeper for England and Trinidad's heavy-weight boxing champion. On the cricket field he was a superb field, especially at short-leg, a very useful right-handed batsman generally in the lower-half of the order, and a slow off-spin change-bowler round the wicket. He toured England in 1939 as an admirable captain, and appeared at home against

England in 1934/5. He hit his highest Test score of 77 in the fourth match at Kingston, adding 147 with George Headley for the seventh wicket. In England he solved the awkward problem of finding an opening partner for Jeffrey Stollmeyer by undertaking the task himself. His best effort was in the second Test at Old Trafford; after England declared at 164 for 7 wickets on a worsening wicket for the batsmen, he proceeded to hit 47 out of 56 in thirty-eight minutes, including 3 sixes off Tom Goddard.

First-class career (1932-39): 1,883 runs (28.53) including 1 century, and 79 wickets (25.17)
Test matches (7): 220 runs (22.00), 11 wickets (32.09) and 13 catches

GREENIDGE, Alvin Talbert (b.1956)

Barbados

A right-handed batsman, like his namesakes Gordon and Geoffrey, but no relation to either, Alvin Greenidge, a tall man, had an impressive season for Barbados in 1977/8, scoring consistently in the Shell Shield and making a fine 96 for the island against the touring Australian team. When the Packer players left the West Indies team after two Tests of that series, Greenidge fitted well into the Test atmosphere despite his inexperience, scoring 56 in his first innings in the third Test and 69 in the second innings of the fourth, but in India the following year he was a disappointment, making only 80 runs in four Tests. A professional in Holland, he was top scorer for Barbados in the 1982 Shell Shield, scoring 172 against Jamaica.

First-class career (1974-): 1,994 runs (32.68) including 4 centuries, 5 wickets (29.20) and 28 catches
Test matches (6): 222 runs (22.20) and 5 catches

GREENIDGE, Cuthbert Gordon (b.1951)

Barbados and Hampshire

Gordon Greenidge moved with his parents to England at the age of twelve, was brought up and educated in Reading and was once approached on the initiative of Ray Illingworth to play for England. But he preferred to await his chance in his native West Indies and developed into one of the finest players. A compact, strong right-handed opening batsman with a marvellous temperament, Greenidge has grafted onto his natural West Indian flair the fruits of a wide experience and become a magnificent and mature batsman with an immaculate technique who always seeks to take immediate control at the start of an innings yet will seldom give his wicket away. His driving in the arc between cover and mid-wicket is his special glory. A loyal servant of Hampshire, the club

Gordon Greenidge

which gave him his start in cricket, he also owes a debt to county cricket generally and in particular to his regular opening partner for Hampshire, the South African Barry Richards. Not so much a natural genius as Richards, Greenidge has improved each year, and in the later years of his partnership with the South African he seldom suffered by comparison, performing many spectacular deeds, including 259 against Sussex in 1975; 136 and 120 (in ninety-one minutes) against Kent in 1978; 177 in a 60-over Gillette match against Glamorgan in 1975; a record 173 not out in 55 overs in the Benson and Hedges Cup against the Minor Counties South in 1973 and a record 163 not out in 40 overs in the John Player League in 1979, an innings which included 10 sixes. Having played for Hampshire since 1970, he made a relatively late Test appearance but made 93 and 107 in his first match against India at Bangalore in 1974/5. In this series he scored 371 runs (41.22) and on the tour, 909 runs (45.45). In England in 1976 he made 1,952 runs in a season of brilliant batting, hitting 9 centuries and averaging 55.77. In the Tests his 592 runs (65.77) were topped only by Viv Richards. On an awkward pitch at Old Trafford in the third Test he produced the most masterly performance of his career, making 134 and 101, his 134 coming out of a total of only 211. He followed this with a brilliant 115 in the fourth Test at Headingley. Against Pakistan in the West Indies in 1976/7 he was the supreme West Indian batsman with 536 runs (53.60), which included, strangely enough, only one century, 100 in the fifth Test at Kingston. When his Test career was interrupted by his signing for World Series Cricket he had shared in eight century opening partnerships. He continued to play with success for West Indies after the disbandment of WSC, despite an increasing proneness to injury. In Australia in 1979/80, however, it seemed that the more he limped with a knee strain, the harder he hit the ball. He made 80 and 98 not out against England in the finals of the one-day Triangular tournament. In New Zealand later in the tour he scored 274 runs in three Tests (45.66). He had a benefit with Hampshire in 1982. Throughout his career he has been a dependable slip catcher.

First-class career (1970-): 21,989 runs (42.69) including 48 centuries, 16 wickets (27.37) and 340 catches
Test matches (36): 2,569 runs (42.81) including 5 centuries, 0-4 and 39 catches

GREENIDGE, Geoffrey Alan (b.1948)

Barbados and Sussex

A sound, right-handed opening batsman and occasional leg-break bowler, Geoff Greenidge had an amazing first-class debut for Barbados in 1966/7, hitting 205 against Jamaica at Bridgetown and taking 7 for 124 in the first innings. In his first Test, against New Zealand at Georgetown in 1971/2 (a match of bottle-throwing incidents), he scored a good-looking 50 and 35 not out but, although he received other opportunities, he did not make his Test place secure. From 1968 until 1975 he played for Sussex, usefully if unpredictably.

First-class career (1966-76): 9,112 runs (29.29) including 16 centuries, and 13 wickets (72.92)
Test matches (5): 209 runs (29.85), 0-75 and 3 catches

GRELL, Mervyn George (1899-1976)

Trinidad

A sound right-handed batsman and medium-pace bowler, Mervyn Grell's sole Test was the second against England at Port of Spain in 1929/30 when he scored 21 and 13, took 0 for 17 and held 1 catch.

First-class career (1929-38): 489 runs (28.76)

GRIFFITH, Charles Christopher (b.1938)

Barbados

One of the most feared fast bowlers of his time, Charlie Griffith began as a right-arm spinner. But he once filled a gap for his new club side as a fast bowler and, after taking 7 wickets for 1 run with his new mode of attack, seldom looked back. The fast bowling partnership of Griffith and Hall became one of the finest and fastest of all time in international cricket. Griffith was 6ft 2ins tall, of massive build with powerful legs and shoulders, clean-living and very fit. He thundered along his twenty yard run to the wicket and delivered the ball with a chest-on action, which caused some controversy. His deadly ball was a fast yorker but it was his bouncer which caused greater consternation, especially after an incident in Barbados in 1961/2 when Nari Contractor, India's captain, was knocked

Charlie Griffith

senseless by one of his balls into which he had ducked: his skull was fractured and for many hours his life was in danger. Happily he recovered, but, in the same match, Griffith was no-balled for 'throwing'. Although some critics (especially the Australians) considered that he sometimes threw his faster ball, which batsmen found difficult to sight, he was only called in one other first-class match, by Arthur Fagg at Old Trafford, in the match with Lancashire in 1966. Volatile in his reactions to problems, Griffith gained a reputation as 'the big bad boy of cricket', and provided some good copy for the gossip-writers. He toured England in 1963 and 1966, India in 1966, and Australasia in 1968/9, and at home played against England in 1959/60 and 1967/8, and Australia in 1964/5. On his first-class debut in 1959/60, for Barbados against MCC at Bridgetown, he dismissed Colin Cowdrey, Mike Smith and Peter May in two overs, and soon added Ken Barrington to his 'bag'. In England in 1963 he was often unplayable, heading the bowling with 119 wickets (12.83), including 32 wickets (16.21) in the Tests. In the highly dramatic drawn second Test at Lord's he took 8 wickets, and in the fourth at Headingley and fifth at The Oval 9 wickets each time, including 6 for 36 in the first innings at Headingley. Against Gloucestershire at Bristol, he captured 13 for 58. Against Australia in 1964/5 he took 15 wickets (32.00). Very disconcerted by the continued rumblings over his action, he was not generally as effective on the 1966 England tour and in subsequent Test series.

First-class career (1959-69): 1,502 runs (17.26) and 332 wickets (21.60)
Test matches (28): 530 runs (16.56), 94 wickets (28.54) and 16 catches

GRIFFITH, Herman Clarence (1893-1980)

Barbados

Short in build but also powerful and exuding a sturdy confidence, Herman Griffith was a fast bowler who also bowled brisk medium-fast out-swingers and off-breaks, cleverly changing pace and maintaining a good length. He once clean-bowled Herbert Sutcliffe with a ball which swung from middle-and-leg to the off stump. 'Griff' was the first consistently successful West Indian bowler in Test cricket. No man hated being hit more than he did and he had the reputation of being ready to call anybody anything which seemed to him to apply. Probably because of his temperament, or because he was rumoured to be a communist, Griff was omitted from the 1923 West Indian team to tour England despite causing a sensation with his 7 for 38 against Trinidad in 1921/2. Touring England in 1928, he took 76 wickets (27.89) in first-class matches (103 in all matches). In the third Test at The Oval he took 6 for 103 in England's total of 438. Against England in the first Test series in the Caribbean in 1929/30, he secured 16 wickets (31.75), including 8 for 162 at Port of Spain in the second match. On the first tour of Australia in 1930/31 he headed the Test bowling figures with 14 wickets (28.07), bowling Don Bradman for a duck in the fifth match at Sydney. (As he had dismissed the Don for 4 in an earlier Test, he was fond of referring to the great man as his 'rabbit'.) In his fortieth year, in 1933, he toured England again. He had lost something of his pace and nip off the pitch, though his language remained as pungent as ever.

First-class career (1921-41): 1,214 runs (15.17) and 256 wickets (28.49)
Test matches (13): 91 runs (5.05), 44 wickets (28.25) and 4 catches

GUILLEN, Simpson Clairmonte (b.1924)

Trinidad and Canterbury

A very competent wicket-keeper and useful right-handed batsman, 'Sammy' Guillen toured Australasia in 1951/2, playing in five Tests with success. The tour brought him 34 dismissals (24 caught, 10 stumped) from eleven matches. He became a permanent resident of New Zealand, keeping wicket for Canterbury, and he appeared for New Zealand in three official Tests against West Indies in 1955/6 and three unofficial Tests against Australia in 1956/7. Although the West Indians raised no objections to Sammy playing for New Zealand, it was strictly illegal as he had not then lived for four years in his adopted country. The highest score of his career was 197 for Canterbury against Fiji in 1953/4.

First-class career (1947-61): 2,672 runs (26.97) including 3 centuries, and 134 dismissals (100 ct, 34 st.)
Test matches (West Indies – 5): 104 runs (26.00) and 11 dismissals (9 ct, 2 st.). (New Zealand – 3): 98 runs (16.33) and 5 dismissals (4 ct, 1 st.)

HALL, Wesley Winfield (b.1937)

Barbados, Trinidad and Queensland

The ideal of right-arm fast bowlers, a muscular six-foot-two-inch man with a classical action and good temper, Wes Hall was a fearsome prospect, especially in partnership with Charlie Griffith. Possessing a long, athletic approach, with eyes bulging, gold teeth glinting and a crucifix swinging across his chest, Hall was an aesthetic joy to the spectator, but an intimidating sight to a waiting batsman. He bowled as though he meant to take a wicket with every delivery; his speed was measured as 91 mph and he was consistently fast and hostile. Curiously enough, he was in early days a batsman/wicket-keeper: indeed, when he first toured England in 1957, with moderate results, he had never taken a single wicket in first-class cricket. Success did not come quickly and it was only as a very late replacement that he toured India and Pakistan in 1958/9. Soon establishing his superiority, he took 46 wickets (17.76) from eight Tests and 87 wickets (15.08) on the whole tour, more wickets than anyone else. He captured 11 for 126 in the second Test at Kanpur

Wes Hall

against India and 8 for 77 in the second at Dacca against Pakistan. Against England in 1959/60 his haul was 22 wickets (30.86), including 7 for 69 in the first innings of the third match at Sabina Park. In the great tied match, the first Test at Brisbane in 1960/61, he took 9 for 203. With his shirt hanging out, he bowled the last over when 6 runs were needed for victory with 3 wickets left. He took 1 wicket and there were 2 run-outs. Earlier in the match he had hit 50 in sixty-nine minutes. In this series Hall took 21 wickets (29.33), again more than any of his colleagues. He was again at the centre of the high drama at Lord's in 1963. He brought West Indies back into the game when, in England's second innings, he bowled unchanged throughout the three hours twenty minutes play on the last day, taking 4 for 93. Unintentionally he further ruined England's chances of winning when one of his deliveries broke Colin Cowdrey's forearm. With India as visitors in 1961/2 he was in his best form throughout, taking 27 wickets (15.74), including 5 for 20 in the first innings of the fourth match at Port of Spain. He was a first choice for his country for ten years, and until the later stages of his career he never had a poor series. Altogether, he toured England in 1957, 1963 and 1966, India and Pakistan in 1958/9, Australia in 1960/61 and 1968/9, and New Zealand in 1968/9. At home he played against England in 1959/60 and 1967/8, India in 1961/2, and Australia in 1964/5. He struck the ball hard and was sometimes a useful run-getter. A popular man wherever he played, he had several seasons for Queensland in the Sheffield Shield competition and several also in the Lancashire League. He later became a politician and has for many years been a senator in the Barbados Parliament.

First-class career (1955-71): 2,673 runs (15.10) including 1 century, and 546 wickets (26.14)
Test matches (48): 818 runs (15.73), 192 wickets (26.38) and 11 catches

HAYNES, Desmond Leo (b.1956)

Barbados

A tall and solidly muscled right-handed opening batsman, Desmond Haynes's promising Test career was interrupted when he spent a year with World Series Cricket but he toured Australia in 1979/80. A fine driver, he also hits hard off the back foot, cutting and hooking majestically, as he showed when making 61, 66 and 55 in three Test innings against Australia in 1977/8. At Bridgetown he put on 131 with Gordon Greenidge for the first wicket in the second innings. Indeed he fitted comfortably into the shoes of Roy Fredericks as Greenidge's regular Test opening partner, playing a number of valuable innings in the increasing number of one-day internationals as well as in Tests. Between 1979 and 1982 he toured Australia and England twice (including the 1979 World Cup), Pakistan and also Zimbabwe, with the West Indies Under 26 team, when he was vice-captain. His finest innings to date was played at Lord's in 1980 when he batted 490 minutes for 184, the solid foundation on which West Indies based a first-innings score of 518. A vibrant character, with a broad smile never far away, he is also a fine fielder anywhere.

First-class career (1976-): 4,588 runs (40.60) including 7 centuries, and 1 wicket (10.00)
Test matches (24): 1,431 runs (38.67) including 3 centuries, 1-8 and 13 catches

HEADLEY, George Alphonso (b.1909)

Jamaica

Born in Panama, George Headley was taken to his mother's island of Jamaica at the age of ten and soon revealed a genius for cricket. Known as 'The Black Bradman', although his method was different, he was to become the dominant West Indian batsman from 1929 until 1948. A compact right-hander with every shot at his command, he never failed in a series of Tests. At the age of eighteen he scored 71 and 211 in two matches for Jamaica against the Hon. Lionel Tennyson's side in 1927/8, and, rather than study dentistry in the USA, he played in the first-ever Test on West Indian soil against England at Bridgetown in 1929/30, making 21 and 176. In the third match at Georgetown he made 114 (adding 196 for the second wicket with Clifford Roach) and 112, West Indies winning a Test for the first time. In the next match at Kingston he amassed 223 in six and a half hours, after the West Indies were set 836 runs to win. In this first home series he made 703 runs (87.87), only three men ever having reached a higher aggregate. He became known as 'Atlas' as the rest of his country's batting rested on him. Essentially a back-foot player, he almost always sought to attack the bowling, although he was also a sound defender. He was a fine cutter but his outstanding feature was his powerful and well-placed driving. He occasionally bowled enthusiastic and useful leg-breaks and fielded well anywhere; in his earlier days he would sometimes make a complete somersault in taking catches, Constantine-fashion. It was on the first tour of Australia in 1930/31 that, after mastering Clarrie Grimmett, he was given the sobriquet, 'The Black Bradman'. All first-class matches on this tour brought him 1,066 runs (44.41) including 102 not out (out of 193) in the second Test at Brisbane and 105 in the fifth at Sydney. At Kingston in 1931/2 he made his career-highest score of 344 not out for Jamaica against Lord Tennyson's side, adding a record unbroken 487 for the sixth wicket with C.C. Passailaigue. His other scores against these tourists were 84, 155 not out and 140. In England in 1933 he made 2,320 runs (66.28), including 7 centuries. In hitting 169 not out in the second Test at Old Trafford

George Headley

– the second century by a West Indian in a Test in England – he added 200 for the second wicket with Ivan Barrow who had preceded him to 100 by a few minutes. In the three Tests he made 277 runs (55.40). Once more the heart of the batting against England in 1934/5, he scored 485 runs (97.00), including his Test-highest score of 270 not out in the first Test at Kingston, an outstanding innings, which lasted nearly eight hours. A few days before he had hit 127 for Jamaica against the tourists. On the 1939 England tour he was still master, no one else approaching his total of 1,745 runs (72.70), including 6 centuries. To the Tests he contributed 334 runs (66.80), including 106 and 107 in the first match at Lord's; no West Indian had previously hit two centuries in the same Test. By the time the Second World War had come, George Headley had not missed a Test played by the West Indies for ten years and in the first post-War Test at Bridgetown against England he was appointed captain; the first black man ever to lead the side. Hampered, however, by a bad back, he missed the remaining Tests. In India in 1948/9 he appeared in the first Test at Delhi, but missed most of the tour through injury. His next and final Test was the first against England at Kingston in 1953/4 when, at 44 years and 236 days, he became the oldest-ever West Indian Test cricketer. He coached on behalf of the Government of Jamaica, and is the father of Ron Headley.

First-class career (1927-54): 9,921 runs (69.86) including 33 centuries, and 51 wickets (36.11)
Test matches (22): 2,190 runs (60.83) including 10 centuries, 0-230 and 14 catches

HEADLEY, Ronald George Alphonso (b.1939)

Jamaica, Worcestershire and Derbyshire

Most of Ron Headley's cricket was played in England where in 1973 he joined a West Indian team, which had been depleted by injury, to appear in two Tests, but without luck. An attractive left-handed opening batsman, with a handsome cover-drive, full backlift and high follow-through, he moved on to his front foot as much as possible. He was a brilliant fielder anywhere and an occasional leg-break bowler. He was registered with Worcestershire from 1958 until 1974 and then briefly joined Derbyshire to play in the one-day games. He appeared for Jamaica in the Shell Shield in 1965/6 and 1973/4.

First-class career (1958-74): 21,695 (31.12) including 32 centuries, 12 wickets (49.00) and 357 catches
Test matches (2): 62 runs (15.20) and 2 catches

HENDRIKS, John Leslie (b.1933)

Jamaica

A tall, extrovert wicket-keeper specially adept at taking slow bowling and a useful right-handed batsman, 'Jackie' Hendriks toured Pakistan in 1958/9 and Australia in 1960/61 as reserve 'keeper. When he finally made his Test debut against India in 1961/2 in the first match at Port of Spain, he broke his finger, though he top-scored with 64. He did not regain his place until 1964/5 when, in the fourth Test at Bridgetown against Australia, he was struck by a ball from 'Garth' McKenzie and removed to hospital for brain surgery: his life was in the balance during this series. He recovered completely, touring England in 1966 and 1969, India in 1966/7 and Australasia in 1968/9, playing in fifteen further Tests before Deryck Murray replaced him.

First-class career (1953-69): 1,568 runs (17.42) and 190 dismissals (140 ct, 50 st.)
Test matches (20): 447 runs (18.62) and 47 dismissals (42 ct, 5 st.)

HOAD, Edward Lisle Goldsworthy (b.1896)

Barbados

A sound, defensive right-handed batsman and leg-break change-bowler, Teddy Hoad was a prolific scorer in the West Indies. In the Inter-Colonial Tournament in 1926/7, for instance, he made 115 against British Guiana and 174 not out against Trinidad at Kensington. In England in 1928 he took a long time to find form, playing in only one Test, but finished at the head of the averages with 765 runs (36.42) including 3 centuries. He captained the West Indies in the first-ever Test in the Caribbean, against England at Bridgetown in 1929/30. He toured England again in 1933 as vice-captain, making 1,083 runs (27.76). He was, however, very disappointing in Test cricket.

First-class career (1920-36): 3,518 runs (38.66) including 8 centuries, and 55 wickets (37.09)
Test matches (4): 98 runs (12.25) and 1 catch

HOLDER, Vanburn Alonza (b.1945)

Barbados and Worcestershire

A dignified and sporting cricketer, Vanburn Holder bowled with outstanding consistency during a long career. Tall and raw-boned, he bowled fast-medium with a good high action after a bandy-legged approach, moving his away-swinger dangerously late and seldom getting the luck he deserved. He fielded capably and batted right-handed in textbook manner, sometimes playing such good-looking strokes that it was surprising he did not get more runs, although he did score 122 against Trinidad at Bridgetown in a Shell Shield match in 1974. First playing for Worcestershire in 1968, he was capped in 1970 and was prominent in the county's win in the County Championship in 1974 when he recorded his best first-class bowling figures of 7 for 40 against Glamorgan at Cardiff. With the West Indies he toured England in 1969, 1973 and 1976. On his Test debut at Headingley in 1969 he took 4 for 48 in England's first innings in 26 overs. In 1973 he took 4 for 56 in the first innings of the third Test at Lord's. In 1976 he took 15 wickets (24.46) in four Tests and shared with Holding, Roberts and Daniel in a remorseless attack of fast or fast-medium bowling. On this tour he took 52 wickets in all first-class games at 19.30 each. Against New Zealand in 1971/2 he headed the Test bowling averages with 12 wickets (23.75) including 4 for 41 in 26 overs in the second innings of the fifth Test at Port of Spain where his 42 in the second West Indies innings was top score. In all first-class matches on the tour of India, Sri Lanka and Pakistan in 1974/5 his accuracy and ability to move the ball off the seam on normally unresponsive wickets enabled him to take 40 wickets at 23.42. In four Tests against India he took 17 wickets (18.52), including 6 for 39 in the second innings of the deciding Test, the fifth at Bombay, paving the way for West Indian victory. The arrival of players like Garner and Croft pushed the reliable Holder out of the Test side for a time but when the Packer players left the fold for a time he bounced back to take 6 for 28 in Australia's first innings of 290 in the fourth Test. In India the following winter, however, he was very expensive, age clearly starting to take its toll of a much-respected cricketer.

Vanburn Holder

First-class career (1966-80): 3,559 runs (13.03) including 1 century, and 947 wickets (24.48)
Test matches (40): 682 runs (14.21), 109 wickets (33.28) and 16 catches

HOLDING, Michael Anthony (b.1954)

Jamaica, Lancashire and Tasmania

It is difficult to believe that anyone has made the strenuous business of bowling very fast seem as effortless as has Michael Holding. Tall and slim, with his arms resting comfortably by his sides and his head nodding like a new-born baby's, he approaches the stumps down a long, floating run which has the fragile grace of an antelope, then leaps high and bowls with fearsome speed and exceptionally high bounce. Few of the adjectives normally applied to fast bowlers apply, for Holding is not overtly ferocious and has none of the normal broad-shouldered, muscular power of most great exponents of his art. Since he is also a university graduate, West Indian cricket has been fortunate to hold his interest. The advent of World Series Cricket, however, has made cricket a lucrative business for him. He developed dramatically in England in 1976 after a tour to Australia in 1975/6 when his accuracy did not begin to match his youthful speed. At Brisbane in his first Test he took no wickets for 127 and his 10 wickets in the series cost 61.40 each. Later the same season, however, he headed the Test averages against India on his home pitches, taking 19 wickets (19.89) which included 6 for 65 in the first innings of the third Test at Port of Spain. In England, in the hot summer of 1976, he was the most formidable of a fierce quartet of fast bowlers (Roberts, Daniel and Holder being the others), taking 55 wickets on the tour at only 14.38 and 28 in the Tests at 12.71. Early in the season, playing against MCC at Lord's, he bowled with awesome pace, once splitting open the side of Dennis Amiss's head with a bouncer. His 5 for 17 in 14.5 overs in the Old Trafford Test on a treacherous pitch hustled out England for 71. In the final Test, in totally different conditions at The Oval on a slow and lifeless pitch, he produced one of the most remarkable fast bowling feats in modern times, taking 14 for 149 in the match by unforgettable bowling which was simply very fast and very straight. His 8 for 92 was the best analysis by

Michael Holding

a West Indian against England and his match figures the best by any West Indian in a Test. He bowled with further success against England in the World Cup of 1979, on tour in 1980 (44 first-class wickets on the tour and 20 in the Tests) and at home in 1981/2 (17 wickets in four Tests at 18.52). Despite his relatively slender build he also stood up well to tours of Australia (twice), New Zealand, and Pakistan between 1979 and 1981, although he fell from grace when expressing his displeasure with the New Zealand umpires by kicking over the stumps. (Even this he did with elegance!) He split his time between county cricket and the Lancashire League in 1981/2, and in 1982/3 played with success for Tasmania. Capable of batting usefully when required to do so, he hit 58 not out in a Test against England at Antigua in 1981. Not the least remarkable fact about a very unusual bowler is that the umpires say that they cannot hear him approaching behind them, so light-footed is the approach.

First-class career (1972-): 1,192 runs (13.24), 308 wickets (22.91) and 31 catches
Test matches (31): 434 runs (12.05), 139 wickets (22.97) and 9 catches

HOLFORD, David Anthony Jerome (b.1940)

Barbados

A tall, slim right-arm leg-break bowler with a generally good command of length, David Holford developed more as a reliable right-handed batsman with a superb drive. Throughout, he was a fine close field and a cheerful and attractive cricketer. He toured England in 1966, India in 1966/7, and Australasia in 1968/9, and at home played against England in 1967/8, India in 1970/71 and 1975/6, New Zealand in 1971/2 and Pakistan in 1976/7. His finest hour came early, at Lord's in his second Test, in 1966; with the West Indies only 9 runs ahead and 5 second-innings wickets gone, he joined his cousin Gary Sobers, and they added 274 in an unbroken partnership – a West Indian record against England – in 5 hours 20 minutes. Holford made a fighting 105 not out. On the tour he made 759 runs (37.95) and took 51 wickets (28.60). The series brought him 227 runs (37.83). Against India in the first Test at Bombay in 1966/7 he made a determined 80 and took 5 wickets, but soon afterwards an attack of pleurisy kept him out of the rest of the tour. In the first Test against India at Bridgetown in 1975/6 he took 5 for 23. These successes tended to come spasmodically, and although consistently a respected and successful all-rounder for Barbados, whom he captained, he never fully established himself in Tests.

First-class career (1960-79): 3,821 runs (31.31) including 3 centuries, and 253 wickets (32.00)
Test matches (24): 768 runs (22.58) including 1 century, 51 wickets (39.39) and 18 catches

HOLT, John Kenneth, junior (b.1923)

Jamaica

Unlike his father, J.K., senior, who made the trip in 1923, John Holt did not visit England but he toured India and Pakistan in 1958/9, and at home played against England in 1953/4 and Australia in 1954/5. A right-handed batsman with strokes all round the wicket, he scored 94 in his first Test against England at Kingston in 1953/4 before being given out lbw to Statham by umpire P. Burke, whose wife and son were assaulted by spectators in reaction to the decision. In the next Test, at Bridgetown, he hit 166, adding 222 with Frank Worrell for the second wicket. In the series Holt made 432 runs (54.00). In India and Pakistan in 1958/9 he made 1,001 runs (43.52), including 3 centuries, one of which was 123 in the first Test against India at Delhi, when, in facing a total of 415, he and Conrad Hunte put on 159 for the first wicket.

First-class career (1946-62): 4,256 runs (41.32) including 9 centuries
Test matches (17): 1,066 runs (36.75) including 2 centuries, 1-20 and 8 catches

HOWARD, Anthony Bourne (b.1946)

Barbados

Tony Howard was a right-arm off-break bowler who bowled well for his island against the New Zealand touring team in 1971/2. He played in one Test, the fourth against New Zealand at Georgetown, when he did not bat and took 2 for 140 in 62 overs in one innings.

First-class career (1965-75): 310 runs (10.00) and 85 wickets (27.30)

HUNTE, Conrad Cleophas (b.1932)

Barbados

By inclination an aggressive right-handed batsman who loved to let his natural talent flow, Conrad Hunte realized, as an opener, that it was more important for West Indies to be given a sound, solid start, and he adapted his technique accordingly. He was very reliable, though he seldom had a completely satisfactory partner. His strength was primarily off his legs, either glancing fine or punching to mid-wicket, but he also hooked with power and timed his off-drive perfectly. He was a fine fielder, especially close to the bat, and occasionally bowled slow-medium cutters. He toured India and Pakistan in 1958/9, Australia in 1960/61, England in 1963 and 1966, and India in 1966/7. At home he played against Pakistan in 1957/8, England in 1959/60, India in 1962/3 and Australia in 1964/5. Although making his first-class debut in 1950/51, he waited seven years before being selected for Tests and in his first series, against Pakistan in 1957/8, amassed 622 runs (77.75), including 142 in the first match at Bridgetown, 260 in the third at Kingston – his highest in Tests, when he added 446 for the second wicket with Gary Sobers (365 not out), a record stand for West Indies – and 114 in the fourth at Georgetown. In Australia in 1960/61 he hit 110 in a total of 233 in the second Test at Melbourne; and in England in 1963 he was at his peak, making more runs than anyone else, 1,367 runs (44.09), including 471 runs (58.87) in the Tests, when he headed the averages. He scored 182 in the first Test at Old Trafford and 108 not out in the fifth at The Oval. Against Australia in 1964/5 he was the outstanding batsman with 550 runs (61.11) and a highest score of 89: consistency personified. On his second tour of England in 1966, as vice-captain, he was not as dominant as before, but, again in the first Test at Old Trafford, he made a century – 108. The highest of his three double centuries was 263 for Barbados against Jamaica at Georgetown in 1961/2. He now works for the Moral Rearmament movement.

First-class career (1950-67): 8,916 runs (43.92) including 16 centuries, and 17 wickets (37.88)
Test matches (44): 3,245 runs (45.06) including 8 centuries, 2 wickets (55.00) and 16 catches

HUNTE, Errol Ashton Clarimore (1905-67)

Trinidad

A good opening batsman and useful wicket-keeper, Errol Hunte toured Australia in 1930/31 but all his Test cricket was played at home against England in 1929/30. In his second Test at Port of Spain he kept wicket and hit 58 and 30.

Test matches (3): 166 runs (33.20) and 5 catches

HYLTON, Leslie George (1905-55)

Jamaica

Heavy-set, Leslie Hylton delivered the ball at great pace. Learie Constantine, Manny Martindale and he were ranked the most formidable right-arm fast-bowling trio in the world when MCC toured the Caribbean in 1934/5; the trio secured 47 wickets between them in the four Tests, of which Hylton's 'bag' was 13. Touring England in 1939, however, he could rarely find his form. He was executed for the murder of his wife.

First-class career (1926-39): 843 runs (18.73) and 120 wickets (25.62)
Test matches (6): 70 runs (11.66), 16 wickets (26.12) and 1 catch

JOHNSON, Hophie Horace Hines (b.1910)

Jamaica

A six-foot-three-inch right-arm fast bowler, Hines Johnson toured England in 1950 with moderate success. His best performance in Tests was in his first match, against England at Kingston in 1947/8, when he took 5 for 41 and 5 for 55, maintaining a great pace and never attempting to intimidate by pitching short.

First-class career (1934-51): 316 runs (17.52) and 68 wickets (23.36)
Test matches (3): 38 runs (9.50) and 13 wickets (18.30)

JOHNSON, Tyrell Francis (b.1917)

Trinidad

A very tall left-arm fast bowler, Johnson toured England in 1939 and looked better than a meagre reward proved him to be. In his sole Test, the third at The Oval, he scored 9 not out, took 3 for 129 and held one catch. He took a wicket with his first ball of the tour and also his first ball in a Test.

First-class career (1935-9): 90 runs (9.00) and 50 wickets (21.50)

JONES, Charles M. (no details available)

British Guiana

A competent left-handed batsman and left-arm slow bowler, Charles Jones played against England in 1929/30 and 1934/5 without much success.

First-class career (1925–39): 917 runs (21.83) and 24 wickets (44.12)
Test matches (4): 63 runs (9.00), 0-11 and 3 catches

JONES, Prior Erskine (b.1917)

Trinidad

Prior Jones was a strong, persevering right-arm fast bowler who moved the ball either way, both in the air and off the seam. He was a stubborn tail-end batsman and a fine slip field with a terrific throw and was expected to be a successful spearhead in England in 1950, but received few opportunities in 'Ramadhin and Valentine's year'. He played against England at home in 1947/8 and toured India in 1948/9, taking 51 wickets (18.54) on the slowish wickets, including 17 in the Tests. In Australasia in 1951/2, however, as a veteran, he was virtually bowled into the ground.

First-class career (1940–52): 775 runs (14.09) and 169 wickets (26.81)
Test matches (9): 47 runs (5.22), 25 wickets (30.04) and 4 catches

JULIEN, Bernard Denis (b.1950)

Trinidad and Kent

A typical West Indian all-rounder, Bernard Julien is a quickish left-arm seam bowler of wiry build, who swings the ball both ways and can also bowl slow orthodox or unorthodox spin. He is also an exhilarating and ebullient right-handed stroke-maker, lacking consistency, and an excellent fielder anywhere. A happy-go-lucky character, with an unerring eye for pretty girls, he has not quite fulfilled the early promise he showed in West Indian youth cricket. His first-class debut was for North Trinidad against South Trinidad in 1967/8. Playing for Kent between 1970 and 1977, he was always doing something useful, though seldom sustaining his performances for long. He took 7 for 66 against Sussex at Hove in 1975 and 7 for 78 against the same opponents a year later when playing for the West Indian touring team. By now, however, his inconsistency had lost him his more-or-less regular place in the West Indies team. He played the first two Tests in England in 1976 but only once more represented the West Indies, against Pakistan at home later that year. He toured England twice in all, 1973 and 1976, went to India, Sri Lanka and Pakistan in 1974/5 and Australia in 1975/6. His most brilliant performance in four Tests was a superb innings of 121 against England at Lord's in 1973 off only 127 balls. He added a second Test century against Pakistan at Karachi but he was more often successful in Test cricket as a dangerous swing bowler, especially with the new ball. His 16 wickets against England at home in the 1973/4 series included 5 for 57 at Bridgetown in an England total of 395. He returned to the Trinidad team in the 1981/2 season and bowled with success, taking 9-97 against Jamaica, his best figures.

First-class career (1967–): 5,673 runs (24.45) including 3 centuries, 479 wickets (28.50) and 124 catches
Test matches (24): 866 runs (30.92) including 2 centuries, 50 wickets (37.36) and 14 catches

JUMADEEN, Raphick Rasif (b.1948)

Trinidad

An accurate slow left-arm orthodox bowler who turns the ball a good deal on helpful pitches, Raphick Jumadeen is basically a steady rather than a venomous bowler. He had little chance to shine in England in 1976 because the fast bowlers dominated a hot summer (when spin, in theory, should have proved fruitful). In all first class matches on the tour he took 58 wickets (30.00). However, he took 11 wickets in two Tests against Australia in 1977/8, including 4 for 72 in a first innings of 343 at Kingston. At home against India in 1976 he took only 9 wickets (31.00) in four Tests. In two more Tests against India in 1978/9, he took only 3 wickets but bowled long, economical spells.

First-class career (1966–): 604 runs (8.50) and 347 wickets (27.91)
Test matches (12): 84 runs (21.00), 29 wickets (39.34) and 4 catches

KALLICHARRAN, Alvin Isaac (b.1949)

Guyana, Warwickshire, Queensland and Transvaal

One of the many great cricketers to prove that a lack of inches need be no disadvantage, Alvin Kallicharran, comes from the same area as Rohan Kanhai, Berbice in Guyana. A brilliant, natural left-handed batsman, fine fielder with a deceptively strong throw from the deep, and an occasional slow right-arm bowler, he developed a straight, textbook technique at an early age and this, plus his natural flair and an excellent temperament, has enabled him to score attractive runs round the world. He is a determined competitor with a full armoury of strokes and immaculate timing whether driving, hooking, cutting or glancing. Off the field he is a sunny, smiling character. His Test career began in Georgetown against New Zealand in 1971/2 when he hit 100 not out on a lifeless pitch, his last 41 coming in an hour after part of his innings had been interrupted by bottle-throwing. In the next Test, and his own second Test innings, he made 101 at Port of Spain. He played his first full Test series against Australia in the West Indies in 1972/3, scoring 294 runs in the series at 36.75. In England in 1973 he hit three hundreds against county sides and 889 runs (64.78) on the tour, although his highest score in the Test matches was 80. A shoulder injury restricted him on his second official tour of England in 1976, although

Alvin Kallicharran

he made a valuable 97 at Trent Bridge. Despite consistent batting for Warwickshire, for whom he scored 1,000 or more runs in five of his first seven seasons, his major successes have been on harder pitches away from England. In India, Sri Lanka and Pakistan in 1974/5 he made 1,249 runs (56.77) and 454 runs in the Tests at 56.75, including 124 in the first Test at Bangalore. In two Tests against Pakistan his scores were 94, 44 and 115. At home against England in 1973/4 he made 397 runs (56.71), never playing so well again after his brilliant hundred in the first Test at Port of Spain where, after Julien had played the last ball of the first day to Greig at short-leg, Kallicharran carried on walking towards the pavilion from the non-striker's end, never having grounded his bat. On Greig's throwing down of his wicket, he was given run out by umpire Douglas Sang Hue, although some of the fielders had turned towards the pavilion unaware of what had happened. After tempestuous scenes and in a heated atmosphere of crisis, Sang Hue diplomatically allowed his (technically corrrect) decision to be overruled. Not out 142 over night, 'Kalli' was out for 158 the next day. He made 119 in the third Test at Bridgetown, adding 249 for the second wicket with Lawrence Rowe, a record for that wicket against England. In Australia in 1975/6 he scored 730 runs (36.50) and 421 in the Tests at 38.27. Later that season against India he scored 237 runs (47.40) with 103 not out at Port of Spain. Less successful against Pakistan at home in 1976/7, he signed without conviction for Kerry Packer's team, then later discovered that this contravened a contract which he had already signed with a radio station in Queensland. He escaped from his contract with Mr Packer's company, thus splitting with the main body of top West Indies players and assuming his country's captaincy in 1977/8 when Clive Lloyd resigned over the Packer issue on the eve of the third Test at Georgetown. 'Kalli' had already scored his customary hundred at Port of Spain in the first Test and he added 126 at Kingston in the fifth when a riot ended play early. On a happier tour of India in 1978/9 Kallicharran learned quickly the difficult art of captaincy and led by example with 538 runs (59.77), once again scoring a century in the first Test of a rubber, 187 at Bombay. Ignoring criticisms, he began playing, with great success, for Transvaal in 1981/2.

First-class career (1966-): 22,781 runs (44.49) including 57 centuries, 52 wickets (47.50) and 233 catches

Test matches (66): 4,399 runs (44.43) including 12 centuries, 4 wickets (39.50) and 51 catches

KANHAI, Rohan Babulal (b.1935)

Guyana, Trinidad, Warwickshire, Western Australia and Tasmania

Rohan Kanhai had a natural genius for batting. A small, neat right-hander with every cricket stroke and a few inventive ones of his own (notably a full-blooded sweep to leg-side – half-volleys which swung him off his feet and the ball out of the ground), he possessed a wonderful gift of timing and scored runs consistently all over the world. A steely determination and huge appetite for runs made him one of the most consistent of batsmen to come from the Caribbean and he did much personally to dispel the general impression that West Indies batsmen would waste their natural brilliance from time to time and either throw their wickets away or fold up quickly in a crisis. Though he was not a particularly successful captain when that honour came his way, his occasionally stormy temperament being wrong for the job, Rohan Kanhai was in this sense highly significant in the development of West Indian cricket at international level. He made his first appearance for British Guiana in 1954/5, for Western Australia in 1961/2, for Warwickshire in 1968, for Tasmania in 1969/70 and for the West Indies in 1957. He played, indeed, in sixty-one of his seventy-nine Tests without a break from his first series on the tour of England in 1957 when he was used as a makeshift wicket-keeper. Apart from his 15 Test centuries, he passed 50 on 28 other occasions, averaging 50 every third innings. On his second tour of England in 1963 he scored 1,149 runs (41.03) and 497 runs (55.22) in the Tests. In 1966 he scored a century at The Oval in the only Test of the series which the West Indies lost and in 1973, as captain, made 223 runs (44.60), including 157 in the third Test at Lord's. He had a prolific winter's cricket in 1958/9, scoring 538 runs (67.25) in five Tests in India, including his highest score of 256 at Calcutta. This was also his

Rohan Kanhai

maiden Test century and the entire innings occupied only six and a half hours. It included 42 fours and remains the highest score in a Test in India. Moving to Pakistan, Kanhai hit 217 in the third Test at Lahore, helping to inflict Pakistan's first home defeat. At home against England the following season he scored 110 out of 244 in the second innings of one of the bottle-throwing Tests, the second at Port of Spain, England winning an infamous contest. In Australia in 1960/61 he scored 117 and 115 at Adelaide to become the first West Indian to reach hundreds in both innings of a Test match. This series brought him 503 runs (50.30) and the tour 1,093 runs at 64.29 with four centuries. The following year, at home against India, he made two Test centuries and an aggregate of 495 runs (70.71), more than anyone else on either side. Against Australia at home in 1964/5 he made big scores in each of the last three Tests – 89, 129 and 121, but he showed he was capable of a loss of form in India in 1966/7. He scored only 463 runs on the tour, although 227 of these came in the three Tests at 56.75. He played in several English (and Scottish) leagues, and married a Lancashire girl. He became a more reliable player as his experience grew and his temperament became less volatile. In the West Indies in 1967/8 he scored 535 runs in the Tests against England at an average of 59.44, including 143 in the fourth Test at Port of Spain, and 150 in the last at Georgetown. As successor to Sobers as captain in Australia in 1972/3, he had successive Test scores of 84, 105 and 56, finishing with 433 runs (54.12), but Australia won the series. A successful series followed in the second half of the English summer of 1973, Kanhai's 653 runs helping his side to two Test wins out of three, but at home the following winter he personally had a poor series and his team failed to follow up several apparently winning situations against England who, having lost the first Test at Port of Spain, squared the rubber by winning the last on the same ground. His sequence of sixty-one Tests was broken only because he had to return to England for a cartilage operation. He was immensely valuable to Warwickshire for ten years, scoring 1,000 runs ten times, his best aggregate being 1,894 runs (57.39) in 1970 and in 1972 he scored 8 centuries to equal the county record. In 1968 at Trent Bridge against Nottinghamshire, he added 402 with Billy Ibadulla, a record for Warwickshire's fourth wicket (Kanhai making 253), and in 1974 put on a world record second-wicket stand of 465 with John Jameson against Gloucestershire at Edgbaston, his own contribution being 213 not out.

First-class career (1955-77): 28,639 runs (49.29) including 83 centuries, 18 wickets (55.11), 315 catches and 7 stumpings
Test matches (79): 6,227 runs (47.53) including 15 centuries, 0-85 and 50 catches

KENTISH, Esmond Seymour Maurice (b.1916)

Jamaica and Oxford University

A well-built right-arm fast bowler, Esmond Kentish played in two Tests against England, one in 1947/8 and the other in 1953/4. At Kingston in his second match he took 5 for 49 in 29 overs in the second innings, by bowling medium-fast at or outside the leg-stump to an on-side arc of seven men.

First-class career (1947-57): 109 runs (13.62) and 78 wickets (26.71)
Test matches (2): 1 run (1.00), 8 wickets (22.25) and 1 catch

KING, Collis Llewellyn (b.1951)

Barbados and Glamorgan

Though he played in four Test matches by the time of the 1979 Prudential World Cup Final at Lords, it was not until that occasion that many people outside Barbados appreciated quite what an explosive hitter of a cricket ball Collis King could be. Coming in when the West Indies were struggling at 99 for 4, he made a superb 86 in 66 balls, adding 139 with Viv Richards in 21 spectacular overs and quite outshining his partner, probably the finest contemporary batsman. A right-hander who, whatever the contest, wastes little time before launching a tallish, spare but muscular frame into all kinds of exotic drives, cuts, hooks and pulls, King also bowls useful medium pace with a busy but far from classical action. He fields well, with that infectious enthusiasm he brings to any match. He first appeared for Barbados in 1972/3, and played as a specially registered player for Glamorgan in 1977. On his first tour of England in 1976, King hit 6 centuries in his 1,320 runs (55.00), the highest being 163 at Northampton, and took 27 wickets (34.37). In three Tests he made 167 runs (41.75), in the second Test at Headingley making a valuable 58 (50 off 39 balls) in the second innings out of 196. In 1979 he was banned from playing for Ponthlyddyn in the North Wales League because he was too good! In one afternoon match in 1978 he made 283.

First-class career (1972-): 5,030 runs (38.99) including 11 centuries, and 113 wickets (31.25)
Test matches (4): 211 runs (35.16), 2 wickets (56.50) and 3 catches

KING, Frank McDonald (b.1926)

Barbados and Trinidad

A right-arm fast bowler, Frank King received his opportunities but failed to establish himself. He toured India in 1952/3 and New Zealand in 1955/6, and at home played against England in 1953/4 and Australia in 1954/5. He possessed much stamina and bowled a considerable number of bumpers but only in his first series, against India in 1952/3, was he consistently effective, taking 17 wickets (28.23); at Port of Spain, in the third match, he took 5 for 74 in the first innings.

First-class career (1947-57): 237 runs (9.11) and 90 wickets (28.75)
Test matches (14): 116 runs (8.28), 29 wickets (39.96) and 5 catches

KING, Lester Anthony (b.1939)

Jamaica and Bengal

A bustling right-arm fast-medium bowler, Lester King had a short but productive Test career. He appeared twice against India in 1961/2 and once against England in 1967/8, in the former match, at Kingston, facing a total of 253, India lost 5 wickets for 26 runs in about an hour, all to King, who finished with 5 for 46. He toured England in 1963, taking 47 wickets (27.31) but, overshadowed by Charlie Griffith and Wes Hall, was not selected for any of the Tests. He also toured India in 1966/7 and Australia and New Zealand in 1968/9.

First-class career (1961-9): 1,404 runs (20.64) and 142 wickets (31.42)
Test matches (2): 41 runs (10.25), 9 wickets (17.11) and 2 catches

LASHLEY, Patrick Douglas (b.1937)

Barbados

A slightly built left-handed batsman, very restricted in his forcing strokes, an occasional medium-pace bowler and an excellent field, 'Peter' Lashley scored 200 for Barbados against Guyana at Bridgetown in 1959/60, thus earning a place to Australia in 1960/61, but he was not a success, averaging only 19.40 although he made 41 in the very exciting fifth Test at Melbourne. He toured England in 1966 and in the third Test at Trent Bridge took over three hours for 49.

First-class career (1957-75): 4,932 runs (41.44) including 8 centuries and 27 wickets (35.48)
Test matches (4): 159 runs (22.71), 1-1 and 4 catches

LEGALL, Ralph Archibald (b.1926)

Barbados and Trinidad

A competent wicket-keeper and right-handed batsman, Legall's sole Test experience was against India in the Caribbean in 1952/3.

First-class career (1946-58): 485 runs (22.04) and 42 dismissals (32 ct, 10 st.)
Test matches (4): 50 runs (10.00) and 9 dismissals (8 ct, 1 st.)

LEWIS, Desmond Michael (b.1946)

Jamaica

An accomplished right-handed batsman and wicket-keeper of high potential, Desmond Lewis had a meteoric Test career. His sole Test series was against India in the Caribbean in 1970/71 when his diligent batting was more than useful. In his first Test, at Georgetown, he made 81 not out; in his second, at Bridgetown, 88 as opening partner for Roy Fredericks; and in his third, at Port of Spain, 72, again as opening batsman. In the next series he was superseded by Deryck Murray.

First-class career (1970-76): 1,623 runs (31.82) and 78 dismissals (67 ct, 11 st.)
Test matches (3): 259 runs (86.33) and 8 dismissals (8 ct.)

LLOYD, Clive Hubert (b.1944)

Guyana and Lancashire

A tall and commanding left-handed batsman and useful right-arm medium-paced bowler, Clive Lloyd revealed a quite phenomenal speed and reach in the covers in his early days and he has throughout a distinguished career thrilled spectators all over the world with his batting and, indeed, with his sheer presence. Instantly recognizable with his heavy spectacles, short curly hair, lean gangling figure and loping walk with head bowed, he explodes into sudden exciting action – whether swooping to cut off an apparent four and throw down the wicket, diving to take a slip catch, or hitting the ball with murderous

Clive Lloyd

power, using a heavy bat to bludgeon fours and sixes with basically orthodox drives, hooks and cuts. Despite persistent pain in his knees – which caused him to move from the covers to the slips in his later years – he remained a most successful batsman, especially on the big occasion, and he became a calm and able captain who usually got the most from a talented side and who twice led West Indies to success in the Prudential World Cup Final at Lord's. A cousin of Lance Gibbs, 'Hubert' first appeared in first-class cricket for British Guiana in 1963/4 and first played for Lancashire in 1968. His first Test series was in India in 1966/7 and in his first game at Bombay scored 82 and 78 not out. His second innings was a masterly performance by one so young – he added 102 with Gary Sobers to win the match on a turning wicket. In the three Tests he scored 227 runs (56.75). Lloyd has toured England in 1969, 1973 and 1976. His 904 runs (56.50) in 1969 included 201 not out against Glamorgan at Swansea and, although he disappointed in the Test matches, his fielding was always worth scores of runs. In 1973 he made 318 runs (63.60) in the three Tests and hit 1,128 runs on the entire tour (59.36). His 132 in the first Test at The Oval ended a period of twenty Tests in which the West Indies had failed to win. During the World Cup Final at Lord's in 1975 Lloyd scored a superb matchwinning century, and a year later made 1,363 first-class runs (61.95) on the tour but only 296 runs (32.88) in the Test series. For the second time he scored 201 not out against Glamorgan at Swansea, on this occasion in 120 minutes, equalling the record for the fastest double hundred in first-class cricket. He had first met England at home in 1967/8, making 369 runs (52.71), which included 118 in the first Test at Port of Spain and 113 not out at Bridgetown. He marked his first appearance against Australia in 1968/9 by scoring 129 at Brisbane and against Australia at home in 1972/3 he made 178 out of 366 at Georgetown. His most prolific series was his first as captain in India in 1974/5 when he scored 636 runs in the Tests (79.50) including 163 in the first match at Bangalore, reaching his century in only 85 balls, and a superb 242 not out in the fifth Test at Bombay. This was the true Clive Lloyd – an explosive matchwinner, but never a consistent grinder out of records. Captaincy had added responsibility to his batting and, although defeated heavily by Australia in 1975/6, Lloyd scored 469 runs (46.90) in the six Tests, including 149 at Perth and 102 at Melbourne. His tenth Test hundred came in his fiftieth Test, against India at Bridgetown in 1975/6, and the following year he made 151 on the same ground against Pakistan, hitting 3 sixes and 21 fours. He resigned as captain on the eve of the third Test at Georgetown against Australia in 1977/8 after disagreement with the selectors over the bitter Packer issue, but returned successfully in the World Cup in 1979 and led the West Indies again in Australia the following winter. A knee operation in Australia during the tour successfully dealt with a recurring problem, and for the next three years he played as well as he had ever done. He hit a beautiful hundred in Adelaide, and in England in 1980 also scored one in the Old Trafford Test, a performance which, as Lancashire was his second home, he was especially pleased with. In the 1980/81 season, following a successful tour of Pakistan, he played nine first-class innings in the West Indies and failed to reach 50 only once: when he was run out for 49! He averaged 76 in the Test series against England – hitting a marvellous 100 in the Barbados Test – and 172.50 in the Shell Shield. He held seven catches in the Tests, all in the slips, to show that his reactions were as quick and his hands as sure as ever. When the period of West Indian supremacy in world cricket, which had coincided with his captaincy, seemed in danger of being threatened during the final Test against Australia at Adelaide in 1981/2, Lloyd added a matchwinning 77 not out to his first-innings 58 and was carried off the field on the shoulders of his fast bowlers, the main cause of the team's extraordinary run of success. The action, however, signified the importance of Lloyd's calm captaincy. By the end of this series, Lloyd had led the West Indies in 46 Tests, the record for all countries. In England he has frequently been a matchwinner for Lancashire, notably in the Gillette Cup. He became captain of Lancashire in 1981 and continued to make the county his domestic base. He has scored 1,000 runs in a season 14 times (10 in England).

First-class career (1963-): 27,334 runs (48.98) including 70 centuries, 114 wickets (36.00) and 325 catches
Test matches (85): 5,831 runs (43.84) including 14 centuries, 10 wickets (62.20) and 63 catches

McMORRIS, Easton Dudley Ashton St John (b.1935)

Jamaica

A right-handed opening batsman who could be difficult to dismiss when well set, McMorris did not quite fulfil expectations for West Indies; he was inclined to weakness against high-class swing bowling. A year after his first-class debut he scored 114 for Jamaica against the strong Duke of Norfolk's side at Kingston in 1956/7. He toured England in 1963 and 1966, and at home played against Pakistan in 1957/8, England in 1959/60 and India in 1961/2. In England he made 878 runs (36.58) in 1966, but each time he fared poorly in the Tests. By far his best series was against India in 1961/2: he made 439 runs (58.16), including 125 at Kingston when he added 255 in a record second-wicket stand with Rohan Kanhai.

First-class career (1956-72): 5,906 runs (42.18) including 18 centuries
Test matches (13): 564 runs (26.85) including 1 century, and 5 catches

McWATT, Clifford Aubrey (b.1922)

British Guiana

A competent wicket-keeper, Clifford McWatt was a left-handed batsman who could hit brilliantly, as when scoring 56 and 123 not out for British Guiana against Trinidad at Port of Spain in 1946/7. He appeared as first-string 'keeper against England in 1953/4 and Australia in 1954/5.

First-class career (1943-57): 1,673 runs (28.84) including 2 centuries, and 51 dismissals (45 ct, 6 st.)
Test matches (6): 202 runs (28.85) and 10 dismissals (9 ct, 1 st.)

MADRAY, Ivan Samuel (b.1934)

British Guiana

A useful all-rounder, being a right-handed batsman and leg-break bowler, Madray's only Tests were against Pakistan in the Caribbean in 1957/8.

First-class career (1954-8): 73 runs (9.12) and 16 wickets (38.87)
Test matches (2): 3 runs (1.00), 0-108 and 2 catches

MARSHALL, Malcolm Denzil (b.1958)

Barbados and Hampshire

A lithe, whippy fast bowler with great potential, and an improving right-handed batsman, Malcolm Marshall made his first appearance for Barbados in the final match of the 1977/8 Shell Shield competition and took 6 for 77 against Jamaica at Bridgetown. His ability was such that he was taken to India in 1978/9 with only this one first-class match behind him and played in three Tests although the slow wickets drew all his youthful sting. However, his success for Barbados in the 1978/9 Shell Shield persuaded the West Indian selectors to prefer him to Wayne Daniel in their Prudential World Cup squad. Marshall was not selected for any of the matches but in his first season of county cricket he several times bowled with genuine pace and hostility to show that he would be a worthy successor to Andy Roberts as a matchwinning opening bowler. His right-arm action lacks a classical final stretch and is not quite side-on enough to satisfy the purists but he has a natural rhythm which gives him the pace to hustle the batsman. By the end of 1982 he had been on five major tours for the West Indies, plus one to Zimbabwe, but played in only 12 Tests, being considered only first reserve for the quartet of Roberts, Holding, Croft and Garner. However, after his performance for Hampshire in 1982 there was little doubt that he would become a regular member of the West Indies side through the eighties. He was easily the most successful bowler in county cricket that season with 134 wickets, the most ever taken by a county bowler in a 22-match Championship. His only

Malcolm Marshall

full Test series before this had been a successful one on the slow wickets of Pakistan in 1980/81, when he took 25 wickets on the tour and 13 in the Tests at 24 each. His batting has steadily improved and he could attain the status of a true all-rounder. His 633 runs for Hampshire in 1982 suggested that he would thrive on greater batting responsibility.

First-class career (1978-): 2,666 runs (19.60) including 2 centuries, and 492 wickets (17.94)
Test matches (12): 126 runs (8.40), 34 wickets (31.85) and 5 catches

MARSHALL, Norman Edgar (b.1924)

Barbados and Trinidad

A useful right-handed batsman and off-break bowler, Norman Marshall's sole Test was the third against Australia at Georgetown in 1954/5 when he scored 0 and 8 and took 2 for 62. In a short first-class career confined to the Caribbean, he made 1,110 runs (27.75) and took 78 wickets (33.51). He is elder brother of the better known Roy Marshall.

First-class career (1940-59): 1,337 runs (30.38) including 2 centuries, and 90 wickets (31.72)

MARSHALL, Roy Edwin (b.1930)

Barbados and Hampshire

An attractive and forceful right-handed opening batsman with a variety of strokes, the tall and bespectacled Roy Marshall was also a useful change-bowler of off-breaks and a very good field. He made his debut for Barbados at fifteen, and at nineteen he scored 191 for Barbados against British Guiana at Bridgetown in 1949/50. He toured England in 1950 with much success, as the youngest member, making 1,117 runs (39.89), including 188 at Leicester but, owing to the great strength of the batting, was not selected for any of the Tests. In Australasia in 1951/2 his best score from Tests was 30, although he scored 114 against New South Wales at Sydney and 102 not out against Otago at Dunedin. In 1951 he became professional to Lowerhouse in the Lancashire League, two years later began his qualification for Hampshire and his international career was ended at twenty-one since at that time the West Indies did not call on players engaged in English first-class cricket. For nearly twenty years, as an essentially adventurous batsman, he was a 'box-office' draw for his adopted county and, on his day, the best bowlers in the world found it difficult to bowl to him; against anyone of less than high calibre, he was a complete destroyer.

First-class career (1945-72): 35,725 runs (35.94) including 68 centuries, 176 wickets (28.93) and 293 catches
Test matches (4): 143 runs (20.42), 0-15 and 1 catch

MARTIN, Frank Reginald (1893-1967)

Jamaica

A left-handed opening batsman, 'Freddie' Martin watched the ball closely and hit hard off the back foot. Steady, calm and sober, he was a difficult man to dislodge; and his slow bowling often kept down the runs. On his first-class debut for Jamaica in 1925/6 he scored 195 against Barbados at Bridgetown and, the following year, made his career-highest, 204 not out, against the Hon. Lionel Tennyson's team at Kingston. He toured England in 1928 and 1933, and Australia in 1930/31, and played at home against England in 1929/30. In the former year he headed the batting in the first-ever Test series with 175 runs (29.16) and on the tour scored more runs than any of his colleagues, 1,481 (34.44), besides taking 22 wickets. In Australia he carried his bat for 123 in the fifth Test at Sydney, batting for about six hours, adding 152 with George Headley for the second wicket, and showing marked skill with the wicket becoming treacherous; Australia lost for the first time to West Indies. During his second visit to England, after scoring well and taking wickets in his first six matches, he wrenched an ankle and missed the Tests.

First-class career (1925-33): 3,589 runs (37.78) including 6 centuries, and 74 wickets (42.55)
Test matches (9): 486 runs (28.58) including 1 century, 8 wickets (77.37) and 2 catches

MARTINDALE, Emmanuel Alfred (1909-72)

Barbados

A small man for a fast bowler – 5ft 8½ins – 'Manny' Martindale was an impressive spearhead with an excellent right-arm action and a dangerous in-swinger; his pace could be terrific. He toured England in 1933 and 1939, and played against England at home in 1934/5. In the second Test at Old Trafford in 1933 he and Learie Constantine caused a sensation by bowling a form of bodyline – short-pitched bowling towards the batsman's body with an accompanying arc of leg-side fieldsmen – 'Manny' taking 5 for 73 and splitting Walter Hammond's chin in the process. In this series he took 14 wickets (17.92) and on the tour, 103 wickets (20.98), three times taking 8 wickets in an innings. He captured 19 wickets (12.57) against England in 1934/5. In the first Test at Bridgetown his 'haul' was 3 for 39 and 5 for 22. In England in 1939 he fell away in pace and accuracy and endured a poor season. By far his best performance as a batsman was a well-struck 134 against Trinidad at Bridgetown in 1935/6, when he added 255 with E.A.V. Williams for the eighth wicket which remains a West Indian record. For some years he was a professional with Burnley in the Lancashire League, and on his return to Barbados, became a coach.

First-class career (1931-39): 972 runs (15.18) including 1 century, and 205 wickets (25.64)
Test matches (10): 58 runs (5.27), 37 wickets (21.72) and 5 catches

MATTIS, Everton Hugh (b.1957)

Jamaica

Tall, a cultured right-hand batsman, particularly strong off the back foot, and a useful off-break bowler, Everton Mattis did not quite live up to his distinguished West Indian Christian name, nor the high hopes held of him, when selected to replace Alvin Kallicharan in the West Indian team against England in the home series of 1980/81. His best effort in the four Test series was a solid 71 at Antigua. He had served an apprenticeship in Shield cricket, scoring an impressive 132 against Guyana in 1980 and, although not selected to tour Australia in 1981/2, he was Jamaica's highest scorer in the Shell Shield in both 1980/81 and 1981/2. He threw away any further chance of playing Test cricket by agreeing to tour South Africa in 1982/3, pleading financial hardship as his reason for going.

First-class career (1977-): 1,840 runs (38.33) including 3 centuries, and 8 wickets (11.12)
Test matches (4): 145 runs (29.00), 0-14 and 3 catches

MENDONCA, Ivor Leon (b.1934)

British Guiana

A capable wicket-keeper and right-handed batsman, Ivor Mendonca replaced the injured Jackie Hendriks as 'keeper in two Tests against India in 1961/2 and, in his first Test at Kingston, hit 78, adding 127 for the seventh wicket with Gary Sobers. He also claimed 5 dismissals (4 caught and 1 stumped), but he never represented West Indies again, there being an abundance of wicket-keeping batsmen available.

First-class career (1958-62): 407 runs (31.30) and 30 dismissals (25 ct, 5 st.)
Test matches (2): 81 runs (40.50) and 10 dismissals (8 ct, 2 st.)

MERRY, Cyril Arthur (1911-64)

Trinidad

At his best a brilliant right-handed batsman, Cyril Merry toured England in 1933, making 856 runs (28.53) which included 146 against Warwickshire at Edgbaston when, by exhilarating batting, he and George Headley added 228 in two hours for the fifth wicket. He met with little success, however, in the Tests.

First-class career (1929-39): 1,547 runs (27.14) including 1 century, and 33 wickets (22.60)
Test matches (2): 34 runs (8.50) and 1 catch

MILLER, Roy (1924-)

Jamaica

A competent all-rounder, a right-handed batsman and fast-medium bowler, Roy Miller's sole Test appearance was in the fourth match at Georgetown against India in 1952/3 when he scored 23 and took 0 for 28.

First-class career (1950-54): 231 runs (25.66) and 14 wickets (45.00)

MOODIE (or MUDIE), George H. (b.1915)

Jamaica

A left-handed batsman and medium paced or slow spin bowler, George Moodie scored 94 and 60 not out respectively in Jamaica's two matches against MCC in 1934/5; and his sole Test was the fourth at Kingston on this tour, when he scored 5 and took 3 for 40.

First-class career (1931-52): 578 runs (22.23) and 42 wickets (35.45)

MURRAY, David Anthony (b.1950)

Barbados

A right-handed wicket-keeper/batsman with cricketing blood of high pedigree in his veins, David Murray has only been prevented from playing a substantial number of Tests by the rivalry of his namesake Deryck. First choice for Barbados for many seasons, he toured England in 1973 and in the short tour scored 285 runs (35.62), including 107 not out against Kent at Canterbury. In twenty games on the tour he took 26 catches and made 5 stumpings. Belatedly given a chance in Test cricket in 1978 when his namesake was dropped because of the row about the Packer players being unavailable to tour India, David caught 6 and stumped 3 in a capable display behind the stumps in the last three Tests against Australia, and again proved his ability in India in 1978/9 with 18 victims. In this series of six Tests he scored 261 runs (29.00), including 84 in the first Test at Bombay when he added 167 for the fifth wicket with Alvin Kalicharran after an early batting collapse. In India's only innings in the fifth Test at Delhi, he took 5 catches. Against Central Zone at Jamshedpur, he made his career-highest score: 206 not out. He finally took over from his namesake Deryck as senior West Indies wicket-keeper in 1980/81, playing a useful part in successes against Pakistan away, and England at home. Against Pakistan he scored 142 runs in six innings, despite a pair at Multan, having started with a valuable 50 in the first Test at Lahore.

First-class career (1970-): 4,158 runs (31.98) including 7 centuries, and 285 dismissals (254 ct, 31 st.)
Test matches (19): 601 runs (21.46) and 62 dismissals (57 ct, 5 st.)

Deryck Murray

MURRAY, Deryck Lance (b.1943)

Trinidad, Cambridge University, Nottinghamshire and Warwickshire

A cricketer of marvellous composure, Deryck Murray was a steady member of the West Indies team for upwards of fifteen years and a strong influence on the game in the Caribbean as the leader of a movement to increase the earnings of leading West Indian players and to give them a greater say in cricketing affairs at home. Quiet, reserved, diminutive and boyish, Murray looked barely out of his school clothes when Frank Worrell entrusted him with the duties of the main wicket-keeper/batsman role in England in 1963. He responded with a record 24 victims in the series (22 caught and 2 stumped) and afterwards proved a reliable wicket-keeper who seldom missed a chance, though without approaching the effervescent brilliance of many of the finest 'keepers. As a right-handed batsman he was a watchful, determined player, limited in the power if not the range of his strokes, but always liable to get runs when they were needed. He played for Cambridge University in his two years there in 1965 and 1966, proving more successful in the middle at Fenner's than he was in the examination room. However he later got his degree at Nottingham University and played for the county from 1966 to 1969. He three times scored 1,000 runs in an English season, including 1,358 runs in 1966 when he made his highest score of 166 not out against Surrey at The Oval. His highest score in a Test was 91 against India in the fifth Test at Bombay in 1974/5 when he added 250 with Clive Lloyd, the West Indian record for the sixth wicket against India. For a short while he opened the batting for West Indies but the experiment was not a success. Nevertheless Deryck Murray was an outstanding case of a cricketer making the most of his ability: behind the calm, gentle and almost retiring exterior lay a calculating and determined character. He was the first secretary of the West Indian Cricketers Association and he is the only West Indian to have claimed over 100 Test victims behind the stumps. When he was left out of the side against England at Port of Spain in 1980/81, local spectators boycotted the match, and vandals damaged the pitch in protest.

First-class career (1960-81): 13,289 runs (28.33) including 10 centuries, and 849 dismissals (741 ct, 108 st.)
Test matches (62): 1,993 runs (22.90) and 189 dismissals (181 ct, 8 st.)

NANAN, Ranjie (b.1953)

Trinidad

A right-arm off-break bowler and useful right-hand batsman, Ranjie Nanan is a policeman who would have been seen in more cricket for West Indies than his one Test in Faisalabad in 1980/81, had he not played in an era when the islands produced a phenomenal number of outstanding fast bowlers. In 1981/2 he had a record number of wickets in the Shell Shield, 32 from five matches, taking all his wickets away from the relaid pitch at the Queens Park Oval, once a haven for the spinner. In his sole Test to date at Faisalabad, he scored 8 and 8, took 2 for 54 and 2 for 37, and held 2 catches, playing a valuable part in the West Indies victory.

First-class career (1973-): 1,111 runs (19.15) and 193 wickets (21.76)

NEBLETT, James M. (1901-deceased)

Barbados and British Guiana

A competent all-rounder, batting left-handed, bowling medium pace and invariably keeping a good length, James Neblett toured England in 1928 but with little success, and his sole Test appearance was in the third match at Georgetown against England in 1934/5 when he scored 11 not out and 5 and took 1 for 75.

First-class career (1925-39): 526 runs (18.78) and 29 wickets (41.55)

NOREIGA, Jack Mollison (b.1936)

Trinidad

As an ageing right-arm off-break bowler, Jack Noreiga replaced Lance Gibbs – temporarily out of form – in the series against India in 1970/71 with dramatic success. In the second match at Port of Spain, which was dominated by spin bowlers, he captured 9 for 95 in 49.4 overs in the first innings of 352. In the second innings of the fifth match he took 5 for 129 in 53.4 overs on a turning wicket, most of the runs being scored by Sunil Gavaskar. He did not represent West Indies again.

First-class career (1961-75): 181 runs (9.05) and 68 wickets (29.67)
Test matches (4): 11 runs (3.66), 17 wickets (29.00) and 2 catches

NUNES, Robert Karl (1894-1958)

Jamaica

A fine left-handed opening batsman with a sound defence and plenty of stroke power, Karl Nunes was in the eleven at Dulwich College. He toured England with the 1923 West Indian team as vice-captain and again in 1928 as captain and wicket-keeper, when West Indies was first accorded Test status, but scored only 87 in six Test innings. At home in 1926/7, he hit 200 not out and 108 in successive games for Jamaica against the Hon. Lionel Tennyson's team. His was a notable swan-song: in the fourth Test against England at Kingston in 1929/30, when he was again captain (each Test saw a different West Indian captain), he scored 66 and 92 as opener. When West Indies were set 836 runs to win, he added a gallant 228 with George Headley for the second wicket; then the clouds began banking over the Blue Mountains, the rains came and the match was saved. A member of the Jamaica Board of Control from its inception in 1926, and president of the West Indies Board of Control from 1945 until 1952, he received the CBE for public services.

First-class career (1920-30): 2,695 runs (31.34) including 6 centuries
Test matches (4): 245 runs (30.62) and 2 catches

NURSE, Seymour McDonald (b.1933)

Barbados

A tall, powerfully built right-handed stroke-playing batsman, a superb driver off the back foot, an occasional off-spin bowler and a specialist close-to-the-wicket field, Seymour Nurse made a considerable impact on West Indian cricket early in his career, lost his place for a time, then re-emerged as a Test cricketer worthy to rank with the best of his generation. He made 128 not out in his second first-class match, against Jamaica at Kingston in 1957/8; and 213 against MCC at Bridgetown in 1959/60, when in his first Test he hit 70 against England at Kingston. He toured Australia in 1960/61, England in 1963 and 1966, India in 1966/7 and Australasia in 1968/9, and at home played against England in 1967/8 besides 1959/60, India in 1961/2 and Australia in 1964/5. Injured and taking to crutches in Australia in 1960/61, he pulled a muscle early in the 1963 England tour and did not make the Test side. In the fourth Test against Australia at Bridgetown in 1964/5 he scored 201 and finally established himself in England in 1966 with 1,105 runs (44.20), including 501 runs (62.62) in the Tests; in the fourth match at Headingley he made 137. Against England at home in 1967/8 he made 434 runs (43.40) and, the next winter in Australia, he registered 348 runs (34.80) in the series, followed by complete dominance of New Zealand's attack: in the first match at Auckland he hit 95 and 168 (in 3 hours 35 minutes) and in the third at Christchurch, 258, his career-highest, a magnificent eight hour innings in a total of 417. On this final tour he made 1,520 runs (52.41), including 4 centuries.

First-class career (1958-72): 9,489 runs (43.93) including 26 centuries, and 12 wickets (32.41)
Test matches (29): 2,523 runs (47.60) including 6 centuries, 0-7 and 21 catches

PADMORE, Albert Leroy (b.1946)

Barbados

A tall off-spinner with an action clearly reminiscent of, and modelled on, that of the great Lance Gibbs, Albert Padmore was unfortunate to become the best off-spinner in the Caribbean at a time when the islands were producing an unprecedented number of top-class fast bowlers. After making his Test debut against India at home in 1975/6 he toured England as the main spinner in 1976 but, in a very dry summer when spinners were prospering, he played in only one Test and even then was granted only 3 overs! Padmore, however, took 59 wickets (23.40) on the tour and became contracted along with bigger names to World Series Cricket.

First-class career (1972-): 544 runs (12.95) and 188 wickets (29.27)
Test matches (2): 8 runs (8.00) and 1-135

PAIRAUDEAU, Bruce Hamilton (b.1931)

British Guiana and Northern Districts

A bespectacled and stylish right-handed opening batsman, Bruce Pairaudeau scored his maiden century, 130, against Jamaica in 1947/8 aged 16 years 5 months: his first-class debut had been the previous season, a month before his sixteenth birthday. He hit 3 consecutive centuries in 1952/3, including 115 at Port of Spain against India on his Test debut. Subsequently, although he remained quite a heavy scorer for British Guiana and toured New Zealand in 1955/6 and England in 1957, and at home played against England and India, he did not fulfil his early promise in Tests. He had several seasons as a professional in the Lancashire League, and from 1958 until 1967 he played for Northern Districts in New Zealand.

First-class career (1946-67): 4,930 runs (32.01) including 11 centuries
Test matches (13): 454 runs (21.61) including 1 century, 0-3 and 6 catches

PARRY, Derek Ricaldo (b.1954)

Leeward Islands and Cambridgeshire

A right-arm off-spin bowler who turns the ball prodigiously and a determined right-handed batsman, Derek Parry comes from the tiny island of Nevis, only 36 square miles in size, and was the second man from this Leeward island to represent the West Indies. First representing the Combined Leeward and Windward Islands in the Shell Shield in 1977, he had an outstanding season in 1978, taking 9 wickets in the first Shield match against Barbados (7 for 100 in the first innings) and making 94 in the same match. He had a nightmarish start to his Test career, being out first ball in the first 1978 Test against Australia and bowling a wide first ball when called on to turn his arm. Returning to Port of Spain for the fourth Test, however, after the World Series players had left the team, Parry made sure that West Indies would win the series by making 65 in the second innings and then by taking 5 for 15 in 10.3 overs, helping to bowl out Australia for 94. All 5 wickets were taken in a single spell of 4.4 overs, 4 of them bowled. In India in 1978/9 he scored 193 runs in the six Tests but his 9 wickets were very expensive. In further tours of England, Australia and Pakistan from 1979 to 1981, he suffered the frustration of never being seriously considered for the Test team because of the policy of playing four fast bowlers, and even his 40 wickets at a cost of only 20 each against the English counties in 1980 did not change things. He was, at least, well paid for his role as a reserve.

First-class career (1975-): 2,263 runs (26.31) and 231 wickets (28.76)
Test matches (12): 381 runs (22.41), 23 wickets (40.69) and 4 catches

PASSAILAIGUE, Clarence C. (1902-72)

Jamaica

A very good right-handed forcing batsman, Clarence Passailaigue was unfortunate in missing selection for the first team to visit Australia in 1930/31 because in the previous home season he had hit 183 for Jamaica against MCC at Kingston and in his sole Test, the fourth match against England, also at Kingston, had made 44 and 2 not out, held 3 catches and taken 0 for 15. He is best remembered, however, for his outstanding performance of 261 not out for All Jamaica against the Hon. Lionel Tennyson's side again at Kingston in 1931/2. The Island amassed 702 for 5 wickets and with George Headley he added 487 in an unfinished sixth-wicket partnership, which remains the world record for that wicket.

First-class career (1929-39): 788 runs (56.53) including 2 centuries

PHILLIP, Norbert (b.1949)

Windward Islands and Essex

A tall, fit and spirited all-rounder, Norbert Phillip is a lively fast-medium right-arm bowler and hard hitting right-handed batsman. Spare-framed and seldom injured, he has performed with great consistency for his native Dominica, the Windward Islands, the Combined Islands and for Essex, since first appearing in first-class cricket in 1970. But his great advance really came in 1978: he averaged 76.66 in scoring 230 runs in the Shell Shield, took 21 wickets (17.71), including 10 in the match against Guyana when he also scored 70 and 90 not out, won his Test cap against Australia, and had an excellent first season with Essex. To crown a hectic year he had a successful tour of India in 1978/9, taking 19 wickets in six Tests at 34.21, including 4 for 48 and 3 for 37 on the fast Madras wicket, besides making 177 runs (35.40). This followed a successful Test debut against Australia at Georgetown where he took 6 for 140 in the match. For Essex Norbert Phillip has fitted comfortably into the shoes left behind by his fellow West Indian Keith Boyce, taking 71 wickets (22.40) in 1978 and scoring 645 runs (26.87), including 134 against Gloucestershire, and in 1979 playing a prominent all-round role in Essex's double of Schweppes County Championship and Benson and Hedges Cup. None of this sudden success has gone to the head of a likeable, capable and widely experienced cricketer. He also played a prominent role in Essex's John Player League success in 1981, hitting violently to play the matchwinning innings in the decisive last match at The Oval and, when the Windward Islands entered the Shell Shield under their own banner for the first time in 1982, he took 21 wickets at 16 and averaged 31 with the bat. A whole-hearted cricketer and a true all-rounder.

First-class career (1969-): 5,672 runs (24.87) including 1 century, and 530 wickets (24.85)
Test matches (9): 297 runs (29.70), 28 wickets (37.18) and 5 catches

PIERRE, Lance Richard (b.1921)

Trinidad

A tall, well-built right-arm seam bowler, Lance Pierre moved the ball either way, mostly out-swinging. He toured England in 1950 but was not selected for any of the Tests. His sole Test was in the third match against England at Georgetown in 1947/8 when he did not bat and took 0 for 28.

First-class career (1940-50): 131 runs (6.23) and 102 wickets (24.76)

RAE, Allan Fitzroy (b.1922)

Jamaica

A modest, friendly and generous-hearted man and a patient and wholly commendable left-handed opening batsman, very safe in defence and a strong driver, Allan Rae provided solidity at the start of West Indies' innings from 1948 until 1953, when the claims of his legal career caused his early retirement from the first-class game. Quite tall and broad-shouldered, he toured India in 1948/9, England in 1950 and Australasia in 1951/2, and at home played against India in 1952/3. Before touring England in 1950, he had batted in only three first-class innings in the Caribbean, and against Trinidad at Port of Spain in 1946/7 he had scored 111 and 128. His initial Test century, 104, was in the second Test against India at Bombay in 1948/9; in the fourth match at Madras he contributed 109, sharing in an opening partnership of 239 with Jeff Stollmeyer, which led to an innings victory. This was the first victory over India, and the opening stand has never been bettered by West Indies. In the series Rae made 374 runs (53.42). In the 1950 series against England – when West Indian cricket 'came of age' – he reached 377 runs (62.83) in the series, including 106 in the second match at Lord's, when the West Indies won their first Test in England, and 109 in the fourth match at The Oval, when he added 172 with Frank Worrell for the second wicket. In all first-class matches on this tour Rae made 1,330 runs (39.11), including 4 centuries, the highest of which was 179 against Sussex at Hove, which remained his career-highest. He had a rather disappointing series in Australia in 1951/2. In the second Test against New Zealand at Auckland, however, he hit 99, and his opening stand with Stollmeyer was worth 197 in less than three and a half hours. His father, E.A. Rae, toured England in 1928, but was not selected for the Tests. A barrister, he has been a prominent figure in Jamaican and West Indies cricket administration since retirement. In November 1981 he was appointed president of the West Indies Cricket Board.

Allan Rae (right) with Jeffrey Stollmeyer

First-class career (1946-60): 4,798 runs (39.65) including 17 centuries
Test matches (15): 1,016 runs (46.18) including 4 centuries, and 10 catches

RAMADHIN, Sonny (b.1930)

Trinidad, Lancashire and Lincolnshire

With Alf Valentine, Sonny Ramadhin gripped the attention of the world of cricket on the 1950 England tour, when West Indies won her first-ever series here. A friendless orphan, he was helped as a budding cricketer and in other ways by a Barbadian Inter-Colonial cricketer. The first East Indian to represent the West Indies, and only 5ft 4in tall, he was a right-arm off-break and leg-break bowler of impeccable length and line, excellent flight and subtle variations of pace, who could hide his intentions so well that wicket-keepers could rarely tell which way he would turn the ball; sometimes he would even succeed with the plain straight ball. Both his leg-break and the off-break, his more regular ball, were finger spun rather than wrist spun, yet appeared to come from the back of the hand. Two trial games before the 1950 England tour were his only experience of first-class cricket, yet he took 135 wickets (14.88), and in the Tests alone his 'haul' was 26 wickets (23.23) from the four matches. When West Indies won for the first time in England – at Lord's in the second match – Ramadhin took 11 for 152 in 115 overs, 50 of which were maidens. His bowling (and that of Valentine) was brilliant, and once the success had been gained on the final afternoon, there was impromptu calypso singing and dancing on the hallowed turf. 'Those two little pals of mine, Ramadhin and Valentine' became a widely sung calypso. Until 1961, when he was supplanted by Lance Gibbs, he was regular choice for his country. He toured Australasia in 1951/2, New Zealand in 1955/6, England again in 1957, India and Pakistan in 1958/9 and Australia in 1960/61, and at home he played against India in 1952/3, England in 1953/4 and 1959/60, and Australia in 1954/5. He tended to be more effective the first time that he came up against an

Sonny Ramadhin

opposing country, although Pakistan and New Zealand never mastered him. In New Zealand in 1955/6 he took more wickets in the Tests and all first-class games than anyone else – 20 wickets (15.80) and 40 wickets (16.40) respectively. In the first innings of the first Test at Dunedin he took 6 for 23 in 21.2 overs. Against England in 1953/4 he was the most successful bowler on either side, in the five matches taking 23 wickets (24.30) in 304.3 overs, of which 133 were maidens. In England in 1957 he took 7 for 49 in 31 overs in the first innings of the first Test at Edgbaston, being as mesmeric as ever, but in the second innings he had a traumatic experience at the hands of Peter May and Colin Cowdrey who decided to play him as an off-spinner and added 411 in one of the most famous stands in Test history. Ramadhin bowled a record 98 overs and England almost won a match they had appeared certain to lose. Ramadhin was never so effective in Test cricket again, although he did take 17 wickets (28.88) against England in the 1959/60 series. He continued to master the lesser batsmen: indeed, in 1957, he headed the bowling in all first-class matches in England with 119 wickets (13.98). Altogether, in the first Test at Edgbaston, he sent down 774 balls (129 overs): no one has ever bowled more in a Test. After several years of Lancashire League cricket, he appeared for Lancashire with some success in 1964 and 1965 and later for Lincolnshire, and in 1979, his fiftieth year, was still operating in the Bolton Association. He first played in the Central Lancashire League in the early 1950s.

First-class career (1949-65): 1,106 runs (8.77) and 758 wickets (20.24)
Test matches (43): 361 runs (8.20), 158 wickets (28.98) and 9 catches

RICHARDS, Isaac Vivian Alexander (b. 1952)

Leeward Islands, Somerset and Queensland

'Viv' Richards is the finest contemporary West Indian batsman and will go down in cricket history as one of the greatest batsmen of all time. Both in looks and in build he is reminiscent of the American world heavyweight boxing champion Joc Frazier. At the time when he joined the other West Indian Test stars and signed for Kerry Packer's World Series Cricket, Richards was batting with a dominance which perhaps only Sir Donald Bradman had hitherto revealed. In eight months of 1976 he scored 1,710 runs (90.00) in Tests, a record for a calendar year. In the last three Tests of a losing series against an Australia spear-headed by Lillee and Thomson he scored 44, 2, 30, 101, 50 and 98: against India, when he got back home to the Caribbean, he scored 142, 130, 20 not out, 177, 23 and 64. Then against England in England and against an attack which at different times included Snow, Willis, Underwood, Pocock, Old and Hendrick, he made a further 829 runs in seven innings: 232 and 63 at Trent Bridge; 4 and 135 at Old Trafford; 66 and 38 at Headingley; and 291 in 472 minutes off 386 balls at The Oval. He missed the Lord's Test through illness. His average in the series was 118.42. On the tour he hit 4 other centuries and totalled 1,724 runs (71.83). He was simply magnificent. Basically an orthodox right-handed batsman with perfect timing and immense power, he almost always looks to attack from the very first ball of his innings and possesses such an amazing range of strokes that he is practically never tied down. More often than not he gets himself out but, frequently, miscued strokes which would be fatal to others are struck by Richards with such force that they clear the field. An imperious driver through extra cover, and a fearless and brilliant hooker, he will unfailingly hit any ball of fullish length which strays anywhere to legward of his middle-stump for four runs between square-leg and mid-on, according to the positioning of the field, casually placing the full face of the bat through the intended line. He is the most likely matchwinner in any contest, whoever he may be representing. The son of Malcolm Richards, who was for many years Antigua's leading fast bowler, he has two brothers who have also played for the island. Viv himself did so both at cricket and football while still at school and was so much the idol of the crowd that, when he was given out caught behind at the age of seventeen in a Leeward Island tournament, they protested, stopped play and forced local officials to overrule the umpire's decision. He was subsequently given a two year suspension – a harsh lesson that cricketers must try to keep their feelings to themselves – so it was not until 1972 that he made his first-class debut, at once scoring freely. A new maturity came with his qualification for Somerset. In his first season for the county in 1974, under shrewd advice and roughly affectionate encouragement from Brian Close, Richards scored 1,223 runs and has scored 1,000 runs or more every English season since, including 2,161 runs (65.48) in 1977. In 1979 Richards helped Somerset win their first major trophies in the Gillette Cup and the John Player League, which gave him as much pleasure as his matchwinning hundred (138 not out) in the Prudential World Cup Final against England. His Test experience began in India, Sri Lanka and Pakistan in 1974/5. Picked largely to be blooded for the future, he in fact replaced the injured Lawrence Rowe, scoring 192 not out in his third Test innings at Delhi. In the 1980s, partly owing to an eye complaint, there were signs of at least a temporary bending beneath the heavy load he carried as the potential matchwinner in each game he played. Yet he seldom failed to produce something memorable on the big occasion. In England in 1980 he was the leading batsman in both the Tests and first-class matches, hitting a superb 145 in the Lord's Test with a six and 25 fours. He hit 120 not out, out of 249, against Pakistan at Multan in 1980/81 and later in the same season, almost inevitably, marked the first ever Test in his native Antigua with a century against England. In the previous Test he had scored 182 not out in Barbados. He was totally dominant in Australia in 1979/80, magnificent in both Tests and one-day internationals and scored 1,077 runs (71.09) in 15 matches on the tour. In the Tests his scores were 140, 96, 76, and 74 – 386 runs at an average of 91. But he was much less successful on a similar tour of Australia two years later. He was clearly in need of a rest and wisely took a long one after the end of his successful benefit season in England in 1982. Either close to the wicket or in the covers, he is a fielder of the highest class and also a capable off-spinner who can bowl seam-up if necessary. All this marvellous, bubbling talent is never boastfully used. At the crease he is relaxed to the point of insouciance; off the field a quiet, charming and justly popular figure, who enjoys the fruits of his success in a relaxed fashion. When he married his childhood sweetheart at St John's in Antigua in 1980, the ceremony was given as much attention as a royal wedding. Richards is, indeed, the island's unofficial king.

Viv Richards

First-class career (1971-): 21,099 runs (48.95) including 63 centuries, 123 wickets (42.10), 266 catches and 1 stumping
Test matches (47): 4,129 runs (58.98) including 13 centuries, 13 wickets (54.07) and 48 catches

RICKARDS, Kenneth Roy (b.1923)

Jamaica and Essex

A confident right-handed batsman, Kenneth Rickards scored 67 in his first Test at Kingston against England in 1947/8 and toured Australasia in 1951/2, but had little success. He played one game for Essex in 1953.

First-class career (1946-58): 2,065 runs (38.96) including 2 centuries
Test matches (2): 104 runs (34.66)

ROACH, Clifford Archibald (b.1904)

Trinidad

Possessing a reasonably strong defence and a variety of dazzling strokes, powerful drives, hooks and crisp cuts, Clifford Roach was a right-handed opening batsman and a brilliant field, especially at cover-point. He stood as the second best batsman to George Headley in the early Test series engaged in by West Indies. In the Tests he hit 50 in the second against England at Old Trafford in 1928; 122 and 77 in the first against England at Kensington Oval, Barbados, and 209, his career highest, which included 3 sixes and 22 fours in less than five hours, in the fourth match at Georgetown in 1929/30. In the first series against England in the Caribbean, he finished second to Headley, with 467 runs (58.37). Though inconsistent, he reached 1,000 runs in each of his 1928 and 1933 tours – 1,222 runs (26.56) and 1,286 runs (25.72) respectively, including, in the latter year, a characteristically free 180 in two hours fifty minutes against Surrey at The Oval, when he reached his century before lunch on the first day. In Australia in 1930/31 he made 637 runs (24.50).

First-class career (1925-35): 4,851 runs (28.04) including 5 centuries
Test matches (16): 952 runs (30.70) including 2 centuries, 2 wickets (51.50) and 5 catches

ROBERTS, Alphonso Theodore (b.1937)

Windward Islands and Trinidad

Slim and rather frail-looking, a steady right-handed batsman, Roberts toured New Zealand in 1955/6 and, in his sole Test, the fourth at Auckland, aged 18 years 173 days, he made 28 and 0. He was the first player from the 'small islands' to play in a Test. He made only 137 runs (19.55) on the tour and was not selected for West Indies again.

First-class career (1955-60): 153 runs (13.90)

ROBERTS, Anderson Montgomery Everton (b.1951)

Leeward Islands, Hampshire, New South Wales and Leicestershire

From 1974 to 1980, a period of intense activity throughout the cricket world, Andy Roberts was one of the most feared bowlers in the world, and between the English winter of 1974 and summer of 1976 he took 100 wickets in nineteen Tests, the fastest in terms of time (two years, 142 days) until Ian Botham surpassed him. A tall, strong Antiguan with exceptionally broad shoulders, he has an action which is the perfect example of speed through economy: a quick sprint to the stumps, a spring into the air and a powerful thrust of the body, sending the ball very fast and very straight to its target. He uses the bouncer frugally but intelligently. Behind a bland, expressionless exterior lies a cool cricketing brain. A teetotaller, who favours a special orange-flavoured soft drink from Antigua, he is as phlegmatic off the field as he is on, where a wicket merits only a quick, hastily dismissed smile, and a near miss no apparent frustration or excitement. At the age of nineteen in January 1970, he made his first-class debut for the Leeward Islands, taking 4 for 50 from 29 overs in the first innings. He played his first Test, against England, in Barbados early in 1974, taking 1 for 75 and 2 for 49 on a good batting wicket, and the fact that he was discarded for the rest of the series had much to do with England managing to draw a series in which they were much the weaker side. However, he was now on his way to the top, the first Antiguan to play for the West Indies. In England in 1974 Roberts took 119 wickets in twenty-one matches for Hampshire at an average of only 13.62, besides being a prolific wicket-taker in limited-over matches. The following winter he was by far the most successful West Indian bowler in India, Sri Lanka and Pakistan, with 32 wickets in five Tests against India and 12 more in two matches against Pakistan. At Madras he took 12 for 121 (7 for 64 and 5 for 57). In Australia in 1975/6 Roberts was again the best West Indies bowler, with 22 wickets (26.36). In England in 1976 he had better fast bowling support and took 28 Test wickets (19.17) in a triumphant tour for his team. Already, however, the strain of bowling fast for more than one team was beginning to dull the keen edge of his pace. At home against Pakistan in 1976/7 his 19 Test wickets were expensively gained (40.15). For Hampshire he remained a potential matchwinner in each game that he played but, never one to convey great enjoyment, he often began to give an impression of a jaded and disillusioned man, and he left the county halfway through the 1978 season to concentrate on cricket for Kerry Packer. Bowling for West Indies in the Prudential World Cup in England in 1979 he looked like a fast bowler whose best days were already behind him. However, he learned to take wickets through movement, and thoughtful probing of a batsman's weakness, as well as through speed and bounce. He held his place as Holding's new-ball partner in Australia (1979/80 and 1980/81) and in England in 1980 but was dropped for the final home Test against England in 1980/81. He was also left out in the second of three Tests in Australia in 1981/2 but returned in the final match to take 4 for 43 in the first innings at Adelaide and set up a win for his side. Later in that season he took 24 wickets in only four matches for the Leeward Islands in the Shell Shield, including 6 for 54 against Jamaica, and he continued to prove that he was not yet to be written off as a spent force by bowling well for Leicestershire in 1982, his second year at the county on a part-time contract. No more than a capable fielder, he can be a useful right-hand bat, as he showed especially in the 1975 Prudential World Cup when he saved his side from elimination at the hands of Pakistan.

Andy Roberts

First-class career (1970-): 2,872 runs (15.11) and 754 wickets (20.93)
Test matches (40): 610 runs (13.55), 173 wickets (25.90) and 8 catches

RODRIGUEZ, William Vincente (b.1934)

Trinidad

A competent and steady right-handed batsman and useful leg-break bowler, Willie Rodriguez toured England in 1963 and went down with cartilage trouble before the first Test, but he was fit enough to appear in the fifth at The Oval when he helped to lay a solid foundation with an opening stand of 78 with Conrad Hunte. At home he played in occasional Tests against India in 1961/2, Australia in 1964/5 and England in 1967/8. He managed the West Indies side in Australia and New Zealand in 1979/80.

First-class career (1953-70): 2,061 runs (24.83) including 1 century, and 119 wickets (28.08)
Test matches (5): 96 runs (13.71), 7 wickets (53.42) and 3 catches

Lawrence Rowe

ROWE, Lawrence George (b.1949)

Jamaica and Derbyshire

One of the enigmas of Test cricket, Lawrence Rowe has had an extraordinary career, the zenith of which was an unforgettable triple century against England in Barbados, one of only eleven scores of 300 or more in Tests. Soon after he spent several seasons in the wilderness due to trouble with his eyesight, injuries and, most eccentric of cricketing complaints, an allergy to grass! Nurtured as a rare talent in his native Kingston, Rowe first played for Jamaica in 1968/9, toured England with the Jamaican side in 1970 and in 1971/2 broke through dramatically with 4 consecutive centuries, all at Kingston, including the unique achievement of a century and a double century on his Test debut – 214 and 100 not out against New Zealand. Probably a more nervous character than his cool, casual appearance at the crease would suggest – he infuriated opposing bowlers by humming or whistling a tune to aid his concentration – he was much less successful for a time outside his beloved Sabina Park. Against New Zealand he averaged 69.83, scoring 419 runs, but missed the later part of the 1972/3 series against Australia after scores of 76, 4 and 16, and a knee injury again caused him to miss the series against England in 1973. But it was England who learned the true quality of his batting the following winter in the Caribbean. A beautifully balanced right-handed batsman who either opens or goes in at number three or four, he has a lazy-looking backswing of the bat, and drives with graceful certainty and impeccable timing through the covers or wide of mid-on, but the bulk of his runs come from strokes off the back foot. At his best, he is thrillingly quick to pick up the short ball and hook it to some distant part of the leg-side boundary. After making 120 in Kingston against England in the second Test of the 1974 series, he played an innings at Bridgetown which none who saw it can forget. His 302 out of 596 for 8 declared was his eleventh first-class century but the first away from Sabina Park. Conditions were all in the batsman's favour and England subsequently drew the game, but Rowe batted for 612 minutes in an impeccable display of masterly batting, hitting a six and 36 fours in 302, made off 430 balls. In the fifth Test of the series, which the West Indies lost, he played the England spinners with cool skill, making 123 in the first innings (opening the innings, as he did throughout the series). His aggregate in the five Tests was 616 runs at 88.00. After a century in the Brisbane Test of 1975/6 he fell away, scoring only 270 runs in the series (24.54). His first season for Derbyshire in 1974 was quite successful, but in 1975 the problems with his eyesight began and, although he played in two Tests in 1976 in England, scoring a fifty in each, he never again seemed to be without some sort of ailment. However, after some success in World Series Cricket he toured Australia and did well in 1979/80, only to miss most of the tour to England in 1980 because of yet another injury. He became captain of Jamaica in 1981.

First-class career (1968-) 8,290 runs (38.37) including 17 centuries, 2 wickets (107.50) and 111 catches
Test matches (30): 2,047 runs (43.55) including 7 centuries, 0-44 and 17 catches

ST HILL, Edwin Lloyd (1904-57)

Trinidad

A right-arm medium-paced bowler and useful batsman, Edwin St Hill played in two Tests against England in 1929/30 with moderate success. He toured Australia in 1930/31, but was not selected for any of the Tests: he took the field in four games, taking 16 wickets (29.81).

First-class career (1923-31): 274 runs (11.91) and 64 wickets (28.62)
Test matches (2): 18 runs (4.50) and 3 wickets (73.66)

ST HILL, Wilton H. (1893-deceased before 1957)

Trinidad

About six feet tall, slim and elegant, but with forearms like whipcord, Wilton St Hill was a strong back-foot player, a superb late-cutter and leg-glancer, and the possessor of some splendid off-side strokes. He scored 105 in two hours and a half at Port of Spain for Trinidad against MCC in 1926/7, and Lord Harris considered that he was the best batsman in the West Indies. In 1929/30 he made a more cautious 102 on the same ground against MCC and in his only Test of the series, the second at Port of Spain, he opened with steady efforts of 33 and 30. On the 1928 England tour he had been selected for the first two Tests ever between the two countries, but he was a big disappointment, in first-class matches making only 262 runs (10.91). He vanished into obscurity, and it is believed he is now dead. His career batting average was 27.15.

First-class career (1911-30): 1,928 runs (27.15) including 5 centuries
Test matches (3): 117 runs (19.50), 0-9 and 1 catch

SCARLETT, Reginald G. (b.1934)

Jamaica

A mountainous figure of a man, Reg Scarlett was a useful right-handed batsman and off-break bowler, who hit 2 fifties and took 3 good wickets for Jamaica against MCC at Kingston in 1959/60, and appeared in three Tests that season against England.

First-class career (1951-60): 477 runs (23.85) and 48 wickets (34.12)
Test matches (3): 54 runs (18.00), 2 wickets (104.50) and 2 catches

SCOTT, Alfred P.H. (b.1934)

Jamaica

A right-arm leg-break bowler who dismayed the Indian tourists by taking 7 wickets for Jamaica against them at Kingston in 1952/3, Alf Scott played in his sole Test against India at Kingston that season, scoring 5 and taking 0 for 140. He is a son of O.C. Scott.

First-class career (1952-54): 38 runs (12.66) and 18 wickets (33.00)

SCOTT, Oscar Charles (1893-1961)

Jamaica

A genuine all-rounder, being a very useful right-handed batsman and slow leg-break bowler, 'Tommy' Scott toured England in 1928 and Australia in 1930/31, and played at home against England in 1929/30. His performances were rather moderate in England – 322 runs (20.12) and 25 wickets (36.24), although he finished second in the batting averages in the Tests with 74 runs (24.66) – but his leg-spin worked in Australia, where he took 40 wickets (33.22), including 11 wickets in the Tests. In the first Test at Adelaide he finished off the first innings by dismissing 4 batsmen in nine deliveries without cost. In the fourth Test against England at Kingston in 1929/30, he took 9 for 374, including figures of 80.2-13-266-5 in a total of 849 in the first innings.

First-class career (1910-35): 1,317 runs (24.38) and 182 wickets (30.47)
Test matches (8): 171 runs (17.10) and 22 wickets (42.04)

SEALEY, Benjamin James (1899-1963)

Trinidad

A lively, hard-hitting right-handed batsman, medium-paced leg-break bowler and sound field anywhere – he was one of the fastest runners in Trinidad – Ben Sealey was in his late twenties before playing first-class cricket for the first time and soon became an all-round 'treasure of his island'. He toured England in 1933, scoring 1,072 runs (39.70), including 3 centuries, and taking 19 wickets (38.15). In his sole Test, the last at The Oval, he made 29, the highest score in a total of 100, and 12, and took 1 for 10.

First-class career (1922-41): 2,115 runs (29.37) including 4 centuries, and 78 wickets (25.97)

SEALY, James Edward Derek (1912-82)

Barbados and Trinidad

A powerfully built and polished right-handed batsman, with a strong defence and forcing strokes all round the wicket, Derek Sealy was also a useful medium-paced bowler with unusual nip off the pitch, and a brilliant and versatile fielder who sometimes served as reserve wicket-keeper. He became the (then) youngest Test Player in history, when, at 17 years 122 days, he played in the first match at home against England at Bridgetown in 1929/30, scoring 58 and 15. He remains the youngest West Indian to have played in Tests. In Australia in 1930/31 he failed in the Tests, but he was at his best against England in 1934/5 when he made 92 in the second Test at Port of Spain, scoring 270 runs (45.00) in the series. Touring in England in 1939, he achieved little in the Tests, but in all first-class matches reached 948 runs (27.88), including a brilliant 181, his career-highest, in three hours and a half against Middlesex at Lord's. For Barbados against Trinidad in 1942 he bowled brilliantly on a wet pitch to take 8 for 8, the best analysis in a first-class match in the West Indies. He moved to Trinidad after teaching games at his old school, Combermere, in Barbados, where one of his pupils was Frank Worrell.

First-class career (1929-48): 3,831 runs (30.40) including 8 centuries, 63 wickets (28.60), 67 catches and 13 stumpings
Test matches (11): 478 runs (28.11), 3 wickets (31.33), 6 catches and 1 stumping

SHEPHERD, John Neil (b.1943)

Barbados, Rhodesia, Kent and Gloucestershire

An irresistibly enthusiastic all-round cricketer, John Shepherd has given much of his best cricket to Kent, since joining in 1965. A vigorous right-arm medium-fast bowler and very hard-hitting right-hand batsman, his stocky powerful frame has been the key to his success, although since slipping in the field in the Lord's Test of 1969 he has been plagued with a back injury. This has not prevented him from remaining a brilliant fielder. His first-class debut for Barbados was in 1964/5, his debut for Kent in 1966 and his first full season for them, 1967, when he won his county cap and Kent won the Gillette Cup. His Test career was all too brief: he played three games in England in 1969 when he bowled excellently with consistent hostility and movement through the air and off the seam, taking 12 wickets (22.16), including 5 for 104 in 58.5 overs in England's first innings of 413 at Lord's. At home the following winter he played in two Tests against India. He became the first black cricketer to tour South Africa, in 1973 with the Derrick Robins team, stirring up much opposition in the Caribbean, and has played in the Currie Cup for Rhodesia (1975/6) as well as having two very successful seasons playing Grade Cricket for the Melbourne club, Footscray. Outstanding performances for Kent include 170 against Northamptonshire in 1968, at Folkestone, and 8 for 83 against Lancashire at Tunbridge Wells in 1977.

First-class career (1964-): 11,444 runs (25.71) including 8 centuries, 1,016 wickets (27.22) and 261 catches
Test matches (5): 77 runs (9.62), 19 wickets (25.21) and 4 catches

SHILLINGFORD, Grayson Cleophas (b.1946)

Windward Islands

An enthusiastic right-arm fast-medium bowler who batted left, Grayson Shillingford toured England in 1969 and 1973. Despite a torn muscle, which kept him idle for a month during his first tour, he took 36 wickets (18.58) and bowled well in two Tests. At home he played against India in 1970/71 and New Zealand in 1971/2, but failed to establish himself.

First-class career (1967-79): 791 runs (10.14) and 217 wickets (26.54)
Test matches (7): 57 runs (8.14), 15 wickets (35.80) and 2 catches

SHILLINGFORD, Irvine Theodore (b.1944)

Windward Islands

The first cousin of Grayson Shillingford, with whom he played for many seasons for Dominica and the Windward Islands, Irvine Shillingford is a fine, orthodox right-handed batsman who has been a consistent high scorer since making his debut against the Australians in 1965. He played three Tests against Pakistan in 1976/7, scoring 120 in his second Test at Georgetown. In 1978 he scored 238 against the Leeward Islands at Castries but was dropped after only one Test against Australia, the third at Georgetown.

First-class career (1961-) 5,449 runs (36.57) including 11 centuries, and 1 wicket (85.00)
Test matches (4): 218 runs (31.14) including 1 century, and 1 catch

SHIVNARINE, Sew (b.1952)

Guyana

A gifted little cricketer, Sew Shivnarine bowls slow left-arm orthodox, bats right-handed and made the transition to Test cricket without difficulty when suddenly elevated in 1978 after the withdrawal of the Packer players in the middle of the series against Australia. His scores in the series included 53 and 63 on his debut at Georgetown and 53 at Kingston, but in India in 1978/9 he was disappointing, and his bowling proved to be not up to Test standards.

First-class career (1970-): 2,182 runs (32.56) including 3 centuries, and 67 wickets (36.52)
Test matches (8): 379 runs (29.15), 1-167 and 6 catches

SINGH, Charran K. (b.1938)

Trinidad

A left-arm slow-bowler, Charran Singh had an unusual Test debut against England as a 'local boy' on his home ground, Port of Spain, in the second Test of 1959/60. It was when he was given run out for 0 to make the West Indies total 98 for 8 against England's total of 382, that the crowd's shattered emotions got the better of them: bottles and missiles rained onto the field, spectators invaded the playing area and riot police had to quell the mob. A few weeks earlier Singh had taken 5 for 57 in 34 overs in the MCC first innings against Trinidad.

First-class career (1959-62): 102 runs (8.50) and 48 wickets (23.93)
Test matches (2): 11 runs (3.66), 5 wickets (33.20) and 2 catches

SMALL, Joseph A. (1892-1958)

Trinidad

Joe Small was a tall, loose-limbed all-rounder, being a dashing right-handed batsman, who off-drove, cut and glanced fluently, a medium-pace off-break bowler, and an agile slip fielder. He toured England in 1923 making 776 runs (31.04), including a classic 94 off Lancashire at Old Trafford, and taking 19 wickets (33.47). In the 1928 tour he totalled 595 runs (18.59) and was more successful as a bowler, taking 50 wickets (28.88). In the first Test between West Indies and England, at Lord's, he made a defiant 52 in a losing cause. He played his last Test, the second at Port of Spain against England, in 1929/30.

First-class career (1920-30): 3,063 runs (26.18) including 3 centuries, and 165 wickets (27.69)
Test matches (3): 79 runs (13.16), 3 wickets (61.33) and 3 catches

SMITH, Cameron Wilberforce (b.1933)

Barbados

An ever-smiling insurance salesman, 'Cammie' Smith was a very competent right-handed opening batsman and wicket-keeper, who toured Australia in 1960/61 and scored 55 in the third Test at Sydney. He kept wicket in the first Test at Port of Spain against India in 1961/2 after Jackie Hendriks had broken a finger on the first day.

First-class career (1951-65): 2,277 runs (37.32) including 5 centuries
Test matches (5): 222 runs (24.66) and 5 dismissals (4 ct, 1 st.)

SMITH, O'Neil Gordon (1933-59)

Jamaica

Stocky and strong, 'Collie' Smith decided as a schoolboy to give up fast bowling and become an off-break bowler, like his hero, Jim Laker; so, for a time, he was called 'Jim'. He developed as a punishing right-handed batsman, a scintillating stroke-maker, and a brilliant versatile field. After only two games for Jamaica he hit 169 against the front-line Australian attack at Kingston in 1954/5, and a few days later, also at Kingston, he made 44 and 104 in his first Test against Australia. In his second match, however, he failed to score in either innings and, after being dropped for one match, returned with variable success for the remainder of his tragically curtailed career. A very cheerful and optimistic cricketer, he toured New Zealand in 1955/6, taking 13 wickets (18.53) in the four Tests, but achieving little with the bat. He consolidated his place in England in 1957, and scored more in the Tests than any of his colleagues, 396 runs (39.60), including 161 at Edgbaston in the first Test and 168 at Trent Bridge in the third. At home against Pakistan in 1957/8 he was the best all-rounder with 283 runs (47.16) and 13 wickets (38.00). Touring India and Pakistan in 1958/9, he scored 901 runs (34.65) and took 25 wickets (26.44) in all first-class matches. In the eight Tests he was second as an all-rounder to Gary Sobers, making 368 runs (28.30) and taking 12 wickets (27.25), although he was not particularly successful against Pakistan. In the first Test against India at Delhi he hit 100 in less than three hours and took 8 for 184. During 1958 and 1959 he was highly successful as professional to Burnley in the Lancashire League. His batting had now matured, his exciting stroke-play was now used with greater discrimination and he had not yet reached his prime when in September 1959 he died of injuries received in a car accident involving also his great friend Gary Sobers. Smith's body was taken back to Jamaica, where 60,000 people attended the funeral.

First-class career (1954-9): 4,031 runs (40.31) including 10 centuries, and 121 wickets (31.02)
Test matches (26): 1,331 runs (31.69) including 4 centuries, 48 wickets (33.85) and 9 catches

SOBERS, Sir Garfield St Aubrun (b.1936)

Barbados, South Australia and Nottinghamshire

Generally considered to be the greatest-ever all-round cricketer, the achievements of Gary, later Sir Garfield, Sobers stand alone. Blessed with every necessary attribute for greatness as a cricketer, he had rare natural genius, determination, stamina, and a remarkable capacity to continue to produce high-quality performances despite an exceptionally heavy workload, intense pressure from publicity, and the burden of always being the player whom the crowd most wanted to see and the opposition feared most. Tall, supple, athletic and strong, with a buck-toothed smile never far away, he enjoyed his cricket and conveyed this to crowds, team-mates and opponents,

Gary Sobers

and though he played the game with a proper competitiveness and never lost his appetite for runs and wickets until late in his career, he made no enemies. His immortality rests on his all-round success, the style and panache with which he compiled the dazzling figures, and on his unique versatility. A left-hander, he was one of the greatest batsmen of all time and a marvellous new-ball fast-medium left-arm over-the-wicket bowler, who was equally good as a slow left-arm orthodox bowler (although he bowled much less in this style in later years), and also capable of bowling high-quality left-arm unorthodox (back of the hand) spin. As a fielder he was brilliant, with feline reflexes close to the wicket, especially on the leg-side. His very walk was internationally famous: a graceful, relaxed, long-striding walk, leaning forward, bent at the knees. He was born in Barbados with five fingers instead of four on each hand. The extra two were removed in boyhood. One of seven children of a merchant seaman, he was brought up by his mother after his father had died at sea in the war when Gary was only five. Encouraged by a number of people who at once appreciated his genius, first shown in cricket matches played with other youngsters with a tennis ball, Sobers played golf, soccer and basketball for Barbados and in 1953 first appeared for the island at cricket against the Indian touring team, aged sixteen. He made his first Test appearance at the age of seventeen at the end of March 1954, in the fifth Test against England at Kingston, taking 4 for 75 in England's first innings of 414. Four years later, having steadily established himself, he made the final step from a highly promising player to a great one when he scored 365 not out at Kingston against Pakistan (1957/8). It was his first three figure score in a Test, made at the age of twenty-one, and it surpassed by one run Sir Leonard Hutton's record 364 which had stood since 1938. Gerry Alexander, the West Indies' captain, declared when the achievement was complete, at 790 for 3. Sobers batted for just over ten hours, three hours less than Hutton, hit 38 fours and shared a stand of 446 for the second wicket with Conrad Hunte. In this series Sobers made 824 runs (137.33) and hit 2 other centuries. He scored more than 500 runs in five other series: against India in 1958/9 (557 at 92.83); England in 1959/60 (709 at 101.28); England in 1966 (722 at 103.14); England in 1967/8 (545 at 90.83); India in 1971 (597 at 74.62). In thirteen of the twenty-two Test series in which he played for the West Indies he took 10 or more wickets and in three series held more than 10 catches. In England in 1966, as captain of the touring team, in addition to his 722 runs in five Tests at an average of 103, he took 20 wickets at 27.25, bowling 269.4 overs and often taking the new ball in an attack which also included Hall and Griffith, and he held 10 catches. He made 161 in the first Test at Old Trafford, saved his side with 163 not out in the second at Lord's, and at Leeds, in the match which decided the rubber, hit 174 and took 8 wickets for 80 in the match. Something of the man's intense competitiveness may be gleaned from his performance in the final match of this series. He made 81 in the first innings, and, when he might have been expected to relax a little, with the series already won, he bowled no fewer than 54 overs, 10 more than anyone else, in England's innings of 527. As a Test captain he was enterprising, once allowing England to win the decisive match of the series with a bold declaration at Port of Spain in 1967/8, but his attacking gestures often had happier results. He had one less successful tour as captain in Australia, although his loss of form and concentration was probably due to falling in love: he married a pretty Australian girl whom he had first met in England. But he is as much a legend in Australia as anywhere else: he is the only man to have achieved the double of 1,000 runs and 50 wickets in an Australian season, and he did it twice. He also played an innings of 254 for the Rest of the World against Australia at Melbourne in 1971/2, which was one of the most magnificent and masterly ever seen in a big match. In domestic cricket in England he was as inspirational for Nottinghamshire as he had been for South Australia. He captained the county from 1968 until 1974, although by the time of his retirement in the latter year, damaged knees and staleness had reduced his effectiveness. Against Glamorgan at Swansea in 1968 he hit Malcolm Nash, bowling slow left-arm, for 6 sixes in one six-ball over. This feat is unlikely ever to be repeated in a first-class match and in a serious competitive situation. Nor is it likely that one man will again possess so wide a variety of cricketing skills as Sir Gary, who was knighted by the Queen in Barbados for his services to cricket in 1975.

First-class career (1953-74): 28,315 runs (54.87) including 86 centuries, 1,043 wickets (27.74) and 407 catches
Test matches (93): 8,032 runs (57.78) including 26 centuries, 235 wickets (34.03) and 109 catches

SOLOMON, Joseph Stanislaus (b.1930)

British Guiana

A steady right-handed batsman whose ability to shut up one end could stem a possible collapse, Joe Solomon was also a useful medium-pace leg-break change-bowler and excellent field. A slim East Indian, he batted around number six, though he twice opened for West Indies with Conrad Hunte, without success. He toured India and Pakistan in 1958/9, Australia in 1960/61 and England in 1963; and at home played against England in 1959/60, India in 1961/2 and Australia in 1964/5. His one outstanding series was his first, against India in 1958/9 when in four Tests he headed the batting averages with 351 runs (117.00), including 100 not out in the fifth match at Delhi, which remained his sole Test century. On his Test debut at Kanpur in the second match he had made 45 and 86. Thereafter he was always useful in the West Indies team, often when the need was greatest, for example in the dramatic Test at Lord's in 1963 when he hit a valuable 56 and in the famous tied Test at Brisbane when he ran out two Australian batsmen in the final crisis. His career-highest was 201 not out for Berbice against MCC at Blairmont in 1959/60.

First-class career (1956-69): 5,318 runs (41.54) including 12 centuries, and 51 wickets (38.23)
Test matches (27): 1,326 runs (34.00) including 1 century, 4 wickets (67.00) and 13 catches

STAYERS, Sven Conrad (b.1937)

British Guiana

A tall all-rounder, being a good right-handed batsman and fast-medium bowler of loose, somewhat gangling action, 'Charlie' Stayers played with moderate success in Tests against India in 1961/2.

First-class career (1957-63): 485 runs (28.52) including 1 century, and 68 wickets (26.10)
Test matches (4): 58 runs (19.33) and 9 wickets (40.44)

STOLLMEYER, Jeffrey Baxter (b.1921)

Trinidad

Captain of West Indies in fourteen Tests from 1951 until 1955 and the holder of the highest score in Inter-Colonial matches, 324 against British Guiana in 1946/7 when he added a record 434 for the third wicket with Gerry Gomez, Jeffrey Stollmeyer was a tall, elegant and stylish right-handed opening batsman, particularly strong on the on-side, a useful leg-break bowler and a fine fielder. He first toured England at eighteen in 1939, making 59 in his first Test innings. In the first post-war Test against England at Bridgetown in 1947/8 he scored 78 and 31, but he missed half the series through injury. In India in 1948/9 he made 342 runs (68.40) in the Tests, including his maiden century, a faultless 160 at Madras in the fourth match, when he laid the foundations of victory by sharing in a record first-wicket stand of 239 with Allan Rae. He hit 244 not out against South Zone at Madras, and in all reached 1,091 runs (64.17) for the tour. In England in 1950, again with Rae as his opening partner, he shared in first-wicket stands worth 52, 32, 37, 48, 77, 103 unbroken and 72 in the four Tests, thus paving the way for 'the three Ws' in the year that West Indian cricket 'came of age'. In this series he scored 305 runs (50.83), including a highest score of 78 at Old Trafford on a poor pitch. In all first-class matches he made 1,334 runs (37.05) including 198 against Sussex at Hove, when he engaged in another record-breaking opening stand with Rae – 355 in four hours and forty minutes. As captain he batted well against Australia and New Zealand in 1951/2, against England in 1953/4 (a drawn series), and against Australia in 1954/5. In Australia in 1951/2 he hit a splendid 104 in the fifth Test at Sydney in a losing cause. He led West Indies to victory over India in 1952/3, scoring 354 runs (59.00) including 104 not out in the third match at Port of Spain. A senator in the Trinidad Legislature, he is the widely respected president of the West Indies Cricket Board of Control and is prominent in the councils of the International Cricket Conference.

First-class career (1938-56): 7,942 runs (44.61) including 14 centuries, and 55 wickets (45.13)
Test matches (32): 2,159 runs (42.33) including 4 centuries, 13 wickets (39.00) and 20 catches

STOLLMEYER, Victor Humphrey (b.1916)

Trinidad

A stylish, stroke-making, fast-scoring right-handed batsman, Vic Stollmeyer was troubled by illness on his sole England tour in 1939, but he made 542 runs (30.11). In his only Test, the third at The Oval, he hit his tour-highest, a brilliant 96 in two and a half hours. It was his only innings at the highest level. He was a prolific scorer in Inter-Colonial cricket and is the elder brother of Jeff Stollmeyer.

First-class career (1936-46): 2,108 runs (41.33) including 4 centuries

TAYLOR, Jaswick Ossie (b.1932)

Trinidad

A right-arm fast-medium bowler, Jaswick Taylor toured India and Pakistan in 1958/9 but, although he captured 35 wickets (18.31), he appeared in only two Tests. At home, in the previous season, he made his Test debut against Pakistan at Port of Spain in the fifth match when, by dint of pace and persistency, he took 5 for 109 in a total of 496.

First-class career (1953-60): 62 runs (5.63) and 50 wickets (26.22)
Test matches (3): 4 runs (2.00) and 10 wickets (27.30)

TRIM, John (1915-60)

British Guiana

A right-arm fast-medium bowler, John Trim toured India in 1948/9 and Australia in 1951/2, and at home played against England in 1947/8, after taking 4 for 68 and 5 for 36 for British Guiana against MCC. On his few Test appearances he was almost invariably inexpensive and penetrative. In the fourth Test at Melbourne in 1951/2 he broke through with the new ball, taking 5 for 34 in the first innings. On the Indian tour he took 37 wickets (22.10), including 7 for 76 in the fourth Test at Madras, bowling throughout with life and pace.

First-class career (1943-53): 386 runs (11.69) and 96 wickets (30.01)
Test matches (4): 21 runs (5.25), 18 wickets (16.16) and 2 catches

VALENTINE, Alfred Lewis (b.1930)

Jamaica

Alf Valentine was coached in Jamaica by Jack Mercer of Glamorgan, Sussex and Northants, who taught him the value of spin, and he soon became one of the best left-arm slow bowlers since the Second World War. Fairly tall and slim, with sloping shoulders, and always bespectacled, he took a few steps and delivered easily, almost square to the batsman, keeping an immaculate length and giving the ball a sharp finger tweak, treating his often very sore spinning finger regularly after play with surgical spirit. Prior to touring England in 1950 as the youngest member, he had taken only 2 wickets at 95 runs each in two first-class matches in the Caribbean, but in an historic parnership with Sonny Ramadhin he enjoyed a triumphant tour, securing 123 wickets (17.94), including 33 wickets (20.42) from 422.3 overs in the four Tests, three times dismissing Len Hutton when he was looking set for a long innings. Ramadhin and Valentine captured 59 wickets between them in the series. After a disappointing start Alf Valentine took 13 for 67 against Lancashire at Old Trafford, followed by 8 for 104 in the first innings of the first Test on that ground and he did not look back – he had 7 wickets at Lord's and 10 for 160 (6 for 39 in the second innings) at The Oval. West Indian cricket 'came of age' in 1950 with its first win in England and the names 'Ramadhin and Valentine' were on everyone's lips. He toured England again in 1957 and 1963, Australasia in 1951/2, New Zealand in 1955/6, and Australia in 1960/61, and at home played against India in 1952/3 and 1961/2, England in 1953/4, Australia in 1954/5 and Pakistan in 1957/8. In Australia in 1951/2 he maintained his high skill, securing 24 wickets (28.79) in the Tests – more than anyone else on either side – and 61 wickets (23.83) in all first-class matches. In the third Test at Adelaide he took 6 for 102 in the second innings, West Indies enjoying a comfortable win. Then he had a relatively lean period though he took his one hundredth wicket in Tests in only 3 years 263 days. In England in 1957 he was plagued by ill health and injury. After three years out of favour he toured Australia in 1960/61 and his bowling was always valuable. On his last tour of England in 1963 Garfield Sobers kept him out of the Test team.

First-class career (1949-65): 470 runs (5.00) and 475 wickets (26.20)
Test matches (36): 141 runs (4.70), 139 wickets (30.32) and 13 catches

VALENTINE, Vincent A. (1908-presumed dead)

Jamaica

A right-arm fast-medium bowler of a congenial disposition, Vincent Valentine made the batsman play every ball, keeping a perfect length, turning the ball both ways and swinging it astutely. He was also a forcing lower-order batsman and a reliable field. He toured England in 1933 as a substitute for Learie Constantine (who had League commitments), taking 36 wickets (42.80) and making 391 runs (17.00): he played in two of the Tests without distinction.

First-class career (1931-39): 500 runs (17.85) and 49 wickets (40.40)
Test matches (2): 35 runs (11.66) and 1-104

WALCOTT, Clyde Leopold (b.1926)

Barbados and British Guiana

With his schoolmate, Frank Worrell, Clyde Walcott added an unbroken 574 for the fourth wicket for Barbados against Trinidad at Port of Spain in 1945/6 which remains the record West Indian stand for any wicket; he was just twenty years of age and his score of 314 not out remained his career-highest. From 1947/8 for a decade, this brilliant and compellingly attractive cricketer was an integral part of the Test team, immortalized as one of 'the Three Ws' – Walcott, Weekes and Worrell. Standing 6ft 2in and weighing about fifteen stone, Clyde Walcott had a commanding presence though a crouching stance, and his powerful physique enabled him to drive with tremendous force; right-handed, he had a strong defence, a peerless off-drive and a dazzling square-cut. He was rarely lost for a stroke. Off either foot he bombarded fielders from mid-on to covers. He served reliably either as a wicketkeeper or first slip and he was a very useful fast-medium change-bowler. He toured India in 1948/9, England in 1950 and 1957 and Australia in 1951/2; and at home played against England in 1947/8, 1953/4 and 1959/60, India in 1952/3, Australia in 1954/5 and Pakistan in 1957/8. Originally, his wicket-keeping kept him in the Test side, but in India in 1948/9 he made 452 runs (64.57) in the Tests and 1,366 runs (75.88), including 5 centuries, in all first-class matches. On the 1950 England tour he made 1,674 runs (55.80), including 7 centuries, the highest being 168 not out in the second Test at Lord's when he put on a record 211 for the sixth wicket with Gerry Gomez. After a lean period against the Australian shock attack of Lindwall and Miller in 1951/2, it was in the West Indies against England in 1953/4 and Australia in 1954/5 that he assumed an unrivalled supremacy. Against England he scored 698 runs (87.25), including 3 centuries, the highest, 220, being his own Test-highest, scored at Bridgetown in the second match. Against Australia he achieved the then-record West Indian aggregate of 827 runs (82.70), including no fewer than 5 centuries in three Tests, 126 and 110 in the second match at Port of Spain and 155 and 110 in the fifth at Kingston; with Everton Weekes he added 242 for the third wicket at Port of Spain, which remains a record. He started the 1957 season in England in fine form, but injured himself in the first Test at Edgbaston when scoring 90, and, though he ended the tour with 1,414 runs (45.61), he seemed like a massive machine not quite functioning as it should. Back in the West Indies, against Pakistan in 1957/8, he returned to his best form, making 385 runs (96.25), including 145 in the fourth Test at Georgetown. At one time in his career he had hit 12 centuries in twelve consecutive Tests. He was a great favourite in the Lancashire League from 1951 until 1954, has managed several West Indies touring teams in the 1970s, and was awarded the OBE for his services to cricket.

First-class career (1941-63): 11,820 runs (56.55) including 40 centuries, 35 wickets (36.25) and 208 dismissals (175 ct, 33 st.)
Test matches (44): 3,798 runs (56.68) including 15 centuries, 11 wickets (37.09) and 64 dismissals (53 ct, 11 st.)

WALCOTT, Leslie Arthur (b.1894)

Barbados

A competent all-rounder, right-handed batsman and quickish off-break bowler, Leslie Walcott's sole Test was the first ever played in the Caribbean, against England at Bridgetown in 1929/30, when he scored 24 and 16 not out and took 1 for 32.

First-class career (1925-36): 555 runs (30.83) and 16 wickets (29.50)

WATSON, Chester (b.1939)

Jamaica and Delhi

A right-arm fast bowler, specially awkward because of his wristy action which made him faster than his run-up suggested, Chester Watson toured Australia in 1960/61 but with poor results. His only full series was against England at home in 1959/60 when he secured 16 wickets (37.06), including 4 for 62 in the second innings of the third match at Kingston.

First-class career (1958-64): 197 runs (7.57) and 85 wickets (32.07)
Test matches (7): 12 runs (2.40), 19 wickets (38.10) and 1 catch

WEEKES, Everton De Courcey (b.1925)

Barbados

Short and thickset with an engaging charm, number two of 'the Three Ws' – Walcott, Weekes and Worrell – Everton Weekes was immensely quick on his feet and possessed a whole armoury of attacking strokes on both sides of the wicket. For long periods he attacked all bowlers in the same relentless manner as Don Bradman; and he was a brilliant versatile field. He toured India in 1948/9, England in 1950 and 1957, Australasia in 1951/2 and New Zealand in 1955/6; and at home he played against England in 1947/8 and 1953/4, India in 1952/3, Australia in 1954/5 and Pakistan in 1957/8. His 141 against England in the fourth Test at Kingston in 1947/8 earned him a place to India in 1948/9 where he hit the then-record West Indian aggregate in a series, 779 runs (111.28), including 4 centuries in succession – 128 at New Delhi, 194 at Bombay and 162 and 101 both at Calcutta – and he only missed the fifth when he was run out for 90 at Madras. In England in 1950, when 'the Three Ws' were a tremendous draw, he again headed the batting, with 2,310 runs (79.65) and 7 centuries, including 304 not out, his career-highest, against Cambridge at Fenner's, 279, 246 not out, 232 and 200 not out. In the Tests he registerd 338 runs (56.33), including 129 at Trent Bridge in the third match. He fell below his own high standards in Australia in 1951/2 and in England in 1957, but otherwise he continued to score heavily. At home, against England in 1953/4, he made 487 runs (69.57), including 206 at Port of Spain in the fourth match when he and Worrell added 338 for the third wicket, a record for any wicket against England. Against India in 1952/3 he was far above anyone else, making 716 runs (102.28), including 207 at Port of Spain in the first match, 161 at Bridgetown in the third and 109 at Kingston in the fifth. Against Pakistan in 1957/8 he contributed 455 runs (65.00), including 197 at Bridgetown in the first match. In New Zealand in 1955/6 he was completely dominant, hitting 940 runs (104.44), including 6 centuries, in eight first-class matches. In the Tests alone he made 418 runs (83.60), which included 123 at Dunedin in the first match, 103 at Christchurch in the second and 156 at Wellington in the third. He also played in English League cricket, toured with various Commonwealth sides, coached in Barbados and was awarded the OBE.

First-class career (1944-64): 12,010 runs (52.90) including 36 centuries, 125 catches and 1 stumping
Test matches (48): 4,455 runs (58.61) including 15 centuries, 1-77 and 49 catches

WEEKES, Kenneth Hunnell (b.1912)

Jamaica

A barrel-chested, stylish and fast-scoring, though unorthodox, left-handed batsman, with a good variety of stroke-play all round the wicket, 'Bam Bam' Weekes was also a good reserve wicket-keeper. He toured England in 1939. He made 803 runs (29.74), which included 146 against Surrey, his career-highest, and a buccaneering 137 in two and a quarter hours against England in the third Test, both at The Oval.

First-class career (1938-47): 1,731 runs (40.26) including 3 centuries
Test matches (2): 173 runs (57.66) including 1 century

WHITE, Winston Anthony (b.1938)

Barbados

A competent and tenacious all-rounder, Tony White was a robust right-handed hitter, a purveyor of stock medium-pace or off-break bowling and a good field. He joined the team in England in 1963 as a replacement for an injured player but, although he collected 228 runs and 28 wickets from nine matches, he did not appear in a Test on this tour. His sole apearances for West Indies were against Australia in 1964/5; he hit 57 not out in his first at Kingston.

First-class career (1958-66): 996 runs (25.53) and 95 wickets (28.05)
Test matches (2): 71 runs (23.66), 3 wickets (50.66) and 1 catch

WIGHT, Claude Vibart (1902-deceased)

British Guiana

A good right-handed batsman, Vibart Wight was appointed vice-captain of the team to England in 1928 although he had never captained a first-class side. He made only 343 runs (20.17) but played in the third Test at The Oval, when he scored 35 in the match for once out. At home he appeared once against England in 1929/30, again reaching double figures in each innings. His overall average in first-class cricket was 30.94. He was the senior member of a well-known British Guiana cricketing family.

First-class career (1925-39): 1,547 runs (30.94) including 3 centuries
Test matches (2): 67 runs (22.33) and 0-6

WIGHT, George Leslie (b.1929)

British Guiana

Leslie Wight was a dour, defensive right-handed batsman whose sole Test apearance was against India in the fourth Test at Georgetown in 1952/3 when he scored a very slow 21 in his only innings. Against Barbados at Georgetown in 1951/2 he amassed 262 not out, putting on 390 for the first wicket with G. Gibbs, which remains the record in the West Indies. He is related to C.V., O.S. and Norman Wight.

First-class career (1949-53): 1,260 runs (66.31) including 4 centuries

WILES, C. Archibald (b.1892)

Barbados and Trinidad

A sound, stylish, defensive right-handed batsman, Archie Wiles had some good performances against MCC in 1925/6 and helped Trinidad to win the Inter-Colonial Tournament in 1931/2. Touring England in 1933, however, he was disappointing. He was aged 40 years 346 days when, at Old Trafford in his sole Test appearance, he scored 0 and 2. His overall average in first-class cricket was 27.16.

First-class career (1919-36): 1,766 runs (27.16) including 2 centuries

WILLETT, Elquemedo Tonito (b.1953)

Leeward Islands

A steady slow left-arm orthodox spin bowler, Willett toured England in 1973 and, although taking 30 wickets (23.13), did not make the Test eleven. At home he appeared against Australia in 1972/3 at the age of only nineteen and toured India and Pakistan in 1974/5 with some success. Coming from the tiny island of Nevis (36 square miles, population about 15,000), Willett was the first Leeward Islander to represent the West Indies, and his success was a much-needed inspiration to many others from the smaller West Indian islands.

First-class career (1970-): 874 runs (12.66) and 228 wickets (27.83)
Test matches (5): 74 runs (14.80) and 11 wickets (43.81)

WILLIAMS, Alvadon Basil (b.1949)

Jamaica

An attractive right-handed opening batsman with plenty of strokes, Basil Williams had an outstanding season in 1977/8, making 399 runs in the Shell Shield for Jamaica at an average of 79.80. He had his reward with a place in the Test side earlier than he might have hoped, when the World Series Cricket players were dropped before the Third Test against Australia at Georgetown. He showed both his ability and his temperament by hitting a century in the second innings of his first Test and in three matches made 257 runs (42.83). In India in 1978/9 he scored 212 runs (35.33), including 111 in the third Test at Calcutta.

First-class career (1969-): 2,099 runs (36.82) including 4 centuries
Test matches (7): 469 runs (39.08) including 2 centuries, and 5 catches

WILLIAMS, Edward Albert Vivian (b.1914)

Barbados

'Foffie' Williams was a very sound, hard-hitting right-handed batsman with a specially powerful drive, a fast-medium bowler who attacked the stumps at all times and could bowl at speed for long periods, and a fine, athletic field. His career was seriously impeded by the Second World War. He hit 131 not out against Trinidad at Bridgetown in 1935/6, adding 255 for the eighth wicket with 'Manny' Martindale, which remains a West Indian record, and toured England in 1939, playing in one Test. In the first Test after the war, against England at Bridgetown in 1947/8, he scored 72 – opening his scoring with 6, 6, 4 and 4 off the first four balls from Jim Laker and 4 and 4 off the next balls from Jack Ikin, a unique opening to an innings in Test cricket. When he bowled, his first spell was 11-8-3-1 and he finished with 3 for 51 off 33 overs. He had only joined the team for this match because Frank Worrell was down with food poisoning.

First-class career (1934-48): 1,479 runs (28.69) including 2 centuries, and 116 wickets (29.20)
Test matches (4): 113 runs (18.83), 9 wickets (26.77) and 2 catches

WISHART, Kenneth Leslie (1908-72)

British Guiana

A careful left-handed opening batsman, Ken Wishart scored 88 and 77 in successive games for British Guiana against MCC at Georgetown in 1929/30 against heavy odds each time, but did not represent West Indies until the third Test at Georgetown against England in 1934/5 when he made a dogged 52 (followed by 0 in the second innings), and he was not tried again. He was British Guiana's (later Guyana's) representative on the West Indies Board of Control from 1949 to 1971.

First-class career (1928-47): 706 runs (23.53)

WORRELL, Sir Frank Mortimore Maglinne (1924-67)

Barbados and Jamaica

Three years before he died of leukaemia Frank Worrell was knighted for his services to cricket. He was a great cricketer, a great captain, an exemplary ambassador for West Indies cricket and a man of strong convictions. Had he lived he would surely have become a statesman in world affairs. His captaining and his cricket always conveyed a monumental calm, even at the height of a crisis, and, as captain, he was involved in two of the most breathtaking finishes in Test history – at Brisbane in 1961 and Lord's in 1963. He first played for Barbados in 1941/2 at eighteen as a slow left-arm bowler. The following season, as night-watchman, he carried his bat for 64 and was soon opening the innings. In the same month he scored 188 (in five hours) and 68 against Trinidad at Port of Spain. At nineteen in 1943/4, he amassed 308 not out, his career-highest, against Trinidad at Bridgetown, adding 502 for the fourth wicket with John Goddard in just under six and a half hours without being separated. This world record for the fourth wicket was broken again by Worrell with 255 not out when he put on 574, again unbroken in less than six hours, this time with Clyde Walcott against Trinidad at Port of Spain in 1945/6; it remains the West Indian record for any wicket. Modestly, he dismissed both achievements: 'The conditions were loaded in our favour. I wasn't all that delighted about it.' Modelling himself on the youngest-ever West Indian Test cricketer, Derek Sealy, a master at his school, Frank Worrell was slim, lithely built, elegant and stylish. A right-handed batsman, he commanded every orthodox stroke, was perfectly balanced and possessed quick judgment and footwork. His timing was exquisite and he would sometimes embark upon an onslaught at once furious and yet graceful. As a left-arm bowler, he could be either a spinner or, more often, a fast-medium swing bowler with an easy, relaxed action. He was accomplished at cover or in the close catching positions. He toured England in 1950, 1957 and 1963, Australasia in 1951/2 and Australia in 1960/61; and at home he played against England in 1947/8, 1953/4 and 1959/60, India in 1952/3 and 1961/2 and Australia in 1954. He captained the West Indies in fifteen Tests between 1960 and 1963, on his third tour of England and second of Australia and at home in his second series against India (when West Indies won all five Tests). Altogether nine of these matches were won. He was a quietly authoritative and yet dynamic leader who earned the respect of all with whom he played. In 1947/8 he scored 97 on his Test debut at Port of Spain and in his next at Georgetown, 131 not out against England: thanks partly to not-outs he averaged the record 147 in this series. In 1950 when 'the Three Ws' legend was born, he was above everyone else in the Tests, making 539 runs (89.93), including his scintillating Test-highest of 261 in five hours thirty-five minutes at Trent Bridge in the third match, sharing in seven records, including the partnership of 283 for the fourth wicket with Weekes. On the whole tour he took 39 wickets and made 1,775 runs (68.26) which included 6 centuries and a record stand of 350 for the third wicket with Weekes against Cambridge University at Fenner's. In the Tests against Australia in 1951/2 he was the heaviest scorer with 337 Test runs (33.70), including 108 in the fourth match at Melbourne, and in the two Tests against New Zealand, he made 71, 62 not out and 100 (at Auckland). He captured 19 wickets (21.57) in the Australian Tests, including 6 for 38 in the first innings of the third match at Adelaide, when he bowled throughout and Australia collapsed for 82. Against India in 1952/3 he had one great innings of 237 in the fifth match at Kingston, adding 197 and 213 respectively with Weekes and Walcott. After several years of inconsistency he returned to his best form in England in 1957, heading the batting in all first-class matches with 1,470 runs (58.80), including 4 centuries, and taking 39 wickets (24.33); in the Tests he registered 350 runs (38.88), including a masterly 191 not out in the third match at Trent Bridge, carrying his bat through the innings of 372. At Headingley in the fourth match he captured 7 for 70 in England's sole innings. At his best on an uncertain pitch at Lord's against Middlesex, he hit 66 not out in a total of 176 and 61 in a total of 143 for 8 – besides taking 5 for 34 in the first innings. Against England at Bridgetown in the first Test of 1959/60 he scored 197 not out in 11 hours 29 minutes and, with Gary Sobers, added 399 for the fourth wicket. His immortal fame as a captain dates from the tour of Australia in 1960/61 when the popular West Indies side helped to revive flagging interest in the game in Australia. In the classic tie at Brisbane, the first Test, Worrell encouraged an attacking approach and himself made two hard-hit scores of 65 in the match. He led West Indies to a 5-0 victory over India in 1961/2 (only three times had this decisive margin been achieved in Test history) and headed the averages with 332 runs (88.00), making 98 not out in the fifth Test at Kingston, batting at number six which was now his usual position. In England in 1963, although he was none too fit throughout, he continued as a remarkably effective captain, West Indies winning the rubber 3-1. He retired from regular first-class cricket at the end of this tour, and was knighted the following year. Sir Frank Worrell had been a professional in the Lancashire League; studied sociology at Manchester University; been appointed Warden of the University College of the West Indies and elected a senator in the Jamaican Parliament. When he died in 1967, a memorial service was held in Westminster Abbey.

'The Three Ws' – Frank Worrell (left), Clyde Walcott (centre) and Everton Weekes

First-class career (1941-64): 15,025 runs (54.24) including 39 centuries, 349 wickets (29.03) and 139 catches
Test matches (51): 3,860 runs (49.48) including 9 centuries, 69 wickets (38.73) and 43 catches

NEW ZEALAND

ALABASTER, John Chaloner (b.1930)

Otago

A right-arm leg-break bowler and occasionally useful batsman, John Alabaster toured India and Pakistan in 1955/6, England in 1958, South Africa in 1961/2 and West Indies in 1971/2. At home he played against the West Indies in 1955/6, England in 1962/3 and India in 1967/8. He reached his peak in South Africa, where, in all first-class matches, he took 86 wickets (25.80), more than anyone else, and scored 296 runs (16.44). In the five Tests he took 22 wickets (28.04), helping New Zealand to square a series for the first time.

First-class career (1955-72): 2,427 runs (13.33) and 500 wickets (25.37)
Test matches (21): 272 runs (9.71), 49 wickets (38.02) and 7 catches

ALCOTT, Cyril Francis Walter (1896-1973)

Hawke's Bay, Auckland and Otago

A very good all-rounder, a left-handed batsman and left-arm orthodox slow bowler, Cyril Alcott visited England in 1927 and 1931 and at home played against England in 1929/30 and South Africa in 1931/2. In 1927 he hit his highest score, 131 against Warwickshire at Edgbaston, putting on 301 for the second wicket with C.S. Dempster, and one of his best pieces of bowling was also in 1927, at Weston-super-Mare, when Somerset, seeking 162 to win, collapsed for 67, Cyril Alcott taking 5 for 3 in five overs. He was very disappointing in Tests.

First-class career (1920-46): 2,514 runs (27.93) including 5 centuries, and 220 wickets (26.78)
Test matches (6): 113 runs (22.60), 6 wickets (90.16) and 3 catches

ANDERSON, Robert Wickham (b.1948)

Canterbury, Northern Districts, Otago and Central Districts

At his best a handsome and hard-hitting player, a tall, strongly built right-handed opening batsman, and athletic fielder, Robert Anderson is the son of W.M. Anderson who played in one Test for New Zealand. Anderson Junior played his early first-class cricket for Canterbury but has since played for three other provinces in his determination to get to the top. Chosen to tour England in 1973, he did not make the Test side, but when he won his first cap at Lahore against Pakistan in 1976/7 he scored 92 in the second innings. He lost his place at the end of this three-Test series but returned to play with some success at home against England in 1978, making 28 and 26 in the low scoring match at Wellington, when New Zealand defeated England for the first time, and 62, 15, 17 and 55 in his subsequent innings in the series. In England later that year he could make only 42 runs in six Test innings against top-class seam bowling.

First-class career (1967-): 5,609 runs (30.65) including 8 centuries, and 5 wickets (30.80)
Test matches (12): 381 runs (31.75) and 1 catch

ANDERSON, William McDougall (1919-79)

Canterbury

A left-handed opening batsman and change-bowler, Bill Anderson's sole Test was against Australia at Wellington in 1945/6, when he scored 4 and 1 and held a catch. Lindwall dismissed him both times. His career-highest was 137 against Otago in 1945/6.

First-class career (1938-50): 1,973 runs (34.61) including 2 centuries, and 18 wickets (38.16)

ANDREWS, Bryan (b.1945)

Canterbury, Central Districts and Otago

For more than a decade a very useful right-arm medium-pace bowler, Bryan Andrews toured Australia in 1973/4, where he played in two Tests.

First-class career (1963-74): 474 runs (9.11) and 198 wickets (23.23)
Test matches (2): 22 runs (22.00), 2 wickets (77.00) and 1 catch

BADCOCK, Frederick Theodore (b.1898)

Wellington and Otago

Born in India and having left England soon after the First World War, Ted Badcock devoted many years to playing and coaching in New Zealand. There was a suggestion of Keith Miller in the dark lock flopping over his right eye, and in his dashing right-handed batting. As a bowler he had an easy, fluent action: his best ball was the medium-pace in-swinger which cut back slightly from leg and, although of a more leisurely pace, he was as accurate as Alec Bedser at his best. He played against England in the first-ever Test in New Zealand in 1929/30, again in 1932/3 and also against South Africa in 1931/2. Surprisingly he never toured England with New Zealand teams, although he was domiciled here during the Second World War, when he occasionally represented Northamptonshire with success. However, against South Africa at Christchurch and Wellington he made 64 and 53 respectively. For Wellington he enjoyed such performances as 5 for 54 and 7 for 59 against Otago in 1926/7, 7 for 50 against Canterbury in 1924/5 and 7 for 55 against Auckland in 1925/6.

First-class career (1924-45): 2,383 runs (25.62) including 4 centuries, and 221 wickets (23.57)
Test matches (7): 137 runs (19.57), 16 wickets (38.12) and 1 catch

BARBER, Richard Trevor (b.1925)

Wellington and Central Districts

A right-handed batsman, Trevor Barber played in only one Test, against the West Indies at Wellington in 1955/6, scoring 12 and 5 and catching the great Gary Sobers.

First-class career (1945-60): 1,966 runs (23.12) including 1 century

BARTLETT, Gary Alexander (b.1941)

Central Districts and Canterbury

A right-arm fast bowler whose pace off the pitch could be very disconcerting despite an action which did not satisfy some purists, Gary Bartlett was a useful batsman and a safe field. He toured South Africa in 1961/2 and played against Pakistan at home in 1964/5, England in 1965/6 and India in 1967/8 with mixed success. In the five Tests against South Africa he scored 215 runs (23.88) but took only 8 wickets (40.75). Against India, however, at Christchurch he took 6 for 38 in the second innings of 301, helping New Zealand to her fourth victory from 81 official Tests. At the age of nineteen in an unofficial Test against Australia at Wellington in 1959/60, he put on an aggressive 71 in forty-five minutes with John Reid and then took 5 for 51 in Australia's first innings.

First-class career (1958-70): 1,504 runs (16.71) and 150 wickets (28.33)
Test matches (10): 263 runs (15.47), 24 wickets (33.00) and 8 catches

BARTON, Paul Thomas (b.1935)

Wellington

A composed, correct and polished right-handed batsman, Paul Barton made a cultured 109 in the fifth Test against South Africa at Port Elizabeth in 1961/2, reaching his century with his nineteenth boundary despite a dislocated shoulder, and in all first-class matches on the tour made 675 runs (27.00). He achieved little in two Tests against England in 1962/3.

First-class career (1954-68): 2,824 runs (23.93) including 3 centuries
Test matches (7): 285 runs (20.35) including 1 century, and 4 catches

BEARD, Donald Derek (1920-82)

Central Districts, Northern Districts and Wellington

A run-saving, right-arm medium-pace bowler who rushed in to deliver the ball and who was by nature and physique a flamboyant hitter, Donald Beard played against the West Indies in New Zealand in 1951/2 and 1955/6. His persistent swing bowling in the fourth Test at Auckland in the latter season helped New Zealand to achieve her first-ever official Test victory. An All-Black Rugby trialist as a flank forward, he became Principal at Te Aroha College.

First-class career (1945-65): 2,166 runs (22.10) and 278 wickets (21.58)
Test matches (4): 101 runs (20.20), 9 wickets (33.55) and 2 catches

BECK, John Edward Francis (b.1934)

Wellington

A hard-hitting left-handed batsman with rippling off and square drives but a reputedly flawed back-foot technique, John Beck toured South Africa in 1953/4 without having played in a first-class match. In his second Test at Cape Town he was run out for 99, having enjoyed four 'lives'. In the first Test against the West Indies at Dunedin in 1955/6 he scored an aggressive 66 to counter Ramadhin and Valentine.

First-class career (1953-62): 1,508 runs (23.93) including 2 centuries
Test matches (8): 394 runs (26.26)

BELL, William (b.1931)

Canterbury

A right-arm leg-break bowler, William Bell toured

South Africa in 1953/4 taking 12 wickets (52.66) and was ineffective in the two Tests he played.

First-class career (1949-59): 170 runs (10.00) and 44 wickets (40.52)
Test matches (2): 21 runs (—), 2 wickets (117.50) and 1 catch

BILBY, Grahame Paul (b.1941)

Wellington

A competent right-handed opening batsman who scored 161 against Otago in 1965/6, Grahame Bilby made an appearance in two Tests against England that season.

First-class career (1962-77): 2,936 runs (32.62), including 3 centuries
Test matches (2): 55 runs (13.75) and 3 catches

BLAIR, Robert William (b.1932)

Wellington and Central Districts

A hostile and accurate right-arm fast bowler and occasionally useful late-order batsman, Bob Blair toured South Africa in 1953/4 taking 30 wickets (25.40) and hitting 79 against Griqualand West at Kimberley, which remained his career-highest score. On the day that he heard his fiancée had been killed in a Christmas Eve train disaster back in New Zealand, he kept his end up bravely in the second Test at Johannesburg, adding 33 for the last wicket when everyone had to fight hard for runs. On the first day of his Test debut, against South Africa at Wellington in 1952/3, he secured the wickets of Waite, Endean and McLean on a batsman's wicket at a personal cost of eight runs. He toured England in 1958, taking 51 wickets (23.58), which included 6 for 19 when Cambridge were routed for 46 at Fenner's, but he achieved little in the Tests. Against South Africa at Auckland in the third Test of 1963/4 his match analysis was 7 for 141. He also played at home against England in 1954/5, 1958/9 and 1962/3 and the West Indies in 1955/6. His best bowling feats in an innings were 9 for 72 for Wellington against Auckland and 9 for 75 (14 for 136 in the match) against Canterbury in 1956/7, in which season he captured 46 wickets (9.47), the greatest number taken in a Plunket Shield season. When injury eventually forced him out of the game, Bob Blair had taken more wickets in first-class cricket than any other New Zealand player. His batting put him amongst an elite company of players who have suffered the indignity of scoring three pairs of noughts in Test matches!

First-class career (1951-65): 1,672 runs (12.26) and 537 wickets (18.54)
Test matches (19): 189 runs (6.75), 43 wickets (35.23) and 5 catches

BLUNT, Roger Charles (1900-1966)

Canterbury and Otago

Dark and lithe, beginning his career in first-class cricket as a schoolboy, Roger Blunt was a very useful right-arm leg-break bowler who developed into a fine, stylish and adaptable batsman. He hit 42 from one eight-ball over for West Christchurch against Riccarton in 1923 (including 7 sixes) and made 3 centuries in succession for Otago the following season. He toured England on the first-ever tour in 1927 and, as the most effective all-rounder, scored 1,540 runs (44.00) and took 78 wickets (24.97) in first-class matches. In 1929/30 he headed the bowling with 9 wickets (19.00) in New Zealand's first Test series, against England. The first match at Christchurch brought him the top score of 45 not out in a total of 112 on the first day, besides a match record of 5 for 34. In England in 1931 he made 1,592 runs (43.02), and also took 34 wickets (34.76). In the first Test in England, at Lord's, a very watchful 96 helped to make an honourable draw. He played in the two Tests against South Africa in 1931/2 without distinguishing himself. In a dazzling display, however, in 1931/2 for Otago against Canterbury at Christchurch, he hit 338 not out at a run-a-minute, at that time the highest score by a New Zealander. Until Bert Sutcliffe surpassed him in 1953, he was the most prolific batsman in New Zealand cricket.

First-class career (1917-35): 7,953 runs (40.99) including 15 centuries, and 214 wickets (31.01)
Test matches (9): 330 runs (27.50), 12 wickets (39.33) and 5 catches

BOLTON, Bruce Alfred (b.1935)

Canterbury and Wellington

A right-handed opening batsman with a sound defence and a useful leg-break bowler, Bruce Bolton played twice against England in 1958/9.

First-class career (1955-71): 2,092 runs (20.30) including 1 century, and 96 wickets (22.32)
Test matches (2): 59 runs (19.66) and 1 catch

BOOCK, Stephen Lewis (b.1951)

Otago and Canterbury

Tall and curly haired Stephen Boock is a slow left-arm orthodox spin bowler with excellent control and considerable power of spin. Also an outstanding short-leg fieldsman, Boock (who pronounces his name to rhyme with 'Hock') became in 1977/8 only the third New Zealand bowler to take more than fifty wickets in a season and, by claiming 66 wickets at 16.45 in thirteen matches, he surpassed the previous record of 57 wickets in a New Zealand season set by G.J. Thompson of Lord Hawke's 1902/3 touring team. After a debut for Otago in 1973/4, he transferred to

Canterbury in 1975/6. However, it was not until two years later that he came to prominence; he had the thrill of winning a Test cap at Wellington in February 1978 when New Zealand beat England for the first time. In the third Test in Auckland he took 5 for 67 in England's innings of 429 and in England a few months later took 39 wickets (22.17) in thirteen matches on the tour. At Trent Bridge in an England innings of 429, he returned remarkable figures of 28-18-29-2. He toured Australia in 1980/81 but played only two first-class matches.

First-class career (1973-): 516 runs (8.06) and 333 wickets (20.96)
Test matches (12): 37 runs (2.84), 19 wickets (37.15) and 8 catches

BRACEWELL, Brendon Paul (b.1959)

Central Districts and Otago

Brendon Bracewell is a right-arm fast bowler who was chosen for the 1978 tour of England on the strength of his performances in only three matches. So well did he bowl that the selectors were handsomely rewarded for their gamble, but he suffered for his hard work on the tour and had a disappointing 1978/9 season in New Zealand, partly because of injury. About 5ft 9in and of wiry build, with a hostile action in which every fibre of body and soul is thrown into the leaping delivery, his career has been interrupted by back trouble, but he did well at home in 1981/2. Playing his first Test at The Oval at the age of eighteen, he took the wicket of Graham Gooch with his third ball and followed up with the wicket of Mike Brearley. Called in to play for New Zealand while playing in Western Australia in 1980/81, he did not take a wicket.

First-class career (1977-): 239 runs (7.96) and 69 wickets (29.73)
Test matches (5): 17 runs (2.12), 10 wickets (45.60) and 1 catch

BRACEWELL, John Garry (b.1959)

Otago

The brother of Brendon Bracewell, John is a tall, quickish off-break bowler with a high action and a useful late-order batsman. When he toured Australia in 1980/81 he bowled with great confidence. His sharp spin and high bounce make him a matchwinner on helpful wickets, as his seven wickets for nine runs for Otago against Canterbury in 1981/2 prove. Making his first-class debut in 1978/9, he had twelve times taken more than five wickets in an innings and three times more than ten in a match by the end of the 1981/2 season. In three Test matches in Australia he made little impact, but he took 5 for 75 and 4 for 61 against India at Auckland in 1980/81.

First-class career (1978-): 825 runs (19.18) and 124 wickets (20.82)
Test matches (4): 29 runs (5.80), 11 wickets (26.36) and 2 catches

BRADBURN, Wynne Pennell (b.1939)

Northern Districts

A sound right-handed opening batsman and slow-medium change in-swing bowler, Wynne Bradburn played in two Tests at home against South Africa in 1963/4.

First-class career (1957-69): 2,077 runs (20.36) including 1 century, and 19 wickets (42.31)
Test matches (2): 62 runs (15.50) and 2 catches

BURGESS, Mark Gordon (b.1944)

Auckland

Mark Burgess, a friendly, level-headed character and a fine cricketer, had been a Test player for more than a decade when he achieved the singular distinction of captaining New Zealand to their first victory over England at Wellington in 1978. In 1979 he led New Zealand into the semi-final of the Prudential World Cup when they lost only narrowly to England in their meeting at Old Trafford. Making his initial first-class appearance for the New Zealand Under 23 side against his own province in 1963/4, Mark Burgess first played for Auckland three years later and in 1967/8 made his Test debut against India, scoring 50 and 39 at Dunedin. A fair-haired right-hander with a sound technique and some handsome attacking strokes, especially adept at driving in the arc between cover and mid-wicket, he toured England in 1969, 1973, and 1978 (also appearing in the Prudential World Cup in 1975 and 1979) as well as going to the West Indies, India and Pakistan (twice). His first Test hundred was 119 not out against Pakistan at Dacca in 1969/70, and he hit a memorable 104 against England at Auckland in his next Test innings. Further centuries followed against the West Indies at Kingston in 1971/2 and Pakistan in Lahore in 1976/7, but his finest innings was a sparkling 105 against England on the Saturday of the Lord's Test in 1973. New Zealand ought subsequently to have won the game but let England off the hook. There was no such failure in 1978 when, amidst great excitement at the Basin Reserve, Burgess directed his fast bowlers Collinge and Richard Hadlee in a sensational demolition of England's second innings. Burgess's batting in Tests seemed to suffer from the extra responsibility of captaincy but he was popular with both his own team and his opponents. Essentially a dedicated amateur cricketer in a professional age, his attitude was that winning or losing was not life or death. Earlier in his career, as an occasional medium-paced bowler, he took 3 for 23 and 1 for 18

Mark Burgess

against India at Nagpur in 1969/70, during New Zealand's first Test win in India. He toured Australia under Geoff Howarth's captaincy in 1980/81, having some success.

First-class career (1963-81): 10,281 runs (35.82) including 20 centuries, 30 wickets (38.26) and 151 catches
Test matches (50): 2,684 runs (31.20) including 5 centuries, 6 wickets (35.33) and 34 catches

BURKE, Cecil (b.1914)

Auckland

A right-arm leg-break bowler consistent in length who delivered with plenty of 'air', Cec Burke or 'the Burglar' was also a useful batsman and a safe fielder in the gully or at third man. He toured England in 1949, securing 54 wickets (29.83) – including 6 for 23 in the first innings at Derby – but he was not selected for any of the Tests. His sole Test was the first after the Second World War, against Australia at Wellington in 1945/6, when he scored 1 and 3 and took 2 for 30. A rather fiery man, he was full of good fellowship and homespun philosophy.

First-class career (1937-54): 935 runs (17.64) and 194 wickets (26.01)

BURTT, Thomas Browning (b.1915)

Canterbury

With his square, thickset figure, easy smile and general air of busy bustle, Tom Burtt was a favourite on many cricket grounds. A left-arm slow bowler of accurate length and flight with the ability to bowl to his field, he once said: 'I could bowl all day; I love it!' A useful and rugged batsman, he was prone to use his 'hockey-shot', a powerful cross-bat crack. He toured England in 1949, his only overseas tour, taking 128 wickets (22.88) in the dry summer, a record number for a New Zealander. Of his 1,245 overs, a third were maidens. In the Tests he took 17 wickets (33.41). At home he appeared against England in 1946/7 and 1950/51, against South Africa in 1952/3 and against the West Indies in 1951/2. He took 8 for 35 in an innings for Canterbury against Otago in 1953/4.

First-class career (1943-55): 1,644 runs (17.30) and 408 wickets (22.19)
Test matches (10): 252 runs (21.00), 33 wickets (35.45) and 2 catches

BUTTERFIELD, Leonard Arthur (b.1913)

Canterbury

A good all-rounder who was not able to play regular first-class cricket, Leonard Butterfield was a right-handed batsman and fast-medium bowler, whose sole Test was the first after the Second World War, against Australia at Wellington in 1945/6, when he made a pair and took 0 for 24.

First-class career (1934-46): 589 runs (22.65) and 38 wickets (19.65)

CAIRNS, Bernard Lance (b.1949)

Central Districts, Otago, Northern Districts and Durham

A massively built and enthusiastic medium-fast bowler with enormous hands, Lance Cairns is primarily a right-arm medium-pace bowler. He swings the ball considerably in a heavy atmosphere, with a hopping, open-chested action reminiscent of a slow-motion Mike Procter. However, he can be equally valuable as a late-order batsman who hits the ball vast distances with a blacksmith's might and relish. In 1979/80 he hit a century in 52 minutes against Wellington for Otago – the fastest ever in New Zealand. He first played for Central Districts in 1972/3 and four years later moved to Otago. At Test level it was some time before he commanded a regular place because his bowling lacked penetration on good wickets, but he has played Tests on tours to Australia in 1973/4, Pakistan and India in 1976/7, England in 1978 and Australia in 1980/81. His outstanding performance was to take 5 for 55 in 33.1 overs in India's first innings of 298 at Madras in 1976. He also took 6 for 85 against West Indies in 1979/80. He played for Durham in 1979 after proving an invaluable all-round member of the New Zealand side which reached the semi-final of the 1979

Lance Cairns

Prudential World Cup. He took 13 wickets in three Tests against Australia in 1980/81.

First-class career (1971-): 2,953 runs (20.08) including 1 century, and 348 wickets (26.05)
Test matches (26): 575 runs (15.97), 72 wickets (34.41) and 19 catches

CAMERON, Francis James (b.1932)

Otago

A wily right-arm medium-fast bowler, able to swing the ball both ways, Frank Cameron toured South Africa in 1961/2, India and Pakistan in 1964/5 and England in 1965. In South Africa his tenacity as a stock bowler brought him 62 wickets (22.77) in first-class matches, including 20 wickets (24.65) in the Tests. His 5 for 48 in the first innings of the third Test at Cape Town materially assisted New Zealand's victory. In England, however, although he captured 47 wickets (24.42) he failed in the Tests. Usually a moderate number eleven batsman, he played twelve careful not-out innings out of fourteen and finished at the top of the tour batting averages with 45! When Pakistan toured New Zealand in 1964/5, he headed the bowling in the three Tests with 13 wickets (15.61). At home he also played against England in 1962/3 and South Africa in 1963/4. On his way to South Africa in 1961/2, he took 7 for 27 in the first innings against Western Australia at Perth. He was later chairman of the New Zealand selectors.

First-class career (1952-67): 993 runs (11.82) and 447 wickets (21.60)
Test matches (19): 116 runs (11.60), 61 wickets (30.31) and 2 catches

CAVE, Henry Butler (b.1922)

Wellington and Central Districts

The best of a large family of cricketers – known as 'the Cavemen' – Harry Cave was an economical right-arm medium-pace bowler who was able to swing the new ball with a high, windmill-type action and was prepared to bowl until exhausted. He was a reliable and adaptable late-order batsman and a very good fielder. He toured England in 1949 and 1958 and India and Pakistan in 1955/6 and, at home, played against England in 1954/5 and the West Indies in 1955/6. He captained the team to India and Pakistan, and led New Zealand in one Test against the West Indies. In England in 1949 his four Test wickets cost 465 runs but he was much less expensive in 1958, taking 50 wickets (22.02) on the tour although he again lacked penetration in the Tests. In India and Pakistan he bowled with remarkable economy, taking 14 wickets in the Tests. Against India alone, 118 of his 255 overs were maidens. In his two Tests against England in 1954/5 at Dunedin and Auckland respectively, his figures were: 48-25-52-3. His most successful series was against the West Indies in 1955/6, when he took 12 wickets (15.50). In the fourth Test at Auckland he bowled New Zealand to their first-ever victory in Tests, by 190 runs, taking 4 for 22 (in 27.3 overs) and 4 for 21 (in 13.1 overs) with his hostile swing bowling. In three unofficial Tests against Australia in 1956/7, he captured 17 wickets (16.70). His highest score was 118 for Central Districts against Otago in 1952/3, and his most effective bowling 7 for 31 and 6 for 33 against Auckland – in a single day – during the same season.

First-class career (1945-59): 2,187 runs (16.08) including 2 centuries, and 362 wickets (23.93)
Test matches (19): 229 runs (8.80), 34 wickets (43.14) and 8 catches

CHAPPLE, Murray Ernest (b.1930)

Canterbury and Central Districts

A steady, stroke-making right-handed batsman, who frequently opened the batting, and a left-arm change slow bowler, Murray Chapple toured South Africa in 1953/4 and 1961/2 and, at home, played against South Africa in 1952/3 and 1963/4, England in 1954/5 and, as captain in one match in 1965/6, and the West Indies in 1955/6. However, despite his experience, he had a disappointing Test record; his best effort was 76 at Cape Town in the third Test against South Africa in 1953/4, when he shared in an opening stand of 126 with G.O. Rabone. For Canterbury against the South

Africans at Christchurch in 1952/3 he hit a fluent 165, his career-highest, and 88. He became involved in the national administration of the game and has managed New Zealand touring teams.

First-class career (1949-72): 5,344 runs (28.88) including 4 centuries, and 142 wickets (25.06)
Test matches (14): 497 runs (19.11), 1-84 and 10 catches

CHATFIELD, Ewen John (b.1951)

Wellington

A hard working, but rather bland medium-fast bowler, Ewen Chatfield had a tragic experience on his Test debut against England at Auckland in 1974/5. In a stubborn defensive innings at number eleven, he was struck on the temple by a ball from Peter Lever; his heart stopped and he swallowed his tongue. Following mouth to mouth resuscitation and heart massage by England's physiotherapist Bernard Thomas, he was taken to hospital and, happily, regained consciousness an hour later. Not selected for the Prudential World Cup in England a few months later, he was fit enough to represent his country against Australia in 1976/7 and England in 1977/8, bowling steadily and industriously. He toured England with New Zealand's 1979 Prudential World Cup team.

First-class career (1973-): 320 runs (8.64), and 309 wickets (19.01)
Test matches (5): 31 runs (7.75) and 8 wickets (61.50)

CLEVERLEY, Donald Charles (b.1909)

Auckland and Central Districts

A right-arm fast-medium bowler who could make the ball fly head-high, Donald Cleverley played in the first Test against South Africa at Christchurch in 1931/2 and also against Australia in the first Test after the Second World War at Wellington in 1945/6, but had little success. He was a national amateur boxing champion.

First-class career (1930-53): 157 runs (5.60) and 90 wickets (30.21)
Test matches (2): 19 runs (19.00) and 0-130

COLLINGE, Richard Owen (b.1946)

Central Districts, Northern Districts and Wellington

When he retired, the most prolific wicket-taker in New Zealand Test cricket, Richard Collinge was at 6ft 5in a menacing prospect for any batsman. He approached the wicket off a notoriously lengthy, long-striding run, hands clawing the air, bowling left-arm fast medium deliveries of consistent accuracy at a length full enough to make good use of any swing. He made his first-class debut in 1963/4 and the following season at

Richard Collinge

the age of eighteen played in the three Tests against Pakistan, taking 15 wickets (24.33). A committed family man, later in his career he was sometimes a reluctant tourist and in 1971/2 had to return home early from the West Indies because of the illness of one of his children. However, he was almost always an automatic selection when he was available because his height and strength made him an opponent all batsmen respected though he was seldom genuinely fast, and sometimes looked rather ordinary on true batting pitches. Apart from the West Indies he toured Pakistan and India and England four times, in 1965, 1969, 1973 and as a replacement for the injured Dayle Hadlee in 1978. A determined and possibly underrated right-handed tail-end batsman, he had one great hour of glory against Pakistan in Auckland in 1972/3, when he made 68 not out, the highest score by a number eleven batsman in Test cricket, and shared a last wicket stand of 151 with Brian Hastings, still a record tenth-wicket stand in Tests. But Collinge's proudest moments must have been his participation in the first defeats ever inflicted by New Zealand on Australia and England. The victory by five wickets at Christchurch in March 1974 was New Zealand's first against Australia in 113 official Tests, and only the eighth in all Tests, Collinge taking 3 for 70 and 2 for 37. In the following match, which Australia won to level the series, he took 5 for 82 and 4 for 84. Three years and eleven months later, at Wellington, Collinge took 3 for 42 and 3 for 35 in the famous 72 run victory over England. The fast in-swinger with which he bowled Geoff Boycott for 1 in the second innings started the collapse of England to 64 all out amidst feverish excitement. It was entirely appropriate that this modest, calm stalwart of New Zealand cricket for fifteen years should have had a strong hand in one of his country's finest cricketing hours.

First-class career (1963-78): 1,848 runs (14.43) and 524 wickets (24.41)
Test matches (35): 533 runs (14.40), 116 wickets (29.25) and 10 catches

COLQUHOUN, Ian Alexander (b.1924)

Central Districts

A competent wicket-keeper and useful right-handed batsman, Ian Colquhoun appeared in two Tests against England in 1954/5.

First-class career (1953-64): 768 runs (14.76) and 136 dismissals (108 ct, 28 st.)
Test matches (2): 1 run (0.50) and 4 dismissals (4 ct)

CONEY, Jeremy Vernon (b.1952)

Wellington

A very tall, fit and enthusiastic all-rounder, Jeremy Coney is a competent right-handed batsman, steady medium-paced bowler and fine fielder. He has appeared in several Tests against Australia, playing two while on tour in 1973/4, two at home in the same season, two more in Australia in 1980/81, when for a struggling side he scored 71 at Perth and 55 not out at Melbourne, and three at home in 1981/2 when he made 73 at Auckland. He also played three against Pakistan in 1978/9. His Test-highest score is 82 in the third match against Pakistan at Auckland in 1978/9, in which series he was his country's most successful batsman, heading the averages with 242 runs (48.40). Also outstanding as captain of Wellington in the Shell Series, Coney, a convivial family man, was named New Zealand's cricketer of the year and was an important member of the 1979 Prudential World Cup team which reached the semi-final and lost only narrowly to England.

First-class career (1970-): 3,961 runs (30.70) including 4 centuries, 63 wickets (29.22) and 102 catches
Test matches (18): 805 runs (30.96), 10 wickets (36.00) and 18 catches

CONGDON, Bevan Ernest (b.1938)

Central Districts, Wellington, Otago and Canterbury

One of the finest all-round cricketers produced by his country, Bev Congdon was a player of immense character and a fine ambassador for New Zealand. Thin, of medium height, and with a slightly stooping walk, he was a right-handed batsman who usually went in first wicket down. He had a sound technique, exceptional depths of concentration and determination, and delightful timing, notably when driving on the offside off either foot. A fine fielder anywhere, he was also a canny medium-paced bowler who swung the ball both ways and expected a wicket with every delivery. As a captain he was orthodox, tough, but never mean, and often shrewd. He led New Zealand in the first win against Australia and, had his fielders held their chances at Lord's in 1973, would also have inspired the first success against England. As it was, though no longer captain, he was a member of the team which eventually beat England for the first time in 1978. He played in more Tests and scored more runs for his country than any other New Zealand cricketer. Of his 7 Test centuries, three were scores of more than 150 and as captain of New Zealand in seventeen Tests between 1971/2 and 1974/5 his batting actually seemed to grow in stature, rather than to suffer under the strain of captaincy. In 1973, in between scoring 176 and 175 in successive Tests, he cheerfully gave up his Sunday to play against a village side in Surrey. He made his debut for Central Districts in 1960/61 and his first Test appearance in 1964/5. On the first of four official tours of England in 1965 he scored 1,040 runs as an opening batsman, and in the West Indies and Bermuda in 1971/2, he was a major success on a happy tour, scoring 992 runs at 82.66. In the second Test in Port of Spain, going in number three, he scored 166 not out and 82, and in the following Test at Bridgetown, taking over the captaincy from the injured Graham Dowling, he scored 126 not out. Scores of 61 not out, 11 and 58 followed, as New Zealand drew a series they had been expected to lose. It was really only in the 1970s that New Zealand went into Test matches without being considered the inevitable underdogs and Congdon's determined captaincy had much to do with this. In England in 1973 he scored a courageous 176, leading his side from the imminence of a crushing loss to one of the most honourable defeats in Test

Bev Congdon – Norman Gifford (England) fielding

cricket. Facing a huge target and standing at 130 for four at one point on the fourth day, Congdon and Vic Pollard put on 177 for the fifth wicket. They amassed what was then the highest fourth innings score by a losing Test side (440) and New Zealand lost by only 38 runs. At Lord's ten days later New Zealand replied to England's 253 with 551, of which Congdon scored 175, but New Zealand's bowlers just failed to bowl England out a second time. The following winter (1973/4), after Congdon had scored 132 at Wellington in the first (drawn) Test against Australia, he led New Zealand to victory by five wickets at Christchurch. Of course Bev Congdon suffered reverses as well, but he accepted the ups and downs with the same good grace. He retired after a disappointing tour of England in 1978.

First-class career (1960-78): 13,101 runs (34.84) including 23 centuries, 204 wickets (30.02) and 201 catches
Test matches (61): 3,448 runs (32.22) including 7 centuries, 59 wickets (36.50) and 44 catches

COWIE, John (b.1912)

Auckland

A well-built right-arm fast bowler, Jack Cowie, nicknamed 'The Bull', displayed invariable determination, stamina, accuracy and outstanding skill. He could get the ball up from the most unresponsive turf, commanded the late out-swinger and, from time to time, could make the ball snap back from the off viciously. For much of his career he was the one 'class' bowler in the New Zealand team. He toured England in 1937 and 1949 and, at home, played against Australia in 1945/6 and England in 1946/7. On his first England tour, he took 114 wickets (19.95) overall and in the Tests 19 wickets (20.78). Despite dropped catches, he took 10 for 140 in the second match at Old Trafford. At Wellington in 1945/6 he took 6 for 40 in Australia's sole innings (after New Zealand had been routed for 42); and in the sole England innings at Christchurch in 1946/7 he captured 6 for 83, besides hitting 45, by far his best score in Tests. His best analysis was 6 for 3 against Ireland at Dublin in 1937.

First-class career (1932-50): 762 runs (10.16) and 359 wickets (22.28)
Test matches (9): 90 runs (10.00), 45 wickets (21.53) and 3 catches

CRESSWELL, George Fenwick (1915-66)

Wellington and Central Districts

Although he did not play in first-class cricket until he was thirty-four, 'Fen' Cresswell toured England in 1949 after one trial match, taking 62 wickets (26.09). A right-arm medium-pace leg-theory bowler with an unusual chest-on delivery, he was invariably steady with his length and could swing or cut the ball either way. A rather poor left-handed batsman, he was nicknamed 'the ferret' because he went in after 'the rabbits' but also answered to 'Fritzy' because he stood to attention before bowling. In his sole Test on the 1949 tour, the last at The Oval, he took 6 for 168 in England's total of 482. He also played against England twice in 1950/51, taking 3 for 18 in 15 overs at Wellington. For a New Zealand XI against Australia at Dunedin in 1949/50 he took 8 for 100 in a total of 299. The soul of good fellowship in his cricketing days, he was found dead with a shotgun at his side.

First-class career (1949-55): 124 wickets (22.52)
Test matches (3): 14 runs (7.00) and 13 wickets (22.46)

CROMB, Ian Burns (b.1905)

Canterbury

Well-built, loose-limbed and high-spirited, Ian Cromb was a right-arm fast-medium bowler, whose action, though rather slingy, was likened to Maurice Tate's. He could swing the ball late, especially in England's heavy atmosphere and cut the ball a little, but his main asset was the ability to hurry the ball on to the bat. Unlike many New Zealand bowlers he could work up a 'hate' against the batsman. He was also a useful late-order batsman and good field. In England in 1931, he took 58 wickets (26.29) and scored 448 runs. At Wellington, in the second Test against South Africa in 1931/2, he hit a valuable 51 not out at number ten. He captained New Zealand in the unofficial Tests against MCC in 1935/6. His career-highest score was 171 for Canterbury against Wellington in 1939/40 and his most productive bowling 7 for 21 and 7 for 74 for South Island Army against North Island Army in 1942/3. He was a professional for several years in the East Lancashire League and in his fifties he played senior club championship cricket in Christchurch.

First-class career (1929-47): 3,950 runs (29.04) including 3 centuries, and 222 wickets (27.71)
Test matches (5): 123 runs (20.50), 8 wickets (55.25) and 1 catch

CROWE, Martin David (b.1962)

Auckland

The son of a first-class cricketer and younger brother of Jeffrey Crowe, a talented batsman who played with success for South Australia for six seasons, Martin Crowe became the first of his family to play Test cricket for New Zealand when at the age of 19 he was selected at home against Australia at the end of the 1981/2 season. Consistent performances for Auckland after his first appearance for them in 1979/80 earned him a place in three Tests against Australia. He failed, but still looked a useful prospect. A strongly-built, 14-stone, curly-haired, right-handed batsman with plenty of shots, and a fine catcher, he toured Australia for a tour of one-day internationals 1982/3.

First-class career (1979-): 1,023 runs (31.96) including 1 century, and 4 wickets (46.75)
Test matches (3): 20 runs (5.0), 0-14 and 3 catches

CUNIS, Robert Smith (b.1941)

Auckland and Northern Districts

Although once described as 'neither one thing nor the other', Bob Cunis was a useful all-rounder. Broad-shouldered, he was a right-arm workaday fast-medium bowler apt to berate the batsman by word or look for some streaky shot, and a determined, steady batsman. He toured England in 1969, India and Pakistan in 1969/70 and the West Indies in 1971/2 and, at home, played against South Africa in 1963/4, England in 1965/6 and 1970/71 and the West Indies in 1968/9. Despite the rain, riots and rows which marred the third Test against India at Hyderabad in 1969/70 he returned a match analysis of 6 for 24. In the third match against Pakistan at Dacca he took 4 for 21, after adding 96 with Mark Burgess for the ninth wicket, saving New Zealand from defeat. On this 1969/70 tour he took 15 wickets (19.93) in the Tests. In 1970/71 Test at Auckland against England he took 9 for 128, but he had to work hard for little reward in both Australia and the West Indies. He was also a Rugby centre-three-quarter of some reputation.

First-class career (1960-77): 1,849 runs (16.50) including 1 century, and 386 wickets (26.65)
Test matches (20): 295 runs (12.82), 51 wickets (37.00) and 1 catch

D'ARCY, John William (b.1936)

Canterbury, Wellington and Otago

One of several young players 'blooded' on the 1958 England tour, John D'Arcy was a right-handed opening batsman of tremendous determination and concentration. He often defended admirably, but an absence of forcing strokes, due partly to an unorthodox grip, reduced his effectiveness. His 522 runs in twenty-two matches included his career-highest score, 89 in about five hours against Glamorgan at Swansea.

First-class career (1955-62): 2,009 runs (23.09)
Test matches (5): 136 runs (13.60)

DEMPSTER, Charles Stewart (1903-74)

Wellington, Wanganui, Leicestershire, Scotland and Warwickshire

'Stewie' Dempster was generally an opening batsman and certainly one of the best players to have been produced by New Zealand. Indeed, at his best he was superb and amongst the finest batsmen in the world. Rather short and stocky, he was a right-hander who drove with tremendous power, rarely lifting the ball. He was always alert and reliable in the field. Never coached, he toured England with the first New Zealand team in 1927 – when he said that he really learned cricket – heading the batting with 1,430 runs (44.68) in first-class matches and 2,165 runs (54.12) in all matches, including six centuries. During his 180 against Warwickshire at Edgbaston he hit W.G. Quaife for 5 fours in an over. In the first Test series in New Zealand, against England in 1929/30, when he headed the batting with 341 runs (85.25), he scored 136 at Wellington in the second match, putting on 276 for the first wicket with J.E. Mills, which remains his country's highest stand for any wicket against England. This was the first century in a Test for New Zealand and he followed it with 80 not out in the second innings. In England in 1931 he was brilliant, making 1,778 runs (59.26) in first-class matches, including 7 centuries, his 212 against Essex at Leyton remaining his career-highest. In the first Test in England, at Lord's, he scored 53 and 120. Although not as dominant in the first series against South Africa in 1931/2, he hit 64 in the second match at Wellington; and in what was to be his last Test, at Auckland against England in 1932/3, coming in with 2 wickets down for 0, he hit 83 not out in a total of 156. After taking up a business appointment with Sir Julien Cahn, he played for his patron's team and qualified for Leicestershire, playing for the county from 1935 until 1939 – as captain in 1936-8 – making 4,659 runs (49.04), including 18 centuries and heading the county's batting averages each year.

First-class career (1921-48): 12,145 runs (44.98) including 35 centuries
Test matches (10): 723 runs (65.72) including 2 centuries, 0-10 and 2 catches

DEMPSTER, Eric Wiiam (b.1925)

Wellington

A competent left-handed batsman and slow bowler, Eric Dempster toured South Africa in 1953/4, making 348 runs (21.75) and taking 22 wickets (32.00), and at home played against South Africa in 1952/3.

First-class career (1947-61): 1,592 runs (22.42) including 1 century, and 102 wickets (30.80)
Test matches (5): 106 runs (17.66), 2 wickets (109.50) and 1 catch

DICK, Arthur Edward (b.1936)

Otago and Wellington

An outstanding wicket-keeper and competent right-handed batsman, 'Art' Dick toured South Africa in 1961/2, England in 1965 and Pakistan in 1965/6 and, at home, played against England in 1962/3, South Africa in 1963/4 and Pakistan in 1964/5. In the series against South Africa in 1961/2 he equalled the then world record number of dismissals in a rubber – 23 (21 caught, 2 stumped). On his Test debut, at Durban, his 7 dismissals (6 caught, 1 stumped) equalled the New Zealand record. In England in 1965, he had 27 dismissals from 13 first-class matches.

First-class career (1959-69): 2,315 runs (20.30) including 1 century, and 169 dismissals (148 ct, 21 st.)
Test matches (17): 370 runs (14.23) and 51 dismissals (47 ct, 4 st.)

DICKINSON, George Ritchie (1903-78)

Otago

This right-arm bowler and often useful batsman was, at his best, as fast a bowler as New Zealand has boasted, though when trying for top speed his arm would drop a little. He appeared in the first and second Tests in New Zealand against England in 1929/30, dismissing Frank Woolley twice, and once against South Africa in 1931/2. He took 11 for 89 against Canterbury in 1924/5.

First-class career (1921-44): 1.013 runs (18.75) including 1 century, and 150 wickets (26.96)
Test matches (3): 31 runs (6.20), 8 wickets (30.62) and 3 catches

DONNELLY, Martin Paterson (b.1917)

Taranaki, Wellington, Canterbury, Oxford University, Middlesex and Warwickshire

Despite his lack of inches, Martin Donnelly was the best left-handed batsman in the world immediately after the Second World War and C.B. Fry volunteered that not one of the left-handers of his own day was superior. A complete batsman, he drove with punishing power and was merciless in pulling and cutting anything short. His footwork was superb. In the field he had speed, as befitted a Rugby footballer, and a powerful, accurate throw: he was equally valuable at cover-point, gully or in the leg-trap. First playing in the Plunket Shield at the age of 19, he was selected for the 1937 England tour, and was outstanding with 1,414 runs (37.21), though he started quietly in Test Cricket with 121 runs from three matches. Whilst serving as a Major, after war service in Egypt and Italy, he played a famous matchwinning innings of 133 for the Dominions against England at Lord's. Already a graduate of University Collge, Canterbury, he went up to Oxford to read history in 1946 and won blues for cricket and Rugby. Against Cambridge at Lord's that year, he hit a memorable 142 in a total of 261. He captained Oxford the following season and his feats in The Parks became legendary. In 1947 he scored a brilliant 162 not out in only three hours for Gentlemen against Players at Lord's. His career-highest, 208 not out for MCC against Yorkshire at Scarborough in 1948, took a mere 180 minutes. But he reached the zenith of a great career on New Zealand's England tour of 1949. He headed the batting with 2,287 runs (61.81), including 5 centuries. In the Tests, he made 462 runs (77.00), passing 50 in five out of six innings. In the second Test at his beloved Lord's, he scored 206, taking complete control of the attack. After coming down from Oxford he went into business and played only a little more first-class cricket – twenty games for Warwickshire and one for Middlesex. In 1946/7 he represented England against Ireland at Rugby football in Dublin. He now lives in Australia unchanged by success. He was always equably tempered and treated cricket as a game , not a war.

First-class career (1937-61): 9,250 runs (47.44) including 23 centuries, and 43 wickets (39.14)
Test matches (7): 582 runs (52.90) including 1 century, 0-20 and 7 catches

DOWLING, Graham Thorne (b.1937)

Canterbury

Graham Dowling was a studious, methodical, and accomplished right-handed opening batsman, a brilliant field, usually at leg-slip, a proficient reserve wicket-keeper and a regular Test choice from 1961 until 1972. He became a thoughtful captain who led New Zealand in nineteen Tests, and was victor in four. He toured widely: to South Africa in 1961/2, India and Pakistan in 1964/5 and 1969/70, England in 1965 and 1969 and the West Indies in 1971/2. At home he played against England in 1962/3, and 1970/71, South Africa in 1963/4, Pakistan in 1964/5, India in 1967/8 and the West Indies in 1968/9. On both England tours – he was captain on the second – he made over 700 runs but, like his colleagues, struggled in the Tests. His three Test centuries were made against India: 129 in a total of 297 in the third match at Bombay in 1964/5; 143 in the first match at Dunedin and 239 in the second at Christchurch in 1967/8, when he led New Zealand to victory over India for the first time. His innings included 5 sixes and lasted 556 minutes. In this series against India he headed the batting with 471 runs (58.87), and in the season as a whole made 966 runs in ten first-class matches, a New Zealand record for a domestic season. During the tour of the West Indies in 1971/2 he was captain until back trouble forced his early return home and retirement from first-class cricket.

First-class career (1958-72): 9,399 runs (34.94) including 16 centuries
Test matches (39): 2,306 runs (31.16) including 3 centuries, 1-19 and 23 catches

DUNNING, John Angus (1903-71)

Oxford University and Otago

A right-arm medium-fast bowler of off-cutters with an unlovely action but considerable heart, John Dunning toured England in 1937, taking 83 wickets (30.10) in 941.3 overs, the lion's share of the bowling. He captured 7 for 67 against Middlesex at Lord's, 9 for 64 against Cambridge at Fenner's and 10 for 170 against Essex at Chelmsford; but in Tests against England between 1932/3 and 1937, his wickets were very costly. Though given a trial for Oxford in 1928, when he was a Rhodes scholar, he did not get a blue. He became a member of the Australian Cricket Board of Control.

First-class career (1923-38): 1,057 runs (13.04) and 228 wickets (27.58)
Test matches (4): 38 runs (7.60), 5 wickets (98.60) and 2 catches

EDGAR, Bruce Adrian (b.1956)

Wellington

On his first tour, to England in 1978, Bruce Edgar looked a player in the high tradition of New Zealand left-handers, worthy to follow in the footsteps of Donnelly and Sutcliffe. These were early days in his career, but this dark left-handed batsman played the rampant England fast bowlers with cool assurance, a very straight bat and the timing of a high class player in the making. His selection for the tour followed a successful season in New Zealand domestic cricket in which he scored 612 runs (34.00), having made his first appearance for Wellington in 1975/6. In his first three Tests in England he scored 147 runs for a heavily defeated side at an average of 24.50 and did a capable job in the last Test as a stand-in wicket-keeper. On the tour he hit a maiden first-class hundred against Scotland and with 823 runs (37.40) in fifteen matches was his side's highest scorer. He scored his first Test century against Pakistan in 1978/9 with 129, and got his own back for a relatively disappointing tour of Australia in 1980/81 by making 161 against Australia at Auckland the following season, the basis for a New Zealand victory and the highest score by a New Zealander against Australia. During the match he passed 1,000 Test runs in only his 17th match. In that 1981/2 season he scored 934 runs (51.88) in 19 innings. In one-day internationals he has been consistently effective. He is a chartered accountant.

First-class career (1975-): 5,012 runs (37.68) including 9 centuries
Test matches (18): 1,049 runs (33.83) including 3 centuries, and 11 catches

Bruce Edgar – Bob Taylor (England) keeping wicket

EDWARDS, Graham Neil (b.1955)

Central Districts

A short, heavily built wicket-keeper, very hard-hitting right-handed batsman and natural comic, 'Jock' Edwards first appeared for Central Districts in 1973/4 and was a useful member of the New Zealand side which participated in, and won, the 1974/5 Gillette Cup in Australia. He made his Test debut against Australia in 1976/7 as a specialist batsman, but was selected for his wicket-keeping in 1977/8 and, on his return to the New Zealand side, celebrated with 55 and 54 in the drawn third match against England at Auckland. In England in 1978, however, he was rather disappointing, having an awkward match behind the stumps at Trent Bridge and losing his place for the third Test. On the tour he made 401 runs (22.27) and took 22 catches and a stumping. Somewhat harshly treated by some English critics, he nevertheless enjoyed himself and kept the spirits of a beaten team high.

First-class career (1973-): 4,585 runs (29.58) including 5 centuries, and 142 dismissals (126 ct, 16 st.)
Test matches (8): 377 runs (25.13) and 7 dismissals (7 ct.)

EMERY, Raymond William George (1915-82)

Auckland and Canterbury

A competent right-handed opening batsman and occasional medium-pace bowler, Raymond Emery played in two Tests against the West Indies in 1951/2.

First-class career (1936-54): 1,177 runs (29.42) including 3 centuries, and 22 wickets (34.27)
Test matches (2): 46 runs (11.50) and 2 wickets (26.00)

FISHER, Frederick Eric (b.1924)

Wellington and Central Districts

A useful all-rounder, a steady right-handed batsman and left-arm medium-pace bowler, Frederick Fisher played in a sole Test against South Africa at Wellington in 1952/3, scoring 9 and 14 and taking 1 for 78.

First-class career (1951-5): 485 runs (21.08) and 53 wickets (23.24)

FOLEY, Henry (1906-48)

Wellington

A very sound left-handed opening batsman of limitless patience and a good slip fielder, Henry Foley played in a sole Test, the first ever in New Zealand, against England at Christchurch in 1929/30 scoring 2 and 2. Ill-health curtailed his career.

First-class career (1927-33): 670 runs (33.50) including 1 century

FREEMAN, Douglas Linford (b.1914)

Nelson and Wellington

Australian by birth and a right-arm googly bowler Doug Freeman appeared in only five first-class matches, two of which were Tests against England in 1932/3, at Christchurch and Auckland, when he had the misfortune to come up against Wally Hammond in supreme run-getting form. In his first Test, at 18 years 197 days, he became the youngest player to represent New Zealand, a record he still holds. On his first-class debut in 1932/3, he took 9 for 187 in the match for Wellington against Auckland.

First-class career (1932-4): 28 runs (4.66) and 14 wickets (35.35)
Test matches (2): 2 runs (1.00) and 1-169

GALLICHAN, Norman (1906-69)

Manawatu and Wellington

Over six feet tall, Norman Gallichan was a hard-hitting, lower-order right-handed batsman and a steady, slow left-arm bowler who toured England in 1937, taking 59 wickets (23.94) and averaging 16.94 with the bat. In his sole Test, the second at Old Trafford, he scored 30 and 2 and took 3 for 113.

First-class career (1927-39): 636 runs (18.17) and 86 wickets (26.09)

GEDYE, Sydney Graham (b.1929)

Auckland

A competent right-handed opening batsman, Graham Gedye scored 52 on his Test debut against South Africa at Wellington in 1963/4; and an equally fine 55 at Auckland in the same series. In that season he also scored 104 and 101 for Auckland against Central Districts. He played against Pakistan (once) in 1964/5.

First-class career (1956-65): 2,387 runs (30.21) including 3 centuries
Test matches (4): 193 runs (24.12)

GUILLEN, Simpson Clairmonte (b.1924)

Trinidad and Canterbury

See West Indies section.

GUY, John Williams (b.1934)

Central Districts, Wellington, Canterbury, Otago, Northern Districts and Northamptonshire

A fleet left-handed batsman of very sound defence and concentration, John Guy hit the ball clearly, relishing the lofted straight drive. At the age of nineteen he scored 57 and 115, which remained his career highest – hitting A.M. Moir for 36 in four overs – for Central Districts against Otago in 1953/4. He toured India and Pakistan in 1955/6, coping well with the dominant leg-spin and making 313 runs (34.77) in the Tests against India, including a stonewalling 102 in over seven hours in the first match at Hyderabad on a perfect batting surface. His other tour was at South Africa in 1961/2, when he reached 533 runs (26.65) in all first-class matches, but failed in the Tests. At home he played against the West Indies in 1955/6 and England in 1958/9, scoring a bright 56 at Christchurch.

First-class career (1953-73): 3,923 runs (25.80) including 3 centuries
Test matches (12): 440 runs (20.95) including 1 century, and 2 catches

HADLEE, Dayle Robert (b.1948)

Canterbury

One of five sons of Walter Hadlee, Dayle Hadlee was a right-arm fast-medium bowler in his youth. Forced by back trouble to reduce his pace, he became a fine swing bowler, but finally lost his battle against back pain and was able to play in only one match of his third tour of England in 1978. Keen and determined, like all the Hadlees, Dayle made his debut for the Under 23 XI against Central Districts in 1966/7, and in 1969 played in two Tests in England, followed by six in India and Pakistan. Performing with great consistency, his best Test was at Hyderabad where, in a match spoiled by poor weather, umpiring problems and some bad feeling, he took 4 for 30 and 3 for 31. India, bowled out for 89 and 76 for 7 in their second innings, escaped with a draw. In 1973 he played in all three Tests against England, taking 10 wickets, showing characteristic accuracy and persistency and often swinging the ball a good deal. A safe fielder, he took a quite remarkable catch off his own bowling to dismiss Alan Knott at Lord's in 1969.

First-class career (1966-80): 1,810 runs (17.07) and 327 wickets (25.78)
Test matches (26): 530 runs (14.32), 71 wickets (33.64) and 8 catches

Richard Hadlee

HADLEE, Richard John (b.1951)

Canterbury, Nottinghamshire and Tasmania

Undoubtedly one of the best fast bowlers to have come from New Zealand and easily his country's highest wicket-taker in Test cricket, Richard Hadlee has all the attributes of a top-class fast bowler and gave New Zealand sides of the 1970s a chance to hold their own against the rest in an era increasingly dominated by fast bowlers. He is also a capable fielder and often useful hard-hitting left-hander, though like most fast bowlers uncomfortable when tasting his own medicine. Wiry rather than muscular in build, six feet tall and determined to the point of fierce hostility towards any batsman, his good right-arm side-on action engenders speed, lift and late outswing. One of five sons of Walter Hadlee, he first played for Canterbury in 1971/2, forming an effective opening partnership with his elder brother Dayle, whom he surpassed in speed, though at first not in accuracy. Touring in England in 1973 as the baby of the New Zealand party, Richard Hadlee's potential was clear, though he played in only one Test. The next time that he met England, in February 1978, he was the acknowledged spearhead of the New Zealand attack and it was his hostile bowling at the Basin Reserve which did most to bring New Zealand victory over England for the first time. Hadlee took 10 for 100 in the match, and with 6 for 26 bowled England out for 64 in the second innings. In the series he took 15 wickets in three matches and in the three Tests in England later in the year was again easily England's biggest danger, taking 13 wickets at 20.76. Throughout the tour of Pakistan and India in 1976/7, he was New Zealand's main weapon during an unsuccessful tour, although only at Madras where he took 3 for 37 and 2 for 52 did he have a pitch with much pace in it. He found a good deal more help from the conditions in England in 1978 when he joined Nottinghamshire, taking 36 wickets in six Championship matches at 14.47 (in the 1978 English season he took 78 wickets at 16.26). He also hit a sparkling 101 not out against Derbyshire and continued to be a highly effective county cricketer, taking 105 wickets (14.89) in 1981, and scoring 745 runs (32.39), including 142 not out against Yorkshire. He and Clive Rice won the Championship for Notts after a fifty-two-year wait. His finest Test figures are 7 for 23 against India at Wellington in 1975/6, finishing with 11 for 58 in the match. Significantly, Richard Hadlee was also prominent in his country's first win against Australia at Christchurch in March 1974, when he took 3 for 59 and 4 for 71. In Australia in 1979/80 he was heroic in a losing cause in the three Tests but helped New Zealand to reach the finals of the International Triangular one-day tournament. In three Tests against West Indies earlier in 1980 he had taken 19 wickets (19.00) and hit his first Test hundred at Christchurch, a typically hard-driving, aggressive innings. Despite the heavy responsibilities he faces, he continues to be New Zealand's outstanding player, the first to do the Test double. In Australia in 1980/81 he took 19 wickets in three Tests.

First-class career (1971-): 5,461 runs (25.75) including 5 centuries, and 743 wickets (19.87)
Test matches (38): 1,241 runs (21.39) including 1 century, 169 wickets (26.41) and 20 catches

HADLEE, Walter Arnold (b.1915)

Canterbury and Otago

A tall and bespectacled right-handed batsman who frequently opened the batting, Walter or 'Wally' Hadlee could score rapidly with a variety of strokes or defend dourly. His most attractive shot was the off-drive, made either off his back foot or with the front foot planted firmly down the pitch and a graceful arc of the bat. In the field he was an inspiration, moving quickly and catching surely. He toured England in 1937 and returned as the enterprising and sporting captain of the 1949 side. He led New Zealand at home against Australia in 1945/6, and against England in 1946/7 and 1950/51. Pipe-smoking and kindly, he did all his work as leader without showmanship and fuss; he was fair-minded but could be ruthless with his team on the field, while driving himself hardest of all. In 1937 he made 1,225 runs (29.87) in first-class matches, and in the second Test at Old Trafford a dominating 93 in two and a quarter hours until he had the misfortune to slip and tread on his wicket. In 1949 he made 1,439 runs (35.97), being at his best in difficult situations. Although he made only one Test century he never failed to reach double figures. Against England at Christchurch he scored 116 in two and a half hours, opening with Bert Sutcliffe in a stand of 133. His highest-ever score was 198 in a total of 347 for Otago against the Australians at Dunedin in 1945/6. Very prominent in the administration of the game, Walter Hadlee has been an efficient Chairman of the New Zealand Board of Control. He is the father of five cricketing sons, two of whom, Dayle and Richard, have appeared in Tests, while Barry represented New Zealand in the Prudential World Cup.

First-class career (1933-52): 7,421 runs (40.11) including 17 centuries
Test matches (11): 543 runs (30.16) including 1 century, and 6 catches

HARFORD, Noel Sherwin (1930-81)

Central Districts and Auckland

A neat, well-balanced right-handed batsman who possessed a sparkling drive and pull but was rather unsound in defence, especially against spin bowlers, Noel Harford toured India and Pakistan in 1955/6 and England in 1958. On his Test debut, against Pakistan at Lahore, he scored 93 and 64. Although he made 1,067 runs (26.02) in England he was very disappointing in the Tests. However, in making his maiden century, against Oxford University in The Parks, he added 204 brilliantly with John Reid in little more than two hours for the third wicket. He was a useful right-arm medium-pace swing bowler.

First-class career (1953-67): 3,149 runs (27.62) including 3 centuries, and 18 wickets (26.55)
Test matches (8): 229 runs (15.26)

HARFORD, Roy Ivan (b.1936)

Auckland

A good wicket-keeper and moderate tail-end left-handed batsman, Roy Harford, born in London and no relation of Noel, played in Tests against India in 1967/8 in a short career. In his last Test, at Wellington, he dismissed 7, all through catches, of the 12 wickets to fall.

First-class career (1965-8): 143 runs (7.94) and 68 dismissals (60 ct, 8 st.)
Test matches (3): 7 runs (2.33) and 11 dismissals (11 ct)

HARRIS, Parke Gerald Zinzan (b.1927)

Canterbury

A right-handed batsman who could force the pace or defend stoutly, and a useful change-bowler, 'Zin' Harris toured India and Pakistan in 1955/6 without much success and South Africa in 1961/2, when he made 284 runs (31.55) in the Tests, including 74 in the first match at Durban and 101 in the third match at Cape Town. At home he played once against Pakistan in 1964/5.

First-class career (1949-65): 3,122 runs (28.11) including 5 centuries, and 21 wickets (30.80)
Test matches (9): 378 runs (22.23) including 1 century, 0-14 and 6 catches

HARRIS, Roger Meredith (b.1933)

Auckland

A right-handed opening batsman and medium-pace change-bowler, Roger Harris played in two Tests against England in 1958/9, but was outclassed by the opposition's bowlers, such as Fred Trueman and Frank Tyson.

First-class career (1955-74): 3,863 runs (30.90) including 3 centuries, and 14 wickets (42.50)
Test matches (2): 31 runs (10.33)

HASTINGS, Brian Frederick (b.1940)

Wellington, Central Districts and Canterbury

A right-handed batsman, Brian Hastings was a delightful timer of the ball, quick to take any opportunity to cut or hook, or to clip medium-fast bowling off his legs. A superb gully, he was a regular choice at number four in the New Zealand order in the early 1970s, yet took a long time to convince the Test selectors of his ability, not being picked until eleven years after making his debut for Wellington in 1957/8 at the age of seventeen. He played one season for Central Districts in 1960/61 and then transferred to Canterbury the following season. When he did win his Test cap against the West Indies in 1968/9, his scores were 21, 31, 8, 62 not out, 0 and 117 not out (at Christchurch). Equally consistent in the next few years, he toured England in 1969 and 1973, India in 1969/70, and the West Indies in 1971/2 where he scored an attractive 105 in the Bridgetown Test. He added further centuries against Pakistan at Auckland in 1972/3 (sharing in a record last wicket stand of 151 with Richard Collinge). His highest first-class innings was 226 for Canterbury against New Zealand Under 23 at Christchurch in 1964/5.

First-class career (1957-77): 7,686 runs (31.86) including 15 centuries, and 112 catches
Test matches (31): 1,510 runs (30.20) including 4 centuries, 0-9 and 23 catches

HAYES, John Arthur (b.1927)

Auckland and Canterbury

A tall, right-arm genuinely fast bowler with a glorious action, much enthusiasm and a late out-swing, Johnny Hayes or 'Haybag' toured England in 1949, but an injured groin muscle made him a passenger for half the tour. When he toured again in 1958, he headed the bowling with 62 wickets (20.20), although he captured only six in four Tests. Early in the tour he took 5 for 29 in the first innings against Essex at Ilford and 4 for 40 and 7 for 49 against MCC at Lord's. Later, at Cheltenham, he routed Gloucestershire, taking 4 wickets in 5 overs. He also toured India and Pakistan in 1955/6, and at home played against England in 1950/51 and 1954/5 and the West Indies in 1951/2. On the India and Pakistan tour he made good use of the new ball, taking 35 wickets (32.11) in the first-class matches, but his 13 Test wickets were very expensive. In New Zealand, his most memorable piece of bowling was in the first Test at Christchurch against the West Indies in 1951/2, when he disposed of Worrell, Walcott and Gomez in eight balls. For Auckland against Wellington in 1957/8 he captured 14 for 65 (7 for 28 and 7 for 37).

First-class career (1946-61): 611 runs (9.54) and 292 wickets (23.14)
Test matches (15): 73 runs (4.86), 30 wickets (40.56) and 3 catches

HENDERSON, Matthew (1895-1970)

Wellington

A left-arm fast bowler, often wayward but also unfortunate, Matthew Henderson toured England with the first New Zealand team in 1927, taking 33 wickets (24.21) in first-class matches. He played in the first-ever Test, against England at Christchurch in 1929/30, scoring 6 and 2 not out, taking 2 for 64 and 1 catch.

First-class career (1921-32): 495 runs (14.14) and 107 wickets (29.90)

HOUGH, Kenneth William (b.1928)

Auckland and Northern Districts

A lively right-arm medium-pace bowler, Kenneth Hough's only Tests were against England in 1958/9, when he dismissed Cowdrey (twice), Watson and Graveney, among others, for low scores. In his first Test at Christchurch he amused the crowd vastly by his impudent snatching of singles with E.C. Petrie when New Zealand were bordering on defeat by an innings. He took 12 for 146 against Central Districts in 1959/60, the same season in which he made his career-highest score of 91 against Otago.

First-class career (1956-60): 624 runs (16.42) and 119 wickets (20.87)
Test matches (2): 62 runs (62.00), 6 wickets (29.16) and 1 catch

HOWARTH, Geoffrey Philip (b.1951)

Northern Districts, Auckland and Surrey

One of New Zealand's first fully professional cricketers, Geoff Howarth overcame many disappointments to become what he had always wanted to be, a successful Test batsman. A neat right-hander with some delightful offside strokes, and especially severe on the half volley which he will drive unerringly, he is

Geoff Howarth – Ian Botham (England) fielding

also a fine fielder anywhere and a useful off-spin bowler. The younger brother of Hedley Howarth, he made his first-class debut for New Zealand's Under 23 XI in 1968/9 and, a few months after, came to England to join the Surrey ground staff. There he served a long and often frustrating apprenticeship. He eventually played for Surrey's first eleven in 1971, was capped in 1974 and in 1976 scored 1,554 runs in the dry summer at an average of 37.90. Not until 1972/3 did he represent a New Zealand provincial side, Auckland, and he subsequently transferred to Northern Districts in 1974/5 when he made his first Test appearances against England. After performing usefully in the 1975 Prudential World Cup, he was very disappointing on the 1976/7 tour of India and Pakistan but at last revealed his true ability when given possibly a final chance against England at Auckland in March 1978 (after playing only a minor role in the first New Zealand win against England at Wellington). He scored 122 and 102, saving New Zealand on a worsening pitch in the second innings and becoming only the second New Zealander after Glenn Turner to score two centuries in a Test. Confident, and sure of a place at last, he time and again kept New Zealand's boat afloat in a seething tide of English seamers in 1978, scoring a fine 123 not out at Lord's and 296 runs (74.00) in the three Tests, the most runs at the best average on either side. With a tour tally of 816 runs (45.33), this likeable and determined character finally justified his dedication to cricket. In the second of three Tests against Pakistan in 1979, he scored 114, his fourth century in six Test matches. He captained New Zealand against West Indies with outstanding success in 1980, scoring 239 runs (47.80) in the three-match series which New Zealand won one-nil, having led Northern Districts to the domestic double. Again captain in Australia in 1980/81, he led his side to the finals of the limited-overs competition but New Zealand were outplayed in the Test series. However, at Auckland in 1981/2 he led New Zealand to a rare Test win over Australia. He was awarded the MBE in 1981 for his services to the game.

First-class career (1968-): 13,928 runs (33.32) including 27 centuries, 107 wickets (30.44) and 176 catches
Test matches (28): 1,788 runs (38.86) including 6 centuries, 3 wickets (78.33) and 14 catches

HOWARTH, Hedley John (b.1943)

Auckland

The elder brother of Geoff, Hedley Howarth was for many years New Zealand's leading slow bowler, and only Richard Hadlee has exceeded his 541 first-class wickets. He was an orthodox left-arm spinner who flighted the ball well, had good control and turned the ball enough to make the most of favourable conditions.

Hedley Howarth

He made his first appearance in first-class cricket in 1962/3 for New Zealand Under 23 and the following season began a long career with Auckland. His first Test was at Lord's in 1969, the start of an unbroken sequence of nineteen Tests in which he took 65 wickets by dint of steady reliability rather than any spectacular performances. He only twice took 5 wickets in a Test innings, both times during a successful tour of India and Pakistan in 1969/70 (on the way back from his first tour of England). His best performance came in the only Test ever played at Nagpur where Howarth, with 4 for 66 and 5 for 34, outbowled the more highly rated Indian spinners and New Zealand gained their first success on Indian soil. Howarth was also in the team which beat Australia for the first time at Christchurch in 1974. In England, however, after taking 57 wickets on the 1969 tour, his return, as a senior member of the side, in 1973 was less successful. His best analysis was 7 for 43 against Essex at Westcliff in 1969. A patient and philosophical temperament kept him smiling through many long and less fruitful bowling stints, notably a marathon one at Lord's in 1973 when, after taking 3 for 42 in the first England innings to set up a winning chance for his team, he battled away for 70 overs in England's second innings of 463 for 9, finishing with 4 for 144. As a batsman he would have a swing if asked to do so and often defended stubbornly and in the field his hands were as safe as anyone's.

First-class career (1962-79): 1,668 runs (13.78), 541 wickets (25.27) and 138 catches
Test matches (30): 291 runs (12.12), 86 wickets (36.95) and 33 catches

JAMES, Kenneth Cecil (1904-76)

Wellington and Northamptonshire

Coming to England in 1927 as a second-string wicket-keeper to captain Tom Lowry, Ken James made the post his own, claiming 85 dismissals (43 caught, 42 stumped), including eight victims at Derby. In a match at Colombo, on the way home, he had a hat-trick of catches off Bill Merritt's bowling. In all James caught or stumped 65 of Merritt's victims. Previously Ken had toured Australia with a new Zealand side in 1925/6 and, on his return, hit 107 not out, engaging in a record last-wicket stand of 138 with W.S. Brice for Wellington against Otago. He kept wicket for New Zealand in the first Tests in New Zealand, against England in 1929/30, and returning to England in 1931 had an immense amount of work to do but did the job with rare skill: his catching of Eddie Paynter in the third Test at Old Trafford being a classic. He kept against South Africa in 1931/2 and England in 1932/3 and then, coming to live in England, he qualified for Northamptonshire and played for the county from 1935 until 1939. In 1936 he had 65 dismissals and his batting improved considerably. In the four seasons he made 3,428 runs, besides collecting 173 catches and 45 stumpings. He was one of the first of the leading wicket-keepers habitually to stand back to medium-pace bowling. On the field he derived every possible scrap of enjoyment from every game he played. He later became a publican.

First-class career (1923-47): 6,413 runs (22.19) including 7 centuries, and 418 dismissals (310 ct, 108 st.)
Test matches (11): 52 runs (4.72) and 16 dismissals (11 ct, 5 st.)

JARVIS, Terrence Wayne (b.1944)

Auckland and Canterbury

A ginger-headed, befreckled right-handed opening batsman, Terry Jarvis was an elegant stroke-maker with a tendency to get stranded between back and front foot, and a fine fielder. He toured India and Pakistan in 1964/5, making 263 runs (32.87) in the Tests, but in England in 1965 was plagued by illness contracted in India. In the West Indies in 1971/2, with his captain Graham Dowling out of action through injury, he became Glenn Turner's opening partner and, in the fourth Test at Georgetown, hit his career-highest score of 182, putting on 387 for the first wicket with Turner, a New Zealand record. In this series Jarvis made 277 runs (46.16). He played against Pakistan at home in 1972/3, but unfortunately made a pair in the first match of the series, at Wellington.

First-class career (1964-77): 4,666 runs (29.34) including 6 centuries, and 102 catches
Test matches (13): 625 runs (29.76) including 1 century, 0-3 and 3 catches

KERR, John Lambert (b.1910)

Canterbury

A right-handed opening batsman of sound technique and stubborn defence, a good driver and strong on the leg-side, John Kerr was also a very good fielder. He toured England in 1931 and 1937. In the former year he made 804 runs (22.97) and played in the first Test in England, at Lord's. In the latter year he made 1,205 runs (31.71), almost 500 of them in his last seven matches, which included two of his three centuries. At home he played against South Africa in 1931/2 and England in 1932/3, when he made his highest Test score, 59 at Christchurch. More effective in the Plunket Shield competition, his career-highest was 192 against Wellington in 1932/3. He has been much involved in the administration of the game.

First-class career (1929-43): 4,289 runs (32.19) including 8 centuries
Test matches (7): 212 runs (19.27) and 4 catches

LEES, Warren Kenneth (b.1952)

Otago

Warren Lees had the difficult job of following Ken Wadsworth into the New Zealand side as wicket-keeper/batsman but immediately proved himself equal to the task playing a resilient and determined role during his side's arduous and unsuccessful tour of Pakistan and India in 1976/7. In only his third Test, against Pakistan at Karachi, Lees came to the wicket when New Zealand were 104 for 5 in reply to a Pakistan total of 565. He responded by scoring 152, the highest individual score by a New Zealander against Pakistan, and sharing in a record seventh wicket stand of 186 with Richard Hadlee. It was a heroic innings, followed by 46 in the second innings which helped save the game. A bold hooker and driver, Lees is a right-hander whose record suggests that he might be capable of earning a Test place as a batsman alone. Certainly he was extremely unfortunate to have been left out of the touring team to England in 1978, especially as his wicket-keeping is seldom less that proficient. He was however, a vital member of the 1979 Prudential World Cup team which reached the semi-finals. He lost his place to I.D.S. Smith in Australia in 1980/81 but was chosen ahead of Smith for the one-day internationals in Australia two years later.

First-class career (1970-): 3,244 runs (23.50) including 4 centuries, and 200 dismissals (173 ct, 27 st.)
Test matches (17): 642 runs (22.92) including 1 century, 0-4 and 42 dismissals (35 ct, 7 st.)

LEGGAT, Ian Bruce (b.1930)

Nelson and Central Districts

A useful right-handed batsman and medium-pace

bowler, Ian Leggat toured South Africa in 1953/4, but never found his true form. In eight first-class matches he scored 138 runs and took 5 wickets. In his sole Test, the third at Cape Town, he failed to score, took 0 for 6 and held 2 catches.

First-class career (1950-62): 1,319 runs (20.29) including 2 centuries, and 58 wickets (35.46)

LEGGAT, John Gordon (1926-73)

Canterbury

A burly, determined and sound right-handed opening batsman, Gordon Leggat toured India and Pakistan in 1955/6 and at home played against the West Indies in 1951/2 and 1955/6, South Africa in 1952/3 and England in 1954/5. Uniquely, he appeared against four different countries in his first four Tests. At his best on the India and Pakistan tour he made 652 runs (34.31), including 275 runs (27.88) in the Tests; his Test-highest was 61 at Madras in the fifth match. His career-highest was 166 against Central Districts in 1952/3. A highly successful manager in South Africa in 1961/2, he became chairman of the New Zealand Cricket Board of Control, but died suddenly.

First-class career (1944-56): 3,550 runs (36.97) including 7 centuries
Test matches (9): 351 runs (21.93)

LISSETTE, Alan Fisher (1919-73)

Waikato, Auckland and Northern Districts

A competent left-arm slow bowler, Alan Lissette played in two Tests against the West Indies in 1955/6 with moderate results. His best performance was 7 for 45 (12 for 109 in the match) for Northern Districts against Otago in 1959/60. He was awarded the MBE for services to the Air Training Corps.

First-class career (1954-63): 476 runs (10.81) and 116 wickets (25.89)
Test matches (2): 2 runs (1.00), 3 wickets (41.33) and 1 catch

LOWRY, Thomas Coleman (1898-1976)

Hawke's Bay, Rangitikei, Wellington, Cambridge University and Somerset

Born at Fernhill, Napier, Tom Lowry was a natural leader. Reserved but approachable, he was lion-hearted and a great sportsman. He captained New Zealand in her first two Tests against England – away in 1931 and at home in 1929/30. He always aimed at winning not drawing, abhorring any waste of time. A large, powerful man, he was a fine attacking right-handed batsman, who materially strengthened his defence over the years, always at his best in a crisis, ignoring frequent bruises to his hands. He could be either a very useful wicket-keeper or a good fielder close to the wicket; and he was a useful slow bowler, not afraid to give the ball plenty of 'air' if required. He promoted Ken James as first-string wicket-keeper on the 1927 tour in place of himself and, concentrating largely on captaincy and batting, made 1,277 runs (38.69), including 4 centuries. In the 1929/30 series he made a fighting 80 at Auckland in the fourth match in 210 minutes, and in 1931, when he made 1,290 runs (31.46) and took 15 wickets (18.26) on the tour, he contributed a gritty 62 in the second Test at The Oval. He came back in 1937 as player/manager and at Trent Bridge against Nottinghamshire hit 121 in 105 minutes. He did not appear, however, in the Tests. The highest score of his career was 181 for Wellington against Auckland in 1927/8. For several seasons he appeared with success for Somerset, and tradition has it that his sole qualification to play for the county was that he was 'born at Wellington'. Later, Tom was President of the New Zealand Cricket Council.

First-class career (1917-37): 9,421 runs (31.19) including 18 centuries, and 49 wickets (24.85)
Test matches (7): 223 runs (27.87), 0-5 and 8 catches

McEWAN, Paul Ernest (b.1953)

Canterbury

A slim and very stylish right-handed batsman and good fielder, Paul McEwan made his first appearance for Canterbury in 1976/77. After a modest Test debut against the West Indies in 1979/80, he went to Australia in 1980/81. Here he failed against fast bowling in both the Tests and the one-day internationals. Such a disappointment might have set back one of less equable temperament, but he continued to bat usefully for Canterbury without doing quite enough to merit another chance at Test level.

First-class career (1976-): 1,811 runs (28.29) including 3 centuries, and 22 wickets (27.72)
Test matches (3): 56 runs (9.33) and 3 catches

MacGIBBON, Anthony Roy (b.1924)

Canterbury

Tony MacGibbon spearheaded New Zealand's attack from 1950 until 1958, and proved himself a tremendous trier in a lean period in his country's cricket. A right-arm fast-medium bowler with a longish run, he could swing the ball either way and used his 6ft 5ins to make it lift awkwardly. He was also a useful late-order batsman and a superb slip. He toured South Africa in 1953/4, India and Pakistan in 1955/6 and England in 1958, and, at home, played against England in 1950/51 and 1954/5, South Africa in 1952/3, and the West Indies in 1955/6. In South Africa in 1953/4 he was handicapped by enteritis, but still took 22 Test wickets (20.63). At Auckland in the fourth match against India in 1955/6, his 4 for 44 in the first innings and his knock of 35 in a low-scoring match contributed considerably to New Zealand's first-ever victory in an official Test (after twenty-six years and forty-five matches). Playing at his best for the weak 1958 side in England, he took most wickets, 73 (21.35), on the tour and in the Tests, 20 (19.45). He made 670 runs (19.70), including a vigorous 66 at Old Trafford in the fourth Test, which was the highest score by a New Zealander in the series. On the first day of the first match at Edgbaston, he took 5 for 64 and England were all out for 221, only for New Zealand to collapse for 94. At the end of the tour, he remained in England to read Civil Engineering at Durham University. He briefly returned to New Zealand's team. His best return in an innings remained 7 for 56 for Canterbury against Auckland in 1954/5.

First-class career (1947-62): 3,611 runs (19.62) and 352 wickets (26.21)
Test matches (26): 814 runs (19.85), 70 wickets (30.85) and 13 catches

McGIRR, Herbert Mendelson (1891-1964)

Wellington

A dashing right-handed batsman and stock medium-pace bowler, Herb McGirr toured England with the first New Zealand team in 1927, making 737 runs (24.56) and taking 49 wickets (27.67). He played in two Tests against England in 1929/30, hitting 51 in his second at Auckland. His career-highest score was 141 for Wellington against Otago in 1930/31 and his best bowling figures in an innings were 7 for 45 against Canterbury in 1921/2. He continued playing club cricket until, after scoring 70 at the age of sixty-seven, he slipped when taking in the milk at home the following morning and had to give up the game.

First-class career (1913-33): 3,992 runs (28.71) including 5 centuries, and 239 wickets (27.49)
Test matches (2): 51 runs (51.00) and 1-115

McGREGOR, Spencer Noel (b.1931)

Otago

A right-handed batsman, Noel McGregor had a wide range of strokes, including a handsome drive off the back foot, and he was a reliable deep fielder. He toured India and Pakistan in 1955/6 and South Africa in 1961/2. At home he played against England in 1954/5 and 1958/9, the West Indies in 1955/6, South Africa in 1963/4 and Pakistan in 1964/5. In India and Pakistan he established himself with 300 runs (25.00) in the Tests. In the second match against Pakistan at Lahore he made a painstaking 111 in 5 hours 40 minutes. He was disappointing against England, but when the 1963/4 South Africans toured he came second in the Test averages with 168 runs (28.00), including a fighting 62 at Auckland in the third match. On visiting South Africa in 1961/2 he made 709 runs (25.32) and contributed 242 runs (24.20) to the tied Test series. Often opening the batting he scored 68 at Cape Town in the third Test, a vital innings in his country's first-ever Test victory abroad. His career-highest was 114 not out against Wellington in 1959/60.

First-class career (1948-69): 6,487 runs (25.33) including 5 centuries
Test matches (25): 892 runs (19.82) including 1 century, and 9 catches

McLEOD, Edwin George (b.1900)

Auckland and Wellington

A competent left-handed batsman and occasional leg-break bowler, Edwin McLeod played in only one Test, the second at Wellington against England in 1929/30, when he scored 16 and 2 not out and took 0 for 5.

First-class career (1920-41): 1,407 runs (32.72) including 1 century, and 20 wickets (33.20)

McMAHON, Trevor George (b.1929)

Wellington

Played mainly for his wicket-keeping, Trevor McMahon toured India and Pakistan in 1955/6, keeping adequately but failing with the bat. His sole Test experience was during this tour.

First-class career (1953-65): 449 runs (9.97) and 98 dismissals (84 ct, 14 st.)
Test matches (5): 7 runs (2.33) and 8 dismissals (7 ct, 1 st.)

McRAE, Donald Alexander Noel (b.1912)

Canterbury

A competent left-handed batsman and medium-pace bowler, Donald McRae played in one Test match, against Australia at Wellington in 1945/6 – the first after the War – scoring 0 and 8 and returning figures of 0 for 44.

First-class career (1937-46): 354 runs (15.39) and 56 wickets (22.51)

MATHESON, Alexander Malcolm (b.1906)

Auckland

A right-arm medium-pace bowler, always likely to whip in an unexpected quicker ball, and a useful tail-end batsman, Alexander Matheson played against England in the fourth Test at Auckland in 1929/30. He also toured England in 1931 when, despite being handicapped by a strained leg muscle, he took 44 wickets (23.81). In New Zealand, every Friday night, he motored a hundred miles over rough country roads in order to play four hours' cricket in Auckland for his club.

First-class career (1926-47): 1,844 runs (23.64) including 1 century, and 194 wickets (28.53)
Test matches (2): 7 runs (7.00), 2 wickets (68.00) and 2 catches

MEALE, Trevor (b.1928)

Wellington

A tall left-handed opening batsman who concentrated grimly, Trevor Meale was a surprise choice for the 1958 England tour: he had appeared with success in London club cricket, but failed in his attempt to qualify for Kent. He made 502 runs (21.82) on the tour, playing in two Tests without distinction.

First-class career (1951-8): 1,352 runs (27.59) including 2 centuries
Test matches (2): 21 runs (5.25)

MERRITT, William Edward (1908-77)

Canterbury and Northamptonshire

A cheerful and skilful right-arm leg-break and googly bowler of great stamina – perhaps the best of his kind produced by New Zealand – Bill Merritt had no great command of length but frequently had good batsmen in trouble. As a batsman he was rugged, unorthodox but effective and he was a fine fielder. He represented Canterbury for the first time at eighteen, taking 8 for 68 in the match with Otago in 1926/7, and he toured England with the first New Zealand team in 1927 as its youngest and most successful bowler. He took 107 wickets (23.64), besides scoring 538 runs (26.90). In 1931 he again took most wickets in England, 99 (26.48), though he was less consistent, and scored 545 runs (18.79). In the two Tests he played, however, he failed. Likewise, in the first-ever series against England in 1929/30, he took only 8 very expensive wickets and made few runs. He joined Rishton in the Lancashire League as a professional and later moved to Dudley. Recommended to Northamptonshire by his colleague, Ken James, he qualified for the county in 1939, but, because of the War, played for them only in 1939 and 1946. In 1939 he took 87 wickets (28.63) and made 926 runs (22.58). At his best he was a true matchwinner. Figures of 13 for 181 for Canterbury against Otago in 1935/6; 12 for 161 for Northamptonshire against Cambridge University in 1939, when the county won a first-class match for the first time since 1935; 12 for 130 for New Zealand against Essex; and 7 for 28 (second innings) at Lord's against MCC in 1931 illustrate his abilities. His highest score was a whirlwind 87 for Northants against Sussex in fifty-seven minutes, including 3 sixes and 10 fours, in 1939.

First-class career (1926-46): 3,147 runs (19.91) and 536 wickets (25.50)
Test matches (6): 73 runs (10.42), 12 wickets (51.41) and 2 catches

MEULI, Edgar Milton (b.1926)

Central Districts

A competent right-handed opening batsman and occasional leg-break bowler, he played against South Africa in the first Test at Wellington in 1952/3, scoring 15 and 23, in his only Test appearance.

First-class career (1945-60): 1,914 runs (26.21) including 2 centuries, and 11 wickets (29.90)

MILBURN, Barry Douglas (b.1943)

Otago

A neat, energetic and reliable wicket-keeper but moderate right-handed batsman, Barry Milburn toured England in 1969 and India and Pakistan in 1969/70, but Ken Wadsworth was preferred to him in the Tests. He represented New Zealand, however, at home in the series against the West Indies in 1968/9. He retired in 1974 but came back for the 1980/81 season.

First-class career (1963-81): 705 runs (12.15) including 1 century, and 173 dismissals (155 ct, 18 st.)
Test matches (3): 8 runs (8.00) and 8 dismissals (6 ct, 2 st.)

MILLER, Lawrence Somerville Martin (b.1923)

Central Districts and Wellington

A tall and likeable left-handed opening batsman, Lawrie Miller possessed a long reach and plenty of courage and, though seldom very impressive on a pitch with much life in it, he knew how to punish anything loose. Also a good field in the deep, he toured South Africa in 1953/4 and England in 1958 and, at home, played against South Africa in 1952/3 and the West Indies in 1953/4. Only coming into first-class cricket at twenty-seven, he was thirty-five when he toured England. He made 1,148 runs (30.21) with a highest of 76, but failed in the Tests there as he had in South Africa five years before. His best score in Tests, 47, was made in the fourth match against the West Indies at Auckland in 1955/6, when New Zealand won a Test for the first time. His career-highest, 144 against Auckland, was scored in the same season.

First-class career (1950-60): 4,777 runs (37.61) including 5 centuries
Test matches (13): 346 runs (13.84), 0-1 and 1 catch

MILLS, John Ernest (1905-72)

Auckland

An artist to his fingertips, John Mills was a left-handed opening batsman who played with a straight bat, drove beautifully and cut superbly, but tended to give the bowler a chance. He toured England with the first touring side in 1927, making 1,251 runs (37.90) and again in 1931, when he made 1,368 runs (31.81), being an effective opener with Stewie Dempster. On his Test debut, the second match against England at Wellington in 1929/30, he scored 117 and with Dempster put on 276 for the first wicket, which remains the highest stand for any New Zealand wicket against England. His career-highest was 185 against Otago in 1929/30.

First-class career (1924-38): 5,025 runs (32.84) including 11 centuries
Test matches (7): 241 runs (26.77) including 1 century, and 1 catch

MOIR, Alexander McKenzie (b.1919)

Otago

A right-arm leg-break and googly bowler, Alex Moir delivered the ball, fingers snapping, with a studious air. As well as his slow bowling, often to a close-set attacking field, he doubled as a useful lower-order batsman. He toured India and Pakistan in 1955/6 and England in 1958. At home he played against England in 1950/51, 1954/5 and 1958/9, the West Indies in 1951/2 and 1955/6 and South Africa in 1952/3. In India and Pakistan his bowling failed against batsmen thoroughly comfortable in their home conditions; and in England, although he took 35 wickets (26.20), his increasingly unfashionable bowling proved ineffective in the Tests. His first Test was his best, against England at Christchurch in 1950/51, when he took 6 for 155 in 56.3 overs in a total of 550. Against Central Districts in 1953/4 he had a match record of 15 for 203 (7 for 84 and 8 for 119).

First-class career (1949-62): 2,102 runs (16.42) and 368 wickets (24.56)
Test matches (17): 327 runs (14.86), 28 wickets (50.64) and 2 catches

MOLONEY, Denis Andrew Robert (1910-42)

Manawatu, Wellington, Otago and Canterbury

Denis Moloney was the leading all-rounder on the 1937 England tour. As well as being a bespectacled right-handed batsman, who often exercised a steadying influence, he was a useful medium-pace change-bowler and a fine field. He made 1,463 runs (34.83) and took 57 wickets (26.88). In the first Test at Lord's, his debut, with his country 248 runs behind and 7 wickets down, he hit a plucky 64. His career-highest was 190 for Wellington against Auckland in 1936/7. He died of wounds while a prisoner of war at El Alamein in 1942.

First-class career (1929-41): 3,219 runs (28.64) including 2 centuries, and 95 wickets (33.16)
Test matches (3): 156 runs (26.00), 0-9 and 3 catches

MOONEY, Francis Leonard Hugh (b.1921)

Wellington

A wicket-keeper without fuss or showmanship who was neat, clean and efficient, sometimes stumping 'like a rattlesnake striking', Frank Mooney concentrated so hard, whether 'keeping or batting, that he rarely spoke or smiled. In the evenings, however, his energetic socializing and dancing helped to earn him the nickname 'Starlight'. A limited but extremely useful right-handed stroke-maker, he could drive hard straight back or through the coves. He toured England in 1949 – his selection causing a strike among the Dunedin waterside workers who preferred one of their own number – and in the second first-class match at Worcester claimed 7 dismissals (6 in the second innings) and had a hand in a run out. He ended the tour with 66 victims (46 caught, 20 stumped), including 10 from three Tests, and 774 runs (22.76). He toured South Africa in 1953/4, having 9 victims in the five Tests, and at home played against England in 1950/51, the West Indies in 1951/2 and South Africa in 1952/3. His career-highest score was 180 against Auckland in 1943/4.

First-class career (1941-55): 3,134 runs (23.38) including 2 centuries, and 213 dismissals (161 ct, 52 st.)
Test matches (14): 343 runs (17.15), 0-0 and 30 dismissals (22 ct, 8 st.)

MORGAN, Ross Winston (b.1941)

Auckland

A sound right-hander whose favourite shot was a 'cuff' through mid-wicket, Ross Morgan was also an off-spin change-bowler with an exotic hop-skip run in and a reliable field. He toured India and Pakistan in 1964/5, England in 1965 and the West Indies in 1971/2. At home he played against Pakistan in 1964/5, England in 1965/6 and 1970/71, and the West Indies in 1968/9. His international career ended on a low note in the Caribbean, but at home in 1964/5 he headed the batting from two Tests with 187 runs (46.75). This included the top score, 66, in his first match at Auckland and an innings of 97 at Christchurch, when he was hitting hard in a vain attempt to force a win. His career-highest was 166 against Canterbury in 1968/9 and best bowling 6 for 40 against Central Districts in 1964/5.

First-class career (1957-77): 5,940 runs (27.50) including 8 centuries, and 108 wickets (32.94)
Test matches (20): 734 runs (22.24), 5 wickets (121.80) and 12 catches

MORRISON, Bruce Donald (b.1933)

Wellington

A combative right-arm medium-pace bowler and a left-handed batsman with an earnest (but, generally, unfulfilled) desire to hit boundaries, Bruce Morrison appeared in only one Test, at Wellington in the second match against England in 1962/3. Selected as replacement for the injured J.C. Alabaster, he scored 10 and 0, took 2 for 129 and held 1 catch.

First-class career (1953-65): 374 runs (9.35) and 167 wickets (24.16)

MORRISON, John Francis Maclean (b.1947)

Central Districts and Wellington

A very competent right-handed batsman, left-arm spin change-bowler and reliable field, John Morrison toured Australia twice, England (1979) and India and Pakistan (1976/7); and played at home against Australia in 1973/4 and 1981/2, England in 1974/5 and India in 1975/6. Over the years, his form has been uneven, but on succeeding the injured Glenn Turner as opening batsman, he hit 117 in his second Test match, against Australia at Sydney, and headed the batting for the series with 249 runs (41.50). Two months later, in the first match at Wellington against Australia, he scored 66, sharing in a century stand for the second wicket with Turner. Against England in the first match at Auckland in 1974/5 he fought well in a losing cause, making 58 and 58 but in the next Test at Christchurch he was caught at third slip off the first ball of the match. His career-highest is 180 not out for Wellington against Northern Districts in 1972/3. In 1981/2 he was recalled at home against Australia to play his first Test cricket for five years. Although only modestly successful at number three, he bowled his slow left arm with remarkable economy, especially at Auckland where his second innings figures of 35-16-52-2 helped his country to win.

First-class career (1965-): 5,889 runs (30.51) including 7 centuries, 43 wickets (31.32) and 128 catches
Test matches (17): 656 runs (22.62) including 1 century, 2 wickets (35.50) and 9 catches

MOTZ, Richard Charles (b.1940)

Canterbury

Although not of startling speed, Dick Motz was a tenacious right-arm fast bowler who combined lively pace with an outswinger and movement off the pitch and was prepared to bowl until he dropped. He was also a late-order batsman who loved hitting sixes. Strongly built, he was a cricketer of great character. On his first-class debut in the Plunket Shield competition in 1957/8 he took a wicket in his second over and two in his third. He toured South Africa in 1961/2, England in 1965 and 1969 and India and Pakistan in 1965/6. At home he played against England in 1962/3 and 1965/6, South Africa in 1963/4, Pakistan in 1964/5, India in 1967/8 and the West Indies in 1968/9. On his first tour, to South Africa, he headed the bowling with 81 wickets (17.77), including 19 wickets (26.57) in his country's most successful official Test series. In England in 1965 he was the attacking spearhead with 54 wickets (22.98) from fourteen matches, including 11 wickets from the three Tests. Against the 1967/8 Indians, he captured 15 wickets (28.86) in the four matches, and at Christchurch in the second match, he broke through to take 6 for 63 in the first innings and helped New Zealand to victory over India for the first time. In England in 1969, he had lost some of his edge but – in the last Test at The Oval – he became the first 'Kiwi' to take 100 wickets in official Tests. Near the end of the summer, it was discovered that he had been bowling for eighteen months with a displaced vertebra, an injury which caused his retirement from first-class cricket on his return home. His best bowling in an innings was 8 for 61 against Wellington in 1966/7. His career-highest

Dick Motz

score was 103 not out against Otago in 1967/8 in fifty-three minutes, including 7 sixes and 8 fours, the fastest century ever recorded in New Zealand first-class cricket. He also hit 94 in as many minutes, including 6 sixes and 10 fours for New Zealand against South Australia at Adelaide in 1967/8.

First-class career (1957-69): 3,494 runs (17.12) including 1 century, and 518 wickets (22.72)
Test matches (32): 612 runs (11.54), 100 wickets (31.48) and 9 catches

MURRAY, Bruce Alexander Grenfell (b.1940)

Wellington

A tall, calm and cautious right-handed opening batsman with a long reach, an occasional leg-break bowler and safe fielder, Bruce Murray toured England in 1969 and India and Pakistan in 1969/70. At home he played against India in 1967/8 and England in 1970/71. He scored 54 in his first Test against India at Dunedin and on his England tour made more runs than anyone else, 800 (40.00), although he had no substantial scores in the Tests. In India and Pakistan he was again prominent with 641 runs (37.70), including 329 runs (27.41) in the six Tests. At Lahore in the third Test against Pakistan he hit 90, his highest Test score, helping New Zealand to win for the first time against Pakistan. His career-highest was 213 against Otago in 1968/9.

First-class career (1958-73): 6,257 runs (35.55) including 6 centuries, and 30 wickets (28.93)
Test matches (13): 598 runs (23.92), 1-0 and 21 catches

NEWMAN, Sir Jack (b.1902)

Wellington, Canterbury and Nelson

A left-arm medium-pace bowler, Jack Newman played against South Africa in 1931/2, the first match between the two countries at Christchurch, and against England in 1932/3. Unfortunate to meet Wally Hammond in supreme form, he was hit for sixes off three successive deliveries in the second Test at Auckland. For Wellington against Otago in 1931/2 he took 10 for 96 in the match. He was President of the New Zealand Cricket Council from 1965 until 1967 and was knighted in 1978.

First-class career (1922-36): 206 runs (8.95) and 69 wickets (24.76)
Test matches (3): 33 runs (8.25) and 2 wickets (127.00)

O'SULLIVAN, David Robert (b.1944)

Central Districts, Hampshire and Durham

An excellent slow left-arm bowler and often useful right-handed batsman, David O'Sullivan has been a prolific wicket-taker in New Zealand domestic cricket. He also had one very successful season with Hampshire and, but for rivalry from two good, slow left-armers in Hedley Howarth and Stephen Boock and doubts about a slight kink in his action, he would have played more Tests. A sharp turner of the ball, he is particularly effective when conditions are wet or very dry. Born and educated in Palmerston North, he moved to England in 1969, and in 1971 made his first appearance as a specially registered overseas player with Hampshire. After taking 29 wickets in eleven Championship matches in 1972, his 47 wickets (20.59) in 1973 had much to do with Hampshire's success in the County Championship as he repeatedly bowled sides out late in the season. Ironically the county had to choose between O'Sullivan and Andy Roberts as their overseas bowler the following year and reluctantly dispensed with the services of the spinner. O'Sullivan's Test debut was an unsuccessful one against Pakistan at Dunedin in February 1973 and it was not until his fourth Test, against Australia at Adelaide in 1973/4, that he took a wicket! His 5 for 148 in Australia's first innings in this match remain his best Test figures.

First-class career (1971-): 1,812 runs (14.73) and 424 wickets (25.50)
Test matches (11): 158 runs (9.29), 18 wickets (67.83) and 2 catches

OVERTON, Guy William Fitzroy (b.1919)

Southland and Otago

A right-arm bowler of considerable pace, able to swing the ball both ways, Guy Overton toured South Africa in 1953/4, taking 26 wickets (30.53). At Johannesburg in the fourth Test he had a spell of 3 wickets for 1 run in 13 balls. In all first-class matches he took more wickets than he scored runs.

First-class career (1945-56): 137 runs (4.15) and 169 wickets (25.14)
Test matches (3): 8 runs (1.60), 9 wickets (28.66) and 1 catch

PAGE, Milford Laurenson (b.1902)

Canterbury

A sound but painstaking right-handed batsman, strong on the leg-side, a useful slow change-bowler and reliable slip field, 'Curly' Page toured England with the first touring team of 1927 and also went with the second of 1931 as chief lieutenant to Tom Lowry before captaining the 1937 side to England. At home he played in the first-ever Tests against England in 1929/30 and as captain in 1932/3; he was leader against South Africa in 1931/2 also. He succeeded Lowry as a sporting, popular but firm skipper. He once said, 'People think more of a good sportsman who loses than a bad sportsman who wins.' A responsible middle-order batsman who restricted himself in the interests of the team, he made 1,154 runs (34.96) and took 23 wickets (21.65) in 1927; 990 runs (26.75) in 1931; and 666 runs (22.20) in 1937. At Lord's in 1931 he scored 104 in New Zealand's first official Test in England, helping New Zealand to an honourable draw by sharing in two century partnerships. His career-highest was 206 against Wellington in 1931/2. A double international, he was also an All Black Rugby half-back.

First-class career (1920-43): 5,857 runs (29.88) including 9 centuries, and 73 wickets (32.32)
Test matches (14): 492 runs (24.60) including 1 century, 5 wickets (46.20) and 6 catches

PARKER, John Morton (b.1951)

Northern Districts and Worcestershire

The youngest of three brothers who have all played first-class cricket in New Zealand, John Parker made up his mind to follow the footsteps of Glenn Turner. A most determined, if limited, right-handed batsman with a short backlift and plenty of pluck, and a fine fielder, who can also keep wicket, he paid his way to England in 1971 and had a successful trial at Worcester, making 91 when he first appeared for them in that year against the Indian touring team. As a qualified player in 1972 he scored 869 runs (39.80) and remained a useful, if seldom a matchwinning, performer, for Worcestershire until 1975. In his first season in New Zealand in 1972/3 he batted outstandingly well to make 452 runs (45.20). He gained his first Test cap that season against Pakistan, but broke a bone in his hand while fielding, was unable to bat and took no further part in the series. Although on the 1973 tour of England he scored well in matches against the counties (648 runs on the tour at 29.45), he had a miserable three Tests against England's seam bowlers, failing to get into double figures in any one of his five innings. He redeemed himself by making 108 against Australia at Sydney a few months later and he was a member of the side which in the same season beat Australia for the first time, at Christchurch. However, he was inconsistent as an opener and did better when he dropped down the batting order. Touring Pakistan and India in 1976/7 as Glenn Turner's vice-captain, Parker led his country against Pakistan in the third Test at Karachi, which New Zealand did well to save, and in the following Test against India at Bombay he made 104 before being run out. His highest score for New Zealand was 121 against England at Auckland in 1974/5, but, although he again scored freely against the counties in the tour of England in 1978, his four Test innings brought him only 55 runs. He was again

John Parker

disappointing in Australia in 1980/81, but the following season he averaged over 100 in the Shell Shield and scored centuries in both innings against Central Districts.

First-class career (1971-): 10,188 runs (34.53) including 20 centuries, 14 wickets (46.07), 165 catches and 5 stumpings
Test matches (36): 1,498 runs (24.55) including 3 centuries, 1-24 and 30 catches

PARKER, Norman Murray (b.1948)

Otago and Canterbury

A right-handed batsman and good fielder, Murray Parker was chosen for the tough tour of Pakistan and India in 1976/7 and won his first Test cap in the Third Test against Pakistan at Karachi when his younger brother John was captaining New Zealand for the first time. Opening the batting, he scored a steady 40 in the second innings which helped to save the game, but, although he played in New Zealand's next two Tests against India, he was not selected again.

First-class career (1967-79): 2,102 runs (25.02) including 1 century
Test matches (3): 89 runs (14.83) and 2 catches

PETHERICK, Peter James (b.1942)

Otago and Wellington

An off-spinner who made his belated debut for Otago in 1975/6, Peter Petherick assured himself of a permanent place in the record books by taking a hat-trick in his first Test match. He is one of only two people to have achieved this unlikely feat, M.J.C. Allom of England being the other. His victims were all distinguished Pakistani cricketers – Javed Miandad, Wasim Raja and Intikhab Alam – in the first innings of the first Test at Lahore in October 1976. Petherick finished with 3 for 103 in the innings of 417. He has been unfortunate to have been given little opportunity since, missing the 1978 tour of England and playing only one home Test, against Australia at Auckland in 1976/7, when he bowled only 4 overs.

First-class career (1975-): 200 runs (5.88) and 189 wickets (24.47)
Test matches (6): 34 runs (4.85), 16 wickets (42.93) and 4 catches

PETRIE, Eric Charlton (b.1927)

Auckland and Northern Districts

A neat reliable wicket-keeper, Eric Petrie improved greatly during his tour of England in 1958, when he had 49 victims in twenty matches and played for Gentlemen against Players at Scarborough; he was one of the few real successes on the tour, and immensely popular. As a right-handed batsman good enough to hit 2 centuries, he was disappointing in representative cricket. In the Test at Christchurch during the 1965/6 tour, after an absence of five years from Test cricket, he hit 55 – his top score in Tests.

First-class career (1950-67): 2,788 runs (17.98) including 2 centuries, and 231 dismissals (194 ct, 37 st.)
Test matches (14): 258 runs (12.90) and 25 dismissals (25 ct)

PLAYLE, William Rodger (b.1938)

Auckland and Western Australia

A right-handed batsman with a wide range of strokes, and a good field, Bill Playle was a surprise choice for the 1958 England tour. In a less wet summer his stylish batting might have been more effective, but he failed in the Tests and twenty-three first-class matches brought him only 414 runs, despite 96 in the second match at Leicester. In his only other series, in 1962/3, against England at Wellington he made 65 in a losing cause, his best effort in Tests. Settling in Australia, his career-highest was 122 for Western Australia against Queensland at Perth in 1965/6.

First-class career (1956-68): 2,888 runs (21.87) including 4 centuries
Test matches (8): 151 runs (10.06) and 4 catches

POLLARD, Victor (b.1945)

Central Districts and Canterbury

Born in Lancashire, Vic Pollard grew up in New

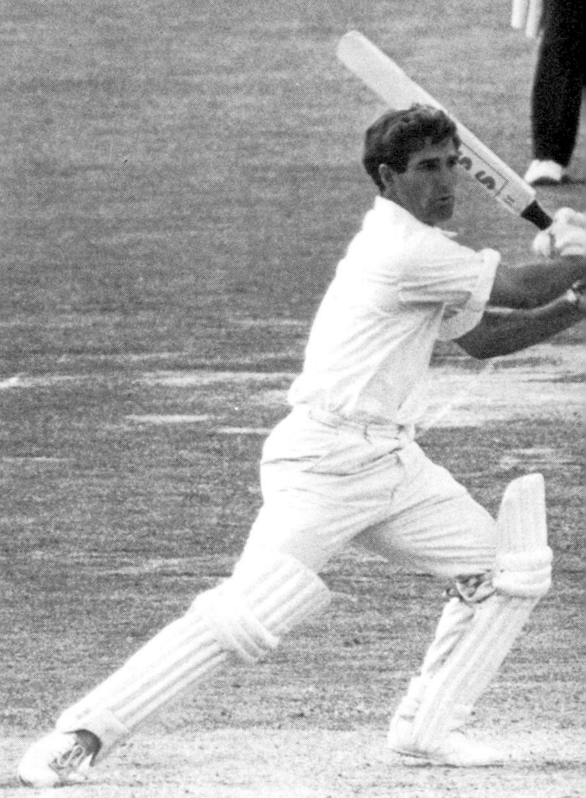

Vic Pollard

Zealand. Short and stocky with short-cut dark hair, he became a stubborn right-handed batsman capable of nimble attacking stroke-play, square-cutting, off-driving and hooking with relish. He was, too, a very useful off-spin bowler and brilliant field, especially at cover. He toured India and Pakistan in 1964/5 and 1969/70, and England in 1965, 1969 and 1973, and at home he played against England in 1965/6 and 1970/71, India in 1967/8 and the West Indies in 1968/9. Making his first tour of England a year after leaving school, having been chosen primarily for his bowling, he was batting 'find' of the year, making 652 runs (31.31), including most runs in the Tests, 281 runs at 56.20. At Edgbaston, with New Zealand being out-played, he scored 81 not out, and at Lord's (twice) and Headingley he also passed 50. His bowling successes were negligible and for several years he did not fulfil his great promise. He made several fifties, and took 23 wickets (16.26) in matches against an Australian B team in 1966/7 but in England in 1969 as vice-captain he achieved very little in the Tests. On his third tour, however, in 1973, he performed nobly: he scored 629 runs (48.38) in all first-class matches and headed the Test averages with 302 runs (100.66) in the 3 matches. At Trent Bridge, when New Zealand, seeking 479 to win, lost four men cheaply, he scored 116 (including only 9 fours), adding 177 with Bev Congdon for the fifth wicket. At Lord's in the next Test, when England came close to being beaten by the Kiwis for the first time, he contributed 105 not out, running out to hit Geoff Arnold and John Snow, and adding 117 for the sixth wicket with Mark Burgess, a New Zealand record. Finally at Headingley, with 4 wickets down for 78 on the first day, he added 106 for the fifth wicket with Burgess, this time making 62. He retired from international cricket after this tour. A teacher and Baptist lay-preacher, he was strongly opposed to the playing of first-class cricket on Sundays.

First-class career (1964-75): 5,314 runs (30.54) including 6 centuries, and 224 wickets (30.94)
Test matches (32): 1,266 runs (24.34) including 2 centuries, 40 wickets (46.32) and 19 catches

POORE, Matt Beresford (b.1930)

Canterbury

A competent right-handed batsman and useful off-spin change-bowler, Matt Poore toured South Africa in 1953/4 and India and Pakistan in 1955/6, and at home played against South Africa in 1952/3 and England in 1954/5. In South Africa he made 550 runs (22.91) including 170 in the five Tests, but in India and Pakistan he was not quite so successful. Played mainly for his batting, he never reached a 50 in Tests. His career-highest was 142 against Central Districts in 1954/5.

First-class career (1950-62): 2,336 runs (23.12) including 2 centuries, and 68 wickets (26.67)
Test matches (14): 354 runs (15.43), 9 wickets (40.77) and 1 catch

PUNA, Narotam (b.1929)

Northern Districts

Born at Surat near Bombay, Narotam Puna was a very good right-arm off-spin bowler and brilliant field, but a rather moderate batsman. He played in the three Tests against England in 1965/6, in which season he captured no fewer than 34 wickets in the Plunket Shield competition. His best bowling in an innings was 6 for 43 against Auckland in 1959/60.

First-class career (1956-69): 1,305 runs (14.81) and 229 wickets (24.43)
Test matches (3): 31 runs (15.50), 4 wickets (60.00) and 1 catch

RABONE, Geoffrey Osbourne (b.1921)

Wellington and Auckland

Geoff Rabone was a forceful right-handed batsman, an off-spin bowler who could turn to leg-spinners or stock medium-pace as well, and a superb slip field who made extremely difficult catches look comparatively simple. Rabone, otherwise 'Bones' or 'Boney', toured England in 1949 and at home played against West Indies in 1951/2 and South Africa in 1952/3. He succeeded Mervyn Wallace to the regular captaincy, and was leader in South Africa in 1953/4 and at home against England in 1954/5. A sensitive, intelligent, genial and courageous captain, he nevertheless lost four and drew one of the Tests during his captaincy. In England he was the best all-rounder, sometimes opening both batting and bowling, and collecting 1,021 runs (32.93), 50 wickets (35.70) and 24 catches; in the Tests his highest score was only 39 not out but he averaged 29.60. In the first three Tests in South Africa he was the most effective New Zealand batsman scoring 254 runs (50.80), including an exemplary innings of 107 lasting over six hours in the first match at Durban. He took 6 for 68 in 38.7 overs in a total of 326 in the third Test at Cape Town. When he broke a bone in his foot and had to return home, thirteen matches had brought him 547 runs and 28 wickets. His last Test as captain saw his country routed by England in the second match at Auckland in 1954/5, the second innings of 26 remaining the lowest total in Test cricket. His career-highest was 125 for Auckland against Central Districts in 1951/2 and best bowling in an innings 8 for 65 for Auckland against Australia B at Auckland in 1956/7.

First-class career (1940-61): 3,425 runs (28.30) including 3 centuries, and 173 wickets (27.94)
Test matches (12): 562 runs (31.22) including 1 century, 16 wickets (39.68) and 5 catches

REDMOND, Rodney Ernest (b.1944)

Wellington and Auckland

Rodney Redmond was a tall, left-handed, opening batsman who drove, cut and pulled off the front foot with tremendous confidence. Also a useful spin bowler and good field, he had a tremendous debut against Pakistan in the third match at Auckland in 1972/3 when he made scintillating scores of 107 and 56 – putting on opening stands with Glenn Turner of 159 and 80. His century came in 2 hours 12 minutes. However, he never appeared again in a Test. He toured England in 1973, but he had trouble with new contact lenses and his aggressive methods at the wicket were only rarely successful: in first-class matches he made 483 runs (28.41) and was not selected for the Tests. His career-highest was 141 not out for Auckland against Wellington in 1970/71 and best bowling in a match 10 for 110 for the New Zealand Under-23 XI against Wellington in 1965/6. His troublesome eyesight caused early retirement.

First-class career (1963-76): 3,134 runs (33.69) including 5 centuries, and 17 wickets (28.29)

REID, John Fulton (b.1958)

Auckland

A neat and attractive left-handed batsman, John Reid

is no relation to his famous namesake. A schoolmaster, he rose smoothly to the top of New Zealand cricket, enjoying steady success in all grades of cricket until his Test debut in 1978/9 against Pakistan at Auckland. Dropped after one match, he came back to score 123 not out against India in 1980/81. Also an accomplished wicket-keeper, he played his early Tests as a batting specialist.

First-class career (1975-): 3,390 runs (38.08) including 4 centuries, 5 wickets (22.00) and 93 dismissals (84 ct, 9 st.)
Test matches (4): 269 runs (44.83) including 1 century, and 2 catches

REID, John Richard (b.1928)

Wellington and Otago

The best all-rounder and captain yet produced by New Zealand, John Reid, or 'Bogo', appeared in fifty-eight consecutive official Tests, a world record. For thirty-four of these matches he was captain and he led New Zealand to her first three victories. He was a very strong, sturdily built, natural forcing right-handed batsman; a powerful driver and a sure hooker and cutter who never liked wasting time at the crease. Regularly having to face the job of redeeming lost causes, he often hit his side out of trouble. A medium-fast outswing bowler, he turned sometimes to off-cutters, pitching an immaculate length. He was also a magnificent fielder, who sometimes served competently as a deputy wicket-keeper. At one time he held the New Zealand records simultaneously for making most runs, taking most wickets, holding most catches, scoring most centuries, and playing for and captaining the country most times, besides having made most runs in all first-class matches. He toured England in 1949, 1958 and 1965, South Africa in 1953/4 and 1961/2 and India and Pakistan in 1955/6 and 1965/6. At home he played against England in 1950/51, 1954/5, 1958/9 and 1962/3, West Indies in 1951/2 and 1955/6, South Africa in 1952/3 and 1963/4 and Pakistan in 1964/5. Altogether, he captained New Zealand in ten series between 1956 and 1965, several of unofficial standing. In England in 1949, his 1,488 runs (41.33) included four centuries, a 50 in his first Test, at Old Trafford, and an innings of 93 in his second, at The Oval. In the weak side of 1958, he stood head and shoulders above everyone else, amassing 1,429 runs (39.69), again including 4 centuries, besides taking 39 wickets (22.74). In South Africa in 1953/4 he became the first player to make a thousand runs and take fifty wickets in a South African first-class season – 1,012 runs (37.48) and 51 wickets (19.33). He also collected the first of his 6 Test centuries, 135 in the third match at Cape Town, when he added 176 with J.E.F. Beck for the fifth wicket in less than two and a half hours. Against England in the first match at Dunedin in

John Reid

1954/5, he took 4 for 36 in 27 overs. On the 1955/6 tour of India and Pakistan he headed the batting with 1,032 runs (54.31) and took 39 wickets (23.87), more wickets and runs than anyone else. Of this total, 493 runs (70.42) were made against India, including 119 not out in the third match, at Delhi, in which 222 was added in an unbroken stand for the third wicket with Bert Sutcliffe. When New Zealand won her first-ever official Test in the fourth match at Auckland against the West Indies in 1955/6, John Reid was top scorer with 84. In subsequent victories over South Africa in the third match at Cape Town and the fifth at Port Elizabeth in 1961/2, he again played a major part, making 92 at Cape Town and 69 at Port Elizabeth, besides taking 8 wickets. In this series, he was by far the most successful all-rounder, making 546 runs (60.64) and taking 11 wickets (19.72), heading the bowling averages. On the whole first-class segment of the tour he eclipsed Denis Compton's record in South Africa, making 1,915 runs (68.39), including 7 centuries, and taking 27 wickets (29.00). He continued to be the bane of South Africa, taking 6 for 60 in 35 overs against them in the second match at Dunedin in 1963/4. His career-highest was 296 for Wellington against Northern Districts in 1962/3 – the second highest number of runs scored by one man in a day's play in New Zealand – and his best bowling in an innings 7 for 20 for Otago against Central Districts in 1956/7.

First-class career (1947-65): 16,128 runs (41.35) including 39 centuries, 466 wickets (22.60), 239 catches and 7 stumpings
Test matches (58): 3,428 runs (33.28) including 6 centuries, 85 wickets (33.41), 43 catches and 1 stumping

ROBERTS, Albert William (1909-78)

Canterbury and Otago

Albert Roberts was a right-arm medium-pace bowler who kept a good length, swung the ball and made it 'whip' off the pitch. As well as being a brilliant slip, he was also an effective batsman despite his peculiar technique – knees sagging, head apparently up – and represented New Zealand as a batsman in the first-ever Test at Christchurch. He was also selected for the first Test against South Africa in 1931/2 at Christchurch as a batsman when he scored 54. He toured England in 1937 primarily as a bowler, however, and, despite shoulder and finger injuries, captured 62 wickets (26.20), but also made 510 runs (25.50) and headed the Test averages with 142 runs (47.33). His career-highest was 181 for Canterbury against Wellington in 1931/2.

First-class career (1927-51): 3,645 runs (30.88) including 3 centuries, and 167 wickets (28.51)
Test matches (5): 248 runs (27.55), 7 wickets (29.85) and 4 catches

ROBERTS, Andrew Duncan Glenn (b.1947)

Northern Districts

A right-handed all-rounder who bats in the middle order and bowls medium-pace, Andy Roberts made his Test debut against India at Christchurch in 1976. His performances in this and the following Test were modest, but during the tour of Pakistan and India in 1976/7 he forced himself back into the side after missing the first Test against Pakistan. He played in the five remaining Tests of the tour, scoring 125 runs (31.25) against Pakistan and 112 (22.40) against India, which included his highest Test score, a determined 84 not out in the first innings of the second Test at Kanpur. In 1979 he hit 76 and 100 not out against the Pakistan touring team but was not selected for the Tests.

First-class career (1967-): 4,937 runs (34.28) including 7 centuries, and 70 wickets (28.88)
Test matches (7): 254 runs (23.09), 4 wickets (45.50) and 4 catches

ROWE, Charles Gordon (b.1915)

Wellington and Central Districts

Born in Glasgow, Gordon Rowe was a right-handed batsman and medium-pace change-bowler whose sole Test appearance was in the first Test after the Second World War against Australia at Wellington in 1945/6, when he made a pair and held a catch. In a modest career he averaged 20.00 with the bat.

First-class career (1944-53): 380 runs (20.00)

SCOTT, Roy Hamilton (b.1917)

Canterbury

A competent right-handed batsman and medium-pace bowler, Roy Scott made his sole Test appearance against England at Christchurch in 1946/7, when he scored 18 and took 1 for 74.

First-class career (1940-55): 874 runs (24.97) and 94 wickets (25.47)

SCOTT, Verdun John (1916-80)

Auckland

A tall, fidgety, right-handed opening batsman with the straight back of a guardsman, 'Scotty' or 'The Scotsman' had a short backlift but he was a fine on-side player, delivering most of his power from his huge wrists and forearms. This quiet, drily humorous man was also a good fielder, especially at first slip. He toured England in 1949, and at home played against Australia in 1945/6, England in 1946/7 and 1950/51 and the West Indies in 1951/2. On his England tour he made 1,572 runs (40.30), including 4 centuries, and contributed 178 runs (25.42) in the Tests. Together with Bert Sutcliffe he gave New Zealand many good starts. His highest score in Tests was his last; a defiant 84 in over four hours in the second match at Auckland against the West Indies in 1951/2, which averted a rout. His career-highest was 204 against Otago in 1947/8. He also represented his country at Rugby League.

First-class career (1938-53): 5,575 runs (49.13) including 16 centuries
Test matches (10): 458 runs (28.62), 0-14 and 7 catches

SHRIMPTON, Michael John Froud (b.1940)

Hawke's Bay, Central Districts and Northern Districts

A painstaking and confident right-handed batsman and occasional leg-break bowler, Michael Shrimpton toured Australia in 1973/4, and at home played against England in 1962/3, 1965/6, and 1970/71 and South Africa in 1963/4. In Australia he headed both batting and bowling averages with 426 runs (42.60) and 7 wickets (24.28), but achieved little in the Tests. His highest Test score was 46 in the second match at Auckland against England in 1970/71, when he added 141 for the fifth wicket with Mark Burgess, a New Zealand record against England, but in his irregular Test career he failed to score on six occasions. His career-highest was 150 for Central Districts in 1962/3 and best bowling figures in an innings were 6 for 40 against Otago in 1969/70.

First-class career (1961-80): 5,812 runs (29.80) including 7 centuries, and 81 wickets (29.45)
Test matches (10): 265 runs (13.94), 5 wickets (31.60) and 2 catches

SINCLAIR, Barry Whitley (b.1936)

Wellington

Fair-haired and one of the smallest cricketers ever to appear in New Zealand, Barry Sinclair was a sound and often fluent right-handed batsman with an indomitable spirit and an excellent field at cover. He was the immovable object of New Zealand's early middle batting for five concentrated seasons and captained the country against England and India. He toured India and Pakistan in 1964/5 and England in 1965, and at home played against England in 1962/3 and 1965/6 (captain), South Africa in 1963/4, Pakistan in 1964/5 and India in 1967/8 (captain). He established himself against South Africa in 1963/4, preventing a heavy defeat in the second match at Dunedin by scoring 52 out of 149. In the next Test, at Auckland, he made his Test highest, 138 (in a total of 263) in five and three-quarter hours. In India and Pakistan in 1964/5 he was rather disappointing with only 250 runs from 6 Tests, though he made 130 in the high-scoring second Test against Pakistan at Lahore. In England in 1965 he made 807 runs (36.68), but his only substantial Test innings was in the first match at Lord's, when runs were badly needed and he made 72 in less than two and a half hours. In the third Test against England at Auckland in 1965/6 he scored 114 in 229 minutes when eight batsmen failed to reach 20, and headed the batting in the series with 218 runs (36.33).

First-class career (1955-71): 6,114 runs (32.87) including 6 centuries
Test matches (21): 1,148 runs (29.43) including 3 centuries, 2 wickets (16.00) and 8 catches

SINCLAIR, Ian McKay (b.1933)

Canterbury

In a short first-class career as a right-arm off-break bowler and left-handed batsman Ian Sinclair played in two Tests against the West Indies in 1955/6.

First-class career (1953-7): 264 runs (14.66) and 41 wickets (27.34)
Test matches (2): 25 runs (8.33), 1-120 and 1 catch

SMITH, Frank Brunton (b.1922)

Canterbury

A stocky, cheerful, wristy right-handed batsman, Brun or 'Runty' Smith was a quick-eyed natural hitter, who tended to play with a cross-bat and his left foot insufficiently close to the ball; most of his runs came from cuts, hooks and pulls. He was an excellent fielder, reliable in his catching and remorseless in pursuit of the hardest hit ball. He toured England in 1949, and at home played against England in 1946/7 and the West Indies in 1951/2. In England he made 1,008 runs (28.00) and at Headingley hit 96 in two hours and 54 not out in fifty minutes in the first Test.

First-class career (1943-53): 2,588 runs (33.17) including 4 centuries
Test matches (4): 237 runs (47.40) and 1 catch

SMITH, Horace Dennis (b.1913)

Otago and Canterbury

A right-arm fast bowler from Queensland, Horace Smith played in only one Test, the first at Christchurch against England in 1932/3, scoring 4 and taking 1 for 113, something of an anti-climax after clean bowling Eddie Paynter with the first ball of his first over. His was a short first-class career.

First-class career (1931-4): 404 runs (22.44) and 17 wickets (33.52)

SMITH, Ian David Stockley (b.1957)

Hawke's Bay and Central Districts

A neat wicket-keeper and useful right-handed batsman, Ian Smith took over from Warren Lees as New Zealand's first-choice wicket-keeper on the tour of Australia in 1980/81. Some spirited innings in both the Tests and the one-day internationals justified his selection, as did his competent wicket-keeping, and not until he broke his finger during the Test in Christchurch against Australia in 1981/2 did his career suffer a setback.

First-class career (1977-): 1,238 runs (19.34) and 97 dismissals (90 ct, 7 st.)
Test matches (7): 86 runs (10.75) and 19 dismissals (19 ct.)

SNEDDEN, Colin Alexander (b.1918)

Auckland

A medium-pace right-arm off-break bowler, Colin Snedden played his sole Test against England at Christchurch in 1946/7, not batting and taking 0 for 46.

First-class career (1938-49): 44 runs (8.80) and 31 wickets (25.41)

SNEDDEN, Martin Colin (b.1958)

Auckland

Dark-haired and built for hard work, Martin Snedden bowls accurate, medium-fast and right-arm, but bats usefully left-handed, as his 70 runs at an average of 35 in two Tests at home against Australia in 1981/2 showed. In these two games his lively medium pace also accounted for 11 Australian wickets. He toured Australia in successive seasons (1981/2 and 1982/3) to play as an all-rounder in the one-day internationals. Also a keen Rugby player, he is a qualified lawyer.

First-class career (1977-): 530 runs (22.08) and 93 wickets (25.90)
Test matches (6): 72 runs (18.00), 11 wickets (38.72) and 2 catches

SPARLING, John Trevor (b.1938)

Auckland

A short, fair-haired all-rounder, John Sparling was a gallant and dogged right-handed batsman, a useful off-spin bowler and very good field. He toured England in 1958 and South Africa in 1961/2, and at home played against England in 1958/9 and 1962/3, and South Africa in 1963/4. Showing promise on his England tour – making 513 runs, taking 38 wickets and holding 13 catches in twenty-one matches – he had his twentieth birthday on the first day of the fourth Test at Old Trafford, when he made a dour 50 in about three hours. Never again did he reach 50, or even achieve a bowling breakthrough in official Tests. His career-highest score was 105 against Canterbury in 1959/60, in which match he also took 7 for 98.

First-class career (1956-71): 4,606 runs (24.37) including 2 centuries, and 318 wickets (22.71)
Test matches (11): 229 runs (12.72), 5 wickets (65.40) and 3 catches

SUTCLIFFE, Bert (b.1923)

Auckland, Otago and Northern Districts

Craggy-jawed and fair-haired, Bert Sutcliffe was probably, with Neil Harvey, the best left-handed batsman of his generation in the world. His stroke-play was at once enterprising and cultured: his off- and cover-driving, hooking and pulling were models for a copy-book. This great opening batsman was genuinely modest yet also a character of sunny optimism. A left-arm slow bowler with a deceptive quicker ball, he was also rapid, clean and safe in the field. He became famous overnight by scoring 197 and 128 for Otago against MCC at Dunedin in 1946/7; and the following week, at Christchurch in his first Test, he made 58. During the next twenty years he proceeded to collect one New Zealand batting record after another. He toured England in 1949, 1958 and 1965, South Africa in 1953/4, and India and Pakistan in 1955/6 and 1965/6. At home he played against England in 1946/7, 1950/51, 1954/5 and 1958/9, the West Indies in 1951/2 and 1955/6 and South Africa in 1953/4. He was soon concerned in several records in New Zealand first-class cricket: for Auckland against Canterbury in 1948/9, he shared in opening stands of 220 and 286 with Don Taylor, a world record. Another record was an opening partnership of 373 with L. Watt, for Otago against Auckland in 1950/51. He made 355 for Otago against Auckland in 1949/50 only to exceed this score with 385 against Canterbury in 1952/3, which remains the highest-ever by a New Zealander. For more than a decade his 230 not out (in nine hours) against India in the third Test at New Delhi in 1955/6, when he added 222 unbroken for the third wicket with John Reid, remained the highest score by a New Zealander in a Test. And in England in 1949 he amassed 2,627 runs (59.70), another New Zealand record on a tour, including seven centuries. When he hit 243 and 100 not out against Essex at Southend, it was the fourth time he had hit a century in each innings of a match. At

Bert Sutcliffe

Worcester in the opening match of the 1958 tour he hit 139, but a broken wrist – incurred while fielding against MCC at Lord's – impeded his progress. He emerged from retirement a few months before the 1965 tour, having made 151 not out brilliantly against India in the second Test at Calcutta. In the first Test at Edgbaston he was hit on the ear, while ducking into a ball from Fred Trueman and, although he returned after treatment to score 53, he had to miss most of the remainder of the tour. His only Test century at home against England was 116 in the first match at Christchurch in 1950/51. He captained New Zealand against the visiting West Indies in 1951/2 with little success. On touring South Africa in 1953/4, he took over the captaincy when Geoff Rabone became incapacitated. Specializing as a middle-order batsman at that time in order to counteract the weakness there, he made more runs than anyone else: in all first-class matches he scored 1,155 runs (46.20) including 305 (38.12) in the Tests. Opening the batting again in the five Tests in India in 1955 he amassed 611 runs (87.28). Successive Test innings brought him 137 not out, 73, 37 and 230 not out! In retirement Bert Sutcliffe has proved himself a superb coach.

First-class career (1941-66): 17,283 runs (47.44) including 44 centuries, and 86 wickets (37.95)
Test matches (42): 2,727 runs (40.10) including 5 centuries, 4 wickets (86.00) and 20 catches

TAYLOR, Bruce Richard (b.1943)

Canterbury and Wellington

A 6 foot 3 inch all-rounder of outstanding quality, Bruce Taylor was an attractive, punishing left-handed batsman and an accurate right-arm fast-medium bowler with a command of swing both ways and a nasty bouncer. No matter what the state of the pitch or the ball, he would, with his high action, coax out at least a little movement. He was also an eager and determined field, and a character who enjoyed life to the full off the field. On his Test debut against India at Calcutta in 1964/5 he created a sensation, hitting 105 freely in 158 minutes, adding 163 with Bert Sutcliffe for the seventh wicket, and then proceeding to take 5 for 86 in India's first innings. Not only was this his first century in first-class cricket, but he achieved the record of being the only player to score a hundred and take 5 wickets in an innings in his first Test. In the next match at Bombay he secured 5 for 26, India being routed for 88, and in his first Test against Pakistan at Rawalpindi he slammed 76 in eighty-eight minutes on a total of 175. He visited England in 1965, 1969 and 1973, India and Pakistan again in 1969/70 and the West Indies in 1971/2. At home he played against England in 1965/6, India in 1967/8, West Indies in 1968/9 and Pakistan in 1972/3. He endured mixed fortune in his three England tours. Each time he exceeded 30 wickets in the short first-class programmes, but only in 1969 was his bowling a vital force in the Tests, especially in the last match at The Oval when, after injury had curtailed his appearances, he took 4 for 47 in the first innings. His best batting was at Lord's in 1965, his first Test in England, when he hit 51 after coming in with the score 62 for 6. When the West Indies visited New Zealand in 1968/9 he failed as a bowler, but headed the batting averages with 209 runs (69.66), including a swashbuckling 124 in the first Test at Auckland after 6 wickets had gone cheaply. His first 50 took thirty minutes and his century, reached with a six into the stand, eighty-six minutes. In the West Indies his bowling accounted for 27 wickets (17.70) in four Tests, including 7 for 74 in the first innings at Bridgetown. At home against Pakistan he took 13 wickets in three Tests, taking his tally past 100. He 'retired' in 1973, but returned successfully in 1978/9. His career-highest score was 173 for Wellington against Otago in 1972/3.

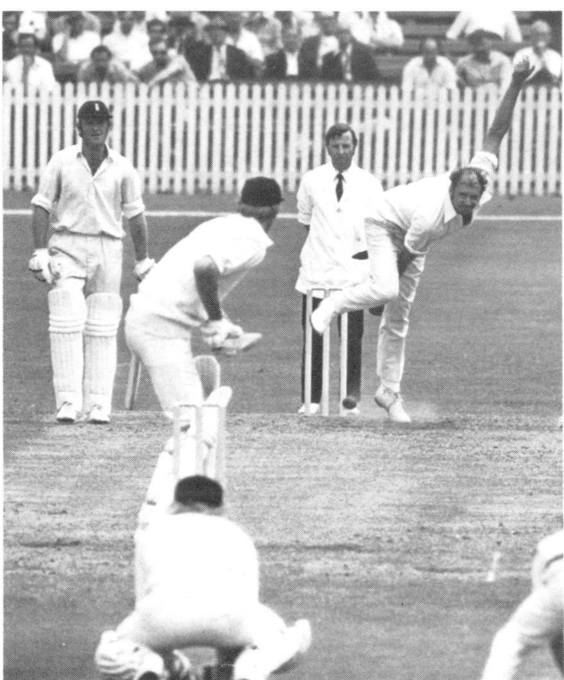

Bruce Taylor, bowling to England's Tony Greig, with Dennis Amiss at the other end. Ken Wadsworth is the wicket-keeper.

First-class career (1963-80): 4,579 runs (24.75) including 4 centuries, and 422 wickets (25.13)
Test matches (30): 898 runs (20.40) including 2 centuries, 111 wickets (26.60) and 10 catches

TAYLOR, Donald Dougald (1923-80)

Auckland and Warwickshire

An attractive, enterprising right-handed batsman with strokes all round the wicket, occasional off-break bowler and good field, Don Taylor played against England in 1946/7 and the West Indies in 1955/6. Against the latter in the third match at Wellington, when he had been recalled to Tests after an interval of nine years, he scored 43 and 77 enterprisingly when runs were badly needed. For Auckland against Canterbury in 1948/9 he made 99 and 143, his career-highest, sharing in opening stands of 220 and 286 with Bert Sutcliffe, a world record. He appeared for Warwickshire as a professional from 1949 until 1953.

First-class career (1946-61): 3,734 runs (23.63) including 1 century, and 30 wickets (33.96)
Test matches (3): 159 runs (31.80) and 2 catches

THOMSON, Keith (b.1941)

Canterbury

A solid right-handed batsman, Keith Thomson played in two Tests against India in 1967/8, making 69 on his debut at Christchurch. His career-highest was 136 not out against Northern Districts in 1968/9. He represented his country also at hockey.

First-class career (1959-74): 3,134 runs (28.23) including 5 centuries
Test matches (2): 94 runs (31.33) and 1-9

TINDILL, Eric William Thomas (b.1910)

Wellington

A lively left-handed batsman who often opened the innings, and a very competent wicket-keeper, Eric Tindill toured England in 1937, and at home played against Australia in 1945/6 and England in 1946/7. In first-class matches on his England tour, he averaged 18.34 with the bat and claimed 45 dismissals. The highest score of his career was 149 against Auckland in 1948/9. A versatile games player, he achieved his greatest renown as an All Black Rugby footballer.

First-class career (1933-50): 3,091 runs (30.60) including 6 centuries, and 119 dismissals (87 ct, 32 st.)
Test matches (5): 73 runs (9.12) and 7 dismissals (6 ct, 1 st.)

TROUP, Gary Bertram (b.1952)

Auckland

Tall and strong, a left-arm fast-medium bowler, Gary Troup toured India and Pakistan in 1976/7. In his sole Test on the tour, the second against India at Kanpur, he took 1 for 116, and was also unsuccessful at home against Pakistan in 1978, but his steady line and length proved useful to New Zealand in the 1979 Prudential World Cup and in the semi-final against England he was New Zealand's second most economical bowler. In 1979/80 he was outstanding against the West Indies, taking 18 wickets in three Tests. Injured after a good start to the 1980/81 tour of Australia, he returned there for the 1982/3 one-day internationals.

First-class career (1974-): 543 runs (12.06) and 167 wickets (28.85)
Test matches (12): 43 runs (4.77), 34 wickets (32.76) and 2 catches

TRUSCOTT, Peter Bennetts (b.1941)

Wellington

In a short first-class career as a right-handed opening batsman Peter Truscott made a single Test appearance against Pakistan in the third match at Christchurch in 1964/5, scoring 3 and 26 and holding 1 catch. His career-highest was 165 for New Zealand Under 23 against Auckland in 1963/4.

First-class career (1961-6): 904 runs (25.82) including 1 century

TURNER, Glenn Maitland (b.1947)

Otago and Worcestershire

In two senses the most professional cricketer ever produced by New Zealand, Glenn Turner made himself a household name throughout the cricket world by dedicating himself to cricket from an early age and making best possible use of a considerable natural ability. Unswervingly single-minded in his pursuit of runs, unashamedly ambitious and often impatient of amateur administrators in New Zealand, his career with Worcestershire has been the key to his success everywhere else. He deliberately enrolled in the hard school of county cricket, learned his lessons quickly and has never forgotten them. Almost frail-looking, pale-faced, and serious-minded, Turner is a right-handed opening batsman who plays immaculately straight, defends with a solidity of technique which few contemporary players have matched, and, although a limited attacking batsman in his earlier days, can now play every shot on demand and scores as fast as anyone when necessary. His most characteristic strokes are the off-drive and a beautifully timed drive to mid-wicket with the face of the bat turned on impact. He is also a high-class fielder either at slip or in the covers. Making his debut for Otago in 1964/5 while still a schoolboy, he was recommended to Warwickshire by Billy Ibadulla, who coaches in New Zealand, but was accepted by Worcestershire because their neighbours already had a full supply of overseas players. Worcestershire have never had a more consistent performer than Glenn Turner, whose loyalty to his county has been total. First appearing for them in 1967, he was qualified to play regularly in 1968, scored 10 centuries in making 2,379 runs in 1970 (a county record), and has hit centuries against the sixteen other counties plus one for New Zealand against his own! In 1973 he scored 2,416 runs (67.11), including 1,018 runs (78.30) for the New Zealand touring team by the end of May, the first time this had been achieved in England since Bill Edrich did it in 1938. His Test career began against the West Indies in Auckland in February 1969 with a duck but he was soon scoring at the highest level as consistently as he did in all other forms of cricket. The broader canvas of the five-day match suits his tempo and his temperament, giving a painstaking and cultured craftsman the opportunity to build his innings steadily, soberly and coolly. He has twice carried his bat through the completed innings of a Test match, and on a third occasion was last man out. He scored 43 not out in a total of 131 against England at Lord's in 1969, and 223 not out in a total of 386 against the West Indies at Kingston in 1971/2. On this tour of the Caribbean Turner hit four double centuries including two innings of 259 in successive matches at Georgetown, first against Guyana and then against the West Indies. Apart from this tour and his official visits to England in 1969, 1973 and for the Prudential World Cups of 1975 and 1979 (he missed the 1978 tour because he wanted to concentrate on his benefit with Worcestershire), he has toured Australia twice (1973/4 and 1982/3) and India and Pakistan twice (1976/7 as captain). He has captained New Zealand in ten Tests, relinquishing the job after a disagreement with cricket officials. He has hit two centuries in the same match on four occasions: 122 and 128 against Warwickshire at Edgbaston in 1972; 101 and 110 not out for New Zealand against Australia at Christchurch in 1974 when Australia lost to New Zealand for the first time; 135 and 108 for Otago against Northern Districts in 1974/5 at Gisborne, and 105 and 186 not out for Otago against Central Districts at Dunedin in the same season. In 1975/6 he scored 1,244 runs (77.75), a record aggregate for a New Zealand season. Against Glamorgan at Swansea in 1977 he scored 141 not out of Worcestershire's total of 169, 83.4 per cent of the total, a first-class record. In 1982 he became only the nineteenth player, and only the second non-Englishman, to score 100 first-class hundreds. He did so in style, making 311 not out against Warwickshire at Worcester, where 33 of his 100 centuries had been scored. His goal achieved, he retired from county cricket, but has now made himself available again to New Zealand's selectors and toured Australia in 1982/3. He has scored 1,000 runs in a season eighteen times (fifteen in England). He has been New Zealand's most prolific player, yet if you passed this slight, pale figure in a crowd you might think him rather downtrodden.

Glenn Turner

First-class career (1964-): 34,213 runs (49.87) including 103 centuries, 5 wickets (37.80) and 406 catches

Test matches (39): 2,920 runs (45.62) including 7 centuries, 0-5 and 40 catches

VIVIAN, Graham Ellery (b.1946)

Auckland

A left-handed stroke-playing batsman, superb deep fielder and a leg-spin bowler with a jerky action who delivered an exotic mixture of orthodox leg-breaks, sharp 'wrong 'uns' and the occasional double-bouncer, Graham Vivian toured England in 1965 at the age of nineteen. His selection followed a late search for a leg-spinner, but he found the pitches unsuitable and did not earn a Test place. He toured India and Pakistan in 1964/5 and in his first and only Test against India, in the second match at Calcutta, hit 43, adding 81 in eighty-three minutes with Vic Pollard for the eighth wicket. In the West Indies in 1971/2 he set a new high standard in fielding, but in nine matches made only 204 runs and took only 4 wickets, his Test record being particularly disappointing. Problems with his eyesight caused his retirement in 1979. His career-highest was 137 not out for New Zealand against Victoria in 1969/70 and best bowling in an innings 5 for 59 for Auckland against Central Districts in 1967/8. An excellent captain of Auckland, he came close to captaining New Zealand as well. He is the son of H.G. Vivian, also a Test player.

First-class career (1964-79): 3,259 runs (28.33) including 3 centuries, and 58 wickets (38.00)
Test matches (5): 110 runs (18.33), 1-107 and 3 catches

VIVIAN, Henry Gifford (b.1912)

Auckland

This attractive left-handed batsman had a sound defence and superb drive, and was particularly quick to punish the loose ball. A left-arm leg-spin bowler with an easy and rhythmical action and able to turn the ball sharply from a very good length, he was also a very alert field. Giff Vivian toured England in 1931 and made his Test debut, the second match at The Oval, at the age of 18 years and 267 days. He took the wickets of Sutcliffe and Ames and top-scored with 51 in the second innings, when New Zealand were losing by an innings, hitting a six off Hedley Verity. On the tour he made 1,002 runs (30.36). This included 136 against Oxford and 101 (including 4 sixes) against the Champions, Yorkshire. He also took 64 wickets (23.75) on the tour. In his first and only Test against South Africa, in the second match at Wellington in 1931/2, he hit 100 and 73, the highest score in each innings. He also took 4 for 68 in a total of 410, but the South Africans won comfortably. Back in England in 1937 he made 1,118 runs (29.42) and took 49 wickets (36.91) and as an opener made 194 runs in the Tests (32.33), but his 8 wickets (42.25) were expensive. His career-highest was 165 against Wellington in 1931/2 and best bowling 6 for 49 (10 for 108 in the match) against Wellington in 1938/9.

First-class career (1930-39): 4,443 runs (34.71) including 6 centuries, and 223 wickets (27.62)
Test matches (7): 421 runs (42.10) including 1 century, 17 wickets (37.23) and 4 catches

WADSWORTH, Kenneth John (1946-76)

Central Districts and Canterbury

A wicket-keeper who was made not born, but who was a safe athletic catcher standing back and who improved steadily, Ken Wadsworth was also a confident and aggressive right-handed batsman, who could, however, defend doggedly if necessary. Strongly built with a mass of fair hair, he was a pugnacious cricketer who hated losing. He was his country's regular 'keeper from 1969 until 1976, and when he died of cancer at the age of twenty-nine he had not reached his peak. He toured England in 1969 and 1973, India and Pakistan in 1969/70, the West Indies in 1971/2 and Australia in 1973/4. At home he played against England in 1970/71 and 1974/5, Pakistan in 1973/4, Australia in 1973/4 and India in 1975/6. He was particularly successful behind the stumps on his two England tours, capturing 17 victims in the six Tests. His highest score in Tests was 80 in the first match at Melbourne against Australia in 1973/4. In the first match against the West Indies at Kingston in 1971/2, he made 78, with Glenn Turner adding 220 doggedly in about five hours, the country's record for the sixth wicket. His number of dismissals both in first-class and Test matches constituted records for New Zealand. His highest innings brought him into prominence for the first time when he scored 103 for South Island against the West Indies at Dunedin in 1968/9. Ken Wadsworth was an inspiration to all those with whom he played, and his funeral at Nelson was attended by cricketers from the length and breadth of the country.

First-class career (1968-76): 3,664 runs (25.62) including 2 centuries, and 282 dismissals (256 ct, 26 st.)
Test matches (33): 1,010 runs (21.48) and 96 dismissals (92 ct, 4 st.)

WALLACE, Walter Mervyn (b.1916)

Auckland

Under average height and of hawklike visage, Mervyn Wallace, or 'Flip', was a right-handed attacking batsman with a wide range of attractive strokes, his cover-driving being immaculate, and his pulling and hooking exuberant, and an excellent field, particularly at cover-point. He toured England in 1937 and as vice-captain in 1949, and at home played against Australia in 1945/6, England in 1946/7 and 1950/51, and also captained the tour of South Africa in 1952/3. He headed the batting on the 1937 tour with 1,641 runs (41.02), and at Lord's on his Test debut made 52 (including two pulls for six) and 56. On the 1949 tour he hit 910 runs before the end of May, but fell away so much that he did not reach his thousand runs until early July. Altogether on that tour he made 1,722 runs (49.20), including 5 centuries. In the last Test at The Oval his 55 and 58 were considerable factors in staving off defeat. His Test-highest was a solid 66 against England in the first match at Christchurch in 1950/51 in a high-scoring match. Despite his disappointments in Tests, he remained a cheerful enthusiast. His first-class career was more fruitful, with a career-highest of 211 against Canterbury in 1939/40.

First-class career (1933-61): 7,609 runs (43.98) including 16 centuries
Test matches (13): 439 runs (20.90), 0-5 and 5 catches

WARD, John Thomas (b.1937)

Canterbury

A capable specialist wicket-keeper and, for his moderate capabilities, often an effective night-watchman, John Ward toured England in 1958 and 1965 as a reserve 'keeper playing in only one Test. He also went to India in 1964/5, when he played in four Tests before injury prevented him from continuing on the Pakistan leg of the tour. At home he appeared once each against South Africa in 1963/4, Pakistan in 1964/5 and India in 1967/8. He made his first tour, to South Africa, after only two first-class matches, including one for South Island in a trial match when he held five catches in the first innings.

First-class career (1957-71): 1,117 runs (12.41) and 257 dismissals (230 ct, 27 st.)
Test matches (8): 75 runs (12.50) and 17 dismissals (16 ct, 1 st.)

WATT, Leslie (b.1924)

Otago

A right-handed batsman of monumental patience, Leslie Watt expected the same quality to be shown by spectators! He played in a sole Test, the first match against England at Dunedin in 1954/5, scoring 0 and 2. He achieved fame when he made his career-highest, 96 in six hours, against Auckland in 1950/51, establishing the record first-wicket stand of 373 with Bert Sutcliffe.

First-class career (1942-63): 1,972 runs (23.47)

WEBB, Murray George (b.1947)

Otago and Canterbury

Bounding in ferociously, tall and long-haired, Murray Webb was a hostile right-arm fast bowler who toured the West Indies in 1971/2, when the heat and heartless pitches took the sting out of his bowling. Off the field he devoted much of his time to a thesis for an MA degree. He played also at home against England in 1970/71 and Australia in 1973/4 but was superseded by the Hadlee brothers. His best bowling in an innings was 7 for 49 for Otago against Wellington in 1971/2.

First-class career (1969-74): 202 runs (10.10) and 133 wickets (23.39)
Test matches (3): 12 runs (6.00) and 4 wickets (117.75)

WEBB, Peter Neil (b.1957)

Auckland

Neatly built, Peter Webb is a right-handed batsman, excellent fielder and occasional wicket-keeper who has not fully developed his potential. He played his first two Tests against the West Indies in 1979/80, then returned to international cricket in 1982/3 when selected to tour Australia.

First-class career (1976-): 2,008 runs (27.88) including 4 centuries
Test matches (2): 11 runs (3.66) and 2 catches

WEIR, Gordon Lindsay (b.1908)

Auckland

Although thinning hair and a serious mien made him look older then his years, Lindsay, or 'Dad', Weir was an active as well as a sound right-handed batsman, and a medium-pace change-bowler who was unfailingly energetic in the field. He toured England in 1931 and 1937, and at home played against England in 1929/30 and 1932/3 and South Africa in 1931/2. On his first England tour he made 1,035 runs (25.87) and took 27 wickets (34.70), including knocks of 37 and 40 and 3 for 38 (as opening bowler with Ian Cromb at Lord's). In 1937, although he did not do himself justice in making 893 runs (26.26) and taking 14 wickets (73.75), he hit 134 not out (including 4 sixes) at Worcester in two hours and three quarters in a losing cause. At Auckland in the fourth match against England in 1929/30 he scored 63 in a run feast. In New Zealand's first Test against South Africa, at Christchurch in 1931/2, he hit 46 and, on a worn pitch, 74 not out in a total of 146. His career-highest was 191 against Otago in 1935/6 and his best bowling figures in an innings, 6 for 56 against Wellington in 1940/41.

First-class career (1928-47): 5,022 runs (32.19) including 10 centuries, and 107 wickets (37.35)
Test matches (11): 416 runs (29.71), 7 wickets (29.85) and 3 catches

WHITELAW, Paul Erskine (b.1910)

Auckland

A sound and attractive right-handed opening batsman, Paul Whitelaw played in the two Tests against England in 1932/3 and, although he did not fail, was never tried again. In 1936/7, on a rain-damaged wicket, he made his career-highest, 195, in five and a half hours, for Auckland against Otago. He added 445 for the third wicket with W.N. Carson in 268 minutes, which remained a world record for that wicket for forty years.

First-class career (1928-47): 2,739 runs (37.52) including 5 centuries
Test matches (2): 64 runs (32.00)

WRIGHT, John Geoffrey (b.1954)

Northern Districts and Derbyshire

John Wright, an outstanding cricketer at Christ's

College, Christchurch, and at Otago University, quickly came to the fore in New Zealand first-class cricket after representing Northern Districts for the first time in 1974/5. He was so successful on trial with Derbyshire and Kent in England in 1976 that the former county signed him as a specially registered overseas player in preference to two outstanding South African cricketers. Wright entirely justified the confidence shown in him by making 1,080 runs (32.70) for Derbyshire in his first season for them in 1977 and has continued to bat with impressive consistency since. A left-handed opening batsman of great determination with deep powers of concentration and fine fielder, he has a sound defence and a full array of strokes, being notably strong, like many good left-handers, in punching the ball away to the on-side whenever a ball is pitched up near to his leg stump. Making his first appearances for his country against England, at home and away, in 1978, he started with a solid 55 in the first Test at Wellington, the highest score for the New Zealand side in their first defeat of England. In England his best Test score was 62 in the first Test at The Oval, but against Pakistan in 1979 he batted consistently, scoring 88 in the second Test at Napier. More recently, he scored 110 against India at Auckland in 1980/81 and 141 against Australia at Christchurch in 1981/2. In county cricket he has scored over 1,000 runs in each full season he has played, including 1,504 runs (48.51) in 1980 and 1,830 runs (55.45) with 7 centuries in 1982.

First-class career (1975-): 5,369 runs (34.86) including 10 centuries
Test matches (20): 976 runs (27.88) including 2 centuries, 0-2 and 8 catches

YUILE, Bryan William (b.1941)

Manawatu and Central Districts

Under average height, Bryan Yuile was a fair-haired left-arm slow bowler who relied much on flight and an immaculate length, a sturdy middle-order, right-handed batsman and a good field, especially at leg-slip. He toured South Africa in 1961/2, India and Pakistan in 1964/5 and 1969/70 and England in 1965 and 1969. At home he played against England in 1962/3, India in 1967/8 and the West Indies in 1968/9. He was rarely assured of a Test place. On his first England tour he headed the bowling averages with 24 wickets (22.91), and appeared in two Tests. On his second tour, however, although he headed the batting averages with 383 runs (63.83) and took 24 wickets (25.87), he was not selected for any of the Tests. On his second tour of India and Pakistan he captured 21 wickets (20.33), but played in only three Tests. He hit his Test-highest score of 64 in the first match against England at Auckland in 1962/3. He took 12 wickets (20.25) in the three Tests against Pakistan in 1964/5, including 6 for 112 in the third match at Christchurch. He also took 9 wickets (27.11) in the three matches against the West Indies in 1968/9. In Tests he was rarely given the opportunity to dominate the scene, but, at least, was very good at the 'bits and pieces'. His career-highest was 146 for Central Districts against Canterbury in 1966/7 and his best bowling in an innings, 9 for 101 in a total of 311 against Canterbury in 1965/6.

First-class career (1959-72): 3,850 runs (24.67) including 1 century, and 375 wickets (21.89)
Test matches (17): 481 runs (17.81), 34 wickets (35.67) and 12 catches

INDIA

ABDUL HAFEEZ (b.1925)

Northern India, Oxford University and Warwickshire
See Kardar, A.H.

ABID ALI, Syed (b.1941)

Hyderabad
A stocky, barrel-chested all-rounder with a military moustache, Abid Ali was a careful stroke-maker who showed the full face of the bat to the ball and could drive well; he was also a medium-fast opening bowler who used the new ball particularly well in England but who in India merely fired a few preliminary shots before the army of spinners took over. Quick-moving and safe in the field, he also served as a deputy 'keeper. He toured England in 1971 and 1974, Australasia in 1967/8 and the West Indies in 1970/71, and at home he played against Australia in 1969/70, New Zealand in 1969/70, England in 1972/3 and West Indies in 1974/5. On his Test debut in the first match at Adelaide he took 6 for 55 in the first innings total of 335. In England in 1971 he dismissed four of England's top batsmen for 15 runs on the first day of the Old Trafford Test. Less than three weeks later, in the final Test at The Oval, he cut the winning boundary when India defeated England for the first time on English soil. In the Ranji Trophy competition he scored more than 2,500 runs and took over 100 wickets. His career-highest was 173 not out for Hyderabad against Kerala in 1968/9 and his best bowling in an innings 6 for 23 against Surrey at The Oval in 1974.

First-class career (1959-79): 8,741 runs (29.23) including 13 centuries, 397 wickets (28.55), 179 catches and 5 stumpings
Test matches (29): 1,018 runs (20.36), 47 wickets (42.12) and 33 catches

ADHIKARI, Lt-Col. Hemu Ramchandra (b.1919)

Gujerat, Baroda and Services
Under average height, Hemu Adhikari was a neat, attractive right-handed batsman with a sound defence and specially good in a crisis, an occasional leg-break bowler and a brilliant cover or close field. He toured Australia in 1947/8 and England (as vice-captain) in 1952, and at home played against West Indies in 1948/9 and (once as captain) in 1958/9, against England in 1951/2, Pakistan in 1952/3 and Australia in 1956/7; but his duties as an officer in the Indian Army often prevented him appearing regularly. He achieved little in Tests on his two tours, but scored 114 not out against West Indies at New Delhi in his first Test in India, and against England in the fourth match at Kanpur in 1951/2, he helped to stave off an innings defeat with 60 in a total of 157. When Pakistan played India for the first time in official Tests in 1952/3, he hit 81 not out at number eight in the first Test, adding a record 109 in eighty minutes with Ghulam Ahmed for the last wicket. In his last Test against the West Indies at New Delhi in 1958/9, when he was skipper, he scored 63 and 40, sharing in a century partnership in each innings with Chandra Borde (besides taking 3 for 68), and steering India clear of defeat. His career highest was 230 not out for Services against Rajputana in 1951/2. Lt-Col. Adhikari has been a popular and efficient manager of touring teams.

First-class career (1936-60): 8,628 runs (41.88) including 18 centuries
Test matches (21): 872 runs (31.12) including 1 century, 3 wickets (27.33) and 8 catches

AMARNATH, Lala (b.1911)

Southern Punjab, Gujerat, Patiala, United Provinces and Railways
Described as a 'pure romantic, the Byron of Indian cricket', Lala Amarnath at his best was an all-rounder of international class and a bold and aggressive captain. A right-handed batsman whose driving and cutting were a rare delight, he would 'explode' with strokes all round the wicket. As a medium-pace bowler, he took an easy, alert run of four paces, gave a double hop as he delivered but maintained an almost

impeccable length, moving his in-swingers greatly and mixing them with venomous leg-cutters. He was always desperately keen to get on with the game and could hardly wait for the ball to be returned to him before heading back for his next run-up. A reliable close fielder, he was also a useful deputy wicket-keeper. He toured England in 1936 and 1946 and Australia in 1947/8, and at home played against England in 1933/4 and 1951/2, West Indies in 1948/9 and Pakistan in 1952/3. For Southern Punjab against MCC in 1933/4 he scored 109 brilliantly, and in the first Test against England at Bombay he made 38 and 118 in three and a half hours. He was the first Indian centurion in Tests, and his bowling talent was discovered at the nets before the start of this match. In England in 1936 the Indian team were rent by divisions and, although he had scored more runs – 613 – than anyone else and taken 32 wickets, he was sent home for disciplinary reasons before the first Test. After a special enquiry months later, he was exonerated, and he toured England again in 1946. In the first Test at Lord's he scored 50 and took 5 for 118 in the first innings, and in the second at Old Trafford he returned a match analysis of 8 for 167 in 81 overs. He captained India on the first visit to Australia in 1947/8, but although successive innings brought him 144, 94 not out and 228 not out and subsequently he hit 172 not out, 171 and 135, he fared moderately with the bat in the Tests. At least he took most wickets in the series at lowest cost – 13 wickets (28.15), twice taking 4 wickets in an innings, and at Melbourne in the third match 7 for 130. Against the first West Indian side in 1948/9, he led India with flair, and scored 294 runs (36.75). No longer captain, he played once against England in 1951/2, but failed to score or to take a wicket. Restored to the captaincy, he led India successfully in the first series against Pakistan in 1952/3. A prolific all-rounder in India, he made 2,162 runs (39.50) and took 190 wickets (14.54) in the Ranji Trophy championship. The highest score of his career was 262 for India-in-England against Rest of India at Calcutta in 1946/7 and his best bowling figures in an innings, 7 for 30 for Patiala against Services in 1956/7. He served on the Indian Selection Committee from 1952 until 1960, for two years as chairman. He is the father of Surinder and Mohinder, both Test cricketers.

First-class career (1929-64): 10,323 runs (41.62) including 31 centuries, and 457 wickets (22.93)
Test matches (24): 878 runs (24.38) including 1 century, 45 wickets (32.91) and 13 catches

AMARNATH, Mohinder Bharadwaj
(b.1950)

Punjab, Delhi and Durham

Trim-figured, boyishly good-looking and of medium height, Mohinder Amarnath, Lala's younger son, is, like his father, a right-handed batsman and medium-paced bowler. With a short, relaxed run-up and good body action, he moves the ball through the air and off the pitch in helpful conditions, and he is an impressively solid orthodox batsman who drives handsomely. He made his first Test appearance in the fifth Test against Australia at Madras in 1969/70, having played for the Punjab when still a schoolboy three years before. Despite a promising start he didn't reappear in Tests until 1975/6 when he quickly established himself. At Auckland he made 64 and followed with 4 for 63 in New Zealand's first innings of the next Test at Christchurch. He averaged 35.60 against New Zealand and 39.71 against the West Indies, including 85 in the second innings at Port of Spain when India defied the odds to score 406 for 4 to win. In Australia in 1977/8, following a disappointing series at home to England the previous year, Amarnath scored 90 and 100 in the second Test at Perth, and in the series made 445 runs (49.44). On the tour he was top scorer with 731 runs (48.73). A second Test century followed against West Indies at Kanpur in 1978/9, 101 not out, but he was desperately unlucky in England in 1979, missing the second and fourth Tests, at first because of an injured back and then more seriously because of a hairline fracture of the skull after being hit by a bouncer. This was a setback from which he took time to recover, but he continued to do well for Delhi and captained them to an incredible success in the final of the Ranji Trophy of 1981/2 when Delhi overhauled Karnataka's first-innings score of 705 thanks primarily to Amarnath's heroic 185, the highest of six centuries in the first innings of either side! He returned to favour with India's selectors when picked to tour Pakistan in 1982/3.

First-class career (1966-): 7,278 runs (37.32) including 11 centuries, and 227 wickets (31.48)
Test matches (26): 1,466 runs (34.90) including 2 centuries, 23 wickets (50.47) and 23 catches

AMARNATH, Surinder Bharadwaj
(b.1948)

Punjab and Delhi

The elder son of Lala Amarnath, Surinder is a skilful left-handed batsman and occasional right-arm medium-pace bowler. In 1963/4 he made his debut for the Punjab while still a schoolboy. In 1972/3 he hit 202 not out for the Punjab against Delhi in the Ranji Trophy and in the same season made his unofficial Test debut against Sri Lanka, scoring 118 at Ahmedabad. On his first appearance in an official Test he scored 124 against New Zealand at Auckland in 1975/6. A neat, wristy left-hander with aggressive instincts, he cover-drives and cuts particularly well and it is surprising that he has not maintained a regular place in India's Test team having stiffened up the batting against England in 1976/7. He was injured during the 1977/8 Australian tour and had to return home. But he was unlucky not to be picked for the next tour of Australia, in 1979/80, after scoring 235 not out against the Rest of India for Delhi in the Irani Trophy.

First-class career (1963–): 6,729 runs (39.12) including 12 centuries
Test matches (10): 550 runs (30.55) including 1 century, 1-5 and 4 catches

AMAR SINGH, Ladha (1910-40)

Nawanagar and Western India

Tall, of strapping build and an entertaining, masterly all-rounder, Ladha Amar Singh could change the course of a game in a matter of minutes. Off a comparatively short, untidy run, climaxed with a sudden, almost frenzied action, he bowled right-arm fast-medium with an easy delivery, maintaining an immaculate length. Always bowling to his field, he could swing and cut the ball – especially in the heavier atmosphere of England – but it was his pace off the pitch which was most disconcerting to the batsman: 'he came off the pitch like the crack of doom', said Wally Hammond. A right-handed hitter, he could score at a rapid pace off the best bowlers; and he was a very agile field in the close positions. He toured England in 1932 taking 111 wickets (20.78) and making 641 runs (22.89) in first-class matches. He took 12 for 211 against Gloucestershire at Bristol, and 11 wickets each against Cambridge and Worcestershire. He hit a rapacious 131 not out at number ten against Lancashire at Blackpool. At Lord's in India's first-ever Test, he took 4 wickets and, in an uphill fight, hit 51 at number ten in the second innings. Against England at Madras in 1933/4, he captured 7 for 86 (44.4 overs) in the first innings of 335 and hit 48 in the second innings. By now a popular and well-paid Lancashire League professional, he could be released only for a few games on the 1936 England tour, but made 143 runs and took 10 wickets in the three Tests. In the first Test at Lord's, he took 6 for 35 in 25.1 overs in the first innings, and at Old Trafford in the second match saved India from suffering an innings defeat when he hit 48 not out. Against Lord Tennyson's team in 1937/8 he captured 36 wickets (16.66) in the five unofficial Tests. He died of pneumonia two years later.

First-class career (1930-40): 3,241 runs (24.18) including 5 centuries, and 484 wickets (18.63)
Test matches (7): 292 runs (22.46), 28 wickets (30.64) and 3 catches

AMIR ELAHI (1908-80)

Baroda, Northern India and Southern Punjab

Touring England with the 1936 team, Amir Elahi was not selected for the Tests, and on the 1947/8 Australia tour he played in one Test, as a bowler, yet was not called upon to bowl! He was in Pakistan's first team to visit India for an official series in 1952/3, but eight first-class matches brought him only 13 wickets. A right-arm medium-pace bowler who turned to leg-breaks and googlies, he was a prolific wicket-taker in the Ranji Trophy championship, taking 193 wickets (24.72). A lovable character, he was the first Pakistan Test player to die.

First-class career (1934-54): 2,469 runs (16.79) and 501 wickets (25.71)
Test matches (India – 1): 17 runs (8.50). (Pakistan – 5): 65 runs (10.83) and 7 wickets (35.42)

APTE, Arvind Laxmanrao (b.1934)

Bombay

A right-handed opening batsman with an array of brilliant strokes, Arvind Apte toured England in 1959, scoring 881 runs (27.53), including 3 centuries, but played in only one Test, at Headingley, when he scored 8 and 7.

First-class career (1955-71): 2,782 runs (33.51) including 6 centuries

APTE, Madhav Laxmanrao (b.1932)

Bombay

A sound right-handed batsman who opened for Bombay with his brother Arvind, Madhav Apte played in two Tests against Pakistan in 1952/3 and toured the West Indies in 1952/3. Second to 'Polly' Umrigar in the West Indian Tests, making 460 runs (51.11), he reached 50 three times in the first two Tests and in the third, at Port of Spain, made 163 not out. After this tour he was discarded, although he continued for several years in Ranji Trophy championship matches, in all making 2,070 runs (39.80).

First-class career (1951-68): 3,336 runs (38.79) including 6 centuries
Test matches (7): 542 runs (49.27) including 1 century, 0-3 and 2 catches

ARUN LAL, Jagdishlal (b.1955)

Delhi and Bengal

Showing his promise early, Arun Lal scored 102 in his first match for Delhi, against Services in 1975/6, and became a Test reserve for a whole season four years later, but in the end he had to move to Bengal to establish himself. A compact, sound right-handed opening batsman and brilliant slip fielder, he tends to be a nervous starter. He was a reserve for the Test side during the 1979/80 series against Australia but his first international experience did not come until 1981/2 when he played in a one-day international against

England at Cuttack. After his Bengali opening partner Pronob Roy failed in England, Arun Lal was given his first Test opportunity against Sri Lanka at Madras. His scores of 63 and 1 plus 2 catches were good enough to earn him a place on the tour to Pakistan in 1982/3, when he strove to establish himself as Gavaskar's regular opening partner.

First-class career (1975-): 2,074 runs (32.40) including 4 centuries

AZAD, Kirti Bagwat Jha (b.1959)

Delhi

A nonconformist in life and in cricket, Kirti Azad, the son of an Indian Government minister, is an attacking right-hand batsman, quickish off-spinner and fine outfielder. After an uneventful debut against England for Combined Universities in 1976/7, he made his first Ranji Trophy appearance the following season and toured Australia and New Zealand in 1980/81. He played his first Test against New Zealand at Wellington, and back at home in 1981/2, he had an extended chance when playing in the first three Tests against England. Although he scored useful runs, and more elegantly than some of his colleagues, his bowling lacked guile or variety.

First-class career (1976-): 1,593 runs (33.18) and 55 wickets (25.32)
Test matches (4): 107 runs (17.83), 1-158 and 2 catches

BAIG, Abbas Ali (b.1939)

Hyderabad, Oxford University and Somerset

Of aristocratic Muslim lineage, Abbas Ali Baig was of small build yet could hit powerfully all round the wicket and his ability to hook fast bowling stamped him as a potentially great player. Equally sprightly in the field, his throwing was fast and accurate. As a teenager, he scored a century against Mysore in the Ranji Trophy competition, and in 1959 made 1,148 runs (45.92) as a freshman at Oxford. During the long vacation he replaced the injured Vijay Manjrekar in the rather weak Indian team touring England, making 102 in his first match against Middlesex at Lord's and 26 and 112 in his first Test, at Old Trafford, when he added 109 with Nari Contractor for the second wicket; at 20 years 131 days he became the youngest Indian to score a Test century. Subsequently, he played against Australia in 1959/60, Pakistan in 1960/61 and West Indies in 1966/7, but his 50 and 58 against Australia in the third match at Bombay were his only other significant performances for his country. He toured England again in 1971, but was left out of the Tests. In all first-class cricket he scored over 7,000 runs, with a career-highest of 224 not out for South Zone against North Zone in 1966/7.

First-class career (1954-76): 12,367 runs (34.16) including 21 centuries
Test matches (10): 428 runs (23.77) including 1 century, 0-15 and 6 catches

BANERJEE, Shute Nath (1913-80)

Bengal, Nawangar and Bihar

The first Bengali to win a place in international cricket, Shute Banerjee was a right-arm fast bowler who thrived on hard work and was a generally useful tail-end batsman who defended with an honest straight bat and hit hard in front of the wicket. His sole Test was the fifth against West Indies at Bombay in 1948, when he scored 5 and 8 and took 5 for 127. He toured England in 1936 and 1946 when he shared in India's record tenth-wicket stand, against Surrey at The Oval. Coming in at number 11, with the score at 205 for 9, to join C.T. Sarwate, he hit 121, the two bowlers adding 249 in three hours ten minutes in masterly fashion. His best bowling in an innings was 8 for 25 for Nawanagar against Maharashtra in 1941/2 and his career-highest, 138 for Bihar against Bengal out of 235 in 1952/3. He led Bihar from 1942 to 1958.

First-class career (1931-60): 3,671 runs (20.50) including 5 centuries, and 381 wickets (26.61)

BANERJEE, Sudangsu Abinash (b.1919)

Bengal, Bihar and Maharashtra

A right-arm medium-pace bowler, 'Montu' Banerjee played in a sole Test against West Indies, at Calcutta in 1948/9, scoring 0, taking 5 for 181 and holding 3 catches.

First-class career (1941-54): 232 runs (7.03) and 92 wickets (23.28)

BAQA JILANI, Mohammed (1911-41)

Northern India

In the course of taking 5 for 7 in twenty-five balls for Northern India against Southern Punjab (who totalled 22) in 1934/5, Baqa Jilani performed the first-recorded hat-trick in Ranji Trophy matches. A right-arm fast-medium bowler and useful lower-order batsman, he toured England in 1936, and in his sole Test, the last at The Oval, he scored 4 not out and 12 and took 0 for 55. He died before reaching the age of thirty.

First-class career (1934-9): 896 runs (18.28) including 1 century, and 81 wickets (1.44)

BEDI, Bishen Singh (b.1946)

Punjab, Delhi and Northamptonshire

One of the most popular cricketers of all time, Bishen

Singh Bedi was for twelve years an almost indispensable bulwark of Indian cricket and also an aesthetic joy to watch. A very solidly built Sikh from Amritsar whose gaily coloured patkas adorned cricket grounds the world over and made him instantly recognizable, 'Bishy' was slim as a youth but filled out without losing an extraordinary looseness of limb and a balletic grace in movement. In the field he constantly flexed muscles and fingers to keep himself supple for the supreme moment when he delivered the ball. Easily the most subtle and artistic slow left-arm orthodox bowler of his generation, he ran in on the balls of his feet – they appeared indeed almost to be ball-bearings – and delivered from the highest possible point with a balance and poise which would catch the breath of the connoisseur. Every nuance of the spinner's art was at Bedi's command at his peak: changes of pace; variations both of flight, and of degrees of spin; curve and loop through the air; the ball swinging in with the arm; the sudden faster one; and the orthodox leg-break to the right-hander, bouncing high because of the perfection of the action. He made his first-class debut for Northern Punjab in the Ranji Trophy in 1961/2 at the age of fifteen and subsequently transferred to Delhi. He played with success for Northamptonshire from 1972 to 1977 and captained India in twenty-two Tests from 1975/6, winning six. He created headlines more than once: objecting to the use of vaseline gauzes by two England bowlers in the Madras Test in 1976/7, and at Kingston, Jamaica in 1976 declaring India's first and second innings closed as a protest against the intimidatory tactics of the West Indian fast bowlers. Bedi has been a consistent wicket-taker since playing his first Test in 1966/7. Against England at home in 1972/3 he took 25 wickets (25.28) including 5 for 63 in 40 overs in the second innings of the second Test at Calcutta. In the first innings of the fourth and fifth Tests of the series he delivered 68.5 and 69 overs respectively, having begun the series with figures of 86-43-109-5 in the match at Delhi. Against England in 1976/7 (when captain) he took 25 wickets again at 22.96, taking 6 for 71 in the second innings at Bangalore, where India won for the only time. Earlier the same season he had taken 22 wickets at 13.18 in three Tests against New Zealand. Thus in one Indian season he took 47 wickets in 8 Tests. His most prolific series, again as captain, was in Australia in 1977/8 when he took 31 wickets (23.87) including 10 for 194 in the second Test at Perth. On his first encounter with Australia in 1969/70 he had headed the bowling averages with 21 wickets (20.57), following match figures of 9 for 108 at Delhi in the third Test with 7 for 98 in Australia's first innings in the fourth match, at Calcutta. He took more wickets for India than any other bowler, and, batting right-handed in spectacles, often contributed some hard-hitting innings at number ten in the order. He twice took 100 wickets in an English season with Northants and his best figures in first-class cricket were 7 for 5 (13 for 34 in the match) for Delhi against Jammu and Kashmir in 1974/5. He was pushed out of first-class cricket earlier than he would have wished, and was involved in disputes over the captaincy of Delhi before regaining a position of authority and not only continuing to play until 1981, but also fulfilling his wish to give something back to Indian cricket by coaching young players.

Bishen Bedi

First-class career (1961-81): 3,564 runs (11.42), 1,547 wickets (21.64) and 172 catches
Test matches (67): 656 runs (8.98), 266 wickets (28.71) and 26 catches

BHANDARI, Prakash (b.1935)

Delhi and Bengal

An exciting, hard-hitting right-handed batsman and useful off-break bowler, Prakash Bhandari toured Pakistan in 1954/5, and at home played against New Zealand in 1955/6 and Australia in 1956/7, but did not establish himself in the Test team. He recorded the fastest century in Indian first-class cricket in sixty minutes for Bengal against Rajasthan at Udaipur in 1961/2; and his career-highest was 227 for Delhi against Patiala in 1957/8.

First-class career (1952-71): 2,453 runs (32.70) including 4 centuries, and 122 wickets (28.17)
Test matches (3): 77 runs (19.25), 0-39 and 1 catch

BINNY, Roger Michael Humphrey (b.1955)

Karnataka

The only Anglo-Indian to play for India, Roger Binny is an adaptable all-round cricketer. Quite tall, he bowls steadily, right-arm and medium fast, fields well, and bats capably in any position. As an opener for Delhi he scored 115, the first of six centuries in the two first innings of the historic 1981/2 Ranji Trophy final. Binny appeared first in first-class cricket in 1975/6, and a year later made a good impression for a Universities side against the MCC touring team at Nagpur. In the 1977/8 Ranji Trophy he proved his class as a batsman, scoring 563 runs (56.30) including an innings of 211 not out against Kerala when he shared an unbroken opening stand of 451 with S. Desai, a record in Indian cricket. He played in the full series of six Tests against the touring Pakistan team in 1979/80, scoring 143 runs (17.87) and taking 11 wickets at a cost of 36 each: he bowled the occasional good spell but on true pitches lacked the necessary control for a bowler of relatively mild pace. He opened the batting in the Golden Jubilee Test against England in Bombay (1979/80) and the following season toured Australia and New Zealand, playing a Test in each country without, however, making a really substantial contribution.

First-class career (1975-): 2,277 runs (27.43) including 3 centuries, and 75 wickets (41.32)
Test matches (9): 198 runs (15.23), 15 wickets (42.13) and 7 catches

BORDE, Chandrakant Gulabrao (b.1934)

Maharashtra and Baroda

An attractive and unruffled right-handed batsman who showed no fear of fast bowling and drove and pulled to leg with assurance, a leg-break and googly bowler of excellent length, and a brilliant slip field, Chandra Borde made 55 and 61 not out for Maharashtra against Bombay in 1952/3 on his first-class debut as a schoolboy, and from 1959 until 1967 played in fifty-five Tests. He toured England in 1959 and 1967, West Indies in 1961/2, and Australasia in 1967/8, and at home played against West Indies in 1958/9 and 1966/7, Australia in 1959/60, 1964/5 and 1969/70, Pakistan in 1960/61, England in 1961/2 and 1963/4 and New Zealand in 1964/5. In his first Test series, against West Indies in 1958/9, he made 109 and 96 in the fifth match at Delhi. In 1960/61 he headed the batting averages against Pakistan with 330 runs (82.50), including 177 not out in nine hours (his Test-highest) in the fourth match at Madras. He tended to bowl less with time but his cultured (if sometimes slow) batting remained valuably consistent. Against England in 1961/2 he made 314 runs (44.85) and took 16 wickets (28.75); in the fourth match at Calcutta, when India defeated England for only the second time, he hit 68 and 61 – top-scoring each time – and captured 4 for 65 in the first innings. In 1964/5 against New Zealand he made more runs than anyone, 371 (61.83), and in 1966/7 against the West Indies easily headed the batting averages with 346 runs (57.66). In his last tour, to Australasia in 1967/8, he was consistency personified, with 408 runs (31.38) in the Tests, although his highest score was a mere 69 in the first Test at Adelaide, when he captained India, unsuccessfully, for the only time. He was a prolific all-rounder in the Ranji Trophy competition, exceeding 4,500 runs (average 51) and 100 wickets. His career-highest was 202 for Maharashtra against Baroda in 1969/70 and his best bowling 7 for 44 for Baroda against Maharashtra in 1958/9.

First-class career (1952-74): 12,821 runs (40.96) including 30 centuries, and 331 wickets (27.32)
Test matches (55): 3.061 runs (35.59) including 5 centuries, 52 wickets (46.48) and 37 catches

CHANDRASEKHAR, Bhagwat Subrahmanya (b.1945)

Mysore

Chandrasekhar, universally shortened to 'Chandra', is unique in style and, in his own era, in achievement too. No other leg-spinner, in an age when the art has gradually become almost extinct, has been consistently a matchwinner. This slim, handsome, bearded South Indian, undoubtedly one of the worst batsmen ever to play Test cricket (he alone has 'achieved' four pairs of noughts), gave Indian cricket many of its finest hours, notably when he bowled his country to their first success both in England (he took 6 for 38 in England's second innings at The Oval in 1971, bowling them out for 101) and in Australia, when in

Bhagwat Chandrasekhar

the New Year Test of 1978 he took 12 for 104 in the match at Melbourne. Always likely to bowl an unplayable ball, Chandra's snake-like venom came partly from the extraordinary speed with which he turned his arm over. Right-handed, although he threw in with his left arm, his bowling arm was withered by polio at the age of five but he turned the handicap into an advantage. After a relatively lengthy run-up of some ten yards, beginning with the ball held in front of his face in both hands as if he were taking aim at the stumps, the wasted limb twirled past his right ear in a vertical plane and the ball hummed out of the back of the hand, sending down googlies, fizzing top-spinners and occasional leg-breaks at near medium pace. Full tosses and long-hops were not infrequent, yet such was his unorthodoxy and unpredictability that batsmen frequently missed the chance to put away his bad balls and indeed often hit them into the hands of a waiting fielder. Chandra first came to light for Mysore in the Ranji Trophy at the age of seventeen. Making his Test debut against England at Bombay in 1963/4, he took 4 for 67 in 40 overs on a slow pitch. The following year against Australia he bowled India to victory on the same Bombay ground with 8 for 123 in the match. In 1966/7 he took 18 wickets (28.5) against the West Indies and in England in 1967 16 wickets (27.18) in the series and 57 wickets on the tour. In 1971 he took 50 wickets on the tour. His peak, however, was reached in India in 1972/3 when he took 35 wickets in five Tests against England, the most by an Indian in any series, at a cost of 18.91, beginning the series with 8 for 79 in England's first innings at Delhi. Having taken 17 wickets in three Tests against New Zealand in 1976/7, he lost form against England but it was significant that the moment that he recaptured his unique bite India did better. His 5 for 50 in the second innings at Madras came too late, but at Bangalore in the fourth match he took 6 for 76 and 3 for 75 as India won. Against Australia in 1977/8 he took 28 wickets (25.14) taking his 200th wicket in his forty-eighth Test in the historic win at Melbourne. However, a recurring injury in his left heel restricted him the following season, and in England in 1979 he appeared to have lost his magic. He did not play Test cricket again and, after a little more domestic cricket, retired to the relative obscurity of work in a bank.

First-class career (1963-80): 600 runs (4.61), 1,063 wickets (24.04) and 106 catches
Test matches (58): 167 runs (4.07), 242 wickets (29.74) and 25 catches

CHAUHAN, Chetandra Pratap Singh
(b.1947)

Maharashtra and Delhi

A small, solid, determined and unflappable right-handed opening batsman, who cuts vigorously and has played in several successful opening stands with Sunil Gavaskar, Chetan Chauhan is also a fine fielder at short-leg, with very quick reflexes. After fleeting appearances against Australia and New Zealand in 1969/70 and England in 1972/3 he established himself on the 1977/8 tour of Australia, scoring 88 in the second Test at Perth, averaging 32.41 in the Tests and making 577 runs at 36.06 in all first-class games on the tour. Against Pakistan in 1978/9 he made 212 runs in three Tests, making 93 at Lahore and sharing with Gavaskar in an opening stand of 192. In six Tests against the West Indies in the same year he scored 331 runs, including 52 and 84 at Bombay, averaging 41.37 in the series. He batted steadily in England in 1979, his top score, in a series interrupted by rain, being 80 at The Oval when his partnership of 213 for the first wicket with Gavaskar passed the previous highest Indian opening stand in England and made possible India's remarkable attempt to score 438 in the fourth innings to win, although they eventually fell nine runs short. More valuable and consistent batting, not least in Australia in 1980/81 when Gavaskar was out of form, made him the only Test player to have scored more than 2,000 Test runs without scoring a century. When he was unaccountably dropped from the side before the series against England in 1981/2 (amid dark allegations of 'cricket politics') he had made 16 Test fifties with a highest score of 97. He is an occasional off-spin bowler.

Chetan Chauhan

First-class career (1967-): 9,451 runs (41.27) including 20 centuries, 47 wickets (33.55) and 161 catches
Test matches (40): 2,084 runs (31.57), 2 wickets (53.00) and 38 catches

CHOWDHURY, Nirode Ranjan (1923-79)

Bengal

A lively right-arm medium-pace bowler, Nirode Chowdhury toured England in 1952, taking 24 wickets (31.00) but not being selected for the Tests. At home he played one Test against West Indies in 1948/9 and one against England in 1951/2.

First-class career (1941-59): 424 runs (7.06) and 200 wickets (25.15)
Test matches (2): 3 runs (3.00) and 1-205

COLAH, Sorabji Hormasji M. (1902-50)

Western India and Nawanager

A fast-scoring right-handed batsman, medium-pace change-bowler and brilliant fielder, Sorabji Colah toured England in 1932, playing in the Lord's Test. He also appeared in the first Test in India, against England at Bombay in 1933/4.

First-class career (1922-42): 3,374 runs (28.11) including 5 centuries
Test matches (2): 69 runs (17.25) and 2 catches

CONTRACTOR, Nariman Jamshedji (b.1934)

Gujerat and Railways

A watchful left-handed opening batsman, Nari Contractor's timing and crisp stroke-play could be superb. He was an occasional right-arm medium-pace bowler and a very good close field. He captained India on twelve occasions with mixed success, until the match with Barbados at Bridgetown in 1961/2, when he was knocked senseless by a ball from Charlie Griffith into which he ducked: the back of his skull was fractured and for many hours he was gravely ill. Though he recovered, Contractor never played international cricket again; he had toured England in 1959, and at home played against New Zealand in 1955/6, Australia in 1956/7 and 1959/60, West Indies in 1958/9, Pakistan in 1960/61 and England in 1961/2. It was in 1959/60, in the home series against Australia, that he blossomed, scoring 438 runs (43.80), including 108 in the third match at Bombay. In 1960/61 against Pakistan he made 319 runs (53.16) in consistent vein. Although he made only 180 runs (22.50) in the 1961/2 series, he had the pleasure of leading India to their first win in a rubber against England. On his debut in first-class cricket in 1952/3 he scored 152 and 102 not out for Gujerat against Baroda (equalling Arthur Morris's debut record). His career-highest was 176 for Gujerat against Bombay in 1956/7, and the following season he made four hundreds in successive innings in the Ranji Trophy competition. In first-class cricket from 1952 until 1971 – he captained Gujerat for some ten years – he made over 8,000 runs.

First-class career (1952-71): 8,611 runs (39.86) including 22 centuries, and 26 wickets (40.00)
Test matches (31): 1,611 runs (31.58) including 1 century, 1-80 and 18 catches

DANI, Hemchandra Tukaram (b.1933)

Maharashtra and Services

A sound right-handed batsman and a fast-medium in-swing bowler who developed off-breaks and leg-breaks, 'Bal' Dani toured Pakistan in 1954/5 without being selected for the Tests. His sole Test appearance was the third against Pakistan at Bombay in 1952/3, when he did not bat, took 1 for 19 and held 1 catch. He has served on the Indian Board's Committee for Test Matches and Tours.

First-class career (1951-73): 6,459 runs (44.54) including 17 centuries, and 198 wickets (21.97)

DESAI, Ramakant Bhikaji (b.1939)

Bombay

In an outstanding first season in the Ranji Trophy in 1958/9 'Tiny' Desai took 50 wickets (11.10) and on his Test debut in the final match at Delhi against West Indies took 4 for 169 in 49 overs in a total of 644 for 8. He was a slightly built but lissom right-arm fast-medium out-swing bowler who opened India's attack with endless liveliness, courage and stamina. Though overworked on the 1959 England tour, he returned to India a much improved bowler. He also toured the West Indies in 1961/2 and Australasia in 1967/8; at home he played against Australia in 1959/60, Pakistan in 1960/61, England in 1961/2 and 1963/4, and New Zealand in 1964/5. Against Pakistan he took 21 wickets (29.80) including 8 for 190 in the match at Delhi. Against New Zealand in 1964/5 he took 6 for 56 in the first innings at Bombay. A very popular man, he was often bowled into the ground, but usually came up smiling! Sometimes an equally spirited batsman, he made 85 at number ten against Pakistan in the first match at Pakistan in 1960/61. His best bowling figures were 7 for 46 (11 for 120 in the match) against Rajasthan in 1960/61.

First-class career (1958-76): 2,384 runs (18.19) including 1 century and 467 wickets (24.15)
Test matches (28): 418 runs (13.48), 74 wickets (37.31) and 9 catches

DILAWAR HUSSAIN, Dr (1907-67)

Central India

Of big physique, a wicket-keeper and right-handed defensive batsman, Dilawar Hussain had an ungainly crouching batting stance but possessed unwearying patience and admirable determination. A Cambridge undergraduate, he assisted India on the 1936 England tour, when the two other wicket-keepers were unfit; he made 620 runs (44.28) and, in his only Test at The Oval, scored 35 and 54. Yet he never represented the university in first-class cricket. On his Test debut in India, against England in the second match at Calcutta, he opened the batting and made 59 and 57, the top score in each innings. Principal of M.A.O. College, Lahore, Dr Hussain was a founder-member of the Board of Control of Cricket in Pakistan and a Test selector.

First-class career (1924-41): 2,261 runs (27.24) including 4 centuries, and 98 dismissals (69 ct, 29 st.)
Test matches (3): 254 runs (42.33) and 7 dismissals (6 ct, 1 st.)

DIVECHA, Ramesh Vithaldao (b.1923)

Bombay, Northamptonshire and Oxford University

A well-built and versatile right-arm bowler, either fast-medium or off-break, and a useful batsman, 'Buck' Divecha played once for Northamptonshire against Australia in 1948. Touring England with the 1952 India team, he took 50 wickets (25.88), but achieved little in the Tests. At home he played against England in 1951/2 and Pakistan in 1952/3, also disappointingly.

First-class career (1946-63): 1,423 runs (20.92) and 217 wickets (24.88)
Test matches (5): 60 runs (12.00), 11 wickets (32.81) and 5 catches

DOSHI, Dilip Razaklal (b.1947)

Bengal, Nottinghamshire, Warwickshire, Northumberland and Hertfordshire

A gentle, intelligent character, philosophical and humorous behind a studious front, Dilip Doshi's greatest virtue is patience. He needed it when waiting years after making his first-class debut before getting his chance to succeed Bishen Bedi as India's first choice left-arm orthodox spinner, and he uses it to great effect as a bowler. Playing cricket in glasses, and less liquid of movement than the great Bedi, Doshi nevertheless has an easy action, turning the ball sharply, and bowls with exceptional accuracy. Mixing flight and pace thoughtfully, he has lured batsmen to destruction in a wide variety of cricket, not least in Test matches. He quickly made his mark at the highest level, reaching 100 wickets in his 28th Test, against Sri Lanka in 1982/3. His first series was against Australia in 1979/80 when he took 27 wickets (23.33) with eight wickets in both the first and last Tests of the series. A further 18 wickets at 28 each followed in another series against Pakistan the same season and at last Doshi, eleven years after his debut, was on his way. He remained an automatic selection until 1982/3, doing well against England at home and away in 1981/2 when he took 35 wickets in nine Tests. His wide experience of cricket in England includes first-class cricket for Nottinghamshire and Warwickshire, second-eleven appearances for two other counties and minor county cricket with Hertfordshire (in 1976, when he bowled them to a notable Gillette Cup triumph over Essex) and Northumberland. His best season was in 1980 when he took 101 wickets for Warwickshire at 26.73. Although apparently a rabbit with the bat, which he wields left-handed, he has been known to surprise opposing bowlers with stubborn defence or a few long-handled blows.

Dilip Doshi

First-class career (1968-): 1,264 runs (8.10) and 803 wickets (25.79)
Test matches (28): 108 runs (5.14), 105 wickets (28.21) and 10 catches

DURANI, Salim Aziz (b.1934)

Saurashtra, Gujerat and Rajasthan

An erratically brilliant left-handed batsman who could hit courageously or defend dourly, Salim Durani was a slow left-arm bowler who, despite his rather lazy-looking action, could extract nip from the pitch and subtly vary changes of flight and line. Always aggressive, he often produced balls that beat batsmen at the top of their form. Tall and good-looking, he was offered the chance to become a film star. As a schoolboy, he made 108 and 41 on his first-class debut for

Saurashtra against Gujerat. He toured the West Indies in 1961/2 and 1970/71, and at home played against Australia in 1959/60 and 1964/5, England in 1961/2, 1963/4 and 1972/3 and New Zealand in 1964/5. His only visit to England was in 1960 to play for Stockport in the Lancashire League. Against England in 1961/2 he took 23 wickets (27.04), besides making 199 runs (24.87). In the fourth match at Calcutta his match analysis was 8 for 113, and in the fifth at Madras 10 for 177. A few months later in the Caribbean he again took most wickets in the Tests, 17 (35.29) and finished third in the batting with 259 runs (28.77), which included his sole Test century, 104 in the fourth match at Port of Spain. In his second series against England he took only 11 wickets (42.81), but scored 230 runs (28.75). Losing his spinning place to Bishen Bedi, he came back in the early seventies and in his final series, against England, made 243 runs (40.50).

First-class career (1953-78): 8,545 runs (33.37) including 14 centuries, and 484 wickets (26.09)
Test matches (29): 1,202 runs (25.04) including 1 century, 75 wickets (35.42) and 14 catches

ENGINEER, Farokh Maneksha (b.1938)

Bombay and Lancashire

One of the best wicket-keepers India has produced, Farokh Engineer, known in England as 'Rooky', was a cricketer of immense character. Everything he did on a cricket field was alert and keen. He was an unorthodox right-handed batsman who either opened or went in between six and nine and his whole approach was brisk, confident and aggressive. A good square-cutter and strong driver, his great strength was on the leg-side: he could 'work' practically any delivery to mid-wicket. As a wicket-keeper he was brash and brilliant, the enthusiastic pivot of all that went on in the field. He could reach the widest leg-glances with an acrobatic dive and have the bails off in an instant if the batsman's back foot was raised. He clearly revelled in taking and then disposing of the ball in the slickest and most stylish manner possible. He made his first-class debut for Combined Universities against the West Indian touring team in 1958/9 and played for Lancashire from 1968 to 1976, later becoming a marketing executive with a textile firm. In his first Test series against England in 1961/2 he scored 65 batting at number nine in the Kanpur Test, and in the second Test against the West Indies later the same season he made 53 and 40 (top score against a rampant Wes Hall) at Kingston. However, he was not an automatic selection, facing strong rivalry from Budhi Kunderan and others. Not until 1965 did he finally play through a whole series, at home to New Zealand, making 90 in the first Test at Madras in only 115 minutes. Thereafter he began to move up the batting order and,

Farokh Engineer

opening for the first time at Madras in the third Test against the West Indies in 1966/7, he hit 109, 94 coming before lunch, on the first day against an attack comprising Hall, Griffith, Sobers and Gibbs. On the England tour of 1967 he opened with a different partner in each of the three Tests. On the 1971 tour of England he batted down the order, scoring 172 runs at 43.00 in three Tests. In 1974 he headed the averages with 195 runs in three Tests at 39.00, opening the batting at Lord's where he scored 86 in the first innings and shared an opening stand of 131 with Gavaskar. English opposition seemed to inspire his best form: opening the batting for the only time in the 1972/3 series, he scored 121 and 66 at Bombay. He headed the batting averages in the series with 415 runs (41.50) but he was discarded after a less successful series against West Indies in 1974/5. His highest score was 192 for the Rest of the World against A Combined XI at Hobart in 1971/2. He made his home in Lancashire and became a highly successful business executive.

First-class career (1958-76): 13,436 runs (29.52) including 13 centuries, and 824 dismissals (703 ct, 121 st.)
Test matches (46): 2,611 runs (31.08) including 2 centuries, and 82 dismissals (66 ct, 16 st.)

GADKARI, Chandrasekhar Vaman (b.1928)

Maharashtra and Services

An attacking right-handed batsman, medium-pace bowler and brilliant outfield, Gadkari toured the West Indies in 1952/3 and Pakistan in 1954/5, and made a defiant 50 not out in the fourth match at Georgetown against West Indies, rescuing his team from collapse. Most of his cricket from 1947 until 1960 was in the

Ranji Trophy competition, in which he averaged 49.60 with the bat, but, as an officer in the Army, he could not appear regularly.

First-class career (1947-65): 3,024 runs (40.32) including 7 centuries, and 48 wickets (31.06)
Test matches (6): 129 runs (21.50), 0-45 and 6 catches

GAEKWAD, Anshuman Dattajirao (b.1952)

Baroda

The son of the former Indian captain, D.K., Anshuman Gaekwad is a tall, bespectacled right-handed batsman with plenty of guts and determination, a fine fielder in the gully and an occasional off-break bowler, good enough to take 6 for 49 against Saurashtra in 1971/2. A charming, gentle character, he was full of strokes in his youth but the stern demands of Test cricket have taken much of the gaiety out of his batting and he has become a steady but sometimes colourless player who, nevertheless, often produces a thoroughbred stroke through the covers off the back foot. He made his first-class debut for Baroda in 1969/70 and became captain in 1975. An innings of 155 against Maharashtra in 1973/4 helped his selection for India against West Indies the following season when he made 80 at Madras in his second Test. He was disappointing on the tour of New Zealand and West Indies in 1975/6, yet played a most courageous innings on a dangerous pitch at Sabina Park, making 81 against Michael Holding at his most fearsome before retiring after being hit on the head. In 1976/7, after making 173 runs in three home Tests against New Zealand (43.25), he could not get going against the England fast bowlers, but in 1978/9, playing once as an opener and three other Tests lower in the order, he scored 293 runs (41.85) against the West Indies at home, including his first Test century, 102 at Kanpur. He could not maintain this form in England in 1979. A prolific 1982/3 season earned him a Test recall.

First-class career (1969-): 5,796 runs (35.77) including 13 centuries, and 78 wickets (33.32)
Test matches (21): 1,089 runs (32.02) including 1 century, 0-80 and 5 catches

GAEKWAD, Dattajirao Krishnarao (b.1928)

Baroda

Although under average height, Datta Gaekwad possessed a sure defence and delightfully crisp strokes, especially through the covers. He was a right-handed opening batsman of quiet efficiency. An occasional leg-break bowler, he was also an agile and fearless field. He toured England in 1952 and 1959 and the West Indies in 1952/3, and at home played against Pakistan in 1952/3 and 1960/61 and West Indies in 1958/9. When he was captain on his second England tour his side was heavily beaten, but he scored 1,174 runs (34.52) in all first-class matches. Modest and retiring, he did not have the verve and drive which are desirable in a captain and sometimes found the job a strain. His career-highest was 249 not out against Maharashtra in 1959/60. In the Ranji Trophy competition, from 1947 until 1961, he made 3,139 runs (47.56), including 14 centuries. He is the father of A.D. Gaekwad.

First-class career (1947-64): 5,783 runs (36.60) including 17 centuries, and 24 wickets (40.79)
Test matches (11): 350 runs (18.42), 0-12 and 5 catches

GAEKWAD, Hiralal Ghasulal (b.1923)

Central Provinces and Berar, and Holkar

A cheerful personality known as 'C.K. Nayudu's devoted Gunga Din', Hiralal Gaekwad was India's short-term replacement for Vinoo Mankad; a left-arm medium or slow bowler of great stamina who could swing the new ball, he was also a hard-hitting batsman. He toured England in 1952 without appearing in Tests. His sole Test was the second at Lucknow in 1952/3 against Pakistan, when he scored 14 and 8 and took 0 for 47.

First-class career (1941-64): 2,484 runs (19.40) and 374 wickets (23.60)

GANDOTRA, Ashok (b.1948)

Delhi

Born in Rio de Janeiro, Ashok Gandotra was a left-handed batsman and slow bowler who played in one Test each against Australia and New Zealand in 1969/70 and was then discarded.

First-class career (1965-75): 2,121 runs (28.66) including 2 centuries, and 21 wickets (26.71)
Test matches (2): 54 runs (13.50), 0-5 and 1 catch

GAVASKAR, Sunil Manohar (b.1949)

Bombay and Somerset

A masterful little right-hand opening batsman of only 5ft 4¾ins, 'Sunny' Gavaskar has proved himself the best and most consistent opening batsman in the world. By the finish of the 1979 tour of England he had scored 20 centuries in 50 Tests: only Bradman has had a higher ratio. Despite his limited height he is a fine player of fast bowling, compact, balanced, patient, and a ruthless destroyer of the bad ball. With full use of the crease either forward or back he is also able to make what might be good-length balls to some players into short ones deserving of punishment. He seldom

Sunil Gavaskar watched by Bob Taylor

hooks, but cuts, drives, pulls and glances with power and without flaw. Allied to his impeccable technique is an ability to set his hand on distant targets and concentrate for long periods. Since making a sensational start to his Test career after proving himself to be something exceptional in schools and representative cricket in Bombay, he has been the Indian batsman whom opposing bowlers most want to dismiss. He has twice amassed more than 1,000 Test runs in a calendar year: in eleven Tests in 1976 he scored 1,024 runs and in only nine Tests in 1978, 1,044 runs. Selected to tour the West Indies in 1970/71 he began with a mere 65 and 67 not out after missing the first Test but soon put such setbacks aside. His second Test brought 116 and 64 not out, his third, at Barbados, 1 and 117 not out and his fourth, at Port of Spain, Trinidad, 124 and 220 not out. His performance enabled India to win a rubber against West Indies for the first time and no Indian has scored more than the 774 runs he made in his first rubber. On the tour he scored 5 centuries, 1,169 runs and averaged 97.41. The tour to England in 1971 was an anticlimax, though he showed his ability with fifties at Lord's and Old Trafford, and he still made 1,141 runs, including 2 centuries. Even at home against England, in 1972/3, he was disappointing, but he made his first century against England at Old Trafford in 1974 in conditions ideal for seam bowling. (In the match he scored 101 and 58 in totals of 246 and 182.) He broke a finger after the first Test against West Indies in 1974/5 and did not play again until the fifth. He was back to his prolific self in New Zealand in 1975 and in the West Indies the same season, scoring 921 runs (41.86) including Test centuries at Auckland, and two at Port of Spain, 156 in the second Test and 102 in the second innings of the third Test, helping India to a remarkable 404 for 4 which won them the match against the odds. Next in the Gavaskar saga came centuries at home against New Zealand and England in 1976/7, both at Bombay. On the tour of Australia in 1977/8 Gavaskar scored 113 in the first Test at Brisbane, 127 in the second at Perth, and 118 in the third at Melbourne. At home to the West Indies in 1978/9 he assumed the captaincy of India, after scoring 447 runs at 89.40 against Pakistan, and the new responsibility merely increased his prodigious appetite for runs. In the six Tests he scored 732 runs (91.50) including four more centuries, the highest being 205 at his beloved Bombay. Although India won the series one-nil, Gavaskar was replaced as captain for the 1979 tour of England, when he scored 542 runs (77.42) in four Tests. These included one of the greatest innings of modern times, a superlative 221 at The Oval, with 21 fours, when he batted without chance or error for 8 hours 10 minutes, bringing India close to a sensational victory. He regained the captaincy and fully established himself in the position, not just by virtue of his batting supremacy but also by tough and increasingly shrewd tactics. He slipped from grace in Australia in 1980/81 when, having finally contributed a substantial score after a run of failures, he was given out lbw in the Melbourne Test. Furious, Gavaskar ordered his opening partner, Chauhan, to leave the field as well, intending that India should withdraw from the Test, but saner counsels prevailed and India's captain apologized. India lost the series, and the one which followed against New Zealand. But at home against England in 1981/2 India won a turgid series one-nil, Gavaskar making 500 runs (62.50) including 172 in the Bangalore Test: here he batted for 708 minutes and was on the field for all but four minutes of the match. In the Ranji Trophy the same season he hit 340, sharing with Ghulam Parkar in an opening stand of 421, for Bombay against Bengal. In England in 1982 India contributed much on a short tour, though they lost the series one-nil, mainly because Gavaskar was less successful. In the third Test at The Oval he broke his leg when fielding close in on the off side, being hit by a ball struck with tremendous force by Ian Botham. He returned, however, to captain India in a Test against Sri Lanka at Madras, in which he scored his 25th Test hundred. He played for Somerset for one season in 1980, scoring 664 runs (33.20) in 14 matches and making many friends.

First-class career (1966-): 20,424 runs (51.70) including 65 centuries, 21 wickets (53.47) and 234 catches
Test matches (79): 6,951 runs (53.88) including 25 centuries, 1-163 and 71 catches

GHAVRI, Karsan Devjibhai (b.1951)

Saurashtra

Though he came from a relatively poor family, Karsan

Ghavri soon made his mark in Indian cricket, touring Australia with the Indian Schools team in 1968/9. A chunky all-rounder, he bowls left-arm fast-medium, slanting the ball across the right-hander from over the wicket but also sometimes swinging the ball back in, and also bats capably left-handed. A very variable cricketer, he can sometimes look a real threat at Test level, at other times innocuous. There have been allegations that his action is suspect when he bowls a bouncer, and also when he bowls slow left-arm (as at Bombay in 1976/7 when four of his wickets in his 5 for 33 against England were taken bowling slow) but he has not been 'called'. First appearing for India in 1974/5 against the West Indies, he took 4 for 140 in a West Indies total of 604 for 6 at Bombay but was in and out of the side until taking 11 wickets in three Tests in Australia in 1977/8, including 7 for 138 in the fifth Test (in the match) at Adelaide after making 64 useful runs in India's only innings at Sydney. At home against the West Indies in 1978/9 he had by far his most successful series, with 27 wickets (23.48) in six Tests, including 5 for 51 in the second innings of the second Test at Bangalore and 7 wickets in the match at Calcutta. In England in 1979 he was overshadowed by his opening partner Kapil Dev but often bowled well and the two formed as effective a seam attack as India had used for many years.

First-class career (1969-): 3,712 runs (27.49) including 1 century, and 424 wickets (27.62)
Test matches (39): 913 runs (21.23), 109 wickets (33.54) and 16 catches

GHORPADE, Jayasinghrao Mansinghrao (1930-78)

Baroda and Maharashtra

A bespectacled and attacking right-handed batsman, leg-break and googly bowler and outstanding cover-point, Ghorpade toured the West Indies in 1951/2, joining the team as a replacement, and England in 1959, and at home played against New Zealand in 1955/6, Australia in 1956/7 and West Indies in 1958/9, without quite establishing himself. In England he made 833 runs (23.80), including 100 runs in six Test innings, which included his Test-highest, 41 in India's first innings of 168 in the second match at Lord's. His career-highest was 123 for Baroda against Rajasthan in 1957/8 and best bowling in an innings, 6 for 19 for Indian Universities against Pakistan in 1952/3. He was a national selector until his untimely death.

First-class career (1948-65): 2,631 runs (25.54) including 2 centuries, and 114 wickets (30.91)
Test matches (8): 229 runs (15.26), 0-131 and 4 catches

GHULAM AHMED (b.1922)

Hyderabad

A tall, slim, handsome man, Ghulam Ahmed was a right-arm off-break bowler with an easy action and a mastery of subtle flight and variations of length and direction. One could almost feel him 'thinking' a batsman out but, except on certain types of matting pitches, he had to work extremely hard for his wickets in India: on the less helpful turf he was at least Jim Laker's equal. An aggressive tail end batsman, he was also a fair field. He toured England in 1952 and Pakistan in 1954/5, and at home he played against West Indies in 1948/9 and 1958/9, England in 1951/2, Pakistan in 1952/3, New Zealand in 1955/6 and Australia in 1956/7. In England he was the best bowler, taking 80 wickets (21.92), including 15 (24.73) of the 39 wickets to fall to Indian bowlers in the Tests. In the first-ever official Test against Pakistan, at New Delhi in 1952/3, he made 50 at number eleven, adding 109 with H.R. Adhikari for the last wicket, and took 4 for 35 in the second innings. At Calcutta in the third match against Australia in 1956/7 he collected 10 for 130 (7 for 49 in the first innings). He captained India once against New Zealand in 1955/6 and twice against West Indies in 1958/9, his last series, when India were losing and he bowled listlessly. At one time he held the record number of balls bowled in an innings, 555, against Holkar in 1950/51. For many years he has been secretary of the Indian Board of Cricket Control.

First-class career (1939-59): 1,341 runs (13.96) and 407 wickets (22.57)
Test matches (22): 192 runs (8.72), 68 wickets (30.17) and 11 catches

GOPALAN, Morappakam Joysam (b.1909)

Madras

A right-arm fast-medium bowler of good length and stamina, Gopalan toured England in 1936 without much success, and his sole Test appearance was in the second match against England in 1933/4 at Calcutta, when he scored 11 not out and 7, took 1 for 39 and held 3 catches. He has served as a Test selector and he presented the 'Gopalan Trophy' which, since 1953/4, has been fought for by Madras and Sri Lanka.

First-class career (1926-52): 2,916 runs (24.92) including 1 century, and 194 wickets (24.20)

GOPINATH, Coimbatarao Doraikannu (b.1930)

Madras

A stylish right-handed batsman with a sound defence and strong off-side shots, an occasional medium-pace bowler and fast outfield, 'Gopi' bagged 'a pair' on his first-class debut for Madras in 1949/50, but he later captained his State and toured England in 1952 and Pakistan in 1954/5; at home he played against England in 1951/2, Pakistan in 1952/3 and Australia in 1959/60. In his first Test, the second against England at

Bombay, he made 50 not out and 42, batting at number eight, but a few months later in England he was, perhaps, the biggest batting failure on the tour. One of the successes in Pakistan in 1954/5, however, he averaged 58.33 in all first-class matches. A heavy scorer in Ranji Trophy matches, he made 2,349 runs (51.06), including 6 centuries, his career-highest being 234 against Mysore in 1958/9. He has been chairman of the selectors and managed the 1979 tour to England.

First-class career (1949-63): 4,260 runs (42.17) including 9 centuries, and 14 wickets (27.78)
Test matches (8): 242 runs (22.00), 1-11 and 2 catches

GUARD, Ghulam Mustafa (1925-78)

Bombay and Gujerat

A large sub-inspector of Police, Ghulam Guard was a left-arm fast-medium bowler, very useful in Ranji Trophy matches, who appeared once each against West Indies in 1958/9 and Australia in 1959/60.

First-class career (1946-63): 238 runs (11.33) and 124 wickets (20.60)
Test matches (2): 11 runs (5.50), 3 wickets (60.66) and 2 catches

GUHA, Subroto (b.1946)

Bengal

A tidy right-arm fast-medium swing-bowler, Subroto Guha toured England in 1967, taking 22 wickets in 13 matches but, owing to injuries, was available for only one Test. At home he played three times against Australia in 1969/70, but with moderate success.

First-class career (1965-77): 1,067 runs (12.70) and 299 wickets (20.29)
Test matches (4): 17 runs (3.40), 3 wickets (103.66) and 2 catches

GUL MAHOMED (b.1921)

Baroda, Hyderabad and Punjab B

A left-handed batsman with sparkling footwork and a spectacular cover-point and deep field, Gul Mahomed toured England in 1946 and Australia in 1947/8, and at home played against Pakistan in 1952/3, but his batting tended to be disappointing. In Ranji Trophy matches, however, he was a prolific run-getter. He made his career-highest, 319, for Baroda against Holkar in 1946/7 in the final of the Ranji Trophy, adding 577 with Vijay Hazare, which remains the world record for the fourth wicket. In Trophy matches he made 1,842 runs (37.38) until he took Pakistan citizenship in 1955. He played for Pakistan once, in the first match against Australia at Karachi in 1956/7, a low-scoring contest, in which he scored 12 and 27 not out, including the winning hit.

First-class career (1938-59): 5,600 runs (33.93) including 12 centuries, and 107 wickets (27.18)
Test matches (India – 8): 166 runs (11.06), 2 wickets (12.00) and 3 catches. (Pakistan – 1): 39 runs (39.00)

GUPTE, Balkrishna Pandharinath (b.1934)

Bombay, Bengal and Railways

Tall and sturdy, 'Baloo' Gupte was a right-arm leg-break and googly bowler of great stamina, whose flight and length were excellent. He once bowled more than a hundred overs in an innings for Bombay against Delhi, in 1956/7, his match analysis being 15 for 302. Although in Ranji Trophy matches alone he took 237 wickets (22.41), he received few opportunities in Tests, playing once each against Pakistan in 1960/61, England in 1963/4 and New Zealand in 1964/5. He is the brother of S.P. Gupte.

First-class career (1953-70): 587 runs (9.17) and 414 wickets (24.95)
Test matches (3): 28 runs (28.00) and 3 wickets (116.33)

GUPTE, Subhash Pandharinath (b.1929)

Bombay, Bengal and Trinidad

The first of the world-class post-1946 Indian spin-bowlers, 'Fergie' Gupte was a slightly built right-arm leg-break bowler, supremely confident because of the control he developed; he flighted and spun the ball cleverly, his length remaining immaculate, though he was constantly experimenting in order to deceive. Despite an unpromising start against England in 1951/2, he toured the West Indies in 1952/3, Pakistan in 1954/5 and England in 1959, and at home also played against England in 1961/2, Pakistan in 1952/3 and 1960/61, New Zealand in 1955/6, Australia in 1956/7 and West Indies in 1958/9. He established himself in the West Indies, taking 50 wickets (23.64), including 27 wickets (29.22) in the Tests. In Pakistan he took 21 Test wickets (22.61) including 5 for 17 at Dacca in the second innings of the first Test, and in the third match at Lahore he sent down 110.2 overs (73.5 in the first innings) for 7 for 167. Shortly before the tour began, he took all 10 wickets in an innings for Bombay against Pakistan Services and Bahawalpur C.C. At his peak against New Zealand, he took 34 wickets (19.67) in the series (his colleagues took 34 wickets between them) including 7 for 128, in 76.4 overs in the first innings of the first Test at Hyderabad. Against West Indies he took 22 of the 53 wickets that fell in the Tests; and in England he captured 95 wickets (26.58) in all first-class matches. In 1981/2 a benefit match was held for him in Sharjah, United Arab Emirates.

First-class career (1947-64): 761 runs (8.18) and 530 wickets (23.71)
Test matches (36): 183 runs (6.31), 149 wickets (29.55) and 14 catches

HANUMANT SINGH (Maharajkumar of Banswara) (b.1939)

Madhya Pradesh and Rajasthan

Hanumant Singh was a prince and bank executive to whom cricket was almost a religion. He was a charming man and a small, consistent right-handed batsman with a large repertoire of strokes, who was always ready to attack; he was also a useful leg-break bowler and a brilliant field in the deep. In the Ranji Trophy competition alone he scored over 5,000 runs for an average exceeding 50. He touched greatness in domestic cricket in 1966/7, scoring 869 runs (124.14) in Trophy matches, including his career-highest, 213 not out for Rajasthan against Bombay. In 1961/2, when Uttar Pradesh were outplaying Rajasthan, he stopped the rot with a flawless unbeaten 200. He toured England in 1967, and at home played in Tests against England in 1963/4, Australia in 1964/5, New Zealand in 1964/5 and 1969/70 and West Indies in 1966/7. As late as 1976 he captained Central Zone against the MCC touring team. On his Test debut against England, in the fourth match at New Delhi in 1963/4, he made 105, never being afraid to play his strokes; he became the only Indian to make a century in his first Test innings. Against Australia he made 94 in a total of 193 in the first match at Madras and against New Zealand in 1964/5 he made 195 runs (48.75), including 75 not out at Bombay and 82 at Delhi.

First-class career (1956-79): 12,338 runs (43.90) including 29 centuries, and 56 wickets (40.92)
Test matches (14): 686 runs (31.18) including 1 century, 0-51 and 11 catches

HARDIKAR, Manohar Shankar (b.1936)

Bombay

A right-handed batsman of sound technique and an occasional bowler of medium-pace or slowish off-breaks, Manohar Hardikar played in two Tests against West Indies in 1958/9 without distinction.

First-class career (1955-68): 3,602 runs (45.59) including 8 centuries, and 74 wickets (31.66)
Test matches (2): 56 runs (18.66), 1-55 and 3 catches

HAZARE, Vijay Samuel (b.1915)

Maharashtra and Baroda

A Roman Catholic and one of India's greatest batsmen, Vijay Hazare was small of stature but had all

Vijay Hazare

the strokes together with a very strong defence. Square-shouldered and with sinewy wrists and forearms, he would move his right foot back outside the leg-stump and hammer his square-cut through the covers. If the circumstances warranted it, he would forget his straight-bat orthodoxy but he rarely lofted the ball. His concentration was intense. He was also a very useful medium-pace bowler and a fine field. Retiring and gentlemanly, he was a conscientious captain of India for three years in the early fifties; he led his country in fourteen Tests (nine against England and five against West Indies). He made his first big impact when scoring 316 not out for Maharashtra against Baroda in 1939/40 and an incredible 309 not out in a total of 387 for The Rest against Hindus in the same season. In 1946/7, when making 288 in two and a half hours for Baroda against Holkar in the final of the Ranji Trophy competition, he added 577 with Gul Mahomed for the fourth wicket, a world record in first-class cricket – and he took 6 for 85 in the first innings. He toured England in 1946 and (as captain) in 1952, Australia in 1947/8 and the West Indies (as captain) in 1952/3, and at home played against West Indies in 1948/9, England in 1951/2 and Pakistan in 1952/3. On his first England tour he scored 344 runs (49.77), besides taking 56 wickets (24.75), but was disappointing in the Tests. In Australia he made most runs in the Tests, 429 runs (47.66), and in all first-class matches reached 1,056 runs (48.00). In the fourth Test at Adelaide he scored 116 and 145 (in a total of 277), the first time an Indian has made two centuries in a Test. Against West Indies in 1948/9 he headed the batting with 543 runs (67.87) in the Tests, his solid 134 not out in the second match at Bombay saving India from defeat after following on, and in the fifth match at Bombay his 122 nearly brought victory. At the top of the batting against England in 1951/2 with 347 runs (57.83), he hit dogged centuries in the first two Tests, 164 not out in 8 hours 35 minutes at Delhi, his Test-highest, and 155 at Bombay in five hours. As captain of a weak side in England, he was supreme in the Tests with 333 runs (55.50). In the first-ever Test against Pakistan, at Lucknow in 1953/4, he made 76, and in the third at Bombay, on turf that was far from easy, he contributed a steady 146 not out in four and a quarter hours, adding 188 with 'Polly' Umrigar for the fourth wicket. After a not particularly successful tour of the West Indies, he was discarded both as captain and Test cricketer, but he had scored at least one Test century against each country. His brother also played in Ranji Trophy cricket.

First-class career (1934-67): 18,635 runs (57.87) including 60 centuries, and 592 wickets (24.49)
Test matches (30): 2,192 runs (47.65) including 7 centuries, 20 wickets (61.00) and 11 catches

HINDLEKAR, Dattaram Dharmaji (1909-49)

Bombay

Never spectacular but always cheerful and sound, both behind the stumps and when batting, Dattaram Hindlekar toured England in 1936 and 1946. Despite suffering at different times from chipped fingers, blurred vision and many strains and bruises, he was India's first-string wicket-keeper. He was also a calm and courageous right-handed batsman who wore his cap at a bewildered angle, and stood with his left toe pointing up at an angle of forty-five degrees. In 1936 he opened the batting in the Test at Lord's; ten years later at Old Trafford as number eleven he stood firm for fifteen minutes with S.W. Sohoni to ward off defeat.

First-class career (1934-47): 2,411 runs (17.34) including 1 century, and 181 dismissals (124 ct, 57 st.)
Test matches (4): 71 runs (14.20) and 3 catches

IBRAHIM, Khanmohammed Cassumbhoy (b.1919)

Bombay

A very sound right-handed opening batsman who scored prolifically in domestic cricket, Ibrahim played in four Tests against West Indies in 1948/9, scoring 85 and 44 in the first at Delhi. Soon afterwards, however, he dropped out of first-class cricket. In fourteen years he had made 2,329 runs (66.50) in Ranji Trophy matches alone.

First-class matches (1938-50): 4,716 runs (61.24) including 14 centuries
Test matches (4): 169 runs (21.12)

INDRAJITSINHJI, Kumar Shri (b.1937)

Saurashtra, Madras and Delhi

A sound wicket-keeper and determined right-handed tail-end batsman who sometimes also opened, Prince Indrajitsinhji toured Australasia in 1967/8 without being selected for the Tests, but at home played against Australia in 1964/5 and New Zealand in 1969/70. For Delhi in the Ranji Trophy matches of 1960/61, while still a student, he gained 23 dismissals, then a record. He was unfortunate to have both Budhi Kunderan and Farokh Engineer as his rivals for a Test place.

First-class career (1954-73): 3,694 runs (26.76) including 5 centuries, and 210 dismissals (133 ct, 77 st.)
Test matches (4): 51 runs (8.50) and 9 dismissals (6 ct, 3 st.)

IRANI, Jahangir Khan (b.1923)

Sind

A very sound wicket-keeper, Irani won two caps on the first Indian tour of Australia in 1947/8, but did not represent his country again.

First-class career (1937-48): 399 runs (17.34) and 27 dismissals (21 ct, 6 st.)
Test matches (2): 3 runs (3.00) and 3 dismissals (2 ct, 1 st.)

JAHANGIR KHAN, Dr Mohammed (b.1910)

Northern India and Cambridge University

Prominent among the Moslem cricketers, Jahangir Khan was a hard-hitting right-handed batsman, a tall, fast-medium bowler with a very effective 'flip' at the moment of delivery which made the ball kick off the pitch, and an alert field. He made 448 runs (19.47) and took 53 wickets (29.05) on his first tour of England in 1932 and in the first-ever Test at Lord's took 4 for 60 in the second innings. Going up to Cambridge, he won four blues between 1933 and 1936. He joined the 1936 Indians in England but was a failure in the Tests. His son is Majid Jahangir Khan of Pakistan.

First-class career (1928-56): 3,319 runs (22.12) including 4 centuries, and 347 wickets (23.66)
Test matches (4): 39 runs (5.57), 4 wickets (63.75) and 4 catches

JAI, Laxmidas Purshottamdas (1902-68)

Bombay

Jai was a graceful right-handed stroke-making batsman whose footwork was superb; his heyday coincided with that of the Bombay Quadrangular tournament. Selected for the 1932 tour of England, he refused on political grounds, most of the leaders of the National movement being in jail. His sole Test was the first-ever in India, against England at Bombay in 1933/4, when he scored 19 and 0. He did tour England in 1936, but a broken finger impeded his progress. For some years he was a Test selector.

First-class career (1920-42): 3,101 runs (31.32) including 5 centuries

JAISIMHA, Motganhalli Lakshminarsu (b.1939)

Hyderabad

A slim, stylish, wristy and usually forceful right-handed batsman, a useful medium-pace bowler of out-swingers and off-breaks and a brilliant field in any position, Jaisimha, or 'Jai', opened both batting and bowling for his State, which he captained for many years. An extrovert by nature, he was considered too 'flashy' sometimes to open in Tests and consequently often strengthened the middle batting instead, learning discretion with experience. On his first-class debut at fifteen, against Andhra in 1954/5, he made 90 and took 3 for 56. He toured England in 1959, the West Indies in 1961/2 and 1970/71, and Australasia in 1967/8, and at home played against Australia in 1959/60 and 1964/5, Pakistan in 1960/61, England in 1961/2 and 1963/4, New Zealand in 1964/5 and 1969/70 and West Indies in 1966/7. In England he made only one unimpressive Test appearance, but in his next Test, the fifth against Australia, at Calcutta, in 1959/60, he hit 20 not out and 74. Two years later, in a battle of attrition with Pakistan in the second Test at Kanpur, he opened and was run out for 99, after 8 hours 20 minutes at the crease: he had made only five scoring strokes in the pre-lunch session on the third day. Against England in 1961/2 he impressed as an opening batsman with consecutive scores of 56, 51, 70 and 127, and made 399 runs (49.87) in the series. Against England in 1963/4 he was again very consistent, with 444 runs (44.40), including 129 in the third match at Calcutta. Flown out to join the team in Australia in 1967/8, he was pressed into service immediately for the third Test at Brisbane and kept the match alive at number six with dogged knocks of 74 and 101, India getting to within 39 runs of victory. But on his last tour, to the West Indies in 1970/71, he failed in the Tests. He has scored over 4,000 runs and taken over 200 wickets in Ranji Trophy matches.

First-class career (1954-77): 13,515 runs (37.54) including 33 centuries, and 431 wickets (29.86)
Test matches (39): 2,056 runs (30.68) including 3 centuries, 9 wickets (92.11) and 17 catches

JAMSHEDJI, Rustomji Jamshedji Dorabji (1892-1976)

Bombay

A slow left-arm bowler, aged 41 years 27 days, Jamshedji played at Bombay in the first-ever Test in India against England. In this, his sole Test (he is still the oldest Indian to have made a Test debut), he scored 4 not out and 1 not out, took 3 for 137 and held 2 catches.

First-class career (1922-39): 291 runs (11.19) and 134 wickets (22.11)

JAYANTILAL, Kenia (b.1948)

Hyderabad

Stockily built and slightly heavy on his feet, Jayantilal is a confident right-handed opening batsman partial to the off-side shots and the pull, and a fine field at slip. He made 153 against Andhra in 1967/8 on his debut in the Ranji Trophy competition, and toured the West Indies in 1970/71 with the triumphant Indian team, coming fourth in the batting averages with 506 runs (56.22). However, he appeared in only one Test, the first at Kingston, scoring 5. In England in 1971 he disappointed and was not selected for any of the Tests.

First-class career (1967-): 4,685 (36.31) including 8 centuries

JOSHI, Padmanabh Govind (b.1926)

Maharashtra

A stalwart who captained his State for several years, 'Nana' Joshi was a very sound wicket-keeper and useful right-handed batsman who opened the batting regularly during his early first-class years. He toured the West Indies in 1952/3 and England in 1959, and at home played against England in 1951/2, Pakistan in 1952/3 and 1960/61, West Indies in 1958/9 and Australia in 1959/60. On his Test debut against England at New Delhi, he had two catches and two stumpings in the first innings.

First-class career (1946-65): 1,724 runs (17.06) including 1 century, and 180 dismissals (119 ct, 61 st.)
Test matches (12): 207 runs (10.89) and 27 dismissals (18 ct, 9 st.)

KANITKAR, Hemant Shamsunder (b.1942)

Maharashtra

Hemant Kanitkar learned cricket at college and was a stocky right-handed batsman of disciplined technique who played the late cut particularly well. He was also a competent deputy wicket-keeper but when not keeping was rather a liability in the field. In his first

Test, against West Indies at Bangalore in 1974/5, he scored an adventurous 65 but he was discarded after the second match.

First-class career (1963-78): 5,007 runs (42.79) including 13 centuries, and 87 dismissals (68 ct, 19 st.)
Test matches (2): 111 runs (27.75)

KAPIL DEV, Ramial Nikhanj (b.1959)

Haryana and Northamptonshire

The best fast bowler produced by India for many years, a gifted batsman and a fine, athletic outfielder, Kapil Dev is a strong six footer who bowls fast-medium with an excellent action. A slow walk back to his mark is followed by a springy approach from some twenty yards culminating in a leap and a sideways-on delivery. His pace is lively, his length full and the late out-swinger comes naturally. Making his debut for Haryana against Punjab in the Ranji Trophy in 1975/6, he took 6 for 39 in the first innings. In 1976/7 he took 7 for 20 against Bengal and in 1977/8 went one better with 8 for 38 against Services and 11 for 61 in the match. It was therefore no surprise when he made his Test debut in Pakistan in 1978/9, although he soon learned to be philosophical about bowling on shirt-fronts against high-class batsmen. His seven wickets in three Tests against Pakistan cost 60.85 but his promise was clear and against the West Indies he took 17 wickets in six Tests at 33.00. Moreover, after making 59 in a run-feast at Karachi he revealed class and immense power with the bat against the West Indies, scoring 329 runs in the series at 65.80 including a magnificent 126 not out at Delhi, hard on the heels of some fine bowling on the fast pitch at Madras where he took 4 for 38 and 3 for 46. In England in 1979 he revelled in the bowling conditions, but failed to show the necessary restraint as a batsman against high-class English seamers, despite making a superb century in 74 minutes against Northamptonshire at Northampton. In each of the four Tests his bowling was both persistent and dangerous, even at Edgbaston where England scored 633 for 5 declared in their only innings, Kapil Dev taking all five for 146 in 48 overs. Back in India in 1979/80 he was again outstanding in two home series aganst Australia (28 wickets at 22) and Pakistan (32 wickets at 17 and 278 runs at 30). At 21 years, 27 days, in his 25th Test, he became the youngest man of any nationality to complete the Test double of 1,000 runs and 100 wickets. Against England at home in 1981/2 and away in 1982 he was India's key player – even ahead of Gavaskar – making 318 runs (53.00) in the home series and hitting 116 at Kanpur, taking 22 wickets in the series. In England his whole-hearted and clean-hitting batting was a joy: his Test innings were 41, 89, 65 and 97. At Lord's, he also took 8 of the 13 England wickets which fell.

Kapil Dev

First-class career (1975-): 3,803 runs (28.17) including 6 centuries and 338 wickets (28.06)
Test matches (42): 1,821 runs (33.11) including 2 centuries, 165 wickets (29.25) and 15 catches

KARDAR, Abdul Hafeez (b.1925)

Northern India, Oxford University and Warwickshire

Abdul Kardar is best remembered as the quiet, determined and orthodox captain of Pakistan in her first twenty-three Tests – quickly leading his country to a position of respect in the cricket world – and subsequently as an administrator of great, almost unimpeachable authority. He toured England with modest success for the 1946 Indian team as 'Abdul Hafeez', after hitting 173 – his career-highest – for North Zone and 161 for Combined Universities against Australian Services in 1945/6. He was an attacking left-handed batsman, willing to back his eye against the bowler; tall, he had good wrists and a fine sense of timing. He bowled accurate left-arm slow or medium-slow and never relaxed in the field. At Partition in 1947 he became a citizen of Pakistan and, on the country's first tour of India in 1952/3, he made 416 runs (37.81), including 79 in the Madras Test, and took 13 wickets (23.53). The peak of his playing career was his successful leadership of Pakistan's first tour of England in 1954, when the rubber was tied. He knew English conditions extremely well, for besides his 1946 tour with India, he had won his blue at Oxford and played for Warwickshire from 1948 until 1950 with success. In the last Test at The Oval in 1954 he top-scored in the first innings with 36 in a total of 133 – and led Pakistan to their first victory over England. In the indecisive 'war of attrition' with India on her first tour of Pakistan in 1954/5 he made 207 runs (25.87), including his highest score in Tests, 93 in the fifth match at Karachi. Again under his command Pakistan won the rubber against New Zealand in 1955/6, when he headed the bowling averages with 10 wickets (15.00). In the sole match against Australia at Karachi in 1956, which Pakistan won, he top-scored with 69. In the West Indies in 1957/8 Pakistan lost a rubber for the first time under his captaincy, but he made 253 runs (31.62). He went into the third match at Kingston against doctor's orders with a broken finger, scoring 57 and bowling 37 overs. Subsequently, he has been active for many years in cricket politics both in Pakistan and in the councils of ICC.

First-class career (1943-58): 6,814 runs (29.75) including 8 centuries, 344 wickets (24.55) and 108 catches
Test matches (India – 3): 80 runs (16.00) and 1 catch. (Pakistan – 23): 847 runs (24.91), 21 wickets (45.42) and 15 catches

KENNY, Ramnath Bhaura (b.1930)

Bombay and Cumberland

A protégé of Duleepsinhji's, Ramnath Kenny was an elegant right-handed batsman, essentially a front-foot player with a sound defence, and an occasional off-break bowler. In 1956/7 he hit three successive centuries in Ranji Trophy matches, including 218 against Madras, his career-highest. He played in one Test against West Indies in 1958/9 and four against Australia in 1959/60, finishing third in the averages with 229 runs (32.71), his highest score being a well-fought 62 in the third Test at Calcutta. He hit three fifties against Australia, but did not represent India again.

First-class career (1950-64): 3,079 runs (50.47) including 11 centuries, and 15 wickets (31.20)
Test matches (5): 245 runs (27.22) and 1 catch

KIRMANI, Syed Mujtaba Hussain (b.1949)

Mysore

At his best a scintillating wicket-keeper and a sparkling and stylish right-handed batsman, Syed Kirmani spent many years as understudy to Farokh Engineer, touring England in 1971, 1974 (and for the World Cup in 1975) without playing a Test. His first Test appearance for India was at Auckland in the first Test of 1975/6 and in the following game, the second Test at Christchurch, he equalled the Test record of 6 victims in an innings, 5 caught and 1 stumped. In the following Test he claimed four victims in New Zealand's only innings and also 49 in adding 116 for the seventh wicket with B.P. Patel. His highest Test score is 101 not out against Australia in the sixth Test at Bombay, 1979/80. His best series with the bat was

Syed Kirmani

against New Zealand in 1976/7 when he headed the Indian averages with 196 runs (65.33), and in the five Tests against England which followed he kept wicket impressively, making 6 stumpings. In Australia in 1977/8 he made 411 runs (41.10) in first-class matches, batting with great consistency, his highest score being only 59 not out, 305 of his runs coming in Tests at 33.88. He lost form behind the stumps in the series against Pakistan and West Indies in 1978/9 and was omitted from the 1979 tour to England, but returned successfully at home to Australia in 1979/80. Outstanding against England both at home and away in 1981/2, he did not concede a bye for three successive Tests in the home series, while England scored 1,964 runs. In both series he made useful runs.

First-class career (1967-): 5,561 runs (27.39) including 3 centuries, and 324 dismissals (239 ct, 85 st.)
Test matches (58): 1,889 runs (26.98) including 1 century, and 137 dismissals (107 ct, 30 st.)

KISCHENCHAND, Gogumal (b.1925)

Delhi, Sind, Gujerat and Baroda

A diminutive right-hander with an ungainly crouching stance, Kischenchand's footwork was excellent and he could be a highly effective hooker and driver. He was a hardworking outfield and occasional leg-break bowler. He toured Australia in 1947/8, achieving little in the Tests, other than 44 on a difficult wicket at Sydney. At home he played in one Test against Pakistan in 1952/3; and for several seasons showed to good account in representative matches against Commonwealth sides, but his career faded. In Ranji

Trophy matches he made 4,223 runs (53.45), including 10 centuries; and for Hindus in three seasons of the Pentangular Tournament, early in his career, he amassed 611 runs (101.83).

First-class career (1940-70): 6,983 (46.86) including 14 centuries, and 37 wickets (31.16)
Test matches (5): 89 runs (8.90) and 1 catch

KRIPAL SINGH, Amritsar Govindsingh (b.1933)

Madras (Tamil Nadu)

An orthodox, fluent and aggressive right-handed batsman, a useful off-break bowler and a good field, Kripal Singh scored 636 runs (106.00) in the Ranji Trophy in 1953/4, including 208 against Travencore-Cochin, his career-highest. He toured England in 1959, and at home played against New Zealand in 1955/6, Australia in 1956/7 and 1964/5, West Indies in 1958/9, and England in 1961/2 and 1963/4. On his Test debut – the first match between the two countries – he scored 100 not out against New Zealand at Hyderabad, and in the three Tests of his first series he averaged 99.50. But in England, although he made 879 runs (33.80), he appeared in only one Test, and was a disappointment, spending much time in the doctor's hands. Suffering from a sore spinning finger (he took 10 wickets) he seldom looked happy in the field; this was his only overseas tour. Against West Indies in the fourth Test at Madras in 1958/9, facing a large total, he top-scored with 53, but the remainder of his Test career was anti-climax. He captained his State for several years, and in the Ranji Trophy competition made 2,581 runs (49.63) and took 115 wickets (20.53). His father was A.G. Ram Singh and his brother is A.G. Milkha Singh.

First-class career (1950-66): 4,947 runs (40.88) including 10 centuries, and 177 wickets (28.42)
Test matches (14): 422 runs (28.13) including 1 century, 10 wickets (58.40) and 4 catches

KRISHNAMURTHY, Pollamani (b.1947)

Hyderabad and Services

A quietly efficient, lanky, quick-thinking wicket-keeper, who stood up to even the fastest bowlers, Krishnamurthy first appeared in the Ranji Trophy competition at seventeen and toured the West Indies in 1970/71 and England in 1971. In the Caribbean he played in all the Tests, but in England, although he had 24 dismissals in nine first-class matches, he was displaced in the Tests by Farokh Engineer.

First-class career (1966-79): 1,559 runs (14.34) and 218 dismissals (150 ct, 68 st.)
Test matches (5): 33 runs (5.50) and 8 dismissals (7 ct, 1 st.)

KULKARNI, Umesh Narayan (b.1942)

Bombay

A right-arm fast-medium bowler, Kulkarni appeared suddenly but disappeared almost as quickly, like many others in India blunted by the prevailing slow wickets. He toured Australasia in 1967/8 but, despite the generally firm pitches, was innocuous. A left-handed batsman, he batted doggedly in the third Test at Brisbane for 1 not out in a last-wicket stand with M.L. Jaisimha which brought India within 39 runs of victory.

First-class career (1963-70): 158 runs (7.90) and 40 wickets (39.95)
Test matches (4): 13 runs (4.33) and 5 wickets (47.60)

KUMAR, Vaman Vishwanath (b.1935)

Madras (Tamil Nadu)

A gifted right-arm leg-break bowler, Vaman Kumar played in only two Tests, in the first of which against Pakistan at New Delhi in 1960/61 he took 5 for 64 and 2 for 68, which brought India very close to victory. Believed by some critics to be the best leg-spinner in the country, his prime coincided with that of S.P. Gupte and the advent of B.S. Chandrasekhar. On his debut in the Ranji Trophy competition in 1955/6 he took 7 wickets against Andhra, and in each of five seasons exceeded 25 wickets. In 1974/5 he became the first bowler to capture 400 wickets in the competition.

First-class career (1955-77): 673 runs (7.64) and 599 wickets (19.98)
Test matches (2): 6 runs (3.00), 7 wickets (28.85) and 2 catches

KUNDERAN, Budhisagar Krishnappa (b.1939)

Railways and Mysore

A product of India's new mass-coaching scheme, 'Budhi' Kunderan was a sound and exciting right-handed batsman who could fit in anywhere in the order, a very capable wicket-keeper and occasional medium-pace bowler. He toured the West Indies in 1961/2 and England in 1967, and at home played against Australia in 1959/60, Pakistan in 1960/61, England in 1961/2 and 1963/4, New Zealand in 1964/5 and West Indies in 1966/7. As an opener, against Australia in the fourth Test at Madras, he hit a confident 71 in a total of 149 in a losing cause; and in the first match against England at Bombay in 1961/2, he caught 3 and stumped 2 in the first innings when only 8 wickets fell – a record for an Indian 'keeper – yet was superseded by Farokh Engineer for the rest of the series. Opening against England in the first match at Madras in 1963/4 when Engineer was unfit, he was man of the match, making the then Indian highest score against England, a solid 192 in 6 hours 50 minutes, and of England's 15 wickets to fall, he caught 3 and stumped 3. In this series he made more runs than anyone on either side, 525 runs (52.50) but claimed only 8 dismissals. Later, when batting at number nine, with runs badly needed, he hit 79 in ninety-two minutes off the powerful West Indian attack in the first match at Bombay in 1966/7. In England in 1967 Engineer kept in the Tests, although Kunderan opened the batting with him in the third match at Edgbaston with some success. Stricken by injuries, India called on him to open the bowling on the first day of this Test; he had not bowled before on the tour and did not do so again. He thus became one of the few men who have opened both the batting and bowling in the same Test – even more surprising for a wicket-keeper who often batted low in the order! Prolific in the Ranji Trophy competition, he made 2,637 runs (48.83). He served as a professional in the North Lancashire League, before becoming a successful and popular professional at Drumpellier in the Western Union in Scotland.

First-class career (1958-76): 5,708 runs (28.47) including 12 centuries, and 251 dismissals (167 ct, 84 st.)
Test matches (18): 981 runs (32.70) including 2 centuries, 0-13 and 30 dismissals (23 ct, 7 st.)

LALL SINGH (b.1909)

Southern Punjab

An enterprising and aggressive right-handed batsman of rather uncertain defence, born in Malaya, Lall Singh was an extraordinarily quick mover in the field. It was said that he glided over the ground like a snake. He toured England in 1932, his sole Test being the first ever, at Lord's, when he scored 15 and 29 and held 1 catch. He has for many years worked for the Cricket Club in Kuala Lumpur.

First-class career (1931-6): 1,059 runs (24.06) including 1 century

MADAN LAL, Udhouram Sharma (b.1951)

Delhi and Punjab

A likeable and enthusiastic cricketer, Madan Lal bowls fast-medium with an excellent action, although lacking the physical strength to be a regular threat at Test level, and bats vigorously, being effective againt all but good fast bowling which he has never relished. He made his first Test appearance against England at Old Trafford in 1974 having taken 7 for 95 in an innings against Worcestershire, six of his victims being Test players. Though he had a good tour generally with 399 runs (33.25) and 31 wickets (40.74) he was a failure in the two Tests he played. On his return to the Indian side against West Indies at Calcutta in 1974/5 he took 4 for 22 in the first innings. The following year

Madan Lal

he took 5 for 134 in an innings of 403 in the second Test against New Zealand at Christchurch, and batted well on the tour of the West Indies, making 189 in the Tests at 47.25. He went on another tour to Australia in 1977/8, taking 9 wickets at 21.88 in the two Tests he played, including 5 for 72 in the second innings of the first Test at Brisbane, but failing against fast bowling. The arrival of the helmet as an acceptable form of cricket equipment, however, helped him greatly, and after consistent performances in Ranji and Duleep Trophy cricket he returned successfully to Test cricket against England in 1981/2, when his powers of swing were mainly responsible for the Indian victory in the only one of six Tests to reach a decision: he took 5 for 23 in England's second innings at Bombay. In England in 1982 he made 309 runs on tour (61.80), but as a bowler was accurate rather than dangerous.

First-class career (1968-): 7,536 runs (44.32) including 18 centuries, 428 wickets (25.33) and 101 catches
Test matches (26): 595 runs (18.59), 51 wickets (35.59) and 12 catches

MAKA, Ebrahim Suleman (b.1922)

Bombay

A competent second-string wicket-keeper, Ebrahim Maka toured the West Indies in 1952/3 and at home played against Pakistan in 1952/3, without much distinction.

First-class career (1941-63): 607 runs (15.56) and 85 dismissals (59 ct, 26 st.)
Test matches (2): 2 runs (—) and 3 dismissals (2 ct, 1 st.)

MALHOTRA, Ashok (b.1957)

Haryana

A wristy, adventurous and attractive little right-handed batsman cast in the mould of Viswanath, Ashok Malhotra twirls the bat like a spinning top before settling for each new ball. He announced his ability by scoring 724 Ranji Trophy runs (72.40) in 1979/80, including an innings of 224 not out against Jammu and Kashmir, and followed up with 515 runs (73.57) in 1980/81. He made his first Test appearance against England in the last two Tests of the 1981/2 series, but he was unluckily run out after making an impressive 31 at Madras and failed in his only innings at Kanpur. In England in 1982 he failed in the first Test at Lord's, lost his place and remained out of favour at home the following season.

First-class career (1973-): 3,639 runs (42.31) including 7 centuries
Test matches (3): 36 runs (9.00) and 2 catches

MANJREKAR, Vijay Laxman (b.1931)

Bombay, Bengal, Andhra, Uttar Pradesh, Rajasthan and Maharashtra

Vijay Manjrekar was one of the finest batsmen to represent India, a correct, fluent right-handed stroke-player, with a sterling defence and a wide repertoire of strokes, who refused to be overawed by the big matches; he was also an occasional off-break bowler and, in his early days, a splendidly versatile field who could keep wicket when necessary. He toured England in 1952 and 1959, Pakistan in 1954/5, and the West Indies in 1952/3 and 1961/2, and at home he played against England in 1951/2, 1961/2 and 1963/4, Pakistan in 1952/3 and 1960/61, New Zealand in 19655/6 and 1964/5, West Indies in 1958/9 and Australia in 1956/7 and 1964/5. He first played in the Ranji Trophy competition at eighteen and made 48 on his Test debut against England in the third Test at Calcutta. As the youngest member on his first tour of England he hit 133 in the first Test, at Headingley (despite Fred Trueman), adding 222 with Vijay Hazare for the fourth wicket. In all first-class matches he made 1,059 runs (39.22). On his first West Indian tour he made 681 runs (56.75), including 118 at Kingston in the final Test when he added 237 for the second wicket with Pankaj Roy, an Indian record. In his first home series against Pakistan he made 270 runs (45.00) and in his first against New Zealand, 386 runs (77.20), including 118 in the first match at Hyderabad, adding 238 for the third wicket with 'Polly' Umrigar, an Indian record. In a low-scoring series at home against Australia he scored most runs – 197 in six innings – and after a moderate series against Pakistan, he toured England for the second time. Although overweight and having to undergo an operation for the removal of a knee-cap after the second Test at Lord's,

Vijay Manjrekar

he was still the most attractive and prolific scorer for a weak side, scoring 755 runs (68.68) in nine matches. He again headed the batting averages in his second series at home against Pakistan, with 247 runs (49.40); and, when India defeated England for the first time in a series in 1961/2, he was the outstanding batsman on either side, with 586 runs (83.71), including a flawless 189 not out at Delhi. He did not enhance his career on his second visit to the Caribbean and his only long innings against England, in 1963/4, was an over-defensive 108 in the first match, at Madras; but against Australia in 1964/5 he made 59 and 39 in the second match, at Bombay, when at 122 for 6 wickets India looked beaten, but he and the Nawab of Pataudi turned the tide and India won by two wickets. In his final Test innings, against New Zealand in the first match at Madras in 1964/5, he hit a classic 102 not out. In the Ranji Trophy he made 3,734 runs (57.44), including 12 centuries.

First-class career (1949-73): 12,832 runs (49.92) including 38 centuries, and 20 wickets (32.95)
Test matches (55): 3,208 runs (39.12) including 7 centuries, 1-43, 19 catches and 2 stumpings

MANKAD, Ashok Vinoo (b.1946)

Bombay

Flat-footed and cuddly-figured, Ashok Mankad, the eldest son of Vinoo Mankad, did not at first look as though seeds of greatness had created him. But though he never rose to the heights of his father, he became a very accomplished right-handed batsman with a good range of neat and well-timed strokes; always looking cheerful, he had a sound temperament and plenty of determination and concentration. Making his first Test appearance against New Zealand in 1969/70, he did not secure a place for India until scoring 74, 8, 64, 68, and 97 in successive innings in the first three Tests against Australia in 1969/70. In this, his first full series, he scored 357 runs as an opening batsman at

35.70, but the Test century he narrowly missed at Delhi never came so close again. In 1970/71 he was equally sound against the West Indies at home, making 180 runs in three Tests at 36.00, but though he scored 795 runs (41.84) in first-class matches on the 1971 tour of England, he failed in the Tests. His best Test score in England, 43 at Edgbaston in 1974, was most unluckily ended when his cap fell on the wicket as he tried to fend off a ball from Chris Old. In Australia in 1977/8 he headed the first-class averages with 508 runs (50.80) with a highest score of 92 but three Tests brought only 119 runs (23.80) and he has not since been picked for India. However, having made his first-class debut in 1963/4 he has made over 6,000 Ranji Trophy runs, and over 12,000 in all first-class cricket, including 265 for Bombay against Delhi in 1980/81.

First-class career (1963-): 12,518 runs (50.88) including 30 centuries, and 76 wickets (40.98)
Test matches (22): 991 runs (25.41), 0-43 and 12 catches

MANKAD, Mulvantrai Himatial (1917-78)

Western India, Nawanagar, Maharashtra, Gujerat, Bengal, Bombay and Rajasthan

A team-man at all times and, perhaps, the greatest all-rounder produced by India, 'Vinoo' (his schoolboy nickname) was a right-handed batsman who varied from the stolid to the adventurous according to the state of the game: watchful in defence, the late-cut (or dab), leg-hit and cover-drive earned him most of his runs. He was a high quality, left-arm orthodox slow bowler with a slightly round-arm action who spun the ball unusually strongly and his flight and length were almost invariably perfect. His over would last little more than a minute; he never allowed a batsman to rest. He fielded beautifully. He captained India in six Tests (losing one and drawing five). Coached by A.F. Wensley (Sussex), he announced himself against Lord Tennyson's team in 1937/8 when he made 376 runs (62.66) and took 15 wickets (14.53) in the unofficial Tests. Touring England in 1946, he became the only Indian to achieve the double; as utility batsman, either at number one or anywhere else in the order, he made 1,120 runs (28.00) and he took 129 wickets (20.76) in 1,160.1 overs. In the Tests he captured 7 for 146 in the second match, at Old Trafford, and scored 63 in his first, at Lord's. He toured Australia in 1947/8, England in 1952 (Tests only), the West Indies in 1952/3 and Pakistan in 1954/5, and at home he played against West Indies in 1948/9 and 1958/9, England in 1951/2, Pakistan in 1952/3, New Zealand in 1955/6 and Australia in 1956/7. In Australia he was again the outstanding all-rounder, making 889 runs (38.65) and taking 61 wickets (26.14). In the Tests he made 116 in the third match at Melbourne to become the first

Vinoo Mankad with Godfrey Evans and Len Hutton

centurion for India against Australia. Against England at home he took 34 (16.97) Test wickets, collecting 8 for 55 (in 38.5 overs) and 4 for 53 (in 30.5 overs) at Madras where India won her first Test. On his second England tour his Lancashire League commitments allowed him to appear only in three Tests, including a historic performance at Lord's when he made 72 and 184 and bowled 97 overs for 231 runs and 5 wickets. In the first home series against Pakistan four Tests brought him 25 wickets (20.56) including a matchwinning 13 for 131 in the first-ever match between the two countries at Delhi. Against New Zealand he scored 526 runs (105.20), and took 12 wickets (27.33); in the fifth Test at Madras he made 231 in eight and three-quarter hours, putting on 413 for the first wicket with Pankaj Roy which remains a world record for all Tests. He also took 4 for 65 in 40 overs in the second innings. In the second match at Bombay he had made 223 in eight hours in a total of 421 for 8 wickets declared, after an early batting collapse. Until Ian Botham of England did so in 21 Tests, no one had completed the Test double of 1,000 runs and 100 wickets in fewer games – he needed 23 – and a few years later he joined two others with a tally of 2,000 runs and 100 wickets.

First-class career (1935-64): 11,558 (34.91) including 26 centuries, and 776 wickets (24.61)
Test matches (44): 2,109 runs (31.47) including 5 centuries, 162 wickets (32.32) and 33 catches

MANSUR ALI KHAN (b.1941)

Oxford University, Sussex and Hyderabad

See Pataudi, Nawab of, Junior.

MANTRI, Madhav Krishnaji (b.1921)

Maharashtra and Bombay

The uncle of India's greatest modern batsman, Sunil

Gavaskar, M.K. Mantri was himself a sound opening batsman and a neat wicket-keeper, who toured England in 1952 and at home played against England in 1951/2 and Pakistan in 1954/5, without quite establishing himself. In England he made 550 runs (22.91) and had 39 dismissals. In the Ranji Trophy competition he was consistently successful: he hit his highest score, 200, for Bombay against Maharashtra in 1948/9, the third of three centuries in successive matches; altogether in the competition he made 2,787 runs (50.67).

First-class career (1941-68): 4,403 runs (33.86) including 7 centuries, and 193 dismissals (137 ct, 56 st.)
Test matches (4): 67 runs (9.57) and 9 dismissals (8 ct, 1 st.)

MEHERHOMJI, Kharshed Rustom (1911-82)

Western India and Bombay

As a competent deputy wicket-keeper, Meherhomji toured England in 1936, in his sole Test, the second, at Old Trafford, scoring 0 not out and holding 1 catch. He also played for the Parsees in the Bombay tournament. His uncle, Rustomji Meherhomji, was a batsman who toured England with All India in 1911.

First-class career (1933-46): 645 runs (16.12) and 64 dismissals (54 ct, 10 st.)

MEHRA, Vijay Laxman (b.1938)

Eastern Punjab and Railways

A small but strong man, Vijay Mehra was a solid, crisp right-handed opening batsman, who represented India for the first time in 1955/6 in the second Test against New Zealand at Bombay aged 17 years 265 days, the youngest ever to appear for the country. After two Tests against New Zealand he had to wait eight years before being selected again for his country – against England in the fourth match at Calcutta in 1961/2, when he made 62 and India defeated England for only the second time. He toured the West Indies in 1961/2, when his only real success was another 62 in the fourth Test at Port of Spain; and he played twice against England in 1963/4 with little success. His career faded, but in Ranji Trophy matches he amassed 3,222 runs (37.90), including 10 centuries. He became a Test selector.

First-class career (1953-75): 5,636 runs (34.36) including 13 centuries, and 26 wickets (30.84)
Test matches (8): 329 runs (25.30), 0-6 and 1 catch

MERCHANT, Vijay Madhavji (b.1911)

Bombay

India's first outstanding Test batsman, Vijay Merchant's comparatively small physique did not handicap him, for what he lacked in reach he compensated for by perfect footwork and quick eye. Right-handed, his cutting, both square and late, was brilliant, and he hooked, drove (especially the fast bowlers) and played the ball off his legs with masterly certainty. He was a careful builder of an innings and there was something softly feline about him at the wicket although, strangely enough, he appeared rather heavy-footed in the outfield. He appeared for Hindus in the Bombay Pentangular or Quadrangular tournaments (1929-46) and Bombay in the Ranji Trophy competition (1933-52); and he represented India in the first home Test series, against England in 1933/4, making 178 runs in three matches. In England in the wet summer of 1936, he was the outstanding batsman, with 1,745 runs (51.32), his 282 runs (47.00) in the Tests including a superb 114 at Old Trafford. In India he made his career highest, 359 not out, against Maharashtra in 1943/4. Back in England in 1946 as vice-captain, another wet summer, he was superb with 2,385 runs (74.53), his 7 centuries including 2 doubles – 242 not out against Lancashire and 205 against Sussex. In the Tests he made 245 runs (49.00), with 128 in the rain-spoiled final Oval match as his highest. In his final Test, the first against England at Delhi in 1951/2, he scored 154, adding 211 for the third wicket

Vijay Merchant (left) and Mushtaq Ali

with Vijay Hazare, a new Indian record for any wicket against England. It was felt, however, that the two were such rivals that they batted more for themselves than their team: England were able to save a match they seemed sure to lose. A recurrence of an old shoulder injury in this match, throwing himself full length while fielding, led to his retirement from active participation in the game, but he became a very prominent and outspoken administrator and writer. In Ranji Trophy matches he made 3,639 runs (98.75), including 16 centuries in only 47 innings

First-class career (1929-52): 13,228 runs (71.11) including 44 centuries, and 65 wickets (31.87)
Test matches (10): 859 runs (47.72) including 3 centuries, 0-40 and 7 catches

MILKHA SINGH, Amritsar Govindsingh (b.1941)

Madras (Tamil Nadu)

A sound left-handed batsman and occasional right-arm medium-pace bowler in the sixties, Milkha Singh was the mainstay of the Madras (later Tamil Nadu) batting, together with his brother, A.G. Kripal Singh. He had a short Test career, playing at home against Australia in 1959/60, Pakistan 1960/61 and England 1961/2 without establishing himself. In the Ranji Trophy competition he made over 2,000 runs, averaging over 40 runs an innings.

First-class career (1958-69): 4,324 runs (35.44) including 8 centuries
Test matches (4): 92 runs (15.33), 0-2 and 2 catches

MODI, Rusi Sheriyar (b.1924)

Bombay

Tall and almost painfully thin, Rusi Modi was a careful, patient and wristy right-handed batsman with a sound defence, an elegant mover at the crease, who was beautifully light on his feet and quick to throw his whole body behind the ball and strike it to the boundary. He was an occasional bowler of medium-pace in-swingers. He toured England in 1946, and at home played against West Indies in 1948/9, England in 1951/2 and Pakistan in 1952/3. After scoring a record 215 for Parsees against Europeans in the Bombay Pentangular tournament in 1943/4, he made only one run on his debut in the Ranji Trophy competition in 1944/5 but followed with a sequence of 168, 128, 160, 210, 245 not out (his career-highest against Baroda), 31 not out and 113. That season he had the record aggregate of 1,008 runs (201.00). In England in 1946, a wet summer, he scored 1,196 runs (37.37). Against West Indies he was the outstanding run-getter with 560 runs (56.00) in the Tests including his sole Test century, 112 in the second match at Bombay, when he added 156 for the third wicket and saved the match. His Test career came to an end, however, on a regrettable note of anticlimax. In Ranji Trophy matches he made 2,696 runs (81.69), including 10 centuries.

First-class career (1941-62): 7,509 runs (53.63) including 20 centuries, and 32 wickets (38.28)
Test matches (10): 736 runs (46.00) including 1 century, 0-14 and 3 catches

MUDDIAH, Venatappa Musandra (b.1929)

Services

A right-arm off-spin bowler, Venatappa Muddiah toured England in 1959 taking 30 wickets (29.46), but was not selected for the Tests. At home he played once each against Australia in 1959/60 and Pakistan in 1960/61 with little success. In Ranji Trophy matches he captured 101 wickets (23.49).

First-class career (1949-63): 805 runs (13.87) and 169 wickets (24.42)
Test matches (2): 11 runs (5.50) and 3 wickets (44.66)

MUSHTAQ ALI (b.1914)

Holkar

Despite sudden rushes of blood to the head – he had a tendency to jump out and hoist the ball straight to a fielder – Mushtaq Ali was a right-handed opening batsman of brilliance, flair and a loose, easy grace. Very quick on his feet, he always introduced a spirit of adventure into his play. In his earlier days he was better-known as a slow left-arm bowler, and he appeared as such in his first two Tests against England in 1933/4. In England in 1936 he made 1,078 runs (25.06), including 4 centuries, and formed a strong opening partnership with Vijay Merchant: in the second Test at Old Trafford, when India batted again 368 behind, they opened with a lively 203, Mushtaq hitting 112 in two and a quarter hours. In the unofficial Test series against Lord Tennyson's team in 1937/8 he scored 101 and 55 at Calcutta. Back in England in 1946 he seemed too often to throw away his wicket attempting the impossible but he proved that he could bat with responsibility against the West Indies in 1948/9 when he came back as opener in the third Test at Calcutta, and scored 54 and 106, batting out of character for India to save the game. In a long career in the Ranji Trophy competition he made 5,013 runs (49.14), including 17 centuries, his career-highest being 233 against United Provinces in 1947/8.

First-class career (1930-64): 13,009 runs (34.78) including 30 centuries, and 155 wickets (29.47)
Test matches (11): 612 runs (32.21) including 2 centuries, 3 wickets (67.33) and 7 catches

NADKARNI, Raghunath Gangaram (b.1932)

Maharashtra and Bombay

A genuine all-rounder, 'Bapu' Nadkarni was a steady and determined left-handed batsman, a patient slow bowler of immaculate length and studious variations, and a courageous close field. He toured England in 1959, the West Indies in 1962/3 and Australasia in 1967/8, and at home played against New Zealand in 1955/6 and 1964/5, West Indies in 1958/9 and 1966/7, Australia in 1959/60 and 1964/5, Pakistan in 1960/61 and England in 1961/2 and 1963/4. A tall, neat cricketer who always bowled and batted with shirt-sleeves buttoned at the wrist, he was the most improved player on the otherwise ill-fated England tour of 1959 making 945 runs (23.62), taking 55 wickets (28.41) and holding 23 catches. In the last match at The Oval he fought for four hours for 76 in a vain attempt to avert defeat. In 1960/61 against Pakistan at Delhi he captured 5 for 67 in 84.4 overs (62 maidens). In the West Indies in 1961/2, when all 5 Tests were lost, he scored 286 runs (33.71) and also took 9 wickets (35.11). Against England in 1963/4 he headed the batting with 294 runs (98.00 – thanks to five not outs) and took 9 wickets (30.88). In the fifth match at Kanpur he spent a total of eleven hours over 52 and 122, both times undefeated. In the first match at Madras his analysis read: 32-27-5-0, and he created a world Test record by bowling 131 balls (21.5 overs) without conceding a run. In 1964/5 against Australia he was the most successful bowler on either side with 17 wickets (13.70) in the three Tests: in the first at Madras he captured 5 for 31 and 6 for 91. Rather ineffective as a bowler against New Zealand in 1959/60, he hit 75 quickly in the first match at Madras but when he visited New Zealand he took 6 for 43 in the second innings of the third Test, at Wellington. In the Ranji Trophy competition he made 3,993 runs (62.39), his 12 centuries including 283 not out for Bombay against Delhi, 1960/61, and took 181 wickets (17.52). Captain of his two State teams, he later wrote about the allegedly shabby treatment meted out by the Board of Control to Indian Test players of his day.

Bapu Nadkarni

First-class career (1951-72): 8,880 runs (40.36) including 14 centuries, and 500 wickets (21.37)
Test matches (41): 1,414 runs (25.70) including 1 century, 88 wickets (29.07) and 22 catches

NAIK, Sudhir Sakharam (b.1946)

Bombay

A gritty right-handed batsman, whose main strength lay on the leg-side, Sudhir Naik toured England in 1974, making 730 runs (40.55) and, on his Test debut at Edgbaston, scored 77. He also played against West Indies in 1974/5.

First-class career (1966-78): 4,398 runs (35.18) including 7 centuries
Test matches (3): 141 runs (23.50)

NAOOMAL, Jeoomal (1904-80)

Sind

A diminutive and watchful right-handed batsman, who could defend doggedly and cut neatly, Naoomal was also a left-arm change slow bowler, and an outstanding fielder or deputy wicket-keeper. He toured England in 1932, making 1,297 runs (30.88), and 33 and 25 in the only Test, at Lord's. He played in two Tests against England in 1933/4. In 1938/9 he hit his career-highest, 203 not out in four and a half hours against Nawanagar in the Ranji Trophy.

First-class career (1926-45): 4,056 runs (33.52) including 7 centuries and 102 wickets (27.00)
Test matches (3): 108 runs (27.00) and 2 wickets (34.00)

NARASIMHA RAO, Modireddy Venkat (b.1954)

Hyderabad

A tall right-hander with a sound technique and a useful leg-spinner with a high action, Rao played in two Tests against West Indies in 1978/9, making only 11 runs in 3 innings, taking 1 for 107 and holding 5 catches. He has been a popular and successful professional in Ireland.

First-class career (1971-): 2,334 runs (38.90) including 6 centuries, and 93 wickets (30.46)

NAVLE, Janardhan Gnanoba (1902-79)

Gwalior

A diminutive wicket-keeper, very quick, neat and safe in all that he did, and considered by Jack Hobbs to be in the same class as George Duckworth and Bert Oldfield, Navle was also a competent right-handed opening batsman. For many years he kept for Hindus in the Bombay Tournament and, touring England in 1932, he made 600 runs (15.78) and claimed 36 dismissals. He played for India in the first Test against England at Lord's in 1932 and at Bombay in 1933/4.

First-class career (1918-44): 1,958 runs (19.00) and 135 dismissals (100 ct, 35 st.)
Test matches (2): 42 runs (10.50) and 1 catch

NAYAK, Suvendra Vithal (b.1954)

Bombay

With a smile never far away, 'Suru' Nayak conveys his enjoyment of the game. He is a most capable all-round cricketer: a brilliant cover fielder with a strong throw; a stroke-playing right-hand batsman; and a bowler who specializes in medium-paced in-swing but can also bowl useful leg-breaks. Steady performances for Bombay and for West Zone earned him two appearances for India in one-day internationals against England at home in 1981/2. Touring England in 1982, he batted steadily in county matches and played in the second and third Tests with limited success.

First-class career (1977-): 1,131 runs (29.76) including 2 centuries, and 81 wickets (30.19)
Test matches (2): 19 runs (9.50), 1-132 and 1 catch

NAYUDU, Col. Cottari Kankaiya (1895-1967)

Madras, Central Provinces and Berar, Holkar and United Provinces

India's first captain in Test cricket and the best all-rounder at that time, 'C.K.' Nayudu was a tall and well-proportioned right-handed batsman, a front-foot player who hit the ball tremendously hard and was strong in driving on both sides of the wicket; he was also a more than useful slow-medium change-bowler, whose length was superb and spin well-controlled. An all-round sportsman, retiring and modest but with a majestic gait, he proved an admirable leader in England in 1932, when he was the best batsman with 1,618 runs (40.45), including 5 centuries, besides taking 65 wickets (25.53). In the first home series against England in 1933/4 he made 160 runs (26.66) and, as captain, was exacting and thorough. In England in 1936, as vice-captain, he scored 1,102 runs (26.23) and took 51 wickets (31.78). In the third Test at The Oval, though hit on the solar plexus by a ball from 'Gubby' Allen, he refused to retire and hit 81, his highest in Tests, in two and a half hours. He was in his prime before the advent of Tests. From 1916 he played in the Bombay Quadrangular matches, making 155 for Hindus against Mohammedans in 1928/9. He hit 153 for Hindus against MCC in 1926/7, including 11 sixes and 13 fours, in just over a hundred minutes. In the Ranji Trophy he made his career-highest, 200 for Holkar against Baroda in 1945/6. His best bowling figures were 7 for 63 for Central India against Bengal in 1935/6. In his sixty-ninth year he returned to play in one first-class match. He became the elder statesman of Indian cricket, especially as Test selector and vice-president of the Indian Cricket Board of Control. His son, Prakash, played for Madhya Pradesh, and his brother, C.S., for India.

First-class career (1916-64): 11,069 runs (36.41) including 26 centuries, and 402 wickets (29.11)
Test matches (7): 350 runs (25.00), 9 wickets (42.88) and 4 catches

NAYUDU, Cottari Subbanna (b.1914)

Central India, Baroda, Holkar, Bengal, Andhra Pradesh, Uttar Pradesh and Madhya Pradesh

A bundle of energy, 'C.S.' Nayudu was a right-arm leg-break and googly bowler who was like a flail, spinning the ball fiercely. As a right-handed batsman, he was inelegant but waited for the right ball and then hit it hard; and in the deep he was brilliant. Between 1934 and 1961 he had an excellent record in the Ranji Trophy competition – 2,575 runs (30.20) and 295 wickets (23.49), once taking 14 wickets in a match and twice exceeding 30 wickets in a season. But, despite his opportunities, he was very disappointing for India. He holds a record for bowling more balls in one match than anyone. For Holkar v. Bombay in 1944/5 he bowled 152.5 overs (917 balls).

First-class career (1931-61): 5,664 runs (23.69) including 3 centuries, and 636 wickets (26.66)
Test matches (11): 147 runs (9.18), 2 wickets (179.50) and 3 catches

NAZIR ALI, Syed (1906-75)

Southern Punjab and Sussex

An attacking right-handed batsman, who was a particularly fine driver, a fast-medium bowler who could move the ball both ways, and a splendid fielder, Nazir Ali attracted attention with good batting and even better bowling against MCC in India in 1926/7, and Arthur Gilligan suggested that he should qualify for Sussex. Some months later the secretary of Sussex was awakened at 1 a.m. by Nazir Ali asking for hospitality or to be sent where he could obtain it! Subsequently, he played once for the county and much cricket around London. He was a successful member of the Indian team in England in 1932 – making 1,020 runs (31.87) and taking 23 wickets (21.78) – and played in the first-ever Test between the two countries, at Lord's. In 1933/4 he appeared in the final Test of the first series in India against England. In later years he was prominent in the administration of the game in Pakistan. He was younger brother of S. Wazir Ali.

First-class career (1923-48): 3,379 runs (30.71) including 7 centuries, and 151 wickets (25.56)
Test matches (2): 30 runs (7.50) and 4 wickets (20.75)

NISSAR, Mahomed (1910-63)

Southern Punjab

A tall, strapping man from the Punjabi hills, Mahomed Nissar was a right-arm fast bowler with a good, easy action who was able to make the ball swing and break back viciously. He came up a long way from park cricket, although hampered by the salwar he wore in his early days instead of a pair of flannels. In England in 1932 he and Amar Singh formed the attacking spearhead, Nissar heading the bowling with 71 wickets (18.09) and in the first-ever Test, at Lord's, he took 5 for 93 in the first innings. In the first innings of the first-ever Test in India, against England at Bombay in 1933/4, he took 5 for 90. Back in England in 1936, he took 66 wickets (25.13) and headed the bowling in Tests with 12 wickets (28.58). For several years until 1940 he opened Muslims' attack in the Bombay Pentangular Tournament, and it was said that he could master all the batsmen except the Hindu, C.K. Nayudu, who would walk down the wicket before the ball left his hand.

First-class career (1928-42): 1,027 runs (10.58) and 384 wickets (17.69)
Test matches (6): 55 runs (6.87), 25 wickets (28.28) and 2 catches

NYALCHAND, Shah (b.1919)

Kathiawar

A persistent, nagging left-arm medium-pace bowler, Nyalchand's sole Test was the second against Pakistan at Lucknow in 1952/3, when he scored 6 not out and 1 and took 3 for 97 in 64 overs (33 maidens) in the visitors' only innings.

First-class career (1939-64): 420 runs (7.63) and 235 wickets (22.57)

PAI, Ajit Manohar (b.1945)

Bombay

Tall, wiry and fiery, a left-handed batsman and right-arm fast-medium bowler, Ajit Pai packed a terrific wallop in his shots off the back foot and could bowl at a stinging pace. He met with some success in both Ranji and Duleep Trophy competitions, but played in only a sole Test, the first against New Zealand at Bombay in 1969/70, scoring 1 and 9 and taking 2 for 31.

First-class career (1968-76): 872 runs (24.22) and 85 wickets (25.22)

PALIA, Phiroz Edulji (1910-81)

United Provinces and Mysore

An attractive left-handed batsman, useful slow bowler and quick fielder, Palia toured England in 1932 and 1936, playing in India's first-ever Test, at Lord's, and again at Lord's four years later. In 1932 he made 476 runs (21.63) and took 24 wickets (31.00). His highest score was also the best ever for United Provinces in the Ranji Trophy competition, 216 against Maharashtra in 1939/40. In this competition he made 1,501 runs (39.50). He was prominent for Parsees in the Bombay Quadrangular Tournament.

First-class career (1928-54): 4,455 runs (32.05) including 8 centuries, and 204 wickets (24.12)
Test matches (2): 29 runs (9.66) and 0-13

PARKAR, Ghulam Ahmed Hasan Mohamed (b.1955)

Bombay

A strict Moslem and a dedicated right-handed opening batsman, Parkar is one of the finest cover fieldsmen produced by India and appeared on the field as substitute several times against England at home in 1981/2 before making his first Test appearances officially in England in 1982. Unable, however, to deal with the awkward bounce of Bob Willis's best deliveries, he failed in the one-day internationals and in his only Test, at Lord's, where he scored 6 and 1 and held 1 catch. Opening partner with Sunil Gavaskar for Bombay, he shared in a first-wicket stand of 421 in the quarter-final of the 1981/2 Ranji Trophy against Bengal.

First-class career (1978-): 2,227 runs (41.24) including 7 centuries, and 2 wickets (30.50)

PARKAR, Ramnath Dhondu (b.1946)

Bombay

Ramnath Parkar is a dapper and flowing stroke-making right-handed batsman, very light on his feet, who usually opens, and a fine cover-point. But his opportunities for India have been limited to only two Tests against England in 1972/3.

First-class career (1964-): 4,253 runs (34.21) including 8 centuries
Test matches (2): 80 runs (20.00)

PARSANA, Dhiraj Devshibhai (b.1947)

Saurashtra, Railways, Guyerat and Durham

An accurate left-arm seam bowler capable of swinging the new ball considerably and a useful left-handed batsman, Dhiraj Parsana was discarded after two unsuccessful Tests against the West Indies in 1978/9.

First-class career (1965-): 2,906 runs (27.67) including 2 centuries, and 299 wickets (21.46)
Test matches (2): 1 run (0.50) and 1 wicket (50.00)

PATANKAR, Chandrakant Trimbak (b.1930)

Bombay

A very competent wicket-keeper and useful right-handed batsman, Patankar's sole Test was the fourth at Calcutta against New Zealand in 1955/6. He dismissed 4 (3 caught and 1 stumped), all in the first innings, and scored 13 and 1 not out.

First-class career (1945-68): 503 runs (15.71) including 1 century, and 58 dismissals (38 ct, 20 st.)

PATAUDI, NAWAB OF, Senior (1910-52)

Oxford University, Worcestershire and Southern Punjab

See England section.

PATAUDI, NAWAB OF, Junior (now Mansur Ali Khan) (b.1941)

Oxford University, Sussex and Hyderabad

Recapturing for a time the aristocratic strain in Indian cricket, 'Tiger' Pataudi was a brave, vigorous and adventurous right-handed batsman who attached greater importance to the productiveness of a stroke than its attractiveness. He was strong on the leg-side and not afraid to loft the ball, and he would have been much more prolific in Tests but for an accident before he had reached his prime. As a freshman at Oxford in 1960, he hit 131 against Cambridge at Lord's and also made his debut for Sussex, but the following year just before the Varsity match, when he was the first Indian to captain Oxford, he was involved in a car accident and lost the sight of his right eye. Having set his heart on playing for India, within a month he was back at the nets facing the bowling again, refocusing, adjusting his stance, experimenting with a contact lens and practising very hard. He returned to Oxford's side in 1963, and went on to captain India in forty of his forty-six Tests. He also captained Sussex in 1966. He toured the West Indies in 1961/2, England in 1967 and Australasia in 1967/8, and at home played against England in 1961/2, 1963/4 and 1972/3, Australia in 1964/5 and 1969/70, New Zealand in 1964/5 and

The Nawab of Pataudi, Junior

1969/70 and West Indies in 1966/7 and 1974/5. In his third Test, against England at Madras in 1961/2, he hit 103 in only 2 hours 35 minutes. He succeeded to the Indian captaincy during the disappointing tour of the West Indies following Nari Contractor's serious injury, but made no large scores. He had a poor series against England in 1963/4 but a year later against Australia he was back in top form, scoring 270 runs (67.50), including a splendid 128 not out in a total of 276 in the first match at Madras and 86 and 53 at Bombay, when India beat Australia. A few weeks later he was equally effective against New Zealand with 317 runs (52.83), including 153 in the second match, at Calcutta, and 113 in the fourth, at Delhi. He led India to victory against New Zealand in two series. On his sole England tour, despite his shrewd captaincy and fine batting, his team suffered many misfortunes: he made 777 runs (35.31), including 269 runs (44.83) in the Tests, when he stood out by himself, scoring 74 and 148 in a masterly fight-back in the first at Headingley. In Australia, batting under considerable personal and team difficulties, he headed the Test averages with 339 runs (56.50). Under his new name, Mansur Ali Khan, having been deprived by the Indian Government of his title, he returned to Tests against England in 1972/3 (but not as captain), making 147 runs (36.75) in three matches. Reappointed leader against West Indies in 1974/5, he was injured while fielding in the first Test and could not find his form. He was prolific in the Duleep Trophy competition, and he also made over 2,000 runs in the Ranji Trophy.

First-class career (1957-76): 15,425 runs (33.67) including 33 centuries, and 207 catches
Test matches (46): 2,793 runs (34.91) including 6 centuries, 1-88 and 27 catches

PATEL, Brijesh Parsuram (b.1952)

Karnataka (Mysore)

Capable on his day of touching the heights of batting,

Brijesh Patel is a right-hander with a scintillating array of strokes played wristily and with a rare panache, but his best has been all too seldom displayed at the highest level. It took him a long time to establish a regular place in the Indian team following failures in the Tests in England in 1974. He made 73 not out in a losing cause against West Indies at Bombay in the fifth Test of 1974/5, 81 in similar circumstances against New Zealand at Wellington in 1975/6, and 115 not out against the West Indies at Port of Spain in the second Test of 1976. In four innings in this series he scored 207 runs, three times not out (average 207!). In 1975/6 he earned his place against New Zealand and England by scoring 601 runs in the Ranji Trophy (100.16) and, in the Tests, scoring 172 runs at 43.00 against New Zealand and 286 at 28.60 against England. These included a sparkling 83 in the fifth Test against England at Bombay. But he was disappointing both in Australia in 1977/8 and in England in 1979.

First-class career (1969-): 8,604 runs (43.02) including 26 centuries
Test matches (21): 972 runs (29.45) including 1 century and 17 catches

PATEL, Jasubhai Motibhai (b.1924)

Gujerat

A right-arm off-break bowler who really spun the ball, Jasubhai Patel toured Pakistan in 1954/5 and headed the bowling averages with 35 wickets (10.68), but was selected for only one Test: indeed he had a chequered career in representative cricket. At home he played against New Zealand in 1955/6, Australia in 1956/7 and 1959/60. A wrist injury sustained as a boy gave him a somewhat jerky action. His best series was against Australia in 1959/60, when he captured 19 wickets (17.21) in three matches; at Kanpur he came in at the last moment and, on newly laid turf, took 14 for 124 (9 for 69 and 5 for 55), the best-ever bowling performance for India, which made possible the first-ever win over Australia. In the Ranji Trophy competition he secured 140 wickets (20.19).

First-class career (1943-64): 787 runs (13.16) including 1 century, and 248 wickets (21.83)
Test matches (7): 25 runs (2.77), 29 wickets (21.96) and 2 catches

PATIALA, YUVRAJ OF (Lt-Gen. Yadavendra Singh) (1913-74)

Patiala and Southern Punjab

A great patron of the game, like his father, who donated the Ranji Trophy, the Yuvraj of Patiala was a tall, graceful right-handed batsman who played in a single Test, the third against England, at Madras, in 1933/4, scoring 24 and 60 and holding two catches. He was invited to tour England in 1936, but State business caused him to decline. He was India's Ambassador to Holland from 1971 until his death.

First-class career (1931-58): 1,602 runs (20.80) including 2 centuries, and 48 wickets (31.93)

PATIL, Sadashiv Raoji (b.1934)

Maharashtra

A right-arm fast-medium bowler, Sadashiv Patil played in a single Test, the second against New Zealand, at Bombay, in 1955/6, scoring 14 not out, taking 2 for 51 and holding 1 catch.

First-class career (1952-64): 859 runs (26.84) and 83 wickets (30.60)

PATIL, Sandeep Madhusudan (b.1956)

Bombay

Tall and talented, a successful pop singer as well as a brilliant attacking right-hand batsman, Sandeep Patil is a national idol whose first two Test centuries were absolute gems, the product of a player of very unusual flair. Having made his mark strongly for Bombay, and also in London club cricket, where his dominant batting led to Edmonton being voted out of the Middlesex League for playing 'guest artists', he toured Australia in 1980/81, and at Adelaide, despite being hit on the head by a ball from Pascoe in the previous Test, he hit a dazzling 174. On the tour he scored 802 runs (53.46). His powerful driving, cutting and hooking was even more impressive against England at Old Trafford in 1982. After a run of failures, his Test future was at stake, but with no sign of nerves he hit India out of danger. His 129 not out included 18 fours, six of them coming off one over from Willis which included a no-ball. This equalled the highest number of runs scored off one Test over of six legitimate balls. Two Tests later, against Sri Lanka at Madras, he hit another rapid century, 114 not out. His Ranji Trophy debut was made in 1975/6, and four seasons later he hit his highest score, 210 against Saurashtra. Also a useful medium-paced bowler despite an awkward action, he swings the ball and even at Test level can be a worthwhile change bowler. He played for the Surrey second eleven in 1979.

First-class career (1975-): 2,977 runs (39.17) including 7 centuries and 34 wickets (35.50)
Test matches (16): 1,081 runs (49.14) including 3 centuries, 9 wickets (26.44) and 8 catches

PHADKAR, Dattaray Gajaran (b.1925)

Maharashtra, Bombay, Bengal and Railways

A genuine all-rounder of excellent temperament, Dattaray Phadkar was an attacking right-handed middle-order batsman, especially good against fast bowling, and a fast-medium bowler who could swing the ball either way, extract much life from the pitch and exploit a bad wicket with slower off-breaks. He toured Australia in 1947/8, England in 1952, the West Indies in 1952/3 and Pakistan in 1954/5, and at home played against West Indies in 1948/9 and 1958/9, England in 1951/2, Pakistan in 1952/3, New Zealand in 1955/6 and Australia in 1956/7. On the first tour of Australia he headed the batting in the Tests with 314 runs (52.33), in each of his four matches making at least one fifty, and took 8 wickets (31.75). On his Test debut at Sydney in the second match he hit 51 and took 3 for 14, and in the fourth match at Adelaide he scored 123, adding 188 with Vijay Hazare for the sixth wicket after a batting collapse. Against West Indies in 1948/9 he made 240 runs (40.00) and took 14 wickets (29.35), in the fourth match, at Madras, collecting 7 for 159 in a total of 582. His only real success, however, against England in 1951/2 was in the third match, at Calcutta, when he scored 115 and took 4 wickets. In England the following season he did not do as well as expected, his only significant contribution to the Tests being a defiant 64 in the second innings of the first match at Headingley after Fred Trueman had broken through; joining Hazare at 26 for 5, these two added 105. Not helped by the lifeless matting pitches in the Caribbean in 1952/3, he yet headed the bowling in the Tests with 9 wickets (25.55). Making his debut in the Ranji Trophy competition at seventeen, he later captained Bombay and, altogether, made 1,920 runs (46.82) and took 216 wickets (16.61), with a highest of 217 for Bombay against Maharashtra in 1950/51 and best bowling in an innings, 7 for 37 for Bengal against Bihar in 1956/7.

First-class career (1942-60): 5,377 runs (36.08) including 8 centuries and 464 wickets (22.13)
Test matches (31): 1,229 runs (32.34) including 2 centuries, 62 wickets (36.85) and 21 catches

PRASANNA, Erapally Anantharao Srinivasa (b.1940)

Mysore (Karnataka)

One of the famous quartet of Indian spin bowlers who graced their country's cricket in the 1960s and 1970s, Erapally Prasanna was a true artist, a subtle and flowing off-spin bowler with a neat, brisk, high action and marvellous control of line, length and flight. Unlike his great rival, Venkataraghavan, he spun the ball in a classic high loop towards the batsman, increasing his chances of beating his adversary through the air. Moreover, through tossing the ball so high, Prasanna also made it bounce higher than expected. On the other hand the bold driver could attack him more easily than spinners with a flatter arc. His Test debut was at Madras against England in 1961/2 in the fifth Test and as late as 1976/7 he was the leading Indian bowler in another series against England. His first overseas tour to the West Indies in 1961/2 proved a tough one and he did not play another Test for five years. He gained a regular place at last in England in 1967, where he took 7 for 111 in the Edgbaston Test and 45 wickets on the tour at 23.91. Against Australia and New Zealand away in 1967/8 he took 25 wickets (27.44) and 24 wickets (18.79) and was throughout the tour the leading Indian bowler. In successive Tests at Wellington and Auckland he took 8 for 88 and 8 for 84 (in the match). There followed 20 more Test wickets at home to New Zealand in 1969/70 and 26 at home to Australia also in 1969/70. A finger injury temporarily lost him his place in the West Indies in 1970/71 and thereafter he was never sure whether he or Venkat would earn the selectors' choice. His next full series were against the West Indies at home in 1974/5, when he took 15 wickets (40.06), including a matchwinning 9 for 111 in the fourth game at Madras, and New Zealand away in 1975/6 when at Auckland he took 8 for 76 in the first innings and 11 for 140 in the match. Against England at home in 1976/7 he played in four of the five Tests and claimed 18 wickets at 21.61 including 4 for 93 in 57.4 overs at Calcutta but he gradually faded with youth and fitness no longer on his side. In domestic cricket he played first for Mysore (now Karnataka) in 1961/2, and captained them after 1969/70.

Erapally Prasanna

First-class career (1961-79): 2,476 runs (11.90) and 957 wickets (23.45)
Test matches (49): 735 runs (11.48), 189 wickets (30.39) and 18 catches

PUNJABI, Pananmal Hotchand (b.1921)

Gujerat

A competent right-handed opening batsman who could keep wicket, Punjabi toured Pakistan in 1954/5, scoring 393 runs (23.11), but was disappointing in his sole Test series.

First-class career (1943-60): 1,953 runs (38.21) including 6 centuries
Test matches (5): 164 runs (16.40) and 5 catches

RAI SINGH, Kanwar (b.1922)

Southern Punjab

A capable right-handed batsman, Rai Singh toured Australia in 1947/8 with little success, and in his sole Test, the third at Melbourne, scored 2 and 24.

First-class career (1940-61): 1,778 runs (30.13) including 4 centuries, and 21 wickets (33.33)

RAJINDERNATH, V. (b.1928)

Southern Punjab and Bihar

A competent wicket-keeper and right-handed batsman, Rajindernath's sole Test was the third against Pakistan at Bombay in 1952/3, when he did not bat and made 4 stumpings (3 off S.P. Gupte).

First-class career (1943-59); 844 runs (22.21) and 59 dismissals (36 ct, 23 st.)

RAJINDER PAL (b.1937)

Southern Punjab and Delhi

A right-arm fast-medium bowler who met with much success in the Ranji Trophy competition, Rajinder Pal's sole Test was the second against England at Bombay in 1963/4, scoring 3 and 3 not out and taking 0 for 22.

First-class career (1954-74): 1,072 runs (11.28) and 339 wickets (21.88)

RAMASWAMI, Cota (b.1896)

Madras

A sturdily built son of a pioneer of the game in Madras, Cota Ramaswami is the second oldest Indian to make a Test debut, at 40 years 37 days. In his prime, a free-scoring left-handed batsman and a fine driver on both sides of the wicket, he represented Hindus in the Bombay Tournament and toured England in 1936, though he claimed modestly that he had been chosen 'for other than cricket reasons' as he had become 'bulky and slow'. On the tour, however, he made 737 runs (30.70), and 40 and 60 on his Test debut, at Old Trafford.

First-class career (1915-41) 2,261 runs (28.26) including 2 centuries, and 30 wickets (33.06)
Test matches (2): 170 runs (56.66)

RAMCHAND, Gulabrai Sipahahimalani (b.1927)

Sind and Bombay

Powerfully built, the whole-hearted 'Ram' Ramchand was a genuine all-rounder, a hard-hitting right-handed batsman, particularly forceful when playing off the back foot, and a medium-paced in-swinging bowler of very accurate length. He toured England in 1952, the West Indies in 1952/3 and Pakistan in 1954/5, and at home played against Pakistan in 1952/3, New Zealand in 1955/6, Australia in 1956/7 and 1959/60 and West Indies in 1958/9. He was captain in the five matches against Australia in 1959/60, his final series, winning one and losing two. A surprise choice for the England tour, he made 644 runs (24.76), took 64 wickets (25.85) and held 20 catches for a weak side, though he achieved little in the Tests, indeed being dismissed for a pair on his debut at Headingley. In the Caribbean he made 249 runs (24.90) in the Tests, but his bowling was not penetrative. Against the Commonwealth team in 1953/4 he made 410 runs (58.57) in the unofficial Tests, and in Pakistan he headed the Test bowling averages with 10 wickets (20.00), besides averaging 29.40 with the bat. At Bahawalpur in the second match, after India had lost 7 wickets for 107 on the first day, he made 53 doggedly, and in the fifth match at Karachi he took 6 for 49 in 28 overs in the first innings, his best performance in Tests. His first century for India was a sparkling 106 not out against New Zealand in the third match at Calcutta in 1955/6. Against Australia in the second match, at Bombay, in 1956/7 he played a rescuing innings of 109. In his final series – as captain against Australia – he was disappointing with bat and ball but led his country to her first-ever win over Australia, in the second match at Kanpur. In the Ranji Trophy competition he made 2,569 runs (75.55), including 10 centuries; he scored a century in each of the last four finals he played. He also took 73 wickets (22.27). His career-highest was 230 not out for Bombay against Maharashtra in 1950/51 and his best bowling in an innings, 8 for 12 against Saurashtra in 1959/60.

First-class career (1945-68): 6,027 runs (36.30) including 16 centuries, and 258 wickets (29.32)
Test matches (33): 1,180 runs (24.58) including 2 centuries, 41 wickets (46.34) and 20 catches

RAMJI, Ladha (1900-48)

Western India

A simple fellow with a massive physique and reckless love of the game, Ladha Ramji was a right-arm fast-bowler who put everything into his opening overs and achieved considerable success for Hindus in the Bombay Quadrangular Tournament. His sole Test was the first ever in India against England at Bombay in 1933/4, when he scored 1 and 0, took 0 for 64 and held 1 catch. He was the brother of Amar Singh.

First-class career (1923-36): 316 runs (8.77) and 111 wickets (18.80)

RANGACHARI, Commandur Rajagopalachari (b.1916)

Madras

A strongly built police officer, Rangachari was a right-arm fast bowler with a round-arm flaying action and, always pacey, he had a useful out-swinger. No mean late-order batsman, he was an intrepid fielder at close quarters, swooping and tumbling near the bat. He toured Australia in 1947/8, but found that speed was not enough. At home against West Indies in 1948/9, he took 5 for 107 in a total of 631 in the first Test, at Delhi. In the next match, however, he conceded 148 runs without taking a wicket, and was not selected for India again. When he retired five years later, he had taken 104 wickets (20.79) in the Ranji Trophy competition.

First-class career (1938-54): 480 runs (7.74) and 200 wickets (25.98)
Test matches (4): 8 runs (2.66) and 9 wickets (54.77)

RANGNEKAR, Khanderao Moreshwar (b.1917)

Maharashtra, Bombay, Madhya Pradesh and Holkar

An attacking left-handed batsman, occasional right-arm medium-pace bowler and excellent field at cover, Rangnekar made 107 and 17 not out on his debut in first-class cricket for Maharashtra against Western India in 1939/40. Touring Australia in 1947/8, he played in three Tests but could average only 10.81 for the tour and he was not selected for his country again. In a career of some twenty years he made 2,548 runs (49.10) in the Ranji Trophy competition.

First-class career (1939-64): 4,602 runs (41.45) including 15 centuries, and 21 wickets (40.95)
Test matches (3): 33 runs (5.50) and 1 catch

RANJANE, Vasant Baburao (b.1937)

Maharashtra and Railways

A very useful right-arm fast-medium bowler, able to swing both ways and cut the ball off the seam when the shine had gone, Ranjane made a sensational debut in first-class cricket in 1956/7, taking 9 for 35 (including a hat-trick) and 4 for 36 for Maharashtra against Saurashtra in the Ranji Trophy competition. He toured the West Indies in 1961/2, and at home played against West Indies in 1958/9, England in 1961/2 and 1963/4 and Australia in 1964/5 without establishing himself. Altogether in the Ranji Trophy competition he took 116 wickets (22.11).

First-class career (1956-71): 698 runs (14.85) and 175 wickets (27.79)
Test matches (7): 40 runs (6.66), 19 wickets (34.15) and 1 catch

REDDY, Bharath (b.1954)

Tamil Nadu (Madras)

A tall, slim wicket-keeper and competent right-handed batsman, who plays fast bowling calmly and with courage, Bharath Reddy has spent much time in the shadow of Syed Kirmani but took over temporarily as India's first-choice wicket-keeper for the 1979 tour of England. An enthusiastic cricketer, his approach to keeping wicket is nevertheless calm and he does the job steadily and undemonstratively.

First-class career (1973-): 1,231 runs (17.58) and 160 dismissals (126 ct, 34 st.)
Test matches (4): 38 runs (9.50) and 11 dismissals (9 ct, 2 st.)

REGE, Madhusudan Ramchandra (b.1924)

Maharashtra

A competent right-handed opening batsman, Madhusudan Rege made a sole appearance in Tests, against West Indies in the fourth match at Madras in 1948/9, when he scored 15 and 0 and held 1 catch.

First-class career (1944-55): 2,348 runs (37.26) including 6 centuries, and 33 wickets (42.96)

ROY, Ambar (b.1945)

Bengal

A sound and consistent left-handed batsman who captained Bengal in the Ranji Trophy competition, Ambar Roy played in Tests against New Zealand and Australia in 1969/70. He made 3,817 runs (49.57) in the Ranji Trophy matches. Also a useful right-arm medium-pace bowler, he is a nephew of Pankaj Roy.

First-class career (1960-78): 7,163 runs (43.15) including 18 centuries, and 29 wickets (34.86)
Test matches (4): 91 runs (13.00)

ROY, Pankaj (b.1928)

Bengal

A stocky, determined opening right-handed batsman

Pankaj Roy, with Arthur McIntyre (England)

and a forceful player off the back foot, Pankaj Roy never quite fulfilled his tremendous promise as a youth: he made 112 not out for Bengal against United Provinces on his debut in the Ranji Trophy competition in 1946/7. He toured England in 1952 and 1959, the West Indies in 1952/3 and Pakistan in 1954/5, and at home he played against England in 1951/2, Pakistan in 1952/3 and 1960/61, New Zealand in 1955/6, Australia in 1956/7 and 1959/60 and West Indies in 1958/9. In his first series, against England, he batted excellently to score 387 runs (55.28), including 140 in his second match at Bombay and 111 in the fifth match at Madras, when India recorded her first-ever Test victory. The following English season, however, he suffered five 'ducks' in his seven Test innings, including 'spectacles' at Old Trafford. He rediscovered his touch against West Indies in 1952/3 when he made 383 runs (47.87), incuding 85 and 150 in the final run-feast at Kingston, adding 237 in 4 hours and 15 minutes with Vijay Manjrekar, India's highest for the second wicket in Tests. In India's inaugural series in Pakistan, 1954/5, he made most runs, 272 (34.00) and again in a first series, against New Zealand in 1955/6, scored 301 runs (72.25), including 100 in the fourth match at Calcutta, followed by 173 at Madras, when he put on 413 in a day and a half for the first wicket with Vinoo Mankad, which remains a record for all Tests. Against West Indies in 1958/9 he made 334 runs (33.40), including 90 in 7 hours 25 minutes in the first match, at Bombay, as the mainstay of a negative policy; and in England the following season he scored 1,207 runs (28.73), though failing in all the Tests, bar the first at Trent Bridge, when he top-scored each time in an Indian debacle with 54 and 49. In his last full series, against Australia, he made 263 runs (26.30). Much more consistent in the Ranji Trophy competition, he made 5,149 runs (66.01), including 21 centuries, his career-highest being 202 not out against Orissa in 1963/4.

First-class career (1946-68): 11,868 runs (42.38) including 33 centuries, and 21 wickets (30.85)
Test matches (43): 2,442 runs (32.56), including 5 centuries, 1-66 and 16 catches

ROY, Pronob Pankaj (b.1957)

Bengal

Son of Pankaj, Pronob is also a right-handed opening batsman from Bengal. A patient and technically correct player, he announced himself as a possible Test player by scoring 140 against a strong Commonwealth team in 1980/81 in a match to raise funds for flood relief. His chance for India came the following season against England at Madras, when he was out for six in a large Indian total of 481-4. He had, however, spent 82 minutes wearing down the new-ball fast bowlers, so if this was no success it was not a failure either. A confident 60 not out in the second innings confirmed that he could be at home in Test cricket; but in England in 1982 he could find no form at all, scoring only 174 runs from 12 first-class innings.

First-class career (1978-): 1,599 runs (34.76) including 5 centuries, and 12 catches
Test matches (2): 71 runs (33.50) and 1 catch

SARDESAI, Dilip Narayan (b.1940)

Bombay

A cool-headed right-handed batsman of sound technique, Dilip Sardesai was a wristy exponent of cover-drives and rippling glances, and a good gully or outfield. He was a very heavy scorer in the Ranji Trophy competition. On his debut in first-class cricket in 1960/61 he scored 87 for Combined Universities against Pakistan. In 1961/2 he made the highest score of his career, 281 against Gujerat. He toured the West Indies in 1961/2 and 1970/71, England in 1967 and 1971 and Australia in 1967/8, and at home he played against England in 1961/2, 1963/4 and 1972/3, Australia in 1964/5 and 1969/70, New Zealand in 1964/5 and West Indies in 1966/7. His first success in Tests was not until his visit to the Caribbean in 1961/2 when, in the third match, at Bridgetown, he opened and scored 60 in a total of 187. Against England in 1963/4, he made 449 runs (44.90), five times exceeding 50. He accomplished little against Australia the following season, but he led the averages against New Zealand soon afterwards, with 359 runs (119.66); dismissed for 88 – 209 behind – in the third match, at Bombay, India were indebted to his 200 not out in the second innings, an effort which saved the match and almost made a victory possible. He had no luck in England in 1967, when after falling down the stairs at Lord's he had to miss the first Test, and he then broke a finger in the second which necessitated his return home. A poor tour of Australasia followed and he lost his regular place for India until he came back as his country's rescuer in every crisis during the series in the West Indies in 1970/71, his Test record being 642 runs (80.25); but for his partnerships with Eknath Solkar, India could well have lost the first, second and fourth Tests. He made his Test-highest at Kingston, 212 in a total of 387, and also scored 112 at Port of Spain and 150 at Bridgetown. However, on his last tour, of England in 1971, he did not recapture this form, scoring 144 runs (29.40) in the Tests. After one match against England in 1972/3 he dropped out of Test cricket, but continued in the Ranji Trophy competition, reaching 3,599 runs (54.53).

First-class career (1960-73) 10,231 runs (41.75) including 25 centuries
Test matches (30): 2,001 runs (39.23) including 5 centuries, 0-45 and 4 catches

SARWATE, Chandrasekhar Trimbak (b.1920)

Central Provinces and Berar, Maharashtra, Bombay and Holkar

For one of his slight stature, Chandra Sarwate was a powerful right-handed batsman, often opening for his State, hitting hard between mid-on and mid-off and to square-leg. He was also a leg-break bowler with a generally low trajectory, able to turn the ball sharply. He toured England in 1946 and Australia in 1947/8, and at home he played against West Indies in 1948/9 and England in 1951/2. In England he took 37 wickets (25.37) and, usually batting at number ten, made 382 runs (23.87), appearing in one Test without distinction. His great match was against Surrey at The Oval when, with the score faltering at 205 for 9 wickets, he and Shute Banerjee added 249 in three hours ten minutes for the last wicket, which remains a record in England. Sarwate made 124 not out and took 5 for 54 in Surrey's second innings. In Australia he opened the batting regularly, in the third Test, at Melbourne, putting on 124 for the first wicket with Vinoo Mankad. At home, however, he achieved little in Tests. Making his debut in the Ranji Trophy competition at sixteen, he took 5 for 33 for C.P. and Berar against Hyderabad, and subsequently became a prolific run-getter and wicket-taker, captaining Holkar (Madhya Pradesh) in due course. His career-highest was 246 for Holkar against Bengal in 1950/51. Against Mysore in 1945/6 he took 9 for 61 in an innings. In Ranji Trophy matches he made 4,923 runs (43.18), including 12 centuries, and took 281 wickets (27.42). By profession he is a fingerprint expert.

First-class career (1936-69): 7,430 runs (32.73) including 14 centuries, and 494 wickets (23.42)
Test matches (9): 208 runs (13.00) and 3 wickets (124.66)

SAXENA, Ramesh Chand (b.1944)

Delhi and Bengal

A right-handed batsman of natural grace and skill, who made 113 aged sixteen against Southern Punjab in 1960/61 on his debut in the Ranji Trophy competition, Ram Saxena was also an occasional leg-break bowler and a good field at cover. He toured England in 1967, scoring 238 runs (23.80), in his sole Test, the first, at Headingley, scoring 9 and 16 and taking 0 for 11.

First-class career (1960-): 7,796 runs (40.18) including 16 centuries, and 33 wickets (28.21)

SEN, Probir (1926-70)

Bengal

Rather stockily built, 'Khokhan' Sen's uncanny anticipation and nimble footwork as wicket-keeper led to catches and stumpings that altered the courses of many matches. A useful right-handed batsman, he was also an occasional bowler, and once, as captain of his State, performed a first-class hat-trick against Orissa in 1954/5 in the very last over, having given his gloves to a fielder. He toured Australia in 1947/8 and England in 1952, and at home played against West Indies in 1948/9, England in 1951/2 and Pakistan in 1952/3. In the fifth Test, at Melbourne, in 1947/8 he took 4 catches in Australia's sole innings of 575 for 8 declared – and let through only 4 byes. In the last Test at Madras against England in 1951/2, when India defeated England for the first time, he stumped 5 (4 in the first innings), all off Mankad. Although he scored 1,796 runs (30.44) in the Ranji Trophy competition, he made no long scores in Tests. He died after a heart attack, following a day's cricket at Calcutta.

First-class career (1943-58): 2,580 runs (23.24) including 3 centuries, and 143 dismissals (107 ct, 36 st.)
Test matches (14): 165 runs (11.78) and 31 dismissals (20 ct, 11 st.)

SENGUPTA, A.K. (b.1939)

Services

A very good all-rounder, right-handed opening batsman, leg-break and googly bowler and slip field, Sengupta made his debut in first-class cricket as a military cadet for Services against West Indies in 1958/9, scoring 35 and 100 not out, and in his first Ranji Trophy match – in the same season – he took 6 for 32 against Delhi. In his first season he played in the third Test, at Madras, against West Indies, scoring 1 and 8. After this bright start his career faded.

First-class career (1958-68): 1,695 runs (26.48) including 2 centuries, and 21 wickets (31.14)

SHARMA, Parthasarthy (b.1948)

Rajasthan

A solidly built and sound right-handed batsman, Sharma first played for India in one Test against the West Indies at Delhi in 1974/5 when he did well, scoring 54 and 49. In another Test in the West Indies in 1975/6 he was less successful, although on the tour he averaged 43.50. Against England's fast bowlers at home in 1976/7 he did as well as most after regaining his Test place with a century (111) at Ahmedabad against the touring team, but 62 runs in four innings were not enough and, after two Indian defeats, Sharma was one of the casualties. He has, however, been a consistent batsman in domestic cricket, and a useful right-arm medium-paced bowler.

First-class career (1964-) 7,341 runs (39.25) including 14 centuries, and 152 wickets (25.31)
Test matches (5): 187 runs (18.70), 0-8 and 1 catch

SHASTRI, Ravishankar Jayadritha (b.1962)

Bombay

At the age of 19 Ravi Shastri made a sensational start to his Test career. Pulled out of a Ranji Trophy match to fly to New Zealand to take the place of two injured spinners, he arrived on the eve of the Wellington Test and took six wickets for 63 runs in the match, including a spell of three wickets in four balls. Nine more wickets followed in the next two Tests. A tall, gangling figure, he bowls very accurate, rather flat, slow left-arm orthodox and bats right-handed with solid calm. He captained India's Under 19 side in Sri Lanka in 1980/81 and could well be a future Test captain. At home against England in 1981/2 he played in all six Tests and was consistently useful with bat or ball. His 12 wickets, however, cost 38 runs each and he lacked the flight and subtlety of his spinning partner, Doshi. In the third Test in Delhi, batting at number eight, he made 93. In the final of the 1981/2 Duleep Trophy he confirmed his growing authority with the bat, scoring a valuable 66 in The Oval Test. His four Test wickets, however, were gained at 68 runs apiece. He was omitted from India's side in a Test against Sri Lanka in 1982/3, but subsequently toured the West Indies.

First-class career (1979-): 988 runs (24.70) including 1 century, and 112 wickets (25.16)
Test matches (12): 281 runs (21.61), 31 wickets (32.70) and 7 catches

SHINDE, Sadashiv Garpatrao (1923-55)

Baroda and Bombay

Tall and rather frail in appearance, Sadu Shinde was a very thoughtful right-arm leg-break bowler whose googly – delivered in two different ways – was difficult to detect, but who tended to lose his length after punishment. He was also a useful tail-end batsman. He toured England in 1946 and 1952, playing in three Tests, and at home played against West Indies in 1948/9 and England in 1951/2 when, in the first Test, at Delhi, his flight and spin kept everyone struggling; he took 6 for 91 in 35.3 overs in the first innings. In the Ranji Trophy competition his most succesful bowling was 8 for 162 for Bombay against Gujerat in 1950/51. He died suddenly of typhoid.

First-class career (1940- 55): 871 runs (14.04) and 230 wickets (32.59)
Test matches (7): 85 runs (14.16) and 12 wickets (59.75)

SHODHAN, Roshan Harshadial (b.1928)

Gujerat and Baroda

A competent left-handed batsman and medium-pace bowler, 'Deepak' Shodhan scored a spirited 110 in his first Test, the fifth against Pakistan, at Calcutta, in 1952/3, when runs were badly needed. He toured the West Indies a few months later but, although he hit 45 in the first Test at Port of Spain, he achieved little else and was not persevered with by the Indian selectors. In some sixteen years in the Ranji Trophy competition he made 1,235 runs (33.37) and took 59 wickets (30.32).

First-class career (1946-62): 1,821 runs (31.94) including 4 centuries, and 73 wickets (34.05)
Test matches (3): 181 runs (60.33) including 1 century, 0-26 and 1 catch

SHUKLA, Rakesh (b.*c*.1951)

Delhi and Bihar

A tidy and skilful right-arm leg-break and googly bowler, Rakesh Shukla has been unlucky not to receive greater recognition for his useful all-round cricket over several years. His most heroic effort came in the 1981/2 Ranji Trophy final against Karnataka when, going in at number nine with the score at 548 for 7, he shared a ninth-wicket stand of 118 with Rajesh Peter to win the match on first innings. His sole Test to date was played against Sri Lanka at Madras in 1982/3. He did not bat but in a high-scoring draw took 0-70 and 2-82.

First-class career (1969-): 2,411 runs (28.36) including 4 centuries, and 211 wickets (23.14)

SOHONI, Sriranga Wasudeo (b.1918)

Maharashtra, Baroda and Bombay

Not tall, but exceptionally broad-shouldered and

moving with a back straight as a guardsman's, 'Ranga' Sohoni was a right-arm fast-medium bowler with an effectively accelerating run and a good sideways action, who preferred bowling with the old ball. Confident and free-scoring, he usually opened the batting for his State, although in Tests he generally batted in the lower reaches. He was also an excellent outfield. He toured England in 1946 and Australia in 1947/8, and at home played against England in 1951/2. On the England tour he was rarely successful and also achieved little in Australia. Making his debut in the Ranji Trophy competition at seventeen, he later captained Maharashtra and Bombay in turn, and altogether in the competition made 2,162 runs (34.87), including 7 centuries, and took 139 wickets (24.49).

First-class career (1935-64): 4,245 runs (28.68) including 8 centuries, and 232 wickets (32.34)
Test matches (4): 83 runs (16.60), 2 wickets (101.00) and 2 catches

SOLKAR, Eknath Dhondu (b.1948)

Bombay and Sussex

Eknath Solkar was a solid, dogged and courageous left-handed batsman, sound in technique, a left-arm medium-pace bowler and a brilliant, agile and fearless short-leg fieldsman. He rose from changing the score-boards at Bombay Hindu Gymkhana (where his father was an employee) to being coached at twelve by Vinoo Mankad, helping Bombay to win the Ranji Trophy for the tenth time in a row, and becoming first choice for India for six packed years. The figures he produced in runs and wickets were often less important than his fielding close to the leg-side to the Indian spinners. He toured the West Indies in 1970/71 and 1975/6 and England in 1971 and 1974, and at home played against Australia in 1969/70, New Zealand in 1969/70, England in 1972/3 and 1976/7 and West Indies in 1974/5. He first impressed as a batsman of Test calibre in the Caribbean on his first visit, with 224 runs from the five matches. With Dilip Sardesai he time and again rescued India from perilous positions. By now he was opening the bowling (with moderate results) with Abid Ali; and in England in 1971 these two gentle medium-pacers saw the shine off the ball before the famous spin bowlers took over. In the Tests Solkar made 168 runs (42.00) and took 6 wickets (22.83); at Lord's he scored 67, sharing in a partnership of monumental patience with Gundappa Viswanath of 92 that saw India gain a first innings lead for only the second time in a Test in England, and at The Oval he bowled tightly in the first innings for 3 for 28 (his best for India) and hit 44, his country ultimately winning her first Test in England. Continuing to open the bowling with Abid Ali against England in 1972/3 – although he failed to take a wicket in any of the five Tests – he hit 75 in the first, at Delhi. On his second England tour, although he was, perhaps, the best fielder on the side, he achieved little beyond taking the wicket of Geoffrey Boycott three times in successive innings. Against West Indies, in the fifth Test at Bombay in 1974/5, he made a dour 102 – his sole Test century. The rest of his Test career was anticlimactic but he remained a force in the Ranji Trophy competition. Recommended to Sussex as a professional by the younger Nawab of Pataudi, he played for the second XI for two seasons. With no vacancy for a further overseas player, his registration was then terminated.

First-class career (1965-81): 6,851 runs (29.27) including 8 centuries, 276 wickets (30.01) and 182 catches
Test matches (27): 1,068 runs (25.42) including 1 century, 18 wickets (59.44) and 53 catches

SOOD, Man Mohan (b.1939)

Delhi

A competent right-handed batsman, Sood's sole Test was the fourth against Australia, at Madras, in 1959/60, when he scored 0 and 3.

First-class career (1956-66): 1,214 runs (28.23) including 1 century

SRIKKANTH-KRISHNAMACHARI (b.1959)

Tamil Nadu

A smiling cavalier of a batsman with a wide array of brilliant strokes, Srikkanth was a controversial choice to open India's innings against England in the first four Tests of 1981/82. He made a delightful 65 at Bangalore but his technique was more that of a gifted club cricketer than a hardened professional, and he temporarily lost his place. Srikkanth made his first-class debut in 1978/9, and scored 90 and 37 against the Pakistan touring team a season later. In 1980/81 he scored more than 50 in five of his six Ranji Trophy innings, including 172 against Karnataka. He missed selection for the Indian tour of England in 1982, but again showed his ability when hitting 57, 95, 92 against Sri Lanka in three one-day internationals in 1982/3, and he was selected for India's tour of Pakistan.

First-class career (1978-): 1,467 runs (39.64) including 2 centuries
Test matches (4): 119 runs (19.83), 0-10 and 1 catch

SRINIVASAN, Thirumalai Echambadi (b.1950)

Tamil Nadu

A sales executive with a Madras piston firm,

Srinivasan was an unexpected choice as a utility batsman on the tour of Australia and New Zealand in 1980/81. A dashing right-hander, he gained his place with a century in the Irani Trophy. In his sole Test, against New Zealand at Auckland, he scored 29 and 19, but he distinguished himself in several appearances in one-day internationals on the tour, batting usefully and fielding brilliantly. Also an occasional leg-spinner, Srinivasan played league cricket for Woodhouse in the Yorkshire League, and has played Grade cricket in New South Wales.

First-class career (1970-): 2,998 runs (35.69) including 4 centuries

SUBRAMANYAM, Venkatraman (b.1936)

Mysore (Karnataka)

A tall, adventurous right-handed batsman with a good eye and powerful wrists, a medium-pace leg-break change-bowler and a reliable field, Subramanyam toured England in 1967 and Australasia in 1967/8, and at home played against New Zealand in 1964/5 and West Indies in 1966/7. In the third match, at Madras, against West Indies he hit 61 courageously without inspiring much confidence. Generally disappointing overseas, his best effort in Tests was at Adelaide in the first Test of 1967/8 when he hit a gallant 75 in a losing cause. A prolific batsman in both Ranji and Duleep Trophy competitions, he made 213 not out against Madras in 1966/7. He made 2,261 runs (39.67) in the Ranji Trophy competition.

First-class career (1959-70): 4,219 runs (31.72) including 8 centuries, and 70 wickets (44.18)
Test matches (9): 263 runs (18.78), 3 wickets (67.00) and 9 catches

SUNDERAM, Gundibail Rama (b.1930)

Bombay

A competent right-arm fast-medium bowler and useful tail-end batsman, Sunderam played in two Tests against New Zealand in 1955/6 with little success.

First-class career (1951-68): 558 runs (14.68) and 127 wickets (26.10)
Test matches (2): 3 runs (—) and 3 wickets (54.66)

SURENDRANATH, R. (b.1937)

Services

A happy cricketer, Surendranath was a slimly built right-arm fast-medium in-swinging bowler who had great stamina but tended to bowl too much down the leg-side, a tail-end batsman of good sense and a very good close field. He toured England in 1959, and at home played against West Indies in 1958/9, Australia in 1959/60 and Pakistan in 1960/61. His best series was in England, when he headed the Test averages with 16 wickets (36.62). Swinging the ball in a sweltering atmosphere at Old Trafford in the fourth Test, he captured 5 for 115 in 47.1 overs (in a total of 490). Again in hot weather in the next match at The Oval, he took 5 for 75 in 51.3 overs (25 maidens) in a total of 361. In the Ranji Trophy competition he took 178 wickets (20.67).

First-class career (1955-69): 1,351 runs (15.70) including 1 century, and 284 wickets (24.95)
Test matches (11): 136 runs (10.46), 26 wickets (40.50) and 4 catches

SURTI, Rusi Framroz (b.1936)

Gujerat, Rajasthan and Queensland

An exuberant character, Rusi Surti was a forceful left-handed batsman especially at the expense of fast bowlers, a useful left-arm medium-pace or slow bowler who sometimes opened India's attack, and an excellent field at cover, often picking up the ball beautifully and hitting the wicket with an unerring throw. He toured the West Indies in 1961/2, England in 1967 and Australasia in 1967/8, and at home played against Pakistan in 1960/61, England in 1963/4, New Zealand in 1964/5 and 1969/70, Australia in 1964/5 and 1969/70 and West Indies in 1966/7. Outstanding for his ground fielding in the Caribbean, he made 246 runs (24.60) in the Tests. The climax of his career came in Australasia, when he scored more runs than anybody else, 967 (37.19), and took 42 wickets (29.73); in the Tests against Australia and New Zealand he was the most successful run-maker with 688 runs (45.50), besides taking 18 wickets (35.77). In the fourth Test at Auckland he was missed twice on 99 and was then caught still one short of his century (it remained his Test-highest). He was not considered for Tests after 1969 as he was, by then, living in Australia. His career-highest was 246 not out for Rajasthan against Uttar Pradesh in 1959/60. In all Ranji Trophy matches he scored 2,293 runs (32.75).

First-class career (1956-73): 8,066 runs (30.90) including 6 centuries, and 285 wickets (36.94)
Test matches (26): 1,263 runs (28.70), 42 wickets (46.71) and 26 catches

SWAMY, V. N. (b.1924)

Services

A competent right-handed batsman and fast-medium bowler, Swamy's sole Test was the first ever against New Zealand at Hyderabad in 1955/6, when he did not bat and took 0 for 45.

First-class career (1951-9): 201 runs (14.35) and 68 wickets (22.16)

TAMHANE, Narendra Shanker (b.1931)

Bombay

Originally a right-arm slow bowler, Tamhane became wicket-keeper in an emergency and developed as one of the best in India. His virtues were safe hands and neatness of execution. He was also a useful batsman. While still a Bombay student, he caught 3 and stumped 4 in the first unofficial Test against the Commonwealth at New Delhi in 1953/4, and he was a regular choice for official Tests from 1954 until 1960. He toured Pakistan in 1954/5 and England in 1959, and at home played against New Zealand in 1955/6, Australia in 1956/7 and 1959/60, West Indies in 1958/9 and Pakistan in 1960/61. Against Pakistan at Bahawalpur in the second Test he top-scored with 54 not out, his only substantial score in Tests. In the first match, at Dacca – his debut – he had 5 victims; in the third at Lahore 5; and in this (his first) series 19 victims. In England he dismissed 49; in the two Tests he played he accounted for 6 of the 18 wickets to fall. On his debut in the Ranji Trophy competition, against Baroda in 1953/4, he had 7 victims (6 caught, 1 stumped). He collected 253 dismissals in first-class cricket between 1951 and 1969; and his career-highest was 109 not out against Baroda in 1958/9.

First-class career (1951-69): 1,460 runs (18.25) including 1 century, and 253 dismissals (175 ct, 78 st.)
Test matches (21): 225 runs (10.22) and 51 dismissals (35 ct, 16 st.)

TARAPORE, Keki Khursedji (b.1910)

Bombay

A competent right-handed batsman and slow left-arm bowler, Tarapore's sole Test was the first against West Indies, at Delhi, in 1948/9, when he scored 2 and took 0 for 72. Active in cricket administration, he managed the Indian team to England in 1967.

First-class career (1937-49): 441 runs (11.30) and 148 wickets (28.77)

UMRIGAR, Pahlan Ratanji (b.1926)

Bombay and Gujerat

A tall, powerful right-handed batsman, 'Polly' Umrigar was especially strong in front of the wicket and could demoralize all but the fastest bowlers; he was also a medium-pace bowler of out-swing and off-cut who was dangerous on a helpful wicket, a brilliantly versatile field, and a sometimes very shrewd captain, especially when leading Bombay to five successive Ranji Trophy victories commencing in 1958/9. He scored 115 not out for Indian Universities against West Indies in 1948/9, and by the mid-fifties had become the sheet-anchor of India's batting. When he retired he had scored more runs for his country than any other

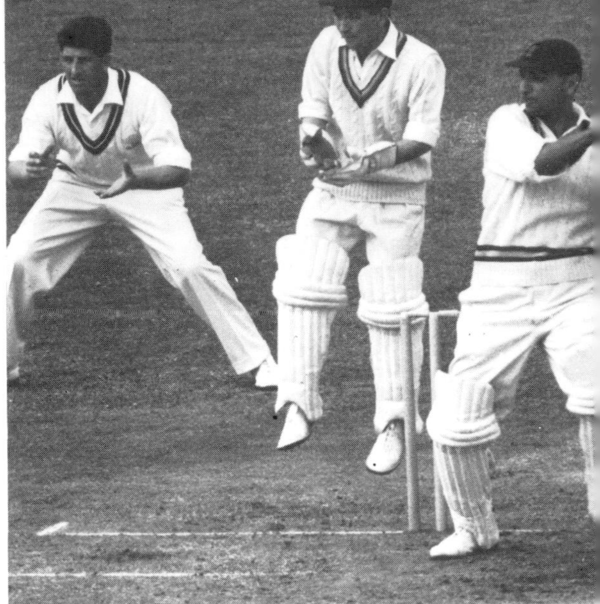

Polly Umrigar – Roy Swetman keeping wicket and Ken Barrington at slip (England)

batsman. He toured England in 1952 and 1959, the West Indies in 1952/3 and 1961/2, and Pakistan in 1954/5, and at home played against West Indies in 1948/9 and 1958/9, England in 1951/2 and 1961/2, Pakistan in 1952/3 and 1960/61, New Zealand in 1955/6, and Australia in 1956/7 and 1959/60. A heavy scorer against three Commonwealth sides, he first made his mark in official Tests, after several disappointing performances, in the fifth match against England, at Madras, in 1951/2 when he made 130 not out and India recorded their first-ever Test victory. On his first England tour he was easily the best batsman, in all first-class matches reaching 1,688 runs (48.22), including 5 centuries, 3 exceeding 200, but he was a failure in the Tests. On his first visit to the Caribbean, he made 560 runs (62.22) in the Tests, including 130 and 69 in the first Test at Port of Spain. On the first visit to Pakistan he again headed the batting, in the Tests alone making 271 runs (54.20), including 108 in a total of 245 in the fourth match at Peshawar, besides taking 8 wickets (30.37), including 6 for 74 in 59 overs in the second match at Bahawalpur. In India's first Test against New Zealand at Hyderabad he hit 223, his Test-highest, in about eight and a half hours, adding 238 for the third wicket with Vijay Manjrekar. In this series he scored 351 runs (70.20), and succeeded to the captaincy after the first match. Altogether, he led his country eight times against New Zealand, West Indies and Australia, winning two games and losing two. On his second England tour he started in a blaze of glory, scoring over 800 runs, including two double centuries, in May, but was overwhelmed by fast bowling more than once in the Tests and missed the last few matches through injury. Despite this, he was the heaviest run-getter with 1,826 runs (55.33), including three double centuries and in four Tests he made 230 runs, including 118 in the fourth, at Old Trafford. A set-back against Australia was followed by 382 runs (63.66) against Pakistan including 115 at Kanpur, 117 at Madras and 112 at Delhi. In the second Test, at Kanpur, against England, he made 147 not out, his third century in successive Test innings; in this series he made 254 runs (50.80). On his second West Indies tour he headed the batting with 445 runs (49.44), besides taking 9 wickets (27.66). In the fourth match, at Port of Spain, he scored 56 and 172 not out (the latter in about four hours) and captured 5 for 107 in 56 overs. A prolific all-rounder in the Ranji Trophy competition, he made 4,102 runs (70.72), including 14 centuries, the highest being 245 against Saurashtra in 1957/8, and took 138 wickets (19.72). He was a national selector and team manager.

First-class career (1944-68): 16,154 runs (52.27) including 49 centuries, and 326 wickets (25.61)
Test matches (59): 3,631 runs (42.22) including 12 centuries, 35 wickets (42.08) and 33 catches

VENGSARKAR, Dilip Balwant (b.1956)

Bombay

A tall, slim, orthodox right-handed batsman, who early in his career often opened the batting but who developed into India's regular number three, Dilip Vengsarkar times the ball with the skill of a high-class player. He drives, glances and hooks gracefully and he confirmed the great ability he has shown at home by playing exceptionally well in England in 1979. He first toured New Zealand and the West Indies in 1975/6 as a very inexperienced batsman, with modest success. He showed his courage briefly against England in 1976/7, when his hand was broken by a ball from Bob Willis in the Madras Test, and established himself as a Test cricketer in Australia in 1977/8, making 589 runs (32.72) in first-class matches and 320 in the Tests at 35.55. At home against the West Indies in 1978/9, he became a senior player after making 83 and 76 in the course of three Tests in Pakistan. In the six Tests against the West Indies he made 417 runs (59.57), including 2 centuries, 157 not out at Calcutta and 109 in the fifth match, at Delhi. In England in 1979 he retained the number three position in the Indian order, hitting 103, including 13 attractive fours, in the second innings of the Lord's Test and adding 210 for the third wicket with Viswanath to help save the match. In the series he scored 249 runs at 41.50 in four Tests. Further Test hundreds followed in 1979/80: 146 not out against Pakistan at Delhi, and 112 against Australia at Bangalore. He had a disappointing tour of Australia and New Zealand in 1980/81, but batted consistently well against England both at home and away in 1981/2, scoring 157 at Lord's.

First-class career (1975-): 8,344 runs (47.14) including 22 centuries, and 105 catches
Test matches (52): 2,964 runs (38.49) including 6 centuries, 0-13 and 42 catches

Venkat

VENKATARAGHAVAN, Srinivasaraghavan (b.1946)

Tamil Nadu (Madras) and Derbyshire

A charming, intelligent man with a natural dignity, 'Venkat' has been internationally popular except with commentators who do not like tongue-twisters. A slim, sinewy man with long fingers which he always brushes through his long dark hair as he walks back before each delivery, Venkat is an orthodox and very accurate off-spinner; making a brief approach to the stumps before delivering with a high arm, he turns the ball more than most of his kind and is always liable to run through a side when conditions help him. He has taken more than 1,300 first-class wickets and has bowled effectively and tidily all round the world. He captained India in England in 1979 and proved a calm, sensible and shrewd leader, but was replaced as captain for the following series against Australia. Although beaten by an innings in the first Test at Edgbaston, India came close to what would have been the most glorious victory in all Test cricket when falling only nine runs short of the 438 they needed to win in the fourth innings at The Oval. Venkat had called for a 'positive attitude' from his batsmen and, partly as a result, a hitherto disappointing tour ended on a very high note. He made his first Test appearance against New Zealand in 1964/5 at Madras. In the following game at Calcutta he took 3 for 86 and 3 for 15 in 17 overs and in the fourth Test at Delhi he took 8 for 72 in the first innings and 12 for 152 in the match. Expensive against the West Indies at home in 1966/7, he toured England in 1967, playing in two Tests but taking only 20 wickets on the tour. A home series against New Zealand in 1969/70 again brought the best out of him, notably at Nagpur where he took 9 for 133. In the Hyderabad Test he top-scored with 25 in India's total of 89. At home against Australia in the same season he was under-bowled but took 12 wickets at 26.66, and on the bland wickets of the Caribbean in 1970/71 he was outstanding, taking 22 Test wickets at 33.81. In the fifth Test at Port of Spain he not only took 6 for 111 but made 51 and 21. In 1971 in England he was preferred to Prasanna in all three Tests, taking 13 wickets at 26.92 and 63 in first-class matches. Against England at home in 1972/3 and 1976/7 and away in 1974 he was disappointing, and was overshadowed by Prasanna, yet against New Zealand in 1976/7 he took 11 wickets (28.00) in three Tests, and at Madràs in the third made 64, his highest Test score. In 1978/9 he re-established himself as the first choice off-spinner, taking 20 wickets in the six Tests at home to the West Indies. Apart from his sensible captaincy in England in 1979, he had once earlier captained India when they were defeated by an innings by the West Indies at Delhi in 1974/5. Such mercurial ups and downs have been typical of his career. Away from Tests, Venkat also captained India in the 1975 Prudential World Cup and has captained Tamil Nadu since 1970. He had taken 5 or more wickets in an innings 64 times by the start of the 1979/80 season, his best figures being 9 for 93 against Hampshire at Bournemouth for the 1971 Indian team. In his three seasons in county cricket he took 154 Championship wickets for Derbyshire. As a batsman, his best score to date is 137 runs, made against Kerala in the 1970/71 season.

First-class career (1963-   ): 6,566 runs (17.84) including 1 century, and 1,320 wickets (24.65)
Test matches (47): 722 runs (13.12), 139 wickets (33.35) and 36 catches

VISWANATH, Gundappa Ranganath (b.1949)

Mysore (Karnataka)

The man with the most consecutive Test appearances and the first Indian to score a century against all India's Test opponents, Gundappa Viswanath has had a glittering Test career and has seldom looked back for long since the day in Kanpur in November 1969 when, having made nought in his first Test innings, he scored 137 in the second, becoming the sixth Indian to record a century in his first Test. A scintillating little player, 'Vishy', who married the sister of India's other little master, Sunil Gavaskar, is a right-handed number four batsman with wrists of steel who hits the ball with a wondrous touch and timing, especially through the covers off either foot. Like Gavaskar his judgement of length, his footwork and his balance are superb, but Vishy is the more likely

Gundappa Viswanath

to give the bowler a chance by flashing unwisely outside his off-stump. Vishy stands only 5ft 4ins high, a dark-eyed genius with a drooping black moustache. A leg-break bowler strictly in the nets only, he is a safe slip fielder and a determined but philosophical competitor. After making 334 runs in his first Test series he toured the West Indies in 1970/71 and England in 1971 with relatively modest results. At home against England in 1972/3 he scored 365 runs (40.55) including 113 and 48 at Bombay, and after averaging 33 in the series in England in 1974 he hit 568 runs in ten Test innings in 1974/5 against the West Indies, including 139 at Calcutta and 97 not out in a total of 190 at Madras. In the West Indies a year later he made 255 runs (42.50), including 112 at Port of Spain on the famous occasion when India scored 406 for 4 to win the match. In 1976/7 India played three Tests against New Zealand, in which Viswanath scored 324 runs at 64.80 with 103 not out at Kanpur, but in the five Tests against England which followed he suffered an inexplicable loss of form, his only substantial innings – 79 at Bangalore – coinciding with India's only win in the series. Back to his best in Australia in 1977/8, he made 473 runs in six Tests at 52.55, with a highest score of only 89. However he scored 145 against Pakistan at Faisalabad in 1978/9 in the first Test between the two countries since 1961, and against the West Indies at home the same season he made 124 out of 255 at Madras in the fourth Test and 179 at Kanpur in the sixth. In the series he scored 497 runs at 71.00 and he continued his good form in England in 1979 when he batted consistently throughout the series for 341 runs (48.71), scoring 113 to save India from defeat at Lord's. He remained an automatic selection for India in the early 1980s, though there were clear signs that his concentration and speed of footwork were waning and his performances became increasingly inconsistent. Yet he enjoyed a successful home series against Australia in 1979/80, scoring 518 runs (74.00) in the six Tests, making 161 not out at Bangalore and 131 at Delhi. In Australia and

New Zealand in 1980/81 he played only one major innings in six Tests, a brilliant 114 at Melbourne, but at home against England the following year he countered a threat to his place by hitting 107 when India were in trouble in Delhi and a dazzling 222 at Madras, his highest Test score, sharing a stand of 415 for the third wicket with Yashpal Sharma. He not only scored a century on his Test debut but also in his first appearance in a first-class match, when, for Karnataka against Andhra in 1967/8, he made 230. He surpassed this exactly ten years later with 247 against Uttar Pradesh.

First-class career (1967-): 16,162 runs (42.08) including 40 centuries, 15 wickets (44.86) and 201 catches
Test matches (85): 5,946 runs (43.40) including 14 centuries, 1-46 and 62 catches

VIZIANAGRAM, Maharajah Sir Vijaya (1905-65)

United Provinces

A well-built, bespectacled right-handed batsman who was able to cut and hit to leg effectively, 'Vizzy' was a great patron though never a really first-class player. He formed his own team to tour India in 1930/31; made handsome donations to the Indian Board of Cricket Control; was appointed vice-captain of the Indian team to England in 1932 and then withdrew at the eleventh hour; and eventually captained the 1936 team to England. It was not a particularly happy side, and just before the first Test he sent home the outstanding all-rounder Lala Amarnath for alleged indiscipline. 'Vizzy' himself achieved little in the three Tests. He was successively a broadcaster, politician and administrator of the game.

First-class career (1930-36): 1,228 runs (18.32)
Test matches (3): 33 runs (8.25) and 1 catch

WADEKAR, Ajit Laxman (b.1941)

Bombay

Standing a little over six feet and strongly built, Ajit Wadekar, or 'Professor', was a cool, reserved character. A stylish left-handed batsman with a sound temperament, he was a hard-hitting stroke-player despite a short backlift, who treated each ball on its merits and seldom missed the chance to drive a half-volley. An occasional slow bowler, he was also an excellent close field and a calm and determined captain. He toured England in 1967, 1971 (captain) and 1974 (captain), Australasia in 1967/8 and the West Indies in 1970/71 (captain), and at home he played against West Indies in 1966/7, New Zealand in 1969/70, Australia in 1969/70 and England in 1972/3 (captain). Altogether he led India in sixteen Tests. After a modest start to his Test career in 1966/7 he scored well in the Tests making 242 runs (40.33) for the weaker side, his best effort being 91 in the second at Lord's after India had followed on. In Australasia he scored freely but had only one notable Test innings – a brisk 99 in the second match, at Melbourne. In New Zealand, however, he made his maiden Test century, 143 in six and a quarter hours, in the third match, at Wellington. He had dominated the bowlers in the first match at Dunedin with 80 and 71, India winning abroad for the first time. In a bowlers' series at home against New Zealand he was chief batsman with 167 runs (27.83); and again made most runs, 336 (37.33), when Australia toured soon afterwards. As skipper in the Caribbean, he made 625 runs (44.64) in all first-class matches, but was below his best in the Tests, though India won their first rubber against West Indies. In England in 1971 he scored 204 runs (34.00) in the Tests, more than anyone else, including 85 in the first match at Lord's, and 48 and 45 invaluably at The Oval when India won their first Test in England. At home a life-size statue was erected in his honour. In all first-class matches on the tour he made 1,057 runs (40.65) and held 23 catches. Against England in India – another victorious rubber – he made 312 runs (34.66) in the Tests. Captain for the last time against England in 1974, his team remained undefeated by any county, but lost all three Tests. At the end of this tour he retired from first-class cricket, having been deposed as captain of Bombay. He had won three series and lost one. Ajit Wadekar's highest score was 323 against Mysore in 1966/7 in a Ranji Trophy match, and in this competition he amassed more than 4,000 runs.

First-class career (1958-75): 15,380 runs (47.03) including 36 centuries, 21 wickets (43.23) and 270 catches
Test matches (37): 2,113 runs (31.07) including 1 century, 0-55 and 46 catches

Ajit Wadekar

WAZIR ALI, Syed (1903-50)

Southern Punjab

An attractive right-handed batsman with a keen eye and plenty of powerful strokes, including a splendid off-drive, a medium-pace change-bowler who maintained an excellent length and a good field, Wazir Ali toured England in 1932 and 1936, and at home played in the 1933/4 series against England. He led India against the unofficial Australians in 1935/6. He was the elder brother of S. Nazir Ali and the father of Khalid Wazir of Pakistan.

First-class career (1922-41): 6,906 runs (38.36) including 20 centuries, and 33 wickets (29.81)
Test matches (7): 237 runs (16.92), 0-25 and 1 catch

YADAV, Nandlal Shivlal (b.1957)

Hyderabad

A steady off-spinner, Shivlal Yadav has a good action and has never been afraid to give the ball air, but lacks any vicious spin and has found taking wickets hard at top level – despite an auspicious first Test against Australia at Bangalore in 1979/80 when he took seven wickets for 81. He finished the series with 24 wickets at 24 runs each but was given little opportunity in Australia in 1980/81, playing in two Tests and breaking his toe while batting in the third and last game. He was disappointing against England, playing against them in the Golden Jubilee Test of 1979/80 and in one of the 1981/2 Tests without taking a wicket. In England in 1982 he took only 7 wickets at 86 each and was not chosen for the Tests.

First-class career (1977-): 602 runs (18.81) and 110 wickets (35.12)
Test matches (15): 207 runs (15.92), 41 wickets (35.34) and 4 catches

YAJURVINDRA SINGH, Jaswantsingh (b.1952)

Maharashtra and Saurashtra

A capable right-handed batsman, medium-pace change-bowler and brilliant close field, Yajurvindra Singh played twice against England in 1976/7, in his first Test at Bangalore taking 7 catches at short-leg, and equalling the innings and match catching records for non-wicket-keepers. Despite few opportunities on the 1979 tour of England, he took over from the injured Mohinder Amarnath at The Oval for the fourth and final Test and again showed his brilliance at short-leg, standing fearlessly still by the batsman's hip pocket.

First-class career (1971-): 3,445 runs (42.01) including 7 centuries, and 48 wickets (31.50)
Test matches (3): 94 runs (18.80), 0-21 and 10 catches

YASHPAL SHARMA (b.1954)

Punjab

Small but wiry, Yashpal Sharma is a neat and attractive right-handed batsman with good balance and timing, and a fine array of strokes, especially to the on-side. He was given little opportunity when he toured Pakistan at the end of 1978, but an innings of 135 not out for North Zone against the West Indies touring team at Jullunder early in 1979 helped him to earn a place in the touring team to England and he made rapid strides towards establishing himself as a regular Test batsman, making 884 runs at 58.93 on the tour and playing in the last three Tests of the series, scoring 102 runs at 25.50. He maintained consistent form against Pakistan at home in 1979/80, averaging 39 in the six Tests although a big score eluded him, and later in the same season scored his first Test century in his seventh Test, against Australia at Delhi. In Australia in 1980/81 he was a failure in the three Tests, despite scoring 201 not out against Victoria at Geelong, and at the end of the tour was dropped after one further failure against New Zealand. It was believed that he was particularly vulnerable to short-pitched fast bowling, but he seemed to lay that bogey against England at home in 1981/2, when he made a comeback to the Test team for the last two matches. In three innings he scored 220 runs, including a very determined 140 at Madras when he shared a record third-wicket stand of 415 with Viswanath. Less successful against England in 1982, he nevertheless held his place against Sri Lanka and on the 1982/3 tour of Pakistan.

First-class career (1973-): 5,376 runs (47.57) including 12 centuries, and 20 wickets (31.65)
Test matches (26): 1,217 runs (35.79) including 2 centuries, 0-1 and 8 catches

YOGRAJ SINGH, Bhagsingh Bhundel (b.1958)

Haryana

A well-built right-arm fast-medium bowler and useful late-order batsman, Yograj was given an early chance at a representative level when playing for Combined Universities against MCC at Nagpur in 1976/7. For two years thereafter injury and poor form kept him out of first-class cricket but he re-emerged to win a place on the 1980/81 tour of Australia and New Zealand. He took 13 wickets in seven first-class matches on a disappointing tour for him. His sole Test to date, against New Zealand at Wellington, was relatively unsuccessful. He scored 6 and 4, and took 1 for 63. In 1979/80 he produced his best figures: 7 for 36 against Jammu and Kashmir.

First-class career (1976-): 184 runs (11.50) and 39 wickets (28.48)

PAKISTAN

ABDUL KADIR (b.1944)

Karachi

A wicket-keeper and sound right-handed batsman, Abdul Kadir had a memorable Test debut, against Australia at Karachi in 1964/5, when he was run out for 95, having put on 249 for the first wicket with Khalid Ibadulla on the first day. But in the first match ever between the two countries in Australia, at Melbourne six weeks later, he was dismissed for a duck. He also played against New Zealand in 1964/5, putting together a careful innings of 58 in the second match at Auckland.

First-class career (1961-72): 1,523 runs (28.73) including 1 century, and 59 dismissals (46 ct, 13 st.)
Test matches (4): 272 runs (34.00) and 1 stumping

ABDUL QADIR (b.1955)

Lahore and Habib Bank

A stocky leg-spin and googly bowler of high class with a quirky, bounding action, an authentic looping flight and well disguised 'wrong 'un', Abdul Qadir can be a true matchwinner, as he was when taking 8 for 29 and 4 for 86 for Habib Bank against Universities at Lahore in 1977/8. In this same season he made his Test debut against England at Lahore and in the second Test at Hyderabad took 6 for for 44 to bowl England out for 191 in the first innings. In the series he took 12 wickets at 25.41 but, plagued by an injury early in the tour, he was a great disappointment in England in 1978, taking only 6 wickets on the tour at 66.00. He had been hampered by a shoulder injury which continued to worry him for some time; but it was a very different story when next he visited England four summers later. Then, he was the sensation of the tour, bamboozling county batsmen quite unfamiliar with a good leg-break bowler, embarrassing England's best players too at times and always entertaining the crowd with his idiosyncratic approach to the stumps and boyish enthusiasm. With a flipper and two different top spinners to add to his basic repertoire of leg break and googly he was too much even for Australians brought up on a larger diet of this type of bowler. Following his 57 wickets in 12 matches in England, taken at 20.82 (his 10 wickets in three Tests cost double this but had an effect of unsettling the batsmen which the figures do not reveal) he took 22 wickets in three home Tests against Australia, all won, later in 1982, more than seven Australian bowlers could manage between them. His return to international cricket came as a result of an outstanding home season in 1981/2 when he took 87 wickets (18.49). A useful, right-handed batsman, he scored a century in his second first-class match.

First-class career (1975-): 1,987 runs (20.69) including 1 century, and 470 wickets (19.08)
Test matches (14): 217 runs (13.56), 54 wickets (30.93) and 6 catches

Abdul Qadir

AFAQ HUSSAIN (b.1939)

Karachi Blues and Pakistan International Airlines

A useful right-arm off-break bowler and batsman, Afaq Hussain played in the first official Test against England in Pakistan at Lahore in 1961/2, top-scoring with 35 not out in the second innings. He toured Australasia in 1964/5 with little success.

First-class career (1957-74): 1,448 runs (24.54) including 1 century, and 214 wickets (19.42)
Test matches (2): 64 runs (—), 1-106 and 2 catches

AFTAB BALOCH (b.1953)

National Bank of Pakistan and Pakistan International Airlines, Karachi and Sind

A prolific batsman in domestic cricket, Aftab Baloch will no doubt be best remembered for his monumental innings of 428 for Sind against Baluchistan in 1973/4, the sixth highest first-class score ever. A very sound right-handed batsman and occasional off-break bowler, he played in two Tests five years apart, against New Zealand at Dacca in 1969/70, when at 16 years 191 days, he became the second youngest Test cricketer ever, and against West Indies in 1974/5, when he hit 60 not out. He was an outstanding captain of the National Bank side in the Qaid-e-Azam Trophy.

First-class career (1969-): 7,607 runs (43.46) including 19 centuries, 179 wickets (30.35), 115 catches and 3 stumpings
Test matches (2): 97 runs (48.50) and 0-17

AFTAB GUL (b.1946)

Lahore

A stocky, right-handed opener, Aftab Gul, although over-impetuous on occasions, was often a reliable and effective batsman. He toured England in 1971, coming second in the batting with 1,154 runs (46.16), sharing in some splendid attacking opening partnerships with Sadiq Mohammad, but his highest score in the Tests was only 33. At home he played against England in 1968/9 and New Zealand in 1969/70 without much success. In 1968/9, while a Law student at Punjab University, he became the first player to appear in first-class cricket while on bail for alleged political activities. Such was his following, indeed, as a student leader that it was said that Pakistan officials did not dare to play the Lahore Test without him.

First-class career (1964-78): 6,129 runs (36.92) including 11 centuries, and 14 wickets (33.21)
Test matches (6): 182 runs (22.75), 0-4 and 3 catches

AGHA SAADAT ALI (b.1929)

Bahawalpur, Lahore

A sound right-handed batsman and reliable fielder, Agha Saadat Ali played in a single Test, the third against New Zealand at Dacca in 1955/6, scoring 8 not out and holding 3 catches.

First-class career (1949-62): 325 runs (14.13)

AGHA ZAHID (b.1953)

Lahore University

A sound right-handed opening batsman and occasional medium-pace bowler, Agha Zahid played in a single Test, the first against West Indies, at Lahore, in 1974/5, scoring 14 and 1.

First-class career (1970-): 8,205 runs (42.73) including 21 centuries, and 39 wickets (28.43)

ALIMUDDIN (or Alim-ud-Din) (b.1930)

Rajasthan, Gujerat and Karachi

A stocky right-handed opening batsman, always ready to play his strokes, and a magnificent fielder, Alimuddin was amongst the earliest prominent Pakistani cricketers. He represented Rajasthan (Rajputana) in India's Ranji Trophy competition in 1942/3 aged twelve! He hit 85 for Pakistan against Ceylon at Karachi in 1949/50 and toured England with the Pakistan Eaglets in 1953. In England, with the first Pakistan Test team in 1954, he started in tremendous form, scoring 142 at Worcester and 51 and 100 not out against Cambridge University at Fenner's in the opening matches and, although he failed in the Tests, he made 1,083 runs (30.94). Afterwards, he toured the West Indies in 1957/8, India in 1960/61 and England again in 1962, and at home played against India in 1954/5, New Zealand in 1955/6, Australia in 1956/7 and 1959/60, West Indies in 1958/9, and England in 1961/2. In the first official series in Pakistan, against India, he was the best batsman on either side, with 332 runs (41.50), including 103 not out in the fifth match at Karachi. In the West Indies he failed to find his best form but, after losing his place, he came back with 50, 109 and 53 in successive innings against England at Dacca and Karachi in 1961/2. On his second Test tour of England, his only notable achievement was in the third Test, at Headingley, when he scored 50 and 60 out of totals of 131 and 180 respectively. After captaining Karachi 'B', he became for a while National Cricket Coach.

First-class career (1942-68): 7,276 runs (32.77) including 14 centuries, and 40 wickets (24.00)
Test matches (25): 1,091 runs (25.37) including 2 centuries, 1-75 and 8 catches

AMIR ELAHI (1908-80)

Baroda, Northern India and Southern Punjab

See India section.

ANWAR HUSSAIN (b.1920)

Northern India, Bombay and Karachi

A sound right-handed batsman and fast-medium seam bowler, Anwar Hussain appeared in the Ranji Trophy before Partition – making his debut for Northern India in 1940/41 – and he played in Pakistan's first official home series, against India, in 1952/3, without much success.

First-class career (1940-55): 1,466 runs (27.14) and 34 wickets (36.32)
Test matches (4): 42 runs (7.00) and 1-29

ANWAR KHAN (b.1955)

Sind, National Bank and Karachi

A tall right-arm fast-medium bowler, Anwar Khan is a lower-order carefree batsman. Touring New Zealand and Australia in 1979, he played in one Test at Christchurch as substitute for the absent Imran Khan, making 12 and 3 not out and bowling only four overs without taking a wicket.

First-class career (1972-): 1,878 runs (24.71) including 1 century, and 172 wickets (27.15)

ARIF BUTT (b.1944)

Lahore

A persevering right-arm fast-medium bowler and useful tail-end batsman, Arif Butt was a member of the first-ever Pakistan team to visit Australasia, in 1964/5, when, despite an injury, he took 31 wickets (23.32) in nine matches, including 6 for 89 in the first innings of the first Test in Australia at Melbourne and 6 for 108 in the first match that was played against New Zealand, at Wellington.

First-class career (1960-78): 4,017 runs (29.10) including 4 centuries, and 201 wickets (26.79)
Test matches (3): 59 runs (11.80) and 14 wickets (20.57)

ASHRAF ALI (b.1958)

Railways

Beefy of build, and unusually large for a wicket-keeper, Ashraf Ali came to national prominence in 1980/81 when, in addition to 37 dismissals, he scored 1,053 runs, topping the batting averages in the Qaid-e-Azam Trophy (49.19). A right-hander with considerable flair, his highest score in that season was 137 and he was chosen to tour Australia where, because of his superior batting, he was preferred to Wasim Bari as wicket-keeper in several one-day internationals. He made his first Test appearances in the last two games of Pakistan's inaugural (home) series against Sri Lanka. He was a great success as a batsman, scoring 58, 29 not out, and 45 not out in a total of 500 runs at Lahore. In the circumstances it was quite surprising that he was not selected for the subsequent tour of England.

First-class career (1974-): 2,317 runs (38.61) including 1 century, and 93 dismissals (65 ct, 28 st.)
Test matches (2): 132 runs (132.00) and 5 dismissals (3 ct, 2 st.)

ASIF IQBAL RAZVI (b.1943)

Hyderabad, Karachi, Pakistan International Airlines, National Bank and Kent

An exciting stroke-playing right-handed batsman, graceful, attacking and very quick on his feet, Asif Iqbal was also a useful second-line seamer, brilliant all-purpose field and shrewd captain who led Kent for more than one successful season and brought Pakistan close to the semi-final of the 1979 Prudential World Cup. A smiling cavalier figure, there was charm in every action he made. Asif was at the forefront of the fight for better pay for Pakistan's professional cricketers, and a leading light in Kerry Packer's World Series Cricket, who came back to Test cricket after announcing his retirement. A nephew of Ghulam Ahmed, the Indian off-spinner, Asif was brought up in Hyderabad in Southern India and played for them in the Ranji Trophy from 1959 before emigrating to Pakistan in 1961. On his Test debut for Pakistan against Australia at Karachi in 1964/5 he went in number ten, scoring 41 and 36, and formed a rather unlikely opening bowling partnership with Majid Khan: both became much better known for their batting. Asif, however, continued to be a serious bowler, taking 18 Test wickets in three matches in New Zealand in 1964/5, at Wellington taking 5 for 48 and 7 for 33. It was really in England in 1967 that he showed for the first time that he could be a batsman of world class, making 76 at number nine in the Lord's Test, sharing a stand of 130 with Hanif Mohammad (still a Pakistani record for the eighth wicket), and then at The Oval, when Pakistan were 65 for 8 in their second innings and still 159 behind England, sharing a dazzling stand of 190 in 175 minutes with Intikhab Alam for the ninth wicket and scoring himself 146 not out, including 2 sixes and 21 fours. In the first innings of the same match, still taking the new ball, he had taken 3 for 66 in 42 overs. When he next met England at home in 1968/9 he batted at number four. But much of his best form over the years has been shown in England, both for Kent and Pakistan. He joined Kent in 1968, playing a prominent role in many county successes, and scoring more than 1,000 runs in a season six times. His second Test century against England came at Edgbaston in 1971, 104 not out. He made two more Test centuries in the 1972/3 season, 175 against New Zealand at Dunedin and 102 against

Asif Iqbal

England at Lahore. But his best season was the busy one of 1976/7 when in three different series he hit 4 centuries. Touring Australia that season he made 313 runs in three Tests at 78.25, including 152 not out at Adelaide, and 120 in the third Test at Sydney when Pakistan defeated Australia away from home for the first time. The Pakistan team moved on to the Caribbean where Asif was less successful, yet still scored 135 in the fifth Test at Kingston. In 1978/9, returning to Test cricket after the Pakistan Packer players had been recalled, he made 104 at Napier to rescue his side against New Zealand and 134 not out in a total of 285 at Perth. Almost all Asif's greatest innings were played in perfect tune with the occasion and the position of the match. His stance at the crease became more open with the years and some of his strokes to the leg-side grew more rugged than graceful but the exceptional speed of eye and feet remained. He ran superbly between wickets.

First-class career (1959-82): 23,375 runs (37.28) including 45 centuries, 291 wickets (30.15) and 304 catches
Test matches (52): 3,308 runs (39.85) including 11 centuries, 51 wickets (28.03) and 32 catches

ASIF MASOOD (b.1946)

Lahore and Northumberland

Tall, well-built and with a flowing moustache and long black hair, Asif Masood was a right-arm fast-medium bowler, hostile with the new ball, who started his run with an eccentric double-chassis. His swing and movement off the pitch could have the best batsmen groping but he relied mainly on varying his angle of attack, using the full width of the crease. He toured England in 1971 and 1974 and Australia in 1972/3 and 1976/7, and at home he played against England in 1968/9 and 1972/3, New Zealand in 1969/70 and West Indies in 1974/5. His Test debut was the first against England, at Lahore, in 1968/9 when, in a riotous atmosphere, he broke through the batting in the second innings, taking 3 good wickets. On his first England tour he took 13 Test wickets (26.46) but on his second England tour he was less effective. His Test career ended disappointingly on his second Australian tour. Among his best feats were 8 for 65 for Punjab University against Rawalpindi in 1970/71 and 5 for 65 for Pakistan against Rest of the World at Karachi the same season.

First-class career (1963-77): 635 runs (8.69) and 305 wickets (29.02)
Test matches (16): 93 runs (10.33), 38 wickets (41.26) and 5 catches

AZHAR KHAN (b.1955)

Lahore, Punjab, Combined Universities, Pakistan International Airlines and Habib Bank

A reliable and talented all-rounder, by the end of 1981/2 Azhar Khan had included a 209 not out among his nine first-class hundreds. He has also on three occasions taken 5 or more wickets in an innings. A right-handed batsman and right-arm off-break bowler, he first played for Lahore in 1971/2. His sole Test was played against Australia at Lahore in 1979/80. In his only innings he scored 14 and, in his three overs in the game, took one wicket for two runs.

First-class career (1971-): 4,193 runs (37.10) including 9 centuries, and 74 wickets (23.13)

AZMAT RANA (b.1951)

Bahawalpur, Pakistan International Airlines, Lahore and Muslim Commercial Bank

The younger brother of Shafqat Rana, Azmat is a neat and consistent left-hand batsman who has played with steady success in Pakistan domestic cricket since his first appearance in 1969/70. His 14 centuries include one of 206 not out, and also a century in each innings (100 and 100 not out) for MCB against Rawalpindi at 'Pindi in 1981/2. His only Test was played at Lahore against Australia in 1979/80. He scored 49 in his sole innings, did not bowl and took no catches.

First-class career (1969-): 5,102 runs (48.13) including 14 centuries

D'SOUZA, Antao (b.1939)

Karachi and Pakistan International Airlines

A very useful right-arm medium-fast bowler who

sometimes bowled slower off-breaks, and a tail-end batsman difficult to dismiss. Antao d'Souza toured England in 1962, taking 58 wickets (34.79), though he was ineffective in the Tests. Undefeated in five of his six innings in the Tests, he headed the averages with 53. Against England at home in 1961/2 he took 9 wickets (22.88) from two Tests, in the third at Karachi capturing 5 for 112 in 57.5 overs in a total of 507. He played once against West Indies in 1958/9.

First-class career (1956-66): 815 runs (18.95) and 190 wickets (26.03)
Test matches (6): 76 runs (38.00), 17 wickets (43.82) and 3 catches

EHTESHAM-UD-DIN (b.1950)

Lahore, Punjab, Pakistan International Airlines and National Bank

A right-arm medium-paced bowler of portly build, but with a good action, Ehtesham belied his unathletic appearance with some steady performances for Pakistan until a tragi-comic appearance in the 1982 Leeds Test when, called from the Bolton Association as a late replacement but hopelessly overweight and unfit, he pulled a muscle in the field and limped painfully out of the game. A record-breaker in the League, with 128 wickets in 1981 and 127 in 1982, he had been due to play in his own benefit match that same weekend, but instead of being a local hero he became something of a public laughing-stock. This was a shame for, in his previous Tests against Australia and India, he had performed a valuable stock bowling role, taking 14 wickets in three Tests at 19.28 against India in 1979/80. In domestic cricket in 1981/2 he took 77 wickets (18.18) in only 13 matches.

First-class career (1969-): 1,008 runs (12.14) and 399 wickets (20.43)
Test matches (5): 2 runs (1.00), 16 wickets (23.43) and 2 catches

FAROOQ HAMID (b.1945)

Lahore

A competent right-arm fast-medium bowler, Farooq Hamid toured Australasia in 1964/5, in all first-class matches collecting 11 wickets (33.09) and in his sole Test, against Australia at Melbourne, scoring 0 and 3 and taking 1 for 107.

First-class career (1961-70): 546 runs (13.00) and 111 wickets (25.16)

FARRUKH ZAMAN (b.1956)

North West Frontier Province

A left-arm spinner, Farrukh Zaman took 3 for 80 and 4 for 37 for the NWFP Chief Minister's XI against New Zealand's touring team in 1976/7 and was impressive enough in winning the match to appear in the second Test at Hyderabad. However he was given very little chance, bowling only ten overs in the match, taking none for 15, not batting and not taking any catches. This has been his sole Test.

First-class career (1971-): 537 runs (11.42) and 123 wickets (32.76)

FAZAL MAHMOOD (b.1927)

Northern India, Punjab and Lahore

Solid in build and character, with striking green eyes, Fazal Mahmood was known as 'the Alec Bedser of Pakistan' and was the most successful right-arm fast-medium bowler produced by his country before the 1970s. Now a senior Police Inspector, he was not so massive as Bedser in build, but his methods bore a distinct similarity. Both were masters of nagging, persistent length and concentrated on varied swing and a mixture of leg-cutters and break-backs. Fazal had no equal on matting and could be equally devastating on grass; determined, disciplined and demanding, but always cheerful, he was also a hard-hitting lower-order batsman and very good field. Before Partition he represented Northern India in the Ranji Trophy competition. A certainty for the tour of Australia in 1947/8, he stood down owing to the announcement of Partition. In 1949/50 he was the leading bowler on Pakistan's visit to Ceylon, and, when Ceylon returned the visit in 1950, he took 20 wickets in two representative matches. In 1951/2 he captured 6 for 40 in 26 overs for Pakistan against MCC at Karachi, helping his country to victory. Once official Tests began, he toured India in 1952/3 and 1960/61, England in 1954 and 1962, and the West Indies in 1957/8, and at home played against India in 1954/5, New Zealand in 1955/6, Australia in 1956/7 and 1959/60, West Indies in 1958/9 and England in 1961/2. In the first official tour of India he was dominant with 20 wickets (25.51) in the Tests, besides making 173 runs (28.83). In the second match, at Lucknow, he had matchwinning figures of 5 for 52 and 7 for 42. On the first tour of England he took 77 wickets (17.53) from sixteen first-class games, the four Tests bringing him 20 wickets (20.40), half of Pakistan's total of wickets. In the famous Pakistan victory at The Oval, Fazal took 12 for 99 (6 for 53 and 6 for 46). In the first official series at home against India, he captured 15 wickets (22.06) in four Tests. At Karachi against Australia in 1956/7 he was never mastered, taking 6 for 34 in 27 overs and 7 for 80 in 48 overs (13 for 114 in 75 overs), and Pakistan defeated Australia in their first-ever encounter. In a losing cause in the Caribbean he captured 20 wickets (38.20) in the Tests – in the third match at Kingston sending down 85.2 overs and taking

Fazal Mahmood

2 for 247 – and hit a determined 60, his Test-highest, in the second match at Port of Spain. From 1958/9 until 1960/61 he led Pakistan in ten Tests against West Indies, Australia and India as A.H. Kardar's successor – winning two and losing two; he was dropped from the captaincy when all five Tests with India (in 1960/61) were drawn. Earlier he had led Pakistan to success against the West Indies at home, taking 12 wickets (15.85) from his three Tests. In his final series as captain his bowling had lost penetration and he was severely criticized as leader. He played once against England in 1961/2; and, on the 1962 England tour, after two opening bowlers had broken down, he was flown over as replacement but, by this time, he was only a shadow of his former self and could not live up to expectations.

First-class career (1943-64): 2,602 runs (23.02) including 1 century, and 460 wickets (19.18)
Test matches (34): 620 runs (14.09), 139 wickets (24.70) and 11 catches

GHAZALI, Mohammed Ebrahim Zainuddin (b.1924)

Services

A forcing right-handed batsman, useful off-break bowler and an excellent field, Mohammed Ghazali toured England in 1954, making 601 runs (28.61) and taking 17 wickets (39.64); he also played in two Tests, in his second at Old Trafford being dismissed for a pair and not taking a wicket.

First-class career (1942-56): 1,569 runs (25.72) including 2 centuries, and 62 wickets (33.11)
Test matches (2): 32 runs (8.00) and 0-18

GHULAM ABBAS (b.1947)

Karachi

A left-handed batsman, strong off the back foot and a splendid cover-driver, an occasional slow bowler and reliable field, Ghulam Abbas was a student when he toured Ceylon in 1964, Australasia in 1964/5 and England in 1967. In England he made 871 runs (34.84), in his sole Test, his third, at The Oval, scoring 12 and 0.

First-class career (1962-80): 5,249 runs (36.20) including 9 centuries

GUL MAHOMED (b.1921)

Baroda, Hyderabad and Punjab 'B'

See India section.

HANIF MOHAMMAD (b.1934)

Bahawalpur and Pakistan International Airlines

Perhaps the best of four brilliantly gifted brothers who played cricket for Pakistan (Mushtaq, Sadiq and Wazir were the others), Hanif Mohammad has been not just a national hero but a legend in Pakistan. Curly haired, with an open, boyish face, he was a small, compact, strong right-handed opening batsman with nearly all the shots in the use of which a rigid discipline was applied. He is one of only ten men to score a triple hundred in a Test match and has played both the longest and the highest innings in all first-class cricket. The latter was an innings of 499 for Karachi against Bahawalpur at Karachi in 1958/9. Always balanced and an unerring judge of the length of a ball, Hanif's bat often seemed impassable, certainly so even to the finest bowlers on the bland surfaces of his own land. But he proved his patience and skill all round the world. He scored 12 centuries in fifty-five Tests and 55 centuries in his career. He captained Pakistan in eleven Tests, winning two, losing two and drawing seven. He seldom took a risk, seldom gave an opponent a chance. Prolific even as a schoolboy, he first played for Pakistan at the age of 17 years 300 days against India at Delhi in 1952/3, scoring 287 runs (35.87) in the series and hitting 4 centuries on the tour, including 203 against the Bombay Cricket Association. He toured England for the first time in 1954, making 1,623 runs in first-class games but only 181 in the four Tests. He showed English spectators something of his monumental patience in making 59 in 314 minutes in the Lord's Test. Back at home he scored his first Test century, 142, against India at Bahawalpur in 1954/5 and the following season made 103 against New Zealand at Dacca. In the West Indies in 1957/8, in the same series in which Sobers scored his 365, he batted the record time of 16 hours 10 minutes to make 337 in a Pakistan total of 657 after they had followed on 473 runs behind. He shared in four century partnerships in

Hanif Mohammad

that innings and his score is the third highest in Test cricket. In the series Hanif made 628 runs at 69.77. When he injured his knee in the first Test against the West Indies at Karachi in 1958/9, after scoring 103 in the first innings, he was forced to miss the rest of the rubber: he had to this point played in each of the twenty-four Tests played by Pakistan. The following season he scored 304 runs (60.80) at home against Australia (including 101 not out in a total of 194 for 8 declared in the third Test) and he was prolific in India in 1960/61, amassing 410 runs (51.25) in the series, including 160 in the first Test at Bombay. Against England in 1981/2 he drove bowlers to distraction, making 407 runs (67.83) including 111 and 104 in the second Test at Dacca when he batted in all for 14 hours and 53 minutes. English bowlers avenged themselves at home in 1962, when Hanif for once failed in the Tests. He captained Pakistan for the first time against Australia at Karachi in 1964/5 and later the same season at Melbourne he not only led the side but scored 104 and 93 and kept wicket throughout in place of Abdul Kadir, who had injured himself batting, taking five catches, four in one innings! On the same tour he hit 100 not out at Christchurch to mark Pakistan's first visit to New Zealand, and when New Zealand paid a return visit in 1964/5 Hanif made 203 not out in a total of 385 for 7 at Lahore. He added 217 for the sixth wicket with Majid Khan. Captain in England in 1967 he made 187 not out at Lord's off 556 balls in 542 minutes, by now batting at number four. His last appearance in a Test, against New Zealand at Karachi in 1969/70, marked the first appearance of his youngest brother Sadiq, with whom he opened the batting. Mushtaq also played, only the third time that three brothers have played in the same Test. (The others were the Graces and the Hearnes.) There were some internal politics, according to some accounts, in his final departure.

First-class career (1951-76): 17,059 runs (52.32) including 55 centuries, 53 wickets (28.58), 177 catches and 12 stumpings
Test matches (55): 3,915 runs (43.98) including 12 centuries, 1-95 and 40 catches

HAROON RASHID (b.1953)

Karachi, Sind, National Bank, Pakistan International Airways and United Bank

A tall, strapping man with heavy jowls and striking eyes, Haroon Rashid is a powerful right-handed batsman and a devastating destroyer on good wickets, but so far a failure in England where the ball moves so much. A magnificent stroke-player, he first made his mark with an innings of 130 for National Bank against Bahawalpur at Bahawalpur in 1972/3. He toured Australia and West Indies in 1976/7, scoring an impressive 57 in his first Test innings at Sydney where, in the third Test, Pakistan won a Test in Australia for the first time. He moved up the order to number three or four, playing in all five Tests against the West Indies and making some useful scores. Against England at home the following season he became a senior batsman in the absence of players contracted to Kerry Packer, and Haroon responded with scores of 122, 45 not out (at Lahore), 108, 35 (at Hyderabad) and 27 in his only innings at Karachi. However in England in 1978, Haroon's hitherto concealed technical deficiencies

Haroon Rashid

were exposed and he never mastered England's seam attack, making only 33 runs in five Test innings. Even then, however, he hit one majestic hooked six into the Lord's Grandstand which will not be forgotten by those who saw it. He failed again in two home Tests against Australia in 1979/80; but a players' dispute over the national captaincy enabled him to rehabilitate himself in 1981/2 by scoring 153, a commanding innings, in the first Test against Sri Lanka at Karachi. He played only one Test in England in 1982 but had a useful middle-order role against Australia in 1982/3, scoring 148 runs in three innings at 49.33. He is an outstanding fielder, especially at short-leg.

First-class career (1971-): 5,749 runs (35.93) including 14 centuries, 8 wickets (31.12) and 96 catches
Test matches (22): 1,217 runs (35.79) including 3 centuries, 0-3 and 16 catches

HASEEB AHSAN (b.1939)

Peshawar and Karachi

A very capable, patient and accurate right-arm off-break bowler in university and trophy cricket, Haseeb Ahsan toured the West Indies in 1957/8, India in 1960/61 and England in 1962, and at home played against West Indies in 1958/9, Australia in 1959/60 and England in 1961/2. His best tour was that of India, when he took most wickets in the Tests, 15 (32.66). He never relaxed his grip when India made 404 in the second match at Kanpur, bowling 5 for 121 in 56 overs. In England he suffered a foot injury in the opening match at Worcester and soon had to return home without playing in a Test.

First-class career (1955-63): 242 runs (5.62) and 142 wickets (27.70)
Test matches (12): 61 runs (6.77), 27 wickets (49.25) and 1 catch

IJAZ BUTT (b.1938)

Rawalpindi

A sound and enterprising right-handed batsman and deputy wicket-keeper, Ijaz Butt opened the batting in his first Test, against West Indies at Karachi in 1958/9, and with 41 not out helped to hit off the runs needed for a ten-wicket victory. His Test-highest was 58 against Australia in the third match, at Karachi, in 1959/60. When he toured England in 1962, he made 21 dismissals and 1,016 runs (28.22), which included a century before lunch against Kent at Canterbury; he achieved little, however, in the Tests. He captained Rawalpindi for several years.

First-class career (1955-68): 3,842 runs (34.30) including 7 centuries, and 71 dismissals (51 ct, 20 st.)
Test matches (8): 279 runs (19.92) and 5 catches

IJAZ FAQIH (b.1956)

Karachi, Sind, Public Works Department and Muslim Commercial Bank

A skilful all-round cricketer, Ijaz is a forceful right-handed batsman and an off-break bowler with subtle variations on a steady theme. His promise was evident at home against the West Indies in 1980/81 when he played his first Test at Karachi, though with little success. He toured with a BCCP XI in England in 1981 and played another Test in Australia in 1981/2, when he also bowled economically in the one-day internationals. In Pakistan he has a highest score of 183, in 1977/8, and in the following season he took 8 for 51 in an innings.

First-class career (1973-): 2,206 runs (30.21) including 3 centuries, and 210 wickets (26.70)
Test matches (2): 63 runs (15.75) and 1 wicket (85.00)

IMRAN KHAN (b.1952)

Lahore, Pakistan International Airways, Oxford University, Worcestershire and Sussex

One of Pakistan's greatest players and most successful captains, Imran is the cousin of Majid Khan. Handsome and immensely gifted, he can bowl genuinely fast for long periods with a long run and leaping action; he picks up and throws magnificently from the deep and is a batsman of high class. At Oxford University he won blues from 1973 to 1975, captaining in 1974, and he was very much the outstanding Oxford cricketer of his generation, scoring 117 not out and 106 in the match against Nottinghamshire in the Parks in 1974, and on the same ground that season hitting 170 against Northamptonshire. He first played for Worcestershire in 1971, was capped in 1976 but in 1977 moved to Sussex whom he greatly helped to win the Gillette Cup in 1978. Although a genuine all-rounder, his fast bowling has gradually assumed greater significance than his batting, although he often produces matchwinning performances in both roles, as at Worcester in 1976 when he scored 111 not out and took 13 for 99 in the match against Lancashire. He played first for his country in England in 1971, toured the United Kingdom again in 1974, Australia and the West Indies in 1976/7 and New Zealand and Australia in 1978/9. He was a prominent all-round figure in Kerry Packer's 'World XI' in 1977/8 and 1978/9. His first great triumph in Tests was his fast bowling performance at Sydney in 1976/7 when his superbly hostile efforts earned him 12 wickets for 165 in the third Test, enabling Pakistan to win on Australian soil for the first time. He has consistently taken wickets as Pakistan's main strike bowler, for many years forming an effective partnership with Sarfraz Nawaz, and would have scored still more prolifically in Tests if the batting strength above him had not been so great. He rescued Pakistan with his first Test century, 123

Imran Khan

against West Indies at Lahore in 1979/80, and the early 1980s saw him fitter, stronger and prouder than ever, reaching new peaks. In Australia in 1981/2 he was heroic in a losing cause, taking 16 wickets in three Tests at 19.50 and comparing favourably with all the Australian fast bowlers. He also made a valuable 70 not out at Melbourne, where Pakistan won. Back home at the end of the same season he returned after a players' dispute to devastate Sri Lanka at Lahore, taking 14 wickets for 116 in the match including 8 for 58, his best Test figures, in the first innings. Asked to captain Pakistan for the first time in England in 1982, he led from the front, learning from defeat in the one-day internationals and inspiring Pakistan to a memorable victory at Lord's. Pakistan were unlucky to lose the series 1-2, despite Imran's 21 wickets (18.57) including 7 for 52 at Edgbaston, and 212 runs (53.00); but at home against Australia he led his country to a crushing three-nil win early in the 1982/3 series. In three innings the triumphant captain averaged 64 with the bat and took 13 wickets at 13 each; but his was no longer a one-man show. Thanks greatly to him, Pakistan were at last really achieving what they were capable of.

First-class career (1969-   ): 11,534 runs (33.04) including 19 centuries, and 930 wickets (22.77)
Test matches (43): 1,606 runs (27.69) including 1 century, 192 wickets (24.78) and 12 catches

IMTIAZ AHMED (b.1928)

Northern India and Services

A shy man but one of the rocks on which Pakistan cricket was built, Imtiaz Ahmed missed only one of the first forty-two Tests played by his country. A right-handed batsman of great fighting qualities and a crowd-puller when in top form, he indulged in delightful sweeps and powerful hooks, especially against the best fast bowlers, but he was not always consistent. Safe and sound as a wicket-keeper, he played for Northern India at sixteen in the Ranji Trophy competition. For Pakistan he toured India in 1952/3 and 1960/61, England in 1954 and 1962, and the West Indies in 1957/8, and at home played against India in 1954/5, New Zealand in 1955/6, Australia in 1956/7 and 1959/60, West Indies in 1958/9 and England in 1961/2. On the first tour of England, he had 86 victims (80 while keeping wicket), the record for a visiting team. In the final match at The Oval, when England were beaten for the first time, he caught 7 behind the stumps – all off Fazal Mahmood. At home against India he made 233 runs (25.88) and disposed of 12 victims – mostly off Fazal. Against New Zealand he headed the batting with 284 runs (71.00), including the highest-ever made by a wicket-keeper in a Test, 209 in the second match at Lahore in six and a half hours. Facing a total of 348, Pakistan had been struggling at 111 for 6 when he and Waqar Hassan added 308 for the seventh wicket, which remains Pakistan's highest for that wicket. In the Caribbean he made 344 runs (38.22) in the Tests, including 122 as an opener in the third Test at Kingston. In India in 1960/61 he scored 375 runs (41.66) in the Tests. He was the rubber-losing captain against England in 1961/2, his only good score in the series being 86 in the third match at Karachi, but his 'keeping was as good as ever. In England the following season, though very disappointed at losing the captaincy, his Test record was 282 runs (35.25) and 7 victims. He came out of retirement to lead Pakistan against the 1963 Commonwealth side and Ceylon in 1964. His career-highest was a forceful 300 not out for The Prime Minister's XI against Commonwealth at Bombay in 1950/51. He has been Chairman of the Test selectors and has also had a book of poems published.

First-class career (1944-74): 10,383 runs (37.21) including 22 centuries, and 391 dismissals (315 ct, 76 st.)
Test matches (41): 2,079 runs 29.28) including 3 centuries, 0-0 and 93 dismissals (77 ct, 16 st.)

INTIKHAB ALAM (b.1941)

Karachi, Pakistan International Airlines and Surrey

A shy but engaging and universally popular character, Intikhab Alam, or 'Inti', was a high-class leg-spin and googly bowler and exceptionally hard-hitting right-hand batsman in the late middle-order. With receding hair, just under medium height, and built, it seems, of solid muscle, he was seldom injured. Intikhab first played in a first-class match for Karachi in 1957/8 aged 16 years 9 months, and apart from his wide experience

Intikhab Alam

with Surrey, where he was capped in his first year, 1969, he also played as a professional for West of Scotland. He captained Pakistan in seventeen Tests and with notable success in England in 1974 when the Pakistan team not only held their own in three drawn Tests but went through the seventeen matches of the tour without defeat, the only side to have achieved this since Sir Donald Bradman's of 1948. He had also been captain on the 1971 tour to England and he went on two earlier tours to England in 1962 and 1967. With other official Pakistan sides he toured Ceylon in 1964, Australia and New Zealand in 1964/5 and 1972/3, the second visit as captain, and Australia and the West Indies in 1976/7 where, after a split with other leading players who had demanded greater remuneration, he was a sad, isolated figure, given little opportunity. He had made a happier visit to Australia as vice-captain of the Rest of the World touring team in 1971/2. His long Test career began auspiciously when he bowled the redoubtable Colin McDonald of Australia with his first ball, but he was run out for nought in his first innings. In his second Test, the third against India at Calcutta a year later, he hit 56 as well as taking 4 for 68 in the match, but it took a long time for him to establish a regular place in the Pakistan side, and not until he took 7 for 92 in the third Test against New Zealand, at Karachi, in 1964/5 can he be said to have been a matchwinner as a leg-spinner. Test cricket was changing: the pitches in his native Pakistan were usually too slow to make him a real danger and in other countries often too green to allow the luxury of a flighty back-of-the-hand bowler. But his all-round efforts continued to be useful: 51 in a stand of 190 with Asif Iqbal at The Oval in 1967, the highest ninth-wicket stand in a Test; 4 for 117 in England's first innings at Lahore in 1968/9 and, as captain against New Zealand the following year, 10 for 182 (5 for 91 in each innings) in the third Test at Dacca. He led Pakistan to their first win in a rubber overseas in New Zealand in 1972/3 when his own role was decisive. At Dunedin in the second Test he took 7 for 52 (his best Test figures) and 4 for 78, and at Auckland in the next match 6 for 127. In March 1973 he also made his highest Test score, 138, against England at Hyderabad, including 4 sixes, in a match in which he also took 7 wickets. These early years of the seventies saw him at his peak. He took 104 wickets (28.36) in England in 1971, 32 of them for Surrey in the County Championship, which they won after a long break. The following season he recorded career-best figures of 8 for 54 for Pakistan against Tasmania at Hobart. He retired from Surrey after the 1981 season and a year later became official manager of Pakistan. Simultaneously Imran Khan became captain and the partnership of the two at the helm of Pakistan cricket proved all-conquering. The role of 'Inti' in this success was often overlooked.

First-class career (1957-81): 14,331 runs (22.14) including 9 centuries, 1,571 wickets (27.67) and 228 catches

Test matches (47): 1,493 runs (22.28) including 1 century, 125 wickets (35.93) and 20 catches

IQBAL QASIM (b.1953)

Karachi, Sind and National Bank

Only 5ft 6ins, Mohammed Iqbal Qasim is a very accurate left-arm spin bowler and fine close fielder. He toured Australia and the West Indies in 1976/7, taking 4 for 84 in 30 overs in the second innings of his first Test at Adelaide. At Melbourne in the next match Qasim took 4 for 111 and 3 for 19. In the West Indies he played with little success in the two Tests at Port of Spain, but the following season in Pakistan he played in all three Tests against England, taking 10 wickets. Disappointing in England in 1978, he took only 4 wickets in the three Tests and 7 on the short tour in nine matches. He was a regular member of the side at home to India in 1978/9, but though he toured New Zealand and Australia early in 1979 he was left out of the Test side. He made amends with 7 for 49 against Australia at Karachi in 1979/80 and 7 for 148 in the match against Australia at Melbourne in 1981/2. At home against Sri Lanka the same season he took 15 wickets in three Tests at 21.93 and, although he lost form in England in 1982, he returned to the side for two of the three home wins against Australia (1982/3).

First-class career (1971–): 1,170 runs (12.71) and 463 wickets (22.11)
Test matches (34): 269 runs (9.61), 112 wickets (29.47) and 25 catches

ISRAR ALI (b.1927)

Southern Punjab, Multan and Bahawalpur

A competent left-handed batsman, fast-medium bowler and close field, Israr Ali made his debut for South Punjab in the Ranji Trophy competition in 1946/7 before Partition. He toured India with the Pakistan side in 1952/3 but achieved little in two Tests. At home he appeared in two more Tests against Australia in 1959/60, taking 5 wickets inexpensively. Playing for Bahawalpur against Dacca University in 1957, he made 79 and took 6 for 1 in 11 overs, and took 9 for 58 against Punjab 'A' in the same season.

First-class career (1946–61): 1,132 runs (20.58) and 114 wickets (22.64)
Test matches (4): 33 runs (4.71) 6 wickets (27.50) and 1 catch

JALAL-UD-DIN (b.1959)

Industrial Development Bank of Pakistan

A right-arm fast-medium bowler who plays in glasses, Jalal-ud-Din had an outstanding season in 1981/2. He was called into the 1982 Pakistan touring team to England as a replacement and was prevented only by injury from playing in the Headingley Test. He made his first Test appearance, however, against Australia at Lahore in 1982/3, taking 5 for 92 in the match. He did not bat. Both his father and his brother played first-class cricket.

First-class career (1978–): 543 runs (16.68) and 124 wickets (22.48)

JAVED AKHTAR (b.1940)

Rawalpindi

A tall, well-built right-arm off-break bowler, Javed Akhtar flew to England on the eve of the third Test at Headingley in 1962 as replacement for the injured Haseeb Ahsan, but he met with little success and in his sole Test (at Headingley) scored 2 and 2 not out and took 0 for 52

First-class career (1959–76): 835 runs (15.75) and 187 wickets (18.16)

JAVED BURKI (b.1938)

Oxford University and Karachi

A solid and reliable right-handed middle-order batsman and an occasional medium-pace bowler, Javed Burki was an Oxford blue from 1958 to 1960. He toured India in 1960/61, England in 1962 and 1967, and Australasia in 1964/5, and at home he played against England in 1961/2, New Zealand in 1964/5 and 1969/70 and Australia in 1964/5. In his first series against India he made 325 runs (46.42) and in his second, against England in Pakistan, he was second to Hanif Mohammad with 340 runs (56.66), which included 138 in the first match at Lahore and 140 in the second at Dacca, both rather slow, painstaking knocks. Captain of the 1962 side in England, he played attractive cricket, making 1,257 runs (33.07), but his only success in the Tests was in the second match at Lord's when Pakistan, 270 behind on the first innings, lost four wickets cheaply and he made a defiant 101, adding 197 with Nasim-ul-Ghani. In Australasia he had a handsome tour aggregate of 843 runs (36.65), but failed in the Tests apart from a 'safety-first' 63 in the second match against New Zealand, at Auckland. On his second tour of England he had a lean time – 582 runs from 29 innings. His career-highest was 227 for Karachi Whites against Khairpur in 1963/4.

First-class career (1955–75): 9,426 runs (36.39) including 22 centuries, and 35 wickets (44.40)
Test matches (25): 1,341 runs (30.47) including 3 centuries, 0–23 and 7 catches

JAVED MIANDAD KHAN (b.1957)

Karachi, Sind, Habib Bank, Sussex and Glamorgan

A brilliant right-handed batsman with the full array of strokes and a buccaneering aggression, Javed Miandad may become one of the world's great batsmen in the 1980s. Small but wiry, a fine athletic cover fielder and useful leg-spin bowler, he is a most glorious cover-driver and square-cutter, and so precocious was his talent that he had scored 6 Test centuries before his twenty-second birthday. He appeared for the first time in first-class cricket for Karachi Whites in the Patron Trophy tournament at the age of sixteen and a half. While qualifying for Sussex in 1975 he scored 227 against Hampshire at Hove for Sussex 2nd XI, sending his opponents home gasping at his ability. Because of the glut of overseas players at Hove, however, his opportunities for Sussex were limited and in 1980 he moved to Glamorgan, captaining them for half the 1982 season. A more than useful member of the 1975 Pakistan Prudential World Cup side, he was accurate enough to bowl twelve overs of leg-spin for 42 runs against the might of the West Indies batsmen, but since his first Test in 1976/7 it has been his batting which has made headlines. He scored 163 against New Zealand in his first Test, at Lahore, and then in his third match made 206 to become, at 19 years 4 months, the youngest ever to hit a double century in a Test. Already, at the age of seventeen, he had scored 311 for Karachi Whites against National Bank. A relatively

Javed Miandad watched by Kapil Dev

lean period followed his magnificent start in Test cricket, especially in England in 1978, but in 1978/9 he scored four more Test centuries: 154 not out against India at Faisalabad; 100 at Karachi in the third Test of the same series; 160 not out at Christchurch against New Zealand; and 129 not out against Australia at Perth. Prematurely made captain of his country, he was not helped by his volatile temperament during 13 Tests as captain between 1979 and 1982, and he was deposed as a result of a players' revolt. He was involved in a flare-up with Dennis Lillee in Australia in 1981/2, when Pakistan lost the first two Tests, but won the last at Melbourne. Javed, with 205 runs in the Tests and 682 (75.77) in the first-class matches of a badly arranged tour, was the side's leading scorer. Not at his best in England, after being replaced as captain by Imran Khan in 1982, he returned to form with 138 against Australia at Lahore in 1982/3, although this was an uncharacteristically dogged innings.

First-class career (1973-): 17,169 runs (51.25) including 47 centuries, 181 wickets (32.49), 243 catches and 3 stumpings
Test matches (46): 3,398 runs (53.09) including 8 centuries, 17 wickets (36.65), 46 catches and 1 stumping

KARDAR, Abdul Hafeez (b.1925)

Northern India, Oxford University and Warwickshire
See India section.

KHALID HASSAN (b.1937)

Punjab
A promising right-arm leg-break and googly bowler and fine field, Khalid Hassan toured England with the first team in 1954, but never settled down, appearing to bowl a little too fast so that his length and direction suffered. In his sole Test, the second, at Trent Bridge, he scored 10 and 7 not out and took 2 for 116 (in 21 overs). At 16 years 352 days he remained for three years the youngest-ever to have played in a Test anywhere. He was not tried again for Pakistan.

First-class career (1953-62): 199 runs (13.27) and 31 wickets (40.87)

KHALID IBADULLA (b.1935)

Lahore, Warwickshire, Tasmania and Otago
Although never possessing the rare talent which could take a match or an innings and shape it as he wished, 'Billy' Ibadulla proved himself a serviceable cricketer for many different teams. He played for Pakistan in New Zealand in 1964/5 and England in 1967, toured India in 1952/3 without playing in Tests, and at home played once against Australia in 1964/5. He represented Warwickshire for sixteen years as a professional, and Tasmania and Otago as player/coach. A highly useful right-handed opening or middle-order batsman, medium-paced change-bowler and deputy wicket-keeper, he is a person of great natural dignity who has become an outstanding coach. He appeared in one match without success for Pakistan in India in 1952/3, but hit a splendid 166 on his official Test debut against Australia at Karachi in 1964/5, having been specially called from England. His score equalled the Pakistan record against Australia, and his opening partnership of 249 with Abdul Kadir set a new record for his country and remains the first-class record for Pakistan. Essentially associated with Warwickshire (from 1956 until 1972), he exceeded 1,000 runs in a season six times, with 2,098 runs (33.83) in 1962 as his best; and shared in two record partnerships for the county: 377 unbroken for the first wicket with N.F. Horner against Surrey at The Oval in 1960, and 402 for the fourth wicket with Rohan Kanhai against Nottinghamshire at Trent Bridge in 1968. His best bowling figures were 7 for 22 against Derbyshire at Chesterfield in 1967. He settled as a coach in New Zealand, and in 1982 joined the English first-class umpires' panel. His son has played first-class cricket.

First-class career (1952-72): 17,039 runs (27.31) including 22 centuries, 462 wickets (30.87) and 337 catches
Test matches (4): 253 runs (31.62) including 1 century, 1-99 and 3 catches

KHALID WAZIR (b.1936)

Karachi
A useful hard-hitting right-handed batsman, medium-pace change-bowler and good field, Khalid Wazir toured England with the first team in 1954 while a student, but achieved little; he played in two Tests but was not tried again for Pakistan. He is son of S. Wazir Ali (India).

First-class career (1952-4): 271 runs (15.05) and 14 wickets (53.28)
Test matches (2): 14 runs (7.00)

KHAN MOHAMMAD (b.1928)

Bahawalpur and Somerset

Helping to establish Pakistan cricket in company with his fast-medium bowling partner, Fazal Mahmood, Khan was also right-arm but, though steady and accurate and able to swing the ball considerably in a heavy atmosphere, was subject to strains, injuries and other cricket engagements. Soon after the commencement of the first tour of India in 1952/3, Pakistan lost him through injury and in the Caribbean in 1958/9 he could appear in only two Tests. On the first England tour in 1954 his Lancashire League engagement precluded him from playing in more than a handful of matches. However, in the first Test, at Lord's, bowling unchanged with Fazal, he took 5 for 61. In the first official series at home, against India in 1954/5, he was the most effective bowler on either side, securing 22 wickets (15.86) in four Tests. Specially penetrative in the first innings, he took 4 for 42 in 26.5 overs at Dacca, 5 for 74 at Bahawalpur, 4 for 79 at Peshawar and 5 for 72 at Karachi. Against New Zealand in 1955/6 he captured 13 wickets (16.00). In the third match at Dacca with the ball swinging and keeping low on the soaked matting, he was unplayable with 6 for 21 in 16.2 overs and 2 for 20 in 30 overs (19 maidens). In his last home Test, the first against Australia, at Karachi in 1956/7, he bowled unchanged with Fazal in the first innings of 80, finished with a record 7 for 112, and Pakistan won comfortably. However, his last series, against West Indies in the Caribbean in 1957/8, he played in two Tests, at Kingston in the third sending down 54 overs and taking 0 for 259. He became a professional in the Lancashire League; captained Bahawalpur; and later became a professional in Canada.

First-class career (1946-61): 524 runs (11.39) and 212 wickets (23.29)
Test matches (13): 100 runs (10.00), 54 wickets (23.92) and 4 catches

LIAQAT ALI KHAN (b.1955)

Karachi, Habib Bank and Sind

A left-arm medium-paced seam bowler, Liaqat Ali toured England in 1975 for the Prudential World Cup after making one appearance against West Indies at Karachi in 1974/5. But it was not until Imran Khan left Pakistan's side during Kerry Packer's two-year World Series Cricket experiment that he got his chance at Test level with any regularity. However, in four Tests against England in 1978/9, two at home and two away, he took only 6 wickets.

First-class career (1970-): 627 runs (7.83), 379 wickets (23.74) and 45 catches
Test matches (5): 28 runs (7.00), 6 wickets (59.83) and 1 catch

MAHMOOD HUSSAIN (b.1932)

Karachi Whites

Faster than Fazal Mahmood, Mahmood Hussain was a tall, confident, fast-medium in-swinging bowler who could obtain lift from any type of wicket but tended to waste much energy with leg-theory and was subject to physical breakdowns. He toured India in 1952/3 and 1960/61, England in 1954 and 1962, and the West Indies in 1957/8, and at home played against India in 1954/5, New Zealand in 1955/6, West Indies in 1958/9 and England in 1961/2. At his best in England in 1954 he took 72 wickets (21.30), including 4 for 58 in the first innings of the last Test at The Oval – sharing the 10 wickets with Fazal – when Pakistan beat England for the first time. On his second England tour, however, he was overbowled and was not very successful in the Tests. In the first home series against India he took 14 wickets (26.57), including 6 for 67 in the first match at Dacca. In the Caribbean he was bowled into the ground, conceding at least 120 runs in each of the first three innings of the Tests, and then broke down after pulling a thigh muscle, having bowled only five balls in the next Test at Kingston. Against West Indies in the second Test at Dacca, his 4 for 48 in the second innings helped Pakistan to a narrow victory. Against India in the first Test, at Bombay, 1960/61, he sent down 51.4 overs and took 5 for 129 in the sole innings. His best bowling in an innings was 8 for 93 for Karachi Whites against Karachi Greens in 1956/7. He has been active in cricket administration and managed the ill-starred 1978 touring team to England.

First-class career (1949-69): 1,107 runs (9.06) and 322 wickets (25.13)
Test matches (27): 336 runs (10.18), 68 wickets (38.64) and 5 catches

MAJID JAHANGIR KHAN (b.1946)

Lahore, Pakistan International Airways, Punjab, Cambridge University, Glamorgan and Queensland

A dignified, intelligent and amiably sleepy character, Majid Khan is a richly gifted all-round cricketer with a composed, quietly confident approach. A brilliant attacking batsman, he is a powerful driver, cutter and hooker, who in the later years of his career has become an opener. He is also a fine close fielder and a natural bowler who once opened for Pakistan but now bowls flat, curling off-spinners which drift awkwardly away from the right-handed batsman. At Cambridge he was the most successful captain for years and, until he lost

Majid Khan

his enthusiasm and left the county in 1975 in an atmosphere of discord, he was also a good captain of Glamorgan, so it is surprising that he has captained his country in ony three Tests. The son of Dr Jahangir Khan, the former Indian Test cap and Cambridge blue, Majid was born at Jullunder in the year before Partition and at the age of fifteen was making 111 not out and taking 6 for 67 on his first appearance for Lahore 'B'. That he comes from thoroughbred cricketing stock is underlined by the success of his cousin Imran Khan, his brother Asad, and another cousin Javed Burki, who also captained Pakistan. Batting for Punjab University against Karachi, Majid scored a double century – undefeated – after his side had been 5 for 4! He was 18 years 26 days when he made his first Test appearance, against Australia at Karachi. He made 0 in his only innings but as an opening bowler took 3 wickets. However, it seems there was some suspicion about the bouncer which got him the wickets and Majid, who had so many strings to his bow, made his own decision to alter his bowling style. On his first visit to England with an official Pakistan side, he managed only 38 runs in Tests, but he showed his quality and power in scoring 973 runs (42.30) in other games including an amazing 147 not out in 89 minutes at Swansea, where he hit the off-spinner Roger Davis for 5 sixes in one six-ball over and in all hit 13 sixes. Glamorgan soon signed him and after making 1,258 runs in his first season, he scored 1,547 (39.66) in 1969. It was partly because he was already such a mature cricketer that his influence was so great when he arrived at Cambridge. Captaining the side in 1971 and 1972, he led them to the first victory against Oxford for fourteen years. He captained by calm and confident example both in technique and spirit. In Australia, Queensland, eager for the same charisma to go to work, employed him for the 1973/4 Sheffield Shield season. He hit centuries in his first two matches but later lost form. The previous season Majid had scored a memorable 158 at Melbourne against Australia in his twentieth Test innings, the highest score by a Pakistan player in Australia, and against New Zealand on the same visit his scores were 79, 79, 26, 110 and 33. Further Test centuries now began to flow: one against West Indies at Karachi in 1974/5; against New Zealand at Karachi and against West Indies at Georgetown, both in 1976/7, and against New Zealand at Napier and against Australia at Melbourne in 1978/9. He scored 89 and 110 not out in his only two Test innings at home against Australia in 1979/80. His brilliance shone more fitfully for Pakistan in the early 1980s, though he was at his best in making 74 in the third Test at Melbourne in 1981/2. He followed this with 63 against Sri Lanka at Lahore in the same season; but in England in 1982 he was a shadow of the magisterial player he had been for so many years. But his Test at Headingley in 1982 was not to be his last.

First-class career (1961-): 26,699 runs (42.65) including 70 centuries, 224 wickets (32.11) and 404 catches
Test matches (62): 3,931 runs (39.31) including 8 centuries, 27 wickets (53.77) and 70 catches

MANSOOR AKHTAR (b.1956)

Karachi and United Bank

With Waheed Mirza, Mansoor holds the record for the highest ever opening stand: 561 against Quetta for Karachi Whites in 1976/7. Mansoor's share was 224 not out. He has since proved himself an exceptionally gifted right-handed batsman with a wide range of strokes. He was not quite ready for Test cricket when playing in Australia in 1980/81 after making his first two appearances at home against the West Indies. In seven first-class innings in Australia he scored 345 runs (49.28) and he was even more successful in the tour of England in 1982, scoring 595 runs (39.66) in the first-class games and doing a useful job at number three in the Tests, top scoring with 58 in the first innings at Edgbaston and 57 in the first innings at Lord's. He appeared to have cemented his place at number three against Australia in 1982/3, hooking and driving brilliantly to score 111 at Faisalabad, but lost his place again soon afterwards. When asked what his ambition was, he replied, 'To be a superstar.'

First-class career (1974-): 3,765 runs (40.05) including 4 centuries, and 3 wickets (60.66)
Test matches (10): 444 runs (27.75) including 1 century, and 7 catches

MAQSOOD AHMED (b.1925)

Bahawalpur

Maqsood was a stylish, attractive right-handed batsman, a natural hitter with a good eye, an occasional medium-pace bowler and a good field. He scored 137 for Pakistan against MCC at Lahore in 1951/2, came to England as a professional in the Staffordshire League, and toured India and England with the first Pakistan sides in 1952/3 and 1954 respectively. At home he played against India in 1954/5 and New Zealand in 1955/6. On the England tour he was second to Hanif Mohammad in the batting, making 1,314 runs (34.57) and often delighting the crowds, besides taking 20 wickets (43.95) and holding 14 catches; in the opening match at Worcester he hit a chanceless 111 in two and a quarter hours. After his country had made a very shaky start against the visiting Indians at Lahore in the third Test, he added 136 with A.H. Kardar for the fourth wicket before he was stumped on 99.

First-class career (1944-64): 3,716 runs (32.03) including 6 centuries, and 120 wickets (28.43)
Test matches (16): 507 runs (19.50), 3 wickets (63.66) and 13 catches

MATHIAS, Wallis (b.1935)

Karachi

An attractive and generally fast-scoring right-handed batsman, occasional medium-pace bowler and a fine slip, Wallis Mathias toured the West Indies in 1957/8, India in 1960/61 and England in 1962, and at home played against New Zealand in 1955/6, Australia in 1956/7 and 1959/60, West Indies in 1958/9 and England in 1961/2. In his first Test, against New Zealand at Dacca in 1955/6, he hit 41 not out in a rain-spoiled match, adding 96 in as many minutes with Hanif Mohammad for the sixth wicket. In the Caribbean he enjoyed his best series with 251 runs (27.88). When the West Indies toured Pakistan, he was at his best in the second Test at Dacca which Pakistan won narrowly; the first day he made 64 in a total of 145 and on the third day 45 in a total of 144. Afterwards, his career faded and, although he toured England, making 734 runs (30.58), he achieved little in his final series.

First-class career (1953-77): 7,508 runs (44.69) including 16 centuries, and 13 wickets (42.69)
Test matches (21): 783 runs (23.72), 0-20 and 22 catches

MIRAN BUX (b.1907)

Punjab, Rawalpindi and Services

A competent right-arm off-break bowler, Miran Bux played in two Tests against India in 1954/5 – his final season of first-class cricket – and on his debut in the third match at Lahore, he was, at 47 years and 275 days, the second oldest Test debutant ever.

First-class career (1949-54): 53 runs (3.31) and 48 wickets (19.45)
Test matches (2): 1 run (1.00) and 2 wickets (57.50)

MOHAMMAD ASLAM KHOKHAR (b.1920)

Railways and Quetta

A very good right-handed, stroke-playing batsman, occasional leg-break and googly bowler and brilliant outfield, Mohammad Aslam Khokhar toured England with the first team in 1954, making 421 runs (28.06), and in his sole Test, the second, at Trent Bridge, scored 16 and 18.

First-class career (1941-64): 1,693 runs (26.87) including 1 century, and 21 wickets (30.47)

MOHAMMAD FAROOQ (b.1938)

Karachi

A hardworking right-arm fast-medium bowler who, in a short Test career, was one of the quickest of Pakistan's bowlers, and a hard-hitting tail-end batsman, Mohammad Farooq toured India in 1960/61 and England in 1962, and at home played against New Zealand in 1964/5. Although he took 33 wickets (26.42) from eight first-class matches in England, he broke down and could not complete the tour. When New Zealand were defeated in the first match at Rawalpindi by an innings, he flogged the bowling at number eleven, hitting 47 out of 65 for the last wicket with Pervez Sajjad in less than an hour, and in the match captured 5 for 82. He took 10 wickets (25.30) in the three Tests against New Zealand.

First-class career (1959-65): 173 runs (12.35) and 123 wickets (26.98)
Test matches (7): 85 runs (17.00), 21 wickets (32.47) and 1 catch

MOHAMMAD ILYAS (b.1946)

Pakistan International Airlines

An attacking right-handed opening batsman and useful leg-break and googly bowler, Mohammad Ilyas toured Australasia in 1964/5 and 1972/3, and England in 1967, and at home played against New Zealand in 1964/5 and England in 1968/9. On his first tour of Australasia he made 781 runs (31.24), including 154 against South Australia and 126 against Queensland, but his only notable Test performance was 88 in the third match against New Zealand on a tricky pitch. Against New Zealand in India he made 223 runs (44.60) in the three Tests. In the third match, at Karachi, as opening batsman, he raced to 126 in the second innings, having hit R.W. Morgan for four consecutive fours when his score was 97. In England, however, he shone only spasmodically until a foot injury laid him low. His Test career against England ended in 1968/9 on a low key against a background of rioting and chaos. Then, early in his second tour of Australia, a severe blow in the face by a bowler's delivery prevented him playing for his country again, and he was accused of indiscipline. Instead of flying home, however, he applied for Australian citizenship and before the end of the season (1972/3) was playing first-grade cricket for Waverley in Sydney.

First-class career (1961-76): 4,607 runs (35.71) including 12 centuries, and 53 wickets (31.00)
Test matches (10): 441 runs (23.21) including 1 century, 0-63 and 6 catches

MOHAMMAD MUNAF (b.1935)

Karachi and Pakistan International Airlines

A competent right-arm fast-medium bowler, a useful late-order batsman and a good close field, Mohammad Munaf toured the West Indies in 1957/8 and India in 1960/61 without appearing in any Tests, but at home he played against Australia in 1959/60 and England in 1961/2 with some success. At Lahore in the first Test against England he took 4 wickets for 42 in a total of 380.

First-class career (1953-71): 1,356 runs (17.61) and 180 wickets (34.22)
Test matches (4): 63 runs (12.60) and 11 wickets (31.00)

MOHAMMAD NAZIR, Junior (b.1946)

Pakistan Western Railways

A cleverly flighting right-arm off-break bowler and useful tail-end batsman and agile field, Mohammad Nazir took 10 wickets (28.20) in the three Tests of his first series, against New Zealand in 1969/70 and, curiously, by virtue of three not out innings, headed the batting averages with 61. Joining the team late in England in 1971, he headed the averages with 20 wickets (19.80), but did not appear in any Tests. In his first and only match against England, at Hyderabad in 1972/3, he conceded 125 runs in 52 overs and failed to take a wicket. However, he made a successful return to Test cricket in 1979/80, playing a full home series against the West Indies and taking 5-44 and 3-76 in the second Test at Faisalabad. With 56 wickets (14.67) he topped Pakistan's national averages in 1981/2, but was ignored by the national selectors and his best Test figure remains his 7-99 on his first appearance against New Zealand at Karachi.

First-class career (1964-): 3,119 runs (23.62) including 2 centuries, and 534 wickets (19.94)
Test matches (8): 89 runs (22.25), 26 wickets (24.42) and 2 catches

Mohsin Khan

MOHSIN KHAN (b.1954)

Railways and Habib Bank

Mohsin Khan is a tall right-handed batsman with a wide range of graceful strokes, though early in his career he did not always play them at the right time. He earned a place in Pakistan's side against England in 1977/8 in the absence of several established batsmen who had signed to play for Kerry Packer in Australia. A determined, painstaking 97 for the Punjab XI against the England team earned him his first chance at Test level in the third Test, at Karachi, when he made an attractive 44 in Pakistan's only innings. In England in 1978 he played in all three Tests and batted consistently for a struggling, unsettled side, making 191 runs in five innings at 38.20, going in first wicket down and scoring more than 30 each time. Not selected against India on the return of the Packer players, Mohsin toured New Zealand and Australia in 1978/9 but played in only one Test in each country. His career suddenly blossomed anew in 1981/2 when he scored 1,160 runs (61.05) in the domestic season, flew to Australia as a replacement and reformed a highly successful Test opening partnership with Mudassar Nazar. Against Sri Lanka in the same season he scored 215 runs in three Test innings, including 129 at Lahore, his first Test hundred. In England in 1982 he played magnificently, scoring 1,248 runs in 20 innings on the tour at 73.41. He scored 203 not out against Leicestershire, and in the second Test at Lord's set up a famous win for Pakistan by hitting 200, with graceful driving and unerring hitting off his legs. He hit a third Test century, 135, against Australia at Lahore in 1982/3 as well as scoring 104 in the first one-day international at Hyderabad. In the first innings of the Karachi Test he was given out 'handled the ball' after illicitly using his glove to prevent the ball hitting his stumps.

First-class career (1970-): 8,670 runs (40.32) including 24 centuries, 11 wickets (41.81) and 106 catches
Test matches (16): 1,175 runs (47.00) including 3 centuries, 0-6 and 15 catches

MUDASSAR NAZAR (b.1956)

Lahore, Punjab, Combined Universities, Habib Bank, Pakistan International Airlines and United Bank

The son of another Test cricketer, Nazar Mohammad, Mudassar is a small and determined right-hand opening batsman, useful bustling medium-pace bowler and a good close-field. He carved a reputation as one of history's great stonewallers when in his third Test innings at Lahore in December 1977 he scored the slowest-ever Test hundred in 9 hours 17 minutes. He proved later that he has plenty of strokes when in the remainder of the series against England he scored consistently finishing with 309 runs from 5 innings. Like the other young players, bereft of experienced support because of the 'defections' to World Series Cricket, Mudassar struggled to find form in England in 1978. In the three Tests he scored only 86 runs (17.20), but on the tour made 677 runs from 21 innings and did enough to suggest a successful future. In 1979/80 he played further Tests against India, New Zealand and Australia and he was a member of the Pakistan team in the 1979 Prudential World Cup. Against India at Bangalore in 1979/80 he scored 126, and in Australia in 1981/2 he showed how useful a bowler he could be when taking 12 wickets at a cost of only 13 each in one-day internationals against Australia and West Indies. Anyone doubting the worth of this performance had to keep quiet in England in 1982 when in the Lord's Test Mudassar, a man inspired, took 6 for 32 in England's second innings to win the match for Pakistan. His ten wickets in the series cost only 10 runs each and although he had only one substantial Test score with the bat he was unlucky. He formed an opening partnership of genuine Test quality with Mohsin Khan and on the tour averaged 82.50 with four hundreds, including 211 not out against Sussex at Hove. At home against Australia in 1982/3 he scored 198 runs in three Tests (66.00). A cheerful, irrepressible character, he has played a good deal of league cricket in the north of England.

First-class career (1971-): 9,009 runs (45.04) including 27 centuries, and 82 wickets (28.69)
Test matches (29): 1,377 runs (32.02) including 2 centuries, 22 wickets (31.45) and 21 catches

Mudassar Nazar

MUFASIR-UL-HAQ (b.1944)

Karachi

A steady left-arm fast-medium bowler, Mufasir-ul-Haq toured Australasia in 1964/5 but with moderate success, and in his sole Test, the third at Christchurch against New Zealand, he scored 8 not out, took 3 for 84 and held 1 catch.

First-class career (1960-76): 286 runs (7.15) and 105 wickets (26.78)

MUNIR MALIK (b.1934)

Rawalpindi

A big-hearted right-arm fast-medium bowler, Munir Malik toured England in 1962, and at home played against Australia in 1959/60. In England he was overbowled, taking 43 wickets (39.93); in the third Test, at Headingley, he bowled without relief from 3 p.m. on the Thursday until 1.30 p.m. on the Friday, taking 5 for 128 in 49 overs in an innings of 428.

First-class career (1956-66): 675 runs (11.06) and 197 wickets (21.75)
Test matches (3): 7 runs (2.33), 9 wickets (39.77) and 1 catch

MUSHTAQ MOHAMMAD (b.1943)

Pakistan International Airlines, Karachi, Northamptonshire and Staffordshire

The most versatile and, in all-round terms, the most

prolific of the famous Mohammad brotherhood, five of whom played first-class cricket and four Test cricket for Pakistan, Mushtaq Mohammad disciplined his brilliant natural talent to become one of the most consistently successful Test cricketers of any nation in a long and very full career. He has scored over 30,000 runs and 70 centuries and was the first Pakistan player to have scored more than 25,000 first-class runs. A stocky right-handed batsman, he can play any stroke with superb timing, his wrists strong as steel yet flexible as a willow branch. Like his brother Hanif, his concentration and application are immense, but Mushtaq has often played fine attacking innings as well as dour defensive ones. As a leg-break bowler he has been one of the best in the world of a dying breed, taking his Test wickets much less expensively than most leg-spin contemporaries and, possessing a good googly, a genuine matchwinner in the right conditions. The fourth of the brothers, Mushtaq showed unbelievable maturity at the age of 13 years 41 days by scoring 87 and taking 5 for 28 on his first-class debut for Karachi Whites against Hyderabad, 1956/7. Two years later he became the youngest player ever to earn a Test cap, when in March 1959, at the age of 15 years 124 days, he played at Lahore in the third Test against the West Indies. Pakistan lost by an innings, Mushtaq made 14 and 4 and took no wickets but he was not in any way overawed and before the age of nineteen he had scored 101 against India at Delhi and 100 not out against England at Trent Bridge in 1962. He played for Northamptonshire from 1966 to 1977, when after some criticism he resigned the captaincy which he had held for two years. Mushtaq had led Northamptonshire in 1976 to their first success in any major competition, the Gillette Cup, and also to second place in the Championship. In all matches for the county he had scored almost 16,000 runs (1,000 or more in a season 12 times) and taken 550 wickets. The Pakistan selectors restored him as captain for the tour to New Zealand and Australia in 1978/9 when those players who had signed contracts with World Series Cricket, Mushtaq amongst them, were recalled. Mushtaq, in fact, had travelled from Australia with Imran and Zaheer the previous season, apparently to play in the third Test at Karachi but, after much politicking from both sides, the three 'stars' returned to Australia without playing. All missed the subsequent tour of England, where Mushtaq had played with official Pakistan sides in 1962, 1967, 1971 and 1974. His second tour as captain began on a high note with victory over New Zealand at Christchurch when Mushtaq's leg-breaks were the main instrument of victory: he took 4 for 60 and 5 for 59. He batted steadily in the two drawn games which completed the series, but as captain took responsibility for much of the acrimony in the two Tests in Australia, one won by each country, when, according to the spirit though not the letter of cricket, two Australian and one Pakistan player were 'cheated' out. He tried in vain to have one of the decisions reversed. But there can be no quibbling about Mushtaq's immense contributions to Pakistan cricket. Often more consistent than other more sparkling batsmen around him in the strong Pakistan batting sides of the seventies, especially on green wickets in England, he scored 121 against Australia at Sydney in 1972/3, 201 against New Zealand at Dunedin on the same tour and later the same season 157 against England at Hyderabad. In 1974/5 he made his first century against a West Indian attack, 123 at Lahore, followed by 121 at Port of Spain in 1976/7, when he also hit 101 and 107 in Tests at Hyderabad and Karachi against New Zealand. Apart from his skill on tricky pitches, it is hard to think of a more difficult batsman to dislodge than Mushtaq in the right mood on a good pitch. He continues to play a good deal including minor county cricket and tours to the Middle East and North America.

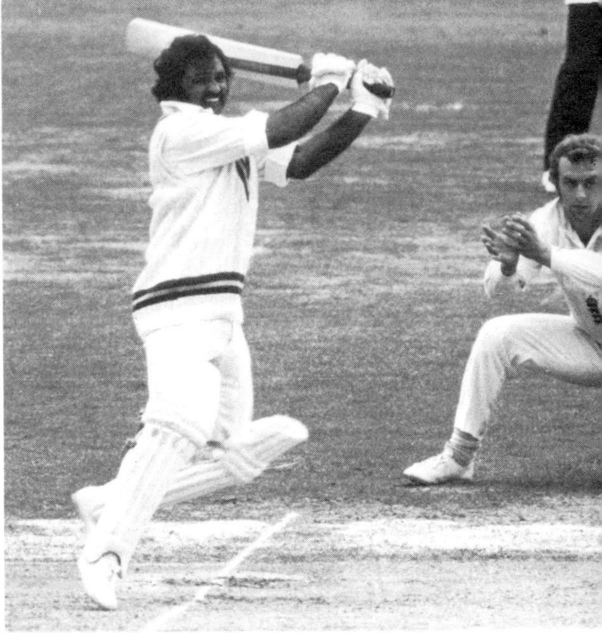

Mushtaq Mohammad, with David Lloyd (England)

First-class career (1956-): 30,974 runs (42.14) including 72 centuries, 935 wickets (24.23) and 345 catches
Test matches (57): 3,643 runs (39.17) including 10 centuries, 79 wickets (29.24) and 42 catches

NASIM-UL-GHANI (b.1941)

Karachi and Staffordshire

A left-handed batsman, Nasim-ul-Ghani went for his strokes whenever possible in his younger, more cavalier days, but, on becoming a professional, tended to eschew risk; he was also a versatile, orthodox slow left-arm bowler, remarkably mature as a young player, of consistent length and much spin, and a good short-leg. He made his first-class debut in 1956/7 at fifteen, bowling 79 overs in an innings (79-19-184-3) for Karachi Blues against Karachi Whites; and at 16 years

248 days, became the youngest Test player ever at that time on his debut against West Indies in the first match at Barbados in 1957/8. He also toured India in 1960/61, England in 1962 and 1967 and Australasia in 1964/5 and 1972/3, and at home played against West Indies in 1958/9, Australia in 1959/60 and 1964/5 and England in 1961/2. In the Caribbean he headed the bowling in the Tests with 19 wickets (26.73), 6 for 67 in the second innings of the fifth match, at Port of Spain, which won the match with an innings to spare – Pakistan's first victory over West Indies. He did not then enhance his career until his first England tour, when he scored 247 runs (27.44) in the Tests, including a fine, stroke-making maiden century in the second match at Lord's. Pakistan were 77 for 4, 270 behind, when Nasim and his captain, Javed Burki, came together; in three hours they added 197 (Nasim 101), which remains the Pakistan record for the fifth wicket against England. On his second England tour he made spasmodic appearances without distinction, whenever his professional engagements allowed, and on his second tour of Australasia he made 200 runs (50.00) but rarely bowled on this unhappy visit. Among his best feats was 6 for 24 (12 for 54 in the match) for Karachi Whites against East Pakistan in 1961/2. For several years a professional in League cricket, he also played minor county cricket for Staffordshire. In 1967 his 50 wickets for Longton cost only 12.32 each and included a hat-trick against Norton.

First-class career (1956-75): 4,490 runs (28.41) including 7 centuries, and 343 wickets (25.16)
Test matches (29): 747 runs (16.60) including 1 century, 52 wickets (37.67) and 11 catches

NAUSHAD ALI (b.1943)

Karachi

A sound wicket-keeper and useful opening right-handed batsman, Naushad Ali toured England with Pakistan Eaglets in 1963 and Australasia in 1964/5, and at home played against New Zealand in 1964/5, his best score being 39.

First-class career (1960-79): 4,136 runs (36.28) including 8 centuries, and 165 dismissals (131 ct, 34 st.)
Test matches (6): 156 runs (14.18) and 9 dismissals (9 ct)

NAZAR MOHAMMAD (b.1921)

Northern India, Karachi and Sind

A generally attractive right-handed opening batsman and reliable close field, Nazar Mohammad played for Northern India in the Ranji Trophy competition from 1940/41 until Partition in 1947, and, when he toured India in 1952/3 on Pakistan's entry into official Test cricket, he was second to his opening partner Hanif Mohammad in the batting, making 687 runs (45.80), including 3 centuries. In his sole Test series, on this tour, he carried his bat through the innings of 331 for 124 not out in the second Test, at Lucknow, batting painstakingly for 8 hours 35 minutes. He retired from first-class cricket in 1953 after suffering a serious arm injury but became a National Cricket Coach, coaching his own son, Mudassar, who has also played for Pakistan.

First-class career (1940-53): 2,484 runs (40.06) including 7 centuries
Test matches (5): 277 runs (39.57) including 1 century, 0-4 and 7 catches

NIAZ AHMAD (b.1945)

East Pakistan

A competent right-arm fast-medium bowler and later-order batsman who could drive fearlessly and snick luckily, Niaz Ahmad toured England in 1967 and at home played against England in 1968/9. In England he took 25 wickets (34.52) and made 104 runs (20.80), but achieved nothing in his sole Test on the tour. He was the first indigenous East Pakistani to win a Test cap.

First-class career (1965-74): 466 runs (14.56) and 62 wickets (38.45)
Test matches (2): 17 runs (—), 3 wickets (31.33) and 1 catch

PERVEZ SAJJAD (b.1942)

Pakistan International Airlines

A graduate in psychology and a cunning slow left-arm leg-break bowler of accuracy and penetration even in unhelpful conditions, a rather moderate right-handed batsman but a good field, Pervez Sajjad toured Australasia in 1964/5 and 1972/3 and England in 1971, and at home played against Australia in 1964/5, New Zealand in 1964/5 and 1969/70 and England in 1968/9 and 1972/3. On his first visit to New Zealand he took 12 wickets (22.66) in the three Tests, including 5 for 42 in the second innings of the second match at Auckland, when he took 4 wickets in 10 deliveries without cost. When Pakistan gained their first victory at home for six years, over New Zealand at Rawalpindi in 1964/5, he was prominent with 4 for 42 and 4 for 5 in 12 overs. In the three Tests against New Zealand five years later he was the outstanding bowler with 22 wickets (15.63); at Karachi he struck telling blows in the second innings with 5 for 33 in 24 overs, and at Lahore he took 7 for 74 in the first innings. In New Zealand, however, in 1972/3 his bowling was mastered. Including his visit with Pakistan Eaglets in 1963, he toured England three times – because of injury, joining the 1971 party later in the tour – and was not as effective as was hoped. His brother is Waqar Hassan.

First-class career (1961-74): 786 runs (10.48) and 493 wickets (21.80)
Test matches (19): 123 runs (13.66), 59 wickets (23.89) and 9 catches

RASHID KHAN (b.1959)

Pakistan International Airlines, Public Works Department and Karachi

Making his first-class debut in 1975/6, Rashid Khan was picked as a medium-fast right-arm bowler for two Tests against Sri Lanka in 1981/2, mainly because a players' revolt had deprived Pakistan of several top cricketers. Curiously, however, it was as a tail-end batsman that he made most mark, scoring 59 and 43 not out when batting at number ten in his first two Test innings. He also bowled steadily and picked up three wickets in Pakistan's victory in the first Test, but just missed selection to England in 1982. He had well deserved his chance after an outstanding performance for PIA in 1979/80.

First-class career (1975-): 414 runs (21.78) and 111 wickets (26.54)
Test matches (2): 105 runs (105.00), 3 wickets (44.66) and 1 catch

REHMAN, Sheikh Fazalur (b.1935)

Lahore

A sound right-handed batsman and leg-break bowler, Sheikh Rehman was flown out very late to the West Indies in 1957/8 as a reinforcement, Pakistan suffering at least three casualties, and in his sole Test, the fourth at Georgetown, scored 8 and 2, took 1 for 99 and held 1 catch.

First-class career (1954-62): 721 runs (19.51) and 91 wickets (21.65)

RIZWAN-UZ-ZAMAN (b.1962)

Pakistan International Airlines

Quiet, soft-spoken and dedicated to cricket, an assiduous practiser, Rizwan is a small right-handed opening batsman with a good temperament and excellent technique. He came to prominence after touring India in 1978/9 with Pakistan's Under 19 side. topping the averages with 701 runs at 40.23. On his first senior tour, however, to Australia in 1981/2, he was less successful. Picked for the first Test in Perth he was lbw first ball to Alderman, the start of a collapse. He finished the tour with 431 first-class runs (43.10) and was not selected to tour England in 1982.

First-class career (1976-): 2,748 runs (36.64) including 6 centuries, and 15 wickets (21.33)
Test matches (3): 112 runs (18.66), 3 wickets (13.00) and 1 catch

Sadiq Mohammad

SADIQ MOHAMMAD (b.1945)

Karachi, Pakistan International Airlines, United Bank, Gloucestershire and Tasmania

The youngest of the famous Mohammad brothers, Sadiq is a left-handed opening batsman who hits the ball with a wristy brilliance and whose approach is generally speaking more aggressive than that of his even more prolific brothers Hanif and Mushtaq. Good-looking, small, stocky, and a shy but personable character, Sadiq cuts and glances with crisp assurance, drives generally square of the wickets on the off-side and defends with determination when necessary, but tends to get himself caught by slips or gully flashing outside his off-stump. With Zaheer Abbas he has adorned Gloucestershire cricket since joining the county in 1972, the year after his first tour to England. He came with other official Pakistan sides in 1974 and 1978 and has also toured Australia and New Zealand in 1972/3 and Australia and West Indies in 1976/7. More than most batsmen he seems to be prone to peaks and troughs. Nevertheless, he has consistently proved his quality in England, scoring more than 1,000 runs in six separate seasons. Like his brothers he was playing first-class cricket as a schoolboy, making his debut in 1959/60 at the age of 14 years 9 months. In addition to several sides in Pakistan he also played for Tasmania, where he was a player-coach. A useful leg-spinner, though seldom called upon in Test cricket, he took 5 for 29 for Karachi Blues against Lahore Greens in 1970/71 and 5 for 37 for Gloucestershire against Kent at Bristol in 1973. He scored 4 centuries in successive innings in 1976, including 163 not out and 150 in the match against Derbyshire at Bristol. In Test cricket he made his first appearance for Pakistan in 1969/70 against New Zealand, winning his first cap at Karachi in the same match as his future Gloucestershire colleague, Zaheer, also made his first Test appearance; Sadiq on this occasion did better with scores of 69 and 37 as opening partner for the only time with his elder brother Hanif. He scored the first of 5 Test centuries against Australia at Melbourne in 1972/3, following up later in the same tour with 166 against New Zealand at Wellington and then making 119 against England at Lahore when he got back home. In 1976/7 he hit 103 not out against New Zealand at Hyderabad and 10 against Australia at Melbourne. He narrowly missed another Test hundred at Headingley in 1978 when, with 210 runs from five Test innings, his skill and experience saved an unsettled Pakistan side from even heavier defeat by England. It was, therefore, surprising, despite the return of the Packer players, that he should have lost his Test place after one appearance against India in 1978/9. He returned for three more Tests in India in 1979/80 but has not appeared since. He had a benefit with Gloucestershire in 1982.

First-class career (1959-): 22,096 runs (37.01) including 44 centuries, 221 wickets (31.99) and 297 catches
Test matches (41): 2,579 runs (35.81) including 5 centuries, 0-98 and 28 catches

SAEED AHMED (b.1937)

Lahore and Pakistan International Airlines

Though often in dispute with the Board of Control for Cricket in Pakistan, Saeed Ahmed was a resplendent stroke-making right-handed batsman of an upright stance with a particularly hard drive who thrived especially on firm pitches. He was also a useful slow to medium off-break bowler and a fine field at cover. Captain successively of Punjab University, Lahore and – briefly – of Pakistan, he toured the West Indies in 1957/8, India in 1960/61, England in 1962, 1967 and 1971, and Australasia in 1964/5 and 1972/3, and at home played against West Indies in 1958/9, Australia in 1959/60 and 1964/5, England in 1961/2 and 1968/9 and New Zealand in 1964/5. He enjoyed a highly successful first series, against West Indies in the Caribbean, making 508 runs (56.44) in the five Tests; on his debut at Bridgetown he hit 65, and in other Tests he scored 64, 52, 44, 150 (at Georgetown in the fourth match), 12 and 97 in consecutive innings. When the West Indies toured Pakistan, he was the chief run-getter with 199 runs (39.80) from the three matches, including 78 in the first at Karachi, sharing in a then-record second-wicket stand of 178 with Hanif; and he was also foremost in his first series against Australia, making 334 runs (55.66), which included a classic 166 in over six hours in the second match, at Lahore. In India he again scored most in a war of attrition, making 460 runs (51.11), including a painstaking 121 in the first match at Bombay, when he added 246 with Hanif in a then-record second-wicket stand, and a dull

Saeed Ahmed

103 in the fourth match at Madras. Although he faded rather against England at home, on his first England tour he was the second best batsman, reaching 1,294 runs (34.97), including 3 centuries, making 302 runs (30.20) in the Tests. For Pakistan against the Commonwealth in 1963/4, he was head and shoulders above most of the other batsmen, but he was below his best on his first tour of Australasia. At home against New Zealand, however, in 1964/5 he made most runs, 286 (71.50), including a glorious 172 out of 307 for 8 wickets declared – his Test-highest – in the third match, at Karachi, when he battled for 5 hours 40 minutes, and saved his country from disaster, leading them, instead, to ultimate victory in both match and rubber. Generally competent in England on his second tour, he made 845 runs (33.80) altogether, and top-scored with two outstanding Test innings – 44 out of 140 and 68 out of 114. Against a background of civil disorder he captained his country against England in 1968/9 in the three matches, the third being abandoned through rioting. He lost his place in the team against New Zealand and on his third England tour he did not find his form until late and played in the final Test only because Majid Khan was unable to appear. On the unhappy tour of Australia in 1972/3, he made 50 in the second Test at Melbourne, in which he had furious words with Dennis Lillee (who had Saeed uppermost in his thoughts for the series), claimed he was too unfit to appear in the third and final Test and was sent home for alleged indiscipline, ending his Test career. Younis Ahmed is his half-brother.

First-class career (1954-78): 12,847 runs (40.02) including 34 centuries, and 332 wickets (24.74)
Test matches (41): 2,991 runs (40.42) including 5 centuries, 22 wickets (36.45) and 13 catches

SALAH-UD-DIN (b.1947)

Karachi

A stylish right-handed batsman with a specially good on-drive, a useful slow off-break bowler and good close field, Salah-ud-Din made his Test debut at the age of eighteen after only six first-class matches. Against New Zealand in the first match at Rawalpindi in 1964/5 he scored 34 not out and took 3 for 52 and 1 catch, but did not improve on this during the rest of his short Test career. He played against England in 1968/9 and New Zealand in 1969/70, and toured England in 1967 without appearing in a Test.

First-class career (1964-80): 5,729 runs (41.81) including 14 centuries, and 155 wickets (28.45)
Test matches (5): 117 (19.50), 7 wickets (26.71) and 3 catches

SALEEM ALTAF (b.1944)

Pakistan International Airlines

A very lively fast-medium right-arm bowler, using both in- and out-swingers, and an uninhibited batsman, generally at number eight, Saleem Altaf appeared in Test trials three times before being selected for his first Test against England in 1967. He toured England again in 1971, Australasia in 1972/3, Australia in 1976/7 and the West Indies in 1976/7, and at home played against New Zealand in 1969/70, England in 1972/3 and India in 1978/9. The fastest bowler of the 1967 side in England, he was handicapped by a torn muscle in the first Test, at Lord's. On his second England tour he was always dangerous with the new ball but suffered from illness. In the second innings of the third Test at Headingley he swept through the tail, taking 4 for 11 in 14.3 overs. In Australasia, swinging and seaming disconcertingly, he took 16 wickets (31.68) in the Tests, and in the third match at Sydney brought Australia close to defeat, taking 4 for 60 in the second innings. In the first Test against New Zealand at Wellington, he broke through in the second innings again, capturing 3 for 11 from his first 21 balls. In the final match at Auckland, he hit a steady 53 not out, his Test-highest, sharing in a last-wicket stand with Pervez Sajjad of 48. He played in one further Test against India at Lahore in 1978.

First-class career (1963-79): 3,067 runs (22.88) including 1 century and 334 wickets (28.38)
Test matches (21): 276 runs (14.52), 46 wickets (37.17) and 3 catches

SALEEM MALIK (b.1963)

Lahore

A cricketer who bubbles over with keenness, Saleem Malik is a fine fielder and brilliant natural right-handed batsman with all the wristy strokes of the best Pakistan players. He was chosen to tour Australia in 1981/2 at the age of 18 and scored 159 runs (39.75) in the only three first-class matches he played in. Later in the season he captained Pakistan's Under 19 touring team in Australia and played his first Tests against Sri Lanka, making 100 not out in the second innings of his debut Test at Karachi. He toured England in 1982 without making the Test team.

First-class career (1978-): 1,543 runs (36.73) including 4 centuries
Test matches (2): 139 runs (46.33) including 1 century, and 4 catches

SALEEM YOUSUF (b.1959)

Sind, Karachi and Industrial Development Bank of Pakistan

An agile wicket-keeper and skilful right-handed batsman, Saleem Yousuf conveys tremendous enthusiasm for the game and has the ability to become the regular Test wicket-keeper. After making his first Test appearance in 1981/2 against Sri Lanka at Karachi – he scored 4 and took 5 catches and 2 stumpings – he toured England in 1982 but got little chance. In the home season of 1981/2 he had scored three centuries.

First-class career (1978-): 1,699 runs (34.67) including 4 centuries, 1-16 and 84 dismissals (74 ct, 10 st.)

SARFRAZ NAWAZ (b.1948)

Lahore, United Bank and Northamptonshire

An amusing, unpredictable character, sometimes genial, sometimes liable to stormy tempers, Sarfraz Nawaz has proved himself a fast-medium bowler of high class and has often been extremely useful as a rugged, hard-driving, late-order batsman. Very tall and strong, he allied with Imran Khan and Asif Masood in the 1970s to give Pakistan considerable seam-bowling strength. After a straight-backed wooden-legged run-up, he has a good high action and bowls at sharp pace, making the ball bounce and swing disconcertingly, and cutting it both ways off the seam. Not lacking courage (or is it foolhardiness?!) he once bowled a succession of bouncers for Northamptonshire against the Australian fast bowler Jeff Thomson. Although Thomson treated it as a joke and did not retaliate, Sarfraz found the massive West Indian Joel Garner less accommodating when he 'bounced' him in the 1979 Gillette Cup Final. Sarfraz's idiosyncrasies went further than this in 1977/8 when he flew from Pakistan to England in the middle of a Test series between the two countries (in Pakistan) as part of a one-man protest against the payment he was receiving, and the following winter he successfully appealed against Australian batsman Andrew Hilditch for handling the ball – Hilditch had picked up a gentle

Sarfraz Nawaz

return from a fielder and thrown it back to Sarfraz, the bowler. Pakistan went on to lose the match and this incident marked a sad end to what had been for Sarfraz a highly successful tour, whose highlight had been a sensational spell at Melbourne on 15 March 1979 when he became the first visiting bowler to take 9 wickets in a Test innings in Australia. His figures for the innings were 9 for 86 and, when Pakistan took the new ball at the start of the final day, Australia with seven wickets left needed only 99 to win. Cutting down his run and bowling seam up, Sarfraz took 7 wickets for one run with the last 33 balls of his final spell. Pakistan won miraculously by 71 runs. Yet Sarfraz's career has also had its darker moments. He was not re-engaged by Northamptonshire in 1972, after first playing for them in 1969, but rejoined the county in 1974, was capped a year later and was a vital member of their team until 1982. First playing for Pakistan in 1968/9, he toured England in 1971, 1974 1978 and 1982, Australia and New Zealand in 1972/3, 1978/9 and 1981/2 and Australia and the West Indies in 1976/7. Before his Melbourne performance his best figures in Test cricket were 6 for 89 against West Indies at Lahore in 1974/5. Troubled by injuries in England in 1982, he played only in the Lord's Test, taking 3-56 in the first innings. He was not re-engaged by Northants after 1982.

First-class career (1967-): 5,342 runs (19.42), 941 wickets (24.04) and 156 catches
Test matches (43): 760 runs (15.51), 136 wickets (32.25) and 24 catches

SHAFIQ AHMED (b.1949)

Punjab University and National Bank

An attractive right-handed opening batsman or number three and occasional medium-pace bowler, Shafiq Ahmed is a vigorous driver and cutter with a handsome, upright style, and he has been a successful member of the strong National Bank team in Pakistan's domestic cricket. At Test level, however, he has been disappointing, though unfortunate to be competing with many brilliant players for a batting place. After hitting 68 and a dominating 100 not out in the opening match of Pakistan's 1974 tour of England – against Leicestershire – he won his first cap at Leeds, making 7 and 18, but subsequently lost his place. In three Tests as a number three batsman at home against England in 1977/8 his highest score was 27 not out.

First-class career (1967-): 11,481 runs (51.95) including 36 centuries, 69 wickets (35.14) and 138 catches
Test matches (6): 99 runs (11.00) and 0-1

SHAFQAT RANA (b.1943)

Pakistan International Airlines

A very good right-handed batsman adept at the cut and the drive, and an occasional off-break bowler, Shafqat Rana had a chequered Test career, playing five Tests over six years. He played at home against Australia in 1964/5, England in 1968/9 and New Zealand in 1969/70, and toured Australasia in 1964/5 and England in 1971 without appearing in a Test. His final series, against New Zealand, was his best: he made 167 runs (41.75) including his highest, 95, in the third match at Lahore, and 65 at Dacca in the next, his last, Test, on a pitch made of pounded mud. Minor rioting caused this match to be abandoned.

First-class career (1959-79): 4,947 runs (35.33) including 9 centuries, and 16 wickets (35.00)
Test matches (5): 221 runs (31.57), 1-9 and 5 catches

SHAHID ISRAR (b.1950)

Karachi

A wicket-keeper, Shahid Israr scored 7 not out at number eleven and held 2 catches in his sole Test, the third against New Zealand at Karachi in 1976/7. Catches dropped by himself and others prevented Pakistan from translating their vast superiority into a victory in this match.

First-class career (1968-79): 847 runs (28.23) and 81 dismissals (61 ct, 20 st.)

SHAHID MAHMOOD (b.1939)

Karachi

A competent left-handed opening batsman and medium-pace bowler, Shahid Mahmood toured England with the 1962 Pakistan team. Insufficient use, perhaps, was made of his talents; his confidence suffered and in his sole Test, the fourth, at Trent Bridge, he scored 16 and 9 and took 0 for 23. Playing for Karachi Whites v. Khairpur at Karachi in 1969/70, he took all 10 wickets for 58.

First-class career (1956-70): 3,117 runs (31.80) including 5 centuries, and 89 wickets (21.69)

SHARPE, Duncan (b.1937)

Quetta, Railways, Lahore and South Australia

An Anglo-Pakistani, Duncan Sharpe was an aggressive right-handed batsman and useful wicket-keeper, who top-scored in each innings of his first Test against Australia at Dacca in 1959/60, scoring 56 out of 200, and 35 out of 134 – but after this series did not represent Pakistan again. He emigrated to Australia in 1960, and played for South Australia in the Sheffield Shield competition with success.

First-class career (1955-66): 1,532 runs (27.35) including 2 centuries

Test matches (3): 134 runs (22.33) and 2 catches

SHUJA-UD-DIN, Lt-Col. (b.1930)

Northern India and Services

A very painstaking right-handed batsman and a useful slow left-arm bowler of great stamina who never hesitated to 'buy' his wickets, Shuja-ud-Din made his debut at sixteen for Northern India in the Ranji Trophy competition in 1946/7 before Partition. He toured England with the first Pakistan team in 1954 (and appeared in one match on the 1962 tour), and at home played against India in 1954/5, New Zealand in 1955/6, West Indies in 1958/9, Australia in 1959/60 and England in 1961/2. In the pioneering England tour, he accomplished little in the Tests, but in all first-class matches he was prominent with 67 wickets (28.85) and 366 runs (19.26), including his initial century, 135, against Somerset at Taunton. His highest in Tests was a determined 47 in the first match against New Zealand at Karachi, and in the second innings he captured 3 for 22 in 22 overs. With Pakistan heading for defeat at Lahore against Australia in the second Test in 1959/60, he made a grim 45 in 6 hours 18 minutes, adding 169 with Saeed Ahmed for the third wicket. Among his best scores was 147 for Services against MCC at Sargodha in 1955/6 and his best bowling was 8 for 53 (12 for 61 in the match) for Services against Lahore in 1961/2. He took 47 wickets in the 1961/2 Qaid-e-Azam matches, then a record. A Lieutenant-Colonel in the Pakistan Army, he was taken prisoner in the Indo-Pakistan War.

First-class career (1946-70): 3,342 runs (24.75) including 6 centuries, and 298 wickets (22.44)

Test matches (19): 395 runs (15.19), 20 wickets (40.05) and 8 catches

SIKANDER BAKHT (b.1957)

Sind, Karachi and United Bank

A tall, pencil-thin, fast-medium bowler with tremendous enthusiasm and a good, high action after a long, zestful approach, Sikander Bakht can get lively pace from most pitches and out-swing in most atmospheres. Though competing with sturdier fast bowlers like Imran, Sarfraz, Masood and Saleem, Sikander played a prominent role in several Tests in the late 1970s and has tended to be underestimated. After a respectable debut as third seamer against New Zealand at Karachi in 1976/7, he toured Australia and the West Indies, and took the new ball for the first time during the 'Packer Interregnum' in 1977/8 when he appeared in Tests at home and away against England. He hit the headlines by breaking the arm of the England captain Mike Brearley when one of his deliveries 'reared' during a one-day match at Karachi. His figures at home were disappointing, 3 for 136 in two Tests, but in England he took 7 wickets in three Tests, and he missed only one of eight Tests played by Pakistan against India, New Zealand and Australia in 1978/9. He performed manfully in India in 1979/80, taking 24 wickets in five Tests, including 11 in the second Test at Delhi where he had his best figures of 8 for 69 in the first innings. But on tours of Australia and England during 1981 and 1982 he was disappointing.

First-class career (1974-): 925 runs (13.40) and 310 wickets (26.67)

Test matches (25): 137 runs (6.22), 66 wickets (34.92) and 6 catches

TAHIR NAQQASH (b.1959)

Punjab, Lahore and Muslim Commercial Bank

A tall, wiry right-handed all-rounder, Tahir bats aggressively in the middle order; but his main strength is as a bowler, fast-medium and with a busy action, tending to fall away as he delivers, thus making the in-swinger his stock delivery. The son of a high-ranking journalist in Lahore, he began his career as an off-spinner but soon realized that he had natural ability as a quicker bowler. He made his first-class debut in 1975/6, and in 1981/2 he toured Australia, making some appearances in the many one-day internationals on that tour. His first opportunity at Test level came when he returned home to play in all three Tests against Sri Lanka following a captaincy struggle in which several senior players refused to play under Javed Miandad. Tahir hit 57 in his first Test but took only seven wickets in the series at 50 each. Against England at Edgbaston in 1982, however, he took 5 for 41 in the second innings, in one hostile spell removing five reputable batsmen in 43 balls at a cost of 20, including Ian Botham first ball. He became the first choice as Imran Khan's opening partner with the new ball, and again performed well against Australia in 1982/3.

First-class career (1975-): 595 runs (19.83), 69 wickets (29.94) and 14 catches
Test matches (8): 197 runs (28.14) and 21 wickets (33.29)

TALAT ALI (b.1950)

Pakistan International Airlines

A determined right-handed opening batsman and occasional medium-pace bowler, Talat Ali had a most unfortunate start to his Test career against Australia at Adelaide in 1972/3 when in his first innings his right thumb was fractured by a ball from Dennis Lillee. He retired hurt for 7 but in the second innings batted one-handed at number eleven to take the match into the last day. He played one further Test on the tour of Australasia, against New Zealand, again with little success, but in 1978/9 he returned and enjoyed his most successful match against New Zealand at Christchurch where he had scores of 40 and 61 in the first Test. He fell to Richard Hadlee in all his five innings in this series; on one occasion he claimed that he had been deceived by the latter's grunt as he delivered, thinking the grunt was a 'no ball' call by the umpire. He lost his place when the team moved to Australia. Having toured England in 1971 without playing a Test, he played a full series at home against England in 1972/3. He also appeared in two Tests in England in 1978. His highest score was 258 for PIA against Rawalpindi in 1975/6.

First-class career (1967-79): 7,296 runs (38.00) including 14 centuries
Test matches (10): 370 runs (23.12), 0-7 and 4 catches

TASLIM ARIF (b.1954)

Karachi, Sind and National Bank

In only his third Test match, against Australia at Faisalabad in 1979/80, Taslim Arif batted over seven hours to hit an outstanding 210 not out, out of a Pakistan total of 382 for 2. He was on the field throughout the match. A wicket-keeper, opening batsman and occasional right-arm medium paced bowler, he made a youthful first appearance in first-class cricket in 1967/8 and played his first Test at Calcutta in the last match of the series against India in 1979/80. He started brilliantly, scoring 90 and 46, though he did not keep wicket in a Test until the following series against Australia. Playing two more home Tests against West Indies in 1980/81, he was less prolific.

First-class career (1967-): 5,605 runs (34.81) including 10 centuries, 3 wickets (29.00) and 254 dismissals (214 ct, 40 st.)
Test matches (6): 501 runs (62.62) including 1 century, 1-28 and 9 dismissals (6 ct, 3 st.)

TAUSEEF AHMED (b.1960)

Public Works Department and United Bank

An off-spinner in the classical mould, Tauseef gives the ball a big tweak, and turns it sharply on helpful pitches. His promise was quickly recognized when he made his Test debut as a teenager a season after his first appearances in first-class cricket. In three Tests against Australia at home in 1979/80 he took 12 wickets (29.66), including 7 for 126 in his first match at Karachi. He also played against Sri Lanka in 1981/2 and, although he was left out of the subsequent tour of England, he played with success in one-day internationals against Australia in 1982/3.

First-class career (1978-): 337 runs (16.85) and 186 wickets (20.33)
Test matches (6): 23 runs (11.50), 23 wickets (26.95) and 3 catches

WAQAR HASSAN (b.1932)

Services and Karachi

Appropriately, Waqar Hassan was an attractive stroke-making right-handed batsman, who was ideal in a crisis and a fine field either at cover or in the outfield. He made his debut in first-class cricket at seventeen and toured India in 1952/3, England in 1954 and West Indies in 1957/8. At home he played against India in 1954/5, New Zealand in 1955/6, Australia in 1956/7 and 1959/60 and West Indies in 1958/9. At Bombay in the third Test against India, when Pakistan were faltering at 60 for 6 on the first day, he made a stubborn 81, but even his 65 in the second innings failed to avert defeat. At Calcutta, however, in the fifth match his determined 97 in five hours saved Pakistan. In this first series he made most runs, 357 (44.62). On his England tour he scored 1,263 runs (32.38) in all first-class matches but, except for 53 in the first Test at Lord's, disappointed in the Tests. In the first official series in Pakistan, against India, he made 244 runs (30.50). Against New Zealand he finished second to Imtiaz Ahmed with 231 runs (57.75), including 189 in the second match at Lahore – his highest in Tests – when, after 6 wickets had fallen for 111, he and Imtiaz added a brilliant 308, which remains Pakistan's highest for that wicket in all Tests; New Zealand were beaten rather narrowly amid intense excitement. His highest score in the first-class game was 201 not out for A.V.M. Cannon's XI against Hasan Mahmood's XI at Karachi in 1953/4.

First-class career (1948-66): 4,620 runs (35.54) including 8 centuries
Test matches (21): 1,071 runs (31.50) including 1 century, 0-10 and 10 catches

WASIM BARI (b.1948)

Pakistan International Airlines, Karachi and Sind

An outstanding natural wicket-keeper and most

Wasim Bari

capable, late middle-order, right-handed batsman, Wasim Bari has been his country's automatic choice behind the stumps since making his first Test appearance at Edgbaston in 1967. He has proved marvellously reliable behind the stumps and, twelve years after that first match, he set a new world record when, in the first New Zealand innings at Auckland, he caught seven of the first eight batsmen. Strangely enough he did not claim another victim in the match, so, although breaking the record for an innings, he fell one short of his best match haul of eight (all caught) against England at Leeds in 1971. Five foot nine inches, Wasim is both balanced and agile, always ready to dive if necessary, but, unlike many, only if necessary. Few wicket-keepers have had a safer pair of hands and he is better than most close to the stumps, having much more practice at keeping to spin bowlers in his native Pakistan than do the majority of contemporary Test wicket-keepers. He has toured Australia (three times), New Zealand and the West Indies (twice) and England in 1967, 1971, 1974 and 1978, when he captained an inexperienced side, unsettled by the ripples of the Packer affair, with commendable calm. As a batsman he is good enough to have scored 177 for PIA against Sind at Karachi in 1976/7 and in Tests has often played useful innings at around number eight in the Pakistan order, notably at Headingley in 1971 when, apart from his eight catches, he made 63, and at Adelaide in 1972/3 when his 72 was top score for Pakistan. Going in as night-watchman at number three in Lahore against India in 1978/9, he made 85, his highest Test score. He continued to hold off challenges by younger wicket-keepers, although not immediately regaining his place after joining a players' revolt against the captaincy of Javed Miandad following the tour of Australia in 1981/2. Back in the side in England in 1982 he did not always keep wicket at his best, but he nevertheless remained first choice against Australia in the series won three-nil early in the 1982/3 season.

First-class career (1964-): 5,462 runs (22.02) including 2 centuries, and 759 dismissals (620 ct, 139 st.)

Test matches (67): 1,191 runs (16.32), 0-2 and 184 dismissals (160 ct, 24 st.)

WASIM HASAN RAJA (b.1952)

Lahore, Sargodha, Punjab University, Combined Universities, Pakistan International Airlines, Punjab, National Bank, Durham and Northumberland

An explosive left-handed batsman, Wasim Raja is a dashing, popular and attractive cricketer of super-abundant talent, although often lacking in application, especially in English conditions; he is also a gifted right-arm bowler of top-spinners and leg-breaks. Driving with a full flow-through of the bat or pulling ferocious, soaring shots whenever the bowler pitches short anywhere to the leg-side of middle, he plays in such an uninhibited manner that he is always likely to be inconsistent. Yet in one series at least he has already disproved this, in the West Indies in 1976/7 when he scored 517 runs in five Tests at 54.44, as well as taking 7 useful wickets at 18.71 each. He played in his usual free, indeed carefree way, though he often faced and overcame a crisis. Hitting no fewer than 14 sixes in the series, he was consistency itself, top-scoring in five of Pakistan's ten innings in the series and hitting his highest, 117 not out, in the first Test at Bridgetown. Wasim first played for Pakistan in New Zealand, 1972/3, quickly establishing himself as a useful member of the side as a batsman at number 6 in the

Wasim Raja

order, as a change-bowler, and as a brilliant fielder in the covers. His only other Test century was also against the West Indies, 107 not out at Karachi in 1974/5 when he put on a record 128 with Wasim Bari for the seventh wicket. But on his two tours of England in 1974 and, especially, in 1978 he was disappointing, although he was a key member of Pakistan's Prudential World Cup teams in England in 1975 and 1979. He again shone against India in 1979/80 (450 runs at 56.25) and against West Indies at home in 1980/81, scoring 246 runs in four Tests (61.50). He batted consistently in Australia in 1981/2; but both in this series and the subsequent one at home against Sri Lanka the big score eluded him and he lost his place after one Test in England in 1982. The impression remained of a talented hard-wicket player never quite at his best when the ball is moving about.

First-class career (1967-): 9,826 runs (35.47) including 13 centuries, 490 wickets (28.32) and 129 catches
Test matches (44): 2,311 runs (37.88) including 2 centuries, 39 wickets (36.20) and 12 catches

WAZIR MOHAMMAD (b.1929)

Bahawalpur and Karachi

The eldest of the Test-playing Mohammad brotherhood, Wazir was a determined, middle-order, right-handed batsman with a strong defence – invaluable in the early days of his country in international cricket – and an excellent outfield. He toured India in 1952/3, England in 1954 and West Indies in 1957/8 – the first three tours ever made by Pakistan – and at home he played against India in 1954/5, New Zealand in 1955/6, Australia in 1956/7 and 1959/60 and West Indies in 1958/9. In England he broke a finger in his second innings, but recovered well to head the averages with 628 runs (39.25). A defiant 42 not out in two and three-quarter hours in the last Test at The Oval contributed to Pakistan's first and only win against England. In the first official series in Pakistan his only valuable contribution was 55 in the third match at Lahore. After several failures in representative matches, he played against Australia at Karachi in 1956/7 and hit 67, adding 104 for the sixth wicket with A.H. Kardar after five men had fallen for 70; Pakistan defeated Australia in the first match between the two countries. Back in good form in the West Indies, he headed the averages in all first-class matches with 70.83 from 850 runs, including 440 runs (55.00) in the Tests; he attempted gallantly to avert defeat in the third Test, at Kingston, scoring 106 in a total of 288; hit 97 not out in another losing cause at Georgetown; and in the final match at Port of Spain, which Pakistan won by an innings, he top-scored with 189 – his career-highest – in six and three-quarter hours. The remainder of his Test career was an anticlimax.

First-class career (1949-64): 4,952 runs (40.26) including 11 centuries
Test matches (20): 801 runs (27.62) including 2 centuries, 0-15 and 5 catches

YOUNIS AHMED (b.1947)

Pakistan International Airlines, Surrey, Worcestershire and South Australia

Thickset and strong, a dashing left-handed batsman with a large repertoire of strokes, including a magnificent off-drive, and an occasional bowler of either slow left-arm spin or medium pace, Younis Ahmed played in two Tests against New Zealand in 1969/70, in the first of which at Karachi he made 62. One of the youngest players ever to appear in first-class cricket, he made his debut in 1961/2 aged 14 years 4 months for Pakistan Inter-Board Schools against South Zone; but subsequently, despite his fleeting Test appearances, his cricket was for many years identified with Surrey for whom he played from 1965 until 1978. His quiet ambition was to qualify for England's Test team, but new qualification rules prevented this. He grew steadily less happy and less successful for Surrey but a move to Worcestershire in 1979 proved mutually beneficial, and he hit 1,539 runs at 69.95 in a triumphant season, including one score of 221 not out against his old county at Guildford.

First-class career (1961-): 21,708 runs (38.90) including 36 centuries, 39 wickets (41.15) and 219 catches
Test matches (2): 89 runs (22.25)

ZAHEER ABBAS (b.1947)

Karachi, Public Works Department, Sind, Pakistan International Airlines and Gloucestershire

A cricket genius, Zaheer Abbas would have found a batting place in most people's imaginary 'World XI' for most of his career. Tall and lean, he has batted for a long time in spectacles which he changed for contact lenses in the late 1970s. Both as batsman and a fine slip fielder he has proved that a natural handicap to the sight need be no disadvantage. Only on bouncy wickets with a tinge of green in them, of a type which became more common in Australia in the 1970s, has he ever looked unlikely to dominate the finest bowlers. But that he is a batsman of rare quality cannot be doubted, whether he is judged by figures or by style: calm, swift to judge line and length, very straight, moving easily either backwards or forwards, his strokes have a rippling, flowing grace all their own. So loose-wristed is he at the moment of impact that he seems able to steer the ball at will through gaps in the covers or the leg-side, a high proportion of his runs tending to come in boundaries. Even on slow wickets he hits the ball very hard, especially off the back foot.

Zaheer Abbas

Often in recent years he has worn a floppy white sun-hat on sunny days which has increased the impression of cool, casual command. Zaheer, born at Sialkot, first played for Karachi Whites in 1965/6. His average in the Qaid-e-Azam Trophy in 1967 was 93.00, including an innings of 197 against East Pakistan, but he did not announce himself to a wider world until his second Test match, and his first in England, at Edgbaston in 1971 when he made a superlative 274; the mastery of his batting then was as remarkable as his unwavering concentration. He batted for 9 hours 10 minutes and hit 38 fours. It was strange that he had hitherto played only one Test, against New Zealand in 1969 at Karachi, but after his performance at Edgbaston Zaheer became an automatic selection at number three or four in the Pakistan order. He has scored two more Test double centuries, 240 against England at The Oval in 1974, when he never looked like getting out, and a majestic 235 not out against India at Lahore in October 1978. In the previous match Zaheer had scored 176 and 96 at Faisalabad in the first Test to have been played between Pakistan and India for seventeen years. He has scored Test centuries also in Australia – 101 at Adelaide in 1976/7 – and New Zealand – 135 at Auckland in 1979. But nowhere is the name Zaheer more revered than in Gloucestershire where he is known by his team-mates simply as 'Z', a modest, gentle, affable destroyer of opposing bowlers. First playing for the county in 1972, he has eleven times scored in excess of 1,000 runs, including 2,554 at an average of 75.11 in the dry summer of 1976. Eight times, a world record, he has scored hundreds in both innings of a match and four times, also a world record, he has scored a double century and a century in the same match. He performed this unlikely feat twice in 1976, 216 not out and 156 not out against Surrey at The Oval and 230 not out and 104 not out against Kent at Canterbury, and did it again with 205 not out and 108 not out against Sussex at Cheltenham in 1977, and 215 not out and 150 not out against Somerset at Bath in 1981. He also scored four centuries in successive innings in 1970/71 and his aggregate of 1,597 runs (84.05) in 1973/4 is the record for a Pakistan season. In 1981 he scored 2,305 runs (88.69) in the English season. Early in the 1982/3 home season, he became only the twentieth man to score more than 100 centuries.

First-class career (1965-): 30,069 runs (52.84) including 95 centuries, 25 wickets (33.12) and 242 catches
Test matches (52): 3,423 runs (41.74) including 8 centuries, 0-10 and 29 catches

ZULFIQAR AHMED (b.1926)

Bahawalpur and Pakistan International Airlines

Primarily a right-arm, off-break bowler of great perseverance with a peculiarly deceptive action, Zulfiqar Ahmed would also try an occasional leg-break and there seemed such a slight change in his delivery that he could confuse even the best batsman; he was also a reliable late-order batsman. In a short but successful Test career he toured India in 1952/3 and England in 1954, and at home played against New Zealand in 1955/6 and Australia in 1956/7. In the first official tour of India he made 179 runs (59.66), including 108 runs in the Tests at an average of 108, thanks to several not out innings. His Test-highest was a hard-hitting 63 not out in the fourth match at Madras, when he shared in a last-wicket partnership of 104 in eighty-five minutes with Amir Elahi. The most successful spin bowler on the first England tour, he took 64 wickets (18.50), though his bowling was rarely used in the Tests. Second in the Test batting with 61 runs (20.33), however, he showed where the weakness of the team lay. His 34 was an essential ingredient to his country's first (and only) victory over England at The Oval, by 24 runs. In the first series against New Zealand he was the best bowler, securing 19 wickets (15.10) in the three matches. In the first match at Karachi he was largely instrumental in the innings victory on a true matting pitch, capturing 5 for 37 in 37.2 overs and 6 for 42 in 46.3 overs, his best ever performance.

First-class career (1946-65): 973 runs (19.87) and 163 wickets (21.65)
Test matches (9): 200 runs (33.33), 20 wickets (18.30) and 5 catches

SRI LANKA

De MEL, Asantha Lakdasa Francis (b.1959)

Sinhalese

A product of Colombo's Royal College, and the best Sri Lankan fast bowler of his generation, Asantha de Mel was fortunate in reaching the top just as his country's long battle to attain Test status had been won. Fast-medium rather than genuinely quick, but with a free, high action and a good out-swinger, he toured England in 1981 with only modest success but quickly made his mark in Sri Lanka's first official Test, against England at Colombo in February 1982. He took 4-70 in England's first innings, including the first three batsmen. He then went to Pakistan and picked up more wickets than many more vaunted fast bowlers in that land of slow pitches, including 11 in the three Test matches. A useful late-order right-handed batsman with aggressive instincts, he is a genuine all-rounder in anything other than the highest level.

Asantha de Mel

First-class career (1980-): 438 runs (33.69) and 36 wickets (50.47)
Test matches (5): 125 runs (15.62), 23 wickets (34.43) and 5 catches

De SILVA, Dandeniyage Somachandra (b.1944)

Moratuwa, Lincolnshire and Shropshire

The younger brother of D.P. de Silva, who played for Ceylon, Somachandra, known familiarly as D.S. to distinguish him from his unrelated spinning partner Ajith, was born in Galle and was already a well-known and widely respected right-arm leg-break bowler when the era of Test cricket dawned for Sri Lanka. He had made his initial first-class appearance as early as 1966/7 for the Ceylon Board President's XI against the Hyderabad Blues of India and toured England in 1975, 1979 and 1981 as well as Pakistan in 1973/4 and 1981/2 and India in 1975/6 and 1982/3. Also a very useful right-handed late middle-order batsman, he was an automatic choice for Sri Lanka's representative teams from the mid 1970s, his well-flighted leg-spinners and googlies commanding respect from even the finest batsmen. He became a popular figure and a respected bowler in the English Minor Counties Championship, playing for Lincolnshire from 1975 to 1979, and for Shropshire from 1980. Playing for the Sri Lankan touring team against Oxford University at Guildford in 1979, he took 8 for 46 in an innings and 12 for 59 in the match. Though wickets came less easily to him in official Tests, he still picked up his share in 1981/2, including 3 for 54 in the first innings against England in the inaugural Test in Colombo and 17 wickets in three Tests against Pakistan.

First-class career (1966-): 1,248 runs (20.12) and 201 wickets (25.09)
Test matches (5): 213 runs (26.62), 23 wickets (30.21) and 1 catch

D.S. de Silva

De SILVA, Ginigalgodange Ramba Ajith (b.1952)

Bloomfield

Born and educated in Ambalangoda, Ajith de Silva is a very steady, orthodox slow left-arm bowler and useful late-order left-handed batsman. He was already an experienced cricketer when picked for Sri Lanka's early Test matches in the 1980s. He toured Pakistan in 1973/4 and 1981/2, England in 1975 and 1979 (playing in the Prudential World Cup in those years), India in 1975/6 and Bangladesh in 1977/8. An effective bowler in one-day cricket because of his commendable accuracy, he disappointed his supporters in the inaugural Test in Colombo, being reluctant to take chances by flighting the ball on a pitch taking some spin. Nevertheless, he took four wickets; but in Pakistan he played in the first two Tests, taking only three wickets at 69 each. These were disappointing returns for so highly rated a bowler and one who in 1975/6 dismissed Viswanath of India in six successive innings, four times in Sri Lanka and twice in India.

First-class career (1973-): 260 runs (7.64) and 159 wickets (25.77)
Test matches (4): 41 runs (8.20) and 7 wickets (55.00)

DIAS, Roy Luke (b.1952)

Sinhalese

A slim, elegant and exceptionally gifted right-handed batsman with a marvellous sense of timing and a style a little reminiscent of Rohan Kanhai, Roy Dias was an automatic selection in Sri Lankan sides in the second half of the 1970s and in the team which played his country's first Test matches. Also a fine cover-point fielder and occasional right-arm medium-paced bowler, he toured India in 1975/6, Bangladesh in 1977/8, Pakistan in 1981/2, India in 1982/3, and England in 1979 and 1981 when he scored 608 runs (40.55). His experience was further widened by three seasons in England between 1977 and 1979 playing in League cricket. Against England in Sri Lanka's first ever Test he scored a brilliant 77 in the second innings, and he went on to make 295 runs in three Tests against Pakistan, including 109 in the third Test at Lahore.

First-class career (1974-): 2,316 runs (35.63) including 2 centuries
Test matches (5): 529 runs (52.90) including 1 century, and 2 catches

Roy Dias

GOONATILLEKE, Hettiarachige Mahes (b.1952)

Kandy

Born in Kandy and educated at St Anthony's College, Mahes Goonatilleke is an accomplished wicket-keeper, polished and swift, and a stolid right-handed batsman good enough to be given the responsibility of opening the innings in Test cricket. Picked to tour India in 1975/6, his first-class debut was made on that tour. He toured Bangladesh two years later and England in 1981, by which time he had made himself first-choice wicket-keeper. Although not an automatic selection for one-day internationals, he played in five of Sri Lanka's early Tests.

First-class career (1975-): 308 runs (14.69) and 47 dismissals (32 ct, 15 st.)
Test matches (5): 177 runs (22.12) and 13 dismissals (10 ct, 3 st.)

JAYASEKERA, Rohan Stanley Amarasiriwardena (b.1957)

Tamil Union

An aggressive right-handed opening batsman and dependable wicket-keeper, Stanley Jayasekera, a product of Royal College, had a successful tour of England in the World Cup year of 1979, scoring 205 at an average of 51 in five innings. He narrowly missed selection for the first ever Sri Lankan Test against England as a specialist batsman, but played in that role in the third Test against Pakistan at Lahore in March 1982. Going in at number three, he was bowled by Imran Khan for 0 and 2.

First-class career (1978-): 359 runs (29.21) and 8 dismissals (6 ct, 2 st.)

KALUPERUMA, Lalith Wasantha (b.1949)

Bloomfield

A skilful right-arm off-break bowler, gritty late-order right-handed batsman and good close fielder, Lalith Kaluperuma dismissed the Indian captain Ajit Wadekar with the first ball he bowled in an unofficial 'Test', in 1975/6, and by the time that Sri Lanka's Test status was recognized he had firmly established himself as a steady off-spinner with good control of flight. However, he was disappointing when asked to dismiss good batsmen on good pitches, failing to take a wicket in his first two Tests, against England (Colombo) and Pakistan (Faisalabad).

First-class career (1970-): 894 runs (16.86) and 125 wickets (28.32)
Test matches (2): 12 runs (4.00) and 2 catches

MADUGALLE, Ranjan Senerath (b.1959)

Nondescripts

Born in Kandy but educated at Royal College in Colombo, Ranjan Madugalle was an effective off-spin bowler as a schoolboy. But he developed into a specialist right-handed batsman of high quality and, having gained experience in the Saddleworth League in England and on the Sri Lankan tours to England of 1979 and 1981, he was ready to claim a batting place in the Test side with a delightful innings of 142 not out for the President's XI against Keith Fletcher's touring team at Kandy in 1981/2. In the inaugural Test his 65 helped to bail out Sri Lanka after a disastrous start to their Test 'career' and he went on to enjoy a successful tour of Pakistan, scoring 91 not out in the second Test at Faisalabad.

First-class career (1978-): 948 runs (27.08) including 1 century
Test matches (5): 273 runs (30.33) and 5 catches

MENDIS, Louis Rohan Duleep (b.1952)

Sinhalese

A strong, wristy right-handed batsman of exceptional talent, Duleep Mendis was vice-captain of Sri Lanka

Duleep Mendis

in the country's early Tests and took over as captain for the second Test against Pakistan in Faisalabad in 1981/2 when Warnapura was injured. A fine fielder, he can also bowl right-arm medium pace and keep wicket when required. Born in Moratuwa, he was a key member of Sri Lankan sides to England in 1975, 1979 and 1981, and also toured Pakistan and India in the 1970s, producing ample evidence of his quality both in first-class cricket and in one-day internationals. His start to his official Test career was disappointing until, in September 1982, he hit 105 runs in both innings in the first Test against India at Madras, thus becoming only the third batsman ever to score hundreds in both innings against India, after Bradman and Weekes.

First-class career (1971-): 3,595 runs (34.89) including 7 centuries
Test matches (5): 370 runs (37.00) including 2 centuries, and 4 catches

Arjuna Ranatunge

RANASINGHE, Anura Nandana (b.1956)

Bloomfield

Twelfth man in Sri Lanka's first official Test, Anura Ranasinghe is a fighting all-round cricketer with considerable experience in the leagues of the north of England. He first played for Sri Lanka in 1974/5 when still a schoolboy, but has not fully lived up to the high expectations held of his right-handed batting and medium-pace left-arm seamers. He toured England three times and India once before making the country's first official tour to Pakistan where he played in one Test, at Faisalabad, making 6 and 5 and taking one wicket in the match for 40 runs.

First-class career (1974-): 983 runs (22.83) and 32 wickets (39.65)
Test matches (2): 88 runs (22.00), 1-52 and 1 stumping

RANATUNGE, Arjuna (b.1963)

Sinhalese

When picked against England for Sri Lanka's first ever Test, the then 18-year-old Ranatunge played with nerveless skill to score an attractive 54 when his side was in trouble. Subsequent efforts were less successful, but this elegant left-hander clearly has a glowing future.

First-class career (1980-): 192 runs (21.33)
Test matches (4): 144 runs (18.00), 0-12 and 1 catch

RATNAYAKE, Joseph Ravindran (b.1960)

Nondescripts

A wiry right-arm fast-medium bowler and left-handed tail-end batsman, 'Ravi' Ratnayake was born in Colombo, but went to school at Trinity College in Kandy. He played against both Pakistan and Australia at Under 19 level and came close to selection for Sri Lanka's first Test after taking five wickets for 120 against England at Kandy for the President's XI. However, his first Test appearances were made in Pakistan where he played in two Tests in 1981/2, and on unresponsive wickets plugged away with determination to take four wickets for 180.

First-class career (1981-): 97 runs (8.81) and 21 wickets (40.80)
Test matches (3): 54 runs (10.80) and 5 wickets (60.20)

WARNAPURA, Bandula (b.1953)

Bloomfield

A popular and respected cricketer, Bandula Warnapura succeeded the prolific Anura Tennekoon as captain of Sri Lanka after some consistent performances as an opening batsman in the years leading up to the achievement of Test status. He thus had the honour of leading his country in her first official Tests. Also a steady right-arm medium paced bowler and good fielder, Warnapura shows balanced and correct right-hand batting, and he was an automatic selection for most of Sri Lanka's representative teams through the 1970s, touring England in 1975, 1979 and 1981 (the latter tour as captain), India in 1975/6 and Pakistan in 1973/4 and 1981/2. In this last tour Sri Lanka were beaten but not disgraced in two matches and Warnapura, who missed the second Test through injury, did not show his best form. He made 106 in a one-day international against Australia in 1980. He fell from grace when choosing to tour South Africa, a decision which cost him and several colleagues a life ban from Sri Lankan cricket.

First-class career (1970-): 2,140 runs (26.09) including 2 centuries, and 11 wickets (47.09)
Test matches (4): 96 runs (12.00), 0-46 and 2 catches

Bandula Warnapura

WETTIMUNY, Sidath (b.1956)

Sinhalese

The younger brother of another Sri Lankan opening batsman, Sunil, Sidath Wettimuny made a most promising start to his Test career as a sound but attractive right-handed opener, who also bowls occasional right-arm seamers. After making his initial first-class appearance in 1975/6 against Pakistan at Kandy, when he was dismissed for a pair, he enjoyed a successful tour of England in 1981 and played (without success) in the inaugural Test at Colombo. But in Pakistan he made his mark firmly on the history of the game by becoming the first Sri Lankan ever to hit a hundred in an official Test when he scored 157 against a crestfallen Pakistan at Faisalabad.

First-class career (1975-): 967 runs (33.34) including 1 century
Test matches (4): 331 runs (41.37) including 1 century, 0-21 and 2 catches

WIJESURIYA, Roger Gerrard Christopher Ediriweera (b.1960)

Sinhalese

A slow left-arm bowler and right-handed tail-ender, Roger Wijesuriya played in all five games that the Sri Lankan Under 19 side played against the Pakistan touring team of 1978/9, taking 25 wickets. But when he visited Pakistan with the senior Sri Lankan side three years later, he was less successful and was discarded by the selectors for Sri Lanka's next tour, of India. In Pakistan he played his only Test to date, taking no wickets for 105 at Lahore and making nought and 3.

First-class career (1978-): 65 runs (9.29) and 31 wickets (36.69)
Test matches (1): 3 runs (1.50), 0-105 and 2 catches